Twentieth-Century Literary Criticism

Guide to Gale Literary Criticism Series

When you need to review criticism of literary works, these are the Gale series to use:

If the author's death date is: **You should turn to:**

After Dec. 31, 1959
(or author is still living)

CONTEMPORARY LITERARY CRITICISM

for example: Jorge Luis Borges, William Faulkner,
Ernest Hemingway, Iris Murdoch

1900 through 1959

TWENTIETH-CENTURY LITERARY CRITICISM

for example: Willa Cather, F. Scott Fitzgerald,
Henry James, Mark Twain, Virginia Woolf

1800 through 1899

NINETEENTH-CENTURY LITERATURE CRITICISM

for example: Fyodor Dostoevsky, Nathaniel Hawthorne,
George Sand, William Wordsworth

1400 through 1799

LITERATURE CRITICISM FROM 1400 TO 1800
(excluding Shakespeare)

for example: Anne Bradstreet, Daniel Defoe,
Alexander Pope, François Rabelais,
Jonathan Swift, Phillis Wheatley

SHAKESPEAREAN CRITICISM

Shakespeare's plays and poetry

Antiquity through 1399

CLASSICAL AND MEDIEVAL LITERATURE CRITICISM

for example: Dante, Homer, Plato, Sophocles, Vergil

Gale also publishes related criticism series:

BLACK LITERATURE CRITICISM

Covers the most significant Black authors of the past 200 years

CHILDREN'S LITERATURE REVIEW

Covers authors of all eras who have written for the preschool
through high school audience

SHORT STORY CRITICISM

Covers the major short fiction writers of all nationalities and
periods of literary history

POETRY CRITICISM

Covers poets of all nationalities and periods of literary history

DRAMA CRITICISM

Covers dramatists of all nationalities and periods of literary
history

ISSN 0276-8178

Volume 44

Twentieth-Century Literary Criticism

**Excerpts from Criticism of the
Works of Novelists, Poets, Playwrights,
Short Story Writers, and Other Creative Writers
Who Lived between 1900 and 1960,
from the First Published Critical
Appraisals to Current Evaluations**

**Laurie DiMauro
Editor**

**Marie Lazzari
Thomas Ligotti
David Segal
Bridget Travers
Associate Editors**

 **Gale Research Inc.** · DETROIT · LONDON

STAFF

Laurie DiMauro, *Editor*

Marie Lazzari, Thomas Ligotti, David Segal, Bridget Travers, *Associate Editors*

Jennifer Brostrom, Christopher Giroux, Ian A. Goodhall, Elizabeth P. Henry, Andrew M. Kalasky, Kyung-Sun Lim, Johannah Rodgers, Debra A. Wells, Janet M. Witalec, *Assistant Editors*

Jeanne A. Gough, *Permissions & Production Manager*

Linda M. Pugliese, *Production Supervisor*
Paul Lewon, Maureen Puhl, Camille Robinson,
Jennifer VanSickle, *Editorial Associates*
Donna Craft, Brandy C. Johnson, Sheila Walencewicz, *Editorial Assistants*

Maureen Richards, *Research Supervisor*
Mary Beth McElmeel, Tamara C. Nott, *Editorial Associates*
Daniel J. Jankowski, Kathleen Jozwiak, Amy Kaechele, Julie K. Karmazin, Julie Synkonis, *Editorial Assistants*

Sandra C. Davis, *Permissions Supervisor (Text)*
Maria L. Franklin, Josephine M. Keene, Denise M. Singleton, Kimberly F. Smilay, *Permissions Associates*
Rebecca A. Hartford, Michele Lonoconus, Shelly Rakoczy, Shalice Shah, *Permissions Assistants*

Margaret A. Chamberlain, *Permissions Supervisor (Pictures)*
Pamela A. Hayes, *Permissions Associate*
Amy Lynn Emrich, Karla Kulkis, Nancy Rattenbury, Keith Reed, *Permissions Assistants*

Mary Beth Trimper, *Production Manager*
Mary Winterhalter, *Production Assistant*

Arthur Chartow, *Art Director*
Nicholas Jakubiak, C. J. Jonik, *Keyliners*

Contents

Preface   vii

Acknowledgments   xi

Preface

Since its inception more than ten years ago, *Twentieth-Century Literary Criticism* has been purchased and used by nearly 10,000 school, public, and college or university libraries. *TCLC* has covered more than 500 authors, representing 58 nationalities, and over 25,000 titles. No other reference source has surveyed the critical response to twentieth-century authors and literature as thoroughly as *TCLC*. In the words of one reviewer, "there is nothing comparable available." *TCLC* "is a gold mine of information—dates, pseudonyms, biographical information, and criticism from books and periodicals—which many libraries would have difficulty assembling on their own."

Scope of the Series

TCLC is designed to serve as an introduction to authors who died between 1900 and 1960 and to the most significant interpretations of these authors' works. The great poets, novelists, short story writers, playwrights, and philosophers of this period are frequently studied in high school and college literature courses. In organizing and excerpting the vast amount of critical material written on these authors, *TCLC* helps students develop valuable insight into literary history, promotes a better understanding of the texts, and sparks ideas for papers and assignments. Each entry in *TCLC* presents a comprehensive survey of an author's career or an individual work of literature and provides the user with a multiplicity of interpretations and assessments. Such variety allows students to pursue their own interests; furthermore, it fosters an awareness that literature is dynamic and responsive to many different opinions.

Every fourth volume of *TCLC* is devoted to literary topics that cannot be covered under the author approach used in the rest of the series. Such topics include literary movements, prominent themes in twentieth-century literature, literary reaction to political and historical events, significant eras in literary history, prominent literary anniversaries, and the literatures of cultures that are often overlooked by English-speaking readers.

TCLC is designed as a companion series to Gale's *Contemporary Literary Criticism*, which reprints commentary on authors now living or who have died since 1960. Because of the different periods under consideration, there is no duplication of material between *CLC* and *TCLC*. For additional information about *CLC* and Gale's other criticism titles, users should consult the Guide to Gale Literary Criticism Series preceding the title page in this volume.

Coverage

Each volume of *TCLC* is carefully compiled to present:

- criticism of authors, or literary topics, representing a variety of genres and nationalities

- both major and lesser-known writers and literary works of the period

- 11-15 authors or 4-6 topics per volume

- individual entries that survey critical response to each author's work or each topic in literary history, including early criticism to reflect initial reactions; later criticism to represent any rise or decline in reputation; and current retrospective analyses.

Organization of This Book

An author entry consists of the following elements: author heading, biographical and critical introduction, list of principal works, excerpts of criticism (each preceded by an annotation and followed by a bibliographic citation), and a bibliography of further reading.

- The **author heading** consists of the name under which the author most commonly wrote, followed by birth and death dates. If an author wrote consistently under a pseudonym, the pseudonym will be listed in the author heading and the real name given in parentheses on the first line of the biographical and critical introduction. Also located at the beginning of the introduction to the author entry are any name variations under which an author wrote, including transliterated forms for authors whose languages use nonroman alphabets.

name variations under which an author wrote, including transliterated forms for authors whose languages use nonroman alphabets.

- The **biographical and critical introduction** outlines the author's life and career, as well as the critical issues surrounding his or her work. References to past volumes of *TCLC* are provided at the beginning of the introduction. Additional sources of information in other biographical and critical reference series published by Gale, including *Short Story Criticism, Children's Literature Review, Contemporary Authors, Dictionary of Literary Biography,* and *Something about the Author,* are listed in a box at the end of the entry

- Most *TCLC* entries include **portraits** of the author. Many entries also contain reproductions of materials pertinent to an author's career, including manuscript pages, title pages, dust jackets, letters, and drawings, as well as photographs of important people, places, and events in an author's life.

- The **list of principal works** is chronological by date of first book publication and identifies the genre of each work. In the case of foreign authors with both foreign-language publications and English translations, the title and date of the first English-language edition are given in brackets. Unless otherwise indicated, dramas are dated by first performance, not first publication.

- **Criticism** is arranged chronologically in each author entry to provide a perspective on changes in critical evaluation over the years. All titles of works by the author featured in the entry are printed in boldface type to enable the user to easily locate discussion of particular works. Also for purposes of easier identification, the critic's name and the publication date of the essay are given at the beginning of each piece of criticism. Unsigned criticism is preceded by the title of the journal in which it appeared. Some of the excerpts in *TCLC* also contain translated material. Unless otherwise noted, translations in brackets are by the editors; translations in parentheses or continuous with the text are by the critic. Publication information (such as publisher names and book prices) and parenthetical numerical references (such as footnotes or page and line references to specific editions of works) have been deleted at the editors' discretion to provide smoother reading of the text.

- Critical excerpts are prefaced by **annotations** providing the reader with information about both the critic and the criticism that follows. Included are the critic's reputation, individual approach to literary criticism, and particular expertise in an author's works. Also noted are the relative importance of a work of criticism, the scope of the excerpt, and the growth of critical controversy or changes in critical trends regarding an author. In some cases, these annotations cross-reference excerpts by critics who discuss each other's commentary.

- A complete **bibliographic citation** designed to facilitate location of the original essay or book follows each piece of criticism.

- An annotated list of **further reading** appearing at the end of each author entry suggests secondary sources on the author. In some cases it includes essays for which the editors could not obtain reprint rights.

Cumulative Indexes

- Each volume of *TCLC* contains a cumulative **author index** listing all authors who have appeared in Gale's Literary Criticism Series, along with cross-references to such biographical series as *Contemporary Authors* and *Dictionary of Literary Biography.* For readers' convenience, a complete list of Gale titles included appears on the first page of the author index. Useful for locating authors within the various series, this index is particularly valuable for those authors who are identified by a certain period but who, because of their death dates, are placed in another, or for those authors whose careers span two periods. For example, F. Scott Fitzgerald is found in *TCLC,* yet a writer often associated with him, Ernest Hemingway, is found in *CLC.*

- Each *TCLC* volume includes a cumulative **nationality index** which lists all authors who have appeared in *TCLC* volumes, arranged alphabetically under their respective nationalities, as well as Topics volume entries devoted to particular national literatures.

- Each new volume in Gale's Literary Criticism Series includes a cumulative **topic index,** which lists all literary topics treated in *NCLC, TCLC, LC 1400-1800,* and the *CLC* Yearbook.

- Each new volume of *TCLC,* with the exception of the Topics volumes, contains a **title index** listing the titles of all literary works discussed in the volume. In response to numerous suggestions from librarians, Gale has also produced a **special paperbound edition** of the *TCLC* title index. This annual cumulation lists all titles discussed in the series since its inception and is issued with the first volume of *TCLC* published each year. Additional copies of the index are available on request. Librarians and patrons will welcome this separate index: it saves shelf space, is easy to use, and is disposable upon receipt of the following year's cumulation. Titles discussed in the Topics volume entries are not included in the *TCLC* cumulative index.

A Note to the Reader

When writing papers, students who quote directly from any volume in Gale's Literary Criticism Series may use the following general forms to footnote reprinted criticism. The first example pertains to material drawn from periodicals, the second to material reprinted from books.

[1] T. S. Eliot, "John Donne," *The Nation and the Athenaeum,* 33 (9 June 1923), 321-32; excerpted and reprinted in *Literature Criticism from 1400 to 1800,* Vol. 10, ed. James E. Person, Jr. (Detroit: Gale Research, 1989), pp. 28-9.

[2] Clara G. Stillman, *Samuel Butler: A Mid-Victorian Modern* (Viking Press, 1932); excerpted and reprinted in *Twentieth-Century Literary Criticism,* Vol. 33, ed. Paula Kepos (Detroit: Gale Research, 1989), pp. 43-5.

Suggestions Are Welcome

In response to suggestions, several features have been added to *TCLC* since the series began, including annotations to excerpted criticism, a cumulative index to authors in all Gale literary criticism series, entries devoted to criticism on a single work by a major author, more extensive illustrations, and a title index listing all literary works discussed in the series since its inception.

Readers who wish to suggest authors or topics to appear in future volumes, or who have other suggestions, are cordially invited to write the editors.

Acknowledgments

The editors wish to thank the copyright holders of the excerpted criticism included in this volume, the permission managers of many book and magazine publishing companies for assisting us in securing reprint rights, and Anthony Bogucki for assistance with copyright research. We are also grateful to the staffs of the Detroit Public Library, Wayne State University Purdy/Kresge Library Complex, and the University of Michigan Libraries for making their resources available to us. Following is a list of the copyright holders who have granted us permission to reprint material in this volume of *TCLC*. Every effort has been made to trace copyright, but if omissions have been made, please let us know.

COPYRIGHTED EXCERPTS IN *TCLC*, VOLUME 44, WERE REPRINTED FROM THE FOLLOWING PERIODICALS:

American Literary Realism 1870-1910, v. XIII, Autumn, 1980. Copyright © 1980 by the Department of English, The University of Texas at Arlington. Reprinted by permission of the publisher.—*The Armchair Detective,* v. 17, Fall, 1984. Copyright © 1984 by *The Armchair Detective.* Reprinted by permission of the publisher.—*Books Abroad,* v. 42, Summer, 1968. Copyright 1968 by the University of Oklahoma Press. Reprinted by permission of the publisher.—*The Christian Century,* v. LXXIV, April 24, 1957. Copyright 1957, renewed 1985 Christian Century Foundation. Reprinted by permission from *The Christian Century.*—*Discourse: A Review of the Liberal Arts,* v. IX, Autumn, 1966 for "The Role of the Theological, Themes in Thomas Mann's 'Dr. Faustus' " by John Peterson. © 1966 Concordia College. Reprinted by permission of the author.—*The Durham University Journal,* v. LXXX, December, 1987. Reprinted by permission of the publisher.—*The Gypsy Scholar,* v. 7, Winter, 1980 for "Ambrose Bierce: The Esthetics of a Derelict Romance" by Brad Hayden. Copyright 1980 by *The Gypsy Scholar.* Reprinted by permission of the author.—*ICLA Congress Proceedings,* v. 23, 1959 for "The Chalk Circle: A Legend in Four Cultures" by E. F. C. Ludowyck. Copyright 1959, renewed 1987 The University of North Carolina Press. Reprinted by permission of the publisher.—*The Iowa Review,* v. 8, Winter, 1972 for "The Problem of Language in 'Miss Lonelyhearts' " by Jeffrey L. Duncan. Copyright © 1972 by The University of Iowa. Reprinted by permission of the publisher and the author.—*The Journal of Aesthetics and Art Criticism,* v. XXXI, Fall, 1972. Copyright © 1972 by The American Society for Aesthetics. Reprinted by permission of the publisher.—*Journal of Popular Culture,* v. 15, Fall, 1981. Copyright © 1981 by Ray B. Browne. Reprinted by permission of the publisher.—*Literature and Psychology,* v. XXXIII, 1987. Copyright © Literature and Psychology, 1987. Reprinted by permission of the publisher.—*Melbourne Slavonic Studies,* n. 2, 1968. Reprinted by permission of the publisher.—*Modern Languages,* v. LIII, March, 1972. Reprinted by permission of the publisher.—*The Modern Language Review,* v. 76, July, 1981, for "From Individual To Universal: Tolstoy's 'Smert' Ivana Il'icha' " by Robert Russell. © Modern Humanities Research Association 1981. Reprinted by permission of the publisher and the author.—*The New Criterion,* v. V, October, 1986 for "The Worldly and Unworldly Fortunes of Rose Macaulay" by Gloria G. Fromm. Copyright © 1986 by The Foundation for Cultural Review. Reprinted by permission of the author.—*New York Herald Tribune Books,* April 24, 1927, April 30, 1933. Copyright 1927, renewed 1955; copyright 1933, renewed 1961, *The Washington Post.* Both reprinted with permission of the publisher.—*The New York Times Book Review,* October 31, 1920, October 27, 1929. Copyright 1920, renewed 1948; copyright 1929, renewed 1957 by The New York Times Company. Both reprinted by permission of the publisher.—*Panorama of Czech Literature,* v. 9, 1987.—*Prairie Schooner,* v. XXXIV, Spring, 1960. © 1960 by University of Nebraska Press. Reprinted from *Prairie Schooner* by permission of the Univeristy of Nebraska Press.—*Slavic and East-European Journal,* v. 23, Winter, 1979; v. 30, Spring, 1986. © 1979, 1986 by AATSEEL of the U.S., Inc. Both reprinted by permission of the publisher.—*The Southern Review,* Louisiana State University, v. V, Spring, 1969 for " 'Art at the Edge of Impossibility': Mann's 'Dr. Fautus' by Joyce Carol Oates. Copyright, 1969, by Louisiana State University. Reprinted by permission of the author.—*Studies in Short Fiction,* v. 21, Summer, 1984. Copyright 1984 by Newberry College. Reprinted by permission of the publisher.—*Twentieth Century Literature,* v. 33, Spring, 1987. Copyright 1987, Hofstra University Press. Reprinted by permission of the publisher.

COPYRIGHTED EXCERPTS IN *TCLC*, VOLUME 44, WERE REPRINTED FROM THE FOLLOWING BOOKS:

Aaron, Daniel. From "Ambrose Bierce and the American Civil War," in *Uses of Literature.* Edited by Monroe Engel. Cambridge, Mass.: Harvard University Press, 1973. Copyright © 1973 by the President and Fellows of Har-

of the publisher.—Usborne, Richard. From *Clubland Heroes: A Nostalgic Study of Some Recurrent Characters in the Romantic Fiction of Dornford Yates, John Buchan and Sapper.* Revised edition. Barrie & Jenkins Limited, 1974. Copyright © Richard Usborne, 1953, 1974. All rights reserved. Reprinted by permission of the publisher.—Walker, Janet A. From *The Japanese Novel of the Meiji Period and the Ideal of Individualism.* Princeton University Press, 1979. Copyright © 1979 by Princeton University Press. All rights reserved. Reprinted by permission of the publisher.—Wasiolek, Edward. From *Tolstoy's Major Fiction.* The University of Chicago Press, 1978. © 1978 by The University of Chicago. All rights reserved. Reprinted by permission of the publisher.—Watson, Colin. From *Snobbery with Violence: Crime Stories and Their Audience.* Eyre & Spottiswoode (Publishers) Ltd., 1971. Copyright © 1971 Colin Watson. All rights reserved. Reprinted by permission of John Farquharson Ltd (New York). In Canada by Methuen London.—Widmer, Kingsley. From *Nathanael West.* Twayne, 1982. Copyright © 1982 by G. K. Hall & Company. All rights reserved. Reprinted with the permission of Twayne Publishers, an imprint of Macmillan Publishing Company.—Wilson, Christopher P. From *The Labor of Words: Literary Professionalism in the Progressive Era.* University of Georgia Press, 1985. © 1985 by the University of Georgia Press. All rights reserved. Reprinted by permission of the publisher.—Yamanouchi, Hisaaki. From *The Search for Authenticity in Modern Japanese Literature.* Cambridge University Press, 1978. © Cambridge University Press 1978. Reprinted with the permission of the publisher.

PHOTOGRAPHS AND ILLUSTRATIONS APPEARING IN *TCLC*, VOLUME 44, WERE RECEIVED FROM THE FOLLOWING SOURCES:

The Bettmann Archive: **pp. 10, 54, 325;** AP/Wide World Photos: **pp. 64, 203;** Dr. Gustav Wieszner, Nuremberg: **p. 110;** Photograph by Roloff Beny: **p. 114;** Thomas Mann Archive, Zurich, Switzerland: **pp. 143, 151, 182;** Foto CTK: **p. 236;** Courtesy of Otto Penzler: **p. 305;** Cover of *The Death of Ivan Ilych, and Other Stories,* by Leo Tolstoy, translated by Aylmer Maude and J. D. Duff. New American Library, 1960. Translation copyright. Used by permission of New American Library, a division of Penguin Books USA Inc.: **p. 347;** Engraving by David Schorr: **p. 411.**

Ambrose Bierce

1842-1914?

(Full name Ambrose Gwinnett Bierce; also wrote under the pseudonyms Dod Grile and William Herman) American short story writer, journalist, poet, essayist, and critic.

For further information on Bierce's career, see *TCLC,* Volumes 1 and 7.

INTRODUCTION

Bierce's literary reputation is based primarily on his short stories of the Civil War and of the supernatural, most prominently "An Occurrence at Owl Creek Bridge," "Chickamauga," and "The Death of Halpin Frayser." Often compared to the tales of Edgar Allan Poe, Bierce's stories share a similar attraction to death in its more bizarre forms: they feature uncanny manifestations and depictions of mental deterioration, and express the horror of existence in a meaningless universe. Like Poe, Bierce was concerned with the pure artistry of his work; at the same time he was intent on conveying his personal attitudes of misanthropy and pessimism.

Bierce was born in Meigs County, Ohio. His parents were farmers, and he was the tenth of thirteen children, all of whom were given names beginning with "A." In 1846 the family moved to Indiana, where Bierce attended primary and secondary school. He entered the Kentucky Military Institute in 1859, and at the outbreak of the Civil War enlisted in the Union army, serving in such units as the Ninth Indiana Infantry Regiment and Buell's Army of the Ohio. Bierce fought bravely and extensively in numerous military engagements, including the battles of Shiloh and Chickamauga and in Sherman's March to the Sea. After the war Bierce traveled with a military expedition to San Francisco, where he left the army in 1867.

Bierce's early poetry and prose appeared in the *Californian* magazine. In 1868 he was hired as the editor of the *News Letter,* for which he wrote his famous "Town Crier" column. Bierce became something of a noted figure in California literary society, establishing friendships with Mark Twain, Bret Harte, and Joaquin Miller. In 1872 Bierce moved to England, where during a three-year stay he wrote for *Fun* and *Figaro* magazines and acquired the nickname "Bitter Bierce." His first three books of sketches, *Nuggets and Dust Panned Out in California, The Fiend's Delight,* and *Cobwebs from an Empty Skull,* were published during this period. He returned to San Francisco and worked in a government mint office for one year before becoming associate editor of the *Argonaut* in 1877. Bierce worked for a mining company in South Dakota for two years, but he returned in 1881 to become editor of the weekly *Wasp.* In 1887 Bierce began writing for William Randolph Hearst's *San Francisco Examiner,* continuing

the "Prattler" column he had done for the *Argonaut* and the *Wasp.* This provided him with a regular outlet for his essays, epigrams, and many of the short stories subsequently collected in *Tales of Soldiers and Civilians* in 1891 and *Can Such Things Be?* in 1893. A committed opponent of hypocrisy, prejudice, and corruption, Bierce acquired fame as a journalist, becoming an admired but often hated public figure, a man of contradiction and mystery. In 1914 he informed some of his correspondents that he intended to travel to Mexico and join Pancho Villa's forces as an observer during that country's civil war. He was never heard from again, and the circumstances of his death are uncertain.

Bierce's major fiction was collected in *Can Such Things Be?* and *Tales of Soldiers and Civilians.* Many of his stories draw upon his experiences in the Civil War, earning him a reputation as a realistic author of war fiction. However, Bierce was not striving for documentary realism, as critics have pointed out and as he himself admitted, for his narratives often fail to supply sufficient verisimilitude. Rather, Bierce focused on the adept manipulation of the reader's viewpoint: a bloody battlefield seen through the eyes of a deaf child in "Chickamauga," the deceptive escape dreamed by a man about to be hanged in "An Occurrence at Owl Creek Bridge," and the shifting perspectives of "The Death of Halpin Frayser." The structure of Bierce's tales commonly hinges on an ironic, surprise conclusion; as Alfred Kazin has noted, "There is invariably a sudden reversal, usually in a few lines near the end, that takes the story away from the reader, as it were, that overthrows his confidence in the nature of what he has been reading, that indeed overthrows his confidence." Similarly Bierce's tales of the supernatural often feature unexpected conclusions that allow the events of the narrative to be interpreted as both the effect of a supernatural agency and the result of hallucination or other psychological phenomena. In *The Devil's Dictionary,* a lexicon of its author's witticisms, Bierce defines *Ghost* as "the outward and visible sign of an inward fear"—clarifying his fundamentally psychological approach to the supernatural. For instance, the eponymous protagonist of "The Death of Halpin Frayser" dies on his mother's grave either by the hand of her widowed husband or in a symbolic, mysterious struggle with the ghost of his mother. Critics have maintained that "An Occurrence at Owl Creek Bridge" plumbs the depths of a condemned man's psyche during execution; though ostensibly a war story, it is sometimes included in supernatural anthologies for its depiction of abnormal phenomenon and has been cited as an early and significant exploration of psychology in fiction.

Bierce's narrative methods have sometimes caused critics to view his works as little more than technical exercises. "Too many of his stories," David Weimer has stated, "lean heavily on crafty mechanics, on a kind of literary gadgeteering." Yet, according to H. E. Bates, the structure of Bierce's stories is significant because "Bierce began to shorten the short story; he began to bring to it a sharper, more compressed method: the touch of impressionism." In addition, Bierce's stories typically display a marked use of black humor, particularly in the ironic deaths the characters often suffer. For example, several stories center on a protagonist who, through a confusion of identities or circumstances, is responsible for the murder of a beloved family member. While critics have both condemned and praised Bierce's imagination, along with Poe's, as among the most vicious and morbid in American literature, his works are counted among the most memorable depictions of human existence as a precarious, ironic, and often futile condition.

PRINCIPAL WORKS

Nuggets and Dust Panned Out in California [as Dod Grile] (sketches) 1872

The Fiend's Delight [as Dod Grile] (sketches) 1873

Cobwebs from an Empty Skull [as Dod Grile] (sketches) 1874

The Dance of Death [with Thomas A. Harcourt under the joint pseudonym of William Herman] (satire) 1877

Tales of Soldiers and Civilians (short stories) 1891; published in England as *In the Midst of Life,* 1892

Black Beetles in Amber (poetry) 1892

The Monk and the Hangman's Daughter [translator; with Gustav Adolph Danzinger] (novel) 1892

Can Such Things Be? (short stories) 1893

Fantastic Fables (satire) 1899

Shapes of Clay (poetry) 1903

The Cynic's Word Book (satire) 1906; also published as *The Devil's Dictionary,* 1911

The Shadow on the Dial, and Other Essays (essays) 1909

The Collected Works of Ambrose Bierce. 12 vols. (short stories, sketches, poetry, essays, and satire) 1912

Frederic Taber Cooper (essay date 1911)

[*Cooper was an American educator, biographer, and critic. In the following excerpt, he discusses Bierce as a critic, satirist, and short story writer.*]

In the preface to the fourth volume of his collected works, the volume containing under the title of **Shapes of Clay** the major portion of purely personal satiric verse, Mr. Ambrose Bierce emphatically expresses his belief in the right of any author "to have his fugitive work in newspapers and periodicals put into a more permanent form during his lifetime if he can." No one is likely to dispute Mr. Bierce's contention; but it is often a grave question how far it is wise for the individual to exercise his inalienable rights. And in the case of authors the question comes down to this: How far is it to their own best interests to dilute their finer and more enduring work with that which is mediocre and ephemeral? For it is unfortunately true that no author is measured by his high lights alone, but by the resultant impression of blended light and shade; and there is many a writer among the recognized classics who to-day would take a higher rank had a kindly and discriminating fate assigned three-quarters of his life-work to a merciful oblivion.

To the student of American letters, however, the comprehensive edition of Ambrose Bierce's writings recently issued in ten portly and well-made volumes cannot fail to be welcome. It places at once within convenient reach a great mass of material which, good, bad or indifferent, as the case may be, all helps to throw suggestive side lights upon the author, his methods and his outlook upon life. It forces the reader who perchance has hitherto known Mr. Bierce solely as a master of the short story, to realize that this part of his work has been, throughout a long and busy life, a sort of side issue and that the great measure of his activities has been expended upon social and political satire. And similarly, those who have known him best as the fluent producer of stinging satiric verse suddenly recognize how versatile and many-sided are his literary gifts. The ten volumes are divided as follows: three volumes of prose fiction; two volumes of satiric verse; two volumes of literary and miscellaneous essays; and three volumes consisting mainly of satiric prose, including a greatly amplified edition of that curiously caustic piece of irony, **The Cynic's Word Book,** now for the first time published under the title of Mr. Bierce's own choosing, **The**

Devil's Dictionary. It seems, therefore, most convenient to consider Mr. Bierce, the Man of Letters, under three separate aspects: the Critic, the Satirist and the Master of the Short Story.

Regarding literary criticism, Mr. Bierce says quite frankly "the saddest thing about the trade of writing is that the writer can never know, nor hope to know, if he is a good workman. In literary criticism, there are no criteria, no accepted standards of excellence by which to test the work." Now there is just enough truth in this attitude of mind to make it a rather dangerous one. If there were literally no accepted standards in any of the arts, no principles to which a certain influential majority of critical minds had given their adhesion, then literature and all the arts would be in a state of perennial anarchy. But of course any writer who believes in his heart that there are no criteria will necessarily remain in lifelong ignorance regarding his own worth; for it is only through learning how to criticise others sanely and justly that one acquires even the rudiments of self-criticism. And incidentally, it may be observed that no better proof of Mr. Bierce's fundamental lack of this valuable asset could be asked than the retention in these ten volumes of a considerable amount of journalistic rubbish side by side with flashes of undoubted genius. Mr. Bierce's entire essay on the subject of criticism is a sort of literary agnosticism, a gloomy denial of faith. He has no confidence in the judgment of the general public nor in that of the professional critic. He admits that "in a few centuries, more or less, there may arrive a critic that we call 'Posterity' "; but Posterity, he complains, is a trifle slow. Accordingly, since the worth of any contemporary writer is reduced to mere guesswork, he, Ambrose Bierce, has scant use for his contemporaries. He has very definite ideas regarding the training of young writers and tells us at some length the course through which he would like to put an imaginary pupil, but he adds:

> If I caught him reading a newly published book, save by way of penance, it would go hard with him. Of our modern education he should have enough to read the ancients: Plato, Aristotle, Marcus Aurelius, Seneca and that lot— custodians of most of what is worth knowing.

In spite of the pains to which Mr. Bierce goes to deny that he is a *laudator temporis acti,* the term fits him admirably—and nowhere is this attitude of mind more conspicuous than in his treatment of the modern novel. It is important, however, to get clearly in mind the arbitrary sense in which he uses the word novel as distinguished from what he chooses to call romance. His occasional half-definitions are somewhat confusing; but apparently by the novel he means realistic fiction as distinguished from romantic fiction—a distinction complicated by the further idiosyncrasy that by realism he understands almost exclusively the commonplaces of actuality and by romanticism any happening which is out of the ordinary. The novel, then, in his sense of the word is "a snow plant; it has no root in the permanent soil of literature, and does not long hold its place; it is of the lowest form of imagination." And again: "The novel bears the same relation to literature that the panorama bears to painting; with whatever skill and feeling the panorama is painted, it must lack that basic quality in all art, unity, totality of effect." He seems utterly unaware that the great gain in modern fiction, the one indisputable factor that separates it from the fiction of half a century ago, is precisely the basic quality of unity. The modern novel whose technique most nearly approaches perfection is the one which when read rapidly with "a virgin attention at a single sitting"—to borrow Mr. Bierce's own phrase—gives an impression of as single-hearted a purpose as one finds in the most faultless of Maupassant's three-thousand-word masterpieces. It is quite possible for any well-trained reader to go through even the longest of novels at a single sitting. The present writer would feel himself grievously at fault if he interrupted his first reading of any novel that had been given him for the purpose of review; and he well remembers that in only two recent cases did he become conscious of the prolonged strain: namely, Mr. Kipling's *Kim,* which required an uninterrupted attention of eight and one-half hours, and *The Golden Bowl,* of Mr. James, which required somewhat more than eleven. Mr. Bierce's attitude, however, is partly explained by his *obiter dictum* that "no man who has anything else to do can critically read more than two or three books in a month"—and of course, if you are going to allow an average of ten days to a book, the most perfect unity of purpose is inevitably going to drop out of sight.

All of this helps us to understand how it happens that Mr. Bierce, otherwise a man of intelligence, can say in all seriousness that "in England and America the art of novel writing is as dead as Queen Anne." Listen also to the following literary blasphemy:

> So far as I am able to judge, no good novels are now "made in Germany," nor in France, nor in any European country except Russia. The Russians are writing novels which so far as one may venture to judge . . . are in their way admirable; full of fire and light, like an opal . . . ; in their hands the novel grew great—as it did in those of Richardson and Fielding, and as it would have done in those of Thackeray and Pater if greatness in that form of fiction had been longer possible in England.

Or again:

> Not only is the novel . . . a faulty form of art, but because of its faultiness it has no permanent place in literature. In England it flourished less than a century and a half, beginning with Richardson and ending with Thackeray, since whose death no novels, probably, have been written that are worth attention.

Think for a moment what this means. Here is a man who has ventured to speak seriously about the modern novel, and who confessedly is unaware of the importance of Trollope and Meredith and Hardy, of Henry James and Rudyard Kipling and Maurice Hewlett—and who deliberately ignores the existence of Flaubert and Maupassant and Zola, Galdos and Valdés, Verga and d'Annunzio! It is not astonishing after that to find Mr. Bierce seriously questioning the value of epic poetry: "What more than they gave," he asks, "might we not have had from Virgil (*sic*), Dante, Tasso, Camoëns and Milton, if they had not found the epic poem ready to their misguided hands?"

The fact is that Mr. Bierce as a critic is of the iconoclastic variety. He breaks down but does not build up. He has no patience with the historical form of criticism that traces the intellectual genealogy of authorship, showing, for instance, Maupassant's debt to Poe or Bourget's debt to Stendhal. He is equally intolerant of that analytical method—the fairest of them all—that judges every written work by its author's purpose as nearly as this may be read between the lines. Nothing is more certain, he says, than if a writer of genius should bring to his task the purposes which the critics trace in the completed work, "the book would remain forever unwritten, to the unspeakable advantage of letters and morals." Yes, he tears down the recognized methods of criticism but suggests nothing better in their place. And when he himself undertakes to to criticise, it is hardly ever for the purpose of paying tribute to excellence—with the noteworthy exception, *mirabile dictu,* of his extraordinary praise of George Stirling's poetic orgy of words, "The Wine of Wizardry." Tolstoy, for instance, he defines as a literary giant: "He has a giant's strength and has unfortunately learned to use it like a giant—which means not necessarily with conscious cruelty, but with stupidity." The journal of Marie Bashkirtseff—the last book on earth that one would expect Mr. Bierce to discuss—he sums up as "morbid, hysterical and unpleasant beyond anything of its kind in literature." Among modern critics he pronounces Mr. Howells "the most mischievous, because the ablest, of all this sycophantic crew."

The truth is that the value of Mr. Bierce as a critic lies solely in his fearlessness and downright sincerity, his unswerving conviction that he is right. He has to a rather greater extent than many a better critic the quality of consistency; and no matter how widely we are forced to disagree with his conclusions there is not one of them that does not throw an interesting side light upon Mr. Bierce, the man.

The short stories and the serious critical papers of Mr. Bierce have appeared in a spasmodic and desultory way, but from first to last he has been at heart a satirist of the school of Lucilius and Juvenal, eager to scourge the follies and the foibles of mankind at large. The fact that Mr. Bierce is absolutely in earnest, that he is destitute of fear and confessedly incorruptible accounts for the oft-repeated statement that he was for years the best loved and the most hated man on the Pacific Coast. Now the ability to use a stinging lash of words is all very well in itself; it is a gift that is none too common. But to be effective it must not be used too freely. The two ample volumes of Mr. Bierce's poetical invectives form a striking object lesson of the wisdom in Hamlet's contention that unless you treat men better than they deserve none will escape a whipping. And when fresh from a perusal of the contents of **Shapes of Clay** and **Black Beetles in Amber,** one has become so accustomed to seeing men flayed alive that a whole skin possesses something of a novelty. Now there is no question that there is a good deal wrong with the world, just as there always has been, if one takes the trouble to look for it. But when any one man takes upon himself the task of reprimanding the universe, it is not unreasonable that we should ask ourselves in the first instance:

What manner of man is this? What are his standards and beliefs? And, if he had his way, what new lamps would he give us in place of the old? In the case of Mr. Bierce it is a little difficult to make answer with full assurance. Somewhere in his preface he has said that he has not attempted to classify his writings under the separate heads of serious, ironical, humorous and the like, assuming that his readers have sufficient intelligence to recognize the difference for themselves. But this is not always easy to do, because in satire these different qualities and moods overlap each other so that there is always the danger of taking too literally what is really an ironical exaggeration. Here, however, is a rather significant passage taken from a serious essay entitled **"To Train a Writer"**; it sets forth the convictions and the general attitude toward life which Mr. Bierce believes are essential to any young author before he can hope for success—and it is only fair to infer that they represent his own personal views:

> He should, for example, forget that he is an American and remember that he is a Man. He should be neither Christian nor Jew, nor Buddhist, nor Mahometan, nor Snake Worshiper. To local standards of right and wrong he should be civilly indifferent. In the virtues, so called, he should discern only the rough notes of a general expediency; in fixed moral principles only time-saving predecisions of cases not yet before the court of conscience. Happiness should disclose itself to his enlarging intelligence as the end and purpose of life; art and love as the only means to happiness. He should free himself of all doctrines, theories, etiquettes, politics, simplifying his life and mind, attaining clarity with breadth and unity with height. To him a continent should not seem wide, nor a century long. And it would be needful that he know and have an ever-present consciousness that this is a world of fools and rogues, blind with superstition, tormented with envy, consumed with vanity, selfish, false, cruel, cursed with illusions—frothing mad!

Now this strikes the average fair-minded person as a rather wholesale indictment of what on the whole has proved to be a pretty good world to live in. In fact, it is difficult to conceive of any one honestly and literally holding so extreme a view and yet of his own volition remaining in such an unpleasant place any longer than the time required to obtain the amount of gunpowder or strychnine sufficient for an effective exit. But of course Mr. Bierce does not find life half so unpleasant as he professes: in fact, he gives the impression of hugely enjoying himself by voluntarily looking out upon a world grotesquely distorted by the lenses of his imagination. He has of course a perfect right to have as much or as little faith as he chooses in any human religion or philosophy, moral doctrine or political code—only it is well when studying Mr. Bierce as a satirist and reformer to understand clearly his limitations in this respect and to discount his view accordingly. It is well, for instance, to keep in mind, when reading some of his scathing lines directed at small offenders who at most have left the world not much worse off for having lived in it, that Mr. Bierce once eulogized that wholesale destroyer of faith, Robert Ingersoll, as: "a man who taught all the virtues as a duty and a delight—who stood, as no other man among his countrymen has stood, for liberty, for honor, for good will toward men, for truth as it was given him to see it."

To the present writer there is much that is keenly irritating in Mr. Bierce's satiric verse for the reasons above implied. It is, of course, highly uncritical to find fault with a writer for no better reason than because you find yourself out of harmony with his religious and moral faith, or his lack of it—for an author's personal beliefs should have no bearing upon the artistic value of what he produces. But putting aside personal prejudice, it may be said in all fairness that Mr. Bierce made a mistake in giving a permanent form to so large a body of his fugitive verses. It is not quite true that satiric poetry is read with the same interest after the people at whom it was directed are forgotten. Aristophanes and Horace and Juvenal cannot be greatly enjoyed to-day without a good deal of patient delving for the explanation of local and temporal allusions; and in modern times Pope's *Dunciad,* for instance, is probably to-day the least important and the least read of all his writings. It is impossible to take much interest in vitriolic attacks made twenty years ago upon various obscure Californians whose names mean nothing at all to the world at large. But, on the other hand, any one can understand and enjoy the sweeping irony as well as the sheer verbal cleverness of a parody like the following:

A Rational Anthem

My country, 'tis of thee,
Sweet land of felony,
   Of thee I sing—
Land where my fathers fried
Young witches and applied
Whips to the Quaker's hide
   And made him spring.

My knavish country, thee,
Land where the thief is free,
   Thy laws I love;
I love thy thieving bills
That tap the people's tills;
I love thy mob whose will's
   All laws above.

Let Federal employees
And rings rob all they please,
   The whole year long.
Let office-holders make
Their piles and judges rake
Our coin. For Jesus' sake,
   Let's *all* go wrong!

One is tempted to devote considerably more space than is warranted to that extremely clever collection of satiric definitions, *The Devil's Dictionary.* It represents a deliberate pose consistently maintained, it is pervaded with a spirit of what a large proportion of readers in a Christian country would pronounce irreverent, it tells us nothing new and can hardly be conceived of as an inspiration for higher and nobler living. But it is undeniably entertaining reading. Almost any one must smile over such specimens as the following, taken almost at random:

> MONDAY, *n.* In Christian countries, the day
> after the baseball game.

> BACCHUS, *n.* A convenient deity invented by the
> ancients as an excuse for getting drunk.
> POSITIVE, *adj.* Mistaken at the top of one's
> voice.

But it is as a writer of short stories that Mr. Bierce's future fame rests upon a firm foundation. It is not too much to say that within his own chosen field—the grim, uncompromising horror story, whether actual or supernatural—he stands among American writers second only to Edgar Allan Poe. And this is all the more remarkable when we consider his expressed scorn of new books and modern methods and his implied indifference to the development of modern technique. He does understand and consciously seeks for that unity of effect which is the foundation stone of every good short story; yet in sheer technical skill there is scarcely one among the recognized masters of the short story to-day, Mr. Kipling, for instance, and the late O. Henry, Jack London and a score of his contemporaries, from whom he might not learn something to his profit. What Mr. Bierce's habits of workmanship may be the present writer does not happen to know; it is possible that he has always striven as hard to build an underlying structure, a preliminary scaffolding, for each story as ever Edgar Allan Poe did. But if so he has been singularly successful in practising the art which so artfully all things conceals. He gives the impression of one telling a story with a certain easy spontaneity and attaining his results through sheer instinct. He seldom attempts anything like a unity of time and place; and many of his short tales have the same fault which he criticises in the modern novel: namely, that of having a panoramic quality, of being shown to us in a succession of more or less widely separated scenes and incidents.

Nevertheless, in most cases his stories are their own best justification. We may not agree with the method that he has chosen to use, but we cannot escape from the strange, haunting power of them, the grim, boding sense of their having happened—even the most weird, most supernatural, most grotesquely impossible of them—in precisely the way that he has told them.

The stories, such of them at least as really count and represent Mr. Bierce at his best, divide themselves into two groups: first, the Civil War stories, based upon his own four years' experience as a soldier during the Rebellion, and unsurpassed in American fiction for the unsparing clearness of their visualization of war. And secondly, the frankly supernatural stories contained in the volume entitled *Can Such Things Be?*—stories in which the setting is immaterial because if *such things could be* they would be independent of time and space. The war stories range through the entire gamut of heroism, suffering and carnage. They are stamped in all their physical details with a pitiless realism unequaled by Stendhal in the famous Waterloo episode in the *Chartreuse de Parme* and at least unsurpassed by Tolstoy or by Zola. Indeed, there is nothing fulsome or extravagant in the statement that has more than once been made that Mr. Bierce is a sort of American Maupassant. And what is most remarkable about these stories is that they never fail of a certain crescendo effect. Keyed as they are to a high pitch of human tragedy, there is always one last turn of the screw, one crowning horror held in reserve until the crucial moment. Take, for example, **"A Horseman in the Sky."** A sentinel whose duty it is to watch from a point of vantage overlooking a deep gorge and a vast plain beyond, to see that no scout of the Southern army shall discover a trail down the precipitous sides of the opposite slope, suddenly perceives a solitary horseman making his way along the verge of the precipice within easy range of fire. The sentinel watches and hesitates; takes aim and delays his fire. The scene shifts with the disconcerting suddenness of a modern moving picture and we see the sentinel back in his Southern home at the outbreak of the war; and we overhear the controlled bitterness of his parting with his Southern father after declaring his intention to fight for the Union. A modern story teller would consider this shifting of scene bad art; nevertheless, Mr. Bierce, in theatrical parlance, "gets it over." Back again he shifts us with a rush to the lonely horseman, shows him for a moment motionless upon the brink and the next instant launched into space, a wonderful, miraculous, awe-inspiring figure, proudly erect upon a stricken and dying horse, whose legs spasmodically continue their mad gallop throughout the downward flight to the inevitable annihilation below. This in itself, told with Ambrose Bierce's compelling art, is sufficiently harrowing, but he has something more in reserve. Listen to this:

"Did you fire?" the sergeant whispered.

"Yes."

"At what?"

"A horse. It was standing on yonder rock—pretty far out. You see it is no longer there. It went over the cliff."

The man's face was white, but he showed no other signs of emotion. Having answered, he turned away his eyes and said no more. The sergeant did not understand.

"See here, Druce," he said, after a moment's silence, "it's no use making a mystery. I order you to report. Was there anybody on the horse?"

"Yes."

"Well?"

"My father."

And again, there is that extraordinary *tour de force* entitled **"An Occurrence at Owl Creek Bridge."** It is the story of a spy caught and about to be hanged by the simple expedient of allowing the board on which he stands to tilt up and drop him between the cross-beams of the bridge. The story is of considerable length. It details with singular and compelling vividness what follows from the instant that the spy feels himself dropped, feels the rope tighten around his neck and its fibers strain and snap under his weight. His plunge into the stream below, his dash for life under cover of the water, his flight, torn and bleeding, through thorns and brambles, his miraculous dodging of outposts and his passing unscathed through volleys of rapid fire, all read like a hideous nightmare—and so in fact they are, because the entire story of his rush for safety lasting long hours and days in reality is accomplished in a

mere fraction of time, the instant of final dissolution—because, as it happened, the rope did not break and at the moment that he thought he had attained safety his body ceased to struggle and dangled limply beneath the Owl Creek Bridge. Variations upon this theme of the rapidity of human thought in the moment of death are numerous. There is, for instance, a memorable story by Morgan Robertson called, if memory is not at fault, "From the Main Top," in which a lifetime is crowded into the fraction of time required for the action of gravity. But no one has ever used it more effectually than Mr. Bierce.

But it is in his supernatural stories that Mr. Bierce shows even more forcefully his wizardry of word and phrase, his almost magnetic power to make the absurd, the grotesque, the impossible, carry an overwhelming conviction. He will tell you, for instance, a story of a man watching at night alone by the dead body of an old woman; a cat makes its way into the room and springs upon the corpse; and to the man's overwrought imagination it seems as though that dead woman seized the cat by the neck and flung it violently from her. "Of course you imagined it," says the friend to whom he afterwards tells the tale. "I thought so, too," rejoins the man, "but the next morning her stiffened fingers still held a handful of black fur."

For sheer mad humor there is nothing more original than the tale called **"A Jug of Syrup."** A certain old and respected village grocer, who through a lengthy life has never missed a day at his desk, dies and his shop is closed. One night the village banker and leading citizen on his way home drops in from force of habit at the grocery, finding the door wide open, and buys a jug of syrup, absent-mindedly forgetting that the grocer who serves him has been dead three weeks. The jug is a heavy weight to carry; yet when he reaches home he has nothing in his hand. The tale spreads like wildfire through the village and the next night a vast throng is assembled in front of the brightly lit-up grocery, breathlessly watching the shadowy form of the deceased methodically casting up accounts. One by one, they pluck up courage and make their way into the grocery—all but the banker. Riveted to the spot by the grotesque horror of the sight he stands and watches, while pandemonium breaks loose. To him in the road the shop is still brilliantly lighted but to those who have gone within it presents the darkness of eternal night and in their unreasoning fear they kick and scratch and bite and trample upon one another with the primordial savageness of the mob. And all the while the shadowy figure of the dead grocer continues undisturbed to balance his accounts.

It is a temptation to linger beyond all reason over one after another of these extraordinary and haunting imaginings, such for instance, as **"Moxon's Master,"** in which an inventor, having made a a mechanical chess-player, makes the mistake of beating it at the game and is promptly strangled to death by the revengeful puppet of his own creation. But it is impossible to do justice to all these stories separately and it remains only to single out one typical example in which perhaps he reached the very pinnacle of his strange fantastic genius, **"The Death of Halpin Frayser."** The theme of the story is this: it is sufficiently horrible to be confronted with a disembodied spirit, but there is one degree of horror beyond this, namely, to have to face the reanimated body of some one long dead from whom the soul has departed—because, so Mr. Bierce tells us, with the departure of the soul all natural affection, all kindliness has departed also, leaving only the base instincts of brutality and revenge. Now in the case of Halpin Frayser, it happens that the body which he is fated to encounter under these hideously unnatural conditions is that of his own mother; and in a setting as curiously and poetically unreal as any part of "Kubla Khan" he is forced to realize that this mother whom he had in life worshiped as she worshiped him is now, in spite of her undiminished beauty, a foul and bestial thing intent only upon taking his life. In all imaginative literature it would be difficult to find a parallel for this story in sheer, unadulterated hideousness.

Mr. Ambrose Bierce as a story teller can never achieve a wide popularity, at least among the Angle-Saxon race. His writings have too much the flavor of the hospital and the morgue. There is a stale odor of moldy cerements about them. But to the connoisseur of what is rare, unique and very perfect in any branch of fiction he must appeal strongly as one entitled to hearty recognition as an enduring figure in American letters. No matter how strongly he may offend individual convictions and prejudices with the flippant irreverence of his satiric writings, it is easy to forgive him all this and much more besides for the sake of any single one of a score or more of his best stories. (pp. 331-53)

Frederic Taber Cooper, "Ambrose Bierce," in his Some American Story Tellers, *1911. Reprint by Books for Libraries Press, 1968, pp. 331-53.*

Wilson Follett (essay date 1918)

[*In the following essay, Follett regards Bierce as a preeminent modern satirist whose talent has been largely unappreciated.*]

The historical function of Ambrose Bierce in American letters can be indicated by saying that he was the long inhibited, yet basic and inalienable, part of Mark Twain—a timely and adequate expression of the pessimistic misanthropy which at last, in *The Mysterious Stranger* and *What is Man?* found posthumous release from the speech-bound surveillance of a lifetime.

In setting down this observation I mean something more than a mere conceit, and something less than an actual comparison of personalities. What I wish to record is not any impression of a debt of influence or of inspiration owed by either great man to the other. Neither is supplementary to the other. But there is a sense, important to a grasp of the historical pertinence of both if not to æsthetic appreciation, in which they are complementary. Their generation—more or less distorted and belied in the work of either, since it led the one to suppress an important part of his attitude toward it, and the other to express his attitude chiefly in truculence—speaks to us with authoritative clarity from their combined achievement.

Mr. Van Wyck Brooks, whose recent admirable article in *The Dial* "On Creating a Usable Past," stops just short of suggesting a pragmatic method to match the pragmatic end sought, would perhaps agree that some fraction of that past usable in the present and in the future can be constructed out of the deliberate synthesis, in one's mind, of contemporary historical or literary phenomena so dissimilar, so utterly opposed, as Bierce and Clemens. What any age expresses to us with the most vivid immediacy is a series of contradictions, out of which we must manufacture our own unity unless we are to go without. The past of English letters embodies itself in pairs of contrasting names—Richardson, sentimentalist, and Fielding, satirist; Dickens, instinctive democrat, and Thackeray, instinctive snob (with a complicating contempt, it is true, for all snobbery less subtle than his own); Tennyson, provincial æsthete, and Browning, cosmopolitan humanist; Meredith, optimist of naturalism, and Hardy, pessimist of the same; and so on. And Ambrose Bierce, misanthropic ironist sticking to his trade, faithfully responsive to the conditions imposed on his temperament by his time, is by this law a natural coeval of Mark Twain, a born wit who chose on the whole to be a humorist, a disillusioned thinker who found it possible to let people imagine he was chuckling—or guffawing—sympathetically with them, while in truth he was laughing sardonically at them.

Now the usable past of Mr. Brooks's phrase, the only immediate American past which makes an adequate tradition for the creative liberalism of the present, is that richer and more untrammeled past, nonexistent in literal history, in which both authors would have been left free to be themselves without the penalty of losing their audience; in which Mark Twain could have signed as well as published *What is Man?* and published as well as written *The Mysterious Stranger*; in which Bierce need not have been driven to journalism, political muck-raking, and various sensational forms of modern knight-errantry to capture the attention of a public which simply ignored **"Ashes of the Beacon"** and *In the Midst of Life.* This past, had it existed, might have served both authors as an automatic corrective and balance-weight. Mark Twain would have been spared the seeming necessity of his enormous self-suppression and the cynicism of his outward contentment—the posture of an artist who found himself applauded for what he said, knowing that he would have been hissed if he had said what he meant; Ambrose Bierce would have been spared the extremity of his bitterness, which became that of a man who shrieks imprecations because no one will listen to his normal utterance. And Mr. Brooks need not have asked, among other like questions, "Why did Ambrose Bierce go wrong?"

"Our greatest humorists, including even Mark Twain," says Mr. H. L. Mencken in *A Book of Prefaces,* "have had to take protective coloration, whether willingly or unwillingly, from the prevailing ethical foliage, and so one finds them levelling their darts, not at the stupidities of the Puritan majority, but at the evidences of lessening stupidity in the anti-Puritan minority. In other words, they have done battle, not against, but *for* Philistinism." "For all our professed delight in and capacity for jocosity, we have produced so far but one genuine wit—Ambrose Bierce—and, save to a small circle, he remains unknown to-day." The genuineness of the wit is not more astounding than the smallness of the circle—a circle mainly, so far as I can find, of writers and artists, and containing very few members of the class of professional academic custodians of the accredited in letters. For example, the most elaborate cis-atlantic history of the short story, *The Short Story in English,* by Professor Henry Seidel Canby, reaches its hundred-thousandth word and the year 1907 without so much as the mention of Bierce's name, even among the appendixed "many below the best," though there are ten solid pages about Bret Harte and forty-three index references to him. This eminent representative of the "Puritan majority" on its academic side helps prove Mr. Mencken's case, and justify Mr. Mencken's rancor, when he says that "Bret Harte was certainly not the author of the best English stories of the nineteenth century, but it is a question whether, on the whole, his tales have not been the most widely read." When acknowledged authority sets out so frankly as this to turn criticism from a search for distinction into the recorded vote of a majority which reads Harte and is oblivious of Bierce, I do not see how we are to revile Mr. Mencken for naming us "a commonwealth of peasants and small traders, a paradise of the third-rate," and for saying that our national philosophy is "almost wholly unchecked by the more sophisticated and civilized ideas of an aristocracy."

It is the function of such more civilized ideas that Ambrose Bierce discharges in his generation; and nearly all of his most salient qualities derive their saliency from the fact that he who exhibited them was the aristocrat half extinguished in the mob, half inflamed by it. All that is most graceful in his acceptance of life and in his expression of it is a product of his innate aristocracy; and all that is most graceless, vociferous, exaggerated, and raucous is a product of the inflammation. For it is not given to the aristocrat to thrive on opposition. It is his business to be a graceful embodiment of a tradition that leaves him free for expression. As a malcontent, he does not shine: it is only the revolutionary who gains in dignity when he answers persecution with articulate protest. Even the satiric mode, in which Bierce mostly wrought and of which he remains the one great exemplar produced on this continent, is protest which has always depended for its success on the existence of aristocratic qualities—such as wit—in a shared, socialized form; like Meredith's "Comedy," satire has flourished only where there was a society, however small, of true distinction, in which ideas were at home and had free circulation.

But it was Ambrose Bierce's misfortune to be a satirist alone. His wit, the one brilliant display of its kind in America, and perhaps the most brilliant anywhere since Voltaire, coruscates almost in vacuo; and his animus against the existence of certain realities which he loathed tends more and more to become converted into animus against the non-existence of everything that he valued. Unlike the first Samuel Butler, he found no sharp social contrast to draw; all he could see in America was a perfect homogeneity of smugness; and therefore, like the second Samuel Butler, he was forced to create fictitious worlds to be the media for his criticism of the real one, as in **"Ashes**

of the Beacon" and **"The Land Beyond the Blow."** The struggle he reproduces is not that of folly against wisdom or of knavery against rectitude: it is simply that of knavery contending with folly for material spoils, in a world where everything else is crowded to the wall. He is the universal cynic.

Even in some of his best tales of the ghastly and the ghostly, such as **"The Death of Halpin Frayser," "Killed at Resaca,"** and **"A Baby Tramp,"** he steps out of the path of the story to belabor indiscriminately everything he can reach, in sentences like these: "Science had as many explanations as there were scientists who knew nothing about it"; "They had a child which they named Joseph and dearly loved, as was then the fashion among parents in all that region." In fact the most inartistic thing Bierce ever does, as a teller of tales, is to substitute his own plastered-on irony for the inherent irony of the nature of things; and too often he merely rasps where he would horrify. The one thing he seriously and sympathetically believes in is the artist's disinterested search for beauty; yet, because he saw this one thing as outlawed in the America he knew, his praise of it is constantly inverted into disgust and rage at its enemies. He rejects everything, becomes intellectually the most homeless man of our time. In **"Ashes of the Beacon,"** his satiric history of the decline and fall of America, in the form of "an historical monograph written in 4930" by a savant living under a monarchy, he riddles one after another the bases, the customs and institutions, the traditions and the hopes of our Western experiment in democracy—but he also riddles his own assumed point of view, for the posture of his imagined historian is one of bootlicking servility to a king. Under "self-government" the successful individual is a knave; under a government by authority imposed, he is a sycophant. This is the choice which Ambrose Bierce saw. But he did not take his choice: he despised and hated both halves of the alternative and got on as best he could with art and friendship.

Even of the struggle in which he had served gloriously and shed his own blood, he said in the end:

> I know what uniform I wore—
> O, that I knew which side I fought for!

He writes some of the most glorious pictures of battle in our language—witness the sketch called **"What I Saw of Antietam"**—and he also writes:

> . . . somewhat lamely the conception runs
> Of a brass-buttoned Jesus, firing guns.

He reviles Oscar Wilde; he writes an admirable defiance of the post-mortem critics of Ingersoll. By his mere aversions, you can prove him on the side of the strong against the weak, also on that of the weak against the strong; for Philistinism, and also against it; a friend of freedom, and a friend of tyrants. For his aversions cover everything.

> His eyes were so untrained and dim
> All politics, religions,
> Arts, sciences, appeared to him
> But modes of plucking pigeons.

A born fighter, he finds in his generation no hopeful cause clear enough or illustrious enough to claim all his fighting energy. Therefore he vents his rage on little things, such as the human liking for dogs, which he loathes as some men do snakes. And he comes out of all his lesser battles the perfect cynic, the complete misanthropist.

There is the threat of tragic unfulfillment in the very composition of the man: a mind of first-rate clarity encompassed by the mediocre and the futile, and achieving a stoic resignation, but mismated with a temperament to which resignation was forever impossible. Surveying life without illusion, he knew that his fighting was vain; being himself, he could but fight the harder. He was denied a great thing, the hope that his two aristocratic divinities, reason and beauty, could ever prevail with the mass of men. But he won, and kept, the greatest thing of all; for he knew that reason was reason whatever multitude preferred folly, and that beauty was beautiful whoever had no eyes in his head. History and his own make-up may partly have thwarted his utility as the social satirist of Philistia; but he paid in full the debt to himself.

It is in the fight for his own identity, and in the aristocratic graces thereby exhibited, that he becomes unsurpassed and, during our time, unequaled. We are all part of a regimen which puts its premium on our common qualities and subtly encourages us to sink our differences. Ambrose Bierce stood almost alone in holding that our individual non-conformity is the one thing worth expression, because through it alone can we make any contribution to the common stock. He fought for his differences; and the gaiety and gallantry of his onset restore to satire its old heroic kinship with knight-errantry and the personal duel. Our coldly intellectual modern charity for everything seemed to him sterile, noncreative; and if he is in one sense unmodern it is because, with Lucian and Juvenal, Dryden and Pope, Swift and Voltaire, he chose to explore the possibilities of hate as a form of creative energy. He is a magnificent barbarian in whom the joy of battle replaces the joy which other artists have taken in their fellow men. His hate is in itself excoriating, terrible, monstrous; his sense of life is, at its sweetest, bitter-sweet, and at its bitterest more bitter than gall. But, after all, the most momentous thing in him, and the most memorable, is an artist's exultation in his art, in the polish and the unique precision of his weapons, in the lightning gleam of his own sword of wit. The fact that he despises life pales before his joy in wreaking himself upon it. Even his personal victims seem not so much contemptible for what they are as admirably accommodating to have been there at all, exposing themselves to him.

In short, Ambrose Bierce is primarily and, I think, most permanently a certain quality of wit. And his embodiment of that quality is above all a style. His personal style has the species of greatness which is felt as much in a phrase as in a volume; he would have proved himself a great man if he had written nothing more than two or three titles such as *Cobwebs from an Empty Skull, Black Beetles in Amber,* and **"Ashes of the Beacon."** The marvel is that he can keep up for whole pages, chapters, essays, volumes this fusion of imagination with accuracy into a homogeneous distillate of sheer wit. His precision alone is a constantly recurring thrill. Literature expresses "the virtues

and other vices" of an age. Crime is "stupidiate of opportunity." A wind thunders in the chimney "like the sound of clods upon a coffin." A trivial utterance at a terrible moment makes the situation more ghastly, "as the fire of a cigar might light up a tomb." A certain commander is

> So brave that if his army got a beating
> None dared to face him when he was retreating.

The popular "godlets" of fiction are to Tolstoi as "slugs; their brilliant work is a shine of slime which dulls behind them even as they creep."

And consider, as a final example, what he has to say to these same "godlets"—"these little fellows, the so-called realists"—in affirmation of his own non-realistic creed:

> It is to him of widest knowledge, of deepest feeling, of sharpest observation and insight, that life is most crowded with figures of heroic stature, with spirits of dream, with demons of the pit, with graves that yawn in pathways leading to the light, with existences not of earth, both malign and benign—ministers of grace and ministers of doom. The truest eye is that which discerns the shadow and the portent, the dead hands reaching, the light that is the heart of the darkness, the sky "with dreadful faces thronged and fiery arms." The truest ear is that which hears
>
> Celestial voices to the midnight air,
> Sole, or responsive each to the other's note,
> Singing—
>
> not "their great Creator," but not a negro melody, either; no, nor the latest favorite of the drawingroom. In short, he to whom life is not picturesque, enchanting, astonishing, terrible, is denied the gift and faculty divine, and being no poet can write no prose.

This is the very organ-note of wit, whereas his epigrams are but its over-tones; they have the same relation to the fundamental that his several hundred "Fantastic Fables" have to ***The Monk and the Hangman's Daughter,*** or to his strange tales of the death which is everywhere in the midst of life. He has surface brilliance, but he has also depth; the gleams shine against a central glow, not against a darkness. The adequate symbol of all his other distinctions together is this distinction of style. Being, by his own definition, a poet, he wrote noble prose.

It is not his fault if there are few to understand that kind of nobility. It is his misfortune—and the more serious misfortune of those who do not understand. (pp. 49-52)

> *Wilson Follett, "America's Neglected Satirist," in* The Dial, *Vol. LXV, Chicago, July 18, 1918, pp. 49-52.*

Eric Partridge   (essay date 1927)

[*Partridge was an American educator and critic whose works include studies of Ben Jonson and Oscar Wilde. In the following essay, he surveys Bierce's work and finds his accomplishments highly undervalued.*]

> How many times, and during a period of how many years, must one's unexplainable obscurity

be pointed out to constitute fame? Not knowing, I am almost disposed to consider myself the most famous of authors. I have pretty nearly ceased to be "discovered," but my notoriety as an obscurian may be said to be world-wide and everlasting.

Those words occur in a letter written by Ambrose Bierce in 1908. Although the various terms of that declaration would now be stated less emphatically and although he is now fairly well known in the United States, yet comparatively few persons in England have read more than the two collections of short stories, while a surprising number have never heard of him. He found a place in Tauchnitz years ago.

His first three volumes were published in England; there have been several English editions of *In the Midst of Life,* a selection of his stories was made by Mr. A. J. A. Symons in 1925, an issue of *Can Such Things Be?* appeared in 1926; one of his military tales figured in the second series of *Selected English Short Stories.* English criticisms of his work are few, and the ball was set rolling by the *Anti-Philistine* (in which some of Bierce's fables and stories were reprinted) when, in 1897, its editor, one Cowley-Brown, launched him in a glowing eulogy tempered with regret. This was a "Periodical of Protest," which was described by a contemporary thus: "There are several big guns in the critical press of Great Britain, but none of them goes off with such a show of militant ardour, or with such a decided bang, as *The Anti-Philistine*"; unfortunately it ran for only four months. The cause of its cessation will probably be found to be the same with that of Cowley's failure to fulfil his project of publishing *Can Such Things Be?* Ten years later, Sir Arthur Conan Doyle, in that pleasant book, *Through the Open Door,* said of Bierce's short stories: "This man had (*sic*) a flavour quite his own, and was (*sic*) a great artist in his way." In 1909 Mr. Arnold Bennett, in an otherwise excellent review in *The New Age,* was responsible for one of those exaggerated statements which do the writer criticised more harm than good; this exaggeration has been quoted on the inside of the jacket covering the recent English edition of *Can Such Things Be?* Mr. Harold Williams accorded Bierce a paragraph in *Modern English Literature* (1918), but, while admitting that he was a master of the macabre tale, considered him too fond of the horrible; of the merely horrible, there is very little in his stories. Mr. A. J. A. Symons prefaced *Ten Tales* (1925) with a provocative short account of Bierce's life and work. A somewhat misleading pronouncement on his stories was made in *Great Short Stories of the World.* Of American criticisms the best are to be found in the Introduction and Memoir in *The Letters of Ambrose Bierce* (1922).

Bierce once stated that biography "obscured counsel" in literary criticism, but so adventurous a life and so unusual a character as his explain certain aspects of his work. He was born on June 24, 1842, in Ohio. He served in the Civil War from 1861 as a lieutenant on the Northern side, performed several gallant deeds, and was brevetted a major for distinguished service. He seems to have remained in the army until 1866, as we judge from "Bits of Autobiography." After a brief employment in the Mint at San Fran-

cisco, he there took up journalism, writing paragraphs for *The Argonaut* and *The News-Letter,* of the latter of which he became editor; its founder was an Englishman, Frederick Marriott.

In 1872 he came to England. In that year and in 1873 he contributed frequently to *Fun.* Of this amusing weekly, Tom Hood the Younger was editor, while the usual writers about this time included W. S. Gilbert (who sent much of his early work), Tom Robertson, Arthur Sketchley, Harry Leigh, Nicholas Prowse, Savile Clark, Brough; among the casual contributors were G. A. Sala, Ashby Sterry, Rands, and Clement Scott. In fact *Fun* was during the years 1865-1875 a serious rival to *Punch; Fun* was more boisterous, more given to verbal wit, than its survivor; the cartoons (many were by Barnard) were very good; in addition to paragraphs and short articles, there were occasionally serial articles, as for example the "Mrs Brown" set of comments. Those fables "translated from the Persian by Dod Grile" which appeared in *Fun* from July, 1872 until March, 1873 were afterwards published in book form, *Cobwebs from an Empty Skull,* which also included twenty-seven "Divers Tales"; of these latter, all had figured in *Fun,* mostly in 1873; moreover, to this year belong the **"Brief Seasons of Intellectual Dissipation,"** likewise contained in *Cobwebs* (1874). About 1873, Bierce wrote also for *Figaro,* edited by an American named James Mortimer, but this journal seems to have disappeared. We know, however, that it was "a small weekly publication, semi-humorous, semi-theatrical." Bierce is supposed to have contributed in 1873 or 1874 to *The Bat* and *The Cuckoo,* audacious periodicals directed by one "Jimmy" Davis; the British Museum lacks both these audacities. In

A caricature of Bierce in the Wasp *early in the 1890s, when he was no longer working for the journal.*

1874, he wrote the two numbers of *The Lantern,* which, in the service of the Ex-Empress Eugénie, he edited in order to undermine the influence of Henri Rochefort. That adventurer published in London a periodical of the same title, the first numbers being in both English and French; begun in July, 1874, it continued until early the next year. Now, only two numbers of Bierce's *Lantern* were issued (May 18 and July 15, 1874), but the story that these two caused Rochefort to quit England is probably true. Rochefort's journal survives, Bierce's has been lost, but we at least know that each number of the latter consisted of twelve pages, four consisting of illustrations; the American once remarked that his paper was one of the finest things ever done "in the field of chromatic journalism," and from what we know of him we would say that "chromatic" bore two meanings. He tells us that "the expenses of the *Lantern*—including a generous douceur to myself— were all defrayed by the Empress. She was the sole owner." It is indeed a pity that so much of the work published in England is inaccessible, but we can still consult two of the three books issued in the early 'seventies. It is also a pity that his English friends, G. A. Sala, Henry Sampson, Tom Hood, and Mayne Reid (long settled in England) have left no record; a younger man, who knew him well in 1874-1876, has given us a few details of his London career. G. R. Sims, in his autobiography, remarks of Bierce: "In San Francisco his humour was occasionally staggering. On this side of the Atlantic it had to be diluted to the capacity of the English digestion," and he relates an episode concerning Bierce and John Camden Hotten that reads like an incident from one of the former's grim stories. Sims remained in touch with him for some years.

Bierce returned to America in 1876 and settled as a journalist in San Francisco, where, with the exception of a brief but strenuous managership of a mining company, he remained about twenty years. He wrote special articles for the aptly named *Wasp,* and, from 1886, for *The Examiner;* in the latter he became notorious for "Prattle" (a title revived from his *Lantern*), which, to quote an American critic, was "the most wickedly clever, the most audaciously personal, and the most eagerly devoured column of *causerie* that ever was printed in this country," and which, lashing the wealthy and the powerful if they offended, "scattered weekly thunderbolts" on the hypocrite, the pretender, the knave. As a journalist, he was not only, like Whistler, an adept at the gentle art of making enemies but also, like Laurent Tailhade, a "fire-eater" ready to give satisfaction in a duel. If his journalism was entertaining, his short stories attained to greatness; while in San Francisco he published *Tales of Soldiers and Civilians* (later known as *In the Midst of Life*) and *Can Such Things Be?*

In 1896 he went to Washington as a political journalist, and returned thither in the following year to remain for the rest of his active days, principally as correspondent for the New York *American,* the *Cosmopolitan* also entrusting him with a department. In 1903 he published *Shapes of Clay,* the better of his two volumes of verse; in 1907-1910 he wrote or rewrote much, to fill in gaps in his *Collected Works,* which were issued in 1909-1912; after 1910 he took things comparatively quietly. But in October, 1913, this restless spirit left Washington to travel through the

Southern States; he revisited some of the old battle-fields; at New Orleans, when questioned about the war in Mexico, he said: "I like the fighting; I want to see it." The last letter came from Chihuahua in December: nothing definite was heard afterwards, although a careful enquiry was made. But since, in that last note, he mentioned that he had attached himself unofficially to Villa's army, we may easily be right in assuming that, rather than with fever, he met with a fate such as he wished, such as he had hinted in a letter written a day before he left Washington: "If you hear of my being stood up against a Mexican stone wall and shot to rags, please know that I think that a pretty good way to depart this life. It beats old age, disease, or falling down the cellar stairs. To be a Gringo in Mexico— ah, that is euthanasia!" Whatever the end, it was in the spirit that George Sterling expressed so finely in his elegy:

> Be sure that heart and head were laid
> In wisdom down, content to die;
> Be sure he faced the Starless Sky
> Unduped, unmurmuring, unafraid.

Courage and clear-sightedness were indeed characteristic no less of Bierce's life than of his work. "A man at once more hated and more adored than any on the Pacific coast . . . ", he was the blend of a fierce satirist and a merciful sage. Sarcastic and ironic to all, bitter and sometimes brutal towards his enemies, most loyal to his friends, he exacted a high standard of friendship. To the deserving needy and the unfortunate, he gave freely but almost secretly. Pretending to be, and creating the general impression that he was, exceedingly "hard-boiled," he had a tender heart that keenly felt the sufferings of humanity. In general, very reserved; to his intimates, charming. Truth he set before all else, and next to truth, beauty; if he felt it necessary, he spoke out with graphic phrase and unflinching courage, as we note especially in *Actors and Acting* (an article written in 1893). Mere brains, if there were no heart or soul, he considered of little worth, and in his last years he remarked: "All that is worth while in life is the love you have had for a few people near to you." Recognising his own weaknesses, he strove for the higher planes.

> I am for preserving the ancient, primitive distinction between right and wrong [he declares in 1893]. The virtues of Socrates, the wisdom of Aristotle, the examples of Marcus Aurelius and Jesus Christ are enough to engage my admiration and rebuke my life. From my fog-scourged and plague-smitten morass I lift reverent eyes to the shining summits of eternal truth, where they stand; I strain my senses to catch the law that they deliver.

Such a quest explains much of his bitterness at the futility of his tilting at vice, hypocrisy, and cruelty, and it lends a distinctive flavour to that satire for which he was chiefly noted during his life, as after it he has become obscurely famous for his short stories. His first three books were mainly satirical. The earliest appeared in 1872, but this work—*Nuggets and Dust*—is now almost unprocurable and cannot be had even at the British Museum. Like the next, it consisted for the most part of articles from the *San Francisco News-Letter,* and, of *Nuggets and Dust* as of *The*

Fiend's Delight (1873), Bierce said in 1907 to a publisher, who wished to reprint them, that they were "youthful indiscretions" and were "better dead"; except for an article or two, dead they remained. *The Fiend's Delight* has an ironical dedication to "the immutable and infallible goddess Good Taste" and a brief preface that is a masterpiece of diabolism:

> In writing, as in compiling, I have been ably assisted by my scholarly friend Mr. Satan; and to this worthy gentleman must be attributed most of the views herein set forth. While the plan of my work is partly my own, its spirit is wholly his; and this illustrates the ascendency of the creative over the merely imitative mind. *Palmam qui meruit ferat*—I shall be content with the profit. DOD GRILE.

(That was Bierce's pseudonym in his early works.) *The Fiend's Delight* is a mixture of parodies, tall talk, witty commentaries, epigrams, sardonic verse. The satirist is there at full strength, the wonderful stylist is yet a little to seek.

In 1874, he issued *Cobwebs from an Empty Skull* under the imprint of Messrs. George Routledge, the two earlier works having been published by Messrs. Chatto & Windus; in 1887 there came another edition of *Cobwebs,* with a slightly different title and from the *Fun* office; every "cobweb" had appeared in that periodical. In the amusing preface, Bierce says that his wise and truthful contributions tended to "diminish the levity of that jocund sheet." The greater part of the volume consisted of the "Fables of Zambri," some of which, like some of the other constituents, were written to suit various old wood-cuts owned by Tom Hood. Among the admirers of *Cobwebs* was Gladstone, who, picking up the book second-hand, was delighted with their cleverness. Nevertheless, Bierce's publications of 1872-1874 remained practically unknown to the general public, while either very few or no reviews were to be seen in the pages of the leading periodicals of that time.

On his return to California, he continued with journalism for some time, but in the 'eighties wrote many short stories, which he managed only with difficulty to get published; editors and publishers admired his style and power, shrank from their supernaturalism and terror. Moreover, he was unfortunate in the first three American firms.

In 1891, a friend brought out **"Tales of Soldiers and Civilians"** at his own risk. There are several different arrangements of these stories, and the one assumed here is that of the edition issued by Messrs. Hodder and Stoughton in 1919. Certain stories stand out from the rest (though the level is high): **"An Occurrence at Owl Creek Bridge"** is a remarkable psychological story; **"A Son of the Gods"** represents an apotheosis of military courage and should be compared with **"Killed at Resaca,"** the latter containing also a merciless sketch of a selfish woman; sacrifice of personal feeling to military duty makes the splendour of those two tragic stories, **"The Affair at Coulter's Gulch"** and **"A Horseman on the Sky Line,"** the second being admirably written and constructed; **"Parker Adderson, Philosopher"** shows Bierce's love and searching analysis of

human nature; **"The Man and the Snake"** is a powerful tale of auto-suggestion and the force of imagination; **"A Holy Terror"** is one of those complicated stories of crime and supernaturalism which the author handles so surely and convincingly; **"Haïta the Shepherd"** is such a story as Dr. Garnett (imitated in this matter by Anatole France) liked to tell, the brief fictional treatment of ancient legend. **"A Watcher by the Dead"** is less interesting in itself than for several parallels: the conclusion of Stanley Houghton's one-act play, *The Master of the House,* would seem to be indebted to Bierce's story of the influence of solitude; on the other hand, it is possible that the American had read *La Confession d'un Enfant du Siècle,* in which occurs this paragraph:—

> Un homme se vantait un jour d'être inaccessible aux craintes superstitieuses et de n'avoir peur de rien; ses amis mirent dans son lit un squelette humain, puis se postèrent dans une chambre voisine pour le guetter lorsqu'il rentrerait. Ils n'entendirent aucun bruit; mais, le lendemain matin, lorsqu'ils entrèrent dans sa chambre, ils le trouvèrent dressé sur son séant et jouant avec les ossements: il avait perdu la raison.

Of the stories not in the edition of 1919 but in the *Collected Works* (there are eleven in all), the best are **"An Affair of Outposts," "The Mocking Bird"**—notable for its beauty and its pathos (and for a haunting resemblance to **"A Tough Tussle,"**), and **"The Eyes of the Panther,"** a terrible story of a panther's influence on a girl's life. Now, if we look at the 1919 edition as a whole, we notice that every story but one fulfils the title, that in almost every instance it is the principal character (without exception a man) who dies or goes mad or suffers both fates. The death or the madness takes place in circumstances unfailingly tragic; the tragedy either has its origin in macabre environment or strange incident or is picturesque, grippingly dramatic. The macabre resides often in the actually or, still more often, in the potentially supernatural; true, this potentially supernatural element frequently depends on the force of imagination acting in unusual surroundings. Bierce appears as a master of the "atmospheric," the dramatic, the terrible, the suggestively fascinating, as well as of the adequacy of phrase to meaning and context, the maintenance of an air or "note" both by incident and description and by dialogue and psychology, and in many of these stories he combines and fuses all or most of these features. The humour is sparse and grim, but the humanity is far-stretching, profound, general, kindly. Bierce narrates easily, tersely, convincingly and, at need, vividly. The characters are sketched rather than drawn, but every sketch is life-like, for in a few words the author conveys just so much as we should know in order to respond fully to the human significance and to the rich, complex psychology. The stories often conclude unexpectedly, both the end and the means disclosing an unusually powerful imagination in the writer, who likes the ghostly and the ghastly, the weird and the terrible; yet an air of probability is everywhere produced. Throughout this and the later collection of short stories, we perceive Bierce's conviction that everything happens according to a divine plan, as intricate as it is merciless, but merciless because cruelty must sometimes subserve that all-powerful purpose: a whole life may have relevance at only one point, but the previous parts have moved gradually toward that point—a view somewhat like that of Mr. G. B. Shaw, who holds that we are all sent into the world "to do a particular job"; Mr. Shaw, however, implies that the performer of this purpose rejoices in the performance, whereas Bierce makes him act as in a dream, without a sense of "duty well done," indeed without consciousness that this is the "particular job." But quite apart from the fascinating sub-interests, these stories carry one along and leave a strong, lasting impression. Even when the theme is tragic or grimly pathetic (and it is usually the one or the other), one has that sense of elevation which is a hall-mark of great tragic art. A certain deliberate sameness of subject is relieved by artistic inventiveness.

In 1892 appeared Bierce's one attempt at a novel, *The Monk and the Hangman's Daughter,* and that was an adaptation. He recast and enlarged Dr. Danziger's imperfect English version of Richard Voss's German tale; Danziger later became well known as a poet, essayist and novelist. In this middle-length story of a young monk's love for a hangman's daughter whom the hero slays to save from an imaginary passion and who actually loves him, Bierce employs an excellent style, leisurely, pure, crystal-clear and often beautiful. There is a recent English reprint.

In the same year he issued **Blackbeetles in Amber,** a volume of satirical poems reprinted from Californian periodicals. Obviously he had studied the methods of the great satirists, chiefly Horace, Juvenal, Dryden and Pope. He satirizes types and fashions, but usually persons—whom he names; he excels in verve and bitter strength.

In 1893 he prefaced a collection of Rearden's essays with a charming, dignified memoir, and published a group of stories under the title of *Can Such Things Be?* In this volume the proportion of supernatural stories is considerably higher than in the earlier set of tales: in the English edition of *Can Such Things Be?*, there are twenty-four stories, of which thirteen are definitely supernatural, five are within the range of experience enjoyed by most of us, while the remainder deal with psychological phenomena so extraordinary as to verge on the supernatural. It is a splendid collection of unusual stories. **"A Baby Tramp"** is notable for much shrewd comment on life and for the quietly, charmingly pathetic treatment of the main character. An arresting pathos marks also **"Beyond the Wall,"** which is utterly delightful and which should be studied for the admirable restraint shown in a sentimental theme that might so easily have degenerated into sentimentality. Bierce displays restraint of another kind in such terrible stories as **"One of Twins"** and **"Fleming's Hallucination,"** where he verges on the melodramatic; here, as elsewhere, he causes us to ask if melodrama depends not on the nature but on the treatment of the subject. **"A Resumed Identity"** sets forth a case of lost memory: many of his stories have great psychological interest, as, indeed, all good introspective or analytical "tales of wonder" must have. **"The Moonlit Road"** is both an attempt to describe the lives of ghosts and a hint as to how frail may be a "circumstantial proof." **"Moxon's Master,"** powerful and dramatic, recalls *Frankenstein* and anticipates *R.U.R.* In **"Mortonson's Funer-**

al," a masterpiece, the incidents are due to Leigh Bierce, the son of Ambrose, who died in 1901, but most of the power, together with the consummate art of the conclusion, must be attributed to the father, who, in a letter of March 12, 1906, remarks: "Of course I had to rewrite it; it was very crude and too horrible. A story may be terrible, but must not be horrible,"—an illuminating commentary on his own short stories. In **"The Secret of Macarger's Gulch,"** he leaves us to puzzle out the solution, which is better worth the effort than "cross words." **"The Death of Halpin Frayser,"** ranking with almost the best of his stories, is intricate, skilfully developed, and with an atmosphere unerringly conveyed. **"The Damned Thing"** is, in its way, the most weird of a collection of weird tales, and it is admirably told. One can but wonder at the imagination that hits upon such a central idea and one must prize the art that gives thereto a masterly form. Several parts of **"The Damned Thing"** remind one of these lines in Browning's *Childe Roland*:

> What made these holes and rents
> In the dock's harsh swarth leaves—bruised as to
> baulk
> All hope of greenness? 'Tis a brute must walk
> Pashing their life out, with a brute's intents.

In the Midst of Life and *Can Such Things Be?* made Bierce a marked man, but the editors asked him for happy endings; to one he replied that he would not write thus, "so long as stealing is more honourable and interesting." And in that declaration we may be right in seeing the reason why, after 1893, he wrote very few short stories.

In 1899, he issued *Fantastic Fables,* which included both a section with that title and "Aesopus Emendatus" and "Old Saws with New Teeth." The fables are mostly cynical, but the cynicism is directed at the dishonest, the unjust, and the cruel. Some are humorous, and as neat as they are brief, as for example "Environment":

> "Prisoner," said the Judge, austerely, "you are
> justly convicted of murder. Are you guilty, or
> were you brought up in Kentucky?"

Four years later, there appeared *Shapes of Clay,* a volume of verse, chiefly satirical and aimed at individuals. In fact, Bierce somewhere writes:

> Great poets fire the world with fagots big
> That make a crackling racket,
> But I'm content with but a whispering twig
> To warm some single jacket.

A few poems, however, display a wider range. **"Invocation"** is splendid and, at several points, it anticipates Mr. Kipling's *Recessional;* the love-poems are simple and fresh; of his sonnets, which were praised by Mrs. Atherton, we may give the following example:—

> Not as two errant spheres together grind
> With monstrous ruin in the vast of space,
> Destruction born of that malign embrace,
> Their hapless peoples all to death consigned—
> Not so when our intangible worlds of mind,
> Even mine and yours, each with its spirit race
> Of beings shadowy in form and face,
> Shall drift together on some blessed wind.

No, in that marriage of gloom and light
   All miracles of beauty shall be wrought,
     Attesting a diviner faith than man's;
For all my sad-eyed daughters of the night
   Shall smile on your sweet seraphim of
     thought,
     Nor any jealous god forbid the banns.

It is a pity that the satirical verse should so heavily preponderate, but then it is an even greater pity that in the complete output, satire should take so large a place. Nor are we to be comforted by the remark that he is America's greatest satirist, for we had a right to expect far more imaginative work.

In 1906, Bierce brought out *The Cynic's Word Book,* which had been begun in periodicals in the early 'eighties and which, even in book-form, went only to *L.* He completed the "dictionary" during the years 1907-1910 and gave it the title that he preferred, *The Devil's Word Book*; the continuation is slightly inferior on the average to the earlier part. The definitions were plagiarised far and wide, as one would expect. In the author's words, the book was written for those who "prefer dry wines to sweet, sense to sentiment, wit to humour, and clean English to slang." From this garner of brilliance, we take but a few examples:—

Garter:	An elastic band intended to keep a woman from coming out of her stockings and desolating the country.
Logic:	The art of thinking and reasoning in strict accordance with the limitations and incapacities of the human misunderstanding.
Man:	An animal so lost in rapturous contemplation of what he thinks he is as to overlook what he indubitably ought to be.
Phonograph:	An irritating toy that restores life to dead noises.
Ritualism:	A Dutch Garden of God where He may walk in rectilinear freedom, keeping off the grass.

In 1909 came not only *Write it Right* (a book of *Don'ts* for journalists) but also *The Shadow on the Dial,* a volume of essays. The latter became volume XI of the *Collected Works,* thanks to the courtesy of the original publisher. The essays concern life and literature, politics and science, the titular one being a long and scathing attack on anarchy, **"Civilisation"** very suggestive of possibilities, **"Some Features of the Law"** forming a searching and bitter analysis of American justice, **"Writers of Dialect"** representing Bierce's formal protest against these sinners.

During the years 1909-1912 appeared the *Collected Works of Ambrose Bierce,* which omitted *Write It Right* as well as much of his journalism. In a letter of August 14, 1908, he says: "I peg away at compilation and revision. I'm cutting about my stuff a good deal—changing things from one book to another, adding, subtracting and dividing." Certain of the writings not published previously in book form deserve mention. **"Ashes of the Beacon,"** apparently written in 1907-08, deals, from the vantage point of the year 4930, with the destruction of the U.S.A. by anarchy and greed. In **"The Land beyond the Blow,"** Bierce presents a series of Swiftian pictures of various imaginary lands, the satire being aimed at his own country; wit and humour abound, as in the remark that "the literature of Ug is copious and of high merit, but consists altogether of fiction—mainly history, biography, theology and novels." "Bits of Autobiography" makes fascinating reading, the battle-pieces being magnificent—vivid, realistic, touched here and there with poetry; the best of all the "bits" is **"What I Saw of Shiloh,"** which is as fine as anything he did. In **"The Ways of Ghosts," "Some Haunted Houses,"** and **"Mysterious Disappearances,"** we see a briefer, more casual treatment of themes present, in essence, in his two collections of stories. "Negligible Tales" and "The Parenticide Club" (the latter containing that grim masterpiece, **"My Favourite Murder"**) are intentionally crude and graceless, the humour being exceedingly "tough." "Tangential Views" is a selection of articles on life, art, literature, politics and science, and all are fresh and vigorous, some provocative, some pleasant, some lashingly satirical. "The Opinionator" consists of sixteen short essays on literature and shows to advantage Bierce's extensive and catholic reading; "The Reviewer" allows us to see the capable and admirable manner of his notices on books and the hardness of his hitting when he thought frankness necessary; and "The Controversialist" proves that he was a doughty opponent on literary matters. "Kings of Beasts" are laughably naïve and "innocent" descriptions. In "Two Administrations" we have a set of dialogues on political themes, caustic, witty, penetrating. "Miscellaneous" consists of sketches that are mostly humorous and lively, some being brilliant, the majority cheerful: in "The Counter," Bierce parodies briefly the manner of historical and of sentimental novels with a skill that suggests an origin for Mr. Leacock's *Nonsense Novels.*

In 1922, his letters were edited with excellent prefatory matter. They cover the years 1892-1894, 1901-1913, and most of them are written to George Sterling. That they are vivid and interesting is to state the obvious, but it is permissible to wonder when, if ever, he recalled his ban on their publication. And finally we may mention the selection made from his fiction by Mr. A. J. A. Symons in 1925: *Ten Tales,* sound in choice, happy in the Introduction.

In so varied a mass of writing, it is by no means easy to point to the constant characteristics. But certain of Bierce's beliefs disengage themselves and may be stated thus: there is an "element of hereditary superstition from which none of us is altogether free"; life is an insoluble mystery; "old science nosing in its prideful straw" (to quote Francis Thompson) treats of little beyond the natural and cannot properly explain even that; undreamt-of forces are at work in the physical as in the mental and spiritual world; although many terrible powers are abroad, the truly good man is the spiritual victor, while the bad man (overt or covert) falls sooner or later into the power of malignant forces that often represent a modern equivalent of the Erinnyes. In his civilian stories, Bierce deals usually with the supernatural, only occasionally with such themes as hypnotism. He handles the supernatural with convincing power and dignity, with striking details and suggestive asides, and he surrenders himself completely to the subject. Yet we are not surprised to learn from his critical pronouncements—the article of 1902, **"The Clothing of Ghosts,"** and the passages on "ghosts" and "ghoul" in the *Word Book*—that he did not himself believe in ghosts ("Ghosts: the outward and visible sign of an inward fear"; "a ghost never comes naked"); he did, however, maintain that without them, literature and art would be greatly impoverished. Where he treats life as we ordinarily know it, he is at times humorous in his observations, and in his letters humour occurs frequently, as for example when, speaking of a serious illness, he says: "I am now able to sit up and take notice, and there are even fears for my recovery." In the *Word Book,* famous rather for its wit than its humour, we find instances of the latter, which we may exemplify by his definition of a gnu as

> An animal, which in its domesticated state resembles a horse, a buffalo and a stag. In its wild condition it is something like a thunderbolt, an earthquake and a cyclone.
>
> A hunter from Kew caught a distant view
> Of a peacefully meditative gnu,
> And he said: "I'll pursue, and my hands imbrue
> In its blood at a closer interview."
> But that beast did ensue and the hunter it threw
> O'er the top of a palm that adjacent grew;
> And he said as he flew: "It is well I withdrew
> Ere, losing my temper, I wickedly slew
> That really meritorious gnu."

The passage on a mouse is very different, but quite as good. That fearsome creature is defined as "an animal which strews its path with fainting women. As in Rome Christians were thrown to the lions, so centuries earlier in Otumwee, the most ancient and famous city of the world, female heretics were thrown to the mice. . . . The mice . . . enjoyed the pleasures of the chase with composure." Needless to say, Bierce's humour is often grim as in the definition of *Kill,* "to create a vacancy without nominating a successor."

Irony and sarcasm abound; both are incisive. They are freely employed by this satirist, and to give examples were supererogatory. The wit, however, depends less upon context. Mr. Mencken once acclaimed Bierce as the greatest American wit, nor can one see any reason to dispute the verdict. The tone of entire articles and fables is largely due to this wit of a penetrating thinker, but such wit can be illustrated only at length. Bierce's epigrams are numerous: we find them as early as 1872, they occur at intervals in his serious stories, they appear in the articles, they sparkle here and there in the letters, and in the *Collected Works* they occupy almost forty pages. So many are excellent that it were difficult to choose. But four may be taken as representative:

> Before undergoing a surgical operation, arrange your temporal affairs. You may live.
> Twice we see Paradise. In youth we name it Life; in age, Youth.
> When God saw how faulty was man, He tried again and made woman. As to why He then stopped, there are two opinions. One of them is woman's.

> God dreamed—the suns sprang flaming into place,
> And sailing worlds with many a venturous race.
> He woke—His smile alone illumined space.

Keen wit, keen psychology. Bierce goes right to the heart of things, as we might judge from two brief examples: "The soldier never becomes wholly familiar with the conception of his foes as men like himself," and all who have fought will corroborate his observation. "That which we do not wish to see," he remarks elsewhere, "has a strange fascination, sometimes almost irresistible. Of the woman who covers her face with her hands, and looks between the fingers, let it be said that the wits have dealt with her not altogether justly." And in more abstruse psychology he is equally proficient, for, as the editor of the *Anti-Philistine* once remarked, "his skill in recording those thousand and one strange impulses that tug for the soul of men and women is almost diabolical." Bierce was a powerful thinker and conversant with philosophical writings; **"Moxon's Master," "Beyond the Wall," "The Damned Thing"** will suffice to prove both facts; moreover, something of his philosophy might be gauged from his definition of an accident as "an inevitable occurrence due to the action of immutable natural laws."

Nature he loved and examined. He describes her with fine sweep and delicate touch, as in **"The Middle Toe," "A Tough Tussle," "Chickamauga,"** and his agreeable article on **"The Moon in Letters,"** and he displays her charm, her power, her seeming cruelty. Towards human nature, he was difficult, for he was exceedingly fastidious in taste; "he had the aristocrat's contempt for mass-feeling," and needless cruelty, hypocrisy, injustice threw him into a fervour of indignation, his hatred of these things being intense. For anarchy he has nothing but searing curses, for socialism as it is practised little but contempt. But to the charge that there is in his tales a lack of human interest, we may reply that he detested sentimental stories, he disliked the novel and was thus precluded from dealing with character at any length; that nevertheless he sympathised deeply with the deserving part of humanity, and that he deliberately chose a kind of fiction in which human nature does appear considerably but not in the conventional manner; and in a few instances (*e.g.,* **"Beyond the Wall," "A Baby Tramp"**) he gave ample space to "the human interest," which, in his life, he understood so well.

Yet he was a great reader. With the English poets he was familiar; saturated with Shakespeare and Milton, he also warmly admired Coleridge and Keats. Among the English novelists, he favoured Defoe, Swift, Scott, and Thackeray. He was steeped in Hugo, Goethe, and Heine; quotations from Omar Khayyam are frequent; and he admired the ancient classics, especially Homer, Plato, the Greek dramatists, Virgil and Horace. Like Poe, he "pondered . . . over many a quaint and curious volume of forgotten lore," and he dipped into such strange, quaint writers as Morryster, Denneker, and Glanvill. His titles are telling and felicitous, his citations very neat.

Bierce himself, as a writer, would repay study. While he insists on the necessity of clear thought, the preservation of truth and obedience to the basic principles of art, he says that what finally counts is "not the What but the How." In a most interesting letter, dated July 31, 1892, he inveighs against literature being regarded as a means of social service; Tolstoi and his like are "missionaries" not artists; "*helpful* writing is dull reading." And in his article, **"To Train a Writer"** (written in 1899), he sets forth his creed:—

> To local standards of right and wrong he should be civilly indifferent. In the virtues, so-called, he should discern only the rough notes of a general expediency; in fixed moral principles only time-saving predecisions of cases not yet before the court of conscience. Happiness should disclose itself to his enlarging intelligence as the end and purpose of life; art and love as the only means of happiness. He should free himself of all doctrines, theories, etiquettes, politics, simplifying his heart and mind, attaining clarity with breadth and unity with height. To him a continent should not seem wide nor a century long.

In his stories, something of this detachment appears. The events are narrated with restraint, the descriptions have no excessive details, for the various details are "constituents" of the atmosphere and nearly every word is necessary for the realisation of the detail. As a rule, Bierce aims to obtain the total and enduring effect by means of atmosphere, and in many stories it would be unsafe to say that the narrative has greater importance than the impression or the conviction that he wishes to "flow" from the stories; in some instances, he allows us to view an action from several points of vantage. He has a delicate sense of the shades of meaning and of strength in words; therefore, he puts the right word in the right place. The style, in brief, is excellent. Even in the description of the invisible and the unknown he is precise; he never leaves us in doubt as to his meaning. He makes a scene live before our eyes, persons vivid, complex movements clear; his battle-pieces are not inferior to those of Napier, Carlyle, Tolstoi and Zola. In his descriptions he is economical, in his narratives vigorous: as every detail tells in the one, so every incident counts in the other. In the words of George Sterling, "Bierce was a sculptor who worked in hardest marble." Yet he can invest a lovely, haunting scene from Nature with that luminous poetry which lay at the back of his apparent asperities; beauty of all kinds draws from him a powerful lyricism that on several occasions affects his prose (for example, the latter part of the third paragraph of **"Halpin Frayser"**).

His gifts of style and composition may have been more suitable to the short story than to the novel. He condemned the novel on many counts, but thought that the romance holds out great possibilities. In both these respects he resembles Poe, who wrote no novels and only one romance; compare what Poe says in *Marginalia* on Brevity with what Bierce says on the novel in the **Word Book** and in his article, **"The Novel."** Like Poe, and in his wake, Bierce considered that "there is no such thing as a *long* poem." This is not to suggest that the later writer imitated the earlier! But some reference to the possibility is advisable. The game of chess in **"Moxon's Master"** may have been drawn from Poe's article, **"Maelzel's Chess-Player,"** for several gestures and the manner of the au-

tomaton in the article are repeated or diversified in the story. Nevertheless, the animal-mechanism of the strange creature in **"Moxon's Master"** and the process of its invention recall, much more definitely, the early chapters of Mrs. Shelley's *Frankenstein.* Bierce combines and improves on the two "sources" and introduces a larger human element, and, in turn, he has indubitably influenced Capek, for the central idea of *R. U. R.* is explicit, several of its most important incidents are implicit, in **"Moxon's Master,"** while at other points of the play we can indicate what look like developments from suggestions made by Bierce. The Baltimore case in Poe's "Premature Burial" presents several details that may, just possibly, have given rise to the incident of the broken ribbon in **"The Boarded Window."** Those debts are few, slight, problematic, and, in his essay **"On Literary Criticism,"** Bierce formally rejects the paternity of Poe in his supernatural and his gruesome stories, and in the article on **"Some Disadvantages of Genius,"** written in 1909, he refers to those critics of Poe who "have made his area of activity a veritable *mare clausum*" and pungently adds that "it was not an unknown sea"; of "tales of the tragic and the supernatural" he says that, "tapping, as they do, two of the three great mother-lodes of human interest, these tales are a constant phenomenon—the most permanent, because the most fascinating, element in letters." Moreover, where the two deal with similar themes, Bierce, the more robust and healthy, maintains a higher level of genius; although he did not quite attain to a "House of Usher," he composed half a dozen stories better than anything else done by Poe.

An interesting writer, Bierce's poetical springs of inspiration have been rather neglected. We may take leave of him in the passage in which he refers, in a letter of about 1903, to the scenes of his soldiering days, recalled with a touch of allegory:—

> The element of enchantment in that forest is supplied by my wandering and dreaming in it forty-one years ago when I was a-soldiering and there were new things under a new sun. It is miles away, but from a near-by summit I can overlook the entire region—ridge beyond ridge, parted by purple valleys full of sleep. Unlike me, it has not visibly altered in all these years, except that I miss, here and there, a thin blue ghost of smoke from an enemy's camp. Can you guess my feelings when I view this Dreamland—my Realm of Adventure, inhabited by memories that beckon me from every valley? I shall go; I shall retrace my old routes and lines of march; stand in my old camps; inspect my battlefields to see that all is right and undisturbed. I shall go to the Enchanted Forest.

(pp. 625-38)

Eric Partridge, "Ambrose Bierce," in The London Mercury, *Vol. XVI, No. 96, October, 1927, pp. 625-38.*

Van Wyck Brooks   (essay date 1927)

[*An American critic and biographer, Brooks is noted chiefly for his biographical and critical studies of such writers as Mark Twain, Henry James, and Ralph Waldo Emerson, and for his influential commentary on the history of American Literature. In the following essay, he comments on a collection of Bierce's letters and praises the author's sincerity and equanimity.*]

The Book Club of California has done a service to all lovers of good writing and fine printing in issuing a collection of the letters of Ambrose Bierce, and I wish it were possible for more readers to possess themselves of the book. Few better craftsmen in words than Bierce have lived in this country, and his letters might well have introduced him to the larger public that, even now, scarcely knows his name. A public of four hundred, however, if it happens to be a picked public, is a possession not to be despised, for the cause of an author's reputation is safer in the hands of a few Greeks than in those of a multitude of Persians. "It is not the least pleasing of my reflections," Bierce himself remarks, "that my friends have always liked my work—or me—well enough to want to publish my books at their own expense." His wonderful volume of tales, *In the Midst of Life,* was rejected by virtually every publisher in the country: the list of the sponsors of his other books is a catalogue of unknown names, and the collected edition of his writings might almost have been regarded as a secret among friends. "Among what I may term 'underground reputations'," Mr. Arnold Bennett once observed, "that of Ambrose Bierce is perhaps the most striking example." The taste, the skill and the devotion with which his letters have been edited indicate, however, that, limited as this reputation is, it is destined for a long and healthy life.

It must be said at once that all the letters in the volume were written after the author's fiftieth year. They thus throw no light upon his early career, upon his development, or even upon the most active period of his creative life, for in 1893 he had already ceased to write stories. Moreover, virtually all these letters are addressed to his pupils, as he called them, young men and women who were interested in writing, and to whom he liked nothing better than to give advice. We never see him among his equals, his intimates or his contemporaries; he appears as the benevolent uncle of the gifted beginner, and we receive a perhaps quite erroneous impression that this, in his later life, was Bierce's habitual rôle. Had he no companions of his own age, no ties, no society? A lonelier man, if we are to accept the testimony of this book, never existed. He speaks of having met Mark Twain, and he refers to two or three Californian writers of the older generation; he lived for many years in Washington, chiefly, as one gathers, in the company of other old army men, few of whom had ever heard that he had written a line; he mentions Percival Pollard. Otherwise he appears to have had no friends in the East, while with the West, with San Francisco at least, he seems to have been on the worst conceivable terms. San Francisco, his home for a quarter of a century, he describes as "the paradise of ignorance, anarchy and general yellowness. . . . It needs," he remarks elsewhere, "another quake, another whiff of fire, and—more than all else—a steady trade-wind of grapeshot." It was this latter—grapeshot is just the word—that Bierce himself poured into that "moral penal colony," the worst, as he avers, "of all the Sodoms and Gomorrahs in our modern

world"; and his collection of satirical epigrams shows us how much he detested it. To him San Francisco was all that London was to Pope, the Pope of "The Dunciad"; but it was a London without any delectable Twickenham villas or learned Dr. Arbuthnots or gay visiting Voltaires.

To the barrenness of his environment is to be attributed, no doubt, the trivial and ephemeral character of so much of his work; for while his interests were parochial, his outlook, as these letters reveal it, was broadly human. With his air of a somewhat dandified Strindberg he combined what might be described as a temperament of the eighteenth century. It was natural to him to write in the manner of Pope: lucidity, precision, "correctness" were the qualities he adored. He was full of the pride of individuality; and the same man who spent so much of his energy "exploring the ways of hate" was, in his personal life, the serenest of stoics. The son of an Ohio farmer, he had had no formal education. How did he acquire such firmness and clarity of mind? He was a natural aristocrat, and he developed a rudimentary philosophy of aristocracy which, under happier circumstances, might have made him a great figure in the world of American thought. But the America of his day was too chaotic. It has remained for Mr. Mencken to develop and popularize, with more learning but with less refinement, the views that Bierce expressed in *The Shadow on the Dial.*

Some of these views appear in his letters, enough to show us how complete was his antipathy to the dominant spirit of the age. He disliked humanitarianism as much as he liked humanism, or would have liked it if he had had the opportunity. He invented the word peasant in Mr. Mencken's sense, as applied, that is, to such worthies as James Whitcomb Riley. "The world does not wish to be helped," he says. "The poor wish only to be rich, which is impossible, not to be better. They would like to be rich in order to be worse, generally speaking." His contempt for socialism was unbounded. Of literary men holding Tolstoy's views he remarks that they are not artists at all: "They are 'missionaries' who, in their zeal to lay about them, do not scruple to seize any weapon that they can lay their hands on; they would grab a crucifix to beat a dog. The dog is well beaten, no doubt (which makes him a worse dog than he was before), but note the condition of the crucifix!" All this in defence of literature and what he regards as its proper function. Of Shaw and, curiously, Ibsen, he observes that they are "very small men, pets of the drawing-room and gods of the hour"; he abhors Whitman, on the score equally of sentiment and form; and of Mr. Upton Sinclair's early hero he writes as follows:

> I suppose there are Arthur Sterlings among the little fellows, but if genius is not serenity, fortitude and reasonableness I don't know what it is. One cannot even imagine Shakespeare or Goethe bleeding over his work and howling when "in the fell clutch of circumstance." The great ones are figured in my mind as ever smiling—a little sadly at times, perhaps, but always with conscious inaccessibility to the pinpricking little Titans that would storm their Olympus armed with ineffectual disasters and popgun misfortunes. Fancy a fellow wanting, like Arthur Ster-

ling, to be supported by his fellows in order that he may write what they don't want to read!

Bierce was consistent: his comments on his own failure to achieve recognition are all in the spirit of this last contemptuous remark. "I have pretty nearly ceased to be 'discovered',", he writes to one of his friends, "but my notoriety as an obscurian may be said to be worldwide and apparently everlasting." Elsewhere, however, he says:

> It has never seemed to me that the 'unappreciated genius' had a good case to go into court with, and I think he should be promptly nonsuited. . . . Nobody compels us to make things that the world does not want. We merely choose to because the pay, *plus* the satisfaction, exceeds the pay alone that we get from work that the world does want. Then where is our grievance? We get what we prefer when we do good work; for the lesser wage we do easier work.

Sombre and at times both angry and cynical as Bierce's writing may seem, no man was ever freer from personal bitterness. If he was out of sympathy with the life of his time and with most of its literature, he adored literature itself, according to his lights. It is this dry and at the same time whole-souled enthusiasm that makes his letters so charming. Fortunate was the circle of young writers that possessed so genial and so severe a master.

One forms the most engaging picture of the old man "wearing out the paper and the patience" of his friends, reading to them Mr. Ezra Pound's "Ballade of the Goodly Fere." Where poetry is in question, no detail is too small to escape his attention, no day long enough for the counsel and the appreciation he has to give. "I don't worry about what my contemporaries think of me," he writes to his favorite pupil. "I made 'em think of *you*—that's glory enough for one." Every page of his book bears witness to the sincerity of this remark. Whether he is advising his "little group of gifted obscurians" to read Landor, Pope, Lucian, or Burke, or elucidating some point of style, or lecturing them on the rudiments of grammar, or warning them against the misuse of literature as an instrument of reform, or conjuring them not to "edit" their thought for somebody whom it may pain, he exemplifies his own dicta, that, on the one hand, "literature and art are about all that the world really cares for in the end," and on the other that, in considering the work of his friends, a critic should "keep his heart out of his head." Let me quote two or three other observations:

> One cannot be trusted to feel until one has learned to think.

> Must one be judged by his average, or may he be judged, on occasion, by his highest? He is strongest who can lift the greatest weight, not he who habitually lifts lesser ones.

> A writer should, for example, forget that he is an American and remember that he is a man. He should be neither Christian, nor Jew, nor Buddhist, nor Mohammedan, nor Snake Worshipper. To local standards of right and wrong he should be civilly indifferent. In the virtues, so-called, he should discern only the rough notes of

a general expediency; in fixed moral principles only time-saving predecisions of cases not yet before the court of conscience. Happiness should disclose itself to his enlarging intelligence as the end and purpose of life; art and love as the only means to happiness. He should free himself of all doctrines, theories, etiquettes, politics, simplifying his life and mind, attaining clarity with breadth and unity with height.

This is evidently a "set piece"; but behind its rhetoric one discerns the feeling of a genuine humanist.

In certain ways, to be sure, this is a sad book.

At seventy-one Bierce set out for Mexico "with a pretty definite purpose," as he wrote, "which, however, is not at present disclosable." From this journey he never returned, nor since 1913, has any word ever been received from him. What was that definite purpose? What prompted him to undertake so mysterious an expedition? Was it the hope of exchanging death by "old age, disease, or falling down the cellar stairs" for the "euthanasia" of death in action? He had come to loathe the civilization in which he lived, and his career had been a long tale of defeat. Of journalism he said that it is "a thing so low that it cannot be mentioned in the same breath with literature"; nevertheless, to journalism he had given nine-tenths of his energy. It is impossible to read his letters without feeling that he was a starved man; but certainly it can be said that, if his generation gave him very little, he succeeded in retaining in his own life the poise of an Olympian. (pp. 149-57)

> *Van Wyck Brooks, "The Letters of Ambrose Bierce," in his* Emerson and Others, *E. P. Dutton & Company, 1927, pp. 147-57.*

Daniel Aaron (essay date 1973)

[*Aaron is an American critic. In the following excerpt, he discusses the Civil War as the single greatest influence on Bierce.*]

Most northern writers who lived through the years of the American Civil War hated slavery, despised southern traitors, and welcomed the integrated nation destined to emerge after the federal victory, but their self-appointed roles as bards and prophets removed them too effectually from theaters of conflict. For reasons of age (many were in their thirties), temperament, health, family responsibilities, they disqualified themselves from military service and supported the Great Cause as soldiers of the pen. (p. 116)

The dream of a nation directed by an ideal aristocracy gave them an elevated view of the war and encouraged them not only to write poetic exhortations but also to campaign on the home front against Copperheads, to write and disseminate "correct" opinion to the nation's press, to address meetings and assemblies. Toward the southern enemy they presented a stern collective face. None would have disagreed with Charles Eliot Norton's description of enemy leaders as "men in whom passions have usurped the place of reason, and whose understanding has been perverted, and well nigh, in moral matters, extinguished by long training in the seclusion of barbarism, and long use in the arts of self-deception." All looked upon slavery as the ugly stigma of that barbarism, and while differing in their notions of the Negro and his capacities, they were ready to prolong the war if necessary to assure slavery's extinction. All, after first misgivings about the "ignorant, ungainly, silly, Western Hoosier" [Charles Leland, *Memoirs*], Abraham Lincoln, eventually backed him and in the end exalted him. He figured in their poems and orations as a benign distillation of the common man, but it is hard to imagine them any more at ease with Uncle Abe than with the common soldiers they sincerely but distantly applauded.

When Walt Whitman made his famous prediction that the real Civil War would never get into "the books," he was thinking, perhaps, of these genteel writers whose "perpetual, pistareen, pastepot work" omitted the terrors of the field and camp. A few writers, however (probably unknown to him) had a first-hand acquaintance with mass killing and organized atrocity and did put the "real War" into their books—the war that choked several millions with blood. One of them was Ambrose Bierce.

Ambrose Bierce not only choked on the blood of the Civil War. He practically drowned in it. For the remainder of his life it bubbled in his imagination and stained his prose.

Toward Grant, the "Butcher," in some of whose campaigns he had taken a microscopic part and whom he had seen shedding "the blood of the grape and grain abundantly" with his staff during the battle of Missionary Ridge, Bierce maintained a reserved respect. He knew from experience, as Grant's toadies did not, that the General blundered on occasion. Nonetheless, in 1886 he memorialized the "admirable soldier" as a hard and cruel agent for a hard and cruel God. Presumptuous civilians might try to invest the Civil War with divine intentions, to see "what the prophets say they saw." Too "simply wise" to dispute chance or fate, Grant submitted without any inward struggle to duty:

> The cannon syllabled his name;
>   His shadow shifted o'er the land,
>   Portentous, as at his demand
> Successive bastions sprang to flame!
>
> He flared the continent with fire,
>   The rivers ran in lines of light!
>   Thy will be done on earth—if right
> Or wrong he cared not to inquire.
>
> His was the heavy hand, and his
>   The service of the despot blade;
>   His the soft answer that allayed
> War's giant animosities.

The eighteen-year-old Ambrose Bierce from northern Indiana, the second in his county to enlist after Lincoln's call to arms, was not the author Ambrose Bierce who wrote these lines. "When I ask myself what has become of Ambrose Bierce the youth, who fought at Chickamauga," he told a friend, "I am bound to answer that he is dead. Some little of him survives in my memory, but many of him are absolutely dead and gone." The "deceased" Bierce was a country boy with a patchy education. Possibly some of the bookishness of his father, an ineffectual farmer, rubbed off on the son. A two-year apprenticeship as a printer's devil

and several terms in a Kentucky military school may also have disciplined his mind. But when he was mustered into the Ninth Regiment of the Indiana Volunteers, nobody expected very much from him. His friends and neighbors knew him only as a solitary, undemonstrative boy who preferred books to games and who showed few signs of ambition or ability.

"At one time in my green and salad days," he later recalled, "I was sufficiently zealous for Freedom to be engaged in a four years' battle for its promotion. There were other issues, but they did not count much for me." That was Bierce's way of saying he had once had illusions. The Bierce clan was antislavery, and none more so than Lucius Verus Bierce, Ambrose's favorite uncle and the only member of the family of any public distinction. It was this same General Bierce of Akron who furnished his friend John Brown with supplies and weapons for Brown's Kansas business. On the evening of Brown's execution, Lucius Bierce addressed a mass meeting in which he equated the martyr's alleged fanaticism, folly, madness, and wickedness with virtue, divine wisdom, obedience to God, and piety. John Brown, he predicted, would "rise up before the world with his calm, marble features, more terrible in death, and defeat, than in life and victory." Whether or not his nephew read the oration, he applauded its sentiments. Eventually an older and disenchanted Bierce conjured up some retributive ghosts of his own.

Bierce's biographers agree the war was the central experience of his life to which he constantly returned, a time of bale and bliss, and an ordeal that brought some coherence to the hitherto random pattern of his youth. Of all the literary combatants of the Civil War, none saw more action or steeped himself so completely in the essence of battle. For no other writer did it remain such an obsessive presence. "To this day," he wrote in 1887, "I cannot look over a landscape without noting the advantages of a ground for attack or defense . . . I never hear a rifle-shot without a thrill in my veins. I never catch the peculiar odor of gunpowder without having visions of the dead and dying." The sight of Richmond in 1912 dejected him as it had Henry James when the author of *The American Scene* visited the city several years before. "True, the history is some fifty years old, but it is always with me when I am there, making solemn eyes at me." There is no reason to question his quiet assertion that prefaces a recollection of Chickamauga, the graveyard of his idealistic youth: "I had served at the front from the beginning of the trouble, and had seen enough of war to give me a fair understanding of it."

Outside a few letters and diary notes, very little remains of Bierce's on-the-spot recording of the war years. His account of them is largely restrospective, often glazed with nostalgia and set down after he had trained himself to write. Yet thanks to an almost uncanny visual sense cultivated by his wartime duties as topographical engineer, he managed to fix in his mind the terrain he had traversed and to map his stories and sketches so that the reader can visualize every copse or ravine or stream he mentions. He also absorbed the business of war, the details of the soldier's trade conspicuously missing from the war chronicles of those who picked up their information second-hand. This "solidity of specification," as Henry James might say, gave his war fiction the "illusion of reality."

The word *illusion* is used advisedly here, because Bierce's tales of war are not in the least realistic; they are, as he doubtless intended them to be, incredible events occurring in credible surroundings. Triggered like traps, they abound in coincidences and are as contemptuous of the probable as any of Poe's most bizarre experiments. Bierce's soldiers move in a trance through a prefigured universe. Father and son, brother and brother, husband and wife, child and servant, separated by chance or conviction, murderously collide in accidental encounters. The playthings of some power, they follow a course "decreed from the beginning of time." Ill-matched against the outside forces assailing them, they are also victimized by atavistic ones. Bierce's uncomplicated men-at-arms, suddenly commandeered by compulsive fear or wounded by shame, destroy themselves.

Yet each of Bierce's preposterous tales is framed in fact and touched with what Poe called "the potent magic of verisimilitude." Transitions from reality to sur-reality seem believable not only because the Civil War was filled with romantic and implausible episodes, but also because of the writer's intense scrutiny of war itself. The issues of the war no longer concerned him by the time he came to write his soldier stories. They had practically disappeared in the wake of history. But the physical and psychological consequences of constant exposure to suffering and death, the way men behaved in the stress of battle—these matters powerfully worked his imagination, for the war was only meaningful to Bierce as a personal experience. If war in general became his parable of pitifully accoutered man attacked by heavily armored natural forces, the Civil War dramatized his private obsessions.

Like John W. De Forest, Bierce smuggled personal experiences into his fiction (the tales are usually laid in localities he had fought over), but he left no personal records so complete as De Forest's *A Volunteer's Adventures*. "Bits of Autobiography," composed some time after the events described, touches only a few of the high points in Bierce's career as a soldier. All the same, it complements the war fiction and hints of his fiery initiation.

From the moment he enlisted, Bierce conducted himself like the trusty and competent soldiers who figure in his stories. The sketches are not self-celebrations, however, and tell little of his personal exploits; they are the emotion-tinted memories of an untranquil man. He looks back to "the autumn of that 'most immemorial year,' the 1861st of our Lord, and of our Heroic Age" when his regiment from the Indiana lowlands encamped in the Great Mountain country of West Virginia. During the first months of his " 'prentice days of warfare," he and his friends in the "Delectable Mountains" assumed the responsibility of personally subduing the rebel fiends. They felt omnipotent and free, in charge of their respective destinies. The proximity of the enemy added just the necessary "spice of danger." Only a few incongruities marred the idyll: a soldier named Abbott killed by "a nearly spent cannon shot" on which his name was stamped (an incident scarcely less im-

Bierce during his military service with the Ninth Indiana Infantry.

probable than one of Bierce's horrendous fictional coincidences) and the discovery of "some things—lying by the way side" whose "yellow-clay faces" would soon be made anonymous by rooting swine.

Subsequent campaigns in the West seasoned the green recruit, and unremitting encounters with death raised first doubts in his mind about the propriety of dying "for a cause which may be right and may be wrong." Bierce was attached to the Army of the Ohio under General Buell and took part in the dash from Nashville to assist Grant's mauled divisions at Pittsburg Landing. Shiloh, his first major battle, began with a sequence of exhilarating bugle calls, reached a climax in a tempest of hissing lead and "spouting fires" and ended in "desolation" and "awful silence." War was no longer new to him, but his surcharged recollection of confusion, of troops demented by shell-shock, of the night march when he and his men, soaked to the skin, stumbled in darkness over the bodies of the dead and near dead, testify to the sustained intensity of the impact:

> Knapsacks, canteens, haversacks distended with soaken [sic] and swollen biscuits, gaping to disgorge, blankets beaten into the soil by the rain, rifles with bent barrels or splintered stocks,

waist-belts, hats and the omnipresent sardine-box—all the wretched debris of the battle still littered the spongy earth as far as one could see, in every direction. Dead horses were everywhere; a few disabled caissons, or limbers, reclining on one elbow, as it were; ammunition wagons standing disconsolate behind four or six sprawling mules. Men? There were men enough; all dead, apparently, except one, who lay near where I had halted my platoon to await the slower movement of the line—a Federal sergeant, variously hurt, who had been a fine giant in his time. He lay face upward, taking in his breath in convulsive, rattling snorts, and blowing it out in sputters of froth which crawled creamily down his cheeks, piling itself alongside his neck and ears. A bullet had clipped a groove in his skull, above the temple; from this the brain protruded in bosses, dropping off in flakes and streams. I had not previously known one could get on, even in this unsatisfactory fashion, with so little brain. One of my men, whom I knew for a womanish fellow, asked if he should put his bayonett through him. Inexpressibly shocked by the cold-blooded proposal, I told him I thought not; it was unusual, and too many were looking.

When Bierce wrote **"What I Saw at Shiloh,"** he was already practicing to disguise the violence of his revulsion from organized killing by irony, understatement, and bravado. He succeeded no better than Hemingway. Like Sergeant Byring in **"A Tough Tussle,"** the repugnance he felt toward the mangled dead was at once physical and spiritual, and his bitter joking about spilled guts and brains, his facetiousness in the presence of corrupted flesh, was his response "to his unusually acute sensibilities—his keen sense of the beautiful, which these hideous things outraged." Neither Bierce nor his sergeant found any dignity in death. "[It] was a thing to be hated. It was not picturesque, it had no tender and solemn side—a dismal thing, hideous in all its manifestations and suggestions." The half-buried corpses at Shiloh angered him:

> Their clothing was half burnt away—their hair and beard entirely; the rain had come too late to save their nails. Some were swollen to double girth; others shriveled to manikins. According to degree of exposure, their faces were bloated and black or yellow and shrunken. The contraction of muscles which had given them claws for hands had cursed each countenance with a hideous grin.

And at the conclusion of this disgusting tableau, he burst out: "Faugh! I cannot catalogue the charms of these gallant gentlemen who had got what they enlisted for."

The sight of men tumbling over like tenpins as the lead thudded against flesh, the piling up of bodies in "a very pretty line of dead," the postures of soldiers flattened out beneath "showers of shrapnel darting divergent from the unassailable sky," parodied the fracas between men and nature. Their fate and his was to wait "meekly to be blown out of life by level gusts of grape—to clench our teeth and shrink helpless before big shot pushing noisily through the consenting air." Neither Blue nor Gray was made to stand up to this kind of chastisement. In Bierce's Civil War, lead

always scores "its old-time victory over steel," and the heroic invariably breaks "its great heart against the commonplace."

At Chickamauga, the setting of one of his most macabre and powerful tales, he observed a fragment of the fierce, seesaw battle as a staff officer in General W. B. Hazen's command. And at Pickett's Mill, too minor a disaster to find a place in Sherman's memoirs but important enough to be "related by the enemy," he stored up additional facts about the art of war. Here ignorant armies clashed by day. The Indiana veterans, unaware of what was going on in front of or behind them, fought alongside regiments of strangers. Their commander—"aggressive, arrogant, tyrannical, honorable, truthful, courageous"—had not flinched at the criminal order that would sacrifice his feeble brigade. His valorous troops, though virtually cut to pieces, pushed to the "dead-line," the stretch of "clear space—neutral ground, devoid of dead" beyond which men vulnerable to bullets could not pass. Veterans of this caliber and experience had by now learned almost instinctively to divine the hopeless and to retire in good order.

Bierce survived a number of other engagements, only some of which he wrote about. "There are many battles in a war," he remarked, "and many incidents in battle: one does not recollect everything." The war itself, however, had pressed so deeply into his consciousness that he did not need to recollect it. Again and again he came back to it, sometimes to the accompaniment of rhetorical music. "Is it not strange," he asked, "that the phantoms of a blood-stained period have so airy a grace and look with so tender eyes?—that I recall with difficulty the danger and death and horrors of the time, and without effort all that was gracious and picturesque?" One suspects that it was not all that difficult for him to recall the terrors so meticulously and relentlessly recorded in his prose. What he desperately yearned for were his adventurous youth and his lost illusions. ("Ah, Youth, there is no such wizard as thou! Give me but one touch of thine artist hand upon the dull canvas of the Present; gild for but one moment the drear and somber scenes of today, and I will willingly surrender an other life than the one that I should have thrown away at Shiloh.") But he could not reproduce the ecstasy as authentically as the pain.

The war left Ambrose Bierce stranded in a civilian world. He ungraciously adjusted to it, but between his retirement from the army and his disappearance into Mexico in 1913, he remained a prickly alien. The unformed (and he would have said "misinformed") youth emerged after four years of fighting as one of those "hardened and impenitent man-killers to whom death in its awfulest forms is a fact familiar to their every-day observation; who sleep on hills trembling with the thunder of great guns, dine in the midst of streaming missiles, and play cards among the dead faces of their dearest friends" [**"A Son of the Gods"**]. In short, he was a veteran, and no civilian who had not undergone this terrific initiation could claim membership in Bierce's mystic company.

The civilian—untested, insulated from the quintessential experience of violence and death—inhabited a different country and spoke in a different tongue. He was likely to be a patriot, an idealist, an amateur; he believed in God and Providence, hated the enemy, and had not an inkling of the soldier's austere trade.

"An Affair of the Outposts" personifies the civilian in the governor who for strictly political reasons comes from the "peaceful lands beyond the sea of strife" to visit Grant's bedraggled army after the battle of Pittsburg Landing. The governor misreads the hieroglyphics of war. To his unpracticed eye, the apparent disorder of the camp suggests "carelessness, confusion, indifference" whereas "a soldier would have observed expectancy and readiness." Trapped in a melee, he is just unterrified enough to appreciate "the composure and precision" of the troops, but he is more shocked than enlightened by the sordidness of battle: "Even in his distress and peril the helpless civilian could not forbear to contrast it with the gorgeous parades and reviews held in honor of himself—with the brilliant uniforms, the music, the banners, and marching. It was an ugly and sickening business: to all that was artistic in his nature, revolting, brutal, in bad taste." The great man is rescued from capture by the heroic sacrifices of the Tenth Company but passes off his near misadventure with a witicism whose irony he is too obtuse to recognize: "At present—if you will permit an allusion to the horrors of peace—I am 'in the hands of my friends.' "

In a society where such men held high place, war seemed superior to the indecencies of peace. The veterans, bestialized by battle and forced into the imbecile business of killing, evoked in Bierce a tenderness notably absent in his dealings with the rest of the world. It made no difference to him whether they broke under the ordeal or survived it; they contended against the uncontendable. The strong in his stories are always broken in any case. The men he most admired were stern paternal figures, like General Hazen, who made a religion out of duty, lived what they preached, and shared the fate of all who lived "a life of strife and animosities." Such men were out of place in postwar America where civilian precepts and values suffocated the soldierly ones.

Bierce's idealism, although not completely extinguished at the end of the war, was already guttering. His work as a government treasury agent in Alabama in 1865 and a glimpse of corruption in New Orleans snuffed it out. Once he had believed in "a set of infinitely precious 'principles'—infallible criteria—moral solvents, mordant to all base materials." The carpetbaggers who enriched themselves and the ex-soldiers who looted "the people their comrades had offered their lives to bring back into the Union," helped to rout such fancies from his mind. "O Father of Battles," he begged in later years, "pray give us release / From the horrors of peace, the horrors of peace!"

Corrupt civilians aroused his contempt, bloody-minded civilians his rage. Bierce never sympathized with the southern cause, but like Whitman he honored Confederate veterans as unfeignedly as he did his northern comrades in arms, for they belonged to his bloodied fraternity. "What glorious fellows they were . . . These my late antagonists of the dark days when, God forgive us, we were trying to cut one another's throat." So Bierce wrote long after when battle seemed to him a "criminal insanity." He regretted his role of death-dealer and looked upon his former enemies as superior to the breed who survived them:

> They were honest and courageous foemen, having little in common with the political madmen who persuaded them to their doom and the literary bearers of false witness in the aftertime. They did not live through the period of honorable strife into the period of vilification—did not pass from the iron age to the brazen—from the era of the sword to that of the tongue and pen. Among them is no member of the Southern Historical Society. Their valor was not the duty of the non-combatants; they have no voice in the thunder of civilians and the shouting. Not by them are impaired the dignity and infinite pathos of the Lost Cause. Give them, these blameless gentlemen, their rightful part in all the pomp that fills the circuit of the summer hills.

Bierce's tribute concluded his plea to provide markers for the shallow and forgotten graves of the Confederate dead. "Is there a man, North or South," he asked, "who would begrudge the expense of giving to these fallen brothers the tribute of green graves?" Apparently there were, just as there were the "Vindictives" of the Bloody-Shirt unwilling to return captured Rebel flags. He gently chided GAR veterans for fearing that concessions to old foes smacked of treason. He and his fellow soldiers had not fought to capture banners but to teach the South better manners. Let kings keep trophies, he said. "The freeman's trophy is the foeman's love, / Despite war's ravage."

> Give back the foolish flags whose bearers fell,
>   Too valiant to forsake them.
> Is it presumptuous, this counsel? Well,
>   I helped to take them.

He was less genial to the superpatriots and self-righteous moralists, inflexible judges of right and wrong. Rejected ideas, he warned them, constantly double back to "mock the new"; they run "recurrent in an endless track." And angered by one who opposed the decorating of Confederate graves, Bierce wrote:

> The wretch, whate'er his life and lot,
>   Who does not love the harmless dead
>   With all his heart, and all his head—
> May God forgive him, *I* shall not.

The war educated Bierce, enlightened or undeceived him in the same sense that Melville's shattered veterans were enlightened by exploding shells and undeceived by bullets. It also left him a casualty, permanently warped and seared like one of Hawthorne's damned seekers who is crushed rather than tempered by revelation. A universe where such atrocities could happen remained hostile to him as did the God who allegedly managed human affairs. Once he had swallowed the "fascinating fallacy that all men are born equal," had believed that words meant what the dictionary said they did. He had heard the cry for help when he was "young and full of faith" and in keeping with others of that "sentimental generation" had willingly taken more than his fair share of hard knocks. But **"The Hesitating Veteran"** asked himself in the light of the aftermath whether it had been worth it:

That all is over now—the reign
  Of love and trade still all dissensions,
And the clear heavens arch again
  Above a land of peace and pensions.
The black chap—at the last we gave
  Him everything that he had cried for,
Though many white chaps in the grave
  'Twould puzzle to say what they died for.

I hope he's better off—I trust
  That his society and his master's
Are worth the price we paid, and must
  Continue paying, in disasters;
But sometimes doubts press thronging round
  ('Tis mostly when my hurts are aching)
If war for Union was a sound
  and profitable undertaking.

No mortal man can Truth restore
  Or say where she is to be sought for.
I know what uniform I wore—
  O, that I knew which side I fought for!

Bierce the veteran did know what side he fought for even though Bierce the devil's lexicographer might treat the pastime of war with Biercean irreverence. If he knew little about the controversies leading up to the war when he enlisted, according to his friend and confidant Walter Neale [in his *Life of Ambrose Bierce*], he decided "after he had reached years of discretion . . . that he had fought on the right side." But the war turned him into a "hired assassin" and a bleak determinist. In his last visits to the battlefields—once in 1903 and again in 1913—retracing "old routes and lines of march" and standing "in my old camps," he tried but only partially succeeded in recapturing the elation of what he called "my Realm of Adventure." The ache of despair overmatched the pleasures of nostalgia.

By this time, Bierce's misanthropy was not "a reasoned philosophy of despair but a conditioned reflex" [S. C. Woodruff, *The Short Stories of Ambrose Bierce: A Study in Polarity*]. His response to the war had always been intensely personal, never philosophical, and he generalized his pessimism into universal law. The war remained for Bierce hardly more than a lurid stage set for a private

---

Bierce on fear during wartime:

Nothing more frightful (and fascinating) than a great battle can be conceived, but it is not frightful in just the way that its historians love to describe it. Men do not fight as heroically as they are said to fight; they are not as brave as they are said to be. If they were, two hostile lines would fight until all of one were down. As long as a man is not disabled he can go forward or stand his ground. When two lines of battle are fighting face to face on even terms and one is "forced back" (which always occurs unless it is ordered back) it is fear that forces it: the men could have stood if they had wanted to.

Ambrose Bierce in an Examiner *column, 23 December 1888.*

---

drama. It left the grander spectacle untouched and unfelt, but few writers registered the shock of war's terrors with a comparable fidelity. (pp. 117-31)

> *Daniel Aaron, "Ambrose Bierce and the American Civil War," in* Uses of Literature, *edited by Monroe Engel, Cambridge, Mass.: Harvard University Press, 1973, pp. 115-31.*

John R. Brazil   (essay date 1980)

[*In the following essay, Brazil documents Bierce's aesthetic theory and finds that it ultimately derives from a nihilistic outlook.*]

Several excellent studies have been written on the life and work of Ambrose Bierce. Strangely, however, they seem incomplete, their various explanations of the man and his art not fully satisfying. Insights remain discrete, discontinuous, the integrating principle elusive. The reason, I think, lies not in what has been said about Bierce or his writing, but in what has not been said. What has been called his "rigid aesthetic" [Kevin Starr, *Americans and the California Dream, 1850-1915*], has been described, but its internal inconsistencies not accounted for nor its psychological functions probed. His inconsistency, that widely oscillating absolutism which makes his opinions seem "less like thinking than like emotional caprice" [Paul Fatout, *Ambrose Bierce: The Devil's Lexicographer*], has been noted, but not traced to its cultural roots. And his personal experience in the Civil War and afterward has been closely delineated but remains unconnected to his intertwined artistic and social attitudes. It is in these missing links, in the unanalyzed interrelationships between aesthetic and political ideologies, between historical circumstance and personal psychology, and between psychological configuration and aesthetic and political ideologies that Bierce is to be found.

Bierce was heir to two literary styles. On the one hand were the traditions of western journalism and the frontier humorist. On the other were the traditions of Victorian belles-lettres, especially as championed by Bret Harte. The former drew heavily on dialect, hyperbole, informal syntax, crude diction and crude humor. The other enjoined restraint, latinate language, formal rigor, and sentimental refinement. As a contributor to both the frontier *News Letter* and Harte's sophisticated *Californian,* Bierce from early in his career hoped to steer a middle passage by "trying to avoid, on the one hand, the Scylla of Bret-Hartism and on the other, the Charydis [sic] of the Town Crier." His subsequent experience in British literary circles from 1872-1875 increased his respect for vigorous stylistic exactitude, but also exhibits attachment to his past associations. Upon returning to the U.S., for example, he said of his British friends, "The good fellows were clever no end but they were one-sided. They had English wit and English humor, but they knew very little of the fast-growing national humor of America."

Despite such sentiments and his middle-of-the-road intentions, Bierce increasingly inclined to the strict standards of Harte's Victorianism. In fact, as Hartley Grattan noted [in his *Bitter Bierce: A Mystery of American Letters*], his aesthetic range underwent a "narrowing and hardening" that ended by the turn of the century in adamantine rejection of the frontier style—those "Writers of Dialect," that "Plague of Asses"—and a defense of formalism that was almost ferocious. Hence, his deservedly dubbed "rigid aesthetic."

Amidst the din of his critical pronouncements, however, one can hear discordant indications that Bierce was only being positive, a word he defined as meaning being mistaken at the top of one's voice. He would say, for example, that "there are dialects which in literary work are legitimate and acceptable—to those who understand." Or he would deride the excessive formalism of "syllable counters." Or he would argue that

> in writing "correctly" there is always the danger of getting too far from the speech of the people. . . . One has to exercise judgement, taste, instinct, always governed more or less unconsciously, by considerations of fitness that are not always capable of clear exposition.
>
> A language is a capricious and illogical thing. It does not always give reasons for what it is about. If one would use only such locutions as are obviously reasonable one would have a singularly hard and juiceless style.

Bierce's aesthetic, then, was not as consistent, nor as rigid as it has appeared. Furthermore, it was less solidly based. Stylistic prescriptions rest implicitly on more basic judgments and perceptions, and his espousal of the "refined" style notwithstanding, Bierce had the strongest objections to those who supported Harte's—and more generally America's—attenuated version of Victorian aesthetics. Uppermost in his mind was the relationship between literature and behavior.

Style was developed from reading, Bierce maintained, telling those who sought his advice, "Read—but that will do at present. And as you read don't forget that the rules of the literary art are deduced from the work of the masters." But significant subject matter had to grow from authentic personal experience, not the recultivation of previously worked soil. "For this I *know:* the good writer (supposing him to be born to the trade) is not made by reading, but by observing and experiencing." Experiences and emotions, "these are necessaries of the literary life."

Bierce had experienced a world quite different from that depicted in Harte's romanticized versions of the frontier. To begin with, the physical and psychological reality of his Civil War experiences had uprooted romantic apprehensions of life, apprehensions that had been fed by sentimental literature. He had joined the Union Army with illusions of noble heroism and war's chivalric cleanliness. He found their opposites. He learned to "begrudge the foolish blood / That in the far heroic days [he] didst . . . pour from [his] riven vein / In testimony to [his] patriotic zeal." As do so many of the characters in his short stories—most notably, perhaps, the deaf-mute child in **"Chickamauga"**—Bierce, nurtured by the "warrior-fire" of his race, his imagination fed by romantic "military works and pictures," played at war until its tragic reality penetrated his perceptual barriers.

Bierce emerged from the War with what Paul Fatout has termed a "defective emotional vision"—a vision that constricted his perception to the vicious in life. Bierce seemed to see only the depravity, the avarice, and the violence of Reconstruction while serving in the ravaged South after the War. On his trip with General Hazen to the West, he was preoccupied with the poverty and pain of the dispossessed throughout the country, including the American Indians. And in California, Bierce found no Elysian Fields. He was confronted with the violence and hardships of a frontier society that grew from the turbulent gold rush, a society in which "daily violence was a living memory" [Larzer Ziff, *The American 1890's: Life and Times of a Lost Generation*], which suffered through a series of depressions in the seventies and which was, according to Kevin Starr, "on the brink of a violent social upheaval." Bierce's post-war experiences, in brief, seemed to confirm the lessons of his "frightful baptism of fire" [Carey McWilliams, *Ambrose Bierce: A Biography*].

As a result, Bierce rejected the historicism and sentimental nostalgia of Harte's school of frontier romance. In the **"Age Romantic"** he argued, "A picturesque period is always remote in time; a picturesque land, in distance." He labled attempts to depict the dignity of poverty, of back-breaking labor, or of ignorance "coarse, rank sentimentality." Such distortions, he concluded, could only be the product of ignorance or selective perception: "It is of the essence of the picturesque that it be unfamiliar." No, to Bierce "books do not give you the truth of life and character." The world and "men and women are certainly not what books represent them to be."

It was not simply to Harte's romance that Bierce objected, and it was more than a literary objection he was making. Bierce believed, "Conduct is of character, character is of thought, and thought is of unspoken speech." In other words, there is a causal relationship between word, thought, and behavior. The causal flow, however, is not entirely from deed to word. True, "a literature rather accurately reflects all the virtues and other vices of its period and country, and its tendencies are but the matching of thought with action." But the reverse is also true. Words, literature, affect action. The two exist in a state of mutual interaction: "Shakespeare says act and word / Should match together true. / For what you've seen and heard, / How can you doubt they do?" Art, conduct, and, inferentially, society are dynamically interactive, and Bierce knew the language of sentimental romance was his society's principal fodder. "We ate that fiction."

> The effect of this diet was not unpleasant but remarkable. Physically, it sustained us; mentally, it exalted us; morally, it made us but a trifle worse than we were. We talked as no human beings ever talked before. Our wit was polished but without point.

Bierce's ultimate objection to Harte's aesthetic was based on fear. He was afraid that people would attempt to deal with the "real" world on the basis of the "language" of romantic Victorian literature, that its portrayal would infect their political—in the largest sense of the word—perception. He saw its reality becoming their reality. The problem, obviously, was that it was not his reality, and above all else, Bierce was a realist.

Despite its importance, when used about Bierce, the word "realist" is inherently ambiguous. As an artist, he wanted his work to be grounded in truth, to represent reality accurately; and in this sense he was a "realist" (thus, his rejection of Harte's historicism and sentimentality). Such was the meaning of realist, for example, that H. L. Mencken had in mind when he said [in his *Prejudices: Sixth Series*] that Bierce's war stories are "plain realism," that he was the first writer to treat war realistically. For Bierce and his critics, however, "realist" had another meaning: one who wrote within the conventions of the genre of literary realism, especially as defined by William Dean Howells. Bierce's feud with Howells is well known. Howells was, in Alfred Kazin's words, one of the "custodians of orthodoxy," but it was really less Howells's preeminence than his literary theories that Bierce could not accept. The subjects, conventions, and language of Howells's realism were, to Bierce, anathema because they enforced distortions of reality. In brief, he rejected the genre of realism because he rejected the realism of the genre.

Bierce's understanding of realism is simplistic, but instructive. To him it was what might be called a literature of artifacts, of "external trappings," dedicated to depiction of physical facts, of external reality. The external and the artifactual Bierce thought to be superficial and impermanent. They were merely part of the "passing show," not part of the "great mother-lode of human interest" which, in his eyes, was the proper subject of art. "It is of the nature of realism never to stop till it gets to the bottom," he wrote.

> If we endure a play in which a man is pitched out of a window we must perforce endure the window; but the cornice, curtains and tassels; the three or four similar windows with nobody pitched out of them; the ancestral portrait on the wall and the suit of armor in the niche; what have they to do with the matter?

Such externalities were factitious additions. Realists were more reporters than artists, more historians of the transitory than revealers of profound truth. Art must provide its own defense; it can not be "authenticated by enumeration of inanimate objects." It was Bierce's belief that literature must be "founded on something permanent in human nature or the constitution of things, and constructed on principles of art which are themselves eternal." Human nature, the constitution of things, and the principles of art were to him, in essence unchanging. They were unaffected by the "passing show," and the permanence in them was alone a fit literary subject.

If the term "realist" has caused confusion in discussions of Bierce's aesthetic position, his own dual usage of key critical terms has exacerbated the problem. "Supernatural," "novel," and "romance" have proved particularly troublesome. Although this distinction is never explicitly made by Bierce, it underlies much of his writing: there are two realities. One is the phenomenal, mundane, external, "natural" world, the world of sensory perception. The other is noumenal, an internal, "supernatural" world, as accessible to the spirit of the artist as the other is to the inquiries of the reporter. The first is without an essential, necessary nature. Its present form is the result of "accident." The supernatural world, on the other hand, the world of "things forbidden to the senses," is the product of inexorable hidden laws and is based on the unchanging core of human nature. As such, it is permanent and ubiquitous. Bierce used "supernatural" in its conventional sense to refer to wraiths and goblins, but he also used it to refer to the essential reality that permeates the "natural" world.

Bierce's use of "romance" and "novel" is like his use of "supernatural" in that each has two different, though inseparable meanings. On occasion he uses "romance" as a term of disparagement to designate sentimental, maudlin literature. More often, he uses it as the name of a literary mode, a mode he wishes to distinguish from the novel. Similarly, Bierce uses "novel" frequently to mean a long piece of fiction. More often, however, he uses it as a shorthand for "the novel of realism."

Bierce had a general objection to long works of literature that is similar to Poe's. In **"The Short Story"** he argues that literature is subject to the "law and limitations of human attention," and the novel, like the painted mural, is too long to produce a coherent, cohesive effect. Elsewhere he makes the same point in greater detail:

> The novel bears the same relation to literature that the panorama bears to painting. With whatever skill and feeling the panorama is painted, it must lack that basic quality in all art, unity, totality of effect. As it can not all be seen at once, its parts must be seen successively, each effacing the one seen before; and at the last there remains no coherent and harmonious memory of the work. It is the same with a story too long to be read with a virgin attention at a single sitting.

Even with such sentiments, Bierce did not, as some have suggested, write-off long fiction altogether. He thought "great work has been done in novels. . . . But many great writers may err in their choice of literary media, or may choose them willfully for something else than their artistic possibilities." He argued that Russian novels were particularly good because they resisted literary fads and rigid conventionalization. In Russia, "the novel," Bierce maintained, "holds something of the elemental passions of the race, unsophisticated by introspection, analysis of motive, problemism, dissection of character, and all the other 'odious subtleties' that go before a fall." The Russian novel, in brief, had not strayed from the portrayal of the "elemental" to portrayal of the transient.

Bierce harbored a more pronounced objection to novels when he used the term to refer to the genre advocated by Howells. The nature of his objection has already been suggested. The novelist's work is conditional; it rests on depiction of cultural situations and characters in social context. The romanticist's work does not. It "knows no law but that of its own artistic development; his incidents do not require the authenticating hand. . . . He taps the great permanent motherlode of human interest. . . . He is lord of two worlds and may select his characters from both."

> And so it comes about [Bierce argued] that while the novel is accidental and transient, the romance is essential and permanent. The novelist, whatever his ability, writes in the shifting sand; the only age that understands his work is that which has not forgotten the social conditions environing his characters—namely their own period; but the romanticist has cut his work into the living rock.

It was Howells's and the realists' reliance on cultural setting, on the external, phenomenal world, their restriction of plot and characterization to the probabilities of social conditions that separated them "from the golden realm of art—the sun and shadow land of fancy."

A corollary to Bierce's rejection of realism was his feeling about the place of politics in literature. In an exchange of letters with Blanche Partington in 1892 he made this rejection explicit. Partington wrote to him, saying she wished to become a writer and giving her reasons. Bierce responded that she had chosen a literary career,

> But, alas, not for the love of the art, but for the purpose of helping God repair his botchwork world. You want to "reform things," poor girl. . . . [I]n such aims (worthy as they are) I would do nothing to assist you; . . . such ambitions are not only impracticable but incompatible with the spirit that gives success in art; . . . such ends are a prostitution of art. . . . Literature (I don't mean journalism) is an *art;*—it is not a form of benevolence. It has nothing to do with "reform," and when used as a means of reform suffers accordingly and justly.

By the end of the century, Bierce had come to feel that a writer should "learn to take comprehensive views, hold large convictions and make wide generalizations. . . . He should free himself from all doctrines, theories, etiquettes, politics. . . ."

Like sentiments are evidenced in Bierce's reactions to major poems written by two of his protégés, George Sterling and Edwin Markham. In *Cosmopolitan,* in September 1907, Bierce defended Sterling's *Testimony of the Suns and Other Poems* against the virtually united assault of its reviewers, and defended it in the very terms with which it was attacked. It was good "despite its absolute destitution of what contemporary taste insists on having—the 'human interest'." He made much the same defense of Sterling's second major work, "A Wine of Wizardry." One could, he wrote with evident pleasure, "look in vain for the 'practical,' the 'helpful.' The verses serve no cause, tell no story, point no morals." In those two poems Sterling had sounded the music of the spheres, and Bierce admonished him, "If you descend from Arcturus to Earth, from your nebulae to your neighbors, from Life to lives, from the measureless immensities of space to the petty passions of us poor insects won't you incur the peril of anti-climax? I doubt if you can touch the 'human interest' after those high themes without an awful tumble."

In 1899 he feared that the fate he warned Sterling about

had befallen Edwin Markham. Bierce objected strenuously to Markham's "The Man with The Hoe" on several grounds, but chiefly to "the sentiment of the piece, the thought that work carries." The sentiment of the poem was explicitly political and in what must be seen as a significant redistribution of emphasis in his critical framework, Bierce argued that

> although thought is no part of the poetry conveying it, and, indeed, is almost altogether absent from some of the most precious pieces (lyrical, of course) in our language, no elevated composition has the right to be called great if the message that it delivers is neither true nor just.

He believed that unless Markham could be persuaded to turn "from the murmurs of 'Labor' to the music of the spheres—the 'surge and thunder' of the universe—the end of his good literary repute is in sight." Eventually, he broke with Markham, in part because Markham no longer seemed content, "as once he seemed to be, with interpreting [the] fluting and warbling and sweet jargoning" of poetry itself. He now insisted on interpreting man's miserable lot.

Bierce's refusal to allow politics a place in literature was intimately interrelated to the development of his "rigid aesthetic," to his rejection of Harte's romanticism, and to his preference for the romantic above the novel of realism. All were to a large degree a function of his response to social and cultural changes that threatened to overwhelm him psychologically; all were intended to help him deal with historical trends he could neither understand nor control. Perhaps a closer look at the substance of Bierce's historical perceptions and political ideas would best illuminate this point.

Bierce grew up in the West and came to San Francisco during an individualistic era. As in any community there were forces to be reckoned with, but the region was still essentially free of the stranglehold of entrenched political, economic, and artistic monopolies. It was, as Paul Fatout argues, an era of "easy toleration." Collective action and formal community organization were minimal. Each man was expected to look after his own affairs. To Bierce, this was as it should be. Integral to his—indeed to most Americans'—frontier credo was a presumption that the individual could and should look after his own affairs, that he was the determining element in the course of his life. Ability and industry made a difference. Underlying Bierce's personal mythology was a belief in the efficacy of the individual.

But in Kevin Starr's words, the gold rush had thrown San Francisco "up for grabs." In the highest cultural strata, which had previously supported journals as disparate as the *News Letter* and *Californian,* a fastidious Victorian refinement was becoming the exclusive orthodoxy. Corporate giants, principally in agriculture, banking, and transportation, were beginning to dominate California's economy. The region's captive labor force was swollen daily by the arrival of miners and farmers who had failed or who were forced out of business, and by thousands of new immigrants who were pursuing the California Dream. A progressively stronger sense of the individual's impotence, his inability to assert himself effectively against the region's looming cultural and economic powers, developed among many—a sense that two severe depressions in the last thirty years of the century raised to the level of a consciously examined doctrine.

One manifestation of changing perceptions of the status of the individual was political, taking the form of debates on the justifications for collective action, on the role the government should play in regulating the size and power of economic combines, and on the methods of adjudicating disputes between employees and employers. As was the pattern so often, Bierce entered these controversies prejudiced by attitudes and assumptions developed in an earlier era, made partial concessions to new cultural realities, and when he could not finally resolve the tension between past and present, retreated to a rigid, but only superficially coherent, absolutism. His early statements on politics roughly correspond to those on literature. They are elitist, stress restraint and form rather than substantive issues. They are also reiterations of the conservative social Darwinism popular in his day. A belief that Bierce never entirely lost was that poverty "may be due to one or more of many causes, but in a large, general way it is Nature's punishment for incapacity and improvidence." He consequently opposed systems of private and public charity because they tended to preserve "the incapables whom Nature is trying to 'weed out'."

Increasingly, however, by the 1890s Bierce had to contend with an incipient awareness that there might be problems inherent in the economic and political system, that the reformers—those agitators whose proposals he had termed some years before a "confection of sin in a diction of solecism"—might have a point. During the national resurrection of Malthusian theory in the 1880s, for example, he began to notice there were too many people and too few jobs. Low wages and unemployment, he came to assert, were the result of overpopulation, and began to argue, "It is not true, though, that relief interferes with Nature's beneficent law of the survival of the fittest. . . . I am still a devotee of the homely primitive doctrine that mischance, disability or even unthrift is not a capital crime justly and profitably punishable by starvation. . . . Who is more truly 'deserving' than an able-bodied man out of work through no delinquency of will and no default of effort?" In March 1894 Bierce went so far as to propose a quasi-socialist program that implicitly recognized the helplessness of the individual confronting concentrations of wealth and power. He proposed: (1) abolishing the private ownership of land, (2) ceasing the importation of cheap labor, (3) preventing control of property by the dead, (4) requiring the state to provide work during hard times, (5) limiting fortunes by taxation, and (6) abolishing wage competition. In 1895 he reaffirmed similar positions on several occasions, and admitted, "I am something of a Socialist myself." He confided to Markham that "Nothing so needs disturbance as our social system," and thought that "most of the best features of our present system are purely socialistic."

But Bierce never wore his reformism comfortably. Somehow he could never make it properly fit his most basic attitudes about life and human nature. By the first decade of the twentieth century, his early assumptions had weakened his ability to adapt. He partially perceived that changes had taken place in the American landscape, many of which he found deeply disquieting. But he could never finally come to terms with them or with what they implied. By 1906 he was at war with reform in general and socialism in particular. Early in that year he took part in a debate, which was subsequently published in *Cosmopolitan,* in which he unequivocally rejected socialistic solutions to society's problems. The proximate reason for his rejection was that he had come to equate socialism with anarchism. In "some countries Socialism is clean, but not in this." Here it is cat's-paw to anarchism. The socialist's "part of the business," he thought, "is to talk away the country's attention while the Anarchist places the bomb."

More importantly, Bierce's experience of social agitation, like his experience of the Civil War, reinforced the Calvinist definition of human nature that had dominated his earliest upbringing. Though eventually denuded of its theological language and implications, Bierce's Calvinist heritage was very strong and its continuing influence has, I think, been underestimated. To him, the human heart was the "lair of a ferocious animal," human nature grounded in an "essential folly and badness." It was this "general moral and intellectual delinquency," this "depravity of human nature," that made government necessary and authoritarian government desirable. Bierce favored a powerful government controlled by those who could control themselves and who could act disinterestedly in the interest of society's larger goals: "Who governs himself needs no government, has no government, is not governed. If government has any meaning it means the restraint of the many by the few—the subordination of numbers to brains."

The confluence of modern political "isms" and malignant human nature could have but one result, Bierce felt—chaos. Chief among its adumbrations were the weakening restraints of civilized behavior and chief among those were the disorder and violence accompanying industrial discontent.

> . . . the relations between those who are able to live without physical toil and those who are not are a long way from final adjustment, but are about to undergo a profound and essential alteration. That this is to come by peaceful evolution is a hope which has nothing in history to sustain it.

"Our labor troubles—our strikes, boycotts, riots, dynamitation," Bierce was convinced, "can have but one outcome. We are not exempt from the inexorable."

As late as 1890 Bierce had rejected as a "captivating absurdity" the notion "that human events occur without human agency, individual will counting for no more in the ordering of affairs than does a floating chip in determining the course of the river." Thereafter, gradually, perceptibly, irresistibly, it seems, he grew less sure. He became less confident that even the superior individual could effectively assert his will. Things were becoming too complex, too big, the current too swift. Social and historical forces had grown too powerful. "We may dislike the direction—may clamor against the current that seems to be affecting a particular interest, but we can neither stay nor turn it."

"The entire trend of our modern civilization . . . toward combination and aggregation," for example, inherently abnegated the individual, Bierce felt. In the economic world, combination produced trusts and, in the political world, what he termed enlarged "units of control." Both conduced to temporary social stability but foreshadowed upheaval. Trusts led necessarily to strikes and class warfare, in which the individual was a nameless cipher, caught up in surging forces beyond his control or influence. Combination in government was the result of population growth, and population growth was integrally a part of the economic pressures that Bierce feared. Of greater significance, population growth was also responsible for the transformation of frontier America into urban America.

Cities to Bierce, to the man who "lamented the passing of the pioneer age" [Elsie Whitaker Martinez, *San Francisco Bay Writers and Artists*], were the most visible reminders of society's snowballing complexity. As such, they were the single most important symbol of the individual's waxing impotence and waning importance. Bierce saw the workings of urban society and the causes of its ills as "complex constant and obscure." His favorite metaphor for urban life was warfare. As in war, in the modern world of the city, things were "beset with accident and dependent upon the unknowable and incalculable." As these and allied sentiments grew in strength, Bierce in his stories and political rhetoric made ever more frequent genuflections to the determining influence on man's life of "fate," "destiny," "chance," "circumstance," and "fortune." Convenient substitutes for a process he could not penetrate, these words served him as synonyms for "accident," defined in his ***Devil's Dictionary*** as an "inevitable occurrence due to the action of immutable natural laws." Together they comprise his analysis of historical causality, his explanation of the working of the world.

Much has been written about the enormous significance of Bierce's war experiences. In truth, modern warfare became a symbol of pervading psychological importance for him. At one level it represented in distilled essence what he could not reconcile himself to accepting in modern society. In life as in war, "moral causation bore no relation to events" [Ziff]; life and death were largely the result of chance, of accident. Individual virtue (in the multiple meaning of that word) played little role. The man with "brains" who controlled the animal in his heart was as much a victim as the "brute tramp [who] welters in his grime." Modern urban life, like warfare, abounded in violent reversals. Events seemed to spin crazily out of control. War and city life destroyed Bierce's belief, in Larzer Ziff's fine phrase, "in the rational continuity of experience."

The great flow of Bierce's best stories lasted from the early 1880s to the late 1890s during a "concitation of his creative energies" [M. E. Grenander, *Ambrose Bierce*]. In those years, when the scars of his war experiences still throbbed, he suffered several great personal tragedies, including the death of a son, and witnessed the most dramat-

ic stages of modernity's accelerating impact. It is an irresistible inference that the historical and personal converged in Bierce's mind and that that convergence significantly contributed to the shape of his aesthetic and political ideas and to the thematic preoccupation of his best fiction. His stories from that period depict a capricious fate; they abound in reasonless, almost pointless, reversals of fortune that usually entail a violent assault by fate on the protagonist. Simply stated, the "abnormal" became Bierce's stock in trade, because he believed it more real than the normal. Howells's realism, which relied on probability, which demanded adherence to the common course of fortune and described experience "in terms of some immediately recognizable causal pattern" [Ziff], he thought banal and deceptive, as perverse as Harte's sanitary romance.

Bierce's nihilistic perception of causality was, of course, reflective of a concomitant ontological confusion. Not knowing why things happened, he could not know what they meant. Not knowing what they meant, he found it impossible to assure himself what they were worth. The volume of his judgments, then, was compensatory—the product of a man who searched ever more frantically for some bedrock reality, some final permanent, immutable proposition that would "authenticate" art, politics, and civilization. He failed in that search. As his acceptance of the comfortable assumption that there is a necessary relationship between intention and result eroded, as he lost confidence that there is an affirmative relationship between moral character and the shape of events, he despaired not only of finding such authentication, but of finding meaning in life. Again, war was the metaphor that expressed his despair: "No mortal man can truth restore. / Or say where she is to be sought for. / I know what uniform I wore— / O, that I knew which side I fought for." Even in death, he was sure, there would be no answers:

> Unbidden still the awful slope
> 　Walling us in we climb to gain
> 　Assurance of the shining plain
> That faith has certified to hope.
>
> In vain!—beyond the circling hill
> 　The shadow and the cloud abide.

Sufficiently rational to distrust faith, not sufficiently faithful to distrust rationality, he mistook his failure for the answers he sought. Because his aesthetic and political imaginations were unable to create a stable, orderly, homogeneous, and meaningful world, he could, at the end, formulate his "entire philosophy in two words: 'Nothing matters'." This sense was always present to some degree in Bierce, and became even more pronounced as he grew older. It is this sense that underlies what Jay Martin [in his *Harvests of Change: American Literature 1865-1914*] has called "the complete obliteration of value discrimination in his stories." For some these may have been the confident years. But for Bierce they were not.

His stentorian aesthetic and political assaults were camouflage for a crumbling defense. Torn by contradictory values that refused to be harmonized or ignored, Bierce's reflex-like reaction was consistent: he sought escape. By championing the romance against the novel of realism he tried to escape, not so much "into aesthetic repose" [Starr]—his themes are seldom pacific—as from inexorable changes in aesthetic form and focus. Inherently, in *the same act,* he sought to escape the social and political realities that so confused him. The romance focused only on the permanent, the immutable. The novel involved its author in contemporary culture, and was, in the most literal sense, historical. His aesthetic, like his political posture, was not only based on control and restraint, it was in itself an *instrument* of control. It protected him from the vagaries and mind-threatening confusion of a modern society that would not conform to his Victorian assumptions and presumptive frontier values. Even his more astute contemporaries saw that he had "withdrawn behind his barricade of classicism" [Porter Garnett, "Poetics, Bierce and Sterling," *The Pacific Monthly* (1907)].

Bierce also eventually sought to escape the locality most closely associated with his confusion by leaving California. And, finally, perhaps inevitably, he sought the ultimate escape. He wandered into Mexico and oblivion. He had decided that "for most of the evils of life, the only remedy is death." He could find true permanence and order only by escaping life. He tried the surrogate of inter-animating political and aesthetic theories that denied time and events, but history, like death, is inescapable. Those who run from it always seem to run to it. (pp. 225-35)

> John R. Brazil, "Behind the Bitterness: Ambrose Bierce in Text and Context," in American Literary Realism 1870-1910, Vol. XIII, No. 2, Autumn, 1980, pp. 225-37.

Brad Hayden   (essay date 1980)

[*In the following essay, Hayden asserts that Bierce was a Romantic writer whose work embodies the essentially modern struggle to apprehend a world perceived as chaotic.*]

Ambrose Bierce was at times a disgruntled romantic confined by an age dominated by literary realism. "Ranked" by reviewers of *The Fiend's Delight* (1892) with writers like Poe and Hawthorne, Bierce's esthetic parallels the sentiments of Hawthorne's essay, "The Custom House." Bierce called not for realism in letters but for a romantic concept of truth, which relies upon imagination rather than upon the creation of a consistent and objective natural world. His romantic esthetics placed him in direct opposition to the critical mainstream of the period during which he lived. Yet his esthetic theories should not, I think, be viewed as an abberation or throwback in American literary history; following in the path of Nathaniel Hawthorne and Edgar Allan Poe, Bierce's writing served to keep alive an important romantic tradition in American letters.

Like the Transcendentalists, Bierce was, at times, inspired by nature, but, like the romantics, he believed nature was not necessarily benign. As in much of our modern literature, nature for Bierce could be indifferent; often his themes naturalistically concern human isolation and fragmentation. Much of his fiction ("**An Occurrence at the Owl Creek Bridge**" and *The Monk and the Hangman's Daughter,* 1891) describes a single, estranged, rather Byronic protagonist who struggles with an unfriendly world. In addition, this solitary vision in literature often becomes impressionistic or surreal because of its inherent focus upon perception (**"My Favorite Murder,"** 1888, and **"Oil of Dog,"** 1911).

Ambrose Bierce was very interested in dreams and had recurrent nightmares. "The monstrous, the preposterous, the unnatural," he wrote, "these are the simple, right and reasonable. The ludicrous does not amuse, nor the impossible amaze. The dreamer is your only true poet; he is 'of imagination all compact.' " Dreams to Bierce were just as much a reality as nature; in fact, they were more so because they represented the type of spontaneous vision in which many romantic writers express interest. In **"Visions of the Night"** he writes: "I hold the belief that the gift of dreams is a valuable literary endowment. . . . By taming our dreams we shall double our working hours. . . . Even as matters are, dreamland is a tributary province, as witness 'Kubla Khan.' "

Dreams are a source of inspiration for Bierce but are not art; art requires a concrete form. "Nothing new is to be learned in any of the great arts," he says, "the ancients looted the whole field. . . . It is the lower order of intelligence that is ingenious, inventive, alert for the original methods and forms. . . . Originality strikes and dazzles only when displayed within the limiting lines of form." Bierce obviously did not consider himself a stylistic innovator; although we might call him a Classicist on this point, like traditional romantics he defined form as organic. For example, one might look at the method Bierce used to describe one of his most persistent nightmares:

> I was walking at dusk through a great forest of unfamiliar trees. . . . I came at length to a brook that flowed darkly and sluggishly across my path, and saw that it was blood. Turning to the right, I followed it . . . and soon came to a small circular opening in the forest . . . by which I saw in the center of the opening a deep tank of white marble. It was filled with blood, and the stream that I had followed up was its outlet. All around the tank . . . were the dead bodies of men. . . . Each lay upon its back, its throat cut, blood slowly dripping from the wound.

The dream represents the raw material of vision or inspiration. Form makes the concepts concrete and gives them esthetic permanence.

Later Bierce describes the dream as a logical and necessary consequence of a crime he imagined himself to have committed; he views the dream as a projection of guilt. Biographers have produced a quantity of speculation on this issue. [In his *Ambrose Bierce: The Devil's Lexicographer*], Paul Fatout, for example, makes much of Bierce's dreams, the violence of his stories and his supposed hatred of his parents. But what is most important about this dream to his theories of esthetics is the grotesque perception of nature which Bierce uses to reveal himself. It is a recurring motif in his literature, typically represented by **"An Occurrence at the Owl Creek Bridge."** The dream vision allows Bierce to interpret the subjective or psychological makeup of a character through that character's response to objects. Bierce analyzes crimes he feels himself to have committed because in his dream Bierce (as well as anyone) totally and ultimately creates his world. The process of creating the world, then, also becomes the method of explaining it. Distilled to its most basic, Bierce's romantic concern is with "seeing": "The truest eye is that which discerns the shadow and the portent, the dead hands reaching, the light that is the heart of darkness, the sky 'with dreadful faces thronged and fiery arms.' "

In a short, critical piece entitled **"The Novel"** Bierce pleads his case for the short story as an art form and for romanticism as an esthetic:

> The novel is a snow plant; it has no root in the permanent soil of literature . . . [the novelist's] chains are heavier than himself. The line that bounds his little Dutch garden of probability, separating it from the golden realm of art—the sun and shadow land of fancy—is to him a deadline. Let him transgress it at his peril.

He also suggests that "He [an author] can represent life, not as it is, but as it might be; character, not as he finds it, but as he wants it. His plot knows no law but that of its own artistic development his incidents do not require the authenticating hand and seal of any censorship but that of taste. The vitality of his art is eternal . . . [because its author] taps the great motherlode of human interest."

At times, Bierce becomes sentimentally fond of nature; such lines are not a typical:

> . . . through the haze of near half a century, I see that region as a veritable realm of enchantment; the Alleghenies as the Delectable Mountains. I note again their dim, blue billows, ridge after ridge interminable, beyond purple valleys full of sleep 'in which it seemed always afternoon.'(**"On a Mountain"**)

> I had not before seen a dawn so glorious! The mountains were rose-red and seemed almost transparent. The atmosphere was of a silvery lucidity and so fresh and pure that with every breath I seemed to be taking new life. The dew, heavy and white, clung to the scanty grassblades like rain and dripped from the sides of the rocks. (*The Monk and the Hangman's Daughter*)

But it is important in a study of Bierce's esthetics that we recognize the falseness, or rather the valuelessness, of nature as an object. Nature for Bierce merely conducts the energy of the human imagination; the solitary individual (either Bierce the writer or one of his estranged characters) provides meaning for an experience in the natural world.

On the point of amorality of nature, writers of the twentieth century have aligned themselves most completely with the romantics. Only through an individual perception is the chaos of nature capable of being ordered: art, even in the Jamesian sense, is the process by which we give form to such experience. For Bierce, man and artist are locked into their own consciousness. Nature when it is perceived to be benign is enchantment; it is a dream. When nature is viewed as malignant, either physically harsh or ironical-ly cruel because of its capacity to be beautiful and indifferent, it is the product of a mind experiencing a nightmare.

Bierce was certainly capable of appreciating nature—but not as a transcendentalist. He was too much concerned with particular evils to envision any kind of ultimate good:

> To thoroughly enjoy a country life, one must be something of a savage, with a savage's simple wants, and something of a god, with a god's means of satisfying such as he has. . . . It is, of course, very delightful to be alone with nature; but it is, at best, but a selfish pleasure to sit upon a rock and smash the pinching ants, clammy worms and stinging bugs which come to dispute your empire.

For Bierce, repose in nature is only temporary; Bierce preferred to view nature from a distance. But most importantly, his allusion to the relationship between art and nature being one of method suggests that nature is a process which the mind can emulate. Natural objects exist for Bierce phenomenologically. The mind interprets nature by using the imagination. "Imagination is merely memory," he wrote; dreams are imagination at its most spontaneous. At this point Bierce again echoes Hawthorne who discovered a moral vision (moral in the sense of discerning form in chaos) in a dead world of objects: whatever Bierce the dreamer sees in the forest is a part of his own nature.

Bierce disliked the novel as a literary form primarily because, like Poe—whom Bierce considered one of the greatest of men—he thought that literature should strive for a "totality of effect," available only in less lengthy literary modes:

> . . . there remains no coherent and harmonious memory of the work It is the same with a story too long to be read with a virgin attention of a single sitting. A novel is a diluted story—a story encumbered with trivialities and non-essentials. . . . It is the lowest form of imagination—imagination chained to the perch of probability.

This of course placed him in direct contrast with such realists as William Dean Howells, about whom Bierce also wrote: " . . . but as a rule he distributes the distinctions that he has to confer according to a system—to those namely, whose work in fiction most nearly resembles his own. That is his way of propagating the Realistic faith which his poverty of imagination has compelled him to adopt."

Bierce also mistrusted matters of the intellect, which he considered the fragmentation accompanying analysis:

> What could be more important and striking than the matter of Darwin's books, or Spencer's? Does anyone think of Darwin and Spencer as men of letters? Their manner, too, is admirable for its purpose—to convince. Conviction, though, is not a literary purpose.

He specifically objected to the "introspection, analysis of motive problemism, dissection of character, and the other 'odious subtleties' that go before a fall," elements which Bierce felt defined the Howellsian Realist and his novel.

Much like his dream perspective Bierce's primary objection to the novel and to realism centers around his interest in the primitive and more spontaneous aspects of life and personality.

In his attempt to unify the writing of a story with its effect upon a reader, for example, Bierce preferred to use emotions and sensibilities that were undiluted by analysis; he also wanted to be able to leave the romantic mystery of life a mystery. Bierce did acknowledge the work of Russian novelists because in his perspective they had not yet depleted their material. But along with praising the novels of "Turgenieff, Pushkin, Gogol and the early Tolstoi" because "we find simple, primitive conditions, and the novel holds something of the elemental passions of the race," Bierce must have indeed felt the novel as a literary form was capable of at least some unity of effect. *The Monk and the Hangman's Daughter,* for example, might very well be considered a novella—even though Bierce only took credit for the language of the work and not for the subject matter, it does have his mark of approval.

Bierce's esthetic theory, then, emphasizes the notion that life to a romantic centers around mystery and that a romantic writer can do no more than to suggest that mystery. Of course, this essential mystery of life (which is the keystone of all romanticism) is arbitrarily defined. For Bierce a certain amount of evil originates in the human mind, and certainly the mystery of life does not connote benevolence.

Another reason why Bierce objected to the novel was because he considered it at best a cumbersome form. Whatever the perception, for example, Bierce believed that symbols and images work just as well as lengthy photographic descriptions more prevalent in realistic works. Bierce wrote, in **"The Matter of Manner,"** "A word is a crystalized thought; . . . we think in words; we cannot think without them. Shallowness or obscurity of speech means shallowness or obscurity of thought." This becomes the basis for much of his criticism of Howells. Even though the novel is capable of creating a limited effect upon a reader, Bierce's praise of the Russians suggests that the very verbosity of a long narrative creates the opportunity for words to become agents of obscurity instead of being agents of "crystalized" thinking:

> The singular inability to distinguish between the novel and the romance is one of criticism's capital ineptitudes. It is like that of a naturalist who should make a single species of the squirrels and the larks. Equally with the novel, the short story may drag at each remove a lengthening chain of probability, but there are fewer removes. The short story does not, at least, cloy attention, confuse with overlaid impressions and efface its own effect.

He praises the work of the Russians on the strength of their use of emotion, not because of their control over technique.

In *A Study of English Romanticism,* Northrop Frye suggests that the romantic perspective, such as Bierce's, often becomes aligned with what he labels the "grotesque":

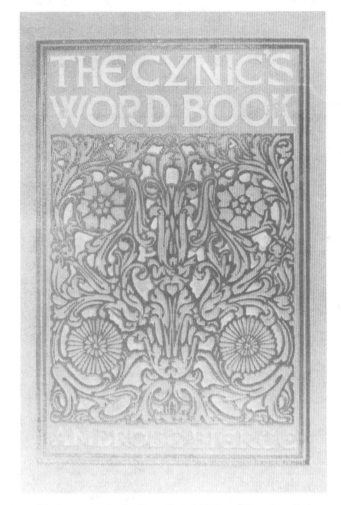

The front cover for the first collected edition of Bierce's cynical definitions.

> The root of the conception of the grotesque is the sense of the simultaneous presence of life and death. . . . The grotesque is also the expression in literature of the nauseated vision, man's contemplating of himself as a mortal body who returns to nature as 'dung and death.' . . . Man is the only animal that knows he is going to die: this consciousness is now regarded as the source of anxiety (*Angst*).

Frye's definition is, I think, as succinct and as well qualified as any. In fiction Bierce adopts a romantic frame of reference and method to which he combines an overriding concern with death. In a world in which human perception is dominated by alienation, the presence of death is what must define life; death becomes the only concrete truth, which is very much a link between Bierce and the writers of the latter twentieth century.

Colin Wilson offers a similar perspective. In a historical study of the psychology of murder, *Order of Assassins,* he suggests that violent acts are a form of repressed creativity. In a simplified manner, murder becomes a distortion of creative impulses in human beings; but the motivations behind murderer and artist are the same. In a chapter entitled "Murder and Romanticism" Wilson writes:

> In *The Outsider,* I tried to show the connection between creative frustration and violence. In a state of mental strain—which sprang from frustration of his creative needs—Nijinsky pushed his wife downstairs, Van Gogh attempted to murder Gauguin, then cut off his own ear; other "outsiders" went insane, like Nietzsche, or behave with "calculated irrationality," . . . Philip O'Conner, an ex-tramp, put his finger on the problem in his book on vagrancy: "My [tramping] excursions were motivated by what psychiatrists would call neurosis. But in truth it was a sane attempt . . . to get out of a positively neurotic convention of living 'respectively.' "

In essence, Wilson suggests that when the esthetic drive to envision order and beauty becomes overwhelmed by the more hideous elements of society and human motivations (when the dream becomes a nightmare) the result is the grotesque. Death exists as a dominant concern in literature of this kind because it is a synthesis between the horror of dissolution (the uncertainty of chaos and disunity) and the unity of what Frye calls a "return to the nitrogen cycle." Like all art, it is a means of reconciliation.

On the art of the grotesque Wilson also writes,

> When he [H. P. Lovecraft, although the same holds true for Ambrose Bierce] talks about a "blasphemous" dream landscape, he does not mean that it contains indecent mockery of the Christian religion, but something horrible, frightening, nauseating, something like those odd fungus-like creatures in the paintings of Hieronymous Bosch. His work is romanticism gone sour and bitter; instead of turning away, like Shelley and Keats, to visionary dreamworlds, he creates nightmares that help to relieve his loathing of modern western civilization.

In this respect Bierce is an artist, like Lovecraft, who uses his imagination to recreate the insanity of a growing technocratic, dehumanized society. Like his dreams, art is a defense; it is, like all art, an attempt to create meaning and morality by creating form.

In the **"Grizzly Papers V"** Bierce discusses the moral problems associated with living in a modern civilization. "When a favorite dog has an incurable pain, you 'put him out of his misery' with a bullet or an axe," he writes, "A favorite child similarly afflicted is preserved as long as possible, in torment. I do not claim that is not right; I claim only that it is inconsistent." In fiction Bierce offers consistency in a morally chaotic and absurd world, through the solitary voice of an estranged character.

In **"An Occurrence at the Owl Creek Bridge,"** the protagonist images a world which suits his desires; in **"My Favorite Murder"** the protagonist carries out his revenge by brutally murdering his uncle; the protagonist of **"Oil of Dog"** describes his parents' deaths while manufacturing a patent medicine comprised of the bodies of stray animals, children and an occasional tramp as the failure of a small American business. In each story Bierce orders negative aspects of the world around him; in a word, he

structures the bizarre. In his most surrealistic stories the effect is achieved through understatement—the method by which social norms are consistently applied, even to the ridiculous. R. D. Laing defines a similar perception in *The Politics of Experience:*

> The "ego" is the instrument for living in *this* world. If the "ego" is broken up or destroyed (by the insurmountable contradictions of certain life situations . . .), then the person may be exposed to other worlds, "real" in different ways. . . . Our time has been distinguished, more than anything else, by a drive to control the external world. . . . If one estimates human evolution from the point of view of knowledge of the external world [of objects] then we are in many respects progressing. . . . If one estimate is from the point of view of the internal world and of oneness of internal and external [an imaginative perspective], then the judgement must be different.

In his sentiments Bierce was a romantic: he favored what Laing calls the inner world. Bierce's art is a union of both the inner and the external because he presents a world of dead objects perceived through the imagination. Bierce's imagination, however, led him not to a vision of man's ascension but rather to a vision of dissolution and of the grotesque.

Most of Bierce's theories, as well as his connection with modern literature, can be seen in his short story **"An Occurrence at the Owl Creek Bridge."** The story is Bierce's most well-known work; indeed with the possible exception of *The Devil's Dictionary* (1906), it is really the only work for which Bierce is known at all. The story deals with the two recurring Bierce themes: death and a character's perception of life. The plot is simple: a man who is about to be executed dreams that he is reprieved by fate and allowed to return to his wife and home. The form is organic: the movement of the story is psychological—the protagonist struggles to imagine his escape from hanging. Finally, the success of the story relies upon the reader's believing in the reality of the life-wish. Bierce creates effect when subjective and objective realities collide, when the reader perceives that what he has been led to believe is a distortion.

As in many of Bierce's stories, the central element of **"An Occurrence at the Owl Creek Bridge"** is the existence of an isolated man in nature. Peyton Farquhar is a man who fancied himself as a hero as most men do. An Alabama farmer during the Civil War, he attempted to sabotage a bridge that was occupied by Union troops. Bierce emphasizes that Farquhar was not a spy and that there is nothing of the cloak and dagger to be associated with the execution. "Evidently this [Farquhar] was no vulgar assassin. The liberal military code makes provision for hanging many kinds of persons, and gentlemen are not excluded." (Discussing realists and probability Bierce wrote that "Nothing is so improbable as what is true"; the mystery of **"An Occurrence at the Owl Creek Bridge"**—typical of the majority of Bierce's stories—is a mystery of the human mind). When Northern troops capture Farquhar (his plan having been doomed to failure from the beginning), he is sentenced to be hanged from the bridge he ironically hoped to destroy.

One of the first sentiments Bierce provokes regards the very commonness of the execution. It is an everyday military event; on the surface there is nothing peculiar about it or about Farquhar:

> A sentinel at each end of the bridge stood with his rifle in the position known as "support," that is to say, vertical in front of the left shoulder, the hammer resting on the forearm thrown straight across the chest—a formal and unnatural position, enforcing an erect carriage of the body. It did not appear to be the duty of these two men to know what was occurring at the centre of the bridge; they merely blockaded the two ends of the foot planking that traversed it (**"Occurrence"**).

The story begins while preparations are being made for the killing; what we know of the protagonist's life before that moment is told to us in a flashback by an omniscient narrator; a voice interprets both the world surrounding the bridge and the world within Farquhar's mind.

The most crucial aspect of Bierce's story is his manipulation of time. The majority of the story takes place in the moment after Farquhar is suspended by his neck and before he dies. Within this moment Farquhar imagines an escape which takes approximately twenty-four hours. This is the world of Bierce's "sun and shadow land of fancy"; this is the region in which the solitary individual is the creator of the world that surrounds him. It is a moment of vision and of spontaneous and instinctual expression of imagination.

The moment before his death Farquhar's perceptions are heightened, and his consciousness of objects in the world is acute:

> He was now in full possession of his physical senses. They were, indeed, preternaturally keen and alert. Something in the awful disturbance of his organic system had so exalted and refined them that they made record of things never before perceived. He felt the ripples upon his face and heard their separate sound as they struck. He looked at the forest on the bank of the stream, saw the individual trees, the leaves and veining of each leaf—saw the insects upon them: the locusts, the brilliant-bodied flies, the gray spiders stretching their webs from twig to twig. He noted the prismatic colors in all the dewdrops upon a million blades of grass. The humming of the gnats . . . the water-spiders' legs. . . . A fish slid along beneath his eyes and he heard the rush of its body (**"Occurrence"**).

The force of the description is deceptive. We are bombarded with physical details in support of the concreteness of Farquhar's perception. We are led to believe that his sharpened consciousness is the result of his escape from death, his zest for a life renewed. But it is too much; no one perceives with such a heightened awareness.

This heightened consciousness creates the tension throughout the remainder of the story. Ultimately, Far-

quhar's experience becomes surreal, and the fallacious sense of time begins to fade. In the beginning of the story he is able to distinguish between the ticks of a pocket watch; at the end, however, he cannot recollect the hours of night. At the moment his perceptions lead him to his home, his senses break down:

> His neck was in pain and lifting his hand to it he found it horribly swollen. . . . His eyes felt congested; he could no longer close them. His tongue was swollen with thirst. . . . How softly the turf had carpeted the untraveled avenue—he could no longer feel the roadway beneath his feet (**"Occurrence"**).

Thematically, Peyton Farquhar is much like Prometheus in Shelley's *Prometheus Unbound;* the emphasis is upon the characters' abilities to perceive a world. Shelley's world is more arbitrary: Prometheus is capable of affirming or negating whatever perception he desires. His mind is like Emerson's in the "Experience" essay: when Emerson's "bark sinks," it is sinking "to another sea"—it is going to wherever Emerson wants it to. The world in Bierce's fiction is not so arbitrary. He is a romantic because he advocates the use of imagination in art rather than the portrayal of a reality of objects. But Bierce also believes that there is an ultimate truth: death, dissolution and decay. Bierce's brand of platonism presents man, perception and death.

In **"An Occurrence at the Owl Creek Bridge"** Bierce simply presents the particulars of an imagined world—the world in which all of us live because of the very process of perception itself. Consequently, Bierce's primary emphasis in the story is upon description rather than upon comment; we appropriately "see" through Farquhar's mind, until the moment at which death annihilates the imagination and transforms life into nothingness. For example, in **"My Favorite Murder,"** the protagonist describes ham-stringing his uncle and hanging him in a sack from a tree to be butted to death by a "grandfatherly" old ram; in **"The Death of Halpin Frayser,"** Frayser's love for his murdered mother drives him through a bloody vision (very much like Bierce's nightmare) and a confrontation with her ghost—he dies on her grave; in the story **"Oil of Dog,"** the narrator describes his mother as "having a studio in the shadow of the village church, where she disposed of unwelcome babies."

In a short essay entitled **"Poetry and Verse"** Bierce wrote that the value of an artist is determined by his ability to "anticipate the verdict of posterity." Many standard anthologies of American literature (*The American Tradition in Literature,* for example) overlook Bierce's work. But Bierce is a significant American writer. His concern with perception and the imagination carried on a romantic tradition in American letters, and his concern with understating the grotesque aspect of life anticipated the black humor and nihilism of the twentieth century. As a romantic he sought to be "the lord of two worlds." Perhaps that is the way literary history should remember him: as an author whose romantic roots grew out of the ashes of one age and whose concern for the grotesque anticipated another. (pp. 3-14)

Brad Hayden, "Ambrose Bierce: The Esthetics of a Derelict Romantic," in The Gypsy Scholar, Vol. 7, No. 1, Winter, 1980, pp. 3-14.

Lawrence I. Berkove   (essay date 1981)

[*An American critic and author who specializes in the study of late nineteenth- and early twentieth-century American authors, Berkove generally examines the way literature embodies and reflects the religious and ethical values of authors. In the following essay, he portrays Bierce as a defender of truth and a model journalist.*]

In his time, Ambrose Bierce was one of America's most distinguished journalists. This facet of his talents has been neglected until recently but it now shows signs of being a major find for students of American culture at the turn of the century. In the past few years, it has become possible to gain access to this material and Bierce's journalism should soon emerge as a uniquely detailed and penetrating commentary upon American events and values during a confused period of transition in our history.

Although it is not a secret that Bierce was a journalist, this fact has never been fully appreciated. Bierce did not dabble in journalism nor use it as a stepping stone to a literary career. Journalism was Bierce's *only* career, and his sole livelihood for the central forty years of his life. He did not abandon it, even temporarily, to produce his famous stories and other literary compositions. The great majority of everything he wrote appeared within the context of the columns he published regularly—usually once or twice a week—in the periodicals which employed him. Today, we know Bierce largely by the exceptional—i.e. literary—material of these columns, but they also contain some of the best and most important writing he ever did.

No account of Bierce's career can afford to omit reference to his seminal years in the crucible of the Civil War. "Among American writers none had a Civil War record of active service in any way comparable to Ambrose Bierce," writes Carey McWilliams. Bierce enlisted in the Union army as a private in immediate response to the first call for volunteers in 1861, and was mustered out as a first lieutenant in 1865 to recover from wounds. He subsequently served in the Reconstruction in Alabama and was retroactively awarded a brevet commission as major in recognition of his distinguished combat service. What he saw and experienced in the war permanently and profoundly changed him. At the deepest level, he achieved a revelation of the poignant tragedy of human existence. But the war also burned away the illusory ideals of his youth and left him with a lifelong bitter hatred of the shams, self-deceptions and remediable follies, errors and vices that add to the inherent injustices and tribulations of existence.

Bierce began his journalistic career around 1867, within a year or two of his arrival in San Francisco. He submitted short feature articles to local newspapers and journals. One of them, the *San Francisco News-Letter and California Advertiser,* had an editor, James Watkins, who was especially impressed by Bierce's potential, and gave him useful advice about improving his style. So rapidly did Bierce progress that when Watkins left the *News-Letter* in De-

cember, 1868, he was able to persuade the owner to make Bierce the new editor. Besides editing the paper, Bierce also wrote for it a regular feature called "The Town Crier," a column of short comments, usually witty or sarcastic, on miscellaneous subjects, usually local personalities or events. This early feature established the basic format that he was to follow the rest of his life. At the same time, he began to send off contributions to the *Alta California* and Bret Harte's *Overland Monthly* and to enlarge his reputation as an up and coming writer.

His style was to grow more trenchant and concise with the passing years, but even in his early articles it was apparent that Bierce was a writer of unusual talent and of strong and deeply thought out convictions. From the start, he was controversial. He had a gift for satire; his satire bit, and the pain lasted. One of his favorite targets described him as "this man with the burning pen." His enemies complained that he was cruel and indiscriminate in his attacks but the record will bear out that he was in fact careful and deliberate about whom or what he scored. And he repeatedly defended such social pariahs as Chinese, Mormons, and Jews from the rampant bigots of the town. Summing up his record in 1872, Bierce described himself in the third person as follows: "The only talents he [the Town Crier] has are a knack at hating hypocrisy, cant, and all sham, and a trick of expressing his hatred. What wider field than San Francisco does God's green earth present?"

Men can be known by whom and what they hate, as well as love, and Bierce was a talented and fearless hater. He largely restricted himself, in the early days, to satirizing the petty politicians and demagogues of San Francisco, and to ridiculing the local clergy for their hypocrisies and factional prejudices. His fearlessness and irreverence attracted much notice and he was no doubt invited to be discreet. But while writing for the *News-Letter,* he rejected the notion that "satire should not be like a saw, but a sword; it should cut, not mangle," and the advice of William Dean Howells that good satire is "so subtle as to leave a half doubt of its intent." "Let us mangle!" he cried, and turned deliberately away from the neat model of Horace to the examples of "that coarse Juvenal, and that horrid Swift." He wrote with the fresh bitterness of one who truly hated what he attacked and much of his power derives from this sincerity; he *was* morally incensed by the arrogance of the wicked and the oppression of the fool.

In 1872, Bierce married and went to England with his wife for an extended stay. While there, he wrote for the magazine *Figaro* and contributed articles to *Fun,* a satirical journal. A publisher was attracted by his work and published his first two books, **The Fiend's Delight** and **Nuggets & Dust,** both collections of the various pieces he had published in several journals.

Bierce returned to San Francisco in 1875, free-lanced for some months, and then found employment in 1877 on the *Argonaut,* a well-known San Francisco magazine. Bierce experimented in it with a variety of literary genres: editorials, poems, fables, stories, and articles, and he also returned to the format of the column of miscellaneous short comments he had written for the *News-Letter.* He self-mockingly named his new column "Prattle: A Transient Record of Individual Opinion."

Bierce left the *Argonaut* in 1880 to work a gold mine in South Dakota but returned to San Francisco in a few months, free-lanced again for a short time, and was then hired by the *Wasp,* an attractive magazine of humor and fiction. Bierce brought "Prattle" to the *Wasp,* as well as contributing other short pieces. He quit the *Wasp* in 1886, and was without steady work for a year until a fateful visit:

> One day as I lounged in my lodging there was a gentle, hesitating rap at the door and, opening it, I found a young man, the youngest young man, it seemed to me, that I had ever confronted. His appearance, his attitude, his manner, his entire personality suggested extreme diffidence. I did not ask him in, instate [sic] him in my better chair (I had but two) and inquire how we could serve each other. If my memory is not at fault I merely said:
>
> "Well," and awaited the result.
>
> "I am from the *San Francisco Examiner,*" he explained in a voice like the fragrance of violets made audible, and backed a little away.
>
> "O," I said, "you come from Mr. Hearst."
>
> Then that unearthly child lifted its blue eyes and cooed: "I am Mr. Hearst."

William Randolph Hearst's father had just bought him a local newspaper. No one knew what potential talent Hearst had, what dreams and ambitions. No one could have guessed that the *Examiner* was to be the first unit of one of the largest and most powerful newspaper empires in America. Young Hearst, however, had decided that to build the *Examiner* into something important, he needed the finest writers he could hire. Bierce was one of the first writers Hearst hired, and without a doubt the finest, one whose reputation would enhance the *Examiner.*

Bierce brought "Prattle" with him to the *Examiner* on two conditions: that the column would always appear either on the editorial page or in the prominent Sunday feature supplement that Hearst shortly inaugurated, and that he not be censored in any way and his copy never altered. Hearst agreed and kept his word for the twenty-two years Bierce worked for him. In 1896, when Hearst bought the *New York Journal* and turned it into the potent newspaper that vied with Pulitzer's *World* for dominance, Bierce's columns ran in it as a syndicated feature once or twice a week, including Sunday. When Bierce moved permanently in 1899 to Washington, D.C., he continued to write for the Hearst papers. "Prattle," however, was given a new title: "The Passing Show: A Record of Personal Opinion and Dissent." This name change lasted about a year. The column then began to appear less frequently and was often shorter. It appeared, furthermore, under a succession of new titles: "Ambrose Bierce Says," "Town Talk," "The Curmudgeon Philosopher" (c. 1901-02), "Views of the Melancholy Author" (c. 1902), "The Bald Campaigner" (c. 1902), and "The Views of One" (c. 1905). Despite Bierce's reduced output—by 1902 he was sixty years of age and frequently incapacitated by illness—Hearst kept

him on his staff and permitted him to contribute at his own pace. From 1905 to 1909 Bierce wrote stories, articles, and collections of newly-minted aphorisms for Hearst's monthly magazine, *Cosmopolitan.* In 1909, Bierce finally retired permanently from the Hearst organization, and from journalism. He spent the next three years collecting and revising his writings for a twelve-volume edition of his collected works which has since become, to all intents and purposes, the standard and definitive edition of Bierce. It fairly represents his fiction, verse and such miscellaneous literary forms as epigrams, fables and definitions, but the sample of his journalism included is both so small and so revised as to fundamentally distort the picture of his achievements in this field. Today, therefore, though Bierce has a secure reputation as a literary figure, it has been forgotten that he was one of the foremost journalists of his time, and one of the great journalists of the nation.

Bierce's "Prattle," and its successors, were among the most popular and influential feature columns of the turn of the century—and the least typical. For years, it has been customary to allude to Bierce's "underground" reputation, but this notion is mistaken. In his biography of Bierce, Carey McWilliams reports that not only did Bierce dominate all writing in the San Francisco area for a quarter of a century but that his fame had spread over the entire West and, in fact, to New York as well. As early as 1883, for example, when Bierce exposed the historian Hubert Howe Bancroft for farming out research work so that he could turn out more histories, at least one New York magazine followed up on the story. Bailey Millard, a Hearst editor, reportedly described "Prattle" as " 'the most wickedly clever, the most audaciously personal and the most eagerly devoured column that was ever published in this country' " The official notice of Bierce's move to Washington that appeared in the *Examiner* testifies to Bierce's wide-spread appeal in the strongest terms. It speaks of an appallingly heavy correspondence to Bierce over the years—mostly favorable—from common people much more often than from literary. Once Hearst syndicated Bierce in the *New York Journal,* his reputation spread even wider, and several scrapbooks of clippings in the Bierce Collection of the University of Virginia's Barrett Library show that Bierce was known and respected in his lifetime over the entire English-speaking world.

Bierce is justly famed for his "burning pen," but style is only a part of what made Bierce so popular and influential in his day. Even if his journalism had been less vivid, it would still merit study by subsequent generations of Americans for it constitutes one of the most extensive and able critiques of America in print. Bierce gradually raised his sights in "Prattle" from local issues and personalities to those of national and even international importance. Typically he supported his opinions with facts and reasoning. As a consequence, he did more than challenge his readers; he engaged them in debate and forced them to re-examine what they had too often thought were self-evident conclusions. Bierce was obviously one of the writers Hearst relied upon to raise the intellectual tone of his publications.

It is common to categorize Bierce as a sort of curmudgeon.

But this seriously misjudges a man who regarded America not with a jaundiced, but with a thoughtful eye. It is true that Bierce was a maverick, and criticized his time, his place, and his countrymen in almost every column he wrote, but what emerges from a sustained reading of his columns is not at all a catalogue of pungent petulancies but rather a coherent history of his own time which for all its bite is surprisingly accurate. Bierce was biased, but not partisan. His bias was for truth and he did not believe it came ready packaged for all time in convenient dogmas or doctrines. His censures, therefore, fell heavily upon those whose worshipful absolutism about a political, economic, social or religious theory blinded them to some phenomenon or consequence ungrateful to their belief. The Civil War had taught Bierce the fatal danger of relying too heavily on theory, and if his countrymen had not learned to be more skeptical, he instructed them.

It is also too easy to label Bierce either as a conservative or a disappointed liberal. It is generally well-known, for example, that Bierce detested socialism. Frequently, he is criticized for his economic or social naivete. But here are his objections to socialism:

> I am something of a Socialist myself; most of the best features of our present system are purely socialist and the trend is toward their extension. But even if Socialism were carried out as nearly to its ultimate implication and logical conclusion as is compatible with individual identity we should be no happier than we are at present, for we should be not better. Any system that human ingenuity can devise human ingenuity can pervert to selfish ends.

Bierce's argument, it will be noticed, is not so much about economic or social theory as about human nature. His main concern is not about the distribution of wealth but about the quality of life, the reality behind the theory. When confronting practical abuses of capitalism, Bierce could pass as a socialist to the uninitiated. He flatly maintained in "Prattle," for example, that government could not be excused for failing to provide work for men who are willing to work. Though he opposed labor which took the law into their own hands, he equally turned upon merchants who intruded upon their employees' private affairs, and upon large corporations which fleeced the public. He despised the doctrine *vox populi, vox dei.* He considered it patently false, the worst sort of self-deception, and an inducement to mobocracy. Bierce believed passionately in morality, but thought that majority votes had no bearing on it. He equally despised the rationalizations of the mighty, the individuals or parties in power. "Prattle" shows Bierce not to be naive, but complex and thoughtful.

On two occasions, Bierce's championing of integrity resulted in outstanding journalism. The first occurred in 1896, when he went to Washington to oppose the Funding Bill, which would have remitted about $130,000,000 of federal money to the railroads which had borrowed it. The railroads naturally supported the bill and Collis Huntington, president of the Southern Pacific, went to Washington to lobby for it. Many thought it futile to oppose so powerful and well-financed a lobby but by dint of extraordinary investigative reporting and bold and forceful writing,

Bierce brought about the defeat of the bill. Ten years later, when the muckrakers began their exposes of big business, Bierce's example guided them.

The second occasion was the three-year period of 1898-1901, when America suddenly became a world power by defeating Spain. It is now generally agreed that the Spanish-American War was unnecessary, and that a major part of the responsibility for it rests upon the yellow journalism of the age, particularly that of the Pulitzer and Hearst newspapers. Bierce was one of the few Americans of the time who saw clearly what was happening and opposed it, though he worked for Hearst. As early as 1895, he wrote "War—horrid war!—between the United States and Spain has already broken out like a red rash in the newspapers. . . . " In 1897, he warned bluntly against being dragged into a manufactured war, and when the war began, only Finley Peter Dunne among journalists was as critical of it as Bierce was. In a column reminiscent of *Lysistrata,* Bierce denounced war and urged women to exercise their power to end it simply by not supporting it. Further, though he wrote from San Francisco, there is no better contemporary critique of the war than Bierce's columns. Many of the nation's best journalists covered the war in Cuba: e.g. Richard Harding Davis, Stephen Crane, Frank Norris, Frederick Remington, Julian Hawthorne, James Creelman, and even William Randolph Hearst himself, but none of them had Bierce's personal expertise in military matters let alone a disposition to be skeptical of military claims. It is instructive to compare their accounts with his. They reported the event; Bierce corrected them. They reported the moment; Bierce explained what the moment meant. His columns are still exciting and interesting to read today, and his analyses convincing.

Just as Bierce was clear-eyed about the causes of the war and the amateurish prosecution of it, so was he able to see what few of his contemporaries even thought to look at—its consequences. He foresaw that America would pursue an expansionist policy and he was right. The Spanish-American War blended into the Filipino Insurrection, the Vietnam of its day. Troubled by a perception of a danger to the freedom of the press, he devoted an entire column to "The Tagalog Insurrection and the Right of Free Speech." Bierce also wrote perceptive columns on American jingoism, our involvement in the Boxer Rebellion, the trans-isthmian canal, the popular doctrines of Manifest Destiny and Anglo-American racial superiority, President McKinley, and the Boer War. On most of the issues of those troubled years, Bierce's journalism ran against the current of popular opinion, but history has vindicated most of his stands and his reasoning.

Not the least of Bierce's journalistic achievements was his maintaining his complete independence of expression while working for Hearst. Bierce detested Hearst and wrote "If ever two men were born to be enemies he and I are they. Each stands for everything that is most disagreeable to each other. . . . " "Prattle" frequently advanced positions in direct conflict with adjacent editorials. Hearst idealized the public, for example; Bierce denounced it. Hearst favored McKinley; Bierce ridiculed him. Hearst promoted the Spanish-American War; Bierce opposed it. Hearst favored the annexation of the Philipines; Bierce wanted them set free. Hearst was sympathetic to socialism; Bierce thought it folly. Bierce was aware of the incongruities attendant upon his working for Hearst; he resigned a number of times yet Hearst always persuaded him to return. The full story of this unlikely association is still not known, but that it existed was important for American journalism. In the final analysis, the relationship of Bierce and Hearst was eminently professional. Hearst was wise enough to know that a modern newspaper needed wide circulation, and that it was more important to present good writers that the public wanted to read than writers who only parroted editorial policy. And Bierce certainly knew that if he wished to reach a large audience—and he did—he had to be associated with a paper that had a large circulation. Thus, this unlikely symbiotic relationship of antipathies provided a model for what is now standard practice in American journalism. The publication of most feature columnists in modern newspapers is essentially a business arrangement that has much more to do with mutual financial benefit than with ideological agreement.

Few journalists have been as widely respected as Bierce, and it is easy to see why. Though some of his writing is spent on ephemeral issues, a great part of it remains vital, full of acute and provoking insights on interesting topics. No other contemporary journalist wrote so extensively and so informatively as he. None of his colleagues were as fearless and exciting, nor able to match him for clarity of thought and incisiveness of language. Yet the standard history of American journalism [by Frank Luther Mott] dismisses him with a single sentence: "Ambrose Bierce ran a column." In our own interests it is time to recall that column to active service. (pp. 34-40)

> Lawrence I. Berkove, "The Man with the Burning Pen: Ambrose Bierce as Journalist," in Journal of Popular Culture, Vol. 15, No. 2, Fall, 1981, pp. 34-40.

William Keough (essay date 1990)

[*In the following excerpt, Keough discusses Bierce as a practitioner of a particularly violent form of humor.*]

> May you live as long as you want to, and then
>   pass
> smilingly into the darkness—the good, kind
>   darkness.
> > —Ambrose Bierce in a letter to Jo
> > McCrackin, September 13, 1913

Less than four months after his wry fare-thee-well to Jo McCrackin, Ambrose Bierce himself passed into the "good, kind darkness"—perhaps in Mexico—perhaps even smilingly. Not many mourned.

As devil's lexicographer and self-appointed gadfly to three generations of political thieves and literary poseurs, Bierce had stood practically alone on the outermost crags of misanthropy. Yet he was also a man of high idealism and ruthless honesty who well knew the price one paid for telling uncomfortable truths. The cynic, as he once observed in *The Devil's Dictionary,* is "a blackguard whose faulty

vision sees things as they are, not as they ought to be. Hence the custom among the Scythians of plucking out a cynic's eyes to improve his vision."

Born in 1842 at the backwoods settlement of Horse Creek Cave in Meigs County, Ohio, Bierce was the tenth child of parents he later referred to as "unwashed savages." He scorned the rudimentary education offered by intinerant schoolmasters and, like Huck Finn, ran wild on the nearby shores of the Tippecanoe River. Like Sam Clemens, seven years his junior, Bierce drifted into journalism in his teens, working as "printer's devil" (how apt a phrase for Bierce!) on the *Northern Indianan,* but after being accused of theft he "absquatulated" to the Kentucky Military Academy.

His military schooling was to be short-lived. On April 19, 1861, in a burst of patriotism, Bierce volunteered for the Ninth Indiana Volunteer Infantry of the Union Army. His service during the Civil War was the key event of his life; and he later recalled, almost with relish, the many grotesque scenes he witnessed in it. After the battle of Cheat Mountain he saw pigs eating dead soldiers: "They had eaten our fallen," he later wrote, "but—touching magnanimity!—we did not eat theirs." Bierce distinguished himself in battle, but sustained "a dangerous and complicated" head wound while directing a charge at Kennesaw Mountain. Later, Bierce was to recall feeling "broken like a walnut." His brother Albert agreed: "He was never the same after that. Some of the iron of that shell seemed to stick in his brain, and he became bitter and suspicious, especially of his close friends. He would remember each failing and slight, fancied or otherwise . . . say nothing of it at the time, and then, many years afterward, release the stored-up poison in a flood." Though he took pride in having been the only American writer of importance to have fought for the Union cause, he came out of the war with no illusions about the United States which he later defined as "a great, broad blackness with two or three small points of light struggling and flickering in the universal blank of ignorance, crudity, conceit, tobacco-chewing, ill-dressing, unmannerly manners, and general barbarity." (Certainly not as many points of light as George Bush has seen, alas.)

But besides becoming prone to long, withering silences and explosions that frightened friend and family alike, Bierce came out of the war with an admiration for clearcut, life-and-death decisions. Death was constantly on his mind, and often on his lips. For this ex-soldier, the struggle for survival was no metaphor; and his ramrod-straight military bearing and "extraordinary vitality" inspired respect, even fear. After a distasteful term as a federal administrator in Alabama, Bierce joined General Hazen's 1866 campaign against the Western Indians—a "masterstroke of military humor" as he later put it. But the one-sided savagery quickly disgusted him, and he continued on to San Francisco, where he took up work as a staff writer. His crisp venom found ready outlets in the newspapers of the Far West which, as we have seen, often delighted in invective. "In the evolution of the comic spirit," as Bertha Clark Pope, editor of Bierce's letters, has noted, "the lowest stage, that of delight in inflicting pain on others, is clearly manifest in savages, small boys, and early American journalism." Bierce was as much at home in the cockpits of San Francisco as on the battlefield, and he described their daily horrors with relish. "The Italians continue their cheerful national recreation of stabbing one another," he wrote in one of his columns. "On Monday evening one was found badly gashed in the stomach going about his business with his entrails thrown over his arm."

Like Twain, Bierce was fond of drunken hijinks. After one memorable drinking bout, Bierce and two of his buddies tried to remove a cross atop a hillside in Golden Gate Park, but somehow got themselves enmeshed in ropes and had to be rescued. But even among fellow journalists, Bierce, despite his high spirits, was regarded as something of a "lizard," only too willing to deal with the darker side of man's nature. "All is worms," he proclaimed; the joke was on any fool who thought differently, and he wielded his pen like a cleaver. To be sure, Reconstructionist America afforded Bierce a host of tempting targets, and he attacked with relish. "To say of a man," he growled, "that he is like his contemporaries is to say that he is a scoundrel without excuse. The virtues are accessible to all. Athens was vicious, yet Socrates was virtuous." He wanted men to stand up—and keep standing. "Christians and camels," he scoffed, "receive their burdens kneeling."

For Bierce, wit, not "vile humor," was of value; and he championed wit despite the unpopularity of his position: "Vituperation—Satire, as understood by dunces and all such as suffer from an impediment in their wit." To a reviewer who criticized him for the indelicacy of his humor, he replied:

> O certainly humor should be "delicate." Every man of correct literary taste will tell you that it should be delicate; and so will every scoundrel that fears it. A man who is exposed to satire must not be made unhappy—O dear, no! Don't mangle the man like that coarse Juvenal, and that horrid Swift, but touch him up neatly, like Horace or a modern magazinist.

Bierce insisted on going for the jugular rather than the funny bone, and he defended the violent underpinnings of his basic comic mode:

> The wittiest man that we ever knew never said but one funny thing in his life, and that killed him—of which we were very glad. We hold that the true function of wit is not to make one writhe with merriment, but with anguish; it is not a sportive cow gamboling absurdly in a pasture, but a vicious horse latent in a stall, who kicks you in the bowels as you pass unconsciously behind him. Somebody has said that humor was but pathos masquerading. That is our idea of it; it is something to make a man cry.

Bierce sneered at Howells's suggestion that American authors should concentrate on "the more smiling aspects of life" and called Howells and Henry James "two eminent triflers and cameo-cutters-in-chief to Her Littleness the Bostonese small virgin . . . complacently enamored of their own invirility and pouring like sponges the vocal incense of a valleyful of idiots." For Bierce, a writer was "sinner, saint, hero and wretch"; and he opposed the genteel tradition by hurling insults at the motley mass of Panglosses he saw spreading across the land like rancid butter from Beacon Street to the Napa Valley. For Bierce, wit was a useful scourge. "Humor is tolerant, tender; its ridicule caresses. Wit stabs, begs pardon—and turns the weapon in the wound. Invective, a secular curse, consists of direct assault to obliterate its object through abuse. I am not a poet but an abuser." Of one local hoodlum he wrote:

> Chuck him overboard! Let him suffocate in slime and stenches, the riddances of sewers and the wash of slums. Give his carcass to the crabs utterly, and let the restless shrimp embed its body in his eye-socket, or wave its delicate antennae from his pale nostril. Let globes and tangles of eels replace his bowels, and the muscular squid lay coils of clammy tentacles about the legs of him. Over with him!

A Juvenal among Horaces as he saw it, Bierce also disdained the camp of native humorists—Twain and Artemus Ward in particular. He regarded what he called the "dialect industry" as "the grunt of the human hog with an audible memory." As for American satire, it was a fantastic and imaginary beast, which

> never had more than a sickly and uncertain existence, for the soul of it is wit, wherein we are dolefully deficient, the humor that we mistake for it being tolerant and sympathetic. Moreover, although Americans are "endowed by the Creator" with abundant vice and folly, it is not generally known that these are reprehensible qualities, wherefore the satirist is popularly regarded as a sour-spirited knave, and his every victim's outcry for codefendants evokes a national assent.

At every opportunity Bierce disdained the poker face of American humor and called for "savage indignation." Stylistically, too, Bierce declared war. Where Twain insisted that the success of American humor depended upon the teller's seeming to lose the point and wander about, Bierce found such tomfoolery not only insufferable but sloppy. He offered to match his "lethiferous" (i.e., lethal) wit against Twain's "bovine humor" and belabored Twain, Petroleum V. Nasby, and Bret Harte for their long-windedness; and he contended that native reading habits consisted usually of "Indian novels, stories in dialect, and humor in slang." Bierce bowed his own head toward Rome and "Augustan" England, and took as models Juvenal, Catullus, Tacitus, and Marcus Aurelius; also Swift, Gibbon, and Macaulay. Like Irving, Cooper, and Hawthorne before him, Bierce took the "high road" of English. (Which may account for the stilted quality of much of his dialogue. Americans, after all, do *not* speak "English.")

For a man of these predilections, there was little room in the literary establishment of late-nineteenth-century America, but Bierce courted his unpopularity assiduously. Rejecting the genteel practitioners and the "phunny phellows" both, Bierce was doomed to be an outsider. But he enjoyed his outcast state, and he relished personal invective. After hearing of Twain's fortuitous marriage to Olivia Langdon, Bierce wrote:

> It was not the act of a desperate man—it was not committed while laboring under temporary in-

sanity; his insanity is not of that type. It was the cool, methodical culmination of human nature working in the heart of an orphan hankering for someone with a fortune to love—someone with a bank account to caress.

Eventually he came under the wing (or talon, as the case may be) of William Randolph Hearst, and wrote for several Hearst publications and such quasi-literary journals as *The Wasp* and *The Prattle,* where he was encouraged to attack whatever prevailing foolishness caught his eye. There, with his poison pen and black ink in endless supply, Bitter Bierce, as many called him, came into his element. Though he wrote too much (over eight million words) and never did quite manage to free himself from the journalistic yoke, there is a bristly integrity to his best work. No Frostian lover's quarrel, Bierce's relationship with the world can more fairly be described as a long divorce proceeding, and much of what he wrote has fallen into deserved limbo. Yet there still is much of worth. Bierce might have been a casualty, but he was no man's fool.

Bierce's wit is probably his most enduring legacy. His serious stories, "Tales of Soldiers" and "Tales of Civilians [in *Tales of Soldiers and Civilians*], praised for technical excellence and economy, seem now overly dependent on plot and coincidence. His one novel, a collaboration *cum* translation of a German Gothic tale, *The Monk and the Hangman's Daughter,* is an overwrought and inadvertent parody of the genre, notable for its curious preoccupation with female purity. His longer pieces, too, in "Tangential Tales" and *Shadow on the Dial,* now seem repetitious and tedious.

Bierce excelled in the short form, and his "ante-mortem" epitaphs and terse newspaper items testify to his mordant wit. Many a Bierce neologism, "futilitarianism" or "femininnies," sparkles like an epigram. Many pithy entries to his *Devil's Dictionary* offer ample evidence of his quirky genius:

> *Bride,* a woman with a fine prospect
> of happiness behind her.
> *Brute,* see husband.
> *Novel,* a short story padded.

Within the short form, only Mark Twain and Dorothy Parker rival Bierce, but neither of them was able to invent so aptly or consistently. Typically, Bierce worked through inversion. He reverses an old saw, for example, to give it a new twist: "To forgive is to err, to be human divine." Absurdity is "the argument of an opponent"; Christmas, "a day set apart and consecrated to gluttony, drunkenness, maudlin sentiment, gift-taking, public dullness, and domestic behavior."

Bierce viewed any notion of the natural goodness of man or the providential integrity of the state as naive and hypocritical. Optimism was but "the doctrine that everything is beautiful, including what is ugly, everything good, especially the bad, and everything right that is wrong"; cheerfulness was "the religion of the little." Bierce saw his own pessimism corroborated in racist California laws and in the hypocrisies of corrupt capitalists such as railroad baron Collis P. Huntington. As Bierce understood the function of wit to be the unmasking of society's crimes, he

intended his *Devil's Dictionary* to expose injustice through the topicality of its definitions:

Amnesty,	The state's magnanimity to those offenders it would be too expensive to punish.
Beggar,	A pest unkindly inflicted upon the suffering rich.
Compulsion,	The eloquence of power.
Love,	Temporary insanity curable by marriage.
Recreation,	Stoning Chinamen.

Unlike Twain or other humorists, "Almighty God" Bierce refused to pull his punches. He wrote purposely to shock, and those he most wanted to shock were the smug and self-certain, or the stupid, his pet aversion. Bierce did shock, sometimes in Swiftian fashion:

> Last week was the best week for dead babies we have ever had. Of the seventy-four deaths occurring in the city, more than half were of infants under two years of age. Thirty were under one year. Whom the gods love die young, particularly if their parents get drunk and neglect them.

Such joking is strong meat, and not for every taste.

Bierce worried little about offending the soft-throated public with his jugular humor. As a coat of arms for American letters, he proposed an illiterate hoodlum rampant on a field of dead authors with the motto, "To Hell with Literature." Bierce dedicated his *Dictionary* to "those enlightened souls who prefer dry wines to sweet, sense to sentiment, wit to humor and clean English to slang." He also predicted "it will have no sale, for it has no slang, no dialect, and no grinning through a horse-collar," and therefore would not appeal to the common reader who was a Philistine "sometimes learned, frequently prosperous, commonly clean and always solemn."

Not all of Bierce's jests still glow; some chestnuts have indeed staled, and as a kind of perverse Pangloss he can be cantankerous to a fault. Even the *Devil's Dictionary* is very uneven work. His techniques—invective, rhetorical overkill, and comic deflation—become repetitive, and as the subjects of his invective have passed on, their crimes sealed up in the petty-cash box of time, we are left with merely the blue streaks. Also, as one becomes acquainted with the Bierce philosophy, his quips and witticisms, unfailingly pessimistic, seem not only formulaic but a bit oppressive:

Defenseless,	Unable to attack.
Noncombatant,	A dead Quaker.
Congratulation,	The civility of envy.
Birth,	First and direst of all disasters.
Year,	A period of three-hundred and sixty-five disappointments.

Yet, for all the cavils, there is, as Mrs. Pope has said, "enough audacity to startle, enough paradox to charm."

Bierce's fiercest thunderbolts were reserved for the political system around him; and as the Gilded Age began to tarnish, many Americans came to doubt the providential implications of the New Zion. California politics in particular inspired many of Bierce's most cynical entries:

Bribe,	That which enables a member of the California legislature to live on his pay without any dishonest economies.
Presidency,	The greased pig in the field of American politics.
Diplomacy,	The patriotic art of lying for one's country.

The law seemed but a matter of caprice. The legal, Bierce rued, was that which was "compatible with the will of a judge having jurisdiction" and a lawyer but "one skilled in circumvention of the law." As Richard O'Connor observes, "In their treatment of the Western frontier Bret Harte made the prevalent contempt for the law picturesque and Mark Twain found it humorous, but Bierce labelled it for what it was—murder, armed robbery, and intent to kill." Indeed, Bierce sneered at the grand legend of the West as "bosh." Juries were the greatest joke of all: "In the McFarland case the defendant set up the plea of insanity, and succeeded in proving himself a fool. And he was acquitted by a jury of his peers." Bierce went on to compose his own **"Rational Anthem"**:

My country, 'tis of thee,
Sweet land of felony,
　　Of thee I sing—
Land where my fathers fried
Young witches and applied
Whips to the Quaker's hide
　　And made him spring.

My knavish country, thee,
Land where the thief is free,
　　Thy laws I love;
I love thy thieving bills
That top the people's tills;
I love thy mob whose will's
　　All laws above.

Bierce was also a hard-liner on crime, and he advocated harsh prison discipline and the death penalty to keep the rabble in line. Strict adherence to Roman law, he argued, would cauterize society and help sweep the rabble from the streets. Anarchists incensed him: "I favor mutilation for anarchists convicted of killing or inciting to kill," he wrote, "mutilation followed by death."

Bierce was no admirer of the so-called "common man." Once, looking out at a crowd, he remarked, "Wouldn't it be fun to turn loose a machine gun into that?" And he was scornful of optimistic claims for the "voice of the people":

Sum up the intelligence of the country and divide it by the number of inhabitants: the quotient represents the intelligence of the average man. It would be found to be considerably greater than that of a soft-shelled crab, and considerably less than that of a hippopotamus. Its expression in bad English is "vox populi," and calling this "vox Dei" is besetting blasphemy.

Bierce proposed "a despotism of brains to save civilization from the mob," but he was not sanguine about its prospects. Democracy was an illusion, and equality "an imaginary condition in which skulls are counted, instead of brains, and merit determined by lot and punished by preferment." Of a "republic," Bierce expected only "the foundation of public order in the ever-lessening habit of submission."

Bierce was a defender of classicism in art, honesty in human dealings, and high-mindedness in government. However (always, with Bierce, a however), though he knew the crimes of capitalists only too well, he also hated socialists and reformers; though he insisted on (and practiced) chivalry toward women, he reviled the sex in print; and though defending the rights of the common man vigorously, he attacked the common man's stupidity constantly. One can, of course, find many glaring contradictions in his writings, but Bierce's attacks do seem a healthy antidote to that ostrich mentality which refuses to recognize problems or register alarm.

Bierce also excelled at the humor of horror. As Clifton Fadiman has noted, "Bierce's morbidity was exceptionally fertile—he made it produce humor as well as chills. I should say in this extremely narrow field of the sardonic, of the ludicrous ghost story, and the comical murder, he is unrivalled. He begins by somehow making you accept his basic premise: death is a joke." And murder high comedy, we might add. We have seen something of this in *Roughing It*, where Twain uses such stories for change of pace, but in Bierce it is the ghoulishness which seems the entire point.

In "Negligible Tales," Bierce's humor is not without a touch of grisly zaniness, and the absurdity set off by the flat style. **"A Revolt of the Gods"** begins calmly: "My father was a deodorizer of dead dogs, my mother kept the only shop for the sale of cat's-meat in my native city. They did not live happily; the difference in social rank was a chasm which would not be bridged by the vows of marriage." Other stories are spiced with similarly gratuitous observations, such as this form **"A Bottomless Grave"**: "I was immediately arrested and thrown into jail, where I passed a most uncomfortable night, being unable to sleep because of the profanity of my fellow-prisoners, two clergymen, whose theological training had given them a fertility of impious ideas and a command of blasphemous language altogether unparalleled." Blithely thumbing his nose—at realism, at any and all offended sensibilities—Bierce seems to be offering these tales as catchbasins of graveyard humor; and they seem the most relaxed, the least tendentious of his works.

The humor of another volume of tales, "The Parenticide Club," however, borders on the pathological. **"Oil of Dog,"** for instance, starts off deceptively, suggesting Dickens—for a sentence and a half: "My name is Boiffer Bings. I was born of honest parents in one of the humbler walks of life, my father being a manufacturer of dog-oil and my mother having a small studio in the shadow of the village-church, where she disposed of unwelcome babes." Again, the style lulls, though underneath lingers a wormy ghoulishness. **"An Imperfect Conflagration"** begins, "Early one June morning in 1872 I murdered my father—an act which made a deep impression on me at the time." Another tale, **"My Favorite Murder"** recounts the torture of an unloved uncle at inordinate length, and is sheer sadism. In these stories we again confront the Bierce who is only too happy to shock or repulse; and (perhaps appropriately) these tales were awarded the first "Prix de l'Humeur Noir" in 1956.

Bierce's obsession with death (an obsession he shared with the late Twain, who could rip off one-liners such as, "Pity is for the living, envy is for the dead.") remained with him throughout his life. For Bierce, death was "the greatest good for the greatest number" and suicide was "courageous"; and he courted danger with an unnatural fondness. Just as, as a young soldier, he had distinguished himself for bravery (some said foolhardiness), later, as a civilian and a journalist, he insulted rival after rival, avoiding challenge only because of his reputation as a crack marksman. It was even rumored that he had acquired the asthma that plagued him by sleeping off his hangovers in graveyards after drinking bouts with the likes of Jack London.

But Bierce claimed that his preoccupation was essentially moral in that death was the final leveler and thus the thought of death should, he felt, encourage modesty. He regarded war as the righteous sword of the Avenging Angel cutting through the mess and fat of civilian life. Certainly, his own life had its share of tragedy. In 1888, Bierce himself left his faithful (and no doubt long-

Bierce in Washington, D.C.

suffering) wife Molly after finding a love-letter to her from an amorous Dane. In 1889, Day, his teenage son, killed his wife's suitor and turned the gun on himself. In 1901 his son Leigh, a reporter, died at twenty-seven in New York. Bierce did not complain; it was as if he expected nothing more from life. Death, on the other hand, he seemed to view as an amiable companion; and he spoke admiringly of the little death-skull cookies Mexican children are given, *memento mori*.

Late in life Bierce took to wearing a suit of black—as naturally, it seems, as Twain took to his famous white suit; and one fellow newspaperman described his forlorn figure, "dressed in black from head to foot [with] a walking cane, black as ebony and unrelieved by gold or silver," like a Puritan minister or Poe's raven, wandering from one Civil War battlefield to another, squatting on gravestones, the sounds of distant thunder awash in his inner ear, the battle sites now quiet and empty except for an occasional cow. Bierce confessed to some remorse about his own role in the war. "They found a Confederate soldier the other day with his rifle alongside," he once said to a friend, "and I'm going over to beg his pardon." With his two sons and estranged wife dead, Bierce became ever more morbid and found the twentieth century even less to his liking. "Why should I remain in this country," he wrote his daughter Helen in 1913, "that is on the eve of prohibition and woman's suffrage? In America you can't go east or west any more, or north; the only avenue of escape is south . . . I want to go down and see if these Mexicans shoot straight."

Go south he did—right into the teeth of the political hurricane that was Mexico torn by a bloody civil war. In his "last piece of humor" as Jay Martin puts it, Bierce crossed over at Ciudad Juárez in November carrying $1500 in American currency and bearing credentials as an observer to Pancho Villa's rebel army, and disappeared into the chaos. On December 16, he arrived in Chihuahua as General Huerta fled; and in his last letter to Connie Christiansen (dated December 26, 1913) Bierce spoke of going to Ojinaga by rail. But nothing more was heard of the old man—the rest is silence, as they say.

But not quite.

The mystery of Bierce's disappearance has never been solved—though theories abound. One theory has it that Bierce died at the hands of Pancho Villa's henchmen; another that he was shot while fighting for Villa at the battle of Ojinaga; still another has him executed by General Urbina farther south. One Charles Fort, who devoted his life to strange phenomena, has noted that an Ambrose Small disappeared at the same time and theorized that some "demonic force" was collecting Ambroses. But by far the most bizarre theory is that of Sibley S. Morrill in *Ambrose Bierce, F. A. Mitchell-Hedges, and the Crystal Skull.* Morrill posits a melange of spies, intrigue, and primitive Indian tribes to explain Bierce's disappearance. Because Bierce worked as a journalist in Washington and was carrying a money belt, Morrill lumps him together with three other foreign "spies" in the Yalbic area of Guatemala, and concludes that Bierce, like the others, must have been "disappeared" because he had seen "the Crystal Skull" in a sacred cave used by the Charro Indians. Morrill's final "proof" is that a British businessman, Mitchell-Hedges, has refused to tell where he found the Crystal Skull, thereby confirming that he was also a spy unable to breach the British Official Secrets Act.

Morrill's odd conspiracy theories extend to Bierce's final letter: "What seems more likely is that if it did, in fact, mention that he was going to Ojinaga, the letter was designed to throw anyone off the scent of where he did go." Morrill's logic, in effect, argues that two plus two must equal five because four is such an obvious answer. *Ambrose Bierce, F. A. Mitchell-Hedges, and the Crystal Skull* is a marvelously absurdist book, amortizing two thousand years of Central American history, an erstwhile British adventurer, a second-string crystal skull, and a lost American satirist into a hilarious concoction of the completely impalpable. Bierce, needless to say, would have delighted in this extra idiocy. Even final ironies, it seems, have final ironies.

The truth seems far less fanciful. Elias Torres, who served with Pancho Villa, says that Villa had Bierce shot before remarking, "Let's see if this damned American tells his last joke to the buzzards on the mountain."

More recently, Mexican novelist Carlos Fuentes has "imagined" Bierce's fate in *The Old Gringo,* a dark and moving novel in which Bierce, "an erect old man, stiff as a ramrod," crosses the border because, as the Mexicans all understand, he has "come to die." Bierce involves himself in the protection of a young, idealistic American woman, Harriet Winslow, to whom he reveals himself as "Old Bitters . . . a contemptible muckraking reporter" whose name is "synonymous with coldness, with anti-sentimentality." Our man, all right.

Fuentes's Bierce speculates about his family, who feared him

> [because] he had mocked God, his Homeland, Money; for God's sake, then, when would it be their turn? They must have asked themselves then: when will it be our turn? When will our accursed father turn against us, judging us, telling us you're no exception, you prove the rule, and you, too, wife and you, my beautiful daughter, and you, my sons, you are all a part of the ludicrous filth, the farts of God, we call humanity.
>
> I shall destroy you all with my ridicule. I shall bury you all beneath my poisonous laughter. I shall laugh at you as I laugh at the United States, at its ridiculous army and flag," the old man said breathlessly, choking with asthma.

He offers the commandments of a New Decalogue:

> Adore no images save those the coinage of the country shows; Kill not, for death liberates your foe from persecution's constant woe;
>
> Honor thy parents, and perchance their wills thy fortune may advance.

But, as he also admits, he might have betrayed his ideals by allowing himself to be used:

> I saw myself as a kind of avenging angel, you see.

> I was the bitter and sardonic disciple of the devil because I was trying to be as sanctimonious as the people I scorned.
>
> I stoutly insisted I was the friend of Truth, not of Plato while my lord and master of the press [Hearst] cannibalized my anger for the greater glory of his political interests and his massive circulation and his massive bank accounts. Oh, what a fool I was, Miss Harriet. But that's what they paid me for, for being the idiot, the buffoon, in the pay of my lord and master on this earth.

This is an interesting observation—one echoed more recently by Kurt Vonnegut and editorial cartoonist Herblock, who also come to question if, in fact, humor does more than just serve as a safety valve for righteous anger against the powerful.

Later, Bierce mutters, with a smile, "To be a gringo in Mexico . . . ah, that is euthanasia." Eventually, he is granted his wish to be "a good-looking corpse." Betrayed and shot in the back, he is then dug up and shot in the front for appearance's sake.

So, even in his grave it seems, wherever that might be, Bierce continues to intrigue. The themes of *The Old Gringo* include the misuse of anger, the apparent futility of goodness, and the sorrow of our imperfections: all of Bierce's darkest and most heartfelt themes. Yet, interestingly, Fuentes has managed to soften—to humanize—some of the edges to create an appealing Bierce.

Bierce continues to occupy a niche, albeit narrow, in the American literary grotto; and there are those who find refreshment in the cutting edge of his satire. "Bierce is good," James Agee wrote Father Flye, "Irony and savage anger and even certain planes of cynicism are, used right, nearly as good instruments as love, and not by any means incompatible with it; good lens wipers and good auxiliaries. . . . I care a lot for smaller, sharp intelligent soreheads like Bierce." We must agree that there is a hard, thorny sincerity to the man. H. L. Mencken, a tough hombre himself, admires his ferocity and fearlessness:

> His disbelief in man went even further than Mark Twain's; he was quite unable to imagine the heroic in any ordinary sense. . . . Man, to him, was the most stupid and ignoble of animals. But at the same time the most amusing. Out of the spectacle of life about him he got an unflagging and Gargantuan joy. The obscene farce of politics delighted him. He was an almost amorous connoisseur of theology and theologians. He howled with mirth whenever he thought of a professor, a doctor, or a husband.
>
> His stories are not a transcript of life. The people in them simply do not live or breathe. Ring Lardner, whose manner Ambrose Bierce would have detested, did a hundred times better in that direction. . . . The timorousness of Mark Twain was not in him; no head was lofty enough to escape his furious thwack. Such berserk men have been rare in history; the normal Americano shows considerable discretion.

Bierce was a dutiful "town crier," faithful to his calling,

raising a loud hue and cry at the crimes he saw. And Bierce was proud of what he was. As he wrote Walter Neale: "My independence is my wealth; it is my literature. I have written to please myself, no matter who should be hurt." Convinced that the image of reality around him was false, Bierce tried to preserve his own mind by ridiculing the crazed world that questioned his sense and sensibility. His grotesque humor presages Nathanael West's extravagant satire, Mencken's own attacks on the "booboisee," and the work of such black humorists as Terry Southern, Joseph Heller, and Thomas Pynchon. In many ways, too, Bierce stands as a precursor to contemporary comedians like Lenny Bruce and Don Rickles, who assault their audiences. By deliberately flinging away the restraint of manners, Bierce pointed a finger at naked human fraud; and his insults offer the release of truth.

But no matter how much one "explains" Bierce, there is still something unsavory about him. Perhaps it is simply that we don't wish our jokes quite that raw. Bierce seems too much the wolf, excessively diabolical. If, in his sardonic couplet, "Forgive, O Lord, the little jokes I play on Thee, / And I'll forgive Thy great big one on me," Robert Frost implies a wry acceptance. Bierce, on the other hand, could never bring himself to forgive or forget that "great big joke." Life, to Bierce, seemed but an empty parenthesis upon the black sheet of eternity.

Since no flower could flourish under the withering gaze of his basilisk eye, Bierce's garden grew only cacti, and thus he seems destined to remain a cult figure. His contribution to the grand concert of American humor may best be summed up as a catcall from the balcony. Though such writers as Hemingway, Mencken, and Stephen Crane (whom he detested) have praised him, no important American writer has claimed Bierce as mentor. Clifton Fadiman has called him "a Swift minus true intellectual powers, Rochefoucauld with a bludgeon, Voltaire with stomach ulcers." Edmund Wilson branded him a "fascist."

Whatever his "value," Bierce is proof-positive of the comic dilemma. As a gleeful paymaster of invective, Bierce attacked his violent society violently; his is the comic mask stripped of pretense, ugly and accusatory. If Mark Twain often shone as the blazing sun of American humor, Bierce seems more its dark shadow. Even if the humorist or satirist, on pain of blandness, must not pull his punches, he must also provide his audience with some tentative comfort, some possible joy. "The danger," as Kurt Vonnegut has shrewdly noted, "is spilling over into misanthropy like Bierce and the late Twain."

Yet the extreme has value. Bierce's critical comments on the general run of American humor do much to illuminate its special nature. Praising the "crank and curio," Bierce might well have been writing his own epitaph: "What would life be without its mullahs and its dervishes? A matter of merchants and camel-drivers—no one to laugh with and at." A harsh, frowning mullah in ministerial black, Bierce reminds us of the limits of humor—even American humor. He stands poised, like a fierce and implacable eagle, on the edge of the abyss. On the very edge. (pp. 61-77)

William Keough, "The Bottled Bile of Ambrose Bierce," in his Punchlines: The Violence of American Humor, *Paragon House, 1990, pp. 61-77.*

Bierce on the nature of his verse:

I am not, properly speaking, a poet—the writing of a few desultory poems gives one but little title to that distinction. The greater part, by far, of my verse is satirical and intended to be; not poetical, but witty. The taste for that kind of thing is like that for dry wines—it comes of cultivation. It is not understood in this country, nor will it be, probably, for generations. It is thought malicious and ascribed to personal rancor. Humor our people understand (if it is coarse enough) but not wit. Nevertheless, following the line of least resistance, I have commonly gone that way.

Ambrose Bierce in a letter to American critic Edmund Stedman, 19 March 1899.

S. T. Joshi   (essay date 1990)

[*An American critic, Joshi is the leading figure in the criticism of weird fiction writers. In the following excerpt from his study* The Weird Tale, *he discusses the importance of Bierce's stories in the genre of weird fiction.*]

[Bierce] had very pronounced views on writing, in particular on writing the short story. Here we are concerned with three essays—**"The Novel"** (1897), **"The Short Story"** (1897), and **"To Train a Writer."** One passage from the first will suffice:

> The novel bears the same relation to literature that the panorama bears to painting. With whatever skill and feeling the panorama is painted, it must lack that basic quality in all art, unity, totality of effect. As it can not be seen at once, its parts must be seen successively, each effacing the one seen before; and at the last there remains no coherent and harmonious memory of the work. It is the same with a story too long to be read with a virgin attention at a single sitting.

This sounds very much like a mechanical adaptation of Poe's theory of poetry and probably is; but it is Bierce's view, and he stuck to it. Certain other of Bierce's remarks—his contempt for literary realism ("imagination chained to the perch of probability"—), his preference for the romance (Scott, Hawthorne) over the novel, and his implicit scorn of Edgar Fawcett's criticism of the short story because " 'it can not express the one greatest thing in all literature—intercommunication of human characters' "—are, taken together, all we need to know of Bierce's literary theory.

Of greater interest is what Bierce's views may have been on the theory of weird fiction. His remarks on romance are suggestive, but we can learn much more on this matter in a rather unusual way—by examining his remarkable and radical reorganization of the contents of his two principal collections of horror tales, *Tales of Soldiers and Civilians* and *Can Such Things Be?* This act of rearrangement has apparently gone almost entirely unnoticed by Bierce scholars, but it is of vital importance to Bierce's aesthetic of horror, for the dominant motive at work is the segregation of his supernatural and his nonsupernatural tales.

The first edition of *Tales of Soldiers and Civilians* (San Francisco: E. L. G. Steele, 1891) contained the following tales: Soldiers: **"A Horseman in the Sky"**; **"An Occurrence at Owl Creek Bridge"**; **"Chickamauga"**; **"A Son of the Gods"**; **"One of the Missing"**; **"Killed at Resaca"**; **"The Affair at Coulter's Notch"**; **"A Tough Tussle"***; **"The Coup de Grâce"**; **"Parker Adderson, Philosopher"**; Civilians: **"A Watcher by the Dead"**; **"The Man and the Snake"**; **"A Holy Terror"**; **"The Suitable Surroundings"**; **"An Inhabitant of Carcosa"***; **"The Middle Toe of the Right Foot"***; **"Haïta the Shepherd"***; and **"An Heiress from Red Horse."** The reissue of 1898 (New York: G. P. Putnam's Sons), now titled *In the Midst of Life* (taken from the British edition of 1892), adds the following three tales: **"An Affair of Outposts"**; **"The Damned Thing"***; and **"The Eyes of the Panther."** When, however, the collection was reprinted as volume 2 of the *Collected Works* (1909), the tales I have marked with an asterisk were removed and placed in volume 3 (*Can Such Things Be?* 1910), and **"The Boarded Window"** was added. It is obvious that Bierce wished to exclude any overtly supernatural tales from this collection—hence the exclusion of the two otherworldly fantasies, **"An Inhabitant of Carcosa"** and **"Haïta the Shepherd,"** and the definitely supernatural **"Middle Toe of the Right Foot"**; **"The Damned Thing"** might be considered supernatural, but more on this later.

Two stories—**"The Boarded Window"** and **"The Eyes of the Panther"**—hint of the supernatural but do not actually involve it. Let us consider the former. A man and his wife live in an isolated cabin near Cincinnati. The wife falls ill and, in spite of attempts by her husband to nurse her back to health, lapses into unconsciousness and "apparently" dies after three days. The man is prostrated with shock and falls asleep. He is awakened in the dark by the sound of a scuffle, and learns that a panther has crawled through a window and is dragging the woman's body away. The man shoots his rifle at the animal and scares it away. Although the woman's body is now mutilated by lacerations at her throat, "between [her] teeth was a fragment of the animal's ear." Probably we are to understand that the woman was not in reality dead but merely in a sort of coma, from which she revived when the animal attacked her—otherwise a "pool of blood" could not have issued from her throat at the animal's attack.

"The Eyes of the Panther" is an extraordinarily difficult tale, and many . . . have declared flatly that this is the story of a shape-changer, and hence supernatural; but there are suggestions to the contrary. Jenner Brading wishes to marry Irene Marlowe; she loves him but claims that she cannot marry him because she is insane. She tells him a story in which her mother, left alone in a cabin by her husband, was frightened to madness by the "luminous orbs" of a panther looking into the window. Irene was born a few months later, and she maintains that these circumstances warrant the belief that she is insane. Jenner,

who has heard stories of a panther peering into people's houses at night, believes that Irene is indeed insane, but that she has fantasized her own past from these accounts. Jenner withdraws, letting it be known that he has been rejected in matrimony by the daughter of the recluse Old Man Marlowe. One evening he sees at his window "two gleaming eyes that burned with a malignant lustre inexpressibly terrible!" He shoots the object with a gun and of course finds that it is Irene.

The key is what we are to make of all these shining eyes. Does Irene's mere possession of such eyes imply that she is herself a sort of werewolf—sometimes human, sometimes a panther? This is possible, for details like this are frequently used in weird tales to signal the supernatural. But Bierce on two occasions goes out of his way to emphasize that, although shining eyes were seen, no actual panther was present. First, when Irene departs after her last meeting with Jenner, he "caught a quick, brief glimpse of shining eyes"; but "no panther was visible." Second, after Jenner shoots Irene and follows her as she drags her fatally wounded body into the forest, he comes upon the victim: "But it was no panther." The bluntness of these utterances seems to suggest that Bierce is signaling a nonsupernatural resolution to the story.

But if the tale is nonsupernatural, is it that Irene is simply insane? that she *fancies* herself occasionally a panther? This is the solution I had adopted until Susan Michaud suggested to me an entirely different interpretation: *it is Jenner who is insane.* He had been incensed at Irene's rejection of his proposal, to the point that he wished to strangle her. When Jenner sees the shining eyes at his window, he may be playing out some subconscious desire to kill Irene—and he in fact does so. Michaud believes that Irene refused to marry Jenner because she did not wish to abandon her reclusive father and therefore made up the tale about her mother and the panther; she came to Jenner's window not to harm him but out of genuine love and concern. I like this reconstruction because it makes the tale fall into a pattern of several Bierce works involving the central irony of individuals talking and acting at cross-purposes, whereby each party is unaware of the other's real motivations. We shall see this exemplified supernaturally in **"The Moonlit Road."**

The only thing that puzzles me about the tales omitted from *In the Midst of Life* is the removal of **"A Tough Tussle,"** a perfectly good (nonsupernatural) war story. I can only suppose that Bierce thought it too similar in basic plot to **"A Watcher by the Dead,"** although other such parallelisms (**"The Affair at Coulter's Notch"** is very close in conception to **"A Horseman in the Sky,"** and **"The Man and the Snake"** bears resemblances to **"One of the Missing"**) do not seem to have bothered him.

The case with *Can Such Things Be?* is considerably more complicated. The first edition (New York: Cassell, 1893) contained **"The Death of Halpin Frayser"**; **"The Mocking-Bird"***; **"My Favorite Murder"****; **"One Officer, One Man"***; **"The Man out of the Nose"***, **"An Occurrence at Brownville"***; **"Jupiter Doke, Brigadier-General"****; **"The Famous Gilson Bequest"***; **"The Story of a Conscience"***; **"The Secret of Macarger's Gulch"**; **"The**

Major's Tale"**; "A Psychological Shipwreck"; "One Kind of Officer"*; "The Applicant"*; "One of Twins"; "The Night-Doings at 'Deadman's' "; "The Widower Turmore"**; "George Thurston"*; "Three Episodes in the Life of a Brave Man"; "John Bartine's Watch"; "The Realm of the Unreal"; "A Baby Tramp"; "Some Haunted Houses"; "Bodies of the Dead"; and "Mysterious Disappearances." The stories marked with one asterisk were transferred to volume 2 of the *Collected Works* (*In the Midst of Life*), and for fairly obvious reasons: "The Mocking-Bird," "One Officer, One Man," "The Story of a Conscience," "One Kind of Officer," and "George Thurston" are war stories; "The Man out of the Nose," "An Occurrence at Brownville" (retitled "An Adventure at Brownville"), and "The Applicant" are clearly nonsupernatural. "The Famous Gilson Bequest" seems to involve a ghost at its conclusion, but it is probable that the apparition is in the mind of the protagonist, Mr. Brentshaw: Bierce lets himself off the hook by noting that Brentshaw "could . . . perceive, or think he perceived" the ghost. In any case, the ghost—if it is that—is not central to the plot, which involves a purely human feud between Brentshaw and Gilson.

The four stories marked with two asterisks were transferred from *Can Such Things Bc?* to volume 8 of the *Collected Works* (1911), containing Bierce's obviously farcical or grotesque tales, now grouped under the headings "Negligible Tales," "The Parenticide Club," "The Fourth Estate," and "The Ocean Wave" (also included in this volume are an odd series of sketches called " 'On with the Dance!' A Review," which ironically recommends dancing as morally uplifting, and a long string of epigrams). Again, the reason for the transfer of these tales is very clear, as they are all more obviously humorous than the other tales in the collection.

In addition, the following tales were added to volume 3 of the *Collected Works:* "One Summer Night"; "The Moonlit Road"; "A Diagnosis of Death"; "Moxon's Master"; "The Haunted Valley"; "A Jug of Sirup"; "Staley Fleming's Hallucination"; "A Resumed Identity"; "Beyond the Wall"; "John Mortonson's Funeral"; "The Stranger"; The Ways of Ghosts (including "Present at a Hanging," "A Cold Greeting," "A Wireless Message," and "An Arrest"), Soldier-Folk (including "A Man with Two Lives," "Three and One Are One," "A Baffled Ambuscade," and "Two Military Executions").

The final contents of volumes 2, 3, and 8 of the *Collected Works* represent virtually the totality of Bierce's short stories. Volume 2 (*In the Midst of Life*) contains Soldiers: "A Horseman in the Sky"; "An Occurrence at Owl Creek Bridge"; "Chickamauga"; "A Son of the Gods"; "One of the Missing"; "Killed at Resaca"; "The Affair at Coulter's Notch"; "The Coup de Grâce"; "Parker Adderson, Philosopher"; "An Affair of Outposts"; "The Story of a Conscience"; "One Kind of Officer"; "One Officer, One Man"; "George Thurston"; "The Mocking-Bird"; Civilians: "The Man out of the Nose"; "An Adventure at Brownville"; "The Famous Gilson Bequest"; "The Applicant"; "A Watcher by the Dead"; "The Man and the Snake"; "A Holy Terror"; "The Suitable Surroundings";

"The Boarded Window"; "A Lady from Red Horse"; and "The Eyes of the Panther."

Volume 3 (*Can Such Things Be?*) contains "The Death of Halpin Frayser"; "The Secret of Macarger's Gulch"; "One Summer Night"; "The Moonlit Road"; "A Diagnosis of Death"; "Moxon's Master"; "A Tough Tussle"; "One of Twins"; "The Haunted Valley"; "A Jug of Sirup"; "Staley Fleming's Hallucination"; "A Resumed Identity"; "The Night-Doings at 'Deadman's' "; "Beyond the Wall"; "A Psychological Shipwreck"; "The Middle Toe of the Right Foot"; "John Mortonson's Funeral"; "The Realm of the Unreal"; "John Bartine's Watch"; "The Damned Thing"; "Haïta the Shepherd"; "An Inhabitant of Carcosa"; "The Stranger"; "The Ways of Ghosts"; "Soldier-Folk"; "Some Haunted Houses" (now incorporating "Bodies of the Dead" and " 'Mysterious Disappearances' ").

Volume 8 contains Negligible Tales: "A Bottomless Grave"; "Jupiter Doke, Brigadier-General"; "The Widower Turmore"; "The City of the Gone Away"; "The Major's Tale"; "Curried Cow"; "A Revolt of the Gods"; "The Baptism of Dobsho"; "The Race at Left Bower"; "The Failure of Hope & Wandel"; "Perry Chumly's Eclipse"; "A Providential Intimation"; "Mr. Swiddler's Flip-Flap"; "The Little Story"; The Parenticide Club: "My Favorite Murder"; "Oil of Dog"; "An Imperfect Conflagration"; "The Hypnotist"; The Fourth Estate: "Mr. Masthead, Journalist"; "Why I Am Not Editing 'The Stinger' "; "Corrupting the Press"; " 'The Bubble of Reputation' "; The Ocean Wave: "A Shipwreckollection"; "The Captain of 'The Camel' "; "The Man Overboard"; "A Cargo of Cat"; " 'On with the Dance!' A Review"; and various epigrams.

I have gone into all this at some length and tedium to show that Bierce put an unusual amount of thought into this process of rearrangement. The finalized *In the Midst of Life* does not contain a single supernatural tale; the finalized *Can Such Things Be?* contains almost no nonsupernatural tales (for the one exception, see below); volume 8 of the *Collected Works* contains nothing but farces, most nonsupernatural. I think that Bierce was planning such a distinction all along but perhaps was compelled to violate it when first putting his collections together simply to fill the volumes. "The Night-Doings at 'Deadman's,' " a clearly supernatural tale, had been published as early as 1877, but Bierce did not include it in *Tales of Soldiers and Civilians* (1891), instead reserving it for *Can Such Things Be?* (1893). "The Damned Thing" was first published in a magazine in 1893, the same year as the first edition of *Can Such Things Be?* But that volume, not nearly as popular as its predecessor, was never reprinted until the *Collected Works,* and so Bierce evidently felt he might as well include the story in the revised *In the Midst of Life* (1898), since the chance to include it in a collection might never occur otherwise. The case of "Soldier-Folk," a series of four brief tales, is interesting. This is the only instance of overt supernaturalism combined with the war story. I do not know when these stories were written, but it is interesting that Bierce chose to include them in the finalized *Can Such Things Be?* rather than the finalized *In the*

Midst of Life: the supernatural aspect of these tales evidently took precedence over the war aspect in Bierce's mind.

Certain curious remarks in some stories we have hitherto deemed supernatural shed further light on Bierce's theory of weird fiction. In an attempt to account for the phenomena observed in **"The Damned Thing,"** a character remarks: " 'We so rely upon the orderly operation of familiar natural laws that any seeming suspension of them is noted as a menace to our safety, a warning of unthinkable calamity." And, at the end:

> "At each end of the solar spectrum the chemist can detect the presence of what are known as 'actinic' rays. They represent colors—integral colors in the composition of light—which we are unable to discern. The human eye is an imperfect instrument; its range is but a few octaves of the real 'chromatic scale.' I am not mad; there are colors that we cannot see.

> "And, God help me! the Damned Thing is of such a color!"

This attempt at a quasi-scientific explanation of seemingly supernatural phenomena, apart from being a startling anticipation of a cardinal tenet in Lovecraft's theory of weird fiction, is of momentous significance because it removes the tale from the rubric of supernaturalism altogether and places it in the realm of science fiction. This is not an isolated reference in Bierce: in **"The Boarded Window"** we again find mention of the "suspension of familiar natural laws," and in **"One of Twins"** we read of "the natural laws of which we have acquaintance." Bierce adds, as if the implication were not obvious, that "perhaps we have not all acquaintance with the same natural laws." This stupendous notion that "natural laws" are in the domain of epistemology, not ontology, is a startling antidote to the positivism of the late nineteenth century and in a dim way even anticipates Heisenberg's Indeterminacy Principle.

Although such tales as **"The Realm of the Unreal"** (in which the bizarre incidents are explained away by hypnosis) and **"A Diagnosis of Death"** (in which a pseudoscientific air is maintained throughout in the discussion of whether it is possible to forecast a person's death) approach science fiction, Bierce comes closest to it in **"Moxon's Master,"** which must be one of the earliest tales (Poe's "Maelzel's Chess-Player" not excluded) genuinely to deal with the question of artificial intelligence. Moxon, the inventor, reveals himself to be a vitalist in the extreme:

> "Doubtless you do not hold with those (I need not name them to a man of your reading) who have taught that all matter is sentient, that every atom is a living, feeling, conscious being. *I* do. There is no such thing as dead, inert matter: it is all alive; all instinct with force, actual and potential; all sensitive to the same forces in its environment and susceptible to the contagion of higher and subtler ones residing in such superior organisms as it may be brought into relation with, as those of man when he is fashioning it into an instrument of his will. It absorbs something of his intelligence and purpose—more of

them in proportion to the complexity of the resulting machine and that of its work."

He finds Herbert Spencer's definition of life ("Life is a definite combination of heterogeneous changes, both simultaneous and successive, in correspondence with external coexistences and experiences") as applicable to machines as to people. (It apparently does not occur to Moxon, or to Bierce, that this may be because the definition is flawed rather than because machines are in fact not different in kind from people.) And although the ending is predictable—the machine, an automation chessplayer, kills Moxon after being defeated by him in a match—the way in which Bierce gradually and subtly hints at the machine's acquisition of human emotions (the shuddersomely suggestive remark that the machine moved the chess pieces "with a slow, uniform, mechanical and, I thought, somewhat theatrical movement of the arm" is masterful. Written more than fifty years before Dunsany's very similar novel, *The Last Revolution* (1952), **"Moxon's Master"** is much more effective and intellectually sound. And yet I suspect that the point of the tale is principally satiric or even misanthropic: if machines are people, then people are machines. La Mettrie is vindicated.

I want to return to the distinction between supernaturalism and nonsupernaturalism and its possible importance to Bierce, because I think it will help to explain why Bierce's war tales can be regarded as authentic horror stories. I cannot believe that Bierce, in arranging *Tales of Soldiers and Civilians,* wished us to regard the two groups of tales as discrete entities, although the title might be thought to suggest it. I am afraid that Lovecraft is (along with many others) almost entirely wrong when he says in passing of the war stories that they "form the most vivid and realistic expression which [the Civil War] has yet received in fiction" [*Supernatural Horror in Literature*]: vivid they are, but realistic they are not—Bierce was not a realist and did not wish to be. In particular, his characters are not "realistic" in any meaningful sense of the term. Edmund Wilson—whether in praise or censure I cannot quite tell, although I suspect the latter—remarked aptly that "in all Bierce's fiction, there are no men or women who are interesting as men or women—that is, by reason of their passions, their aspirations or their personalities. They figure only as the helpless butts of sadistic practical jokes, and their higher faculties are so little involved that they might almost as well be trapped animals." But all this is precisely in accord with Bierce's aesthetic of fiction: this is how Bierce *wanted* to portray men and women. What "realism" there is in Bierce is the higher realism of romance—the realism, say, of **"A Horseman in the Sky"** or **"The Affair at Coulter's Notch,"** in which the tragedy of the Civil War in splitting up families into enemy factions is unforgettably etched; but the characters and incidents Bierce uses to convey this realism are, quite frankly, highly artificial.

Even more artificial—or, perhaps, artificial in a different way—would be the intrusion of supernaturalism into the war story. Yes, he did just this in the "Soldier-Folk" section of *Can Such Things Be?* but these stories are slight and not especially effective. In all the war stories in *Tales of Soldiers and Civilians* it was important to Bierce to establish that the events are *not* supernatural, that nothing in them happens contrary to nature—either cosmic nature or human nature. Peyton Farquhar's arduous escape from the execution committee at Owl Creek Bridge is only a hallucination in the split second before he dies by hanging. An air of dreamlike fantasy pervades **"Chickamauga,"** even when the boy protagonist comes into contact with the grotesque band of men coming out of the forest: "He now approached one of these crawling figures from behind and with an agile movement mounted it astride. The man sank upon his breast, recovered, flung the small boy fiercely to the ground as an unbroken colt might have done, then turned upon him a face that lacked a lower jaw—from the upper teeth to the throat was a great red gap fringed with hanging shreds of flesh and splinters of bone." But they are nothing but the (very real) survivors of one of the bloodiest battles of the Civil War. Carter Druse in **"A Horseman in the Sky"** seems to see the horseman flying through the air:

> Straight upright sat the rider, in military fashion, with a firm seat in the saddle, a strong clutch upon the reins to hold his charger from too impetuous a plunge. From his bare head his long hair streamed upward, waving like a plume. His hands were concealed in the cloud of the horse's lifted mane. The animal's body was as level as if every hoof-stroke encountered the resistant earth. Its motions were those of a wild gallop, but even as the officer looked they ceased, with all the legs thrown sharply forward as in the act of alighting from a leap. But this was a flight!

I would not be surprised if Lovecraft were influenced by this in his own description of fantastic horsemen in "Celephaïs":

> Just as they galloped up the rising ground to the precipice a golden glare came somewhere out of the east and hid all the landscape in its effulgent draperies. The abyss was now a seething chaos of roseate and cerulean splendour, and invisible voices sang exultantly as the knightly entourage plunged over the edge and floated gracefully down past glittering clouds and silvery coruscations. Endlessly down the horsemen floated, their chargers pawing the aether as if galloping over golden sands. . . .

But Lovecraft's tale is an otherworldly fantasy; in Bierce it is only Carter Druse's mind that has slowed the horseman's crash from the cliff to the woods below, since he knows he has killed his own father. In **"A Tough Tussle"** Brainerd Byring feels "a sense of the supernatural" as he obsessively stares at an enemy body he has come upon—but it is only a corpse, and it is Byring's fear of death that kills him.

Many critics have noted the principal feature of all the war stories—the isolation of the central characters. But there is more to it than that: they are not merely isolated but in a state of *compulsion*. It is because they are placed in intolerable situations, and are unable to escape them, that they meet their doom, whether it be death or madness. Carter Druse cannot abandon his post as a sentry lest he betray his entire army: he has no choice but to kill his father, a

scout on the enemy side. In a very similar tale, **"The Affair at Coulter's Notch,"** Coulter is placed inescapably in an excruciating position: he must man the tiny pass singlehandedly and destroy the house on the other side, even though it is his house and his wife and child are inside. In **"An Occurrence at Owl Creek Bridge"** Peyton Farquhar, although surrounded by enemy soldiers, is hideously alone as the hangman's noose slips around his neck; and it is significant that virtually the last image in his delusion of escape is the sight of his wife, "looking fresh and cool and sweet," on the verandah of his house. Farquhar years to return to his family, but it is all an illusion. In **"One of the Missing"** Jerome Searing is physically immobile as he is caught in the collapse of a house, his gun falling in such a position that its barrel is pointing directly at his forehead. But, as with all these tales, this physical fixity is a thin symbol for the psychological paralysis that overcomes the characters in the face of death. This is made explicit in **"A Tough Tussle,"** in which Byring can simply walk away from the corpse at his feet, but his mind will not let him.

It is worth establishing that in several of Bierce's war stories the actual war element is not intrinsic to the plot—this is what makes them nonsupernatural horror tales rather than war tales. To be sure, the crazy sort of bravery we find in **"A Son of the Gods"** or **"Killed at Resaca"** could only be exhibited in war, while we have already noted the tragic splitting of families caused by the Civil War portrayed in **"A Horseman in the Sky"** and **"The Affair at Coulter's Notch"**; but in several other tales the war is only a phantasmagoric backdrop. Once again I point to the similarity in plot of **"A Tough Tussle"** and **"A Watcher by the Dead"**—the former a "soldier" tale, the latter a "civilian" tale. Peyton Farquhar could be any criminal convicted of a capital crime. Jerome Searing could have been a huntsman caught in a shanty where he was camping out.

The degree to which characters in the war stories *observe* phenomena in a strangely objective way—Carter Druse observing his father on the cliff; Peyton Farquhar noting carefully all the paraphernalia of his execution; Jerome Searing taking minute stock of the detritus all around him in the shack—links them in a suggestive way to another body of Bierce's work that has gone relatively unnoticed, "Bits of Autobiography." These sketches of his years during and slightly after the war are similarly filled with observation, but it is Bierce who finds himself suddenly stepping back and looking at a war in which he is supposed to be participating:

> My regiment having at last been relieved at the guns and moved over to the heights above this ravine for no obvious purpose, I obtained leave to go down into the valley of death and gratify a reprehensible curiosity. . . .
>
> Looking across the fields in our rear (rather longingly) I had the happy distinction of a discoverer. What I saw was the shimmer of sunlight on metal; lines of troops were coming in behind us! . . .
>
> I observed this phenomenon at Pickett's Mill. Standing at the right of the line I had an unob-

structed view of the narrow, open space across which the two lines fought. . . .

> As a member of Colonel Post's staff, I was naturally favored with a good view of the performance. . . .

I suspect that Bierce—both as a soldier and later as a journalist—rather liked this role as objective spectator upon the anthill of life. We are not, I think, to understand that, because of this, Bierce's characters in the war stories are autobiographical, especially since they do not retain their objectivity very long; but it is an interesting phenomenon. As it is, probably more work could be done in tracing links between "Bits of Autobiography"—which, incidentally, contains some of Bierce's finest writing, especially the poignant and kaleidoscopic **"What I Saw of Shiloh"**—and the war tales.

In all Bierce, but especially in these war stories, we cannot help feeling that coincidence has been used a little too neatly in setting up these artificially dramatic situations. One of the most powerful and shocking of Bierce's tales is **"The Coup de Grâce."** Captain Downing Madwell is a devoted friend to Caffal Halcrow, but Caffal's brother Creede maintains a furious hatred of Madwell. During a battle Caffal falls at Madwell's feet, evidently mortally wounded. It does not seem that Madwell can do anything but put him out of his misery. He places his gun next to Caffal's forehead and fires; it is empty. In desperation he takes his sword and finally dispatches his friend.

> At that moment three men stepped silently forward from behind the clump of young trees which had concealed their approach. Two were hospital attendants and carried a stretcher.
>
> The third was Major Creede Halcrow.

This is undeniably effective, but there is a suggestion of authorial trickery here—we have been manipulated in some O. Henry—like fashion. How would Bierce respond to this charge? I am not sure that he would, save again to assert his freedom, as a romancer, from the mechanical conventions of realism. But there are hints of another answer in some of the tales. I suspect that Bierce adhered to the view (expounded first by Democritus) that we are not merely creatures of fate, but that what we call chance or coincidence is nothing but fate itself working in ways we do not perceive or understand. A very long and curious passage to this effect in **"One of the Missing"** is worth quoting in this regard:

> But it was decreed from the beginning of time that Private Searing was not to murder anybody that bright summer morning, nor was the Confederate retreat to be announced by him. For countless ages events had been so matching themselves together in that wondrous mosaic to some parts of which, dimly discernible, we give the name of history, that the acts which he had in will would have marred the harmony of the pattern. Some twenty-five years previously the Power charged with the execution of the work according to the design had provided against that mischance by causing the birth of a certain male child in a little village at the foot of the Car-

pathian Mountains, had carefully reared it, supervised its education, directed its desires into a military channel, and in due time made it an officer of artillery. By the concurrence of an infinite number of favoring influences and their preponderance over an infinite number of opposing ones, this officer of artillery had been made to avoid punishment. He had been directed to New Orleans (instead of New York), where a recruiting officer awaited him on the wharf. He was enlisted and promoted, and things were so ordered that he now commanded a Confederate battery some two miles along the line from where Jerome Searing, the Federal scout, stood cocking his rifle. Nothing had been neglected—at every step in the progress of both these men's lives, and in the lives of their contemporaries and ancestors, and in the lives of the contemporaries of their ancestors, the right thing had been done to bring about the desired result. Had anything in all this vast concatenation been overlooked Private Searing might have fired on the retreating Confederates that morning, and would perhaps have missed. As it fell out, a Confederate captain of artillery, having nothing better to do while awaiting his turn to pull out and be off, amused himself by sighting a field-piece obliquely to his right at what he mistook for some Federal officers on the crest of a hill, and discharged it. The shot flew high of its mark.

There is, certainly, a bantering or even parodic tone to this passage; but the idea it expresses—and this is what makes Edmund Wilson's criticism of Bierce for his failure in characterization irrelevant—is found in more compressed form in all Bierce's stories: we are pawns in the hands of fate.

The same sort of compulsion that we found in the war tales can be found in the "civilian" tales. The corpse-watcher in **"A Watcher by the Dead"** is affected in very much the same manner as Byring in **"A Tough Tussle"** while **"The Man and the Snake,"** in which Harker Brayton is frightened to death by what proves to be a toy snake, is one of Bierce's most carefully written tales. Here again the compulsion is entirely psychological: Brayton can simply walk out of the room if he wishes—but he cannot. Bierce's mastery both of style and of psychological perception is encapsulated in a single paragraph: "The snake had not moved and appeared somewhat to have lost its power upon the imagination; the gorgeous illusions of a few moments before were not repeated. Beneath that flat and brainless brow its black, beady eyes simply glittered as at first with an expression unspeakably malignant. It was as if the creature, assured of its triumph, had determined to practise no more alluring wiles." Here nearly every other phrase alternates between what is in fact realistic description of the toy snake (it does not move because it is not alive; its eyes glitter because they are made of shoe buttons) and Brayton's erroneous perception of it. The snake really is "brainless," but Brayton does not know that. Only at the end do all the pieces fall into place, and we come to realize the significance of the telltale phrases ("appeared," "illusions," "it was as if") that reveal what Brayton's imagination is adding to the stuffed snake.

In the tales in *Can Such Things Be?* Bierce is just as careful in using the supernatural as he is in avoiding it in *Tales of Soldiers and Civilians.* We have already noted the tales that approach science fiction: what they represent is an extension of the boundaries of the natural world to encompass what, given our current state of scientific knowledge, appear to be supernatural events. Many other tales—perhaps the most effective is **"The Middle Toe of the Right Foot,"** although **"Staley Fleming's Hallucination," "The Night-Doings at 'Deadman's,' "** and **"Beyond the Wall"** all fit the pattern—are simply tales of revenge in which the supernatural is a scarcely veiled metaphor for the conscience of the guilty.

Perhaps Bierce's most remarkable supernatural tale is the much-discussed **"Death of Halpin Frayser."** Recently a controversy has arisen over what actually happens in this tale and whether the supernatural comes into play at all. In a brilliant and ingenious essay ["The Deaths in Ambrose Bierce's 'Halpin Frayser',” *Papers on Language and Literature,* 1974], Robert C. Maclean has argued that it is possible to explain all the events of the tale naturally, with the conclusion that the murderer of Halpin Frayser is his own father, disguised as the private detective Jaralson. Maclean's work is too involved to discuss in detail here, but both he and William Bysshe Stein, who discussed the problem earlier ["Bierce's 'The Death of Halpin Frayser': The Poetics of Gothic Consciousness," *ESQ,* 1972], reject the obvious supernatural "explanation" of the events of the tale—that Frayser is killed by his own deceased mother. But I sense that they and other critics do so because they are unwarrantedly embarrassed at the mere existence of the supernatural, which in any case does not preclude other (e.g., psychoanalytical) interpretations. Bierce leaves hardly any doubt of Frayser's incestuous love for his mother (a love that she reciprocates), and it appears—thus far Maclean is correct—that we are to understand that Frayser and his mother fled separately west and lived as man and wife. Frayser kills his wife/mother, but she comes back from the dead and murders her son as he lurks by her grave. Any other reconstruction of events will make the epigraph—a passage from the sage Hali—inexplicable: "Whereas in general the spirit that removed cometh back upon occasion, and is sometimes seen of those in flesh (appearing in the form of the body it bore) yet it hath happened that the veritable body without the spirit hath walked. And it is attested of those encountering who have lived to speak thereon that a lich so raised up hath no natural affection, nor remembrance thereof, but only hate." Frayser's mother is the "lich so raised up." The phrase "natural affection" is interesting; for the mother it suggests merely the blind destructiveness of the undead, but for Frayser it is meant to convey his profoundly unnatural love of his mother. At the end of the story the detective and a sheriff, standing over the murdered body of Halpin Frayser as it lies atop his mother's grave, hear "the sound of a laugh, a low, deliberate, *soulless* laugh . . . a laugh so *unnatural,* so *unhuman,* so devilish, that it filled those hardy man-hunters with a sense of dread unspeakable!" Now unless Bierce is deliberately trying to deceive us (something he never does in this precise way) or is suggesting that the two characters are victims of a collective hallucination, this can only be the laugh of the

"body without the spirit" that is Halpin Frayser's mother. To say that this is merely a tale about "zombies" (as Mary Elizabeth Grenander does in dismissing the supernatural interpretation) is both to imply that there is something inherently subliterary about zombies (itself a questionable assertion) and to misconstrue the role of the supernatural here. What we have is a *double* irony: Halpin Frayser is killed by his own murder victim, not out of simple revenge (for his mother has no "remembrance" of the crime), but by sheer chance—the same sort of chance that trapped Cthulhu in the sinking R'lyeh in Lovecraft's "The Call of Cthulhu." It is the haplessness (and hopelessness) of human beings against the inexorable course of fate that is at the heart of this story.

The clarity and precision, both of diction and imagery, that are central to Bierce's actual methodology of writing—his scorn of slang and dialect is too well documented for citation—frequently augment and in some senses even create the sense of horror in his work. Lovecraft censures Bierce for his "prosaic angularity," remarking that "many of the stories are . . . marred by a jaunty and commonplacely artificial style derived from journalistic models." I regret to say that the entirety of this statement is false. Oh, Lovecraft is free to regret the lack of "atmosphere" in Bierce, but he seems not to have understood that the harrowing and pitiless clarity of Bierce's images is the secret to much of his effectiveness. More surprisingly, Lovecraft appears to have been unaware that Bierce's style is, fundamentally, modeled upon the same eighteenth-century idiom that served as the basis for his own style. But whereas Lovecraft's Asiatic, densely textured prose drew from Addison and Johnson, the spare, laconic, Attic style of Bierce derives from Swift and Gibbon. Clarity was Bierce's hallmark. There is never an imprecise sentence or image in his work, never a time when we do not know exactly what is going on. One tale in particular, **"The Moonlit Road,"** emphasizes this tendency in an especially satisfying way. [In his *Elegant Nightmares*] Jack Sullivan remarks—rather oddly, I think—that the story "achieves an almost mind-numbing complexity by emerging from three fragmented points of view." but Sullivan is mistaken if he thinks obfuscation is Bierce's aim. Each character—even the murdered Julia Hetman, "through the medium Bayrolles"—tells his or her side of the story, and only by combining these three accounts can we arrive at the truth of the matter. Joel Hetman, Julia's son, begins the tale. He has been summoned home from college because, as his father says, his mother has been murdered by an intruder who was seen entering the house but escaped undetected. Later, as he and his father walk along a moonlit road, the father sees an apparition but the son sees nothing; the father then disappears. The father (under the pseudonym Caspar Grattan) then takes up the narrative. He is a jealous man and wishes to test his wife's faithfulness. He tells his wife he will be away until the next afternoon, but returns home in the evening to see someone enter through the back door. Enraged, he bursts in and kills his wife, who is cowering in a corner of a room. It is the apparition of his wife that he sees on the moonlit road, and he flees in terror. Julia Hetman now reports that the intruder was just that—not a lover but a burglar who was frightened away by the return of her husband. But she, imagining that the burglar has returned, tries to hide in the dark. She does not know who killed her, and when her spirit meets her husband and son on the moonlit road it is to express her "great love and poignant pity," not her hatred or revenge. Here again the supernatural is used in almost a clinically precise way to fill in the missing gaps in the story. And yet this tale finally becomes a testament to Bierce's authorial supremacy: only he (and, now, the reader) knows the true circumstances of the story; each of the characters is missing some vital element of the picture, even the deceased Julia Hetman, since "the sum of what we know at death is the measure of what we know afterward of all that went before."

Clarity of expression is the key to another story, **"An Occurrence at Owl Creek Bridge."** This tale is a masterwork because of the almost mathematically exact way in which the style leads us to reverse the period of waking and dreaming in Peyton Farquhar. The first section of the tale is the "waking" part, with the grim preparations for an all too real execution; but Bierce presents it almost as if it were a dream (or nightmare) of Farquhar's: we are not told here the crime for which he is being executed; Farquhar's sensations seem both dulled ("A piece of dancing driftwood caught his attention and his eyes followed it down the current. How slowly it appeared to move! What a sluggish stream!"—) and preternaturally heightened (the ticking of his watch sounds like "the stroke of a blacksmith's hammer upon the anvil"—). But in the brief second section we learn that Farquhar was convicted of passing on information to the enemy, and in the third section (Farquhar's delusion) every image is crystal clear: he feels a "sharp pain in his wrist" from the ropes; as he struggles in the water to free himself "his whole body was racked and wrenched with an insupportable anguish!" Freed, he finds himself

> now in full possession of his physical senses. They were, indeed, preternaturally keen and alert. Something in the awful disturbance of his organic system had so exalted and refined them that they made record of things never before perceived. He felt the ripples upon his face and heard their separate sounds as they struck. He looked at the forest on the bank of the stream, saw the individual trees, the leaves and the veining of each leaf—saw the very insects upon them: the locusts, the brilliant-bodied flies, the gray spiders stretching their webs from twig to twig. He noted the prismatic colors in all the dewdrops upon a million blades of grass. The humming of the gnats that danced above the eddies of the stream, the beating of the dragonflies' wings, the strokes of the water-spiders' legs, like oars which had lifted their boat—all these made audible music. A fish slid along beneath his eyes and he heard the rush of its body parting the water.

And it goes on—in the split second before his death Farquhar's mind conjures up images far more lucid and precise than in the minutes before his execution.

Bierce was a satirist, and a great one. In the final analysis, I am not sure that Bierce's satire—or any satire—requires a philosophical justification: it will be valid insofar as it is

skillfully manipulated. For Bierce, satire *is* philosophy; his whole world view can be inferred from it. More, it is satire that links the whole of his literary work—war stories, Swiftian satires, supernatural tales, journalism, poetry, and those two masterpieces of wit, *Fantastic Fables* and *The Devil's Dictionary.* This overarching satiric tendency may help to explain certain anomalies in the horror tales as well as to redeem certain of Bierce's lesser stories. But first a curiosity about Bierce's satiric method: all Bierce's satire has an undercurrent of violence. In a sense, of course, this may be said of satire generally, but even to call Bierce's satire Juvenalian is a little mild. Note the degree of viciousness in even so harmless a thing as a parody of conventional greetings in *The Land beyond the Blow:*

> The tigerherd having perceived me, now came striding forward, brandishing his crook and shaking his fists with great vehemence, gestures which I soon learned were, in that country, signs of amity and good-will. But before knowing that fact I had risen to my feet and thrown myself into a posture of defense, and as he approached I led for his head with my left, following with a stiff right upon his solar plexus, which sent him rolling on the grass in great pain. After learning something of the social customs of the country I felt extreme mortification in recollecting this breach of etiquette, and even to this day I cannot think upon it without a blush.

Bierce's satire is always of this sort: it is just on this side of gratuitous nastiness. When, in **"An Occurrence at Owl Creek Bridge,"** Peyton Farquhar is struggling in his mind to free himself from his bonds, Bierce obtrudes this incredible aside: "What splendid effort!—what magnificent, what superhuman strength! Ah, that was a fine endeavor! Bravo!" This would be bad enough for one who is actually fighting for his life but is particularly unnerving for one who is only hallucinating. **"The Applicant,"** in *Tales of Soldiers and Civilians,* is neither a war story nor a horror tale but a satire: it paints the grim picture of a man turned away from a "Home for Old Men" (" 'The trustees,' Mr. Tilbody said, closing more doors than one, and cutting off two kinds of light, 'have agreed that your application disagrees with them' "—), for the man is the once-prosperous benefactor of the home. The mere inclusion of this tale may point to the fact that satire is the real underlying body of unity in this collection.

Two tales in *Can Such Things Be?* illustrate Bierce's graveyard humor at its best. One is supernatural, the other nonsupernatural; but the horror is produced by satire, not the supernatural or the lack of it. **"One Summer Night"** tells the grisly tale of two graverobbers who plunder the tomb of the recently deceased Henry Armstrong. Armstrong, however, refuses to acknowledge the fact of his death and sits up in his grave when it is unearthed. One robber flees, but the other "was of another breed": he kills the corpse again with his shovel, takes it to the local medical college that uses his services, and calmly demands his pay. In **"John Mortonson's Funeral"** (actually a tale by Bierce's son Leigh, but one which Bierce extensively polished and prepared for publication) the somber obsequies of Mortonson are rudely interrupted when the mourners flee in terror at the sight of the deceased's face. The coffin falls over and the glass shatters: "From the opening crawled John Mortonson's cat, which lazily leapt to the floor, sat up, tranquilly wiped its crimson muzzle with a forepaw, then walked with dignity from the room." There is nothing supernatural about this; it is merely a macabre joke. This lone exception to the supernaturalism of *Can Such Things Be?* is again explicable only if we regard satire as the unifying feature of the volume. **"One Summer Night"** is also a macabre joke, but the supernaturalism is not an important component of it. Or, rather, while the supernatural itself is significant (the joke depends on the double death of Henry Armstrong), there is no need—and Bierce makes no attempt—to account for the supernaturalism, either pseudoscientifically or in any other way.

But Bierce has gained the greatest notoriety—and, indeed, opprobrium—for the graveyard humor of the four tales included in volume 8 of the *Collected Works* under the heading "The Parenticide Club." Perhaps the most amusing thing about them is the outrage they have elicited among some of Bierce's critics. But we will not understand these tales unless we ascertain whom the satire is directed against. **"My Favorite Murder"** opens with "Having murdered my mother under circumstances of singular atrocity . . . "; in **"Oil of Dog"** we learn that the narrator "was born of honest parents in one of the humbler walks of life, my father being a manufacturer of dog-oil and my mother having a small studio in the shadow of the village church, where she disposed of unwelcome babies"; and so on. Who is being satirized here? Who but the reader? It is as if Bierce is daring us to find these things funny. Bierce can't lose: if we are revolted, then he can merely chuckle and heap contempt upon us for our squeamishness; if we laugh, we stand self-condemned as sadists. I do not know whether any other works of literature offer an experience parallel to this. It could even be said that this sort of thing—in milder (or subtler) form—colors the whole of Bierce's fiction. What varies, of course, is tone. The bizarre authorial intrusion we noted in **"An Occurrence at Owl Creek Bridge"** is unusual in its bluntness; in the other war tales Bierce's ice-cold style alone produces shock and horror. Perhaps the trick ending we noted in **"The Coup de Grâce,"** and which in various forms occurs frequently in Bierce, can be accounted for by appealing to his satiric intent: all Bierce is interested in is a certain type of tableau in which a character is pitilessly placed in a grotesque or unbearable position. This is why so many of Bierce's tales—whether of war or of the supernatural—have irony as their central feature: the irony of a man killing his own father in battle; the irony of a husband killing his wife on a false suspicion of adultery; the irony of a man frightened to death by a stuffed snake. It is clear that these are the focal images which came to Bierce's mind at the moment of inspiration; and he concocted a scenario of events—whether plausibly or not—to work these images into a narrative.

If Bierce is to be termed a misanthrope, it will not be from his avowedly philosophical utterances but from the philosophy that is implicit in his tales. When faced with a crisis, his characters always fail; they fear what should not be feared, act with irrational violence, and collapse in weakness when they should hold firm. If this is Bierce's picture of humanity, then it is a sufficiently bleak one, and the rapier strokes of his prose seem to take a perverse glee in augmenting the horror of his conceptions. Bierce's importance in weird fiction rests upon his role as a satiric horror writer—or a horrific satirist. As such he simultaneously founded and closed a genre; he has no successors. (pp. 147-67)

> S. T. Joshi, "Ambrose Bierce: Horror as Satire," in his The Weird Tale, *University of Texas Press, 1990, pp. 143-67.*

FURTHER READING

Biography

Harding, Ruth Guthrie. "Mr. Boythorn-Bierce." *The Bookman* (New York) 61, No. 6 (1925): 636-43.

Reflects on her personal relationship with Bierce. Harding states that "he was my friend; there is none who knew better than I his kindness, none who came closer to knowledge of his weariness and pain, none who believes more tenderly in his vision, his wisdom, and his integrity."

Walker, Dale L. "A Last Laugh for Ambrose Bierce: The Enigmatic Life—and Mysterious Death—of the Noted Cynic, Author, and 'Wickedest Man in San Francisco.' " *The American West* X, No. 6 (November 1973): 34-9, 63.

Biographical sketch.

Criticism

Berkove, Lawrence I. "Arms and the Man: Ambrose Bierce's Response to War." *The Michigan Academian* 1, No. 1 (Winter 1969): 21-30.

Argues that Bierce was not insensitive to the brutality of war, concluding that "far from being callous to the carnage of the Civil War or objectively detached from the sufferings of individual soldiers, Bierce actually tended toward the other extreme, toward being painfully sensitive."

————. Introduction to *Skepticism and Dissent: Selected Journalism from 1898-1901,* by Ambrose Bierce, pp. i-xxiv. Edited by Lawrence I. Berkove. Ann Arbor, Mich.: Delmas, 1980.

Discusses Bierce's journalism as it relates to American military and diplomatic action during 1898-1901, and examines his relationship with William Randolph Hearst.

————. " 'A Strange Adventure': The Story behind a Bierce Tale." *American Literary Realism 1870-1910* XIV, No. 1 (Spring 1981): 70-6.

Offers the anecdote "A Strange Adventure" by William Chambers Morrow as evidence that Bierce was "kind, considerate and friendly" as well as " 'a romantic and fascinating figure.' "

————. "Two Impossible Dreams: Ambrose Bierce on Utopia and America." *Huntington Library Quarterly* XLIV, No. 4 (Autumn 1981): 283-92.

Examines Bierce's rejection of both utopian experiments and republican democracy in America, noting that "outright utopian communities he considered foolish; republican democracy he thought insidiously dangerous."

Cheatham, George, and Cheatham, Judy. "Bierce's 'An Occurrence at Owl Creek Bridge.'" *The Explicator* 43, No. 1 (Fall 1984): 45-7.

Discusses the significance of the name Peyton Farquhar in Bierce's "An Occurrence at Owl Creek Bridge," concluding that "Peyton Farquhar's name itself—not only meaning patrician and manly but also actually sounding somehow aristocratic, genteel—is woven into the texture of the story, heightening the ironic contrast between a civilian's romantic fantasies and the realities of war."

Crane, John Kenny. "Crossing the Bar Twice: Post-Mortem Consciousness in Bierce, Hemingway, and Golding." *Studies in Short Fiction* VI, No. 4 (Summer 1969): 361-76.

Compares the treatment of post-mortem consciousness in Bierce's "An Occurrence at Owl Creek Bridge" to subsequent treatments of the same phenomenon in Ernest Hemingway's "The Snows of Kilimanjaro" and William Golding's *Pincher Martin.*

Davidson, Cathy N. *The Experimental Fictions of Ambrose Bierce: Structuring the Ineffable.* Lincoln: University of Nebraska Press, 1984, 166 p.

Assesses Bierce as "a fictional experimentalist who elaborated in his stories surprisingly modern views on the nature of language and the interrelationships between language, perception, and fictional forms."

Follett, Wilson. "Ambrose Bierce: An Analysis of the Perverse Wit that Shaped His Work." *The Bookman* (New York) 68, No. 3 (November 1928): 284-89.

Maintains that the power, wit, and form of Bierce's writing was determined by the significance and attention he gave to the individual sentence.

———. "Ambrose, Son of Marcus Aurelius." *The Atlantic Monthly* 160, No. 1 (July 1937): 32-42.

Finds that the perennial significance of Bierce's thought has been lost amid both his mass of less notable work and excessive fascination with his personality.

Grenander, M. E. *Ambrose Bierce.* New York: Twayne Publishers, 1971, 193 p.

Analysis of Bierce's fiction aimed at an "understanding of a limited number of works, rather than a superficial coverage of everything he wrote."

———. "'Five Blushes, Ten Shudders and a Vomit': Mark Twain on Ambrose Bierce's *Nuggets and Dust.*" *American Literary Realism 1870-1910* XVII, No. 2 (Autumn 1984): 169-79.

Examines the merit of Mark Twain's negative review of Bierce's *Nuggets and Dust.* Grenander finds that *"Nuggets and Dust* was not humor, and [Twain] was exactly the wrong person to evaluate it." She adds that Twain's assessment "reveals a great deal about himself, but it is worse than useless as a critical appraisal of Bierce's second work."

Hartwell, Ronald. "Fallen Timbers—A Death Trap: A Comparison of Bierce and Munro." *Research Studies* 49, No. 1 (March 1981): 61-6.

Compares Bierce's "One of the Missing" and H. H.

Munro's "The Interlopers," observing that "at the very moment when Jerome Searing, Ulrich von Gradwitz, and Georg Znayem are ready to kill someone else . . . they are caught and imprisoned by a sudden force totally unexpected and surprisingly powerful."

Kunz, Don. "Arthur Barron & Bitter Bierce." *Literature/Film Quarterly* 15, No. 1 (1987): 64-8.

Discusses Arthur Barron's film adaptation of Bierce's "Parker Adderson, Philosopher." Kunz observes that "Bierce's story lends itself nicely to adaptation because it is more dramatic than narrative."

Langleben, Maria M. "Phonology as a Pattern of Analysis: The Deep Message of the Thrillers by Ambrose Bierce." *The Prague School and Its Legacy in Linguistics, Literature, Semiotics, Folklore, and the Arts,* edited by Yishai Tobin, pp. 205-15. Philadelphia: John Benjamins, 1988.

Studies several of Bierce's stories in order to "come closer to the subconscious personal motivation of his work and life, to the source of the internal discomfort that he fought with, a discomfort that he masked by misanthropy."

Martin, Jay. "Ambrose Bierce." In *The Comic Imagination in American Literature,* edited by Louis D. Rubin, Jr., pp. 207-17. New Brunswick, N.J.: Rutgers University Press, 1973.

Contends that Bierce "employed humor to expose the absurdities of his deluded contemporaries and the institutions delusions created and perpetuated. In short, he preserved his own mind by ridiculing the crazed world that questioned his sense and sensibility."

Nickell, Joe. "Ambrose Bierce and Those 'Mysterious Disappearances' Legends." *Indiana Folklore* XIII, No. 1-2 (1980): 112-22.

Suggests that Bierce was fascinated with stories of mysterious disappearances. Nickell examines the influence of Bierce on the genre of "mysterious disappearance" literature.

O'Brien, Matthew C. "Ambrose Bierce and the Civil War: 1865." *American Literature* 48, No. 3 (November 1976): 377-81.

Comments on a discrepancy in biographical accounts of Bierce's action during the Civil War. O'Brien maintains that extant documentary material indicates that Bierce never participated in Sherman's march toward Richmond but had been discharged and remained in Alabama.

Roth, Russell. "Ambrose Bierce's 'Detestable Creature.'" *Western American Literature* 9, No. 3 (November 1974): 169-76.

Drawing evidence from Bierce's work, Roth asserts that the author was a misogynist.

Scholnick, Robert J. "'My Humble Muse': Some New Bierce Letters." *The Markham Review* 5 (Summer 1976): 71-5.

Reprints and discusses five previously unpublished letters from Ambrose Bierce. Scholnick finds the letters valuable as statements by Bierce on topics related to his literary career and also "for providing us with an opportunity to watch this combative man in action."

Wiggins, Robert A. "Ambrose Bierce: A Romantic in an Age

of Realism." *American Literary Realism* 4, No. 1 (Winter 1971): 1-10.

    Surveys Bierce's career and evaluates his literary significance.

Winn, Ralph B. "Ambrose Bierce." In *American Philosophy,* edited by Ralph B. Winn, pp. 280-82. New York: Philosophical Library, 1955.

    Cites definitions from *The Devil's Dictionary* as evidence that "Bierce's philosophical work reminds us of Voltaire, except that it was much more fragmentary, mainly isolated comments upon life and social criticisms."

Zarro, Joseph A. "Understanding Zap." *English Journal* 57, No. 5 (May 1968): 654-56, 669.

    Discusses "An Occurrence at Owl Creek Bridge" as "unquestionably a well-constructed piece of prose" and a rewarding subject for student study.

Maxwell Bodenheim

1892-1954

(Born Maxwell Bodenheimer) American poet, novelist, dramatist, and editor.

INTRODUCTION

Bodenheim is best remembered for his poetry and novels depicting moral corruption and the hardship of urban life in the United States during the early twentieth century. Regarded as a promising poet at the beginning of his career, Bodenheim gained more attention during his later years for his self-destructive behavior than for his literary works. Biographer Jack B. Moore has asserted: "I believe it true of Bodenheim's life and art that rarely has an American writer of any historic significance committed more obvious and sometimes more disastrous mistakes: but it is also true that rarely have the virtues and the accomplishments of such a writer been so clearly misrepresented and so quickly forgotten."

Bodenheim was born in Hermanville, Mississippi. His father was a clothing store clerk and a traveling whiskey salesman whose frequent business failures and job changes contributed to an unhappy marriage and the family's severe financial difficulties. As an adolescent Bodenheim rejected the middle-class values which his parents embraced, and he began writing poetry partly as an act of defiance. The family moved to Chicago in 1900. At age sixteen Bodenheim was expelled from high school for an undisclosed infraction. He then left home and joined the army but deserted when he became frustrated with the strict regulations of military life. Bodenheim was apprehended and spent the remainder of his term of enlistment jailed in Fort Leavenworth, Kansas. Upon his release he traveled in the Southwest for two years, working at various unskilled jobs, before returning to Chicago. Bodenheim contributed works to *Poetry* magazine and was soon recognized as a talented poet. His career flourished following his move to New York City in 1915, when he became an editor of the literary magazine *Others* and formed friendships with such writers as Conrad Aiken, William Carlos Williams, and Malcolm Cowley. Critics concur that Bodenheim wrote his most successful works during the 1920s, when he published such acclaimed poetry collections as *Minna and Myself, Advice, Introducing Irony, The Sardonic Arm,* and *Returning to Emotion,* as well as several popular novels, including *Replenishing Jessica* and *Georgie May.*

During the 1930s Bodenheim's works declined in both quality and quantity, a development that biographers attribute to his worsening alcoholism. He spent most of his time in Greenwich Village bars, often selling his poems to passersby for drinks. In 1938 he divorced Minna, his wife of twenty years, who had inspired many of the poems in

his collection *Minna and Myself.* He was hired to write his memoirs but did not complete the task, and *My Life and Loves in Greenwich Village* was ghost-written. Following the death of his second wife in 1950, Bodenheim married Ruth Fagan, a young woman with a history of mental instability. By this time Bodenheim was becoming increasingly debilitated by alcoholism, and the two were impoverished and often homeless. Vincent Starrett described Bodenheim's deteriorating health during this period: "[Bodenheim] looked as if he had been buried, or drowned for some weeks: a sort of living dead man." In 1954 Bodenheim and his wife befriended Harold Weinberg, a young man who had been discharged from the army as mentally unfit. Weinberg's attraction to Ruth and antagonism toward Bodenheim have been suggested as motives for his murder of the couple during a night of drinking when he shot Bodenheim in the heart and stabbed Ruth to death.

Bodenheim established his literary reputation as a poet, and throughout his career critics generally considered his poetry superior to his fiction. Many of his early poems focus on nature. "A Hillside Tree," from his first collection, *Minna and Myself,* describes a tree squatting "like a drowsy, rain-browned saint" and states that its voice "in which the wind takes no part, / Is like mists of music wedding each other." While critics praised Bodenheim's evocative use of language, many found the dreamlike quality of his imagery unnecessarily obscure. Bodenheim defended his intensely subjective poetic style, and, in *Introducing Irony,* he berated the poetry of his contemporaries as dry, passive, and overly concerned with surface appearances. The pervasive theme of Bodenheim's poetry throughout his career was the desensitizing and alienating effects of urban life on city dwellers in New York and Chicago. Each of his collections contains poems depicting life in cities as bleak and impersonal, often focusing on working-class characters who are defeated by their surroundings: "Afternoon has fallen on this street, / Like an imbecilic organ-grinder / Grinning over his discords" ("North Clark Street, Chicago").

In Bodenheim's fiction the most prominent theme is rebellion against authority. The protagonists of his novels are often young, assertive characters who reject parental authority and the values of bourgeois society. For example, his autobiographical first novel, *Blackguard,* chronicles the artistic development and social defiance of a young man who turns to writing poetry as an escape from the constrictions of his parents' middle-class way of life. Rebellion is joined to an unconventional moral code in *Crazy Man,* which relates the story of a thief named John Carley who steals in order to free people from materialism and possessiveness. Critics considered Carley a foolish but endearing protagonist whose criminal acts are mitigated by his liberated, accepting, and gentle qualities. Bodenheim's female protagonists also reject the established values of society, displaying their defiance in the form of sexual rebellion. *Replenishing Jessica,* for example, chronicles an heiress's repudiation of repression and hypocrisy in upper-class society through a series of romantic adventures. Although some critics have faulted Bodenheim's characterization as superficial and underdeveloped, they have also noted that Bodenheim portrayed women sympathetically, often depicting them as victims of an oppressive and intolerant society. *Georgie May,* another of his popular novels, has been praised for its effective characterization of a prostitute living in Memphis during the early 1900s. Despising her sleazy, often violent, life-style and entrapped by her social status, Georgie May ultimately commits suicide, an act that critics have interpreted as symbolizing her only option for self-determination.

Bodenheim's later works were strongly influenced by the economic hardship he witnessed during the Depression. A tone of failure and disillusionment with the American system pervades his last novel, *Slow Vision,* which portrays a series of numbed and poverty-stricken people as victims of capitalism. This novel and other politically charged works, including *Run, Sheep, Run* and *Lights in the Valley,* incorporate forceful critiques of capitalism and reveal Marxist convictions. Critics have observed that rather than propagandizing a communist ideology, these works, like those written throughout his career, express the high value Bodenheim placed on individualism.

PRINCIPAL WORKS

Minna and Myself (poetry) 1918
Advice (poetry) 1920
Introducing Irony (poetry) 1922
Against This Age (poetry) 1923
Blackguard (novel) 1923
The Sardonic Arm (poetry) 1923
Crazy Man (novel) 1924
Replenishing Jessica (novel) 1925
Ninth Avenue (novel) 1926
Returning to Emotion (poetry) 1927
Georgie May (novel) 1928
The King of Spain (poetry) 1928
Sixty Seconds (novel) 1929
Bringing Jazz! (poetry) 1930
Naked on Roller Skates (novel) 1930
A Virtuous Girl (novel) 1930
Duke Herring (novel) 1931
Run, Sheep, Run (novel) 1932
New York Madness (novel) 1933
Slow Vision (novel) 1933
Lights in the Valley (poetry) 1942
Selected Poems (poetry) 1946

Conrad Aiken (essay date 1919)

[*An American poet, Aiken was deeply influenced by the psychological and literary theories of Sigmund Freud, Havelock Ellis, Edgar Allan Poe, and Henri Bergson, among others, and is considered a master of literary stream of consciousness. In the following excerpt, he discusses the presentation of mood and emotion in Bodenheim's poetry.*]

It will be recalled that when the Imagists first came upon us they carried banners, and that upon one of them was inscribed their detestation of the "cosmic," and of the "cosmic" poet, who (they added) "seems to us to shirk the real difficulties of his art." . . . It was not unnatural that those of our poetic revolutionaries who, tired of the verbose sentimentalities and ineptitudes of the more mediocre among their predecessors, determined to achieve a sharper picturism in poetry should in the first excited survey of the situation decide that anything "cosmic," or let us say philosophic, was obviously beyond the focus of their poetic camera—could not be "picturized." It appeared that thought would have to be excluded—and in fact for a year or more, under the influence of the Imagists, the markets were flooded with a free verse in which thought was conspicuously at a minimum. "Pure, sensation!" was the cry—a cry which has been heard before, and will be heard again; it arises from a question almost as old as poetry itself—the question whether the poet should be only a drifting sensorium, and merely feel, or whether he should be permitted to think. Should he be a voice, simply—or something beside? Should he occasionally, to put it colloquially, say something? Or should he be merely a magic lantern, casting colored pictures forever on a screen?

The question is put perhaps too starkly, and purposely leaves out of account all of the minute gradations by which one passes from the one extreme to the other. And the occasion for the question is Mr. Maxwell Bodenheim, who, though already well known as a poet, has just published his first book, *Minna and Myself.* Mr. Bodenheim might well, it appears, have been one of the Imagists. None of them, with perhaps the exception of "H. D.," can equal his delicate precision of phrasing. None of them is more subtly pictorial. Moreover Mr. Bodenheim's theories as to the nature of poetry (for which he has adroitly argued), such as that it should be a "colored grace" and that it should bear no relation to "human beliefs and fundamental human feelings," might seem even more clearly to define that affinity. Yet it would be a great mistake to ticket Mr. Bodenheim as an Imagist merely because his poetry is sharply pictorial, or because he has declared that poetry should not deal with fundamental human emotions. As a matter of fact his theory and performance are two very different things. One has not gone very far before detecting in him a curious dualism of personality.

It is obvious, of course, that Mr. Bodenheim has taken out of the air much that the Imagists and other radicals have set in circulation. His poems are in the freest of free verse: they are indeed quite candidly without rhyme or metrical rhythm, and resolve themselves for the most part into series of lucid and delicate statements, of which the crisp cadences are only perhaps the cadences of a very sensitive prose. It is to Mr. Bodenheim's credit that despite the heavy handicap of such a form he makes poems. How does he do this? Not merely by evoking sharp-edged images—if he did only that he would be indeed simply an exponent of "colored grace" or Imagism—but precisely because his exquisite pictures are not merely pictures, but symbols. And the things they symbolize are, oddly enough, these flouted "fundamental feelings."

Mr. Bodenheim is, in short, a symbolist. His poems are almost invariably presentations of mood, evanescent and tenuous—tenuous, frequently, to the point of impalpability—in terms of the visual or tactile; and if it would be an exaggeration to say that they differ from the purely imagistic type of poetry by being, for this reason, essentially emotional, nevertheless such a statement approximates the truth. Perhaps rather one should say that they are the ghosts of emotions, or the perfumes of them. It is at this point that one guesses Mr. Bodenheim's dualism. For it seems as if the poet were at odds with the theorist: as if the poet desired to betray these "fundamental emotions" to a greater extent than the severe theorist will permit. In consequence one feels that Mr. Bodenheim has cheated not only his reader but also himself. He gives us enough to show us that he is one of the most original of contemporary poets, but one feels that out of sheer perversity he has withheld even more than he has given. There are many poets who have the *vox et praeterea nihil* of poetry, and who wisely therefore cultivate that kind of charm; but it is a tragedy when a poet such as Mr. Bodenheim, possessing other riches as well, ignores these riches in credulous obeisance to the theory that, since it is the voice, the hover, the overtone, the perfume alone which is important in poetry, therefore poetry is to be sought rather in the gossamer than in the rock. Mr. Bodenheim has taken the first step: he has found that moods can be magically described—no less than dew and roses. But poetic magic, as George Santayana has said, is chiefly a matter of perspective—it is the revelation of "sweep in the concise and depth in the clear"—and, as Santayana points out, if this is true we need not be surprised to perceive that the poet will find greatest scope for this faculty in dealing with ideas, particularly with philosophic ideas. . . . And we return to our old friend the "cosmic."

Nor need Mr. Bodenheim be unduly alarmed. For when one suggests that the contemplation of life as a whole, or the recognition of its items as merely minute sand-grains of that whole, or an occasional recollection of man's twinkling unimportance, or a fleeting glimpse of the cruel perfection of the order of things are among the finest headlands from which the poet may seek an outlook, one is certainly not suggesting that poets should be logicians. It is not the paraphernalia but the vision of philosophy which is sublime. If the poet's business is vision, he can ill afford to ignore this watch-tower. For if, like Mr. Bodenheim, he desires that poetry shall be a kind of absolute music, "unattached with surface sentiment"—a music in which sensations are the notes, emotions the harmonies, and ideas the counterpoint; a music of detached waver and gleam, which, taking for granted a complete knowledge of all things, will not be so naive as to make statements, or argue a point, or praise the nature of things, or inveigh against it, but will simply employ all such elements as the keys to certain tones—then truly the keyboard of the poet who uses his brain as well as his sensorium will be immensely greater than that, let us say, of the ideal Imagist.

The point has been elaborated because, as has been said, it is one on which Mr. Bodenheim seems to be at odds with himself: the poems in *Minna and Myself* show him to be an adept at playing with moods, an intrepid juggler with sensations, but one who tends to repeat his tricks, and to juggle always with the same set of balls. Of the poems themselves what more needs to be said than that they are among the most delicately tinted and fantastically subtle of contemporary poems in free verse? Mr. Bodenheim's sensibility is as unique in its way as that of Wallace Stevens or of T. S. Eliot or of Alfred Kreymborg. One need not search here for the robust, nor for the seductively rhythmic, nor for the enkindling. Mr. Bodenheim's patterns are cool almost to the point of preciosity; they are, so to speak, only one degree more fused than mosaics. They must be read with sympathy or not at all. And one feels that Mr. Bodenheim is only at his beginning, and that he will eventually free himself of his conventions on the score of rhythm (with which he is experimenting tentatively) and of theme-color. In what direction these broadenings will lead him, only Mr. Bodenheim can discover. One is convinced, however, that he can step out with security. (pp. 356-57)

Conrad Aiken, "Vox—et Praeterea?" in The Dial, *Chicago, Vol. 66, April 5, 1919, pp. 356-57.*

Malcolm Cowley (essay date 1922)

[*Cowley was a prominent American critic and editor. His literary criticism does not attempt a systematic philosophical view of life and art, nor is it representative of a neatly defined school of critical thought. In the following excerpt, he considers stylistic and technical elements of* Introducing Irony.]

Poetry has been based on rhythm, rhyme, syllable-counting, alliteration, repetition, and some fifty other linguistic devices. Bodenheim makes it depend almost wholly on figures of speech. His poems are a dictionary of metaphor, arranged in unalphabetical order. If he had chosen to write, "When she played too loudly a man in the next room knocked on the wall," he would be writing prose. He says instead, "An acrimonious man in the next room often remonstrated with the wall when her piano conversed too impulsively." He says, "When swung to him the voices were insolent enigmas, tripping him as he stood midway between fright and indifference. . . . His rages were false and sprang from aloof thoughts chanting over their chains." Sometimes a pentameter line which is the accidental essence of the eighteenth century. "The stunted messengers of trembling thought." Oftener his accumulation of images resembles Shakespeare, and still more often that early and underestimated model of Shakespeare's, John Lyly. Only, Bodenheim is if possible more euphuistic.

Maxwell Bodenheim . . . Euphues . . . not "a second Euphues"—for he is no imitator—but Euphues simply; American prophet of the new preciosity (and with many disciples). If I were Max Beerbohm and making his caricature, I should draw him in mandarin robes, posing on a torn dictionary and somehow leading a cotillion of empty champagne bottles and tomato cans. It would not be a very consistent portrait.

In [***Introducing Irony***] Bodenheim has included, in addition to the poems, a number of "poetic short stories." The word poetic, as usual with him, means "full of metaphor," but here it carries another meaning also; it means that these stories are fantastic, improbable, ironic. Furthermore they are remarkable for containing no real characters and for distilling no emotions except wonder and (I borrow the word) a sort of windy sadness. They are not an attempt at creating or reproducing life, but a literary criticism with faint unimitative memories of Jules Laforgue. They are an impromptu banquet of words, a verbal pyrotechnic: pin-wheels, Roman candles, sky-rockets, giant firecrackers that hiss and sometimes explode; afterwards the memory of a boy's Fourth of July with green apple colic and the smell of burned powder. They are by no means negligible stories.

Another innovation in this latter book is rhyme, which Bodenheim once utterly despised. He rhymes awkwardly sometimes, as if he were the captain of the P.H.S. eleven making his first tentative verses. He puts "boy" at the end of one line and "toy" at the end of the next; he peppers half a dozen words before each of them without much regard for rhythm or metre, and calls the result a couplet:

> Of undesired love, to quiet a boy

> Who wept inanely for his favorite toy.

Sometimes the facture of his verses is impeccable, as if he were T. S. Eliot. One would allow ten years between the two quotations, and yet they may have been written on the same day:

> Above the sprightly insolence of plates
> Men sit and feign industrious respect,
> With eye-brows often slightly ill at ease—
> Cats in an argument are more erect.

No poem attains a lyrical perfection (he has a contempt for lyricists) and no poem is without its excellences:

> Take your cocaine. It leaves a blistering stain,
> But phantom diamonds are immune from greed.
> You pluck them from the buttons of your vest,
> Wildly apologizing for your need.

> . . . . .

> Two figures on a subway platform
> Pieced together by an old complaint.

> . . . . .

> If one mutters, "I shall go to Euston Road,"
> Imagination is relieved of all errands
> And, decently ticketed, enters the omnibus.

Evidently there is no consistency to his work; it cannot be catalogued under any of the epithets which he so abuses; there is no place for him in the files. He is good and bad at once; brilliant and boring; awkward and skilful. He has all the insufferability of genius, and a very little of the genius which alone can justify it. He will be known some day wherever an adjective meets a strange adverb and where they bow distantly to each other; that is, he will be known in the literary circles where such introductions are made. Elsewhere he will never need to be forgotten. (pp. 446-48)

> *Malcolm Cowley, "Euphues," in* The Dial, *Chicago, Vol. 73, October, 1922, pp. 446-48.*

Mark Van Doren (essay date 1923)

[*Van Doren was one of the most prolific authors in twentieth-century American literature. His work includes poetry (for which he won the Pulitzer Prize in 1940), novels, short stories, drama criticism, and social commentary. In addition, he edited a number of popular anthologies and served as the literary editor and film critic for the* Nation *during the 1920s and 1930s. Aimed at the general reader rather than the scholar or specialist, Van Doren's criticism is noted for its lively perception and wide interest. Like his poetry and fiction, his criticism consistently examines the inner, idealistic life of the individual. In the following review of* The Sardonic Arm, *Van Doren discusses the limited appeal of Bodenheim's poetry.*]

The laconism of this title-page [***The Sardonic Arm***] implies not so much an increase in Mr. Bodenheim's vanity as a strengthening of his determination, a renewal of his most militant mood. His kind of poetry has not been welcome in the world; therefore he will assault the citadel and clear a space where he can stand and be himself. A "Reluctant Foreward" enumerates the qualities which he believes we neglect when we neglect him.

> That tantalizing obscurity of words, luring the nimbleness of mental regard—subtlety—and those deliberate acrobatics that form an original style—both are waiting for the melodrama, comedy and lecture to subside. Alas, what a long waiting is before them—pity these two aristocrats and admire their isolated tenacity. Drop the trivial gift of a tear, also, upon a wilted, elaborate figure thrown into cell number thirty-two and trying to remember that his name was once Intellect. Then deposit the lengthened confession of a sigh upon another drooping form known as Delicate Fantasy—an elusive liar who ravishes colors without mentioning their names (not the endless blue, green, white, yellow, red, lavender, mauve, pink, brown, cerise, golden, orange, and purple of American Imagists). They have kicked him into the cellar, damn them. Recognize the importance of his bruises. And also, spy, in the loosely naive tumult, an agile, self-possessed pilgrim known as Irony. They have kicked him in the stomach, these symbols of earth triumphant.

Mr. Bodenheim is as scornful of his contemporaries as Marlowe, Jonson, Pope, Wordsworth, and Whitman were of theirs. Like them he wants to begin the game again.

He will continue to meet resistance for several reasons. The difficulty of reading him may be the most obvious of these, though it is not the most important. Difficulty after all is a relative term, and if Mr. Bodenheim is read three times, or ten, he will be clear. A more serious reason is the abstractness of his language—or rather its new kind of abstractness. It has long been a question whether terms like pool, wood, sky, ground, grass, smile, kiss, rain, flower, stone are not abstractions in poetry. But at least they are familiar, and are believed to mean something. Now comes Mr. Bodenheim with new terms—"the identity of sternness," "the delicate anti-climax of a mental caper," "the persistent shudder of emotion," "the rancid importance of flesh," "the ritual of disappointment," "the recalcitrant antics of words," "the opium of innuendoes." These to be sure mean a good deal in their contexts. Yet how often is it clear, to others than their maker, precisely what they mean?

Another reason, not unconnected with the foregoing, is contained in the fact that Mr. Bodenheim's intellect is an implacable enemy of both sensuous and sensual things. The aim of his least poem is to dissolve the flesh of appearances and discover the small, insoluble deposit of thought beneath—the fine, silver wire of irony that eats like a worm at the center. Even then there is disillusion. Surfaces bore him; so does the space within. Outwardly life is dull; inwardly it is meaningless. The world is a heap of rubbish for his wit to penetrate and refine. Nothing will result, of course, but his mind is restless, and this will have been something for it to do. Nature learned the lesson long ago.

> The countless vagaries of maple leaves,
> Elastic humbleness of flowers and weeds,
> The hill, a placid stoic to all creeds,
> They use an obvious language that deceives

> The subtle theories of human ears.
> Their tongue is motion and they scorn the rhyme
> And meter made by men to soothe their fears.

> Beneath the warm strength of each August hour
> They spurn cohesion and the plans of thought,
> With quick simplicity that seems confused
> Because it signals mystic whims that tower
> Above the thoughts and loves that men have caught:
> Beyond the futile words that men have used.

Mr. Bodenheim is content to chatter with the trees against the pitiful formulas of men. For him "the lurking emptiness behind life separates into little, curious divisions of sound." And that is all.

That, it goes without saying, will continue to be unpopular. Most men like appearances, and most of the remainder like to believe that there is much behind them. Mr. Bodenheim must be content to address a very small band. But they will call him excellent, and they will be right. It is something to have reduced the universe "to a speck of quivering clarity," to have looked until "an unearthly laugh peered through the crevices of our eyes." Mr. Bodenheim has learned to put all his brains, and he has many, into each line. He has developed a subtle and brittle rhythm; he has chastened his style until its accuracy is uncanny—perhaps unreal. Wrenched as his diction sounds at first, it has a way of sticking in the memory, as gargoyles do. And in the midst of so much dryness and desolation of phrase, occasionally something comes that can be seen or heard, that crackles in the stillness.

> Earth, the men who scrape at your flanks
> Can never stop to examine
> The thin line of speech that goes adventuring
> Where your brown hills bite the sky.

> *Mark Van Doren, "Bodenheim," in* The Nation, *New York, Vol. CXVI, No. 3022, June 6, 1923, p. 668.*

Louis Untermeyer   (essay date 1923)

[*A poet during his early career, Untermeyer is better known as an anthologist of poetry and short fiction, an editor, and a master parodist. He was a contributing editor to* The Liberator *and the* Seven Arts, *and served as poetry editor of the* American Mercury *from 1934 to 1937. In the following essay, he focuses on expressionism in Bodenheim's poetry.*]

Minna and Myself (1918) contains the first hints of Bodenheim's expressionism. But his later intensities are only foreshadowed in the precise delicacies of this volume. . . . Bodenheim has an extreme sensitivity to the power of words, an understanding which, in his use of the verbal *nuance*, results in effects that are little short of dazzling. Words, under his adroit manipulation, bear strange blossoms and stranger fruit; fantastic adjectives are grafted upon startled nouns and the consequent hybrid is like no other contemporary growth.

Hill-Side Tree

Like a drowsy, rain-browned saint,

You squat, and sometimes your voice
In which the wind takes no part,
Is like mists of music wedding each other.
A drunken, odor-laced peddler is the morning
   wind.
He brings you golden-scarfed cities
Whose voices are swirls of bells burdened with
   summer;
And maidens whose hearts are galloping
   princes.
And you raise your branches to the sky,
With a whisper that holds the smile you cannot
   shape.

Bodenheim has no superior in these shifting pictures, the depiction of tenuous moods in which one figure blurs into another. In the realm of the whimsical-grotesque, he walks with a light and nimble step; the black and whites of Beardsley are scarcely more decorative than such fantasies as **"Old Age," "To One Dead," "Interlude,"** several of the love poems and this gracefully *macabre* drawing:

Death

I shall walk down the road.
I shall turn and feel upon my feet
The kisses of death like scented rain.
For death is a black slave with little silver birds
Perched in a sleeping wreath upon his head.
He will tell me, his voice like jewels
Dropped into a satin bag,
How he has tiptoed after me down the road,
His heart made a dark whirlpool with longing
   for me.
Then he will graze me with his hands;
And I shall be one of the sleeping silver birds
Between the cold waves of his hair, as he tiptoes
   on. . . .

In *Advice* (1920) the tone is sharper, the figures more intricate. Sometimes Bodenheim packs his similes so close that they become inextricably mixed; sometimes he spins his ideas so thin that the cord of coherence snaps and leaves the reader only a handful of colored ravellings. More frequently still, he allows his poems to sink beneath the weight of ornaments with which he has tricked out designs that, in themselves, are essentially simple. But Bodenheim is not fundamentally interested in simplicity. He analyzes his sensations, using realism only as a point of departure, intellectualizing every gesture, putting every figment of thought through a rigid examination. Thus, what Bodenheim loses in spontaneity he gains in intensive exaggeration. The first poem in *Advice* is indicative.

Advice to a Street-Pavement

Lacerated grey has bitten
Into your shapeless humility.
Little episodes of roving
Strew their hieroglyphics on your muteness.
Life has given you heavy stains
Like an ointment growing stale.
Endless feet tap over you
With a maniac insistence.

O unresisting street-pavement,
Keep your passive insolence
At the dwarfs who scorn you with their feet.
Only one who lies upon his back

Can disregard the stars.

A desire to pack his lines beyond their capacity, to make word-relations which have an old antipathy for each other occupy the same space at the same time, causes him to strain and dislocate his mental musculature. Instead of enriching his utterance, he merely macerates it; in the midst of cunning disguises, he can be as baldly *gauche* as in the lines which begin his address to **"Track-Workers,"** the metaphorical absurdity of the sixth line being a triumph of the ridiculous.

The rails you carry cut into your hands,
Like the sharp lips of an unsought lover.
As you stumble over the ties
Sunlight is clinging, yellow spit
Raining down upon your faces.
You are the living cuspidors of day.

Introducing Irony (1922) is the essence of Bodenheim; acridity acidified. Here he allows his ironic expressionism to dictate its harshest accents and, true to the technic of a race which has fed on frustration, intensifies it by the very bitterness of his coldly picked epigrams. It is an excessive elegance, almost a mincing nicety of language that Bodenheim affects; a diction that startles with its apparently wild but precisely calculated leaps. In *Introducing Irony,* Bodenheim's transilient euphuism is greater than ever. His is an acrobatic mind that juggles a dozen mixed metaphors during its flight, a mind that, when it is not leaving one high trapeze for a giddier one, tosses up glittering knives, balancing itself upon the points of emotion with a mordant grimace. He slips from one posture to the other with peculiar agility, and he fascinates by the very precariousness of his position. It is a fascination which is not necessarily charming; he is often garrulous, grotesque, narcistic, verbally dandified, frequently irritating, seldom unintelligible. He may be—and, at times, is—so wedded to strangeness of speech that he brings his oddities even beyond the borders of preciosity, but he is, none the less (possibly all the more) provocative. Let those who find Bodenheim merely a malicious phrase-twister read such clear though intricate mood analyses as **"Jack Rose," "Turmoil in a Morgue," "Two Sonnets to My Wife,"** the second and seventh of **"Finalities";** let a scoffer of this poetry examine the brutal vividness of **"Summer Evening: New York Subway Station,"** matched by the light satire of **"Uneasy Reflections."** Let him observe the peculiar texture of the prose that concludes the volume (and, incidentally, his novel, *Blackguard,* published in 1923) or the deftness of some of the monologues which, like **"Meditations in a Cemetery,"** contain reflections as sharpened as:

The tombstones around my path
Have been crisply visited by names
To which they bear no relation.
Imagine the perturbation
Of a stone removed
From the comprehension of a mountain
And branded with the name of A. Rozinsky!

This volume has an added interest because of its closer approximation of solidity; Bodenheim struggles here with the "hard fashion," he fights with "the resisting mass." Although he is not uniformly successful, several of the sonnets triumph over their own restrictions without either distorting the pattern or Bodenheim's attention to his own thoughts. The second of the **"Sonnets to My Wife"** is significant.

> My wife relents to life and does not speak
> Each moment with a deft and rapid note.
> Sometimes a clumsy weirdness finds her throat
> And ushers in a music that is weak
> And bargains with the groping of her heart.
> But even then she plays with graver tones
> That do not sell themselves to laughs and moans
> But seek the counsel of a deeper art.
>
> She drapes her loud emotions in a shroud
> Of glistening thought that waves above their
>   dance
> And sometimes parts to show their startled eyes.
> The depths of mind within her have not bowed
> To sleek emotion with its amorous glance.
> She slaps its face and laughs at its surprise!

Such examples and the still more patent brilliance of too cleverly constructed chains of epigrams (**"Impulsive Dialogue"** is one of the most arresting), cannot disguise the admission that their poet is in continual danger of being his own parodist. He coddles and croons over his idiom. He enjoys a little too much and somewhat too self-consciously the paradoxical mating of adverbs and adjectives, of adjectives and nouns that ordinarily would shrink from each other. He delights in such forced marriages as "cold elation," "meek verbosity," "noisy thinness," "deftly tepid," "tactful lustres," "animated mausoleum," "stagnant buffoon," "limpid warehouse." Technically, too, his rhythms often betray him. He is not quite at ease in the formal measures, a piece like **"Seaweed from Mars,"** jarring with an intrusion of flat feet and false quantities, is a tumbling of awkwardly interfering metres. But, however special his talent may be, this poet is an original. Within his self-sharpened limitation, Bodenheim is mordantly himself. (pp. 334-39)

> *Louis Untermeyer, "The Expressionists," in his* American Poetry Since 1900, *Henry Holt and Company, 1923, pp. 333-39.*

Harry Hansen   (essay date 1924)

[*Hansen was an American editor, critic, and war correspondent. In the following essay, he praises the characterization and narrative technique in* Crazy Man.]

Crazy Man, by Maxwell Bodenheim, is a novel of breadth and distinction that makes the reviewer pause before he begins to wave aloft the usual adjectives that serve as traffic signals on the literary highroad. It is the author's seventh book, and with its publication he seems to rise like one of the peaks that dominate the plain in the American scene. It is, broadly speaking, realistic—at least the reviewer may be pardoned for designating it so, after beholding a flying wedge of bouncers in a cheap New York dance hall converge upon a lame duck and throw him downstairs. But the lame duck disseminates a doctrine of non-resistance in the most romantic manner, and now and then the author contributes such unrealistic bits as "the kiss was belief, seeking to be full born against his skin," something that reads like an entry out of a diary that might have been kept by Richard Feverel in his trysting days.

The story of *Crazy Man* has to do with the petty world viewed by Selma Thallinger, who worked during the day as a milliner and at night sold her services as a dancing partner in Ravanni's "Academy" in lower New York. Twice every week Selma gave herself to the same pair of men, the owners of the dance hall, but the custom had long ago become meaningless and tiresome. Mr. Bodenheim has read her mind with marked insight; in fact, she is the most clearly visualized character in the book and absolutely convincing. Her revolt against the blandishments of Ravanni had already begun when John Carley appeared at the dance hall. His pleading manner and his clothes—tieless and patched—were breaks from normality and a challenge to Ravanni and his cohorts; so he was thrown out. But because he followed a philosophy of non-resistance he returned again and again, to be beaten to a pulp, but to conquer in the end through his gameness. It was natural that Selma, surfeited with her meaningless life, should turn to Carley and seek to understand the strange philosophy that had been born in him by much reading. "Every book I read tells me something different, but all the people I meet, they say the same things all the time," says Carley. He has become convinced that men must emancipate themselves from the claims of the flesh and give more thought to their intellects.

He believes that only too often men are the "duped, evanescent trustees of property," the slaves of its bulk. To free men from its tyranny he robs the rich to give to the poor—that is, he specializes in stealing furs out of large stores, and then distributes the money gained by their sale to indigent strangers. His view of religions is that

> they ask you to take care of your feelings and treat men like you'd want them to treat you, but they don't pay any attention to your mind, to what's going on inside of your head.

And as for human beings:

> They've got to teach their minds and their feelings to have more respect for each other, and when they do they don't take each other's bodies so often because that's not the only thing that they're interested in. It's all right for them to take each other if they're taking something else besides their flesh, if they're really trying to get into each other's minds and hearts and look for the secrets that are hidden there.

It is natural that most of the men Carley talks to cannot comprehend, and Selma, too, is confused because his principal occupation is talk when her body is longing for his embraces. Society, too, has its doubts, and eventually pronounces Carley the victim of an exalted paranoia and sends him to the state insane asylum. Carley breaks out, but he is convinced that permanent incarceration is not far off. "I will be arrested again," he says, "and when that happens they will undoubtedly keep me in an asylum for the rest of my life, as an incurable case of intelligence."

Mr. Bodenheim has a clearness in portraiture due in part to the fact that he expresses himself with much precision and economy of language; he makes words carry the burden of his ideas with a keen perception of their powers and capacities. This imparts a feeling of surety and accelerates movement; it commends his work to judgment in company with that of the few stylists in America. But Mr. Bodenheim's clarity in expression is set off by an individual and sometimes irritating mannerism. He turns easily to simile and metaphor; one never knows when he is going to breathe life into inanimate objects and consult their feelings in such conspicuously original terms as the "chin advised her face," or the "wound communing with hostility," or the "sawdust waiting to be teased by feet." A man careful of his diction does not fling these figures about nonchalantly; one may conjecture that Mr. Bodenheim does so with intent and after much deliberation; have we not proof elsewhere in his ironical poem **"Hatred of Metaphor and Simile"?** Here he depicts an audience crying: "Give us earth and logic!" "Down with metaphor and simile!" and then evicting two forlorn poets who show their contempt by "flicking the ashes carefully into the rage of faces around them." Bodenheim, striving for clarity in his novel, eliminated all extraneous matter from his plot and wove a story of a few simple characters and a single theme; the book is nearly one-third under way before the first incident is disposed of. But Bodenheim, the poet, kept looking in the casement and dictating a disturbing line here and there, and thus produced this strange conglomeration of styles which reminds us of a description Witter Bynner once wrote of Bodenheim's lines: "It is a drunken thief's hand, still deft in the poetic treasury." We find such circumlocutions as these: "His face . . . was firmly framed by the outward adventure of a jaw," "Emotionally, a Negro revival meeting was hurling its cries from the curves of his heart"; "invading their nearness by the tragical mirage of distance"; "the sunshine of a warm spring day waltzed with this curiosity in ever-narrowing circles."

But these are the inequalities that stand out from the body of this author's prose like gargoyles on a cathedral and lead one to the belief that the poet is fighting for survival against a young novelist who is gaining in strength. The rest of the prose has many conspicuous qualities, not the least of which is its honesty and clarity. Mr. Bodenheim conveys the vernacular of Selma, Ravanni, and others of a coarser social stratum without ever becoming the literal reporter, and he is coherent throughout, thereby breaking with the younger experimenters, who cannot hope to be understood outside a narrow circle without a glossary. (pp. 441-42)

Harry Hansen, "Incurable Intelligence," in The Nation, *New York, Vol. CXVIII, No. 3067, April 16, 1924, pp. 441-42.*

Marianne Moore   (essay date 1924)

[*Moore was an American poet, translator, essayist, and editor whose poetry is characterized by the technical and linguistic precision with which she reveals her acute observations of human character. In the following excerpt, she questions the validity of Bodenheim's language and ideas.*]

Maxwell Bodenheim's work has been honoured in almost every notable type of current publication; in that published for the politically conservative seriously cultured person, in the contumaciously aesthetic uncompromisingly intellectual magazine, in the "poets' garland," in newspapers, and in the fashionable woman's Lady-Book-and-Shopping-Guide. As is to be expected of a writer for many persons, Mr Bodenheim is many things: social philosopher, literary critic, novelist, and poet; but it is to be regretted that as a critic of modern life, he goes but part of the way, sparing himself accurate exposition of the things he advocates, impetuously dogmatizing so that one is forced in certain instances to conclude that he is self-deceived or willingly a charlatan. Our anger is stirred by his epitome of Christ's "mistakes" in emancipating humanity. He says Christ approved the repressing of instinct and that he "told people to believe with their feelings and let their minds go on a vacation." As it were in passing, Mr Bodenheim offers definitions which detain without enriching. In comparison with Chesterton's compact, expansive consideration of mysticism, his definition of it is not thorough, nor are his definitions indeed definitions, but assertions. When he says to a grass blade,

> You reach the sky because your face
> Is not turned toward it,

one feels a shrewdness of which the logic is not sound; eventually one doubts the authoritativeness of opinions which have the effect of being aphorisms; aphorisms in which there is often the mischievousness of half-statement or a slovenly abandoning of what at first had seemed to the author to be interesting. "Modern poets . . . frequently sneer at philistines, hypocrisies, and conservative postures," says Mr Bodenheim, "and this reiterated attitude reveals a baffled longing for vengeance." Can a poet sneer? Is not Mr Bodenheim's interest in retaliation at variance with creative power? Moreover, side by side with much candour, sensitiveness, and emancipated judgement, this author's concept of woman puzzles one. Surely there is false perspicacity in an analysis which results always in the exhibiting of woman's "enticing inferiority"; which finds her an embarrassing adjunct, "cooing and crawling for your money," a creature of perfumed effeteness, of "interminable evasions," "waving surrender in the foreground," never other than a receiver of "men's ornaments and poverties." The writer's altitude of pronouncement reaches its apex in the statement made by one of his *dramatis personae,* that there is zest in bagging a woman who is one's equal in wits; the possibility of bagging a superior in wits not being allowed to confuse the issue. Suspecting that Mr Bodenheim has but half sifted the facts in his observations as cited above, one feels a false approach to life in certain of his ironies. "Highly imaginative men are accused of being demented, and consequently belittled," he says. If they are, it is perhaps because they are not laborious—not so severe in judging themselves as in judging others. In his interpretation of Christ, his attitude to woman, his impatience with his readers, one feels a grudging view, a lack of breadth, of noble reverie, of the detachment of faith.

There is more for us, however, in Mr Bodenheim's writing than cause for objection. In one of his poems he makes the crystal statement that "simplicity demands one gesture and men give it endless thousands," and he is in his own fiction somewhat stark and emphatic, showing dispatch and quick firm action, with that condensed finality of implication which is an attribute of the genuine narrator. There is too, an acid penetration which recalls James Joyce's *Dubliners* in the statement, "[his] eyes greeted the darkness as if it were an advancing mob." One values the compactness of, "the sea had lent her its skin," the power of accurate observation in the poem, **"Old Man,"**

> You turn your hammock and surrender limbs
> To sunlight, and increase the hammock's swing,

and the pliant irony of some of Mr Bodenheim's underworld vernacular:

> "He asks me to please keep quiet! I said, 'Gee,
> you've got a big opinion of yourself, haven't
> you? . . . and he answers, 'No, it's not that, but
> I know in advance everything that you're going
> to say so there's no need of me hearing it.' "

But again we disagree with him when he says, "The novel should be far more interested in style than in message." It is Mr Bodenheim's misfortune that he has attained this ideal, since in his work, there is much to arrest one yet not enough to detain; his work lacks substance—his unscientifically careless pronouncement for the bettering of fiction, explaining the lack on his own part of a genuine triumph; for is not style invariably a concomitant of content—the prototype of personality? Mr Bodenheim says, "Man has a far more plaintive interior than the sexologist dares to admit." We agree, and apropos of his further statement that "intellectual curiosity, emotional whimsicality, the decorative poetic touch, ironical strength, and even a plausible realism are . . . absent from American novels of the present," are hopeful of what he may give us, only to be astounded in his proffer of *Crazy Man*—a staggering dream of fleshly discontent.

It is to his poetry that we owe most; although in it, as in his prose, there is the elected right to be superficial. Aboriginal enticing femininity has been completely written of by the Greeks; again with freshness, by Restoration poets. Such subject-matter requires magical treatment if it is to receive a second glance. Emotion, truth, intellect, revenge, money, are topics about which universal sciences have been built. How then, can we accept a stinginess of content in certain of Mr Bodenheim's poems which deal with these themes, the poet deifying "the workshop of his mind," the matter in hand eluding him?

The mechanism of Mr Bodenheim's mind is delicate and his predilection for "tombstones, skulls, and lilies" is by no means ridiculous, nor is it surprising that he should be alive to the beauty of death; but among poems of distinction, there are some self-consciously macabre conceits, for example **"Emotional Monologue"**—a weightless, miasmal, brittle, "studio" extravaganza in which we have the hobby for death at its worst.

Waiving the matter of content, Mr Bodenheim's technique varies in soundness. He says, "No longer do poets linger over their output, seeming to emulate the men who turn out collars and automobiles." Then why when expectation has been awakened by the piquancy and proper reserve of

opening lines such as "Gingerly the poets sit," is it not fulfilled? And how is it that in what one ventures to call a very bad poem, such strokes of excellence occur, as:

> Men sit and feign industrious respect,
> With eye-brows often slightly ill at ease—
> Cats in an argument are more erect?

Mr Bodenheim's aloofness from the faults of the day would not lead one to expect the weak last lines which mar many of his poems—in some lines, a not sustained effortful crispness of implication which seems an evasion, a faith in words rather than in logic, and that pitfall of aesthetic natures, the convention of the bizarre in which poetry instantaneously and disaffectingly becomes prose. Mr Bodenheim invents with firmness:

> Black angels and muscular contortions
> On panels of taffeta,

and inquires with what is to the reviewer, engaging *esprit,*

> Maiden, where are you going,
> With impudence that makes your arms and legs
> Unnecessary feathers?

Admitting such a thing as exotic diction, one can sometimes applaud Mr Bodenheim's "madness" although feeling his most daring prose to be not entirely cohesive or transparently accurate. As has been said of his "tall adjectives" and verbal sleights, in one of those gentle and distinguished analyses that have been accorded him by literary experts: "Such tricks, although they often steal distinction from surprise, wear out the power of the brain to respond, and eventually develop a resentment toward the kind of verse that leaves us jaded." A certain form of soliloquy resorted to by Mr Bodenheim has not one's entire sanction. The soliloquy is, at its best, creatively a make-shift, and when not used with consummate address, has the effect of being a not quite natural, ripe vehicle for conveying meaning; for example, **"Turmoil in a Morgue," "Impulsive Dialogue," "Dialogue Between a Past and Present Poet," "When Spirits Speak of Life," "A Chorus Girl Speaks in a Dream to a Former Lover."** Perfect diction we have, in **"Advice to a Blue-Bird:"**

> Who can make a delicate adventure
> Of walking on the ground,

in that allusion to the "woman in penitent lavender," and in this interpretation of despair:

> She killed herself, believing
> That he might become to her in death
> A figure less remote and careful.

Yet why, in prose that is the work of a precisian, should one encounter unintentional rhymes: "Their heads cleared and the past night reappeared," "the sickly brawls and vapid scandals of streets and halls"? Why in either verse or prose, the words "boresome," "peeked," "glimpsed," "tawdrily," the phrase "apt to induce," and the effete one, "moments of rare insight"?

There is that in Mr Bodenheim's work which is delicately moving, as when he calls the butterfly, "aimless petal of the wind" and in

> . . . you will have a wife

Like a thistle dipped in frost.

> . . . your life will
> Stand in a desperate majesty.

And far beyond mere sensibility, in certain work, a laconic violence with exactness persuades one of more than sensory impressionableness, as in the lines:

> An effervescence of noises
> Depends upon cement for its madness.

Dissatisfied with the irony and unrest of Mr Bodenheim's spirit, we await an exposition of that which to him would make life satisfactory. He writes in one of his poems of a man who in 1962:

> . . . died with a grin at the fact
> That literature and art in America
> Were still presenting a mildewed, decorous
> mien.

Is the implication accurate? And if it is, is not the best corrective, an exemplifying at white heat of the accuser's indigenous, individual genius? (pp. 251-56)

> *Marianne Moore, "Thistles Dipped in Frost,"
> in* The Dial, *Chicago, Vol. LXXVII, No. 3,
> September, 1924, pp. 251-56.*

Harriet Monroe   (essay date 1925)

[*As the founder and editor of* Poetry, *Monroe was a key figure in the American "poetry renaissance" that took place in the early twentieth century.* Poetry *was the first periodical devoted primarily to the works of new poets and to poetry criticism, and from 1912 until her death Monroe maintained an editorial policy of printing "the best English verse which is being written today, regardless of where, by whom, or under what theory of art it is written." In the following essay, Monroe offers an overview of Bodenheim's achievement as a poet.*]

In nineteen-thirteen and fourteen, when *Poetry* was in its first and second years, a blond youth used to appear at the office now and then, bearing innocent young rhymes written out in an incredibly large round babyish hand. Of all the young poets who have called on us—so numerous, and of so many aspects, origins, and degrees of fortune—this usually silent figure was perhaps the most unpromising and forlorn. He always looked hunted and haunted, as if half-starved and half-ill. Nor had his manner acquired its later audacity.

At that time Helen Hoyt was the "subscription department" of *Poetry,* and Alice Corbin Henderson the associate editor, and we all used to feel sorry for this pale young prentice-poet, to the point of inviting him to stay and read the books and magazines which were already bringing us new voices from all over the world. We wished we might accept his rhymes—alas that we did not preserve a few to confirm or deny the justice of those early rejections! Now probably they are lost forever, for the author himself has rejected them.

So it was a pleasure to "the staff" when this frail pale visitor surprised us one day with some free-verse experiments which we were able to print. At last Maxwell Bodenheim had caught on to "the new movement"—it was new indeed at that time—and these *Sketches,* in *Poetry* for August, 1914, were a not inadequate introduction of his inquisitive ironic mind and his slantingly searching art. One finds in them some of his characteristic phrases—"the surliness of the ditch," the miner "bending under thick knowledge," the steel rail's "stiff smile at Time—a smile which men call rust." And his irony is there, though serious and inherent, not uttered with a smile.

Well, after that Mr. Bodenheim's rise was rapid and his hitherto subdued manner became adventurous—nay, insistent and emphatic. His bitter childhood and youth urged him to a dark literary revenge—letters full of malign, carefully sculptured phrases of denunciation, began to descend upon his recent friends—a harmless pirouetting which kept his mind agile for the more serious exercise of his art. Life was a theatre for Mr. Bodenheim, in which, as a proud poet, he felt bound to play his heroic role jauntily, let the sword-play fall where it might. And of course the stage was none too stable—financial props and pillars were very shaky if not utterly lacking, and the social background of his little scene—the great rough-and-tumble world whose commands he ignored—was unsympathetically discordant. Thus the drama came to many a point of strain, with Comedy and Tragedy offering their masks in the wings.

He fell in with Ben Hecht, and they were friends at intervals between pranks and rages. He was one of the early contributors to that high-stepping and gaily careering periodical, *The Little Review.* He discoursed and read poems at the Dill Pickle and other gathering-places of storm-tossed souls. In short, he sharpened his keen wits against whatever he could find of adroit and sophisticated in Chicago before he shook its dust from his feet and its smoke from his eyes, and made off to New York to become a contributor to *The Century* and a prickly pillar of the Poetry Society of America.

Meantime, while he was lifting himself by such contacts out of the slums and stupidities which fate had tried to assign him to, what was he achieving in his art? From the first the critics began to notice his phrase-making, his adroit manipulation of words. It is true that he has a caressing way with words, that he turns them to strange uses, making the familiar old coins seem newly minted and patterned. He is a lover of words; he studies their color and savors their "bouquet" like a winebibber. But this is not his whole story, though perhaps it is more of it than truly great art would confess. If words have been an intense preoccupation with him, that is a consistent detail of a spirit keen, narrow and ironic rather than rich, big and generous.

Though his sensitive feeling for words betrays him sometimes into preciosity, mostly he makes it serve his purpose. For his is an art of veiled and egoistic emotions, in which the immediate subject, be it a lady or a buttercup or the rear porch of an apartment building, reflects, like an actor's practice-mirror, the poet's swiftly changing expressions and attitudes. This is not said in dispraise—there is a sense in which it is true of every artist; indeed, one's self is so important that the most outward-gazing soul can not escape it. But with Mr. Bodenheim it is the one all-engrossing phenomenon of the universe. Standing before the mirror, he is kindled to frozen fires of passion over the ever-changing aspects of his thought in its mortal sheath; he is intrigued—nay, moved to the white heat of ice by the subtle workings of his mind, trailing off from the central unreal reality there visible out to nebulous remote circumferences of an ego-starred philosophy. The eyes he looks into are his own; the bluebird flies with his own wings; the planets whirl through space to "drop little gestures upon my forehead."

The inevitable answer of egoism to the world's enormous disregard is irony—Mr. Bodenheim's artistic motive is ironic always. Sometimes the irony is veiled and delicate, almost invisible, like that of a man blowing bubbles against the pitiless destructive sunlight:

> Your cheeks are spent diminuendos
> Sheering into the rose-veiled silence of your lips!

he cries, and with sarcastic satisfaction he watches the gossamer words dissolve unheeded. His "Minna whose smile is my throne" is as theoretic an abstraction as the Elizabethan lady whose gallant sang,

> Her eyes are sapphires set in snow,
> Refining heaven with every wink.

But he celebrates his literary loves with a dark modern seriousness and intensity unknown to Lodge and Lyly.

One watches the development of his art with much the same feeling which a gaping crowd lavishes on a tight-rope athlete dancing over perilous abysses. Graceful and marvellously expert are the steps he wastes in merely asserting his expertness. A paradox is to him an irresistible temptation—he must set out to prove it though truth freezes on her mountain-top. At first, when beauty was his paradox, some of the proofs he offered had an exquisite grace. The poems in free verse in *Minna and Myself* on death and **"To Our Dead,"** one called **"Love,"** the lovely **"Make of Your Voice a Dawn,"** and a few others, are gestures so beautiful that one forgets the attitude. Their rhythms are his own, dangerous but perfectly achieved, like the disembodied figures of speech which he plucks somewhere out of the soaring air. Here, as rarely elsewhere, he achieves ease.

But ease cannot be maintained on a tight-rope, and proving the paradox does not produce great art. The super-athletic attitude becomes a strain. Already in Mr. Bodenheim's second book, *Advice,* one feels weariness; the rhythms are not so sure, and the motives are much more perfunctory. The best poem in it, **"Advice to a Bluebird,"** is deliberate rather than spontaneous, and bears no comparison with the earlier lyrics above mentioned. In later publications he quite silences the lyric note; and when, in certain rather expository poems, he experiments with rhyme and metrics, even to the point of writing sonnets, one is forced to wonder how a rhythmic instinct once sensitive and original could become so tame.

But the later books are mostly confessedly satiric—the irony hitherto implied is now stated. In *Introducing Irony*

Bodenheim selling his poems in Washington Square, 1948.

and *The Sardonic Arm* the super-athletic attitude is frankly maintained, but with an engaging and insolent humor. The unexpected is ushered in with a flourish, the fantastic is gaudily paraded. Wit is so agile that one misses half its leaps and bounds. Life circles around us like a three-ringed circus whose countless stunts have agility but neither motive nor meaning. Mr. Bodenheim, as ringmaster, greets his whirling world with a wild malicious grin, and whips it cruelly along on its path of pain. Always, here also, the behold-me attitude; always the super-athlete putting words, characters, conceptions through incredible impossible paces.

Sometimes one responds with a grin to the delightfully demoniac topsiturviness of it all. The heroin-peddler,

> Immersed in that brisk midnight known as
>   crime.

The lively dead in a morgue, whose talk

> Accepts the jest of a universe.

The acrobat, violinist and chambermaid celebrating the "geometry of souls." Even

> Death,
> Grandiosely hackneyed subject,

does not escape this sardonic jester. In his cemetery, where Shaw and Maeterlinck are put lightly underground with Shakespeare, the poet reflects:

Being finalities, the grass and trees
Find no need for rules of etiquette.

He salutes "the old gravediggers"—

From their faces adjectives have fled,
Leaving the essential noun.

And he bids us

Imagine the perturbation
Of a stone removed
From the comprehension of a mountain,
And branded with the name of A. Rozinsky!

But witty lines, brief extracts, slander this poet by seeming more humane than his intention. To get the sardonic flavor of his satirical accusation of life one must read entire poems, entire books. Of late he has written two novels: the first one, **Blackguard,** has not reached me; the second, **Crazy Man,** I have just read. Following its keen and sympathetic portrait of the dance-hall girl, with its marvellous use of her swift-winged slang, I wondered whether at last Mr. Bodenheim had forgotten his pose, abandoned his quest of the paradox. But no—enter the noble thief, who, being handled with a singularly voluble prosiness, turns the tale to sentimental bunk quite unworthy of our defiant satirist, our usually accomplished artist.

What drop of poison in this poet's blood, embittering his thought, threatens to nullify the higher reaches of his art? One thinks of the great satirists, of Cervantes, Aristophanes, of Swift and Gay—men bigger, more generous than their private grudges at untoward fate; men whose laughter is rich and round as it still rolls heartily over the world. What Freudian tragedy of suppression and deprivation through this poet's childhood may have turned his blood to gall, and the wine of his satire to vinegar? Will he never work himself free of the inferiority complex which twists his art? (pp. 320-27)

Harriet Monroe, "Maxwell Bodenheim," in Poetry, *Vol. XXV, No. 6, March, 1925, pp. 320-27.*

William Carlos Williams on Bodenheim:

Bodenheim pretends to hate most people, including Pound and Kreymborg, but that he really goes to this trouble I cannot imagine. He seems rather to me to have the virtue of self-absorption so fully developed that hate is made impossible. Due to this, also, he is an unbelievable physical stoic. I know of no one who lives so completely in his pretenses as Bogie does. Having formulated his world neither toothache nor the misery to which his indolence reduces him can make head against the force of his imagination. Because of this he remains for me a heroic figure, which, after all, is quite apart from the stuff he writes and which only concerns him. He is an Isaiah of the butterflies.

William Carlos Williams, in his essay "Prologue to Kora in Hell," 1920.

E. S. Forgotson   (essay date 1942)

[*In the essay excerpted below, Forgotson discusses the relationship between Bodenheim's political ideology and the poems in* Lights in the Valley.]

The poems in [*Lights in the Valley*], divided according to subject matter, fall into two chief categories: those which seek to "dramatize" sympathetically the experience of the proletariat; and those which argue the ideological case of the proletarian artist or intellectual, either by a direct advocacy of the preferred values, attitudes, and ways of behavior, or indirectly, through satirical attacks upon the opposition. Within the second category might be included a third sub-class, that of the "conversion" poem, where we are shown the artist or intellectual caught in the crucial experience which teaches him a new "view of life."

The poems of the first category are in the minority, at least in the present collection, but they deserve examination for the reason that they represent the fruits of the poetic ideology set forth in the formally argumentative poems of the second category. I will serve up a specimen of the fruits, and then make a brief inspection of the ideological tree that has borne them. (As a matter of fact, the argumentative poems themselves are, in their technical aspect, also products of the ideology they contain; but it suits my limited approach to consider them merely as "tracts." Presumably, too, their subject is looked upon by the author as a relatively temporary preoccupation—that is, the prescriptions of the ideology are aimed at persuading poets to begin writing in a certain way about proletarian experience, not about the ideology of proletarian poetry). The first example is taken from *Southern Labor Organizer;* I quote the opening twelve lines.

What is the limit of a man's
Control when torture rips the breast
Until, almost insane, it fans
A groveling desire for rest?
You know the answer, you were bound
To cypress tree that night. They made
Your blood gush to the swampy ground,
They hacked your flesh with whip and blade.
Their hope was that you would confess
Sharecroppers' names, throw year-long friends
To quick death or a crouching press
Where copperheads and slime contend.

The features of this passage, and of the whole poem from which it is taken, are consonant with the requirements of Mr. Bodenheim's moral and literary "convictions" as these emerge from the polemical poems. Mr. Bodenheim does not approve of ironizing the bourgeois without investigating the economic incitements of its vulgarity, and without having a clear, positive and practicable program of reform; this is the accusation he levels against himself and his fellow-intellectuals of the twenties and thirties in **"One Generation"**. He does not approve of speculation about the "meaning of the universe," particularly when it is accompanied by only a vague and fishy awareness of the immediate exigencies of the actual world (**"Renunciation"**). He would like to see poets arise who will be more interested in materials drawn from the common fund of experience of the proletariat, than in those that spring from the highly specialized or subjectively perverted experience of the isolated or the neurotic. This summary does a very rough justice to Mr. Bodenheim's congeries of values—and to the frequent acuteness of the analytical statements upon which the values are psychologically based; but it may be enough to show his moral and intellectual outlines, which are of course Marxian.

What I have to say against Mr. Bodenheim's poetic practice, therefore, does not call into question the consistency of his application of the ideology to the practice. Again, it does not debate the "correctness" of the value-premises of the ideology. They are as "correct" as they can be; as "right" as anybody else's—and no righter. (The strictly empirical and logical elements of the ideology nonetheless remain separately submissible to their established rules.) And finally, it does not consist in any major rejection on my part of Mr. Bodenheim's avowed values, poetic or moral; indeed, I am willing in the main to accept the values which he *avows*. My demurrer attaches to certain values, implied by the poetic practice, but which pass by and large without attention in the overtly critical poems, and which may or may not be consciously maintained by the poet. What these values are can partly be demonstrated by an analysis of the metaphoric technique of the lines cited above. In line two, "torture" is an instrument that does physical damage. In the next line, however, the image of the ripped breast moves rapidly through a reference to a purely psychological and impalpable condition ("almost insane"), which shares none of the attributes of the opening metaphor, into a second metaphor of the wounded breast itself "fanning" a desire for rest, as doubtless a fire is fanned into growth. But the presence of the word "groveling" in modification of the flame-like desire is metaphorically at odds, for a growing fire does not grovel. And exactly how are we to picture the "breast"—already, in its metaphoric status, "ripped"—as "fanning" a vaguely located internal fire? Also, in the last three lines of the passage, we find the press crouching like a beast of prey—and straightway somehow metamorphosed into a combination of poisonous snakes and slime; the confusion is one which the additional sense of "copperhead" does nothing to relieve. Moreover, by the terms of the metaphor, the alternatives ("quick death *or* a crouching press") are not really different, since to be delivered to the poet's mysterious compound monster would surely mean a death as quick as quick death itself.

Such metaphoric usage is prevalent in Mr. Bodenheim's volume. And in most other technical respects—metrically, for example—he is, by my reading, dull, imitative, and obvious. One infers, from the last poem in this book **"Advice to a Man,"** that there have been critics who dispose of such a poet as Mr. Bodenheim by calling him a "talent dispersed in the lowlands." I am not of this haughty group, as I have meant to indicate. I am prepared to admire a poetry written out of Mr. Bodenheim's stated sympathies and intellectual position, but I see no reason why that poetry should not have, or could not have, as full a measure of technical rigor and interest as any other. I might add that if Mr. Bodenheim thinks his work already *is* technically rigorous and interesting, the last word is his. (pp. 219-23)

E. S. Forgotson, *"The New Line and the Old Bottle,"* in Poetry, *Vol. LX, No. 4, July, 1942, pp. 219-23.*

Allen Churchill on the decline of Bodenheim's career:

Like other writers, Bodenheim went on the WPA, but his personal demons kept pushing him ever downward. At the San Remo he began writing poems on scraps of paper and selling them for drinks, asking first one dollar, then fifty cents, and finally a ten-cent beer. He would drink anything bought for him, then go raging through the streets of the Village "shouting imprecations at a society that returned his hate by ignoring him." Those who bought his scribbled poetry found it more doggerel than verse, clever rhymes with pretentious thoughts, as empty, really, as his oft-repeated epigram, "Greenwich Village is the Coney Island of the soul."

Bodenheim was not unaware of his decline. Often his battle cry, "I have a malady of the soul," would ring over the bardin at the San Remo or Minetta. To anyone who bought him a drink, he might confess, "I am a scarecrow body and a dead soul." To Ben Hecht, who on a visit to New York sought out his old friend, Bodenheim said, "I know of no sensible reason why I should not commit suicide and put an end to the whole stupid nonsense."

Allen Churchill, in The Improper Bohemians: A Re-creation of Greenwich Village in Its Heyday, *1959.*

Jack B. Moore   (essay date 1970)

[*An educator and critic specializing in American literature, Moore is the author of a book on Bodenheim's life and literary career. In the following excerpt from that work, he characterizes Bodenheim's approach to writing and provides an overview of his most prominent poetry collections and novels.*]

Bodenheim's blossoming as a poet roughly coincides with that of Imagism's birth and sway, and many of the poets with whom he was friendly—William Carlos Williams, for example—are usually thought of as Imagists. But Bodenheim's art paralleled without ever really intersecting much of the Imagist poetry. He is, in fact, in many ways a curiously old-fashioned poet, so old-fashioned that he seemed clearly one of the most original poets of his day. He wrote like no one else around him, and surely no one after him wrote precisely as he did. He claimed upon his first publication in the *Little Review* in September, 1914, that he was "an intense admirer of Ezra Pound's. . . . I worship him"; but neither Pound nor any other contemporary influenced him more than generally. His own character, his stance, was stamped into every poem he wrote, for good or bad.

Bodenheim was a poet of sensibility, in the old sense of the word. Through an impressionistic, though often highly controlled, investigation of his emotional responses to the people and world about him, he apparently hoped to reveal to his audience the essential truths about those people and that world. As a poet, he left rational, objective surfaces of the mind and object unexposed; he preferred to scrutinize his own highly intense, highly personal world view. He rarely attempted to render accurately the thing in itself, but rather rhapsodized upon the emotional re-creation of the thing within himself. At his best, he achieved sparkling and remarkable insights; at his worst, a temporarily catchy vagueness or flat sentimentality. In his poetry, as in his novels and in his life, he shied from disciplined factuality and from responsibility to rational or recognized authority. In all things, Bodenheim was the measure.

He ordinarily did not emphasize Imagist aims: concreteness, simplicity, concentration, natural speech rhythms (though in one strange, personal way he did, for he came to speak as he wrote), colloquial diction, or firmly outlined images. Often his poems suggested rather than stated overtly; but this diffusion of thought results more from the difficulties involved in registering the individual strands of reaction evoked by the response to some object, idea, or person than from any desire to avoid telling the reader exactly what is being felt or described. He tended to mannerism in reporting his reactions, since he claimed that "originality, therefore, can only occur in the style and not the content of man's creations. In literature, the way in which a man shifts and contrasts his words, and not what he actually says, determines his freshness."

And he constantly switched significance back from the thing observed to himself; for, as he wrote, "I deny that vision is any part of the poet's business. Let him leave that to the philosopher, novelist and political-economist—those people who are forever engaged in explaining and pigeon-holing life and individuals, and concern himself with the many, unrealized possibilities of word-combinations: possibilities by means of which he may discover adroitly hidden threads within himself and within the life about him. The luxury of looking ahead and pointing a confident finger at what in reality is but a plausible mirage, or of generalizing about an insoluble melée, is one that does not appeal to me."

One of the complexities involved in reading Bodenheim's poetry—and elsewhere in the just quoted letter he stated his aim was a "delicate complexity"—stems from his theory. Naturally, he registers his own perception of an object or situation or emotion, so that the reader must be prepared to analyse not only the quality or final result of perception, but the emotional and intellectual lens through which Bodenheim perceives. That is, his response to what is outside himself is significant, but it is often meaningful only if the apparatus through which he responds is understood. Bodenheim did not clearly distinguish in his own mind between reality and illusion, and in his response to the real and the illusory he is apt to place both on the same plane of being.

To him, a thought, a color, and a sound are equally substantial—or insubstantial. When he refers in one of his early poems to a voice composed of "cool rubies of sound" in which the lover bathes, he is not speaking metaphorically since he is describing a feeling and not an objective reali-

ty. The various levels of sense and substance equally affect the poet's response and in that way are equally real and substantial. The imagined feeling of coolness, the imagined hard, beautiful ruby, the real sound of the voice, and the imagined cool wetness of bathing all merge into one emotionally actual response. To the reader this kind of imagery may be meaningless beyond what it vaguely suggests because it lacks visual or any other sensory concreteness. How can one bathe in rubies of sound? Synesthesia would explain bathing in sound, but not rubies of sound. What is even the figurative sense of rubies of sound?

Bodenheim does not always maintain consistency in recognizing levels and kinds of substances and essences that provoke a response within him. Such a poet as Shelley maintains remarkable control over the varying tangible and intangible objects and qualities imaged throughout the song from *Prometheus Unbound* beginning "My soul is an enchanted boat, / Which, like a sleeping swan doth float / Upon the silver waves of thy sweet singing." Shelley achieves a delicate but wholly recognizable balance between what is outward and what is inward, what is imagined and what is real. Bodenheim does not always achieve that balance and, moreover, does not seem to recognize the boundaries between variant sensuous and illusory perceptions. What would be synesthesia for another poet seems more for him simple expository comparison.

Bodenheim's poetic practice was drawn from his attitude toward reality. One of his closest friends, the poet Louis Grudin, writes [in an unpublished letter]:

> The extreme Platonism of Max's imagery in speech as well as in his verse carried through to a total commitment, as in compulsive religious mania, a flight into systematic myth. It was as if Poe's cosmic parable of the verbal genesis of the physical world had possessed Max's mind. He believed inflexibly in the casual primacy of "intangibles," ideas and emotions were like individual persons to him, as autonomous realities within the "illusion" of the actual world. . . . A number of times Max solemnly confessed meetings with a woman he had once loved and who had died. . . . She kept trysts with him to hold long conversations in a language of pure poetry; and these were as actual as the visits of the Angel Gabriel who would come in person to pose for Blake. This was not feigned, and Max would be beside himself with rage when I hinted at skepticism.

Concerning the poet's function, Bodenheim was of two minds. First, as already noted, the poet was honestly to report his response to the surrounding world of people and ideas. By fresh and original phrasing, he is to perceive "adroitly hidden threads within himself and within the life about him." He also claimed that "poetry has no utilitarian or instructive function." But it is impossible not to watch throughout Bodenheim's poetry the delivering of various messages concerning how man should view himself and his world. His second volume of poetry is, after all, titled *Advice;* and, knowingly or not, he was constantly advising his readers, not always dogmatically perhaps, but nonetheless explaining to them many of the concepts directly promulgated in his novels. His early poetry then shows a second, perhaps unconscious function of the poet as a legislator of the world. His later poetry, when he becomes more and more politically involved, shows the poet as acknowledged legislator.

But even early in his career he tries to make the instructional poet compatible with the pure artist. The poet, he wrote in 1920, "exists to show other men what lies beneath their hard outer skin; to reveal to them the complexities and unfoldings which life has denied them." He admits that, with this concept of the poet, the writer is preaching; but the poet is "not a preacher in the ordinary sense of the word." The poet is "the mad, insulted preacher among men . . . one who indirectly tells men what they could have been, by holding his heart and mind up to them like an unconcerned child." The preaching is supposedly indirect, by display rather than by demand, and is performed with almost disregard for the audience.

Bodenheim sought purity of personal revelation, not of observation. This pure revelation was to portray for the reader in "bare words, expressions, forms, and colors of life . . . the nearest possible approach to the sum total of their essence." The poet's expression tells only about itself, while indirectly engaging the reader's response to something similar within himself. And elsewhere Bodenheim praises the dispassionate eye that seeks poetry which "need have no direct connection with the salient motifs of human nature, and need only paint a picture without comment, or supplemented by the poet's purely spiritual reaction." Interestingly enough, Bodenheim uses as an example of the dispassionate eye Walt Whitman, who was as involved with didactic poetry as was Bodenheim.

Bodenheim thought that through the "abstracted, impersonal glare of eyes that do not seek to judge, praise or blame," the poet would arrive at essential truths about men and their world. The presentation of such truths would not in itself constitute didactic poetry; for the artist was merely, through subjective analysis, arriving at ideal reality. The poet would not lecture his audience, but would try to approximate pure poetry, "the vibrant expression of everything clearly delicate and unattached with surface sentiment in the emotions of men toward themselves and nature." But as will be seen, he was increasingly neither dispassionate nor uncommitted in his poetry—in some of his best poetry—as his reputation waned and as the economic system of the country buckled along with his personal resources.

As the title to his first volume of poems [*Minna and Myself*] suggests, young Bodenheim divides his attention in the volume between "Minna" and "Myself." The poems to Minna are love poems anatomizing her physical presence and his emotions concerning her. The poems in the "Myself" section fall into four main categories: love poems, poems about death, poems of city life, and nature poems. Generally, Bodenheim does least well with nature poems. He is often clearly not concerned with the object to be described, but with his emotional reaction expressed in ingenious language. A tree or a flower, no more than glanced at or vaguely imagined in reverie, becomes an excuse for displaying the poet's verbal resources. Occasionally, though the phrasing itself is arresting, the original object of the poet's attention disappears beneath the superstructure of imagery. (pp. 36-41)

[*Advice*, Bodenheim's next book of poetry, has] a solidity of accomplishment that progresses beyond the higher-flying but shorter-spanned talent of *Minna and Myself*. *Advice* contains, for example, a number of Bodenheim's best city poems portraying the sights and moods and people of the modern, industrial city. The greatest deficiency of *Advice* is unfortunately in the title series of poems. These comprise ten clearly related poems, placed sporadically throughout the book's first half, offering advice to some object or person.

Bodenheim is more interested in the opportunity for giving advice, and for suggesting the emotional reaction evoked within him by the object or person, than he is in observing what the entity advised really is and what its symbolic point of reference might be. Therefore, the resulting advice does not always seem to have any poetically logical connection to its ostensible subject. Bodenheim himself must have been uncertain of this relationship. One poem titled **"Advice to a Street-Pavement"** concludes originally "Only one who lies upon his back / Can disregard the stars." In the *Selected Poems* he switches the advice to "Only one too long upon his back / Can appreciate the stars above him." Worse, however, Bodenheim never overcomes a basic error of strategy indicated by the titles of some of the poems: he writes "Advice" to a bluebird, to a butterfly, to a buttercup, to a forest, to a grass blade, to maple trees, to a pool, and to a horned toad. Bodenheim was never particularly strong in nature poems anyway, but surely anyone presumptuously offering advice to a forest or grass blade should have some startling information; and advising butterflies and buttercups also seems a dubious proposition for a grown poet. (pp. 48-9)

Introducing Irony revealed a few slight shifts in Bodenheim's poetry, though irony exists in his published works from the start. He writes a number of poems answering his critics and he also includes more poems employing orthodox meter and rhyme. As though in compensation, he includes several poems dealing with esoteric characters, sights, and situations. He also presents familiar types: love poems to Minna and a collection of city poems. (p. 56)

The least effective poems of *Introducing Irony* are imaginative flights that, rather than soar into some empyrean of absolute truth, simply spin off nowhere near reality. Several of these begin with complex stage directions indicating that Bodenheim could not get everything into the poem that he wanted to. The directions also recall closet dramas that cumbersomely mix the ethereal and the all too solid: Shelley's *Prometheus Unbound* has a scene that opens with Ocean reclining close to shore. Bodenheim's **"When Spirits Speak of Life"** is prefaced by a paragraph explaining that three spirits are sitting on a low stone wall on top of a hill. After further explanation, the reader is told "the wall, the hill, and the figures exist only to the spirits who have created them." (p. 58)

Perhaps the most significant new direction in *Introducing Irony* is taken in **"Seaweed from Mars."** Bodenheim is able in this poem to portray a world of superior emotional existence in wildly fanciful, synesthetic images that are organic to his subject, since the visitor from Mars who relates the poem finds our language and senses hopelessly inadequate to explain life on his planet. What would be synesthesia on earth is simply a rough translation of sensuous life on Mars. Mars is an emotional alternative to conventional, mundane human existence, a world of essential intensity reached, one supposes, through escaping from what seems the crust of reality. (p. 62)

Against This Age shows little change and no decline from Bodenheim's previous three volumes. The poems generally indict modern society as sordid and mean, but do so with little of the figurative tenderness of his earliest work. **"New York City,"** in iambic pentameter couplets, contrasts the city's daytime ugliness with the dangerous beauty it achieves when masked by night. His impressions of bleak New York, its "undistinguished crates of stone / And wood, the wounded dwarfs who walk alone— / The chorus-girls whose indiscretions hang / Between the scavengers of rouge and slang," are more effective than his depiction of what occurs when "The night, with black hands, gathers each mistake / And strokes a mystic challenge from each ache. / The night, New York, sardonic and alert, / Offers a soul to your reluctant dirt." The "black hands" of night are a cliché, and the image of stroking a "mystic challenge" from aches means less and less the more it is studied. (pp. 64-5)

One of the few poems in *Against This Age* showing development of interest is **"Regarding an American Village,"**— Bodenheim's first full-scale employment of American small-town life. In the tradition of Masters' *Spoon River Anthology,* Sherwood Anderson's prose *Winesburg, Ohio,* and Edwin Arlington Robinson's "Tilbury Town" poems, the work presents character vignettes of village life. The poem is possibly the immediate result of Bodenheim's friendship at the MacDowell Colony with Robinson, whom he admired. The first section of Bodenheim's poem states that he will follow a middle course in his portrayals: "I have not contempt or praise / To give you—no desire / To rip off, discovering / Skin, and undulations known as sin, / And no desire to revise you / With glamorous endearments of rhyme." (p. 66)

The poems in Bodenheim's second book of 1923, *The Sardonic Arm,* are less sharp in outline than those in *Against This Age;* they are some of his most suggestive and some of his most diffuse verse. In the series "Portraits," his images sometimes blur what are really simple statements: in **"Stenographer"** the secretary's superiority over the "droning man beside her" is announced by the lines "Intellect, / You are an electrical conspiracy / Between the advance guards of soul and mind"; a shop girl's beauty in **"Shop Girl"** becomes metaphysically significant— "Yellow roses in your black hair / Hold the significance / Of stifled mystics defying time." (p. 67)

Just as *The Sardonic Arm* continues the earlier style of Bodenheim's images and repeats his standard themes, it displays no real prosodic experimentation. Few poems are rhymed, and few feature manipulation of line length or meter in any consistent, meaningful fashion. Bodenheim's free verse of the period is often structurally similar to the patterns of newspaper headlines, but this resemblance may not be planned. Such lines as those introducing **"Woman"** do, however, resemble a page-one head:

> They worship musical sound
> Protecting the breast of emotion.
> Their feelings pose as fortune-tellers. . . .

The short, relatively even, and journalistically direct rhythm contrasts with the highly unjournalistic diction Bodenheim ordinarily employs; and it provides an ironic framework for his ideas.

The volume does contain, if nothing technically new, a few poems that reaffirm old ideas in a fresh way. In at least three poems, Bodenheim investigates the interplay of essence and shadow, the meaning that impersonal object and death impart to life: he discusses what is real and what is not, what is the real significance of seeming unreality. (p. 70)

Bodenheim's autobiographical first novel, *Blackguard,* showed the growth of a young poet in lower-middle-class Chicago, and presents him as an esthete and a miscreant. While not the best-fashioned of Bodenheim's books, it displays a comic self-portrait and a nostalgic pathos rare in the usually bitter writer: tonally, the work is similar to O'Neill's *Ah Wilderness.* The book's defects were repeated in his novels throughout Bodenheim's career: authorial intrusions, shaky handling of point of view (often a talky omniscience), lack of focus, and sometimes subservience to irrelevant matter. At their worst, Bodenheim's novels seem tracts designed for revenge.

Examples of Bodenheim's characteristic obtrusions are numerous in *Blackguard.* When his hero, Carl Felman, walks down a Chicago street observing children's games, Bodenheim comments that the play masks feelings created by summer's "sensual madness"; and he adds: "most people are incapable of actual thought, and thinking to them is merely emotion that calmly plots for more concrete rewards and visions." Another repeated fault in Bodenheim's fiction is his penchant for artily self-conscious dialogue or reverie. "The shadows gave your face," young Carl's girlfriend says, "a soft excuse, and you looked half like a sprite and half like a martyr. There was an indelicately impish weariness on your face." And the young woman is not being satirized.

But Bodenheim's novelistic defects should not obscure his accomplishments. His fiction offers keen social analysis and sometimes powerful investigations of contemporary urban life and of mainly disaffected urban types. In *Blackguard* he employs one of the central myths of American fiction: a youth's education in the city. Beginning with Charles Brockden Brown's *Arthur Mervyn* and continuing through J. D. Salinger's *The Catcher in the Rye* and Ralph Ellison's *Invisible Man* and beyond, the city has provided urban landscapes dangerous as the wilderness to test the sensitive young man. The American quest is a city quest: a major theme of much native fiction and of *Blackguard;* for the city is the dominant force in young Carl Felman's growing up.

Bodenheim fuses the myth of the city quest with the career of a now-familiar American city type, the marginal Jew.

Carl Felman must combat two enemies, the cold, brutalizing city and what he considers a crumbling tradition. Combined with the story of a poet's growth, the themes produce a touching, comic portrait of the silly, dedicated artist who collides with the husk of a devitalized establishment. (pp. 74-5)

Bodenheim later wrote better novels, but he never again displayed so much raw autobiographical material. He learned to pay more attention to the matter and manner of his work, less to his own personal philosophy. He learned to pare peripheral comment and action from the urban themes he dealt with and to limit purely personal revelation. But he never again captured the sad and bitter comedy of youth as he did in *Blackguard.*

Bodenheim's next novel, *Crazy Man,* constitutes a considerable advancement over *Blackguard* in that it is less uneven and less awkward technically. Its action is divided into three parts: in the first, the life of Selma Thallinger is described in all its drab meaninglessness until she meets the crazy man John Carley. In the second, Carley's life is described; his slow development as a Christ-Robin Hood is depicted to the time when he is brutally beaten at the dance hall where Selma works. The third section shows the effect of the two on each other: Carley's strange Christ-like example initiates Selma into a meaningful existence, and Carley gains his first female disciple. (pp. 79-80)

Bodenheim is still gabbily omniscient in the book, but his simple three-part structure produces orderly progression; and, as a result, his philosophic interpolations are short; and he focuses effectively on key scenes. He . . . reveals a good ear for the depressingly banal tedium of poverty-stricken minds and for the equally petty and habitual language of family squabbling. "Now you stop jokin' with me," Selma's mother shouts; "I've always been a modest woman and I'm not ashamed of it either but you sure didn't inherit none of it from me. Go on, now, put your nightgown on." Bodenheim's rococo descriptions are also frequently bright: "Lucille, in the atrocity of her pink dress with a melee of ruffles, and one hundred and seventy pounds of pale brown flesh that might have been used as a sail for some grotesque ship, for it presented a light and adventurous appearance in spite of its weight, and curved loosely outward."

The book's investigation of the viciousness of contemporary urban life is sharp, and its revelation of city behavior patterns, especially sexual, are significant and in greater part valid. The crippling effect of enforced closeness on the rootless yet circumscribed city dweller, the futile and frenzied habitual search for "kicks," the ugliness of city life and bleakness of city hopes, continue Bodenheim's portrait of the American wilderness. (p. 86)

The book that contributed most to Bodenheim's reputation as a libertine was *Replenishing Jessica.* Jessica's erotic rebellion is her chief weapon against an immoral society. But, unlike Selma Thallinger, she is essentially corrupted by her behavior; and Bodenheim portrays her decline with increasing distaste. Jessica, a sexual Lanny Budd, sleeps with over a dozen men from two continents and various social worlds, attempts to split her sex life

from the rest of her existence, but becomes increasingly coarsened and degraded. Occasionally, a bright phrase shines through the repetitious and frequently dull narration of Jessica's sex life—for example, the book's most notorious image: "his fingers enveloped the fullness of her breasts quite as a boy grasps soap-bubbles and marvels at their intact resistance"—but generally the book is disappointing unless perhaps read as "hot stuff" in very early adolescence.

The book's main failure is Bodenheim's strange social and psychological naïveté. For all its quasi-mystical meandering, *Crazy Man* was solidly rooted in a drab and oppressive milieu that exerted a strong force over its characters. Carley himself could be analyzed as a case of dementia praecox, or as a kind of holy bum. In *Replenishing Jessica* Bodenheim does not present a credible world to warp Jessica into her rebellion. The picture Bodenheim gives of the rich is thin and unconvincing, certainly too weak to account for Jessica's intense promiscuity. Jessica herself is worth four million dollars, and this fact simply does not function in the novel. The weight of so much money should seriously be accounted for in such a supposedly gorgeously crippled life. And Bodenheim's chronic disregard of Freudian psychology permits him to neatly separate from the causes of Jessica's dilemma the facts that she was the only child of a millionaire father and that her mother had been dead for several years. Though she is sexually attracted to her father and has censored out remembrance of her mother, Jessica's relationship to her parents "had little effect on [her] make-up," Bodenheim tells us. (pp. 94-5)

His next novel was less sensational and far better written. *Ninth Avenue* provides what Bodenheim had been heading toward in his first three fictions, an almost classic example of the American city novel. Urban ugliness frames and dominates the book, which opens in the concrete-hard light of a city Sunday morning and closes with its heroine Blanche and her Negro lover gazing hopefully beyond the dirty green swells of the Hudson River. In between, the city forces its imprint on all characters and events. The novel's first paragraph describes the "smudged, flat fronts" of tenements that seem like "warehouses stretching down both sides of the street . . . holding commodities rather than human beings." Through this depersonalized squalor roams the Ninth Avenue elevated train, mechanical, saurian, overpowering, yet itself dwarfed by the cold towers surrounding it. And its tracks do not lead beyond the city, only through it. It goes nowhere. (pp. 95-6)

Cruelty abounds in such a world, for the male can assert his individuality only through violence or by some other display of power, especially through sex domination. The women seek temporary escape through titillations and thrills, but they must be careful not to succumb too easily to the predatory male. Girls and boys are wise in the ways of grasping pleasure and are sexually knowledgeable too young. Blanche's sister Mabel is at eighteen "stuffed with tricks, and informations, and cool wiles picked up on streets and cabarets." Older standards of value have largely disappeared, and institutions such as church and family have little pressure to exert. Ritual is conventionalized and trivialized: somewhat like Alexander Pope's Belinda, Blanche "combed her dark red, bobbed hair, as though it were a sacred and perilous performance." She performs these rites on Sunday morning. Sunday has become in fact a travesty. Blanche's family is stolidly content together once a week, after Sunday dinner, when they are physically if not spiritually full. (p. 96)

Bodenheim returned to poetry for his next book, *Returning to Emotion.* In this work most of the limpness and flabby precocity that haunt his lesser poetry is gone. His lines are relatively firmer, tougher, more disciplined. The second poem in a series called "Chinese Gifts" suggests the poetically mature artist writing simply, unsentimentally, imaginatively. "Only fools believe / That breezes shift the roses / Within the valley of Hang Tso. / With lengthy whispers of perfume / The roses command each breeze / To tilt them in six directions." The poet sees a self-contained beauty in the roses so inspiriting that they appear to control the subservient wind. Only the ideally and not literally realistic poet can master this beauty: "Most poets in the valley / Swear that the roses are tender, / Frail, and smoothly amorous." The younger Bodenheim might have said this. However, "most poets" are wrong. "But one poet, derided by the rest, / Insists that they are cold, / Indiscreetly strong, and careless. / The roses alone bow to him." (p. 102)

Returning to Emotion is often esthetically triumphant and demonstrates a poetically mature variety. Even in ordinarily less valuable areas, as with **"Sonnet to Elinor Wylie,"** Bodenheim displays a hard, tight accomplishment. Among his early volumes, *Returning to Emotion* ranks high.

The King of Spain reveals a general decline, however, from the arresting versatility of *Returning to Emotion.* Bodenheim reworks many old subjects with more gesture than force, and he is trapped at least once, in **"Baseball Game,"** into revealing a style made pretentious by faulty application. In **"Baseball Game"** the pitcher views the batter "With a morbid cogitation / Dressed in unconcern." At ball two, "The batter's scowl / Remains but lessens to admit / The lighter poise of confidence, / And the pitcher surveys him / With chagrin and anger— / Twin playthings for his patient soul." The title poem, an overly long story of almost a hundred and fifty lines, concerns attempted regal assassination with ponderously allegoric overtones not really worth deciphering. Occasionally an attractive image flashes out, but it is too surrounded by bombast. One wonders if the plot were to talk the king to death, and then fondly hopes for its quick success. **"Two Salvation Army Women"** patronizingly points out that the wrong people have sponsored Christianity and describes one of these a fat, middle-aged worker whose "lips are sensual moans / Visible beneath the pretext / Of your singing love for Christ." (pp. 105-06)

Among the books of this period [the late 1920s], *Georgie May* was Bodenheim's most successful fusion of action, style, and message. Georgie is a pre-World War I Memphis whore who wanders from one tough lover to another. Like many of Bodenheim's central women characters, she is sensitive and dreamy, but uneducated: an emotionally complex, quicksilver woman vulnerable to fits of deep despondency, since she exposes herself to greater emotional risks than the dumb, complaisant "chippies" about her. After the mother of her last, wealthy, upper-class lover throws in her face the folly of continuing such an impossible affair, Georgie decides "living was jus' a stinkin', bahstahd mess, and what in hell did a few yeahs moah oah less amount to anyway," and swallows poison. Every element in the book converges relentlessly toward this depressing climax. The conclusion is real and inevitable, not sentimentally melodramatic. Clearly seeing her fate and clearly recognizing the impassive cruelty of her world, she achieves a self-revelation that demands as a conscious act of will, her destruction. Her death becomes an act of self-assertion. (p. 110)

Like much of Bodenheim's best fiction, *Georgie May* is a city novel. It is one of the relatively few Southern city novels in a tradition dominated, as Gelfant's *The American City Novel* shows, by fiction about New York and Chicago. Bodenheim's ugly, cluttered Memphis weighs like a huge, heavy machine upon those crowded and trapped within; and it stamps out almost identically sordid lives. Drink, violence, and occasional flashes of lust temporarily relieve the oppressive tedium of the city's cage-weary animals. (p. 111)

Sixty Seconds reveals Bodenheim's dissatisfaction with the technically old-fashioned novel form he had regularly employed. For example, the book uses a sometimes double time frame to focus on his protagonist's reminiscences. Thematically, the book is standard, for its hero, John Musselman, is another young city dweller rebelling from restrictive parents and environment. As in **Blackguard** and in **Crazy Man,** the central character is a criminal; he is in jail awaiting execution. In each of four sections Musselman looks out his cell window or around his narrow room and sees something that reminds him of earlier times. Each memory concerns a woman, and each woman helps define a stage in his education. First, Musselman looks at the sky, which reminds him of when he was eighteen in Chicago, walking along the rails. As the eighteen-year-old Musselman walks, he in turn remembers his initiation in sex, and the next twenty pages chronicle this initiation. Then the double flashback fades, and Bodenheim returns to the single flashback of Musselman mooning along the railroad tracks. He looks up from his reveries to see a young girl being attacked by dogs, and he chases and kills a dog. Then for over a hundred pages Bodenheim narrates John's affair with this girl, arranging the events chronologically. The now single flashback proceeds to where the girl, Elizabeth, departs. John decides to " 'bo" it on the road since the octoroon Elizabeth has been taken away from him by her parents. The section concludes with the condemned man still looking out his cell window, watching a robin. Ten seconds have passed since he saw the sky. (p. 116)

As always, Bodenheim fleshes out his basic narrative with philosophic asides. His generalizations do not attack the heart of his real enemy but rather prick a child's balloon he has himself blown up. When he shouts against the "spurious mystics" who "almost two thousand years ago" pronounced the "clean, powerful, springy flesh of human being . . . unclean and evil," one wonders precisely whom he is talking about. These same "mystics . . . manufactured" the words "sin" and "sinful." Bodenheim sees the antagonist in terms of a handy cartoon figure, like the spirit of prohibition so frequently portrayed in the 1920's. Such pseudo-philosophizing obscures more about the nature of man than it reveals.

And the book has other shortcomings. More clumsy sentences exist than should at this stage of Bodenheim's development. Once he writes: "when hair is clipped from a head, an essential sincerity shows itself openly on this head." His running battle with the critics is irrelevant. His interpolated veracity is questionable; he says: "once I saw a college Dean of Sociology turn to a berserk creature when some one called him a god-damn bastard." And he repeats an earlier fault in permitting his characters to think sometimes in terms they clearly would not have employed. He once interjects: "these precise adjectives did not emerge in his mind, but a wordless approach to them fought in his head." In *Georgie May* the omniscient author became an immediately concerned participant evoked by the horror of contemporary society. The unmistakable odor of what Bodenheim thought his personal failure permeates *Sixty Seconds*. (pp. 120-21)

A Virtuous Girl employs essentially the same theme as *Sixty Seconds:* a youthful rebel frees herself from the oppressive morality of communal and parental authority. Emmy Lou Wilkins expresses her rebellion through complete sexual liberation. In sleeping with whomever she wants when she wants she achieves, if not happiness, then what seems in the novel even better—freedom. Emmy does not, like Jessica Maringold, become jaded or corrupted by her erotic adventures. She remains throughout the novel untainted, "a virtuous girl." Though a virgin at the book's start and sexually inexperienced, she already knows that sex is "bee-oo-ti-iful, oh so bee-o-oo-ti-iful, and warmly spiced"; and she wonders "dimly, in the chime-laden, palpitantly unequipped depths of her virginal heart . . . why people made it, oh, kind of ugly."

Bodenheim's thesis—that society's sex attitudes are foolish, that young erotic impulses are strong and basically healthy and should be permitted freer expression—is placed in a fictional context sometimes difficult to examine seriously. His failure casts doubt on his corollary thesis, that Emmy Lou can be a sexual cornucopia and remain virtuous. Bodenheim, who tells a good deal about Emmy's sexual beliefs, often agrees with them. But her thinking is too often ludicrous, and her actions are so tailored by Bodenheim to demonstrate the proof of her erotic philosophy that the pattern of her life emerges in gross and unrealistic over-simplification. We are simply told that Emmy's "heart was not carnal but fearlessly bird-like in the flutterings of a longing for . . . space-erasing, sweetly vowing sex." Emmy is described as unmoral but never coarsely lustful, promiscuous but choosy and always innocent. Her sexual behavior is so unrealistically stripped of probable concomitants that she is unbelievable in action. Half-pursuer, half-pursued, pulling her first lover down upon her, she appears utterly passionless and unheated, a merry little rebel. (pp. 121-22)

The flaws in *A Virtuous Girl* are especially disappointing since the book begins so promisingly, and since it contains throughout much effective material. Apart from the sexual bravado forced upon her, Emmy Lou is an interesting turn-of-the-century girl, a rebellious miss caught in a period of transitional stress, both historically and personally. When she and her young friends flirt with sex, the book offers interesting and entertaining insights into adolescent behavior. Bodenheim's re-evoking of the time is often effective, for scraps of dialogue and snapshots of life as it was then lived illuminate much of the book. And Bodenheim continues to have a surer command of technique—when he keeps himself out of the book's texture. He employs extensively for the first time stream-of-consciousness, and he again handles flashback sequences competently. His description of those supposedly good years is filled with technically well-put-forth details of character and place. But, when he propagandizes, and does so shakily, the book is marred.

The versatile Bodenheim changed directions in his next book, [*Naked on Roller Skates*]. The seriousness of his tone had increased steadily from his first book, *Blackguard,* and in *A Virtuous Girl* his philosophizing had become quite heavy-handed. As the title suggests, *Naked on Roller Skates* is not only one of Bodenheim's more sensational novels but also one of his most comic. The book is in fact comic to the degree that it is sensational in its parodying of young and old frantically searching for "kicks" in the last years of the Jazz Age. Bodenheim provides his readers with an extraordinary number of thrills in presenting a descent into the underworld by his life-tasting hero and heroine. He describes several bloody fights, near murders, the obligatory trip to a Harlem nightclub—no sensational New York novel would be complete without one—miscegenation, a fifty-six-year-old man being seduced by a seventeen-year-old girl he has just met, a sixteen-year-old blonde necking in a den of thieves with a forty-year-old man, near kidnapping, a crooked poker game exploding into a free-for-all, latent incest, gangsters, and a protection racket. In fact, Bodenheim reduces to absurdity the sensationalistic city novel of crime and sex.

Bodenheim once again employs as his hero a liberated male who has wandered on the road experiencing life fully, but this time he is one capable of triumphing over all situations, no matter how difficult or dangerous. The hero, Terry Barberlit, is matched with a blundering young woman, Ruth Riatt, who wants to wallow in the mud of life just to see what doing so is like. As the novel proceeds, it grows increasingly apparent that Ruth really wants Terry and a wild but definite domesticity. While Bodenheim leaves himself room to philosophize over favorite themes within this comic and picaresque frame-work, he speaks sparingly. Certain weaknesses of *Sixty Seconds* and *A Virtuous Girl* are therefore minimized. (pp. 124-26)

Basically a simple, exuberant work, *Naked on Roller Skates* makes many of its points more tellingly than some of Bodenheim's more portentous and pretentious fictions. The book is comic, but says that the darker side of life must be experienced, that the individual must liberate himself from society's foolish restraints. It attacks the mechanized drabness of comtemporary life and the magnetic viciousness of the city. Bodenheim preaches less and relates his style to his matter: the romantic posturings of his freed superman are matched by Bodenheim's comic prose. "Hey, big boy," Ruth says, "put the brakes on for a minute. You'll be skidding into the furniture. You're speeding on a wet road, big boy." Terry answers "Speeding hell, I'll be stalled on the turnpike if I don't get better service at this filling station." Though certain crudities of phrasing and technique are not parodies or burlesques but simply bad writing, the book remains a comic success and shows once more that Bodenheim was at his best when sticking in sight of reality. He had an eye for the significant detail or turn of speech, and the ability to re-create what he saw and heard.

If *Naked on Roller Skates* is Bodenheim's most free-wheeling fiction, *Bringing Jazz!* is his most exuberant book of poems. Published in 1930, it belongs more to the wild decade Bodenheim had just lived through, the 1920's, than to the sad one he approached. The book is difficult to evaluate, since its poems vary from comic doggerel to jazz lyrics for as yet unwritten melodies, to impressionistic jazz tone poems. Bodenheim prefaced the poems by saying that "these poems were written to be set to music, and a jazz composer is earnestly invited," but not many of the individual works can be treated as potential lyrics for songs. Some could only with difficulty be accompanied by a subordinate jazz background, while others, such as the title poem, would make very good jazz entertainment pieces for poetry and jazz readings. Bodenheim uses the term "jazz" loosely, seeming to suggest by it "low down" music and lyrics, highly colloquial diction, frequent and playful rhymes, but not any well-defined technical or rhythmic mode. He does not distinguish consistently between "blues," Dixieland (with all its varieties), rag time, Mickey Mouse, syncopated dance band, or other specific subcategories of jazz. He uses the term broadly, producing a kind of "pop"-art poetry. That the book lacks philosophic depth and artistic intensity is perhaps inherent in the nature of his limited concept of popular poetry. (pp. 130-31)

• • • • •

Before composing his final novels of social consciousness, Bodenheim published his thinly disguised satiric attack on Ben Hecht, *Duke Herring.* The Depression had not yet awakened his political inclinations enough for him to forgo retaliating to Hecht's *Count Bruga* (1926), [a novel satirizing Bodenheim's life]. *Duke Herring* is Bodenheim's only completely comic novel. As such, it contains several effectively humorous situations and an acid portrait of Hecht. But the personal jest pales occasionally. The book does not offer enough overall comic detail that is independent of the Hecht-Bodenheim squabble, nor is the satire applicable enough to the general follies of mankind to have much pervasive relevance. The Duke is shown a ridiculous figure, and the caricature of Hecht must have satisfied Bodenheim, for it cuts deep. The question of the novel's success perhaps rests on whether Hecht was worth demolishing. Bodenheim performed a good

hatchet job, but maybe on a cigar-store Indian. (pp. 139-40)

After *Duke Herring,* only incidental portions of his novels are comic. The country was of course in the midst of the Depression, and Bodenheim was having personal difficulties, artistic and otherwise. *Run, Sheep, Run* is his first radical novel. The book develops three of the four basic areas Walter Rideout claims are the essential categories of the American radical novel. The work documents an individual's increasing knowledge of class-consciousness; deals in part with the life of "bottom dogs," the lowest layers of society; and portrays middle-class decadence. *Run, Sheep, Run* does not describe a strike (the fourth category), though it does report anti-state riots. Part of Bodenheim's point in the book is that the oppressed workers who should be striking are not yet aware of this beginning solution to their troubles or, if aware, are incapable of instigating agitation. (p. 142)

While *Run, Sheep, Run* is a serious attempt to portray the Depression conditions, *New York Madness* (1933) is not. The book is filled with violence and sensationalism, but both seem calculated, and inapposite to a historic evaluation of the contemporary conditions. The book is curiously old-fashioned in tone, revealing little true social consciousness or political awareness. Although several passing references are made to the Depression, the major characters are well-fed and economically content. In portraying Alicia McCulley's quest for satisfaction—an almost purely sexual search—Bodenheim travels around New York City and Greenwich Village, occasionally presenting a fight or a seduction, taking time out to attack his critics, and etching sometimes amusing, sometimes compulsively insulting pictures of fellow New Yorkers. His sentences are occasionally incoherent: "Alicia McCulley was bored, mournful, even gangrenous, but in every accidental collision between conditions, each one became less convinced of its reality and strove to strengthen itself in the confusion of mutual insult." The characters and situations are too clearly worked from earlier material: Alicia has the intellect and yearnings of Blanche Palmer with the sexual precosity of Jessica Maringold. The man she ultimately finds happiness with is a sensitive cripple as was Ernest Maller in *Replenishing Jessica.* (pp. 148-49)

Bodenheim's last novel, *Slow Vision,* resembles *Georgie May* in its powerful delineation of individual and social decay, and *Run, Sheep, Run* in its vigorously anti-capitalistic stance. *Slow Vision* also shows more than any of Bodenheim's other works the terrible strain under which he was working. The book reeks of disillusionment and failure, and it depicts a hopeless parade of numbed Depression derelicts. Though written from a generally radical point of view, the book offers no true way out of the economic chamber of horrors shown. *Slow Vision* represents a blind corner in Bodenheim's career that he never worked himself out of; for he never again published fiction. (pp. 149-50)

Lights in the Valley and Bodenheim's portion of *Seven Poets in Search of an Answer* are combined in the *Selected Poems* as "Poems of Social Message," and must be treated together as such. His work is generally competent, and less rhetorically flamboyant than his earlier poems. Gone are the flashy metaphors driven together by sheer poetic verve. Instead, the poetry shows the desire to communicate social messages to other artists and men. Bodenheim seems compelled to employ rhythms and rhymes that do not call attention to themselves. He even avoids free verse: poem after poem uses iambics, with *abab* exact rhyme.

Three concerns dominate his work: criticism of his generation of artists and of himself for lacking social consciousness; direct social criticism of the American scene; and attacks on war. His point of view is not formally Communistic, and no coherent social theory emerges from the various poems. They are, instead, the work of a man who is sometimes emotionally attracted to the movement, who thinks he sees a society gone mad, who sees himself alone and a failure, who knows something, everything, is wrong and wants to attack. But the poems have only the most general relevance to the basic tenets of communism. They reveal little militancy, no suggestion of American class warfare, no investigation of economic forces invariably in dialectic confrontation. Even at the height of the Popular Front movement his social message is that war is evil, that inequality is unjust, and that artists cannot afford to remain aloof in a world out of whack, but that they must concern themselves with the social obligations of art. (pp. 161-62)

• • • • •

Any conclusions concerning Maxwell Bodenheim's contribution to American life and letters must mention his own life, since unfortunately that has so far been his major known contribution: Bodenheim as symbolic of the Bohemian free spirit or of some ancient obscene Huck Finn rebelling with whiskey on his breath against civilization. Bodenheim as myth perverts what he actually was: a talented and wretched man who added to whatever warping force he experienced as a young man his own bundle of self-destructive impulses. (p. 174)

Bodenheim's fiction, though it clearly suffers from lack of technical skill and errors in diction, and from what Marianne Moore pinpointed in the September, 1924, *Dial* as his "interest in retaliation," contributed more to American literature than most slighting references to it indicate. *Blackguard* shows what it must have been like to be a young foolish poet in the early years of one of America's greatest literary periods. Works such as *Ninth Avenue* reveal the materialistic frauds and sexual hypocrisies in American life, and they also portray the individual struggle against a bleak and corrosive urban civilization to which man, to his own near-destruction has habituated himself. He exhibits an unfaltering ability to describe the viciousness and tedium of what he termed "upper proletarian" family life in its constant disintegration. Books such as *Crazy Man* and even the generally unsuccessful *Replenishing Jessica* show an exact touch in portraying the sick city's fourth and fifth raters—cheap comics, taxi dancers, fake artists. Often his sense of locale presents how it was in a dance hall like the Merry Grotto and how the metallic floors burned in a Memphis jail. He describes scenes eminently suited to their marginal inhabitants, the losers and *schlemiels,* the whores and jobless, the trapped

outsiders of contemporary life. Occasionally, as in *Naked on Roller Skates* and in parts of *Blackguard* and *Duke Herring,* he wrote of modern city life comically, creating rough satire whose bludgeon sometimes concealed a fine point.

Stylistically, he could simply evoke the numbing torpor of Depression life as in *Slow Vision,* or impressionistically depict the exploding and then sputtering-out of a riot, as in *Run, Sheep, Run.* His critical prose could be cold and reasoned, as, for example, when defending free verse in his **"Reply to A. C. H.,"** or comic and colorful, as in most of his work for the Chicago *Literary Times.* And no style but Bodenheim's would describe the effect of poison in the blood of a beautiful girl as he did in **"The Master Poisoner"**: "The skin becomes a milk-tinted pond, in which wine-ghosts timidly bathe."

In **"American Novels,"** Bodenheim wrote that the novel should be "more concerned with inward investigation and less immersed with outward, colloquial and visual fidelities." His major difficulty as a novelist is perhaps that he never achieved a completely adequate technique for presenting the "inward investigation." Yet where he apparently did not care to succeed, "with outward, colloquial and visual fidelities," he had significant potential as novelist. Even relatively doctrinaire books like *Slow Vision* and *Run, Sheep, Run* show an ability to root ideas in realistic detail.

Bodenheim's achievements in poetry are, however, more constant and definite than his achievements in prose. Each of his successive volumes has its flaws, but each offers at least three or four poems of high value that arrest the reader's attention and make him linger over lines and phrases, that offer a variety of poetry no one else, precisely, was writing. **"Death," "Seaweed from Mars," "Rattle-Snake Mountain Fable I," "Summer Evening: New York Subway Station," "Platonic Narrative," "Fairy-Tale," "Bringing Jazz,"** and **"Dear Noel Coward"** are only a random handful of Bodenheim's poems that deserve attention. These are intensely his own. He worked in his own stylistic areas and, for good or bad, presented his unique manner and vision.

He also achieved variety in the nature of his poetry. His work was esoteric, and popular; made no compromises to public taste; and dealt with materials springing directly from the public domain. He wrote fragile and erotic love poems; tender realistic and naturalistic poems of urban life; poems describing imaginary worlds of mind and matter; jazz poems; humorous poems; and poems whose commentary on history (such as the war poems) are horrifying; and he wrote poems of art's independence and of art's social obligations. His accomplishment in these areas is uneven: everything he did was uneven. His esthetic, as expressed in **"Esthetics, Criticism, and Life"** almost guarantees unevenness: "etshetics recognizes laws of the moment" only; is "unruly"; shows "disorder."

But, from the outset of his career, he was not content to view poetry narrowly, and so he incorporated much of his own person and his own interests at any one time into his work and had also perhaps a great need and urge to let the poetry justify the life, so that the craft of his poetry became somewhat neglected in the poetry's self-involvement. To him, the self was not narrow but very broad; unfortunately for his work and life, he himself was chaotically organized. His gift for phrasing and his keen original intellect, properly disciplined and cautiously focused, might have produced a skilled craftsman of high order—but discipline and caution could have also produced a bland journeyman, which Bodenheim certainly was not. He was an interesting and often striking poet.

I believe it true of Bodenheim's life and art that rarely has an American writer of any historic significance committed more obvious and sometimes more disastrous mistakes: but it is also true that rarely have the virtues and the accomplishments of such a writer been so clearly misrepresented and so quickly forgotten. (pp. 174-77)

> *Jack B. Moore, in his* Maxwell Bodenheim, *Twayne Publishers, Inc., 1970, 193 p.*

FURTHER READING

Aiken, Conrad. "Candidly Speaking." *The New Republic* LI, No. 652 (1 June 1927): 54.
> Review of *Returning to Emotion.* Aiken maintains that Bodenheim's "approach to the writing of verse is studiously cerebral."

Benét, William Rose. "Poet and Novelist." *The Saturday Review of Literature* V, No. 4 (18 August 1928): 52.
> Review of *The King of Spain* and *Georgie May,* asserting that when Bodenheim's "manner is adapted to prose one realizes that the impact of his peculiar images and metaphors is often far greater in the stringent speed of verse than on the balder page of prose."

Gorman, Herbert S. "Poets of Today and Yesterday." *The New York Times Book Review* (26 December 1920): 22.
> Review praising *Advice* and affirming that Bodenheim

"is one of the most original poets writing in America, if not the most original."

Grudin, Louis. "Maxwell Bodenheim: Mathematician." *Poetry: A Magazine of Verse* XXI, No. II (November 1922): 100-04.
> Critical discussion of *Introducing Irony.* According to Grudin, the work "is a book in which new territories of the imagination have been surveyed by an intelligence direct, modern and impersonal as a flashlight."

Krutch, J. W. "Devil's Disciple." *The Nation* CXVI, No. 3016 (25 April 1923): 496-97.
> Discusses *Blackguard,* comparing its theme of individualism to the rebellion presented in works by Sinclair Lewis. According to Krutch, "[Lewis] seeks a new social order, [Bodenheim] seeks only the chaos within and the dancing star."

"Crazy Man." *The New York Times Book Review* (10 February 1924): 8.
> Review of *Crazy Man* discussing its plot, characters, and themes.

"An Underworld Story." *The New York Times Book Review* (10 June 1928): 8.
> Review focusing on the plot of *Georgie May.*

"Bruga's Brother." *The New York Times Book Review* (26 July 1931): 6.
> Discussion of *Duke Herring* praising its satirical plot but finding its structure weak.

"Intangible Paraphrases." *Poetry: A Magazine of Verse* XXX, No. 2 (May 1927): 104-08.
> Discussion of *Returning to Emotion* asserting that the collection lacks the inventiveness of Bodenheim's previous works.

Ridge, Lola. *"Minna and Myself." Twice a Year* (Summer-Fall 1945): 430-31.
> Review of *Minna and Myself.* According to Ridge, "many of these poems will endure though they will probably not be widely popular for the principal reason that they are too distinguished,—too peculiar."

Additional coverage of Bodenheim's life and career is contained in the following sources published by Gale Research: *Contemporary Authors,* Vol. 110; and *Dictionary of Literary Biography,* Vols. 9 and 45.

Futabatei Shimei

1864-1909

(Pseudonym of Hasegawa Tatsunosuke) Japanese novelist, translator, and journalist.

INTRODUCTION

Futabatei is best remembered as the author of *Ukigumo* (*The Drifting Clouds*), which is considered the first modern Japanese novel. Representing a radical departure from the allegorical narratives and character types of traditional Japanese literature, *The Drifting Clouds* features realistic descriptions of everyday Japanese life and convincing psychological portraits. A student and translator of Russian literature, Futabatei was influenced by the work of Fyodor Dostoevsky, Vissarion Belinsky, and other Russian novelists and critics of the mid-nineteenth century who emphasized realism in fiction. He is especially noted for his detailed rendering of the emotional life of isolated, often troubled characters.

Futabatei was born in the Edo district of Tokyo. Because his family belonged to the aristocratic samurai class, he received a superior education at prestigious schools. Due to his nationalistic feelings, the potential threat of war with Russia, and a desire to serve his country, Futabatei applied to the Tokyo Military Academy. Failing to meet the requisites for admission to the academy, he then studied Russian, anticipating the need for translators in wartime. While rendering into Japanese the fiction of Dostoevsky, Nikolai Gogol, Ivan Goncharov, and Ivan Turgenev and the critical writings of Belinsky, Nikolai Dobrolyubov, and Mikhail N. Katkov, Futabatei perceived a need for realism in the literature of his country, and in 1886 he began writing *The Drifting Clouds*. Tsubouchi Shōyō, a friend and a prominent Japanese novelist, acted as his editor for the novel, and the first installments of the book, published serially between 1887 and 1889, were attributed to him. Believing fiction-writing was unworthy of a samurai, Futabatei chose the pseudonym by which he is known today. In Japanese the name sounds very similar to the expression "die and be done with," which his father is rumored to have uttered when informed his son was a novelist. Despite critical acclaim, Futabatei abandoned fiction writing, finding employment as a teacher, translator, and, eventually, a correspondent for *Asahi shimbun,* a newspaper based in Ōsaka. In 1906 Futabatei began to write fiction again, publishing *Sono omokage* (*An Adopted Husband*) and *Heibon* (*Mediocrity*) within the next two years. Journalism assignments led him to St. Petersburg in 1908, but declining health and a nervous breakdown precipitated his return home. Futabatei died while traveling back to Japan.

In "Shōsetsu sōron" ("A Theory of the Novel") Futabatei stated that "the novel perceives directly the ideal of Nature in the various phenomena of the world; what is perceived must be conveyed directly. Such direct communication is possible only by means of realism. Accordingly, realism is obviously the essence of the novel." By rejecting the didacticism prevalent in Japanese literature of the period, which manifested itself in fantastic plots and characters who were the allegorical embodiment of vice and virtue, and by incorporating interior monologues, settings with an identifiable time and place, and *gembun itchi,* or colloquial language, Futabatei found a means to depict his experience of the world. His first book, *The Drifting Clouds,* focuses on Bunzō, a member of the samurai class whose principles are challenged by the dramatic social changes of the Meiji Restoration (1868-1912), when the Japanese abandoned an archaic social order based on feudal governors in order to admit the social, political, and technological innovations of Western countries. Bunzō's adherence to the past is manifested in his proud, reserved manner, his assumption that virtue will be rewarded, and his belief in the innate superiority of the samurai. These qualities and convictions are presented as liabilities in a society that no longer appreciates traditional values, bringing Bunzō into conflict with the people around him, specifically his boss, who fires him; his materialistic aunt, who considers an unemployed nephew unworthy; his cousin Osei, whom he wishes to marry; and Noboru, a sycophantic and ambitious coworker whose successes contrast with Bunzō's failures. These individuals represent the changes Bunzō is unwilling to accept as the Meiji government attempted to westernize Japan. Commentators have viewed Bunzō as an antihero engaged in a futile resistance to change, intelligent enough to recognize his problem but not mature enough to realistically evaluate the situation, find an appropriate solution, and act on that solution. Although some early critics contended that *The Drifting Clouds* was flawed by a lack of narrative resolution, most deemed Futabatei's examination of Bunzō's psychological and social predicament a success. Tsubouchi praised the narrative innovations Futabatei introduced in the book, particularly his use of colloquial language. Another contemporary, Tokutomi Soho, noted that *The Drifting Clouds* "is a banal, domestic novel. But the author must be recognized as an amazingly talented writer in that he can make men grieve or hate, be surprised or fascinated in such a banal context. . . . In another way of speaking, the light which shines from the author's eye illuminates the mundane world and in the end creates characters and events in the image of reality."

Futabatei's later works, *An Adopted Husband* and *Mediocrity,* also focus on realistic representations of individuals. The protagonist of *An Adopted Husband,* a university lecturer, experiences an identity crisis when he assumes his domineering wife's surname to ensure that her family name will survive. His confusion increases when he compromises his integrity by initiating an affair with his wife's illegitimate stepsister and when he recognizes his incompetence as a professor. Ultimately he is left bankrupt, unemployed, homeless, and wandering the streets of Peking in an alcoholic stupor. Less esteemed by critics than *The Drifting Clouds, An Adopted Husband* is often considered technically superior to the earlier novel. *Mediocrity* is a collection of autobiographical sketches that mirror many of the events recounted in Futabatei's novels and illustrate his deftness at describing and fictionalizing personal anguish.

Although his books were popular with readers, Futabatei was virtually ignored by scholars during his lifetime and did not influence the writing of his peers. Eventually, in the years after his death, realism became widely accepted and practiced in Japanese literature, and Futabatei's work began to be reexamined, firmly establishing his reputation as the author of the first modern Japanese novel and the forerunner of the *shi-shōsetsu,* or autobiographical novel.

PRINCIPAL WORKS

Ukigumo (novel) 1887-89
  [*The Drifting Clouds,* 1967]
Sono omokage (novel) 1906
  [*An Adopted Husband,* 1919]
Heibon (novel) 1907
  [*Mediocrity,* 1927]
Futabatei Shimei zenshū. 16 vols.   (novels, essays, translations, and journalism) 1953-54

Marleigh Grayer Ryan   (essay date 1965)

[*Ryan, an American critic and specialist in Japanese literature, was the first translator to render* Ukigumo *into English. In the following excerpt from* Japan's First Modern Novel: Ukigumo *of Futabatei Shimei (1967), she examines how Futabatei applied the techniques of literary realism as practiced by such Russian novelists as Ivan Turgenev and Ivan Goncharov in order to achieve a balanced depiction of Japanese society, particularly in the portrayal of the alienated individual, or "superfluous hero."*]

Philosophic speculation in nineteenth-century Russia led the literary world into a protracted debate on certain key problems of aesthetic theory. This debate centered on the question of whether or not it was desirable or indeed even permissible for a novelist to make use of the vacillating, impotent hero portrayed by many great Russian writers beginning with Pushkin. This issue was fought in the salons and journals by critics and novelists. Virtually every leading writer was involved on one side or the other. The "superfluous" or alienated man of fiction was pitted against the "new" man, the positive hero. Each type symbolized the more significant issue underlying the debate: Was art to be allowed to remain free of political considerations or was it to be used for the expression and advancement of specific political goals? Writers on both sides fa-

vored extensive changes in the Russian social and economic system. Most had been imprisoned or exiled for their views. But men like Goncharov, Turgenev, and Dostoevsky demanded the right to depict life as they saw it; to reveal evil even in those whose political motives were commendable; to show the foolishness of revolutionary radicalism in a society which was not ready for it. These views were opposed by the radical, didactic critics, and their novels were frequently damned as empty and meaningless, if not positively dangerous. (pp. 149-50)

Futabatei was greatly interested in Russian theories of social reform, but he did not consider political problems as legitimate subjects for fiction. He discovered that by following the example of writers like Turgenev and Goncharov he could replace simple social protest with what was for him a more significant device. He learned that through describing Japanese society as accurately as he could, he might uncover truths no man had ever revealed before.

Objective realism, he believed, would portray the soul of Meiji Japan, and this picture of itself would serve to enlighten the reader. He felt it would be wrong to select only those aspects of reality which might prove a point of view desirable in the political or social sense. If an evil exists, it would be apparent from the total picture. In truth, no human being is entirely good or entirely evil. Each man must be analyzed and appreciated individually, and each literary type, while perhaps symbolizing a characteristic of broad social significance, must be human, vibrant, and, above all, believable.

Bunzo, the hero of *Ukigumo,* is a superfluous man, a direct literary descendant of the Russian type. The novel also has its new man in the person of Honda Noboru. The four main characters of the novel each symbolize certain aspects of modern Japan as Futabatei saw them, but they are all eminently human and fallible. Furthermore, it would be as foolish to treat *Ukigumo* exclusively as a social allegory as it would be to describe *Crime and Punishment* solely as a symbolic representation of the dangers of irresponsible radicalism. *Ukigumo* reflects Japanese life in the 1880s, but more than that, it attempts to go beyond the limitations of nation and time and deal with universal questions that pertain to the entire society of man.

Futabatei's conception of the purpose and scope of a novel had its origin in Russian literary criticism, which in turn was based on German romantic philosophy. He was extremely interested in German philosophic reasoning and read and translated Russian works based on it. Of all the critics and theorists he studied, none fascinated him more than the brilliant, erratic Vissarion Belinsky (1811-48). (pp. 150-51)

Futabatei, captivated by Belinsky's writing, was anxious to have his work read and accepted in Japan. Early in 1886 he translated an essay by Belinsky entitled "The Idea of Art" in order to help Tsubouchi and his other friends understand the Russian critic's theories. The translation, not published during his lifetime, was virtually incomprehensible to his contemporaries, not because it was poorly executed, but because the material is fundamentally so difficult. (p. 153)

Although "The Idea of Art" is fragmentary and disorganized, it is probably Belinsky's most positive statement on the nature of the primordial essence, variously called the Idea or the Essence or the Thought, which is the focal point of the Hegelian cosmology. The Idea is said to have existed since the beginning of time and is contained in greater or lesser quantities in every material object. All of life, all of history, is an inexorable progression caused by the interaction of the Idea with the Material from which it is constantly trying to emerge. There are periods of quiescence when the struggle between the two is suspended, but they are only temporary. The movement will inevitably begin again and continue until at last it reaches its ultimate goal, the moment when the Idea finds complete expression: "the first movement of primordial matter striving to become . . . our planet and the last rational word of intelligent man are merely one and the same being at different moments of its evolution."

Man, said Belinsky, is the end product of a long evolutionary process, the result of continuous action and interaction within Nature. Through him, through his mind and his creations, history takes form and progresses. Like every other object, man is composed of the Idea within him, and the Material, his outer form. He has the great gift of being able to perceive the Idea in himself and in the whole universe. He can perceive this instantly, spontaneously, without the benefit of reason, but he can also discover it by rational processes. The great man is one who grasps the Idea clearly, instinctively, and lives in terms of his perception. He may be conscious of the need for his actions, but that is not what makes his actions great. It is his contact with the Idea, his awareness of it as it shines forth from his actions, which determines their worth. Actions which emerge from this awareness are creations; those which grow from calculation alone are base and mechanical. The products of inspired awareness, the creative, artistic products, are the perfect manifestations of the Idea; they need form to be expressed, just as man needs form to exist. In the universe "we perceive two apparently opposite but actually cognate and identical aspects: spirit and matter. The spirit is divine thought, the source of life; matter is the form without which thought cannot manifest itself. Obviously both these elements need each other: without thought all form is dead, without form thought is merely that which may be, but is not."

Implicit in this discourse is a definition of the artist's function. Hegel had conceived of each phase of world history as having a specific configuration. As history progresses, so the form of every society progresses and everything within it changes. At any given moment in any one society there are distinct, discernible elements which are peculiar to that society. They will never be repeated; they are the embodiment of the Idea at that one time. The artist can perceive those elements more readily than ordinary men and can record them for posterity.

Belinsky and his successors accepted this as a creed for the artist; he not only was capable of perceiving, it was his moral duty. Given the talent or insight to analyze the spe-

cial characteristics of his society, the writer had to devote his total energy to the study of the world around him. Only the artist who satisfied this requirement could be considered great. (pp. 153-55)

These are the thoughts which formed the basis of Futabatei's first literary essay, **"Shōsetsu sōron"** ["The Elements of the Novel"], published in April of 1886 in the magazine *Chūo gakujutsu zasshi*. Futabatei wrote **"Shōsetsu sōron"** at Tsubouchi's suggestion, in an attempt to state Belinsky's theories in language simpler than he had used in his translation of "The Idea of Art." (pp. 155-56)

"Shōsetsu sōron" begins with an explanation of the Idea. Futabatei states that the Idea is present in all material objects and abstract concepts, and that it expresses the true nature of those things. The Idea is eternal and immutable and would exist even without any Form. The outward Form assumed by objects or concepts, in fact, tends to disguise the Idea and prevents our being clearly aware of its universality. Man is compelled by his nature to search out the unchanging factor among all the changing Forms of the world; scientists and scholars do this with the aid of their intellect, artists with their emotions or instincts. Both methods are necessary for complete understanding, but it is the great gift of Art that it can make the existence of the universal Idea, buried as it is in an infinite amount of Forms, clearly apparent to the most ordinary human being.

Futabatei then proceeded to demonstrate how these deductions apply to the construction of a novel. He rejected moral instruction as the purpose of fiction. Its function is rather to perceive the Idea in all the numberless Forms in the world directly, instantaneously, and to transmit this perception to mankind. Realism, the only technique which can achieve this, should be adopted. However, it is difficult to write a successful realistic novel. It requires much insight on the part of the writer to sense the Idea in the events of the everyday world and to incorporate this knowledge adequately into his book. He must write in a vital, dynamic style suited to his theme and develop his plot as logically and sensibly as it would have evolved in real life. Otherwise the Idea will not be revealed and the story will seem pointless and insipid, no matter how valid the original germs of the plot. (pp. 156-57)

Futabatei directed his arguments to writers; it was the novelist, as an artist, who was obliged to extract the all-pervasive, eternal Essence or Idea and convey it to the reader. Japanese writers in the 1880s, however, were not concerned with such abstract arguments. They were fascinated by Western material culture, Western literary forms, and practical political and economic theories, but not by abstract philosophic speculation. Nothing in **"Shōsetsu sōron"** was sufficiently novel or intriguing to hold their interest long enough for them to see its value.

The concept of realism had already been well expressed by Tsubouchi [Shōyō] in his *Shōsetsu shinzui,* and those predisposed to accept realism had done so. On the surface, the only difference between Futabatei's arguments and Tsubouchi's was the theory of the Idea underlying Form. The obligation of the artist to reveal the Idea is the rationale for realism, but to a writer who had already accepted realism, such a rationale might easily seem unimportant. In any case, Futabatei's **"Shōsetsu sōron"** failed to find an interested audience, but he continued to study and translate Russian criticism which advanced similar theories. (pp. 157-58)

In May 1889 another translation by Futabatei appeared, his last published work on aesthetic theory from the period while he was writing *Ukigumo.* It is a selection from a long review by the radical critic Nikolai Dobrolyubov (1836-61). In his brief introduction to the translation Futabatei explained that he chose the portion most directly concerned with the author's main thesis, the relation between the common people and the development of Russian literature. "I made this translation because I felt this essay contained theories pertinent to evil conditions in Japan," he wrote.

The concept of the importance of the "common people" in literature was an essential element of Dobrolyubov's philosophy. Dobrolyubov idolized Belinsky. Not only was he educated on Belinsky, but he considered his own theories a logical outgrowth of those of his master. However, a striking difference divided the aesthetic views of the two men: Belinsky argued for the creation of realistic characters; he did not speak as if they existed outside the work of art. He did not expect the characters in a novel to maintain a fixed moral standard as if they themselves had some choice in the matter, nor did he set an ideal level of accomplishment and then demand that the characters attain it. In other words, his criticism did not tamper with the intrinsic unity of the work of art, which remains whole, each segment inseparable from the others. The integrity of a work of art was, in a real sense, sacred to him. This was not true of Dobrolyubov. His criticism attributed to the characters of a novel or play a life of their own. He held them morally responsible for their actions; he judged them as people and not as part of an artistic unit. This technique was displayed in his most famous essay, "What is Oblomovism?" in which he blamed the heroes of Russian fiction for their inadequacy in coping with problems they faced as a man might accuse an acquaintance of failing to live up to his obligations.

In his other writing Dobrolyubov applied the same standards in judging historical figures and, by extension, groups of men and nations. Their worth is determined by the amount of constructive work they completed or at least attempted to complete. Constructive work, in Dobrolyubov's thinking, is often what we would define as progressive: social and economic reforms including education for more people, expanded economic opportunities, greater freedom for women, right of redress for wrongs, and the like. The evidence he accumulated in his militant attacks on past and contemporary societies is specious. His writing is filled with facile and often highly inaccurate generalizations about world history. Still it is difficult to deny his sincerity. He obviously wanted reform, change, and progress in whatever disguise. In championing action over inaction, he frequently drew the comparison between the producer and the parasite. It is the common people,

the Russian peasant classes, who are active and productive; their social superiors are, with certain rare exceptions, the parasites. Dobrolyubov was not as idealistic on the subject of the virtues of the peasantry as some of his contemporaries, but he clearly saw in them the source of hope for future progress, excusing their boorishness by their condition of life. (pp. 161-63)

Modern literature, Dobrolyubov goes on to state, is the product of privileged groups concerned only with portraying themselves and virtually never with the lower classes. This indifference to the common people was found not only in the arts but in the social sciences. No field of study is devoted to analyzing the accomplishments or failures of the common man; none describes the world from his point of view. Those social sciences like political economy, which pretend to deal with the people, are only concerned with them as they affect the capitalist class. Only two or three geniuses in the history of the world have been able to put aside their own interests and concern themselves truly with the question of the dignity of the whole human family and not of any one class.

Although no mention of the neglect of the common man in literature occurred in Futabatei's earlier writings, he had undoubtedly been concerned with this question from his days in Gaigo Gakkō, [the Tokyo School of Foreign Languages], as his interest in socialism indicates. With the exception of the brief mention of "evil conditions" in his introduction and his agreement with Dobrolyubov's theories implicit in the fact that he published the translation, Futabatei made no public statement on this question in these years. His choice of plot and characters in *Ukigumo,* however, has been interpreted as an attempt to bring the common people into literature by showing the conflict between the bureaucracy and the oppressed employee. Marxist critics have praised Futabatei's boldness in introducing the subject into a novel but have been disappointed that he showed more interest in investigating the psychology of his "common man," Bunzō, than in describing the cruel machinations of the government in more detail.

Dobrolyubov's essay also contains a protracted attack on the belief that literature invents issues or causes and, further, that theories expressed in a work of literature can have any effect on the course of events in real life. The problems exposed in literature must have existed in his society before the author wrote about them. He could not have thought of them if they had not. Art does not create situations; it merely describes them. Careful observation of the conditions of real life and its accurate reproduction in a work of art are an author's greatest obligations. A writer likes to think of himself as a teacher. He wants to believe that his words will expose social evils and bring about their rectification, but he must not forget that what he says will affect only a very small number of people, and they are most likely to be those who would have agreed with his point of view even before he expressed it.

Futabatei voiced ideas similar to these earlier; in **"Shōsetsu sōron"** he speaks of the value of realism and attacks the didactic writers of the East who wrote novels to prove moral lessons. By translating this portion of Dobrolyubov's essay he reasserted his faith in the power of realism to describe a society thoroughly. Futabatei believed in fiction concerned with nonaristocratic men and women incapable of great acts of heroism. The "evils" in the society would be revealed by realism; no other device was necessary.

Futabatei's conception of art is expressed in these translations from Russian criticism and in "Shōsetsu sōron." It is essentially mystical, depending on intuition and insight for its success. The artist is to peel away the outer layers of reality, find beneath it the buried spirit which gives it its particular shape and meaning, and expose that spirit in the work of art. Because it contains that spirit, the completed work will lend both the artist and his audience understanding and enlightenment. The novelist is described as an observer, an especially sensitive, astute observer, equipped by his superior intelligence and special training to see more in the world about him than ordinary men. His duty is to portray reality, to capture his moment in time as exactly as possible.

The novelist should study his society and determine its essential characteristics; then he should construct his plot and define his characters so that they may illustrate these characteristics. "Present day novelists and critics," Futabatei wrote in his journal in June 1889, "occupy themselves with questions of stylistics and are forgetful of their obligation to depict the characteristics of men and paint the conditions of their country." The novelist, he felt, "Takes up his pen and depicts the characteristics, the customs, and the aspirations of the people of his nation. He paints the conditions of his country and personifies the lives of the people. In doing so, he discovers truth untouched by the scholar or novelist and helps his people through his suffering."

Futabatei rejected Russian didacticism as he rejected Japanese didacticism and chose to study and investigate rather than teach. The lessons to be learned from literature would, he felt, emerge naturally. In this, he followed Tsubouchi's opinions. Tsubouchi stated in *Shōsetsu shinzui* that whatever advantages came from literature, they were merely the products of greater enlightenment. In writing *Ukigumo,* Futabatei used his four characters to symbolize his time and hoped to convey his feelings about contemporary Japanese society through their actions. As his title indicates, he saw the people of his nation as drifting clouds, torn loose by the force of Western ideas and material development from the foundations on which they had rested for hundreds of years, wavering uncertainly between clinging to the old and adopting the new, unsure of the value of their traditional moral code and not yet ready to accept Western philosophy and religion.

In some instances Futabatei's criticism of his society is lighthearted. He saw the foolishness of superficial Westernization; the vogue for learning foreign languages, wearing foreign dress, adopting foreign customs, all seemed to him ridiculous. Other flaws in Meiji Japan moved him more deeply. Futabatei was disturbed by the loss of the old standards of loyalty and courtesy, the disappearance of the respect for education which had for centuries characterized Japanese society, and the success of the vulgar man over his more restrained counterpart. He reveals these flaws through the plot of *Ukigumo;* by what his characters say and do, and even by what they fail to do.

In *Ukigumo* Futabatei describes a society where many of the traditional values are lost and a new ethic predominates, With his small cast of characters he attempts to symbolize the profound changes which had already taken place in Japan by 1886 and to forecast the path his nation would take in the future. He did not admire the changes, but even at that early date he knew that there was no holding them back and that, for better or worse, the society he describes was permanently established.

All the major characters in *Ukigumo* are members of the samurai class or at least pretend to that distinction. It was the group in society which was most gravely affected by the political reforms following the Restoration of 1868, and therefore Futabatei's choice was particularly appropriate. In Tokugawa times the samurai together with the 140 families of the Imperial courtiers (*kuge*) constituted the hereditary aristocracy. The samurai were supported by stipends allotted to them by their domain lords or, in the case of those living on lands governed by the Tokugawa shoguns, by the shogunate itself. Beneath the shogun ranks within the samurai class ranged from the daimyo, the lord of the domain, often an extremely rich and powerful man, down to the low-ranking samurai, whose stipend barely supported a small family. (pp. 163-67)

Whether rich or poor, however, in theory at least they shared a common ethical and moral code. This code had as its basic tenets a belief in loyalty to one's family and superiors, faith in the efficacy of education and hard work, devotion to propriety and restraint in social behavior. An insistence on modesty and humility ruled out all forms of display, and the study of both literary and martial arts was considered more important than the acquisition of practical knowledge which might result in greater material success.

In addition to his stipend a samurai enjoyed other privileges which set him apart from the rest of society. Most offices within the government were reserved for the samurai, either by law or by custom, and most officially sponsored schools were maintained exclusively for the children of the samurai. Samurai also had the privilege of wearing swords, symbolic of their duties—now largely fallen into abeyance—as soldiers, and emblematic of their superiority over the commoners. Membership in the class was largely hereditary, and the stipend of a samurai was transmitted to his son. With the advent of the Meiji period, the privileges of the class were stripped away. By 1876 the samurai ceased to receive stipends and were no longer permitted to carry swords. Generally, a samurai would not succeed to a post merely because his father had previously held it.

Among the commoners in the Tokugawa period, the wealthiest people were the merchants of the large towns and cities. Although they were in some danger of having their money confiscated or their trade ruined by restrictive laws, some amassed great fortunes and were, in fact, reasonably powerful in the society. There were numerous cases of merchant children marrying into samurai families, but the fiction of a separation between the samurai class and the commoner merchants was maintained until the 1870s. The samurai aristocracy believed itself superior to the merchants and claimed to scorn the aggressiveness, shrewdness, and avariciousness which it felt characterized the businessmen.

With the advent of the Meiji period, it became a practical impossibility for the samurai to maintain this ethic. It was an age of opportunity unprecedented in Japanese history. The acquisition of a new, Western-style education—knowledge of Western languages, science, or mathematics—allowed a young man to rise quickly to fame and fortune. Changes in government administration were sudden and frequent; the clever man might seize his opportunity and find himself in a high-ranking position. Even in the far more rigid Tokugawa era there had been brilliant young men who rose through the ranks to positions of power, but never before had it been so easy for so many to succeed. The new generation of samurai, or *shizoku* [gentlemen] as they were called, could no longer be content with a life of classical studies and simple devotion to family and superiors. There were to be few hereditary jobs in the new Japan; a man had to make his own arrangements for his livelihood. The vast range of opportunities awaiting in government and finance combined with the removal of hereditary posts and ranks forced the shizoku to come to grips at last with the competitive world. (pp. 167-69)

Ukigumo is in part the story of two branches of the same family; one is successful in adjusting to the life of the new Japan, the other fails. Magobei went to Tokyo and, after some initial difficulties, established himself as a businessman. His brother, Bunzō's father, remained in the family home in Shizuoka, used up his savings, and barely managed to eke out a living with his salary as a minor bureaucrat. His death left his wife and son destitute. Only Magobei's intervention offered Bunzō hope of salvation from a fate similar to his father's, but in the end, despite his Tokyo education and his knowledge of English, he too fails. Bunzō's brave and resolute mother is left alone in Shizuoka, waiting only for an opportunity to join her son and escape her loneliness.

Bunzō does not belong to the city. He cannot exchange his belief in sincerity, honesty, and restraint for sycophancy and aggressiveness. He is not witty and would not be able to join in an evening's festivities in a teahouse. He could not spend his time playing games or going to the theater. His are the traditional Confucian values: devotion to his family, hard work, and study. It is impossible for him to yield to the fashions of his time, and, as a consequence, he is crushed by the age.

Magobei never appears in the novel. His branch of the family is represented by Omasa, his second wife, a woman of the city. Shrewd, aggressive, calculating, Omasa conducts a successful business on her own. She deals in moneylending and real estate. Education, the most esteemed of all accomplishments in traditional Japan, is valueless to Omasa unless it can produce some material return. She is scornful of Bunzō because he is incapable of currying favor with anyone. By contrast, she admires Noboru; he

is obviously going to be a great success in the new bureaucracy and he knows how to flatter her.

Noboru is in step with the modern world; he has the qualities associated even in Tokugawa times with the *edokko,* or child of Edo. He loves to banter in puns or off-color jokes. He enjoys drinking and flirting with pretty women and can talk of money and business with considerable authority.

He is also of samurai stock, but he does not subscribe to any of the traditional beliefs. Having no family, he is free to pursue his own success ruthlessly. He spends his Sundays making himself useful to his superior and his superior's wife and sees an opportunity to establish himself permanently by marrying the chief's sister-in-law. Far from presenting a model of diligence for those who work under him, as Confucian morality would suggest, he is concerned only with pretending to his superiors that he is working. He even permits himself to play the fool, mimicking the chief at every turn to show the admiration in which he holds his model, acquiescing in every decision. Noboru never contradicts his superiors and leaves no stone unturned in attempting to win their favor. He ridicules Bunzō's bookishness. Furthermore, he lacks any sense of loyalty to his friends. It is apparent that he fails to help Bunzō's cause, for he could easily have prevented his dismissal. Sycophantic, opportunistic, materialistic, Noboru is the very antithesis of the Confucian gentleman. He has learned well the lesson taught by such monuments to success as Samuel Smiles's *Self Help.*

Noboru represents success, Bunzō failure. Noboru never questions his actions. He believes that what he does is right because it is successful. Aiming only at material gain, he is not torn by any conflicts over the ethics of his way of life. Bunzō cannot accept success as a goal; money or position mean nothing to him except as a means to pay necessary expenses for himself, his future wife, and his mother. Not valuing wealth, he does not even consider sacrificing his moral code for it. It is only when he is in danger of losing the girl he loves that he is first tortured with doubts, and then the struggle becomes profound. In the end he does not yield; he clings to his belief in the old virtues.

The head of the department in which Bunzō and Noboru work is another symbol of success. Here Futabatei paints a brief but bold picture of a fool. The chief has been abroad and spouts modern, democratic ideas while, in fact, being totally undemocratic in conducting his department's affairs. He is completely taken in by Noboru's sycophancy and greatly admires the young man. The reader knows him primarily through Noboru's confident remarks regarding his influence with the older man and through Bunzō's utter loathing of him. Success in the bureaucracy, then, can be obtained by a stupid man who has been abroad. Intelligence, ability, or hard work have little to do with making one's way in the bureaucratic world of Meiji Japan. (pp. 170-72)

Futabatei was . . . critical of the way his countrymen admired the Western world without understanding it. He touched upon this in the characterization of the chief but developed it more fully in the portrait of Ishida, Bunzō's old teacher, to whom he goes for help when he loses his job. Ishida has lived in England and claims to know Herbert Spencer and many other influential Englishmen. Ishida is an economist, by his own account, but he has been teaching English for eight years since his return to Japan and has not made any reputation for himself despite his foreign education.

Ishida, who may well be a fictional representation of Ichikawa, Futabatei's teacher at Gaigo Gakkō, is a pathetic figure. Not having achieved fame, it is difficult to resent his empty boasts of contacts in England, and his claim to knowing so much of the West because he can speak of boots and roll cigarettes is more touching than annoying. Through this highly exaggerated caricature, Futabatei captured another tragic but unavoidable failing in his nation. Futabatei felt that in trying so earnestly to learn, the Japanese were permitting themselves to accept virtually anything to which the word foreign could be applied. And the danger was that too many of his people would, like Ishida, avoid anything "preceded by the adjective 'Japanese,' be it object or idea."

The hazard of exchanging the new for the old is exemplified by the course Osei's life takes as the novel develops. By the shift in her affections, she demonstrates how Japan was turning away from the traditional values and replacing them with the new formula for success. At first she is infatuated with Bunzō and tries futilely to make him propose, but soon after his dismissal she turns to the cheerful, flattering Noboru. Although for a few days she clings to her defense of Bunzō when Omasa blames him for being fired, she soon loses interest in the whole problem and tries instead to capture Noboru's full attention. She forgets that she once thought of Noboru as crude and ignorant and is dazzled by his worldly manner. The shift is too rapid to be anything but metaphoric, but here Futabatei is describing the change his nation had made in a single generation.

Osei also epitomizes the vogue for things Western. She follows the current fads—European languages, Western clothes, "progressive" ideas of female equality—and forgets each in turn. She is a spoiled and willful girl, cruel and insulting to her mother when the mood strikes her, soft and affectionate when she wants something. But she is suffering from growing pains, and as the novel progresses, her youth and immaturity become her predominating characteristics. Like her nation, Futabatei saw Osei as a naïve child, buffeted about by a confusion of ideas, lacking guidance from the previous generation, unable to distinguish between the superficial and the genuine.

Futabatei obviously sympathized most with his hero, Bunzō. He lavished the greatest attention on his portrait of this desolate child of the samurai and devoted a major part of his novel to exploring his mind. He knew, however, that the Bunzōs of this world were doomed to a life of obscurity and that men like Noboru would attain rank and fortune. Furthermore, he recognized that Noboru and his kind were in the majority. There would be few men who would dare to defy the current customs; most would concede to necessity and behave as their positions demanded. In an interview Futabatei said:

> I realized that people like Bunzō were actually more intelligent, but that men of Noboru's type were more numerous. They were the ones who enjoyed success and power in modern Japan. No matter how noble their ideas may have been while in school, the attitudes of most modern young people of the day were very superficial; as soon as they went out into the world, they became like Noboru.

Futabatei was not blind to the faults in his hero. At times, he portrayed Bunzō's weaknesses with scathing humor. He showed his hero to be a blundering fool. His uncertainties and inaction are not admirable qualities even if they are pathetic. The Confucian gentleman was enjoined to act as well as to be sincere and honest, and for a considerable portion of the novel Bunzō is incapable of direct action. Futabatei's portrait of Bunzō has depth and dimension; he is at once admirable and foolish. Similarly, Omasa, although crude, vicious, and selfish, captured Futabatei's sympathy. He is openly critical of Osei's nasty manner toward her mother. The frustration Omasa experienced in having her plans for Osei's marriage to Bunzō thwarted is brilliantly depicted. Omasa's efforts to charm Noboru can be interpreted as simply her way of trying to secure a good marriage for Osei. The sympathetic characters in *Ukigumo* are not all good, and the unpleasant ones are not all bad. This is what gives the novel its merit. (pp. 173-76)

Futabatei portrays Bunzō in many dimensions. He is shown alone with his thoughts; a timid, terrified young man, slow to reach decisions and even slower to act. We see him restrained and respectful with Omasa, and shy but somewhat more relaxed with Osei. Toward Noboru he is cold and finally openly belligerent. We also see him through the eyes of the other characters; quiet, retiring, and, in Osei's astute summation, "stodgy." In this many-sided portrait Futabatei depicts his version of the superfluous hero, the alienated man cut off from society. Futabatei learned of this literary type from his study of Russian fiction and, by transferring this hero to Japan, introduced a new facet into modern Japanese literature.

Perhaps no literary type is as difficult to define as the superfluous hero; he must be described almost in terms of what he is not. The superfluous hero is seen most clearly when contrasted to the positive hero, the man of action, assertion, and aggressiveness. The positive hero, himself a conglomerate type, sets a goal for himself—economic, political, moral, or emotional—and proceeds to move toward attainment. He is usually completely successful.

In politics, the positive hero may be a revolutionary or at least a radical, but he may equally be an arch conservative. Whatever his position, he recognizes it, believes in it, and will stop at nothing to bring his objective to fruition. In the world of ideologies or philosophies, his devotion may be to a god or to a system of thought which has captured his faith and from which he will not be dissuaded. His goal may be success in the material sense, perhaps tied to political and philosophic ideals or else entirely unencumbered by intellectual considerations. He may be ruthless in achieving his goal or he may be kind and generous to his colleagues; in any case, it is power and recognition of his superiority which he seeks and often obtains. The positive hero frequently is a man of great physical strength. His strength, coupled with determination, often enables him to lead others. He may, on the other hand, excel only in his good looks and not possess notable strength. He invites devotion from his friends and from women; often they are prepared to sacrifice life and fortune for him.

The superfluous hero is a man who lacks these qualities. If he attempts to lead others, something is bound to thwart his success. When he falls in love, the love either falls short of fruition or dissolves into blind passion devoid of continued respect and admiration. No matter how sincerely he may believe in a cause or philosophic system, sooner or later he will reject it or find it deficient. Either his gods abandon him, or he turns his back on them. What had seemed most important in life will sooner or later slip into the background with no new faith to replace it. If he is a rich landowner, his attempts at modernization of his estates are often misguided; if he is a salaried clerk, the promotions he hopes for never materialize.

In some cases the superfluous hero is foolish, but usually he is both intelligent and sensitive and acts as a fictional representation of the artistic personality. Life buffets him and his intelligence rarely achieves maturity, but originally he possessed considerable talent. He was able then to think out his problems with reasonable clarity; he could see the foibles of those about him accurately and even perceptively. Misfortunes, however, are likely to frustrate his abilities. Failure, either material or spiritual, may so darken his outlook that he appears stupid to others and finally even to himself. He will not take the kind of action which for the positive hero would be obvious. He waits for his chance, but when it comes, he cannot seize it. (pp. 178-80)

The superfluous hero has become a symbol of the sensitive, intellectual, or artistic man who lives outside the mainstream of modern life. He cannot find faith or philosophy or love in his world because the old beliefs have proved mortal and the new ones are not yet acceptable. The faith he seeks may be religious, intellectual, or emotional. The love he needs will take him from his confined universe, that is, from himself, and bring him closer to other people or even to one other person. He must learn to give—to a cause, to an ideal, or to a person. He must learn to sympathize, to see why the positive man wants what he wants. The superfluous man pictures all life as a reflection of himself, as if he were somehow looking at a distorted mirror in which his image filled every inch. As a consequence he cannot fully appreciate anyone else; in some cases he is led to reject everyone completely. Some superfluous heroes are merely quiet and ineffectual; others are completely mad, exhibiting the whole range of classic paranoiac symptoms favored by the literary world. Most are situated somewhere in between.

Bunzō is a superfluous hero. He is neither completely lazy nor utterly stupid nor insane, but he is weak, uncertain, unsuccessful, overly cautious, indirect, and not without neurotic symptoms. He is also gentle, tender, and completely sympathetic. Critics are fond of saying that Bunzō is an ordinary man, an average, everyday man, in contrast to the dashing heroes of earlier fiction. However, he is ordinary only in the sense that he is not extreme; he is nei-

ther very rich nor abysmally poor, brave nor exceedingly cowardly, fiercely intellectual nor totally ignorant. He is no more ordinary than any of the heroes of modern literature from Stephen Dedalus to Edward Albee's George; he in fact shares many qualities with his Western counterparts of the last hundred years.

Dozens of earlier Russian models may be found for Bunzō's endless brooding, his deep concern with others' opinions about himself, and his habit of ascribing the highest virtues to himself and the basest motives to others. Many similar figures abound in later nineteenth- and twentieth-century European, American, and Japanese fiction. Futabatei was not consciously copying any single Russian novel in writing *Ukigumo,* and little evidence suggests that later Japanese authors often modeled their heroes on Bunzō. Futabatei saw the applicability of the Russian type to Japanese fiction and adopted the pattern because of its appropriateness. In Japan, as in the West, this hero or antihero is so closely entwined with realism and naturalism that no one model should ever be cited. It is almost an accident that Futabatei was the first to portray him; another author would surely have created such a hero in any case. The amazing thing is that, being the first, Futabatei succeeded so well.

By centering his plot on Bunzō's difficulties in the bureaucracy, Futabatei established a setting for his superfluous hero already familiar from Russian literature. Bunzō's feelings toward his employers are not as overladen with emotion as those of some Russian heroes. In *Ukigumo,* however, the bureaucracy represents a major part of the cold, impersonal world which finally forces Bunzō into lonely isolation.

The symbolic treatment of the bureaucracy varied between two extremes in Russian fiction. In many Russian novels it assumes no particularly significant role. It is shown as inefficient, corrupt, and manned by fools, but it represents no important object of hate or fear to the hero. This is true, for instance, of the bureaucracy described in [Ivan Turgenev's] *Fathers and Children.* In other stories, however, the Russian government system plays an important part; it becomes the symbol of the larger, unknown, hostile world which the hero cannot enter. For example, in Dostoevsky's early story *The Double,* the government service is represented as a vast, impersonal machine, deaf to the pleas of the desperate hero, who feels himself powerless to combat it. It symbolizes the uninterested modern world which has no place for the weak, discontented, or inept.

Bunzō's attitude toward the bureaucracy lies closer to the second of these extremes. Although Bunzō's hatred of the office where he works never reaches the intensity of emotion experienced by Golyadkin in *The Double,* he too scorns the pettiness and ignorance he finds there. Bunzō's position had been that of a lowly clerk. The work was simple for him, in fact considerably below his intellectual abilities. Unlike Oblomov in Goncharov's most famous novel or Makar in *Poor Folk,* Bunzō committed no foolish error which brought him to the attention of his superiors. His crime was simply that he was too retiring or too dull to interest influential people. Higher-ranking officials did not protect him, perhaps because they had not even noticed him; when someone was to be dismissed, he was the obvious choice. (pp. 181-84)

In common with many of the heroes of Russian fiction, Bunzō finds it difficult to visualize a situation from any point of view other than his own. He does not recognize his essential selfishness because of his conviction that he is morally correct. Sycophancy, he is sure, is wicked; his aloofness, therefore, must be virtuous. He expects to be admired, only to meet with criticism and even ridicule for his stubbornness. Like Golyadkin, Bunzō often imagines himself to be the only man in his world who understands the true meaning of honesty and sincerity, and he convinces himself that he is being persecuted for his virtue.

Bunzō cannot understand the other characters in the novel. Noboru, Futabatei's positive hero, is the mirror opposite of Bunzō. Noboru is ruthless and calculating, and again Bunzō is morally correct in finding nothing to admire in him. However, he does not ever realize that he is jealous of Noboru. Noboru's success in the office is matched by his ability to win a woman's heart. Bunzō fails in both and will not even admit that it might be some inadequacy on his part that causes his failure. He assumes it is only because the world is stupid and vulgar that a man like Noboru can be so esteemed while he is ridiculed. Bunzō never considers that Noboru may, in fact, be a man of ability, or at least that his talent may have some value.

Similarly, Bunzō finds it very difficult to understand Omasa's behavior. Again he quite accurately perceives her lack of morality. She is dishonest in pretending that she had not planned his marriage to Osei. She wants nothing more than to be rid of him permanently and makes him extremely uncomfortable. Instead of offering him sympathy for his plight, she flies at him in fury. Omasa concedes to the traditional system of family loyalty only to the degree that she does not actually turn him out of the house. On the other hand, except for one brief flash of insight, Bunzō does not see why Omasa is driven to such extremes of anger. The reason is obvious to the reader. By wit and will, Omasa has raised herself to a position of respectability. She is determined to see her daughter married well so that her status will be maintained; a poor, unemployed relative is a blight in her home. Bunzō has disappointed her bitterly, and she is convinced that it is because he would not take her advice and be more yielding to the chief. No longer a suitable match for her daughter, he promises to be a persistent burden to her. Bunzō is morally correct in despising her overt materialism, but his failure to understand her position is a serious flaw in his personality. (pp. 184-85)

Bunzō's inability to carry out any of his plans is his most dominant characteristic. Resolutions are broken one after the other. When he is rejected by the bureaucratic world, he determines to find other work, but, in fact, he makes only one feeble effort to gain employment in the many weeks encompassed by the novel. After his visit to Ishida four days after his dismissal, he does not contact anyone else, although he fully realizes that Ishida is not really interested in helping him. Early in the novel Bunzō also resolves to leave the Sonoda household. Initially his realiza-

tion that he would be insulting his mother by being rude to his aunt combined with his affection for Osei prevent him from going. As the days pass, he reaffirms his resolution any number of times but still hesitates. Then he decides that he must save Osei from the degradation into which he is convinced she has fallen. He spends hours, even days, searching for a way to tell her how dreadfully she is behaving. In the end he merely exhausts himself in thinking about acting; he does nothing. In the closing chapters of the novel, Osei loses interest in Noboru and becomes more cheerful, but this owes nothing to Bunzō. He has failed to take any positive action at all.

In the few instances where he carries out one of his resolutions, he blunders badly, and his deeds become a kind of failure in themselves. He twice goes to Osei to seek her support in his despair, and both times she becomes extremely angry with him. He succeeds in telling Noboru that he wants no more of his so-called friendship, but in the course of their argument Bunzō is made a fool of, and subsequently both Osei and Omasa take Noboru's side. Bunzō then is a failure in virtually everything he tries to do in the novel.

Despite many striking similarities between Bunzō and the superfluous heroes of Russian fiction, Futabatei's transfer of the type into a Japanese context is complete. Bunzō's immediate problems, his relations with his mother, aunt, and cousin, as well as with his acquaintances, and the reaction he has to his situation are all consistent with conditions actually existing in Tokyo in the late 1880s. The reader is never conscious of an alien influence in the novel.

Although Futabatei found the theme for *Ukigumo* in Goncharov's work and, as we have seen, greatly admired his style, he did not adopt the Russian novelist's ideas indiscriminately. Oblomov [in *Oblomov*] and Alexander Aduyev in *A Common Story* are members of the landed aristocracy. Their difficulty in adjusting to modern society stems from their unwillingness to part with the comforts of their childhood. They had been brought up to believe that everything would be provided for them and that they would never have to work hard for anything. Both novels are filled with nostalgia for the ease and graciousness of the old life. Nothing of this appears in *Ukigumo*. Bunzō was always poor and, although his family were samurai, they were near the lowest level of the class. Bunzō, raised in the belief that hard work was his duty, never shirked this responsibility. Unlike Oblomov's self-induced pathological inertia, Bunzō's inaction is temporary and precipitated only by the loss of his job. He does not long for the past because, in fact, he has never known anything but poverty and uncertainty. It is death of an ethical system which Bunzō represents and not the end of a social class. Although the code which Bunzō believes in was kept alive by the samurai, it was not dependent for its survival on the continuance of the Tokugawa social structure.

Bunzō is protected against the worst extremes of poverty by the Japanese family system. As long as he stays in Magobei's house, he will be fed and his clothes cared for. He will not exhibit the visible signs of poverty which disgrace Dostoevsky's superfluous heroes. Without an income, Bunzō cannot send his mother any money nor bring her to live with him, and this is his greatest financial concern. However, although his mother's poverty worries him at first, he begins to think less and less about it as the novel progresses. It is possible to assume that Bunzō knows that she too will be cared for in some other way. Therefore Bunzō does not have to face unemployment with the terror which dominates many of the heroes of Russian fiction.

Bunzō is not insane. Although he feels oppressed and misunderstood, his is the variety of neurosis common to modern society. The Japanese bureaucratic world and the materialistic forces represented by Omasa fill Bunzō with disgust, but Futabatei did not follow the example of Dostoevsky and present a hero almost too sick to be brought back to the society of ordinary men.

Finally, it is important to note once again that *Ukigumo* contains no political message. It will be remembered that immediately before starting *Ukigumo,* Futabatei had been translating *Fathers and Children* and that he himself had been quite outspoken on political issues earlier in life. While the contrast between the strong man and the weak which is such a consistent theme in Turgenev's work is repeated in *Ukigumo,* it is impossible to read a political implication into the plot.

The theme which *Ukigumo* shares in common with many Russian novels is the tragedy of separation or isolation. Sympathy, love, or understanding—whatever aspect the emotion takes—is the unchanging, universal, all-pervasive force in human behavior; it is, in Futabatei's terminology, the Idea. *Ukigumo* deals with the absence of that emotion in the lives of its characters and, through the detailed analysis of Bunzō's situation, with the pathetic confusion which accompanies such a loss. Futabatei attempted to capture the qualities which made his time different from any other by telling the story of Noboru's success and Bunzō's failure in the bureaucratic world; he tried to capture the Essence of life by showing how Bunzō was unable to win the sympathy and understanding of Omasa and Osei. (pp. 186-89)

The superiority of *Ukigumo* to Tsubouchi's novels and to many other novels written in the same period lies in Futabatei's attempt to reveal aspects of the human condition which are buried beneath man's daily actions. He gives us a picture of a young man in his solitary hours, away from the probing, critical eyes of his family and friends, free to let his mind wander where it will. The portrait of weakness, vacillation, fear, and uncertainty is a vivid representation of modern man's dilemma. Despite Futabatei's despair over his novel and the unpolished state of Part Three, *Ukigumo* is a powerful, realistic novel.

With the models of the great Russian masters of realism to work from and with his own philosophic conviction in the merit of fiction as a serious form of art, Futabatei was able to create a novel whose plot and characterization symbolized some of the most important conflicts of his time. *Ukigumo* is a statement in fictional form of Futabatei's analysis of Meiji society. He was never successful in putting his literary theories into written form in expository writing; his novel is the positive expression of his

views, and through it and his translations from Russian fiction he influenced generations of Japanese intellectuals. Futabatei was not a good literary critic, although his perception and understanding of Russian and Japanese literature were highly developed. The critical argument for realism was made by Tsubouchi in *Shōsetsu shinzui.* It remained for Futabatei to put that argument into practice. Between them, Tsubouchi and Futabatei established the model for realism which has remained the dominant pattern of Japanese fiction until today. (p. 190)

> *Marleigh Grayer Ryan, "Futabatei's Definition of Realism and the Superfluous Hero," in* Japan's First Modern Novel: "Ukigumo" of Futabatei Shimei, *translated by Marleigh Grayer Ryan, Columbia University Press, 1967, pp. 149-90.*

Masao Miyoshi   (essay date 1974)

[*Miyoshi is a Japanese-born critic and educator who has lived in the United States since the 1950s. In the following excerpt, he focuses on the narrative devices Futabatei employed to delineate the psychology of the protagonist of* The Drifting Clouds.]

[The title of Futabatei's first novel, *Ukigumo (The Drifting Clouds)*], is evidently intended to suggest the hero's uncertain position relative to both his love and his position in society. Besides "drifting," *uki* can be read as either "sad" or "gay," depending on which ideogram is used. When spoken, *uki* at once sets off the paradox inherent in the pun. Also, *ukiyo* (floating world) is a key term in Edo literature, and the most representative arts of the period are called *ukiyo-e* (pictures of the floating world, chiefly woodcut prints), and *ukiyo-zōshi* (stories of the floating world, or the novel). Futabatei's choice of this title, then, at once signifies the tradition he has inherited, while also pointing to the essential ambivalence of sadness and gaiety, tragedy and comedy (or the *carpe diem* of Edo decadence and Buddhist resignation) quite evident in the work itself.

The novel is brief (less than 150 pages in the standard text), which is often the case in Japanese fiction, and the plot . . . is extremely simple. The young man in the story, Bunzō, is laid off from his government job. His aunt Omasa, in whose house he lives, is annoyed and begins to show her contempt for him. Bunzō is in love with his cousin Osei, but the beautiful girl's reaction to this news is rather indefinite. Bunzō has a worldly and aggressive colleague, Noboru, who presents a threat to his marital prospects. What fills the story is the day-to-day family conversations, Bunzō's unending self-analysis, and a few episodes such as Bunzō's efforts to find another job, and Noboru's visit, in the company of Omasa and Osei, to a chrysanthemum show. The chronology of the narrated events is also very short: less than two weeks (October 28 to November 8) in the first sixteen chapters and a few subsequent weeks in the remaining three.

A simple story with a very brief chronology can indicate either trivialization—which is not the case here—or the internalizing of events. And for the author to have worked hard at it for nearly three years suggests the possibility at least of his continual assessment and reassessment of his material. The work is thus doubly psychological in the sense that, while exploring the inner experience of the main characters, it also reveals the author's fluctuating feelings about this experience. And the temporal structure of the novel, reflecting this psychological complexity, is far from simple.

The story opens with a conversation between two men just after one of them has been given notice of dismissal. As yet unnamed, they are singled out from the rush-hour crowd of office workers and government bureaucrats hurrying home. The next two chapters flash back to fill in the background of the man who was fired: his now deceased father, formerly a samurai, his impoverished and helpless mother, his energetic aunt, his beautiful cousin with whom he is in love, and so on. After that, the narrative progression more or less straightforwardly covers the rest of the short duration. Yet a clear outline of the passing time is not what the reader perceives. For one thing, the "events" of the novel are to such a degree internal that, despite numerous temporal references, it is impossible to mark the calendar. Then, too, the portrayal of the vacillating and pusillanimous young introspective is necessarily a little tedious. One reflection leads to another, still to another, then turns back to the original point, such circularity defeating the projection of any clear sense of passing time and in any case retarding the novel's tempo by lengthening the felt time. There is also the matter of grammatical tense. Japanese has no clearly established tense, and forms for past and present are often interchanged without creating any confusion for the reader. *The Drifting Clouds* is for the most part written in such a past-present mixture, and this, though it might on occasion intensify reader involvement in the manner of the "historical present," usually tends to obscure the linear time development. (The author himself is apparently halfhearted in tracing the passage of time, since the very first sentence contains an error: "at 3 p.m., the twenty-eighth of October, leaving only two days to the end of the month." And there are other discrepancies: in chapter 9, for example, "fifth day [since October 28]," ought to read "seventh day.")

As for the repetitiousness, it, too, is deliberate. Take the four successive descriptions of Osei in the first four chapters. The first time the reader hears about her, in chapter I, she is merely referred to as "your sweetheart" by Noboru. In the same chapter, the housemaid reports to Bunzō how Osei looked earlier that day when she went out with her mother. The description is largely of her clothes and not of her total appearance and expression. In the second chapter, the reader is given a brief account of her schooling and Bunzō's growing love for her, but no direct portrayal. In the next chapter, the reader comes a little closer; she is now reported as Bunzō sees her—as it happens, under the moonlight. A full daylight account of her appearance must await chapter 4, where the narrator attempts to provide a more objective view, though in no less admiring terms. The effect of this is twofold. First, the process by which the reader is introduced to Osei parallels the way one often comes to know another person in real

life. Second, the narrative sequence at the same time disrupts the chronology of the events. Chapters 1 and 4 belong to the same day, while chapters 2 and 3 deal with the past. All of this means, simply, that our progress in coming to know Osei does not accord with ordinary temporality, and thus our grasp of the plot is somewhat obscured.

Such temporal obfuscation, however, is not necessarily a disadvantage: in this novel, especially, whose chief movement is "drifting," the absence of a clear linear progression is almost a formal requirement. Even the author's abandonment of definite time references in the last three chapters helps create a sense of temporal dislocation which is the expected consequence of drifting.

This discussion of the novel's narrative sequence leads naturally, I believe, to the question of the language in which the narrative is set forth. The most important feature is the archaism that dominates a fair proportion of this "new" novel. Here is a passage from chapter 2 as Marleigh Ryan translates it:

> Bunzō was so happy he could have danced for joy. He had been terribly overworked by his aunt since coming to her house and had, in addition, very much disliked his role as a dependent nephew. Now that he was back in school, he was able to devote his full time and energy to his studies without any distractions.
>
> But even at school he was continually reminded of his poverty and loneliness. He had no one to spoil and pamper him as the other boys had, no one to give him an allowance. He channeled all his youthful energies into his studies. He was inspired by an overwhelming desire to bring joy to his destitute mother and to repay his great debt to his uncle by being successful at school. And he was. He took either first or second place—but never lower—in every examination. He was the pride of his teachers. His rich and lazy fellow students were very jealous of him.

A perfectly ordinary style, as any translation probably ought to be, but the original is hardly so plain and clean. In fact, the whole of these two paragraphs is originally only one sentence which runs—at the risk of incoherence—like this:

> Till yesterday, in the misery of being but a hanger-on at [his] uncle's home, being slave-driven and anxious, even frightened, to please; today, no longer ordered around by anyone, now able to devote his entire time and energy to study, well, wasn't [he] pleased, so pleased, that [he] jumped up and down in pleasure; but a student though [he] is now, it too being also a life of troubles; of course unlike the spoilt rich sons, having no fancy treats like help from parents, [he] cannot waste even a penny, but then doesn't want to; only being determined that [he] must relieve his helpless, lonely mother, must pay back his uncle for the debt; [his] study—undertaken in struggle and hard work with no wasted time—advancing remarkably; always being ranked the best, not even the second, at every examination; teachers being impressed [by him] as an extraordinary student.

It may be remarked here that since systematic punctuation in Japanese was, in a sense, a new concept developed only a short while earlier, and Futabatei may not yet have learned its full use or significance, it may be a mistake to take his commas and periods too seriously. At the same time Futabatei did learn the concept of syntax from his foreign-language study, as his sentence-by-sentence translation of [Turgenev's] "The Tryst" will bear out. Besides, archaism can be an advantage. The loose sentence, which he inherited from the *yose* storytellers and the Edo *gabuntai* writers, while clearly unsuited to precise statements requiring definite syntactic relationship of subject and predicate, is remarkably effective here where the hero cogitates seemingly endlessly and without explicit logical development. At times the style almost achieves the effect of the interior monologue and stream of consciousness—and this a few decades ahead of Joyce.

Unfortunately, this use of the old style is not generally a happy choice for Futabatei. The very first phrase of the novel, for instance, "Chihayafuru kannazuki," means simply "October," for which the ordinary word is *jūgatsu* (tenth month). The epithet *Chihayafuru* is a vestigial formula-term (*makura kotoba;* "pillow word") from the ancient formulaic tradition; it means "who shakes the world with a thousand rocks (thunder and earthquakes)" and hence "powerful, strong"; it is always applied to deity. *Kannazuki* is an old term from the lunar calendar meaning "the *god*less month" (hence the epithet). This type of formulaic expression, together with puns, might of course intensify poetic ambiguity and irony, and William Empson probably would have approved of it. But after centuries of overuse such verbal techniques began to lose their appeal for the reader, and Meiji writers were by this time actively boycotting a convention they felt was functioning now as mere superficial ornamentation. For instance, Futabatei's readers would hardly pause at "earth-shaking godless-month" to consider a possible religious comment by the author on his "ant-like" crowd of modern bureaucrats; they would quickly gloss over the phrase as a quaint name for October.

Then there is the summer evening scene where Bunzō tries to talk to his flippant cousin, and a description of the moon is given:

> The cool moon rose, outlining the leaves of ten slim bamboo trees which stood in the corner of the garden. There was not a single cloud and its powerful, radiant, white light lit up the face of the sky. Glistening drops of light poured down to the earth below. At first the bamboo fence between the houses held back the moonbeams and they extended only halfway across the garden. As the moon rose in the sky, the moonbeams crept up to the verandah and poured into the room. The water in the miniature garden there shimmered in the light; the windbell glittered and tinkled. Then the moonlight silhouetted the two young people and stole the brightness of the single lamp in the room. Finally it climbed up the wall.

An exquisite film fadeout. But the highly stylized and heavily Chinese texture is not related at all to the real movement of the characters' feelings. It appears that the elegant and archaic passage with its verse-like rhythm (5-7 meter) provides Futabatei with an escape from his job of scrutinizing the actual situation of that moment as it abruptly leaves the level of reality the novel has thus far been negotiating. The "beauty" and "elegance" of the passage do almost nothing to further the psychological drama between the young lovers. It is too easy a way out.

Another passage of this sort is the description of Ueno Park:

> Fall in Ueno Park. Ancient pine trees stood row upon row, their branches interlaced, their needles thick and luxuriant, of a green so deep as to saturate the heart of an onlooker. The fruit trees were desolate in contrast; old and young alike covered with withered leaves. The lonely camellia bushes, their branches laden with flowers, seemed to yearn for companionship. Several of the delicate maple trees had turned a blazing red. The cries of the few remaining birds mirrored the sadness of the season. All at once, the wind blew sharply. The branches of the cherry trees shivered and trembled, shaking free their dead leaves. Fallen leaves strewn on the ground rose as if moved by a spirit and danced about in happy pursuit of one another. Then as if by unanimous accord they lay down again. This bleak and dreary autumn scene cannot compare with a bright and hopeful spring day, but still it had a special magic of its own.

"Branches interlaced," "a green so deep as to saturate the heart of an onlooker," "the lonely camellia bushes," "yearn for companionship"—phrases as cliché as the dance of dead leaves. Futabatei's painterliness is heavy-handed, even in the English. It is a set picture, almost that of a traditional scroll. Compare this with a passage from Turgenev's "The Tryst," which Futabatei translated about this time:

> A slight breeze was faintly humming in the tree-tops. Wet with the rain, the copse in its inmost recesses was for ever changing as the sun shone or hid behind a cloud; at one moment it was all a radiance, as though suddenly everything were smiling in it; the slender stems of the thinly-growing birch-trees took all at once the soft lustre of white silk, the tiny leaves lying on the earth were on a sudden flecked and flaring with purplish gold, and the graceful stalks of the high, curly bracken, decked already in their autumn colour, the hue of an over-ripe grape, seemed interlacing in endless tangling crisscross before one's eyes; then suddenly again everything around was faintly bluish; the glaring tints died away instantaneously, the birch-trees stood all white and lustreless, white as fresh-fallen snow, before the cold rays of the winter sun have caressed it; and slily, stealthily there began drizzling and whispering through the wood the finest rain.

For Turgenev, a tree is a tree, the actual physical existence of which is conveyed through the word. If meaning emerges from his words, it is grounded in the life of the trees. For Futabatei, in contrast, meaning is imposed by his verbal trees—words, or pictures, exist, but not trees. (Partly, this is due to Futabatei's lack of ease with outdoor scenes. His genius being in the dramatic presentation of men and women, whenever he has to describe a scene larger than a room, he escapes into the elegant style which offers the security of a stereotyped convention.)

The Drifting Clouds puts the conventions to occasional good use in its imagery, particularly animal imagery for expressing Bunzō's sexual frustration:

> Since Osei had come home to live, worms had been breeding inside poor, unsuspecting Bunzō's heart. At first they were very small and did not occupy enough space to give him trouble. But once they started actively crawling around, he felt as though he were peacefully departing from this world and entering a blissful paradise. . . . But all too soon the worms grew fat and powerful. By the time Bunzō had begun to suspect that he was infatuated with Osei, they were enormous and were crawling about, anxious to be mated.

The translator is surely in error regarding the plural "worms." Although Japanese nouns can be grammatically either singular or plural, the word here definitely means "the worm"—that is, the snake, the phallic being of Bunzō. In fact, there is a boldly explicit pun, *soitai no ja,* in the passage. The phase literally means "anxious to sleep together," but *-ja,* a nonsignifying verbal suffix, being a homophone with another *ja* that means "snake," the phrase can also mean "the snake that wants to sleep (with someone)." Similarly, there are many feminine symbols—*hamaguri* (clam) and *shijimi* (top shell), for instance—and, all told, a surprising number of fairly explicit sexual and scatological expressions.

Clouds of course are a major part of the book's imagery: the clouds in the sky and "to cloud" in the sense of "to obscure" both appear throughout the novel, reiterating its leitmotif. The reader will recall that Bunzō spends most of his time "upstairs," close to the clouds, and in any case quite cut off from the ground floor where most of the daily activities of life are conducted. The upstairs room, suggesting the paradox of claustrophobic one-room confinement and spatial and psychological indefiniteness, is a fit location for him. And the same sort of symbolic notation system operates in the names of the main characters, which all suggest representative qualities. The Oblomov-like hero is named Uchimi Bunzō, meaning "Inland Sea" and "third son of *Bun* (writing)." The name can also indicate "introspectiveness" and "three letters" (or "three cultures"—Japanese, Chinese, and Western?). Honda Noboru, "main rice field" and "to rise," is a suitable name for an energetic upward mobile in modern Japan. The name of Bunzō's domineering aunt, Omasa, "to govern," is no surprise, while that of Osei, her charming, light-hearted daughter, means the "course of things," though it can also mean "force" and "vigor," which may suggest some untapped strength she inherited from her mother. Given all this, to read a point-by-point allegory of proper names may be overdoing it. We have to keep in mind that Futabatei knew his Dickens and Thackeray well, and

must have learned from their not-so-subtle use of names as a prop to reinforce the orientation of a work.

But beyond this, the most important stylistic feature of the work is, of course, *gembun'itchi,* the kind of colloquialism that both Bimyō and Shōyō wished, but could not themselves begin to write. The quaint elegant style appears quite often in Part One, less frequently in Part Two, and hardly ever in Part Three. The time Futabatei spent working on the novel no doubt explains the change, but his own understanding is that the three parts, written at different periods, were modeled after different writers: Edo novelists for the the first part, Dostoevsky for the second, and Goncharov for the third. But whatever the generic circumstances of the gradual disappearance of archaism in ***The Drifting Clouds,*** it should be noted that the later parts are much more serious in confronting the psychological movement of the characters. Anything that can be called an event in this "novel of no events" occurs in the earlier parts, and toward the end all the action takes place in the minds of Bunzō and Osei. Since the elegant style is linguistically alien to psychological drama, a totally new kind of colloquialism is called for. To twist it around, Dostoevsky and Goncharov—whom Futabatei discovered for Japan—taught him a style that called for a new subject matter. Serious study of an ordinary person's thought and behavior ultimately requires a language rooted in his ordinary life, and a novel written in such a language will of necessity have to deal with the daily life of the ordinary person. Despite Futabatei's occasional successful use of the quaint and unpunctuated style, his real achievement was in forging a plain, ordinary language to be used in the novel of plain, ordinary people.

With regard to the characters in ***The Drifting Clouds,*** Futabatei's best work is in dialogue and the main characters' self-analysis. He is also, however, adept at the swift presentation of minor characters. Both the old teacher and the department head who fires Bunzō are successful caricatures of the kind of "Westernized" men who have been crowding the Japanese literary scene ever since. Though self-convinced connoisseurs of the West, they in truth know very little of it, or of Japan either for that matter. While drawn with broad satiric strokes, these two characters also amplify certain traits shared to some degree by the younger characters—Bunzō, Osei, and Noboru. And they gloss a noticeable contradiction within Bunzō himself, who, though generally a sympathetic figure, self-righteously refuses to "apple-polish" his boss, at the same time doing exactly that to his old teacher. Using minor characters to gloss or amplify the traits of the major figures is a common enough technique in fiction but Futabatei's skillful use of it here gives us impressive and tangible evidence of his knowledge of such novelistic resources.

Omasa is a type character, and what a sardonic portrayal of powerful maternity she is. Utterly unself-conscious and seemingly indefatigable, she snorts and belches along, secreting her venom for her unfavorite people and then letting them have it. Similarly, Noboru, the vulgar but quite self-assured social climber, is very much alive. The verbal exchange between these two big-mouths is a comic masterpiece.

Cover and interior illustration for Futabatei's Ukigumo.

Where Bunzō is concerned, his extreme shyness and taciturnity make the author's good dialogue technique irrelevant. His thoughts must somehow be conveyed, but there is the problem of how to proceed. Since he vacillates so interminably, a third-person narrator's presentation and interpretation would be awkward and boring: how could any other person, particularly the narrator, be interested in his endless does-she-or-doesn't-she and should-I-or-shouldn't-I debate with himself? Bunzō had better speak for himself. He had better, but he doesn't. The novel is not told from the well-focused point of view of its chief character. In fact, the narrator maintains an ironic and rather condescending distance from the character, especially in the earlier parts. Here is his earliest description of Bunzō, for instance: "His complexion was quite poor, pasty and sallow, but his thick eyebrows lent distinction to his face, and the bridge of his nose was straight. His mouth was not very shapely but it was firm and restrained. He had a pointed chin and prominent cheekbones. He was rather drawn and seemed nervous and not particularly appealing." Even at the end of the novel, where Bunzō at long last reaches some sort of resolution, the narrator presents him ironically:

> Restlessly he wandered [back and forth in the corridor]. Eventually he reached a decision. He would try to talk to her when she came back. He would gamble everything on her response. If she would not listen, he would leave that house once and for all. He went back upstairs to wait.

Note his restless movement "back and forth" in the house; also his final move in the novel, which is a return to his upstairs room, an ivory tower of sorts, protected from the context of life. If a novel can be said to judge events and characters, it must certainly be said of *The Drifting Clouds.*

Now, if the narrator seems ironic at both ends of the novel, it is logical to ask what the perspective of this irony might be. And how about other passages, especially in the later parts, where he seems so intensely involved in the hero? In Browning's dramatic monologue, the authorial stance is unambiguous in its irony and the character is made to reveal himself in spite of himself. It is the same in the omniscient-narrator novel: the narrator's comments add up to a definable commitment on the part of the author himself. But what is the narrator's judgment in *The Drifting Clouds?* What does his irony mean? Is this young man—painfully honest and credulous and finally quite ineffectual—an object of pity to the narrator? Or is he somehow praiseworthy as a kind of modern moralist? Or, still another possibility, is the narrator saying that he *is* modern man? And finally, is life "sad" or "gay" in Futabatei's eyes? Is Bunzō tragic or comic? Or a little of each?

I do not believe we shall find a clear answer to these questions. *The Drifting Clouds,* for all the hero's propensity to moral judgment, affords no perspective in which his broodings might take on some significance. Melville's Bartleby, Goncharov's Oblomov, Dickens's Eugene Wrayburne, for instance, all exist in a moral and psychological context in which their paralysis is precisely defined; in Uchimi Bunzō we have a fragmented modern man portrayed without a clue to his broader significance. The narrator is as unsure about Bunzō as Bunzō is about himself. It must be then that the irony in the narrative voice originates in the author's own feeling of fragmentation, his awareness of his inability to organize a coherent judgment vis-à-vis his character.

Osei, pretty and faddish—a flapper, if such an anachronism might be allowed—is similarly ambiguous. Often dismissed by critics as a superficial "new" girl, she is actually extraordinarily charming. She has a shallow sort of crudeness, true, but it is nevertheless balanced by her refreshing temperament and free energy. Osei also undergoes certain changes in the course of the novel. From chapter 12 through chapter 16, she is no longer such a flirt, but rather subdued toward Noboru and her cousin and attentive to her mother. In a rare passage that directly squares with her inner thoughts, there is even a moment of self-realization. But what does it mean? What are we supposed to think of her now? And how does Bunzō see her now? There is no direction coming from the narrator here. To our frustration, he provides no clue to such questions. Just as he was uncertain about his modern young man's predicament in the loss of being, so is he now unsure of the girl in the picture—this time, simply because he does not seem to understand what a girl is. Potentially there is a full-bodied young woman—lively, good-looking, affectionate, shallow, callous, sexy, pretentious—but the narrator does not gather these features into a sharp focus so we can see her clearly. We don't know what to think of her any more than Bunzō does.

The novel is formed by one person's consciousness of another. Each character's understanding of himself is modified by the other's notion of him. And this interlocking of consciousnesses creates the world of the novel, the community of men and women as the novelist perceives it. What is curious about *The Drifting Clouds* is how little the characters seem to understand each other despite the fact that they are living in the same house, having their meals together, and sitting down in the evening together. Their physical world is one small house, and yet the residents are worlds apart, each one isolated with no promise whatever of better understanding in the future. Omasa and Noboru, vulgar-minded as they are, dismiss Bunzō too casually, and that ends the matter right there. Between Osei and Bunzō, there is little promise of any greater insight.

What we begin to suspect after a while is that Bunzō does not know Osei at all. Her sexual energy is obviously attractive to him, but Bunzō, Confucian puritan that he is, is afraid to think very well of sex, which is finally "wantonness," even "obscenity," as he unhesitatingly defines it in relation to his rival Noboru. The moral-psychological terms available to him are neither extensive nor sophisticated enough to apply to a modern young woman who owns her own mind, and, alas, her own body. Bunzō does not see Osei herself but his own restricted image of her, which is mere fantasy and illusion, and he knows it:

> Bunzō was certain that her new attitude toward him contained a significance that he was not yet able to grasp, and he was determined to find out what it was. With an enormous effort he concentrated all his energy on analyzing her behavior to isolate this evasive element. He had little success. He became irritated. And then those devilish worms inside him started their tantalizing dance again, teasing him with one hint after another, and finally tricking him into accepting some absolutely absurd solution. Half realizing how ridiculous it was, he accepted it for the moment anyhow and worked on the idea until he had constructed a whole situation from it. He experienced exactly the same hurt and pain from this artificial hypothesis as he would have if it had been a fact. At last he made himself see it for what it was: a ridiculous fantasy. He was simply looking for trouble. In a rage of self-disgust, he mentally smashed the illusion into a million pieces. He sighed with relief.

And, finally, we suspect that the narrator—indeed the author—shares with his character much the same ambivalence, the same fogginess and irresoluteness. The astonishing lack of mutual understanding among the characters of *The Drifting Clouds* cannot be explained solely in terms of Osei's superficiality or Bunzō's obtuseness. Nor can the surprisingly complete separation of the characters be interpreted as a result of the paradoxical privacy prevailing in the apparently communal Japanese home. There is doubtless something here of Futabatei's personal isolation, which was nearly absolute in a real sense for many periods of his life.

One might connect this moral ambiguity with the technique of temporal obfuscation discussed earlier. *The Drifting Clouds* is a moral and psychological novel in the sense that the hero is possessed of a compelling moral sensibility, and the narrator obviously tries to deal with it. The hero's action must then be anchored in the chain of events arranged from a temporal-causal viewpoint. The novel is, however, quite vague in its temporality, and as a result the hero's action is suspended in its clouds of anxiety without being rooted in the context of everyday temporal sequence. The novel, in short, tries to judge the hero from a point of view, while it has no point of view. The narrative sequence, disrupting the temporal sequence, is both a symptom and a strategy of this frustrated judgmental effort.

The Drifting Clouds neither defines the nature of its own irony nor demonstrates much conviction that irony might turn out a saving grace in a world of grotesque absurdities. And yet it is an important modern work for the way it disdains the crowded panoramas that tease fiction into episodic surveys, and for the way it manages to transform behavior into motivation and action. Similarly, its language, while using the conventions to its advantage, pushes the frontier of the craft of fiction to the border of colloquialism.

Futabatei wrote two more novels after an interval of twenty years. *The Visage* (*Sono omokage,* 1906) describes a married man's love for his wife's sister. The consummation of their love produces an awful guilt in the girl, and the man, a university lecturer, abandons family and career and disappears on the Continent to become eventually a skid-row alcoholic. Here again, the novel suspends judgment on the tormented man. Though the language is plainer, more in tune with other novels being written at the time (which had caught up with *gembun'itchi* by then), this novel lacks the attractive concentration of *The Drifting Clouds.* Futabatei's last work, *Mediocrity* (*Heibon,* 1908: translated into English in 1927), is quite boldly autobiographical. At the beginning of the *shi-shōsetsu* (I-novel), the orthodox tradition in the modern Japanese novel, *Mediocrity,* is interesting to a historian. But from the point of view of art it does not come up to *The Drifting Clouds.* For one thing, it peters out unpleasantly at the end, confirming a tendency already evident in the author's earliest work, but not so damaging there.

Futabatei is one of the few really attractive men of Japan's modern literature. Honest to a fault, he refused to join the Tokyo literati, with their jealousies, petty backbiting, and continually compromised positions. He hated to think of himself as a writer, preferring the man of action as a self-image. In fact, to be true to himself he abandoned his writing career soon after *The Drifting Clouds,* and during the rest of his short life was in turn a journalist, a colonial administrator, and a teacher. Even in these capacities he refused to sell out, and no doubt as a consequence he never really succeeded in his ventures. Now, of course, his genius is recognized, and despite his meager production he is considered a giant among Japanese novelists. (pp. 23-37)

> *Masao Miyoshi, "The New Language," in his*
> Accomplices of Silence: The Modern Japanese Novel, *University of California Press, 1974, pp. 3-37.*

Hisaaki Yamanouchi   (essay date 1978)

[*Yamanouchi is a Japanese critic and educator. Commenting on his* The Search for Authenticity in Modern Japanese Literature *(1978), he wrote that his intention was to trace "the development of Japanese literature since 1868 with reference to some twelve representative writers. The tension they felt between the impact of the West and the claims of a native tradition led to feelings of estrangement which find expression in their work.*

The book attempts to analyze the inner psychological conflicts of the writers concerned and to explain why the careers of many of them ended in mental breakdown or suicide." In the following excerpt from that study, Yamanouchi relates the realism of The Drifting Clouds *to Futabatei's theory of the novel.*]

Futabatei wrote his **'A Theory of the Novel'** and showed it to [Tsubouchi] Shōyō on their first encounter. It is worth comparing Futabatei's **'A Theory of the Novel'** with Shōyō's *The Essence of the Novel:*

> There are two kinds of novels, one didactic, the other realistic; but the latter is what the novel should essentially be. I fully understand the objections raised by one or another of recent scholars [Shōyō certainly was one] against the prevalence of the didactic novel. My aesthetic theories, applied particularly to the novel, are in agreement with this view. The novel perceives directly the ideal of Nature in the various phenomena of the world; what is perceived must be conveyed directly. Such direct communication is possible only by means of realism. Accordingly, realism is obviously the essence of the novel. What is didacticism? It is to slight the phenomena of the world by assuming that good wins over evil. . . . It is nothing but preaching under the guise of the novel. Can it be worthy of being called a novel at all? However, if one did not define the novel as *mosha* or copying, people would become sceptical of it. Generally speaking, imitation means to represent the ideal by means of the real. In the phenomenal world the idea of Nature can be embodied, but it is not always apparent as it is covered by the veil of the accidental. The phenomena copied in the novel are nothing but accidental, but it is possible to represent clearly the idea of Nature in it by means of expression and dramatization—this is the aim of a realistic novel.

It is said that **'A Theory of the Novel'** was intended to be an introductory essay for Futabatei's full-length criticism of Shōyō's *The Temperament of Present-Day Students.* Unfortunately, the manuscripts of the longer essay have been lost. As it stands, **'A Theory of the Novel'** is too short to reveal Futabatei's theory of the novel in its entirety. Since he does not elaborate his points fully, one needs to speculate on what he may have thought about the novel beyond the elliptical remarks in his brief essay. Several points emerge from this questioning. First, Futabatei supports Shōyō's criticism of the doctrine of 'reward virtue, punish vice'. Secondly, however, while Shōyō's theories indicate little more than that the 'artistic novel' aims at copying the phenomenal world, Futabatei's theory seems to suggest a realism based on Aristotelian mimesis, which is not a mere copying of the phenomenal but a representation of the ideal by means of the incidental. From where does this difference between Shōyō and Futabatei derive? Some of the theoretical sources to which Shōyō was indebted were British, whereas some critics have proved that Futabatei was indebted to contemporary Russian literary theorists such as Belinsky, who had fully absorbed Hegelian aesthetics. This accounts for the idealistic undertone in the above quotation. However, among the many British sources he consulted, Shōyō must have come across the Aristotelian conception of mimesis, which called for the synthesis of the ideal and the incidental. Aristotelian poetics had been incorporated into English literary theories of the seventeenth and eighteenth centuries. Possibly, then, the difference between the theories of Shōyō and Futabatei derives from their different literary tastes. Futabatei's theories, elliptical though they are, point more explicitly towards the realistic novel which modern Japanese authors were seeking to write.

Can we make a similar judgment of his novel, **The Drifting Clouds**? It centres round a hero, Utsumi Bunzō, who is frustrated both in his public and private life. A well-educated man of integrity, he was a promising young bureaucrat until his dismissal from office for no particular reason. While staying with his aunt-in-law, O-Masa, he fell in love with his cousin O-Sei. His calculating aunt-in-law first favoured the idea of their marriage because of his promising future, but after Bunzō's dismissal her favour shifted to Honda Noboru, a colleague of Bunzō's, who scaled with ease the office's ladder of success not through his intelligence but through his opportunistic sycophancy. In the projected ending of this unfinished novel, Futabatei seems to have intended that Honda was going to seduce O-Sei, thereby driving Bunzō insane.

Once again, one can profitably compare **The Drifting Clouds** with Shōyō's *The Temperament.* Futabatei is far more successful than Shōyō in modernising the Japanese prose style. Both put into practice their denunciation of the doctrine of 'reward virtue, punish vice': Bunzō, for instance, while embodying moral righteousness, is defeated instead of being rewarded. There are, however, two significant differences between the two novels. While *The Temperament* is a novel without a hero, in **The Drifting Clouds** Bunzō stands out as the hero or, rather, the anti-hero. Furthermore, despite Shōyō's claim in *The Essence* that priority should be given to human sentiment rather than to the ways of the world, *The Temperament* does not probe into the depth of the characters' psychology but only depicts the surface of the varied modes of student life. Futabatei, on the other hand, traces the development of the hero's psychology and achieves what may be called a modern psychological novel even though in crude form.

One of the Russian writers with whose works Futabatei was familiar was Ivan Turgenev. Particularly relevant in this connexion are such works as *The Diary of a Superfluous Man* (1850) and *Fathers and Children* (1862). The characters who crowd these novels are prototypes of Russian intelligentsia at odds with nineteenth-century bourgeois society. The society in which Futabatei's hero Utsumi Bunzō lives had just undergone the Meiji Restoration, but many of the problems that then confronted modern Japan remained unresolved. Like most Meiji intellectuals, and in fact like the author himself, Bunzō is of a samurai, though declining, provincial family. He is well-versed in European culture, but his moral integrity presumably stems from his Confucian education. His difficulty is that the traditional values he embodies do not help him to cope with the bureaucratic system and with society at large. Futabatei does not imply, however, that the traditional values clash with the West *per se,* but rather he stresses the superficial ways in which Western culture has been imported and adopted in Meiji Japan.

Futabatei's hero, of course, is not free of flaws: he lacks the willingness to assert his own righteousness and to overcome the obstacles he confronts. He seems inclined towards defeatism. There is a curious imbalance—so prophetic of the portraits of intellectuals in later Japanese novels—between his intelligence, integrity and introspection on the one hand, and his ineffectualness in practical matters on the other. That the hero, embodying such values, suffers defeat was an inevitable dénouement for Futabatei who had no way of writing didactic novels, even such updated versions as the political novels of early Meiji. In a way Futabatei practised in this novel his theory of realism as laid down in **'A Theory of the Novel'**. The idea of good is not explicitly preached; instead, it emerges from the defeat of the character who suggests this good. Futabatei has thus created a hero who is to some extent the prototype of a character suffering from alienation and insecurity, variations of which are abundant in modern Japanese literature. (pp. 13-17)

> *Hisaaki Yamanouchi, "Two Precursors: Tsubouchi Shōyō and Futabatei Shimei," in his* The Search for Authenticity in Modern Japanese Literature, *Cambridge University Press, 1978, pp. 6-19.*

Ryan on Futabatei's evaluation of *The Drifting Clouds*:

Futabatei's evaluation of literature, based on Russian standards, convinced him that a man should write books not to earn money but to learn and, in turn, to enlighten. A novel written for such an exalted purpose obviously had to be of the highest quality, but Futabatei considered that few novels by his contemporaries attained this standard.

In judging his own achievements, he was also evaluating them in terms of Russian literature. He wanted to write a Japanese novel which would meet the standards set by the masterpieces of Russian fiction, and he knew he had not succeeded. His despair over *Ukigumo* [*The Drifting Clouds*] grew from his realization that he was incapable of portraying life with the skill of Turgenev, Dostoevsky, or Goncharov. He did not think to compare his novel with those of his contemporaries; he thought only in terms of the Russian masters. By such standards, *Ukigumo* was a failure.

> *Marleigh Grayer Ryan in her* Japan's First Modern Novel: *Ukigumo of Futabatei Shimei, 1967.*

Janet A. Walker   (essay date 1979)

[*Walker is an American critic and educator specializing in comparative literature and Asian studies. Commenting on her work as a literary critic, she has stated: "Since I am a comparatist by training and inclination, I am interested in what happened when Japanese writers of the late nineteenth century encountered Western ideas, and in the ways they took Western cultural ideals and literary forms and shaped them to their own purposes. In my [The Japanese Novel of the Meiji Period and the Ideal of Individualism], I showed how certain writers of fiction used the Western ideal of individualism to forge an important new practice of literary confession. But that was not all they did. In some cases they took over this ideal as an ideal to live by; and the ideal has continued to be a problematic one for Japanese, promising freedom from the strictures of the family and tradition on one hand, and threatening the individual with cultural isolation on the other." In the following excerpt from* The Japanese Novel of the Meiji Period and the Ideal of Individualism, *Walker praises* The Drifting Clouds *as "the first Japanese novel that places a high enough value on the individual's inner life to depict it expansively and lovingly."*]

[In 1885 Tsubouchi Shōyō, a well-known critic and novelist, wrote] the first comprehensive theory of the novel in the history of Japanese literature: *Shōsetsu shinzui* (*The Essence of the Novel*). Basing his remarks on nineteenth-century Western theories of the novel, as well as those of earlier Japanese theorists of the novel such as Motoori Norinaga, Tsubouchi took the position that the function of the novel was to reveal truth about life.

The purpose of the novel was not to teach a narrow morality, he urged, but, by opening man's eyes to the wide world of people and events, to "move the heart and stimulate the imagination." The novel ought to have a tightly constructed and believable plot. Furthermore, it ought to portray characters in depth and build up an impression of everyday reality, and the actual speech of different classes should be rendered realistically. Only when these demands were fulfilled could the novel attain the status of an art form and "outdo European novels." It is obvious from Tsubouchi's remarks what were the faults of the Japanese fiction of his time: fantastic plots made up of hastily and incoherently linked episodes; a moralistic tendency to punish vice and reward virtue that utterly removed the works from any connection with the reader's experience of the truth of life; and stilted, unnatural dialogue. However, the worst fault of Japanese fiction, as Tsubouchi saw it, was the inability of writers to depict characters with any depth to them. Tsubouchi criticized the early nineteenth-century novelist Takizawa Bakin (1767-1848), for example, for creating characters that were mere "ghosts of virtues," not real human beings. Indeed, the first translators of Western novels in the 1870s and 1880s frequently omitted from their translations passages analyzing the personalities or motivations of the characters, assuming that the Japanese reader would not be interested in reading about the inner life. Tsubouchi emphasized strongly that the goal of fiction was to depict human emotions. In order to do this, novelists could not just construct a hero to fit a preconceived ideal, but must portray him as he really was. This is the directive of Tsubouchi that was most significant for the development of the novel of the individual's inner life, and Futabatei was the first writer to fulfill it.

Futabatei Shimei wrote **Ukigumo (The Floating Clouds)**, the first Japanese novel to depict a hero in depth, over the years 1886 to 1889. The novel depicts the changes that occur in the relationships between four people over a period of a few weeks in the autumn of one year in the early 1880s. (pp. 31-2)

Ukigumo can be considered a novel of the individual because, though it depicts three characters in addition to Bunzō, only Bunzō is scrutinized at length from the inside; furthermore, the events of the novel are seen largely from his subjective (and distorted) point of view. What makes Futabatei the first writer of modern fiction is his revelation of the inner life of his character. He does this by means of the traditional interior monologue, borrowed from the native dramatic narrative form of the *yose* and made to fit the demands of a more tightly knit narrative, and the Western technique of indirect statement. The former technique is used mainly in the first part of the novel, and its open, extroverted, and even humorous style fits the dramatic character of the earlier parts. After chapter eight (out of nineteen chapters) the main action is over, and the characters—particularly Bunzō, but Osei also—retire to closed, introverted places to think over what has happened. Here the technique of third-person indirect statement is used more and more, and its use induces a serious, contemplative mood. Thought, not action, is the heart of the novel: time is slowed down to a leisurely pace and stretched to accommodate the vacillations of Bunzō's mind, rather than rushing forward to meet the demands of physical action. Similarly, Futabatei contracts space in the novel to suit Bunzō's intense but narrow inner life—the most innovative scenes, to the readers of the time, were those where Bunzō cogitates alone in his ten-by-ten-foot room. Bunzō's mentalized action takes place in this room, located symbolically above the rooms of everyday life, while dramatic action occurs on the ground floor. Bunzō is seen, then, as distant both physically and mentally from the other characters in the novel. The result of all this is that Bunzō comes across to the reader as a person with a unique inner life who is literally and painfully separated from other people.

Without the dissemination of logical thinking in Japan, Futabatei would not have been able to see Bunzō as a separate individual. Logical thinking, which made it possible for Japanese to see the individual for the first time as a being with a social and legal existence apart from others, was the basis for the ideals of independence and human rights that were popularized in early Meiji by Fukuzawa Yukichi and the Enlightenment movement. Essentially, logical thinking meant scientific thinking, the rational observation of things with the intent of discovering their laws. It involved a spirit of doubt and experiment that went directly counter to traditional moral modes of thought that stressed the harmonious unity of man and nature. According to Neo-Confucianism, the philosophical and religious system that influenced all schools of thought during the Tokugawa period, moral principles governed both man and nature and it was on this basis that man and nature were unified. Each thing, including man, had *li*, or an "ideal form or principle that prescribed the norm of its nature." Man's *li* was his *hsing*, or good nature, and consisted of the four virtues of benevolence, righteousness, etiquette, and wisdom. As the mind of Heaven, the underlying principle of unity, expressed itself in man

as these virtues, it expressed itself in nature as the four seasons.

Because man's *hsing* had become obscured by his physicality, however, he was no longer aware of his original nature. It was thought that by investigating the *li* of things other than himself, the *li* of all things being essentially identical, man could learn to become aware of his own *hsing* once more. As a consequence of this belief, when traditional Neo-Confucian scholars spoke of the "investigation of things" (*kakubutsu*), they meant, in essence, a discipline of the mind whereby one meditated on the *li* or nature of a particular thing with the objective of not only understanding the thing itself, but also of regaining an awareness of one's own *hsing*. Thus, "investigation of things" was nothing less than a spiritual discipline that led man to recover a lost sense of unity with things. The observation and investigation of objects in their purely physical aspect, without regard to their *li*, was considered to be useless, false learning—yet this was the kind of observation advocated by Western science. Conservative scholars such as Ōhashi Totsuan (1816-1862) criticized Western scientific learning for this reason, noting that "even with hundreds of microscopes," one could never observe principles. Thus, microscopes, and Western learning as a whole, were irrelevant to the true purpose of learning. Indeed, Western-style observation of things was irreverent as well, since it treated natural phenomena as if they were so many dead things, as if they were unrelated to man, and thus destroyed the harmony existing between man and the universe. Futabatei's technique of observation was posited on this new vision of Western science in which harmony between things no longer existed, and in which, as a consequence, one no longer carried out the discipline of observation in order to become aware of moral principles. For the world after the beginning of Meiji, including man himself, had suddenly acquired a depth and mystery that challenged the novelist to discover and reveal it by means of the microscope of analysis.

That readers of the time were shocked by the first use of psychological analysis in *Ukigumo* is evident from the remarks of Tokutomi Roka on his impressions of *Ukigumo* when he read it as a young man: "I was astounded by (Futabatei's) *Ukigumo*. As if I had been dragged for the first time in my life into a room where human beings were being dissected, I was frightened by the sharpness of his pen, which was like a scalpel." His comment recalls the fact that the origins of the realism and Naturalism of late nineteenth-century Europe—the Western literary movements that influenced Japanese novelists after Futabatei—are in Flaubert, whose foundations as a realistic novelist were perhaps laid when, as a child, he observed his father dissecting corpses with his medical students in the amphitheater of his hospital. Though Flaubert was not one of Futabatei's acknowledged influences, Dostoevsky was—the Dostoevsky who had evolved the dissecting realism of *Crime and Punishment*. Futabatei's appreciation and understanding of Dostoevsky's novels are documented, and it is evident that the self-interrogating interior monologues of parts two and three of *Ukigumo* were influenced by Raskolnikov's monologues in the Dostoevsky novel. Also, though Bunzō is hardly an individual with inner conflicts as destructive as Raskolnikov's, to the readers of the time he must have seemed a man who lacked the comforting, smooth surface of a hero or a villain and, instead of surface qualities, possessed only a rather frightening depth. In effect, what Futabatei had accomplished in *Ukigumo* was to introduce the Japanese reader of his time to a world of the individual that . . . opened up new and sometimes ominous territory.

In the Meiji period, then, logical thinking replaced the old, Neo-Confucian moral observation done as a spiritual discipline with a secular technique of observation that aimed at revealing not unity, but multiplicity and depth. It also undermined the Confucian moral system inherited from the Tokugawa period by insisting that natural laws were unrelated to moral principles. The consequence of this was that morality, which had been seen as linked to spiritual or natural laws under Neo-Confucianism, was now liberated. Individuals who were educated in Western logical thinking were thus free to evolve a morality that was based on their own individual laws. As the collapse of the old morality was reflected in the efforts of individuals in the Meiji period to evolve their own morality, it was also reflected in the new way of depicting characters in fiction. Confucian moral philosophy had viewed each individual as a *mei,* or role, to which various virtues, or vices, belonged. According to this view, a person of high class or a person of high status within one class would invariably be depicted as possessing virtues of strength, lower-class characters as possessing virtues of obedience. Those who did not possess virtues inevitably possessed vices. In the pre-Meiji world where people were unified with one another and with nature through their potential awareness of the common *li* that was inherent in all creatures, it was thought that reading about characters who exemplified the Confucian virtues would influence a person to become aware of his own virtues, and thus to become a better person. Correspondingly, reading about characters who exemplified the lack of Confucian virtues would, ideally, have a cautionary effect on the reader. Under the old Confucian moral system, then, the role of fiction was to affirm the world of Confucian values.

Tsubouchi Shōyō's insistence that the novel present characters that were believably and uniquely human contributed greatly to the destruction of the pre-Meiji view of character. Speaking of the eight heroes of the famous Tokugawa novelist Takizawa Bakin's *Hakkenden (Biography of Eight Dogs,* 1814-1841), Tsubouchi criticized the author for creating his characters, each of whom represents a specific virtue, with a set moral pattern in mind rather than being guided by his observation of real people. Tsubouchi noted that the reliance on formulas rather than on real life resulted in characters who had no depth and underwent no development. Seen from Tsubouchi's viewpoint, the decision to depict a role rather than a character in the traditional novel accounted for all of its defects, for without a character there was no character development and hence no occasion to depict time in a realistic manner. The absence of meaningful, purposive, human time in the novel in turn led to its episodic and fantastic plot structure and to its unrealistic and unhuman ending.

In the Tokugawa period fiction was not able to transcend these defects; only the characters in Chikamatsu's plays were able to overcome the limitation, in terms of realism, of being identified with a particular role and its specific (and static) virtues. The reason for this was that Chikamatsu depicted his characters as fulfilling several roles—Jihei, for example, is a husband, a father, a son-in-law, a brother, and a merchant. As such, he has specific obligations to fill. Yet Chikamatsu also depicted Jihei as a man in love, as a man who betrays his wife, destroys his family, and commits suicide. Seen from the Confucian point of view these acts are manifestations of selfish desires, and Jihei is thus a vicious man, though from a realistic standpoint Jihei is merely an individual who possesses human feelings that are valid in their own right. Because Chikamatsu depicts these virtues and vices as conflicting in Jihei, the latter achieves a dynamism that is akin to development, and time in the play is human time. In a sense, then, Chikamatsu's Jihei, possessing a depth of character that resulted from the sharp division in him between duty and inclination, prefigured the complex morality of the Meiji character.

Futabatei's Bunzō is not primarily one role, nor several roles, not even an identity resulting from the conflict between virtue and vice, but an identity for himself. Presented from the inside rather than from the outside, he gives the impression of being something beyond either a role or a virtue. Bunzō can be said to adhere to certain traditional assumptions about human relations: that there should be harmony among people, chiefly among family members, and that one owes loyalty to the members of one's family no matter what they do. Two further aspects of his morality—his deep respect for and devotion to learning and his belief that it is evil to kowtow before an unworthy superior—seem to stem from the samurai morality of the pre-Meiji era. Indeed, Bunzō's ancestors were samurai. Yet he is not only a samurai in the novel; he is also an individual, and his morality appears as private and individualistic largely because the author depicts his actions and thoughts as springing from an inner center of being. Bunzō's tendency to look inward is a characteristic that does not link him with the old samurai world in which actions were relegated to the category of either virtue or vice, but with a modern world in which the individual's actions are interpreted psychologically. For Bunzō is an introvert: a person who, for better or for worse, acts on the basis of data coming from inside himself.

Futabatei's study of Goncharov's Oblomov, Turgenev's Rudin, and Dostoevsky's Raskolnikov drew him into the world of the introverted person. Yet it was his own ability to observe himself that enabled him to direct his attention to the personality of an imaginary character. It is interesting, then, that Futabatei's friend and mentor, Tsubouchi Shōyō, referred to Futabatei as "timid and introspective—what psychoanalysts call 'introverted,'" Tsubouchi further described Futabatei as a person caught between two conflicting moralities: a Confucian one that demanded allegiance to external norms of behavior and a modern, Western one that made the individual responsible for himself:

As a writer he was a pure realist but in terms of personal conduct he was a Romantic or idealist. It may have been due to his Confucian training, but he was different from the people who came later. He was correct in his manners, humble, and moderate in speech. He abhorred falsehood, pretense, pride, and frivolity. Consequently he considered his own deceitful words and deeds as the greatest sin, and was always engaged in soul-searching and exposure of his personal weaknesses, censuring himself and speaking ill of himself. He was liable to worry unnecessarily, and was prone to world-weariness and pessimism.

It is probable, then, that Futabatei himself was the model for Bunzō's vacillating nature, and his soul-searching the model for Bunzō's constant examination of conscience. Thus, through Futabatei there passed into Japanese literature the nineteenth-century Western type of the brooding, pessimistic, and introspective hero.

The inner world of the individual, whether or not it was valued in pre-Meiji times, was never depicted in literature before Futabatei's *Ukigumo.* In the novel it is depicted as literally separate both from the world of society at large and from the inner worlds of other individuals. The disparity between Bunzō's inner world and the outer world is shown, for example, in the scene where Bunzō is walking the streets after his quarrel with Noboru, gnashing his teeth and wondering how he can get revenge on his rival. He is obviously completely caught up in his own subjective world at this point and becomes aware of the external world only when he suddenly notices that a policeman is looking at him strangely. He had glared at the policeman, and at the whole world, as if they were Noboru. At such times the author sees the distance between the subjective world of the mind and that of other people as comic. However, Futabatei depicts Bunzō's estrangement from the world of other people as neurotic and destructive in the scene where Bunzō becomes more and more irritated at Noboru's kidding, finally telling Noboru to leave his aunt's house. It is obvious to the reader that Bunzō is over-reacting, taking as an insult what was meant only as a slightly nasty jibe on the part of an extroverted person. Yet the author does not blame Bunzō here. Rather, he presents a clash between two psychic worlds that are naturally opposed to one another: the world of the introvert, whose self exists far inside him, resisting any superficial evaluation, and that of the extrovert, whose self is exposed easily on the surface. It is a matter of incompatibility of personalities: the one remains locked inside himself and is easily attacked, the other ventures forth too easily and can be accused of attacking others. But the scene is painful, both for Bunzō and for the reader who has been seduced into identifying with him.

The introverted Bunzō is a shy, reserved person with a strong sense of loyalty; he is a man of principle also. These characteristics sound like virtues, but Futabatei shows how they can look equally like vices. On being dismissed from his job, Bunzō is put in the position of being dependent on his aunt and uncle. Eventually he becomes dependent on Noboru also, for it is Noboru, the successful bureaucrat, who could probably manage to have him re-hired, if Bunzō would only speak up for himself, defend his actions, and kowtow to Noboru. However, just at this point Bunzō's love of principle becomes a stubborn insistence not to toady to an unworthy man (Noboru); his shyness a refusal to defend himself and his interests (in Osei) from encroachment by others; his loyalty a passive hanging onto the affection of his aunt and cousin; and his reserve an unhealthy withdrawal from the world of action. Indeed, from the beginning of the novel when he is dismissed from his job, Bunzō is scarcely depicted as a man of action. As an introvert he had probably always tagged along behind other people, reacting to their actions rather than initiating action himself. When he was protected this did not matter, but now, when he should act to save himself, he does not, and retreats into a dangerous world of fantasy. This period begins during the excursion to Dangozaka, when Bunzō stays home in self-pity as Osei goes off with her mother and Noboru. Bunzō makes the introvert's typical mistake of failing to take into account the demands made on him by the outside world, and thus his existence becomes airless and narrow. Finally, his small room with its shabby furniture and its frying pan with the chipped edge becomes symbolic of the stagnant and dreary consciousness of its occupant.

Neither Jung's definition of introversion, nor Futabatei's view of Bunzō as an introvert, indicates that Bunzō is morally wrong. Rather, Bunzō suffers from a lack of self-knowledge that leads him to undervalue the demands made on him by others. Then, too, an excessive amount of self-pride keeps him from looking too closely at his own motives in his dealings with others. However, Bunzō's fundamental weakness is his lack of awareness of other people's inner lives. He continues to see Noboru as his enemy and dreams of revenge, when Noboru has offered, albeit somewhat condescendingly, to help him. He continues to see Osei as a young, powerless girl who is being led astray by Noboru, though it is clear from the novel that Osei is quite able to manipulate Bunzō to attain her ends. He sees Omasa likewise in distorted fashion, as a cold, cruel woman who has mistreated him. Yet when he retires to his room to think about what she has said to him and places her words and behavior in the framework of the events of the several months he has known her, he is able to see things from her point of view. Bunzō is presented sympathetically as he turns Omasa's behavior and words over and over in his mind, trying to discover their meaning. By the end of his session in his room Bunzō is able to understand her completely to the point of forgetting his own demands on her.

Yet when Bunzō goes out of his room to act he bungles the situation. For example, Bunzō realizes, after reflecting a while, that Omasa must have been disappointed that he lost his job, rather than angry at him, for it meant the failure of her plans to have Osei marry him. Then, moved by Omasa's predicament, he resolves to try to please her, but immediately realizes, after a little further thought, that the only way he could please her would be by getting his job back. To do this, he would have to appeal to Noboru, and the thought of pleading with his rival disgusts him. He decides he cannot bear to sacrifice his pride by speaking to Noboru. To avoid facing the knowledge that by deciding not to speak to Noboru he has in fact given up his plan to regain Omasa's favor, he quickly decides to appeal to Osei. If she too urges him to try to persuade Noboru to get his job back for him, he'll know she is not on his side. Yet he really expects that she will support him in his attitude of lonely pride. Thus, Bunzō's step toward action has ended in an appeal to Osei to justify his nonaction. It is not at all surprising to the reader that Osei, when confronted by Bunzō, urges him to seek Noboru's help. However, when she does so, Bunzō accuses her of disloyalty, failing to understand that for Osei, like himself immersed in her private world of values, his joblessness was a practical problem that required action, not merely something as abstract as sympathy or loyalty. After Osei refuses to confirm Bunzō in his nonaction, he retreats to his room, having once more lost the battle in the world of practicality and action. In this way, Bunzō's resolve to do good, which was the fruit of his sincere attempt to understand another person, has been frittered away by his inability to see action itself as important. This is a consequence of his neurotic introversion.

At one point in the novel, after Bunzō has made one of several decisions to solve everything by appealing to Osei's loyalty, the author remarks: "If he were patient just a little while longer, everything would work out all right. Poor Bunzō—he was living in a dream." Indeed, the dream ended quickly enough when he actually talked to Osei, for he had taken into account neither her touchiness, which was caused by his own earlier angry treatment of her as well as her growing awareness of her own sexual desire, nor his own unconscious desire for her. Thus, when he began to talk, the failure of communication was complete. Bunzō wanted to apologize to Osei, but

> As he struggled to get out the words, Osei suddenly stood up. He was caught completely off guard and the printed pattern of her obi dancing before his eyes awakened an impulse within him. He seized her sleeve.
>
> "What are you doing?" Her voice was harsh.
>
> "I just want to talk to you."
>
> "I have no time now." She pulled her sleeve free and quickly left the room.

Somehow Bunzō is unable to express to Osei what he wants to tell her. Also, it is clear that even if he could have, he is not taking into account her own desires as an independent and separate person. Indeed, he does not really want to take into account Osei's separateness because he wants so badly to see himself as inseparably united with her and Omasa.

Bunzō's vision of harmony and unity becomes clearer in the last chapter, when he has failed to take any decisive action whatever to change the unsatisfactory situation. He thinks about why, in spite of all the humiliation he has suffered in the Sonoda household, he still remains there. He admits that a certain personal irresoluteness, a certain love for Osei, and a certain shame at admitting that he had bungled his relationship with her all keep him there. Yet what holds him there above all these is his sense of obligation to the Sonoda family, who are, after all, his relatives,

and to a dream of harmony between them. He looks back on the period a few months earlier when the three of them—Bunzō, Omasa, and Osei—had existed in perfect harmony together, each in a distinct relationship to the other that promised future happiness. That was all destroyed, first by Bunzō's losing his job, then by the entrance of Noboru. Since that time, the female members of the household have been scheming, each in her own way, to get what they want; they are no longer working either in harmony with one another or with him. For Bunzō this vision of disharmony is extraordinarily painful. It is as though Bunzō, as the first individual in Japanese fiction, is looking at the situation of being an individual and finding it painful. The vision of past harmony is so strong that any development beyond it seems fraught with difficulty and, ultimately, regrettable. This is the tone of the last chapter, at least. Bunzō never gives up his dream of restoring harmony, for the book ends with him waiting to speak with Osei, hoping to save her from Noboru and thereby to restore the lost harmony. It seems clear, however, that Bunzō will not be able to do this. Osei is pictured, at the end, as more friendly to Bunzō, but there is no reason to suppose that she has decided to return to the former harmony of the family after once venturing abroad. Also, Bunzō's posture of waiting to make a last appeal to Osei is a repetition of an action he had taken before, without it resulting in a restoration of harmony.

Ukigumo can be said to imply an unhappy ending, though it closes as Bunzō is fixed in his dream of a happy future. Yet whether Bunzō succeeds or not in this particular effort to restore a lost harmony, what is important for Futabatei is his dream of the restoration of a harmony and love between individuals that had existed under the hierarchical system of the past. Bunzō is the carrier of the author's dream of recovering a lost unity between individuals, much as Oblomov was the carrier of Goncharov's dream of the restoration of a lost hierarchical harmony, in *Oblomov*. Bunzō's worth as a person cannot be measured in the old way, as a carrier of virtues or vices. Rather it is his devotion and loyalty to others that have value for the author. Of all the characters in the novel, Bunzō is the most sympathetic, and it is because of precisely this capacity to dream. As a man of action he is ridiculous; compared to Noboru he is a weakling. Yet as a man with an inner vision, one that, though at times clouded with ignorance, is motivated by love, he is a hero. Even though he will fail to restore either the lost harmony of the Sonoda family or the lost harmony of modern Japan, his dream, made serious by continuous concern and attention, will live on. This, Futabatei seems to be saying, is the value of the inner life: that it allows man to live with hope and dignity and love regardless of what is happening to the world outside.

When we consider Bunzō we should not forget that his clinging to the dream of a restored social harmony is connected to his failure in the world of action. The less he is able to function in the external world the more important his inner world of fantasy becomes for him. Yet Bunzō is not insane. He is an ordinary person. Bunzō is, then, a weak hero, a fact that was noticed by an early reviewer of part one of *Ukigumo* when it appeared in the fall of 1887: "Because the author of *Ukigumo* understands the novel, he purposely makes a mediocre, imperfect man his hero." The critic went on to praise Futabatei's fascinating depiction of his hero's vacillations. Yet later in the same review he appeared to have reservations about the "feminine" character of Bunzō, noting that Futabatei had given the feminine qualities of "timidity, gentleness, indecision, pliancy, agility, modesty" to the male characters, specifically Bunzō. Despite his reservations about Bunzō's "non-masculine" character, however, this reviewer, and most critics of *Ukigumo,* found the novel innovative in its realism of character and approved of this innovation. However, as it turned out, Bunzō forecast the type of hero that was to dominate a large part of subsequent Japanese fiction of the individual. How did Bunzō, an unlikely candidate for heroism in any traditional sense, become the new culture hero of the Meiji period? In order to answer this question one must consider the fate of samurai values in the 1880s.

The lower-ranking samurai had brought about the overthrow of the Tokugawa government and gained power for themselves by acting according to time-honored ideals of their class: loyalty to their lord and heroic service to the state. In making the revolution, these leaders, who had suffered under the stagnant rule of the Tokugawa from the lack of opportunity to serve their country, wished to create a society in which samurai ideals could truly be fulfilled. Thanks to the preponderance of this class in positions of power in all spheres of Meiji rule, the samurai ideal of service to the nation dominated the early Meiji period. Under the influence of the samurai ideal that stressed the development of a strong, ethically oriented personality that would find its highest expression in concrete patriotic action, a new kind of economic heroism was given validation. Samuel Smiles's *Self-Help,* the Bible of such heroism in early Meiji, was interpreted as a manual that would inform young men how to serve their country through their economic efforts. Likewise, Defoe's *Robinson Crusoe,* translated already in 1859, was read as an illustration of how the virtue of independence, accompanied by those of initiative and enterprise, could enable a person alone on an island to build a civilization. Consequently, the culture heroes of early Meiji were not only samurai heroes in the traditional vein such as Fukuzawa Yukichi, a tireless educator of his people, or Ōkuma Shigenobu, a gifted politician. Shibusawa Eiichi, a genial entrepreneur, also fulfilled brilliantly the samurai ideal of usefulness to the nation.

It is worth emphasizing that *Self-Help* and *Robinson Crusoe* were acceptable to a reading public influenced by samurai ideals because they presented an ideal of patriotism that, though new, could be fitted into the old Confucian tradition that stressed loyalty and service to the nation. An aspect of the ideal of individualism that could not easily be fitted into the Confucian heroic ideal of service to the nation was the longing for undefined and limitless freedom from political oppression that dominated Japan in the 1880s, when those interested in the attainment of the ideal of human rights were anxiously awaiting the promulgation of the constitution and the holding of the first elections for parliament. A new sort of novel, the political novel (*seiji-shōsetsu*), sprang up to express this new longing for a freedom that went beyond patriotism. As Nakamura Mitsuo phrased it [in *Nihon no kindai shōsetsu, Nakamura Mitsuo zenshū*], these novels "gave the most direct expression to the 'vitality' of the society—especially the youth—which had been roused from the old refuse of the feudal period by the 'unprecedented upheaval' of the Meiji Restoration, which had been awakened to new ideas and new life." The political novels, both translations from Western novels and novels written by the Japanese themselves, spoke for the ideals of independence and human rights that were the center of the People's Rights movement of the time. Works as diverse and of such varying quality as Schiller's *Wilhelm Tell* (translated as "Tell: Story of Freedom" in 1882) and pamphlets dealing with the sufferings of the Russian Nihilists were received enthusiastically by a wide range of readers. (pp. 34-51)

Ukigumo is the true descendant of the political novels of the 1880s, for while the heroes of the political novels were fantasies, mere projections of the dynamic ideal of freedom, Bunzō represents the reality of freedom in the Meiji period: his freedom is an inner freedom only. Bunzō's departure from public life to live a mentalized existence in his room is highly significant for the development of the Japanese novel of the individual, then, for it marks the failure of the traditional samurai ideal of heroic moral action. The early Meiji ethical ideal of *risshin-shusse* (rising in the world and making a name for oneself) had signified individual heroic action, whether in government or business, in the service of the state—in other words, Fukuzawa's ideal of developing individual independence in order to bring about national independence. What Futabatei demonstrates in *Ukigumo,* however, is that the sudden expansion of economic and social opportunity of the early Meiji period placed pressure on individuals to abandon the old samurai ideals of loyalty, social harmony, and devotion to learning and hard work—in short, values of service to the state—in the rush to advance on the social ladder. In the figure of Noboru, whose name appropriately means "to rise," Futabatei depicts an extreme example of a samurai who possesses the new virtues demanded by bureaucratic life: competitiveness, ruthlessness, sycophancy, and superficiality. Noboru is a caricature of the samurai ethical ideal and a forecast of its complete disintegration, for, lacking the reverence for the ideal of national independence that was linked with the early Meiji ideal of *risshin-shusse,* Noboru's attempts to succeed in his petty bureaucratic position reveal him to be a *seikō-seinen* ("success-seeking youth"). From the example of Noboru, who succeeds in the new style of life centered around the bureaucracy, it is clear that, though the samurai had brought about the Meiji Restoration, ultimately they failed to create a society in which their ideals could be fulfilled.

By contrast, in the character Bunzō, Futabatei has portrayed a person imbued with almost all the true samurai ethical ideals: love of learning, loyalty, desire for social harmony, devotion to principle—yet the corruption of the ethical system, in a time of rapid change, makes it impossible for him to act. For the samurai of the past, the attainment of virtue was useless without the opportunity to manifest it in ethical action. In *Ukigumo* Futabatei portrays a situation in which an individual educated according to samurai ethics is asked to harness his ideals of maintaining high standards and working with devotion for the good of the state to the petty aims of a bureaucracy: carrying out meaningless paper work and serving a petty, ignorant boss. In a situation where action is impossible, virtue becomes useless decoration, and, seen from the samurai point of view, Bunzō becomes a superfluous man. Like the high-principled, educated gentry of the 1840s in Russia who wanted reform but were kept from action and driven to excessive self-absorption by the oppressive atmosphere of tyranny and stagnation in still feudal Russia, Bunzō and members of the samurai class like him can be seen as frustrated by the authoritarian feudal environment of the early Meiji period. As Futabatei created him, Bunzō is a Japanese Oblomov, who, because he does not value his bureaucratic job as a means to manifest his virtues, is not sorry to lose it.

Yet Bunzō is not only a samurai, he is also an individual. Consequently, he has values other than those of his social class. If one looks at him negatively, as a failed samurai, Bunzō conspicuously lacks one of the most important samurai virtues: the desire to do great deeds for the state. Thus, it is not that he is kept from action by the daily minor harassment and pettiness of the bureaucracy, but rather that he lacks interest in action itself. Bunzō does not value action, not even enough to restore the social harmony that is being lost in his very household, a microcosm of Meiji society. His spirit is far from that of Saigō Takamori, the hero that the youthful Futabatei admired because of his attempt to restore a lost feudal harmony. Looked at positively, in terms of his own individualized virtues, Bunzō is an authentic introvert whose talent lies in the contemplative rather than in the active realm. Like Goncharov's Oblomov, he was born not to act but to dream, to feel, and to accomplish small unseen miracles in his heart, which for him is the center of the universe. It is the lack of a tradition of introverted literature that prevented Futabatei from making Bunzō's virtues shine forth more clearly—for where Oblomov, even in the midst of his laziness, inspires his friends Stolz and Olga through his virtues, Bunzō only appears to be a failure. For Omasa he is good-for-nothing, for Noboru he is ridiculous, and for Osei he is old-fashioned. The introvert's existence is a bungled one in *Ukigumo,* as it is not in Futabatei's models, the novels of Goncharov, Turgenev, and Dostoevsky. For Bunzō there is no hope of fruitful interaction with the distant world of the others, as there is no hope of reconciliation between the values of the individual and those of Meiji society.

Futabatei's presentation of Bunzō as the new hero of the age, and the appearance of Bunzō's successors, the introverted heroes of the I-novel after the turn of the century, were signs of the decline of the samurai ideal of heroism. Yet the appearance of a hero whose sphere was not action but feeling, and who was unique rather than virtuous, also meant the end of the hold that Confucian moralism had had on fiction. In the Tokugawa era, fiction was written under a manipulative aesthetic; it was used to enforce certain moral attitudes beneficial to the state: obedience, loyalty, selflessness, ethical heroism. (pp. 53-6)

Futabatei's *Ukigumo* was the first modern Japanese novel to embody a contemplative aesthetic. In the figure of Bunzō the author presents a person whose individual values are at the center of the world: Bunzō fantasizes, analyzes, dreams, and Bunzō is in love. All of these activities are validated by the author in paragraph after paragraph of analysis that is at times loving, at times irritated or amused, but always respectful. Not since the Heian fictional masterpieces had there been a novel where the character's inner world was respected and where eccentricity (here in the modern form of psychological depth) was admired. (p. 57)

> Janet A. Walker, "Futabatei's 'Ukigumo' (The Floating Clouds): The First Novel of the Individual," in her The Japanese Novel of the Meiji Period and the Ideal of Individualism, Princeton University Press, 1979, pp. 30-61.

Donald Keene   (essay date 1984)

[*Keene is one of the foremost American translators and critics of Japanese literature. In the following excerpt, he details how Futabatei's realistic depiction of Japanese culture was an important influence on later Japanese writers, focusing his discussion on* The Drifting Clouds.]

The Drifting Cloud was received with warmth and even acclaim by critics of the day. Although it marked a radical departure from the works hitherto translated from or influenced by Western literature, there was little of the conservative resistance we might have expected. The hero—or perhaps anti-hero—Utsumi Bunzō is a young man of the samurai class living in Tokyo with relatives, waiting for the time when his finances will permit him to send for his mother from the provinces. As the book opens, however, we learn that he has been fired from his job in the government, apparently not because of incompetence but because of his unwillingness to toady to his superior. When he breaks the sad news to the aunt with whom he lives, she is furious. The aunt, Omasa, intended Bunzō to marry her daughter, Osei, but an unemployed son-in-law is out of the question. She contrasts Bunzō with his friend Noboru, an industrious and sociable young man. . . . Noboru has not been fired: on the contrary, he has been given a raise in salary. The girl Osei, though attracted to her timid cousin, a model of samurai morality, falls under the spell of Noboru's glib and confident chatter. For a time it looks as if she will marry him, but the rising young bureaucrat has higher aspirations—the pretty young sister-in-law of his section chief—and his visits become infrequent. The book ends inconclusively. Most critics believe that Futabatei left it unfinished, but perhaps he deliberately wished to leave in the air his hint that Osei might relent toward Bunzō after all.

Unlike the over-plotted novels of the late Tokugawa period, or [Tsubouchi Shōyō's] *Characters of Modern Students,* **The Drifting Cloud** is devoid of scenes of violence, excitement, lovemaking, or any other exceptional circumstances, and the characters seem to typify Meiji society rather than stand out by virtue of their unusual qualities. As in so many Meiji novels, the names of characters were apparently intended to suggest their roles. Bunzō is the man of *bun*, the Confucian-minded literatus; Noboru's name means "to climb"; and one meaning of the character used for Osei's name is "impulse." Nakamura Mitsuo suggested that Futabatei originally meant the fickle Osei to be the principal character of the work: in her superficial Westernisms, her uncertain veering between Bunzō and Noboru (the old and the new), and her lack of any strong will of her own, she is the "drifting cloud" par excellence, and also a symbol of the Japanese people of Futabatei's day. Futabatei's aim in the novel was a criticism of contemporary Japanese culture, and not merely a naturalistic depiction of society. The characters are believable and the details show the marks of careful observation. Above all, Futabatei wanted to express by means of these outward forms, his perceptions of inner truth, a concept of the function of literature that he borrowed from [Vissarions] Belinsky.

But if Futabatei intended to treat Osei as the central, symbolic figure, he clearly changed his mind while writing Part II. The action develops almost entirely in terms of Bunzō's thoughts and his reactions to the other characters. Part III lacks the humor that made the first two parts enjoyable, perhaps because Futabatei had come to identify himself increasingly with the unhappy Bunzō. [In his *Futabatei Shimeiden*] Nakamura Mitsuo wrote, "*The Drifting Cloud,* as far as the author was concerned, may be said to be a novel that began as a criticism of Japanese culture and ended up by being a criticism of himself." Nakamura further suggested that this was the reason why Futabatei had given up the novel: he could not continue merely to describe Bunzō objectively; he had in his own life to find a solution to Bunzō's problems.

This may be why Futabatei could not finish the work. But for all the inconsistencies Nakamura detected in the portrayal of Bunzō, he remains [what Marleigh Grayer Ryan, in her *Japan's First Modern Novel: Ukigumo of Futabatei Shimei* terms] a conspicuously "superfluous hero." His inability at crucial moments to act or speak appropriately may remind readers especially of Goncharov's Oblomov, the supreme example of the lethargic hero. But there is an important difference. Goncharov clearly did not sympathize with or identify himself with Oblomov; he seems instead to have intended the character to serve as an example of the overcivilized, ineffectual aristocracy. Bunzō, for all his ineptitude, is more attractive than the aggressive and successful Noboru, and his refusal to compromise with samurai morality, though it seemed quixotic in the new Meiji era, is affecting, whether expressed in his shyness before his cousin, his timidity before his vulgar, money-minded aunt, or in his refusal to allow Noboru to intercede for him with the section chief. His actions are motivated not by self-seeking but by decency. But he is all the same superfluous in a society that has ceased to prize this kind of virtue. His rival, Noboru, will undoubtedly succeed in his ambitions to get ahead in the world, but this does not make him admirable, let alone endearing. Osei, a girl infatuated with Western ways, vacillates between Bunzō, who is unquestionably devoted to her but ineffectual, and Noboru, who amuses her but is ready to discard her if this will advance his career. Omasa stands for the old Japan at its least attractive; she is a *chōnin,* as seen by a samurai—indifferent to anything besides money.

Futabatei surely had an allegorical intent, but that was not why *The Drifting Cloud* was a success when it appeared, nor what excited the writers of the Naturalist school when they rediscovered the work about 1905, praising it as the first modern novel, a reputation it has retained. It was successful first of all because of the characters. They are of no great profundity or subtlety, certainly when compared to those in the great Russian novels, but they are believable as human beings to a degree unknown in earlier Meiji literature. Realism is apparent, not merely in the use of effective details (in the manner of Saikaku), nor in the exactness of the conversations (in the manner of Shunsui or Ikku), but in the personalities, given the contradictions and ambiguities of real people. They are three-dimensional or, in the words of a Meiji critic, "The characters in most novels these days resemble figures in woodblock prints. The characters in *The Drifting Cloud* however are people in oil paintings." Critic after critic expressed the thrill of discovery that a work written by a Japanese and faithfully describing contemporary Japanese society could possess the depth and intensity of a European novel. Futabatei did not imitate any single Russian writer but, steeping himself in the literary principles of the Russian novel, he addressed himself to his own society. His success can be measured in terms of the kind of praise *The Drifting Cloud* received; it would probably never have occurred to the reviewer of any earlier Japanese novel to write: "*The Drifting Cloud* is a study of the human mind; its author is a master of analyzing human emotions."

The Drifting Cloud was a success for another, no less important reason. It was the first novel written almost entirely in the colloquial. *The Characters of Modern Students* has long passages in the style of Bakin, and even [Tsubouchi's] "The Wife" reserves the colloquial for the conversations, but Futabatei, once past the first few, stylistically uncertain chapters, made superb use of the colloquial, both in narrative and in dialogue. The creation of a literarily acceptable colloquial style cost him enormous efforts, if only because of the universal conviction that the colloquial could not be employed to express poetic or elevated thoughts. Even such an apparently trivial matter as the level of politeness appropriate for the copula verb cost Futabatei much anguish. His experiences as a translator of Russian fiction undoubtedly helped to decide him that the colloquial was capable of a wide variety of literary effects, and on the whole he resisted Tsubouchi's suggestions that the descriptions be heightened by an admixture of classical phrases. Contrary to Tsubouchi's expectations, the occasional lapses into the conventional literary language were the only parts of the book adversely criticized. (pp. 109-13)

During the long period when Futabatei ceased to publish his own fiction, he was nearly forgotten because the quite different kinds of novels associated with the Ken'yūsha group dominated the literary scene. When the reaction against that school came, it took the form of Naturalism. Futabatei was rediscovered and his colloquial style was now acclaimed as the only acceptable literary style. Futabatei was persuaded to write again. He started one manuscript, abandoned it, then began to publish serially *Sono omokage* (*In His Image*) at the end of 1906. This novel is technically superior to *The Drifting Cloud* but it is also more conventional and borders on the melodramatic. The central character, Ono Tetsuya, is a decent, intelligent man but a failure as a professor, seemingly because he has been emasculated by his wife and mother-in-law, who never let him forget that he was adopted into the wife's family and his educational expenses were paid for by the girl's father. His only comfort is his wife's half-sister, Osayo. Gradually he realizes he is in love, a rare instance of middle-aged love in Meiji fiction. He and Osayo become lovers, but Osayo, who has given herself to Ono out of sympathy, is a devout Christian, and when reproached by another Christian for having yielded to the temptations of the flesh, she at once terminates the affair. Ono is broken when this last possibility of happiness is denied him. At the end we see him as a drunken beggar in China, wandering from place to place in filthy rags.

Not only can parallels be drawn between Bunzō and Ono, but between Noboru and Ono's prosperous friend Hamura. The book opens with a scene identical to that of the opening of *The Drifting Cloud:* two men of totally dissimilar natures, technically friends, discuss a matter painful to the more decent of the two—in this case a proposal that Osayo become the mistress of a rich old man. Some critics taxed Futabatei for an insufficiency of creative imagination, pointing at the excessive resemblances between the two novels; but *In His Image* fails not because Ono resembles Bunzō but because the manner is dreary, suggesting the worst of the Naturalist school. *In His Image* lacks the spontaneity and humor that make *The Drifting Cloud* so memorable; it suggests an effort of will rather than of the heart.

It was nevertheless generally well received, and Futabatei was encouraged to write another serialized novel. . . . *Heibon* (*Mediocrity*) began to appear at the end of 1907. It is told in the first person, and scene after scene is reminiscent of incidents in Futabatei's own life, though the circumstances are often twisted. The first visit of the hero, then a struggling and unknown writer, to an older master who lives in squalid surroundings despite his fame, recalls Futabatei's visit to Tsubouchi, though the treatment is satiric. The best part of *Mediocrity,* the section describing a boy's love for his dog, was also based on Futabatei's experience, though given a different meaning by changing the age of the dog's owner from twenty-nine (when Futabatei lost his beloved dog) to eleven. The innocent love of the boy for his dog, contrasted with the sordid circumstances of his affair with a chambermaid years later, is the only example in Futabatei's fiction of pure and wholehearted love, unclouded by selfishness or feelings of guilt. These touching pages end with the dog being wantonly killed, perhaps because he did not distrust men enough.

Futabatei created no heroes in his fiction. Bunzō, Ono, and the narrator of *Mediocrity* are ordinary men. If more talented than most, they are also less effective. The judgment the narrator of *Mediocrity* passes on himself is: "If I live, I am not the least good to the world, and though I die, nobody can lose by it except my wife and child. From the world's point of view, I am a superfluous man whose existence or nonexistence is of no moment." Perhaps that was Futabatei's voice speaking about himself; it was certainly the judgment he passed on Bunzō and Ono. The book ends with the narrator, disgusted with his own writings and even with the praise they have won, expressing his doubts on the value of literature. The final sentence is left unfinished.

Tsubouchi and Futabatei deserve the greatest credit for the creation of modern Japanese literature. Both men turned to the West for inspiration, but not with the thought of mere imitation. They were determined to create a literature true to their new society. When Tsubouchi recognized that he was not Futabatei's equal as a novelist he gave up fiction; Futabatei's conviction that he would never equal Turgenev led to the same decision. Nevertheless, their works of fiction, criticism, and translation not only rank as major products of the Meiji era but served as the foundation for the even more impressive works to come. (pp. 113-15)

> *Donald Keene, "Tsubouchi Shōyō and Futabatei Shimei," in his* Dawn to the West, Japanese Literature of the Modern Era: Fiction, Vol. 1, *Holt, Rinehart and Winston, 1984, pp. 96-118.*

FURTHER READING

Okazaki, Yoshie. *Japanese Literature in the Meiji Period.* Translated by V. H. Viglielmo. Tokyo: Ōbunsha, 1955, 673 p.

> Discusses Futabatei's work in relation to various literary movements of Meiji Japan.

Walker, Janet A. "The Fusion of Japanese and Western Poetic Systems in Two Works of Modern Japanese Fiction." In *Proceedings of the Xth Congress of the International Comparative Literature Association,* edited by Claudio Guillen, pp. 681-86. New York: Garland Publishing, 1985.

> Examines *The Drifting Clouds* and Natsume Sōseki's *Kokoro* (*Human Feeling*) as the first novels of the Meiji period to combine "Western linearity with Japanese sequentiality."

Klabund

1890-1928

(Pseudonym of Alfred Henschke) German novelist, short story writer, poet, dramatist, essayist, lyricist, and journalist.

INTRODUCTION

Klabund was one of the most celebrated German writers during the period between the two world wars. Although he is best known for his works adapted from Chinese literature, particularly his drama *Der Kreidekreis* (*The Circle of Chalk*), Klabund is also noted for novels that are considered exemplary of German Expressionist prose and for autobiographical fiction in which his suffering from tuberculosis is the central subject. While his output was prolific and diverse, ranging from folk poetry to political satire to experimental fiction, critics have observed that Klabund's oeuvre is unified by two constants: his attention to the political and social context in which he was writing and an awareness of his own mortality.

Klabund was born to a middle-class family in Crossen on the Oder River. Diagnosed as tubercular in 1906, he was nonetheless able to pursue his studies of literature and philosophy at universities in Lausanne, Munich, and Berlin. He spent the remainder of his life in Berlin except during periods of treatment at Swiss and Italian sanatoriums. His first published works were erotic poems that appeared in 1913 in the journal *Pan.* The atheist philosophy expressed in one of these poems led to his prosecution for blasphemy. Public attention to the trial and testimony on behalf of Klabund provided by the dramatist Frank Wedekind and the poet Richard Dehmel contributed to the notoriety of Klabund and his writings. Until this time Klabund had published under his given name, Alfred Henschke, but, beginning with *Morgenrot! Klabund! Die Tage dämmern!,* employed the pseudonym under which he would publish all his subsequent works. This pseudonym was formed from (Kla)bautermann ("hobgoblin") and Vaga(bund) ("wanderer") and defined by Klabund as "change." In both his life and work Klabund fulfilled the intentions declared in his pseudonym. During the First World War, he supported German interests and published two collections of patriotic war poetry. Toward the end of the war, however, Klabund became a vocal opponent of the government, publishing his call for the Kaiser's abdication in the Swiss newspaper *Neue Zuricher Zeitung* and serving a prison sentence for his alleged involvement with the revolutionary Spartakus movement. Throughout his career, Klabund's commitment to his writing and his political activities, which were generally expressions of his concern for pacifist causes, were complicated by his tuberculosis. Echoing Klabund's experience, a character in his novel *Die Krankheit* sardonically states, "Everywhere I lived for

my health, as they so nicely put it, but was I not living for my illness?" In 1918 Klabund's wife and daughter died from tuberculosis; he remarried in 1925. In the same year, he achieved popular and literary success with *The Circle of Chalk,* a drama that was widely translated and performed throughout Europe. Klabund died in 1928 at Davos, Switzerland. In 1933, due to Klabund's reputation as a proponent of liberal ideals and the fact that his second wife was Jewish, the Nazis suppressed his works for their "degeneracy."

Klabund's most important works as a poet, dramatist, and novelist focus on contemporary political issues and autobiographical subjects. His poems take their subject matter from a variety of sources, including the Berlin lumpen proletariat, as in the case of *Die Harfenjule,* a political work advocating the plight of the destitute; German folk songs, evident in Klabund's cabaret lyrics; and personal experience, exemplified by the ballad "Totenklage," written in mourning after the death of his first wife. Klabund also found sources for his poetry in Chinese literature. His "translations" were popular with readers and critics, an indication of his dexterity as a writer, since his knowledge of Chinese was rudimentary and he depended almost entirely on French versions of the originals. Klabund's interest in Chinese literature led to his reworking of the parable play *Hoei lan kia,* written by Li Hsingtao during the Yüan Dynasty (1259-1368) and rendered by Klabund as *The Circle of Chalk.* The original play combines verse and prose in representing a young woman's struggle to prove her innocence before a corrupt court controlled by a despotic government. Klabund's drama introduces the melodramatic subplot of the travails of separated lovers and abandons the original stress placed upon the theme of justice. Klabund's romanticized version of the Chinese drama, particularly his investigation of morality and ethics, strongly influenced Bertolt Brecht's play *Der kaukasische Kreidekreis* (1948; *The Caucasian Chalk Circle*).

Like his poetry and drama, Klabund's fiction is concerned with both the personal and political. Along with such autobiographical works as *Spuk* and *Die Krankheit,* Klabund also wrote allegorical novels, including *Pjotr* (*Peter the Czar*), *Borgia* (*The Incredible Borgias*), and *Bracke* (*Brackie, the Fool*), which is considered his greatest prose work. While Klabund's novels make use of historical subjects, they are thinly veiled critiques of the corruption and authoritarianism that he perceived in the Weimar government. In *Brackie, the Fool,* which is set during the Reformation, the vagabond Brackie first becomes an artist and later a political advisor to the German government. Because he is a pacifist and humanist, Brackie's convictions contrast sharply with the government's promotion of force. Klabund capitalizes on irony throughout the narrative of *Brackie, the Fool.* For example, whereas German epics of medieval conquerors and conquests were used in both the late Weimar period and the sixteenth century to justify the advancement of militarism, Klabund undermines governmental propaganda by basing Brackie's utopianism on similar "Blood and Soil" legends. Klabund's other novels, like *Brackie, the Fool,* are regarded as effective satires that avoid sacrificing artistry to ideology.

PRINCIPAL WORKS

Celestina [as Alfred Henschke] (short stories) 1912
Morgenrot! Klabund! Die Tage dämmern! (poetry) 1913
Klabunds Karussel (short stories) 1914
Kleines Bilderbuch vom Krieg (poetry) 1914
Dumpfe Trommel und berauschtes Gong (poetry) 1915
Die Himmelsleiter (poetry) 1916
Li tai-pe (poetry) 1916; enlarged edition, 1923
Moreau (novel) 1916
Das ideale Kaberet (songs) 1917
Die Krankheit (novel) 1917
Mohammed (novel) 1917; revised edition, 1921
Bracke: Ein Eulenspiegel-Roman (novel) 1918; revised editions, 1924 and 1932
　　[*Brackie, the Fool,* 1927]
Die Geisha O-Sen (poetry) 1918
Irene, oder die Gesinnung (songs) 1918

Der himmlische Vagrant: Ein lyrisches Porträt des François Villon (poetry) 1919
Hört! Hört! Ein politisch-satirisches Gedicht (poetry) 1919
Montezuma (poetry) 1919
Die Nachtwandler (drama) 1920
Die Sonette auf Irene (poetry) 1920
Franziskus (novella) 1921
Spuk (novel) 1922
Pjotr (novel) 1923
　　[*Peter the Czar,* 1925]
Der Kreidekreis (drama) 1925
　　[*The Circle of Chalk,* 1929]
Die Harfenjule: Neue Zeit-, Streit- und Leidgedichte (songs) 1927
Borgia (novel) 1928
　　[*The Incredible Borgias,* 1929]
XYZ (drama) 1928
Rasputin (novel) 1929
Gesammelte Werke in Einzelausgaben. 6 vols. (novels, novellas, short stories, poetry, dramas, essays, and songs) 1930

Donald Douglas (essay date 1927)

[*In the following excerpt, Douglas praises* Brackie, the Fool *for its realistic rendering of sixteenth-century Germany.*]

If you have no time or patience for contemporary documents and old histories you can gain no more thrilling entrance to the medieval world than through Klabund's **Peter the Czar** and **Brackie the Fool.** To many it will seem like a nightmare wherein monks and hangmen and emperors and fools utter appalling words of doom and gibber like epileptic saints. Yet it's the world where once men lived before science charted and explained the heavens and the earth and the waters under the earth and the phantasms of the mind. Though now we may not know all things we at least have no cause for fear. We understand how to outwit tempests and no longer think them visitations of divine wrath. When we sicken with plagues we hunt down the bacillus to his lair and more or less know just what to do. We don't jam into churches and beat on our breasts and implore forgiveness for our sins. There has been no sin: some one has sneezed in our face in the subway. We don't shake with fear lest a planet come tumbling upon our cities as a portent of the last judgment. No longer do demons skulk in haunted forests and angels glitter in bright legions in the blue arch of the sky. Death is no longer a cowled skeleton who shambles like a ghost through the narrow streets of the town. We *know.*

These things have been, and there's not much use in pretending that Klabund does no more than just work up a fine poetic frenzy about the Middle Ages. It's not a rhapsody in medieval blues, but a document of the most exact realism of a time where gargoyle and angel sat craggy jowl by downy cheek and emperors renounced the world for the stone cells of a monastery and fools gave out a divine stutter of mystical inspiration. Brackie is both Till Eulenspiegel and medieval saint. He's priest and idiot, philosopher and fool, sin and innocence, lecher and Galahad, who pulls the beards of emperors, keeps company with hangmen and gravediggers, the familiar of heaven and the coadjutor of hell. When the Elector of Brandenburg asks Brackie to train actors for a mystery play of the Nativity Brackie has the parts played by a hangman, a knacker, a murderer and a harlot; and all as a reproof to the sadistic and dissolute life of the Elector. As a privileged fool of the court he plays grotesque tricks on the nobility, waylays and hangs a knight who robs merchants, wanders like an outcast through town and wood and valley, always that he may destroy evil with a fool's paradoxes and weaken the cause of the corrupt aristocracy and bring men and women to the love of nature and animals and to all human kindness and sweetness and tolerance.

In the true and only sense of the word Brackie is a saint. He's no curate of impeccable, flaccid virtue who chides sinners without himself ever having entered the house of sin. Like all the real saints of his time he has been lover and Puritan, warrior and man of peace, the devil's advocate and the friend of God. He scolds the Elector, tells him all the dreadful truth about the license of the court and the oppression of the people; and yet he makes love to the Elector's wife. He loves his own wife dearly and once spends the night with a girl of the streets. He preaches peace and at the last stabs the Elector with his own dagger. The people rise from their mud and destroy the government. The hangman is to lop the head of the Princess-Elector, and at the last moment he marries her by his hereditary right that any hangman may marry his victim if he abstains from his purpose of execution. Can you fancy that sort of thing being done in the modern world? And so the gorgeous and terrible processional goes by, with Popes in gorgeous raiment and monks eaten by hair shirts, with emperors who tolerate fools and fools who do not tolerate emperors, with the world showing like a nightmare, blood and pestilence hanging like a fume in the oozy streets, men crying aloud to God, and the king and the fool knowing each other as brothers of one flesh.

In these later days the world lies before us plumbed and measured and without heart. Good and evil are no longer monsters walking visibly by night. Yet here in **Brackie the Fool** is the old, unhappy, far-off, medieval world wrapped in a fiery garment of pain and terror and splendor woven both of the bright robe of heaven and the worm-devoured cloak of hell.

> *Donald Douglas, "The Gothic World," in* New York Herald Tribune Books, *April 24, 1927, p. 3.*

Ivor Brown   (essay date 1929)

[*Brown was an English essayist, novelist, journalist, dramatist, and critic. In the following excerpt, he reviews a performance of* The Circle of Chalk, *which was produced by Basil Dean from James Laver's translation of Klabund's drama.*]

[**The Circle of Chalk** is] a pigtail feuilleton made succulent

with the romanticism that is more of Chinatown than of China.

As I listened to the piece it seemed to me odd that out of the Ancient East should have come a tale so well calculated to arouse emotional vibrations in the hearts of the modern West. The little victim of the Yellow Slave Traffic who is loved by the Prince and ultimately rescued by him when he has become Emperor so that she can marry the Son of Heaven and be just too frightfully happy ever after, is a figure whom one imagines to be more native to *Peg's Paper* than to Old Peking. On receiving a copy of Mr. Laver's text, I was able to verify my suspicions. Klabund was a German poet and journalist who found a hundred-year-old French translation of **The Circle of Chalk.** The piece was a feature of fourteenth-century Chinese Repertory, but Klabund knew quite well that this is a world of progress and that the simple and ruthless ethics of Oriental medievalism would never do for a Europe in which the combined forces of Censorship, Sob Stuff, and Sex Appeal are the pastors and masters of the Tragic Muse:

> Klabund was compelled, for Western taste, to make two important modifications in the original play—he had to tone down its ruthlessness, and he had to provide what is called "love-interest." Hence the introduction of the Emperor, and (in Chinese eyes) the entirely immoral part which he is called upon to play. The mere fact of Hi-tang's marrying again would be repugnant to Chinese standards; it was enough, for the original author, that she was vindicated—and revenged. The West has substituted Humanitarianism for Morality, and we, being Westerners, can hardly regret that this change is reflected in Klabund's play.

Mr. Laver's parting irony is good. We, being Westerners, must apparently welcome any mawkish nonsense of the "Prince-and-the-Beggar-Maid" order and be glad that a realistic story of ugly passions has been partly romanticized. But the curious fact remains that, while Klabund made the plot safe for the film-fed millions, he (or is it only Mr. Laver?) none the less wrote in an idiom of high-brow humour which will pass by those millions as surely as it will strike a few as deliciously quaint. Take the opening. We are approached by Tong, a fat eunuch, pander, and tea-house proprietor, who soliloquizes thus:

> I have the honour to introduce myself. My despicably low-class name is Tong. It sounds, does it not, as though somebody were striking a gong, slightly out of tune? I am the proprietor of this modest, but really first-class establishment. My "savoir-vivre" and good taste, qualities of mine which are generally acknowledged by the most exalted of my customers, forbid me the importunities of extravagant commendation and the vulgarities of self-advertisement.

Tong, it need hardly be explained, is one of Klabund's creations. Indeed, one can see him leering out of a German cartoon, and he made me thirsty for a mug of Münchener.

I hope I am no pedant and I do not ask of the late Klabund, of Mr. James Laver, or of Mr. Basil Dean an exact and exacting loyalty to the Chinese theatre in the time of

Jenghiz Khan. Let us have our Tongs and our sugar of sentiment too, so it be handsomely done. (p. 390)

> Ivor Brown, "Chin Chon Chino," in The Saturday Review, *London, Vol. 147, No. 3830, March 23, 1929, pp. 390-91.*

The New York Times Book Review   (essay date 1929)

[*In the following excerpt, the critic comments on the lack of historical verisimilitude in* The Incredible Borgias, *a work that he nevertheless recommends for its inventiveness and entertainment value.*]

The title of the latest book by Klabund to be translated into English does not belie its contents. The author succeeds admirably in making the Borgias thoroughly incredible, but since it is meant to be, as the subtitle indicates, "an impressionistic panorama," one cannot quarrel.

Klabund is entirely within his rights in making what use he pleases of the material at his disposal. He deliberately sets out to give a picture of the infamous Borgia family which, while true only in outline to historic fact, will, nevertheless, by suggestion and emphasis on certain traits, render their characters with the same fidelity that a caricature depicts its subject. His success is at best debatable, but in the process a thoroughly enjoyable book is produced, whose pages glow with lust, violence, hatred, greed, corruption.

This is the second of Klabund's biographical studies to be translated into English. He has written others on Mohammed, Moreau, Rasputin and Peter the Great. . . . Klabund, incidentally, is a pseudonym for Alfred Henschke. The book called **Peter the Czar** was written in the same vein as **The Incredible Borgias.** Having only one main character to follow, it was less incoherent than the present book, and the figure of Peter was better adapted to Klabund's violent, distorted method of presentation than the Borgias.

For though their vices were enormous, the Borgias were exceedingly human. In fact, the Renaissance was full of such characters, the great difference being that in the case of the Borgias, the sacredness of the Holy Office with which they were connected tinged their actions with a blasphemy which has horrified succeeding generations, as well as their own. But that sacredness lay in the minds of outsiders—Rodrigo and Cesare and Lucrezia were certainly unconscious of it.

In order, therefore, to give the proper coloring of "incredibility" to their characters, the author is forced to make monsters of them—creatures of unutterable bestiality and viciousness. Nothing is too bad for them in his pages. Except for Lucrezia, who is grudgingly granted a few of the many virtues she undoubtedly possessed, there is not a single ray of light to pierce the gloom and horror of the inferno Klabund makes of their lives.

Every breath of scandal that blew upon them is here given as gospel truth; every rumor of incest, rape, poison and treachery has its place in this book as authentic. Some of the incidents are true; many are false, but the reader is left no choice.

If one takes this book, as it is perhaps meant, purely in the form of entertainment (much as one reads Edgar Saltus's *The Imperial Purple*), it is hard to surpass. It is vivid, colorful, fascinating, and once started is difficult to abandon. The book carries the Borgia family to its extinction. One by one they die—Juan, Alexander, Cesare, Lucrezia. All who bore the name of Borgia are driven from Italy, and then the incredible really happened, for the Borgias actually produced a saint! He was the Jesuit, Juan Borgia, who became General of the society in 1565. After his death he was canonized as Saint Francis Borgia.

It is a strange ending for a strange book, which gives such a fascinating account of the Borgias that one sets it down with a regretful sigh, and the thought: "What a pity it isn't true!"

> "Klabund's Violent Tale of the Borgias," in The New York Times Book Review, *October 27, 1929, p. 4.*

Wolfgang Paulsen   (essay date 1939)

[*Paulsen is a German linguist, critic, and educator. In the following excerpt, he investigates the intimate relationship between Klabund's life and work, particularly as exemplified in* Brackie, the Fool.]

Klabund's spiritual life is determined by two factors which, although diametrically opposed, are nevertheless closely related and must necessarily colour every expression of life, however slight: his fateful experience of death and his wild desire for life. For him art and life were in a very profound sense one. Hence it was impossible for him to create a work of art any less free from dross than the life from which it was drawn. And just as we accept human life as a whole with all its beauties and weaknesses, so we must accept as a whole each work of Klabund's which is drawn from his own experience.

His work is self-experience in the highest sense of the word. The course of the poet's own life, sketched with but a few strokes is sufficient to show that he had no time for trifling. The continual change in which he himself saw the purpose of his life, means nothing else but the continuous advance of a man who wants to grasp every facet of life. As he wrote:

> My name Klabund.
> That means change.
> My father was called phantom
> My mother vision.

Alfred Henschke, a son of a chemist, was born in 1890 in Crossen on the Oder. As early as his sixteenth year tuberculosis became apparent and drove him, hungry for life, from town to town, from country to country.

> From Locarno to Borkum, Bückeberg, Gardone-Riviera, Arco, Swinemünde, Reichenhall, Arosa, Lugano, Davos, Wehrawald and back to Davos again. Everywhere I lived for my health, as they so nicely put it, but was I not living for

my illness? I remember a sanatorium in the Black Forest where our nurse and masseur was also gravedigger in the little village. The restrooms looked out onto the churchyard. A cheerful symbol. With me it is even worse. I am patient, nurse, gravedigger all in one person.

Thus Klabund makes his Sylvester in the story **Illness** speak as though of himself. For twenty-two years he carried death within him, for twenty-two years he struggled, for twenty-two years his ever new farewell lasted—twenty-two years he resisted the deadening of his faculties. But his fate was inevitable. Even for the young man, just becoming conscious of himself, death was an immediate reality, the one essential factor, in the face of which everything else became empty and unreal. Death is destruction, the destruction of the individual—and all he desired was life and creation. The fool Brackie, Klabund's spiritual image, is most profoundly aware of how closely united life and death are, and that one must wish for life in sheer defiance of death: 'Hatred of murder, hymn to life—even in the humblest form. Embrace of masterful hearts—in spite of death, in spite of affliction, in spite of Elector, Emperor and edict.'

Only along these two lines of thought is Klabund able to think: he sees life which is retreating more and more, and death, approaching ever nearer. Indeed, poetic existence is always in some form or other creative reaction to the ex-

Woodcut of Klabund by the expressionist Erich Büttner.

perience of death; but Klabund did not experience death as an idea but as a reality, just as in mediaeval woodcuts the spectre always stands in the background of the picture, waiting. Its outward forms manifold, but for Klabund it is embodied in illness and this illness is for him the basis of his earthly existence. 'Everywhere I lived for my health—but was I not living for my illness?' Illness makes him different from all other men. It makes him susceptible to irritation in a high degree, 'more transparent, more crystal-clear and as it were more inwardly transformed.' 'Since I am slowly dying, I have become a poet. One must take whatever opportunity offers. Men such as I, experience no real adventure because of the trivial adventurings of life!'

Thus he who had the mark of death upon him becomes a glorifier of life, a very fanatic for life in every form and in every degree and the more his strength ebbs, the more insatiable the yearning becomes. For however much he struggles, it is death alone which he holds in his hands, just as a 'horrible fear of transitoriness' takes hold of Brackie directly after his deepest experience of love. 'He looked down at his body and realized he was perishing. He wanted to tear down heaven itself and cried: I will not die! I will not die!'

But was not the whole age, in which the poet lived, standing thus between life and death? Did he not as an individual fatefully repeat on a smaller scale this, his age? The generation of the War and post-War years had experienced death as an immediate reality. The despair of the youth of Klabund's day, this not knowing whither to turn, was a despairing of life in the face of death. The western world seemed to be bleeding to death and not only on the battlefields. There was no longer any sphere of life, where one could take refuge. All forces were paralysed, and however great the longing for something new—their strength was powerless to realize it. Everywhere the same devastating emptiness was evident, for the standards of spiritual values no longer existed. Everything spiritual had proved itself too weak to bring the death and senseless slaughter of the war to a standstill. If you wished therefore to discover life in essence, you had to learn to cast everything aside and seek in naked sensuality alone the pulsating rhythm of life.

That is the meaning of the eroticism which colours the literature of this age. The body becomes life itself. The mere possession of a body brought to each individual the belief that he had found his way back to the springs of human existence and its sources of power. And all Klabund's heroes struggle for the physical life. Only the fact that even for them there is still no rest in mere carnal sensuality, leads the poet back to the secret of hidden powers, without which man's existence would be incomprehensible. Thus Joshua (in the **Novel of a Young Man**), Peter, Rasputin and the Borgias reflect the fervour of an age determined to live to the utmost the life of the body, and yet they cannot disregard the enigma of the interdependence of soul and mind.

It is just in this conflict that Klabund, the poet and the man, was doubly and fatefully enmeshed. It is easy to speak of all these things simply as 'instability', if we forget that the doubt and dissatisfaction with things mundane was of necessity borne in again and again upon one who was so early stigmatized by death. As Klabund could only think and feel in disharmony and paradox, this instability was no more than the effect of his continually unsatisfied approach to life. And yet for Klabund there was in the midst of such chaos, one main stay: his genuine, pure and purifying love of woman. He who most deeply understood that we suffer (leiden) through woman, and that she, as a result, becomes a passion (Leidenschaft) for us (in *Francis*), and who felt sexual intercourse as a 'frantic, destructive urge', finds security in woman. He twice experienced the mystery of love, he married twice and twice inward peace descended upon him and his work, but both times it was death, merely granting a short span of life. 'Irene', as he called her in his poems, was his first wife, and, like him, an invalid. After a year of happiness she died in childbirth. But this one year gave him a supreme vitality, which not only suffused his poetry but also his prose and gave us the story of the incredibly faithful dog 'Francis'. And when 'Irene' died, it was in his grief for her that her figure became for him the symbol of 'upright attitude to life' (Gesinnung).

The second time he is the one who is struck down. And even though the wild, posthumous novel of the Borgias seems to belong to this period, it is above all the orientally coloured dramas of the *Circle of Chalk* and *Cherry Blossom Festival* which he wrote for his wife, the actress, that are the most characteristic of this period.

Klabund is burning with a passion for life, rushes madly through time, but lays hold on nothing, and the more passionately he seeks, the poorer he becomes. Brackie, the fool, who alone retains his calm among men, is his symbol; he is the good and bad conscience of his time and of humanity; he stands free, ready to pour forth his scorn, but also to bestow his pity—only to sink finally into nothingness. Without roots, like Ahasuerus to whom he is akin: 'Earth is not our home. Strangers, we wander there, forever seeking with inflamed senses.' For 'it is Ahasuerus . . . eternal youth . . . this man . . . man must have suffered much, suffered honourably. See, how pure he has remained.' Klabund himself is like him, too. He has suffered much; he plunged continually into new changes and transformations and endeavoured to give them an interpretation. The truth, however, is that life cannot be explained, only lived. But Klabund had no time for that. Death stood there, waiting. In feverish haste he had to achieve in a few years that for which others have a whole lifetime. On this account the poet has again and again wrongly been reproached with superficiality. Life for him is time—and time is *tempo*. He can only comprehend life in time, as *tempo*. Reality as such is only subordinated to it and—senseless venture!—must be reduced to terms of time. Reality is matter, closed besides in a confused mass of traditional conceptions and misleading unrealities which must first of all be cast aside. 'Makeshift!' declares Joshua Klabund in the *Novel of a Young Man*—'Everything is makeshift. Men, poor imitations of their true selves. If only they could really be, even in the lowest, meanest form—but don't you see that they are flying? Foolish men—we never come to earth.' In this one utterance Klabund's whole attitude to reality and therefore to the world can be compre-

hended. Vulgarity is one aspect of life, and life cannot be understood if even one aspect is ignored. At this point even the most unrestrained sexuality has its full right in the picture of the whole. For it is perhaps just the most animal act that is the most enlightening for human nature. Nothing, however, is too long drawn out or dilated upon with degrading lust for detail, only the fact itself speaks— and when the poet has discovered the fact, he lets it drop once more. There is never any pause or rest, what has been attained is never sufficiently near the goal. But such an insatiability as this is baroque in the deepest sense, for in it is combined the longing for a resting-place beyond reality with a drunken love of this earthly life.

It is evident that in spite of all his ardour for life, the attitude of such a man to the world must necessarily be pessimistic. The forces he summons up and lavishes so freely, never stand in any positive relationship to the objects of this world which are so passionately sought after. 'What hour is great? I found them all small and vain,' confesses Brackie at the end of his life. Man remains for him the supreme mystery. Even here a profound love is opposed to a deep contempt. Man as a being, as a divine creature, really has the possibility of attaining goodness. Klabund's men know: We wished for the good and did what was best. And our smile did not always seem genuine. But we had faith in what was good.' But when, in another place, he adds that for 'free men' there are 'no unworthy thoughts nor wicked deeds', this proclamation of the free individual in the person of the poet Klabund, who was otherwise so firmly rooted in the oriental world, this proclamation which he always firmly maintained to the last, shows unquestionably the influence of Nietzsche. And this is only partially transformed by his decisive penetration into the world of Russia (as, for instance, to some extent in *Peter the Czar*). Peter is just such another 'superman', like the Borgias, like Rasputin, Mohamed and above all Moreau, besides whom the remaining mass of men are everlastingly empty.

How meaningless then is the question whether Klabund was by conviction an individualist or not in view of this other antithesis which resolves itself in experience alone. It is only natural that a man who loses everything in this world and cannot attain the next, regards himself as the ultimate reality. However much he may often long to merge himself with the people, with the mass of his many 'brethren'—he will never be able to lose himself in others or even to desire to do so. 'I have not sought after you, for I do not know you,' declares Brackie, 'and I wish for nothing, neither from you nor from anyone else. I only desire myself and even that seems to me too much, since I have only for that reason come into this storm and these mountains.' Even Moreau was ready to draw his sword, 'not for justice, not for you, Madame, but for myself—for myself and myself alone.' For his contempt for the people is unbounded. 'I loathe this people,' he says, 'on whom every master is wasted.' And again Nietzsche's message, so important for the young Klabund, becomes manifest in the form of *Francis*, when he says: 'O how vulgar is their all pervading vulgarity (All-Gemeinheit)!' Indeed, the whole of Klabund's peculiar preference for antithetic play upon words can be wholly set down to Nietzsche's account.

It would almost appear as if Klabund had never decided upon a definite attitude. In the political sense he certainly did not do so, for what he said of his Joshua applied to himself too: 'Politics had become an empty word for him, an empty vessel into which everyone pours his own broth. As in "art".' For him the people were not free enough—and the 'master' in every way weighed down again and again with the curse, the curse of not achieving goodness. He was never really able to recognize the western demand for equality which signifies absolute levelling. And his attitude towards the most extreme consequence of the French Revolution, the Soviet State, is sufficiently shown at the end of the Rasputin-novel, where he sees the face of this amoral dictator of souls assuming during cremation the features of Lenin.

Klabund was always a poet, never in any way a politician. But the vision of a pure and great man hovered before him, that man, who preserves his individuality and yet can call other men his brothers. He alone is a man, who has discovered himself to such a degree. And Brackie, the fool, knows that too, for

> you can teach a man nothing else out of yourself or out of him, but this: to do everything human in a humane fashion. To find for every proper feeling the proper form. Always to be at one and content with oneself in spirit and action. To redeem oneself—thus God redeems you.

And his relationship to men is the same as that to peoples. He was never international in any doctrinaire sense, for he knew that to comprehend the spirit of foreign peoples, one must first completely understand the spirit of one's own. And so we continually find by the side of only too justifiable criticisms of German conditions the most passionate outbursts of painful love. He was a patriot, but never a nationalist. For 'it is thus, when two peoples wage war . . . they are really and essentially one people, separated by war. And whichever of them is victorious—it will just succeed in devouring the other before it perishes itself. Since one cannot live without the other.' *(Brackie)*

It has already been shown how Klabund, this desperate fighter, again excluded from and disappointed by life, was naturally compelled to seek and to find his final stay in religious truths. And even though this religiosity of Klabund's was deeply discordant and joyless, it pointed (just because of this perpetual inner readiness) to a reality, entirely exceeding all confessions. For him, 'God' is not an authority for middle-class security, to which one can righteously appeal at pleasure. For him, God is much rather the symbol of Good in the world which man does not possess as a matter of course but the achievement of which forms an eternal duty. Certainly 'there is nothing more unjust than God', for 'to one he gives little, to another much, while to yet another he gives nothing at all', so that the problem of human equality and imperfection proves to be one of an eternally divine nature; but as a result, the task of every individual to be 'a brother to other men' becomes all the greater and mightier, as Brackie realizes at the end of his life when he continues: 'How easy it is to be good and to do good! What a blessing to gain forgiveness! How much greater to grant it! I will serve my brothers with the vision of perfection always before me and be a pious guardian of my sisters.' Now it is here that Nietzsche's philosophy meets that of Russia. For man's greatness lies not in raising himself brutally above others, but in descending, inspired by boundless love, to struggling humanity. Thus all religious supermen are nothing but criminals against mankind, and only through their fall—the fall of all Peters, Rasputins and Borgias—will divine humanity be able to raise itself.

However, mystery dawns everywhere upon this world. Klabund's world is in continuous dynamic movement, full of monsters, spirits, demons, never explicit, always opening up further depths. The dream is also a part of reality, a very real form of consciousness, which no longer stands apart from and outside of existence, as a kind of pseudo-existence. Man lives in a dream just as he lives in his waking hours, and he cannot separate one from the other. Human intellect in itself is not sufficient, only by the combination of every sense is real life to be savoured to the full. The artist who wishes to give form to his life must raise himself above the rational causality of psychology and must allow himself to be impelled by the dynamic force of his soul into a realm where the laws of causality no longer exist.

And it is not only by means of dreams that the poet is able to portray animate nature. The musical rhythm of his style is in itself sufficient to reflect sweetness and raging, whispering, imploring love. The very old elements of the fairy story open up new vistas, in which evils, joys and anxieties attain unsuspected symbolism. The poet suggests throughout, but he does not analyse. And it is always his own need, his most personal suffering to which he gives form in this manner and raises himself often enough through visionary contemplation into the plane of universal being. He is open to everything that strikes his susceptible senses, and the charm of a plant, or the agony of an animal can move him more deeply than the most passionate of human events.

Klabund was a poet possessed of an elemental urge, a poet in the true sense of the word. Through the art of words, he was able to recreate in most concentrated form life that was so dear to him. But how could this fleeting word itself form a firm element, when everything else was ever slipping through his fingers? Was not even art a new makeshift, a makeshift of most impressive style?

Indeed, this scepticism regarding the worth and sense of art was of necessity inborn in Klabund's generation. The every day problems which weighed so heavily on all, could not be solved by poetic exorcism. The eternal truth that the aim of art could not lie therein, had first to be rediscovered.

Klabund was a poet of our age whose fate he suffered and whose battles he fought to the end. He had no time to spare or to pamper the feelings of his contemporaries. With unswerving constancy he trod the path planned for him by death. Only to one thing did he give his allegiance—to life. But what can an age which values man's life so lightly, find in Klabund? It will have to discover him, as it had to discover Kleist. (pp. 222-30)

Wolfgang Paulsen, "Klabund," in German Life & Letters, *Vol. III, No. 3, April, 1939, pp. 222-30.*

E. F. C. Ludowyk (essay date 1959)

[*In the following essay, Ludowyk explores the four cultural traditions that influenced Klabund's version of* The Circle of Chalk.]

The evolution of the theme of the just judge, who decides which one of two mothers is the rightful claimant to a child, may be used to illustrate the paradigm of change, using what is symbolically the most significant figure in man's image of the world he lives in. The original is probably either Hebrew or Indian, the Biblical judgment of Solomon, or one of the birth stories of the Buddha; another version is the Chinese play entitled *The Chalk Circle;* and recently the story has been treated in German by Bert Brecht and by Klabund.

In both the Hebrew and the Indian versions, the first term of the paradigm is so strongly pervaded by religious values that it may be used to clarify its dominant trait. In the Hebrew story, taken from *I Kings III,* Solomon, the central figure, is the legatee of God who appears to him in a vision and confers a unique power on a faithful devotee. The gift is "a wise and understanding heart; so that there hath been no one like thee before thee, neither after thee shall arise any like unto thee." The figure of the Judge is much more akin to the one God than to the king of the Jews, and the celebrated story of the judgment is an illustration of the power of the deity whose agent is the king. It is not surprising that it concludes with a remark which is both statement and veiled admonition: "All Israel heard of the judgment which the king had judged; and they feared the king: for they saw the wisdom of God was in him, to do judgment."

In the Pali *jataka,* or birth story, the judgment on a claim somewhat similar to that of the two harlots before Solomon is the work of a *Bodhisatta,* not of the Father God. (The Buddha expressly denied the existence of a creator God, and refused to admit any speculations about the creation of the world.) The figure of authority here is the exceptional human being, due in his next birth to become a Buddha, for central in the teaching of the Buddha is the certitude that the human being himself can, if he enters upon the Way and perseveres in it, become enlightened. This *jataka* (variously called the *Ummaga* or *Mahosadha*) thus illustrates a wisdom which does not proceed from a supernatural or divine agency, but one which is based on human logic. The beauty of the story lies in the fact that the *Bodhisatta* does not decide the issue by fiat; instead, he submits the plaintiffs to a test, and elicits the verdict from the audience through their knowledge of a general truth applicable to all human beings. When he is asked how he knew which was the rightful claimant, he says quite simply that he saw certain facts and drew from them logical conclusions. In the opening line of the Buddhist stanza, "When this is . . . that is . . . "

Where the Hebrew sounds the praises of the power of a minatory omniscient God, the Indian stresses the special value placed on the insight which is within the power of all men who can develop their understanding. The difference between the two symbolical figures marks the difference between the two systems—the Hebrew with its background of a jealous father ready to keep his refractory children in check by exhibitions of arbitrary power: "Divide the child in two, and give half to one and half to the other"; the Buddhist, gracious in its understanding of human emotion and confident in the human being's ability to reason. The words of the *Bodhisatta* to the *yakshini* point strongly to the lack of knowledge (*avijja*) which is at the botom of all the world's woes: "O foolish woman! For your former sins you have been born a *Yakshini,* and now do you still sin!"

In the Chinese play of the thirteenth or fourteenth century A.D., the figure of authority is the bureaucrat or civil servant. The emperor's ideal justice and the system of government which he has instituted in his capacity as The Son of Heaven are demonstrated through him, despite the tortures which Hai-T'ang suffers at the hands of the corrupt officials. The chalk circle (or lime barrier, whichever may be the test) is only the accessory through which the power of the emperor and his punishment of the oppressors are manifested. In this picture of an Oriental despot, the heliocentric figure in man's world is the ruler, under whose despotic sway one might still hope for some alleviation of the common accidents of the human condition. At the play's end Hai-T'ang, who has suffered from the vagaries of the system, but who now finds herself able to gloat over the ruin of her enemies, says:

> Honored Sir, this history
> Of the Chalk Circle
> Is worthy of being spread
> Over the four seas
> And over all the kingdoms
> Of the Celestial Empire.

In Klabund's reworking of the old Chinese play which he found in Stanislas Julien's French translation, there are two central figures: a pair of lovers—a prince in disguise and a teashop girl, who meet, and part, and in the end are as romantically united as they romantically met. Love is the absolute, the sole lord of Klabund's piece of *chinoiserie,* which though nonwestern in background, is one with it in its vein of sentimental attachment to the belief in a first and only love, and in the faith that though love's course might not run smooth, its power can surmount the most formidable obstacles. Klabund's play has nothing to do with the Chinese or with the theme of justice. It is a tribute to the dream which makes all sorts of distresses in this life bearable with the assurance that in the end love will find the way. As his false gallop of verse puts it:

> Verborgenes ward durch Liebe offenbar.
> Die Dunkelheit ward durch die Liebe klar.
> Die Liebe macht die Lügner stumm.
> Die Liebe bringt die Hoffart um.
> Die Liebe brennt wie Sonn' so sehr,
> Die Liebe rast wie Sturm im Meer.
> Die Liebe bringt den Tod zu Fall,
> Und Liebe, Liebe überall!

To the title of his play on the same theme Brecht added the adjective "Caucasian", presumably in order to achieve a double effect: he wanted to add depth perspective to the subject while at the same time stressing its relevancy to our time. The play presents us with two figures whom he would have us accept as beings of compelling significance. Both his key personages are humble—Grusha, a more or less illiterate kitchenmaid, and Azdak, an old and highly articulate reprobate. Working men and women have replaced the gods, sages, emperor's deputies and heroes of romance. In order to load his dice as heavily as possible in the interests of his parable, Brecht radically alters the persons of his story which he borrows, as he says, from the Chinese. To the emotionally sanctioned mother of the old legend he prefers the working-class stranger who shows stronger maternal feelings than the child's real parent. The wise judge he turns into an amiable rascal who, in the true pastoral tradition, is a better and juster judge than any god or his deputy in the robes of office. The most interesting effect of Brecht's parable is its affinity, even in its denial of the traditionally accepted generalizations about motherhood and justice, with an ancient mode of paradox which most religious teachers have used. The play promotes no political truth, but it comes to an acceptable conclusion which most systems of ethics would be prepared to sponsor. The words of the Singer which end the play recommend a truth which echoes in many creeds:

> Ihr aber, ihr Zuhörer der Geschichte vom
>   Kreidekreis
> Nehmt zur Kenntnis die Meinung der Alten
> Dass da gehören soll, was da ist, denen, die für
>   es gut sind, also
> Die Kinder den Mütterlichen, damit sie gedei-
>   hen
> Die Wagen den guten Fahrern, damit gut ge-
>   fahren wird
> Und das Tal den Bewässerern, damit es Frucht
>   bringt.

To turn now to a brief inspection of the play in its three versions. The Chinese medieval drama of the fourteenth century was, like most Chinese plays, of poor literary quality. Yet it provides good melodramatic theatre, with a much needed vindication of the system of justice in a despotic country. It is in keeping with a system of aesthetics which, like its Indian counterpart, preferred the combination of the pathetic with a miraculously happy ending to the downright tragic. For this reason the play accumulates on Hai-T'ang's head all the sufferings of which a human being is capable, and then magically rescues her.

The theme of the play stresses the retributive quality of justice, as a warning to the evildoer both on the bench and in the dock. In this respect it is closer to the Hebrew story than to the *jataka*. In *Oriental Despotism,* Karl August Wittfogel makes the point that though *mores* and beliefs were assumed to restrict even the most tyrannical regimes, the potential victims of despotic power found little consolation in this reflection. That is true enough, but at the same time members of the audience, subject though they were to the fickle will of an arbitrary despot, must have derived some slight cheer from the fact that the persecuted Hai-T'ang—the victim of the machinations of a scheming First Wife aided by her Civil Servant lover and condemned to death by a corrupt judge—is in the end freed by the Emperor's deputy. Plays like this must have sweetened the consciousness of the subjects of his Imperial Majesty, embittered by the harshness of their condition in a world full of oppressive wrongs.

That is probably why the relation of the mother to the child, and the actual test used (about which the erudite might dispute)—whether it was a circle drawn with chalk in the centre of which the child was placed, or a lime barrier over which the child had to be drawn—are comparatively unimportant. The play is an occasion for a series of melodramatic situations in which, after a progression of woes, the sufferer has her wrongs righted magically. There is no scene of joyful reunion of child and mother, in fact Hai-T'ang makes not the slightest reference to her child after he is restored to her. Her sole preoccupation is to take revenge on Mrs. Ma and Ch'ao.

Characteristic of Klabund's ***Kreidekreis*** are three sets of commonplaces: the German intelligentsia's stock responses to China; the clichés of contemporary liberal thought; and those of Romantic sentiment. In the thick sweet-sour sauce of the latter float easily distinguishable pieces of *chinoiserie,* together with unexceptionable meaty slices of good humanitarian feeling. Klabund's confection of these three ingredients is attractively served to please the palates of intelligent theatre audiences (which still exist, but which are pretty much on their last legs, except, perhaps, in the University theatre workshops.) It is guaranteed to tax nobody's digestion; in fact there are so many remembered flavours in it that one could enjoy it as that species of Oriental cookery intended solely for Occidental tastes, and much more satisfying than the real thing.

In all three "elements" in his play, Klabund's language, always a trifle mannered, transforms the straight and plain of his original into the whimsical, the quaint, or the decorative. His lyrics are not Chinese, but romanticised German renderings of what was accepted as being Chinese. Allusions, and the over-worked proverbial sayings are all part of the same décor. When Haitang in Act III enumerates her distress to the storm-laden sky, Klabund in a few strokes gives what is supposed to pass for Chinese: "Was ist das für ein weisser Kreis im Himmel, wie mit Kreide gezogen? Zwischen den Wolken, du mildes Angesicht des Mondes, blinke mir Hoffnung zu! Der Schnee fällt, Flocke um Flocke. Wo meine Tränen in den Schnee fallen, färbt sich der Schnee rot . . . "

As for the revolutionary speeches (if they could be so termed) put into the mouth of Tschang-Ling, Haitang's brother, they could appeal to all good liberals who would find it both intelligent, and safe, to echo this sort of reflections on the times: "O Leid! O Zeit! Was kam ich in einem Land zur Welt, wo Gerechtigkeit nur ist für die Reichen, und die Armen ein Spielball sind ihrer herrischen Lüste! In diesem Land gilt gut als böse, and böse als gut." The same sentiments could be echoed almost anywhere, in the Germany of the twenties, in Austria, or in any country in the world, then or now.

The most significant change Klabund made was in the motivation of his characters and in the end of the story. Romantic sentiment would hardly allow Haitang to be intro-

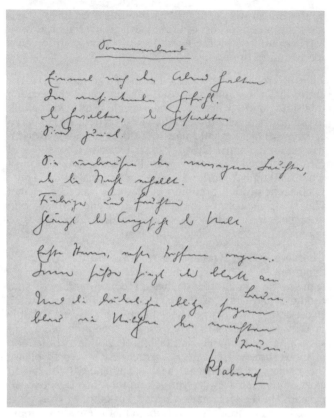

Manuscript of a poem by Klabund.

duced as a regular prostitute, who became the second wife (or concubine) of a rich man, the father of her child, whom she survived, only to be falsely accused by the first wife (who claimed both property and child) of having murdered him. Klabund's Haitang is therefore virginal in her innocence. At her first attempt at prostitution she meets a young lord with whom she falls in love. Bought by Mr. Ma who is able to pay more for her than her lover could, she follows her purchaser to his house, apparently bears *him* a child, but shows him no affection except for one single moment just before his death. Chinese sentiment might have been revolted at the result of the discovery in the last act of Klabund's play that the widowed Haitang then will marry the young lord of the first act who turns out to be the Emperor. But surely a European audience gets a Haitang nearer to its heart's desire in the revelation made by the Emperor, that on that fateful evening when he first met and lost Haitang, it was he who had secretly betaken himself to her pavilion in Mr. Ma's garden, where he, in Haitang's own wilted image, "die Blume meines Parkes pflückte." So he turns out to be the father of her child, and not Mr. Ma, and though the morality of the proceedings might have been difficult for anyone to swallow, Chinese or European, Haitang remains the type of distressed virtue rewarded.

Compared to the thin and anaemic artificiality of Klabund's version, Brecht's reworking of the theme is markedly superior. The energy and the resourcefulness of Brecht's *Schlamperei* in language and situation, the skill with which he stands the old story on its head, and the total effect of his combination of poetry, song, mime and dialogue make *Der Kaukasische Kreidekreis* a parable for our times, with or without the later addition of the *Vorspiel im Kolkhoz.*

His significant figure is Grusha, no mother at all, dumb at the climactic moments of her existence by the stream when Simon returns from the wars (a wonderful piece of realism this last, despite everything Brecht claimed for his *Verfremdungseffekt*). Face to face with Brecht's other important figure, the judge, however, she launches into a torrent of words, the gist of which is blasphemy and contempt of court. Yet in this very blasphemy a timeless truth is revealed—what she says has to do with feeling for one's fellows, and not with the aridities of law or justice. She shouts at Azdak: "Zu einem Beruf wie dem deinen sollte man nur Kinderschänder und Wucherer auswählen zur Strafe, dass sie über ihren Mitmenschen sitzen müssen, was schlimmer ist als am Galgen hängen." When Grusha for the third time has no words to express her meaning, Azdak marks her silence, which the Singer renders in a rough ballad:

> Wird es müssen den Hunger fürchten
> Aber den Hungrigen nicht!
> Wird es müssen die Finsternis fürchten
> Aber nicht das Licht!

Now he can say he thinks he understands. He then proceeds to the test of the chalk circle which will reveal whose is the heart of stone and in whose heart human feelings spring.

In spite of all his venality and rascality Azdak has this quality of warmth of feeling, too. To it he adds a power of speech which distinguishes him from Grusha. His is a justice which is rough, ready, and never inequitable. (It is interesting that in the case of the rape of Ludowika his sentence should have almost coincided with that in the records of a village tribunal in Burma quoted in *Culture Patterns and Technical Change,* edited by Margaret Mead.)

It is good use which justifies everything. So the child, to its real mother only an adjunct to the Abashwili estate, is given to Grusha who had done well by it. The play moves on to its close with the disappearance of the mythical figure of the judge, and the Singer can effectively proclaim its moral.

Brecht proves his paradox through the force of his language and his feeling for the arresting situation. By eliciting the simple humanity of his moral, his version becomes the most moving of all the dramatic developments of the theme.

No one has yet looked at the story from the point of view of the child. Surely here is a field in which a psychologically orientated dramatist could discover new significances. Perhaps this twist to the old story awaits an American playwright. (pp. 249-56)

E. F. C. Ludowyk, "The Chalk Circle: A Legend in Four Cultures," in ICLA *Congress Proceedings, Vol. 23, 1959, pp. 249-56.*

Malcolm Read (essay date 1972)

[In the following excerpt, Read compares The Circle of Chalk *to the classical Chinese drama on which it was based.]*

Of the many foreign influences upon German literature in this century, that of the Orient, and China in particular, has received only limited attention. Yet from the turn of the century German authors have turned in increasing numbers to the East as a source for their creative work, producing numerous examples of Chinese thought, political reality and culture as material for German works. These threads can be traced in Döblin's novel *Die drei Sprünge des Wang-lun,* several of the authors of the Expressionist era, and Loerke, Kasack, Brecht and Hesse, with a high-point in the mode of 'chinoiserie' during the twenties when China became a vogue in popular literature, giving rise to innumerable fanciful, quasi-oriental creations.

The motif of the Chalk Circle can serve to illuminate the recurrence of Chinese themes in German literature, the most famous being undoubtedly Brecht's *Der kaukasische Kreidekreis.* Surprisingly little attention has been given to the sources of Brecht's play and it is not appreciated that an earlier version of the Chalk Circle by Klabund had been a considerable and unqualified theatrical success in Germany.

To find the original material for both these plays one must go back to the China of the Yüan Dynasty (1259-1368) and a collection of 100 plays written during this period, the 64th of these being *Hui-lan-ki* by Li Hsingtao. Like all Chinese classical drama it is a mixture of song and dance, recitation and prose speech, conforming to the highly stylised mode of Chinese acting. It lacks characterisation, dramatic development and tension. Thematically it is constructed around the austere Confucian ethic and includes a veiled comment upon the rule of the foreign overlords in its depiction of the widespread corruption among officials of the court. The motif of the circle is a forensic device employed by the judge Pao, a Solomonic figure amid the corruption, to discover the true mother of the contested child.

Considering its total lack of dramatic qualities, it would seem an unlikely choice for the German stage, yet, in the skilful hands of Klabund, it became *the* theatrical success of the year 1924-25. Klabund, the pseudonym which Alfred Henschke assumed, was primarily a lyric poet and had already received wide public acclaim for his popularisation of other aspects of Chinese culture, despite his lack of knowledge of the Chinese language. His translations of Chinese verse, although very free renditions of translations made by European sinologists, were warmly received by the general public and led others to emulate him. He had also published popular versions of Chinese philosophy, namely excerpts from the *Tao-te-king* and *Wang Siang,* following the same technique of translation and 're-poeticisation'. Further evidence of his interest in China is available in his prose work and in the disparate elements which form the mysticism of a cycle of poems entitled *Dreiklang,* especially the very esoteric section 'I-Hi-Wei', an apostrophisation of the concept of trinity individually interpreted by Klabund. Much of the background to such works is culled from his readings in Chinese philosophy and the dubious interpretations made by the Western commentator Windischmann, in whose work Klabund noted recurring tripartite groupings such as 'Himmel, Erde, Mensch,' 'Sinn, Seele, Sein,' 'Mond, Sonne, Gestirne' which are synthesised with Klabund's essentially mystical belief into a modern syncretism, a fusion of various world religions, in which Laotse, Buddha and Christ appear as manifestations of the Godhead, I-Hi-Wei (Yaweh). Of greater importance than these extremely esoteric utterances, which require knowledge of specific sources to clarify their meaning, is the central motif of regeneration in *Dreiklang,* the stressing of rediscovery of the essence of humanity, recognition of life's animating force, the organic structure of life and attachment to non-material values. Klabund is typical of that group of Expressionists we term the 'Gottsucher'. He refutes the mechanistic and material world-picture which modern science and technology had developed and strives towards a recognition of spiritual values in a world preoccupied with externality and transient trivia. Many of Klabund's generation, realising the ineffectuality of Western religion and critical of its institutionalised form, turned to the East and sought redemption via Eastern spirituality and a personal experience of God.

Klabund's version of the Chalk Circle incorporates many of these features in dramatic form and is far more worthy of investigation than would seem from one critic's summary of its popular, yet undemanding characteristics: the German intelligentsia's stock response to China, the clichés of contemporary thought and Romantic sentiment. This superficial explanation of its outstanding success neglects the more profound qualities of the work.

When prompted by Elizabeth Bergner in 1925 to write a version of the Chinese play, which she had recently read in translation by Wollheim da Fonseca, Klabund turned to a French version *L'histoire du Cercle de Craie* by Stanislas Julien published in 1832. The latter is a precise translation of the Chinese text in which no attempt is made to render the piece suitable for production in the West. Klabund's contribution is to reintroduce elements he felt had been destroyed by literal translation, notably its lyrical features, whilst retaining theatrical techniques which were relatively unknown in the West, particularly the epic device of self-introduction. He also consolidated the philosophical and cultural background, making it a work with universality of theme that rises above the specific action and giving it a solution combining social, political and religious motifs.

In summary, the action of the original is as follows: the father of the young girl Haitang is financially ruined by the Mandarin Ma, and commits suicide. She is then forced to become the Mandarin's concubine in order to support her ageing mother. The Mandarin's wife and her lover conspire to murder him, implicate the concubine and claim the son born to Ma by the concubine is the wife's child, in order to gain the estate. By bribing the judge they ensure that the court rules in their favour and the young girl is sent for judgement. The final act is played out in the court-room of the incorruptible judge Pao who, by means of the now famous chalk circle, reveals the true mother.

Klabund's version is far more elaborate. Haitang, the young girl, is forced into the service of Tong, a tea-house proprietor, due to her father's financial ruination by the Mandarin Ma, and his subsequent suicide. Pao, a vaga-bond prince reminiscent of Büchner's Leonce, meets Hai-tang at this house of ill-repute and falls in love with her; but he has a rival in Ma, a regular customer, whose finan-cial power secures him the prize. She bears Ma a son and he intends promoting her to first wife but is brought to a premature end by the jealous couple, who accuse Haitang and contest her claim to the child. Trial and judgement are secured by liberally bribing the judge and witnesses but a *deus ex machina* in the form of an Imperial messenger brings news of the election of a new emperor and a suspen-sion of all sentences pending re-trial by the Son of Heaven himself. Haitang is transported to the Capital together with her brother, who is to be tried for treason. The re-trial is held before Pao, who employs the chalk circle to ellicit the truth. The final, harmonious, though implausi-ble conclusion is Pao's confession that he is the father of the child, having entered Haitang's bedchamber on the night of their first meeting.

The differences are readily apparent. The action of the original is retreated in the form of a dramatic 'Märchen'. Its affinities with the Romantic tradition of the fairytale are to be seen in the theme of love between the prince and the common girl, the crass contrasts between good and evil and the inevitable victory of the former. It is a trivial story with wider application, incorporating ethics and cos-mology. Formally the play has features which conform to the theory of Romantic irony. The devices of self-introduction and interpolated lyrical passages and song serve to break the illusion of reality and the continuity of action or to comment upon the story. These are techniques which Brecht was to use later, though to radically differ-ent ends.

Within this Romantic form Klabund clearly created a drama typical of Expressionism, utilising the starkly ethi-cal basis of the original and over-laying the didactic motif with contemporary themes. The conclusion is an amalgam of Eastern spirituality and Western humanism, not a naïve 'happy-end'.

The social theme of the corrupt judiciary, a conscious in-clusion in the Chinese, is linked with the degenerating ef-fect of materialism and opposed by the themes of reform and revolution. The conclusion is not the vision of utopian socialism held by many of Klabund's contemporaries but an equally utopian return to the patriarchal state of en-lightened monarchy. A theme more indicative of its adher-ence to the creed of Expressionism is that of 'Wandlung', in this case through the guiding principle of love. Love is seen as the absolute force whose attributes are justice and universal brotherhood.

The cultural and historical background is hinted at, though inaccuracies are numerous. Quotations from the Confucian classics and the Taoist Tao-te-king and the in-troduction of the White Lotus sect add local colour. Simi-larly the language is rich in colourful imagery, an attempt to create stylised, poetic speech which the author consid-ered typically Chinese. It is an image of China and not an authentic picture that emerges from the play: China, the home of mysticism and sublime wisdom, far removed from the political chaos of the historical state.

Before the appearance of Brecht's play other versions were published and performed in Germany with certain suc-cess. Klabund's adaptation became the most widely trans-lated work of its day, being performed in almost every Eu-ropean country, though it was not until the appearance of Brecht's play that the Chalk Circle again aroused public interest. (pp. 28-30)

> *Malcolm Read, "Brecht, Klabund and the Chalk Circle," in* Modern Languages, *Vol. LIII, No. 1, March, 1972, pp. 28-32.*

FURTHER READING

Bibliography

Paulsen, Wolfgang. "Klabund (Alfred Henschke, 1891-1928): A Critical Bibliography." *Philological Quarterly* 37, No. 1 (January 1958): 1-17.

Clarifies the chronology and publishing history of Kla-bund's works.

Criticism

Bithell, Jethro. "The Novel of Expressionism." In his *Mod-ern German Literature: 1880-1950*, pp. 359-76. London: Methuen & Co., 1959.

Briefly describes Klabund's major works. Bithell points out the strengths and weaknesses that characterize Kla-bund's oeuvre.

Schürer, Ernst. Review of *Der himmlische Vagrant: Eine Auswahl aus dem Werk*, edited by Marianne Kesting. *Books Abroad* 43, No. 4 (Autumn 1969): 590-91.

Descriptive review of an edition of Klabund's selected works.

Review of *Peter the Czar*, by Klabund, translated by Herman George Scheffauer. *The Sewanee Review* 34, No. 2 (April 1926): 254.

Negative review criticizing Klabund's departure from historical fact in *Peter the Czar*, which the critic finds "naive and incoherent."

Additional coverage of Klabund's life and career is contained in the following source published by Gale Research: *Dictionary of Literary Biography,* Vol. 66.

Rose Macaulay

1881-1958

(Full name Dame Emilie Rose Macaulay) English novelist, essayist, critic, travel writer, poet, biographer, and short story writer.

For further discussion of Macaulay's works, see *TCLC,* Volume 7.

INTRODUCTION

Macaulay is best known for satirical novels in which she voiced a contempt for the commercialism, hypocrisy, and superficiality of post–World War I England. While she first earned acclaim for her novels written in the 1920s, particularly *Potterism* and *Told by an Idiot,* it is her last novel, *The Towers of Trebizond,* that is considered her greatest literary achievement. A fictional account of her travels through Turkey, the book is an entertaining composite of autobiography, travelogue, and comic novel; on a deeper level, critics have found this work a poignant statement of Macaulay's religious faith.

Macaulay was born in Rugby into a family of eminent intellectuals and clerics; her father was a classical and medieval scholar, a don at Cambridge, and a descendant of the seventeenth-century poet Robert Herrick. Macaulay spent much of her childhood in Italy, but received a traditional English education, eventually studying modern history at Somerville College, Oxford. She was supporting herself as a writer when World War I began.

During the war she worked in Britain's Propaganda Department, where she met Gerald O'Donovan, a married man and minor writer with whom she had a romantic relationship that lasted over twenty years. Macaulay often incorporated these real-life occurrences into her writing: *What-Not: A Prophetic Comedy,* a farcical look at government bureaucracy, and *Mystery at Geneva* mirror events which took place during the War; *The Fabled Shore: From the Pyrenees to Portugal* and *Pleasure of Ruins* reflect on Macaulay's love of travel; and *The World My Wilderness* and *The Towers of Trebizond* are substantially based on Macaulay's relationship with O'Donovan, whom she credited as her literary inspiration, and the sense of loss she felt when he died. Macaulay's genteel ancestry and upbringing are also apparent in much of her work. She perceived her audience as upper-middle class and educated—"Bloomsbury *entre deux guerres,*" as J. V. Guerinot has noted—and her successful, intelligent, and independent heroines are considered thinly disguised self-portraits. A celebrity admired for her wit and intelligence, Macaulay regularly appeared on the B.B.C. program "Brains Trust" and contributed to England's leading newspapers and magazines. Shortly before her death in 1958, she was named a Dame Commander of the British Empire.

Although Macaulay's earliest novels were not well-received, they introduce themes that recur in much of her later fiction and are representative of her ability to infuse her work with satire and wit. *Abbots Verney* and *The Valley Captives* explore the antagonism that exists between family members, generations, and the sexes, while *The Furnace* and *Views and Vagabonds* assert the values of unconventional lifestyles as a possible means to virtuous behavior. With the publication of *Potterism,* a book that was favorably compared to Sinclair Lewis's *Babbitt* (1922), Macaulay gained critical and popular acclaim. Emphasizing the sensationalism of the "yellow journalism" era, this novel ridicules the profit motive of the press as well as the gullibility of the public, and "potterism" became the by-word for all that was hypocritical, superficial, and vulgar in society. In *Potterism* Macaulay also examined sexual stereotypes; the ambitious Jane Potter is encouraged to be a wife and mother while her less-intelligent twin brother pursues a career in business. This theme was further developed in *Dangerous Ages,* the story of a free-spirited mother who attempts to resume her education after her children are grown; in *Mystery at Geneva,* in which a woman disguises herself as a man to find employment; and in *They Were Defeated,* a historical novel wherein the attempts of Julian Coneybeare to oppose the patriarchal traditions of Cambridge ultimately result in her death.

In addition to this focus on the social tribulations of women, Macaulay explored other facets of Western culture. *Orphan Island,* the book Macaulay said she most enjoyed writing, examines how a group of English citizens institute a system of law and order when shipwrecked on a desert isle. Critics have described this novel as an anti-Utopian satire of England's class system. In *Crewe Train* Macaulay employed the theme of the "noble savage" to ridicule London's literary world of rivals and gossips. Another satire, *Told by an Idiot,* which follows three generations of the Garden family through the Victorian, Edwardian, and Georgian periods, has been called by J. W. Krutch a chronicle of "the flux of enthusiasms and absurdities which constitute life. . . . [and] the History of Our Own Times." Other critics emphasize that because Mr. Garden, a clergyman, converts from one religion to another in an attempt to resolve his spiritual disillusionment, *Told by an Idiot* additionally mocks organized religion.

Although *The Towers of Trebizond* also satirizes organized religion, Macaulay had another purpose for writing this book: *The Towers of Trebizond* provided Macaulay with the opportunity to publicly grieve for O'Donovan and come to terms with the guilt she associated with their extramarital romance. Macaulay and O'Donovan's relationship is paralleled in that of Laurie, the protagonist, and her cousin, Vere. Laurie, Macaulay's most fully realized and honest self-portrait, and her Aunt Dot, who is determined to convert the Turks to Anglicanism and liberate the Turkish women, pilgrimage to Trebizond, Turkey. While traveling across the Turkish desert and visiting the ruins where Christian churches and monuments once stood, Laurie realizes that she is both physically and figuratively separated from her homeland and, due to her adulterous affair, the Anglican Church. According to the doctrines of the Church, the affair prohibits Laurie from attaining salvation, and a profound conflict arises from her recognition that her love for Vere is not only inextricably connected to her concept of sin but also to her desire for spiritual grace and communion with others. Noting that *The Towers of Trebizond* transcends Macaulay's earlier works in the depth of her characterizations and portrayal of social institutions, critics have also praised the novel's descriptive prose and called the work a reaffirmation of Macaulay's religious faith. C. V. Wedgwood commented: "Miss Macaulay has evolved a style which reflects Laurie's character—an easy colloquial style, inconsequent but never incoherent, edged and witty, but flowering from time to time into ample passages of description, into dreaming musings, into religious argument. . . . It reads like a gay, learned, eventful, lyrical comedy, with never a dull patch. But it is never a comedy. . . ."

While Macaulay has been praised for her humorous and effective social commentaries, she is generally styled a minor novelist. With the sole exception of *The Towers of Trebizond,* critics fault her novels for their emphasis on the intellect rather than the emotions, and they contend that her characters are types. Nevertheless, Macaulay continues to be appreciated by readers and critics as a witty and entertaining satirist. As Guerinot writes: "Macaulay is a novelist of real distinction, and nothing that she wrote after the First World War is untouched by her urbanity and learned wit, her deeply civilized imagination."

PRINCIPAL WORKS

Abbots Verney　(novel)　1906
The Furnace　(novel)　1907
The Secret River　(novel)　1909
The Valley Captives　(novel)　1911
The Lee Shore　(novel)　1912
Views and Vagabonds　(novel)　1912
The Making of a Bigot　(novel)　1914
The Two Blind Countries　(poetry)　1914
Non-Combatants and Others　(novel)　1916
What-Not: A Prophetic Comedy　(novel)　1918
Three Days　(poetry)　1919
Potterism　(novel)　1920
Dangerous Ages　(novel)　1921
Mystery at Geneva　(novel)　1922
Told by an Idiot　(novel)　1923
Orphan Island　(novel)　1924
A Casual Commentary　(essays)　1925
Crewe Train　(novel)　1926
Keeping Up Appearances　(novel)　1928; also published as *Daisy and Daphne,* 1928
Staying with Relations　(novel)　1930
Some Religious Elements in English Literature　(criticism)　1931
They Were Defeated　(novel)　1932; also published as *The Shadow Flies,* 1932
Going Abroad　(novel)　1934
Milton　(biography)　1934
Personal Pleasures　(essays)　1935
I Would Be Private　(novel)　1937
The Writings of E. M. Forster　(criticism)　1938
And No Man's Wit　(novel)　1940
Fabled Shore: From the Pyrenees to Portugal　(travel diary)　1949
The World My Wilderness　(novel)　1950
Pleasure of Ruins　(nonfiction)　1953
The Towers of Trebizond　(novel)　1956
Letters to a Friend, 1950-1952　(letters)　1961
Last Letters to a Friend, 1952-1958　(letters)　1962
Letters to a Sister　(letters and unfinished novel)　1964

The Nation, New York   (essay date 1920)

[*In the following excerpt, the critic reviews* Potterism, *relating it to Matthew Arnold's concept of philistinism.*]

Potterism has had a very uncommon reception in literary London with Frank Swinnerton leading the chorus of praise; it is quite likely that that reception will be duplicated in New York and Chicago. Whether, on the other hand, the great middle class reading public will be either stirred or stung by Miss Macaulay's gay yet ultimately tragic satire, remains to be seen. To call a man yellow in Peking would cause no commotion though you shouted at the top of your voice. To denounce Potterism in Birmingham or Topeka may leave large and respectable populations unmoved. Matthew Arnold had his battle with Potterism and barely scratched its hide; aesthetes and philosophers innumerable have sped their little arrows. The monster plunges on. Northcliffe or Ochs is in the saddle or—Bulmer or Potter. For Potterism is but another name for Philistinism, the same old human lust for "second-rate sentimentalism and cheap short-cuts and mediocrity" and "muddle and cant." But through the mouth of Arthur Gideon, her central figure, Miss Macaulay gives what is, perhaps, the completest and most incisive brief description on record.

> Potterism has, for one of its surest bases, fear. The other bases are ignorance, vulgarity, mental laziness, sentimentality, and greed. The ignorance which does not know facts, the vulgarity which cannot appreciate values, the laziness which will not try to learn either of these things, the sentimentality which, knowing neither, is stirred by the valueless and the untrue; the greed which grabs and exploits. But fear is the worst. The fear of public opinion, the fear of scandal, the fear of independent thought, of loss of position, of discomfort, of consequences, of truth.

A group of young men and women set out to fight Potterism. Among them, honestly convinced, are John and Jane, offspring of the great newspaper magnate Potter and of his wife Leila Yorke, the novelist, who shares the popularity of Ethel Dell and Florence Barclay. The rest are Juke, who seeks an untrodden path to the ancient goal of Christian freedom, Katherine Varick, a new woman with a very old ache in her soul, and the half Jewish journalist Arthur Gideon, who, having a really incorruptible mind, is forced to play a Laodicean's part amid the fevered factions of the world and is killed because he wears no badge but that of humanity and has no party but the truth itself. Jane and John, though on a slightly higher plane, revert to type. Ease and worldly success seduce both. And that, indeed, is what makes Potterism so supremely insidious. The intoxication of the world's applause, the softness of creature comforts, are on its side. Once in a while the Potterite pays—as in war. But since the child of light pays too, and pays, in addition, for something he never wanted, his earthly reward is reduced to the satisfaction of his own mind. No wonder his kind is rare.

Miss Macaulay's narrative technique shares the keenness and distinction of her intellectual outlook. Each section of the book is told by one of its characters and thus the characterization is of a rare completeness and inwardness. The section written by Leila Yorke is masterly in its revelation of a third-rate mind rendered impenetrable by the shoddy goodness of its own intentions. But from the various narratives there arises not only a picture of these conflicting minds; there arises also a swift and tragic action saved from any taint of melodrama by a constant scrupulousness in the treatment of the psychical values involved. Thus Miss Macaulay's book is both brilliant and skilful, a notable story and an incisive criticism of life.

> L. L., *"Steel and Oak," in* The Nation, *New York, Vol. III, No. 2884, October 13, 1920, p. 428.*

The New York Times Book Review   (essay date 1920)

[*In the following review of* Potterism, *the critic praises the satirical nature of the work.*]

Potterism introduces to the American reading public Rose Macaulay, a young Englishwoman who has clinched the fact that ten-tenths of her fellow-mortals "think" with their hearts and has embodied that conclusion in a first novel brilliant in its exposition of the insincerities and stupidities of the average conventional person.

When our philosophy of life and our emotions clash, says the author, our philosophy is foredoomed to defeat. Hence the amusing and tragic chaos in matters mundane. Her book is appropriately dedicated "to the unsentimental precisions in thought, who have, on this confused, inaccurate and emotional planet, no firm habitation." On one of its front pages appear quotations from five different authors, all of whom succinctly phrased observations on the near-bankruptcy of society's intelligence.

Anatole France called man "that animal with a musket," and the materialistic Cabanis judged him nothing more than "a digestive tube." Miss Macaulay is not quite so sweeping in her contempt; she prefers to divide the world into conventional-minded people and originals, and directs her iron against the former. She admits, however, that the most original of us have some blind spots in our minds. In *Potterism* she dramatizes a number of unflattering thoughts upon man's muddleheadedness, his selfishness and his hypocrisy. All the qualities of humbug, of egocentricity, of cant and of greed that man is prey to the author lumps together under the convenient head of "Potterism" and calls their victims "Potterites." We are not all "Potterites," she says, but even the best of us have a tinge of "Potterism" in our makeup.

The form which Miss Macaulay had adopted as a vehicle for her epigrammatic onslaught upon our self-esteem is unique. The story of a small group who set out to wage war upon "Potterism"—and one by one fall before the monster, to the author's sardonic amusement—is told in six books, the first and last of which are written by Miss Macaulay in her own person and each of the intermediate four by a different character in the story, three of them by "anti-Potterites" and one by an arch "Potterite." This last, by the bye, is a delicious burlesque of the Florence Barclay-Ethel Deil-Ruby Ayres school of fiction.

Miss Macaulay's capacity for "showing us up" and yet

keeping us in high good humor by her sallies against types in which we readily recognize our acquaintances, but oddly enough, do not at first seem to recognize ourselves, gives fine evidence of her skill as a literary artist. One by one we greet with malicious chuckles the vulgarities of other people's minds and souls—their shallowness, their prejudices, their soft-headedness, their habits of slovenly thinking, of shirking facts, their insincerities, their self-seeking, their sentimentality—yet the picture is so dispassionate, so free from the bitterness, despair and malice with which pictures of equal verisimilitude are usually drawn that the reader is forced to smile at human funiosities. When it does finally dawn upon him that he himself is perhaps a member of this unlovely company, he has already assigned so many of his respected friends to it that the fangs have been drawn from the realization of his own membership.

This precision at war with the world of stupidity, telling us to our faces that the great ocean of what we fondly term "thought" is in reality nothing more than incoherent, befuddled emotion, this idealist crying in our ears that abstract truth is something beyond the grasp of our petty intelligences, is gifted with the rare genius for belittling the reader in his own eyes without antagonizing him. In fact, she so many times scores off our own pet abominations for every time she scores off ourselves that our hearts warm to her as do those of beleaguered soldiers to the bearers of fresh ammunition. It is such remarks as the following, selected at random, that make us hail her as a sort of social Daniel come to judgment.

> One lot (strikers), are out to get, and the Potterites to keep. The under-dog is more excusable in its aims, but its methods aren't any more attractive. . . . Artists care for the thing-in-itself; Potterites regard things as railway trains, always going somewhere, getting somewhere. . . . Anarchists are people who disapprove of authority, not wages. . . . Capitalists are merely persons who use what money they have productively instead of hoarding it in a stocking. . . . I have never seen any signs of constructive ability or sound principles in any Bolshevist leader; nothing but enterprise, driving power, vindictiveness, Hebrew cunning and a criminal ruthlessness. . . . He's a Gentile by religion, by the way; an ordinary agnostic. . . . The Russians were without shame and without cant, saw things as they were, and proceeded to make them a great deal worse.

Add to this penetrating observation and trenchancy of expression a finished style and good powers of characterization and it is not difficult to understand why Miss Macaulay's fictional commentary on present day foibles was praisefully acclaimed in London, where it has already run into several editions.

Whoever has the intellectual honesty to relish an unflattering picture of the world we live in—and, of course, you and I have that courage, brother "Potterite"—will revel in Rose Macaulay's satire.

> *"Are You a Potterite?"* in The New York Times Book Review, *October 31, 1920, p. 22.*

Stuart Sherman   (essay date 1924)

[*In the following excerpt from an essay originally published in* New York Herald Tribune Books *in 1924, Sherman discusses Macaulay as a woman writer.*]

Rose Macaulay is one of the wittiest writers going. But she makes me as uncomfortable as a patch of nettles, and very anxious about the future of mankind. I sit here uneasily studying her photograph. I conjecture that she herself has described it under the name of Katherine Varick in **Potterism:** "frosty blue eyes, a pale square-jawed, slightly cynical face, a first in Natural Science, and a chemical research fellowship." I blench under the rapier points of those eyes, so piercing, so ironically mocking, so candid, so caustic, so pitiless.

Is that the way a woman's eyes should rest upon this wounded, weary world? What did Byron say about soft eyes looking love to eyes that spake again in the same soft dialect? Or is that "old stuff"? Have we had rather too many soft eyes healing the wounds our own folly has made?

At any rate, this face knows too much! It knows everything that I know—which is pardonable; and a great deal besides—which is dangerous and disturbing. In seeing through me and all around me, I suppose she is like every well-informed woman that I have met in the last twenty years. I have never imagined that superior women were dull. But she differs from others in making no concealment of her scathing insight. Ever since I can remember I have adored, under the name of "feminine tact," women's readiness and ability to lie imperturbably in order to spare other people's feelings, particularly the feelings of their husbands and other male dependents. But Rose Macaulay rejects "tact." Her intelligence has no reservations. She looks at me without gloves. To the brutal frankness which is English she adds a hard, realistic thrust which is feminine—the special characteristic, it seems, of the full-fledged feminine Intellectual.

Once started on logical courses, women, I surmise, run through them faster than men. Consider the mad speed with which Rose Macaulay has run through the bright hopes of the feminist program. Her course was slowly prepared and her lamp was trimmed by such poor, old, patient plodders as Samuel Butler, G. B. Shaw and H. G. Wells. Forty years it took these fumbling iconoclasts to get the Victorian candelabra thoroughly junked and the clean cinder path laid out for the Ann Veronicas of the present age. With **Potterism,** 1920, Rose Macaulay caught up what for brevity we may call the Wellsian torch, and in four short years she burned it out and tossed us the charred wick in **Told By An Idiot.**

If she had refrained from the race, who knows?—perhaps dear old Mr. Wells with his rich resources of erotic sentiment and his vast social hopefulness might have kept his beloved young people "forward-looking" for another ten years. As it is, Mr. Wells is collecting his works, and closing the great epoch of social expectation, while Rose Macaulay cynically explains to the now tittering young people that before they can get around to reform the world they themselves will be old, and then, of course, it will be useless to try to do anything about it.

With a presentiment that she has now pretty well exhausted the satirical vein, I have been re-reading *Potterism,* 1920. It is a breezy book, and with *Dangerous Ages* contains nearly everything of hers that fans the smoldering ashes of my sanguine years. It is dedicated, a bit pedantically, to *"the unsentimental precisians in thought,* who have, on this confused, inaccurate and emotional planet, no fit habitation." People who hankered to be "unsentimental precisians" were not so few as one feared. In 1921 *Potterism* had run through thirty-five editions.

Just what was it in this first book that cried "come hither" to so many readers? The gospel of Wells, the ideas of Wells, with the rose color rubbed off, the sentiment squeezed out. The Anti-Potterite League for the Investigation of Fact, for the destruction of cant, the slapdash, the second-rate, pomposity, mush, shellacked propriety and every hollow, plausible form of words employed to mask and blur the hard, sharp edges of actuality. Youth was there, shameless, fearless, uncompromising youth, truculently showing up the base compliances of parents. Above all, young women were there, with Cambridge honors, scientifically trained, tempered, edged, going into the world fully prepared to compete with their brothers, and bent on getting some of the important jobs, and demonstrating that "woman's work" is a disgusting Potterism.

Dangerous Ages, which followed hard upon *Potterism* in 1921, is the only book of Rose Macaulay's which wrings the heart, or, indeed, much recognizes the existence of that organ. It is my impression that no dozen novels of my time have given me so much authentic information about womankind as this one.

There are girls of twenty here, clean, fine and candid, who have read Freud and Ellis and don't wish to marry, but, open-eyed, to take the risks of a free companionship, in a "keen, jolly, adventuring business, an ardent thing, full of gallant dreams and endeavors." There are women of thirty who write—experienced, brilliant, gay, with a cynical twist, with no religious illusions, yet "with a queer desire, to put it simply, for goodness, for straight living and generous thinking, even, within reason, for usefulness." There are women of forty-three, with satisfactory husbands and promising young children—women turning, at forty-three, to the medical career interrupted twenty years before, turning back to the career, in horror of the threatening vacancy of the rest of life. There are grandmothers and great-grandmothers who have ceased to rebel at their wrinkles, and who stave off the ennui of age by reading Russian fiction and consulting the psychoanalyst.

Pathos broods over them all. For they are all hungry for some more adequate self-expression than they are ever likely to attain. They are bitten with a desire to leave behind in the world some record more permanent, more personal, less undistinguished than—merely children! They are so sick of this self-sacrificial song! They want to live their own lives—for a little while, before they descend into the eternal nothingness. There is a hard core of egotism in them—just as there is in every *man* who sticks to his

career. But one likes these girls and these women, so deliberately clean and fine and slim and taut; and one pities them, too. The intellectual life? Not many of them, one fears, want it, as men of their class want it—as the first indispensable life choice. And a career chosen on any other basis is bitter with relinquishment.

In *Dangerous Ages* as it appears to me, Rose Macaulay let herself go as in none of her other books. She is more or less in love with all these women who are trying to make something satisfactory out of the little interval which is theirs before the swiftly shifting bright dance of the earth shall know them no more. Consequently she has here for once revealed her poignant emotional as well as her pungent intellectual qualities, and she has expressed intensely and adequately the consciousness of existence which her persons feel within themselves—the courage and verve with which they take up life's gauntlet.

If you scrutinize the story, however, you see that she has few illusions about the capacity of her sex to live the "life of reason." Her perception is lucid that the great majority of her sisters, struggling for "emancipation," are inextricably in the grip of the life-force, the passionate admiration of men remains still the secret ultimate object of their heart's desire and at a pinch they will fight for it with the crude ferocity of savages.

She has seen through them.

From the first, therefore, she has been anxious to make known that she is by no means committed to the positions in which her dramatis personæ are found. In *Potterism,* for example, she gave us a long epigraph from Evelyn Underhill on that "disinterestedness" of the artist which enables him to see things "for their own sakes." The point of view at which she philosophized upon the pangs of the feminine heart at the ages of twenty, thirty, forty, sixty and eighty is indicated by this epigraph in *Dangerous Ages:* "Reflecting how, at the best, human life on this minute and perishing planet is a mere episode and as brief as a dream."

She has, however, a personal register in one of the characters in *Dangerous Ages.* In the final chapter we are told that Pamela has the "key" to the door against which various of the other women bruise their eager hands. The key is not an important job, not a career, nor yet a man, but a philosophic attitude—an attitude of blithe philosophic despair. I will quote a passage which makes a close link between this book and *Told By An Idiot* and *Orphan Island* (1924):

> Pamela, going about her work, keen, debonair
> and detached, ironic, cool and quiet, responsive
> to life and yet a thought disdainful of it, lightly
> holding and easily renouncing, the world's lover,
> yet not its servant, her foot at times carelessly on
> its neck to prove her power over it—Pamela said
> blandly to grandmama, when the old lady com-
> mented one day on her admirable composure,
> 'Life is so short, you see. Can anything which
> lasts such a little while be worth making a fuss
> about?'

One sees at a glance that Rose Macaulay has flung aside

the torch with which Mr. Wells started the Ann Veronicas of 1909 marching toward the earthly kingdom of *God, the Invisible King*. She has reverted to a mood nearer the "blithe paganism" of George Moore and Oscar Wilde and old Samuel Butler, with his seductive maxim: "We have all sinned and come short of the glory of making ourselves as comfortable as we easily might have done."

In 1923 she blithely expressed her political disillusion in *A Mystery at Geneva*—not a satire, she assures us in a prefatory note; no, not a satire, but a simple straightforward "mystery story" about an imaginary League of Nations Assembly which somehow dissolves without much result in a subterranean banquet chamber.

In 1924 she chose as epigraphs for *Told By An Idiot* the walking shadow passage from *Macbeth* and a sentence of Paul Morand's to the effect that "history, like an idiot, mechanically repeats itself." If there was to be laughter at the expense of the feminine Intellectuals Rose Macaulay proposed to herself the pleasure of being the first to laugh!

Told By An Idiot is saturated with the pitiless, disintegrating, depressing irony of one who conceives that she has seen through "the illusion of progress." "Why so hot, little man, little woman?" she seems to inquire, with a frosty detachment which I find extraordinarily exasperating.

> What we are doing and planning and hoping so hotly, with such an elate sense of its novelty, is very old stuff, my children. Come, peep in here at my little puppet show. Here you shall see the generations pass, one by one—Victorian, Fin-de-siècle, Edwardian and Georgian. Mark them well and four times you shall see history mimic the vain spectacle of your anxious progress from the cradle to the grave, with all your empty mouthings and ineffectual gestures. Come, let us amuse ourselves. As the whirligig of dead time spins past us I will mention for you all of the score or so of odd little 'interests' which constituted life and its zest for each of our little marionettes, as, for examples, the untimely death of the Duke of Clarence, the alarming increase of female bicyclists and the prevalent nuisance of that popular song, 'Ta-ra-ra-ra-boomdeay.'

I should like to call *Told By An Idiot* a heartbreaking tale, but if I did that its author would turn her cool, frosty intelligence in my direction and inquire exactly what physiological change I conceived to take place when I spoke of the rupture of that organ. Let us say nothing of the heart. *Told By An Idiot* is a satire of great wit and even of erudition, but I find it horribly depressing, because it systematically belittles life and denies the possibility of progress.

Fancy becoming so superior to mundane events that in a chronicle of forty years you can tuck such an event as the World War into a couple of pages. On a scale of that sort the individual dwindles to a pin point, and births, marriages and deaths become of infinitesimal consequence. I ask, Whose is this sublime point of view? Where does the observer sit who whiffs all our human affairs into the air like a puff of cigarette smoke? No longer, certainly, at the point of view of the artist, according to Evelyn Underhill's definition, for she no longer is making any effort to see people "for their own sakes." She is no longer expressing the consciousness of existence which her persons feel within themselves.

I search again for Rose Macaulay's "register," and I find it in Miss Garden, a wholly disillusioned feminist—"a little cynical, a little blasé, very well dressed, intensely civilized, exquisitely poised, delicately, cleanly fair. She would soon be thirty-nine, and looked just that, neither more nor less." Miss Garden gambles very intelligently at Monte Carlo; she inquires how the wars are going—"the most noticeable wars at the moment were those between America and Spain and between Great Britain and the Sudanese"; she visits the picture galleries and the theaters; she spends some hours in the shops buying a clear jade elephant and a dull jade lump that swings on a platinum chain, a tortoise shell cigarette case, some Irish lace, ivory opera glasses and considering the purchase of a Poltalloch terrier. She understands that to be a little in love is fun and adds a zest, but one must be careful not to be perturbed by it. She philosophizes thus:

> Funny, hustling, strutting, vain, eager little creatures that we are, so clever and so excited about the business of living, so absorbed and intent about it all, so proud of our achievements, so tragically deploring our disasters, so prone to talk about the wreckage of civilization, as if it mattered much, as if civilization had not been wrecked and wrecked all down human history and it all came to the same thing in the end. Nevertheless, thought Rome, we are really rather wonderful little spurts of life.

In *Orphan Island* I find this yawning bright-eyed satire far less of an affliction—on the contrary, decidedly exhilarating, I suppose because it is directed at the Victorians, and I am gradually beginning to see the necessity of proving the Victorians ridiculous in order to fortify my own sense of progress.

According to the ingenious scheme of this anti-Utopia, a kind-hearted evangelical lady, Miss Charlotte Smith, undertaking to conduct some fifty miscellaneous orphans from East London to San Francisco, is wrecked on a coral island, with all the culture of an early Victorian evangelical spinster safe in her head. Seventy years later a scientific and sociological party set out from Cambridge to discover and rescue the survivors, if any.

It transpires that the survivors of the castaways number something like a thousand, and they haven't the faintest desire to be rescued. The island population is divided into two classes, the descendants of the orphans, the working class, and the descendants of Charlotte Smith by the ship's doctor, who are capitalists and land owners. Charlotte herself, aged ninety-eight, and generally tipsy on cocoanut wine, is the recognized source of religion, government and morals. Through the decay of her memory she has almost lost the distinction between herself and Queen Victoria. The society to which she gives the tone is perfectly smug and thoroughly hypocritical. It talks prohibition, chastity, etc., and it does just as it pleases.

For a time I had an awful suspicion that *Orphan Island* was meant for the United States, but I read an article by Robert L. Duffus in the February *Century* on the progress we have made in the last twenty-five years and decided that my surmise was absurd.

Clearly **Orphan Island** is a picture of Victorian England, and how as intelligent a woman as Rose Macaulay can fail to regain her faith in progress after painting it is past my comprehension. As for myself, I find that my faith and hope and charity are all restored to me when I let my imagination dwell for an hour or so with that tippling, pedantic bigot, Charlotte Smith, and then turn swiftly to the description of Neville's forty-third birthday in **Dangerous Ages.**

I see that adorable woman, mother of two grown children, waked from her dream-broken sleep at sunrise of a summer dawn, "roused by the multitudinous silver calling of a world full of birds." She cups her tanned face in her sunburnt hands and, looking out of sleepy violet eyes, she shivers and says, "Another year gone and nothing done yet." She decides to change all that. She hops out of bed, spreads two chunks of bread with marmalade, trots across the lawn in her pajamas and down through the wood to the broad swirling pool in the stream. There she strips, has her swim, eats her bread, "resumes" her pajamas, swarms up the smooth trunk of a beech tree to a limb in the sun and sits there, whistling.

If that doesn't represent progress I give it up. (pp. 83-93)

> Stuart Sherman, "Rose Macaulay and Women," in his Critical Woodcuts, Charles Scribner's Sons, 1926, pp. 83-93.

Frank Swinnerton (essay date 1934)

[*Swinnerton was an English novelist, critic, biographer, and journalist. A prolific writer, he is best known for his novel* Nocturne *(1917), his critical history of English literature entitled* The Georgian Literary Scene, *and the "London Letters" series which he published in* Bookman *using the pseudonym Simon Pure. In the following excerpt, Swinnerton describes Macaulay as a topical satirist and perceptive social critic.*]

Possibly the fact that Rose Macaulay is the daughter of a professor (her father was G. C. Macaulay, a good scholar, and lecturer in English Literature at Cambridge University) is accountable for her detached attitude towards the human species; but whatever the cause she has always, apparently, terrified others by a sort of immunity from weakness and great causticity of comment. I take these items on trust from printed or spoken report: personally, I have not noticed the causticity or indeed any occasion for terror. To me, Rose Macaulay has always seemed one of the kindest and least affected of all English literary women. She does, it is true, bring her mind to bear upon the conversation, and she is a little brisk (as well as indistinct of speech, in the manner of some Cantabs of her generation); but that is all. She is as far as possible from the greatest sin of English women writers—the desire to impress. She is tall, slender to thinness, has very pale blue eyes and a delicate fair complexion, and is a lady.

As I see it, the trouble about Rose Macaulay is that she feels herself, and always has felt herself, to be fully adult in a world of children. Not her own children, and not altogether nasty little brats, but children in whom, for their own good, she takes an auntly interest and to whom she finds it necessary, in print, to administer slightly repressive words of reason. She has a strong moral sense, much scepticism, a great dislike of those who are cruel, thoughtless, stupid, and selfish, and a feeling between pity and contempt for those who are innocently silly. And she cannot restrain her wish to demonstrate the undesirability in a civilized community of the stupid and the silly. At the beginning of her life she thought she could lecture these faults of mankind out of existence. Now she hopes to ridicule them to death. But she has always felt mature and wise; and in her earliest novel [**Abbots Verney**] there is, as now, the strongest possible air of grown-upness and knowing better than others.

Rose Macaulay continued to publish novels—one of them, **The Lee Shore,** winning a thousand pound prize competition—upon themes suggested by the trend of current thought (for she is a commentator upon what she reads in the weekly reviews, and not an originator of ideas); and for several years her books were intelligent, serious, critical, and illuminative of the minds of middle class people of culture. But the War changed many things for this writer, and life, from being a *pis aller,* became something of a futility. Had she preserved the solemnity of her first youthful tales, she no doubt would have become a sort of Mrs. Humphry Ward (cultured, current, and for those of goodwill and breeding highly instructive); but she had a faculty denied to Mrs. Humphry Ward. It was the faculty of derision; and derision became tremendously the fashion among intelligent people immediately after the War. It was a way of shrugging one's shoulders and washing one's hands of the politicians and admitting wryly that life was "a poor business," while at the same time indicating that one knew of much better ways of managing mankind than any that had been tried. Accordingly, after the War (and she now seems to ignore her pre-War novels), Rose Macaulay definitely gave herself to the composition of topical comedies. These faintly extravagant and ridiculing novels follow a formula. They collect a number of cranks and sillies and puzzled people, twist and turn them for our laughter, burlesque common vulgarities by quotation (as Henry Mencken burlesques them in *Americana*) or by merciless ridicule, and are uniformly crushing towards sentimentalists. One pictures these unfortunate characters—who of course are primed with every contemporary cliché—as dashing, full of enthusiasm, like dirty little boys, into the clean, well-aired, slightly under-heated house of a female connection. They are too excited with their fancies to wipe their shoes or their noses; and they run up to Rose Macaulay (in the silly way of thoughtless children) to pour out their fatal nonsense. "And the bull . . . the aeroplane . . . Positivism . . . advertisement . . . amazing . . . Youth . . . "—these are their excitements, the things they have just found. Rose Macaulay listens with a quiet smile, a little remote. Finally she says, crisply: "Yes, very interesting. Now, don't you think you'd better wash your hands and come to luncheon?" Or "Yes, I know; but that was said quite a hundred years ago by William Godwin." Or "You shouldn't say 'mephitic,' darling; you mean 'dense,' don't you? Like yourself." I wonder she is not at times haunted by the poor wretches whom she has so unsparingly made amusing in her books. Perhaps that fate is in store for her. She has sympathy for none but the critically alert, those who stand aside from the follies of man and laugh (not jeer) lest they should weep with exasperation and shame. As her first heroine said—I can hear Rose Macaulay using the words herself: "It always rather riles me . . . to see people behaving in what strikes me—well, as a foolish manner of behaving, you know." She is not really angry, not hot with the passion of a zealot; only impatient with the noisy and self-deceiving and easily-fooled. She cannot endure their idiocy. But for the bystanders who virtuously never make fools of themselves she has a fellow-feeling, because (she says it of Rome, the heroine of *Told By An Idiot*):

> Without opposition and without heat, she had refused to be made an active participant in the business, but had watched it from her seat in the stalls as a curious and entertaining show.

Curious and entertaining. You might have thought she would be a realist? Not at all; for the duffers and cranks and cowards, taken as a matter of course by realists, and as a matter for reverent treatment by defenders of all emasculates from the pressure of machinery and convention, move her but to laughter.

The laughter is without malice. It is the laughter of one quick to notice absurdity and drily to record it. It is the laughter of one who is impatient of vanity and muddle; one who, while up-to-date with news of all intellectual and social movements, and busily aware of all the latest freaks and follies, is incurably conservative; one who, with much kindness and goodness and indeed much sweetness in her temperament, has little pure imagination. (pp. 286-88)

> *Frank Swinnerton, "The Younger Novelists: Rose Macaulay," in his* The Georgian Scene: A Literary Panorama, *Farrar & Rinehart, 1934, pp. 285-88.*

Alfred P. Klausler   (essay date 1957)

[*Klausler is an American educator and critic. In the following excerpt, he favorably reviews* The Towers of Trebizond.]

Perhaps it is because this reviewer finds his theological prejudices confirmed in it that he is willing to shout to everyone that in *The Towers of Trebizond* Rose Macaulay has written one of the most enchanting novels of this season or any season. Here is the plot: Mrs. Dorothy ffoukes-Corbett, high Anglican widow of a high Anglican missionary who committed suicide rather than be boiled alive by hungry Africans, is the possessor of a male white Arabian Dhular (single hump) camel, which she rides to church through the English countryside Sunday after Sunday. Her friend and companion is Fr. Hugh Chantry-Pigg, an even higher Anglican, who is firmly convinced of the inerrancy of his church and the value of the Mass. Poor Fr. Chantry-Pigg's liturgical life is made miserable by "Catholic Commandos" and "Protestant Storm Troopers" who constantly harass his services. This remarkable pair sets out for Turkey, Mount Ararat and Palestine to make an

extensive survey of the progress of Anglo-Catholic mission work.

Accompanied by her niece Laurie, an assortment of relics and the ineffable camel, Aunt Dot and Fr. Chantry-Pigg invade Turkey. Alas, Christianity seems to have made only a minor dent in the Moslem world. Aunt Dot is quite upset over the enslavement of Turkish women, and Fr. Chantry-Pigg discovers to his horror that Seventh-day Adventists and Billy Grahamites are perverting the few Turkish Christians from the one true church, the Anglo-Catholic. Somehow their survey loses its missionary enchantment and soon Aunt Dot and Father Hugh slip through the iron curtain and begin their wanderings through the Soviet Union to spread the gospel.

But this is only part of the novel. In the meantime, Laurie is left with the camel, her aunt's notes for a book and sundry other impedimenta. She wanders about the Middle East, and finally goes back to London to await Aunt Dot's return. There is no lasting joy in Laurie's adventures, for she is bothered about the problem of sin, about her attitude toward the church and, very specifically, about her adultery. Her life is a counterpoint to the absurdly happy life which Aunt Dot and Father Hugh lead. Her conscience aches most grievously:

> Another thing you learn about sin, it is not one deed more than another, though the Church may call some of them mortal and others not, but even the worst ones are only the result of one choice after another and part of a chain, not things by themselves, and adultery, say, is chained with stealing sweets when you are a child, or taking another child's toys, or the largest piece of cake, or letting someone else be thought to have broken something you have broken yourself, or breaking promises and telling secrets, it is all one thing and you are tied up with that chain till you break it . . .

Laurie finds she cannot talk to anyone about wanting to be good and being in a state of grace; people just don't talk about those things nowadays. There was a time when the struggle between good and evil was high drama and heaven and hell seemed round every corner. Today a kind of green corruption, like overripe cheese, a horrible putrescence, is abroad in the world and no one knows or cares that it is sin. Laurie accidentally kills her lover with whom she had been living in adultery for more than ten years. She knows in her heart she has murdered him. She discovers the horror of sin and hell:

> Someone once said that hell would be, and now is, living without God and with evil, and being unable to get used to it. Having to do without God, without love, in utter loneliness and fear, knowing that God is leaving us alone forever; we have driven ourselves out, we have lost God and gained hell. I now live in two hells, for I have lost God and live also without love.

Here is the eternal dilemma of modern man: wanting complete self-gratification without having to reckon with the problem of sin or the existence of God. Here is the modern tragedy: knowing that the glorious towers of Trebizond (the church) shimmer and glitter in the light of eternity, and still not wanting to accept the demands which faith makes of everyone who wants to live within these towers. "Yet I had to be inside . . . there was some pattern that I could not unravel. . . . I turned back from the city and stood outside it, expelled in mortal grief."

There is not room to call attention to the learned discussions on St. Augustine, the problem of original righteousness, the difficulty of teaching conscience and a sense of sin to a Stamboul ape, and dozens of other witty asides on ecclesiasticism, Archbishop Canterbury, fundamentalism. On the surface the novel is sparkling drawing-room comedy causing the reader to double over in laughter. Underneath there is such unutterable sadness that one rediscovers the tragic poignancy of Good Friday. (pp. 533-34)

> *Alfred P. Klausler, "Dilemmas and Tensions,"
> in* The Christian Century, *Vol. LXXIV, No.
> 17, April 24, 1957, pp. 533-34.*

Gloria G. Fromm   (essay date 1986)

[*Fromm is an American educator and critic. In the following excerpt, she asserts that the experiences of Macaulay's female protagonists are autobiographical.*]

In her diary in the mid-Twenties, Virginia Woolf, not yet lionized, railed at Rose Macaulay for being too visible: for speaking at dinners, for giving opinions to newspapers, for writing articles for the American press. "Why should she take the field so unnecessarily?" Woolf wanted to know. Answering her own question, she supposed that the "leading lady novelists," all equally dutiful, simply did as they were asked. She herself, of course, was "not quite one of them."

Woolf's remarks have an uneasy ring, if not an uncertain tone, but there is no doubt about Rose Macaulay's ubiquitous presence in the postwar literary world. She had caused a minor sensation in 1920, with *Potterism: A Tragi-Farcical Tract,* her tenth novel and first best-seller, a brilliant, caustic commentary on the noxious influence of the mass media on contemporary life. Virginia Woolf had pronounced it a "donnish" book, "hard-headed" and "masculine," not to her taste at all. But it had launched Rose Macaulay's career, which Woolf followed with considerable interest through the Twenties and into the Thirties. Even as late as 1956, Macaulay's best-seller, *The Towers of Trebizond,* won her high and discriminating praise, of the sort to gratify the most fastidious writer. Yet now, another thirty years later, when women artists are so much in the public eye, she has virtually disappeared from the scene. A curious state of affairs, it is surely worth an attempt to redress the balance and perhaps uncover in the process a Rose Macaulay who even at her zenith had scarcely been seen at all, and whose personal as well as literary character has suffered in unexpected ways from the stigma of success. (p. 38)

Rose Macaulay's family plays a large, complicated part in her personal history and her career. Her parents were cousins, her mother a devout High Anglican, her father indifferent to religion, perhaps ensuring thereby that his wife's influence would be the stronger. Of their six surviving children, only his second daughter, Rose, was at home in the scholarly world, but she also found it hard—throughout her life—to resist the lure of faith. For she stemmed from a long, distinguished line of clergymen as well as intellectuals—Macaulays, Babingtons, Conybeares, and Roses. The poet Robert Herrick was also one of her ancestors, and his century became her favorite, not least for its extraordinary mixture of poets, scholars, and divines, the secular with the sacred, libertinism with puritanism. Indeed, the conflicts at the heart of seventeenth-century life and literature seem to have been reproduced in Rose Macaulay herself and account for some of the difficulties critics have had getting her into focus. That she was not unaware of this all her work shows, for it, too, is divided between the frivolous or secular and the intensely moral; between the irreverent and the worshipful; between public display and secretiveness; between worldliness and asceticism. In *Keeping Up Appearances* (1928), these opposing sides of her are amusingly depicted in the central character, as though to make light of the theme of divided selves—and thus perhaps to confirm it as an unsolved problem. Her heroine seems at first to be a pair of sisters—one a popular, outgoing, prolific writer, the other scholarly and withdrawn—but then in an arch aside midway through the novel, she is revealed to be one person, a contemporary type of the split personality, a creature of the new Freudian psychology.

Rose Macaulay was certainly conscious of the incompatible strands in her makeup. The vein of skepticism ran as deep as the opposing vein of faith. Perhaps by marrying as cousins, her parents had exacerbated the differences rather than cemented the similarities. She confesses as much with a series of scholarly works in the Thirties that revolve compulsively around the subject of heritage. She may have felt that the reputation gained from her topical satires of the Twenties—that of a clever, freethinking, argumentative middlebrow, addicted to cerebral but transient pleasures—needed to be qualified and offset. She had created by then a narrative form peculiarly hers, a blend of the essay and the novel, presided over by the ironic and sophisticated voice that most readers took to be the author's: a voice ideally suited to the disengaged, unsettled postwar generation. In the early Thirties, however, she began to sound a very different note and turned another side to her public by producing a trio of remarkable books: *Some Religious Elements in English Literature* (1931), which is still readable; *They Were Defeated* (1932), an historical novel set in the seventeenth century; and a short life of John Milton (1934) that displeased his admirers by not allowing the greatness of the poetry to obscure the limitations of the man. She presented him as nothing less than "an arrogant, self-dedicated solitary, a superb and monstrous alien." Her controversial Milton was followed a few years later by a full-length study of E. M. Forster's novels (1938), which she saw as the product of a thoroughly homegrown English sensibility—rational, modest, humane—and which she went out of her way to praise.

Among these books, the one of most value today for what it tells us about Rose Macaulay is the historical novel, *They Were Defeated.* A genuine *tour de force,* its language consists mainly of words actually in use during the seventeenth century. It happens also to be autobiographical fiction of a remarkable kind: a mingling of English, family, and personal history. Set in the period just before the outbreak of the Civil War, the novel's central characters are modeled on her own ancestors—the Conybeares and Robert Herrick, the parson whose limpid love lyrics offended the minds of the Cambridge metaphysicals. Rose Macaulay slips herself into the plot of the novel in the form of the young, intellectually precocious Julian Conybeare, daughter of a bookish physician working on a history of irrationality.

Julian's name as well as her unfortunate fate provide us with a glimpse of yet another Rose Macaulay, neither the one who dominated the novels of the Twenties nor the one emerging from the scholarly works of the Thirties. This one gave to a slew of fictional girls and women masculine or genderless names—Stanley, Rome, Neville, Denham, Laurie—and had them play, beneath the surface, a revealing double role. On the one hand, they certainly represent Rose Macaulay's belligerent view that the only difference worth noting between males and females was intellectual; on the other, they serve—intentionally or not—to minimize the importance of sexuality, in effect refusing to grant it primacy. This impression is reinforced by yet another group of characters—the girls who look and dress like boys and who sometimes come to grief because they fiercely resist growing unequivocally into women. "Sexless," the world would call them, as it was to call Rose Macaulay herself for the tall, bony, casual figure she made: "a withered spindle-shanked virgin," was how Virginia Woolf once put it.

This side of Rose Macaulay few people ever fathomed, least of all Virginia Woolf, who had her own problems about sex but who also knew surprisingly little about Rose Macaulay, even though by the Thirties they were on equal as well as more intimate terms. But only Rose Macaulay's closest friends knew anything at all about the intense relationship at the center of her life, a relationship which endured for a quarter of a century and left its unmistakable mark on the patterns and themes of her fiction.

In her historical novel, Julian Conybeare—for whom sex and mind do not mix—is faced with a variant of Rose Macaulay's own dilemma, one which she wove into her fiction from the early days of her secret affair with Gerald O'Donovan, former priest, married man, father of three children, and minor novelist. (pp. 39-40)

Her long affair with O'Donovan cut her off from the church just when she had begun to take a renewed interest in religious practice. The greater her sense of sin, the more fervent her longing for a communion she felt she did not deserve. And as her writings reveal, the dilemma intensified with time, embedding in her fiction a running argument between the counterclaims of religion and sex. In novel after novel there are traces of the conflicts and contradictions in her personal life that she could not verbalize elsewhere. They constitute an autobiographical dimension that has gone virtually unremarked, mainly because Rose Macaulay herself was bent on concealment but also because she did not believe in tragic emotions for ordinary life. Sadness yes, frustration, of course, and certainly guilt,

but not the heroics of tragedy. Thus, at the end of *They Were Defeated,* with Julian dead and everyone vanquished, the central message of endurance and moderation is contained in the "Epigraph on the Earl of Strafford," a poem whose doubtful authorship left Rose Macaulay free to imagine it as having been written by Julian and found by her lover John Cleveland, to whom the poem is usually ascribed. And she has him take its last lines to contain Julian's forgiveness of his trifling with her love: "Riddles lye heere; and in a worde / Heere lyes bloud; and let it lye / Speechless still, and never crye."

In the novel, the riddles surrounding the execution of Strafford and the ensuing civil war are neither solvable nor cause for tears, resulting as they do from the imperfection we all share, a well-worn yet powerful theme. Rose Macaulay had taken it to heart early on, and blended the appeal of the classical with the attraction of the modern. She was given to the long look and the balanced view, yet taken by the passing show. Human oddities, antiquated words, popular beliefs and customs: all these delighted her and fed her art, which, in the manner of her favorite Latin poet, Catullus, she tried to steer between the comic and the tragic, between satire and epic, even between the subjective and the impersonal. *Told by an Idiot* (1923), for example, is a mixture of genres: in its structure a chronicle novel, in its tone a mock epic, in its content a social history of England from 1879 to 1920. Full of facts and brilliant commentary, and the distinctive gaiety and skepticism with which Rose Macaulay registered the so-called progress of civilization, it also presents the warring elements in her own personality, divided among three characters—Rome, the eldest daughter and clever critic who seems to believe in nothing but has learned to conceal everything; her sister Stanley, the ardent reformer whose enthusiasms weary her aesthete-husband; and their niece Imogen, one of Rose Macaulay's boyish young girls unwilling to grow up.

The contradictory self-images have tended to cancel each other out. For the sake of consistency, nearly everyone has settled for the Rose Macaulay whose fictional voice most resembled the one so often heard in public. But to ignore the free-hand sketches of herself scattered through the novels, is, in fact, to close them off and keep her silent, prevent us from hearing what may turn out to be the most compelling lesson she was driven to work out for herself in fiction: the Blakean one of the marriage of Heaven and Hell.

This was the painful burden of a series of definitive events in the world and her personal life that found their way into her later fiction, testing her anti-romantic vision to its limits. As the Thirties wore on and the Spanish Civil War became a rallying point and a cause for liberals and intellectuals, Rose Macaulay, in their midst, was more in the news than ever. As one of the original sponsors of Canon Sheppard's Peace Pledge Union, whose members renounced war, she wrote a pamphlet, *An Open Letter to a Non-Pacifist,* that was an apologia for a position she nevertheless had trouble defending. At the same time she wrote a novel wryly called *I Would Be Private* (1937) and strenuously objected, in her daily *Spectator* column, to the acquittal of an English lord charged with causing a traffic fatality; he sued both her and the *Spectator* for libel damages, and won.

The libel suit had scarcely been forgotten when Rose Macaulay caused her own traffic accident, injuries included. It went unnoticed by the avid press because the legal name on her driver's license was Emilie Macaulay. The publicity would have been unpleasant indeed, because her passenger was Gerald O'Donovan. On holiday together in the spring of 1939 and driving in her car from the Lakes to the Roman Wall, they were involved in a serious collision. Gerald suffered head injuries and not long afterward a stroke, from which he gradually recovered. The accident was clearly Rose Macaulay's fault; unlike the arrogant lord who had denied culpability even though he had been driving on the wrong side of the road, she took the blame for it on the spot. But shaken by the narrow escape from several kinds of disaster, she could not help meditating on the limits of her own responsibility, and even wondering in what realm or sphere her own life was actually being carried on—with Gerald O'Donovan or with the rest of the world. And just how much did the rest of the world mean to her? The answers to these questions were already taking shape in her fiction.

And No Man's Wit (1940) was her second novel about a civil war—this time the contemporary Spanish one, linked to the earlier work, however, by its title from Donne. In it, she created a puzzling minor character who, far from fitting into the main plot, stands out by seeming arbitrary and contrived. The presence of this disturbing girl, who has always wanted to do nothing but swim, is usually explained away as a lighthearted fantasy, inspired by Rose Macaulay's own familiar English fondness for bathing. But the effect of the girl's character is dark and eerie, with psychoanalytic undertones. In the belief that she has finally rediscovered her natural element—the sea—Ellen Green swims farther and farther out, loses her sense of direction as well as her confidence, and drowns, without anyone knowing what has happened to her. Her "case"— for this is how Rose Macaulay presents it—comes perilously close to an enactment of her author's sense of her own secret and drifting existence between opposing worlds—Gerald O'Donovan's and God's. But it is in God's unplumbed world that she fears she may drown.

Ellen Green's fate seems to sound a note of warning which Rose Macaulay amplified in the story she wrote a year and a half later, one of her rare ventures into short fiction. Called **"Miss Anstruther's Letters,"** and written in the early months of 1942, when London was trying to recover from the great blitz and Gerald O'Donovan was hopelessly ill with cancer, it is about a woman who returns one evening to find her home gone. Rose Macaulay herself, in a bombing attack the previous May, had had the same devastating experience. Miss Anstruther, however, is given an opportunity Rose Macaulay did not have—to remove a few possessions before the fire got too intense and no one was allowed back in. But to her dismay and shock, after retrieving a few relatively insignificant items, she realizes—too late—that she has forgotten the letters from her dead lover, all of them saved for rereading when the world

was quiet again, all now lost forever in a total silence she can scarcely bear to contemplate. There is no comfort possible; and Rose Macaulay allows none, for this is precisely her point. She was looking ahead. The handwriting on the wall told her plainly that when Gerald O'Donovan died nothing would be left—not a single scrap—of the intensely physical relationship that had dominated her life for a quarter of a century. And she wondered what could fill such a void and whether the waters of faith—if she ever reached them—would sustain her.

Gerald O'Donovan died in the summer of 1942, and Rose Macaulay paid her tribute to him in the conventional form of a letter to the *Times,* signed with her initials. But in any number of novels, and known only to him, she had already testified to his overwhelming influence on her life, for good or ill. All the evidence indicates that the astonishing creativity of the Twenties and Thirties was sparked by O'Donovan. Her career seems to have meant more to him than his own, perhaps because hers held greater promise, and he urged her on, but he also encouraged a disposition to dependency that was nearly disastrous. Indeed, her greatest tribute to him would come in *The Towers of Trebizond,* when time had given her back the acerbic fictional voice he had always preferred to any other, and she could spell out in his favorite tones the nature of the bond between them.

Meanwhile she finished out the Forties—once the war had ended—in travel to foreign lands and in writing splendid books about them: *They Went to Portugal* (1946); *Fabled Shore* (1949). But novels seemed impossible until the end of the decade, when she returned to fiction, as though to pick up the emotional threads of her life, and produced *The World My Wilderness* [1950], a novel about the postwar world that many people could not help feeling was her most pessimistic work. They were responding to the vision of the world in physical and moral ruins, to the lost child Barbary—a teenage anarchist—and the cultivated, cynical university graduate, destined, Rose Macaulay feared, to rebuild England in his own image. Yet no one seems to have noticed that she had also created for the first time a central character (Barbary's mother) openly committed to sensuality. Helen Michel dabbles in several arts and specializes in the pleasures of the body. She has never compromised either her unconventionality or her feelings, and, significantly enough, by the end of the novel hers is the most balanced and sympathetic character of all, as though Rose Macaulay had arrived at a strenuously argued conclusion about the efficacy of love and sex. In a book full of moral lapses and ironies, the magnificently amoral figure of Helen Michel becomes the linchpin. A few years later, *The Towers of Trebizond* would revolve around an adulterous affair that is also a vehicle of religious faith.

In between, in characteristic Macaulayan style, came an apparent corrective to *The World My Wilderness* (and its setting amidst London's postwar rubble) in the form of a sumptuous prose work, *Pleasure of Ruins* (1953). She spent four years researching the responses of human beings in all eras to the great ruins, and in the process found her way back to the religion of her ancestors, helped in this by a priest out of her own past. He was one of the Cowley Fathers, a religious community that held an appeal for C. S. Lewis as well as Rose Macaulay. She had met Father Hamilton Cowper Johnson before the First World War but lost track of him when he was sent to the States. Now, in 1950, he wrote to her, compelled to do so after reading her historical novel, *They Were Defeated,* thus initiating an extraordinary correspondence published after her death. These letters show how timely was the entrance of the learned Father Johnson into her life, for he replaced Gerald O'Donovan as the representative of benign, admiring authority. She depended on his answers to all her questions—theological as well as personal—and they invariably came. No one reading the irreverent and satiric novels of Rose Macaulay's middle years—*Potterism, Dangerous Ages, Mystery at Geneva, Told by an Idiot, Orphan Island, Keeping Up Appearances, Staying With Relations*—could have dreamed that the Church would one day come to serve as the cherished companion others seek and find in tangible human relationships.

She had played her worldly role only too well. Even among those who knew her, relatively few were aware of the extent to which, in her last decade, religious practice regulated her life and occupied her mind. This too, like her relationship with Gerald O'Donovan, was her own private affair. She thought people ought to "consume their own smoke." So her appearances in public were as numerous and catholic as ever, their lively character unchanged, but early each morning she might have been found worshipping at Grosvenor Chapel, the little eighteenth-century church near her flat, where the brand of Anglicanism—"high but not 'extreme' "—seemed perfect.

In this state of unworldly contentment, she wrote *The Towers of Trebizond,* one of her funniest and raciest novels: an ingeniously clever first-person narrative that is a travel guide to Turkey as well as a mystery, a fable, and a farce. It was also her most openly religious work of fiction, centering on a longstanding secret liaison, like her own, that provides a beautiful example of the way in which fiction can be so frankly autobiographical that it turns into high and impersonal art. The affair in the novel—between cousins, one of whom (Vere) is married—has been going on for years, with neither party having the slightest intention of giving it up. As Laurie (the narrator) says, there was no way out of the dilemma such love produced—the "discord in the mind, the happiness and the guilt and the remorse pulling in opposite ways so that the mind and soul are torn in two." Here indeed is the marriage of Heaven and Hell. And the only way out—the death of one of the lovers—becomes in fiction a mirror version of reality, reflecting Rose Macaulay's acceptance of equal responsibility in the long-term relationship with Gerald O'Donovan that had been the source, in the same measure, of joy and sorrow. This is why the lovers are made kin in *The Towers of Trebizond;* this is why the narrator's sex is not revealed until the last moment; and this is why Laurie must bring about Vere's death in an automobile accident caused by senseless pride. The novel ends here, with Laurie (female) living "in two hells," without love and without God, the hellish paradise gone forever and insensibility all that remains.

Macaulay on writing:

Heaven never, I think, destined me for a storyteller, and stories are the form of literary activity which gives me the least pleasure. I am one of the world's least efficient novelists; I cannot invent good stories, or care what becomes of the people of whom I write. I have heard novelists complain that their characters run away with their books and do what they like with them. This must be somewhat disconcerting, like driving an omnibus whose steering-wheel, accelerator and brake are liable to be seized by the passengers. My passengers know their places, and that they are there to afford me the art and pleasure of driving . . . I have heard of novelists who say that, while they are creating a novel, the people in it are ever with them, accompanying them on walks, for all I know on drives (though this must be distracting in traffic), to the bath, to bed itself. This must be a terrible experience; rather than allow the people in my novels to worry me like that, I should give up writing novels altogether. No; my people are retiring, elusive, and apt not to come even when I require them. I do not blame them. They no doubt wish that they were the slaves of a more ardent novelist, who would permit them to live with her. To be regarded as of less importance than the etymology and development of the meanest word in the dictionary must be galling.

And so we come to words, those precious gems of queer shapes and gay colours, sharp angles and soft contours, shades of meaning laid one over the other down history, so that for those far back one must delve among the lost and lovely litter that strews the centuries . . . Words, living and ghostly, the quick and the dead, crowd and jostle the otherwise too empty corridors of my mind, to the exclusion, doubtless, of much else that should be there. How charmingly they flit before me, heavy laden with their honey like bees, yet light on the wing; slipping shadowy out from dusty corners, hiding once more, eluding my reach, pirouetting in the air above me, now too light, too quick, to be caught in my net, now floating down, like feathers, like snowflakes, to my hands.

They arrange themselves in the most elegant odd patterns; they sound the strangest sweet euphonious notes; they flute and sing and taber, and disappear, like apparitions, with a curious perfume and a most melodious twang. Or they abide my question; they offer their pedigrees for my inspection; I trace back their ancestry, noting their diverse uses, modes, offspring, kin, transformations, transplantations, somersaults, spellings, dignities, degradations . . . lines and phrases which have enambered them for ever, phrases and lines which they have themselves immortally enkindled. To move among this bright, strange, often fabulous herd of beings, to summon them at my will, to fasten them on to paper like flies, that they may decorate it, this is the pleasure of writing.

Rose Macaulay, quoted in Essays by Divers Hands: Being the Transaction of the Royal Society of Literature, New Series, *Vol. XXXVIII, 1975.*

Yet the novel did not depress its readers as *The World My Wilderness* had done, for many of them heard Rose Macaulay's voice suggesting, through the young and vital Laurie, that the hopelessness would not last, as it had not lasted for Rose Macaulay herself. When she wrote the novel, she had already made her way back to the Church from her own lowest point, after Gerald O'Donovan's death. In fact, *Towers* was an instant success, winning her the James Tait Black Memorial prize in 1957 and prompting her inclusion in the 1958 New Year's Honours. Thus, not long before her sudden death in October of that year, she became—like her friend Ivy Compton-Burnett later on—Dame Commander of the British Empire. (pp. 40-4)

Rose Macaulay's absence from today's critical consciousness, however, is another matter, and not difficult to understand, even though she offers so rewarding a mix of cultural materials for the historian of women and literature. Determinedly anti-romantic to the last, she also blended causticity and piety into a heady modern brew. When you add to this that she turned fiction into a social essay and her social life into a fiction, the end result might well be a disappearing author in the postmodern mode. Given, however, to reconstruction rather than deconstruction, I would argue that Rose Macaulay *is* available to critical scrutiny. The brilliant surfaces of her fiction—the rhetorical flourishes, the linguistic explorations, the witty play of idea against idea—yield only a partial portrait of the artist, a portrait that has held sway for years, in large measure because she wanted it that way. But beyond the verbal facility—and the clear prose persona mistaken for its elusive and polymorphous author—is a rich historical imagination that never failed her and a religious sensibility she could neither wholly suppress nor fully indulge, not even in her old age, when she was free of the personal constraints of the past. An ingrained skepticism always got in the way, so that hers was an art of contrarieties played against each other, at its best in such fictions as *The World My Wilderness* and *The Towers of Trebizond,* supremely balanced achievements that represent the hard-won triumph of classicism and impersonality. (p. 44)

> Gloria G. Fromm, *"The Worldly and Unworldly Fortunes of Rose Macaulay,"* in The New Criterion, *Vol. V, No. 2, October, 1986, pp. 38-44.*

J. V. Guerinot (essay date 1987)

[*In the following excerpt, Guerinot discusses Macaulay's novels and nonfiction.*]

The most revealing comment Rose Macaulay ever made on her art (she took an excessively modest view of her books) was that all she was interested in when she wrote her novels was "the style—the mere English, the cadences etc.; and sometimes when I make a joke." And it is the style, the sentences, and the jokes that make the novels so worth reading. In a Rose Macaulay novel it is not plot, not character, that matter most, but the narrator's prose. She has little interest in making up a plot. Usually she takes a fairly simple idea or situation to focus her special vision of life: a young girl raised as a near illiterate in Andorra is suddenly faced with the London literary world (*Crewe Train,* 1926); a successful young novelist, famous for her grasp of character, goes to visit relatives in the jungles of Guatemala (*Staying with Relations,* 1930); a single family is followed through all the decades from 1879 to 1920 (*Told by an Idiot,* 1923). The framework serves its purpose by allowing the characters to do amusing things, to talk endlessly and the narrator to comment freely. What we enjoy is listening to the voice speaking.

What I am always aware of in reading a Rose Macaulay is that it was written by the woman in the Cecil Beaton photograph. She looks, does this elderly, gaunt, and handsome lady, rather formidable; one believes readily in the tales of her terrible tongue. She looks wise and witty and learned and courageous, a woman one would greatly like to have known. And I often think of what one of her friends said after her death: "If everyone were as good as Rose Macaulay, and also as clever, the world would be a paradise."

What pleasures, then, am I suggesting that, busy as we are, we may find in that long shelf of books? (Writing for a living, she averaged a novel every other year for fifty years.) Primarily, I suggest, a sense of joy. She blesses what there is for being. She thinks the world amazing and comic. People delight her, and their so odd ways. Her books are full of laughter and wit and delight in Abroad, architecture, classical and modern literature, the more peculiar heresies, the England of Laud and the Cambridge Platonists, the Anglican church, and bathing. (She seems to have gone swimming in just about every body of water she saw, including a muddy pond at Sissinghurst, and daily after Mass, in the Serpentine, which rather worried T. S. Eliot.) As Laurie says at the end of *The Towers of Trebizond* (1956), "One finds diversions; these, indeed, confront one at every turn, the world being so full of natural beauties and enchanting artifacts, of adventures and jokes and excitements and romance and remedies for grief." It is natural she should have written books entitled *The Minor Pleasures of Life* (1934), *Personal Pleasures* (1935), and *Pleasure of Ruins* (1953).

Then there is her fastidious care for words, her distaste for what in her Hogarth Pamphlet of that name she called "catchwords and claptrap" (Hogarth Press, 1926). When her library was totally destroyed in the bombing of London, the first volumes she replaced were the *OED*. There are these who like their novelists (and such novelists greatly abound) shirts off, muscles rippling, and those who think that the only muscles a novelist may hint at possessing are those needed to take down the wanted volume of the *OED* from its accustomed shelf.

Her novels are for those who prefer their fiction to smell agreeably of the British Library Reading Room. She was a writer of remarkable learning, as any reader of *Some Religious Elements in English Literature* (1931) or *Pleasure of Ruins* will perceive. The learning, out of the way, surprising, agreeable, gives the novels their special flavor.

The novels are full of recurrent terms of approbation that suggest the quality of spirit she admired: ironic, bland, elegant, detached, celibate, urbane, rakish, scholarly, civilized. Together they compose an attitude very close to what in her excellent book on E. M. Forster (*The Writings of E. M. Forster,* 1938) she conveniently calls "Cambridge." "Cambridge," then, we may call it, or "Bloomsbury *entre deux guerres*" or, more exactly, "Marylebone." Every book presupposes ideal readers, and one way of defining a book is to summon these up. Rose Macaulay novels are for Sir Gilbert Murray, Sir John Betjeman, Archbishop David Mathew, and Elizabeth Bowen (all of them, in fact, ardent admirers).

Wit, learning, and piety, then, I would claim for her. The piety is the hardest to talk about, but all of her books were clearly written by a woman of deep religious conviction. Everyone, I suppose, who knows anything at all about her, knows that because of her love affair over many years with a married man, Gerald O'Donovan, she ceased gradually to be *pratiquante* until, after her lover's death, she returned to the Church under the guidance of the lowly Father, the Rev. John Hamilton Cowper Johnson. A most important fact in her life, but not a fact to concern the reader. She was always a Christian writer, as Robert Liddell has pointed out, correcting Ivy Compton-Burnett. Her standards for her characters, as he observes, are Christian standards. All her books testify to her abiding affection for the Church. All the teasing and joking about Buchmanites, and Billy Graham, and Bishop Colenso's arithmetic book, and Collyridianism, and Cowley fathers biting Nestorian bishops are the jokes of a Benedictine calefactory. *They Were Defeated* (1932) in its brilliant reconstruction of Cambridge before the Civil Wars, the place of special honor in her sacred geography, is only the clearest mark of her passion for the religious thought and worship of the earlier seventeenth century. . . . (pp. 110-12)

Her books are, for the most part, very gay and rather silly, excellent things for books to be in this fallen world. They are also, at times, which is a virtue as well, awash with melancholy. She knows, as does every comic novelist worth reading, that "Everything's terrible, *cara*—in the heart of man." Her heroines, particularly at night, in bed, are engulfed in terror, in accidie, in the bitter waves of fruitless passion. They agree with Raphael that "In loving thou dost well, in passion not," but can find no answer to their grievous plight. Nor can Rose Macaulay, nor can we. The wit, the grace, the poise, the intelligence of high civilization is built on shifting sands, as the ruins she so loved everywhere triumphantly display.

With so many books to choose from, where is one to start? I would recommend beginning with the following four books.

There are not so many good comic novels in the language that a lover of the genre can afford to miss one. *Going Abroad* (1934) is, after *The Towers of Trebizond,* Rose Macaulay's funniest and most endearing novel, a novel, as the dedication promises, "of unredeemed levity." It is the very model of an English comic novel. Against the lovely background of the Basque country and its beaches Rose Macaulay assembles English eccentrics, international crooks, and earnest, deplorably bouncy young Oxford Groupers. It begins splendidly:

> Mrs. Richard Aubrey, the wife of a missionary bishop, sat outside the Café Bar Inoxion, in the Plaza de Armas, Fuenterrabia, one hot eighth of September, reconstructing, as was usual with her the Garden of Eden. . . . While her hus-

band (a very kindly and persuasive clergyman) had striven to convert the uncultivated citizens of Mesopotamia, she, shyer, less fluent, much less convinced, and slightly unbalanced by the Mesopotamian sun, had ridden about on camels, donkeys, and other such creatures, brooding over that lost and lovely garden watered by the Tigris and the Euphrates and now so run to seed. . . . "That the Forbidden Fruit of Paradise was an Apple," she doubted with the late Sir Thomas Browne.

Staying with her in the hotel at Zarauz is her husband, the Bishop of Xanadu, and Sir Arthur Denzil, a retired diplomat. Also at the hotel are Colonel and Mrs. Buckley with their children Hero and the snobbish Giles, the dreadful M. and Mme. Josef, who run an international chain of beauty parlors, and Mrs. Dixon, one of their pathetic victims whose face they long ago destroyed (not a convincing character). And everywhere in evidence is the party of young Oxford Groupers. ("Mrs. Aubrey, being Cambridge, was one of those who liked this name for them." These provide much of the satire, but they are really handled very gently. Ted, their leader, is a likable enough young man, and they have "a kind of bright, touching, barbaric confidence, like that of dogs and boy scouts." What makes them so absurd is that they have arrived to convert the Basques, "Already," as the Bishop justly observes, "among the more religious of European tribes, though of course when you came to absolute honesty, absolute purity, and absolute unselfishness—well, no doubt they would lack all that as much as any one else." (pp. 112-14)

Ted falls in love with the Byronically lovely Hero, one of Rose Macaulay's firmly nonintellectual heroines. Ted related to her his success in beginning to Change a fisherman, Ted speaking Castilian and the fisherman Basque, although the latter thought he was speaking Castilian.

> "But I don't think it got between us. Language doesn't actually matter terribly, do you think? I mean, there are far more important things."
>
> "Nearly everything," Hero agreed.

She shares his simplicity:

> "We happen to think that life matters more than books, I'm afraid. Don't you agree?"
>
> "Oh, yes, I suppose so."
>
> Such comparisons were not natural to Hero. Life. Books. Well, naturally, books scarcely mattered at all. That was easy.

The comedy of the Changing of Hero ensues. Good Macaulayesque heroine that she is, she loves swimming, and Ted and she go swimming a lot while Ted, not without difficulty, attempts to Change her. She is not one to grasp quickly the point of an exemplum, nor does the Argument from Design work well for her. They are looking out over the ocean:

> "Makes one jolly well think, doesn't it? I mean, all that can't be just blind accident." Had it been an accident, Hero understood, there would have been less of it.

"A bit overdone, though," she commented. "I mean, we could have done with less, actually. . . ."

The Oxford Groupers hold a grand meeting at the Miramar over which the kindly Bishop agrees to preside. Sir Arthur sighs on learning that Paris is now full of Groups. How different it must be from the Paris of his diplomatic days. Two young poleta players, thought by the Groupers to be confessing how they have Changed, say a few words in Basque about their national game, and, then, to the exquisite embarrassment of her very well-bred parents, Hero gets up to testify. " 'I've faced up to things,' " she says. " 'That dreadful expression!' moaned the bowed mother. *'Up to . . . so unnecessary, so American. . . .' "

Poor Hero is indeed Changed and writes long letters to her family, sharing her past and present sins. Her parents decide they must get her to St. Jean de Luz at once. But on their return from Loyola all of the English characters and M. and Mme. Josef are kidnapped by Basque smugglers and taken off to a mountain fastness where they are kept, in great discomfort, until the Josefs will agree to pay a large ransom. The Josefs are at last, to everyone's relief, Changed, and Mme. Josef's public confession of her sins in the cosmetic industry, the Sharing we have been looking forward to, is satisfyingly lurid. The Basque kidnappers themselves are not at all Changed and find the Oxford Groupers' continual references to smuggling in the worst of taste.

The scholarly Aubreys with calm good sense make the best of their captivity, Mrs. Aubrey happily using the opportunity to improve her Basque, the bishop finding he can continue work on his book on the survival of ancient heresies among Iraqui tribes:

> "I see I have with me too, my notes on semi-Pelagianism and Priscillianism among the desert Nefudian missionaries. . . . The Priscillianists combined Sabellianism, Manicheeism, and Gnosticism. So did the Nefudian missionaries, whom we met in Basra. But there was also an outbreak of Adamism among them."

All travelers must have dreamed wistfully of those linguistically carefree days when Latin, we are told, was a universal language, and many, driven by desperate circumstances, must at some time have endeavored to communicate in such Latin as they could command, but Rose Macaulay contrives an attempt at Latin conversation which for sheer zaniness has, I think, no peer. The Aubreys and Sir Arthur want very much to talk to the Basque priest who comes to visit their kidnappers to find out why they are being held and to persuade him that they must be released immediately. But the nice village curé speaks no Castilian. Surely, however, he understands Latin. Mrs. Aubrey begins by quoting relevant bits from Milton's *Defensio pro Populo Anglicano*, which she has just been reading. Sir Arthur tries Virgil's first Eclogue: " 'At nos hinc. . . . But we must hence. Some to the thirsty regions of Africa . . . some to where the Britons dwell. . . .' " But Father Ignacio to such surprising and unfamiliar sentiments just keeps replying, "Ita est." The bishop sensibly

decides they should, with such a poor classicist, stick to the Latin of his religious duties.

> "Quare," he gently asked, "fremuerunt gentes, et populi meditati sunt inania?"

> Father Ignacio recognized with pleasure this familiar inquiry of the psalmist despite its un-Vasco pronunciation. He did not, indeed, answer it, but obligingly assisted the bishop in his religious exercise by rapidly and nasally reciting the next verse.

The novel ends amid autumn bonfires in Cambridge gardens as Mrs. Aubrey and the bishop tranquilly pursue their respective speculations on the Garden of Eden and the survival of primitive heresies. Basque fishing villages and wild mountains, baroque churches, brigands, kidnapping, Milton and Sir Thomas Browne, several of her most lovable characters, the vagaries of patristic theology, all irradiated by wit and the most impudent insouciance. It is the perfect book for an August afternoon when we want "only a novel," but a novel that is original, amusing, urbane, and undisturbing. Delightful and wayward characters behave and misbehave against this world's created glories, while the novelist says from time to time to the fools, Deal not so madly; and to the ungodly, Set not up your horn.

Her achievement in *They Were Defeated* (1932, called in the American edition *The Shadow Flies*) is to have recreated convincingly the world of Robert Herrick, to have imagined for us seventeenth-century Devonshire and the Cambridge of the Laudian reform in a novel which is a serious and satisfying work of art. After the light comedy of the Twenties, she found this once in the historical novel—a genre perfectly suited to her temperament and abilities.

Even its divisions suggest its shape and flavor: "Bucolick," "Academick," "Antiplatonick," and "Postscript." We move from Dean Prior to Cambridge, and then back to Devonshire for the sad postscript which spells out the Royalist defeat. As Miss C. V. Wedgwood, in her fine introduction to the 1966 reprinting, accurately observes, Herrick "presides" over the book, but the plot concerns the fifteen-year-old Julian Conybeare, an eager young scholar and poet, reading the classics with her vicar Mr. Herrick since her father believes strongly in female education. Herrick, a not too wildly erring parson, is presented so successfully that we believe easily that the Herrick of the novel wrote Herrick's poems.

Amid the bucolic charm and the harvest festivals the ominous political news, the growing hatred of Laud and fear of the Scots army, Julian dreams of Cambridge where her brother Kit is, of Mr. Cleveland of St. John's, Kit's tutor, who writes "marvelous ingenious verses," of Mr. Richard Crashaw of Peterhouse, but especially of Mr. Abraham Cowley. Sir John Suckling, who comes to visit her beloved tutor, is something of a disappointment, jealous, she suspects of Cowley, finding Herrick's verses distinctly out of fashion, and much more inclined to flirt with the lovely poetess than take her verses seriously.

Her atheistical father, Dr. Conybeare (modeled after Rose

Macaulay's cousin, F. C. Conybeare), takes her with Parson Herrick to Cambridge to visit Kit. The fun Rose Macaulay admitted to having in thinking it up is obvious and catching. We learn what it was like to study at Cambridge in 1640, how the university looked, how it felt. The Cambridge Platonists, the intellectual innovations, the reformed Anglican liturgy, the metaphysical poets, the love of learning, and the desire for God—it all makes for Julian a *hortus conclusus,* a Paradise.

Waking up in the White Horse Inn on a "magical Cambridge All Hallows morning," Julian can hardly wait to get to church:

> Oh, there were a hundred of noble clergymen, Arminian, Calvinian, and Latitudinarian, who must even now be worshipping all the saints in church or chapel, and who would later be walking abroad, and might be catched sight on as they passed. There was Dr. Beale, who had so beautified St. John's Chapel; there were Dr. Whichcote and Dr. Holdsworth and Mr. Cudworth of Emmanuel, Dr. Fuller of Queen's, and a host more.

Giles takes her to Little St. Mary's:

> Kneeling in the little church, so dim, so charmingly aisleless, so reminiscent still of the college chapel for which it had served for three centuries until seven years back, Julian seemed to herself to have entered into another religious country from any she had trodden before. Here was a new Anglicanism, decorated with ornament, lit with tall tapers that flamed softly in brass candlesticks on the high-raised altar; a crucifix hung over the altar, and incense drifted faintly about the church. It seemed to Julian very lovely. . . .

And to make things even better there is Richard Crashaw sitting in the chancel, who is said to watch and pray in the church all the night sometimes and who is only kept from Popery by Little Gidding and Dr. Cosin, the Peterhouse Master.

Conybeare is delighted to send Julian to Mr. More's classes for women on Tuesday afternoons, where he expounds on the universe and the Platonical soul, and reads with them "Plato, Plotinus, Origen, Tully, and Clement, and that eximious little book, *Theologia Germanica*" and hopes to work them up to Descartes. Mr. More is one with Dr. Conybeare in his belief that women should be scholars, as men should, "only, having been neither married, nor having had to minister to female invalids, he had more faith in the female understanding."

Alas, the Antiplatonick part now begins. Cleveland becomes Julian's tutor. He burns the thesis she has written for Henry More on Pythagoras' theory of the soul and sets about to seduce the fifteen-year-old nun of the Platonick quarry who falls blindly in love with him although he cares nothing for her verses and mocks her learning. But Cleveland has immanacl'd her corporal rind, and Julian learns the sadness that there must always be in love.

Then, on the day of the execution of Strafford, she is killed accidentally in a quarrel between Cleveland and her Puritan brother. She had burned all her verse except the poem she had written that morning, "An Epitaph on the Earl of Strafford," which Rose Macaulay borrows for her from its uncertain attribution to Cleveland:

> Riddles lye heere; & in a worde
> Heere lyes bloud; & let it lye
> Speechless still, & never crye.

The Postscript takes place on Midsummer Day 1647, when Herrick seditiously and for the last time reads the Evening Service from the Book of Common Prayer. He is leaving for London. Julian is dead; Dr. Conybeare, despairing of liberty of thought and conscience, has fled to The Hague; Kit lives a hanger-on at the beggared English court in Paris. They are defeated all. Rose Macaulay was justifiably annoyed when the title was changed for American publication. Herrick is left alone to mourn for us "his mutilated Alma Mater in the hands of Vandals, her learned sons exiled and deprived, their places taken by unscholarly usurpers."

> The rose withers, the blossom blasteth,
> The flower fades, the morning hasteth,
> The sun sets, the shadow flies,
> The gourd consumes; and man he dies.

Pleasure of Ruins (1953), written at the height of her powers, is one of the three or four best books Rose Macaulay ever wrote. Polymath, slightly perverse in its subject (a heartless pastime she admits it is, echoing Henry James), at times a mighty maze without a plan, it suggests some anatomy from her beloved seventeenth century. It is a book hard to read seriatim: so many ruins, so many ruin-fanciers, all described with such style and wit and learning, so many places from China to Peru (only North America escapes, having *keine verfallenen Schlösser*), the mind's eye glazes over. But it would be a mistake not to read all of it, in judiciously spaced sittings, because its beauty is cumulative; excerpts can never suggest its rhythm. There is no good reason why it should not have gone on and on with its loving catalog. I, for my part, can wish it longer.

Pleasure of Ruins is both an examination of our pleasure in ruins, its history, and of ruins themselves, their discoverers and visitors. The ruin-seekers are as delightful as the ruins. Caracalla, for example, at the Graeco-Roman Ilium became "Troy-minded to excess," fancied himself Achilles, staged elaborate funeral rites, and ran "naked with his retinue round the hero's tomb." Memorable, too, is the triumphal entry of Lady Hester Stanhope on her white Arab horse into Palmyra. " 'The inhabitants were arranged,' " she wrote, " 'in the most picturesque manner on the different columns leading to the Temple of the Sun.' " Dancing girls, poets singing odes, a whole village singing and dancing—we are frankly envious. "One may say that no one has ever enjoyed himself or herself more in any ruins that did Pitt's niece in Palmyra; it was *Ruinenlust* in its highest, most regal degree."

Easier for the modern tourist to identify with is C. G. setting out for Baalbek. Having learned a little Arabic to speak to her horse, she packed carefully, "not forgetting my nice little spirit-lamp, with apparatus for making tea, some preserves, sardines, biscuits, hard eggs, etc." Having arrived at the village, she paused: "Now for a cup of deli-cious tea, some fresh eggs and splendid grapes. A walk of ten minutes, stumbling over huge stones, leaping or wading . . . I stood among the far-famed ruins of the three temples of Baalbek. Well! this is indeed one of the wonders of the world."

Turks she dislikes and Goths, "those disgusting savages who roamed over Europe sacking other people's cities, who are so praised by German historians, and who ought never to have left the Vistula." Her heroes, on the other hand, are many: the romantic Gregorovius, that "learned, picturesque and ivy-loving historian of the Middle Ages," Baedeker, Cassiodorus, Pope Pius II. Hadrian is her man: "But most he liked to see things: it was his ruling passion . . . and famous ruins, such as Ilium, Thebes, and Nauplia sent him into ecstacies." She greatly admires ar-chaeologists like Sir A. H. Layard and Sir Arthur Evans, who taste "the highest and purest of ruin-pleasures," but appreciates as well the varied sensibilities of Chateaubri-and and Byron and Hobhouse.

Throughout history she selects those who share her ruin-pleasures. The first of these would seem to be the Hebrew prophets, "in those impassioned invectives described mei-otically by commentators as 'discourses against foreign nations.'" Pilgrims to Nineveh can quote Zephaniah

> who, like all prophets, rejoiced over the ruin of great cities, confident that they had richly de-served their fate, for prophets have believed all large cities to be given over to wickedness, and an abomination in the eyes of the Lord, and no doubt they are right. They have been the most single-minded of ruin-lovers, having no use for cities until they fall, and then rejoicing over the shattered remains in ringing words.

> "And he will stretch out his hand against the south and destroy Assyria and will make Nine-veh a desolation . . . everyone that passeth by her shall hiss and wag his hand."

> It may be questioned if Zephaniah would have approved the excavations which have brought the wicked palaces to light, to be marveled at by future generations who neither hiss nor wag their hands, but carefully steal decorations and graven images and store them in museums for the admiration of the world.

Though, as for Nineveh, Rose Macaulay is not greatly en-thusiastic, rightly calling winged bulls "those creatures so little loveable to any but Assyrians."

The ruins themselves and the so varied pleasures they ex-cite are, of course, her central concern. Unable or perhaps only unwilling to organize them at all neatly (only church-es and castles stay put very well), the reader moves back and forth through Greece and Italy, Syria, Turkey, the Barbary Coast, Mesopotamia, Armenia, and India, with excursions to Central and South America and the Far East. On Mycenae she is both reverent and funny:

> Today, like Pausanias, we observe the Lion Gate . . . admire the fragments of the Cyclope-an walls, the Treasury of Atreus, the tombs, the remains of palace and temple, and muse on the

terrible family life led by the royal house of Pe-lops, as Edmond About mused at the Lion Gate on a Sunday morning a century ago, with the shocked pleasure of one reading the more sensa-tional Sunday papers. . . . Indeed, to reflect on the extraordinary goings-on that occurred when the ruins we survey were in their hey-day must ever be among the pleasures that move us, and such reflections have profoundly moved those who have gazed on ruined cities, castles, palaces and abbeys.

On Pompeii she is admirable, on the Neapolitan villas and palaces, on the history of Athens' ruins, on Rome, whose ruining affects her as it did Gibbon. How one envies Hilde-bert of Lavardin and Petrarch for what they were still able to see, and Byron, Shelley, Chateaubriand, Stendhal for the luxuriant conditions in which they could see what was left, half-buried beneath trees and vines, moss and wild flowers, while now every ruin is scrubbed and cleaned. In-evitably, twin laments run through the book, that ruins themselves become more ruined, and that no one can rec-oncile the opposed demands of the Romantic tourist and the archaeologist. One mourns Gauthier's Stamboul, the Carthage Tasso and Chateaubriand saw, the Pozzuoli of Evelyn and Bishop Burnett—all spoiled by urban develop-ment. How little is left of Osney, beloved by Aubrey, lying in the slums near Oxford's (rebuilt) railway station, while Tintern and Netley have been cleaned up by the Ministry of Works.

She prefers her classical temples broken but not entirely prone, finds Byzantine churches more exquisite when en-tire but decayed, and Baroque in ruins the most emotion-stirring of all. The decaying churches of Armenia strike the right note, especially the Byzantine with their conical tiled roofs and apses and broken Roman columns. "About them mutter the eccentric ghosts of the so tenacious, so wrong-headed anti-Chalcedon churchmen who main-tained their monophysite rites and notions in them for so long. . . . There is something reassuring in their ancient-ness, their sturdy frailty, and their spirited, erroneous, martyred history."

She brings to her vast survey a remarkably wide range of response; she is the least narrow-minded of tourists, rejoic-ing at once in classical architecture, in Byzantine, Roman-esque, Gothic, Baroque, in pagan palaces and crusaders' castles and Indian rock temples. Everywhere the reader feels her passionate fondness for the past and delight in its ruined artifacts. Especially does her abiding interest in the history of Christianity come through, her love of its ex-treme beauty and oddity. There is, she tells us, a baptistery in Djemila,

> on whose font an inscription remarks hopefully that in time all nations will be baptised. Be that as it may, the valiant attempts to bring such a state of affairs about has strewn the habitable and unhabitable world with the most enchanting buildings in decay. The Jesuit order in particu-lar, diving into fantastic jungles to baptise the most improbable beings, planted their baroque mission churches in clearings among dense for-ests and cannibal Americans whom they in-structed in the faith against startling odds. . . .

> To come suddenly out of savage forests into such
> a clearing, to see such a church embraced by the
> wild growths of the centuries since its desertion,
> but still civil, still elegantly baroque in its ruin,
> would be an encounter of the most rewarding.

One thinks of Charles Ryder in *Brideshead Revisited.*

What a traveling companion Rose Macaulay would have
been, greeting each ruin with enthusiasm, knowing everything earlier visitors had written, investigating with intelligence each new dig, revisiting ruins loved since childhood,
swimming wherever possible, as, for example, among the
ruins of Roman villas near Naples.

The Towers of Trebizond has one of the three or four best
opening sentences I know: " 'Take my camel, dear,' said
my aunt Dot, as she climbed down from this animal on
her return from High Mass." It is her funniest and wisest
book. She was nearly eighty, with a lifetime of writing behind her, when she achieved her masterpiece.

One can think of several things that help explain the
book's distinction. Her novel has a double focus, one
comic, one tragic. It is full of the most amusing incidents
and dialogue and is at the same time an exploration of a
conscience struggling with sin and faith. She has expanded
the genre of the comic novel.

She achieves this by using a first-person narration which
unifies her novel and by creating for her narrator, Laurie,
a prose style which is a great comic invention, a triumph
of parataxis, rambling, stuck full of surprising odds and
ends of feelings and beliefs, that ranges easily from the
profane to the sacred. It is Laurie's prose which allows
Rose Macaulay to write a novel rich in eccentric characters and a kind of disciplined lunacy, which is also an investigation of the gravest problems of belief, a serious call
to a sober and devout life. Laurie shuttles between describing the funny things that keep happening and recording
her own consciousness. Her imagination lights up the
books with metaphors at once odd and beautiful that fit
the wittily careless prose:

> Dr. Pococke had said that, when he was there,
> Troas was infested by Rogues; that was over two
> centuries ago, but Rogues do go on in the same
> places for ever, as churches do, it seems to have
> something to do with the soil they are on. A
> group of inhabitants stood by the road as we
> drove up; they were dark and sad, and they may
> have been rogues, but I thought they looked
> more like those obscure, dejected, maladjusted
> and calamity-prone characters who come into
> Tenebrae, such as Aleph, Teth, Beth, Caleph,
> Jod, Ghimel, Mem and the rest, and they sound-
> ed as if they were talking in that afflicted strain
> that those characters talk in, and saying things
> like "he has brought me into darkness and not
> into light," "he has compassed me with gall and
> labour," "he has built against me round about,
> that I may not get out, he has upset my paths,"
> and "my eyes have failed with weeping, my bow-
> els are disturbed, my liver is poured out," and
> so on, till all the lights go out and there is noth-
> ing but the dark.

We have been led in two sentences from Turkish vagrants

through the ceremonies of Tenebrae and the Lamentations of Jeremiah to the death of God.

She also hit on the idea of using the form of a travel book.
She had always written splendidly about places and history; now she can do it through her pleasing narrator. The
choice of Turkey (which she had recently visited) makes
possible the double focus. The setting is rich in comic possibilities; the wrecked Byzantine splendor creates the images that carry the religious theme.

Even the stylishness of the prose serves a purpose; it reveals Laurie to us. Never has Macaulay used better her
trick of suddenly embedding a quotation, because here the
mannerism illuminates Laurie's mind; we learn the kinds
of things her memory is stored with: "Some of them [Lau-
rie's clerical ancestors] were thus vanquished by the assaults of Manicheeism, others by the innocent theories of
Pelagius, others again by that kind of pantheism which is
apt to occur in meadows and woods, others by the difficulties of thus thinking of the Trinity, and still more by plain
Doubt."

The plot, with its comic and tragic elements, is easily told.
Laurie goes to Turkey with her aunt Dot and the Hon. the
Rev. Hugh Chantrey-Pigg, who are being sent by the
Anglo-Catholic Missionary Society to see if the neighborhood of Trebizond would be a suitable place to open an
Anglican mission. The amazing and fearless aunt Dot, a
staunch Anglican who, however, sits down during the
Athanasian Creed, is "a cheerful and romantic adventurer" for whom travel is the chief end of life. Father
Chantrey-Pigg, an ancient bigot, had a London church
several inches higher than St. Magnus Martyr, is now retired, and collects relics; in Tiflis he cures a policeman's
wife of lumbago with a relic of St. Jane Frances De Chan-
tal applied on her feast day. When aunt Dot and Father
Hugh disappear quietly behind the Iron Curtain to fish in
the Caspian and see Armenian churches, Laurie returns
alone to Trebizond and then travels, drugged by an en-
chanter's potion, by camel from Trebizond to Jerusalem,
meeting at Alexandretta her married lover, Vere. Back in
England, she anxiously awaits news of aunt Dot who does,
of course, turn up. Laurie goes off for a holiday in Venice
with Vere, and as they drive back from Folkestone, he is
killed when a bus crashes into their car.

It is, then, in part, and this provides the comedy, a Turkey
book, such as so many of their friends are engaged simultaneously in writing, full of adventure and tourism. She invents marvelous complications with passports and the
Turkish language, scattering acerb comments on Mos-
lemism, policemen, and Turks.

They take with them aunt Dot's camel, and not a Land-
rover, and this has many advantages, service garages being
few. But, on the other hand, the camel, the book's most
foolish character, causes much inconvenience, being mental.

> "Has it had mental trouble before? For I think
> that it now has."
>
> Aunt Dot said that she believed that camels usu-
> ally had a certain degree of this, they were born
> with it, and without it they would never lead the

peculiar lives they did, but her camel had, she thought, not yet been actually round the bend.

"It looks odd because it is odd," said Aunt Dot. "Camels are."

Laurie, as accomplished a traveler as aunt Dot, well-up on Byzantine history and architecture and the history of the Greek Church, is, as her prose proves, a complex young woman. The tragic element in the book is her adultery, whose sinfulness she never disguises or denies. She cannot, she thinks, give up her married lover, Vere. The sin comes from a deep meanness and selfishness, but out of these, and this is her problem, flow love and joy and peace. Father Chantrey-Pigg asks her on Whit Sunday how much longer she will go shutting the door against God. Will she come back only when she has nothing to offer but a burnt-out fire? " 'Oh, he'll take it, he'll take anything we offer. It is you who will be impoverished for ever by so poor a gift.' " Has she put herself beyond caring, he asks. "Not quite, never quite, I had tried, but never quite. From time to time I knew what I had lost." And she thinks of Trebizond, "that lost corner of a lost empire, defeated and gone under so long ago that now she scarcely knew or remembered lost Byzantium, having grown unworthy of it, blind, deaf and not caring any more, not even believing, and perhaps that was the ultimate hell."

Slowly Laurie's imagination transforms the dull Trabzon of today into the symbol of her baffled religious longings. Trabzon keeps dissolving into Trebizond, and Trebizond acquires an anagogic level and becomes the City of God. Through metaphor and symbol Rose Macaulay can develop her Christian theme within Laurie's capacious prose, without violating the novel's surface.

The real Trebizond is, she knows, "in the ruined Byzantine citadel, keep and palace on the heights . . . and in the disused, wrecked Byzantine churches that brooded, forlorn, lovely, ravished and apostate ghosts, about the hills and shores of that lost empire." Hidden there is something she wants for herself and could make her own. She has between sleeping and waking, in the central passage of the novel,

> a vision of Trebizond: not Trebizond as I had seen it, but the Trebizond of the world's dreams, of my own dreams, shining towers and domes shimmering on a far horizon, yet close at hand, luminously enspelled in the most fantastic unreality, yet the only reality, a walled and gated city, magic and mystical, standing beyond my reach yet I had to be inside, an alien wanderer yet at home, held in the magical enchantment; and at its heart, at the secret heart of the city and the legend and the glory in which I was caught and held, there was some pattern I could not unravel, some hard core that I could not make my own, and, seeing the pattern and the hard core enshrined within the walls, I turned back from the city and stood outside it, expelled in mortal grief.

She cannot enter the Kingdom because she will not. But her Augustinian restlessness persists, and her vision of the Church:

the gleaming, infrangible, so improbable as to be all but impossible, walled kingdom of the infrangible God. . . . The fact that at present I cannot find my way into it does not lessen, but rather heightens its spell; a magic castle, it changes down the ages its protean form, but on its battlements the *splendor lucis aeternae* inextinguishably down all the ages lies.

Nor does Vere's death allow Laurie to return to the Church. "I live now in two hells, for I have lost God and live also without love, or without the love I want, and I cannot get used to that either. Though people say that in the end one does. To the other, perhaps, never."

The Towers of Trebizond is thus about faith because it is about the loss of faith. The end is left very much open. We are permitted to hope that Laurie, with her great sense of humor and her high romantic dreams, will, ultimately, enter Trebizond, her fortress and her ease.

What else of Rose Macaulay is most worth reading? Of the nonfiction, it would be a pity to miss *Fabled Shore,* (1949) a first-rate travel book on Spain which, most unfortunately, helped begin the destruction of the Costa Brava. Following the route of Avienus' late-fourth-century *Ora Maritima* she drove in 1947 along the eastern and southern seaboards. It took a sense of adventure to do this alone at the age of sixty-six, and although she was never stoned, as nineteenth-century travelers were apt to be, some little boys did throw tomatoes at her once, and everywhere she was greeted with the cry, "una señora que conduce!" Many of the roads were, as Gauthier had found them, "vraiment impracticables," and when the hotels promised by out-of-date guidebooks could not be found, she simply camped out under the stars, alone.

Her letters to Father Johnson, *Letters to a Friend* [1961], and its sequel [*Last Letters to a Friend* (1962)], were received with enthusiasm and are indispensable for our knowledge of her. However right Elizabeth Taylor and Robert Liddell may have been in deploring the violation of privacy in publishing them after her death, it is impossible to regret the publication of books that so many have found comforting and inspiring.

Among the many novels it is possible to list only a few titles. The five early novels one may ignore; she was believed to be planning to steal the copies in the London Library. *The Making of a Bigot* (1914) is the first novel in which she found her mature voice, and although *Potterism* (1920) and *Dangerous Ages* (1921) have most amusing passages and helped establish her reputation, *Told by an Idiot* (1924) is, I think, her first totally assured novel. It begins in 1879 and ends in 1923 and while we follow the lives of Mr. and Mrs. Garden and their six children, and grandchildren, we watch the shift from Late Victorianism to the Twenties, the political situation, the new books, the appearance of bicycles, bloomers, Ping-Pong, nightclubs. Mr. Garden, modeled on Thomas Arnold, is one of her most lovable characters. In the course of the novel he becomes an Ethicist, a Roman Catholic once again, a Theosophist, a Christian Scientist, an Evangelical, a Spiritualist, a disciple of the Higher Thought, and of the New Theology, and at the novel's end he embraces all creeds, believing everything. His granddaughter Imogen dreams of becoming a poet and knows all the ships in the British Navy. At fourteen "she still, and, for many years to come, thought of herself, with hope growing faint and ever fainter, as a brown-skinned, blue-eyed young naval man." Rose Macaulay's father finally had to tell her when she was about thirteen that she really must stop saying she wanted to be a young man and go into the Navy.

Orphan Island (1924) was, she told Father Johnson, except for *They Were Defeated,* the novel she most enjoyed writing. It is both a celebration and a mocking of the myth of the desert island. The Thinkwells, arriving from Cambridge to rescue any survivors of the orphans their grandfather had abandoned on a coral reef sixty-five years before, discover that the orphans under the direction of their guardian, Miss Smith, have reproduced the social, ecclesiastical, and economic arrangements of Victorian Britain. Miss Smith's identification with Queen Victoria is now absolute as she reigns at Balmoral, her cottage among the palm groves. The contrasts between the island splendor and the rigid caste system are wonderful to follow. Primitivist dreams are confounded by what a Miss Smith can do to an island paradise. But not entirely. The island remains memorably beautiful and seductive.

Elizabeth Bowen finely calls *Staying with Relations* (1930) Rose Macaulay's "most dementing novel." It also contains one of her finest inventions, a hacienda set in the clearing of a Guatemalan jungle that had been a Dominican monastery built on Mayan ruins and whose great bedroom is after one of the New Palace rooms at Potsdam while the dining room is Cuvilliés' octagon room in the Amalienburg. Here Catherine Grey comes to visit her relatives, "like so many young females, a novelist" who has been lecturing in the United States on the Creation of Character in Fiction. The first night she firmly characterizes each of her relatives only to discover, as the action of the novel proves, that she has been entirely wrong. Still, she argues, "people must be like something, if only one can discover what."

The World My Wilderness (1950) is, though untypical, certainly one of her two or three best novels. Two children who have lived in France during the war, on the fringes of the Maquis, are brought to England to live with their upper-middle-class families, and for escape and solace they play among the ruined churches near St. Paul's. It was her first novel since the war and the bombing of her flat, the first since the death of Gerald O'Donovan, and it is a somber and moving book. " 'The maquis is within us,' " says Helen, " 'we take our wilderness where we go.' " Her son, like Flaubert, "is aware of irremediable barbarism coming up out of the earth, and of filth flung against the ivory tower" and quotes Burke: "Learning will be cast into the mire and trodden down under the hoofs of a swinish multitude." And yet the ruined churches, St. Alban's and St. Giles's and St. Vedast's, "kept their strange courses, kept their improbable, incommunicable secret" and still stand amid the Waste Land. (pp. 114-27)

J. V. Guerinot, "The Pleasures of Rose Macaulay," in Twentieth Century Literature, *Vol. 33, No. 1, Spring, 1987, pp. 110-28.*

John Coates   (essay date 1987)

[*In the following excerpt, Coates examines* The Towers of Trebizond, *focusing on Macaulay's use of the city of the title as a metaphor for the decline of the traditions of Western civilization.*]

Any account of *The Towers of Trebizond* (1956) must seek to determine why it stands out from the body of Rose Macaulay's sprightly, intelligent and very cultivated novels. What raises her last completed work so far above the level of *Told by an Idiot, Potterism* and the rest, social and intellectual comedies, popular in their time and pleasant to re-read, but less significant, surely, even than early Aldous Huxley? It is likely that *The Towers of Trebizond* wins its very superior station in her work through two striking features; the management of its central metaphor, and the adroit control its author exercises throughout her novel over its particularly complex tone.

It is easy to discern the broad outlines of the novel's key metaphor. Rose Macaulay makes use of the shadowy existence of Trebizond as a Byzantine "empire" after the Latin conquest of 1204 and its survival for a few years after 1453 as the last fragment of Greek Christian Asia Minor, when all the rest had fallen to the Turks. The metaphor defines one of her chief concerns, the problem of cultural fracture or amnesia and the nature of its emotional effects on the individual. At first sight, the novel's central image may seem somewhat esoteric. The scene of *The Towers of Trebizond,* and a symbol drawn from the obscure persistence of some remote Byzantine city in the fifteenth century, looks too *recherché* for the conflicts and tensions the novel purports to handle. In fact, post-Ataturk Turkey and Trebizond, perhaps best considered together, are a peculiarly exact and appropriate metaphor for several reasons. Apart from the much more historically remote example of North Africa, Anatolia is the most important instance of the entire eradication of a formerly flourishing Christian culture. Asia Minor exemplifies the destruction of a language, of a religion, and of art, even of a very landscape, more completely than perhaps any other territory. Moreover, the lost Christianity and the lost culture of the region are not obscure or remote. Anatolia is, of course, the site of the seven churches compared to seven golden candlesticks lighting the world (*Revelation* I, 12-13), of Nicaea where the Christian creed was defined, and the home of the Cappadocian fathers who defended Orthodoxy and shaped monasticism. Less significantly, but still given the wider cultural concerns of *The Towers of Trebizond,* it is important as the setting of the seven Grecian cities which fought for Homer dead and of the Pre-Socratic philosophers. It is the cradle of classical culture and of Western European intellectual speculation.

Rose Macaulay is fortunate in the actual existence of a haunted landscape whose ghosts mean nothing to its inhabitants but which must be full of meaning to a Western visitor educated in the traditions and values of his own culture. Modern Anatolia with its deserted and ignored churches and Greco-Roman ruins is the embodiment of a fracture in civilisation. At the same time, if offers a striking metaphor for another fracture closer to home; the oblivion of the Greek and Latin classics and the culture they sustained and, largely, of Christian traditions and values which has characterised the last hundred years in Britain and in Europe. In *The Towers of Trebizond* religious belief and an acceptance of the value of religious experience are not merely acts of choosing by the individual will and intellect. They are *cultural* facts, bound up with inherited attitudes. Such attitudes may persist only as family traditions and yet such persistence may pose an intriguing personal problem in a secularised society which meets the "outmoded" view with, to use one of yesterday's catch phrases, "repressive tolerance". *The Towers of Trebizond* examines, among much else, the individual psychological tensions created, at least partly, by such a situation. It explores the division set up in the mind which has inherited a set of attitudes, an assumption of certain priorities, a way of seeing, when these are not shared, or even understood by a confident culture, very much at home with itself. Rose Macaulay's novel asks how the individual, troubled besides by personal temptations, can maintain a frame of reference denied, not so much by persecution, which might be stimulating in small doses, but by simply writing it out of the record. It is the deeper denial of historical or cultural amnesia. Claims and a language are passed over not merely as untrue, but as boring, jejune and incomprehensible. As P. L. Berger points out in *A Rumour of Angels,* one of the most interesting modern examples of the sociology of religion, there is bound to be a difficulty in maintaining a minority view or an out of favour model of man which lacks social validation. This is quite apart from the objective truth or falsehood of such a view or such a model. It is also quite apart from the conflict, recorded in *The Towers of Trebizond,* between religious belief and illicit love. In another cultural or intellectual climate, however, such suffering would probably have taken another form.

The Trebizond metaphor, although it defines very broadly an area of conflict and an emotional and intellectual attitude, does not remain constant, still meaning one thing. Trebizond embraces the whole spectrum of emotions evoked by the vanished religion of a secularised world. At one extreme, these touch on a whimsical, slightly patronising antiquarianism. The lost romantic city is, in this guise, the haven of nostalgias, of cultural and historical snobberies, of all the intriguing or tiresome enthusiasm which surrounds lost causes. Trebizond is the religious equivalent of "The Royal Stuart Society" or "The Richard III Society".

At the other extreme, the Towers of Trebizond are the focus of deeper emotions, yearnings much less easily dismissed, of intimations of a heart within the heartless world. In this respect, it is the legendary or archetypal heavenly city from which one is, by one's own actions, cast out. Between the two extremes are many moods, many ambiguous ebbs and flows of thought and emotion. It would be difficult to imagine a metaphor, drawn from an historical event, capable of more supple and versatile use. Trebizond expresses emotions which are frankly absurd and escapist. Yet the lost city is also a fixed point in a world full of shallow restless curiosities, incoherent desires, of momentarily real but fundamentally unsatisfying pleasures. Behind the day-to-day stimuli of Laurie's life

and her more inward sadness and guilt, Trebizond is the continued, if perplexing and half-hearted, affirmation of something nobler which may be beyond the grasp but which ought not to be beyond the reach of humanity. It is a testimony to the fact that religious instincts and needs are so potent that even their ghosts are compelling. Since the power and interest of the Trebizond metaphor consists in the detailed use to which it is put, it will be the object of this paper to examine some of its nuances.

The binding metaphor of Trebizond depends for some of its force and meaning on the tone, the particular speaking voice of Rose Macaulay's novel establishes from the outset for its narrator. The first pages of *The Towers of Trebizond* read like a comic variant, a translation into dottiness, of her own autobiographical comments on that ambience which defined her outlook and interests [in *Letters to a Friend, 1950-1952*]:

> No wonder that I feel an interest in religion, considering how steadily and for how many generations ancestors versed in theology had converged on me from all sides.

In the novel's opening passage a distinguished theological and classical background such as that which formed its author, with its dynasties of clergymen, scholars and scientists, Macaulays and Conybeares, is deliberately rendered comic. Cultural traditions which were once at the heart of the national life seem to advertise themselves as quaint and fey in those first references to Aunt Dot and the camel on which she has been to High Mass, or her car, stolen by an Anglican Bishop outside the Athenaeum and in the whole breathless, slightly gamin, tone of Laurie's narrative. Instead of a world of scholarship and piety which formed an ideal and a standard within English life, we are offered a clique of lovable or not so lovable eccentrics or "characters".

There is something odd and revealing about the sedulous charm, the "playing for laughs", in Laurie's account of her family, staunch in

> that great middle class of the Church of England which is said to be the religious back-bone (so far as it has one) of our nation.

The presenting of serious beliefs as picturesque oddities is often a way for a culture to cope with their obstinate and otherwise irritating persistence. The final crushing answer to any intellectual position is to declare that it is "lovable" or "charmingly eccentric". There is a classic instance in Addison's dealing in this way with Toryism in Sir Roger De Coverley. At the same time, the posture of lovable eccentricity is a tempting one for holders of minority or "reactionary" views to slide into. It disarms a hostility which may be just as wearing to its victims for being tacit and helps to make them acceptable in the face of incomprehension.

Laurie gives an externalised account of her High Anglican family background which seems to concede that beliefs which upheld it were a private and perverse idiosyncrasy:

> We belong to an old Anglican family which suffered under the penal laws of Henry VIII, Mary I and Oliver P . . . Under Elizabeth we dug our-

selves firmly into Anglican life, compelling our Puritan tenants to dance around the Maypole and revel at Christmas.

The opening chord of *The Towers of Trebizond* is the start of what is to be a turning and twisting argument through many phases of belief, half-belief and doubt. Laurie and the novel seem at first to accept the charge levelled at the religious frame of reference. Yes, it is irrelevant and only pardonable because it is picturesque. Having accepted the charge, however, *The Towers of Trebizond* proceeds to subvert it by deft, almost imperceptible changes of tone. The first of these is the long fishing metaphor. Almost all her dotty clerical ancestors, Laurie tells us, were keen fishermen. What looks a mere oddity slides into the image of a gentle civilised religious tradition, which lacking cut and dried dogmas or absolute authority, yet preserves its faith against the "dragon in the path":

> This dragon they would sometimes step over without injury, saved at perhaps the moment of encountering it by a gentle tug at the line.

Those quiet generations were not, in fact, ages of simple complacent acceptance, contrasted with the present. Doubts and intellectual problems were always there.

What it shows of the modern world is, however, the chief way in which the novel tactfully encourages its reader to revalue the discarded religious image of man. Perhaps the best response to the superficially plausible argument that the chief traditions of western culture are merely relative, local and temporary ideologies, is to examine that point of view which claims to stand outside and above them. Modern Turkey is, perhaps, of all the Islamic countries the one which has adopted most uncritically the values of secular progress. In the novel, it is a place where those values unselfconsciously built into our attitudes, may be seen from outside. The Turkish university students on the boat to Trebizond

> knew that the Church, being backward and reactionary, had been left behind in the spectacular progress of Ataturk's modern Turkey. Imams, priests, patriarchs, prophets, Turkey had left them all behind.

They attended lectures at the British Institute in Istanbul on English poetry, ("Dylan Thomas, Spender, MacNeice, Lewis, Eliot, Sitwell, Frost, Charlotte Mew. It is very like ours, yes?"), and are full of views on the Modern Poem, the Modern Novel, and the Modern Woman. What Rose Macaulay suggests is a synthetic culture, patched together from the least interesting notions of material improvement once current in the West. Here, perhaps, the essence of those notions can be seen more clearly. The public buildings of the new Ankara which the young Turks proudly patter off, blur together into the anonymous haze of a modern city which could be anywhere in the world and which was "obviously a bore". Curiously, this "progress" in a given country, Israel, Russia or Turkey is hardly ever interesting to foreign visitors, however much it may interest those who live amid it. This comment, gently subversive and undeniably true, raises a disturbing point. If the values embodied in the physical achievements of secular progress are so convincing, why are their manifestations

abroad so dull and repellent, so "very vile and common", "compared with what was in the country before they got there?" The ideal of the "New Woman" brought about by the Ataturk revolution seems a factitious notion, rooted in nothing and offering nothing to Laurie's intelligent companion Dr. Halide, troubled by a variant of Laurie's conflict between ideals and personal feelings. Dr. Halide tires of her compatriot's "juvenile babble" about the new opportunities:

> Lawyers, doctors, teachers, writers, judges, painters, dancers, modistes, beauticians . . . Some virgins, some wives. In Turkey today, it is no matter. All get about.

The catalogue may be statistically true but it does not give the sense of any quality or depth in the lives it enumerates. By itself this might be mere reactionary prejudice but the mobility of the, probably hypothetical, Turkish Woman takes it place in *The Towers of Trebizond* as another instance of movement without meaning. The keynote of much of the book in its description of the modern world is that feeling of experience without the fruit of experience, of events and encounters without significance, of a continual sipping and hurrying on. Laurie does not like to tell the amiable Turkish students she thinks their modern culture vapid since they "did not know where they truly belonged, and perhaps few of us do".

The English traveller abroad forms a minor but significant aspect of the Turkish metaphor. Modern Turkey is a paradigm of the earth made small by the revolution in communications, known and yet not known. Ubiquitous touring vans from the B.B.C. hurry about the Turkish landscape as, we must assume, they range about other landscapes, seeking "colour", local interest, supposedly picturesque details. The B.B.C.'s interpreters unsuccessfully urge the impassive Turks to break into song and dance so that the result can be recorded:

> They did not take any notice, but no doubt they would be bribed presently and a nice little Home Service programme about Trebizond would emerge.

As Aunt Dot remarks these techniques reduce "abroad" to a stylised uniformity. (pp. 111-13)

The global village promised by mass communications turns out to be a world converted into the material for light entertainment. *The Towers of Trebizond* adopts a casual, almost indulgent tone about the travel programmes, as about their written equivalent, the coffee table volumes almost every character in the novel seems to be writing. Like the B.B.C.'s organising the "natives" into group singing, the "Turkey books" are an industry based on the need, which Rose Macaulay remarked on elsewhere, to kill time by those who liked it better dead. Both Radio programmes and travel books grow from, and try to create, a trivial curiosity, the former by a technique of pseudo-event, the latter by efficient plagiarism from earlier books or as with David and Charles, from the writer's own collaborator.

Turkey offers more than a glimpse through the foreign visitors of a world which has found technologies, of book production and radio, and lost a culture. Travellers of this kind, amusing and interesting as they are, are only the periphery of the novel's Turkey metaphor. As has been suggested, Rose Macaulay is more interested in exploiting the historic role of Asia Minor the palimpsest of cultures, of buried worlds and lost values, as image of a contemporary predicament. The visit of Laurie and her party to the site of Troy offers an early and important instance of the use to which the Turkish landscape is put. We are reminded that

> Turks are not brought up, as Europeans are (or were) on the Trojan legend.

The parenthesis, "or were", is notable. The focal points of reference for Western Man, the "European folk tales", are disappearing from his consciousness. The Trojan cycle, the cycle of Charlemagne, the cycle of Roland, the cycle of Christ, Laurie reflects, are no longer the means of organising and valuing experience and response or the vehicles of emotion and reflection. *We* are like the Turks, inhabiting a landscape purged of associations. Like the Turks, our minds are shaped by alien images and patterns "in so far as they have been shaped at all, which is not much". The point here is not a disdainful dismissal of Turks in themselves, but a comment on the Western European cultural impoverishment of which they are the image, the way in which *we* are strangers in what was once our country.

Stories rich in texture and almost inexhaustible in their nuances have been replaced by shallow and threadbare patterns of behaviour. When Father Chantry-Pigg

> who knew Tennyson started reciting Oenone, about the vale in Ida lovelier than all the valleys of Ionian hills,

Charles, joint writer of yet another coffee table book, merely looks "distant" but makes allowance for the old man's generation. He cannot respond either, to the priest's quotation from Ovid, "corn grows now where Troy once stood":

> "Well, hardly *seges* just grass and things and anyhow Troy had probably never stood there at all."

Jackson Knight has remarked, as one testimony to the influence of Latin literature on the European mind, that the conflicts between love and duty, the moment and the future which are so familiar "have become familiar through Vergil". Equally, one might say, the sense of traumatic loss, *Troia fuit,* and of man sad and dutiful, seeking to rebuild the broken past have become familiar not only through Virgil but through all the Latin poets who touched on The Tale of Troy. In not feeling such resonances, the sophisticated or at least articulate Charles is one with the bored Turkish policemen to whom the site means nothing.

It is not merely that such allusions are interesting, are worth knowing or furnish the mind well. It is not even that such cycles and traditions form the general memory and pattern of response for our culture, that

> Troy was our ancestor, and the centre of a world that Turks could never know.

The point is deeper and more disturbing. Without the knowledge of and therefore the ability to meditate upon the great inherited corpus of moral and imaginative statement and questioning, the quality of the individual's mind is impaired.

Rose Macaulay obliquely suggests the manner of such impairment. Laurie reflects that certain dark sad human figures in the distance look like the bent and twisted Hebrew characters in the Psalms which "come into Tenebrae", the service for Good Friday. She does not share this fancy with Charles who "not being a Christian would not know" about such things. While he is speaking, she reflects on the "afflicted strain" of those Psalms, phrases of mounting grief repeated "till the lights go out and there is nothing but the dark". Her thoughts imply the consciousness which underlies her assumed personality, the grief beneath her fey, jaunty air. She assimilates into the pain of her own bruised conscience, of the regret that her adultery loses her the consolations of a religion in which she believes enough for it to matter, a general sense of the pain and loss recorded in the Tenebrae Psalms, or that suffered at Troy. Suffering and loss change their aspect but not their essence and man has always endured them. Meanwhile Charles, who does not know of or care for such allusions, is busily telling her of his quarrel with David. His flow of words passes over her, hardly heard, much less understood:

> "And then David said . . . and I said . . . and he said"

> It was like women talking near you on the bus— she said, I said, he said. And it was like the B.B.C. news—Mr Attlee has said at Blackpool . . . Mr Dulles said at Washington. Mr Nehru said yesterday in Delhi.

Without the sense of proportion gained from the classical and religious models of man's nature and suffering, experience is rendered shallow. Those "personal relationships" contemporary humanism endeavours to set up in the place of the fading lights of the past seem themselves to die of inanition. Charles' and David's quarrel, despite the fact that Laurie hears both their versions of it, remains as trivial and incomprehensible as it is intense. The relationships, the emotional awareness, the "only connect", taught by E. M. Forster, Rose Macaulay's friend and, years before, the subject of her major critical book, seem, in this unrealised and unrealisable estrangement, to have been reduced to meaningless babble. The bickerings, feuds and egotism which Charles and David call their personal lives are actually on the same level as the slogans, speeches and "events" the B.B.C. News offers as world affairs. Neither personal nor public discourse, the reader is left to assume, offers any food to the spirit. Both are deception and self-deception. The "relationships", with their freight of vanity and of quarrels, so significant to those who enact them (to David, for example, theatrically throwing a glass of hock cup in someone's face, yet so pointless to anyone else, seem part of a pattern of illusion. Charles hurries off to Istanbul to tell people about himself and David, in case they should be getting false ideas.

David then appears and gives his account but a sleepy Laurie gets "the two stories confused". This propaganda of private life is mirrored in the process of public propaganda through the media. As Aunt Dot asks, "Where *is* this free world they all talk about so much?" The lightest, most purely satirical section of *The Towers of Trebizond,* describing the newspaper reaction to Aunt Dot's and Father Chantry-Pigg's disappearance behind the Iron Curtain, seems designed to display the swirl of fictionalised events, of unreal "comment" and "opinion" which hides reality for contemporary man, educated or uneducated. The kind of sensibility from which modern culture and communications grow and which they feed, is not itself wicked or depraved but it is lightweight and shallow, like the girls in bikinis sunbathing who watched Father Chantry-Pigg's religious service and "thought the altar and the candles and the Mass very cute". The inability to dwell on any matter, either in acceptance or rejection, is accompanied by insatiable short-lived curiosity. As well as the B.B.C. vans "collecting a slice of Black Sea Life", Turkey is full of writers, diggers, photographers, spies "tumbling over each other". The novel several times reverts to the image of nomadic migration, like that of the Turks into Anatolia, and of uprooted peoples camping in the ruins of broken civilisations, to symbolise the deracinated mind of modern man. Dr. Halide's metaphor is more alarming and ironic in its implications than she suspects:

> When the masses will also start to advance, it will be as when our ancestors rolled across the Asia hills and plains, nothing could stay them. This will surely be again, when the minds of the Turkish masses roll on like an army and conquer the realms of culture.

So much of European thinking since the Enlightenment has been built around concepts of dynamism and change through the "movement" of the masses towards some ill-defined, allegedly higher goal. The Turkish incursion into Asia Minor is a mischievous, yet exact, visual and historical equivalent of such discourse. Nomadic settlers and destroyers are dynamic enough, but presumably this is not what the rhetoric meant, though, unfortunately, it is what it involves.

The Towers of Trebizond takes as its dominant metaphor one of the half-erased fragments of the past, a town which was a "corner of a lost empire, defeated and gone under long ago". In general, Trebizond represents the remains, uncomprehended and pathetic, of an earlier world view. In the particular terms of Laurie's own mind and predicament, Trebizond is the guttering flame of the religious and moral sense, dying under the habit of deliberate sin, and involvement in the triviality of the world. Early on, Laurie recognizes the town's connection with herself, drawing an explicit parallel between its forgetting of "Byzantium", "having grown unworthy of it", and the agnosticism "blind and deaf and not caring any more" into which she is sliding, as a refuge and relief from her conscience.

Within the basic map of the metaphor, however, there is room for a variety of perceptions. Like Trabzon, the mod-ern Turkish town, the wreck of the historic Christendom disappoints:

> Expecting the majestic, brooding ghost of a fallen empire, we saw, in a magnificent stagey setting, an untidy Turkish port.

The ruins of the Comnenus palace on the hill overlooking the modern city suggest little of the beauty and magnificence which were once there. There is nothing left of the painted walls of Cardinal Bessarion's medieval description. There only remain fig trees "hot in the sun", sprouting from what had once been marble mosaic floors, and "goats all about". By analogy, there is little left of the Christian cultural heritage to suggest its nature and proportions to the uninstructed and uninterested. Laurie, however, broods over the ruins, seeing "something" hidden in the town, that she wanted for herself and could still make her own, "something exiled and defeated but still alive, known long since, but forgotten". *The Towers of Trebizond* hints in this poignant and suggestive way at the survival of religious instincts and needs in a secular culture. To the individual who knows what they stand for the ruins are eloquent. Such knowledge is, perhaps, the essence of the matter. Laurie knows the history of "Trebizond" from the time of Jason, its role of "Queen of the Euxine and apple of the eye of all Asia". For her, it is "a romance" like Troy, Fonterrabia or Venice. Without a sense of the beauty of the Christian past, by analogy, the mind has nothing to work on in considering Christianity. Like the Turks who had not heard of it and called it Trabzon and "supposed it has always been a Turkish town," the modern European mind lacks historical sense and humility before the grandeur of its own past.

It is right to emphasise that *The Towers of Trebizond* is, among much else, a novel about modern European man's obliviousness to religion and only incidentally about Turkey. The "Turks" of the novel are essentially a metaphor for cultural fracture, not is author's ignorant dismissal of an alien culture. A sensitive reader is well aware from many studies, of which E. Said's excellent *Orientalism* is one of the latest, of the degree to which Europeans have used the stereotyped "oriental" as a figure to sustain their own aggression or illusions. At first sight Rose Macaulay seems to run this risk. She avoids it, I would suggest, for two reasons. Her statements about the Turkish migration and its relation to earlier Anatolian civilisation are undeniably accurate as far as they go. Of course, she only emphasises the few features of these past events which establish a parallel with the modern predicament. Such selectiveness is a guarantee of the metaphorical nature of the Turkish material and disinfects it of any racialist overtone.

A historian would almost certainly not quarrel, for instance, with her description of Ottoman culture, the province of a wealthy elite of officials and courtiers, with its own style and language incomprehensible to the masses, the "Turks without money":

> Sultans, Pashas, and Eunuchs and nobles and Tycoons have built palaces and mosques and harems and castles and cities, out of the stones they take from Greek and Roman cities and temples.

At the same time such a statement provides an exact parallel to modern Western synthetic culture, wealthy and materially impressive but thrown together from the uncomprehended fragments of the true civilisations of the past.

If *The Towers of Trebizond* had rested at this point it would have been an impressive conservative analysis or a moving threnody, but it would have begged some vital questions. The novel's basic metaphor is far more subtle and its author much more fair minded. Trebizond, "the ghost that haunted Trabzon", is, like historic Christendom, the ghost haunting modern Europe, highly equivocal. The actual medieval Greek city, as opposed to the Trebizond of romance, had more than its fair share of torture, palace-revolutions and intrigues. Christianity in history, as opposed to Christianity as an ideal, is disfigured by innumerable acts of savagery. But, Rose Macaulay makes Laurie ask, what do we actually feel when we confront the ruins of the city or the ruins of the religious frame of reference? Even when allowance is made for the wickedness which disfigured Trebizond, the moralisings of Finlay's *History of Greece* seem glib. Pat dismissals of the Christian culture of which Trebizond is the image cannot do justice to the haunting sense of beauty and power which has been erased. Admitting all the historic crimes and failures, it is the sense of loss that remains.

The Trapezuntines, or the Christians of the ages of faith of whom they are the figure, did

> behave very corruptly and cruelly and wildly very often, and they no doubt deserved to go under, but not so deeply as Trebizond has gone, becoming Trabzon, with a squalid beach and full of those who do not know the past.

Dismissive moralistic attitudes to vanished cultures, whether Trebizond or the wider wreck of Christendom, ignore the obvious fact that there is little to choose historically between "Byzantine" and Turk, Christian and non-Christian, when it came to "blood-thirstiness, murder, torture, violence and all that". Selective condemnation is pointless. On a more serious note, Laurie remarks that "this failure of the Christian Church" was what happens when a magnificent idea has to be worked out by human beings. Men call their cruelties the will of God, "which they have not grasped". Yet the Church "did grasp something" and Laurie wanted to be inside it, "though this is foolishness to most of my friends".

Acknowledging all the crimes of historic Christianity, the novel still challenges the reader repeatedly with the sight, unique perhaps to just that particular terrain, of ruined churches, "broken up, or used for army stores and things". A landscape in which the churches are not even picturesque survivals but shells, utterly devoid of meaning to inhabitants who hardly notice them, presents the question of the value of Christian culture in a peculiarly acute form.

The church of Hagia Sophia at Trebizond was converted to a Mosque but now "is decayed and redundant". Instead it is a half-derelict store-house for ladders, buckets, tools and oddments, its once glorious Byzantine frescoes peeling. After Laurie has stared at them for some time, the mutilated figures resolve themselves into Adam, Eve and the serpent, the basic mythic statement of human sinfulness. Laurie interprets the Greek inscription around the frieze with some difficulty. (It is quoted in the text, where it is, presumably, incomprehensible to most readers). The words prove to be about "saving me from my sins". Since she cannot give up her illicit love-affair she cannot "say this prayer".

What follows is a reflection on two features of contemporary life, the dulling of the individual's moral sensitivity, and the loss, connected with secularisation, of a language of personal aspiration, words in which to describe a private struggle to be good. The man or woman who, like Laurie, habitually acts against conscience, eventually gets "into a kind of fog, drifting about without clues", in which the sense of right and wrong blurs in "a confused sort of twilight". The prevalence of such relativism in a culture means that the struggle everyone still has about good and evil "cannot now be talked about without embarrassment". Yet from the Ancient World to the nineteenth century the nature of good and evil and the consequences of moral action absorbed the best minds of each generation. Such concerns, once "extremely interesting and exciting", have now become "very dead". The result is that clever wide-ranging, well-informed, inquisitive cast of mind *The Towers of Trebizond* portrays, full of views on "religion, love, people, psycho-analysis, books, art, places, cooking, cars, food, sex and all that", but drifting and at a loss. The novel at this point is not simplistic but it is explicit. If this is not, the reader is asked, what the ruined church of Hagia Sophia, as image of the loss of religious and moral dimension, implies about the texture of the moral and emotional life, what does it mean? What, if any, losses does the obvious process of secularisation involve? The direct question and the stark image demand an answer.

One way of evading the question, both in its wider cultural and its purely personal and intimate bearings, is through the cultivation of quaintness, and of the pleasures of nostalgic but fundamentally unserious historical celebration or pastiche. In one of its aspects Trebizond is a metaphor of this too. The challenge of lost religious values may be escaped by emphasising their utter remoteness from the present, by romanticising them, turning them from a moral and intellectual coherence into an archaic pageant. Laurie is, throughout the novel, a mistress of this technique. The most curious instance of the device, however, is her use of the Greek "sorcerer's" potion.

The episode is introduced by repeated references to the colourful legends and events of which the Euxine has been the setting, the "strange, frightening and romantic drama" of which it has been the "stage". The words "stage" and "drama" are repeated and are linked, in some unspecified way, to Laurie's need to "sort out my own problems", to dig up "some strange hidden meaning." Part of that meaning may be, or may be accompanied by, a vivid sense of beauty. (Interestingly, the legends most frequently referred to in association with the region, the voyage of the Argonauts to Colchis and march of Xenephon and the Ten Thousand are quests to remote regions, but more significantly, epics of successful return *home*).

Trebizond, the last refuge of Christianity, was also and still is, seemingly, the last refuge of sorcery. Magic flourished there during the Middle Ages when it was "a great city for enchanters and magicians". Those "notorious wizards, enchanters and alchemists" offered forms of the supernatural for money and "practised their arts for those who paid for their services". This traffic was specifically Greek and Christian and was driven underground by the down-to-earth Ottomans "who were neither clever nor imaginative". The expulsion of the last Pontic Greeks by Ataturk might have seemed to have killed the trade but, in fact it survives, in corners, among "pseudo Turkish Greeks" who still sell charms and curses.

The mention of Trapezuntine magic illustrates, in little, Rose Macaulay's method with the historical facts of the "lost city". She carefully selects those which develop her novel's binding metaphor for religion in the modern world. Every detail of the passage on sorcery serves a purpose. Magic was related to religion. "Like the fairies, the enchanters were of the old profession". The religious impulse, common among men, on the whole has its higher and lower, its ennobling and illicit manifestations. The city which contains the broken beauty of Hagia Sophia, with its unanswered challenge, contains also the "small elderly man", the "pharmakeus" or sorcerer, who sells Laurie the strange liquid which offers a short cut to that beauty, as it once was. Neither spiritually, nor the dregs of religion in the form of drugs, magic, or superstition, mean anything to the "Turks", types of the secularised consciousness. Interestingly, and perhaps accurately, however, it is suggested that it is the debased variants of religion which prove hardest to kill.

The first meeting with the old man comes immediately before Laurie's visit to the ruined Hagia Sophia. This visit is, of course, the novel's moral crisis. The "pharmakeus" looks round him craftily to see if there are any Turks about and then identifies himself by a few phrases of broken Greek. Laurie tells him they may meet again but for the moment hurries away "lest we should get involved in any expensive sorcery". At this stage, she seems undecided about how to solve her problem, or dig up her secret.

Laurie's refusal of the offer, contained in the inscription round the frieze, of salvation from sin stems from her unwillingness to give up what she knows to be wrong, her adultery with Vere. ("It would make things too difficult and too sad".) There remains the possibility of gaining an acceptable surrogate for the experience on other terms. Already, Laurie has dwelt in loving reverie on "all the centuries of lively Byzantine chatter" which had taken place in the palace ruins. In these earlier reflections she had recognised that those who had lived by the erased "Byzantine" vision had been, above all, alive, "active in mind and tongue, not lethargic like the Turks". After her refusal and her defeat at Hagia Sophia, and running out of money, she sells the medicines belonging to Aunt Dot. As part of the deal the "pharmakeus" offers her in exchange "a bottle full of a green liquid".

It is possible that Rose Macaulay may have intended what follows as a comment on the easy route some had already begun to see in drugs to some kind of "religious vision". Aldous Huxley's experiments with mescalin had already aroused interest. (His account of them in *The Doors of Perception* appeared two years before **The Towers of Trebizond**). What is not speculative is the relationship of Laurie's "vision" to the desires her moral failure had rendered impotent. The religious need becomes transmuted in her dream into a camp historical fantasy in the style of James Elroy Flecker or, more likely, Cecil B. De Mille. Instead of the men of the age of religion, "active in mind and tongue", she sees phantoms "disputing in hieratic gestures about the aphthartocathartic heresy". Sorcerers, jugglers, alchemists, dancing-girls, an ape playing chess with a young man, palace revolutions with ritual blindings, form the ingredients of a scene which ends with the chanting of priests. Laurie's "trip" is to a land of ghosts. The drug pedlar did not cheat her. He asked what she desired and whether she has had pleasant dreaming. He has given her what she presumably wanted but all he can give is meaningless illusion. The beauty of lost Trebizond cannot be had on the cheap. Yet knowing that, Laurie takes the green bottle and says "goodbye to the glories of Byzantium".

The complex metaphor of Trebizond is intimately bound up with the complex mind of Laurie herself, the novel's chief consciousness. That mind has the poignance and may have been formed with a classicist's awareness of Hadrian's "animula vagula blandula", the little soul, elusive and jesting, faced by the terrible ultimate fact of its fate after death. Laurie is so full of a buoyant intellectual curiosity that the reader may miss her deep sadness, the lack of peace of mind suggested in the first half of the novel. What the reader cannot miss, however, is her descent, after the failure at Hagia Sophia and the "vision" bought from the "pharmakeus", into a kind of frantic levity. The speed of the novel increases, the jokes come thick and fast, remaining funny but verging on hysteria. Eventually, there is more than a suspicion of a loss of touch with reality, almost of mental balance.

Laurie's meeting with her lover at Antioch marks a starting point in this final process. We are told little of her affair with another woman's husband. Rose Macaulay emphasises the value of the love to both partners. Besides a consuming sexual passion, Laurie and Vere are bound by a likeness of tastes, sympathies and outlook:

> We laughed at one another's jokes and love was
> our fortress and our peace.

Both lovers know, however, that their love is an act of meanness and robbery. Adultery, as Laurie had earlier remarked, is "chained with stealing sweets when you are a child". Neither Vere nor Laurie want marriage since the "everyday life married people live together" blunts romance. Though finding separation "a sadness and a torment" they conduct their affair through meetings in London and abroad. Vere, on holiday in the eastern Mediterranean in a press lord's yacht, is a distinguished and brilliant intellectual, a writer eminent in the circle of pundits, media personalities, writers of travel books and broadcasters, described elsewhere in the novel. He has achieved the success, fame and wealth humbler practitioners like David and Charles struggle for. *The Towers of Trebizond* is not concerned with the intricacies of Laurie's and Vere's love. Since this part of the novel is, of course, based on Rose Macaulay's own painful and long-lasting predicament, there is much she could not describe in detail. (In London during the First World War Rose Macaulay

> fell deeply in love with a man who, she later learnt, was already married. For some years she struggled to combine their friendship with her now habitual religious practice. In the early twenties, however, their secret attachment deepened and eventually she broke away from the sacramental life of the Church.

The man with whom Rose Macaulay had her affair died in 1942, some years before *The Towers of Trebizond* was written). In any case, such a bodying forth of the relationship is hardly necessary in what is a deliberately honeddown novel. The subject of *The Towers of Trebizond* is not a relationship but a dilemma. Vere is given to the reader as a fact, intelligent, charming, kind and deeply attractive to Laurie. Love, joy and peace flood over her when she thinks of him. Yet all this happiness is rooted in "this selfishness and this lying". Happiness and guilt pull in opposite directions, creating a deep discord "so that mind and soul are pulled in two." After her failure at Hagia Sophia, Laurie, as noted, becomes increasingly brittle and frantic, until her hysteria culminates in the road accident which kills her lover.

The love, partly because of the tension which accompanies it, partly because of Laurie's natural liking for the historical and colourful, seeks heightened and stylised modes of expression and romantic settings. Laurie and Vere meet at Antioch, itself notorious in the ancient world, and drive out to the groves of Daphne, "once the haunt of votaries of pleasure from Greece and Rome, very licentious and a perpetual festival of vice". The whimsical tone here, as in much of the later part of the novel, is forced. Ominously, the trip to the pleasure grove is a failure. The place is "dark" and the Turks have purged it of its old associations. They sit over non-alcoholic drinks, playing tric-trac. If Trebizond and the religious pattern of feeling it symbolises have been erased by time and change, Daphne, the image of splendid pagan indulgence, fares no better. The modern consciousness lacks, perhaps, the capacity for a whole-hearted sensuality or spirituality.

The note of melancholy struck at Daphne is forgotten, for a while. The cascade of almost frenetic vitality and wit continues, reaching a height in the lovers' final assignation at Venice, "the best week we ever had, and there will not be another". This last week, before Vere's death, seems almost taken out of time. Laurie describes it in the style of Restoration comedy, according to Charles Lamb, stylised, precious, deliberately unreal. She and her lover are like Florimel and Olinda in *Secret Love*. The reader is perhaps meant to see that Vere and Laurie need a deliberate heightening of consciousness, as well as blurring of the moral sense.

There is abundant evidence of that blurring in the later

stages of *The Towers of Trebizond,* in the lazy, cheerful, happy-go-lucky way in which Laurie slides into blackmail and betrayal over the dead Charles' manuscript. The manuscript, significantly about Trebizond, is "very good and very detailed". It is a skilful, if derivative work, evoking the lost beauty of the city through quotations from old travellers such as Bessarion and Evliya Effendi and modern authorities like Talbot Rice. Rose Macaulay suggests that, in writings like Charles', the question Trebizond posed and the loveliness it enshrined have become mere fragments of colourful reminiscence, devoid of ultimate significance. Worse still, Charles was a plagiarist, "hoping that people would think he had found it all out for himself". Interestingly, it is from his notes that Laurie discovers the address of the "pharmakeus" who later sells her the drugged "vision" of Trebizond. Moral obliquity, theft and illusion are ultimately connected here, as elsewhere in the novel. It is not enough that the true vision recedes behind a tapestry of stolen words, ready to be marketed. After Charles' death his former friend David publishes the work as his own and desperately seeks to get hold of the manuscript in order to cover his tracks. So cheerful is Laurie's act of blackmail that one might not notice that the light of Trebizond has been refracted through the medium of one more act of betrayal:

> I did not want to torment him, only to keep him on a string a little longer, so that he might do kind acts for me.

After her victim has treated her to an expensive meal and advanced her considerable sums of money, she tells him, in detail, over coffee and liqueurs, how far Christianity has strayed from the spirituality of the early Eastern Fathers. The more she talks, the more she convinces herself that "what was keeping me from the Church was not my own sin but those of the Church". The process of betrayal does not end here, since Laurie is not even true to her blackmailer's bargain. Carelessly, and in her by now prevailing mood of giddy amusement, she reveals the whole business. Reflecting briefly that she "had betrayed David, broken her promise" in spite of the gifts of money and the long, friendly conversations they had had, she dismissed her regret with the thought that he would probably live it down anyway. This last passage is typical, syntactically, of the graceful muddle, the piling up of clauses which qualify and even contradict each other, which forms the prose through which Rose Macaulay conveys Laurie's mind. There is, in the style, an inimitable mixture of upper-class breathlessness, assumed gaucherie and charm, by which the narrator seeks to hide her evident contradiction of feeling and her guilt. The increasingly forced quality of her eccentricity is shown in her act, after returning to England, of taking her pet ape to Mass and trying to teach it to genuflect. More likely this whole episode is a fantasy suggesting she is losing touch with reality. The figure of the half-human ape, in fact, appeared in her drugged "vision" of Trebizond. The car-accident which kills her lover is the work of a woman in an almost manic condition. Laurie's insistence of their right of way, the specific cause of the crash, is the last result of her spiral into wilful egocentricity.

The chief metaphor of *The Towers of Trebizond* is that of

the lost city and the landscape purged of once familiar meanings. However, some of the significance of the book is expressed in other metaphors. The image of a pilgrimage is clearly one of the most important of these. Laurie is literally on a pilgrimage, of course, a journey which is supposed to culminate in Jerusalem. She is engaged, also, in travel through the Christian past and her own past which her companions, and perhaps she with part of her mind, hope will be a spiritual recovery of herself. *The Towers of Trebizond* is, in fact, written within that myth of the spiritual quest or journey towards wisdom or salvation, recurring from *Gilgamesh* to Bunyan and beyond.

Rose Macaulay plays with the possibilities of the genre in interesting ways. Laurie's own pilgrimage fails at Hagia Sophia, as has been noted. Her later journey to Jerusalem is a perfunctory anti-climax, a mere set of holiday snaps and an excellent example of the author's narrative skill. What could have been overwhelming and healing is hurried through as a set of perceptions, amusing or interesting, but in any case fragmentary. *The Towers of Trebizond* is a tragi-comic *Pilgrim's Progress,* written from the point of view of the pilgrim who finds a way to Hell even from the gates of Heaven.

The adventures of Laurie's companions, Aunt Dot and Father Chantry-Pigg offer a more unpredictable variant on the pilgrimage theme. Instead of going to Jerusalem or quietly visiting the archaeological sites, they act in fashions which seem, both to Laurie and others, highly provocative, attempting to proselytise both in Turkey and then in Soviet Russia which they enter illegally. Although many of their modern-minded contemporaries see them as wildly eccentric, they are unconcerned. They are engaged on a pilgrimage of their own but not in an elegiac spirit amid a land where they see only ruins. As one of Rose Macaulay's closest friends and correspondents pointed out, readers at the book's first appearance were wrong to see Father Chantry-Pigg as wholly ridiculous. Much of his and Aunt Dot's apparent oddity stems simply from their being pilgrims in an unbelieving world. Yet they have their own inner joy and confidence and can ignore the ruins made by time. They are not, in fact, the first such pilgrims to move in just that spirit through that landscape, once the Greek Asia Minor of the first missionary journeys.

The actions of the defiant pair as missionaries, whether in Turkey or Soviet Russia, affront the modern secularised consciousness, in a comic variant of *The Acts of the Apostles.* In Rose Macaulay's novel, religious faith encounters something of the same blend of contempt, incomprehension, idle curiosity and hostility, from a similar medley of bewildered officials, worldly cynics and sudden mobs, as in *The New Testament* original. Both Laurie's companions, however, whatever their differences, are anchored to their faith by a firm intellectual understanding of its nature and its demands. Each shows a reasoned certainty beneath a surface eccentricity. Father Chantry-Pigg offers a sudden sharp and terribly cogent statement of Laurie's spiritual condition. Aunt Dot, more gently and charitably, warns her niece not to lose sight of the "hard core" of religion underneath the "aesthetically exciting", the "euphor-

ic drug". It is in such movements from the comic into the serious, as well as the more frequent from the serious to the comic, that the author displays her stylistic control.

Ultimately, nevertheless, the success of *The Towers of Trebizond* rests on the choice of a leading image, based on a series of convenient and unique historic facts and the skill with which Rose Macaulay has exploited every facet of Trebizond to catch the nuances of a very specific psychological and religious problem. Partly this is a case of luck since Trebizond and the history of Turkey have certain qualities the author needed for her novel. But there is audacity in the metaphor, too, since it might have failed simply through its obscurity. Rose Macaulay triumphantly justifies the choice of her key-image, however, by the tightness of her intellectual control over its every detail and by her courage and delicacy in handling very personal material drawn from the experience, years long, of happiness and fun, coupled with guilt and the bitter loss, for many years, of peace of mind. (pp. 113-21)

> *John Coates, "Metaphor and Meaning in 'The Towers of Trebizond',"* in The Durham University Journal, *Vol. LXXX, No. 1, December, 1987, pp. 111-21.*

FURTHER READING

Biography

Babington Smith, Constance. *Rose Macaulay.* London: Collins, 1972, 254 p.
   Biography of Macaulay by her cousin.

Criticism

Babington Smith, Constance. "Rose Macaulay in Her Writings." In *Essays By Divers Hands: Being the Transactions of the Royal Society of Literature, New Series,* Vol. XXXVIII, edited by John Guest, pp. 143-58. London: Oxford University Press, 1975.
   Discusses Macaulay's opinions about her fiction and her desire to be a poet.

Bensen, Alice R. "The Skeptical Balance: A Study of Rose Macaulay's *Going Abroad.*" *Papers of the Michigan Academy of Science, Arts, and Letters* XLVIII (1963): 675-83.
   Discusses the novel *Going Abroad* as both a comedy of manners and a serious examination of modern morality.

————. "The Ironic Aesthete and the Sponsoring of Causes: A Rhetorical Quandary in Novelistic Technique." *English Literature in Transition* 9, No. 1 (1966): 39-43.
   A study of *Views and Vagabonds.* Bensen contends that in this novel Macaulay failed to reconcile her theme of respect for individual lifestyles, no matter how unconventional, with her belief in the importance of traditional values.

————. *Rose Macaulay.* New York: Twayne Publishers, 1969, 184 p.
   Critical and biographical study.

Gould, Gerald. "Sociological: The Long View." In his *The English Novel of Today,* pp. 69-73. New York: The Dial Press, 1925.
    Concludes that both the interest and the limitations of Macaulay's novels derive from her reliance on frequent generalizations in her portrayal of social life.

Passty, Jeanette N. *Eros and Androgyny: The Legacy of Rose Macaulay.* Rutherford, N.J.: Fairleigh Dickinson University Press, 1988, 252 p.
    Examines how the role of women in English society, Macaulay's sexual desires, and her personal relationships influenced her fiction.

Schelling, Felix E. "Potterism." In his *Appraisements and Asperities as to Some Contemporary Writers,* pp. 56-61. Philadelphia: J. B. Lippincott, 1922.
    Describes and defines "potterism" as an inherent quality of modern society.

Tallmer, Jerry. "Tower of Power." *The Village Voice* XXVI, No. 14 (1-7 April 1981): 38.
    Favorable review of *The Towers of Trebizond.* Describes the novel as a comedy and parody that is "deeply, indeed mortally, serious."

"Miss Macaulay's Novels." *The Times Literary Supplement,* No. 2519 (12 May 1950): 292.
    Surveys Macaulay's novels, noting that despite their humor and satirical nature Macaulay's fiction conveys her compassion for humanity.

Additional coverage of Macaulay's life and career is contained in the following sources published by Gale Research: *Contemporary Authors,* Vol. 104; and *Dictionary of Literary Biography,* Vol. 36.

Thomas Mann

Doktor Faustus (Doctor Faustus)

German novelist, short story and novella writer, essayist, and critic.

The following entry presents criticism of Mann's novel *Doktor Faustus: Das Leben des deutschen Tonsetzers Adrian Leverkühn, erzählt von einem Freunde* (1947; *Doctor Faustus: The Life of the German Composer Adrian Leverkühn as Told by a Friend*). For further information on Mann's complete career, see *TCLC*, Volumes 2 and 8. For discussion of *Der Tod in Venedig* (*Death in Venice*), see *TCLC*, Volume 14; *Der Zauberberg* (*The Magic Mountain*), see *TCLC*, Volume 21; and *Buddenbrooks*, see *TCLC*, Volume 35.

INTRODUCTION

Doctor Faustus is considered one of the most complex novels of the twentieth century. A reworking of the Faust myth, a legend that was first published in Germany in 1587 in a version by Johann Spiess and which inspired works by such writers as Christopher Marlowe and Johann Wolfgang von Goethe, Mann's *Doctor Faustus* has been described as both a fictional biography of composer Adrian Leverkühn and an allegorical depiction of the rise of fascism in Germany. In Spiess's original "Faustbook," Dr. Faustus is granted by the devil twenty-four hours of unequivocal knowledge of the universe if he renounces "all living creatures, and the whole heavenly host and all human beings." Mann utilizes this "pact with the devil" theme in *Doctor Faustus* to elucidate the fate of Leverkühn, a musical genius who declines into insanity after composing an oratorio of technical perfection. By paralleling Leverkühn's obsession with creating a perfect musical composition with the Nazis' determination to purify the Teutonic race, Mann explored such myriad themes as the relationship between genius and tyranny, the role of the artist in modern society, the origins of cultural and intellectual decay, the repercussions of ideological rigidity, and the deceptive nature of reality.

Mann wrote *Doctor Faustus* primarily in the United States, where he and his wife Katia settled in 1938 after fleeing Nazi-dominated Europe. After two years as a professor of humanities at Princeton University, Mann decided to move to Pacific Palisades, California, where many German exiles, including his brother Heinrich Mann, Franz Werfel, and Leonhard Frank had already settled. It was here—after finishing *Joseph der Ernahrer* (*Joseph the Provider*), the last novel of a trilogy, and the novella *Das Gesetz* (*The Tables of the Law*)—that Mann began formulating plans for *Doctor Faustus*. In a 1943 letter to Agnes Meyer, he explained: "I am writing again—on the novel for which the war in Europe, alas, will probably give me time. The thing is difficult, weird, uncanny, sad as

life." Mann later wrote that he was setting out "to write nothing less than the novel of my era, disguised as the story of an artist's life." Throughout the war years, Mann continued to work on what he called his "wildest novel," with his narrator documenting the progression of the war and portending Germany's eventual defeat. Mann finished the manuscript for *Doctor Faustus* in January 1947. Shortly after its publication, he began to compile *Die Entstehung des Doktor Faustus: Roman eines Romans* (*The Story of a Novel: The Genesis of Doctor Faustus*), an account of the circumstances under which *Doctor Faustus* had been written. An invaluable source for understanding the various historical, scientific, and musical allusions in *Doctor Faustus, The Story of a Novel* was published shortly before the English edition of *Doctor Faustus* appeared in 1948.

Doctor Faustus is the story of Leverkühn's life as told by his friend Serenus Zeitblom three years after the composer's death in 1940. Zeitblom, a decent and well-meaning professor of literature and classical languages, is self-admittedly incapable of comprehending Leverkühn's musical genius, nor does he recognize the demonic ramifications of the composer's self-destructive approach to creativity. By portraying Zeitblom as a biographer who is often naïve about his subject, Mann hoped to "achieve a certain humorous leavening of the somber material and to make its horrors bearable to myself as well as to the reader." Often described as a "tragic parody" because of Zeitblom's evasiveness with respect to Leverkühn's motivations, *Doctor Faustus* utilizes the traditional biography in order to reveal the ambiguity and subjectivity of this form. While Zeitblom attempts to explicate the events that influenced Leverkühn's musical works and led to his eventual insanity, including the composer's upbringing in the provincial German town of Kaisersaschern, his involvement in various student societies in Munich, his contraction of syphilis from a prostitute, and his conjectured dialogue with the devil, *Doctor Faustus* does not follow a chronological or linear pattern but rather is structured to emphasize the interconnectedness of events and ideas and the complexity of the characters' motivations. To achieve these effects, Mann employed a narrative technique that he described as a "montage" of literary, scientific, historical, and biographical references. *Doctor Faustus* contains specific references to one hundred and thirty-five works, including William Shakespeare's *Much Ado about Nothing* (1598-99), Theodor Adorno's *Philosophie der neuen Musik* (1949), and Fyodor Dostoevsky's *The Brothers Karamazov* (1880). Particularly important are Mann's references to the philosopher Friedrich Nietzsche's *Ecco Homo* (1908) and passages quoted from Paul Deussen's account of his last visit to Nietzsche who, like Leverkühn, became insane as a consequence of advanced syphilis. Mann explains the significance of the parallel fates of Leverkühn and Nietzsche in *The Story of a Novel*: "There is an interweaving of Leverkühn's tragedy with that of Nietzsche, whose name does not appear in the entire book—advisedly, because the euphoric musician has been made so much Nietzsche's substitute that the original is no longer permitted a separate existence." *Doctor Faustus* was also inspired by German composer Arnold Schönberg's form of musical composition known as atonalism, or the twelve-tone system, a technique Mann attributes to Leverkühn in the novel. Although Mann initially did not acknowledge the composer's influence, Schönberg's repeated protests caused him to add a footnote to *Doctor Faustus* in which he admits that he "transferred [Schönberg's] technique in a certain ideational context to the fictitious figure of a musician, the tragic hero of my novel."

Critics generally agree that Mann's greatest achievements in *Doctor Faustus* can be found in Leverkühn's dialogue with the devil, commonly known as the "confession," and in the evolution of Leverkühn's final composition and musical masterpiece, *D. Fausti Weheklag* (*Lamentation of Dr. Faustus*). Determined to conquer the threat of artistic unproductivity and to recover the "objective, binding, and compelling" elements of genuine music, Leverkühn ostensibly makes a pact with the devil during a bout of fever, a condition which could be interpreted as either the result of a communion with demonic forces or as an early symptom of syphilis. Zeitblom, after finding Leverkühn's frenzied forty-page transcription of his dialogue with the devil in which the composer is promised a "work-filled eternity of life," offers a scholarly speculation that the composer made his pact in 1912. Described as the original Faustbook set to music, this oratorio is so rigid and stylistically

ordered that "there is no longer one free note." After completing his *Lamentation,* Leverkühn suffers from mental illness for ten years before dying; during this period he confesses he once spoke with the devil. However, because he admits this while insane, the source of his musical genius remains obscure, allowing Mann to analogously explore the etiology of disease and the moral disintegration of modern civilization. Through its exploration of the causes and nature of evil, *Doctor Faustus* also serves as an allegory for the rise of nazism in Germany. Throughout the 1930s, Mann adamantly opposed the nationalistic fanaticism integral to fascist politics and intermittently warned that Europe was on the brink of war. Mann chose to use Leverkühn's process of musical composition to symbolize the Nazis' obsession with authority and order, explaining that in *Doctor Faustus* music is "only foreground and representation, only a paradigm for something more general, only a means to express the situation of art in general, of culture, even of man and the intellect itself in our so critical era." Through Leverkühn, a uniquely German character who is so intent on composing an original musical masterpiece that he remains oblivious to his own downfall and the well-being of those around him, Mann was able to explore the methodical nature of German atrocities and the Nazis' fixation with creating a "master race."

Initial reaction to *Doctor Faustus* was mixed, with some critics praising the novel's synthesis of aesthetic, philosophical, and social concerns and others castigating Mann's inflated rhetoric and experimental narrative technique. Mann's detractors questioned his decision to employ an unreliable narrator in a novel that was presented as a fictitious biography, stating that Zeitblom's reverent observations were so subjective that *Doctor Faustus* lacked credibility; defenders of Mann's work argued that his method of narration was highly effective because it demonstrated how interpretation is often mythologized and revealed the complexity of Leverkühn's personality through a mosaic of perceptions rather than through straightforward description. Critical commentary on *Doctor Faustus* in the 1950s emphasized Mann's symbolic depiction of the rise of Nazi Germany and the author's exploration of the relationship between creativity and decay. In recent years, scholars have begun to focus on the novel's more subtle narrative and thematic elements, including Mann's use of various German dialects as a means to enrich his characterizations, his self-parody, and his conception of humankind as a collective entity. Despite objections that *Doctor Faustus* is more of an intellectual and rhetorical exercise than a work of fiction, the majority of modern scholars view the novel as a profound vision of twentieth-century life which evidences Mann's mastery of irony and his empathic view of humanity.

H. C. Hatfield (essay date 1949)

[*Hatfield was an American critic, educator, and editor who specialized in German language and literature. In addition to publishing comprehensive studies of Franz Kafka and Johann Wolfgang von Goethe, Hatfield also wrote extensively on Mann, including* Thomas Mann: A Critical Guidebook *(1951) and* Thomas Mann: An Introduction to His Fiction *(1952). In the following excerpt, Hatfield focuses on* Doctor Faustus *within the context of Mann's career.*]

Even to readers thoroughly versed in Thomas Mann's works, certain aspects of his [*Dr. Faustus*] must have come as a considerable surprise. Here the author attempts tasks of a new type: for example, the dialogue with the devil, Adrian Leverkühn's terrible last words to his friends, the brief inserts describing the progress of the war (reminding one from afar of the technique of Dos Passos), the *chronique scandaleuse* of Munich society—the last a type of realistic portrayal somewhat of the sort one associates with Heinrich Mann. Like *Der Zauberberg, Lotte in Weimar,* and *Joseph, Dr. Faustus* is an experimental novel.

Yet for all its experimental tendencies, one is impressed, particularly after several readings, with the close but complex relation between *Dr. Faustus* and Mann's earlier work. Familiar themes and techniques are repeated, varied, and further developed. Briefly to indicate, from this point of view, the place of the novel in Mann's work as a whole is the purpose of this paper.

Adrian Leverkühn represents a new departure in Mann's long series of treatments of the artist. . . . Here Mann has chosen one of the "proud and cold" as a central figure, and treated him, without envy indeed, but with great affection. His position as an artist in a "late" age, who cannot create spontaneously, is explicitly contrasted to that of Goethe. On one level of interpretation Leverkühn is a *Leistungsethiker,* related to a succession of such figures as Aschenbach, Frederick II of Prussia, and the Schiller of "Schwere Stunde."

Mann's familiar belief, inherited from Novalis, that disease can intensify talent or genius, re-occurs. The parallel to Hans Castorp's case is obvious enough; what is characteristic of *Dr. Faustus* is the use of an extreme example: Adrian suffers from a more repulsive and, so to speak, less poetic disease than the tuberculosis of *Der Zauberberg,* realistically though that is portrayed. It is equally typical that love (allied to disease, death, and the anti-social in general) is represented by the prostitute Esmeralda, rather than by such a figure as Clavdia, who is, after all, *salonfähig.*

In his latest novel, far more than elsewhere, Mann gives expression to his passion for music. Convinced that it was a "serious mistake" of the tradition not to have made Faust a musician, he rectifies the error here. In the singing lessons of the boy Adrian and his friend Serenus, the descriptions of musical instruments owned by Adrian's uncle, the eccentric but memorable effusions of Kretzschmar, this theme is increasingly developed; most impressively in the many attempts to reproduce through words the effect of both actual and imaginary works of music. Again, this is no innovation in itself: one remembers Hanno's improvisations in *Buddenbrooks;* the climactic scene in *Tristan;* and the interpretations of Hans Castorp's

favorite gramophone records. Yet the musical passages in *Dr. Faustus* are more ambitious, more technical, far more extensive, and, if a non-musical person may venture an opinion, at their best more successful. If, for instance, one compares the account of Hanno's music, which seems to give the effect which an ideal listener might receive, with the close analysis of some of Adrian's compositions, the difference is clear. In *Buddenbrooks,* the technique is, so to speak, more literary: the primary purpose is apparently to interpret the ideas and emotions associated with the music. In *Dr. Faustus,* while Mann likewise stresses the ideological associations and, of course, the emotional impact, far more attention is devoted to the music *as music.*

The cultural and political role of music is also a familiar theme. As we know from the *Betrachtungen eines Unpolitischen* and from Naptha's remarks in *Der Zauberberg,* Mann has long regarded it as an anti-bourgeois, one might say an anti-political force. Adrian's utter aloofness from the political and civic spheres fits perfectly into the pattern.

Mann's belief (one might almost say his obsession) that music is a dangerous, potentially destructive force reaches back to *Buddenbrooks* and *Tristan.* Music brings release to Hanno and Frau Klöterjahn, but it is a release from life into illness and death. Even such an apparently harmless song as Schubert's "Der Lindenbaum," we are told in *Der Zauberberg,* bears within it the seeds of dissolution. *Dr. Faustus* again carries a tendency to the extreme: music is linked to the diabolic. To be sure, Mann as usual shows us the other side of the coin. Music, in its affinity to mathematics, is the realm of order, harmony, and discipline—and, in Adrian, a realm of inhuman coldness. Either aspect of music can and does lead him towards damnation. Yet by still another characteristic dialectical twist it is in music that Adrian can express, at the very end of his career, a hope which lies beyond despair.

To return to the political level: Mann would seem to have returned to the conviction that Germany is a nation without skill in politics, but his evaluation of this conviction has shifted radically. In the *Betrachtungen,* it will be recalled, to be non-political is a "good thing." In *Der Zauberberg* one senses a certain ambivalence. While Settembrini protests strongly against the German aversion to politics, we can by no means be sure of Mann's own position, for the Italian humanist, after all, generally loses his arguments. Even in *Mario und der Zauberer,* with its clear warning against the fascination of fascism, the German narrator maintains for a while a certain aloofness from what seems at first to be a purely Italian phenomenon. . . . In *Dr. Faustus,* despite its many ironies, there is a clear, unequivocal commitment to the "Western" point of view in matters of politics. Serenus Zeitblom, who for all his foibles and pedantries is no fool, clearly represents a humanistic and ethically very decent strain in German culture. To the extent that he is a non-political *Bürger,* however, he is doomed to tragic frustration, perhaps even to a certain share of responsibility for the general catastrophe. (pp. 13-16)

In manner, as in thought, *Dr. Faustus* shows a further development along lines already laid down by Mann. He seems now less interested in the leitmotif in the narrower sense, but employs the Nietzschean concept of eternal recurrence, as in *Joseph.* One can compare, for instance, the return of the mythical archetype "Eliezer," in various individuals, to the uncanny resemblance between the respective "mothers," maids, and even dogs on the farms where Adrian lives, first as a boy, then as a mature artist. And the way in which Mann introduces a theme, reverts to it again and again, and finally builds it up to a fortissimo, justifies the use of the term "symphonic novel." One notes particularly how the theme of music is introduced with the part-singing directed by the dairymaid Hanne; how the politics of the "irrational" develops from the apparently harmless discourse of the students at Halle to the diabolic; and how the related themes of medievalism, mass hysteria, and utter madness, first adumbrated in the description of Kaisersaschern, and largely supported by Mann's skilful use of a sort of "old-German" style and diction, reach a stunning climax. It is impossible more than to mention here that Mann again demonstrates his virtuosity in dealing with the element of time. . . .

As a symbolic novel, *Dr. Faustus* carries further a tendency apparent in *Der Zauberberg* and *Joseph.* While Mann's symbolism is not of the "private" type, and is far more translucent than that of Joyce, Kafka, or Eliot, it is nevertheless complex; the novel moves on several different levels of meaning. Here a single example must suffice to show the close parallel to *Joseph.* Thus while Joseph is first of all his own complicated, interesting self, he represents a wealth of other entities. In the realm of the divine, in his burial and resurrection, he "is" Adonis-Tammuz, as he is also an anticipation of Jesus. He has a touch of the roguish Hermes as well. Beyond that, he is reminiscent of the young Goethe (as Mann himself has pointed out); accordingly, he is one of the few "marked men" who may be considered relatively happy, for he has realized to a considerable degree a synthesis of Mann's fundamental antitheses, life and spirit. Finally, as a social and economic reformer, he shows the impact on Mann of his stay in this country. Surely, it is difficult to read *Joseph der Ernährer* without thinking of the "ever normal granary" and other innovations of the New Deal. An equal abundance (or overabundance) of associations is centered on Adrian. He is the type of the artist struggling for spontaneity in a "late" age; on another level he recalls characteristics of such composers as Schönberg, Hugo Wolf, and Gustav Mahler. Obviously, he "is" Nietzsche as well as Faustus; indeed he is a symbol of the German intellectual, perhaps of Germany itself. From another point of view, Adrian may be understood as the "late" intellectual or artist of any nation; it is here, I believe, that the novel's most valid claim to general significance lies. In a sense, like all of Mann's artist figures, he is presumably to some degree a portrait of the author. If this is true, must one not agree with the suggestion that Adrian represents what Mann himself might have become had he not freed himself from some of the obsessions of his earlier years? In that case, *Dr. Faustus,* like *Der Tod in Venedig,* must have had the value of a catharsis for the author. The emotional intensity to which the novel rises, towards the end, suggests that such may have been the case.

This intensity is of great importance in Mann's treatment of the myth. Compare for example the fundamental seriousness of his representation of the Devil with the playful attitude towards Hebrew angels and Egyptian gods in *Joseph!* No doubt the use of a native legend also tends to give greater authenticity and force.

To conclude: *Dr. Faustus,* for all of its innovations, falls within the pattern of Mann's work as a whole. It is a late work in the sense that it carries tendencies, both of thought and of style, to new extremes. There is a considerable hypertrophy of digression, reminiscent of [Goethe's] *Faust II;* but in its most successful passages, it is as forceful as anything that Mann has written. (pp. 16-17)

> *H. C. Hatfield, "Two Notes on Thomas Mann's 'Doctor Faustus',"* in Modern Language Forum, *Vol. XXXIV, Nos. 1-2, March-June, 1949, pp. 11-17.*

Carroll E. Reed   (essay date 1952)

[*Reed is an American critic and educator who has written extensively on German language and literature. In the following excerpt, he compares* Doctor Faustus *to previous interpretations of the Faust myth, including the* Faust-Book *(1587) by Johann Spiess and* Faust *(1887) by Johann Wolfgang von Goethe.*]

In his recent novel *Doktor Faustus* Thomas Mann has produced a literary tone-poem, the epic proportions of which are expressed in the principal theme and symbolized by the title itself. The essence of Mann's technique as a novelist is his treatment of literature as music, so that it seems entirely fitting for us to look upon *Doktor Faustus* as comparable to a musical composition—a symphonic arrangement of a descriptive theme. The protagonist of the work, Adrian Leverkühn, has been described by Mann—in the words of Lermontov—as a "hero of our times," hence as a symbolic type. The story of Dr. Faustus has been told and retold so often since the time of the Renaissance that its recital in musical prose may be regarded as epic in scope. As a legend it is timeless, as a symbol, applicable in every age.

Thomas Mann's *Faustus* is pseudo-biographical in form, so that the author might share the more intimately with the reader his enjoyment of an old theme. There are few secrets involved in Mann's use of source materials, since he himself delights in revealing them. In his appreciation and synthesis of these materials, he invites the reader to join him in a literary adventure. With the completion of *Doktor Faustus* he has fulfilled a promise of many years' standing, during which time he has equipped his readers with a keen receptiveness for the work now at hand, and we witness here another appearance of what has come to be regarded as a typically German symbol. For not only the framework of the story itself, but many of the smaller motifs (for which Thomas Mann expresses the greatest preference) correspond to the patterns and episodes of the Faust tradition. At the same time, *Doktor Faustus* is an expression of Mann's attitude toward disease and the life of the artist, so that the novel introduces certain aspects of biological and psychological interpretation that would never have occurred to previous Faust writers. Mann's Faustus is therefore cast in a mold that is as old as the story itself and as new, in its day, as was more than a century ago the one composed by Goethe.

In an essay on Goethe's *Faust* (1938) Thomas Mann reveals very clearly his familiarity with the Faust tradition. Here he takes note of the numerous mythological elements brought together in the "oldest Faust-book," that of the Frankfurt printer, Johannes Spiess, published in 1587. After indicating the fact that the name "Faust" had been closely associated with that of the legendary Simon Magus (the latter, in turn, with the biblical Simon of Acts 8:9 ff., 18 ff.) in the *Clementine Recognitions* (written in about the fourth century), he arrives at a discussion of Faust's erstwhile lady companion, known as Helena. Even in the minds of the early church fathers, she had ceased to be an individual and had become part of a legend. (pp. 17-18)

Although his appreciation of the devil in the role of Faust's advocate contains no . . . historical interpretation, Mann's approach to Goethe's Mephisto begins with a discussion of the details traditionally associated with him: the name as it appears in the old Faust-book, the negative, destructive nature of the devil as a breeder of pestilence and filth, his stewardship over the "Ungeziefer," his *"kalte Teufelsfaust,"* and his ultimate personification of darkness. These and other diabolic attributes he incorporates in his own *Faustus* story, according to tradition. The function of the devil in Faustian lore, however, is a matter which Thomas Mann has defined in terms of his own peculiar background. Another essay that clearly sets the stage for the fictional biography of Adrian Leverkühn is entitled: **"Germany and the Germans."** Here he defines the traditional Faust as a man who, "out of a presumptuous urge for knowledge, surrenders to magic, to the devil." This "presumptuous urge" is then stigmatized as "arrogance of the intellect, mating with the spiritual obsolete and archaic," the "devil's domain." Faust is pictured as a reflection of Germany in the process of self-destruction, bartering its soul to satisfy the "presumptuous urge" for "world enjoyment and world domination." Mann, whose own writings reflect the profound influence of German Romanticism, draws an analogy between the essence of this Faust, this Germany, and the Romantic philosophy of disease, saying:

> The priority over the rational which it grants to the emotional, even in its arcane forms of mystic ecstasy and Dionysiac intoxication, brings it into a peculiar and psychologically highly fruitful relationship to sickness; the late-Romanticist Nietzsche, for example, himself a spirit raised by illness to heights of fatal genius, was profuse in his praise of sickness as a medium of knowledge. In this sense, even psychoanalysis, which represents a great advance towards the understanding of a man from the side of illness, is a branch of Romanticism.

And in connection with this reference to Nietzsche (whose personality may be identified frequently in *Doktor Faustus*), Mann has drawn similar conclusions from the experiences of Dostoyevsky, whom he describes as "a man who has been in Hell." Speaking of Dostoyevsky's "infirmity,

the 'sacred' disease, the pre-eminently mystic disease, epilepsy," he says:

> Two symptoms, according to his [Dostoyevsky's] description, are characteristic of the falling sickness: the incomparable sense of rapture, of inner enlightenment, of harmony, of highest ecstasy, preceding by a few moments the spasm that begins with an inarticulate, no longer human scream—and the state of horrible depression and deep grief, of spiritual ruin and desolation that follows it. This reaction seems to me even more symbolic of the nature of the disease than the exaltation that precedes the attack. Dostoyevsky describes it as a rapture so strong and sweet "that one is ready to exchange ten years of life or even life itself for the bliss of these few seconds."

The philosophy of disease as Mann develops it goes back to the secularized Pietism embodied in the Romantic movement in Germany, in the inspirational moods of Novalis and the inner brilliance of enthusiasm exemplified by Goethe's "Bekenntnisse einer schönen Seele." And in the same way, the Romantic ideas on music find their way into Mann's *Faustus.* Music and disease are concepts that appear as innovations by Mann in the Faust tradition. In criticizing the traditional features, and as a prelude to the writing of *Doktor Faustus,* Mann declares:

> It is a grave error on the part of legend and story not to connect Faust with music. He should have been musical, he should have been a musician. Music is a demonic realm; Kierkegaard, a great Christian, proved that most convincingly in his painfully enthusiastic essay on Mozart's *Don Juan.* Music is Christian art with a negative prefix. Music is calculated order and chaos-breeding irrationality at once, rich in conjuring, incantatory gestures, in magic of numbers, the most unrealistic and yet the most impassioned of arts, mystical and abstract. If Faust is to be the representative of the German soul, he would have to be musical, for the relation of the German to the world is abstract and mystical, that is, musical—the relation of a professor with a touch of demonism, awkward and at the same time filled with arrogant knowledge that he surpasses the world in "depth."

It is with this thought in mind that Mann permits his Faustus to develop an enthusiasm for music; moreover, the demonic character of this particular enthusiasm is exhibited in a desire to exceed the mundane heights of "normal" music and venture into the speculative, mathematical possibilities beyond. Such possibilities were given fragmentary recognition by Novalis in his remarks on mathematics and music. Throughout the Romantic movement in general the characterization of music as a higher emotional realm, a source of ecstasy and intoxication, runs parallel with the philosophy of sickness, and these two features were so remarkably combined in the life of Friedrich Nietzsche that Thomas Mann found it appropriate to endow his hero with Nietzsche's personal life and outlook, his ailing body and his quickened soul.

In drawing together the various interpretations which he

has applied to the Faust tradition, Mann makes extensive use of the old Faust-book. It provides him with the setting, language, and the "smaller motifs" in general, as well as the plot itself. To be sure, his Faustus (Adrian) does not appear as a biological curiosity, like the Johann Faustus of 1587 whose parents are exonerated from blame for the folly of their son. By virtue of certain inherited tendencies, Adrian Leverkühn is particularly well suited for the role of a modern Faustus. His father before him exhibited a proclivity towards the abnormal or, as Thomas Mann suggests, the realm of the demonic. The father's headaches, resembling migraine and occurring "not oftener than once a month," are to be interpreted as signs of the son's more developed sickness, and especially of Adrian's *thirst for darkness.* It is Jonathan Leverkühn's audacious curiosity with regard to the "obscure phenomena" of nature that Mann characterizes as a desire "to speculate the elements." The Faustus prototype of 1587 launches his dangerous adventures with this same desire. . . .

Jonathan Leverkühn's inordinate preoccupation with natural oddities is illustrated, first, in his morbid concern with chemical plants ("Und dabei sind sie tot," he sadly remarks, commenting on their lifelike activity), and again in his interest in the "devouring drop," but above all in his study of the peculiar butterfly, the *hetaera esmeralda,* as it was called. All of these mysterious phenomena transcended in some way the normal bounds of both inorganic and organic nature. The strange butterfly is to be identified as symbolizing the traditional companion of Simon Magus, and the prostitute who (as we shall see) is to be Adrian Leverkühn's contact with the devil: it is a creature of striking beauty, "loving the duskiness of heavy leafage," but with disgusting attributes; for it was poisonous, hence "tragically safe" from its pursuers.

Father Leverkühn's predilection for experimenting with the exotic workings of nature constitutes, according to Mann, a teasing, or "tempting" of nature and, as such, falls within the realm of witchcraft, of the "Tempter." In addition to this inherited tendency, symbolized by the recurrent migraine of both father and son, Adrian Leverkühn exhibits a peculiar relationship to his early environment. Concerning Adrian's home town, the biographer says:

> Kaisersaschern lies in the midst of the native home of the Reformation, in the heart of Lutherland. It is the region of cities with the names Eisleben, Wittenberg, Quedlinburg, likewise Grimma, Wolfenbüttel and Eisenach—all, again, rich with meaning for the inner life of the Lutheran Leverkühn and linked with the direction his studies originally took, the theological one.

This is a setting which has been used by writers on the Faust theme ever since the Spiess *Faustus* of 1587. There it was also the uncle in Wittenberg who raised the young Faustus and sent him to school to study *"theologiam."* Luther's preoccupation with the devil and with the Faust legend itself is not the only reason why Mann makes such pointed references to this great theologian: the identification of Luther with nationalist Germany and the spirit of German music provides Mann with a suitable analogy for the career of Adrian Leverkühn and, simultaneously, for the tragic course of German politics.

As was the case with Johann Faustus, the study of theology is for Adrian Leverkühn no end in itself. In the peculiar Reformation-period idiom which he has acquired, he bids his friends farewell, saying:

> So did I feed my arrogance with sugar, studying divinity at Halla Academie, yet not for the service of God but the other, and my study of divinity was secretly already the beginning of the bond and the disguised move not Biblewards, but to him the great religiosus. For who can hold that will away, and 'twas but a short step from the divinity school over to Leipzig and to music, that I solely and entirely busied myself with *figuris, characteribus, formis coniurationum,* and what other so ever are the names of invocations and magic.

Indeed, even before he gives up the formal study of theology, Adrian is predisposed to musical enchantment. His father's experiments with visible music, in which "the simple and the mysterious, law and miracle," were "so charmingly mingled," the singing stable-girl, whose tuneful ditties moved in "a realm of imitative polyphony, which the fifteenth century had had to discover," uncle Leverkühn, the violin maker who dealt in musical instruments, and who first provided Adrian with the means for "making music"—these were also powerful influences in his early years. The "short step" from divinity studies to music is facilitated by an interest in mathematics—on the religious plane of a Novalis, but with the magical hocus-pocus of "Dr. Faustus" himself.

The most significant thing about Adrian's existence is the manner in which he clings to his strangely archaic medieval environment; even though he exchanges Kaisersaschern for Pfeiffering, the elements about him remain the same:

> [The] scene of his later days bore a curious resemblance to that of his early ones. Not only did the environs of Pfeiffering (or Pfeffering, for the spelling varies) have a hill with a community bench, though it was not called Mount Zion, but the Rohmbühel; not only was there a pond, at somewhat the same distance from the house as the Cow Trough, here called the Klammer Pond, the water of which was strikingly cold; no, for even the house, the courtyard, and the family itself were all very like the Buchel setting. In the yard was a tree, also rather in the way and preserved for sentimental reasons—not a lime tree, but an elm. True, characteristic differences existed between the structure of the Schweigestill house and that of Adrian's parents, for the former was an old cloister, with thick walls, deep-vaulted casements, and rather dank passages. But the odor of pipe tobacco pervaded the air of the lower rooms as it did at Buchel; and the owner and his wife, Herr and Frau Schweigestill, were a father and a mother too. . . . The yard dog in Pfeiffering could laugh, even though he was not called Suso, but Kaschperl.

And the stable-girl, Waltpurgis, looked much like the singing Hanne of Buchel.

In Kaisersaschern "something still hung in the air from the spiritual constitution of the men of the last decades of the fifteenth century: a morbid excitement, a metaphysical epidemic latent since the last years of the Middle Ages." From this town, with all its oddities, Adrian proceeds to Pfeiffering in order to live a life of seclusion in a building which once was a medieval monastery. Thomas Mann plays with the word Pfeiffering in a rather ironic manner; for this obscure place-name occurs in a relatively minor incident in the Faust-book, but its importance has been magnified by the contention of scholars as to how it was spelled (one philologist even suggested that it was really the name of a horse). The dog of Adrian's early days, named Suso, is somehow later reincarnated in Kaschperl, who responds to Adrian's magic charm—a high-frequency whistle, well known to dog trainers, but here almost a demonic feature—and even prefers being called "Suso." The name Kaschperl (as Caspar, Crispin, Harlekin, Hans Wurst) occurs commonly in Faust plays, particularly puppet plays, for a slapstick character who acts either in the place of Faust or as a parody to Faust. The monastery itself, with its vaulted ceiling and deep casements, serves admirably as a Faust study—comparable, in general, to the "high-vaulted, narrow Gothic room" of Goethe's *Faust,* and suggesting the elements of darkness and coldness, with which Adrian's character and tendencies are associated.

The period of transition from Kaisersaschern to Pfeiffering is one in which Adrian Leverkühn's formal relationship with the devil is effected, the signing of the pact in blood, as it were, in keeping with the Faust tradition. First, the music lectures of Wendell Kretschmar bring to Adrian the intriguing story of Conrad Beissel, whose hymnology represents a union of theology and music. Then the Luther-figure, Professor Kumpf, exerts a profound influence upon Adrian's German. His language, from this period on, is a conscious imitation of Kumpf's robust style. He speaks "good old German, without any adornment and smoothing." . . . Kumpf's intimate relation with the devil is reflected in his rich terminology for the "Great Adversary," and his language is precisely the one favored by the devil, who at times "understands only German." Kumpf enjoyed speaking of *der Hellen und ihrer Spelunck*"—which is a phrase repeated by Adrian in his conversation with the devil and commonly found in the Spiess Faust-book.

Still another person who left a subtle impression upon Adrian here at Halle was Privatdozent Eberhard Schleppfuß (who resembles the late Joseph Goebbels). Mann's fondness for descriptive names is especially pointed in the remark: "In my opinion [i.e. that of Adrian's friend, Zeitblom] he actually dragged (*schepple*) one foot (*Fuß*)." In fact, his physical characteristics suggest very strongly the goat-footed monk in whose form Faustian devils frequently appear.

Schleppfuß' psychological approach to religion leads him to dwell upon the extent of the devil's domain and the clarification that "evil, the Evil One himself, is a necessary em-

anation and inevitable accompaniment of the Holy Existence of God," all of which leads him to the subject of sex and the temptation of man by that "*instrumenium of the Tempter*"—woman. The theology of Schleppfuß is presented in a pedantic manner that is characteristic of the informative "Geist" of the old Faust-book, whose dry lecturing on theology and the universe communicated part of the forbidden knowledge Faust so earnestly desired. Moreover, Schleppfuß' curious tales of sex and magic contain motifs and episodes familiar to the Faust tradition. In one such tale an old woman is said to have made a "pact with the Devil," who "had appeared to her in the form of a goat-footed monk," or in the same form in which Mephistopheles visited Faust in the Faust-book. And in this revolting story of Bärbel and Heinz Klopfgeißel, the devil's caprice is held responsible for an ill-fated case of sexual suppression—at least one analogy for which may be found in Faust tradition. This, and other such "theological" lectures, Adrian hears from the "scorner's bench," . . . which he occupies with the devil—according to the conversation later on—and to which the Spiess Faustus was assigned by his particular nemesis.

The "short step" from these "theological" contacts to Leipzig, and to music, is described repeatedly by a phrase from the Faust-book: Faustus "hat die H. Schrifft ein weil hinder die Tür und unter die Banck gelegt." Adrian hesitates momentarily in this act . . . , and in his subsequent conversation with the devil, he is reminded (in the language of Professor Kumpf) of the time when he had not yet laid the holy scripture *vor die Tür und unter die Bank.*

Upon his arrival in Leipzig, Adrian is led (by some strange chance or diabolic fate, and through the agency of a "small time Schleppfuß") to a house of prostitution, much to his surprise and embarrassment, for he has always been oddly aloof from sexual matters. This incident is based on an episode in Nietzsche's life. Adrian (Nietzsche) rushes to a piano, begins to play, and is approached by a dusky wench—designated as an *esmeraldo*—whereupon he leaves in haste. Just as in Nietzsche's case, however, he later seeks out this *hetaera esmeralda* and, deliberately it seems, contracts syphilis. This intentional act corresponds to the traditional signature in blood, or the formal conclusion of Faust's "Promission," according to which a definite period of spiritual enlightenment is granted him and, when the time is up, the devil is to take Faustus off to hell. In the Faust-book this contract, signed by Faust in his own blood, involves a whole list of stipulations constituting the "Promission" (to cover a period of twenty-four years). Goethe's Faust ridicules the whole idea of a written agreement, saying to Mephistopheles: "Auch was Geschriebnes forderst du, Pedant? Hast du noch keinen Mann, nicht Mannes-Wort gekannt?" And in response to Mephistopheles' desire that he sign "mit einem Tröpfchen Blut," Faust replies: "Wenn dies dir völlig G'nüge tut, So mag es bei der Fratze bleiben."

No such conscious formalities are described by Thomas Mann, but the union with disease clearly represents a preservation of the traditional contract. In fact, Hermann Weigand actually anticipated this symbolic reference by some ten years when he spoke of Mann's *Zauberberg* and of another such voluntary surrender to disease: "Hans Castorp's surrendering to disease has the same symbolic significance as Faust's concluding his pact with the devil."

Adrian thus sets his course by means of the fateful embrace; thereafter, he relives the myth of a traditional Faustus, but in the unique style prescribed by his author. Even in Halle, when he was conscious of the affinity of theology and music, where he was afraid of making the "Promission" to art, an inner voice seemed to warn him, saying: "O homo fuge!" (the words which the Spiess Faustus reads in his left hand as he draws the blood from his wrist). After his infection Adrian lives under a spell. The devil protects his own interests by interfering with Adrian's attempts at medication: one doctor dies and another is jailed, whereupon Adrian gives up all pretense and allows the matter to go unattended. In his farewell, or *Oratio ad Studiosos*, twenty-four years later, he refers to this decisive year as follows:

> . . . since my twenty-first year I have been married to Satan, with knowledge of my peril, out of well-considered courage, pride and audacity, because I wished to achieve fame in the world, I made him a bond and vow.

To the traditional features of the pact, from the elaborate details of the Faust-book to the easy-flowing banter of Goethe's *Faust,* Adrian adds a new interpretation:

> Believe not, dear brothers and sisters, that for the promission and conclusion of the pact a crossroads in the wood, many circles and coarse incantations were needed, since already St. Thomas teaches that, for the fall from grace, no words are needed as an invocation, rather any act may be enough, even without express allegiance. For it was only a butterfly, a Hetaera Esmeralda; she charmed me with her touch, the milk-witch, and I followed after her into the twilit shadowy foliage that her transparent nakedness loves, and where I caught her, who in flight is like a wind-blown petal, caught her and caressed her, in spite of her warning, and thus it happened. For as she charmed me, so she bewitched me, yielded to me in love—so was I initiated and the promise made.

Although Adrian has long been destined to exceed the legitimate bounds of normality and to suffer consequent disaster, the fatal act, in this instance, spells the beginning of his twenty-four-year period of privilege—which is the traditionally allotted time. He governs his behavior according to the conditions of the original pact: his immortal soul becomes a pawn, and he is to reject, without reservation, the influence and faith of all Christian believers. He is extremely fascinated by the Andersen fairy tale of the mermaid whose tragic existence grew out of the inordinate desire for an "immortal soul":

> An immortal soul, [says Adrian] but why? An entirely foolish wish! It is much more comforting for one to know that after death he will become foam on the sea, as would befall the little maid by nature.

On at least two significant occasions, his resolution to infringe upon the stipulated rules has extremely disastrous consequences. His belated desire to marry (the corresponding incident occurs very early in the Faust-book) suggests a flagrant violation of the pact. The Spiess Faustus, in face of the devil's ire, quickly accepts a counterproposal involving mere sexual satisfaction, for marriage itself is Christian in essence, as Adrian Leverkühn had long recognized when he said: "But one has to admit that the domestication of sex, which is evil by nature, into Christian marriage was a clever makeshift."

Goethe's Faust also avoids the sanctity of marriage and brings about directly, in this way, Gretchen's tragic death. Distracted by the scenes of the Walpurgisnacht, but still haunted by the memory of Gretchen, he later accepts the devil's paramour, Helena. Although the Gretchen episode involves a motif that is especially peculiar to Goethe's time, and not found in the Faust-book, there is a certain parallel to be noted between the abandonment of Gretchen, in the case of Goethe's Faust, and the substitution of demonic concubines for the wife whom the Spiess Faustus desires. Mann's Faustus turns to thoughts of marriage only a short time before the end of his twenty-four-year period, so that the incident seems to replace, at this point, the Helena marriage which was undertaken by the Spiess Faustus in the last year of his "Promission."

Since this desire to marry is an illicit impulse from the devil's point of view, it results in the violent death of Adrian's friend, Rudi Schwerdtfeger, whom Adrian appointed as a go-between in his marriage negotiations. The actual marriage, however, is never concluded, and it is, in fact, of secondary importance in the episode, for—according to the author—Adrian simply becomes an accessory to the murder of his friend; the devil takes his due. Rudi's friendship for Adrian had passed legitimate bounds and become far too intimate.

In a similar fashion, little Nepomuk Schneidewein becomes a victim of demonic destruction. The torture and death of this completely innocent child is necessitated by Adrian's breach of the pact. His love for such a "divine child," the most remarkable Christian believer, is a thing that is strictly forbidden, as Adrian well realizes when he sees the child go screaming to its death. For Adrian, by virtue of his "Promission," is relegated to sterile solitude. The biographer [Zeitblom] compares Adrian's loneliness to a yawning abyss. Although his physical traits are never revealed, he is surrounded by an air of coldness. It is a coldness that reflects his detachment from human society and his preoccupation with the demonic. It is a little of the coldness that characterizes the devil himself, and which Adrian notices particularly when the devil pays him a visit. In his private account of this singular experience, he says: "Then all at once I felt a bitter cold, as if I sat in a winter-warm room and suddenly a window had opened and let in the frost." The Spiess Faustus had fared similarly . . . . (pp. 18-29)

During the course of this interview, Mann permits his readers to observe the logical implication of the devil's coldness—it enables him to enjoy comfort in the intense heat of his natural habitat. The interview itself is reminiscent of traditional discourses between Faust and the devil, but in its detail the scene is modeled on the nightmare of

Ivan Karamazov, in Dostoyevsky's *The Brothers Karamazov,* where the devil manifests himself in order to convince Ivan of his, the devil's existence. Adrian's devil serves to recapitulate the events of his life in which demonic forces have played a part. The descriptions of the two devils parallel each other, but are not identical. Yet the entire atmosphere is the same: the unwelcome visit, the gaudy clothing of the devil (the trousers too tight, checkered vest), his appearance as a ham actor (for Mann) and as a déclasseé (for Dostoyevsky). Dostoyevsky shows an uncommon appreciation for traditional devils, including Goethe's Mephistopheles. Likewise, Mann's devil is equipped with a number of familiar characteristics. For example, the devil's little creatures, the bugs and vermin (which play their roles in Goethe's *Faust,* and which, according to the Spiess Faust-book, were created in order to plague and injure mankind), now appear as the "Volk der Lebeschräubchen, die lieben Gäste aus Westindien"; in other words, the old *"Unsiffer"* have turned up in the form of *spirochaeta pallida,* and have been entrusted with the function of operating for the devil upon the human brain—in this case for the purpose of creating temporary enlightenment through sickness. In this connection another character, Baptist Spengler, is played off against Adrian, for he too has embraced the *hetaera esmeralda.* The two characters represent, respectively, two aspects of Faustian desire, both of which were incorporated previously, in varying degrees, within a single individual: Spengler possesses here an almost completely sensual appetite, while Adrian craves purely intellectual adventure.

The interview with the devil is punctuated with the doubts and hopes of Adrian Leverkühn that somehow he has lived in a dream of his own making, so that his curiosity in regard to demonic lore gives way to an attempt to trap the devil and deny him. Upon learning of the source of his heightened mental vision, he cries:

> Do I trap you, blockhead? Do you betray yourself and tell me personally of the place in my brain, the fever hearth, that makes me imagine you, and without which you are not?

This is much in the same vein as Ivan Karamazov's declaration: "You are lying, your aim is to convince me you exist apart and are not my nightmare, and now you are asserting you are a dream."

Such delicate irony is lacking in previous Faust tradition, although the attitude of Goethe's Faust toward Mephistopheles shows some of the same contempt that is shared by Adrian and Ivan for their respective devils. The suggestion that the devil's appearance may be a dream and delusion is emphasized, in Adrian's case, by his conscious acceptance of the Faustus role that he knows he is playing, by his deliberate conformance to a Faust *mythos,* from the "Promission" itself to a fanciful story of his descent in a diving bell . . . , and his scientific studies concerning the universe. His musical compositions, entitled *Marvels of the Universe* and *Phosphorescence of the Sea,* are the expressions of these imaginative projections. The conversation with the devil, in fact, shows the typical distortions of dream-pictures, and seems to develop from Adrian's peculiar mental state as he reads Kierkegaard's "painfully

enthusiastic essay" on Mozart's *Don Juan.* The dream-motif was introduced into Faust tradition by Lessing, whose Faust would have experienced a rational sort of dream and awakened a wiser man, but in Mann's *Faustus* we are faced with a familiar Romantic paradox of later design, namely, the question of which is more real—the dream world or its physical counterpart.

Apart from presenting a dramatic conversation (that erupts near the climax in most of Mann's novels), this same chapter also serves to introduce some of the "smaller motifs" of the Faust-book. The miscellaneous collection of proverbs contained in the sixty-fifth chapter of the Spiess Faust-book is found here once again as the devil presses the troubled Faustus with odd, mocking jests and sayings. . . . These very proverbs are then echoed by Adrian in later conversations with his friends. They serve to emphasize the hopelessness of Adrian's situation; they are clearly eschatological and are punctuated from time to time with references to the dwindling sands of the hour glass, particularly during Adrian's farewell speech to his friends. (pp. 29-30)

In the final years of his musical career, Adrian composes the *Apocalipsis cum figuris,* for which he prepares himself from the eschatologies of pre-Christian and early Christian times. The fear of torture and damnation has grown upon him since the conversation with the devil, and he is ever more conscious of the impending doom. The *Apocalipsis* presents a musical impression of the "hellish

Mann in the workroom of his house in California, where much of Doctor Faustus *was written.*

laughter" that has been associated with Adrian before, and which Zeitblom recognizes in the "overwhelming, sardonically yelling, screeching, bawling, bleating, howling, piping, whinnying salvo, the mocking, exulting laughter of the Pit."

The prophetic doom envisioned here finds the expression of its fulfillment in Adrian's musical composition, entitled *D. Fausti Weheklag,* the letter and spirit of which are the same as the woeful laments of the Spiess Faustus. . . . This cantata is compared with the Ninth Symphony of Beethoven as a final work, and is also contrasted to it as an "ode to sorrow," rather than to joy. Thomas Mann steps aside at this point to remind his readers that he has been following the Faust-book, and that the story will end, of necessity, in the manner of the older tradition (not at all like Goethe's *Faust,* or the one Lessing might have written):

> Man erinnert sich ja, daß in dem alten Volksbuch, das Leben und Sterben des Erzmagiers erzählt, und dessen Abschnitte Leverkühn sich mit wenigen entschlossenen Griffen zur Unterlage seiner Sätze zurechtgefügt hat, der Dr. Faustus, als sein Stundenglas ausläuft, seine Freunde und vertrauten Gesellen, "Magistros, Baccalaureos und andere Studenten" nach dem Dorfe Rimlich nahe Wittenberg lädt, sie dort den Tag über freigebig bewirtet, zur Nacht auch noch einen "Johannstrunk" mit ihnen einnimmt und ihnen dann in einer zerknirschten, aber würdigen Rede sein Schicksal, und daß dessen Erfüllung nun unmittelbar bevorsteht, kund und zu wissen tut. In dieser "Oratio Fausti ad Studiosos" bittet er sie, seinen Leib, wenn sie ihn tot und erwürgt finden, barmherzig zur Erde zu bestatten; denn er sterbe, sagt er, als ein böser und guter Christ. . . .

The point of this discourse is not merely to introduce the final scene, in which Adrian emulates his mythical prototype by delivering a modern *Oratio ad Studiosos,* but it is meant to show incidentally that the words, "denn ich sterbe als ein böser und guter Christ," contain twelve syllables corresponding (according to the author) to the twelve-tone scale—which Adrian has developed as a result of his musical adventuring, his *hetaera esmeralda,* as it were, by means of which he has wedded himself to an abnormal and audacious intellectual and emotional spirit. Moreover, the remaining elements of Faustian tradition are here injected into the text. Once again the reference is made to the hourglass as a symbol of the limited time that has now run out. A momentary impulse attracts Adrian to the thought of committing suicide by drowning himself in the "Kuhmulde." . . . But he rejects any such temptation to escape his fate. . . . (pp. 31-3)

Amidst the lamenting of Dr. Faustus, as well as in the choral scherzo of Adrian's *Weheklag,* the evil spirit is heard in overtones with its mocking jests and proverbs. An echo of the devil's own words can be distinguished here again: the following words, similar to one of Luther's *Reimsprüche,* are recited in the Spiess Faust-book:

> Drum schweig, leyd, meyd und vertrag,
> Dein Unglück keinem Menschen klag.

> Es ist zu spät, an Gott verzag,
> Dein Unglück läufft herein all tag.

The chorus of the final scene in the *Weheklag* is described as sounding like the lament of God over the lost state of his world, like the Creator's troubled "I have not willed it so!" In this respect the underlying theme of Goethe's *Faust* is wholly by-passed: here evil, in the form of the abnormal (or "normal madness"), has triumphed and must claim its due. The man of action can make no compromise with humanity. The Titan has lost his balance and must fall. He must await the inevitable consequence of his agreement with the devil in the same way as his Faust prototype in general before Goethe. In this instance, Mann draws a parallel between his own Faustus and the one in the Faust-book, whose pious neighbor makes a last vain attempt to save him. The "temptations" here involved, however, coincide only in so far as Faustus is free to choose (or to refuse) to repent. The Nietzsche-Faustus, Adrian, rejects penitence on the grounds of principle, whereas the old Faustus clearly lacked the courage to hasten his bodily destruction in order to save his soul, even though he continued to hope for redemption after death.

An attitude of resignation is displayed in Mann's Faustus as he plays the role of the traditional Faust, awaiting the running-out of the hourglass and fulfillment of his appointed doom. When Adrian delivers his *Oratio ad Studiosos,* he summarizes the story of his "Promission" with the words of the Faust-book but in the spirit of the new Faustus whom Mann has created. For it becomes increasingly evident to the reader that the Faust theme is here as much a vehicle for an expression of the author's *Weltanschäuung* as it was in the case of Goethe's *Faust.*

A certain irony is to be noted in the fact that even the religious writers dealing with this theme were blissfully aware of its fictional value; Spiess offered the story as a "horrible lesson and example" to "godless persons," but it was really a popular romance that frequently met with official censorship. Yet only since the time of Lessing has the traditional account been separated from religious bias. It then became a moral fable that could be used as a means of enlightenment. The contemporary applications envisioned by Lessing were powerfully utilized in Goethe's *Faust.* Here was represented the author's faith in a triumph of humane idealism, through action and persistent striving towards a sympathetic, divine love. The framework of Protestant dogma that characterized the Spiess Faust-book was replaced by a philosophical scheme which permitted Faust to achieve salvation.

Mann's Faustus, however, while possessing the insatiable intellectual thirst of Goethe's Faust, is still the medieval Faustus of the older tradition. Thus, Adrian Leverkühn exemplifies the danger of temptation engendered by an intellectual arrogance which is—paradoxically—necessary for the revaluation of values and the creation of a higher spiritual order. Mann regards the adventuresome pursuits of the mind as productive and, at the same time, dangerous, for unless they are tempered with a sense of moral reverence, they lead to destruction. With the Romanticists, Mann suggests sickness as an analogy: just as sickness can chasten the soul and give it greater vision, so can it also destroy the body. Hence, Mann has produced a Faustus whose fatal career parallels that of Germany itself. In so doing, he has synthetically adapted the elements of the Faust tradition (avoiding for the most part the reinterpretations of Lessing and Goethe) to his own inherently Romantic philosophy. (pp. 33-4)

Carroll E. Reed, "Thomas Mann and the Faust Tradition," in The Journal of English and Germanic Philology, *Vol. LI, No. 1, January, 1952, pp. 17-34.*

Frank Donald Hirschbach   (essay date 1955)

[*Hirschbach is a German-born American critic and educator who wrote* The Arrow and the Lyre: A Study of the Role of Love in the Works of Thomas Mann. *In the following excerpt from that work, Hirschbach discusses the extent to which Mann's feelings toward Germany and his investigations into the nature of creativity are reflected in his presentation of personal relationships in* Doctor Faustus.]

In *The Making of Doctor Faustus (Die Entstehung des Doktor Faustus)*, that fascinating book which affords the curious a look into a magician's laboratory, Thomas Mann describes how he spent March 14, 1943 in emptying desk drawers and book shelves of the prodigious mass of material which had gone into making *Joseph,* much in the manner of a sick man who after a long illness is able to leave his sickroom for the first time. The final volume of *Joseph and his Brothers* had witnessed profound changes in its author's life as well as in the world in which he lived. After Lübeck, Munich, Palestrina, the regions of the North as well as the Baltic Sea, Switzerland and New Jersey, Mann had chosen the Pacific Ocean coast and the Far West as his home. More important: the World War, dormant in its beginnings, had gathered fury; the powers of darkness continued to gain strength on the seas and on the continent until they were assembling their forces on the plains outside of Moscow. To many, perennial optimists among them, it seemed that the strength of democracy was rapidly crumbling and that the Age of Tyranny was dawning on the horizon.

The scraps of his diary, which Mann published in the companion volume to *Doctor Faustus,* as well as the other products of his pen between March 15, 1943 and January 29, 1946 (roughly the two poles of his work on *Doctor Faustus*), are indicative of his deep concern for the fate of Germany. An entry such as

Excerpts from the Faust book. Read in it during the evening. Second bombing of Berlin within forty-eight hours . . .

speaks for itself.

A passing allusion to Mann's feelings toward Germany and the Germans seems entirely justified in a treatment of erotic relationships in his works, for Mann's attitude toward the country of his birth and its people is definitely a curious love-relationship. Like Goethe, whom he once called "a red-blooded non-patriot", he abhorred flag-waving, and vociferous protestations of loyalty were

anathema to him. But the vigor with which he condemned certain traits in the German character and in those whom he considered responsible for her downfall bears testimony to the love and admiration which he once bore her soul.

Mann's position as an artist was indeed a strange and an unhappy one at this time. After thirty years of writing in a country in which literary criticism is a popular and widespread activity, he was suddenly compelled to live in a country in which the vast majority had never heard of him and even fewer had ever read any of his works. Literary criticism was then and still is confined mainly to the halls of the universities, the pages of the esoteric little magazines and the columns of the book reviews. Moreover, few, except the members of the miniscule clusters of German refugees, ever read Mann in German, a feature which must have seemed especially painful to a man of his linguistic propensities. Many of these difficulties exist even today. Although Mann has recovered much of his reading public in Germany, misunderstanding and rancor toward him still exist in large measure, dulling the eyes of many who read his works today.

Without appreciating this mingled feeling of spurned love, deep disappointment and hope for the future, one cannot possibly fully understand *Doctor Faustus.* There is no doubt that Mann associates himself to a large extent with Zeitblom's opinions on Germany, and many of these, such as the admission that the enthusiasm at Germany's invasion of Belgium in 1914 seems slightly ridiculous in retrospect, are undoubtedly fragments of a concealed confession. Kahler is quite correct when he calls the book a radical confession and adds:

It is as if he were trying to emphasize the fact in retrospect that he, Thomas Mann, belongs and is a part of it, that he includes himself among the fates of Leverkühn and Zeitblom, the fates of Germans and of intellectuals, the fate of modern art.

It is not quite clear whether the lines from Dante's *Inferno* are meant to be included by Zeitblom or whether they are meant to be read as Mann's preface to Zeitblom's account; but certainly Dante's doubt, whether his passion and partisanship allow him to do justice to the work before him, is quite expressive of similar doubts, probably felt by Mann-Zeitblom.

Once before, in 1894, when he published the story **"Fallen,"** Mann had used the narrator technique, the installation of an intermediary between author and audience to carry the burden of telling the story. But there are two important differences in the employment of this technique between **"Fallen"** and *Doctor Faustus.*

While **"Fallen"** is a "framed story" in the best nineteenth century tradition, one can hardly speak of *Doctor Faustus* as a "framed" novel. To be sure, it has a narrator who goes to great lengths to assure us that he is telling the story of a friend and only for the sake of doing just that. But of the forty-seven divisions of *Doctor Faustus,* forty-four begin with a reference of the narrator to himself or to his personal circumstances, generally in the first sentence and varying in length from a few lines to several pages. The surprising insights which Zeitblom exhibits concerning his friend would, of course, not be credible at all if we did not have his constant assurance and testimony that he was Adrian's best friend and intimus, as far as that was possible in the case of a man like Leverkühn. Their stories are in truth interwoven, and if **"Fallen"** can be compared to a framed picture, then *Doctor Faustus* can, perhaps, be likened to an old painting in which the story of Serenus Zeitblom represents the web of vein-like lines which one often finds on old masterpieces.

The second basic difference in technique between **"Fallen"** (and, for that matter, many other nineteenth-century framed stories) and *Doctor Faustus* is that the author treats the narrator of the latter and his style of writing with an all-pervasive, exceedingly skillfully-handled irony whereas a similar attempt in the case of Dr. Selten had been abortive at best. It is often said of the frame, and it has been said of this particular instance that it may be likened to a mask in front of the author's face, the implication being that he does not want the world to see his smiles and his anguish. This would certainly apply to the present book where Mann was dealing with a time and its issues about which he felt most strongly and which were still very much in balance when he wrote the book.

But there is far more involved here. If Zeitblom has been called "dusty" and "pedantic" and a descendant of Faust's Wagner by some of the critics, it is because Mann has chosen to parody in his style the manner in which supposedly a retired German high school teacher of the classics would write about an infinitely greater man in whose shadow he was permitted to walk throughout his life. Similarly, his comments on the era in which he exists are those of a German who is stumbling along toward an end, both unwanted and unforeseen.

Whom does Mann parody in Serenus Zeitblom? The answer can only be: himself and his generation. The young Zeitblom, who participates in the endless hayloft discussions with his fellow students and who volunteers for service in the First World War, partly because he is ashamed of his students and partly because he firmly believes in Germany's cause, certainly has much in common with Thomas Mann who is only eight years older than Zeitblom. Mann frankly admits to a pre-war attitude of mind which, seen in retrospect, had much to do with the rise of Hitler and the coming of the Second World War. In 1948 he recognizes how much of a German he once was, but he has also gained enough distance to parody himself and his fellows.

Such a parody, it may be argued, may be of more importance to the student of political relations in Mann's works than to the student of human relations. But the parallel Zeitblom-Mann can be carried one step further. If we ask ourselves, where in the life of the younger Thomas Mann there existed a man whom he admired with that same mixture of love and fear, of familiarity and non-understanding, of agreement and reservation that characterizes Zeitblom's feelings toward Leverkühn, we can come up with only one answer: Friedrich Nietzsche. The equation Zeitblom: Leverkühn equals Mann: Nietzsche, in turn, opens up interesting vistas of the author's intent in

shaping Leverkühn's life, destiny, and end in the manner in which he did it.

In examining the various types of human relationships in *Doctor Faustus,* let us begin with the one that lasts the longest and about which we hear most: the friendship between Adrian Leverkühn and Serenus Zeitblom. It is perhaps incorrect to call theirs a friendship because the term implies an equal amount of affection exchanged by both parties. Such cases of friendship are quite rare in Mann's works. In the relationships between Thomas Buddenbrook and Stephan Kistenmaker, Hans Castorp and Joachim Ziemssen, Tonio Kröger and Hans Hansen, Schridaman and Nanda, or even the Man and his dog, there are always differences of an intellectual nature between the two partners which preclude a true understanding between the two. Such understanding is possible only when both partners have an artistic penchant (Kai and Hanno, Tonio Kröger and Lisaweta Iwanowna) or in which neither possesses it to a pronounced degree (Hans Hansen and Erwin Jimmerthal). (pp. 115-19)

The relationship between Leverkühn and Zeitblom is that between genius and an exceedingly cultured mediocrity. No one is more conscious of this than the narrator himself. After a life of inculcating the love of classic ideals in generations of students and after having founded a family of five, the man of sixty-three modestly admits:

> My life, insignificant but capable of fascination and devotion, has been dedicated to my love for a great German man and artist. It was always a love full of fear and dread, yet eternally faithful to this German whose inscrutable guiltiness and awful end had no power to affect my feeling for him—such love it may be as is only a reflection of the everlasting mercy.

On the other hand, Zeitblom retains his own independence and integrity to a remarkable degree. It is a mixture of love and anxiety, together with a refusal to care whether his love is returned, which is present whenever Zeitblom speaks of his friend.

> . . . I loved him, with tenderness and terror, with compassion and devoted admiration, and but little questioned whether he in the least returned my feeling.

There are many indications that Leverkühn only tolerates the less imaginative Zeitblom and the latter seizes upon all indications of friendship with a dog-like devotion. Thus, he repeatedly points with some pride to the fact that he is the only one who is called "du" by Adrian, especially in view of the fact that after the student days it is Rüdiger Schildknapp who assumes an increasingly important position in Adrian's life. From the very beginnings of this latter friendship, it is clear that Zeitblom feels intensely jealous toward it and the bond of continence which seems to unite the two men. But Zeitblom is far too unselfish in his friendship to envy Rüdiger or to begrudge Adrian the laughs which he enjoys in Rüdiger's company.

Although he is only two years older, Zeitblom sees himself in the role of Adrian's protector. Although he knows that his friend will always go his own way, he feels that somehow the worst will not happen in his presence. Thus, he attends courses at the university quite without his own curriculum,

> . . . only out of the imperative desire to hear what he heard, know what he learned, to "keep track" of him—for that always seemed to me highly necessary, though at the same time futile.

Very early in their lives—Zeitblom himself is unable to say just when—he feels that he may some day become his friend's biographer, but only after his friend's death does he realize that this biography will lend his own life significance.

Leverkühn's response to this friendship, as has been said before, is one of complete detachment. He likes Zeitblom's temperament and company, and seems to regard him as an intellectual equal whom he can use as a sounding board for his own opinions, but from whom he is not likely to seek opinions. He indicates little faith in the friend's appreciation of creative problems and turns to people like Wendell Kretzschmar or Rüdiger Schildknapp for their discussion. He respects Zeitblom chiefly as a human being, and on two crucial occasions, after the visit to the bordello and before the proposal to Marie Godeau, it is Zeitblom who is apprised first. But here again the artist does not seek an opinion or advice: he merely tells. The few moments when Leverkühn manifests his emotions are shared with others or are spent in loneliness. Like Joseph, Leverkühn must essentially be friendless, and a Joseph motif is repeated when Zeitblom writes:

> There had always been in his nature something of *noli me tangere*. During my visit . . . it was as though the "Touch me not!", the "three paces off," had to some extent altered its meaning, as though it were not so much that an advance was discouraged as that an advance from the other side was shrunk from and avoided . . .

The friendship between Leverkühn and Zeitblom can best be characterized by the latter's statement:

> There are people with whom it is not easy to live; but to leave them is impossible.

Their relationship is a great and positive one which heavily counterbalances all the negative elements surrounding Leverkühn. In the midst of the hopelessness, which seems to be characteristic of his end, this stands out as the one hopeful feature, promising grace and solution.

Serenus Zeitblom, a man of great sensibilities and superior esthetic capabilities, who devotes himself to the analysis of another's genius, has little to say about his own life and emotions when separate from Leverkühn. He writes about them with a meekness which almost seems to indicate that he is ashamed to have a private life apart from the friend. His life with the woman, most prosaically named Helene Ölhafen, appears drab and pedestrian. He generally mentions her in passing and with a superior, though respectful, indulgence. His reasons for marriage were primarily a desire for order, and secondarily, a philologian's love for the name "Helen". The twenty-seven year old finds it necessary to assure his friend, Adrian, that his marriage will not upset his life,

> . . . everything is directed towards the foundation of love and tranquility, a fixed and undisturbed happiness.

Thereafter, Zeitblom makes only occasional references to Helene as "my excellent wife" or "my dear Helene," and she appears on those occasions as serving him cocoa or bearing him children. It is a Buddenbrook marriage, concluded because it is in the best interest of all concerned and having no great emotional effect on either of the partners.

Where Serenus Zeitblom is consciously assuming serious responsibilities, Rüdiger Schildknapp is doing exactly the opposite, a circumstance which undoubtedly contributes to Zeitblom's reserve toward him. Rüdiger, like the younger Buddenbrook, is a great entertainer who regales large audiences with stories about his hypochondriac father, or by speaking and dressing like an Englishman and managing to imitate the members of that nation with telling effect. Schildknapp's motto, just like Christian Buddenbrook's, is the formula "One ought to . . . ," the vain painting of possibilities never to be realized, the apotheosis of the subjunctive. In his relations with other people, among whom he enjoys great popularity, he is—again like his cousin from Lübeck—totally irresponsible. He flees anything that looks like a binding, a tie, an engagement. Women like Schildknapp because he appears athletic without carrying on athletics and because he seems to be a complete gentleman. But Zeitblom adds, somewhat maliciously:

> The women were not quite so lucky with him as he was with them, so far as I saw; at least not individually, for collectively they enjoyed his entire devotion. It was a roving, all-embracing devotion, it referred to the sex as such, and the possibilities for happiness presented to him by the entire world; for the single instance found him inactive, frugal, reserved.

Realizing his potentialities as a lover, he is quite happy to contemplate them as such and to leave well enough alone. The grave and somewhat emasculating responsibilities of being a lover, a husband, and a father—often mentioned by Mann as a somewhat painful by-product of love and marriage—frighten Rüdiger Schildknapp to the point of mania.

Among the few human relationships which do not involve Adrian in some manner, perhaps the most interesting is the triangle Helmut Institoris—Ines Rodde—Rudi Schwerdtfeger. Ines Rodde is one of that type of women in Mann's works whose voice and inner life seem hopelessly drowned out in a man's world. She possesses the knowledge and the resultant melancholy of all the Hamlet-like men and women in Mann's works called to bear a cross which they are not strong enough to carry. Having enjoyed a faultless but mediocre education, she now finds herself rapidly fading away in the salon of her mother, who, on the other hand, is trying very hard to paddle against the current of time. Ines sternly disapproves of her mother's activities and is striving to leave the house peacefully by contracting a secure and respectable marriage,

> . . . for love if possible, but in God's name even without love.

Her courtship and married life with Helmut Institoris is decidedly of the latter type. For Institoris, a reticent and fragile lecturer with a lisp, is physically anything but attractive and represents intellectually all the things which are anathema or of no import to Ines. A lover of the Renaissance, he worships blood and fire, strength and lawlessness, beauty and instinct—in others. For the strange feature in this relationship is that each cherishes in reality the other's ideals. Institoris, conscious of his weakness and general mediocrity, appears to devote his life to a concept totally alien to his nature, but in reality seeks a peaceful, conventional home in which he can be the undisputed master. Ines, on the other hand, perhaps unconscious of the pent-up passion and appetite for living within her, concentrates her hopes for salvation upon one who to her represents life in its glittering freedom and lawlessness: the utterly unattainable Rudi Schwerdtfeger. Thus, Institoris is more or less doing Schwerdtfeger's bidding.

But Rudolf Schwerdtfeger, the object of her passion, is not available. For the young man, though hopelessly addicted to the sport of conquering the hearts of young and older women, has, in truth, strong homosexual leanings and is therefore loath (and perhaps unable) to enter into any binding relationship with any of the women whom he knows. Rudi is a violinist of talent but not of genius. Outwardly at least, he has none of the characteristics of an artist of the Mann school. He is handsome, well-built and healthy; in temperament and outlook he is a boy rather than a man and carefully cultivates that impression. He works hard at being amiable and sometimes labors the point. His immaturity knows no love, only complaisance. In short, the man whom Ines Rodde loves so tragically, is, in turn, eager to gain simultaneously the liking and respect of as many women as possible.

Under such circumstances, it is inevitable that disaster must strike at all corners of this living triangle. Without love, Helmut Institoris and Ines Rodde conclude their marriage, found a home which becomes a fortress of middleclass morality and raise children which become, according to Ines' wishes, "des jeunes filles accomplies." But the fire of Ines' unsatiated passion continues to smolder within this imitation of paradise. Ines carries on for many years, presiding over an exemplary household and moving to progressively lower stages of depravation. Her final act, the murder of Rudi Schwerdtfeger, is by no means a precipitate flash of sudden passion, but, on the contrary, a premeditated, highly logical act which tops a period of years in which lust and desire have gathered until they reach the unbearable point. It is the tragedy of Mut-em-enet relived; it is, in short, "the coming of the stranger god."

The fate of Clarissa Rodde is equally tragic, though perhaps a bit more on the conventional side. Its model is, of course, the fate of Mann's sister, Carla, and in the sketch of his life he had already told many of the exact details which he repeats in this novel. In many respects, Clarissa's end is similar to that of Ines. Disappointed in her artistic career, she too sees in marriage an anchor to help her in fixing her position, and the young Alsatian industrialist who offers her marriage is only little more likable than the Bavarian esthete. Her marriage would not have been unlike that of her sister,

> . . . but now it was her haven, her happiness; a bourgeois happiness, which obviously looked more acceptable because it possessed the charm of novelty; the foreign nationality was a new frame into which she would be transplanted. In fancy she heard her future children prattling in French.

But the proud Clarissa is driven to suicide through blackmail on the part of the man to whom she gave herself on two occasions. Her fate, incidentally, also corresponds to that of Mann's other sister. The full story of her end has never been told.

If we add to all this, for the sake of completeness, the fact that Baptist Spengler is syphilitic, we can conclude that the erotic relationships in *Doctor Faustus* up to this point are fully in keeping with the time in which they take place. They are shallow, lacking in genuineness, abnormal or diseased. We have not yet encountered a single strong and mutual love relationship.

Adrian Leverkühn, the man, and Adrian Leverkühn, the artist, are so closely bound up with each other that one cannot effectively deal with Adrian's entire personality if one separates them. Adrian's childhood and youth clearly show the characteristics of early genius. Until he is fifteen he discharges his school obligations with an ease and a nonchalance which might have aroused the envy of his classmates if it had not been for the fact that the young student himself seemed quite indifferent toward his success. The headaches, which come with increasing frequency from then on, decreased his stature in class somewhat; even then Zeitblom admits:

> Adrian presented the singular phenomenon of a bad student at the head of the class.

But the factor that frightens the friend most is the indifference which Adrian exhibits toward the contents of their schooling, toward the revelations made by their teachers and their books. Zeitblom—who, after all, is a Catholic—believes that faith in absolute values, even if it is a conscious delusion, is mandatory in human affairs.

> But my friend's gifts measured themselves against values the relative character of which seemed to lie open to him, without any visible possibility of any other relation which would have detracted from them as values.

Leverkühn's genius reveals itself early in musical affairs. His two earliest experiences in this field are the singing of rounds under the leadership of "Stable Hanna," one of the maids, and the acquaintence with his uncle's collection of musical instruments. It is here that he first experiments with the harmonium, and the fifteen-year old demonstrates to his older friend the twelve-tone scale which he has discovered on his own. During this year and the following years Adrian attends Wendell Kretzschmar's lectures and receives his first formal musical training from that gifted teacher. From the very beginning, Adrian seems to have little interest in playing the works of past masters, but he is fascinated by musical problems which he both poses and solves in the manner in which one solves an equation, a chess problem, or a crossword puzzle. The sixteen-year old surprises his teacher one day by having arrived at the theory of double counterpoint through experimentation. His views, as he propounds them for Zeitblom's benefit on walks and other occasions, as well as his musical accomplishments, reveal not only an outstanding maturity, but also the tremendous amount of thinking which Leverkühn must have done regarding music.

Under the circumstances, it must seem surprising that Leverkühn's chief interest in school is mathematics, and that later on he chooses theology as his field of study at the university. Is his biographer right in saying,

> Very long, with instinctive persistence, he hid himself from his destiny?

The answer is that Leverkühn, like so many other artists in Mann's works and like Mann himself, is bothered by scruples of conscience toward art. In an address before the citizens of his native city, Mann once defined ethics as the sense for one's duties in life,

> . . .that which inspires an artist to look at art not as a dispensation from life, to found a home and a family, to build his life, which may be adventurous enough in itself, on a firm, dignified, civil basis.

In a more concrete manner, an artist in one of the stories confesses how his conscience bothers him every time he awakes to find that he has slept till noon. "Sleeping till noon" seems a menace to Leverkühn, which he counters with an addiction and adherence to discipline and order, quite like that of Gustav Aschenbach. Beissel's severe musical system, which attempts to force creative genius into a corset of rules and regulations, has at least one redeeming grace in Leverkühn's eyes:

> At least he had a sense of order, and even a silly order is better than none at all.

Adrian's decision to study theology seems to have been due, in part at least, to a desire to find truths which would answer his questions in a valid manner, to find the same faith in absolute values which his friend possesses. After he has become a theology student, he tells some of his fellow students:

> I see in the Church . . . a citadel of order, an institution for objective disciplining, canalizing, banking-up of the religious life, which without her would fall victim to subjectivist demoralization, to a chaos of divine and demonic powers, to a world of fantastic uncanniness, an ocean of demony.

In his letter to Wendell Kretzschmar he makes it clear that he would consider the step from theology to music one from order to disorder, if he were going to be an ordinary musician. Again, he motivates his choice of theology by saying: "I wanted the hair shirt, the spiked girdle beneath," and vows that he will consider music a magic combination of theology and mathematics.

Order, the presence of an iron-clad system, becomes the cardinal artistic principle of this man of genius. The concept of freedom, so dear to the lover of classic antiquity, is treated derisively by the composer, or at least interpreted quite differently by him when he says:

> Freedom always inclines to dialectic reversals. It realizes itself very soon in constraint, fulfills itself in the subordination to law, rule, coercion, system—but to fulfill itself therein does not mean it therefore ceases to be freedom.

One is reminded of Zeitblom's repeated assertion that Leverkühn has won his physical freedom from Kaisersaschern only to be tied to it in a more intense manner through intellectual bonds.

The culmination of Adrian Leverkühn's search for order and systematization is the twelve-tone system, as whose discoverer he is pictured in the conversation with Zeitblom in September of 1910. Its salient feature can be described in the words of Leverkühn as the following:

> Every note of the whole composition, both melody and harmony, would have to show its relation to this fixed fundamental series . . . Not one would be allowed to appear which did not fulfill its function in the whole structure. There would no longer be a free note. That is what I would call "strict composition"!

Zeitblom's objection that under such a system the composer would lose all creative freedom is answered by Leverkühn with a dialectic reversion when he describes his ideal composer as "bound by a self-imposed compulsion to order, hence free." All objections, he claims, melt away in the face of the possibility to fulfill an age-old desire: to define the magic substance of music in terms of human reason. Adrian's symbol is Dürer's magic square which hangs over his desk. Here, just as in his music, the system permits of many possibilities within a definite, humanly defined frame.

Men, like nations, give up their freedom voluntarily when they have become so used to it that it seems worn-out and banal to them. Adrian Leverkühn is acutely conscious of his role as the latest link in a long chain of musical tradition (the names of seventy composers are mentioned in *Doctor Faustus* in some connection with him), and as he looks on this endless chain, stretching out behind him, he despairs of being able to say anything new. It is the resigned feeling of the twentieth-century artist that everything has been said or done at least once before, coupled with a deep dissatisfaction with the existing media which he considers unsuitable or disproportionate to his power of expression and to his subject. In adopting his new system, Leverkühn breaks off all bridges to the past. Never again will he be able to say anything in the manner or even with the means of Bach, Beethoven or Wagner. But until a new body of music exists, until some new tracks have been trodden in the new field, either by himself or others, he is limited to a certain extent to parody, the insincerest form of imitation.

The young student, who has not yet written a single original note, searchingly examines a highly romantic piece of music in a letter to his teacher and laughs at the thinly-veiled manner in which the composer pulls the stops of joy and sadness, gaiety and gravity, loveliness and sublimeness, manipulating the emotions of his audience in a highly refined manner. But at the same time he recognizes the danger which for him personally grows out of the ability to be too clairvoyant.

> I have always had to laugh, most damnably, at the most mysterious and impressive phenomena . . . Why does almost everything seem to me like its own parody? Why must I think that almost all, no, all the methods and conventions of art today are good for parody only?

But this is almost the only instance in which Leverkühn's reluctant attachment to parody is defined and explained in its origin. Hereafter, we are only told that it becomes second nature with him. Thus, his Leipzig letter to Zeitblom, detailing his experiences at the house of prostitution, is written in a style parodying the Luther style of German, employed by Kumpf and Schleppfuss. *Meerleuchten,* the orchestral tone poem written by the twenty-year old, is pictured as bearing parody features. In connection with his projected opera, *Love's Labour Lost,* Adrian speaks of his aim as a revival of the opéra bouffe in a spirit of artificial mockery and parody of the artificial, the ridicule of affected estheticism. Later we are told that Leverkühn's work on the opera is frequently interrupted because he finds it difficult to maintain the parodistic pitch of his own style. A later composition, *The Marvels of the Universe (Die Wunder des Alls),* is still shot through with parody. Its name alone suggests mockery of the pathetic to Zeitblom, who consequently calls it "flippant"; its music—uncanny and formal, monstrous yet mathematical—is a travesty of the praise which humans and especially artists are wont to apply to the clock-like working of the universe. The peak of this trend is reached some time in 1915 in the musical dramatization of parts of the *Gesta Romanorum.* Needless to say, Leverkühn was thoroughly enchanted with these fables which go to such lengths in describing immortality for the sake of morality. It charmed his intellect to impose upon these immorally moral stories an almost invisible net of malice and travesty, to puncture the pomp of priestliness with the subtle needle of irony.

The employment of parody has two closely connected purposes for Adrian Leverkühn: it characterizes his predecessors and their mode of expression as empty and banal in reference to his time, and it exempts him from the necessity of being ponderously sincere. Zeitblom correctly characterizes the style of his friend's letter from Leipzig as "parody as a means of reserve," and of the parodistic element in one of his compositions he says:

> In truth parody was here the proud expedient of a great gift, threatened with sterility by a combination of skepticism, intellectual reserve, and a sense of the deadly extension of the kingdom of the banal.

Leverkühn himself is quite conscious of the fact that parody, as such, while it may be handled ingeniously and artistically, is sterile and basically uncreative. It is interesting to observe that in his dialogue with the Devil he becomes very angry only once: when the Devil asks him whether he really expects greatness or artistic satisfaction from toying with lifeless forms. Leverkühn replies with an indignant "no", and gradually thereafter his work becomes more genuine and original, culminating in *The Lamentation of Dr. Faustus (Doktor Fausti Wehklag)* which lacks all parody. Expressive of Leverkühn's tragic ability to "look through" people and ideas is the laugh which is his characteristic throughout the book.

The clairvoyance which makes him see the shallowness of so many ideas and persons, causes him to appear "superior" and arrogant to others. Herr Michelsen, his first tutor at Buchel, already fears that Adrian's talent signifies a danger for "the modesty of his heart" and may easily lead to arrogance. In high school Leverkühn exhibits complete indifference not only toward his marks, but also toward the curriculum which he conquers with ease. The temptations of talent form the gist of the remarks which the principal directs toward Adrian at his graduation. In Zeitblom's opinion it was arrogance that led his friend to choose theology as his field of study: a desire, perhaps, to master a subject in which no one had thought him very likely to succeed. Leverkühn himself harbors a very definite guilt complex regarding his "arrogance", for in his confession and self-accusation before his collapse, he cites it as one of the main influences of the devil which manifested itself early in his life.

But Leverkühn's reputation for being arrogant is only an outgrowth of the loneliness with which he surrounds himself, because he considers it essential for the development of his art. It was Schopenhauer who said that genius lives essentially alone, and Mann has on occasion quoted this with obvious approbation. Thus, Leverkühn seems to draw a circle about him which no one must trespass without incurring the danger of being treated with contempt. Zeitblom speaks of the coolness and reserve even in the child, and even though he is Leverkühn's best friend, he can never quite overcome it. Leverkühn himself is entirely conscious and far from proud of his coldness which he treats as if it were not of his own making. To Kretzschmar he writes:

> I fear, . . . I am a lost soul, a black sheep; I have no warmth. As the Good Book has it, they shall be cursed and spewed out of the mouth who are neither cold nor warm but lukewarm. Lukewarm I should not call myself. Without a question I am cold; but in my judgment of myself I would pray to dissent from the taste of that power whose it is to apportion blessing and cursing.

And a little later he reserves for himself the adjective "unsocial" and his letter continues:

> This quality, he judged, was the expression of a want of warmth, sympathy, love, and it was very much in question whether one could, lacking them, be a good artist, which after all and always means being a lover and beloved of the world.

Here is a remarkable confession in which the young man and artist expresses doubt in his ability to love and to be loved, a crucial element in his personality.

The frigidity, which surrounds Adrian Leverkühn, is thus composed of two elements: his own indifference toward the reactions of other persons toward him and his awareness of his own inability to make or receive love. It is difficult to speak about Leverkühn's love life because of both his and his biographer's reluctance to discuss the subject. We are given a slight hint that music was Adrian's first outlet for erotic emotions when Zeitblom remarks that his friend began his experiments on the piano at the age of fourteen (as did Hanno Buddenbrook),

> . . . at the time of beginning puberty when one emerges from the shadows of childlike innocence.

Throughout his school days there is never even the slightest mention of any strong affection which the boy harbors for anyone. But even the high school student already declines love theoretically and prefers an intellectual interest. With the words of Wendell Kretzschmar, regarding the martinet of music, Johannes Beissel, still in his ears, young Leverkühn postulates that music has so much "bovine warmth" in it that the chilling effect of the musical law is essential to its enjoyment. His Catholic friend objects not only to this but also to the attempt to explain music and to define it. And then the following short dialogue takes place:

> [Zeitblom speaking about music]: "One must love her." "Do you consider love the strongest emotion?" he asked. "Do you know a stronger?" "Yes, interest." "By which you presumably mean a love from which the animal warmth has been withdrawn." "Let us agree on that definition!" he laughed.

The subject of love and sex is never discussed between the two friends, even though their conversations range over a wide variety of other subjects. But in discussing this conspicuous absence, Zeitblom warns the reader not to infer that Leverkühn was a prude or that he had totally ignored the subject. For love and passion do creep into their discourses on art and literature, and on such occasions Leverkühn manifests an objective, if totally impersonal, knowledge of the matter. In addition, we are told that he has accepted certain teachings of Kretzschmar regarding the necessity of the sensual in art. But throughout his life Adrian remains essentially chaste and untouchable.

Leverkühn loathes everything that smacks of the filthy joke or the *double entendre,* and his friend describes the wry mouth and the contemptuous expression with which he recoils when the subject of sex is treated lasciviously or coarsely. While his fellow theology students in Halle refrain from such an attitude, Adrian occasionally encounters it later, especially in the painter Zink. On the other hand, Leverkühn's sense of parody is quite ready to see something farcical in the erotic, especially when seen against the background of medieval-ecclesiastic morality, as in the case of his adaptation of the *Gesta Romanorum.*

Speaking from experience, Zeitblom confesses that in natures like his own, intellect and animal drives (the "Natur" and "Geist" of the earlier Mann) interpenetrate and appease each other, resulting in a solution which, even if not wholly free from illusion, makes life bearable and even enjoyable. Natures like Adrian Leverkühn, however, lack this ability to combine intellect and instinct.

> It is a fact . . . that the proudest intellectuality stands in the most immediate relation of all to the animal, to naked instinct, is given over most shamelessly to it; hence the anxiety that a person like me must suffer through a nature like Adrian's—hence too my conviction that the accursed adventure of which he had written was in its essence frightfully symbolic.

That is why natures like Leverkühn, Johannes Friedemann or Gustav Aschenbach must suffer a catastrophe when they confront love and affection.

"Proudest intellectually" facing up with "naked instinct": that is Adrian Leverkühn confronting the painted women in the Leipzig house of ill repute. His first thought is of flight, and after a few seconds at the piano he follows his instinct and rushes out. But:

> His intellectual pride had suffered the trauma of contact with soulless instinct.

The knowledge of this house, not as a source for gratification, but as the spot in which he has already been touched, lingers on. Almost a year later Adrian returns to the house, this time of his own volition, to see the girl whom he remembered from his first visit. Again he emerges physically pure because she, whom he sought, is no longer there. He finds her in the Hungarian city of Pressburg and insists on being with her, even though she reveals to him that her body is diseased. Adrian's motive in intentionally contracting syphilis is difficult to understand. It is unlikely that he foresaw the heightening of his artistic genius which it supposedly produced, and his modesty makes it unlikely that this was the reason, even if he had foreseen it. The reason possibly lies in the fact that he felt his chastity compromised by his first and especially by his second visit to the Leipzig brothel, and that the infection is a logical punishment which Leverkühn inflicts upon himself. Together with his monastic existence (Zeitblom reports that there was a noticeable increase in the severity with which Leverkühn regulated his relations with others after the bordello episode) his disease is a way of atoning for the spots on his armor. If we take the infection as punishment, we can also understand why Leverkühn did not desire to lessen or lift the penalty by undertaking a cure.

We will discuss the role of the devil in some greater detail later. Let us say now, however, that he is, of course, a figment of Leverkühn's imagination and that the devil's stern warning to him that he must not love also originates in his own mind and is a further part payment for the sin which he has committed against himself. But, during the twenty-five years which follow his first Leipzig visit, until his insanity sets in, Leverkühn, nevertheless, loves three, and perhaps four times: a man, a woman, a child, and perhaps a prostitute. We cannot say with any certainty whether Adrian loves Hetera Esmeralda. If however, the girl of the Pressburg streets is identical with Frau von Tolna . . . , then his correspondence with her, in which he is said to go to the very limits of his confidence, and his acceptance of her hospitality would indeed seem to indicate an affection for her. If Frau von Tolna, whose ring Adrian wears, is Hetera Esmeralda, then the many compositions which contain the five-tone leitmotif are dedicated to her.

At the age of thirty-nine and in the nineteenth year of his disease Adrian Leverkühn is conquered by Rudi Schwerdtfeger. It must be said, first of all, that the relationship between the composer and the violinist, which begins as a thinly-veiled wooing of the latter for the other's friendship, has its culmination in an affair which is frankly and unequivocally physical and homosexual. It must be added that Leverkühn is at first unaware of the physical character of Rudi's advances, but that he is later quite conscious of it and, in fact, becomes the initiator of the series of meetings with the violinist which finally lead them to Frau von Tolna's castle in Hungary.

Rudi Schwerdtfeger's homosexual leanings become evident early in the book. He is handsome, well-mannered and of a very friendly and even disposition and thus well-liked by most of his many friends. Like many "salon homosexuals" he is dedicated to the flattery of women, perhaps because his successes afford him real satisfaction or perhaps to conceal his true intentions. His boyish naïveté, his frankness, his basic decency, his lack of prejudice and his indifference toward his artistic triumphs make him popular, even with his male acquaintances. A significant incident is described in which young Schwerdtfeger absents himself from a party to visit Leverkühn who is indisposed and to ask him—who is by no means a great asset to a party—whether he could not possibly attend it because it was so dull without him. Who could possibly resist such an approach? Rudi's intentions toward Leverkühn are so evident in the very beginning of their acquaintance, in fact, thirteen years before the consummation, that Ines Rodde warns Leverkühn: "You should not do him that favor. He desires everything." Rudi Schwerdtfeger is, of course, not exclusively Adrian's seducer. He is a talented artist although his talent is one of technique and manipulation rather than of a creative nature. He is truly fond of Adrian, and his friendship puts up with the many rebuffs which he receives. At the same time, he seems quite aware of Adrian's loneliness and utilizes it for his purposes. Thus, when Leverkühn is sick, he devotes a great deal of time to him, and Zeitblom writes:

> It was my impression that he believed he could use the sufferer's reduced and as he probably thought more or less helpless state to exert his quite imperturbable ingratiation, enforced by all his personal charm, to conquer a coolness, dryness, and ironic withdrawal which annoyed him on grounds more or less serious, or hurt him, or wounded his vanity, or possibly some genuine feeling on his part.

Certain responses by Adrian, an occasional use of Rudi's first name or just the more frequent toleration of his company, lead the violinist to the confession—implicit, to be sure—of his erotic tendencies and finally he proposes a violin concerto to which Adrian is to be the father. Rudi promises to be a good mother.

Leverkühn's true surrender to Rudi Schwerdtfeger comes in a conversation during a soirée at the house of the manufacturer Bullinger, where Leverkühn—à propos one of Delila's arias from Saint-Saens' *Samson*—confesses that the intellect is by no means attracted by the intellectual alone, but that it can be most deeply moved by the animal melancholy of sensual beauty. Before this gathering of esthetes and friends, he breaks a lance for broadmindedness in the field of artistic morals, a hint which the agile seducer understands and obeys.

The idea that the assault of Rudi's charm upon Adrian's deep loneliness is successful, is credible and well-motivated. But it is extremely hard to believe that a man of Leverkühn's past and his nature could ever desire or endure the physical proximity of a man. For the sake of the story we must assume that homosexual desires have been slumbering in Adrian for years previous to this event, but the author has certainly given us no inkling of it. In fact, Adrian's and Rudi's trip to Hungary appears as a bit of an afterthought—not very well prepared, hardly credible and easily dispensable.

Leverkühn's tremendous loneliness, his awareness of the impending disaster, his ardent desire to be tied to the world around him in some concrete way, and perhaps an increased confidence arising out of the successful affair with Schwerdtfeger, lead to the astounding marriage proposal to Marie Godeau. On the occasion of his sister's marriage, Leverkühn had mockingly discussed the marriage ceremony which to him seemed but an official sanction of fleshly lust, although he did not disapprove of the latter.

> If all at once the other one's flesh becomes the object of desire and lust, then the relation of the I and the You is altered in a way for which sensuality is only an empty word. No, one cannot get along without the concept of love, even when ostensibly there is nothing spiritual involved.

The distanced manner with which the twenty-five year old speaks makes it clear that he is not suffering from such a desire.

Love and sexual desire do not seem to be involved in Adrian's feelings for Marie Godeau. In her sincerity and seriousness she perhaps conforms to his ideal of womanhood. But more definitely, she offers him a chance to escape from the "inhumanity" with which his life had been endowed. When Rudi Schwerdtfeger rather pointedly reminds him that he perhaps owes his artistic greatness to his isolation, Leverkühn heatedly replies:

> That I have nothing to do with humanity, may have nothing to do with it, that is said to me by the very person who had the amazing patience to win me over for the human and persuaded me to say "du"; the person in whom for the first time in my life I found human warmth.

Human warmth is Adrian's goal and the proposal an experiment to gain it.

Adrian's proposal is declined, and it is likely that he himself never believed that it would be accepted. Zeitblom marvels at Adrian's apparent assurance regarding the outcome and comes to the conclusion that the illusion here conceals deep doubts. A second note of lack of self-confidence can perhaps be seen in the fact that Leverkühn fears to hear the refusal himself and sends Schwerdtfeger, who is not only an almost professional flirt but has also just confessed to amorous sentiments toward the same woman. Untouched by real affection Adrian has made a last attempt to cheat the devil.

Leverkühn's feelings toward Marie Godeau and his proposal of marriage are closely related to similar feelings and a like proposal on the part of Friedrich Nietzsche. The thirty-seven year old Nietzsche, who had lost friends, influence, and publishers through his resignation from the faculty of the University of Basel and his break with Richard Wagner, was introduced in 1882 to the twenty-four year old Russian Lou Andreas-Salomé. This highly cultured and quite unbeautiful woman became his student and for a short six months Nietzsche had visions of having found the ideal intellectual companion, besides what he called in a letter "an intellectual heiress who would continue his thinking." After a short summer, spent in steady communion with her, he sends his friend, Dr. Rée, to her and proposes marriage. Later on, Nietzsche claimed that he had hoped and was sure that he would receive a negative answer, but more likely Brann's analysis is quite correct:

> Under the pressure of Nietzsche's loneliness a strange amalgamation and vicarious displacement of his great intellectual feeling of being left alone and lost and his human, erotic, and sexual frustration took place. As the degree and extent of loneliness increased, there developed also out of the tension and hyper-differentiation of his unfulfilled desires and needs an emotional primitivism which in such cases is unavoidable and is the logical sequence of this overcomplicated state of affairs.

Adrian Leverkühn in the role of a lover, suggesting sleigh rides and hinting at plans for domesticity, appears in a strange light, for which "emotional primitivism" is a charitable term. Interesting, by the way, is the fact that Nietzsche later attempted to talk his intermediary, Dr. Rée, into marrying Lou Salomé. And Nietzsche himself writes to Lou: "I do not want to be lonely any longer and learn to be human." Both Nietzsche and Leverkühn—revolutionaries who do not fundamentally believe in the sacrament of marriage—nevertheless think of companionship with a woman in terms of this civil and ecclesiastic institution. Brann calls Nietzsche "strongly infected by Naumburg morals," the exact counterpart of the Kaisersaschern element in Leverkühn.

It should be added at this point that Leverkühn's bordello experience in Leipzig is analogous to one which Brann reports for the twenty-year old Nietzsche in Köln in February of 1865 (Leverkühn is of the same age), during which a cicerone led him to a similar house in which he stayed only long enough to dart a quick glance at the women surrounding him and to strike a chord on the piano. Just when and where Nietzsche received the germs of the syphilitic infection which led to his end has never been ascertained. A Jena record of Nietzsche as a patient claims that it was 1866, a year after the first experience, and this is evidently the date which Mann accepts. It is generally considered likely that Nietzsche intentionally brought about

this infection, probably in order to punish himself for an imagined sin. Brann reminds his readers of similar acts of self-punishment on the part of Sören Kierkegaard and Otto Weininger.

We need not spend much time on Leverkühn's final love: that for the child, Echo. Suffice it to say that his affection in this case is not entirely one of instinct either. It is rather another attempt to gain a bond with life and humanity through the exercise of conventional sentiments, in this case the avuncular, and an attempt to gain human love as a substitute for grace. This is not to imply that there is anything false or pretended in Leverkühn's love for Echo, only that it lacks complete spontaneity and contains consciousness.

In the case of Adrian Leverkühn, who does not speak to us directly but through the pen of a friend of a totally dissimilar temperament, much is left to guesswork and conjecture. When we speak of his love life, the concrete fact is that he, like Nietzsche, remained basically chaste and innocent throughout his life. He remained true to his chastity, even if he could do so only at the price of self-destruction. But total chastity is never normal and never totally unconditioned, even in the greatest genius. In Leverkühn's case we find at the bottom of it a deep and abiding insecurity toward women and toward human beings in general. It is this feeling of "being different" which is engendered in this case by a complete and utter failure on the part of Leverkühn to comprehend the nature of instinct. Leverkühn is the personification of consciousness, even to the extent of realizing his complete helplessness toward the instinct and the drive which are at the bottom of and a prerequisite for any successful erotic affair. No wonder that Leverkühn is deeply moved when he reads Kleist's essay, *Über das Marionettentheater*, where he finds his problem summed up most pithily by Herr C. . . . . when he says of the dancer's grace,

> . . . that it appears in its purest form in that human body which either has no consciousness at all or else an infinite one, i.e. in the puppet or in God.

And Kleist closes:

> "In other words," I said, somewhat absentmindedly, "we should have to eat again from the tree of knowledge in order to recapture the state of innocence?" "True," he answered, "that constitutes the final chapter in the history of the world."

Coupled with Leverkühn's doubts in his ability as a liver or a lover is an equally strong doubt in his ability as an artist, which stems from the same deficiency. Equipped with a tremendously agile mind, an uncanny understanding of the deepest meaning of art, and an astounding talent for imitation and parody, Leverkühn is nevertheless a tragic artistic failure, because he is basically unoriginal. Unable to pour new content into old forms, he must be satisfied with supplying new forms for old contents or new forms with no contents at all. How aware Leverkühn is of this problem and of his own inability to solve it is shown by his statement:

What we called the purification of the complicated into the simple is at bottom the same as the
winning back of the vital and the power of
feeling . . . Whoever could succeed in the
break-through from intellectual coldness into an
adventurous world of new feeling, should be
called the savior of art.

It is significant that he follows this with a shrug of the
shoulders as if to say that he was not the man for it.

The original Faust legend, as well as almost all of its successors and variations, contained as an unchangeable element the devil's commandment to Faust: Thou shalt not
love. In the Spiess edition of the Volksbuch, Faust's covenant with the Devil specifically includes a promise on
Faust's part to be hostile toward God and Man. Nevertheless, Faust feels a desire to marry a little later but is
brushed off by the devil:

> And the Evil Spirit asked him what he planned
> to do with himself? Also, whether he remem-
> bered his promise? And whether he did not
> mean to keep it? Since he had promised to be
> hostile toward God and all men?

When Faust tries to marry nevertheless, he is forcibly restrained by the devil.

In Marlowe's play, Faust asks for feminine company in
the same elementary fashion:

> . . . let me have a wife
> The fairest maid in Germany;
> For I am wanton and lascivious
> And cannot live without a wife.

Here Mephistopheles plays a little hoax on Faustus by
bringing in a devil, dressed like a woman, who is rejected
by Faustus rather harshly, and the devil consoles the latter
with the words:

> Tut, Faustus,
> Marriage is but a ceremonial toy;
> If thou lovest me, think no more of it.

The general psychological deepening of the Faust legend
which characterizes Goethe's treatment of it, also extends
to this particular element. Faust's inability to love here becomes an inability to love successfully. Faust finds an innocent girl who returns his love (just as Leverkühn encounters his nephew, Echo, at a crucial moment), but in
turn he ruins the object of his love and thereby himself.
The devil's role here is not the prevention of love; on the
contrary, he advocates and abets its consummation as the
quickest way to destruction. (pp. 119-40)

We must keep in mind that in Mann's **Doctor Faustus**
Leverkühn's erotic difficulties, his inability to love or be
loved, begin before he makes the actual acquaintance of
the devil. In fact, the coldness, the temperamental root of
all evil, is his characteristic long before the devil attains
an even indirect influence over him through the infection.
Nevertheless, the three great, unhappy loves—for Rudi,
Marie, and Echo—occur after the devil-dialogue and seem
a direct outgrowth of the devil's admonition.

The devil in **Doctor Faustus** resembles in many respects
God in **Joseph.** Both are represented as pure figments of
the hero's imagination, even though he may not be quite
clear about it. Both conclude a pact with their subject and
watch jealously over its fulfillment. It is perhaps enough
to say that, with a single exception (in **The Magic Mountain**), Mann did not introduce any occult happenings into
his novels, and the exception was accompanied by an essay
"Occult Happenings" ("Okkulte Erlebnisse") in *Be-
mühungen,* expressing strong disapproval of such activities. Thus, we need not assume such a character for the
devil's appearance in **Doctor Faustus.** Leverkühn's apparition (he is himself not entirely sure that he had one) can
be explained entirely by his own tremendous feeling of
guilt, coupled with his artistic despair. Besides, he has always lived in consciousness of the devil from the moment
when his high school principal issued a stern warning
against Satan, who was sure to appear to the arrogant. The
study of theology is in itself a study of demonology; in fact,
both Zeitblom and the sinister guest at Palestrina hint at
the possibility that Leverkühn took up the study of theology only because he was really interested in studying the
devil. The two professors, with whom the young student
is most intimate, are in turn on excellent terms with the
devil, and there is something satanical about the personalities of Kumpf and Schleppfuss. Kumpf possesses many
charming names for him and is able to see him to the extent of hurling a baked roll at him while Schleppfuss, who
in Zeitblom's opinion really drags one foot a little, almost
does the devil's bidding by declaring hell a necessary correlate of heaven, darkness an indispensable component of
light. The description of the Leipzig cicerone, who shows
Leverkühn the way to the bordello, awakens thoughts of
the devil in Zeitblom. In his discussion of marriage,
Leverkühn makes it clear that he considers the sexual the
devil's domain and pokes fun at the theologians (among
whom he includes himself) who believe that sex can be endowed with a holy quality through the sacrament of marriage. Thus, it might be said that the devil was a familiar
figure to Leverkühn long before he "met" him.

On the crucial evening, when the twenty-six year old composer has his devil experience, he is reading Sören Kierkegaard's *Either-Or,* more specifically the chapter entitled:
"The Immediate Stages of the Erotic or the Musical Erotic," containing Kierkegaard's thoughts on Mozart's *Don
Giovanni.* Leverkühn's choice of reading is doubly significant. In the first place, the great Danish philosopher led
a deeply unhappy life, throughout which he was troubled
by doubts and pangs of conscience. The son of a morosely
serious father, he had spent a somber youth under his tute-
lage. His college days had been just the reverse and included a traumatic experience in a house of prostitution. There
is some speculation that Kierkegaard, too, contracted a
venereal disease, but the exact cause of his death at fifty-
five is not known. The rest of his life was spent more or
less in atonement for his "guilt" and included the voluntary dissolution of his engagement.

In his essay on Mozart, whom Kierkegaard loved with an
abiding affection, he confesses deep fascination with the
subject of sensuousness, which he sees represented by Don
Juan. For Don Juan is to him not just the seducer but personifies the inherent power of the erotic drive. His victims
fall to him without reservations or a feeling of guilt be-

Mann and his wife Katia with their grandchildren in California, shortly before the publication of Doctor Faustus.

cause they do not reflect. *Don Giovanni,* to him, portrays this pre-reflective, amoral gaiety of sensuous emotion which, he believes, the post-Mozart opera has been unable to recapture. Such thoughts must strike Leverkühn where he is most sensitive. Both in his personal relations and in his artistic expression he has been seeking just such a synthesis of natural elementality and beauty, i.e. form. Kierkegaard's essay points up the fact that it is Leverkühn's misfortune to be born 130 years later than Mozart. Guilt and the despair over his inability of saying something new well up in Leverkühn as he "sees the devil."

The figure of the devil has always played a large part in Mann's writings. The mysterious men without names in **Death in Venice,** both Settembrini and Naphta in **The Magic Mountain,** the figure of "the stranger god" in **Joseph and his Brothers,** and the various figures in **Doctor Faustus,** already mentioned—all of these have a definite satanical quality about them. Gustav von Aschenbach, Joseph, and Adrian Leverkühn—certainly these are persons to whom Mann's words might apply:

> Where the conceit of intellect marries up with soulful antiquity and ties of old, there is the devil.

Leverkühn's devil appears because he must appear in the old Faustian tradition. But there the similarity stops. For the devil at Palestrina cannot offer any of the things which former devils did. It is most important to note that at no time is there any covenant between Leverkühn and his visitor, no drop of blood, no promise given or extracted. The devil, to be sure, says that such a pact is obviated through the fact that the composer's soul is already his. But the terms are never defined. Adrian attains a mysterious boost in his creative power, attributable to the strength of his disease. He surrenders something which he has never possessed—love. In the manner of God, speaking to Adam and Eve, the devil (in Adrian's mind) thunders:

> Love is forbidden you, in so far as it warms. Thy life shall be cold, therefore thou shalt love no human being . . . Cold we want you to be, that even the fires of creation shall hardly be hot enough to warm you. Into them you will flee out of the cold of your life.

The devil, by the way, shows his relatedness to, if not identity with the God of Joseph, when he gives jealousy as the cause for his demand and says:

> Do you think that jealousy dwells in the height and not also in the depths? To us you are prom-

ised and espoused, you fine, well-created creature. Thou shalt not love.

And in his final talk to his friends, Leverkühn speaks of his "marriage" to the devil. This idea, the identity of God and devil, which had figured strongly in Joseph, is taken up again in **"Germany and the Germans"** where the author says:

> At times, and especially in looking at German history, one has the impression that the universe is not the sole creation of God but rather was created by Him in communion with someone else.

We have tried to show that perhaps the chief function of the devil in the Faust legend is that of forbidding Faust to love. But the particular devil who appears to Adrian Leverkühn at Palestrina has his ancestors in a great Russian novel by an author by whom Mann was always deeply fascinated, Dostoyevski's *The Brothers Karamazov*. In the latter part of that novel, Ivan, the second one of the four brothers, is brought face to face with the devil who is represented as a shabby gentleman of middle age, dressed in checkered trousers (like Settembrini's), sporting a lorgnette and fond of puns and witty stories. The physical circumstances of the visit are quite like those of the visit at Palestrina. Ivan believes that the devil is an hallucination, and the visitor spends much of his time trying to establish his identity. Politely, the devil defers to Ivan, who calls him names, throughout the conversation, leaving no doubt at the same time about who is the true master in this relationship. Ivan's devil, like Adrian's, is neither hating nor hateful: he almost convinces us of his notion that evil is the necessary complement of good in the world, as darkness is of light. Far from denying God, he only modestly admits that he does not know, concedes that he sometimes feels like joining the chorus of the angels, and "solely from a sense of duty and my social position, I was forced to suppress the good moment and to stick to my nasty task."

But while these physical circumstances probably were in Mann's mind when he created the Palestrina surroundings, the devilish element in *Doctor Faustus* has an eminent spokesman in another place in Dostoyevski's novel: the Grand Inquisitor. The circumstances, of course, are quite different: Ivan Karamazov recites a legend to his brother, Aloysha, whom he wishes to disabuse of his blind faith. In his legend, Christ returns to earth in sixteenth-century Seville only to be arrested and cast into the dungeon by the Grand Inquisitor. The latter sharply points out to Christ his supreme error: his insistence on setting and then leaving humanity free, his refusal to compel their obedience and faith. He pictures humanity as suffering from the effects of "the terrible gift of freedom" until finally the Catholic Church rectified Christ's error by taking away man's freedom and replacing it by mystery, miracle and authority, "and men rejoiced that they were once more led like sheep." (pp. 142-46)

The freedom of which the Grand Inquisitor speaks is, of course, the freedom to choose between good and evil. But in its wider ramifications it is also the artist's freedom which Adrian gives up in favor of "order" and "the compulsion of the system." For the order and regularity which

Adrian seeks in theology and Beissel's musical system is born of the same despair of man's ability to handle freedom. Adrian's realization of this inability, his conscious acceptance of non-freedom makes him a leader, and the Grand Inquisitor clearly forecasts his doom:

> And all will be happy, all the millions of creatures except the hundred thousand who rule over them. For only we, we who guard the mystery, shall be unhappy.

Adrian's devil is a figment of his imagination, but his punishment—the descent into insanity—is a very real one and a concrete catastrophe. The final question which we must ask ourselves is: What has Adrian done to deserve his fate? what was his sin? One answer is that Adrian's sin consisted in exactly that quality that rendered his artistic rise possible: the maintenance of an inhuman reserve, a distance from life. When he finds that his art requires contact with life in order to be complete, he can achieve this contact only through what he considers a sin. But Leverkühn's path of life is in reality not of his own choosing. Even though he is a Lutheran by birth, his life is predetermined in a Calvinistic sense. He is condemned from the very beginning. The existence of genius, as such, is his sin, and the great ethical struggle between Faust and Mephisto becomes senseless, because in reality it is Faust's struggle against his inexorable fate.

A much younger Thomas Mann had written:

> At any rate, sin is this: doubt, the trend to the forbidden, the urge to adventure, to lose oneself, surrender, experience, search, know. Sin is the element of seduction and temptation.

But the older Mann had long gotten over the idea that being a genius or an artist must, of necessity, mean loneliness and unhappiness. Thus, Leverkühn's problem, without a doubt also a generally human problem, is primarily artistic. The problem is the question whether art is still possible in a time in which everything points to a cosmic catastrophe, a complete dissolution—the end. It is the question whether in a time, in which complete reality and utter consciousness rule supreme, we can find some little corner into which a last remnant of "Naivität" can flee. Expressed in different terms, it is a question whether realism can exist as a form of art without a touch of romanticism. How can an age which has dissolved, defined, and criticized everything, including itself, ever again find a whole, an inexplicable, an indefinable, a subject to sing about? In short: Is art possible without love?

In *Doctor Faustus* Thomas Mann has adapted the Faustus legend to the requirements and conditions of the twentieth century. Its modern hero is neither Nietzsche, nor Schönberg, nor even Thomas Mann. Its hero is the modern artist who, with centuries of art behind him, faces a wall beyond which there may or may not lie new centuries of art. In previous centuries love had been an essential element of art. In this century an ingenious composer by the name of Adrian Leverkühn has tried to create a new medium without love. He sold his soul to the devil and tried to create without it. Leverkühn failed.

At the end of his greatest novel the author had asked

whether out of the universal feast of death love would one day mount. Twenty-five years later his answer is "no". To be sure, it is a temporary answer; but we may never hear a "yes". (pp. 146-48)

> Frank Donald Hirschbach, in his The Arrow and the Lyre: A Study of the Role of Love in the Works of Thomas Mann, *Martinus Nijhoff, 1955, 195 pp.*

Mann on writing *Doctor Faustus*:

When I began to write [*Doctor Faustus*], my notes were scanty and there was no actual written outline. Yet the book, insofar as the sequence of events was concerned, must have lain plainly before my eyes; I must have had a fairly good over-all view of it to be able at once to take up its entire complex of motifs, to give the beginning the perspective in depth of the whole, and to play the part of the tremulous biographer so filled with his subject that he is always haplessly anticipating and losing himself in later developments. His nervousness was mine; I was parodying my own overbrimming eagerness. And it was a boon to play this part; to let the book be written for me, as it were; to be conscious of the indirectness of my responsibility along with such intense resolve to achieve directness; to fling into the game reality and my private world. How necessary the mask and the playfulness were, in view of the earnestness of my task— and this I was clearly conscious of from the very start.

> *Thomas Mann, in his* The Story of a Novel: The Genesis of "Doctor Faustus," *1961.*

R. Hinton Thomas   (essay date 1956)

[*In the essay excerpted below, Thomas discusses how the ideas and experiences of the philosopher Friedrich Nietzsche are reflected in the characterization of Adrian Leverkühn and considers Mann's association in* Doctor Faustus *of music with evil.*]

On 27 March 1943 Mann wrote in his diary: 'Found the three lines of 1901 containing the plan for Dr. Faust. Contact with the *Tonio Kröger* time, the Munich days, the never completed plan for the novel *The Loved Ones* and *Maja* . . . Embarrassed and touched to encounter once again these sorrows of my youth'. The desire to set about the writing of the long-planned work on the Faust theme was tempered by 'the feeling that there was something not quite proper and in order about the content and that it would cost me much inner suffering to put it into shape'. His wife suggested the possibility of his finishing *Felix Krull:* 'The idea is not altogether unsympathetic', Mann commented in his diary, 'but I consider the plan, which dates from a period when I was dominated by the problem of the opposition of artist and man of affairs, out of date and superseded by *Joseph.* Nevertheless, reading and listening to music yesterday, I was keenly attracted by the thought of resuming it, mainly from the point of view of the unity of existence'. He read through the unfinished manuscript of *Felix Krull*—'with a strange result': 'Realization of its inner relationship with the Faust-material

(based on the *theme of loneliness,* in the latter related to a tragic mysticism, in the former to a humorous criminality); but, if it can be given shape and form, the latter appears to me now the more appropriate, the more topical, the more urgent. On 23 May 1943 Mann thus set about writing his 'wildest' book, completed on 29 January 1947 and published the same year.

The central character of *Doctor Faustus* is a musician, Adrian Leverkühn. He was born in 1885—the same year as Alban Berg—amid the political and cultural prestige of the Hohenzollern Reich. His mind gives way in 1930, on the eve of the advent to power of the Nazis, and twenty-four years after his 'pact' with the Devil. He dies in 1940. Three years later Serenus Zeitblom, his schoolmaster friend, is imagined as beginning his account of Adrian's life and work. This is concluded in 1945 amid the disintegration of Hitler's Reich. Through this account, affectionate and horrified at once, the fate of the composer is brought into association with the tragic course of his country's history. The sixteenth-century German chapbook deals with one who sells his soul to the Devil in return for the enrichment of experience during the twenty-four years before the Devil claims his own. This theme is brought by Mann into relationship with music, long associated by him with disorder and unreason. It is round the figure of a musician that revolves this story of 'flight from the difficulties of the cultural crisis into a pact with the Devil, the thirst of a proud spirit threatened with sterility for release at any price, the paralleling of a doomed euphoria with the fascist intoxication of the peoples'.

The triumph of German fascism had led Mann in 1944 to a critical revaluation of Nietzsche's thought. Its outcome was the address **"Nietzsche in the Light of Our Experience"**, written during work on *Faustus* and standing to this novel in a relationship similar to that of the essays **"Goethe and Tolstoi"** and **"On the Republic"** to *The Magic Mountain* and the study of Freud to *Joseph.* As in the earlier **"Address on Nietzsche"** (1924), Mann stresses the withdrawal of Nietzsche's existence as a process of self-discipline and self-purification, finding this symptomatic of his spiritual struggle against weakness and disorder. It aroused in him 'tragic pity for a soul overburdened with tasks beyond its strength, which is called to knowledge but is not born to it and which, like Hamlet, was thereby shattered'. The description brings to mind Thomas Buddenbrook, Aschenbach, and the rest, in whom a 'heroism of weakness' exerts itself in a struggle against obligations beyond their natural capacity to fulfill. 'Nietzsche and the pity he arouses' . . . was Mann's description of a conversation during the writing of *Doctor Faustus.* Nietzsche, he points out, signed his last notes as 'the Crucified One' and died 'a martyr's death on the cross of thought'. The horror, even the barbarism, of Leverkühn's existence is not allowed to stifle our sense of pity. His face had 'something of spiritualized suffering about it, something Christ-like'. He is engaged 'in the struggle with tasks so highly complicated that one can only imagine their being mastered with the highest and most exclusive concentration'. His being is strained to breaking point by the effort of manipulation of ever more complex musical forms. 'Art has become too difficult', he cries in his tortured confession at the end. He is 'an ideal figure', a 'hero of our time', one who 'bears the sorrows of the age'.

'In the light of experience' Mann fastens attention in the later essay also on another side of Nietzsche's existence. We live, Mann had said in the twenties, not in the times of 'classical balance' but times in which men seek compensation for the shortcomings and unbalance of their nature and situation by resort to instinct and passion—the phrase used in this context closely anticipating the phraseology of this essay. He quotes Nietzsche's question in *Ecce Homo*: 'Has anyone now, at the end of the nineteenth century, an idea of what poets of *strong* ages called inspiration?', and with this question Leverkühn is to be confronted by the Devil in the novel. Mann's comments on it in this essay focus Leverkühn's situation: 'And now begins a description of moments of illumination, rapture, elevation, whispered messages, divine feelings of power and might, which he (Nietzsche) cannot help feeling as something atavistic, at once daemonic and reactionary—belonging to human situations other than our own, "stronger" and nearer to the gods, but beyond the physical possibilities of our weak age of reason. Then he describes . . . a disastrous condition of heightened sensitivity heralding paralytic collapse. Nietzsche's justification of existence as an 'aesthetic phenomenon' is now discussed, not without critical misgivings, as an attitude subordinating truth and morality to a defence of 'life', directed alike against the 'pessimism' of those who believe in the afterworld of the Christian faith and the 'optimism' of those who work for the happiness of all in the here and now. His glorification of barbarism 'is nothing more than the excess of his aesthetic intoxication'. Thus, in Nietzsche Mann finds the dangerous polarity of extreme 'fear of the world' and a 'tragic wisdom' 'baptized in the name of the drunken god', Dionysus. Nietzsche's existence was 'a phenomenon of stupendous cultural fullness and complexity, gathering together within itself the essential elements of the European tradition, a phenomenon which had absorbed much from the past, which it . . . repeated in a mythic manner'.

The characteristic of Leverkühn of which we become most easily aware in the earlier sections of the novel may appear to have little connexion with anything so far suggested. Zeitblom observes: 'His sense of the comical, his yearning for it, and his tendency to laughter, to laugh till tears ran down his face, is something to which I have already drawn attention and I should have given a false picture of him if the reader did not understand how to harmonize such high spirits with his character'. Some features of Leverkühn's 'intoxication of laughter' disquiet the placid humanism of old Zeitblom. They remind him of the story told by St. Augustine in his *De civitate Dei* to the effect that Ham, the son of Noah and father of Zoroaster, was the only person who laughed at his birth, 'something that could only have happened with the help of the Devil'. Leverkühn's proclivity to mocking laughter, contrasting with the 'seriousness' of his father, derives from his scornful impatience with bourgeois standards. He tends to see everything in the light of comedy, just as he expresses himself naturally in parody. His compositions illustrate his conviction that 'an artist can put his best into a thing in

which he no longer believes, and insists on excelling in artistic forms which for him are already hovering on the point of being worn out'. 'Why have I had, from the very beginning', Leverkühn had written as a young man to Zeitblom, 'to laugh, like a soul damned, at the most mysterious and impressive things? Why must it seem to me as if almost all—nay, all—the means and resources of art *nowadays lend themselves only to parody*?' The phrase 'in the manner of a soul damned' (*verdammter Weise*) creeps into his words with an apparent casualness that might conceal a significance beyond its everyday associations. One reason for Leverkühn's choice of theology as his field of study was the belief that it might check his habits of derision and 'stop the itch'. It is a hope disappointed, since theology—which, Zeitblom remarks, stands near to the sphere of demonology—merely opens a further field for the indulgence of his mocking tastes. The answer to Leverkühn's question about parody is suggested by a remark of Wendell Kretschmar, his early teacher and admirer: 'That he does not yet write, does not show a creative urge and set about producing a mass of youthful compositions, does him honour; it is his pride which prevents him from putting into circulation merely imitative music based on past models'.

Leverkühn rejects, and not to his dishonour, the emotional self-gratification of much nineteenth-century music—its 'animal warmth' and 'romantic trash'. His aim is something 'as un-Wagnerian as possible'. His contempt for programme-music may remind us of the attitude of Erik Satie, who gave some of his pieces grotesque titles to protect them 'from persons obsessed with the sublime'. A statement of Schönberg can serve to define Leverkühn's attitude: 'More mature minds resist the temptation to become intoxicated by colours and prefer to be coldly convinced by the transparency of clear-cut ideas'. His choice of the twelve-tone scale suggests a measure of identification with Schönberg, despite the latter's observation that Leverkühn 'does not know the essentials of composing with twelve tones. All he knows has been told him by Mr. Adorno, who knows only the little I was able to tell my pupils'. Leverkühn's early habit of speaking about music impersonally and superciliously might be likened to the description of a poet as 'a kind of chemist who mixed poems out of words, whilst remaining detached from his own feelings', aiming 'not to express a feeling, but to concentrate on the best arrangement that could be derived from the occasion', playing 'a game of impartial objectivity about catastrophes, wars, revolutions, violence, hatreds, loves, and all the forces which move through human lives'. 'For you', Hugo Wolf wrote to a friend in terms seemingly echoed in many of Leverkühn's pronouncements, 'love itself is a vocation. . . . But love alone as a vocation for a man may perhaps be in place in a novel or on the stage. There it may suffice to fill out several volumes or five acts, but in reality it certainly doesn't serve as a calling for a man's whole life'. Leverkühn—who incorporates important features regarded by Mann as characteristic of the modern musician—might say with Hugo Wolf that he is 'only fit for solitude'. It is true that he seeks escape from the chill detachment of his life when, like Nietzsche, he woos by proxy and in vain, while his attempt to adopt a child is frustrated by its death.

Leverkühn's opera *Love's Labour's Lost* set out to be 'a renewal of the *opera buffa* in the spirit of the most sophisticated persiflage and of the persiflage of artistic sophistication, a work of the most playful preciosity'. This approach enabled him 'to place the primitiveness of nature side by side with the comically sublime and to poke fun at each through the other'. By this time his attitude is fast becoming a scepticism about art in general. The word beauty, Zeitblom quotes him as saying while still at school, 'was always half repulsive to me, it has such a silly face and there is something lecherous and rotten about people's mouths when they say it'. Nietzsche's voice is heard in Leverkühn's many references to the emotional subterfuge and pretence of art. Its ambition 'is to make us believe that it is not made but has arisen and sprung into existence, just as Pallas Athene arose in the full splendour of her civilized weapons from the head of Jupiter. But that is illusion. Never has a work of art thus come into being. For it is the result of labour, of the labour of art, in order to create a semblance'. The question, Leverkühn goes on in a crucial passage 'is whether the work of art is still spiritually possible, whether it is to be taken seriously, whether the . . . self-sufficient and harmoniously self-contained pattern of form still stands in any legitimate relationship to the complete insecurity, problematicalness and disharmony of our social conditions, whether all semblance—even the most beautiful, and particularly the most beautiful—has not nowadays become a *lie*'. The work of art is deception, he cries, 'something which the bourgeois would like to imagine still existed. It is in opposition to truth and seriousness'. What then remains valid for the artist? We can answer his question in Schönberg's words: 'Great art must proceed to precision and brevity. It presupposes the alert mind of an educated listener who in a single act of thinking includes with every concept all associations pertaining to the complex'. For Leverkühn a composition only wins respect when it is a work of 'utmost brevity', a concentrated and self-consistent 'musical moment'. Such a work would be, let us say, Anton von Webern's *Five Pieces* for orchestra—one of which lasts only about one-third of a minute—and which fulfil Schönberg's ideal of 'lending every sentence the full pregnancy of meaning of a maxim, a proverb, an aphorism. Leverkühn's aim is the 'severely organized movement' (*strenger Satz*): 'I mean by that the total integration of all musical dimensions, their indifference to each other by virtue of complete organization'. His interest, while at Leipzig, in setting words to music—a taste that ran counter to Kretschmar's doctrine 'that music had found its ultimate and highest form of expression and effect in the orchestral movement'—was connected with his 'scruples about the fate and the historical position of art itself, of the autonomous work of art'. He questioned form as 'mere semblance, mere play', and so the 'small lyrical form of the song' could strike him as the 'most acceptable, the most serious, the truest', best fulfilling his theoretical demand for concentrated brevity. Let Leverkühn's own analysis of his song 'O Maiden Dear' in his song-cycle to the words of Brentano illustrate his intentions:

> It is derived entirely from a basic figure, a sequence of intervals variable in different ways, from the notes B-E-A-E-E Flat (Note: it is important for future reference to observe the German equivalent: H-E-A-E-ES). The horizontal and vertical lines are determined and dominated by it in so far as this is possible with a basic motif with such a limited number of notes. It is like a word, a key word, the signs of which are to be found everywhere in the song and strive to determine its whole character. But it is too short a word and has too little inherent mobility. The tonal range it offers is too limited. One would have to go further and from the twelve stages of the tempered half-tone alphabet form larger words, words of twelve letters, definite combinations and permutations of the twelve half-tones, serial formations from which the piece, the single movement or a whole work in several movements, would have to be strictly derived. Every tone of the whole composition, melodically and harmonically, would have to be able to demonstrate its relationship to this pre-determined basic series. No tone would be allowed to recur before all the others had appeared. None would be permitted to appear which did not fulfil its motivistic function in the total construction. There would be no free note left. That is what I should call the severely organized movement.

What is here enunciated is an essentially mathematical approach to musical composition, abstract and formalistic. It is in keeping, for example, with Leverkühn's early interest in chess, with the style of decoration of his student's room at Halle, with his early experiments with the interpenetration of scales and chords, and with his predilection for theology as a field for intellectual exercise and speculation, as the 'peak of thought'. It recalls the analysis set before him by Kretschmar of the abstract spirituality of Beethoven's music. ('If a mathematician's or a chess player's mind', he might ask with Schönberg, 'can perform such miracles of the brain, why should a musician's mind not be able to do it?') The statement that so concentrated a key-motif has 'too little inherent mobility' acquires fuller significance as Leverkühn is driven to seek escape from his austere intellectualism in less restrictive forms of emotional compensation. He might be described, in a phrase once applied to Webern, as a 'closed composer': 'He opened a particular outlook and on his death it closed up. Any disciple using Webern's manner must surely fail to produce anything individual to himself. Extension or variation of the principle can result only in the negation of the principle itself'. From one point of view Leverkühn's cult of mathematically ordered concentration of form might be attributed, to quote a critic's observations about Hindemith, to 'a weakening of the imaginative vitality of the music and an attempt to replace, or at least control, imagination by reason and calculation'. From another it could be characterized by Schönberg's statement: 'Our sense of form was right when it forced us to counterbalance extreme emotionality with extraordinary shortness'.

Zeitblom is disturbingly conscious of such apparent contradictions in Leverkühn. He is uneasy about the way his remarks suggest magic and astrology. His musical ideal reminds him of a 'magic square'. Leverkühn tells him that his aim is to 'dissolve the magical essence of music into human reason', on which Zeitblom comments with some alarm: 'You want to play on my honour as a human-ist. . . . Human reason! Forgive me, but, when you talk, every third word is "constellation". It belongs more to the sphere of astrology. The rationality you are crying for has a good deal of superstition about it—of belief in something intangibly and vaguely daemonic. . . . Your system is the contrary of what you say, it seems to me to tend rather to dissolve human reason into magic'. He observes quite early that Leverkühn's 'intellectual self-control' is strangely interfused with characteristics of 'slight feverish-ness'. In Leverkühn's nature a fastidious and supercilious intellectualism constantly appears to taste the delights of forms and values whose appeal lies beyond the pale of rea-son. His life is referred to as 'monkish', suggesting mysti-cism and also qualities of continency and austerity. It is the 'life of a saint', the phrase recalling Mann's often re-peated identification, stemming from Schopenhauer, of the dedicated life of the artist with the sphere of holiness. At the same time the monkish life can imply, as in the ac-tion of the monk Luther in throwing an inkpot at the Devil, a contact with medieval demonology. Leverkühn comes from the area associated with the Reformation, looking back to the Dark Ages and forward to the modern world. That is why Zeitblom regards it as significant that both he, as a humanist, and Leverkühn, in his role as a theologian, sprang from Kaisersaschern. At Kaisersasch-ern and at Halle Leverkühn is in an environment where 'one experienced how the ghostly voices from a level of time lying behind the present constantly penetrate into it'.

There is hardly anything in **Faustus,** however external it may seem to the inner world of Leverkühn's soul, which has not its deeper *raison d'être* through reference to it. For instance, he had listened as a student to Kretschmar's ar-gument that Beethoven was the 'supreme master of a pro-fane epoch of music' in which the art of the fugue 'had emancipated itself from cult into culture', a composer who had revealed, in terms applicable to some of Leverkühn's subsequent aspirations, the 'unceasing nostalgic yearnings of liberated music for its origins firmly bound to cult'. In another lecture, again in language bearing on what we later learn about Leverkühn, Kretschmar had spoken about the elemental and the primitive in music which, fashioned through the centuries into a miracle of subtlety and high complexity, 'had never lost its pious desire faith-fully to remember its original situation, solemnly to con-jure up and to celebrate the elements', and he had spoken of music's yearning 'to plunge back into the elemental and to admire itself in its basic beginnings'. Kretschmar had described too the ideas of Johann Conrad Beissel, the founder of a group of German anabaptists in Pennsylvania in the eighteenth century. Among the musical notions at-tributed to him there is the idea, associated by its context in this novel with fascist tendencies, that each scale had to be divided into 'master notes' and 'servant notes'. What instinctively pleased Leverkühn about this, he explains to Zeitblom, defending it against the latter's 'simple rational-ism', was

> something itself instinctive, standing in a naïvely harmonious relationship to the spirit of music: the will, rather comically manifested, to con-struct something in the nature of a severely orga-

nized movement. On a different, less childish level we could do with his like today, with a mas-ter of systematization, a schoolmaster of objec-tivity and organization, sufficiently a genius to combine . . . the archaic with the revolutionary.

Zeitblom laughs at this formulation of a 'revolutionary conservatism' as 'something very German'. Harking back to Mann's own views at the time of the **Reflections of a Non-Political Man,** Leverkühn stands his ground with the comment that such a notion expresses 'something neces-sary at the present time, something promising salvation in this period of the destruction of conventions and the disso-lution of all objective commitments, a period, in short, in which freedom begins to settle on talent like a mildew and to show features of sterility'. For freedom 'is but another word for subjectivity, and one day it will . . . despair of the possibility of itself being a source of creativeness and will seek protection and security in objectivity. Freedom tends towards a 'dialectical reversal'. It will 'fulfil itself in subordination . . . but does not therefore cease to be free-dom'. Zeitblom is horrified at these arguments, not least for the fact that in Leverkühn's presence the threat of the paralysis and crippling of inspiration 'could only be thought of as something positive and proud, something in-timately linked up with high and pure spirituality'.

Leverkühn's music draws on the most modern techniques and sophistications, but from an early stage it looks back—to the variation-form, for instance, and to the bour-rée, characteristic for Leverkühn of the 'playfully archaic element of social integration'. Facing both ways, it is 'music of Kaisersaschern'. Leverkühn's later works com-bine an increasingly revolutionary modernism with a pas-sionate reenactment of earlier features sometimes sugges-tive of primitive barbarism. In the same way Leverkühn's life and habits show the paradox of a lonely form of mod-ern intellectualism relishing the delights of a cruder and more instinctive existence. His conviction, varying the 'circular' idea of time in **The Magic Mountain,** that man must go back in order to advance, reveals its sinister asso-ciations in the light of his statement that 'we must become much more barbaric in order to be capable of culture'. One commentary on such views is the account of Kaisersasch-ern which 'in its external appearance had preserved some-thing strikingly medieval' and in which one would not be surprised to witness scenes more characteristic of the Mid-dle Ages than of the modern world. Zeitblom is prompted to reflect that 'age is the past experienced as the present', 'it is a present only covered over by the past', so that time can produce 'a false and miserable movement of history', 'turning back into past ages and repeating with enthusi-asm symbolical actions which have something dark about them and which are a blow in the face to the spirit of mod-ern times, like burnings of books and such like, which I would rather not mention'. A further commentary is pro-vided by the students whom Leverkühn encounters in the Winfried Circle. In their discussions Mann brilliantly par-odies the language of German nationalism before the First World War, its belief in the inherent 'destiny' of Germany as a 'young' nation moulding itself and its future at what-ever cost in conquest and suffering. To be young, says one of them, 'means to be primitive (*ursprünglich*), to have remained near the springs of life, to be able and to dare to arise and cast off the bonds of an outlived civilization, while others lack the courage to do so, to be submerged once again in the elemental. The courage of youth is the spirit of "dying and becoming", the knowledge of death and resurrection.' In every vital movement 'daemonic forces are found side by side with qualities of order'; 'the daemonic, that means in plain German, instincts'. The deeper aspects here in question are suggested by Mann's phrase about Schönberg (and closely paralleled by his account of pre-1914 Germany), 'the strangest mixture of loyalty to tradition and revolution'.

The most important capacity of a composer, Schönberg once said, 'is to cast a glance into the most remote future of his themes or motives. He has to be able to know beforehand the consequences which derive from the problems existing in his material and to organize everything accordingly'. With reference to the writing of *Doctor Faustus,* and echoing a passage in *The Magic Mountain,* Mann said that one always carries 'the work of art within one as a whole. Aesthetic philosophy may assert that the work constructed of words or tones in contrast to the plastic arts, depends on time and the succession of events in time, but it is nevertheless the case that the former always strives to be present in its entirety at every moment. In its beginning exist its middle and its end, the past permeates the present, and even the most extreme concentration on the present is invaded by concern for the future'. 'Everything is association', Leverkühn remarks, amplifying his conception of musical form, 'and if you want to give it a more precise name, its title is "ambiguity".'

The term characterizes Leverkühn's nature and his music. His father, Jonathan Leverkühn, a loving student of the Bible, was deeply concerned with the spiritual values of life. His tendency to migraine, 'from which he suffered, but only moderately, not more than once a month for a single day and almost without his being interrupted in his job', revealed, however, an emergent weakness associated with sensitivity, foreshadowing his son's more chronic disability. His pious spirituality was accompanied by a 'tendency to magic', a fascination with the 'forbidden sphere', manifested in his preoccupation with exotic moths and marine creatures, 'insects which in their fantastically exaggerated beauty live their ephemeral lives and some of which are regarded by the local population as evil spirits carrying malaria'. The theme of the nearness of beauty and evil, later exemplified in Adrian's life, is here suggested, just as Adrian's later Nietzschean scepticism about the validity of the 'lie' of art is prefigured in his father's explanation that the apparent beauty of some of these creatures was merely the result of the play of light and shade. Others are so made, Jonathan Leverkühn explains, that they become indistinguishable from their surroundings; 'such a butterfly, in its transparent nakedness loving the dusky shade of leaves, was called Hetaera Esmeralda'. Others of these creatures are so fashioned as not to conceal but to demonstrate their presence, giving warning of their approach, 'because they were a horror'. How much, runs the comment, 'was here combined—poison and beauty, poison and magic, but also magic and liturgy'. As a student in Leipzig the young Adrian Leverkühn, in an episode

borrowed from the life of Nietzsche, is maliciously and to his horror misdirected to a prostitute, Esmeralda, from whom he flees in disgust. In due course he returns in order to infect himself with the disease which heightens his powers of inspiration, but which also plants the seeds of his madness. Thereafter, in a way not fortuitously reminiscent of Hugo Wolf's life after his infection with the same disease, Leverkühn's career alternates between periods of despairing uncreativeness and of the most intense inspiration. Esmeralda's first appearance—in the brothel—is described in language evocative of the accounts of his father's butterfly-collection, as when on his return she 'warned him of her body'. The letter in which Leverkühn informed Zeitblom of the incident is dated '1905, Friday after the Purification'. What lured him back to Esmeralda, Zeitblom supposes, was a deep and secret longing for 'daemonic conception (*Empfängnis*)'. From her name is derived Leverkühn's favourite musical motif, woven into work after work and making its appearance first in the setting of Brentano's poem 'O Maiden Dear, How Evil Art Thou'; the phrase, in German notation, is the sequence: H-E-A-E-ES—Hetaera Esmeralda.

When Leverkühn writes to Zeitblom about his original unhappy experience, he does so in a parody of sixteenth-century German. The next use of the language of the Reformation period is in the Pact Scene of the following year, and here Hetaera Esmeralda is identified as the agent of the Devil, giving point to the earlier reference to the brothel as the 'hell of lust'. The scene of the Pact occupies a place in the novel similar to the central scene 'Snow' in *The Magic Mountain.* In a total of forty-seven chapters it is placed twenty-four chapters from the beginning—the number of years granted to Leverkühn (and Faust) in the agreement. It focuses everything that precedes it, enlarging the significance of much which thus far might have seemed often fortuitous references to devilry and temptation—as, for instance, to Zeitblom's conviction of his humanistic immunity to the 'forces below', the 'gods of the depths', and the 'nether kingdom'. Its culminating consequence is Leverkühn's final confession, again in the style of the sixteenth-century folk-book, of his guilt, preceding his 'paralytic collapse'. The Pact Scene comes just after Leverkühn has paid his first visit to Pfeiffering, the Bavarian village which, figuring in the chapbook itself, was to become his retreat until his death. He notes its attractions—the setting 'stood in a relation of strange similarity to that of his childhood; the scene of his later days was a curious repetition of that of his early period':

> Adrian's soul preserved the picture of this locality, but it had not yet determined his decision. He wanted to get away, but further away than a mere hour's journey by rail in the direction of the mountains. Of the music for *Love's Labour Lost* only the piano sketch of the expository scenes was written; but the work was stagnating; the parodistic artificiality of the style was hard to maintain, it produced a recurring eccentricity of mood and aroused a desire for the air of distant places. . . . He was restless. 'I am looking', he wrote to me, . . . 'for a place where I can really bury myself from the world and where undisturbed I can hold conversations with my life

and my fate. . . . ' Strangely ominous words! Is it not enough to make shivers run down my back and to make my hand tremble at the thought of what these conversations, this encounter, and this engagement might be, for which, consciously or unconsciously he was seeking a setting?

The passage recalls the restlessness of Aschenbach at the opening of **Death in Venice** ('desire for the air of distant places') and Mann's difficulties at that time with **Felix Krull** ('the parodistic artificiality of the style was hard to maintain'). It raises a central problem, the problem of failing inspiration, of artistic sterility. It relates by juxtaposition the struggle of the artist with the 'eccentricity of mood', which in Mann's experience springs from the nearness of intellectual concentration to the yearning for release in spiritual adventures. It defines the nature of Leverkühn's discourse with the 'Devil' as self-communion. The reminiscence here of Ivan Karamazov is significant in so far as Dostoyevsky—like Nietzsche—mirrors aspects of the disintegration of established forms and values of traditional bourgeois society. To these we may add a third, Kierkegaard, who figures in the discussions of the Winfried Circle. 'Religiosity, that perhaps is youth itself', remarks one of these smart young intellectuals to Leverkühn, 'it is the experience of the natural and daemonic feature of life which Kierkegaard recalled to our consciousness.' Leverkühn recognizes that 'it is the most intelligent of you people who have read Kierkegaard and who regard truth, even ethical truth, as subjective', but he cannot assent to their separation of Christianity from institutional religion: 'I see in the church . . . a fortress of order, an institution for the objective disciplining, canalization and control of religious life, which without it would fall victim to subjectivistic disorder, to numinous chaos, to a world of fantastic mystery, a sea of daemonic impulses. To separate church and religion means to abandon the separation of religion from madness.' The fact, however, that in conversation with these people Leverkühn slips sometimes into the use of the familiar second-person singular forewarns us that we may expect to find him nearer to their position than this forthright rejection of their enthusiasm for Kierkegaard might suggest. In fact, he is deep in the reading of Kierkegaard when the Devil visits him. The setting is in Rome, 'Via Torre Argentina . . . three stories high'—in short, the very place where Mann himself had sought seclusion at the outset of his career. With appropriate paradox Leverkühn here lives the 'life of a saint'.

Artistic creation, the Devil tells him, is 'accomplished with toil and ill-pleasure'. Composition has become 'too difficult, devilishly difficult'. Art is 'becoming criticism' and sterility threatens. The self-sufficient appearance of music has become impossible, he declares, for what is falling victim to criticism is the 'false character of the bourgeois work of art'. Leverkühn has a quick retort: 'One could impart a heightened potency to the game by playing with forms, from which, one knows, the life has departed.' His adversary knows what he means—parody: 'It could be jolly, if it were not so depressing in its aristocratic nihilism'. Does Leverkühn really 'promise himself much happiness and greatness on this track'?—Leverkühn angrily answers with a simple negative. Leverkühn's arguments

spur the Devil to the observation: 'Your desire, my friend, to seek objectivity, so-called truth, and to be suspicious of subjectivity and pure experience as valueless, is veritably petty-bourgeois and needs to be overcome', like the naïve belief that in this time and hour artistic achievement is compatible with the traditional proprieties of bourgeois order. The artist 'is the brother of the criminal and the lunatic'. Does Leverkühn really believe that an enlivening work has ever come into being 'without its creator having learnt to understand the existence of the criminal and the madman?' Disease which 'imparts creative power and genius', and 'leaps high-seated on its horse over all obstacles in bold frenzy from rock to rock'—the metaphor echoes a favourite image of Goethe—is nearer the heart of things 'than health, shuffling along on foot'. Leverkühn may inwardly resist, but always in this self-communion the Devil speaks to him in terms of yearnings and temptations at home in his own heart—and long known no less to Mann himself. The Devil is right. Leverkühn has 'always longed for the elemental', seeking it in the marriage of 'algebraic magic' with 'cleverness and calculation'. This is the form of his revolt 'against reason and sobriety'. Leverkühn yields in return for the promise of twenty-four years in which to live out to the full all his needs and temptations, heightened and pushed to their extreme; 'you will be enabled to break through this epoch of culture . . . and boldly resort to a barbarism which is twofold because it comes after . . . humanism and bourgeois refinement'. The contract promises Leverkühn only the intensification of existing qualities: 'We do not create anything new . . . we merely release and liberate. We cast away paralysis and timidity, chaste scruples and doubts. With a little stimulus of the blood we loosen and dispel all weariness, small and great, private weariness and the weariness of the age'. It is no use lamenting

> that this man and that man could have life whole, infinite joy and infinite sorrow, without being faced with the hour-glass and without being presented with the reckoning. What was possible in classical times and admittedly without us, today we alone have to offer. And we offer something better . . . but it is no longer the classical, my friend, that we let you experience, it is the archaic, the primeval, that which for long has ceased to be tried. Who knows today, who knew even in classical times, what inspiration is, what true and original enthusiasm is, unsicklied o'er by criticism, paralysed reflection, and the killing control of reason,—in a word, holy rapture?

This is offered to Leverkühn—or rather he bestows it on himself by yielding to the temptations of his inner self—on one condition: 'Love is forbidden you in so far as it warms. Your life is to be cold—therefore you shall love no one'. For

> a complete chilling of your life and your relationship to men lies in the nature of things—or rather it lies already in your nature. We impose, in truth, nothing new upon you, my little minions do not make anything new and strange out of you, they merely cleverly strengthen and exaggerate everything that you are. . . . We want

you cold, so that the flames of artistic production shall be hardly hot enough to warm you in them. To them you will flee from the coldness of your life.

Leverkühn's development thus involves the heightening to the point of crisis of inherent features. His self-infection with disease intensifies a tendency to migraine familiar (but only 'moderately') to his father. Hetaera Esmeralda imparts nothing intrinsically new. The Devil promises merely the opportunity to live out the possible extremes of his being. The Hell that awaits him 'is basically merely a continuation of extravagant existence', its essence is that its inhabitants are only given the choice between extreme cold and a heat sufficient to melt granite—extremes already known to Leverkühn but not to this degree. After the Pact his music accordingly shows an intensification of qualities suggested in the earlier compositions up to *Love's Labour Lost*.

It is now that he composes his puppet-opera based on episodes from the *Gesta Romanorum*. One of these, familiar also in a Middle High German poem of Hartmann von Aue, Mann was to make the theme of his novel **The Holy Sinner;** his account of Leverkühn's work illuminates the irony of his own intentions in this book. The opera is a 'regression to the musical style of *Love's Labour Lost*' and at the same time anticipates features of the later *Apocalypsis con figuris* and the *Lament of Doctor Faustus,* his most barbarous work. Its composition coincided with the initial triumphs of German power in the early stages of the First World War. Its theme was 'in the highest degree calculated to arouse Adrian's sense of parody'. It was his reaction to 'the inflated pathos of an age of art moving to its close'. Sophisticated musical modernism is here allied to the essentially 'popular' form of a puppet-opera in which, in a thoroughly 'destructive' and 'scurrilous' manner, 'a farcical treatment of the erotic' takes the place of 'priestly moralism'. After the performance of this work Zeitblom and Leverkühn have a discussion which throws light on Leverkühn's fusion 'of the advanced and the popular'. Was it mere sentimentality 'that music—and in this respect it stood for everything—yearned with growing consciousness to step out of its respectable isolation, to find community without becoming vulgar?' The means to this goal was not mere sentimentality, 'but rather irony, mockery which, clearing the air, allied itself with the objective and the elemental against pathos and prophecy, tonal intoxication and literature'. The 'longing of art' is to resolve complexity into simplicity, a notion which Leverkühn—talking now with flushed cheeks and bloodshot eyes as in a 'slight fever'—defines as the 'rediscovery of vital power and emotional force', the 'breakthrough . . . from spiritual coldness into a risky world of new feeling'.

Zeitblom had remarked that 'the depressive and the productively heightened conditions of the artist, disease and health, are not sharply separated, that in disease 'and at the same time under its protection, elements of health are at work and elements of disease are carried over into health, heightening genius'. The observation stands immediately before the discussion of Leverkühn's 'first main work', his 'apocalyptic oratorio', *Apocalypsis con figuris.* Long in Leverkühn's mind, it is completed in 1919, by which time his health is markedly deteriorating. Composed 'not without reference back to the archaic fugal form of certain canzoni and ricercari of the pre-Bach period', its theme is summed up in the remark 'that in his incommensurable choral work Leverkühn did not in any way limit himself textually to the Apocalypse of St. John, but so to speak took over into his work that whole chiliastic tradition of which I spoke, so that it ends up as the creation of a new apocalypse of his own, to some extent a résumé of all prophecies of the end of things'. We are now in the early years of the Republic, and in the Kridwiss Circle (a counterpart in the Republic to the Winfried Circle of earlier days) we encounter the aristocratic nihilism of some of its intellectuals indulging in a 'many-sided, embracing criticism of the bourgeois tradition . . . of the values of culture, enlightenment, humanism. . . . ' Like the episodes of the Rodde girls and of Rudi Schwerdtfeger's violent death, these 'essentially fascist discussions' have the aim of 'conjuring up in every sense and accelerando the feeling of the end' and 'basically with every word point in the direction of Leverkühn's decisive and representative work, the apocalyptic oratorio'. In this high-fallutin' talk, in which 'everything tended towards dictatorship and violence', Zeitblom recognizes a 'nose-tilted intellectual commentary' on the composition and character of the *Apocalypsis con figuris.* Its musical technique appears to him as 'a return, full of novelty, via the harmonic art of Bach and Handel to a deeper past of true polyphonic art'. He is disturbingly reminded of the pseudo-learned debates about the 'way round the sphere . . . this way in which reaction and progress, the old and the new, past and future became one'.

Leverkühn's two bids for love, his attempts to win a wife and later to adopt a child, Nepomuk, fall within the settled and hopeful period of the Republic after the Dawes Plan of 1924. The agent of the first is Rudi Schwerdtfeger, with whom Leverkühn enjoys one of his few easy and fairly intimate relationships. Between these episodes come various chamber music works. These include the esoteric string quartet, differing from his other compositions in that 'there is not a sign of traditional forms', though it resembles them in the complexity of its polyphony. The string trio, an 'intellectual feat', a 'unique fantasy of combination' in the 'fury of its construction', and 'the unsuspected mixtures of sound', is 'scarcely playable'. The end of the twenty-four years is now approaching, and Leverkühn's main task is the symphonic cantata, the *Lamentation of Doctor Faustus.* Simultaneously various 'stilizations' of his speech and writing—borrowings from sixteenth-century German and half-concealed references to the practice of magic—force themselves on the attention of the anxious Zeitblom. By this time Leverkühn has had the following conversation with Zeitblom:

> . . . *it shall not be.*
>
> —What, Adrian, shall not be?
>
> —The good and the noble, he answered,—what people call the human, although it is good and noble. What men have fought and stormed citadels for and what those, who have known fulfil-

ment have joyfully proclaimed—it shall not be. It will be cancelled. I will cancel it.

—I don't quite understand you, my friend. What will you cancel?

—The Ninth Symphony, he answered.

The period in which the *Lamentation of Dr. Faustus* was composed was one 'of enormous and excited—one is tempted to say, monstrous—creative activity, sufficient to throw even anyone present into a dizzy reel, and it was impossible to avoid the impression that it served as payment and reward for the deprivation of happiness and the right to love, to which Leverkühn had been subjected'. The now familiar theme of cold intellectualism seeking compensation in emotional frenzy is here restated and in this work—an 'Ecce homo' gesture, with a visionary energy scorning physical decay and spiritual agony—finds its culminating expression in this 'lamentation of the son of Hell, the most frightful lamentation of men and gods . . . ever sounded upon earth'. . . . (pp. 137-60)

Zeitblom recalls that, in describing Leverkühn's 'apocalyptic oratorio', he had drawn attention to 'the substantial identity of the most heavenly features and the most horrible', demonstrated by 'the inner sameness of the chorus of angelic children and the laughter of Hell'. This characteristic, he adds, comes to dominate the Faust cantata. It is an 'enormous work of variations on the theme of lamentation—as such negatively related to the finale of the Ninth Symphony with its variations on the theme of rejoicing'.

With the composition of *The Lamentation of Doctor Faustus* ends the creative career of Adrian Leverkühn. Only madness and damnation await him, just as what remains for Germany is the 'hell of Nazism'. The close of his final work—the high G of a solitary cello, slowly fading into silence—is 'the lamentation of God over His lost world'. In 1930 the twenty-four years now being up, Leverkühn invites a select company of acquaintances—including Zeitblom, Sextus Kridwiss, and members of his circle, among them the Nietzschean anarchist Daniel zur Höhe—to his seclusion in Pfeiffering to hear him play extracts from *The Lamentation of Doctor Faustus,* just as Hugo Wolf had summoned his intimates to his presence that he might play his uncompleted opera 'to all the faithful'. Like Leverkühn, Wolf had then revealed unmistakable symptoms of mental disorder, heralding paralytic collapse. It is a time, Leverkühn announces,

> when no work can be fashioned in goodness and sobriety and art has become impossible without the Devil's help and hellish fire under the pot. . . . Yea verily, dear friends, the fact that art is coming to a standstill and has become too difficult, and that God's poor creature knoweth not where to turn in his distress,—that is the guilt of the age. But if anyone invites the Devil as his guest in order to escape from that situation and to break out, his own soul stands accused and on his head he takes the guilt of his time and is damned.

He goes on:

> For we are commanded: Be sober and watch!

But that does not suit everyone. Instead of wisely attending to what is needful upon earth, in order that it may be better there, and instead of thoughtfully seeing to it that among men such order is established as to restore to the work of beauty a basis on which it may thrive and to enable it once more to exist in honest harmony with life, man plays truant and breaks out into hellish drunkenness; thus he surrenders his soul and ends on the carrion-heap.

Truth and beauty, Mann had said, 'must be brought into relationship with each other', and this, too late for Leverkühn's salvation, is the substance too of this conclusion.

Buddenbrooks, The Magic Mountain, Joseph, and ***Lotte in Weimar*** had all sprung from modest intentions disproportionate to their ultimate scope, but 'this time, in the case of the work of my old age, it was different. This time I knew what I wanted and the task that I was setting myself: it was to be nothing less than the novel of my epoch, dressed up in the story of a highly precarious and sinful artistic life', its basic theme 'the nearness of sterility and innate despair to predisposition to a pact with the Devil'. Reversing the upward and forward movement of history in ***Joseph,*** it concludes—consciously recalling Michelangelo's portrayal of the 'Fall of the Damned'—with the fall of a gifted individual into frenzied madness and of a civilized nation into the pit of Nazi barbarism:

> Germany, with a feverish flush upon her cheeks, was reeling on the heights of her wild triumphs in the process of conquering the world through the strength of the one pact she was mindful to keep and which she had signed with her blood. Today, wrapped round by devils, a hand over one eye and with the other staring into horror, she plunges down from despair to despair. When will she reach the bottom of the pit? When from ultimate hopelessness will there be vouchsafed a miracle transcending all belief, when will the light of hope dawn?

We think back to the end of *The Lamentation of Doctor Faustus;* does it perhaps convey also a message of hope beyond nothingness?

Originally the sub-title was to have been: 'The Strange Life of Adrian Leverkühn, Told by a Friend.' Warned of the danger of 'helping to create a new German myth and of flattering the Germans' belief in a mysterious "destiny" governing their existence', Mann dropped the questionable epithet, replacing it by reference to Leverkühn as the 'German composer'. Leverkühn does not stand for the whole of mankind, doomed to despair or perdition. He is a German composer in a particular set of circumstances at a particular stage of development of a particular society, and the frequent references to actual events, people, and institutions—conductors, orchestras, musical institutions, and so forth—reinforce this most important aspect. However, while the theme of the novel has 'admittedly a very German colouring', its 'criticism of the cultural situation of the age' should be seen in a more than German significance. Leverkühn's mockery and scepticism, his 'delicious horror' of himself and his times, his exaltation of despair, have not, of course, been the prerogative only of German intellectuals in our perplexed and troubled century. It belongs to the perspectives of Mann's analysis that we should see them as part of what he calls the 'European element' in the novel's theme of crisis, even though the German reference stands always in the foreground of the author's, and the reader's, attention.

It was, as Mann remarks, a 'comical' idea to present so 'daemonic' a theme through the eyes of so 'undaemonic' a person as Serenus Zeitblom, 'a humanistic, pious and simple soul, loving and frightened at the same time'. In *Faustus* the role of the narrator is always thrust upon our notice. He appears throughout in conversation and as a commentator. We are admitted to the intimacy of his presence. There is 'not yet the slightest chance', he remarks at the beginning, 'that my work will ever see the light of publicity, unless by some miracle it were enabled to leave our threatened European fortress' and 'bring to those outside a breath of the secrets of loneliness'. Zeitblom writes for himself in the first instance, inspired by the desire to make a loving record of the affairs of a man of whom he alone is fully informed. We follow, as from within his mind, the shaping of his sentences and the whole process by which he orders his material. The reasons why *Faustus* employs a narrator ever in the foreground of the story are twofold and on them we are precisely informed by Mann himself. In the first place, 'the measure was a bitter necessity in order to relieve to some degree the gloom of the material and to make its horrors bearable to myself as also to the reader'; 'it allowed me to present indirectly all the excitement caused by what was of direct and personal concern to me, by the element of personal confession, fundamental to the whole uncanny conception, and to travesty it in the confusion and trembling of that frightened soul'. ('How much *Faustus* contains of my life and feeling! At bottom it is a radical confession. From the outset that was what made the writing of the book so disturbing an experience to me'.) Secondly, 'what I gained through interposing the narrator was, above all, the possibility of letting the story play on two levels of time, of interweaving the experiences, which appal the story-teller as he writes, polyphonically with those which he is recording'.

Zeitblom has lived, so it would seem, by values so different as to render his friendship with Leverkühn surprising and improbable. His standards of life have been guided by the hope that culture and barbarism are distinct spheres and that his own existence has been dedicated to the one and immune from all temptations of the other. His humanism, not untouched by doubt and bewilderment, is as remote from the concrete problems of his time as the long-winded, involved sentences of his style from the manner of expression of the masses of his contemporaries. His faith in the validity of his humanism is weak and full of contradiction. His account of his reactions to the 'glowing August days' of 1914 reveals that his enthusiasm was on occasions neither in quality nor quantity behind that of any average German nationalist of the time. The policy of Hitler repels him. For the sake of conscience and common decency he resigns his post as schoolmaster to pursue an existence of innocent seclusion. But the initial triumphs of the German fascist armies fill him with pride, and his vocabulary

shows that he has absorbed more of the assumptions of fascism than he would care or be able to admit. In the same way he can combine a feeling of horror at the character and development of Leverkühn's work with an affection, even a fascination, inconsistent from all points of view with his stated principles. In *Mario and the Magician* (1929) Mann had drawn a picture of the shortcomings of traditional liberalism in the figure of the 'gentleman from Rome' who wills himself to resist the wiles of hypnotist Cipolla only to fail 'through the negativity of his combat attitude'. Zeitblom is a similar case and Mann's portrayal of him springs from his sense of the crisis of bourgeois humanism, of bourgeois values altogether, in an age which in important parts of Europe had witnessed the triumph of fascism. Mann's anxieties, moreover, were not stilled by the defeat of Hitler. The death of Roosevelt—the 'aristocratic friend of the people', the 'equal of the European dictators as a shrewd guide of the masses, the born antagonist of the dictators, the great politician in the service of good, for whom the popular war against Japan had been a means of defeating the fascism saved by "Munich"', provoked from Mann the comment: 'An epoch is ending. It will no longer be the America to which we came'. The defeat of Hitler and Mussolini did not set his mind at rest. The use of the atom bomb at Nagasaki was necessary 'only to get in first and exclude the Russians from this victory'. Fears of the planning of a 'reactionary' war against the Soviet Union, of the desire to rearm Germany in this cause, of the activities of the Committee on Un-American Activities occupied his mind as the writing of *Faustus* moved on to its conclusion. Faced with the rise and triumph of German fascism Zeitblom is confused, powerless, resigned. The novel ends with his comment: 'A lonely man folds his hands and says: May God be gracious to your soul, my friend, my Fatherland'. (pp. 162-67)

R. Hinton Thomas, in his Thomas Mann: The Mediation of Art, *Oxford at the Clarendon Press, 1956, 188 p.*

Joseph Frank   (essay date 1961)

[*Frank is an American critic and educator who has written on such diverse subjects as biblical themes in literature, English poetry, and McCarthyism. In the following essay, he praises Mann's analysis of the relationship between revolution and tradition, his use of the montage narrative technique, and his representation of the evolution of art and literature in* Doctor Faustus.]

The literary career of Thomas Mann is certainly one of the most remarkable in modern letters. Beginning at the very close of the last century, when Symbolism, Naturalism, and *fin de siècle* decadence were the reigning international artistic movements, Mann has traversed all the peripeties of the first half of the twentieth century—and he is the only writer of his generation who has never ceased to grapple artistically with the chaotic world that replaced the complacent security of pre-1914. Neither Gide nor Shaw, his rivals in longevity, retained sufficient artistic resiliency to renew themselves creatively in the latter period of their lives; and Joyce retreated into a private world of linguistic experimentation whose fascinating ingenuity does not compensate for its total lack of contact with the world of the common reader. But Thomas Mann, after writing one of the great novels to emerge from the holocaust of the first World War (*The Magic Mountain*), has performed the astonishing feat of composing what is unquestionably the greatest work inspired by the degrading and horrifying events culminating in the second World War. For no other work of our time can compete with Mann's *Dr. Faustus* as a sublime and sophisticated esthetic expression of the raw reality of contemporary historical experience.

Mann himself, in a letter to a friend, has called *Dr. Faustus* his "wildest" book, a work in whose light the immediately preceding *Joseph* novels—and, he might have added, *The Magic Mountain* as well—appears as an "operatic pleasantry." *Dr. Faustus,* indeed, is colored by an emotional *chiaroscuro* far removed from the bland narrative poise of Mann's other works. Mann has always conceived of the artist as the mediator between nature and spirit, the all-reconciling *deus ex machina* playfully harmonizing the contraries of which all human life is formed. The appointed role for the artist is thus that of cosmic master of ceremonies or of supreme ironist (irony being understood not as satirical mockery but as clear-eyed and unbenighted love); and Mann's leisurely narrative manner, with its tongue-in-cheek slyness, is the perfect embodiment of this conception. This typical Mannian tone, however, is conspicuous by its absence in *Dr. Faustus;* and it is not difficult to understand why.

In *Die Entstehung des Dr. Faustus* (1949), a little book that he wrote about his own novel, Mann remarks on the "curious and licentious spiritual dissolution" that seemed to accompany the writing of this work, the relaxation of inner barriers that turned it into both a "piece of esoterica and a personal confession." To a large extent *Dr. Faustus* is Thomas Mann's own spiritual autobiography, where he makes an almost unprecedented usage of events drawn directly from his own life. And the tragedy he depicts is not only that of his country and his people, but also that of the cultural heritage from which he has drawn his spiritual sustenance.

This does not mean, however, as many American reviewers thought in 1948, that *Dr. Faustus* is too "German" to have much interest for other readers. The book was conceived, Mann tells us in his commentary, to express "the situation of art in general, of culture, yes, of mankind itself, of the spirit in our thoroughly critical epoch." Adrian Leverkühn is a musician because music has a special symbolic relation to the German spirit; but the cultural situation that his music reflects is that of the Occident as a whole in the past half-century. This situation has often been expressed in Yeats's famous lines:

> The best lack all conviction, while the worst
> Are full of passionate intensity.

But Mann goes considerably deeper by making us aware of the extent to which the best and the worst have become intermingled, linked in a dialectical unity of opposites which incessantly transforms one into the other and blurs all distinctions. How can we any longer tell the primitive from the *avant-garde,* barbarism from civilization, reaction from progress? It was German culture, of course,

which pressed this dialectic to its terrifying practical and political conclusion; but it would be folly and false pride to believe that Thomas Mann's Devil holds no temptations for those raised elsewhere than among the medieval towers of an old German city.

The original plan of *Dr. Faustus* goes back to a note three sentences long that Mann jotted down in 1901, and which, after completing the last volume of *Joseph and His Brothers,* he took up again early in 1943. Even while working on the last volume of his *Joseph* series, Mann reports that he found himself perusing the *Memoirs* of Stravinsky and leafing through a number of long-familiar works about Nietzsche. "Music and Nietzsche" he writes. "I could give no explanation for such a direction to my interests and thoughts at that particular time." But on March 15, 1943, having cleared away all the material of the *Joseph* novels, he began to look through old papers for his note on *Dr. Faust.* What was *Dr. Faust?* He hardly knew himself. "A certain long-existing outline of a very cloudy idea that I pursued. At the moment it concerned the diabolic and fatal *release* of an artistic existence through intoxication." At the same moment as this idea was emerging from the mists of the past, Mann's notebooks (cited in *Die Entstehung*) were also filled with accounts of Nazi atrocities against friends and acquaintances and with comments on the course of the war. Music and Nietzsche, the theme of Faust, the depravations of Nazism and the struggle against it—all these motifs were beginning to focus themselves as part of one artistic complex.

The central action of *Dr. Faustus,* the theme of Faust itself, thus goes back to an early period of Mann's work ("the *Tonio Kröger* period," as he himself calls it); and *Dr. Faustus* takes its place in Mann's famous series of *Künstlernovellen,* dealing with the antinomy between art and life. Mann had played many variations on this theme in the past; one of the most famous is the mortal peril in which the artist places himself by his commerce with the sensuous, the demonic and the irrational. Gustave von Aschenbach, the great writer in *Death in Venice,* had fallen a victim to this danger by confusing the boundaries between art and life. As an artist himself, whose spiritual education had been conducted under the guidance of Schopenhauer, Nietzsche and Wagner, Thomas Mann could hardly ally himself with Philistinism against art and the irrational; but *Death in Venice* reveals his acute consciousness of the possible degradation involved in giving the latter any hegemony over conduct. This theme had been only a private and personal one in 1911—an outgrowth of the tension in Mann himself between the amoralism of art and the ethical responsibility of the burgher. But it is an essential part of Mann's genius that, like all great writers, he has been able to exfoliate his quarrel with himself into a mirror of the universe; and the whole course of modern German history had conspired to give the theme of *Death in Venice* a vaster and much more terrible scope.

It may well be that Mann did not really know why "music and Nietzsche" began to preoccupy him as the *Joseph* novels drew to a close, or why he opened his old packet of notes on *Dr. Faust* (though one suspects him of being a little coquettish on this score). Nevertheless, Mann's political writings of the late Thirties and early Forties are filled with references to demonism and the Devil in speaking of the capitulation of the German people to Hitlerism. The German people, he wrote in 1939—to select only one example among many—had now become the "Enemy of Mankind," i.e., the Devil incarnate; and alluding to the ideals of freedom, truth, and justice, he says: "We hold them out before the Enemy of Mankind, as the medieval monk held out the crucifix before Satan in person." The Faust-theme of a pact with the Devil, as we can see here, had clearly become associated for Mann with the political triumphs of Nazism and the surrender of the German spirit to the irrational forces of blood and soil. But this same surrender, on a higher level, had long before become linked in Mann's sensibility with the work and the figure of Nietzsche.

After the defeat of Germany in the first World War, German culture was inundated by a flood of doctrines and attitudes exemplified by such names as Spengler, Ludwig Klages, Bachofen, Ernst Junger, Stefan George and *tutti quanti.* All these novelists, philosophers and poets, Mann noted in an important article on Freud (1929), stress "the impotence of spirit and reason . . . while by contrast the powers of the lower regions, the dynamic of passion, the irrational, the unconscious, is exhibited with bellicose piety." Whether intentionally or not, the writings of these men served as the intellectual and spiritual precursors of Nazism; and Thomas Mann, who felt this whole movement as a perversion of his own deepest values, recommended Freud as an antidote in the courageous struggle he waged both as publicist and artist against this movement. Freud too had called attention to the dynamism of the irrational and the importance of the instinctive; but he had done so with the ultimate aim of harnessing this dynamism in the service of reason and enlightenment. And while the post-war irrationalists appealed for support to the German Romantics, who had pitted the idealization of the sacred past and the cult of death against the "shallow" reason and clarity of the Enlightenment, Mann points out that the Romantics had never attempted to conceal their reactionary nature by taking the offensive against reason in the name of revolution.

"The word 'revolution'," Mann writes, "is here given a paradoxical and, according to logical usage, inverted sense. For while we are accustomed to link the idea of revolution with the powers of light and the emancipation of reason, in short, with the future, the message proclaimed here sounds quite the opposite. For it points to the great return into the nocturnal, the primevally holy, the fecundity of the pre-conscious, to the mythical, historical and romantic womb." Mann labels this whole movement with a phrase taken from Nietzsche: "Reaction as Progress"—a phrase that Nietzsche had used to characterize German culture as a whole as typified by representatives like Luther and Schopenhauer. Indeed, Nietzsche's own relation to this tendency, as Mann points out, is a highly ambiguous one. For while Nietzsche saw himself as carrying forward the banner of Enlightenment inscribed with the names of Petrarch, Erasmus and Voltaire, there is little doubt that his own work had given a mighty impulse to the counter-Enlightenment holding the field in the Twenties. "Following in Nietzsche's footsteps" Mann writes, "whose battle against Socrates' enmity to instinct so pleases our prophets of the unconscious . . . following in his footsteps all the anti-rational tendencies of the nineteenth century have continued to our own day; in the more extreme cases, of course, not so much in his footsteps as over his body."

This essay is of first importance for *Dr. Faustus;* it shows us how early Mann had begun to equate the growing influence of Nazism with the idea of "reaction as progress"— the typically German transformation of a return to the past into a revolutionary principle. Moreover, this dialectic was not only baptized by Nietzsche but also incarnated by one aspect of his own career. Nietzsche's life and intellectual history, however, also reveal a heroic struggle for the self-conquest and self-transcendence of his own Romantic primitivism. "All its [the present's] conflicts and convulsions" Mann writes, "seem like a satyr-play and a ludicrous repetition of his [Nietzsche's] experience reduced to a trivial, everyday scale . . . in him, through him, they were settled long ago in the grand manner." The two levels of *Dr. Faustus*—the tragically sublime sufferings of Adrian Leverkühn, with their distorted image in the mirror of contemporary German cultural life—are already implicit in these pages. And in the years when Germany rose to her horrible apogee of power, enjoying the fruits of her fatal pact with the chthonic powers of blood and soil, it is little wonder that Mann should have turned to meditate again on the figure of Nietzsche and use his life as scaffolding for his fictional Leverkühn.

It is thus easy to see how the Faust-theme of the demonic fused with the Nietzsche-theme of "reaction as progress" under the pressure of Mann's experiences in the late Thirties and the early war-years. But to these two themes we must add a third—German apoliticism and *Innerlichkeit,* which Thomas Mann has always loved to symbolize under the aspect of music. "If Faust is to represent the German soul" wrote Mann in an essay that serves as an ideological overture to *Dr. Faustus,* "then he must be a musician; for the relation of the German to the world is abstract and mystic, i.e., musical." Nothing has stirred up more antagonism to *Dr. Faustus* than this coupling of music with Faust and the demonic; Mann has been accused both of slandering Germany's most precious spiritual heritage and of distorting the nature of the most seraphic of the arts. To the latter charge, one might reply that *Dr. Faustus* is a novel and not a treatise on esthetics; to the former, that the symbolic value Mann attributes to music is by no means his individual invention.

It was Schopenhauer who first interpreted music as the direct expression on the metaphysical reality of the will; and it was Nietzsche and Wagner, Schopenhauer's disciples, who seized on music as the typically "German" art precisely because of its presumed relation to the tragic, irrational depths of the world-soul. To be sure, Mann himself did a good deal to popularize this symbolism of Germany as the "unliterary land," the land of music, whose rhetorical inarticulateness is a consequence of the sublimity and purity of its emotions. But at least since *The Magic Moun-*

tain he has also been concerned with the dangers involved in German *Innerlichkeit,* the inadaptation of such a "musical" culture to the non-metaphysical and "human" realm of social and political reality. It was thus inevitable and suitable that Mann should place music symbolism at the center of *Dr. Faustus*—not only because of its previous use in his own artistic world, but also because this use coincides with the dominant modern image created for itself by German cultural self-consciousness.

The structure of *Dr. Faustus,* as Mann has noted, is based on a "montage-technique" that he chose to employ for a number of reasons. In the first place, it allowed him to attain a certain distance from the material that he felt was humanly necessary if he were to write the book at all. The history of Adrian Leverkühn, accordingly, is not narrated in the third person by the author; it is written as a biography (with interjected comments) by Leverkühn's boyhood friend Serenus Zeitblom. This narrative method "allowed me," Mann explains, "to divert into indirection all the emotion caused by everything direct, personal and confessional that lay at the root of this uncanny idea. I could portray it in travesty as the perplexity, the trembling hand of that fearful soul." Even more, this technique gave Mann the possibility of constructing his narrative "on a double time-plane," so that "the experiences which shake the narrator as he writes interweave polyphonically with those he is recounting. Hence the trembling of his hand from the vibrations of distant bomb-explosions and from inner terrors can be explained both doubly and yet again unitedly as one." The montage-technique allows the career of Adrian Leverkühn and the catastrophe of the Third Reich mutually to reflect and illuminate each other; but this does not mean that they are to be considered absolutely parallel. Indeed, one of the commonest errors in the interpretation of *Dr. Faustus* is to make this identity more absolute than Mann does himself.

The story, then, is told through the eyes of Serenus Zeitblom, a life-long friend of Leverkühn's and a teacher of Latin, Greek and theology in a German high-school and seminary. Zeitblom's very name, with its faintly grotesque and pedantic mixture of Latin and German, immediately evokes the atmosphere of his character and his symbolic function in the book. By birth and conviction a Catholic humanist, Zeitblom represents a tradition of cultural unity that corresponds to the *via media* of "the human" between the competing extremes of Western civilization. "For my part" he says, "I feel very truly at home in that golden sphere where one called the Holy Virgin *Jovis alma parens.*" And as a human being, too, Zeitblom incarnates a golden (but naturally rather unexciting) mean. For he is a touching and sympathetic but hardly inspiring figure—a decent man revolted by Hitlerism but, for all his personal probity, timorous and ineffectual. There can be little doubt that Thomas Mann's rather pathetic portrait of Zeitblom represents a good deal of what he feels about himself and his relation to Germany—not, to be sure, as a private individual (for Mann was anything but timorous and ineffectual in the fight against Nazism), but as the representative of a German humanism that was impotent to check the course of catastrophe.

If there were any doubt on this score, it would be removed when Zeitblom, in the opening pages of the novel, evokes Hans Castorp's famous vision in the snow from *The Magic Mountain*—the vision of the harmonious fusion of the Apollonian and the Dionysian, the human and the awesomely irrational, in the higher unity of the *Homo Dei:* "When I stood at the place of the initiation itself, in the district of Eubulus at the edge of the Plutonian cleft overhung by rocks, I experienced by divination the rich feeling of life which expresses itself in the initiate veneration of Olympian Greece for the deities of the depths; often, later on, I explained to my pupils that culture is in very truth the pious and regulating, I might say propitiatory entrance of the dark and uncanny into the service of the gods." Zeitblom's point of view is thus the very ideal of Mann himself as expressed in *The Magic Mountain*—and Zeitblom's helplessness, sadness and sense of resignation certainly represents one facet of Mann's own feeling as he describes the defeat of this ideal in the history of Adrian Leverkühn. For instead of the unity he had once envisaged in Hans Castorp's "dream poem of humanity," instead of enlightened human intercourse in silent recognition of the blood-sacrifice, the latter had found its voice and was now shouting its supremacy from the housetops—or, to be more accurate, through the loudspeakers.

Dr. Faustus is thus narrated through the perspective of *The Magic Mountain,* but this perspective, appropriately enough, no longer controls the pattern of the symbolism. In *The Magic Mountain,* the elaborate dialectic play of opposites was intended to reveal the necessity of the higher synthesis embodied in the major theme. Each character, both humanly and ideologically, was driven into self-contradiction by the necessary limits of his being and point of view; all were to be reconciled and transfigured by "life's delicate child," Hans Castorp, who represents the precarious balancing-point of "the human" and is lord of counter-positions. But the world of *Dr. Faustus* is precisely one from which "the human" has been eliminated except as helpless onlooker; and the symbolic structure is thus controlled by the *fusion of extremes without mediation*—exactly as in Naptha's Catholic-Communist "morally chaotic all," in which "God and the Devil were at one in being opposed to life, to bourgeoisiedom, reason and virtue, since they together represented the religious principle." The confusion and identity of "reaction as progress" is the very principle of Naptha; and it is his dialectic (though not in the specific political form that he embodied) which now shapes the entire symbolic structure.

The first chapters of the novel hold up before us an image of unity and harmonious reconciliation; but when we come to the description of the Leverkühn family and Adrian himself, this is replaced by a treacherous process of metamorphosis in which opposites become confused and identified, and extremes merge with each other in such a fashion that one cannot disentangle opposing categories. This symbolism is developed in relation to the experiments in biology and natural science carried on as a hobby by Leverkühn's father. Mann's description here strikes the note of the uncanny, the mysterious and the terrible that swells in volume as the novel proceeds, and which reaches its piercing peak of expression in Adrian Leverkühn's greatest music. For all these experiments hover on the uncertain borderline between the organic and the inorganic, natural law and miracle, science and witchcraft; it is impossible, in any given case, to draw a hard-and-fast line between the two. And Zeitblom speaks of the senior Leverkühn, in medieval terms, as "speculating the elements" (like Faust's doctor-father in Goethe) because "a tinge of mysticism was perceptible in them [the experiments] which would once have been suspect as a leaning to the black arts."

Two points should be made about this episode, aside from its illustration of the diabolic transposition of "reaction as progress" that controls the entire symbolic structure of the book. One is the picture given here of Adrian Leverkühn's supercilious and mockingly distant personality, which is symbolically associated both with Lucifer's Satanic pride and with German national arrogance. Another is the introduction of the motif of a "yearning for life" in connection with one of the experiments in question. The senior Leverkühn takes a group of chemicals and develops them into what appear to be underwater plants: these give all the appearance of life but are really dead. Still, on being exposed to the rays of the sun shining from one direction, they all poignantly turn toward the source of light. "Indeed, they so yearned after warmth and joy that they actually clung to the pane and stuck fast there." Despite Adrian Leverkühn's silent laughter at this spectacle, which moved the other onlookers to tears, this motif, so to speak, remains in the family; Adrian himself will ultimately yearn for "warmth and joy," and for a life and a soul that his nature cannot attain. And this secret, irresistible yearning for "the human" is what saves him in the end, or at least gives his life an aura of self-sacrifice and martyrdom that keeps it quite distinct emotionally from the historical plane of the book.

The background of Leverkühn's early life is masterfully depicted by Mann in chapters where the dialectic of the imagery evokes the interpenetration of late nineteenth-century Germany with the atmosphere of the Reformation. The Reformation is of course the period of the original *Faust* chapbook, whose theme of damnation in return for knowledge and power over nature—the theme taken over and used by Marlowe in *his Dr. Faustus*—expresses the Lutheran opposition to the humanism of the Renaissance. And it is this atmosphere of regressive folk-fanaticism and folk-superstition, of religious ardor reverting to mass hysteria, that Zeitblom feels lingering in the old streets and buildings where one still sensed "a morbid excitement, a metaphysical epidemic latent since the last years of the Middle Ages."

This Reformation atmosphere is an essential element of the symbolism of the book, and, as part of the general coloring of the Faust theme, its employment is explicable enough. Yet since Hitler and Nazism have very little (indeed nothing) directly to do with Luther and the Reformation, one may well wonder why Mann uses it so insistently. The answer is that Mann, along with a good many historians, view Luther's sharp distinction between spiritual and political freedom as having exercised a nefarious influence on German culture. Luther imposed a strict religious obligation to obey political authority; and this accounts for the musical "interiority" of German culture, i.e., the political irresponsibility of its greatest representatives (Nietzsche is the most relevant example) and for German docility to authority of any kind. Luther's extremism in separating the realms of the religious and the social is thus the prototype of the German fusion of opposites, which turns the highest concerns of the spirit into the breeding-ground for the most ruthless tyranny.

Ortega y Gasset once remarked very acutely that most of the radical movements in modern art and literature could be analyzed as quite simple changes in the normal perspective with which the world is seen or described. Depending on whether the artist places himself closer or farther away than the normal distance, or shifts the accepted relation between background and foreground, his work will appear, more or less, startling and daring. One of the secrets of Thomas Mann's art is a mastery of such shifts in perspective—shifts so slight, however, that the normal perspective is never destroyed while we gradually became aware of a reality existing below or beyond or behind the one we are nominally regarding. Every reader of Mann will recall such effects, which are usually obtained by a careful choice of incongruous detail, by the repetition of leit-motifs, and by stylistic stress and insinuation. Nowhere in Mann's work, however, is this palimpsest separation obtained with such mastery and effectiveness as in *Dr. Faustus,* where every step of Adrian Leverkühn's career must be felt both as humanly free and yet as guided by a hidden diabolism working itself out at the same time.

Leverkühn's life is indissolubly linked with music from his earliest days; and the major music symbolism is first expounded in the lectures of Wendell Kretschmar, town organist of Kaisersaschern and Leverkühn's music teacher. Kretschmar sees modern music (his example is Beethoven) as longing to transcend its individualism and romantic subjectivity by a return to its old role as the expression of a collectivity like the church. Not that any simple return is possible—but the way forward would be a re-immersion in the powerful currents of the mythical, the collective and the supernatural under new conditions. These lectures exercise a profound impression on young Leverkühn; but their first result is to drive him to study theology instead of music, as if to ward off the imminent danger he feels in his attraction to the latter.

Leverkühn, in effect, is fleeing from the demon to the protection of God; futilely, as it turns out, because he finds no refuge in the ancient sanctities, which are themselves exposed to the same dialectic that Kretschmar had foreseen in music. When theology is not ridiculous and ludicrous (in the guise of the professor who apes Luther's grossness and vulgarity), it is brilliantly sinister in the lectures of Dr. Schleppfuss (Dragfoot, the Devil), privatdocent in the psychology of religion. For Schleppfuss ingeniously demonstrates the dialectical unity of good and evil, equating "freedom" with the power to sin, "humanity" with the concern for the salvation of the soul shown by the pious witch-burners of the Middle Ages, and belief in the evil eye with a "humanistic" elevation of spirit over matter. Schleppfuss insinuates—without saying so expressly—that theological re-definitions of Enlightenment ideals are far more "advanced" than their ordinary, banal meanings. And in the same way, in the conversations of Leverkühn's student friends, any concern with political matters is immediately "raised" to the level of metaphysics or to speculations about the "folk-soul." All the *clichés* of German high-brow jingoism are rehearsed in these pages; and it is interesting to see how, in this theological atmosphere, they blend with the growing influence of Kierkegaard and his contempt both for "objective" truth and a "herd" existence (Kierkegaard was discovered at the turn of the century by the German *avant-garde*).

Leverkühn finally abandons theology for the study of music; but in doing so he is well aware of the disparity between his own nature and the traditional conception of art. For art like politics is always, in a certain sense, a compromise and reconciliation between genius and convention, between the individual and the social. But Leverkühn writes to Kretschmar: "I am embarrassed at the insipidness which is the supporting structure, the conditioning solid substance of even the work of genius, at the elements thereof which are training and common property, at use and wont in achieving the beautiful." All this seems to Leverkühn's icy haughtiness the peak of absurdity: "Why must I think that almost all, no, all the methods and conventions of *art are good for parody only?*" The answer, within the symbolic structure of the book, can only be found in Leverkühn's incapacity to experience or express feeling except negatively, jeeringly, derisively. And his inability to participate in the median sphere of "the human" would seem to doom his art to be merely "parody and critique" instead of truly creative.

This is the point, however, at which the Devil overtly takes a hand. From whence can a genius with such a nature draw the emotional dynamism necessary for positive creation? Only by a dialectical fusion of the negativity of pure spirit with pure (or rather, impure) flesh; not by love—for love is precisely the "human" mediation of both spirit and flesh—but by sex. And Leverkühn's pact with flesh and the demonic (the two, as Dr. Schleppfuss has luminously explained, have always been traditionally the same) is sealed by a sexual embrace with a prostitute that culminates in a syphilitic infection of the brain. This is the poisoned source from which Leverkühn will draw his inspiration—not from the healthy heat of sun-warmed feeling, but from the smoldering fire cover by crackling in the witch's kitchen. In associating art with disease and genius with illness, Mann is of course returning to one of the omnipresent Nietzschean motifs of his artistic career. But while in the past this linkage had been treated as a piquant though somewhat melancholy paradox, it is now the Devil who announces: "The artist is the brother of the criminal and the madman," and who laughs at the Goethean idea, still clung to by Leverkühn, of "sane and sound greatness." What was once merely a paradox has now become diabolism and the spirit's self-betrayal.

It is only after this event that the musical originality of Leverkühn begins to flower; and he fictively re-invents Schönberg's atonality to solve his musical problem. This system of composition imposes an objective structure on music that rigidly controls both melody and harmony in a manner paralleling—though without duplicating—the "strict style" of early Church polyphony. The harmonic subjectivity, the freedom, of the atonal composer is totally negated; but in relation to harmonic convention his music sounds wildly iconoclastic. "More interesting phenomena" Leverkühn observes to the narrator, "probably always have this double face of past and future, probably are always progressive and regressive in one." And at the midpoint of the book, when Leverkühn's surrender to the demonic has been effectuated both physically (by his contraction of syphilis) and musically (by the invention of atonality, with its inverted relation to early Church music), the Devil in person appears in what Leverkühn tries to convince himself is only a feverish hallucination.

The burning dialogue between the two is obviously modelled on *The Brothers Karamazov;* and it triumphantly survives the burden of such a comparison as one of the greatest scenes in modern literature. Twenty-four years are given Leverkühn in which to create those remarkable works that press so far forward (or backward) along the path he must follow; but he shall create them in icy solitude, denied "the human" and the normal love of other "humans." "Not only will you break through the paralysing difficulties of the time—you will break through time itself," the Devil promises Leverkühn, "by which I mean the cultural epoch and its cult, and dare to be barbaric, twice barbaric indeed, because of coming after the humane. . . . Believe me, barbarism even has more grasp of theology than has a culture fallen away from cult, which even in the religious has seen only culture, only the humane, never excess, paradox, the mystic passion, the utterly unbourgeois ordeal."

Particular attention must be paid in this discussion to a knotty point in theology. Taxing the Devil with a certain shallowness in his approach to the subject, Leverkühn warns him not to be too sure of his bargain; for there is a *"Prideful contritio"* that may work in Leverkühn's favor. "The *contritio* without hope, as a complete disbelief in the possibility of mercy and forgiveness, the rocklike firm conviction of the sinner that he has done too grossly for even the Everlasting Goodness to forgive his sin—only that is the true *contritio*. I call your attention to the fact that it is the nighest to redemption, for Goodness the most irresistible of all." But the Devil replies that precisely such speculations, which testify to Leverkühn's supremely insolent self-possession, will forever prevent him from achieving "the naive recklessness of despair" necessary for "the sinful way to salvation."

After this fateful interview the novel widens into a macabrely grotesque evocation of German culture from the period immediately preceding the first World War up through the final triumph of the values of the demonic-irrational in the Third Reich. This section of the book, in a literal sense, is Thomas Mann's autobiography. He pitilessly weaves in tragic incidents from his own family life (the suicide of his sister Carla is narrated, even to the exact reprinting of her suicide note, in the death of Clarissa Rodde); and in Zeitblom's identification with German hopes of a "breakthrough" to world power in 1914, Mann depicts his own spiritual state at the time he wrote his ***Betrachtungen eines Unpolitischen*** (1918). Mann also settles accounts here with the Munich intelligentsia among whom he lived for so many years, satirizing real figures under assumed names or, in many cases, not even deigning to invent a pseudonym at all.

This does not mean, however, as a good many critics have suggested, that Mann neglects the demands of his major theme at this point for the sake of paying off old scores or unburdening himself of searing memories. On the contrary, each of the major episodes in this section rehearses, on a smaller and less significant scale, some aspect of Leverkühn's grandiose history. Clarissa Rodde is an artist herself, an actress who, like Leverkühn, lacks warmth of feeling, and consequently cannot project herself successfully on the stage. She is finally seduced and driven to suicide by a shabby "pseudo-Mephistopheles" of the backstage coulisses. Her equally ill-fated sister Inez, who ends up by murdering her unfaithful lover, is married to a Renaissance art-historian infatuated by Nietzschean "ruthlessness"; and the tragedy of her life is described in terms of Leverkühn's own opposition between ethics and esthetics. All this part of the book is literally a "satyr-play and ludicrous repetition" of what Leverkühn-Nietzsche is undergoing "on a grand scale"; and the artists and intellectuals of the Kridwiss circle, who vaunt the creative superiority of irrational "myth" over "abstract" ideas like justice and truth, are clearly the very ones against whom Mann launched his article on Freud in 1929.

All through ***Dr. Faustus*** we are given superbly expressive accounts of Leverkühn's music. Far from burdening the novel with a dead weight of unassimilated material, as some critics have contended, these serve as the chief means of characterizing the main figure. Leverkühn's life is as outwardly uneventful as Nietzsche's; and his spiritual history is entirely portrayed by the description of his musical compositions. Every detail of these descriptions is carefully designed to bring out some facet of his inner conflicts, or to express the cultural situation of his time; but the parallel between Leverkühn and German culture, as we have already remarked, is by no means a total identity.

Leverkühn's pact with the demonic is a source of continual spiritual torment, not an occasion for emotional titillation or moral license; it leads both to agonizing physical suffering (whose symptoms are taken largely, though not exclusively, from Nietzsche's letters), and to the inner wrestlings of his god-forsaken conscience as revealed through his music. The "yearning for life" never ceases to haunt even his most bitter and uncompromising scores. This is why he speaks so tenderly of the little sea-maid in Andersen's fairy tale, who, for love of a human prince, enters into the kingdom of the sea-witch to gain human legs instead of a fish's tail; and who wears her human legs despite the knife-sharp pains at every step "perhaps to win, like human beings, an immortal soul." When the accusation of "barbarism" is levelled against one of Leverkühn's compositions with its use of glissando to imitate animal howls, Zeitblom rejects the charge because of certain song-passages that are "like a fervid prayer for a soul . . . to call soullessness the yearning for a soul—the yearning

of the little sea-maid—that is what I would characterize as barbarism, as inhumanity."

This "yearning for a soul," which contravenes the interdiction of the Devil against human love, is reflected in various episodes of the book; but in none more poignantly than in Leverkühn's final devotion to his little nephew Nepomuk, whose nickname is Echo. No pages of Mann's work are more charming and touching than his description of the elfin Echo, whose figure is interwoven with allusions both to the Christ-Child and to Shakespeare's Ariel. Leverkühn's love for Echo, however, precipitates the last personal tragedy in a book weighted with disaster. The child dies a horrible death in the throes of spinal meningitis, an illness whose symptoms and prognosis duplicate those of Leverkühn's syphilitic infection of the meninges. Echo's death is the revenge that the Devil wreaks on his unfaithful accomplice; and this crushing blow wrings from Leverkühn a gigantic cry of despair—his last and greatest composition, a massive symphonic cantata *The Lamentations of Dr. Faustus,* which "takes back" Beethoven's "human" paean to the brotherhood of man in his Ninth Symphony.

In this work, which is described by Zeitblom at the exact moment when the Satanic horrors of Hitler's concentration camps are exposed to the world for the first time, "echo, the favorite device of the baroque, is employed with unspeakably mournful effect." For echo represents the human voice transformed into nature, given back as nature-sound, "Nature's melancholy 'Alas' in view of man, her effort to utter his solitary state." The entire structure of *The Lamentation* is rigidly controlled by the twelve syllables of Faust's confession in the old chapbook: "For I die as a good and as a bad Christian." Yet despite its inflexible atonality, *The Lamentation of Dr. Faustus* represents Leverkühn's "break-through" to pure expressiveness. The very rigidity of the structure, the complete absence of any free note, allows the composer, by a dialectical paradox, to take technique for granted. The uttermost constraint resolves itself into "the free language of feeling, the birth of freedom from bondage"; and there is no trace of parody left in the total negation expressed both by the words and construction of the music.

But in the most often-quoted passage in the book—Zeitblom's concluding paragraph on *The Lamentation*—a further and almost inconceivable paradox is also hinted at:

> No, this dark tone-poem permits up to the very end no consolation, appeasement, transfiguration. But take our artist paradox: grant that expressiveness—expression as lament—is the issue of the whole construction: then may we not parallel with it another, a religious one, and say too (though only in the lowest whisper) that out of the sheerly irremediable hope might germinate? It would be but a hope beyond hopelessness, the transcendence of despair—not betrayal of her, but the miracle that passes belief. For listen to the end, listen with me: one group of instruments after another retires, and what remains, as the work fades on the air, is the high G of a cello, the last word, the last fainting sound, slowly dying in a *pianissimo-fermata.* Then nothing

more: silence and night. But that tone which vibrates in the silence, which is no longer there, to which only the spirit hearkens, and which was the voice of mourning, is no more. It changes its meaning; it abides as a light in the night.

The religious paradox alluded to here is of course that of the *"prideful contritio"*; and it should be clear that Leverkühn's "yearning for a soul" has brought him to the "naive recklessness of despair" that the Devil had thought impossible.

This despair is revealed in Leverkühn's terrible demented address to his assembled "friends," in which he utters all the horror and agony of his demon-haunted spirit, and acknowledges his guilt for not having striven so that "among men such order shall be 'stablished that again for the beautiful work living soil and true harmony be prepared." And then, with a gesture of crucifixion, he sinks into total mental darkness. But this confession is the light abiding in the night of Leverkühn's madness, faintly illuminating his wasted features, from which all intelligence has fled, with the aura of martyrdom. Nothing similar, however, occurs in the world symbolized and foreshadowed by Leverkühn's tragic end; the satyr-play continues its tumultuous course, and its protagonists feel personally untouched by Leverkühn's prophetic collapse. The question remains open whether the German people too can achieve his "naive recklessness of despair"; and perhaps part of the answer may be found in what one hopes (but does not really believe) is only a failure of critical acumen. For ironically enough the most popular accusation made against *Dr. Faustus* in German criticism is that Mann condemns his people to "hopelessness" and leaves them no way of attaining salvation.

Lengthy as this analysis has been, it is far from having begun to exhaust the complexities of *Dr. Faustus.* Hermann J. Wiegand once called *The Magic Mountain* the "most highly integrated" of all novels conceived on so vast a scale; but it is quite likely that the palm must now be awarded to *Dr. Faustus* (the only other possible contestants are *Ulysses* and *Finnegans Wake,* and it may be argued that neither of these are novels in the sense in which Thomas Mann still writes such works). *Dr. Faustus* is clearly composed in the "strict style" that defines Leverkühn's music: every incident, episode and detail is paralleled, varied and transposed in an incredibly elaborate variety of correspondences. But no matter from what angle one approaches *Dr. Faustus*—whether from that of content or of form—the entire work reveals itself as a dialectical transposition of opposites whose paradigm may be found in Mann's original analysis of "reaction as progress." All the thematic material is controlled by this dialectic; and the same is true of the structure. For while the density of its symbolic texture makes *Dr. Faustus* the quintessence of the Symbolist novel, this is combined with the most primitive narrative form of fictitious biography. Or from another perspective, the raw material of historical events, family disasters and real personages are assimilated into the recital of Leverkühn's rarefied esthetic adventures and blended with the Faust myth.

Not the least originality of this remarkable work springs from its endeavor—unique in the history of the novel—to narrate the life of an artist primarily through an account of his creations. With the exception of one or two novellas of Balzac (notably his *Chef d'Oeuvre Inconnu*) nothing similar has ever been attempted. Proust's beautiful analyses of Elstir's paintings and Vinteuil's sonata are the only comparable pages one can think of in modern writing; but Proust strove to communicate the impressions imparted by an art-work to a particular sensibility, rather than to recreate the art-work itself as an objective structure. *Dr. Faustus* is the first great work in which an artist comes to life, not primarily as a special kind of picturesque or exotic personality, but truly and solely as a creator of his art; and it seems, for this reason, the first successful novel about an artist that has ever been written.

All previous works of this kind deal exclusively with what, for any artist, is merely peripheral—namely, the circumstances of his life. The author desperately tries to convince us that the life of his protagonist has overwhelming importance, but this importance is never "realized" as part of the book—it derives from an activity whose quality we are required to take on faith; but nothing about any aspect of an artist's life can really persuade us that he is capable of producing first-rate art. It was no doubt some such thought which impelled Henry James to remark, in the preface to *The Tragic Muse,* that the artist as subject is only interesting to the extent that he is an artist *manqué.* "Any presentation of the artist *in triumph*" James writes, "must be flat in proportion as it really sticks to its subject—it can only smuggle in relief and variety. For, to put the matter in an image, all we then—in his triumph—see of the charm-compeller is the back that he turns to us as he bends over his work." Thomas Mann magisterially solves this problem by expressing the inner "reality" of the artist's life exclusively through a depiction of his work; and the works themselves become an integral part of the dramatic realization of the theme.

As we know from *Die Entstehung,* Mann felt the technical problem outlined above with particular acuity; but the solution he adopted has far more than purely a technical function. It is by maintaining his focus constantly on Leverkühn's music that Mann succeeds, despite the intense "Germany" of *Dr. Faustus,* in raising the book to the level he wished to attain—the level on which he portrays the situation "of mankind itself, of the spirit in our thoroughly critical epoch." Indeed, without wishing to add another paradox to those of the book itself, we may yet argue that *Dr. Faustus* is an "international" novel in a far deeper sense than *The Magic Mountain.* For in spite of the latter's Swiss setting and cosmopolitan cast of characters, the theme depends on a special thesis about German culture that few but Germans would accept. This thesis considered Germany to be "the land of the center," the country destined by fate (or the *Weltgeist*) to reconcile the conflicting cultural antagonisms of Western civilization. The European surface of the book, then, was sustained by a thematic foundation with a strong nationalistic bias. In *Dr. Faustus,* however, the strongly accentuated national coloring of the surface does not conceal the "international" character of Adrian Leverkühn's music; his work bears the characteristic stamp of twentieth-century European culture as a whole. And who can fail to recognize in Leverkühn's compositions a dialectic to which all of modern culture has fallen prey in a greater or lesser degree?

It is hardly possible any longer to overlook the union in modern art of the most daring intellectual and esthetic modernity with a rejection of humanism and liberalism, and a preference—both formally and ideologically—for the primitive, the mythical and the irrational. To be sure, this has not necessarily resulted in an alliance with the forces of political retrogression; nor did it do so, we should remember, in the case of Leverkühn himself, whose music was considered *Kulturbolschewismus* by the masters of the Third Reich. Still, the careers of Knut Hamsun, Ezra Pound and Drieu la Rochelle; the political pronouncements of Yeats, Eliot (in the mid-Thirties), Wyndham Lewis and Gottfried Benn; the proto-Fascist tendencies in the work of D. H. Lawrence and Stefan George—all this reveals to what extent Thomas Mann has managed to raise to the level of sovereign art the problematic nature of modern culture itself. As modern life has become more and more rationalized, mechanized and industrialized, art has been driven into a more and more frenzied and violent assault on a world in which the total dimension of the spirit has been reduced to a stiflingly materialistic utilitarianism. The legitimacy and necessity of such a revolt is beyond question; yet its danger is no less evident. For it is an uncomfortable but inescapable truth that, if some of our noblest artistic expressions were to be translated tomorrow into practical, political terms, the result would only be to play into the hands of some form of tyranny and oppression.

The parallel between Adrian Leverkühn and Nazism has aroused a good deal of criticism, and, even among writers generally friendly to Mann, has been rejected as unconvincing. The gap between the two phenomena, it has been said, is too wide to eliminate an ultimate sense of incongruity. But it seems to me, on the contrary, that the greatness of Mann's book as a symbolic projection of the crisis of modern culture derives precisely from the tension of this incongruity and the dialectic it suggests. The images of our greatness are far more intimately connected with those of our misery than we are willing to admit; and it is the genius of Thomas Mann, sharpened by the tragedy of his culture, which has discerned and portrayed their hidden interconnection. All the significant movements of modern times, whether in art, politics, philosophy, or theology have driven straight for one or another type of extremism; nothing has seemed so paltry and contemptible as counsels of caution or recommendations of prudence. It is only the final paradox that, out of Thomas Mann's "wildest" book, which captures the spirit of our apocalyptic era as no other comparable work, the peaceful, bourgeois *via media* of "the human" should finally emerge as the true Promised Land. (pp. 19-38)

Joseph Frank, "Reaction as Progress: Thomas Mann's 'Dr. Faustus'," in Chicago Review, *Vol. 15, No. 2, Fall, 1961, pp. 19-39.*

Ronald Gray (essay date 1965)

[*Gray is an English educator and critic specializing in German literature. His works include* Kafka's Castle *(1956) and* Brecht the Dramatist *(1976). In the essay excerpted below, Gray analyzes the function and characterization of Serenus Zeitblom, the narrator of* Doctor Faustus.]

The whole of **Doktor Faustus,** directly related in time to the period which gave rise to the Nazis, and indirectly related to it through a symbolism which makes the central character look like the epitome of his age, gives clear evidence of Mann's continued adherence to ambiguity. In the person of Adrian Leverkühn ('Livebold'), the musical composer who plays here also the part of a Faust, disposing of his soul to the devil in return for a new access of creative power, Mann represents the German nation in its self-abandonment to Nazi rule. At the same time, a wide array of further suggestiveness is included. Not only is Leverkühn's childhood upbringing portrayed, but also his university career, and the intellectual circles in which he moved, in short the whole background of German thought which he later came to represent; in addition, hints are woven in, resemblances between his life and that of Nietzsche, and others recalling that of Thomas Mann himself. Indeed, so far as Mann is concerned, Leverkühn is all that part of him which sympathized with Nietzsche and adopted his way of thought.

Leverkühn is not, however, the whole of Mann, any more than he is the whole of Germany. Interposed between him and the reader is the narrator, Serenus Zeitblom ('Time's flower'), the solid pedant and worthy citizen, 'bieder' and 'tüchtig' (to use untranslatable words), in whom other German qualities which Mann admired and shared come to the fore. It is perhaps significant that a narrator appears here for the first time in Mann's novels as a technical device: by this means the author himself remains in the background entirely uninvolved, while at the same time he alternately lives out the implications in the two existences of his protagonists. For Zeitblom is as much a part of Mann as Leverkühn is, and the contradictory natures interlink in a remarkable and sometimes oppressive manner. At the same time, Mann remains, like Tadzio in **Der Tod in Venedig,** 'unverbindlich', attached neither to the one nor the other. Zeitblom may show a reverent and horrified admiration for his daemonic friend, as Mann did for Nietzsche. He may also speak of the path of German history which had led to the concentration camps and the Gestapo as 'wickedly godless ["heillos"] in every respect, at every twist and turn', again as Mann was able to do. Yet admiration and condemnation play into one another's hands, at times seeming even to coalesce.

The choice of Zeitblom as narrator means that the novel cannot be read with aesthetic enjoyment. Zeitblom has no talent for writing a novel, and says so repeatedly; indeed the second sentence of the first chapter becomes so involved that he breaks it off with an apology and begins again—a frank and so far amusing indication that felicitous prose is not the main object. Other sentences, later in the book, become so turgid that they need to be followed with some doggedness if they are read at all—and these too are sometimes offered with an apology. Periphrasis, abstraction, a pedantic show of scrupulousness, redundancy, digression, the complex adjectival phrase, and the lengthy relative clause which withholds its verb till several lines of print have passed—these are some of Zeitblom's favourite devices. All characters speak, with rare exceptions, in the same professorial prose: even the beautiful Marie Godeau refuses a suitor in language more likely to come from a government official, and the greater part of the dialogue is given in reported speech, with its distancing, disillusioning subjunctive. Little of what is said is in the form of conversation: people hold forth for pages at a time, and the first two hundred pages give, in reported speech, the substance of lectures and discussions heard by Leverkühn in his early years. From time to time Zeitblom intervenes . . . to observe what the reader already knows, that he is not writing well, that this is not a novel, that the point of these digressions will be realized later, or that he is afraid the reader may have skipped the last few pages. There is no formal pattern to speak of, almost no plot, and the main character is realized largely by a description of his intellectual background and musical compositions. All this does serve a purpose. By the very fact that Zeitblom is so dull, the dynamism he attributes to Leverkühn looks the more attractive. At the same time, the novel whose deficiencies he so frequently deplores does ironically seem to set forth an interpretation of Leverkühn which would, it might have been thought, be beyond Zeitblom's power to convey.

The bulk of the novel is presented as a foil to the two principal events—Leverkühn's conversation with the devil, and his collapse into madness twenty-four years later. Everything contributes in some way to the understanding of these two moments. German culture is surveyed in almost every aspect: social life, politics, painting, architecture, literature, philosophy, and above all, two of its most notable contributions to civilization, German theology and German music. (There is curiously little about Marxism.) From all this, two features emerge which have the closest relevance to Leverkühn's situation: the tradition of ambiguity and paradox, and an idea best given in its German form, 'Durchbruch', or 'breakthrough'. The first of these is familiar enough. Leverkühn lives in a world where opposites coincide, where theologians are preoccupied with diabolism, musicians speak of the 'sensuality' of their 'most unsensual work', and life and death constantly intermingle. The second is concerned with the sense of isolation which appears to result from this way of seeing things. Where there is unity-in-duality there is also aloneness, from which escape is sought by a breakthrough into a wider world. Politically, German history is seen as the attempt to make this breakthrough, to make contact with other nations even at the price of dominating them. Spiritually, it is seen as the attempt to escape from a fundamentally ambiguous relationship with the world into a true unity.

The dilemma of Leverkühn's situation in his youth, which resembles that of Mann, is that his works are all in some sense parodies. Being parodies, they are twofold: Leverkühn is self-conscious in everything he does. There is the mood he sets out to express, and the ironical contem-

First page from the manuscript of Doctor Faustus.

plation of it which finally makes the work as it emerges parodistic. To escape from parody, to break through into single-hearted feeling, is one of the motives which lead to his meeting with the devil, for with the devil's help he imagines the possibility of at least a temporal success. Ecstasies and terrifying despairs are the offers made, the heights and depths of emotion, and with them the possibility of unheard-of creativity. Damnation is to be the final outcome, intense heat and intense cold, the heights and depths of consciousness, in fact a life after death which will closely resemble, if it is not identical with, the one Leverkühn will lead from now on, so that he observes already that what is being offered is 'hell in advance'. There is nothing enticing about the devil's proposals, nor is Leverkühn deceived by them; he sees them with complete clarity. Nevertheless, like Goethe's Faust, he inserts a proviso into any possible pact that may be made. The devil, for his part, imagines that he will win the bargain, since Leverkühn's pride will never allow him to make the act of contrition which might save him in spite of everything. Leverkühn retorts that the devil's theology is defective. There is such a thing as proud contrition: 'Contrition without hope at all, complete unbelief in the possibility of grace and forgiveness, the unshakable conviction of the sinner that he has been too wicked, and even infinite goodness is insufficient to forgive his sins—only that is true contrition, and I would point out to you that it stands closest of all to redemption, being the most irresistible claim on goodness.' With this in mind, Leverkühn puts forward his proviso: 'A sinfulness so graceless that it makes a man utterly despair of grace, that is the truly theological path to grace.' The devil, it is true, is quick to point out the absurdity of this over-cunning speculation on divine forgiveness. Hell, he says, is full of ingenious contrivers like Leverkühn, who have insured in this way against the fruits of their wickedness. Nevertheless, the narration continues as though Leverkühn's proviso had gone uncountered.

The narration continues, but no pact is made. For the remainder of the novel this can easily be forgotten: everything takes place as though there were a pact, but in reality Leverkühn has done no more than consider the implications of a pact with a devil who is perhaps no more than a projection of his own unconscious desires. The absurdity and fruitlessness of the pact has been observed, even the absurdity of Leverkühn's proviso has been noticed, and he has not committed himself to it. The contrast with the pact of Goethe's play, with its 'Topp!' 'Und Schlag auf Schlag!', is striking. In Mann's work nothing so definite occurs: the devil is a shadow, perhaps not supernatural at all; what he offers is neither accepted nor rejected, what Leverkühn objects is neither affirmed nor denied. The motions of making a pact are gone through, much as Hans Castorp goes through the motions of dying in order to be reborn, but the decisive act is never made in reality. What appears to be a climax is not one. The 'consequences' provide no change in Leverkühn's manner of composition, and his last works are parodistic like his first. Sameness rules throughout, the sameness of ambiguity. This is the more damaging to the novel as a whole, in so far as it reflects an outside world of German history where concrete evil was in no way indecisive. Where the outside world was really committed, Leverkühn remains in an atmosphere of shadowy unreality.

A distinction should be made here between Leverkühn's proviso and the concept of 'abandonment' to the divine will, often mentioned in studies of mystical authors, and especially by de Caussade. Leverkühn's argument is in effect that by the fact of being an extreme sinner he ensures his salvation. He is, as he puts it with seeming arrogance, 'closest of all to redemption'. Contrast with this the conviction of the Cambridge Platonist, Henry More, meditating on the Calvinist doctrine of pre-destination: 'I did thus seriously and deliberately conclude within my self, viz. If I am one of those that are predestinated unto Hell, where all Things are full of nothing but Cursing and Blasphemy, yet will I behave my self there patiently and submissively towards God. . . . Being certainly perswaded, that if I thus demeaned my self, he would hardly keep me long in that place.' More's carefully worked out phrases (not, for instance, claiming salvation for certain, though not doubting it either) are echoed in modern times by Simone Weil, considering her own dilemma that, while baptism would mean salvation for her, she is also irresistibly impelled to feel that it is not God's will for her to be baptized. 'If it were conceivable', she says, 'that in obeying God one should bring about one's own damnation, whilst in disobeying him one could be saved, I should still choose the way of obedience.' The whole difficult concept is treated at length by Ronald Knox, especially in relation to St Francis of Sales, who as a young man made a resolution

to go on loving God, even though he knew himself damned. For St Francis, conditions could be imagined in which a soul ought to throw up its salvation and run eagerly to perdition if, 'par imagination d'une chose impossible', it believed that to be God's intention for it. His most faithful disciple taught that a man should acquiesce in his own damnation, 'la grâce de Dieu toujours sauve, au cas où Dieu le voudrait', and this was incontestable for some of the greatest saints, including Catherine of Siena and Ignatius Loyola. 'Truly humble souls', Knox adds, 'might consent to God's will, even if, on a wholly imaginary supposition, it were his good pleasure to keep them in eternal torment, without the loss of his grace and love.' Leverkühn's contention, in contrast, is avowedly proud and calculating, being more concerned with salvation than with love. It should not be confused with the delicate notions of people who really believe themselves damned and would rather not be.

Like all Mann's work, *Doktor Faustus* rests on nothing: there is no pact and nothing is at stake. To see the whole nature of the novel, however, it will be necessary to ignore this temporarily and pursue the progress of events with which it seems to be concerned. The stage is set as though in illustration of Leverkühn's proviso, that a completely despairing sinfulness, proudly persuaded of its own damnation, is the truly theological path to salvation. The outward events of his life, few as they are, are presented so as to suggest the extent of his sin, and so have the air of bearing out his argument. Like the events in Tonio Kröger's life, however, which equally seemed related to an argument concerning the position of the artist in society, they are delusive. First, before ever the pact with the devil is propounded, comes the incident based on accounts of the life of Nietzsche, where Leverkühn contracts syphilis from a prostitute. This is, perhaps, the beginning of the pact itself, for it is presented as a deliberate act, made by Leverkühn for the same purpose as the one mentioned in his discussion with the devil. In contracting the disease, he looks for that heightening of his creativity in artistic invention which it is supposed to bring: he physically brings about the intense ecstasies and despairs promised to him by his imagined devil. Or so at least Zeitblom is inclined to surmise at times. At other times he puts a different interpretation on his friend's actions. He suggests by remote allusions that it was not such a 'daring temptation of God', not a perverted form of self-aggrandizement, but an act of compassion. Leverkühn was not willing to live a healthy life while others were diseased, and took on himself this evil in order to experience it in his own person to the full. In Blake's lines from 'Silent, silent night', which Zeitblom quotes,

> . . . an honest joy
> Does itself destroy
> For a harlot coy.

With this motive, Leverkühn appears in a different light. But whether or not it was his motive is left obscure. The episode of his journey to meet the prostitute in a remote part of Austria is briefly related, and no more of it is said than that it happened. The rest is Zeitblom's speculation; Leverkühn's thoughts and emotions remain unknown except for the fact that motifs using the letters of the woman's name as musical notes recur throughout his work. Thus the apparently sinful act remains capable of being interpreted in two ways. It is no more possible to say that Leverkühn evilly contracts a disease for the furtherance of his own projects than it is to say that he contracts to serve and be served by the devil. The whole episode, on the face of it so vital for Leverkühn's proviso about extreme sinfulness, is allowed to remain in darkness.

The same is true of the other events of Leverkühn's outward life, after the pact has been propounded. It is, outwardly, a sheltered life, the life of a recluse. Shortly before his final collapse, however—that is, while he still remains sane—Leverkühn accuses himself before his friends of several monstrous sins. He has committed murder and incest, has brought about the death of his young nephew, and has indeed, as he foresaw in his speech with the devil, been so great a sinner that divine forgiveness must remain a perpetual impossibility. In these last words of his sane life, Leverkühn recalls the proviso, and thereby suggests the possibility, though he cannot for himself claim it, that he has in fact found the truly theological path to salvation. The paradox seems to have been driven to its utmost, and the man despairing of grace may yet come to grace despite the absurdity of his speculations. But again, it is only a matter of seeming. The murder of Rudi Schwerdtfeger of which Leverkühn accuses himself is not in fact committed by him, but by a woman, Ines Roddes. It is true that Leverkühn was at one time involved in an intricate love affair, in which Schwerdtfeger and Ines Roddes also played a part, and that he might have helped to bring about a situation in which her jealousy of Schwerdtfeger would not have led to this disastrous end. But his part in the murder is so extremely remote, if indeed it can be said to exist at all, that his self-accusation appears as the exaggeration of an over-scrupulous conscience. One is inclined to feel, because he accuses himself so violently, that he is really innocent. Of the second charge which he brings against himself, incest with his sister, nothing else is said in the novel; certainly it does not form an episode in the narration. What Leverkühn appears to have in mind is the mermaid in Hans Andersen's story, who has always had a strange fascination for him, and whom he confuses with his sister at this point in his confession. Thus once again the accusation looks like a scruple expanded to monstrous proportions by the onset of insanity. And the third charge is equally unrelated to the reality of the novel. Leverkühn's nephew has died at an early age from a horrifying attack of meningitis. This, Leverkühn believes, was a direct outcome of his pact with the devil, who had put venom in his eyes, so that when he gazed lovingly on the boy he unwittingly became the agent of the disease which destroyed him. At this point, no one is likely to feel that this is properly a confession of extreme sinfulness. On the contrary, one is moved rather by the horrifying self-torture of a diseased mind. Leverkühn, one feels, needs to believe himself guilty, whether he is so or not, in order that the very proviso he has made may be fulfilled. For only by fulfilling this proviso can he reach the 'truly theological path to salvation'. More and more strongly comes the feeling that this is a man who may believe himself extremely sinful, but who has in fact led a comparatively blameless life.

With this, of course, the paradox of Leverkühn's proviso is reduced to meaninglessness. If what was meant by sinfulness was not sinful deeds but a subjective conviction of having sinned, whether or not this bore any relation to facts, then no more was affirmed than that a man of blameless life who thought he had done wrong would be saved nevertheless. The paradox becomes a tautology. It did not, however, seem to be presented as one. It looked as though Leverkühn by his pact were being portrayed as a parallel to the evil-doing of the Nazis, as though in some way he were an explanation of what they had done. Later in the novel, the German people are in fact said to have entered on a pact with the devil, and it will be seen that yet further parallels are to be drawn between Leverkühn and them. In portraying Leverkühn, however, Mann has had recourse to his customarily ambiguous technique. A situation is outlined which might be described, though remotely, as evil. At the same time so little definition is provided that an entirely different interpretation is equally possible. This, in a story professedly dealing with diabolical matters, cannot be expected to sustain interest. Mann withdraws here as always from the definite statement, and as he veers away from perfect beauty in *Der Tod in Venedig*, so he veers away here from absolute evil.

Leverkühn's inward life, seen almost entirely through accounts of his music, is lived in terms of a similar ambiguity. It is, however, an ambiguity which does seem to lead, in his final work, to a single, unitive absolute, and to explore the way in which this comes about must be the preoccupation of the next few pages. Unfortunately, whatever may be said in words, these are after all verbal accounts of music, not the realization of music itself, as indeed they could not be unless the novel were issued with an accompanying album of gramophone records. It is taken for granted that the 'meaning' of music can be alternatively expressed in words, so that what is in fact received by the reader is Zeitblom's philosophical interpretation, not the mysterious communications of musical sound. As a result, there is once again not reality—not the reality of witnessing a composition through the ear—but the interpolation of the narrator's speculative point of view. The reader can no more hear for himself what Leverkühn's music was like than he can see the events of his life: both are screened first by Zeitblom. Granted, however, this mode of narration, what emerges from the music is what might be expected. In the oratorio *Apocalipsis*, for example, there seems to be confirmation of Leverkühn's own paradox. Believing (yet not believing) that the extreme, proud, unrepentant, yet contrite sinner is on the right path to salvation, he writes a work which contains both a diabolical chorus and a serene choir of angelic children. They are as different as could well be imagined: the first a 'sardonic gaudy of Gehenna', fifty bars of swelling laughter, screeching, howling and neighing, 'a salvo of the mocking and triumphant laughter of Hell'; the second a piece from the music of the spheres, 'icy, clear, glassily transparent, astringently dissonant, it is true, but full of what I might call a distant, strange, unearthly loveliness of sound, filling the heart with hopeless longing'. Yet Zeitblom notices with a fascinated horror that 'in musical substance' the two sections of the work are identical. The angelic chorus is in an entirely different rhythm, played by entirely different instruments, yet the notes of which it is composed are the same, and follow one another in the same order, as in the laughter of Hell. . . . It may seem strange to describe the mere sequence of notes as musical substance, without regard to rhythm, phrasing, instrumentation, dynamics. It is rather like speaking of two sentences as identical in substance because the words in them have exactly the same sounds. [The critic adds in a footnote: "As, for instance, in these lines by Aragon: Gal, amant de la reine, alla, tour magnanime, Galamment de l'arène à la Tour Magne, à Nimes."] One is more inclined to say that they are substantially different and only superficially alike. Moreover, the implication within the context of the novel, that here a unity in duality exists, suggests a certain contrivedness. However, Zeitblom affirms that for those who had ears to hear, this identity could not only be seen in the score but heard in the performance. Within the novel you can only take his word for it.

This 'substantial identity of the most blissful with the most hideous', this 'inward oneness of the choir of angelic children with the laughter of hell', is preliminary to the realization of Leverkühn's final work, the cantata, *Lament of Dr Faustus,* in which the combination of opposites 'becomes universal'. Here, in the cantata, Leverkühn takes over from the original 'Volksbuch' certain words of the dying Faust, and gives to them a melody, composed of all twelve notes of the chromatic scale and thus itself all-inclusive, which forms the basis of the whole composition. The words are 'For I die as a wicked and a good Christian', and thus themselves express a paradoxical combination. The melody, meanwhile, with its pervasiveness 'creates the identity of extreme multiplicity—that identity which operates between the crystalline angel-choir and the howls of hell in the *Apocalypse.* In this work, however, there is no such contrived identity as there is in the earlier one, if indeed an identity can be spoken of at all in either. On the contrary, it is from first to last a work of lament, a deliberate counterpart to Beethoven's Ode to Joy, and a determined refusal to accept the 'lie', that the world is a blessed creation of God. There is not, however, as might be expected, any hellish laughter on the part of Faust, any laughter which is mysteriously united in substance with the song of angels. On the contrary, there is only Faust's despair and lament over a world which does not fulfil the perfection due to its divine origin—and this is far from being a matter of diabolical concern. The terms of reference have, as in the *Joseph* novels, subtly shifted. Hellish delight at imperfection, and triumphant mockery over it, have become confused with Faust's desperate lament that the world is not perfect as it ought to be. Zeitblom, suggesting that the ambiguity of the *Apocalipsis* carries over into the cantata, makes it impossible to appreciate the later work adequately even through his ears, for his own abstract account contradicts the details as he narrates them. His own purpose, clearly enough, is to indicate the unity of opposites and persuade the reader of its existence in both works. Yet the cantata as he describes it is evidently of a different nature. Here the Leverkühn who perhaps took on the disease of the prostitute out of compassion, not the man who evilly contracted syphilis for its creative gifts, is in the foreground: the figure of Faust in the musical work represents this aspect of the composer. For Zeit-

blom, there is no clear distinction: it is all, vaguely, a pact with the devil, and thus equally vaguely identical with blessedness. In short, Zeitblom himself is inclined to accept the paradox of Leverkühn's proviso in the pact, and to persuade the reader of its value.

While the *Lament of Dr Faustus* thus contains no identity of opposites, it does end on a note which almost permits of hope. There is, Zeitblom says, to the very end no comfort, no reconciliation, no possibility of transfiguration. Nevertheless, in its very hopelessness, there is perhaps a budding hope, if only as the barest suggestion:

> Hört nur den Schluß, hört ihn mit mir: Eine Instrumentengruppe nach der anderen tritt zurück, und was übrig bleibt, womit das Werk verklingt, ist das hohe g eines Cello, das letzte Wort, der letzte verschwebende Laut, im pianissimo-Fermate langsam vergehend. Dann ist nichts mehr,—Schweigen und Nacht. Aber der nachschwingend im Schweigen hängende Ton, der nicht mehr ist, dem nur die Seele noch nachlauscht, und der Ausklang der Trauer war, ist es nicht mehr, wandelt den Sinn, steht als ein Licht in der Nacht.

> [Listen to the end, listen to it with me: one section of instruments after another withdraws, and all that remains, the last note of the work, is the top G of a 'cello, the final word, the last hovering sound, slowly dying away in a sustained pianissimo. Then there is no more—silence and night. But the note that hangs vibrating in the silence, the note that no longer exists, which only the soul goes on hearing, that echo of mourning mourns no more, changes its meaning, stands like a light in the darkness!]

Here there is not identity but change, not reconciliation but something like the mystery of tragedy. From hopelessness comes hope: there is no similarity between the two, though the one could not be known without the other. The idea of a substantial identity is clearly impossible, yet Zeitblom's account continues to speak as though Leverkühn's life and music were still under the sign of the paradox. Zeitblom cannot approve Leverkühn: his feeling towards him is ambivalently one of love and hatred, and he would have preferred, he says, not to hear the dreadful identity of hideousness and bliss. Yet he cannot deny the admiration he feels for a man greater than himself in his probing of heights and depths, nor can he rid himself, despite his own accounts of Leverkühn's *Lament,* of the feeling of a unity of the opposites. In his description of Leverkühn's physical appearance in his final years of sanity, he finds something Christlike. . . . Yet at the same time, he speaks of a habit of rolling the eyeballs in a frightening way, so that a suggestion of diabolical intensity lies not far off. In the light of the *Apocalypse* music, it is easy to suppose that here too some kind of identity is implied. And indeed the whole scene of Leverkühn's final speech, with its suggestion of a 'Pietà' at the end, seems bent on bringing the reader to feel that here is an extreme sinner who is at one and the same moment a saint. The paradox of von Aschenbach, 'iniquitous yet holy', is repeated once more. Leverkühn accuses himself of murder and incest, charges in which Zeitblom apparently believes; he affirms that it was the desire for fame (not compassion with human suffering, which for his part he does not mention) that drove him to make his pact; he makes no repentance, but claims that the spirit of his times compelled him to lead the life he has led, and dies with just such a cry of lament as that which ends the Faust-cantata. Yet by the terms of his proviso, this very pride in the magnitude of his sin—he despises and envies moderate sinners, ordinary men—is the prerequisite of salvation. By his obduracy in proud contrition, if his proviso means anything at all, he does nevertheless ensure his place among the saints. And Zeitblom does what he can to suggest that the paradox does emerge triumphant.

There remain, within the novel, the last links to be forged with the history of Germany in Leverkühn's era. This has already been prepared in the documentation of his earlier life, and in the chronological sequence of dates. Born in 1885, Leverkühn enters on his pact towards the end of the Wilhelmine Empire, eight years before the outbreak of the First World War. He becomes insane in 1930, the year in which the strength of the Nazi party first showed itself in the elections. He dies in 1940, on 25 August, when the Nazi conquest of western Europe was complete. Throughout the novel, Zeitblom has interspersed reports of what has happened in Germany since that time, of the mounting pressure that is bringing her to her knees, and at length, writing in 1944 after the landings in Normandy, he looks back in a final paragraph to the situation at the time of Leverkühn's death:

> Deutschland, die Wangen hektisch gerötet, taumelte dazumal auf der Höhe wüster Triumphe, im Begriffe, die Welt zu gewinnen kraft des einen Vertrages, den es zu halten gesonnen war, und den es mit seinem Blute gezeichnet hatte. Heute stürzt es, von Dämonen umschlungen, über einem Auge die Hand und mit dem andern ins Grauen starrend, hinab von Verzweiflung zu Verzweiflung. Wann wird es des Schlundes Grund erreichen? Wann wird aus letzter Hoffnungslosigkeit, ein Wunder, das über den Glauben geht, das Licht der Hoffnung tagen? Ein einsamer Mann faltet seine Hände und spricht: Gott sei euerer armen Seele gnädig, mein Freund, mein Vaterland.

> [Germany, its cheeks in a hectic flush, was swashbuckling at that time at the height of its savage triumphs, on the point of conquering the world by virtue of the one pact that it was minded to keep, and which it had signed with its blood. Today it plunges down, surrounded by demons and with a hand over one eye as it stares with the other into shuddering horror, down from despair to despair. When will it reach the bottom of the abyss? When will there dawn, from this utter hopelessness, a miracle transcending faith, the light of hope? A lonely man joins his hands together and says: God be merciful to your poor soul, my friend, my Fatherland.]

The phrasing here is identical in places with that used by Zeitblom in writing of the conclusion of Leverkühn's *Lament*. He had spoken there of a hope beyond hopelessness, a miracle transcending faith, expressed through or beyond

the last note of the 'cello, and he now allows his own story, the novel *Doktor Faustus,* to end in the same way. The parallelism is maintained to the end, as if to imply that the pact made by Leverkühn were aligned with that made by Germany—and at the same time to imply that both pacts might end in a miraculous new uprising, that both were the truly theological path to salvation.

The implications of this are absurd or horrible. If they are not taken as meant, the parallelism in the novel can only be regarded as fortuitious: the two 'pacts' are then not to be seen as related at all, and there was no particular point in referring to them both by the same name. Yet if they are taken seriously, with Germany cast in the role of Faust, as everything in the novel seems to imply, a vast national perversion tends to be seen as an ambiguous saintliness. (pp. 208-23)

The confusion of *Doktor Faustus* derives from the fact that Zeitblom operates always with a dual conception of Leverkühn. There is the man who makes no pact, who consorts with the prostitute out of compassion, and who falsely accuses himself of monstrous crimes; and there is the man who somehow does make a pact, who contracts syphilis in order to achieve fame, and commits murder and incest. Neither of these comes to life in described action, both remain possibilities on which Zeitblom can speculate. Equally, he operates with a dual conception of morality. He condemns evil in the strongest terms, espe-

---

Mann on his method of narration in *Doctor Faustus:*

On May 23, 1943, . . . I began writing *Doctor Faustus.* My diary of the period does not record exactly when I made the decision to interpose the medium of the "friend" between myself and my subject; in other words, not to tell the life of Adrian Leverkühn directly but to have it told, and therefore not to write a novel but a biography with all its trappings. Assuredly, recollection of the sham autobiography of Felix Krull influenced me here. Besides, this strategy was a bitter necessity in order to achieve a certain humorous leaving of the somber material and to make its horrors bearable to myself as well as to the reader. To make the demonic strain pass through an undemonic medium, to entrust a harmless and simple soul, well meaning and timid, with the recital of the story, was in itself a comic idea. It removed some of the burden, for it enabled me to escape the turbulence of everything direct, personal, and confessional which underlay the baneful conception, to steer it into indirection and to travesty it as I depicted it through the eyes of this good, unheroic soul, who could only wring his hands and shake his head at these events.

But, above all, the interposition of the narrator made it possible to tell the story on a dual plane of time, to weave together the events which shake the writer as he writes with those he is recounting, so that the quivering of his hand is ambiguously and yet obviously explained both by the vibration of distant bomb hits and by his inner consternation.

Thomas Mann, in his The Story of a Novel: The Genesis of Doctor Faustus, *1961.*

cially the evil committed by Nazi Germany; at other times he suggests, as Mann himself was always prone to do, that evil and good are indistinguishable, or that the one is the proper path to pursue in order to attain the other. To use his own words: 'Belief in absolute values, illusory though it be, seems to me a condition of life.' He feels it necessary to condemn evil as though holding by an absolute distinction between it and good, but he feels at the same time that such a distinction is mere illusion from the standpoint of a Whole which is committed to neither good nor evil. In this way it comes about that a book which seems to be written in condemnation of a whole tradition—the tradition in which Mann stood, and which is here interpreted as leading to disaster—can also be read as providing a seeming justification for the same tradition. A more oppressive conclusion, for Germans and non-Germans alike, to a work by so prominent and as some have thought so representative a figure, can scarcely be imagined. (p. 223)

> Ronald Gray, "Dr. Faustus," in his The German Tradition in Literature, 1871-1945, Cambridge at the University Press, 1965, pp. 208-23.

John Peterson   (essay date 1966)

[*In the following excerpt, Peterson examines how theological themes contribute to the unity of* Doctor Faustus *and enhance its "artist-in-exile" motif.*]

> Wherefore doth a living man complain,
> A man for the punishment of his sins?
> Let us search and try our ways,
> And turn again to the Lord. . . .
> We have transgressed and have rebelled·
> Thou hast not pardoned.
> Thou hast covered with anger
> And persecuted us:
> Thou hast slain, thou hast not pitied. . . .
> Thou hast made us as the offscouring
> And refuse in the midst of the people.

The choral fugue above [from *Doctor Faustus*] is composed of the words of Jeremiah who is a personification of the prophet in exile—a prophet who was forced to tell his people about the fall of their nation. Throughout the recorded history of mankind there have been men capable of isolating themselves from the contemporary world to look objectively at society. Different men have been able to do this in different ways, but the role which they take may still be systematized as the "artist in exile." It is in line with this motif that one of the most gifted novelists of the twentieth century must be seen, Thomas Mann.

Mann experienced a conflict within his own life and saw this dissension existing between the political and social orders of the twentieth century. He became an exile from Germany because of his hatred of the Hitler regime and therefore, as an artist, Mann does not always give an objective account of his times, but, instead, presents the problem of the age as he experienced it. He is an artist who constructs consciously by adding detail to detail until the edifice of a unity and a whole is achieved.

Mann's political exile from Germany during the War represents an artist objectively trying to view the terror of Na-

zism. This exile, although represented even in his earlier works, can be seen explicitly in *Doctor Faustus;* as [Henry] Hatfield maintains, the novel "undertook his most onerous task: to represent in symbolic form the decline and eventual ruin of Germany" [*Thomas Mann: An Introduction to His Fiction*]. (pp. 492-93)

It must never be forgotten that Mann represents his own land of Germany, so that the tragic Faust motif must be seen in affinity with his own nation. Here the Faustus theme takes on an entirely new point of view from the medieval theme of a man selling his soul outright to the devil. Instead of with Satan, Adrian Leverkühn fights his battle with venereal disease which ultimately in the fourth stage takes his life. Still, the novel must be seen from a greater perspective than just the life of Adrian Leverkühn; but the guilt which Germany and ultimately the world has manifested upon her people and the world. The lamentation of Mann is clearly expressed by the horror of Serenus Zeitblom

> Our unhappy nation, undetermined by fear and dread, incapable of understanding, in dazed fatalism lets them pass over its head, and my spirit too, worn with old sorrow, weary with old wrong, is helplessly exposed to them as well.

As can be seen here "no colours could seem too black to represent the moral, political, and cultural catastrophe" which Mann so clearly explicates.

Doctor Faustus: The Life of the German Composer Adrian Leverkühn as told by a Friend—so reads the title of the novel under consideration. The life is revealed of a specific individual who is a musician; therefore the other characters must be seen as an outgrowth of that certain musical motif. Indeed, to discuss *Doctor Faustus* means in more than one respect to discuss the return to the past; but above all Thomas Mann's own life as it is

> recalled by this life of a composer in whom genius and the passion to create are yet threatened with sterility, possessed as he is of the knowledge that the tradition of his medium is so utterly exhausted that to work within it would condemn the artist to banality, and to 'break through' require sacrifices and ingenuities not thought of in Heaven. [Erich Heller, *The Ironic German: A Study of Thomas Mann*]

Mann's love for music is also expressed in other novels—particularly *Buddenbrooks*—but not so intensively and extensively as in *Doctor Faustus.* Besieged as he is "by the belief that music is the realm of danger and death, perhaps even of the diabolic, Mann naturally makes his Faustus a musician." The musical theme which Mann develops throughout the entire novel, represents a more complex composition than he had ever before attempted, one that was to render both ideas and words of music in music. Hatfield points out that this might have been an "impossible task, and one is reminded of the metaphor of the deep-sea diver who ventures more and more boldly until the final descent from which he does not return." We are first introduced to Adrian's early musical training by Zeitblom when he describes Hanne of Buchel, a stable-girl who ran with "bare feet caked with dung":

When we sang with her, she accompanied us in thirds, and from there went down to the lower fifth and lower sixth and left us in the treble, while she ostentatiously and predominantly sang the second. And probably to fix our attention and make us properly value the harmonic enjoyment, she used to stretch her mouth and laugh just like Suso the dog when we brought her her food.

From this point Mann develops more fully the compositions which are both real and imaginary. Through the use of the musical motif, the artist contrives the theme of Doctor Serenus Zeitblom, a "somewhat pedantic teacher and bourgeois humanist living in retirement forced upon him by the Hitler régime, relates in the form of a chronicle the story of the tragic career of Adrian Leverkühn" [J. G. Robertson, *A History of German Literature*]. Into the different strands of music, Mann has woven his own life and work:

> his comprehension of Nietzsche, the growth of modern music, the collapse of Germany, the Bürger and society, the relation of genius and disease, only to name a few. [Robertson]

One must then turn to the theological motifs to see the way in which Mann was influenced by the decay of society.

The four predominant theological themes found in *Doctor Faustus* are instrumental in the development of the theme "artist in exile"—the artist fighting the cultural crisis of Fascism. These four themes (devil, *Apocalypse,* Old Testament, and mythology) play an important role in the understanding of the unity which is achieved throughout the novel. To maintain, however, that Mann was an expert in these four themes along with all of the other motifs used would be an ungrounded fallacy. This is not to distract from the artist's understanding of these different ideas, for Mann read widely and formed notations from the material covered. In *The Story of a Novel* there are endless citations where Mann drew his material—

> Read an excellent article in the *Nation,* a piece by Henry James on Dickens . . . Extensive reading in Niebuhr's book, *The Nature and Destiny of Man . . .* In the evening read *Love's Labour's Lost . . .* Meetings with Schönberg and Stravinsky planned.

Mann was not a scholar, but adapted his material to the portrait he was painting. The tempera which each individual strand added to the characters, can only be seen in respect to the development of the larger whole: the artist in exile motif. Mann gradually saw his role as an artist for the whole of mankind. Although in the *Joseph* tetralogy, the correlation between the religious and exile theme can be seen more easily, the strands presented in *Doctor Faustus* render an understanding to the nature of exile in Adrian Leverkühn. One brief example of this can be developed in the phrase "Watch with me!"

> 'Watch with me!' In his cantata Adrian might if he chose transform that cry of human and divine agony into the masculine pride and self-confidence of his Faust's 'Sleep quietly and fear

nothing!' But the human remains, after all: the instinctive longing, if not for aid, then certainly for the presence of human sympathy, the plea: 'Forsake me not! Be about me at my hour!'

It is here that the four theological themes to be discussed are laid out for us and therefore must be seen in their proper perspective. The cry which was uttered by Jesus Christ was also uttered by the Psalmist of the Old Testament and the correlation carries a greater symbolic meaning when it becomes the final plea of Adrian.

The first theological theme confronted in the novel is that of the devil and the pact which Adrian makes with him. For Mann, Adrian attempts to become human and everytime he tries his payment becomes defeat and suffering. The pact with the devil could only represent "life and experience . . . divorcing them from their common meaning and lending them an aura of horror, which nobody understands who has not learned them in that awful context." The author's use of the devil pact [according to Hatfield] "tells him that future generations will draw health from the products of his illness; and Mann's Devil, it is emphasized, is no liar." Therefore, the decision which Adrian makes appears to be a valiant one as he is sacrificing himself "for the sake of the future, and one can almost speak of vicarious atonement." The devil permeates the entire novel and [Erich] Kahler maintains that "Adrian's Faustian character is constitutional. The demon resides *within him* from the start, in his migraine, in his enormous intelligence which rapidly assimilates all that can be known" ["The Devil Secularized: Thomas Mann's Faust" in *Thomas Mann: A Collection of Critical Essays,* ed. Henry Hatfield]. The demon is continually seen in everything which Adrian comes in contact, and all deviation which he sought turns against him, this resulting in an abyss in his life.

The relationship of the devil's pact and society cannot be limited solely to Adrian, however, because all of mankind is to be seen represented in this setting. The failure to become human is one of the ultimate meanings of the devil's pact. This becomes one of the initial implications to be drawn from the beginning of the novel as Zeitblom explains this failure when describing the coldness on the part of Adrian. Both Serenus and Adrian had grown up together and yet this feeling of coldness is related when Serenus said " . . . I loved him, with tenderness and terror, with compassion and devoted admiration, and but little questioned whether he in the least returned my feeling. That he never did—ah no!" Coldness was also experienced by Adrian because he had loved Maria, but because of the pact, the love resulted ultimately in death. What happened to Adrian embraces not just the fate of modern art and the intellect, but it also portrays the tragedy of Germany "that is enacted in the background, the transgression of the German character, of which Adrian partakes; it comprises the general crisis of our world" [Kahler]. It is then in the musical motif that the theme of the devil's pact must be seen as the theme and variation through the counterpoint continually lets the readers see a broader meaning to the pact: a meaning which is not isolated to a fictitious character by the name of Adrian Leverkühn, but to everyman. Therefore, the cry "Watch with me" takes on a meaning which originally was beyond comprehension of the novel and the lament of Adrian is one of sacrifice for the future. Consequently, specific motifs of the devil must be seen in the relationship to the novel.

The pact follows Mann's rigid plan of showing the internal decay of the German nation which finally resulted in eventual ruin. The tragedy which rose in Germany as the result of Nazism caused the author to refer to the catastrophe of German history as

> such musicality of the soul is dearly bought in another sphere [in contrast to music]—the political, the sphere of human living together. In the baneful light of the Third Reich's descent into hell, Faust's pact with the devil becomes, for the speaker, a metaphor of the real meaning of German history. [Hans Egon Holthusen, "The World without Transcendence," in *Thomas Mann: A Collection of Critical Essays*]

For Mann, the devil was literally taking the soul out of Germany; Adrian was not the only one who had sold his soul.

As the novel progressed so did the war and Mann became more aware of the inhumanity to man which was taking place and the conversations with the devil became more probable as the pictures of hell become more real. Chapter XXVI was written [according to Mann] during a period in which the temporal power was continually changing so "that the downfall of Germany is counterpointed by the catastrophe that draws ever and more balefully closer."

> Leipzig, which played so significant a part in Leverkühn's development and tragedy, has lately been struck with might and main; its famous publishing quarter is, I hear, a heap of rubble, with immeasureable destruction of educational and literary property: a very heavy loss not only for us Germans but altogether for the world which makes culture its concern, but which in blindness or in even-handedness, I will not venture to say which, appears to pocket up the loss.

These chapters blend tragedy and grotesqueness which attempt to point to the final stages of society because of the decay taking place. Mann even sees at the surrender of the Second World War that in reality nothing really ended: "rather, an inexorable process of social, economic, and cultural change, which had begun throughout the world a generation before, rolled on without any actual interruption, pregnant as ever with fantastic possibilities" [Mann].

The eventual ruination which Mann felt so keenly is evident in *The Story of a Novel* as well as in his numerous articles and personal communication. The contrivance of *Doctor Faustus* represents a step in Thomas Mann's life which far supersedes his original ideas on the decay of a country. One finds, for example, in *Buddenbrooks* an artist who is basically concerned with the fall of a Hanseatic family and Mann even portrays ironically how the people cling to the old; however in *Doctor Faustus,* as well as in his memoirs, the devil takes on a role of complete seriousness. The devil's pact then gives one an insight into the literary artist and the strands which Mann used from Schopenhauer and Nietzsche further the understanding of the

demonic. The style and attitude of the artist does not create ambiguities, but only "perspectives which endlessly cross and intersect one another" [Bernhard Blume, "Aspects of Contradiction: On Recent Criticisms of Thomas Mann," in *Thomas Mann: A Collection* of *Critical Essays*]. Here then, a part of Nietzsche's formula can be seen which Mann paid the price:

> To be an artist, man pays the price of experiencing the element which all nonartists call 'form' as *content* as 'the thing itself'!. . . . Thus, to be sure, one becomes part of an *inverted world,* for content becomes something merely formal—and this includes one's own life' [Blume].

The slow process in which this decay takes place is symbolic of the slow death of Adrian. One is immediately made aware of the biological stages encountered in syphilis, and the long process of decay which takes place before the ultimate death. Adrian, himself sees the disease as a private rebelliousness which finally rots away the stomach, kidney, heart and ultimately the brain.

> Disease, indeed I mean repulsive, individual, private disease, makes a certain critical contrast to the world, to life's mean, puts a man in a mood rebellious and ironic against the bourgeois order, makes its man take refuge with the free spirit, with books, in cogitation. . . . He rots away, liver, kidneys, stomach, heart, bowels; some day his voice will be a croak, or he will be deaf, after a few years he will ingloriously shuffle off this coyle, with a cynical quip on his lips— what then? It forceth but little, there was never any illumination, enhancing or enthusiasm, for it was not of the brain, not cerebral, you understand—our little ones in that case made no force of the upper and noble, it had obviously no fascination for them, it did not come to a metastasis into the metaphysical, metavenereal, meta-infectivus.

The stages of syphilis are a unifying factor within the novel, as the disease of Adrian can be seen in respect to his decay and how he tried to overcome the pact which had been placed against him. The treaty which is made by the devil with Adrian, "Thou shalt not love" is in part superfluous for he had already fulfilled it. Actually he is not capable to love; "his purely formal existence in which everything becomes art makes this impossible. This is his guilt, tragic guilt if you will, for it is presupposed in his own being" [Blume].

Because of the autobiographical nature of the novel, it can also be assumed that this is the guilt which Mann felt in his very existence. He nearly experienced death while writing and during his recovery a different perspective was taken on the role of the novel: it was "like an open wound; it needed only to be touched, even with the most loving intent, and in my weakness I would be shaken with unpredictable force." It is during this time, however, that Mann raises questions about the very nature of suffering as can be exemplified when he asks: "Do there exist some vital depths in which, with all the senses shut off, one nevertheless suffers? Is suffering inseparable from enduring in the lowest depths?" Here is a motif which is necessary to be seen in *Doctor Faustus;* the unconscious suffering which man experiences and the correlation which can be drawn between the two lives. The suffering which Mann experienced, both physically and mentally has a direct relationship to Adrian. Firstly, the separation from Germany because he saw what was happening, and secondly, the decay of the people under Hitler. For an artist like Mann, to see a nation gradually decay because of an infection, could only result in his own political exile. On the other hand, Mann also suffered the physical pains—the physical pains of a weakening body, but also the suffering of not being accepted by his own people. Because of the exile, Mann and his works were isolated from his people, having created, in other words, a distance or coldness in life. Here then are the grounds on which Adrian and Mann must be compared.

The death of the idolized child, Echo, caused Mann to question the very ideals on which the culture of classical Germany had been built. Echo or Fridolin had a personal place in Mann's contrivance because he was one of his daughter's sons—a special child to Mann. (pp. 493-99)

In the early planning stages of the novel the author corresponded with Bruno Walter, in which correspondence, the idea was expressed to use Frido in the "musician novel" and Walter replied that he should play the episode of *allegretto moderato*. Mann goes on to point out

> this dear friend and splendid musician had no notion of the cold breath of inhumanity that blows through the book at the end. He could not know that I would be constrained to tell the story of the child of God in quite another spirit from that of *allegretto moderato*.

In the Echo chapter (XLIV), he is described as a frail little boy in all his elfin charm.

> But it always seemed as though one were looking at a fairy princeling. The graceful perfection of the small figure with the slender, shapely legs, the indescribable comeliness of the little head, long in shape, covered with an innocent tumble of light hair; the features despite their childishness with something finished and well-modelled about them; even the upward glance of the long-lashed clear blue eyes, ineffably pure and sweet, at once full of depth and sparkling with mischief—no, it was not even all these together that gave such an impression of faerie, of a guest from some finer, tinier sphere.

Mann took the character of Echo and transformed it into something no longer rational, but with characteristics divine so that people would interpret it as a far away reality. Echo took on the problems which were facing Germany and through the child's speech a memory was restored in the people of Middle High German or the German of Luther. As is pointed out in **The Story of a Novel** the evening prayers of the little child are adopted from Freidank's *Bescheidenheit* which are usually rephrased in the third and fourth verses

> Through sin no let has been,
> Save when some goode be seen.
> Mannes good deede shall serve him wel,
> Save that he were born for hell.

> O that I may and mine I love
> Be borne for blessedness above!

These lines are reflective of Mann's own thoughts and memories which were attached to him as a child. The child Echo was to be taken away from the man who was not able to love; the very nature of Echo's disease was to be seen in correlation to both Adrian's life and Germany. The isolation or coldness of Adrian was ultimately to be reflected in the child as Echo's fatal disease finally was to result in sorrow. The prayers went much beyond the theological speculation as Adrian sees that all of creation was included in his prayers "in order that he himself may be included." Adrian concludes that the "unselfishness is gone as soon as one sees that it is of use." The young life which had lasted only two weeks after the disease had set in, represents the demonic nature of Adrian; this (demonic nature) being seen since everything he touched or tried to love would end in death. In respect to the demonic there is a story which is told by Adrian to Echo which gives a clearer indication of the painful years which must be encountered which Echo could not really comprehend.

> And Adrian told him about the wicked witch Sycorax and her little slave, whom she, because he was a spirit too delicate to obey her earthy and abhorred commands, confined in a cloven pine, in which plight he spent a dozen painful years, until the good master of spells came and freed him. Nepomuk wanted to know how old the little spirit was when he was imprisoned and how old when he was freed, after twelve years. But his uncle said the spirit had no age, that he was the same after as before imprisonment, the same child of air—with which Echo seemed content.

This story carries a further impact into the novel as the correlation of the witch Sycorax and her slave can be seen in respect to the three parts of the counterpoint running throughout the novel: firstly, Adrian's confrontation with selling his soul to the devil; secondly, Germany's outright selling its soul to the slave Fascism, thirdly, the author's exile because of the slave which had caused the German people to be imprisoned since they did not fully understand. Here then the pact must be seen once again in respect to the "artist in exile" and the demonic themes which result.

Mann sees the pact with the devil as a curse for the "artist in exile" as everything that Adrian touches dies; and in the same light, he believes curse extends to him in writing the novel. As has been established, Adrian's touching of little Echo, the boy whom he wanted to love, caused death. The pact with the devil is not limited solely to this example as it can also be seen exemplified in the woman he wanted to love, Maria, and also in the eventual death of Rudy. Maria was the one with whom Adrian thought that he was in love, but he was incapable of winning her admiration. Zeitblom maintained that he (Zeitblom) "doubted that he (Adrian) believed it himself. I thought perhaps he struggled against the feeling and purposely so put it as though his success were a matter of course." Maria was described as a beautiful, friendly, and intellectual individual who could have done a great deal for Adrian Leverkühn as his life partner. Zeitblom makes an interesting correlation when he raises the questions

> Did not 'the world' come near to him in her, the world from which he shrank—and, in an artistic and musical sense, the part of the world which was outside Germany? . . . Did he not love her out of his own world of musical theology, oratorio, mathematical number—magic?

The love which Adrian tried to give Maria could not be, and as a result a further separation Adrian felt in society.

The curse which Mann felt being in political exile must be seen linked to the characters which he contrived in a technical manner as to express his own feelings. Consequently, the artist must face the technical problems and then art becomes a critique when every chord carries the whole story. This is another aspect which Mann sees in respect to the devil's pact: the involved forces acting upon the artist in exile. The artist as an agent is forced to contrive on a rigid device of technique as Beethoven faced in opus III—"the tension between consonance and the harshest dissonance known to him." Therefore, certain musical motifs must be seen in relationship to a specific musical contrivance, that being the *Apocalypsis cum figuris.*

It is here, in the Apocrypha, that one of the ironic elements of the novel must be seen. Basically, as has been established, the novel throughout is one of pessimism of an artist in exile. The *Apocalypsis,* which ultimately resulted from a study of the Apocrypha, points out the failings of people when they had strayed from the teachings they were to have followed; but when the prophetic message of doom was given, a sign of hope gave a revelation into the future. There are many examples of this in Biblical literature when the people of God saw Him as one to judge, yet, on the other hand, as One who would give hope to His people. This is the motif which Mann develops in **Doctor Faustus** and therefore after an understanding of the *Apocalypsis* a new interpretation of the novel must be seen as the ironic element has been added to the *Apocalypsis cum figuris.* Then the comment of Zeitblom about Adrian bears more meaning because of the *Apocalypsis.*

> Everywhere is Adrian Leverkühn great in making unlike the like. One knows his way of modifying rhythmically a fugal subject always in its first answer, in such a way that despite a strict preservation of its thematic essence it is as repetition no longer recognizable. So here—but nowhere else as here is the effective so profound, mysterious and great. Every word that turns into sound the idea of Beyond, of transformation in the mystical sense, and thus of change, transformation, transfiguration, is here exactly reproduced. . . . That is Adrian Leverkühn Utterly. That is the music he represents; and that correspondence is its profound significance, calculation raised to mystery.

Therefore the *Apocalypsis* must be seen as one of the correlating parts of the novel.

The musical themes in the novel play a significant role and the meanings which they portray cannot be isolated to the previous discussion because they go much beyond the original theme and variation and counterpoint. However, the themes of these musical motifs take on a different meaning only when the novel progresses and can be seen as a collective whole. As the character of Adrian is developed, the novel becomes more of an art piece and it is not until the subjective nature is completely removed from the novel that the work can become soulless. The understanding of the nature of Adrian, Mann and Germany is seen when total despair is felt by the characters and then it is out of this suffering that a hope can come for the future. It is here that the *Lamentation of Jeremiah* can be seen more clearly which will be discussed more fully in the next section of this paper.

The title of the oratorio, *Apocalypsis cum figuris,* was in homage to Dürer and "is intended to emphasize the visual and actualizing, the graphic character, the minuteness, the saturation, in short, of space with fantastically exact detail: the feature is common to both works." The words of the *Apocalypsis* were also inspired by the woodcuts of Dürer which underlie the tonal art, but Adrian broadened this concept by

> including also much from the Lamentations in the Psalter, for instance that piercing 'For my soul is full of troubles and my life draweth nigh unto the grave,' as also the expressive denunciations and images of terror from the Apocrypha; then certain fragments from the Lamentations of Jeremiah, today unspeakable offensive in their effect; and even remoter matter still, all of which must contribute to produce the general impression of a view opening into the other world and the final reckoning breaking in; of a journey into hell wherein are worked through the visional representations of the hereafter, in the earlier, shamanistic stages, as well as those developed from antiquity and Christianity, down to Dante.

By seeing this broader outlook into the *Apocalypsis* the prophetic tradition of the Revelation of Saint John must be seen as apocalyptic literature as a whole and of not one specific work. It is here that the nature of the apocrypha can be seen as the ultimate which resulted from the message which was spoken by prophetic men; a message of hope shining in the darkness. This can be correlated with the apocalyptic chapters of **Doctor Faustus** which are a "blend of tragedy and grotesquerie, attempt to paint the final stage of a society, when it lies open to ridicule, totally at the mercy of intellectuals' picayune conspiracies" [Mann].

It is significant that Mann used the musical theme of the Apocrypha to develop the motif of the inner despair that prepares the pact with the devil and the realm of suffering. This oratorio cannot be seen isolated from the rest of the novel as the artistic quality of the *Apocalypsis* makes the painting closer to a unified whole—a whole which represents Adrian, Germany and Mann. For this reason, the Apocalyptic is consistent with the other themes developed. The anguish seen in respect to the demonic conceptions in the *Apocalypsis* is contrived through the use of music. Music becomes a reality and is not an idea. For Leverkühn, it is almost the definition of God. Adrian is driven to the peak of his musical genius by the devil "who has stolen into his entelechy via a syphilitic infection. Music, which Mann expressly praised in the **Reflections,** using Luther's words, as a 'gift of God,' has been stealthily transformed to a gift of the devil" [Holthusen]. Music, therefore, is in

> league with the Evil One . . . of which Luther said that 'Satan was very hostile' to it; music, to which men have always ascribed the power to calm, make blissful, bear them upward; music, which the most ancient wisdom and mythology of mankind has quite decidedly associated with the spirit of joy, with piety and love, with the 'harmony of the spheres,' with the cosmogonic Eros. [Holthusen]

In contrast with the devil, the *Apocalypsis* must be seen beyond the technical aspects of music as theme and variation take over the leading role. The repetitive theme of the ultimate ruination of man, as he sinks further into the abyss of bliss, was overcome by the restoration which the apocalypsis makes in the novel. The use of the images of terror fixes a "firm tonality [which is] reserved for the world of hell, in this context a world of banality and commonplace." Here some of the current religious and political thoughts which influenced the music must be recognized in order that the self-expression of the *Apocalypsis* might be viewed with the subjective element of suffering and despair eliminated from the novel.

Mann knew the religious and political problems which the people were facing and was sure that the devil was the "sole custodian of the theological side of existence" [Heller]. In the **Story of a Novel** Mann makes reference that he had just finished chapter twenty-seven with "Adrian's voyage into the depths of the ocean and 'up among the stars' . . . when news came of 'the first attack on Japan with bombs in which the forces of the fissioned uranium atom are released.'" As previously pointed out, Mann maintains that with the ending of the Second World War nothing had really ended and that the social and cultural changes which had begun a generation before were only continuing at a faster pace. This is reflected in the *Apocalypsis* and ultimately in the theological side of existence. With the final cry of the novel "God be merciful to thy poor soul, my friend, my Fatherland!" a partial interpretation of Mann's understanding of the conclusion of the Second World War can be seen—this cry also reflecting an idea which did not stop with the signing of a specific peace treaty. With Thomas Mann's **Doctor Faustus** one has entered a world which "craves again for theological rigour; but alas, the only true *religiosus* to be found in Leverkühn's world is Satan" [Heller]. Adrian himself maintains that the man who "succeeded in the breakthrough from intellectual coldness into a touch-and-go world of new feeling, him one should call the saviour of art." It is this breakthrough with the Devil that the accomplishments of Leverkühn's later music like the *Apocalypsis* is to be seen. The political banishment which the people were experiencing represents a nation in exile with a disease which gradually saps the country to death. The role of the devil in **Doctor Faustus** then becomes the only humane creature because it is through the devil that a faint

hope remains for the man and nation which had fallen into an abyss.

The *Apocalypsis* is still a "self-expression," as it is the composer's defiance of the devil's demand of decay; but it is through hope in the apocryphic struggle, that the ultimate expression of Adrian must be realized. This, however, can only be done at the end of the novel when all of the subjective elements have been removed and the artistic nature is seen coming out of despair. It is only out of suffering that such a hope can come. Adrian, a man who sought to know too much, has come to full knowledge before this aspect of the *Apocalypsis* can bear any other meaning for him. The ultimate sorrow of the final despair is a self-expression which is spoken to Faust in the last hour and it is here that the *Apocalypsis cum figuris* must be correlated with Adrian's final piece, *The Lament of Doctor Faustus.* Zeitblom describes the Faust cantata as

> stylistically so strongly and unmistakably linked with the seventeenth century and Monteverdi, whose music—again not without significance—favoured the echo-effect, sometimes to the point of being a mannerism. The echo, the giving back of the human voice as nature-sound, and the revelation of it *as* nature-sound, is essentially a lament: Nature's melancholy 'Alas!' in view of man, her effort to utter his solitary state. . . . In Leverkühn's last and loftiest creation, echo, favourite device of the baroque, is employed with unspeakably mournful effect. A lament of such gigantic dimensions is, I say, of necessity an expressive work, a work of expression, and therewith it is a work of liberation; just as the earlier music, to which it links itself across the centuries, sought to be a liberation of expression.

This liberation of the spirit must first be apprehended as Faust's descent into hell and an overwhelming outburst of lamentation "after an orgy of infernal jollity."

A significant clue to the understanding of the meaning of the *Apocalypsis* comes when the distinction is made between that cantata and the *Faust*. The *Faust* is an expression of the statement " 'Thus it is.' But sometimes, like the awful ballet-music of the descent to hell, they also stand for parts of the plot." The orchestral cantata goes into the chorus of lament at the end and it is gradually passed over only to the reverse of joy. It is here that Mann has given an entirely different outlook to the novel and the phrase of Christ "Watch with me" now both assume a deliberate reversal in meaning. The fullness of the novel must be seen in relationship to the question of craftsmanship and the ironic nature of hope which the Apocrypha brings to the novel. This can only be contrived by Mann after all of the subjective has been taken from Adrian as hope can then come from despair.

> In the cantata he is clearly drawn in the character of a tempter; and the tempting of Jesus by Satan is unmistakably suggested; as unmistakably also is the 'Apage!' by the proudly despairing 'No!' uttered to false and flabby middleclass piety. . . . At the end of this work of endless lamentation, softly, above the reason and with the speaking unspokenness given to music alone, it touches the feelings. I mean the closing move-

ments of the piece, where the choir loses itself and which sounds like the lament of God over the lost state of His world, like the Creator's rueful 'I have not willed it.' Here toward the end, I find that the uttermost accents of mourning are reached, the final despair achieves a voice, and—I will not say it, it would mean to disparage the uncompromising character of the work, its irremediable anguish to say that it affords, down to its very last note, any other consolation than what lies in voicing it, in simply giving sorrow words; in the fact, that is, that a voice is given the creature for its woe. . . . It would be but a hope beyond hopelessness, the transcendence of despair—not betrayal to her, but the miracle that passes belief. For listen to the end, listen with me: one group of instruments after another retires, and what remains, as the work fades on the air, is the high G of a cello, the last word, the last fainting sound, slowly dying in a pianissimo fermata. Then nothing more: silence, and night. But the tone which vibrates in the silence, which is no longer there, to which only the spirit hearkens, and which was the voice of mourning, is so no more. It changes its meaning; it abides as a light in the night.

Here the artistic paradox constructs the agony which is expressed in respect to the religious paradox of hope. This is a self-expression which Mann ultimately saw for Germany, but still in a more comprehensive sense for all of mankind, as it is here that the counterpoint becomes a unified whole—"as the work fades on the air, is the high G of a cello, the last word. . . ."

The role of the Old Testament themes in *Doctor Faustus* also reflects the exile of the artist and his land. The theme running throughout the Old Testament is that of a people who believed they were the children of God and how they (the children) interpreted God at work through them in history. This is a consistent theme starting with the Exodus event as they fled under the "outstretched" arm of Moses to the Promised Land. Throughout the Old Testament, this one theme is repeated as the people look back upon Moses and how he led the people out of bondage. Even when the people were suffering the persecutions of the exile (an exile which was a result because they believed they had fallen away from the teachings of Moses) they looked back upon their history for a prophet who would come to give them some hope for their future; the future being a time when they would be able to return home.

Mann was just as familiar with the Old Testament as he was with the Apocrypha; and, therefore, a correlation can be made between the artist and his nation in respect to both the Old Testament and Germany. It is interesting to note that Mann used the *Lament of Jeremiah* in his apocalyptic work and that this lament might go much beyond the cantata, but into his own personal life. When the Lord came to Jeremiah, Jeremiah replied that he was but a youth and pleaded to God not to send him as he did not feel qualified because he was too young.

> I appointed you a prophet to the nations.
> Then I said, 'Ah, Lord God! Behold, I do not know how to speak, for I am only a youth.' But the Lord said to me,

> 'Do not say, 'I am only a youth'
> for to all to whom I send you you shall go,
> and whatever I command you you shall speak.
> Be not afraid of them,
> for I am with you to deliver you, says the Lord.

> Jeremiah 1:5c-8. R.S.V.

A distinct correlation can be drawn between Mann and Jeremiah as they both felt a deep concern for their native land. The artist Mann, loved his country and was driven to a sense of shame for what his country had done to the Jews. Mann felt he was commanded to speak like Jeremiah as he saw his home, Germany, in the same situation that had confronted Judah. The judgement must come, and for Mann, *Doctor Faustus* could only be told through a devil's pact which had been made by him. Men, during the time of Jeremiah could not see that their nation had fallen away and what the ultimate consequences would be. Mann too must have also felt the same when he went into exile and eventually took upon himself the painful task of writing a novel. Therefore, one's attention must turn to what Mann says about the exile and then correlate the "harsh choral fugue to the words of Jeremiah" remembering, there are many other Old Testament motifs which could also be discussed.

Mann maintains that "exile creates a special form of life, and the various reasons for banishment or flight make little difference." He realized because of his exile that he would have "to provide a convincing, precisely realistic description, one of utter verisimilitude, of Leverkühn's apocalyptic oratorio" to show the unhealthy complex of the time. In the novel he expresses the time in which he writes as one of "national collapse, of capitulation, of uprisings due to exhaustion, of helpless surrender into the hands of strangers," and that Germany can be compared to the swollen body which is carried in silence and solitude as Germany has become a "theatre of war" because of the unboundless hatred of the people. With this statement of self-judgement in mind the fugue motif of Jeremiah can be examined. The personal, self-examination is one way in which man can suffer for the wrong which he has committed,

We have transgressed and have rebelled.

The Lamentation of Jeremiah and Mann's Germany must be seen concerning the whole which was revealed, instead of the isolated parts. The clear development of the whole cannot be seen; it is "loosened and in a way reduced *ad absurdum,* to which the artist seems to submit himself." The banishment from life must be in order that the artist is able to view objectively the painfully close cultural movements of the time. Zeitblom maintains to do this it gives him

> needed reassurance, still needed even as it was at time when I was present with horror, amazement, consternation, and pride, at its birth—an experience that I suppose was due to my loving devotion to its author but actually went beyond my mental capacities, so that I trembled and was carried away.

Not enough emphasis can be laid on this correlation between the fugue of Jeremiah and the personal expression of Mann which gradually develops into a much broader sphere by including all of mankind. The scene which Mann saw represents doom and destruction to his nation and this becomes a poignant experience when one is able to see the syphilitic disease take hold on the people.

The exile of the Old Testament can then be correlated to the Apocrypha and particularly to the *Apocalypsis* which represents the final doom upon the nations exiling the Hebrew people. The collapse for the Hebrew people was inevitable and no one had the least doubt that the nation would fall. As the "inevitable" became clearer, it turned into sheer horror as everyone was bound to silence but still the truth could be seen easily. It is interesting to note the references made to the foreign nations in *Doctor Faustus* and how these countries affected the condition of Germany as comparable to the Old Testament themes. For example, the invasion of France was inevitable because of the invention of the bomb, and the threat Russia created only added to the boundless hatred developed by the people. The ultimate was defeat for the nation but

> the defeated must continue somehow to be responsible for themselves; outside leading-strings are there only for the purpose of preventing the Revolution which fills the vacuum after the departure of the old authority from going to extremes and endangering the bourgeois order of things for the victors.

It is here that the Old Testament exile is significant in its development as the defeated nation; since a nation that appears to be without hope must be responsible for themselves. The hope which Jeremiah gives after the judgement prophecy is the same hope of freedom which is expressed by Mann over and against what "those evil men willed"—the hope that Germany will be free "in so far as one may apply the word to a land prostrate and proscribed." The optimism which Mann saw for Germany was not any brighter than Jeremiah's when he cried to his people—"God be merciful."

The contemporary political conditions raised questions about the authority of the Scriptures and the very existence of God. Early in the novel Mann confronts the reader with the decision Adrian is forced to make—whether or not he will continue his education at Halle or will go into music. It is here that an astute criticism of the church is given, because of the hatred which had engulfed it. Zeitblom presents the problems which the Protestant Church was facing and pointed out that they were the same which the Roman Church had encountered. Inside Protestantism there was a "revolution of pious feelings and inner heavenly joy against a petrified orthodoxy from which not even a beggar would any longer want to accept a piece of bread." The church had fallen into a state of indifference and religion was dying; therefore people questioned the value of religion. Zeitblom saw the problem the church was facing in respect to all of the different philosophical theses which tried to explain the existence of God. The ideas of pietism "by virtue of its overemotional nature, would indeed make a sharp division between piety and science, and assert that no movement, no change in the scientific picture, can have any influence on faith." On the other

hand, orthodoxy had let reason into the field of religion, and orthodoxy then sought to prove its position by the use of reason. A compromising position was maintained "that the history and teaching of the Church were in its eyes only a comedy of errors." Without going into further detail, it must be maintained that the dilemma came as a result of reason versing religion and that this was the result of the scientific and political advancements of the day. Mann's criticism ultimately revealed that the people had been blinded by Nazism and could not clearly see any other ethical or religious standard. Mann, through the narration of Zeitblom, makes it clear that the exile was the result of a people blind to the government taking over the power of the state. The church and state had lost the insight into the human needs of man and had covered up a problem of good will with hate. The absence of God from society created the despair which was felt by Jeremiah and also by Mann in the painstaking task of isolation which confronted both of them. The dying of the ideals of mankind caused a total decay of the state which would gradually place both of them in exile. It is in this respect that the Old Testament must be seen in *Doctor Faustus* and to remember the words from the *Lament of Jeremiah* are far from idle.

> Wherefore doth a living man complain,
> A man for the punishment of his sins?
> Let us search and try our ways,
> And turn again to the Lord. . . .
> We have transgressed and have rebelled:
> Thou hast not pardoned.
> Thou hast covered with anger
> And persecuted us:
> Thou hast slain, thou hast not pitied. . . .
> Thou hast made us as the offscouring
> And refuse in the midst of the people.

The last predominant theological motif found in *Doctor Faustus* is that of the mythological. This theme must also be seen centered around the artist in exile. Bernhard Blume presents an interesting study to show how the mythological subject is drawn into the novel. He maintains that "when the devil appears in a novel and God does not, that still does not mean that God is not present." It is well known there are stories in the novel where the devil plays a more significant role than God, but this does not mean the Christian aura of the novel is weakened. The use of the devil is one of the strongest motifs which could have been used as the pact signifies that aesthetic existence which is viewed under guilt. The parody of guilt makes the novel a tragedy in the sense that the devil has the last possible happiness or greatness afforded by the genre. The mythological pact with the demon must not be isolated solely to Adrian's pact with the devil, but with all of the aspects of the novel contained within the pact, and finally this to be seen within the whole of mankind. It is through the mythological motifs that the Christian conceptions must be seen in the novel, for it is through these motifs that the evil has its origins. Adrian believes that the devil does not pass for a man of destructive criticism:

> Slander and again slander, my friend; God's sacrament! If there is anything he cannot abide, if there's one thing in the whole world he cannot stomach, it is destructive criticism. What he

wants and gives is triumph over it, is shining, sparkling, vainglorious unreflectiveness!

Adrian's soul, after it was "sold" to the devil, did not enjoy any appeasement, for the discovered truths which it discovers later "are certainly of little use to the soul, and it is hard not to sympathize with Serenus Zeitblom's observation" [Heller].

> I shall never understand the glory-to-God mental attitude which certain temperaments assume when they contemplate the 'works of God,' meaning by the phrase the physics of the universe.

It is this not-able to "understand theme," which the devil has placed upon Adrian, that makes the mythological so probable as the artist places himself in exile. "I shall never understand" carries the musical theme throughout the novel as the pact becomes the theme of the counterpoint which can only become clear at the end of the novel; Adrian cannot understand until the subjective is laid aside and then it is too late; but the high G of the cello continues in a soft tone—does mankind now understand?

The study of mythology gave Mann an insight into different concepts of life and death and the magnitude of art. As Mann isolated himself, the art which he was creating also had to be withdrawn from the world, but still the dramatic action had to be centered from a personal self-experience. To withdraw from the world creates a power to be able to see more clearly. Mann develops the Faust motif in such a way that it is [according to Kahler] "not only of German but of Western culture, up to date. He treats it with finality, secularizing it and its demon, and integrating it in a purely mundane cosmos." It is as though Mann wished to emphasize that he was a part of the novel, that "the destinies of Leverkühn and Zeitblom as well as of Germany, the intellectual, and modern art, deeply involve him." By using the legend theme of Faust which had been used by Marlowe and Goethe, Mann gave the novel a greater authenticity. The magnitude of art which can be seen in the novel is based on the sixteenth century tale and many of the incidents of the

> folk book are recalled: Faust's parentage, his prowess in theology and mathematics, his 'famulus', his pact with the devil, his scientific investigations, his lapses of remorse, his love for Helen, their mysterious child, the final lamentation, and so on. [Roy Pascal, *The German Novel*]

Even if these analogies were not made, the language and the use of the devil makes the sixteenth century setting more plausible. However, one overlooks the artistic devices which are used to make the concepts of life and death conceivable in *Doctor Faustus.*

The fact that Mann chose a musician to be the representative of Germany to whom he would sell his soul unifies the novel for it was intended to be purely represented in a musical composition. The demonic counterpoint running throughout the three parts of the literary fugue expresses the mythological motif of man selling his soul to the devil. It is here that the ideologies of life and death can be made. Because of the mythological motifs developed, the only

thing which can result is the total collapse of Adrian and ultimately Germany. This death, because it is venereal in nature, is one of long decay, gradually causing insanity to the mind, and, therefore, Mann uses the mythological motif to underline this point.

If one were to end here, there would be no hope for the future, but as established, the theological theme of the *Apocalypsis* and Old Testament gives an insight into what will happen. It is here that the comparison between the mythological and theological must be made. It becomes ironic that in Mann's contrivance the mythological devil becomes the most humane because he is the only one who can understand what ultimately can come out of despair. It is for this reason that the novel takes on such a broad perspective representing all of mankind.

> God be merciful to my poor soul, my friend, my Fatherland.

(pp. 500-13)

> *John Peterson, "The Role of the Theological Themes in Thomas Mann's 'Dr. Faustus',"* in Discourse: A Review of the Liberal Arts, *Vol. IX, No. 4, Autumn, 1966, pp. 492-515.*

Joyce Carol Oates   (essay date 1969)

[*Oates is an American author and critic whose fiction is noted for realistic detail, striking imagination, and evocation of abnormal psychological states. She has also written critical studies on such authors as William Shakespeare and Herman Melville. In the following excerpt, Oates examines narrative technique and existential tragedy in* Doctor Faustus.]

Dr. Faustus, along with **The Magic Mountain** and *Ulysses,* is one of the most complex novels ever written. Mann's extraordinary mind leaves nothing out, resists no opportunity to analyze works of music that do not exist, misses no ironic connection between Adrian and Nietzsche, Adrian and Adam, Adrian and Germany, Adrian and "bourgeois humanism," Adrian and his prototype, Faust, who somehow incorporates in himself his temper and seducer, the Devil. One of the highest products of what Mann calls the reflective-analytic art, **Dr. Faustus** repays many readings and in its ingenious artlessness forces the reader to become a creator himself, a kind of secondary novelist. The artlessness is a result of Mann's technique, which presents us with the long biography of Adrian Leverkühn that is written, or is in the process of being written, by his old associate and admirer, Serenus Zeitblom, Ph.D. Zeitblom has no pretensions to art; if he seems to be respecting form and symbolism it is not because he is "creating" but rather because he is "recording." Zeitblom may, then, quite seriously ask: "For a man who is not an artist the question is intriguing: how serious is the artist in what ought to be . . . his most pressing and earnest concern; how seriously does he take himself in it, and how much tired disillusionment, affectation, flippant sense of the ridiculous is at work?" Mann, at an ironic distance, invites us to ponder the "seriousness" of his Faustian parable. There is a great deal of the "ridiculous" in it—the constant pairing-off of characters, a kind of maniacal parody of Mann's own penchant for the dialectical process—and the very choice of subject matter demands that one think of other Fausts, particularly of Goethe's Faust, and that one make careful comparisons with the hallucinatory devil of Ivan's intellect in *The Brothers Karamazov. Dr. Faustus* exists as one of those apparently terminal works, terminal in a genre, which operates on the verge of self-parody, of an extreme and startling self-consciousness unthinkable in naive art, very nearly one with the composition of Adrian's that is a "tense, sustained, neck-breaking game played by art on the edge of impossibility." We are told by Adrian himself that music and speech belong together and are at bottom the same; language is music, music is language. And music, as the most intellectual of the arts, demands its incorporation into this most intellectual of literary modes. "This is no novel," Zeitblom explains, "in whose composition the author reveals the hearts of his characters indirectly, by the action he portrays." This is true, for all action is predetermined and it is instead "being" that arrests our attention. But the work is a novel, a highly experimental novel cast in the form of a traditional critical biography, the oldest novelistic device for securing a skeptical audience's interest.

Any analysis of *Dr. Faustus* must distort the novel's complexities and subtleties. What is delicate as a strain of music must in criticism be underscored; what is symbolic and perhaps achieves its magical power on an unconscious level must be wrenched into consciousness and connected with other symbols in the work. Symbolism exposed is no longer symbolic in the powerful sense in which Mann intends it to be: not as conscious contrivance, a linking-together of times and themes, but as the unconscious manifestation of destiny, of the mystery of a universe in which nothing is accidental. Mann's strange belief in the power of will accounts for mystifying elements in his novels; it is not to be confused with the desire for a well-written novel whose parts add up to a whole. Indeed, Mann says in his essay, **"Freud and the Future,"** that the "apparently objective and accidental is a matter of the soul's own contriving."

The question of Mann's formal technique is closely related to the question of the meaning of *Dr. Faustus,* for it is out of the apparently accidental meshing of fateful events that the tragedy of will arises—the fulfillment of violent life at the edge of the impossibility of life itself, the point at which life passes over, as Nietzsche's did, into fiction.

Mann's technique in *Dr. Faustus* consists of the layering of experience in concentric circles, rather like circles of hell. What happens once will happen again, and perhaps a third time—it is fated to recur. Nietzsche's mystical conception of the Eternal Recurrence is evoked with a vengeance in Mann's diabolical imagination, as the eternal egoism of Adrian comes to rest ultimately in the most egoistic of all conditions, infantilism, while Adrian's "soul"— that is, Adrian's music, the herald of the twice-barbaric future—is promised to us in the aftermath of the decline of individual worth. Hence the classical rise and fall of the tragic hero, who subsides in the mindlessness from which he came—a true turning of the wheel of fortune, bitterly ironic. As Mann says of **The Magic Mountain,** the novel

is "hermetic"—turning endlessly upon itself, complex and dazzling in its intricacy, representing by its very nearly atrophied difficulty the plight of the decadent bourgeois society with which it deals.

Dr. Faustus is subtitled "The Life of the German Composer Adrian Leverkühn as Told By a Friend." Eighteenth-century in its insistence upon biographical realism, it is also classical in its back-stepping evocation of Dante:

> The day was departing, and the brown air taking the animals, that are on earth, from their toils; and I one alone was preparing myself to bear the war both of the journey and the pity, which memory, that errs not, shall relate. O Muses, O high Genius, now help me! O Memory, that has inscribed what I saw, here will be shown thy nobleness.

It is "Zeitblom" asking for aid here, Mann/Zeitblom asking the Muses for help in his creation of Mann/Leverkühn. Mann's splitting of his impulses toward bourgeois kindliness and order, and toward "barbaric" simplicity and violence, has been anticipated in earlier works of his concerning artists: the melancholy yearning of Tonio Kröger for the blond, blue-eye mediocrities forever beyond the range of his art, the violent yearning of Aschenbach for the beauties of a sensual passion embodied in a spoiled Polish child. The story is Adrian's but from Adrian's point of view there would be no story at all. His "tragedy" takes form only from the point of view of the observer, Zeitblom, who is a representative of ours, and who insists at once upon a dialectical split between types of art (pure and "impure" or acquired) and types of human beings (the ordinary man and the artist). Adrian hates the words "art" and "artist" and "inspiration" excessively; his aristocratic nihilism judges such bourgeois attempts at interpretation and classification as absurd.

In his early essay on Goethe's *Faust,* Mann remarks of Faust's desire for the synthesis of his conflicting impulses toward sensuality and toward spirituality that it is "half-hypocritical"; "for well he knows that dualism is the soil and the mystery of creative fruitfulness." The ceaseless struggle between man's earthliness and his heavenly aspirations accounts for man himself: and it is logical to extend this essentially Schopenhaurian dualism to the clinical Freudian dualism of Id and Ego, the domain of the "other," the primitive, elemental, and unconscious, and the domain of the personal, the thinking, the ever-conscious. The Ego, according to Freud and Mann, does not exist in itself but as the result of violent struggles between the demanding Id and the indifference of the world, its restrictions and suppressions which become partly internalized (in that mysterious part of the Unconscious to which Freud gives the name "super-ego"). All this is to anticipate Mann's conception of the "will," but it is necessary to note at this point the essential split in his imagination, a faith in the restless swerving from pole to pole which has its external and formal manifestation in the series of doubles (whether characters, things, or events) which make up much of the novel's substance.

The basis of the novel is a split in the psychological potentialities of man as an abstract essence: a device freely and successfully used by Conrad, Melville, and Dostoyevsky, among others. Therefore Adrian is released so that he may drift to the farthest boundaries of the human, restrained by nothing, like Conrad's Kurtz with nothing above or below him, having "kicked himself free of the earth"; like Ahab he dares the very fabric of the universe, which Melville has told us early in *Moby-Dick* is simultaneously the fabric of his own soul; like the bizarre Karamazov family he acts out aggression on various levels of consciousness, an aggression that finds its ultimate object in the destruction of the highest and most sensitively developed person in the novel. And Zeitblom, who worries about losing weight during the social chaos following World War I, who loves his wife exceedingly and is faithful to her, yet, in true middle-class hypocritical fashion has experimented with a working class "creature" whom he blithely abandons—Zeitblom remains fixed, predictable, an absolute in a world gone mad, rather prim and prudent and anti-Nazi, yet unable to resist enthusiasm for such humanistic devices as German-developed torpedoes, though of course he is resolutely opposed to the war and German nationalism. Zeitblom, then, is the ordinary man writ large.

The hermetic universe begins at once, though only later in Adrian's life is the symbolic meaning made clear. He and Zeitblom, grow up in a truly Edenic countryside, complete with a height called "certainly from old days and most inappropriately, Mount Zion." The various components of his childhood are repeated at the end of his life, in a similar Edenic setting into which he has withdrawn in a monastic compulsive asceticism, living only in order to create music. Here he has a surrogate mother, Frau Schweigestill (whom he will call *Mutter* and *Sie* in his madness), who at first stands in for and then accompanies his real mother (*Mutter* and *Du*). Eerily, everything returns from his childhood, and yet Adrian himself is not aware, or only half aware, of the coincidences. Zeitblom remarks: "This choice of a place to live, reproducing the earliest one, this burying of oneself in one's earliest, outlived childhood, or at least in the outer circumstances of the same—it might indicate attachment, but in any case, it is psychologically disturbing." Because, in Mann, there is usually an uncanny correspondence between inner logic and outer event, it is no surprise that "at the same age, seventy-five years and strange to say almost on the same day, Max Schweigestill and Jonathan Leverkühn departed this life: the father and proprietor of Adrian's Bavarian asylum and home, and his own father up in Buchel." There are other doubles: the dogs Suso and Kaschperl (dogs of earthly hell in the guise of paradise, who can hear the whistle Adrian makes and who respond to it); the stable girl of childhood who teaches him songs, and the stable girl Waltpurgis. But Adrian synthesizes the two times by remarking sardonically that he incorporates in himself the elements of his earlier life. With Mephistophelian wit he states, "Where I am, there is Kaisersaschern." Not simply psychological, this insight, but mythical as well—for Adrian senses himself as typical, a type, a dehumanized person who must fulfill his destiny as if consciously acting out a role.

In the essay on Goethe's *Faust* Mann gives us a brief background to the Faust legends. Out of the mysterious depths of early Christian history comes the figure of Simon from Samaria, held in abhorrence by the Fathers of the church because he founded a heretical sect, the Simonians, pretended divinity, and took about with him a woman he called Helena. All this, Mann tells us, is "mythological hocus-pocus," but it fascinates him, perhaps, because it anticipates the theory of the individual-passing-into-myth which is the basis of the composition of *Joseph and His Brothers* (discussed at length in **"Freud and the Future"**). Simon and Helena are imposters who survive in a novel of the early Christian age called *Recognitiones;* and it is in this book that Simon becomes Faust, takes on the name "Faust." Centuries later, in 1526, another imposter by the name of Georg Helmstätter sets himself in motion as the successor to this early Faust, even passing out name cards; and he conforms to the original pattern by acquiring a female accomplice whom he names Helena. Fifty years after his death the first Faust-book is composed, in Frankfurt, in honor of his "miracles."

And so it came about that Helena, of antiquity, is matched with the figure of Faustus. This combination, Mann says, "is one of those pregnant inventions which can make a period of two thousand years seem like a single span of human life." And, in this essay written many years before the writing of *Dr. Faustus,* Mann uses the specific term *hetaera* in connection with Helena.

All this history is interesting for its own sake, and it certainly fascinates Mann, who is already moving from the individualistic psychology of Freud to what can only be called a Jungian sense of archetypal experience—the "collective unconscious" of famed unintelligibility. But it is interesting to note that the *hetaera* appears early in Adrian's childhood, not as a woman but as an insect called to Adrian's attention by the investigations of his father, Jonathan—a good man of a typically German nature though afflicted with migraine headaches, with a "taste for research" that according to Zeitblom always leaned in a certain direction—"namely, the mystical or an intuitive half-mystical . . . all this had quite close relations with witchcraft." One butterfly in Father Leverkühn's book is the *Hetaera esmeralda,* an insect of transparent nudity, with only dark spots on her wings. Adrian, who forgets nothing and is sardonically quick to note a chilling relationship between various stages of his life, thinks of the diseased harlot who gives him syphilis as *Hetaera esmeralda* and even dedicates a piece of music to her. But it is not only the fateful harlot who is summoned up, in disguised form, by the father of Adrian; the condition of Adrian's very soul is suggested by the discourse on ice crystals, which vainly imitate the vegetable world of ferns and grasses and flowers, but which do not live ("To the utmost of their icy ability they dabbled in the organic.") And the agents of syphilis itself, years later embarked upon a journey to Adrian's brain, are anticipated in the culture Jonathan Leverkühn grows in a jar, a "confused vegetation of . . . shoots . . . entirely unorganic in their origin"; but through the process of osmotic pressure this crop of pseudo-plants springs forth in imitation of life, yearning for warmth and joy—but "even so they are dead," as Jonathan says, thus reducing his unsentimental son Adrian to laughter and thus anticipating the Devil's remark. When, years later, Adrian comes to understand his predicament, he says to the Devil with a casual dignity that he is being visited by an annunciation. "I am to grow osmotic growths." So, slowly and inevitably, the circles close about Adrian; the drama of a free soul, the embodiment of Nietzsche's ideal of man beyond good and evil, turns bitterly ironic by the process of Mann's intricate hermetic technique.

In Chapter VI, when one is introduced to the rather sinister town of Kaisersaschern, the analogies between the microcosmic world of Adrian and the larger world of significance take shape. For now, reaching beyond the limitations of childhood, we discover a phenomenon: the retention in Kaisersaschern of barbarism simultaneous with the glory of European bourgeois humanism. The roots of Adrian's childhood are in the barbaric, though he is not consciously involved in it. Kaisersaschern (clearly Mann's home town of Lubeck) has a medieval air about it. Its "stamp of old-world, underground neurosis" betrays itself by the many peculiar people who live there, eccentrics and harmlessly half-mad folk. The age itself (and Zeitblom is writing this book during the rise of Hitler) "tends . . . to return to those earlier epochs; it enthusiastically re-enacts symbolic deeds of sinister significance, deeds that strike in the face the spirit of the modern age." Zeitblom, committed to the ego-oriented world of humanism, is frightened by the very concept of the "folk," for there is something anachronistic and evil about it, "this old, folkish layer [that] survives in us all." He does not believe that the institution of religion is sufficient to restrain the passion of the "folk"; "for that, literature alone avails, humanistic science, the ideal of the free and beautiful human being."

In this town, in the strange warehouse of Adrian's uncle, there is a universe of musical instruments, described with leisurely meticulousness by Mann. Everything is present, every instrument except the piano, in this "silent paradise" which so fascinates Adrian. Gravitated toward music, Adrian exhibits precocity not simply in his skill but in his philosophical grasp of music. Hardly more than a child, he replies to his friend Zeitblom's belief in the condition of life as necessarily residing in "belief in absolute values" with his statement, as he plays the harmonium, that *relationship is everything.* "And if you want to give it a more precise name, it is ambiguity." A "double" of Adrian's, a famous predecessor, is summoned up in the form of Beethoven. An anecdote is told about him, surprised in a kind of maniacal creativity and only arbitrarily related to the world of ordinary men when friends unexpectedly visit him. It is Beethoven's Ninth Symphony that will be the ghostly double for Adrian's last work, *The Lamentation of Dr. Faustus,* the ending of which has a choral part that is the reverse of the *Ode to Joy,* the "negative, equally a work of genius, of that transition of the symphony into vocal jubilation." Mann says of Beethoven:

> [his] art had overgrown itself, risen out of the
> habitable regions of tradition, even before the
> startled gaze of human eyes, into spheres of the
> entirely and utterly and nothing-but personal—
> an ego painfully isolated in the absolute, isolated
> too from sense by the loss of his hearing; lonely
> prince of a realm of spirits. . . .

As with Beethoven so with Adrian.

Adrian's sudden desire to study theology, which he admits later is due to his desire to study demonology, brings us into the bizarre world of Halle, medieval spiritually as Kaisersaschern is medieval emotionally. Zeitblom dwells uneasily upon the opposition between theology and humanism. It seems paradoxical that theology is constantly passing over into demonology; but, obsessed as it is with ecclesiastical brawls and self-laceration and the "inward and given psychological fact" which is so far removed from philosophy, it is in danger by its very nature of becoming demonology.

This paradox is borne out by the ludicrous professors Kumpf and Schleppfuss, the one on rowdy, folksy, bawdy terms with the "Divil," the other apparently a manifestation of the Devil himself!—for Privat-docent Schleppfuss lectures for two semesters at Halle and then "disappeared from the scene, I know not whither." In his disturbing, rather sinister lectures he seeks to incorporate the hellish in the divine, declaring the vicious to be a part of the holy and the holy a constant satanic temptation to violation; his Manicheanism has a sound, though obscene, basis in the psychology of the erotic/religious. Fond of saying, "your humble servant," he is reincarnated later when, in Leipzig, a sly porter leads the chaste Adrian to a house of prostitution and thereby brings about his fall.

Adrian's strange longing for the harlot who brushes his cheek with her arm is explained in terms of a love that is madness. Zeitblom sees Adrian's willful possession of her diseased body as a compulsion to combine the punishment in the sin, a "mysterious longing for daemonic conception." He seeks her out in a hospital and insists upon consummating his desire for her, though she warns him of her disease—and such an act, under such circumstances, can indicate nothing but a morbid yearning for the very extremes of experience, the communion with disease, with darkness, with the unknown that Mann sees as necessary in order that great art be created. The Devil asks Adrian rhetorically whether he thinks that "any important work was ever wrought except its maker learned to understand the way of the criminal and the madman." It is unfortunate that Mann conceives of the harlot in abstract terms and that he does not give to this anonymous Helena any of the voluptuousness and intelligence of that other diseased temptress, Clavdia of *The Magic Mountain.* She is hardly realized for us, not at all dramatized, little more than a projection of Adrian's desire for a communion with the unknown and the forbidden, which will unlock his creative powers but ultimately destroy him.

Comically following this episode is the mysterious encounter with the two doctors, Erasmi and Zimbalist, who are sought out to cure Adrian of his disease. But the first doctor dies suddenly and the second doctor is arrested and taken away just as Adrian is climbing the stairs to his office . . . perhaps arrested by the devil's agents, perhaps by ordinary secular police. So Adrian breaks off the treatment.

In the series of "doubles" the most interesting are the Rodde sisters, Clarissa and Inez, the one infatuated with

a bohemian, "artistic" life on the stage and the other mor-
bidly attracted to a bourgeois life complete with an opu-
lent apartment, servants, expensive furniture and silver,
all the heavy accoutrements of a decadent, useless culture.
Clarissa dies, a suicide, and Inez becomes a murderer—
the instrument by which one of Adrian's "loves," albeit
a minor one, is taken from him. The viciousness of Inez
Rodde's egoism is all the more deadly in that it has no object beyond itself, its delight is in acting out behind the
forms of an outmoded society a personal, private, sordid
equation of worth with sensual passion. Adrian, who cannot love, who is chaste out of impurity and eternally
"cold," is indirectly matched with Inez, who cannot love
without gluttonous, selfish desire—the two of them
trapped in a tragic egoism, despairing and doomed, the
hypothetical end-products of a decadent Europe. Between
them the boyish Rudi is destroyed, spurred on to a foolish
proposal of marriage by Adrian's remoteness and destroyed by Inez's unnatural passion.

There are many other dialectical devices used by Mann,
sometimes extravagantly and sometimes subtly. Unforgettable is the Devil as an impresario of avant-garde music,
Saul Fitelberg, or perhaps he is a parody of the Devil himself—lively, airy, with an elegant and engaging patter that
takes up page after page of Chapter XXXVII:

> Enfin, I cashed in on the connections I owed to
> the Fourberies, and they multiplied when I
> opened my agency for the presentation of con-
> temporary music. Best of all, I had found myself,
> for as I stand here, I am a born impresario; I
> can't help it, it is my joy and pride, I find my sat-
> isfaction et mes délices in discovering talent, ge-
> nius, interesting personalities, beating the drum,
> making society mad with enthusiasm or at least
> with excitement. . . .

Adrian, true to his Faustian archetype, talks of a fantastic
descent to the depths of the ocean and speculates about the
cosmic chill of the universe, the immeasurable and inhuman. Zeitblom, the perpetually ordinary man, is uneasy
over these speculations; there is nothing in this "mon-
strousness" that could appeal to him as goodness, beauty,
or greatness. All this is introductory to Adrian's next musical composition, *Marvels of the Universe,* which parallels
the "witchcraft" of Father Leverkühn. The work of music
is mock-pathetic and ironic, bizarre, unpleasant, and grotesque in a solemn, formal, mathematical way.

Now blessed with the Devil's strength, Adrian gravitates
toward the un-human, the cosmic vision before which
man's puny humanism is no more significant than marsh
gas. It is the vision of which Nietzsche so often speaks in
his desire to break through, once and for all, the blinding
human dimension of language and metaphysical pretense.
In an early essay called "On Truth and Lie," Nietzsche
says:

> What, indeed, does man know of himself! Can
> he even once perceive himself completely, laid
> out as if in an illuminated glass case? Does not
> nature keep much the most from him, even
> about his body, to spellbind and confine him in
> a proud, deceptive consciousness, far from the
> coils of the intestines. . . . And woe to the ca-

lamitous curiosity which might peer . . .
through a crack in the chamber of consciousness
and look down, and sense that man rests upon
the merciless, the greedy, the insatiable, the
murderous, in the indifference of his ignorance—hanging in dreams, as it were, upon the
back of a tiger.

Hans Castorp's "dream poem of humanity" in the chapter
"Snow" from *The Magic Mountain* gives us a fanciful
dramatization of Nietzsche's idea. For, having wandered
into the haze, into "nothing," Hans Castorp has a vision
of a lovely Edenic world in which man and nature are
one—with the hideous chapel in which a child is being dis-
membered at its very center, the culminating point of the
hallucination and of the novel itself. Castorp thinks clearly, "I have dreamed of man's state, of his courteous and
enlightened social state; behind which, in the temple, the
horrible blood sacrifice was being consummated. Were
they, those children of the sun, so sweetly courteous to
each other, in silent recognition of that horror?" For man
is "the lord of counter-positions," we are told, made fruitful through his tragic dualism, and raised above the mute
processes of physical nature that embody this dualism.

The dialectical tension within Adrian himself consists of
his passing violently from a period of "coldness" (depression, pain, lethargy) to a period of "heat" (compulsive,
maniacal activity). But, as Zeitblom notes, these periods
"were not separate and without all connection, for the
present state had been preparing in the former one and to
some extent had already been contained in it . . . " He
swings helplessly back and forth between the extremes of
cold and heat, promised by the Devil as one of the punishments of hell. When Adrian finally loses his mind he
comes to resemble Christ, where in his mature being with
his cold, aloof, mocking humor he had resembled the
Devil; does the Devil pass over into Christ, then, absolved
of his evil through his suffering? Or absolved of his evil,
at least, by having lost his mind? At the end of his life
Adrian fulfills his own prediction for man; he is Adam
who has eaten a second time from the tree of knowledge
in order to fall back into innocence. But innocence, ironically, is to be equated with the infantile.

And yet Mann suggests a "hope beyond hopelessness." In
Adrian's greatest work, *The Lamentation of Dr. Faustus,*
there is an ending that is somehow beyond the audible
ending: "one group of instruments after another retires,
and what remains, as the work fades on the air, is the high
G of a cello, the last word, the last fainting sound, slowly
dying. . . . Then nothing more: silence, and night. But
that tone which vibrates in the silence, which is no longer
there, to which only the spirit hearkens, and which was
the voice of mourning, is no more. It changes its meaning;
it abides as a light in the night."

> . . . Who denies that a real breakthrough is
> worth what the tame world calls a crime? . . .
> There is at bottom only one problem in the
> world, and this is its name. How does one break
> through? How does one get into the open? How
> does one burst the cocoon and become a butter-
> fly? Kleist is talking only about the aesthetic,
> charm, free grace, which actually is reserved to

the automaton and the god; that is, to the unconscious or an endless consciousness, whereas every reflection lying between nothing and infinity kills grace. The consciousness must . . . have gone through an infinity in order that grace find itself again therein; and Adam must eat a second time from the tree of knowledge in order to fall back into the state of innocence.

These are Adrian's words, passionate and Nietzschean, the expression of a will seeking its objectification in the world—and how ironic that he should speak of every reflection between nothing and infinity as a killing of grace, dooming mankind (or the man in himself) to a purgatorial world of gracelessness, the burden of mortality torn in two directions and unable to "break through" to either pure unconsciousness or an endless consciousness! For just as Adrian aspires toward the satanic power of a god's consciousness, he is doomed by both his temperament and his physical disease to the infantile unconsciousness of a second childhood. To his icy, brittle imagination everything given is fitted for parody; earlier in the novel he has asked in bewilderment why everything seems to him its own parody. The question may very well have been Hamlet's. And, as in Hamlet's Denmark the fact of social and moral rottenness is unquestionable, so in Adrian's Europe the fact of a larger, folk-based barbarism, a true automaton's unconsciousness, is a catastrophe for the precarious bourgeois order.

Dr. Faustus is a tragedy of will. But is will the seething forces of the Unconscious, or the harnessed energy of that domain which can be controlled by the Ego only at great cost, only at Faustian audacity? And what is Adrian's Devil—hallucination or real devil, or both? The relationship between Adrian's pact with the Devil and Germany's pact with the Devil is fairly clear. Mann is always writing political allegory. The desire for a mysterious breakthrough on Adrian's part, an act that may seem a crime to the "tame world," and the breakthrough on Germany's part is fairly clear—and Adrian's rise and fall precedes the rise and fall of the Third Reich. The time in which the novel is written and the time of which it is written are very important. Zeitblom confesses: "This is a quite extraordinary interweaving of time-units, destined, moreover, to include even a third: namely, the time which one day the courteous reader will take for the reading of what has been written; at which point he will be dealing with a threefold ordering of time: his own, that of the chronicler, and historic time." To which one must add a fourth dimension: the time of Mann's writing of the novel. Certainly this emphasis on time-units, this arranging of concentric circles around the fairly short life span of Adrian Leverkühn, points toward a definite historic and political framework. And, propelled backward into theological history, indeed, invited to consider what Zeitblom calls the epoch of bourgeois humanism beginning at the end of the Middle Ages, the reader understands that Adrian is to bear on his frail shoulders a tremendous symbolic burden, being at once a historical German and an ahistorical Adam, made to serve the cause of political allegory as well as the larger cause of mythical allegory.

Critics who interpret *Dr. Faustus* as a devastating critique of an imperialist epoch surely miss the point: one thinks of the extraordinary claims of the Marxist critic Lukács, who applauds Adrian at one point for discovering "the way which leads to Marx," but writes him off as a victim of the disintegrating values of his society. Certainly the political symbolism of the novel is highly significant: is not little Helmut Institoris, instructor in art and aesthetics and Inez's cuckholded husband, a terrible parody of the age and of Adrian as well? He who celebrates the Italian Renaissance as a time that "reeked of blood and beauty," and who himself must lead a life of scrupulous regularity is a mockery of Adrian's impulse toward the twice-barbaric that will break through to the future. And the various members of the Munich circle (nearly all of them physically diseased or somehow incapacitated for active life) express comically grotesque enthusiasms for the coming era, applauding violence and waste and the elimination of the unfit—though they themselves are obviously unfit. The most despicable character in the novel is the Jewish scholar Dr. Breisacher, whose cultural barbarism and argumentative love of paradox prefigures the glorification of the irrational that will result in wholesale slaughter of the Jews—and, if the reeking of blood and beauty is desired, if a breakthrough is desired, why not a wholesale slaughter of the Jews?

Mann is fascinated by the morbid passivity, the suicidal masochism of the German intellectual community. When insanity becomes history it seems to become sane again; no standards remain. The line between aestheticism and barbarism is uncertain. These intellectuals give themselves over to the new era before it is even upon them, prophesying the violence of the future all too accurately. But to say, as Lukács says, that Adrian's tragedy lies in his attitude toward social and historical reality is to suggest that the problem of the artist is not psychological at all, but simply social. A rearrangement of society will eradicate the artist's sufferings and make his art miraculously *per du* with humanity—a transformation that is very nearly mystical. It is simply not true that the artist's problem in the modern age is tied up with modern bourgeois individualism, which is in its turn a result of imperialism; on the contrary, the very nature of the artist predetermines his isolation—and it is the isolation of the artist that makes possible his art, and his art that justifies his tragic isolation. Nor is it true that the artist searches for truth of any social or moral nature.

"Relationship is everything," Adrian has told Zeitblom. It is ambiguity. To the existential imagination things do not exist except through relationships; they do not, strictly speaking, exist in themselves. As Nietzsche says in *Human, All-Too-Human:*

> Apparently, [the artist] fights for the higher dignity and significance of man; in truth, he does not want to give up the most effective presuppositions of his art: the fantastic, mythical, uncertain, extreme, the sense for the symbolic, the overestimation of the person, the faith in some miraculous element in the genius. Thus he considers the continued existence of his kind of creation more important than scientific devotion to the truth in every form, however plain.

By definition, the artist is asocial; not necessarily antisocial, but asocial. He has no clear relationship with society. Delivered over to an ideology, caught up in a historical certainty, he fails to be faithful to the ambiguous—hence the feverish and unconvincing redemptions in Dostoyevsky, which seem to follow so violently from the convincing nightmares that are his true interest. Erich Kahler interprets Adrian's predicament as the tragic inability to relate, to achieve redemption through relationship with life; "the Faustian drama is revealed as the dialectical predicament of every creature, the inborn paradox of life." And this is surely Mann's point, at least in part: the paradox of life is inborn and not socially determined. But to settle for an interpretation that aligns Adrian with all of mankind—Adrian as simply Adam, desirous of eating once again of the tabooed fruit—is to ignore the worth of Adrian's compositions. And surely Mann has not gone to such extraordinary lengths in analyzing and admiring these non-existent musical works for no purpose?

Adrian is Mann's most exalted embodiment of the artist. Unlike Aschenbach, who is another European genius though a "classical" writer, Adrian makes a conscious choice of nightmares; he arranges and wills his disaster. The strange passivity with which he sends Rudi to his own beloved, to propose for him, is not really strange at all. He does not want to love her, he wants instead to lose her, and so it happens that he loses her—it is a choice, perhaps half-conscious, but a choice nevertheless. When, near the end of his career, he comes to love his nephew and is torn apart by the child's terrible suffering and death, it is clear that he laments his fate but not clear that he would have traded it for another. Adrian becomes Faust: he walks in the footsteps of Faust, in the fulfillment of a destiny which was willed and from which he does not draw back in terror or self-pity. Though Mann has said in a letter that Adrian represents only a single type of artist, this does not exclude the possibility of Adrian's being the highest type of artist; nor does it really exclude the possibility of Mann's remark being quite irrelevant to his own work. If Adrian's life is seen as wasted, then there is no tragedy; but if his musical compositions are truly great, if he is truly a genius who could have fulfilled his genius by no other means than this "pact with the Devil," then his story is a tragedy. It seems obvious from the novel that Mann apotheosizes Adrian as composer (music being the highest art) and makes clear the paradox that his work balances his sufferings, and perhaps even the sufferings of those around him. Existential tragedy may be differentiated from classical tragedy in that no "mistake" occurs; there is not a point at which the tragic hero could have taken another direction. Having chosen another direction he would not have become himself—which, in Nietzschean terms, is the only imperative—and having chosen this particular direction, this particular destiny, he comes to a "tragic" end as a human being but achieves a triumph denied to human beings generally.

Does art in **Dr. Faustus** "tragically lament the loss of its own mystery?" Or is this a question from the point of view of Zeitblom? Art as expression of conscious will, the highest expression of will, discloses not simply the alternatives of the endless unconscious or the endless conscious but

justifies the intermediary realm that Adrian calls graceless. Suffering is justified by its art, and, curiously enough, art is justified by its suffering: "the value of a thing sometimes does not lie in what one attains by it, but in what one pays for it—what it costs us," as Nietzsche says in *The Twilight of the Idols.* There is the slightly repulsive suggestion in both Nietzsche and Mann that the artist expends himself in his art and, having accomplished it, is finished as a human being.

Two central questions: what is will? And what is Adrian's devil, fantasy or reality, or both? Let the Devil exist as a given, not simply as Adrian's eloquent repressed consciousness (in the manner of Dostoyevsky), for otherwise what are we to do with the comic diabolicalism of Saul Fitelberg and of the professor Schleppfuss, "your humble servant"? It is fashionable to insist upon the psychological basis of literary devils, who are an embarrassment to a naturalistic epoch. Therefore it is no surprise to note that the dust-jacket of a popular edition of **Dr. Faustus** shows us Adrian and his tempter facing each other with precisely the same expression and the same face—in short, they are the same person—this is acceptable enough for most readers, indeed it is the only acceptable devil. But Mann is not a writer of naturalism. He deals with historical reality and his bizarre stories take place in real countries and real cities, but he has no commitment to the limitations of naturalism; the "fantastic, mythical, uncertain, extreme, the sense for the symbolic . . . the faith in some miraculous element"—all this is Mann, thoroughly Mann. In **The Magic Mountain** there is a chapter ambiguously titled "Highly Questionable," in which Hans Castorp's dead cousin Joachim appears at a seance. He is wearing a strange uniform, and as Hermann J. Weigand points out in his study of the novel, one must know that "no civilian of prewar days could possibly have brought forth out of his sub-consciousness a vision of a soldier in garb like this." Therefore the novel's walls fall back. It is not Hans Castorp's projection, this fantastic image, but a true prophecy of the future—and so the novel itself breaks through the boundaries of a conventional naturalism. Mann's Devil may be in Adrian's head or outside it.

As Mann says through the Devil, this tendency to insist upon the objective is petty bourgeois. "As you see me, so I exist to you. What serves it to ask whether I really am? Is not "really" what works, is not truth experience and feeling?" The accidents of Dr. Erasmi and Dr. Zimbalist are factually true in the narrative of **Dr. Faustus,** just as certain irrefutable clues in Henry James' *The Turn of the Screw* point toward the existence of the ghosts, disappointing as this may be to argumentative critics. Indeed, the matched improbabilities of Mann and James suggest nothing more than the various improbabilities of any work of art, usually tacitly accepted because they are behind the scenes.

As a drama of will-made-conscious, **Dr. Faustus** is terrifying because it is hermetic, and that which is hermetic excludes all accident, all chance. This is Mann's point precisely. "When I hear of hearing!" Adrian exclaims. "In my view it is quite enough if something has been heard *once;* I mean when the artist thought it out." So, for the composer, the actual written composition is far removed from its original vital reality; it has become material, it exists for others, it has been bypassed. There is no wonder in the fact that Adrian avoids attending presentations of his own work, for his having thought it out, his exercise of original will, precludes any further interest of his in it. Just as the artist's will creates his art in a godly manner, in pure thought, so does the artist's will create itself. As psychology this is bewildering indeed, for it is Sartre's psychology, the theory of "endless consciousness"—one creates one's essence, one makes himself, man has no nature but only a history, etc. Far from the modest speculations of Freud, far into the realm of the mystic and the terrifying—in short, Mann as Schopenhauer.

For behind Nietzsche stands Schopenhauer, the "father of all modern psychology" in Mann's opinion, because he is the first psychologist of the will. *The World as Will and Idea* is an extraordinary accomplishment, says Mann, a work whose meaning is expressed totally in its title and is present in every line. The bipolar nature of man is analyzed without sentiment by Schopenhauer and found to consist of a terrible opposition: the will, the idea; the blind primitive force of will, or life, and the enlightened, would-be autonomous force of the intellect. The struggle is dramatic and endless, though will has its ultimate victory in the reproductive life of the species; man splits in two, drawn by the erotic in one direction and by the principles of the mind in another, unable to synthesize the two. Mann is impatient with fashionable twentieth-century trends of reacting against classical rationalism in favor of the "Unconscious," the deliberate glorification of Instinct. In Schopenhauer's essay "Transcendent Speculations on Apparent Design in the Fate of the Individual," there is developed the extraordinary theory that life, like dreams, is directed by man's will, and that the accidental is only accidental in appearance. "It is our own will," Mann says, "that unconsciously appears as inexorable objective destiny."

It is possible for Mann to believe in and to create more-than-human men like Adrian, then, whose asceticism (a conscious fight against the blinding instinctive will) leads them to a higher consciousness, a refinement of the will to the point at which the will creates itself. Thus Adrian creates himself and his destiny: his fall has depended upon the "disposition, the readiness, the invitation" and it depends also upon his decision, which is a decision for disease. That which is diseased and that which is criminal blend, in Mann as in Nietzsche, the criminal being a type of strength under unfavorable circumstances: "a strong human being made sick." Nietzsche sees society (Christian society) as tame and emasculating, in which a natural human being necessarily degenerates into a criminal. Zeitblom speculates that the process of sublimation is faulty in such a person as Adrian: "the proudest intellectuality stands in the most immediate relation of all to the animal, to naked instinct, is given over most shamefully to it . . . ." This supports Adrian's conviction that intellectual interest, not love, is the strongest human emotion—for love is not possible in a being in whom sublimation does not work. And Zeitblom counters shrewdly with a

definition of Adrian's "interest"—it is a kind of love "from which the animal warmth has been withdrawn."

For the higher human being, then, there is the possibility of utter freedom—of breaking through outmoded forms. The ego is unified with the world; when one perceives that the apparently objective and accidental is a result of the soul's creation, one understands the tragic confinement of this freedom. The existential figure creates himself through his actions; he cannot make mistakes because that is a contradiction in terms. Adrian does not make any mistakes. His ego expands to include a participation in other selves, as Mann believes certain human beings transcend their historical reality through this abrogation of the individual in the "type." Adrian's role as Leverkühn is individual enough, and entirely believable; but his role as Faust is one he grows into, one which his suffering (over the loss of his beloved, of Rudi, and most of all of his nephew) educates him into knowing. Mann was fascinated by the confidence-game of the early Fausts, Simon of one century and Helmstätter of another, not simply because of their audacity and success but because of their apparent ability to transform themselves, to abrogate their selfness in the type. Hence, in 1526, Mann speculates, Helmstätter was not merely the successor of Faustus; in a sense he became Faustus; it was an age of "great sympathetic understanding of the myth." In the famous 1936 essay **"Freud and the Future,"** Mann discusses this mythologizing of the self in relationship to *Joseph and His Brothers.* It is the movement from bourgeois individualism to the mythical and typical, the timeless creation, that characterizes this work; a religious gesture, a celebration, a making present of the past. So with Adrian, unlike "Adrian Leverkühn" he invites a large and varied audience to hear *The Lamentation of Dr. Faustus;* he has become Faust, who likewise invited an audience to whom he confessed his sins.

The paradox in Mann lies in his commitment to and his strenuous approval of the dialectical process as a technical means, and his ultimate mystical belief in the unity of the ego and the world. **Dr. Faustus,** like *The Magic Mountain,* concerns itself with form and formlessness, the discipline of living and the temptation of dying, attempting in its very pages a synthesis of the two which cannot come about except through art, that is, through artifice. The struggle between the will and the ego, or the Id and the Ego, is pathetic and comic and tragic simultaneously; but, viewed as idea alone, viewed as the total creation of man's will represented through art, it makes a "significant spectacle" and transcends mortality to become timeless and immortal, as the inhuman will itself is immortal. For life in the myth, Mann says, is a liberation from the individual and the doomed; "it becomes a feast." (pp. 377-97)

Joyce Carol Oates, " 'Art at the Edge of Impossibility': Mann's 'Dr. Faustus','" in The South-ern Review, Louisiana State University, Vol. V, No. 2, Spring, 1969, pp. 375-97.

T. E. Apter   (essay date 1978)

[In the following excerpt, Apter discusses Mann's depiction of music in Doctor Faustus, *relating music to the*

[development of both demonic and redemptive imagery in the novel.]

Doctor Faustus is subtitled 'The life of the German composer Adrian Leverkühn as told by a friend'. The focus of the novel is on music—German music—and the course of Leverkühn's creative, artistic history is interwoven with and sometimes parallel to the political history of Germany. Leverkühn himself is not involved in the political world but, through his unconscious sympathy with the spirit of his age (through his artistic sensibility) he himself enacts, in his creative life, the tumultuous atmosphere and moral confusion which erupts under Hitler's government. The composer's dissatisfaction with classical forms, his sense that they are unsuited to the expression of the modern soul and that they can no longer be used seriously, but only in parody, mirrors his contemporaries' awareness of their outworn morality. Modern consciousness has become too sophisticated to accept the moral precepts of bourgeois humanism or the shallow view of man as a rational being upon which such moral precepts rest. The Kridwiss circle can only parody the old moral assumptions. They see themselves as exhibiting a characteristically German honesty in facing the multi-dimensional aspects of man; they dismiss as hypocrisy the morality that assumes human nature to be capable of attaining reliability and altruism. If one no longer treats the old humanist morality as an irrefutable premise, they argue, then logic does not compel one to reinstate it. In this circle, the German penchant for tragedy becomes a penchant for sadism, and the prospect of chaos—which will result from the moral revolution advocated in this circle—is welcomed. The old morality must be destroyed, and the ensuing violence is seen as a fine test of the German character.

Alongside Germany's need to establish a national self-definition and alongside society's need to discover a morality that could take into account the modern view of man as a largely irrational and amoral being, is Adrian Leverkühn's need to establish new principles of musical composition. These new principles must satisfy the intellectual demands of music and provide the possibility of objective organisation, an organisation that is necessary to music as communication. At the same time, these forms must allow emotive—sensuous—spiritual expression; they must supply an objective organisation of personal expression, as does a language. The problem is too drastic to be solved simply by developing another musical form—something just a little different from the sonata or rondo. The problem can be solved only by a new conception of form. For essential to classical form is the appearance of ease and fluidity and grace. Classical forms attempt to solve the problem of structure and expression as though the problem never existed. With great care the classical composer presented a work which seemed effortless. Musical forms were thought to be God-given forms, reflecting the logic and harmony of the universe, and the composer used these forms to express a soul that delighted in universal laws. Contemporary man, having no belief in a universe whose ultimate reality can be expressed in elegance, ease and harmony, can only mock classical forms. Mockery, however, is limited; it is purely negative, and the contemporary composer seeks a positive language for the

modern upheaval and violence. The Germans accepted a highly regimented government to provide form for the contemporary glorification of instinct; the National Socialists offered discipline in a time of chaos, and the impression of energy in an atmosphere of hopelessness. In parallel, Leverkühn develops a rigorous method of composition in which no note is free; that is, every note is derived from the original, chosen series, the notes of which always appear in the same order, though they can be ordered vertically [as] well as horizontally and can be varied through inversion, retrograde inversion and crabfigures imitation. This compositional method provides a musical form which—unlike classical forms—is indifferent to harmony and melody. Leverkühn's arbitrarily chosen series undercuts the assumption of an ultimately rational God-given basis for musical form and escapes the pleasing conventions of classical styles.

Adrian Leverkühn's compositional method is of course derived from Schoenberg's serial compositions. While Mann was writing **Doctor Faustus** he and Schoenberg were neighbours in California—both were exiles from Hitler's Germany. Mann had the opportunity to see some of the composer's scores, and Leverkühn's penultimate oratorio, *Apocalypsis cum figuris,* is similar to Schoenberg's *Jakobsleiter,* though this work had not yet been performed. Schoenberg's subsequent quarrel with Mann over this novel involved, more than Mann's presumption that the serial composer had sold his soul to the devil, Mann's attribution of serial composition to a character without explaining that the method was really Schoenberg's. The musician's hostility towards the novelist for the theft was compounded by Schoenberg's belief that what the novelist

Arnold Schönberg, Austrian composer recognized for his method of musical composition with twelve tones, a system Mann attributes to Leverkühn in Doctor Faustus.

had stolen he had not got right; Schoenberg denied that his method was as rigorously determined as Mann made Leverkühn's out to be. Schoenberg was partly to blame for Mann's misinterpretation; for the composer himself over-emphasised the importance of the series as a unifying principle of his works (which are in fact unified by texture and expression and mood at least as much as by the series) and he did not advertise the fact that he frequently deviated from the series when the series did not provide the sound he wanted. Mann was influenced by Theodor Adorno's *Philosophy of Modern Music* in his assessment of the impersonal rigour of serial composition; but though **Doctor Faustus** reveals Mann's misgivings as to the creative flexibility of twelve-tone composition, this method does provide a form for Leverkühn's message; he achieves the artistic breakthrough which supplies a moral-psychological musical expression of the modern soul.

Schopenhauer saw music as a direct expression of the Will, and Mann shared the view that music, of all the arts, had the closest affinity to the seething, preintellectual forces that lie behind life and death. Kierkegaard, too, saw music as primarily an expression of the dæmonic: immediate sensuousness was music's proper subject, and all other uses of music were secondary or derivative. Mann, however, was sensitive to music's ability to combine the utmost sensuousness with the most sublime spirituality, so that if music actually was the devil's language it nonetheless seemed to be God's language. Moreover, he was (unlike Schopenhauer and Kierkegaard) greatly interested in the intellectual aspect of music and in the way this seemed to be at odds with the licence and yearning of music's content. Kretzschmar, Leverkühn's teacher, says that music is a Kundry who wills not what she does: music is primarily intellectual, and its sumptuous sounds defy its essentially intellectual purpose. Music's intellectual purpose is refined spiritual expression, but music's spirituality is always ambiguous, and can be sustained only by overcoming its other sensuous and dæmonic enchantments.

With its double danger of the barbaric will and sensuousness, music presents the Romanticist's most compelling temptations, and only a hero can survive it. Mann saw Nietzsche's struggle in this light. Music, he said, tried the heroic nature of Nietzsche's soul, and through this temptation he found resolution and redemption. Adrian Leverkühn is in many respects modelled on Nietzsche. Some of the incidents in his character's life are drawn directly from Deussen's memoirs of the philosopher. Nietzsche and Leverkühn each tried to escape his emotional isolation by making a proposal of marriage to a highly intelligent, attractive and popular young woman (Nietzsche's woman was Lou Andréas-Salomé, and Leverkühn's was the set designer Marie Godeau), yet each ruined his chances by sending a messenger (Nietzsche sent Paul Rée) who became himself the successful suitor. Leverkühn's trip to the Liepzig brothel, where, unaware, he is led by an anonymous guide, is based upon Nietzsche's experience. The philosopher walked directly to the piano, struck a few chords (chords which echo the Hermit's prayer in *Der Freischütz*), and left the brothel, but, a year later, by some frightful compulsion, he returned to the brothel and contracted syphilis. Both the fictional composer and the

philosopher saw the disease as a means of heightening their creative powers; both, therefore, sacrificed their health and the possibility of a love attachment on the basis of a very cruel assessment of the demands of their work. The composer, like the philosopher, is disdainful of a safe, comfortable morality and both, though themselves physically weak, exult in man's dæmonic strengths and urges. Just as Nietzsche (or, rather Nietzsche edited by his anti-Semitic sister) was used in the political sphere to justify mass cruelty, Leverkühn's denial (through a rejection of classical forms) of the harmony between man's soul and the divine, and his alignment of the modern soul with the devil, is reflected, in the political world, as the abnegation of morality. The results of Nietzsche's work were disastrous; the political reflection of Leverkühn's consciousness is disastrous; yet in both cases Mann saw a hero and, ultimately, a triumphant hero—a Romantic saviour who depicts hope through devastation and despair.

Mann's love for Nietzsche obviously influenced his portrayal of the composer, for, despite Leverkühn's aloofness, the character has a thoroughly convincing magnetism and commands total sympathy. Leverkühn's laughter, his mocking manner and his blue-black eyes continually remind one of his isolating purposefulness and dæmonic intensity; yet this cold vividness presents an extremely appealing character. As a child, when Adrian's father shows him how nature uses deception and illusion as a means for survival (as in camouflage and in mimicry of dangerous animals) his laugh is a slight expulsion of air from the nose and mouth, with

> a toss of the head at the same time, short cool, yes contemptuous, or at the most as though he would say: "Good, that; droll, curious amusing!" But his eyes were taking it in; their gaze was distant and strange, and their darkness, metal-sprinkled, had taken on a deeper shade.

Similarly, when Zeitblom complains that Adrian, in his series of songs taken from the *Purgatorio* and the *Paradiso*, has set only the cruellest passages in Dante to music, Leverkühn responds:

> Mute, veiled, musing, aloof to the point of offensiveness, full of a chilling melancholy [his glance] ended in a smile with closed lips, not unfriendly, yet mocking, and with that gesture of turning away, so long familiar to me.

The laughter, Zeitblom says, is clearly not an expression of humour, but a desire to escape his stern consciousness. Laughter also plays an important part in Adrian's music; it is excitement and mockery in the face of suffering; it is the devil's response to the confusing amalgamation of good and evil and damnation and salvation, which, over and over again, is a theme of Adrian's music, as it was a theme of his professors' theology. In this way Mann uses a personal characteristic to reveal a psychological and moral difficulty. The frequency with which such a description is repeated, and the number of its associations, give it the character of a *leitmotif.*

Mann often compared the structure of his novels to musical structures and when he was satisfied with a book he called it a 'good score'. His use of *leitmotifs*—which is most prominent in **Doctor Faustus** but occurs in works as early as **Buddenbrooks**—was influenced by Wagner, and his juxtaposition of themes has the complexity and intellectual rigour of the juxtaposition of musical themes. The comparison of the structure of a novel to that of a score, however, can be made only in highly metaphorical terms. Musical form, generally, is a question of purely musical principles. The *leitmotif* can be used as a literary device, but Mann's use of it is not like Wagner's. Mann's use is far more rigid than Wagner's, and whereas Wagner transforms and compounds motives to extend their meanings, Mann achieves Leverkühn's vivid portrait through (nearly) straightforward repetition. As a result, the character lacks the volatile power that the dæmonic must have if it is to reveal something more than a tortured human soul. Hagen's motives, for example, have the chilling melancholy attributed to Leverkühn, and his laugh is as cold as hell; his nightwatch, as he wishes Gunther and Siegfried joy on their journey, exhibits a combination of mockery and self-torture that characterises Leverkühn, too; but whereas Leverkühn attracts through the sympathy he commands (and this gives him a distinctly non-dæmonic aspect), Hagen's wickedness can burst forth with an irresistible geniality, blurring the distinctions between friendly and destructive exuberance (as in his call to his vassals), and thus the dæmonic character overwhelms by the way he persuades one, not to sympathise with him, but to participate in his disturbing exuberance. Mann's adoration of Nietzsche, which is sometimes tediously reflected by the narrator's love for Leverkühn, results in a character for whom one can feel affection and admiration alongside a somewhat uncomfortable awareness of ruthlessness and hostility; but Mann does not create a true dæmon.

Indeed, much of Mann's presentation of the dæmonic seems forced. When Zeitblom discovers Adrian at the piano of his uncle's house exploring, with a flushed face which reveals unusual excitement, the ambiguities of the key system and the way enharmonics can be used as modulation, the narrator says he felt amazed and even ashamed at his discovery of a passion of Adrian's. Relationship is everything, Adrian explains to his startled friend; and this remark is supposed to be connected to the breakdown of the old morality that had depended upon the belief in absolute values. 'Relationship is everything' is used to make the implication that 'everything is ambiguous'; but the former does not imply the latter. 'Relationship is everything' might mean that something (a chord, a moral value?) has a determinate form only within a given context, or that what it is, is clear only when the context is known; it does not mean that a chord (or the value of something?) is never determinate and always ambiguous. Moreover, Zeitblom's anxiety about Adrian's discovery overlooks the fact that such key ambiguity was widely used by composers of the classical style; the brightest, healthiest of all composers—Haydn—was a master of enharmonic modulation. It is, then, not at all clear why such harmonic ambiguity should be thought to indicate anything dæmonic in Adrian's musical interests.

The dæmonic elements in nature, too, are presented with unsatisfactory contrivance. Adrian's father, who represents the fine, old German type, with his honest simplicity

and earnest, catholic interests, feels reverence for the oddities of nature, but Zeitblom believes—and his belief is endorsed by the obvious similarity of Jonathan Leverkühn's naturalistic studies to those described in the Faust chapbook—there is something of witchcraft or forbidden magic in the attempt to tease nature into revealing her various techniques: 'Nature itself is too full of obscure phenomena not altogether remote from magic—equivocal moods, weird, half-hidden associations pointing to the unknown—for the disciplined piety not to see therein a rash over-stepping of ordained limits'. The weirdness of various natural phenomena is asserted without qualification or explanation, as though scientific curiosity itself were irreverent. Mann connects this weirdness-of-nature motive to Adrian's pact with the devil, for Adrian calls the prostitute who infects him (and his syphilis represents his pact with the devil, for it is the means whereby he believes he will heighten his powers, but deny the possibility of a good, human life) 'Haetera Esmeralda', which is the name of the clear-winged butterflies Jonathan Leverkühn studied. This name also provides the basis for the note-row of Leverkühn's first serial composition—his first composition, that is, in the style that provides a language for modern, dæmonic reality. The *leitmotif* and its associated themes are tools for insistence rather than a development of the dæmonic image.

The medieval atmosphere is more convincingly achieved. Germany itself is shown to be an essentially backward-looking nation, and the apparently modernistic ruthlessness is shown to be a hearkening back to a medieval consciousness. The substantial criticisms Mann makes of this Gothic-Romanticism pertain to the sadism-based morality and the dæmonic-based religion which underlies it. Leverkühn begins his university studies at Halle, where he belongs to the theology department. One of his teachers—Kumpf—is a parody of Luther, or, rather, of Luther's vulgar simplicity. Kumpf's hatred of the devil is so personal and immediate that it conjures up the devil and makes him a constant companion. Luther threw an inkwell at the devil, and Kumpf throws rolls; the imagination that makes the devil so vivid reveals an imagination that needs the sadistic thrill of the dæmonic image. Leverkühn's other teacher, Schleppfuss, openly acknowledges his affinity, as a man of God, with the devil. Goodness is meaningless, he argues, without the possibility of evil, and good can therefore be understood and appreciated only when evil is understood and appreciated. Like Naphta, the theology professor believes that people crave the cruelty that goes hand in hand with this view of the spiritual struggling up from the dæmonic swamp; he claims that the victims of the Inquisition were actually grateful for their punishments, because such punishments purged them from the evil which they genuinely attributed to themselves. The Inquisition thrived upon the victims' need for such judgements, Schleppfuss insists; and, in modern terms, this is reflected in the National Socialists' view that pain is a purge, a refreshment of the spirit and culture, and that Germany wants to suffer the torture that will give her new life. But the medieval devil does not provide a satisfactory image for the modern dæmonic. When Leverkühn himself adopts a medieval tone and a medieval religious manner, as he does in writing to Zeitblom about the guide who brought him to the Leipzig brothel (the guide reminds him of Schleppfuss and, being lame, he bears the mark of his twin's name), he adopts the tone to mock it; yet, at the same time, the dæmonic-religious atmosphere is unquestionably real, and the mockery is a disguise for his confusion and moral fear. Leverkühn must realise the image of the modern devil; his confusion and fear must become more self-aware and less superstitious; and, thus, he turns from theology to music.

Leverkühn as composer has an affinity with the dæmonic partly through his affinity with music, whose sensuous domination threatens the spirit (though in Leverkühn's works, with their severe intellectual structure, this aspect is not dominant) and whose access to the primitive, destructive—creative will threatens normal life and morality. More specific to his impasse as a contemporary composer is his need to develop a language capable of giving expression to the modern state of man and his world. This modern state consists of chaos, licence and savagery; here the dark, unreflecting forces of life are glorified in their cruellest aspects. The power to express such spiritual deprivation, the capacity to give form to moral chaos and emotional licence, can be provided only by the devil's language, for these states belong to the devil. Thus Leverkühn makes his pact. But what if the use of the devil's language, the exposure of the devil's estate, were to result in horror of evil rather than in celebration? What if, through spiritual deprivation, one discovered an undeniable longing for spirit and a recognition of the necessity of morality? Could not the use of the devil's language be a sacrifice of one's moral and spiritual impulses for the purpose of discovering their ultimate reality, and thus, could not the sacrifice point towards redemption? This is the essentially unanswered question that surrounds Leverkühn's creative endeavours.

The image of the artist as someone who sacrifices himself to his art is not new in Mann's work, but *Doctor Faustus* does present a new conception of the nature of that sacrifice. Tonio Kröger envied the people whose lives he described in his books; he, as an artist, as the discoverer of inward laws and truths, was denied active life. Aschenbach was destroyed as he tried to overstep the boundaries his art drew around his life; as an artist he could not handle the upsurge of immediate life. But *Doctor Faustus,* carrying on from *Mario and the Magician,* in which Cipolla claims to suffer the pain he persuades others to express, presents the artist as someone who bears the burden of life more intensely than the ordinary man. The artist is still not an active participant in life (when the artist steps into life he becomes a pathetic and dangerous figure: Hitler had wanted to be a great architect, and referred to himself as a frustrated artist) but he is nonetheless bound especially close to the forces underlying life. His individuality, his personal emotions and history, are sacrificed to his ability to express the collective psyche. In *Buddenbrooks* and *Tonio Kröger* 'life' was simple, unreflecting activity and immediate, practical desire; it was sometimes banal and sometimes rather fetching, but it was always innocuous. In *Doctor Faustus* the unreflecting activity is the artist's subject, yet it is anything but innocuous. Hanno's death drift has become aggressive; it is active, and there-

fore destructive; the practical world and the artist's world are one, and the mingling is the devil's achievement.

The artist, in this novel too, is still separated from the world of human attachment and affection, and this theme is still portrayed with a good deal of sentimentality. Leverkühn's nephew, who dies from meningitis and whose death Leverkühn sees as his own responsibility (because he loved him in spite of his dæmonic pact) is too sweet and benevolent and innocent to be convincing. Moreover, the connection between Leverkühn's behaviour and the child's illness is too arbitrary to provide any justification for his sense of guilt. The themes of this novel do indeed point to the need to reassess responsibility for disasters one did not foresee or intend; but to make any sense of responsibility some kind of causal link must be argued. Leverkühn's pact with the devil is real because the devil's world is real and because the composer's imagination, with almost exultant determination, explored that world; but the devil does not have the reality of Kumpf's devil, at whom one could throw rolls, nor the reality of an overseer who, like Faust's Mephistopheles, becomes a personal agent in the drama. More convincing—because given an explanation in terms of human motive and desire—is Leverkühn's unwitting instigation of tragedy when he sends Schwertfeger to propose on his behalf to Marie Godeau. Schwertfeger understands his errand to be a travesty, yet he, the flirtatious violinist, is sycophant to the composer. He goes, but the confrontation ends with him suing for Marie Godeau's hand himself, and, as a result of his engagement, his mistress shoots him. Here the artist's emotional awkwardness is seen on a human plane; his coldness is not presented as a privileged quality, but as part of the world's confusion and ignorance.

In *Doctor Faustus* the artist still suffers in isolation, as did Tonio Kröger, but his suffering is no longer narcissistic and self-indulgent. Leverkühn's isolation intensifies the universal element of his art; for in isolation from specific conflicts and desires, he faces the bare bones of the moral problem: he goes to the farthest extreme of evil to warn against that path or to find a way through it. Furthermore, the chilling aspect of Leverkühn's solitary journey makes, dramatically, an important moral point. As Leverkühn explains the meaning of his final composition to his friends (who are all, in various ways, representative of Germany and who, therefore, are ultimately the subjects of his work), they either recoil from him or mock his agony or declare him, when he is revealing their own reality, to be mad. Leverkühn strikes a dissonant chord on the piano and then opens his mouth as though to sing; but instead he utters a horrible, heart-piercing cry. When he collapses even the faithful Zeitblom hesitates to approach him. Only Frau Schweigestill, whose wholesome humanity has remained inviolate, despite the moral decay around her, is free from the egoism which fears contact with illness and injury; only her healthy understanding makes her care effective, and prevents any gap between the perception of suffering and sympathetic action.

This episode reveals a continuing force against evil in traditional humanism—humanism which is importantly different from the shallow, feeble enlightenment of the burgher classes, which the proud Faust, in Leverkühn's final composition, totally rejects. Whereas 'enlightened' society, with its hypocritical restraints, destroys people like the Rodde sisters, Frau Schweigestill offers her lodgers reprieve from the false urban morality. She describes a schizophrenic who had once stayed with her as a woman whose ideas had not been able to fit in with those of the rest of the world: Frau Schweigestill is too sensitive to suffering to be intolerant of madness. She also cared for a pregnant Fräulein, and she sees the young woman's parents' despair as both ridiculous and cruel because it is brought on by finicky social fears and prevents them from giving their daughter the love she needs. Frau Schweigestill does not deny the darker side of human nature because she is not shocked by it. Nor does she dwell upon sin with the fascination of the guilty. The key to her sanity and morality is effective, immediate sympathy.

Towards the end of his life, when he is paralysed as a result of syphilis, Leverkühn has—according to Zeitblom—a Christ-like appearance. Though this association is somewhat simplistic, the novel as a whole supports the conception of the artist as a man who, like no other, explores and suffers the extreme depths of the soul and the psyche. In the grip of passion and pain the artist discovers his ultimate humanity and his ultimate morality. The model is a Romantic one, for gigantic, uncompromising forces are seen as the greatest reality, and the hero is the one who exhausts himself in his struggle with these forces, who is destroyed and redeemed through his destruction. For the Flying Dutchman, caught within the sea's tumultuous yearning and strife, to be drowned is to be freed; and the impetus of this novel is towards spiritual redemption through immersion in the will.

As Romanticism's prime representative, music provides the dramatic focus of the novel. It is music that combines the best and worst impulses: it is music that discovers the devil's language in its supreme suitability for the expression of the chaotic and savage will, and it is also music, which arose from lamentation, that will reveal an irreducible spiritual craving. Leverkühn's world is a musical one; but the artistic bias of his life does not limit him (as it limited Tonio Kröger and Aschenbach). The musical world penetrates the human world and extends it to reveal its deepest sources.

Frau Leverkühn's melodious mezzo-soprano speaking voice, with its instinctive sweetness and warmth, was, from the hour of Adrian's birth, his lullaby. As a child Adrian learned counterpoint from Hanne, the stable girl, who, smelling of her good and useful animals, sang partsongs with him and Zeitblom in the evenings under the linden tree. The songs she sang were often gruesome and mawkish, and her simplicity introduces a sinister element in Adrian's musical world. The folk-songs reveal a taste for cruelty. Their medieval flavour is reflected in the medieval setting of Leverkühn's first disciplined musical instruction—the city of Kaisersaschern—where Adrian is taught by a man who left America because it was too progressive and who clings to the backward-looking conservatism that thrives in the heart of Germany. Despite Kretzschmar's view of music as the human spirit's finest

and most subtle spokesman, it is he who introduces Adrian to the notion that the classical style is at an end. His description of the consummation of the classical style, however, is hardly pessimistic, for it employs a thoroughly positive conception of music as an art that involves one's sensuous and emotional being but at the same time provides a language for the spirit. As Kretzschmar, battling against his stutter, discusses the question as to why Beethoven did not write a third movement to his last piano sonata (opus III), he plays the second and final variations movement:

> The arietta theme, destined to vicissitudes for which in it idyllic innocence it would not seem to have been born, is presented at once, and announced in sixteen bars, reducible to a motif which appears at the end of its first half, like a brief soul-cry . . . What happens now to this mild utterance, to this pensive, subdued formulation rhythmically, harmonically, contrapuntally, with what does its master bless and to what condemns it, into what black nights and dazzling flashes, crystal spheres wherein coldness and heat, repose and ecstasy are one and the same, he flings it down and lifts it up . . .
>
> The characteristic of the movement is of course the wide gap between bass and treble, between the right and left hand, and a moment comes, an utterly extreme situation, when the delicate motif seems to hover alone and forsaken above a giddy yawning abyss—a procedure of awe-inspiring unearthliness, from which then succeeds a distressful diminishing, something like a start of fear that such a thing could happen. Much else happens before the end. But when it ends, and while it is ending, something arrives, after so much rage, persistence, obstinacy, extravagance: something entirely unexpected and touching in its mildness and goodness.

(pp. 139-51)

Despite the vicissitudes to which music itself is shown to be subject in this novel, Kretzschmar's type of musical analysis remains valid. Music expresses man's battle with spiritual and dæmonic forces, and on the musical battlefield the composer seeks his ultimate, heroic resolution in tenderness and lamentation. The Romanticism of Wagner, which Mann saw as a burden of longing, a passive dissolution of the senses and spirit which drifts towards death, has been replaced by the Romantic heroism of Beethoven and Nietzsche, in which resolution is triumph and exultation, and death is a lamenting departure rather than an ecstatic greeting.

In many respects Leverkühn's struggles have a moral clarity those of Hans Castorp and Aschenbach lack. Leverkühn's discovery of hope is through the despair of hell, and Mann shows how the good aspects of the German character and the good aspects of Romanticism have been distorted into the greatest evil; but there is not, in this novel, the moral ambiguity of *The Magic Mountain* in which the most desirable is the most deadly, or of *Death in Venice* in which the abyss provides imagination's richest promise and yet is totally destructive. In *Doctor Faustus* Mann's hell (which is a place in which evil is celebrated rather than a place in which evil is punished) is moral annihilation, and the underworld is not the seductive-dæmonic or fascinating wildness or release from shallow practicality; savagery and licence are deprived of their aura of lush vitality, and hell breeds them in awful isolation. The devil tells Adrian:

> That is the secret delight and security of hell, that it is not to be informed upon, that is is protected from speech, that it just is, but cannot be public in the newspapers, be brought by any word to critical knowledge, wherefore precisely the words "subterranean", "cellar", "thick walls", "soundlessness", "forgottenness", "hopelessness", are poor weak symbols. One must be satisfied by symbolism, my good man, when one is speaking of hell, for there everything ends—not only the true word that describes, but everything altogether . . . Every compassion, every grace, every sparing every last trace of consideration for the incredulous, imploring objection "that verily you cannot do so unto a soul": it is done, it happens, and indeed without being called to any reckoning in words; in a soundless cellar, far down beneath God's hearing, and happens to all eternity.

The horror rather than the fascination of hell is emphasised in **Doctor Faustus.** The devil explains that what are normally referred to as the 'lusts of hell' is excitation from continuous pain, an excitation which destroys the dignity of suffering. Everyone is in pain, yet everyone mocks his neighbour for his pain. Suffering here, in the devil's hell, leads not to compassion but to sadism and jeering. Adrian uses this image of hell in his music, for it is this—this counterpart to Germany's soul—which he must express; but in this hell Adrian discovers his humanity and music discovers its proper subject as lamentation, and the devil's hell is, possibly, redeemed.

Mann's account of the development of musical form is strongly influenced by his moral vision and lacks historical incisiveness. Kretzschmar's view that the second movement of opus III is the consummation and thus the end of sonata form, is based upon the expressive rather than the harmonic or structural aspects of the music: the movement is seen as a leavetaking after which there can be no return. But of course there was a return to this form, though the classical style itself had come to an end. Leverkühn's creative impasse, during the period in which he could write only parodistic works, seems to imply that between Beethoven and possible contemporary styles there was a huge gap; whereas Schumann, Brahms and Debussy (and of course Wagner) formed a bridge without which contemporary music as it is, is unimaginable. Moreover, the devil's explanation as to why the composer needs his dæmonic gifts makes little sense as a musical argument. He tells Adrian that the devil's function is not to destroy value through reductive criticism (as did Goethe's Mephistopheles) but to rule with 'shining, sparkling, vainglorious unreflectingness'. This amoral, instinctive energy must be Adrian's subject matter and, the devil argues, to realise this subject the composer needs a strict and dæmonic style. Again his argument is moral rather than musical: a musical style given by God would allow free-

dom, as God allows freedom, but the devil is a despot; secondly, godly forms appeal to the understanding, whereas the barbaric and elemental subject matter the devil provides, confounds and terrorises the understanding.

The sometimes simplistic, sometimes contrived account of Leverkühn's musical form is mitigated by Mann's masterly descriptions of the compositions themselves. In these descriptions the musical forms chosen by Leverkühn are indeed shown to be necessary to musical expression. *Apocalypsis cum figuris,* Adrian's penultimate oratorio uses the devil's language to reveal a highly disturbing paradox; for in this composition, dissonance is used to express everything lofty, solemn, pious, everything of the spirit, whereas the consonance of classical harmony is reserved for the world of hell. The paradox arises from the fact that the world is now in harmony with hell, and the 'rightness' associated with classical tonality, the sense of its belonging to an objective order, stems from its correspondence with the true nature of the world, which is now the devil's nature.

The awfulness, and the greatness, of this work are frighteningly clear. At the end of the first part of the oratorio there is a hellish laughter which represents the devil's hell: 'for this bliss of hell is like a deep-voiced pitiful jeering and scorn of all the immeasurable anguish'. In the musical work the laughter begins with a single voice and then rapidly gains ground, embracing choir and orchestra, until it explodes in the mocking, exulting laughter of the Pit. Yet this hellish laughter has its counterpart in the beginning of the second part of the oratorio, where a children's choir is accompanied by a chamber orchestra to achieve an icy, cosmic effect, with harsh dissonances, but also with an apparent effect of inaccessible, supernatural and alien loveliness of sound that fills the hearer with a hopeless longing. The spiritual impasse is clear when one understands that this music of the spheres reproduces, note for note, the music of hell's mocking laughter. The devil has usurped heaven, and the longing, which Zeitblom says is felt within the work, the longing for a soul, is a longing without hope.

When Leverkühn discusses the terms of his pact with the devil he proposes the possibility that contrition will eventually save him. The devil answers that contrition for the sake of salvation is worthless. Leverkühn insists he means genuine contrition which is too profound to consider the possibility of salvation: what then? The devil evades Leverkühn's question, and the question re-emerges with Leverkühn's final work, *D. Fausti Weheklag* which, ultimately, defeats the devil. The most profoundly dæmonic aspect of the earlier oratorio was the fact that hell's barbarism gave rise to mockery, that universal suffering was divorced from compassion, that there was absolutely no viable moral position in that ecstasy of chaos and impulse. The initial conception of his final work is equally savage and negative: after the death of his nephew, Leverkühn declares his determination to 'take back' Beethoven's Ninth Symphony. He plans to deny the vision of universal love, joy and communion with which Beethoven's work concludes. But this denial is not a negation of religion; its denial is couched in terms of lamentation, which reveal reverence for the lost vision. Moreover, in this work Leverkühn rediscovers music's first and original manifestation as lamentation; and lamentation is expression, and expression is liberation. The work has a highly determined structure, but the expressive element supersedes this rigour; finally, the cellar walls of hell are broken, and music gives a hearing to man's spiritual needs and offers a recognition of his humanity.

This enormous work is, like the finale of the Ninth Symphony with its variations of exultation, a variation-piece, but it is negatively related to Beethoven's work in that the variations are a series of laments, and there is no spiritual expansion, but always a return to the theme, based upon Faust's saying in the sixteenth-century chapbook, 'For I die as a good and bad Christian'. His goodness stems from his contrition; his badness from his pact with the devil; but Leverkühn changes the notion of a Christian as someone who might be saved. Indeed, the very hope of salvation is the devil's temptation, and, in proud despair, Faust says 'No' to the false and feeble burgher's God.

There is no going back to the traditional religion in which it is supposed that reason and goodwill triumph. In this respect Leverkühn is dæmonic, for he, like Nietzsche, prefers the devil's truth to comforting falsehood. Yet the very strength of his despair and his proud commitment to truth and the genuine assessment of human suffering is a gesture towards redemption:

> at the end of this work of ceaseless lamentation, softly, above reason, and with the speaking unspokenness given to music alone, it touches the feelings. I mean the closing movement of the piece, where the choir loses itself and which sounds like the lament of God over the lost state of His world . . . This dark tone-poem permits up to the very end no consolation, appeasement, transfiguration. But take our artistic paradox: grant that expressiveness—expressiveness as lament—is the issue of the whole construction. Then may we not set it parellel to another conception, a religious one, and ask, but only in the lowest whisper, whether out of the thoroughly irremediable hope might germinate? It would be a hope beyond hopelessness, the transcendence of despair—not a betrayal of it, but the miracle, which goes beyond belief. Listen to the end alone, listen with me. One group of instruments after another retires, and what remains, as the work fades in the air, is the high G of a cello, the last word, the last fainting sound, slowly dying in a pianissimo-fermata. Then nothing more—silence and night. But that tone which vibrates in the silence, which is no more, upon which only the spirit meditates, and which was the voice of mourning, is so no more, it changes its meaning, it remains like a light in the night.

Schopenhauer believed that man discovered a compassion-based morality when he realised the universality of the chaotic forces that lie behind life and death. The horror of the devil's hell is the ignominious thrill of pain and the continuous desire to wound and to mock one's companions in pain. Leverkühn, as he uses the devil's language and presents the devil's world, develops his own human voice—the voice of lamentation—and this is a discovery

of his own humanity, of his participation in all suffering and of the necessity of a new morality. It is a morality based on a thoroughly pessimistic view of the world, as was Schopenhauer's, but it is also the only morality that seemed honest at the time of the composition.

Leverkühn worked on *D. Fausti Weheklag* during the last two years of his rational existence (1929-30), years which bred the disasters that overwhelmed the country, disasters which, as Zeitblom finishes his biography (in the last phase of the Second World War), are being drowned in blood and flame. Adrian dies in 1940, just when, as Zeitblom puts it, Germany, at the height of her corrupt triumphs, was about to gain the whole world by her pact with the devil. And now the country 'embraced by demons, a hand over one eye and with the other staring into horrors, falls down from abyss to abyss. When from the uttermost hopelessness will a miracle, which goes beyond belief, light the day of hope?'

Germany, trying to seek national identity through a political glorification of the Romanticism that was part of the country's art, has discovered herself to be at the mercy of her self-created dæmons. Zeitblom's prayer for his country, which closes the novel, echoes the close of Leverkühn's last work: when the will has its way, when reason and morality are thoroughly overpowered, then man draws his breath and looks at his evil world and rediscovers his need for reason and restraint. But there is no going back to a belief in the possibility of man as a rational being, whose deepest desires and interests lead to goodness and harmony. The irrational, the aggressive and the destructive have been revealed as the largest part of human nature; yet the horror of this revelation is such that some moderation of man's dæmonic reality is seen to be necessary—absolutely necessary.

The moral tale is darker than that of **The Magic Mountain,** with its similar ending, when it is proposed that love might arise from the world-feast of death and destruction. Here the hope is meagre, but for the Romanticist it is a triumph. **Doctor Faustus** exhibits a felt need for a restraining morality in a way that transcends a Romanticist's view—a view in which death and dissolution and the power of passion and impulse are seen as the highest goods. Yet the drama in which this frail but essential moral standpoint is secured, is itself highly Romantic. The notion of redemption from the uttermost point of despair, of building up only from destruction, of finding truth only through forbidden journeys, reveals an abiding sympathy with Romantic extremity and intensity and with the peculiar life-defeat that accompanies them, a life-defeat based upon an enormous vitality that cannot integrate itself with reality. **Doctor Faustus** is a triumph for Mann's imagination in that the necessity of morality is discovered in the depth of a Romanticist's tale, but even this triumph is conceived only as the final, despairing, Romantic gesture. (pp. 151-57)

T. E. Apter, in his Thomas Mann: The Devil's Advocate, *The Macmillan Press Ltd., 1978, 165 p.*

Paul Coates   (essay date 1983)

[*In the essay excerpted below, Coates challenges social and historical interpretations of* Doctor Faustus, *asserting that its central focus is the breakdown of personality and the human tendency to develop myths in response to extreme deprivation and isolation.*]

Doktor Faustus is often described as an allegory that parallels the demonic turn taken by the art of the composer Adrian Leverkühn with Germany's adoption of National Socialism and regression to a barbaric, cultic reality. It is easy to see whence this view stems; Mann himself contributed to it in the form of statements like 'what he inflicts on Rudi is a premeditated murder required of him by the Devil', whilst his anti-war broadcasts and deliberate parallel with Goethe's great drama would lead one to expect an ambitiously programmatic statement. But a 'statement' is just what the work is not. Mann's reference to the 'clear-ambiguous' relationship between Zeitblom's despairing account and the pressures of war should have made readers wary of identifying it as an allegory with point-by-point equivalences in actual historical reality. Ronald Gray teeters on the edge of a subtler understanding, only to retreat; he remarks [in *The German Tradition in Literature, 1871-1945*] that 'the confusion of *Doktor Faustus* derives from the fact that Zeitblom operates always with a dual conception of Leverkühn.' It is almost embarrassing to have to point out the simple fact that this confusion is Zeitblom's and not Mann's and to draw the necessary critical conclusions: namely, that Mann's astonishing, resonant work is neither an allegory nor the failure it is commonly held to be (*pace* T. J. Reed) but rather a close analysis of the conditions under which people resort to myth. It analyses the extreme situations of deprivation and isolation to which people respond by myth-making, and whatever Mann's conscious intentions may have been, the allegories in his work stem from his two narrators (*two*, for Leverkühn narrates the encounter with the presumed Devil) and are so shaped as brilliantly to express their impulsions. It is Leverkühn who mentions the Devil and calls his last work *Doktor Fausti Weheklag*, whilst it is Zeitblom who picks up the cue and terms the music hag-ridden. Leverkühn's full statement of the consequences of his 'pact' is uttered before his gathered acquaintance and is chilling because its conscious recapitulation of a myth sounds insane; indeed, a doctor present remarks that Adrian *is* mad. Adrian's words cannot be taken literally. Mann's description of him in *Die Entstehung des Doktor Faustus* as 'deliberately and darkly playful' suggests that Adrian has donned a mask he is now unable to separate from his face. The central theme of *Doktor Faustus* is the breakdown of personality, which recurs on all levels of the book. Leverkühn sees himself as Faustus, adopts a pseudo-Lutheran dialect and frames his account of his meeting with the Devil in terms borrowed from Dostoevsky. That he does this, and that Mann painstakingly composes his character of fragments of Hugo Wolf, Schoenberg, Nietzsche and various other artists, is less a consequence of Mann's own defective powers of imagination than a means of suggesting the elusiveness of Adrian's personality, which evaporates in the gaps between the echoes. The use of people and places as leitmotifs sends ripples criss-crossing through the entire narrative, reflections of the theme of breakdown. This serves a dual purpose: on one level it expresses the way Zeitblom's obsessions mould and probably distort the material (it is he alone who is alarmed by the similarity between Buchel and Pfeiffering and he who persuades one to consider Adrian as purely and simply demonic by voicing the unease he feels when his friend is too 'human'); on another level it shows how ideas that seem harmless in one context can circle back into history in a virulent form, just as Kretschmar's ideas (and Mann's own?) bear in retrospect an unsettling similarity to those of the Kridwiss group. Thus Modern Germany melts into its medieval forebear, as Kaisersaschern emerges as the kind of place where one expects to see haggard old witches walking the streets, as the habit of book-burning returns, and as intellectuals advocate a cultic civilisation. The nightmare extends from time into space; the Devil moves without transition from one part of Adrian's room to another and seems at moments to be Schleppfuss redivivus, Kretschmar, or even Adrian's own double.

Dualism is a constant feature of Mann's works. Here it is movingly related to the themes of insanity and mutual unknowing, rather than—as usual—being employed to generate a series of endlessly dissipated and reiterated polarities. Here the dualism says that even childhood friends are strangers. Where knowledge is insufficient, myth enters; Leverkühn is no doctor, so he mythologises his disease, of which he exhibits no comprehension; Zeitblom's lack of continual intimacy with his friend makes him use myth to create the illusion of knowledge, both for himself and for others. By dissociating himself from the narrator, Mann underlines that the creation of myth is part of the Teutonic malady. Zeitblom is the child of a myth-making era and cannot escape its fundamental assumptions. Like the later Wittgenstein, Mann traces the bounds of sense by letting his characters overstep them, and lest this seem complacent, he implicates himself in the objects of his critique by attributing many of his own ideas to a generation which becomes lost through seeing itself as lost. That Mann's work was read as a myth or allegory by the civilisation he suspected of being diseased is hardly surprising; the readers projected their own ailment onto the work. Mann breaks the vicious circle by showing how a *present-day* man, even one as apparently sober and unbiased as Zeitblom, is driven to myth as an attempt to explain the inexplicable. Myth is self-hypnotising pseudo-explanation.

Mann remarks that he employed Zeitblom in order to bring about 'a certain lightening of the dark material', but the narrator's deeper function is to relativise Mann's own words and so to preserve him from the presumption of attempting to explain whatever complicities may have obtained between German high culture and National Socialism. By placing the accusation in another's mouth he avoids the fatuity of art about the danger of art: for to question culture truly is to question the questioner who assumes that he can stand outside culture. [T. W.] Adorno has written [in *Noten zur Literatur I*] of the 'enigmatic irony, which cannot be reduced to any conceptual mockery' in Mann's style, and in the earlier novels this tendency often infuriates, for the narrator is perpetually on the verge of becoming a discrete personality but never actually does so, which produces a tantalising sense of the wilfully withheld. The emergence of the narrator as a separate character brings the sub-text of doubt out into the open to make it actually functional in the text. Incorporating non-Mannian ideas into the text becomes the ultimate extension of his realism and represents the dialectical point or border case at which the writer relinquishes control over his characters. Here Mann really does recall Dostoevsky, as was his intention. The narrator's ignorance, which drives him to myth in an attempt to produce a pseudo-explanation, is undermined by the way the ideas held by the characters are more powerful than those of the narrator. Mann gained this effect by inserting many of Adorno's ideas virtually verbatim into his text. Kretschmar's 'Da-wird-die Sprache—nicht mehr von der Floskel—gereinigt, sondern die Floskel—vom Schein—ihrer subjektiven Beherrschtheit' (There—the language—is no longer—cleansed—of flourishes, but the flourish is cleansed—of the illusion—of its subjective—control) is Adorno on Beethoven's late quartets.

Mann's decision to give his narrator his head (or enough rope to hang himself with) makes reading him much more like living with any other person; at times we empathise strongly with him, whilst at others he leaves us lukewarm or even cold. His nature is not fixed and he is no easier to classify than Leverkühn. His moving accounts of the histories of Ines and Clarissa Rodde are rapt and passionate. Similarly impressive is the domino-like collapse of the interdependent characters, in which the final symbol of the community is the apocalyptic image of the Munich tram discharging infernal sparks. But there are also moments when one is suspicious of him, which is why Mann holds the process of narration at arm's length. Zeitblom's frequent references at the end of the paragraphs to his 'Erschütterung' seem in the end to protest too much, and it seems disingenuous of him to feel thus about Adrian's actions whenever his friend behaves 'humanly'; his parallels between Buchel and Pfeiffering, Kaschperl and Suso, and the maids with mud-caked feet, seem in the end like tasteless doodles. Perhaps the area in which he is most suspect is that in which he analyses Adrian's reasons for sending Rudi Schwerdtfeger to present his suit to Marie Godeau. It is at this point that he confesses his absence from these meetings, and so instantly undermines his own claims to authority. And the possibility that the German defeat he is experiencing as he writes predisposes him to a pessimistic, 'demonic' interpretation should also put one on one's guard. Moreover, Leverkühn's enigmatic reserve makes all categorical explanation dubious. Whilst reading these passages, I felt that the account was left open and that it was part of Mann's mastery to present the narrator's relationship to his material as ambiguous whilst allowing one to separate the one from the other and attempt to decide for oneself. Thus I felt convinced that Zeitblom's reading was wrong—partly for the aforementioned reasons, and partly because Leverkühn is drained and dejected when he receives no reply. His action in sending Rudi seems to be a despairing wager to determine whether or not the dice of reality are loaded against him, and it has a child-like magicality. It is as if Leverkühn has said to himself that if, despite everything, a flirt like Rudi proves capable of self-sacrifice and his own belief in Marie

Godeau's love for him proves correct (something his isolation makes it hard for him to determine), then reality will be seen to be beneficent and he will be justified in coming out of isolation. It is Adrian who notices that Marie's voice resembles his mother's, and his suspicion that spiritual incest underlies his fascination by her may make him desire to keep his distance. A romantic, implicitly incestuous love, is the only affection that offers a *Durchbruch* (breakthrough—a key word in the novel) from isolation, but the fixation on the past it establishes relates the self back to an internalised archetype and so consolidates isolation. So devilish is this procedure that one is tempted to see behind it an actual devil who indulges one's desire to escape oneself by immuring one in a tower of obsession. One may be tempted to demonise the whole proceeding, as does Zeitblom, but he has no warrant for believing that Adrian deliberately removed from his presence the only two people who could have mitigated his isolation. Rather, Leverkühn's behaviour here recalls Kafka instructing Max Brod to incinerate his works—he seeks a way of acting without acting, for he is unsure of the legitimacy of any of his impulses. It is this self-uncertainty which has led him to music, which speaks but without committing itself to any meaning.

Only by having his narrator consistantly refer to music that does not exist could Mann establish his structure of ambiguities. The 'speaking unspokenness' attributed to music by Zeitblom is such that when he speaks on the same page of how a certain feature is *unverkennbar* (unmistakable) we suspend assent, for Mann leaves us to choose for ourselves whether to believe or to doubt. The fact that Adrian's music exists for us only in this form stresses the unity between Zeitblom and himself, to whom Mann referred as the two halves of one self (which is why neither of them can be visualised) and whose connectedness is underlined by the *du* with which Adrian addresses both Zeitblom and himself. Had Mann chosen an existing composer (Schoenberg for instance, who clamoured for Mann to credit him in *Doktor Faustus* with the invention of twelve-tone composition) this hostile complicity between narrator and subject would have been impossible. Moreover, he would have violated the general principle of the book, which in its concern to diagnose the Zeitgeist eschews the search for scapegoats. And since all writing about music belongs to mythology in the sense that it is desperately difficult to validate (except on the level of technical analysis), Mann can use music both as an image of the kind of experience that can seem so ineffable as to generate myths as verbal approximations to it (an experience that would render the Germans, 'the musical nation', the nation most prone to myth-making) and as a means of preserving us from an easy scepticism about the nature of Zeitblom's motives. His position is that of the stained glass that both transmits and alters the light. Through him Mann sums up his own life-long obsession with the description of music, since it is in such description that the suggestion of inverted commas worn by his style is most appropriate. He confronts his own critical language with that of actual musicians (the composite figure Schoenberg—Adorno—Leverkühn—Kretschmar), allowing the two languages to complement and criticise each other. Mann develops two opposed forms of virtuosity: he assimilates modern ideas about music and he creates an impressionistic medium to refract its heard complexity. The opposition precludes fetishism, for music is experienced both by professional musicians and by non-musicians.

When at the end of the novel Adrian talks of his pact with the Devil, it is his other-wordliness which is unnerving, not the mention of a possible demonic inspiration, and the chill is intensified by the fact that his understanding of himself is so mythological and so portentous as radically to diverge from the kind of understanding embodied in the biographical novel. Mann refers to Adrian as 'repeating a myth or a cliché with dark, deliberate playfulness'. To suspect that the hero has lost himself to a cliché rather than a myth is to face the frightening possibility that his very heroic self-stylisation is on the same level as a manipulated response to an advertisement, in this case, to an advertisement for 'Kulchur'. In Mann's work, the novel is eroded from two sides by the myth that preceded it and the cliché into which it is degenerating, so it can only yield a negative image of what would constitute an understanding of Adrian; psychology has been leeched of all meaning. Mann once explained his predilection for parody by terming parody the expression of love for a form that is no longer viable. The explanation is plangent and beautiful, but in *Doktor Faustus* Mann comes to terms with the self-indulgence with which it is also tinged. For in Adrian and in Zeitblom, the parodistic fixation on the past becomes a means of amputating oneself from the present. Together, they throw his life away by casting it in the mould of the Faust legend. In Mann's novel, as in Adrian's final work, parody explodes itself from within. Adrian's quotation of Faust's phrase 'for I die as a good and bad Christian' is so ambiguous as finally to burst the mythical framework that has supported it. Ambiguity becomes a means, like music, of talking silently, and represents the paradoxical moment at which the exhausted language of a devastated culture lies fallow before it can be used again. Here the partial, and hence inauthentic, ambiguity of Mann's earlier works becomes total, and it does so through a dissolution of his rigid categories—art versus life and so on—which corresponds to the eerie fusing of characters and ideas. Moreover, the genuinely modernist, dialectical (rather than dualistic) aesthetic at which Mann finally arrives makes it quite possible to see Leverkühn as Zeitblom. This is the most mysterious side of the novel, a radical sub-text that has passed unnoticed in Mann criticism. The identity of the two is possible for the following reasons: (a) both the novel and Leverkühn's music have the density of twelve-tone composition; (b) Zeitblom occasionally remarks that he is recounting scenes from which he was absent (e.g. the scenes between Adrian and Marie Godeau), as if dropping a hint for those who have ears to hear; (c) the co-presence of two ways of writing about music suggests the presence of a dual personality; (d) it seems strange that Zeitblom, the serene humanist, should express unease whenever his friend is too 'human' (here Zeitblom sounds like Nietzsche—'Human all too Human'—and hence like Leverkühn); (e) Leverkühn enjoys composing parodies, as when he apes Lutheran accents in the scene with the Devil; (f) Zeitblom is the only person Adrian ever addresses by the intimate 'du' (thou); and (g) Adrian's fear of the nakedness of the voice may have led him to clothe

himself in the mantle of an alien voice. The novel may be the terrifying spectral after-life of his sanity, its narrator a madman. This would account for the myth-making elements in 'Zeitblom' 's early evocations of Halle as a demonic medieval town whose lengthened shadow extends into the twentieth century. Yet this reading remains only a tantalising possibility, which is why I have relegated it to the end of this essay, rather than pronouncing it 'the true reading of *Doktor Faustus*'. The reader is drawn to participate in the book's making, so he can never be sure. The despair of Mann's book lies in the fact that its definition of sanity and truth is a negative one; its hope is that by embodying inadequate, myth-ridden means of understanding and demonstrating their inadequacy, he can indicate the existence of a point beyond them. He is not so presumptuous as to assume that he can occupy such a point. Novels allow authors both to speak and to remain silent behind the volubility of their characters, the silent image of the page. To exploit this to the full, as Mann does, is to reveal the impotence of art's power, the power of its impotence. For art alone is aware that the language it uses is fictive. By means of self-negation it transcends its own fictions. (pp. 141-48)

Paul Coates, "Fictions of Identity: Modernism in Germany," in his The Realist Fantasy: Fiction and Reality Since "Clarissa," *St. Martin's Press, 1983, pp. 141-89.*

Mann on completing *Doctor Faustus*:

On the morning of January 29, [1947] I wrote the last lines of *Doctor Faustus,* as I had had them framed in my mind for a long time—Zeitblom's silent, fervent prayer for his friend—and looked back over the three years and eight months during which I had lived under the tension of this work, from that May morning in the midst of the war when I had first taken up the pen to begin it. "I am finished," I said to my wife when she fetched me in the car from my usual walk toward the ocean. And she, who had stood by me through many a finishing, how heartily she congratulated me! "With good reason?" the diary asks. And adds: "At least it is a moral accomplishment."

Thomas Mann, in his The Story of a Novel: The Genesis of Doctor Faustus, *1961.*

Jeffrey Meyers   (essay date 1985)

[*Meyers is an American critic, educator, and biographer whose approach to modern English and European literature is what he describes as "interdisciplinary, comparative, and biographical." In the following excerpt, Meyers focuses on disease and its relationship to the creative process in* Doctor Faustus.]

Doctor Faustus is like a palimpsest with multiple layers of meaning: Faustian myth, Lutheran theology, Shakespearean parody, Nietzschean pathology, Dürer's iconography, Schönberg's music theory, Mann's autobiography and Nazi history all coalesce into the complex totality of the work. Mann's immensely complicated literary technique of aesthetic, cultural and historical analogies achieves both subtle artistic effects and profound insights into the possibility of artistic creation in an age of moral chaos and personal disintegration. Mann stimulates the careful reader to recognize "certain correspondences, transposed, as it were, into another but not far removed key." Mann intends his work to "gather up all their elements into one single focus, assemble them in one pregnant, portentous synthesis and in relentless transmission hold up to humanity the mirror of the revelation, that it might see therein what is oncoming and near at hand."

Doctor Faustus concerns the disease of Adrian's body and of his soul, the pathology of his music and his love, and the gift of creativity at the cost of demonic suffering and political destruction. Adrian, from the very beginning of his childhood acquaintance with Serenus Zeitblom, the narrator of his life, is set apart by his refusal to exchange personal glances; his unwillingness to let anyone penetrate his privacy; his reluctance to establish a *Du* relationship; his scepticism and intellectual self-consciousness; his apparent armor of purity, chastity, irony and pride; his lack of human warmth, sympathy and love. Zeitblom attempts to explain Adrian's character as he describes his tragic transformation from the ethos of purity to the pathos of impurity: "There had always been in his nature something of *noli me tangere*. I knew that; his distaste for too great nearness of people. . . . He was in the real sense of the word a man of disinclination, avoidance, reserve, aloofness. Physical cordialities seemed quite impossible to associate with his nature, even his handshake was infrequent and hastily performed. . . . An advance from the other side was shrunk from and avoided and this, undoubtedly, was connected with his abstention from women."

Adrian corrupts his natural gifts, and is unable to exorcise the evil that both possesses and inspires him. Cold—which surrounds him, emanates from him and prevents him from loving (but not desiring love)—is a leitmotif (like his mirthless laughter) that connects Adrian to the devil and symbolizes his hellish isolation in "a country where nobody else lived." Adrian's coldness also emphasizes Mann's characteristic dichotomy between the healthy normality of the bourgeois family and (as the devil demands) the enforced isolation of the artist who must give up all hope of a normal life in order to create. Adrian actually embodies and experiences the fatal consequences of the artist-victim—the decline in health, the corrupted nervous system, the icy ecstasies, the sinister damnation, the agonizing death—that Tonio Kröger merely theorized about with his Russian friend.

Adrian's education reinforces his inhuman characteristics. In Halle he comes under the influence of the two Lutheran fanatics—Kumpf and Schleppfuss—who confirm Zeitblom's Catholic belief that "endless blood-letting and the most horrible self-laceration would have been spared the human race if Martin Luther had not restored the Church." Kumpf goes so far as to fling a roll at the devil lurking in a dark corner of his house, Schleppfuss (an incarnation of the limping devil and symbol of the Nazi clubfoot, Joseph Goebbels) attracts young men by lecturing on the prominent role of sex and the power of demons in human life. He illustrates the diabolic temptation of women with the story of Heinz Klöpfgeissel, who loves the maiden Bärbel and is bewitched by her. Heinz becomes impotent when he visits a Hungarian slut and when a landlord's comely wife caresses his arm to encourage his advances. Bärbel, arrested and examined by the Church, confesses to witchcraft and is burned at the stake.

Adrian's change from theology to music is a flight from the protection of God to the realm of the demonic. It also reveals the crucial antithesis between—rather than synthesis of—ethics (theology) and aesthetics (music): "the elevation of culture as a *substitute* for religion" (or of prostitution as a substitute for love). When the music teacher Kretschmar persuades Adrian's mother (who, like Kumpf, sometimes strums a guitar) to allow Adrian to change his career, she protectively "drew her son's head to her as he sat beside her, in the strangest way," put her arms around his threatened head and leaned it upon her breast—exactly as she does when he returns to Pfeiffering after his mental collapse. Adrian's need for maternal care and his mother's instinctive gesture suggest his similarity to the "outwardly robust and even bearded [man, who] was so highly strung that when he was ill—and he inclined to illness—he wished to be treated only by a child-specialist." After choosing a musical career, Adrian—like the characters in *The Possessed* and *The Turn of the Screw*—becomes demonically possessed, and eventually psychotic. Music forces him to sever his tie with his mother, but he can never replace her love; she intuitively understands this and poignantly tries to defend him from his destiny.

Adrian's career represents a retreat from the spontaneous and sensual to the technical and systematic aspects of music, which confines his emotions to the purely intellectual sphere. This inevitably leads, by way of the twelve-tone system, to serious musical impoverishment: to parody and to stagnation. His interest in polyphonic vocal music, lieder, oratorio and opera; his tendency to marriage with the word; his insistence that music and speech "were at bottom one, language was music, music a language," articulate the sinister meaning of his art. Kretschmar's peculiar mixture of stuttering speech and brilliant oratory is echoed first in Adrian's witty repartee during his verbal pact with Satan and then in his inability to pronounce words during his final confession. Though Adrian yearns to create a more vital, emotional and melodious music, he is never able to transcend his acutely self-conscious intellect, liberate his creative imagination and achieve an "art without anguish, psychologically healthy, not solemn, unsadly confiding, an art *per du* with humanity." Rudolf—whose eye color matches Adrian's just as the butterfly matches the leaf—is murdered shortly after they become *per du* (a pun on the French *perdu*).

Every aspect of Adrian's education suggests his tendency toward disease with Hetaera and a pact with the devil. The beautiful but poisonous butterflies and his father's experiments with osmotic growths prefigure the contagious meningitis that penetrates Adrian's brain and Nepo's spine by fluid diffusion. Medieval Kaisersaschern predisposes him to the temptation of witches and hallucinations of demons. Schleppfuss' stress on the connection between the carnal and the demonic as well as the excess and violence of the Reformation encourage his self-destruction. The wish to retreat into purely intellectual music is balanced by the compensatory, all too-human desire for sexual love.

Adrian's dangerous education is complemented by his hereditary tendency to migraine, which he inherits from his father and which leads from melancholy to madness. Melancholy, symbolized by Dürer's engraving, pervades the novel: the whole nineteenth century, even truth and art itself, are called melancholy in *Doctor Faustus.* Adrian's insanity is foreshadowed by the mad baroness who lived in Pfeiffering before him and eventually had to be placed in professional care; by the weak-headed Amelia Manardi in Palestrina whose repetition of *spiriti, spiriti* anticipates his encounter with the devil; and by the conversation about mad King Ludwig on a visit to Linderhof. (Ludwig's attempt to escape his captors by swimming across the lake parallels Adrian's attempt to escape from life by drowning in the pond.)

Adrian's first migraine attack, which begins during puberty and his early experiments on the piano, is associated with sex and music. He is rejected by the army because of narrow-chestedness (a tendency to tuberculosis) and his habitual headaches. He worries that his proneness to migraine will prevent the fulfillment of his artistic promise. He suffers head pains at his sister's wedding, which drains him emotionally, and while inventing the twelve-tone system, which drains him intellectually. He seems to bear the mark of suffering, the outward sign of his hidden disease; maintains a precarious balance of vitality and informality; swings between penitential paralysis and creative release. He suffers the ordeal of all Mann's artists and is torn by "the conflict between a doctrinaire glorification of 'life' in its splendid unthinkingness, and the pessimistic reverence for suffering, with its depth and wisdom."

The clinical description of Adrian's migraine is based on Nietzsche's life, and on the detailed notes that Mann received from medical friends while writing the novel: "Luetic paralysis results from physical destruction of the brain mass by the spirochetes . . . paralyzation of the pupils . . . headaches. Psychic irritability—to the point of sudden frenzied states. Vague speech—frequent unconscious slips of the tongue, inability to pronounce difficult words. . . . General state of health more or less affected. Headaches, dizziness, lack of appetite, weakness. Periods of improvement even without treatment." These increasingly grave symptoms are the physical penalty that accompany the creation of Adrian's major works. Severe migraine and a sensation of violent seasickness attack him several times a month and force him to remain in bed in a darkened room (Adrian's seasickness recalls his early symphonic fantasy *Ocean Lights,* his descent into the sea in Professor Akercocke's diving bell, his identification with Andersen's little sea-maid and his final attempt to drown himself in the pond at Buchel):

> It was as though he were pinched and plagued
> with hot pincers, without being in immediate

danger of his life. That, however, seemed to have arrived at its nadir, so that he was just prolonging it by dragging on from one day to the next. He had been attacked by a stomach ailment, not yielding to any dietary measures, beginning with violent headache, lasting several days and recurring in a few more; with hours, yes, whole days of retching from an empty stomach, sheer misery, undignified, niggling, humiliating, ending in utter exhaustion and persistent sensitivity to light after the attack had passed.

Adrian's role as sacrificial artist is subtly foreshadowed by the soloist in his setting of the Brentano song-cycle, for when it was performed in the Tonhalle in Zurich, the part "of the boy who 'early broke his leg' was sung by a boy unfortunately really crippled, using a crutch, little Jacob Nägli." And the relationship between pathology, theology and music is emphasized when Adrian identifies with the little sea-maid, who is willing to endure knife-like pains with every step she takes in order "to win, like human beings, an immortal soul."

Mann contrasts the agonizing artistic with the comfortable bourgeois way of life, and increases the subtlety of the novel by making Zeitblom the narrator and forcing the reader to see beyond his imperfect understanding. For Zeitblom's health and temperament prevent him from truly comprehending the full significance of Adrian's allegorical career, despite their long friendship. Zeitblom is intellectual enough to grasp and express the basic issues, but too pedantic and too infatuated with his subject to see the implications of Adrian's evil art. Like Tonio Kröger, Hans Castorp and the devil in *Doctor Faustus,* the conservative Zeitblom (who does not realize that syphilis is the devil's means of inspiring music) expresses the Romantic idea of disease and ironically insists that Adrian's genius grows out of illness rather than out of evil: "The depressive and exalted states of the artist, illness and health, are by no means sharply divided from each other. . . . [In illness] elements of health are at work, and elements of illness, working genius-like, are carried over into health. . . . Genius is a form of vital power deeply experienced in illness, creating out of illness, through illness creative." Zeitblom—but not Mann—would agree with Proust's observation [in *Time Regained*] that "Works of literature are like artesian wells, the deeper the suffering, the higher they rise."

Adrian's encounter with Hetaera esmeralda, anticipated by Heinz's meeting with the Hungarian slut, brilliantly synthesizes the complex pattern of associations and dominant themes of the novel: Nietzsche's syphilis, Jonathan Leverkühn's butterflies, Adrian's two mothers, Schleppfuss' lectures, Faust's temptation, Dürer's woodcut of the great whore, Blake's poetry of poison and pollution, Weber's opera the *Freischütz,* Brentano's folk-songs, Beethoven's sonata, Schönberg's twelve-tone system, Frau von Tolna's mysterious patronage and Nazi Germany's collapse.

Unlike Tonio Kröger, an unwilling artist-victim, Adrian *pursues* disease as a means to creativity. Mann uses repulsive venereal rather than pathetic pulmonary disease not only because *Doctor Faustus* is based on Nietzsche's illness, but also because it is contracted during sexual intercourse and perversely relates Adrian to an infectious prostitute (a very different temptation from Tonio Kröger's attraction to the blond and blue-eyed Ingeborg Holm); because its long phase of apparent remission permits a period of creativity followed by the "punishment" of madness; and because its classically anti-social nature extends the theme of the artist's opposition to society. On the realistic level, syphilis is associated with promiscuity, causes insanity, infects unborn infants and kills new life (like Nepo). On the symbolic level, it creates beauty, redeems corrupt society and destroys the creator.

When Adrian arrives at Leipzig to study music he strikes a bargain with a devilish pimp, a "small-beer-Schleppfuss," who guides him (as Nietzsche had been guided in Cologne) to a whorehouse filled with a half dozen bare-breasted "morphos, clear-wings, esmeraldas." Adrian describes his experience in a letter to Zeitblom written in archaic German:

> I stood, not showing what I was feeling, and there opposite me I see an open piano, a friend, I rush up to it across the carpet and strike a chord or twain . . . as in the hermit's prayer in the finale of the *Freischütz*. . . . A brown wench puts herself nigh me, in a little Spanish jacket, with a big gam [mouth], snub nose, almond eyes, an Esmeralda, she brushed my cheek with her arm. I turn round, push the bench away with my knee, and fling myself back through the lust-hell, across the carpets, past the mincing madam, through the entry and down the steps without touching the brass railing.

Terrified and revolted by this awkward confrontation, Adrian hides his emotions and flees to the refuge of the open piano and the certainty of music—exactly as he had done with the Winfried group: "going straight to the piano, as though that alone were his goal." He breaks the magic spell in the bordello with a chord from the *Freischütz,* in which the hermit prays to give the hero Max a year's probation for dealing with the devil. (Adrian had seen the *Freischütz* with Kretschmar; the devil later alludes to the villain Kaspar and the satanic Samiel—the "angel of death"—in the opera. Kaspar is also associated with folkish—proto-Nazi—elements in the story *Kasperl and Annerl* by Brentano, whose poems Adrian had set, and with the dog Kaschperl in Pfeiffering, a Cerberus who confines Adrian to his hermetic hell.)

The brush on the cheek is an ironic allusion to Kretschmar's explanation of the arietta theme in the second (and final) movement of Beethoven's Sonata in C minor, opus. 111: "an end without any return": "It is like having one's hair or cheek stroked, lovingly, understandingly, like a deep and silent farewell look." This analogy vividly links the flesh and blood experience that Adrian lacks with the artistic creation that he craves. Adrian loses human love when he leaves his mother for music and attempts to recover it with Hetaera. The moving "stroked cheek" motif in Beethoven is typically transformed by Adrian into the coldly coded note-cipher in his setting of Brentano's "O dear maiden, how bad you are" and his *Lamentation of Dr. Faustus:* "h, e, a, e, e-flat: hetaera esmeralda."

"Understanding," which Kretschmar associates with Beethoven's sonata, is the most characteristic trait of Else Schweigestill, Adrian's landlady at Pfeiffering. Both love and understanding merge at the very end of the novel when his real and surrogate mothers finally meet, but can no longer help him: "Adrian trembled for a long time, [characteristically] resting his head on the breast of the woman he called *Mutter* and *Du.* Frau Schweigestill, who kept out of the way, he called *Mutter* and *Sie.*" In the last paragraph of the novel, when Zeitblom identifies Adrian with Germany and prays mercy for "my friend, my Fatherland," he again alludes to Hetaera and speaks of the hectic flush on Germany's cheek during the excitement of her military triumphs.

Zeitblom calls Adrian's profane and dangerous encounter with Hetaera (an extreme version of his own seven-month liaison with a working-class girl) his "toll to nature." He warns that his friend will soon return to the bordello when driven by what Adrian calls "interest," an egoistic, libidinous passion that is even stronger than love: "a love from which the animal warmth has been withdrawn." One year later the rational Adrian irrationally surrenders to instinct and deliberately mortifies himself. Like the medieval religious fanatics described by Leo Naphta—"kings' daughters kissing the stinking wounds of lepers, voluntarily exposing themselves to contagion and calling the ulcers they received their 'roses'; or drinking the water that had been used for the cleansing of abscesses, and vowing that nothing had ever tasted so good"—Adrian, using a musical pretext, abandons himself to an act that is unnatural in its self-destruction, but natural in its pathetic quest for love and attempt to relate the cerebral to the sensual.

Adrian ostensibly goes to Graz to hear the Austrian première of Richard Strauss' opera *Salome*—based on the biblical story of a man ignobly destroyed by a woman's lust. (Strauss was also inspired by Nietzsche's *Zarathustra* and later became a Nazi sympathizer.) Hetaera has left the whorehouse for hospital treatment, but Adrian finds her in Pozsony, across the border in Hungary. She responds with genuine feeling to the second visit of her distinguished client, once again caresses his cheek with her bare arm and transcends her wretched existence by warning him against her syphilitic body. Zeitblom asks: "What madness, what deliberate, reckless tempting of God, what compulsion to comprise the punishment in the sin, finally what deep, deeply mysterious longing for daemonic conception, for a deathly unchaining of chemical change in his nature was at work, that having been warned he despised the warning and insisted upon possession of the flesh?" But it seems clear that Adrian scourges himself and risks the salvation of his soul for a "daemonic conception" that would (as Mann says) "unblock inhibitions at any cost" and lead through disease to productive genius. Hetaera (like Beethoven's Sonata) is "an end without any return". For he consciously chooses the whore as he later chooses the devil; his syphilitic infection produces the hallucination that allows him to sign the pact and forces him to renounce human love.

Adrian throws more light on his experience with Hetaera during the confession he makes to his horrified friends—

who get up and leave throughout his speech like the musicians in Haydn's *Farewell Symphony.* In contrast to Zeitblom's emotional rhetoric, Adrian describes the fatal encounter in an objective and even lyrical fashion that recalls the nudity and caress of the deceptive whore as well as the devouring drop that licks the shellac off the glass stick (like a witch in the form of a cat) before ejecting it from its body:

> For it was but a butterfly, a bright cream-licker, Hetaera Esmeralda, she charmed me with her touch, the milk-witch, and I followed after her into the twilit shadowy foliage that her transparent nakedness loveth, and where I caught her, who in flight is like a wind-blown petal, caught her and caressed with her, defying her warning, so did it befall. For as she charmed me, so she bewitched me and forgave me in love—so I was initiate, and the promise confirmed. . . . Man is made for hell or blessedness, made and foredestined, and I was born for hell.

Adrian's encounter with Hetaera, like his father's scientific experiments, is a temptation of nature in which he fails to buy rather than earn love, to enjoy promiscuous sexual relations without paying the physical penalty and to defy disease without becoming infected.

Heinz's Hungarian slut and Adrian's sexual encounter in Hungary (he is tempted and treated in Leipzig, infected in Pozsony) lead, through an introduction by the Hungarian musicologist Desiderius Fehér (he bears the first name of Erasmus, who disputed with Luther) to the invisible Hungarian noblewoman Frau von Tolna. Like Zeitblom (but unlike the unreliable Schildknapp and the unfaithful Schwerdtfeger), this fabulously wealthy widow of a sexually dissipated nobleman was "the most devoted friend, confidante, and counsellor, unconditionally and unfailingly at his service." She gives him a precious emerald with an engraved prophetic warning from Callimachus, which he ignores; but the ring forms the "precious link of an invisible chain" and he ritualistically wears it while composing. He visits her princely castle (art) in her indescribably filthy village (disease) when she is absent. But Hetaera, who infects Adrian and then "disappears by adaptation" into aristocratic society, is present as a veiled stranger at his grave.

Fehér's first name is connected with the last name of Dr. Erasmi (Adrian composes on a slanting surface "like Erasmus in Holbein's portrait"), who treats him for a local infection five weeks after his return to Leipzig. When Adrian goes back to the unhealthy, red-faced doctor after three visits, he finds his corpse laid out in an open coffin. The name of Adrian's second doctor, Zimbalist, whose office is above a piano warehouse, has musical associations. He has reddish hair and a Hitler moustache, is inclined to dirty jokes and leaves an illustrated history of morals in his office. When Adrian returns for his third visit, he finds the handcuffed Zimbalist being led away by two policemen. Adrian's infection, which does not produce pustulant sores and a worm-eaten nose, spontaneously disappears. When Zeitblom returns to Leipzig just after Adrian sees the doctors, they attend a chamber music recital that ironically includes the "Thanksgiving for Recovery" movement from Beethoven's A-Minor String Quartet.

The dubious doctors have reddish physical characteristics; are associated with the mystical number three, bad health, music and evil; have their seedy practices suddenly terminated. Their sad fates foreshadow the tragic destiny of the two Rodde sisters who, like Adrian, are betrayed and corrupted by love: Clarissa's sudden death by suicide, Inez's criminal murder of Rudolf. Both doctors are clearly associated with the devil, who explains to Adrian that he put the blunderers away before their "quackery and quicksilvery" (mercury was commonly used to treat syphilis) could prevent the syphilis from progressing up the spinal column and penetrating the brain. The devil's description of the disease suggests both the means of infection ("the pulsating column") and its treacherous development: "osmosis, fluid diffusion, the proliferation process—the whole magic intreats of these. You have there the spinal sac with the pulsating column of fluid therein, reaching to the cerebrum, to the meninges, in whose tissues the furtive venereal meningitis is at its soundless stealthy work."

Adrian's pact with the devil (inspired by Ivan's encounter with Satan in *The Brothers Karamazov*) takes place while he is living with the Manardi family in Palestrina and writing his *opéra bouffe* based on *Love's Labour's Lost.* (Giovanni Manardi, a sixteenth-century Professor of Medicine at Ferrara, was the first to isolate the agent of venereal disease.) Adrian's artistic parody, intellectual mockery and aristocratic nihilism are "the proud expedient of a great gift threatened with sterility by a combination of scepticism, intellectual reserve, and a sense of the deadly extension of the kingdom of the banal." His fear of artistic paralysis and sterility is the direct cause of his diabolical pact.

Adrian substitutes love of the devil for love of God (*Agape*) and describes his encounter on music-paper because he cannot find stationery in the shop on the Piazza St. Agapitus. As in Dostoyevsky, it is not clear whether Adrian is made or possessed, whether he imagines the devil or He actually appears. But Adrian, at the time and later on, acts as though the protean apparition were real. The disgusting "brain-maggot" materializes with a wave of cold just after a severe seizure of migraine leaves Adrian retching and spewing. The devil ironically appears in pagan-Catholic Italy, but associates himself with the bloodthirsty fanaticism—with agitation, unrest, anxiety, presentiments—that connects Luther's Reformation to Hitler's Nazism: "bleeding of the Host, famine, Peasants' League, war, the pest at Cologne, meteors, comets, and great omens, nuns with the stigmata . . . divillishly German time!"

The devil links spiritual with physical pathology through an allusion to Dürer's woodcut *The Syphilitic* (1496), which depicts an unfortunate victim in the secondary stage, miserably ragged and completely covered with pustulant ulcers. He calls the spirochetes "flagellants," traces the origin of syphilis from the West Indies to Germany, and develops another complex pattern of associations: from Faust and Nietzsche through osmosis and "breakthrough" to inspiration and destruction; from Esmeralda and Baptist Spengler through Nepo and Adrian to Weimar and the Third Reich. The devil concedes that syphilis "rots away the liver, kidneys, stomach, heart and bowels" of men like Beethoven and Jules Goncourt; but praises the inspirational properties of an illness that pushes the victim into extreme opposition to conventional society: "Disease, indeed I mean repulsive, individual, private disease, makes a certain critical contrast to the world, to life's mean, puts a man in a mood rebellious and ironic against the bourgeois order, makes its man take refuge with the free spirit, with books, in cogitation."

Like Rimbaud and Nietszche, the devil also insists on the sacrificial and penitential aspects of illness, links inspiration with insanity and roots art in pathology: "a man must have been always ill and mad in order that others no longer need be so. . . . The artist is the brother of the criminal and the madman. Do you ween that any important work was ever wrought except its maker learned to understand the way of the criminal and madman? Morbid and healthy! Without the morbid would life all its whole life never have survived." The devil mouths Tonio Kröger's doctrine, but gives Adrian creativity only when he renounces human love. This makes Adrian very different from Mann's earlier anti-social artist-heroes, and stresses the great paradox of his music: it is admired but condemned by Zeitblom, expresses his genius but is icily demonic, is forbidden by the Nazis but representative of their sterile culture. Adrian's place in German history forces him into the impossible position of creating music that is inspired and ignored by a diseased civilization.

Even the manuscript of Zeitblom's biography of Adrian, with its pedantic but treasonable criticism of "Our Führer and his paladins," threatens the author's life. For if it were discovered, Zeitblom's patriotic sons, on leave from service in the Nazi army, would undoubtedly report him to the authorities and have him sent to a concentration camp. Goethe's remark on the ambiguous genius of his friend Schiller applies with equal force to Zeitblom's conception of Adrian: "The higher a man is, the more he is under the influence of the demons, and he must take heed not to let his guiding will counsel him to a wrong path. There was altogether something demonic in my acquaintance with Schiller."

The devil also demands in return for twenty-four years (1906-1930) of "genuine inspiration, immediate, absolute, unquestioned, ravishing," that Adrian renounce the love of all human creatures. The excision of human feeling reveals the analogy between the abandonment of traditional form in atonal music and the abandonment of traditional moral values. Adrian's inability to love intensifies (like his migraine) his tendency to madness and places him in hell while he is still alive. It also emphasizes the connection between Adrian's personal hell and the actual hell on earth of the extermination camps; between the place where all compassion and grace disappear, where tortures and executions take place in soundless cellars, where the stench of human flesh emanates from the crematoria and the disturbing music of the *Apocalypse* oratorio that expresses both Adrian's disease and the barbarous sounds that emerge from those horrible places: "a fortissimo tutti, an overwhelming, sardonically yelling, screeching, bawling, bleating, howling, piping, whinnying salvo, the mocking, exulting laughter of the Pit."

The disease of Adrian is reflected in the corruption of Munich society and the death of Clarissa Rodde (like Adrian, she lacks natural talent as an artist); his diabolical inability to love is reflected in the treacherous triangular wooing of Marie Godeau and his responsibility for the deaths of Rudolf and Nepo. The idea of indirect courtship originates in medieval romance (King Arthur, Lancelot, Guinevere; King Mark, Tristram, Iseult); is portrayed in *Love's Labour's Lost*; based on the Nietzsche, Paul Rée, Lou Salomé triangle; and expressed in the tragic relationships of Henri, the Pforzheim lawyer and Clarissa; Institoris, Rudolf and Inez; Adrian, Rudolf and Marie Godeau.

Marie replaces Hetaera just as Nepo replaces Marie in Adrian's affections. When Adrian breaks his demonic pact, Nepo contracts a fatal disease similar to the syphilis Adrian would have ruthlessly given to Marie if he had persuaded her to marry him (Adrian does not warn Marie as Hetaera warned him). Mann explains that "Adrian *kills* the friend [Rudolf] whom he loves, because in involving his friend with the lady painter [Marie] he exposes him to murderous jealousy." And at the end of the novel Adrian confesses that he "daemonically conceived" a (syphilitic) love-child with Hetaera, thought he could love Nepo because he was not female, and then "coldly murdered the trusting one"—who (like Adrian) was receptive to poisonous influences.

Nepo's spinal resembles Adrian's cerebral meningitis. Adrian's cold look glazes Nepo's clear eyes, he cannot bear light and sound, he retreats into a darkened room. These warning symptoms are followed by fever, vomiting, skull-splitting headaches, violent convulsions, paralysis of the eye muscles, rigidity of the neck and "twenty-two hours of shrieking, writhing torture"—then by a coma and gnashing of teeth.

Adrian seems to have extracted and absorbed Nepo's good health, for after the sacrificial death of the child, his uncle

German philosopher Friedrich Nietzsche, who eventually went mad after contracting syphilis, a fate shared by the protagonist Adrian Leverkühn in Mann's Doctor Faustus.

enjoys the excessive energy and exceptional well-being that enable him to compose his last work, *The Lamentation of Dr. Faustus*—which "takes back" Beethoven's "Ode to Joy" and mourns the destruction of his nephew, his nation and himself. Once this work is completed, his creative period ends, he suffers a paralytic stroke and (like Nietzsche) lapses into hopeless insanity for the last decade of his life.

Doctor Faustus . . . is an allegory of Fascism that portrays the artist-criminal as a demonic dictator. Nazi ideology is prefigured in the jingoistic and proto-Fascist doctrines of the Winfried theological students, the Kridwiss circle and the Jewish Chaim Breisacher, who anticipates his own death by stating: "There was no doubt that in the future, after we had begun to practice large-scale elimination of the unfit, the diseased and the weak-minded, we would justify the policy by similar hygienic arguments for the purification of society and the race." These barbaric Germans are contrasted to the more sympathetic European characters: Luca Cimabue (assistant to Adrian's uncle Nikolaus), the Manardis in Palestrina, Nepo (whose father is Swiss), the French-Swiss Marie Godeau, the frenchified Pole Saul Fitelberg, and the translator of English Rüdiger Schildknapp. Like Nietzsche, who prophetically exclaimed: "Against the *Germans* I here advance on all fronts. . . . This utterly irresponsible race has on its conscience all the great disasters of civilization," Mann also insists that the essence of Germanism, is "a psychology threatened with envelopment, the poison of isolation, provincial boorishness, neurosis, implicit Satanism."

Joseph Frank perceptively calls *Doctor Faustus* "a sublime and sophisticated aesthetic expression of the raw reality of contemporary historical experience." In the "double-time reckoning" of Zeitblom's biography Adrian's career corresponds to the war in Europe, so that, as Mann notes, "the quivering of his hand is ambiguously and yet obviously explained both by the vibration of distant bomb hits and by his inner consternation." Zeitblom draws a deliberate parallel between Adrian's hellish insanity and the political fate of Nazi Germany, "a land self-maddened and psychologically burnt-out": "Little as it was possible to connect his worsening health in any temperamental way with the national misfortune, yet my tendency [was] to see the one in the light of the other and find symbolic parallels in them."

The apotheosis of Adrian's musical genius is expressed in terms of the "break-through" which, like the Hetaera and syphilis motifs, unites the dominant themes of the novel: the attempt to "burst the cocoon and become a butterfly"; the redemptive break-through to human love—if only with Hetaera esmeralda; the osmotic break-through of the spirochetes into the brain; the Faustian break-through to musical creation; the German military break-through to the domination of Europe; the Allied break-through to capture Berlin.

Zeitblom's description of the first performance of *Ocean Lights* in cosmopolitan Switzerland and Adrian's composition of the Brentano song-cycle coincides with the contemporary invasion of Sicily, the fall of Mussolini (July 1943), the surrender of Italy (September 1943), the first

aerial bombardment of Munich and Nuremberg (early 1944), and Zeitblom's realization that the war is lost: that Germany "is marked down for collapse, economic, political, moral, spiritual, in short all-embracing, unparalleled, final collapse." The completion of the *Love's Labour's Lost* opera in Pfeiffering coincides with the recapture of Odessa by the Russians in 1943 and the bombing of Leipzig in April 1944. The *Apocalypse* coincides with the invasion of Normandy in June 1944 and the spread of disease through the Nazi body politic: "Its collapse and abdication result in a situation of permanent hunger and want, progressive depreciation of the currency, progressive laxity and loose speculation, a certain regrettable and unearned dispensing of civilian freedom from all restraint, the degeneration of a national structure." *The Lamentation of Dr. Faustus* follows the attempt to assassinate Hitler in July 1944, coincides with the invasion of Franconia and Bavaria, and the capture of the extermination camp at Buchenwald outside Weimar in April 1945, when "Germany had become a thick-walled underground torture-chamber."

As culture is overwhelmed by barbarism, Adrian's *Apocalypse* prophesies the end of Germany and his *Lamentation* bewails the destruction of the soul of the Germans. The years of Adrian's life (1885-1940) saw Bismarck's Prussianism develop into Hitler's demonology; his madness, damnation and death correspond to the collective insanity and collapse of the Thousand-Year Reich. The musical, military, pathological and political themes brilliantly merge at the end of the novel as the four stages of Adrian's disease—migraines, infection, remission and collapse—tragically fuse with Germany's predisposition to Reformation-inspired demonology, deliberate choice of Nazism, decade of military conquest and apocalyptic destruction. (pp. 67-82)

> *Jeffrey Meyers, "Mann: 'Doctor Faustus',' in his* Disease and the Novel, 1880-1960, *The Macmillan Press Ltd., 1985, pp. 62-82.*

Nina Pelikan Straus   (essay date 1987)

[*In the essay below, Straus provides a psychological analysis of* Doctor Faustus, *asserting that the work in many ways parodies the theories of Sigmund Freud.*]

As one of the "terminal" texts of modernism, *Doctor Faustus* is notable for what Erich Kahler calls its "labyrinthine mathematics," its maze of mythic-metaphoric interconnections through which the "Idiot Questioner" wanders and from which she seeks to cull a center that will hold, at least for as long as the possible differences between a man's reading and a woman's reading of a given text seem relevant to literary criticism. The questions a woman reader may ask about Mann's novel can be considered less idiotic now than they did when it first appeared; and if for some forty years a male-dominated Mann criticism has employed a polite self-censorship, casting [according to Ignace Feuerlicht in the *Germanic Review,* 1982] "only furtive and embarrassed glances at Mann's homoeroticism," for example, a woman reader may be bolder in her gaze at certain elements of the text: she may note that *Doctor Faustus* is not so much a mathematical labyrinth as it is a homocentric, even homosexual labyrinth, and that part of what it both parodies and glorifies is the homocentric nature of art (in this case, music) itself.

The list of what Mann's readers have found him to parody in *Doctor Faustus* is rather long: Walter Muschg finds a parody of the Bible, Goethe, Germany, burgher morality, while for Jonas Lesser the list includes Luther, Schopenhauer, Wolf, and of course, Nietzsche. Even Georg Lukács, whose commentary is short on humor, argues that in *Doctor Faustus* the "angst" which Lukács finds intrinsic to contemporary literary works that contain no socialist elements, is "overcome" by Mann's technique; and he implies [in *The Meaning of Contemporary Realism*] that Mann's work is to some degree a critique of capitalist "present-day society," if not exactly parody. What readers have not yet noticed, however, is the way Mann implicitly critiques one particular element in society—that psychoanalytic hunt for motives and connections, that (as Mann called it) "revolutionary" vision of human character, the Freudian, which the biographer Zeitblom, the novelist-behind-the-biographer, Thomas Mann, and the reader of the biography-novel have all implicitly incorporated as part of their intellectual *gestalt*. That *Doctor Faustus* contains a playful and deliberate deconstruction through parody of some of Freud's most serious notions has become clearer since so much feminist effort has been expended on criticizing Freud and since this effort also reveals the disturbing nature of Freud's ideas themselves. One can argue that Freud's attitude to women is as disturbing to them as Freud's attitude to homosexuality (connecting it to narcissism) might have been to a "homoerotic" writer who also was "never without Freud" [Frederick J. Beharriell, in *Thomas Mann in Context*, ed. Kenneth Hughes] in all but his earliest fiction. Whether Mann's parody of Freudian ideas is complete, suggesting those ideas' limitations, or only partial—and thus either evading the implications of those ideas or acquiescing and thus unable to parody some of them—is the question we address. Is the "Breakthrough" (*Durchbruch*) which Adrian Leverkühn quests in music symbolic of a parodic breaking-through or penetration into a woman's realm? Does Mann take Goethe's idea of Faust's quest for the Eternal Feminine seriously? Or is it that the choice of Esmeralda, whose "friend and cohabitant" is the Devil, as the central female image in the text, is not only a demonic parody of Goethe's pure woman, but an image suggestive of Mann's hidden agenda: namely, his effort, against Freud, to honor homocentricity, to connect it with intellectuality, and to express "his strange belief that homosexuality has very little to do with nature and much more with intellect"? [Feuerlicht]

The whore Esmeralda symbolizes both nature and disease, and as such she is coincident with ideas of growth and development, either of a festering or creative kind. The paradox of the artist Adrian's relation to her is that after an initial and primal contact with her, he is loosened back into the homocentric maze from which he came. His quest and his work, though manifesting traces of her in musical note form, reveal a latent content that is not woman-centered but homocentric; or as Zeitblom suggests about Adrian's Faust *Lamentation,* that is "lacking in development" and composed of "concentric circles made by a

stone thrown into waters spread[ing] ever farther." What then can we also make of Zeitblom's insistence that Adrian's break-through has to do with Esmeralda?

The question can be answered in one sense if we read Mann's text as Lukács does, seriously and without salt, or if we swallow Zeitblom's idea that Adrian moves from his initial coldness to a later warmth in his music so that at the end, "everywhere . . . there is reference to the bond and the vow, the promise and the blood pact" with Esmeralda. This is merely a heterocentric (or pro-heterosexual) version of Lukács' pro-socialist notion that in "Leverkühn's final monologue . . . the perspective of a new society of socialism [is revealed] under which the artist will be free from his former enslavement." The serious reader's "new society" in this case is presumed to be the heterosexual society in which Adrian Leverkühn and Esmeralda (or the little mermaid) are joined in symbolic marriage, indicating Adrian's freedom from the enslavement of a cold narcissism.

Among Mann's female critics, Inta Ezergailis reads *Doctor Faustus* in just this serious way [in *Male and Female: An Approach to Thomas Mann's Dialectics*]. In Mann's work women function as mediators for men, and heterosexual love represents "the highest and strongest form of the expansion of the soul" and "a possible synthesis of the male-female dialectic." Yet Ezergailis does not note that in *Doctor Faustus,* "love"—particularly the heterosexual love to which traditional romantic music may allude—is considered by Adrian Leverkühn to be the very essence of comic belatedness. Indeed, Mann exhibits Adrian as a victim of what (after the fact) Bloom calls the poet's belatedness, his sense that he comes late after a great tradition, and that he can do nothing but imitate it. This "bum, bum, bang!" that Adrian continually hears in traditional music—this familiar, repetitive and ritualistic development towards a climax which makes music sound like an imitation of coitus—strikes Adrian as ludicrous. It makes him laugh; it is that the root of his sense of life as a parody. To put it in the Devil's terms: "bourgeois Nueremberg" heterosexual music (love) is the paradigm for life as a farce:

> "And I, abandoned wretch, I have to laugh, particularly at the grunting supporting notes of the bombardone, Bum, bum, bum, bang! . . . Thus the sonorous melody presses on up to nearly the height of a climax, which, in accordance with the law of economy it avoids at first, gives way . . . postpones . . . then withdraws . . . and it continues, solemnly, to that climax from which it wisely refrained the first time, in order that the surging feeling, the Ah-h-effect, might be greater. . . . Dear friend, why do I have to laugh? Can a man employ the traditional or sanctify the trick with greater genius?"

Like Mann, who writes in **"Freud and the Future"** that "the artist's eye has a mythic slant upon life, which makes it look like a farce," Adrian finds "the desire to laugh . . . irresistible. . . . I fled from this exaggerated sense of the comic into theology, in the hope that it would give relief to the tickling—only to find there too a perfect legion of ludicrous absurdities. Why does almost everything seem to me like its own parody?" Adrian laughs at traditional music because it seems so deterministic, so *Freudian*. Such music sanctifies bourgeois ethics, heterosexual love; it assumes that music can be about nothing but sex. What Mann presents through Adrian is no serious "synthesis of the male-female dialectic," but its parody—a calling into question of Freud's description of the artist's nature and art; of Freud's dictum that "the behaviour of a human being in sexual matters is often a prototype for the whole of his other modes of reaction to life" ("Sexual Morality"). What Mann held against Nietzsche he held even more strongly against Freud: the "misperception of the power relations between instincts and intellect . . . the utterly false relationship . . . establish(ed) between life and morals when [Nietzsche] treats them as opposites. . . . The real opposites are ethics and aesthetics" (**"Philosophy"**). If Adrian's aesthetic ambition is to transcend conventional music through his own apocalyptic break-through, then *Doctor Faustus* is Mann's attempt at a Freudian apocalypse: his revelation of Freud's philosophical limitation as well as Freud's revolutionary truth; his answer to the sort of case Freud makes, for example, in his study of Leonardo da Vinci, "the Italian Faust" ("Leonardo") who, like Adrian Leverkühn, is emotionally cold and loveless, who illustrates for Freud the struggle between intellect and instinct, but for Mann must illustrate the struggle between "ethics and aesthetics"—that is, between art and (bourgeois, heterosexual) morality.

Adrian's question about parody, then, is the key to a text where "everything" is "its own parody" and where the putting of Adrian's case "into the mouth of the good humanist Zeitblom" is, as Mann insisted, "pronouncedly humorous" (**"Humor and Irony"**). In writing his "account of the impressions that moulded [Adrian's] early life" Zeitblom frequently comments on Adrian's need for laughter and connects it with his demonic impulses. Zeitblom's "account" parodies the accounts which link jokes and verbal "slips" to unconscious (demonic) desires made by another researcher, Sigmund Freud. What neither researcher emphasizes, however, is the aesthetic dimension of laughter and the idea that for the artist, the parodic or comedic sense may be a defense against engulfment by the ordinary—engulfment either by science or seriousness. And this implies that it is the researcher's vision of life from which the artist must escape; and that Mann also intends the reader's *view* of Adrian to escape from the humorless fixities that Zeitblom imposes upon him.

While in his early work, particularly *The Magic Mountain* (1927), Mann incorporated Freud's ideas without much skepticism or humor . . . in *Doctor Faustus* Freud seems to have been so thoroughly incorporated into Mann's thinking that Freudianism could seem belated enough and ripe enough to parody. In **"Freud and the Future"** (1936) Mann has already qualified his admiration with a "polemic" against Freud: "He does not esteem philosophy very highly. . . . He reproaches it with . . . believing in intuitions as a source of knowledge . . ., in that it believes in the magic of words and in the influence of thought upon reality. But would philosophy really be thinking too highly of itself on these assumptions?" The fact that Freud excoriates "intuition as a source of knowledge" from his psy-

choanalytic theory serves as a target for Mann's parody of Zeitblom's research into the soul of a musical genius in *Doctor Faustus.* The choice of Zeitblom, a man who has "absolutely no sense of humor" [Hermann J. Wiegand, in *Thomas Mann in Context*], suggests something of Mann's critique of psychoanalytic humorlessness. Like Freud, Zeitblom is fascinated with the abomination of the artist's demonic imagination; like Freud, he is a "doctor" who spends his life scrutinizing the life of others; and like Freud (whom Mann initially misunderstood but came to terms with by 1936), Zeitblom is on the side of the Ego against the Id, and on the side of traditional moral values (what Freud calls, despite his discontent with it, "civilization"). What Zeitblom notices about Adrian is that his

> gifts measured themselves against values the relative character of which seemed to lie open to him, without any visible possibility of any other relation which would have detracted from them as values.

In other words, because Adrian recognizes himself in terms of his belatedness, and recognizes his "gifts" in terms of the gifts of all those others who have come before him, he is not quite civilized. He is beyond the pale of "absolute values." "Belief in absolute values, illusory as it always is, seems to me a condition of life," writes Zeitblom. The values "through which . . . the character is . . . sustained" can only develop, however, "If the relativeness [of these values] remains unrecognized," and Adrian Leverkühn, like Mann himself, recognizes their relativeness all too well. It is this "intuition" which differentiates the mind of the artist from the mind of the moralist; which distinguishes both Mann who considers himself "primarily a humorist" (*Letters*) and Leverkühn who cannot help but laugh, from the serious researchers Zeitblom and Freud. For Mann's artist nothing is either new or absolute; all is belated, a repetition, a relative instance, a farce and therefore comic. Not only is Freud's revolutionary work indebted to, if not a copy of Nietzsche's, Schopenhauer's, Goethe's etc., but Mann understands his own work, "Doctor Faustus" to be a "book . . . based on the principle of montage" and a product of "higher copying" (*Letters*). "There is nothing left for art to do except becomes its own parody" [Mann quoted by Erich Heller in *Thomas Mann: A Collection of Critical Essays,* ed. Henry Hatfield]. "The root of the book's humor," Mann writes to Hesse, "is that it parodies biography and strikes the pompous pose of the researcher" (*Letters*). What is comic about the tragic content of Mann's text is that everything in it is "lifted" (his word) from somewhere else, and that what distinguishes the artist is not his inventiveness but his capacity to identify and articulate the mythic redundancy of life. Mann warrants the parodic technique of *Doctor Faustus* when he writes to Adorno that

> I have developed an inclination in old age to regard life as a cultural product, hence a set of mythic clichés which I prefer, in my calcified dignity, to "independent creation." (*Letters*)

Mann strikes at Freud's refusal to accept myths ("Mythic clichés") as vehicles of "intuition" and knowledge. *Doctor Faustus* interprets the myth of Faust to suggest that Adrian consciously mythologizes himself so that he will transcend belatedness into timelessness and reach the source of art's intuition in myth. Mann's joke is that the loss of woman's love (heterosexual union) is the price paid for timeless art; and despite Zeitblom's bourgeois ethics, it is well worth that price. This suggests that art is an inevitably male phenomenon, that it may exploit but not find its source in women; and that the relationships of *Doctor Faustus* parody a homosexual enclosure, replicated linguistically in the word-labyrinth spun by the men Leverkühn, Zeitblom, the two Rudis, and the Devil.

Through its *omnium gatherum* of German myths, not only of the Superman complex intrinsic to fascistic culture but the Goethe's Faust complex which defines Truth as a break-through into the Eternal Feminine, Mann implicitly goes much further in his diagnosis of civilization than does Freud by indicating (as Mann wrote in his diaries) that "the German nation is homoerotic" and that "homosexuality" is a "characteristic of national socialism" (Feurlicht). Although Zeitblom takes seriously the notion that Adrian's male "calculated coldness" is "convert[ed] into a voice expressive of the soul and warmth and sincerity of creature confidence" in his late music, and that it is expressive of a "break-through" and "work of liberation" which involves the "Hetaera—Esmeralda figure" (thus suggesting that the male-female bond is the solution for the artist's problem)—the homocentric structure of the novel renders this notion suspicious. This may be Zeitblom's own defense against the anti-humanist relativity which would tempt him if he were to recognize, as does Adrian with Rudi, his own homoerotic desires for Adrian. It is part of the joke that what Zeitblom approaches with such solemn reverence is not necessarily a musical break-through but a return or regression to the traditional synthesis, some (modern) version of the "bum, bum, bang!" If we read Zeitblom's encomium to Adrian's *Lamentation of Doctor Faustus* with this in mind, his words seem overdetermined. He seems to protest too much:

> Woe! Woe! A De Profundis, which in my zeal and love I am bound to call matchless. . . . Does it not mean the 'break-through,' of which we so often talked when we were considering the destiny of art, its state and hour? We spoke of it as a problem, a paradoxical possibility: the recovery . . . of expressivism . . . suggesting the Hetaera-Esmeralda figure, first perceived by me . . . everywhere where there is reference to the bond and the vow, the promise and the blood pack.

If Mann is "never without Freud" in his hunt for the origins of a necessarily male art, he also parodies Freud (and notes something about Freud's own psycho-sexual nature) in his revelations of the homosexual origins of the researcher's love for the artist. In *Doctor Faustus,* Zeitblom's relation to Adrian is the vehicle for a confrontation with Freud which Mann may also intend as a homage to Freud. Thus Doctor Faustus is a "Freudian" text which deconstructs itself. Zeitblom's biography of Adrian is a kind of dreamwork that contains its own censorship, but which through its symbolism ("the Esmeralda figure . . . [was] first perceived by me") also reveals the wish for a homosexual love "bond" with Adrian, a "nearness" project-

ed into heterosexual imagery. Clearly, Zeitblom's self-censorship is part of his humanism and stands opposite to Adrian's self-exposure to demonism (the Devil, disease [Esmeralda's syphilis], and homosexuality [Rudi]). The tension between these choices, and the aesthetic and mythic connotations of these choices, serves to deconstruct the psychological determinism implied by Freud's "science": Freud's tendency to reduce human choice to either Pleasure principle or Reality principle. Just as Mann attempts to erase the line Freud inserts between "intuition" and truth, so he indicates in *Doctor Faustus* that the boundary between disease and health has no ontological existence. In "the depressive and the exalted states of the artist, illness and health, are by no means sharply divided from each other. . . . genius is a form of vital power deeply experienced in illness, creating out of illness, through illness creative." Contradicting Freud's idea that "our mental apparatus . . . supp[lies] one of our indispensible satisfactions" so that "pleasure . . . is in general the condition that governs all aesthetic ideation" [*Jokes and Their Relation to the Unconscious*], what Adrian longs for is not pleasure—nor can his contraction of syphilis be ascribed to some masochistic urge—but he longs for genius itself, for a "deathly unchaining of chemical change in his nature" that will produce genius. Because as an artist Adrian perceives Reality as relative and mythic, music ("aesthetic ideation") cannot be governed by the Pleasure principle, but must be governed by a dense spectrum of human impulses and cultural myths. By creating the "mythic cliché" of the Devil's visitation to Adrian, Mann denies the implicit division Freud makes between mind and spirit, between imagination (which Freud relegates to delusion) and necessity (which Freud defines as truth) Experiences of life, Mann suggests, offers no such distinctions, and it is myth which reveals this "intuition." As J. P. Stern argues [in his *Thomas Mann*], in *Doctor Faustus* "spirituality is acknowledged against the greatest odds that [Mann's] imagination can devise"; and we are arguing here that these great odds are the ideas of Sigmund Freud.

The relationship of Serenus Zeitblom and Adrian Leverkühn is constituted by the power of myth as much as by latent homosexual desire, by Zeitblom's belief that Adrian is Faust and by Adrian's disclosure in music that warrants that belief. This holding out of the "intuitive" power of myth and "the magic of words" against Freud's "line" is a plea against a compelling but deterministic psychoanalytic view of life. Threatening to myth by which both literature and imagination enliven themselves, Freud's work stimulates in Mann a Negative Capability. Anxiety about literary influence is transformed into parody of all literary influences; and the " 'melancholy knowledge' that was to trouble Mann for many years, about the neurotic roots of creativity" (Beharriell) is transformed into a celebration of disease. Yet Freud's disturbance continues to be felt in the text even when the spiritual-demonic element of art is intensified. There is no male-female dialectic in this novel of the kind we notice in *The Magic Mountain* between Hans and Clavdia; instead *Doctor Faustus* sustains a homosexual-heterosexual *male* dialectic to which the female element is subsumed, reduced to shadow imagery or to musical notes. The women figures in *Doctor Faustus* seem to censor and distort the nature of the relationships between the men, as if to disguise the nature of the homocentric pattern of art which severs and protects Adrian from the world. Zeitblom is married, for example, and there is the brief episode of Adrian's attempt to marry Marie Godeau; but the "line" between "mind" and "spirit" is not engaged here. Except for the mythic extenuations of Esmeralda, it is difficult to understand what the other women in Mann's text are doing in it.

What they are doing becomes clearer if we argue that the unresolved erotic complexities in Mann's own life enabled him to easily incorporate Freud's idea of the link between sexual repression and art, between sublimation and culture; but made him uncomfortable, indeed "melancholy" with the more buried connections between art, narcissism, and homosexuality which Freud discussed in his "Leonardo: A Memory of his Childhood." The Mann behind Zeitblom may find Freud useful when he writes that Marie's voice is "like Elsbeth Leverkühn's in colour and register but sometimes one might really think, as one listened, that one heard the voice of Adrian's mother;" but he may choose not to make the disturbing connection between the fact that Inez Institoris's erotic object is Rudi Schwerdtfegger and that Rudi's object is Adrian Leverkühn. While Inez's erotic love for Rudi is conceived as pathetic and delusional—(Zeitblom) is at pains to "point out her erotic over-estimation of her love" and her merely "temporary gains" that finally end in suicide—the homosexual love-affair of Rudi and Adrian is presented with confusion. Zeitblom is jealous: watching Rudi embrace Adrian, Zeitblom shouts "Enough!" and puts out his hand "to quench the unquenchable and restrain the unrestrained." But he also finds the affair itself trivial: "Rudi had been *per du* with Adrian, whereas that had only been in carnival time, and even then entirely on Rudi's side." The confusion is compounded by the fact that there are two Rudis in Adrian's circle as well as two Inez (Institoris and Rodde), both of whom love Rudi Schwerdtfegger, who loves Adrian, at one time or another. The duplication of names and the tangle of sexes suggests a knot which only the most assiduous Freudian could entangle, but the fact that it *is* a tangle indicates more than Mann's usual playfulness.

The knot pattern of sexual interrelations in chapters XIX-XXXII indicates where the "threads" of the labyrinth meet, and it is Rudi, the one character to whom Mann assigns a physically homosexual nature, who runs through the whole pattern. Emblematic of the buried desire this pattern creates, the violinist must later be sent by Adrian to Marie and must confirm Adrian's isolation from the world by marrying Marie himself. Adrian's failure to marry results less from the devil's contract than from his artist's compulsion, perhaps symbolizing Mann's own, to remain in the woman-less labyrinth. The women in the text function to blur and confuse this wish, thus acting as censors in much the way that Zeitblom acts as a censor of himself; and they can be understood as Mann's nod to heterosexual continuity, as Mann's shelter from self-exposure. Heterosexual love, then, is a parody of homosexual love in *Doctor Faustus,* although it may not be part of Mann's intention to reveal this. The true bond in the text is not between Adrian and Esmeralda, but between the artist and his bi-

ographer; and neither man is interested in women as anything but *bilt:* image, shadow, symbol, and muse.

Adrian's only sexual fantasy, albeit articulated in diseased rantings, concerns coitus with "the little mermaid"—the woman-fish or woman-serpent whose ancient iconography Mann exploits to link her to the devil. Suggesting the struggle between homosexual and heterosexual impulses, Adrian imagines a woman upon whom the shape of the phallus is grafted, a figure in whom the "line" between male and female parts is undetermined:

> Adrian spoke of the aesthetic advantages of the nixie's shape over that of the forked human kind, of the charm of the lines with which the feminine form flowed from the hips into the smooth-scaled, strong, and supple fish-tail, so well adapted for steering and darting. . . . The sea-wife had a perfectly complete and charming organic reality, beauty, and inevitability; you saw that at once, when she became so pathetically *déclasseé* after she had bought herself legs, which nobody thanked her for.

If there is any break-through in Adrian's music or imagination, it is conceived of in terms of this sexually ambivalent figure, the mermaid, into whom the original Esmeralda has been transformed, and with whom at the end of his life Adrian is able to imagine a traditional heterosexual coitus:

> "For the Devil brought her me to my bed as my bedsister that I gan-woo her and loved her ever more, whether she came to me with the fishes tail or with legs. Oftentimes indeed she came with the tail, for the pains she suffered as with knives in the legs outweighed her lust, and I had much feeling for the wise wherein her tender body went over so sweetly into the scaly tail. But higher was my delight even so in the pure human form and so for my part I had greater lust when she came to me in legs."

The evolution of Adrian's imagination and art from homocentricity to heterosexual symbolism is not complete, however. To Zeitblom's insistent question, "Is that not the 'break-through' "?, an equivocal answer must be given. What is clear, however, is that the imagery to which Adrian himself is addicted involves the serpent, the mermaid, "our pale Venus, the spirochaeta pallida"—the demonization of Freud's "scientific" notion of "dream symbols" as "memory traces" back into their origins in myth. And because Woman is mythic and emblematic, she is ubiquitous, duplicatable, transparent as the wings of the *Hetaera esmeralda* butterly for which the flesh woman is named. As Laurence M. Porter suggests [in *Medicine and Literature,* ed. Enid Rhodes Peshel], Esmeralda is Adrian's "syphillitic muse," and the process of demonic possession of Adrian's soul is "represented metaphorically by a body invaded by the alien microorganisms of an infectious disease." "In this twenty-fifth chapter where the reader hears Adrian's voice direct," or hears, rather, Adrian speak in the Devil's tongue, a crucial element of the Esmeralda imagery and its connection to the knot of names and sexes discussed earlier, is initially and very strangely formulated:

[The Devil]: "Oh, thy father is not so ill-placed in my mouth. He was a shrewd one, always wanting to speculate the elements. The mygrim, the point of attack for the knife-points of the little sea-maid—after all, you have them from him . . . Moreover, I have spoken quite correctly: osmosis, fluid diffusion, the proliferation process—the whole magic intreats of these. You have there the spinal sac with the pulsating column of fluid therein, reaching to the cerebrum, to the meninges, in whose tissues the furtive venereal meningitis is at its soundless stealthy work. But our little ones could not reach into the inside . . . without fluid diffusion, osmosis."

The "pale Venus, the spirochaeta pallida" organism that invades Adrian's tissues is imagined as having, like mermaid tails, "scourges." The phallic imagery is extended in the idea of the mermaid's "knives." An image of microscopic invasion of little sea creatures into Adrians "liquid" is suggested; but more importantly, the penetration into Adrian's body is associated with Adrian's father and with the Devil. The Devil is imagined to have f— Adrian by way of Esmeralda. The fantasy of a coital "attack" that takes place in Adrian's "head region" and has "a passion for the upper story," blurs the relation of the organic to the mythic and the relation of homosexual and heterosexual unions. Both male figures, Adrian's father and the Devil, and a female figure are represented as "penetrating" Adrian's "head," and this "osmosis" between male and female functions serves to erase the line Freud inserts between homocentric narcissism and heterosexual love and the desires they provoke. "The learned gibberish" the Devil speaks is the demonic language of the artist who denies that his art is determined by mere sexual aetiology. He insists, instead, that the origin of art is in myth, the very "German" myth of the Devil—not sex.

If this is so, why is Mann at pains to suggest Adrian's heterosexuality or to suggest that after Marie's refusal of marriage and Nepo's death, Adrian goes into a decline? Mann employs Freud's idea that "memories may arous(e) a wish that finds a fulfillment in the [art] work in question" ("The Poet"); and Mann willingly suggests the connections between Frau Schweigetstill's home, where Adrian lives for nineteen years, and his maternal home; the connections between Adrian's "seawife" and Esmeralda (both associated with "knives," sickness and pain); and the way the word Esmeralda Hetaera is ciphered in Adrian's music (B ["H" in German], E, A, E, and E" ["Es" in German]). The "echo effect" in the Faust Cantata refers to the beloved dead nephew, Nepo ("echo" in German). Adrian's music is thus filled with "memory traces" easily linked to wishes connected, in Freud's terms, with women. Yet there are deliberately no such traces of homosexual wishes in the music, while in Adrian's life such latent wishes seem palpable. Both Mann and Zeitblom ask us to take Adrian's curse seriously: "Thou maist not love," as if it would be woman whom Adrian chose to love if he could love at all.

Adrian's "coldness" is not connected to homosexuality; instead, his possible homosexuality is displaced to Zeitblom who is both "warm" and a humanist. The efforts Mann makes to break the connections between repressed homosexuality and coldness are significant because these are the connections Freud makes in describing such an artist as Leonardo:

> A conversion of psychical instinctual force into various forms of activity can perhaps no more be achieved without loss than a conversion of physical forces.. . . . A man who has won his way to a state of knowledge cannot properly be said to love and hate; he remains beyond love and hatred. He has investigated instead of loving. And that is perhaps why Leonardo's life was so much poorer in love than that of other great men, and of other artists. ("Leonardo")

No doubt Mann was familiar with Freud's idea that "Homosexual object-choice originally lies closer to narcissism than does the heterosexual kind" (*Introductory Lectures*), and in evading Adrian's homosexuality he rationalizes Adrian's *difference* in terms of the *organic* changes that come with syphilis. Describing Leonardo's "manifest, if ideal (sublimated) homosexuality," Freud writes that:

> Homosexual men, who have in our times taken vigorous action against the restrictions imposed by law on their sexual activity, are fond of representing themselves, through their theoretical spokesmen, as being from the outset a distinct sexual species, as an intermediate sexual stage, as a 'third sex.' They are, they claim, men who are innately compelled by *organic determinants* to find pleasure in men and have been debarred from obtaining it in women. Much as one would be glad on grounds of humanity to endorse their claims, one must treat their theories with some reserve, for they have been advanced without regard for the psychical genesis of homosexuality. . . . [that is, their] very intense erotic attachment to . . . the mother. ("Leonardo," my italics)

The presentation of Adrian as a "third" or alternate sex, capable of sexual relations with both sexes, fits Freud's idea of the way homosexuals may defend themselves against (Freud's) theory that their physical "genesis" is peculiar and a variant of the norm. And there is nothing humorous or parodic about the way Mann deliberately obfuscates the issue in *Doctor Faustus.* While Mann's "humorous intention" in his choice of Zeitblom is to unmask the biographer's scholarly interest in Adrian as homosexual love, it is not part of Mann's intention to reveal that, even if Adrian could love, he would love men. Yet this implication is at the center of the labyrinth. Supported by the affair of Adrian and Rudi which, as Feurlicht suggests, is a fictionalized version of Mann's affair with Paul Ehrenberg," Mann's effort to suppress what he cannot parody paradoxically exposes Mann's own homosexual fantasies more powerfully than they are exposed in *Death in Venice.*

The whole demonic apparatus of Adrian's contact with the Devil and syphilis, meant to indicate the origin of Adrian's genius, becomes a symptom, in Freud's sense, of Mann's "disease." The hidden message in the Devil's statement that the "artist is the brother of the criminal and the madman" is that the artist is the brother of the homosexual, whose symbol in *Doctor Faustus* is the Devil himself—that "*strizzi* . . . with reddish lashes and pink lips . . . an actor's voice and eloquence," so reminiscent of the lurid homosexual type encountered in Mann's fictional Venice. It would not go too far if we followed the implications of Mann's choice of having Adrian persecuted and haunted by a Devil figure to arrive at Freud's conclusions, even if these conclusions do not detonate the power of the Faust myth itself:

> *Paranoia persecutoria* is the form of the disease in which a person is defending himself against a homosexual impulse which has become too powerful. . . . it is clear that the person of the same sex whom the patient loved most had, since his illness, been turned into his persecutor. This made a further development possible: namely the replacement of the beloved person . . . by someone else—for instance, a father by a schoolmaster or by some superior. (*Introductory Lectures*)

Adrian's "schoolmaster," Schleppfuss, who carries the Devil's nickname, is just this sort of "replacement," and another sort of figure who is connected with Adrian's suppressed homosexuality. It is he who tells Adrian the story of the sexton's daughter who, through witchcraft, gains control over her husband's potency, is discovered, and is burned at the stake. "No sooner was his love reduced to ashes than he recovered the sinfully alienated free use of his manhood." Although Zeitblom finds Schleppfuss's tale "revolting," Adrian is interested in it because it discloses how the "spiritual" can "affect and modify the organic and corporeal in a decisive way,—again suggesting that Adrian, like the homosexuals in Freud's description, are "fond" of imagining themselves *organically* different from other men.

It is part of Mann's homage to Freud, however, rather than his parody of him, to associate Adrian's spiritual progress with his progress away from homocentricity and towards heterosexuality. An implicit escape from the (homosexual) Devil is suggested in Adrian's final imagining of bedding the Little Mermaid not in "tail" but in "legs," and by the fact that Adrian's music moves from the parodic and demonic *Gesta* to the self-mournful *Lamentation of Doctor Faustus*. In this novel, literary-music-philosophical work is conceived of as spiritual work—but only when tested against the psychoanalytic science which humiliates it.

Mann's opening remarks in **"Freud and the Future,"** considered in retrospect, seem prophetic of the undertaking that is ***Doctor Faustus,*** an undertaking that involves nothing less than an answer to Freud. The "author in his character as artist . . . is by nature more a man of feast-days than the scientist"—that is, he has more humor, more life (not less, as Freud implies in "Leonardo"); and this is a "theme" that Mann would like to enlarge upon but decides not to. Instead, he offers this curious reversal:

> But it is more likely that the sponsors of this evening had something else in mind in their choice; that is to say, the solemn and novel confrontation of object and subject, the object of knowledge [the artist] with the knower [Freud]—a *Saturnalia,* as it were, in which the knower and seer of dreams [Freud] himself becomes, by our

act of homage, the object of dreamlike penetration. And to such a position I could not object, either; particularly because it strikes a *chord capable in the future of great symphonic development.* (my italics)

It is not only that Mann uses the occasion to suggest how Freud will become the object of his analysis, but that such an enterprise has enormous potential for Mann's work in the future. Indeed, ***Doctor Faustus*** contains those elements of the "saturnalia" that accord with the word's definition: "devilry, whoredom, . . . pride, . . . rebellious gestures, into which the Dionysian feeling can flow" [C. L. Barber, *Shakespeare's Festive Comedy*]. As "lord of misrule" Mann enacts a reversal in ***Doctor Faustus*** where the Freudian struggle between "instinct and morals" is replaced, perhaps not wholly consciously, by the struggle between homocentric aesthetics and heterosexual ethics.

Yet considering his struggle with and homage to Freud, it is finally the intrinsic identity between the two writers that is remarkable. Even if Freud could so humiliate artistic invention that Mann was forced to make Adrian cry out—"Why must everything seem like its own parody?"—Freud could only sustain Mann when it came to the use and abuse of women figures and images in his artistic productions. For Freud as for Mann woman is the symbolic "mother" of art when she couples with the demon—in the case of ***Doctor Faustus,*** the Devil with whom Esmeralda "cohabita[tes]," and in the case of Freud's Leonardo, the vulture whose beak is grafted on to the mother's body. The vulture-mother compound of Freud's description bears a similarity to the woman-fish/woman-serpent compound that is Adrian's muse. The memory of the vulture's beak recorded in Leonardo's diary stands in relation to the mouth imagery in his paintings of women (Mona Lisa) as the mermaid-Esmeralda motifs in Adrian's music stand to the pseudo-creatures ("phallic polyp-stalks . . . half-formed limbs") to which Adrian's father exposes him in childhood. Like Leonardo, Adrian conquers "the inhibition in his art . . . with the help of the oldest of erotic impulses," the love of his mother. For Adrian, the disease he contracts from Esmeralda likewise conquers his inhibition, his sense that "art today" has "become a pilgrimage on peas." "Disease," as Mann explains in a letter, "is a means provided by the devil to induce creativity in an artist inhibited by knowledge" (***Letters***)—knowledge, as ***Doctor Faustus*** makes clear, about the condition of the artist in modern times, of his own belatedness, his paralysis, his impotence, if you will. The cure for this impotence is a return to barbarous instinctuality from which art extracts its power. "Not only will you break through the paralysing difficulties of the time," says the Devil, "you will break through time itself, by which I mean the cultural epoch and its cult, and dare to be barbaric, twice barbaric indeed. . . . "

Mann's symbol for this "barbaric" daring, for this "breakthrough" is—as it was for Freud's patients—a visit to a prostitute. Such a visit, as Freud suggests in his "The Most Prevalent Form of Degradation in Erotic Life," is the "principle means of protection used by men against this complaint" (physical or psychical inhibition); and it "consists in *lowering* the sexual object in their own estimation. . . . As soon as the sexual object fulfils (sic) the condition of being degraded, sensual feeling can have free play." In Adrian's case, not sensual but artistic feeling and force achieve free play after the visit to the prostitute Esmeralda. Although Nina Auerbach has recently argued that images of demonic womanhood in Victorian literature suggest how the "disobedient" or degraded woman may be the "demonic savior of the race," this myth does not seem to operate in the case of Freud or Mann. Zietblom makes this clear when he writes of how in this "embrace, . . . one staked his salvation, the other found it." It is in these images and uses of women that Freud and Mann can be understood as literary brothers whose quarrel does *not* extend beyond a homocentric and patriarchal tradition.

In both their work, Woman serves to censor man's homosexual impulses or to fulfill his heterosexual ones, to serve as his muse or mother, to assist art, but never to become, like man, a successful artist herself. For Mann as for Freud, woman's biology is her destiny. Woman may make man a Faust, but she is no Faust herself. The mutual goal exposed here is that Freud and Mann include everything within the homocentric labyrinth of male art and male psychoanalysis in which woman is but a shadow, an echo, or a note; in which the question of her own "breakthrough" does not—until now—come up. (pp. 59-72)

Nina Pelikan Straus, " 'Why Must Everything Seem Like Its Own Parody?': Thomas Mann's Parody of Sigmund Freud in 'Doctor Faustus'," in Literature and Psychology, *Vol. XXXIII, Nos. 3 and 4, 1987, pp. 59-75.*

Dominick LaCapra   (essay date 1987)

[*LaCapra is an American critic and educator whose works combine social history and literary criticism. He states: "My primary objective has been to reconceptualize the way intellectual history is written, in part by employing approaches developed in recent literary criticism and philosophy." In the following excerpt, LaCapra presents a sociohistorical analysis of* Doctor Faustus.]

Who is the devil in *Doctor Faustus*? This is an embarrassingly insistent but unanswerable question, no doubt—one that invites psychological and sociological reduction or, more generally, "cultural" explanations of which the devil himself is the potent and wily critic in spite of his distaste for criticism. But let us start by calling him names, a classical apotropaic device. The names with which we shall hesitantly begin are repetitive temporality; repetition as displacement; the parodic and hyperbolic voice of the unconscious that deceptively promises the transcendence of parody and the breakthrough to the old, the inspired, the original: revolution as reaction, the return of the repressed. But this beginning is not decisive, for the names we have chosen are not identical. They have somewhat different valences. Indeed they threaten diabolically to displace while repeating one another and to be caught up in the wily one's game, the game *Doctor Faustus* itself tries to play and work out without giving full sympathy, to the devil.

The interposed narrator, Serenus Zeitblom—the discursive intermediary between Thomas Mann and the "diabolical" modern genius Adrian Leverkühn—himself has difficulty in beginning. He quite improperly addresses the reader while deferring his formal introduction and the disclosure of his name until the beginning of the second chapter. He spends the first chapter thematizing and enacting the problem of beginning, and he enunciates his fear that he may "be driven beyond [his] proper and becoming level of thought and experience an 'impure' heightening of [his] natural gifts" in undertaking the task of narrating the uncanny story he is driven to tell. He compulsively begins an endless series of excuses for premature anticipations of characters and events which, along with retrospective allusions, mark his far-from-linear account. He repeats and repeats his "sense of artistic shortcomings and lack of self-control." Yet his story is very much "about" repetition, its variations, and the difficulties in coming to terms with it.

On the simplest and most obvious level, the narrative structure involves a tangled web of relations linking Mann as writer, Zeitblom as narrator, Leverkühn as seemingly central figure, Germany as the diabolically hyperbolic embodiment of modernity, and the reader as implicated witness to the story told. Mann has himself referred to his montage technique in piecing together or grafting into the context of the novel components from various literary and existential sources—the Faust chapbooks, letters, theological treatises, recent events, his own earlier writings, and so forth—in a heady interplay of fact and fiction. As is well known, Theodor W. Adorno, who had studied with Schoenberg, was Mann's "privy councilor" in musical matters. And the novel itself interweaves narration, commentary, and theory. It comments on itself and offers theoretical reflections on its problems in ways that threaten, as Erich Heller has wryly observed [in *The Ironic German*], to reduce the commentator to plagiarism in his or her discussion of it. But the text does not become "autonomous" or self-referential in a narcissistic sense that would repress or deny a specific engagement with history. Indeed, it thematizes the problem of the "autonomy" of modern art and its relation to historical issues. The question it opens, in ever so intricate a form, is that of the precise manner in which the novel relates to its relevant contexts without being simply reducible to them.

Zeitblom as narrator is both mediator and supplement as well as a kind of buffer zone positioned between Mann and Leverkühn. He is also situated between Mann and the reader. Zeitblom represents one aspect of Germany often lost sight of in discussions of the Nazi period. His name combines the Latin and the Germanic: *Serenus,* serene; *Zeitblom,* time with a hint of *Blume*—flower of time. He is a Catholic, a humanist, a child of the Enlightenment and of civilization. . . . He is manifestly not a dominant figure; neither is he an insignificant one. But he is clearly not up to the demands of the times and is even occasionally overwhelmed by them. He is pathetic yet noble in the face of problems that are too big for him to handle, given his ideology and his intellect. He has the courage to resign his teaching position when the Nazis come to power, but he can do little to prevent or effectively oppose their rise and their appeal. At times he passively goes along with protofascist views that repel him, and when he does speak out against them, he tends to be reduced to humanistic and rationalistic nostrums. He is not the simple opponent or adversary of revolution as reaction. He is himself infected by the currents of the time; he even threatens to replicate them. The fact that he, like Nietzsche [one model for Leverkühn], is a philologist is one small sign of the complications in his personality. From earliest childhood he has a genuine love for Leverkühn; in his adulthood his love is reinforced by a commitment to his friend and his musical experiments—a commitment that remains steadfast even when it is sorely tested by doubts and the suspicion of affinities between the devilishly disconcerting art form and the frenzied sociopolitical disorientation of the period. Yet he too is at times attracted to extremes, gets carried away, loses control, and succumbs to the excesses from which he tries to keep a critical distance.

I shall later quote references to Germany that should be read as hyperbolic outbursts and indeed are so marked by "alienation effects" in the text. Here I shall simply mention the problem of the relation of the narrator to anti-Semitism. Zeitblom's family name might be seen to have Jewish overtones, and his attitudes toward Jews have at least traces of Jewish self-hatred. His very outrage at the blatant idiocies of Nazi propaganda does not bring with it a full escape from "racial" prejudice and stereotyping. Even as he takes his distance from the Nazis, he lets slip ways in which their ideology is infectious:

> I have never, precisely in the Jewish problem and the way it has been dealt with, been able to agree fully with our Führer and his paladins; and this fact was not without influence on my resignation from the teaching staff here. Certainly specimens of the race have also crossed my path—I need only think of the private scholar Breisacher in Munich, on whose dismayingly unsympathetic character I propose in the proper place to cast some light.

The suspect reference to "specimens of the race" itself is made in a proleptic remark that attests to an absence of full, classical narrative control. Chaim Breisacher himself represents the paradox of the protofascist Jew who espouses a radical, modernistic, archaicizing "conservatism" that is as offensive to traditional conservatives as it is to liberal bourgeois. And he makes repeated appearances—in the Schlaginhaufen salon, "where the social ambitions of the hostess brought people of every stripe together"; in the Kridwiss circle (itself a "mature" repetition of the youthful Winfried society), where the indiscriminate mingling of categories is made to serve the ideological forces of reaction; and finally in the group called together to hear the last words of Adrian Leverkühn where Breisacher (unlike many others) stays to the bitter end, though the reader is given no indication of his reaction to the disquieting event.

An even more complicated and bewildering stereotype of the Jew is provided by the devil himself, for the "Great Adversary" has internalized certain stereotypical and prejudicial features of the Nazi's scapegoated "other." Since Zeitblom recedes from the narrative scene in the central "dialogue" between Adrian and the devil, Mann as writer may be implicating himself here as well. Early in the exchange, the devil objects to the name *Dicis et non facis* on the grounds that he delivers on his promises "more or less as the Jews are the most reliable dealers." In his second metamorphosis as a refined intellectual, "writer on art, on music for the ordinary press, and the theoretician and critic, who himself composes, so far as thinking allows him," he has a hooked nose and black, woolly hair. Later in the text, Saul Fitelberg is an avatar of the devil who at times literally repeats the devil's temptations, but in the mask of the mass-market impresario he tries vainly to convince Adrian to take his show on the road and capitalize on it. Yet Fitelberg is not a representative of crass commercialism. . . . He is genuinely ingratiating and insinuating; he has an intimate knowledge of music and can *causer musique* with someone like Leverkühn. He is a cultured European, and he is Jewish. And it is difficult to decide whether the stereotype he embodies, as well as its affiliates in the text, are symptomatic expressions of prevalent ideological prejudices or critical disclosures of the very fact of their prevalence and the need to counteract them in oneself, not simply in discrete others.

An axial narrative technique of the novel is dependent upon the fact that—except in the central chapter 25—we see Leverkühn only through Zeitblom's words. Thus the "genius" is perceived by the reader only in the indirect lighting provided by the discourse of one who loves, fears, and does not fully understand him. Given this narrative technique, Adrian, the center of the novel—its ideological "dominant"—is decentered. Even in the central chapter, in which the narrator has simply transcribed Adrian's own notes made on sheets of music, the central figure is doubled by his parodic, diabolical alter ego. To this extent, the novel emulates the atonal, non-hierarchical, serial music that Adrian Leverkühn fictively invents. But the return of the polyphonic in the atonal is also countered by the harmonizing and humanizing role of parody in Zeitblom's narrative. The novel is written in intentional parody of a pompous, stuffy, academic style not up to the events it relates and the problems it treats. Yet the parody of this style is telling and at times even moving, and the style itself is not the object of nihilistic attack or radical dismemberment.

For Leverkühn, however, the problem of modern art and of culture in a thoroughly problematic time would seem to pose itself in terms of the transcendence of parody. Yet Leverkühn seems to live to the utmost intensity the extremity of paradox, and parody itself is enmeshed in the unreconciled meeting of incompatible extremes. While the pact with the devil is made to enable the composer to transcend parody and achieve a total breakthrough, his ordinary life falls increasingly into a self-parodic repetition compulsion. And the artistic breakthrough itself courts both existential breakdown and the return to the oldest but now neobarbaric sources of immediate, unconstrained creativity. Leverkühn is thus a "representative" figure insofar as he embodies a parodically and paradoxically unmediated meeting of the extremes that divide modernity, but he is not a simple representative. The one way in which he does seem to get beyond if not entirely transcend parody—at least to drive it to its explosive limit—is in his own uncompromising tragedy, while his historical context descends beneath parody to filthy, self-deceived, and bloody farce. In and of itself, however, his tragedy redeems nothing; it provides no symbolic recompense, either for the characters or for the reader, but remains unsettling both in its indirect relation to history and in its disquieting implications for any present time that has not transcended the basic problems to which it bears witness.

Leverkühn seems a singularly Germanic figure: modeled on Nietzsche, unintentionally reminiscent of Wittgenstein, he provoked Schoenberg . . . to accuse Mann of plagiarism. Yet he is a singularly Germanic figure only insofar as the Germanic is itself a hyperbolic manifestation of modern crisis and extremity—a hyperbole within the hyperbole. He is thus a highly ambivalent figure, a question mark. The very oppositions he embodies are especially troubling because they are not pure opposites. They—like everything with which he comes in contact—are displacements of one another that allow neither for dialectical reconciliation nor for viable interplay and mutual contestation.

Leverkühn experiences a pathos of distance, at times an icy detachment from things. Yet he longs for human closeness, communication, and love. In his life, these forces meet only in an impenetrably obscure economy. In his music the "dehumanization" of art encounters its expressive counterpart only in the most problematic of ways. For him parody seems to be irrevocably on the side of the icy and the distant, and the breakthrough seems to require the transcendence of parody.

As a child Leverkühn is marked by an uncanny precociousness. In an extremely unchildlike manner, he learns so quickly that he becomes bored with everything. His boredom bespeaks the exhaustion of traditional forms and canonical gestures that seem fit only for parody or for a life of unself-conscious self-parody. Phenomena that elicit childlike awe or sacred respect from others—such as the prescientific, quasi-magical attempts of his father to "speculate the elements"—bring forth laughter from him. But his laughter and sense of the ridiculous are eerie rather than carnivalesque. They recall at a slight remove a story from St. Augustine's *De civitate Dei*—the story of the laughter of Ham, "son of Noah and father of Zoroaster the magian . . . the only man who laughed when he was born—which could only have happened by the help of the Devil." This reversal of what occurs at the time of the ordinary infant's "breakthrough" thus moves to the side of the devil and prefigures the later pact. Adrian retains a joking relation with others throughout his life, but it is a relation in which intimacy and commitment are either deferred or engaged at a disastrous price.

Even in Leverkühn's early life, nature itself is not the setting for innocence and authenticity. It cannot be the simple alternative to problems of culture. It poses in its own displaced manner the problems of simulation, dissimulation, and parody. There is, for example, the case of the fluctuating boundary between the organic and the inorganic suggested by his father's experiments with an erotic

"devouring drop." And there is the edible butterfly, nature's charlatan, that cunningly imitates or deceptively simulates another beautiful but distasteful and poisonous butterfly in order to escape predators—a phenomenon that evokes Leverkühn's chilling laughter.

If the boundary between nature and culture is unsettled, a related boundary is recurrently questioned as well: that between culture and cult. Zeitblom would like to disestablish the sharp opposition between culture and civilization as well as the tendency of culture to be belittled in relation to cult. By Leverkühn's time, the opposition of Germanic *Kultur* to Western *Zivilisation* was becoming a mainstay of modern German intellectual history, and the demand that true culture be grounded in prereflective cult was taking the defense of culture from conservative to radical rightest and even protofascist extremes. Early in the text, Zeitblom informs the reader that he often "explained to [his] pupils that culture is in very truth the pious and regulating, I might say propitiatory entrance of the dark and uncanny into the service [*Kultus*] of the gods"; the translation of course loses the wordplay between *Kultur* and *Kultus,* wherein a change of one letter signifies a break between two world views. Zeitblom's humanistic attempt to tame or domesticate cult in the interest of a civilized understanding of culture is resisted, in different but perhaps related ways, by experimental art and by reactionary politics, both of which reaffirm the cultic in its pagan or barbaric force—but a barbaric force that has become, deceptively and questionably, neobarbaric precisely because it comes after and along with a long and intricate history of civilization. For the young Leverkühn, however, the entire system of oppositions upon which Zeitblom would rely calls for deconstruction. After one of the lectures of Leverkühn's music teacher, the enigmatic stutterer Wendell Kretzschmar (the "z" in his name that evokes an affinity with Nietzsche is for some unexplained reason dropped in the English translation), Zeitblom recounts this exchange:

> What principally impressed [Leverkühn], as I heard while we were walking home, and also next day in the school courtyard, was Kret[z]schmar's distinction between cult epochs and cultural epochs, and his remark that the secularization of art, its separation from divine service, bore only a superficial and episodic character. . . . That the cultural idea was a historically transitory phenomenon, that it could lose itself again in another one, that the future did not inevitably belong to it, this thought he had certainly singled out from Kret[z]schmar's lecture.
>
> "But the alternative," I threw in, "to culture is barbarism."
>
> "Permit me," said he. "After all, barbarism is the opposite of culture only within the order of thought which it gives us. Outside of it the opposite may be something quite different or no opposite at all. . . . For a cultural epoch, there seems to me to be a spot too much talk about culture in ours, don't you think? I'd like to know whether epochs that possessed culture knew the word at all, or used it. Naïveté, unconsciousness, taken-for-grantedness, seems to me to be the

first criterion of the constitution to which we give this name. What we are losing is just this naïveté, and this lack, if one may so speak of it, protects us from many a colourful barbarism which altogether perfectly agreed with culture, even with very high culture. I mean: our stage is that of civilization—a very praiseworthy state no doubt, but also neither was there any doubt that we should have to become very much more barbaric to be capable of culture again. Technique and comfort—in that state one talks about culture but one has not got it. Will you prevent me from seeing in the homophonemelodic constitution of our music a condition of musical civilization—in contrast to the old contrapuntal polyphone culture?"

Leverkühn thus seems to regress from the attempted deconstruction of one "humanistic" opposition to the affirmation of another opposition—the "deadly dichotomy" between culture and civilization that performed conservative if not reactionary ideological functions in the celebration of the German nation. The latter binary was of course the very opposition Mann himself tried to defend in a tortured and partially self-questioning way in his early **"Reflections of a Nonpolitical Man"** (1918), only to criticize it in his later polemical writing. Leverkühn himself does not simply rest upon this opposition in his thoughts about culture and modernity but tries in a secularized or displaced theological mode to return to cultic polyphony; he even retains a fascination for the attempt of the religious utopian Beissel to coordinate musical and social patterns, to the extent of conceiving of "master" and "servant" notes. The culture-cult motif is struck in the section on the youthful Winfried Society, and it is elaborated in the section on the Kridwiss circle—an especially significant section, since it forms part of the same threefold chapter as Leverkühn's penultimate masterwork the *Apocalypsis cum figuris*. But it receives its most rending rendition in the exchange with the devil in which Leverkühn is promised his own version of the *felix culpa:*

> You will lead the way, you will strike up the march of the future, the lads will swear by your name, who thanks to your madness will no longer need to be mad. On your madness they will feed in health, and in them you will become healthy. Do you understand? Not only will you break through the paralysing difficulties of the time—you will break through time itself, by which I mean the cultural epoch and its cult, and dare to be barbaric, twice barbaric indeed, because coming after the humane, after all possible root-treatment and bourgeois raffinement. Believe me, barbarism even has more grasp of theology than has a culture fallen away from cult, which even in the religious has seen only culture, only the humane, never excess, paradox, the mystic passion, the utterly unbourgeois ordeal. But I hope that you do not marvel that "the Great Adversary" speaks to you of religion. Gog's nails! Who else, I should like to know, is to speak of it today?—Surely not the liberal theologian! After all I am by now its sole custodian!

Kretzschmar, whose stutter, indicating the difficulty of

culture in transcending nature, is another reminder of the devil, himself poses the problem of "historical exhaustion and the vitiation of the means and appliances of art, boredom and the search for new ways." His lectures are supported from a public fund, yet they are attended by very few and understood by even fewer, perhaps only by Leverkühn. The topic of one of them is why Beethoven did not write a third movement for his piano sonata opus III. The suggested answer is that the sonata form had been exhausted by the second movement and that the third movement would have been superfluous.

Leverkühn does not use the intimate form of address—*du*—even with close friends such as the narrator Zeitblom. Yet he wants to be *per du* with humanity—on an intimate footing with it. He also seeks an art that is *per du* with humanity. (pp. 150-60)

Yet the desire to be *per du* with humanity involves a paradoxical cross-cultural play on words that marks one instance where the translation actually enriches the text. *Per du* (not used in the original German) means in German to be intimately related; in French *perdu* means "lost." And the condition of Leverkühn's pact with the devil is that twenty-four years of creativity (one for each chapter or section after the central chapter) are to be acquired at the price of isolation and the renunciation of human intimacy and love. Yet Leverkühn's pact was initially sealed early in the novel when he (in imitation of a putative act of Nietzsche) intentionally sought out a syphilitic prostitute—the Hetaera Esmeralda, whose name recalls the name of a butterfly and becomes an obsessive motif in his music. His own obsession with her began when she brushed by his cheek, causing him to blush like the marking on the wing of the butterfly, as he sat bewildered, next to a piano in the bordello. He was taken there under false pretenses by a porter, who resembles another of his teachers, who in turn resembles the devil: one Schleppfuss, or drag-foot, professor of theology. But his aleatory encounter turns out to be fatal and to elicit what was in him: the need for a diabolical engagement induced by a sexual act in which human mediation between flesh and spirit in love is hinted at only to be exceeded by blind and almost sacred fascination beyond all calculations of prudence.

Anyone with whom Adrian becomes involved will also be *perdu*. One of these is Rudolf Schwerdtfeger, the violinist who seduces Adrian into composing a concerto for him and toward whom Adrian displays an "ironic eroticism." Schwerdtfeger's name sounds much like that of another close friend of Leverkühn's, Rüdiger Schildknapp. They have similar relations to the composer Leverkühn and are to that extent displacements of each other: Schwerdtfeger as an interpreter and performing artist, and Schildknapp as a translator who is somewhat disgruntled by what he sees as a derivative activity. While the sounds of their names erosively induce the reader to run them together, the meanings bear at least a tenuous difference: Schwerdtfeger as one who himself rubs away hard edges through a facile virtuosity; Schildknapp as a shield bearer whose escutcheon is threatened with effacement by the fall of the hero whose shield he would bear. Schildknapp himself is plagued with the weight of a bridge supported by progressively rotting teeth, while Schwerdtfeger is shot by a jilted lover as he prepares to go off with a woman whom Leverkühn had halfheartedly tried to engage by using Rudi as an *entremetteur*. (The woman's voice, needless to say, reminds Adrian of his mother's.) But the relations with Schildknapp and Schwerdtfeger are only dress rehearsals for Leverkühn's final, disastrous attempt to cheat the devil in his relation with his little nephew, Echo.

Chapter 25, involving Leverkühn's dialogue with the devil, is the displaced center of the novel. And the novel in general enacts a serioparodic relation to numerology. Leverkühn himself has a magic square above his piano; adding numbers in it in any serial direction always gives the same result—thirty-four. The magic square is atonal like the form of music Leverkühn fictively invents; the latter breaks through the dominant key signature and away from hierarchy, yet it offers a strict rule of order whose acoustic result may appear chaotic from a classical perspective. In the organization of the novel itself there are twenty-four chapters before the central one and twenty-four chapters or sections after it. One chapter—appropriately enough, chapter 34—is divided into three sections to indicate the affinity but not the full identity (in other words, the repetitively displaced relation) between its parts (the Kridwiss circle, preceded by a discussion of the biographical context and followed by an "internal" analysis of the *Apocalypsis cum figuris*).

What is the nature of Leverkühn's dialogue or internally dialogized monologue with the devil in chapter 25? The devil parodies the concerns of Leverkühn by practicing a strategy of citation. He literally quotes the unconscious of the genius and thus renders explicit what Leverkühn tries to repress. Leverkühn himself is both the devil's adversary and his advocate who argues with an internalized diabolical other. But the devil is himself up on modern psychology as well as sociology (at the very least he has read the critiques of T. W. Adorno), and he shows the superficiality of attempts to deny what he stands for by simply seeing him as a projection of a sick mind or a sick society: "Don't blame it on social conditions. I am aware you tend to do so, and are in the habit of saying that these conditions produce nothing fixed and stable enough to guarantee the harmony of the self-sufficient work. True, but unimportant. The prohibitive difficulties of the work lie deep in the work itself. The historical movement of the musical material has turned against the self-contained work."

Or again: "We are entering into times, my friend, which will not be hoodwinked by psychology. . . . This *en passant.*" The devil seems to insist upon a status that is neither quite cultic nor altogether secularized—in any case, a status that cannot be explained away. He demands a durability or iterability in and through differences. In his exchange with Leverkühn he changes appearances in an apparent parody of the devil who tempts Christ in the desert, but he retains the same voice in his displaced repetitions. As I have already said, one of the topics of the conversation is, of course, parody.

> I [Leverkühn]: "A man could know that [i.e., that it is all up with the classical tradition] and recognize freedom above and beyond all cri-

tique. He could heighten the play, by playing with forms of art out of which, as he well knew, life has disappeared."

> He [Devil]: "I know, I know. Parody. It might be fun, if it were not so melancholy in its aristocratic nihilism. Would you promise yourself much pleasure and profit from such tricks?"

> I (retort angrily): "No."

Leverkühn's attempted breakthrough beyond parody to renewed objectivity and feeling reaches its highest forms in his last two masterworks, which are intricate displacements of each other: the *Apocalypsis cum figuris* and the *Lamentation of Dr. Faustus*. They are separated by Leverkühn's attempt to cheat the devil through love for his nephew Nepomuk, nicknamed Echo. Leverkühn seeks the love of a seemingly innocent child. His own love is innocent, since he cannot help himself. But it is also guilty because he knows the condition of his pact and the harm he will bring to one he loves. Thus he does not fully master his fate, but he nonetheless feels answerable for it. The child, the seeming embodiment of innocence transcending parody, is himself at least somewhat equivocal, however. He has an undeniable charm and is able to evoke the sincere affection of those around him. But he is almost too perfect to be credible, and he bears the suspect nickname Echo—a name that denies innocence. Reversing the relations in the myth, the child is very narcissistic and even rather affected in his poses. The echo effect itself marks the equivocal place of the human being in nature. An echo, in which the human voice is returned by nature, seems to intimate intersubjectivity and dialogical reciprocity with the other. Yet the only thing the human gets back is the distorted sound of his or her own voice. The revenge of the devil on Adrian is to have the child die cruelly and painfully of spinal meningitis—a disease that is itself a vicious echo or parody of Leverkühn's own syphilis of the meninges.

The composition that precedes Echo's appearance also in paradoxical and obscure ways anticipates it. And in the only tripartite chapter in the novel, which treats the *Apocalypse*, Mann himself explores the relation between thematic contextualization and formal analysis of the artwork. Zeitblom takes the "speechifying" of the Kridwiss circle to heart because it constitutes "a cold-blooded intellectual commentary upon a fervid experience of art and friendship . . . a work which had a peculiar kinship with, was in spirit parallel to, the things I had heard at Kridwiss's table-round." Like the myth-hungry, antimodern, and reactively revolutionary ideologists of the Kridwiss circle, enamored of such works as Georges Sorel's *Reflections on Violence*, Adrian, in his extremely experimental work epitomizing the entire apocalyptic tradition, was also seeking "a state of mind which, no longer interested in the psychological, pressed for the objective, for a language that expressed the absolute, the binding and compulsory, and in consequence by choice laid on itself the pious fetters of pre-classically strict form." The reproach to which Leverkühn's work "did perhaps expose itself . . . in its urge to reveal in the language of music the most hidden things, the beast in man as well as his sublimest stirrings" was "the reproach both of blood-stained barbarism and of bloodless intellectuality." Zeitblom is deeply sensitive to this reproach, which involves the unmediated meeting and mingling of extremes, for he has "experienced in his very soul how near aestheticism and barbarism are to each other: aestheticism as the herald of barbarism." The very attempt to arrive back at cult through the sacrificial dismemberment of culture has for him its dangers; it requires a pact with the magical and the ritual, which are out of place in a profane epoch.

Adrian's *Apocalypse* courts these dangers especially in its relatively indiscriminate use of his preferred glissando effect—"a naturalistic atavism, a barbaric rudiment from pre-musical days . . . the gliding voice . . . a device to be used with the greatest restraint on profoundly cultural grounds." The glissando is "extremely uncanny" in its orchestral uses, but it is "most shattering" in its application to the human voice, for with it the voice loses touch with the human and with meaning to merge with subarticulate noise, particularly in the formless form of howls and shrieks. The *Apocalypse* is not punctuated by orchestral interludes; rather, the orchestra and voices "merge into one another, the chorus is 'instrumentalized,' the orchestra as it were 'vocalized,' to that degree and to that end that the boundary between man and thing seems shifted: an advantage, surely, to artistic unity, yet—at least for my feeling—there is about it something oppressive, dangerous, malignant." Indeed, "the whole work is dominated by the paradox (if it is a paradox) that in it dissonance stands for the expression of everything lofty, solemn, pious, everything of the spirit; while consonance and firm tonality are reserved for the world of hell, in this context a world of banality and commonplace."

Thus Adrian's reversal and generalized displacement of given assumptions invites an extremely serious reproach, one that approximates experimental art and protofascism—a reproach, Zeitblom tells us, "whose plausibility [he] admit[s] though [he] would bite [his] tongue out sooner than recognize its justice: the reproach of barbarism." But before Zeitblom will indicate, in however qualified a manner, what it is in the work that resists the reproach, the halting textual movement first intensifies that reproach by pointing to

> a certain touch, like an icy finger, of mass-modernity in this work of religious vision, which knows the theological almost exclusively as judgment and terror: a touch of 'streamline,' to venture the insulting word. Take the *testis,* the witness and narrator of the horrid happenings: the 'I, Johannes' . . . whose chilly crow, objective, reporterlike, stands in terrifying contrast to the content of his catastrophic announcements.

Zeitblom presses even further in disclosing the complicity of the work with the degraded forms of mass culture it seems to transcend. He offers another "example of easy technical facility in horror, the effect of being at home in it: I mean the loudspeaker effects (in an oratorio!)"—effects which (although Zeitblom refrains from mentioning the point) cannot but recall to the reader the easy technical facility of another manipulator of loud-speaker effects: Hitler. But then Zeitblom draws back at the brink

of the abyss and reveals how the work itself resists too facile a conflation with sociocultural and political resonances:

> Soullessness! I well know this is at bottom what they mean who apply the word "barbaric" to Adrian's creation. Have they ever, even if only with the reading eye, heard certain lyrical parts—or may I only say moments?—of the *Apocalypse:* song passages accompanied by a chamber orchestra, which could bring tears to the eyes of a man more callous than I am, since they are like a fervid prayer for a soul. I shall be forgiven for an argument more or less into the blue; but to call soullessness the yearning for a soul—the yearning of the little sea-maid [in Hans Christian Andersen's story about a mermaid who painfully desires human legs—another obsessive motif in Leverkühn]—that is what I would characterize as barbarism, as inhumanity!

This bolt from the blue is, however, followed by concluding paragraphs in which Zeitblom, in extremely disconcerting fashion, reveals how the work does not transcend parody and even prefigures later events and the final composition motivated by them. For he turns to the question of how the diabolical laughter in the first part of the *Apocalypse*—"an overwhelming, sardonically yelling, screeching, bawling, bleating, howling, piping, whinnying salvo, the mocking, exulting laughter of the Pit"—has its "pendant" [*Gegenstück*] in "the truly extraordinary chorus of children which, accompanied by a chamber orchestra, opens the second part: a piece of cosmic music of the spheres, icily clear, glassily transparent, of brittle dissonances indeed, but withal of an—I would like to say—inaccessibly unearthly and alien beauty of sound, filling the heart with longing without hope." Thus in the music that is Adrian Leverkühn "utterly," the unrestrained laughter of hell "as repetition no longer recognizable" is displaced and merges undecidably with the heavenly chorus of children in a sublime echo effect.

Leverkühn's last work, the *Lamentation of Dr. Faustus,* returns to the echo effect, now given supplementary weight through the death of his nephew; and it seems to indicate, at least to Zeitblom, how longing without hope may engender a glimmer of hope nonetheless. The echo effect, we are told, was a favorite of baroque masters such as Monteverdi, and it is intimately related to the mournful, melancholic theme of lament. With this work, Adrian seems clearly to recognize how the breakthrough must combine tradition and critique. Yet his disarmingly "original" project (so like many others in the modern period) is to invert and take back Beethoven's Ninth Symphony with its culminating ode to joy. The death of a child reveals to him that one no longer deserves the Ninth Symphony, and so he must revoke or erase it, with joy reversed into lament. Beginning chorally and ending orchestrally, the piece plays variations on the words of Faustus: "For I die as a good and a bad Christian." The twelve syllables correspond to the twelve notes or tones used in the composition. The series they form "is the basis of all the music—or rather, it lies almost as key behind everything and is responsible for the identity of the most varied forms—that identity which exists between the crystalline angelic choir and the hellish yelling in the *Apocalypse* and which has now become all-embracing: a formal treatment strict to the last degree, which no longer knows anything unthematic, in which the order of the basic material becomes total, and within which the idea of a fugue rather declines into an absurdity, just because there is no longer any free note. But it serves now a higher purpose; for—oh, marvel, oh, deep diabolic jest!—just by virtue of the absoluteness of the form the music is, as language, freed." Through the moving inexactness of words evoking music, the final work of Leverkühn seems to achieve the tense unity of objective intellectuality and formal strictness not only with the aleatory but also with expressive "warmth and sincerity of creature confidence" in and through the paradoxical medium of lament. Yet after completing this work, Leverkühn calls together a heterogeneous assemblage of friends and acquaintances and, in Reformation German, discusses his composition in the form of a Faustian confession of his sins in allying himself with the devil. At the end of his parodically inverted but genuinely anguished recitation of Christ's own agony, he (recalling Nietzsche) utters a wailful lament, collapses into madness, and—in childlike dependence—must be tended by his mother.

The issue that has been active, either manifestly or latently, in my entire discussion is how the text of **Doctor Faustus,** through modulations of repetitive temporality, itself relates to its historical contexts. That relation is largely a matter of displaced or offset parallels. One of the most questionable of them is between pre-Nazi Germany and the Reformation or *Lutherzeit.* It is assumed in Adrian's use of old German, particularly in his exchange with the devil and in his "mad" confession to his assembled friends and acquaintances. It is explicit, yet marked as perhaps special pleading in the mouth of a humanist and Catholic, in Zietblom's occasional and at times unbalanced comments. He is even led to ask "whether the reformers are not rather to be regarded as backsliding types and bringers of evil. Beyond a doubt, endless blood-letting and the most horrible self-laceration would have been spared the human race if Martin Luther had not re-established [or cured: *wiederhergestellt*] the Church."

The relation between the rise of the Third Reich and Adrian's experimental art is a more pointed but still controversial matter. German history has for Mann perhaps the most concentrated and forceful expression of the problems and paradoxes of modern civilization—the paradoxical meeting of the best and the worst. Yet the way this history relates to the novel is intricate, and it is obvious that the parallel between Adrian and the rise of Hitler's Germany is indirect, in certain ways not a parallel at all. The Nazis themselves condemn Adrian's work as "cultural Bolshevism," and as in the case of the use and abuse of Nietzsche, the Nazi period is for Mann a vicious and low-grade parody of the artist-figure in whom problems attain more genuinely tragic dimensions. Indeed, it is when one tries to make the tragic exception into a rule of putative collective redemption in a time of crisis that one degrades and cheapens tragedy into senseless barbarism.

One form of more direct reference to German history in the novel is through Zeitblom's outbursts where he loses self-control and repeats in his response the excesses of the time that he condemns. What is significant is that these direct references are clearly situated textually as outbursts. Such is the case with the following moving—indeed, all too moving—passage:

> We are lost. In other words, the war is lost; but that means more than a lost campaign, it means in very truth that *we* are lost: our character, our cause, our hope, our history. It is all up with Germany, it will be all up with her. She is marked down for collapse, economic, political, moral, spiritual, in short all-embracing, unparalleled, final collapse. I suppose I have not wished for it, this that threatens, for it is madness and despair. I suppose I have not wished for it, because my pity is too deep, my grief and sympathy are with this unhappy nation, when I think of the exaltation and blind ardour of its uprising, the breaking-out, the breaking-up, the breaking-down; the purifying and fresh start, the national new birth of ten years ago [1933], that seemingly religious intoxication—which then betrayed itself to any intelligent person for what it was by its crudeness, vulgarity, gangsterism, sadism, degradation, filthiness—ah, how unmistakably it bore within itself the seeds of this whole war! My heart contracts painfully at the thought of that enormous investment of faith, zeal, lofty historic emotion; all this we made, all this is now puffed away in a bankruptcy without compare. No, surely I did not want it, and yet—I have been driven to want it and will welcome it, out of hatred for the outrageous contempt of reason, the vicious violation of the truth, the cheap, filthy backstairs mythology, the criminal degradation and confusion of standards; the abuse, corruption, and blackmail of all that was good, genuine, trusting, and trustworthy in our old Germany. For liars and lickspittles mixed us a poison draught and took away our senses. We drank—for we Germans perennially yearn for intoxication—and under its spell, through years of shameful deeds, which now be paid for. With what? I have already used the word, together with the word "despair" I wrote it. I will not repeat it: not twice could I control my horror or my trembling fingers to set it down again.

Mann, with his own intense love-hate relation to Germany, seems very close to Zeitblom in this madly passionate outburst. But then there comes an antidote to the poison draft of intoxicated outrage in the form of an ironic alienation effect. For the passage above is immediately followed by three asterisks and the observation: "Asterisks too are a refreshment for the eye and mind of the reader. One does not always need the greater articulation of a Roman numeral, and I could scarcely give the character of a main section to the above excursus into a present outside of Adrian Leverkühn's life and work." The more considered attitude toward Germany, modulated and intense at the same time, as well as the supreme ambition of the novel itself, comes in the offset parallel between the passage in which Zeitblom describes the effect of the ending of the *Lamentation,* on the one hand, and the ending of **Doctor Faustus,** on the other:

At the end of this work of endless lamentation, softly, above the reason and with the speaking unspokenness given to music alone, it touches the feelings. I mean the closing movement of the piece, where the choir loses itself and which sounds like the lament of God over the lost state of His world, like the Creator's rueful "I have not willed it." Here, towards the end, I find that the uttermost accents of mourning are reached, the final despair achieves a voice, and—I will not say it, it would mean to disparage the uncompromising character of the work, its irremediable anguish to say that it affords, down to its very last note, any other consolation than what lies in voicing it, in simply giving sorrow words; in the fact, that is, that a voice is given the creature for its woe. No, this dark tone poem permits up to the very end no consolation, appeasement, transfiguration. But take our artist paradox: grant that expressiveness—expression as lament—is the issue of the whole construction: then may we not parallel with it another, a religious one, and say too (though only in the lowest whisper) that out of the sheerly irremediable, hope might germinate? It would be but a hope beyond hopelessness, the transcendence of despair—not betrayal to her, but the miracle that passes belief. For listen to the end, listen with me: one group of instruments after another retires, as the work fades on the air, in the high G of a cello, the last word, the last fainting sound, slowly dying in a pianissimo-fermata. Then nothing more: silence, and night. But that tone that vibrates in the silence, which is no longer there, to which only the spirit hearkens, and which was the voice of mourning, is no more. It changes its meaning; it abides as a light in the night.

"Though only in the lowest whisper": this affirmation on the margin of silence reverses while replicating the hushed tones of the exchange with the devil. Compare the high G of the novel itself (which also recalls the painting of the Last Judgment mentioned toward the end of the first section on the *Apocalypse* as well as the recurrent Hetaera-Esmeralda motif):

> Germany, the hectic on her cheek, was reeling then at the height of her dissolute triumphs, about to gain the whole world by virtue of the one pact she was minded to keep, which she had signed with her blood. Today, clung round by demons, a hand over one eye, with the other staring into horrors, down she flings from despair to despair. When will she reach the bottom of the abyss? When, out of the uttermost hopelessness—a miracle beyond the power of belief—will the light of hope dawn? A lonely man [*Mann*] folds his hands and speaks: "God be merciful to thy poor soul, my friend, my Fatherland."

Adrian cannot achieve in his personal life what is at least intimated in his music, for existentially the breakthrough is ironically reversed into compulsive repetition leading to tragic breakdown. Yet the musical ambition is itself displaced onto the narrative with indirect implications for historical life, thereby ironically recalling the devil's

promise that Adrian's venture would enable others (Zeitblom? Mann himself?) to create without madness. Here one may make a pertinent chronological point in the midst of repetitive temporality, its reversals and displacements. Zeitblom like Mann narrates his story during the Second World War, but he speaks of Adrian's life before the First World War and until May 1930, when the musician goes mad and continues a vegetating existence until 1940. Curiously, there is a three-year gap between Adrian's madness and Hitler's accession to power. Does this mean that the game was up in 1930, or that there was still a chance for Germany in that three-year interval? The text provides no answer. Indeed, it even leaves in doubt whether Zeitblom's interpretation of the "high G" of the *Lamentation* is his own projective wish-fulfillment, which resonates with his (Mann's?) concluding prayerlike invocation to Germany, Leverkühn, and the reader.

Nonetheless, it would be questionable to read the final lines as a simple apology for quasi-religious quiescence and fatalistic or apathetic withdrawal. Mann, in other texts written or spoken during the period in which he wrote **Doctor Faustus,** was asserting the need for active commitment to democratic values and opposition to fascism in ways that might be read, to some limited extent, as the counterpart to what he attempts in the novel. Nor should one ignore the fact that Zeitblom, despite his desire for moderation, can assert that "ethically speaking, the only way a people can achieve a higher form of communal life is not by a foreign war, but by a civil one—even with bloodshed" and even that "the dictatorship of the proletariat begins to seem to me, a German burgher, an ideal situation compared with the now possible one of the dictatorship of the scum of the earth"—outbursts indeed, but not modulated by irony. But the most unsettling dimension of the novel—its hyperbole, perhaps its hubris, in any event a sign of both its power and its limits—may be that it almost leads the reader to look at the Nazi period as an offset and distorted displacement of the life and work of Adrian Leverkühn rather than vice versa. It is of course at this point that the novel reaches its limits and, in its seeming attempt to break through them, courts disaster.

One should, however, perhaps end by finally striking the note of Thomas Mann's own skillful use of parody in the novel—a use that cannot be conflated either with Zeitblom's unskilled narrative or with Leverkühn's explicit conception of parody as a chilling dead end. By contrast, Mann's parody, in its liminal position between humane care and diabolical play, is both mediation and supplement relating the interposed narrator's inept but endearing self-parody and the *Tonsetzers* demonically antithetic theoretical reflections and ambivalently poignant musical practice. Nor can Mann's parody be identified with an evasive strategy of containment or with the contorted attempt of a transcendental ego to pat itself on the back for its putative ability to bracket the world and view it from a safe aesthetic perspective. Rather, it is a complex narrative mode involving both implication in the story and critical distance from it: a mode of indirect, self-reflective discourse which, far from becoming fully autonomized or narcissistically speculative, may be one of the most compelling ways to address (by displacing)—possibly to work (if not break) through—certain problems, including one's relation to the demonic, the nearly exhausted, and the compulsively repetitive. (pp. 161-74)

> *Dominick La Capra, "History and the Devil in Mann's 'Doctor Faustus',"* in his History, Politics, and the Novel, *Cornell University Press, 1987, pp. 150-74.*

FURTHER READING

Bibliography

Jonas, Klaus W., and Jonas, Ilsedore B. *Thomas Mann Studies, Volume II: A Bibliography of Criticism.* Philadelphia: University of Pennsylvania Press, 1967, 440 p.

Lists critical works written on Mann between 1954 and 1965, including extensive entries on *Doctor Faustus.* Book is arranged alphabetically according to critic name and includes indexes by specific work, subject, and theme.

Biography

Berendsohn, Walter E. *Thomas Mann: Artist and Partisan in Troubled Times.* Translated by George C. Buck. University: The University of Alabama Press, 1973, 261 p.

Comprehensive biography that emphasizes the influence of social and political conditions in Germany before and after World War II on Mann's personal life and artistic career.

Criticism

Barnes, Jim. "*Doctor Faustus* and *Under the Volcano.*" In his *Fiction of Malcolm Lowry and Thomas Mann: Structural Tradition,* pp. 97-105. Kirksville, Mo.: The Thomas Jefferson Press, 1990.

Examines parallels between *Doctor Faustus* and Lowry's *Under the Volcano,* focusing specifically on the respective protagonists' tendencies toward "self-annihilation."

Blomster, W. V. "Textual Variations in *Doctor Faustus.*" *The Germanic Review* XXXIX, No. 3 (May 1964): 183-91.

Discusses the significance of extensive textual revisions made between the original 1947 publication of *Doctor Faustus* and the 1948 edition published by Bermann-Fischer in Vienna.

Boeninger, H. R. "Zeitblom, Spiritual Descendant of Goethe's Wagner and Wagner's Beckmesser." *German Life & Letters: A Quarterly Review* XIII, No. 1 (October 1959): 38-43.

Analyzes the character of Zeitblom as the "antipode of Leverkühn-Faustus."

Briner, Andres. "Conrad Beissel and Thomas Mann." *The American German Review* XXVI, No. 2 (December 1959-January 1960): 24-5, 38.

Asserts that the technical explications of music in *Doctor Faustus* were influenced in part by the life and work of German-American composer Conrad Beissel.

Brown, Calvin S. "The Entomological Source of Mann's Poisonous Butterfly." *The Germanic Review* XXXVII, No. 2 (March 1961): 116-20.

Maintains that Mann incorporated English naturalist Henry Walter Bates's description of the butterfly *Hetaera esmeralda* into *Doctor Faustus* as a metaphor for sensualism and prostitution.

Butler, E. M. "The First Faust Reborn, 1947." In her *The Fortunes of Faust,* pp. 321-38. Cambridge: The Syndics of the Cambridge University Press, 1952.

Contends that the text of *Doctor Faustus* was highly influenced by the archaic mythology in the first Faustbook.

Charney, Hanna, and Charney, Maurice. "*Doctor Faustus* and *Mon Faust:* An Excursus in Dualism." *Symposium: A Quarterly Journal in Modern Literatures* XVI, No. 1 (Spring 1962): 45-53.

Comparison of the differing characterizations and narrative techniques in *Doctor Faustus* and in Paul Valéry's *Mon Faust.*

Cicora, Mary A. "Wagner Parody in *Doktor Faustus.*" *The Germanic Review* LXIII, No. 3 (Summer 1988): 133-39.

Examines the extent to which Richard Wagner's last music drama, *Parsifal,* influenced *Doctor Faustus.*

Cobley, Evelyn. "Closure and Infinite Semiosis in Mann's *Doctor Faustus* and Eco's *The Name of the Rose.*" *Comparative Literature Studies* 26, No. 4 (1989): 341-62.

Discusses how the two novels "explore similar conflicts between medieval and contemporary semiotics, foreground similar intertextual processes, investigate along similar lines the deconstruction of oppositions, and discuss similar parallels between art, religion, sex, and politics."

Engelberg, Edward. "Thomas Mann's Faust and Beethoven." *Monatschefte* XLVII, No. 2 (February 1955): 112-16.

Relates Beethoven's music theories and his bitterness over his deafness to "the special problems of Leverkühn's artistic conflict."

Fetzer, John Francis. *Music, Love, Death and Mann's "Doctor Faustus."* Columbia, S.C.: Camden House, 1990, 155 p.

Asserts that the "reciprocal links between music, love, and death" provide a sense of unity in *Doctor Faustus.*

Field, G. W. "Music and Morality in Thomas Mann and Hermann Hesse." *University of Toronto Quarterly* XXIV, No. 2 (January 1955): 175-90.

Compares the views on music evidenced in *Doctor Faustus* and in Hesse's *Das Glasperlenspiel.*

Foster, John Burt, Jr. "Enter the Devil: Nietzsche's Presence in *Doctor Faustus.*" In his *Heirs to Dionysus: A Nietzschean Current in Literary Modernism,* pp. 338-402. Princeton: Princeton University Press, 1981.

Attempts to explain why Mann drew so heavily from André Gide's *The Immoralist,* a biographical novel about Friedrich Nietzsche, while writing *Doctor Faustus.*

Hatfield, Henry. "The Magic Square: Thomas Mann's *Doktor Faustus.*" *Euphorion: Zeitschrift für Literaturgeschichte,* 62 (January 1968): 413-20.

Contends that the narrative pattern of *Doctor Faustus* corresponds to the twelve-tone system in musical composition and to the "magic square," a mathematical pattern in which groups of numbers are arranged in a square so that they add up to the same sum, vertically, horizontally, and diagonally.

Heller, Erich. "Faust's Damnation: The Morality of Knowledge: Parts I, II, and III." *The Listener* LXVII, Nos. 1711, 1712, 1713 (11 January 1962; 18 January 1962; 25 January 1962): 59-61, 121-23, 168-70.
    Series of articles in which the critic traces the history and various interpretations of the Faust myth, including Christopher Marlowe's *Dr. Faustus,* Johann Wolfgang von Goethe's *Faust,* and Mann's *Doctor Faustus.*

————. *Thomas Mann: The Ironic German.* Mamaroneck, N.Y.: Paul P. Appel, 1973, 314 p.
    Biographical and critical work that includes discussion of *Doctor Faustus* as a tragic parody of evil.

Hoelzel, Alfred. "Leverkühn, The Mermaid, and Echo: A Tale of Faustian Incest." *Symposium: A Quarterly Journal of Modern Foreign Languages* XLII, No. 1 (Spring 1988): 3-16.
    Focuses on the details and implications of Leverkühn's "confession" in order "to identify their interrelationship, and thus to elucidate their significance for the novel."

Kaufmann, Fritz. "Last Judgment: *Doctor Faustus.*" In his *Thomas Mann: The World as Will and Representation,* pp. 197-238. Boston: Beacon Press, 1957.
    Discusses *Doctor Faustus* as a synthesis of the "Stoic-Christian impulses behind the Enlightenment with the dark mysticism of the romantic counter-revolution." Kaufmann concludes: "*Ecce homo!* Thomas Mann's story is a story of stress and striving in the teeth of death, devil, and temptation. It is the mystery story of the human soul."

Kaye, Julian B. "Conrad's *Under Western Eyes* and Mann's *Doctor Faustus.*" *Comparative Literature* IX, No. 1 (Winter 1957): 60-5.
    Examines how Mann's "method of narration, the relation of the narrator to both 'story' and author, the characterization, [and] the attribution of value to events and themes" in *Doctor Faustus* was influenced by Joseph Conrad's *Under Western Eyes.*

Krieger, Murray. "Disease and Health: The Tragic and the Human Realms of Thomas Mann." In his *The Tragic Vision: Variations on a Theme in Literary Interpretation,* pp. 86-113. New York: Holt, Rinehart, and Winston, 1960.
    Asserts Mann's Faustus figure is a "tragic visionary" who represents the pessimism and despair of the twentieth century.

Lukács, Georg. *Essays on Thomas Mann.* Translated by Stanley Mitchell. London: Merlin Press, 1964, 169 p.
    Maintains *Doctor Faustus* is the greatest achievement of Mann's *oeuvre* because it parallels the social and historical developments of the first half of the twentieth century, including the rise of fascism.

Lyon, James K. "Words and Music: Thomas Mann's Tone-Poem *Doctor Faustus.*" *The Western Humanities Review* XIII, No. 1 (Winter 1959): 99-102.
    Explains German composer Arnold Schönberg's objections to Mann's portrayal of Leverkühn as the originator of the twelve-tone system of musical composition in *Doctor Faustus.*

Mann, Michael. "The Musical Symbolism in Thomas Mann's *Doctor Faustus.*" *The Music Review* XVII, No. 4 (November 1956): 314-22.
    Essay by Mann's son in which he discusses his father's use of the montage narrative technique in *Doctor Faustus,* his literary aesthetic, and his knowledge of the technicalities of music.

Mann, Thomas. *The Story of the Novel: The Genesis of Doctor Faustus.* New York: Alfred A. Knopf, 1961, 242 p.
    Published notes and diary entries written simultaneously with *Doctor Faustus* in which Mann explains the technical, thematic, and philosophical concerns he encountered while writing the novel.

Miller, Leslie L. "Myth and Morality: Reflections on Thomas Mann's *Doktor Faustus.*" In *Essays on German Literature,* edited by Michael S. Batts and Marketa Goetz Stankiewicz, pp. 195-217. Toronto: University of Toronto Press, 1968.
    Connects the characterization of Leverkühn with the problem of morality in *Doctor Faustus.* According to Miller, "The composite life of Leverkühn is . . . Mann's representation of that sad chapter in German history which saw the emergence, triumph, and fall of National Socialism. Thus, the guilt incurred by Leverkühn in concluding his sinful pact must be understood as an interpretation by Mann of German morality in accepting National Socialism."

Morrison, Karl F. "Malevolent Sympathy." In *"I Am You": The Hermeneutics of Empathy in Western Literature, Theology, and Art,* pp. 69-97. Princeton: Princeton University Press, 1988.
    Discusses various ways to interpret Mann's use of "association by contrast" in *Doctor Faustus* and how this technique influenced the author's themes of humanism, self-knowledge, and individualism.

Nemoianu, Virgil. "Adrian Leverkühn, or the Secondary as Victim." In his *A Theory of the Secondary: Literature, Progress, and Reaction,* pp. 43-57. Baltimore: The Johns Hopkins University Press, 1989.
    Contends that the fate of Leverkühn in *Doctor Faustus* does not solely symbolize the political history of Germany because "the reliability of the narrator is severely questionable and his account of Leverkühn is thus gravely distorted."

Parkes-Perret, Ford. B. "Thomas Mann's Silvery Voice of Self-Parody in *Doktor Faustus.*" *The Germanic Review* LXIV, No. 1 (Winter 1989): 20-30.
    Speculates that the viola d'amore in *Doctor Faustus* serves "as a symbol for Zeitblom's love of Leverkühn. But it functions also as a metaphor for the way Zeitblom conceives his relationship with Leverkühn."

Politzer, Heinz. "Of Time and *Doctor Faustus.*" *Monatschefte* LI, No. 4 (April-May 1959): 145-55.
    Traces the development of the various interpretations of the original Faust myth and states that "Mann changes the Faust motif, equating his tragedy with that of the European artist of the twentieth century who sees his heritage exhausted and all possible paths already pursued."

Puknat, S. B., and Puknat, E. M. "Mann's *Doctor Faustus* and Shakespeare." *Research Studies* 35, No. 2 (June 1967): 148-54.

Relates William Shakespeare's explications on the role of the artist and the significance of the written word in his sonnets and play *Love's Labour's Lost* to *Doctor Faustus.*

Reed, T. J. "Reckoning." In his *Thomas Mann: The Uses of Tradition,* pp. 360-402. Oxford: The Clarendon Press, 1974.

Traces the sources of the cultural, historical, biographical, and textual variations that Mann incorporated into *Doctor Faustus.*

Rice, Philip Blair. "The Merging Parallels: Mann's *Doctor Faustus.*" *The Kenyon Review* XI, No. 2 (Spring 1949): 199-217.

Discusses the complexity and innovations in *Doctor Faustus,* focusing on Mann's experiments with form and narrative technique in the novel.

Scher, Steven Paul. "Thomas Mann's 'Verbal Score': Adrian Leverkühn's Symbolic Confession." *Modern Language Notes* 82, No. 4 (October 1967): 403-20.

Musical analysis of *Doctor Faustus* in which the critic discusses how Mann's musical descriptions symbolize Leverkühn's life and correspond to Richard Wagner's Prelude to Act III of *Die Meistersinger von Nürnberg.*

Stout, Harry L. "Lessing's Riccaut and Thomas Mann's Fitelberg." *The German Quarterly* XXXVI, No. 1 (January 1963): 24-30.

Maintains Mann adapted a scene from Gotthold Lessing's novel *Minna von Barnhelm* in order to add comic relief and to enhance the thematic complexities of *Doctor Faustus.*

Swales, Martin. "The Mind's Betrayal: *Mario und der Zauberer, Doktor Faustus.*" In his *Thomas Mann: A Study,* pp. 77-97. Totowa, N.J.: Rowman and Littlefield, 1980.

Psychological analysis of the themes of temptation, self-deception, creativity, and music in *Doctor Faustus.*

Taubes, Jacob. "From Cult to Culture." *Partisan Review* XXI, No. 4 (July-August 1954): 387-400.

Speculates how scholar Chaim Breisacher's "philosophy of culture" in *Doctor Faustus* was adapted from the work of philosopher Oskar Goldberg.

Tuska, Jon. "The Vision of *Doktor Faustus.*" *The Germanic Review* XI, No. 4 (November 1965): 277-309.

Asserts that *Doctor Faustus* should not be read exclusively as a biography of Leverkühn but rather as "a representation of a *Last Judgment* upon Western civilization."

Vogt, Karen Drabek. "*Dr. Faustus.*" In her *Vision and Revision: The Concept of Inspiration in Thomas Mann's Fiction,* pp. 127-59. New York: Peter Lang, 1987.

Maintains that the central focus of *Doctor Faustus* is "the question of how an inspired artist fares in the twentieth century milieu of science and humanism."

Weigand, Hermann J. "An Interview on *Doktor Faustus.*" In *Thomas Mann in Context: Papers of the Clark University Centennial Colloquium,* edited by Kenneth Hughes, pp. 95-126. Worcester, Mass.: Clark University Press, 1978.

Interview with scholar Hermann J. Weigand conducted by Helene Scher and Kenneth Hughes. Weigand discusses his personal relationship with Mann, the narrative and thematic complexity of *Doctor Faustus,* and Mann's artistic motivations.

Williams, W. D. "Thomas Mann's *Dr. Faustus.*" *German Life & Letters: A Quarterly Review* XII, No. 4 (July 1959): 273-81.

Suggests that while *Doctor Faustus* explicates the tragedy of modern Germany, the novel could in fact be considered "an analysis of the whole of contemporary civilization."

Additional coverage of Mann's life and career is contained in the following sources published by Gale Research: *Contemporary Authors,* Vols. 104, 128; *Dictionary of Literary Biography,* Vol. 66; *Major 20th-Century Writers;* and *Short Story Criticism,* Vol. 5.

Vítězslav Nezval

1900-1958

Czechoslovakian poet, novelist, dramatist, critic and translator.

INTRODUCTION

Nezval was one of the most influential poets in Czechoslovakian avant-garde literature of the interwar era. A leading contributor to the literary movements Poetism and Surrealism in Czechoslovakia, he is best remembered for such poetry cycles as *Praha s prsty deště* (*Prague with Fingers of Rain*) and *Básně noci* (*Poems of the Night*) in which he evokes mystical, erotic, and grotesque atmospheres through surrealistic dream imagery.

Nezval was born in western Moravia and grew up in the village of Šemkovice. Although his first artistic interest was musical composition, he turned to poetry as a teenager, when he became dissatisfied with his technical ability as a musician. After attending secondary school in Třebíc, in 1920 he entered the University Charles IV in Prague, where he studied literature and philosophy, and joined Devětsil, a communist literary group which promoted proletarian literature and rejected traditional art forms. Many reviewers have emphasized the Marxist, avantgarde influence of the Devětsil group on Nezval's first volume of poetry, *Most* (*The Bridge*), which rejects conventional poetic structures and addresses proletarian concerns. In 1922 Nezval broke from Devětsil, concluding that its preoccupation with Marxist rhetoric and propaganda impeded artistic expression. He then embraced Poetism, a Czechoslovakian movement which has been likened to Italian Futurism for its celebration of modern technology and its playful approach to art, emphasizing the imagination and direct appeal to the emotions. During the 1930s Nezval became a leading figure in the Czech surrealist movement following his travels in France and Italy, where he associated with such writers as Paul Eluard and André Breton. However, with the outbreak of World War II, Nezval turned to writing intensely political poetry, criticizing the Nazi occupation of his country and praising Communism. Throughout the 1940s he produced such propagandistic works as *Stalin* and *Zpěv míru* (*Song of Peace*), while assuming a prestigious position in the Communist regime's Ministry of Information. Because of its polemical nature, Nezval's later work is often considered artistically inferior to his earlier poetry. However, he has received praise for his verse play *Dnes ještě zapada slunce nad Atlantidou* (*The Sun Still Sets over Atlantis*), which draws inspiration from Greek tragedy, in contrast to the experimental, avant-garde nature of his earlier works. Nezval died in 1958 following a prolonged illness.

Social and spiritual liberation is a prominent theme in Nezval's poetry. While such works as *The Bridge* advocate liberation of the proletariat through Communism, his poetist and surrealist works often focus on emancipating the individual from the psychological oppression of fear and guilt. For example, reflecting the psychoanalytic theories of Sigmund Freud, his epic poem *Podivuhodný kouzelník* (*The Amazing Magician*) depicts the quest of a magician who ventures deep into the unconscious mind where he confronts and overcomes repressed fears, thus liberating the imagination. Many critics have praised the spontaneous tone of the work and assert that the poem was one of the defining expressions of the Poetist movement. Nezval's epic poem *Edison* also celebrates the artist's liberating power, likening the inventor Thomas Edison's ability to generate light from darkness to the creative role of the artist. Noting the opposition of light and dark images throughout the poem, critics have also suggested that *Edison* depicts the conflict between the control achieved by humanity through technology and the more mysterious power of nature. Forces of light and darkness in Nezval's poetry are also interpreted as representing the contrast between life and death. Such imagery has been noted in *Poems of the Night,* which critics find reminiscent of the verse of Edgar Allan Poe. "Neznámá ze Seiny" ("The Unknown Girl of the Seine,") for example, combines macabre and erotic images of death in an account of a drowned girl floating in the Seine river in Paris.

Nezval's surrealist poems are often described as hypnotic, mystical, and erotic, suggesting an overflow of the subconscious and juxtaposing reality with dreams and fantasy. For example, *Prague with Fingers of Rain,* often considered Nezval's most successful surrealist work, presents his impressions of Prague through a collage of colors, aromas, and images in free, unrhymed verse. In addition, critics note his emphasis on the paradoxical and contradictory aspects of experience. Nezval also incorporated such elements of surrealism as automatic writing, free association, and the theme of childhood into several prose works, including his autobiographical trilogy composed of *Kronika z konce století, Posedlost,* and *Dolce far niente.* He described the trilogy as an attempt to record "the forgotten regions of my soul," and to encourage the reader's communication with his or her lost childhood.

PRINCIPAL WORKS

Most (poetry) 1922
Pantomima (poetry) 1924
Menší růžová zahrada (poetry) 1926
Edison (poetry) 1928
Hra v kostky (poetry) 1928
Kronika z konce století (novel) 1929
Básně noci (poetry) 1930
Jan ve smutku (poctry) 1930
Posedlost (novel) 1930
Snídaně v trávě (poetry) 1930
Dolce far niente (novel) 1931
Milenci z kiosku (drama) 1932
Pan Marat (novel) 1932
Skleněný havelok (poetry) 1932
Jak vejce vejci (novel) 1933
Sbohem a šáteček (poetry) 1933
Zpáteční lístek (poetry) 1933
Žena v množném čísle (poetry) 1935
Praha s prsty deště (poetry) 1936
Řetěz Štěstí (novel) 1936
Absolutní hrobař (poetry) 1937
Historický obraz (poetry) 1939
Pět minut za městem (poetry) 1939
Manon Lescaut (drama) 1940
Stalin (poetry) 1949
Dílo. 38 vols. (poetry, drama, and novels) 1950-70
Zpěv míru (poetry) 1950
   [*Song of Peace,* 1951]
Chrpy a města (poetry) 1955
Dnes ještě zapadá slunce nad Atlantidou (drama) 1956
Z mého života (novel) 1959

———

A. French   (essay date 1968)

[*French is an English critic and translator who has written several books on Czech literature. In the following essay, he chronicles the development of Nezval's literary career and presents a detailed analysis of his most prominent works.*]

The end of the first World War marks a turning point in the literary as well as the political history of the Czech people. With the reopening of the frontiers, the pages of Czech journals were invaded from East and West by news and views the novelty and excitement of which were all the greater because of the isolation of Czechs during the war years. Reports of revolution were filtering in from the East. From Paris and Berlin came accounts of revolt against every form of social and artistic tradition. The proclamation in Prague of the new Czechoslovak state seemed to symbolize the opening of a fresh epoch in the world not only of politics but also of ideas. During the war a new generation had grown up, and to these young people the ideas of their fathers seemed suddenly as outdated and ill-fitting as the soldiers' garb in which the latter returned to homes they found strange after their long absence. Impatient of their elders' leadership the young claimed the future for themselves: student journals multiplied, and were filled with the blueprints of a new world untainted by the blindness and folly of the old. In literature a complete change of taste swept into oblivion the intellectualism, subjectivism and "decadence" of pre-war writers, and social questions became the central theme even of lyric poetry. The young writers of Prague, drawing their political programmes from Moscow and their artistic models from the Expressionist art of Paris and Berlin, adapted their literary efforts to the cause of world revolution. Enthusiastically they pressed their talent into the service of the cause, and termed their movement Proletarian literature.

In 1920 the young Vítězslav Nezval left the rural surroundings of his Moravian home to become a student at the Caroline University of Prague: it was here that he met the bohemian set of writers which included J. Wolker, the most talented of all the Proletarian school. Nezval became a frequent visitor at Wolker's lodgings, and spent whole days arguing with him about art and politics. Nezval was startled and excited by the wild radicalism of his new friends, and he entered with enthusiasm into their revolutionary plans. In his own anarchic way he rejoiced at the current tendency to debunk tradition. But the fashionable allegiance of modern art to ideology was far less to his taste, and at first he fought shy of any collective political programme which might clip the wings of the artist. Accordingly he was among the first of the young writers to raise his voice against the idea of Proletarian literature, and his influence turned out to be decisive in the development of post-war Czech writing away from purely social themes.

The inspiration for his early poems had come in fact not from social events or literature, but primarily from dreams. According to his own account he was constantly driven by the urge to express his own sense of terror and horror felt upon waking from the nightmares from which he suffered. Once the content of the dream was forgotten, the obsessive experience which he felt would become divorced from all logic or action, and it was this feeling which he tried to convey, first in music, then in a form of verse which would express mood and atmosphere rather than thought or action. His first models were the so-called

Decadents, that fiery generation which had shaken the dying years of the nineteenth century with their mysticism, their exploration of the inner self, and their cult of death and damnation. As he moved away from their influence Nezval's poems turned from gloom to fantasy and from the nightmare of the graveyard to the free play of the imagination, untrammelled by logic or inhibition.

Nezval shared the political views of the Proletarians, but in matters of art they parted company. Both Nezval and Wolker became members of an intellectual group known as the Devětsil, devoted to revolutionary art, and guided by the brilliant theoretician Karel Teige. Within the group the influence of Nezval gradually rose, while that of Wolker waned. By 1922 Wolker was at the peak of his success, but the cause of Proletarian art was already in decline, and his early and tragic death sealed its fate. Hitherto the future of Czech poetry had hung in the balance: from now on it was clear that the conception of art represented by Nezval was to prevail.

In 1922 Nezval had published his first book of verse, *The Bridge.* The title was suggested by Nezval's vision of Prague by night: the river which runs through the city is crossed by series of bridges, and to the poet, looking over the moving water, each appeared as a flaming rosary connecting two pools of darkness, a symbol of human life in transit between two unknowns. Many of the poems were dream-like fantasies combining the charm and horror of a fairy tale. In the poem 'Death' Nezval strikingly demonstrated his ability to transform into poetry the memories of childhood. Beginning with his future death the scene moves backwards, as in a feverish dream, until suddenly it steadies on a first sharp impression in the poet's life. His father is moving cautiously across the yard of his home; he stops, and the three-year-old child catches his breath. There is a detonation as his father shoots a rat: the fire of the explosion reveals to the poet the ultimate secret; his own heart stops. The wheel has come full circle and the poet is dead. The Czech critic F. X. Salda rightly perceived, even at this early stage, Nezval's inclination towards Surrealism, attracted as he was by the adventurous half-life of subconscious experience. 'It is in the fantastic dream that the individual stamp of Nezval's fancy best appears: he identifies himself with the external world through action of a mythical, fabulous, or fairytale nature, writing into them the image of his own spirit, for the barrier between it and the world has quite disappeared.'

In 1922 Nezval also published the poem '**The Amazing Magician**', an epic of fantasy on an ambitious scale. The poem opens in the half-light of the evening: wandering along the riverside and away from the city the poet reaches a frontier between the real world and that of dreams; a convent rising before him symbolizes the ascetic and unawakened nature of his own country with its conventional morality. Suddenly there appears the vision of a beautiful woman, and from her the magician is born. He is the product of a long line of forebears who stretch, like elements of nature, through successive layers into the depths of the earth. Among the elements is a fountain which is constantly forced upwards towards the light by the relentless pressure from below; yet always it fails to break through

the crust of the earth, and the tumult below echoes a frustrated song of creation. The magician feels, but cannot understand the turmoil within him, and can find no outlet for his magic. He sees a recurring vision, the lake lady, to whom he confides his feeling of imprisonment within himself and his creative impotence; how he is haunted by a memory of some lost paradise; of the nightmares that trouble his sleep with the sight of a grotesque cat watching him through a window; of the death of his childish playmate. He plunges into the world of action and adventure, and finding himself amid the surge of revolution he strikes off the shackles that bind the outer man: thus he accomplishes his social vindication. The solution of his inner conflict comes only when he recognizes the woman of his vision as one who was at once his mother, playmate, and lover. By love he is taught to escape from the limitations of his own personality, which is the product of his past, by merging his individuality in the stream of living things. By death he is released and sees his own petrified body, on which crouches the lady of the vision in the form of a tigress. From his grave springs the fountain, echoing the song of creation and bathing all that lies between the bowels of the earth and the sky in its living stream.

This long, and at first sight chaotic poem gained much of its effect from the constant juxtaposition of the familiar and the unreal, set in a world uninhibited by convention or logical association: as classical poets had explored the world of mythology, so Nezval explored that revealed by psycho-analytical speculation. Nezval was the hero of his own epic; the fountain was the magic of his verse, bursting from his innermost being; the stifling crust of earth was the dead weight of conventional morality, upholding a system riddled with social injustice; but it was also the dead hand of tradition in art. In the poem the social tension was resolved by revolution, the inner conflict by enlightenment and love: on the one hand the call to revolt against the social order, sounded by Wolker and his friends; on the other hand the struggle of modern art against the traditional forms imposed upon it, the recognition that the present is the child, not the slave, of the past.

Nezval explained his methods in an essay included in his new book *Pantomime.* The essay rejected logic as a basis for poetry, whose themes could more properly be connected by associated sounds than by sense. The theory was illustrated by the accompanying poems which often resembled nothing so much as a scrap album of inconsequential pieces, some of which were evidently not to be taken seriously. It was a feature of Nezval's work to exploit the absurd in poetry, and he specialised in setting gay, sophisticated irony next to primitive horror. It was in 1924 that the new style of poetry received a name and a platform. In an article by K. Teige the functional side of modern art (as exemplified in modern architecture) was contrasted with the bizarre and irrational style which was its reverse side. Man lived not by logic alone, but by fantasy, imagination and humour. As Constructivism would satisfy man's artistic taste on a rational plane, so would Poetism (as Teige called it) satisfy man's hunger for the topsyturvy world of the imagination even as the carnival, the harlequinade, the circus and the film provided relief and relaxation from the grimness of life for the masses. Poetry was meant to be enjoyed: but, like the new products of the film industry, it hoped, by revealing new lines and angles of vision and fresh combinations of objects, to give fresh insight into life. The aim of the poet was to catch and portray pure sensation unencumbered by preconception or rational association, to see each object as though through the eyes of a child or a visitor from another planet. A cultivated hedonism was the basis of the new poetry, but this was only part of the story. The dissociation was to extend not only to objects, but also to the words in which they are expressed. 'When words were new they shone out, when set together in their incessant, native intensity. Gradually from their frequent usage was evolved phraseology. It is logic that makes phrases out of illuminating words. Logically there is a proper connexion between the glass and the table, the star and the sky, the door and the stairs: hence these things pass unnoticed. It was necessary to set the star to the table, the glass near to the piano or the angels, the door next to the ocean. The point at issue is how to clarify reality, how to give it its illuminating form, as on the first day of its existence.

Nezval's books now began to appear in rapid succession. *The Smaller Rose Garden, Postcard Poems, Grave Inscriptions,* and *Diabolo* all appeared in 1926; *Twins* in 1927. In the first of these books **'Premier Plan'** produced an astonishing succession of pictures: night like a necklace burning above the green lakes of Bohemia; a bell ringing with alarming suddenness; the rubber ring of sound expanding like the meridian above the rotting woods; and so on. The scene switches in bewildering fashion from the gaming tables of Monte Carlo to Versailles, Italy, the streets of Leningrad, the lotus gardens of Asia, Tokyo city, the Sahara desert and Australia, Luna Park, and Niagara roaring like an organ above the graves of Red Indians. In other poems the scenes are homely, but the switch of thought is bizarre. At times, and for variety, the thought and expression are perfectly clear and simple.

In 1927 Nezval published the poem **'The Acrobat'.** It was a return to the theme of the poet-liberator, as in the earlier **'Amazing Magician'.** The opening scene shows all Europe awaiting the coming of the tumbler, as if the fate of humanity hung upon his skill. As he steps forward along the wire the suspense is unbearable. His faith is unequal to the immense burden, and he falls to his death. This is merely an introduction to the poem, the core of which is a flashback to the acrobat's childhood. As we delve deeper and deeper into the secret life of his memories, which is the workshop of his future art, we find ourselves in a lost world of miracles. It is a child who finally leads the acrobat by the hand to meet his moment of truth, the revelation of himself in the last citadel of unreason, the madhouse, for pure truth is glimpsed only by children and madmen.

In the following year appeared the epic poem **'Edison'.** The theme once more is the liberation of mankind, but now the liberator is no longer the magician but the scientist. It is an epic in a new setting, an elaborate hymn to the technical miracles of the electric age. In this poem Edison is the type of modern hero in an ancient cast; instead of the hero's accoutrements—his horse, lance, or bow—

his weapon of conquest is science itself. He has all the courage and verve of the adventurer; yet behind this brave exterior he is sad, full of doubts, and alone: as a pioneer he is the leader of men; in his loneliness he is the outcast; he is guided by logic in his science; but his own world is full of dreams. It is this that sets him apart from other men, like a hermit or a leper, even amid the acclaim of society: his is the dilemma of the full individual who remains aloof and at tension with the common life of men. Like Galahad in Western, and Styenka Razin in Eastern European epic, he renounces the allegiance to sex which would destroy his heroic isolation. His rejection is symbolized by the burning, for the sake of an experiment, of a Japanese fan, the souvenir of innocent love: thus the fire ordeal, which evokes the mystical associations of suffering and purification, initiates him to his dedicated task. As the man of action he is at the head of his people's forward progress; as the dreamer and hermit he turns away from civilization into the jungle, always struggling, unsure, introspective, like the blinded poet, or the wandering Jew. All through the poem there is the alternation between courage and despair, joy and loneliness. The guide who leads Nezval to the inventor is the suicide who is his other face. The summit of Edison's achievement is the creation of light, which is the symbol of life, and the conquest of darkness, the mirror of death. Seclusion, suffering, and renunciation perfect the maturity of the modern, as of the ancient, hero: suicide is the ultimate mystery which serves as an initiation rite into perpetual heroism: yet by his sacrifice the hero is one with the outcast, for the price of excellence is eternal loneliness.

In 1929 appeared the beautiful poem **'The Unknown Girl taken from the Seine'.** Having taken all the world as his literary province, Nezval finds here his theme in the body of a drowned girl drifting down the river in Paris. In **'Edison'** the ordeal had been by fire; the reward, light: in **'The Unknown Girl'** the ordeal is by water; the prize, and the symbol of triumph, is the death-smile on the maiden's face. The laundrymaids pacing beside the river form a Greek chorus; the objects they carry bear a mystic symbolism which alters as the poem changes its mood. Surprises and contrasts are strikingly painted: the fresh face of a girl turns, in the reflecting water, to the haggard face of an old woman: the enchanting song of the sirens becomes the tolling of a death-knell as the drowned girl comes floating down the stream. The unknown girl is isolated and lost, even to her very name; yet her smile is the expression of knowledge and power unglimpsed by the society which has cast her out. At first the laundrymaids walk gaily, as on holiday, savouring the sensuous charms of the river with all its romantic associations of love and beguilement. Later their walk becomes a sombre funeral procession. At the end it is a ritual parade, honouring the sacrificial victim whose virgin emblem, the pinafore, is picked out by the sunlight as it floats away down the stream.

In the popular language of psychopathic analysis, ritual killing is the collective atonement of society for its individuals' feelings of (sexual) guilt: hence the traditional accoutrements of sacrifice or execution are generally of an elaborate type, often with erotic associations. In **'The Unknown Girl'** Nezval expresses, with very great delicacy, the fascination of the death-theme, combining the macabre with the erotic in a wealth of metaphors and images reminiscent of Freudian free play. The offering to society is the girl's youth and innocence, taken at the moment of physical maturity. But from the sacrifice she alone emerges intact; her vindication and triumph over physical suffering is expressed in the smile which not even the poet can touch, or limit by his description. The spirit of Poetism is at its height; words and dreams are true realities, linking, and drawing sustenance from, the physical world.

Nezval was now at the height of his powers. Still experimenting, he dared to economize in line to the extent of writing in the accents of childish song. Since his aim was to avoid didactic moralizing, the childish ding-dong was an ultimate in the sophisticated manipulation of pure form without pretence at intellectual content. In the collection *Dice* he showed his mastery of the simple idyll. Using all his developed taste for words he was able to produce the effect of spontaneity out of the simplest themes, romantic love, love of nature, the pastoral cameo and so on. There is little free verse, though there is a metrical looseness which emphasizes the intricate sound pattern; the rhyme is generally close. He paints a melancholy picture of the child fingering the faded pages of a family album; the young bride changes into the old woman, shuffling along on a stick to burn a candle at the cemetery to which she already half belongs; the juxtaposition of shining youth and decaying age is by now a familiar motif. In one poem he sees himself through the eyes of the future: his wife, barren of grandchildren, comes stealing into the secret room of his imagination and sees the fantastic, brilliant and theatrical jumble of his inner life.

In 1930 Nezval published a long pastoral poem **'Jan in mourning'**, written in five-line stanzas with a close, rhyming pattern. Two lovers, Jan and Marie, conscious of a growing estrangement, leave their home and walk through the fields, listening to the charming songs of the reapers at work. The sunshine is suddenly replaced by storm and Marie is struck dead by lightning. Amid the weeping sound of a barrel organ the poet espies Jan in mourning; with a mirror he is catching the shifting sunlight, and the poet, seeing him, is strangely transposed to the magic of remembered childhood. The theme of the flash-back to the poet's childhood, and the exploration of his inner life was now becoming embarrassingly familiar, and the poem drew on Nezval's head the wrath of critics who saw in it the beginning of his decline. In 1931 however he returned to his most successful vein with **'Time Signal'**, intended as an epilogue to **'Edison'**. The same energy and lack of restraint with which Nezval had painted the colours of life, he now applied to death; shadows are everywhere, the artist looks at the world with horror:

> Forgive my words, good future generations,
> my life was set in ever-changing rhythm
> in fevers sprung from war's malaria . . .

The poem is punctuated by the time signal which marks the passing of human life. The death of the inventor is the central theme, but the vast emptiness of night and darkness has its fascination for the poet even amid his passionate protests.

In 1932 Nezval published two important collections of verse, **The Glass Cape** and **Five Fingers.** Both books contain many charming lyrics which show Nezval as a master of personal poetry. Both contain sections of entirely different types, between which there is little fusion; on the one hand the poetry of instinct and unconscious, on the other the poetry of revolution. Among the more successful of the first type is the **'History of Six Empty Houses'**, which began in morbid fashion:

> I love empty houses
> resembling thoughts of death . . .

He had returned to free, unrhymed verse: as in a nightmare he feels again as an unborn child, caged by his mother's corset. As his mother kneels at prayer her thoughts stray; she thinks of her son's future sins; she faints, and is revived with holy water: this is the first empty house. Life draws nearer like a Persian carpet spilled with blood, a life in which prison bars are again the fashion. His mother is pale, the church chandelier is suddenly frightening, jutting like a gallows. This fantastic autobiographical poem reveals a new fusion of the real and the dream world; the sixth empty house, towards which he insensibly moves, is identical with the first; death closes the circle. Besides the poems of imagination the poems of revolution seem flat and prosaic. Unlike Wolker, in whom social questions evoked a deeply personal response, Nezval found it hard to express in poetry the ideas to which he intellectually gave assent. Only when a theme could touch, by recollection or association, his personal being, could the electric bells of his poetry be set ringing. He himself claimed that much of his work was an involuntary response from within him: 'Poetry moves within me like that germ of life and death which I swallowed with my first breath.'

In 1933 he made a trip abroad to France and Italy, and the impressions he gathered there were collected in **A Goodbye—a Handkerchief** (1934). The book provides a diary of the poet's views and thoughts, beginning with the train journey from Prague to Vienna, and ending with his home-coming. From Vienna he went to Paris, where he met for the first time leaders of the French Surrealist movement, a meeting which was considerably to affect his poetic development. His impressions of Paris provide a gay and amusing jumble of brightly-coloured word pictures. Paris entirely captured Nezval's imagination, and was, with Venice, to remain one of the great loves of his life. From Paris he travelled through Provence to Marseilles. In one poem **'The Roofs of Marseilles'** the town provides a background to two features on which the poet's eye alights: the Transbordeur overhead line, which stands as an emblem of modern man's inventiveness, and an old woman who lives on in the dream of a fled youthful love.

From Marseilles Nezval went on to Monte Carlo and wrote some amusing and trival cameos about his glimpses of the gaming tables. A woman, her hair dressed in a bun, sits playing all day, while her bun goes out of fashion. She plays and plays until, still unnoticed by her, her bun comes back into fashion. He goes to Beausoleil, whose picturesque surroundings contrast with its poverty and remind him of his revolutionary principles. From France he crosses, via Ventimiglia, to Italy and is unpleasantly impressed with the belligerent atmosphere of the Fascist régime. From Milan he travels to Venice, the beauty of which he can find no words adequate to express. The book ends with a series of pretty poems in childish trochees as he enters again his home country with all its youthful memories.

After his return to Prague, and following a visit by Paul Eluard and André Breton, Nezval openly embraced the cause of Surrealism in poetry and art, and soon became leader of a group of enthusiasts which included some associates from his earlier Poetist phase. The basic stated aims of this new group were to extend the domains of art by removing the barriers which separated the 'real' from the 'unreal' world, the conscious from the sub-conscious experience of man. 'Surrealism, profiting from the discoveries of Freud and others . . . has conceived poetry as being, on the one hand, a perpetual functioning of the psyche, a perpetual flow of irrational thought in the form of images taking place in every human mind and needing only a certain predisposition and discipline in order to be brought to light in the form of written words.

Full of enthusiasm for his new love, Nezval avidly experimented with surrealist methods of dream analysis, automatic writing, and popular psycho-analysis. The results appeared in **Woman in the Plural,** and **Prague with Fingers of Rain** (1936). They marked an advance in the bizarre fantasy of his style. Written as by a medium in a trance they present a series of dizzy inconsequential images, with mystical and erotic over-tones; **Prague with Fingers of Rain** was concerned with the poet's impressions of Prague, amid a jumble of smells, colours and tones, and was written in free unrhymed verse. Nezval followed this up with another collection in 1937, **The Unadulterated Sexton.**

Nezval, still only 36, had been pouring out books at a prodigious rate for fifteen years. In spite of his brilliant successes, too much of his writings gave an unfortunate impression of uncritical irresponsibility. He had received a generous share of brickbats together with bouquets, and his surrealist adventure did him little good with the orthodox critics, who saw a steady decline in his latest phase.

For two years Nezval published no more verse collections under his own name. But in the meantime a book of fifty-two ballads appeared under the pseudonym of Robert David; this was followed by a second book **The Hundred Sonnets of Robert David,** and a third, **Seventy Poems from the Underworld,** also under the name of David. The true authorship of the poems was not released to the general public until 1953, when Nezval included the poems in a volume of his collected works. This interesting trilogy shows the poet in a new light again. He is no longer the surrealist, the poet of wild dreams and borderland fantasies, but a master of classical metres, an elegant experimentalist with metrical exercises drawn mainly from French and Italian poetry, but with incursions into the metres of Spanish, Arabic and Malayan literature. The poems themselves are of variable quality: they include glimpses of Prague in its various moods, sardonic cameos from low life in the style of Villon, satire on the evils of the social order, little love ditties and folksy chats. It was

evident that Nezval was already tiring of Surrealism, and in 1938, after a violent quarrel, the group disintegrated. For Nezval it was a break with many who had been for years his close friends. From this time a change can be detected in his work, which loses the gay and anarchic quality of his early days.

The second World War, which spared Prague from physical destruction, completed the disintegration of its once brilliant literary circle. Under an occupation régime of increasing severity writers found their choice of themes more and more restricted. It was now that Nezval staged his version of **Manon Lescaut,** a free adaptation in verse of [Abbé] Prévost's novel. The success of the play was extraordinary; its charming lyrics, in which the voice of poetry repeatedly and effortlessly exerted itself, swept the country and gained for the poet a wider audience than he had ever known. It is still being successfully revived in Prague.

In 1949 Nezval published a new book, **The Great Clock.** The title poem traces the poet's lineage and connects his living spirit with all material and sentient things in a cosmic, almost pantheistic, spirit reminiscent of **'Time Signal'** of earlier days. The image of his spirit is the great steeple clock of Prague's Old City, whose hands, moving backwards and forwards, tick off the minutes, hours, months and seasons in the life of time. The most charming of the lyrics are those in the section **'June Rains',** while the cycle **'On the Trapeze'** recalls with a certain nostalgia the fantasy of earlier work. Meanwhile a great change had come over the literary atmosphere of Prague, and work was being evaluated solely by the criteria of Marxist aesthetics. **The Great Clock** did not get an altogether enthusiastic reception from critics who considered the pre-war *avant-garde* a particular target for their shafts; works were assessed on their ideological content and from the point of view of their social attitude. Amid the harsh and often senseless polemics of this melancholy era a certain numbness came upon Czech poetry and some of its most brilliant writers fell silent.

In 1951 Nezval suffered a heart attack, and returned for prolonged convalescence to his home in Moravia. Amid the familiar scenes of his childhood he began that revival which added another chapter, unhappily of short duration, to his unpredictable career. Once more the bells began to ring, awakening fresh and long-forgotten echoes along the dark passages of his memory. His new book **From the Home Country** surprised critics and public alike. This charming pastoral captures in nostalgic fashion the scenes and scents of the past; the pine forests, the cherry orchards, and the calm meadows form a backdrop to the living people who populated his village.

In 1955, following a visit to France, Nezval published in the press a new poem which caused a minor sensation among the critics. **'The Sea'** was one of a whole cycle of verses on the theme of Nezval's French visit, and was eventually included in a collection **Cornflowers and Towns.** Although the French cycle formed only one of the seven sections into which the book was divided, it was in many ways the most striking and beautiful, and gave to the collection its peculiar tone. It was here that Nezval returned, more falteringly than in his Poetist phase, yet without the extravagance of earlier days, to the spirit of pure lyricism, enhanced by his maturity. Romance and nostalgia coalesce in the theme of his return to Paris, this time without Paul Eluard. Once Nezval had yearned for his lost childhood, now the years had taken much more— youth, love, happiness, friends. It was the old Nezval, unmistakable even in the transformation of age. Yet his lament for the lost years was in no sense an act of resignation; his melancholy sense of the irretrievably departed, and his dread of the approaching dark were rather an expression of his ruthless hold on life, his adoration of the physical vigour of nature. The glorification of the common world of sensual experience had been among Nezval's most beloved themes, now he returned to it with an ardour and intoxication tempered only by age. Transported to the atmosphere of his earliest poems, he found himself again and looked with nostalgic wonder on the buds swelling along the river banks and the young life stirring in his own son. It was his materialism which had led him to his political faith, for it was this world which he worshipped, not the next. Now surrendering himself once again to the senses, enriched by memory and fertile imagination, he bathed eagerly and lovingly for the last time in their waters.

The last years of his life were clouded with illness, but he worked with feverish vigour, and in 1956 he staged an impressive verse play **Sunset over Atlantis,** set on the classic lines of Greek tragedy. In 1958 he returned from a trip to Italy where he had hoped to regain his failing health. A week later he died, and a whole epoch of Czech literature closed with his death.

The literary output of Nezval's life was, by any standards, prodigious, comprising forty books of verse, a number of novels, plays, literary studies, librettos, and translations from English, French, Italian and Russian. It is hoped to republish the bulk of his work in a collected edition of thirty-five volumes. The enormous scope of his reading and interests has laid on his work a bewildering variety of literary influences. Of the Czech poets, Hlavacek and Deml with their lyrical mysticism, made perhaps the greatest mark on Nezval's early work. Of foreign writers none left a more enduring impression than G. Apollinaire, to whom Nezval was first led by the brilliant translations of Karel Capek. To Capek's anthology of modern French poetry Nezval has paid generous tribute, and it would be hard to over-estimate its effect upon him. He translated into Czech the poems of Poe and Rimbaud, and was translated into Russian by Pasternak.

Few poets can have returned so often in their imagination to the scenes of their childhood as Nezval, both to the Moravian countryside and to the world of his childhood impressions which combined the qualities of innocence, mystery, and horror typical of a fairy tale. Nezval, for most of his life, held vigorously anti-religious views; but the language of religious observance is a striking part of his poetic style and is used by him to convey the sense of the mysterious and the supernatural. The themes on which he chose to write are as varied as life itself, and encompass a fascinating range of objects, cameos, vignettes, dreams, visions,

reflections, word pictures in which ugliness as well as beauty plays a part. Beside freshness, innocence, the promise of Spring, there is decay in many aspects—not only the slow decay foreshadowed in the hour of bloom, but the shadow of apocalyptic ruin, the farewell to life as we know it, symbolized in the recurring glimpses of the waters swirling for ever over the lost continent of Atlantis.

There are few features characteristic of Nezval's poetry throughout his career. In the early days a dominant feature is the search for novelty; the consistent element is inconsistency. Ideologically a rebel against political conservatism, Nezval shared to the full in the aesthetic revolt of the post-war generation of writers against tradition in theme, treatment and technique, a revolt by no means confined to politics and literature. Turning their backs on classical music, they embraced the cult of jazz; instead of concerts, they frequented bars and dancing places; they were fascinated by the primitive nostalgia of Negro melodies, and with enthusiasm they beat out together the rhythm of the tom-toms. Into Prague of the twenties, exhilarating in its new-found freedom, had come a flood of films and music representing the popular culture of the New World. While the youth of Prague was building its camp-fires, wig-wams, and canoes along the banks of Bohemian rivers, new and bizarre motifs were making their appearance in modernist Czech poetry. In Nezval's poetic world Red Indians ride beside Douglas Fairbanks, the pampas and the prairie take their place beside the homely ploughlands of Moravia. He did not make the mistake of abandoning himself entirely to the new motifs; in this case his verse would have been little better than a literary curiosity. It was because he retained so much of the earthy and familiar background of home that the importations are so startling. It was by the juxtaposition of the new and the old that the effect of excitement was achieved.

But the search for fresh and strange themes was but one aspect of the new romanticism. Not only was the strange made familiar, but the familiar was, by the artful exploitation of contrast, made strange. Details of a picture, unnoticed in the general background, spring into sharp focus when they are dissociated from that background. Strangeness is achieved by combining dissimilar elements in description, as in a puzzle picture which contains other pictures hidden in the background; the tree, which in normal focus is but a tree, will be found on close examination to contain the figure of a person or animal, a cloudy sky or a blazing fire will throw up pictures of castles or gigantic birds. The aim is to change the focus. But to show to another person the image glimpsed by oneself is a hard task; he must be led to the new perspective by the unscrambling of the received pattern, the disassociation of its components. Nezval himself described his poetry as a 'joyful organisation of confusion'. His memory, that vast storehouse of poetic inspiration, was likened by him to a still-life, a fantastic and theatrical jumble. His restless mind, ever sorting, discarding, rematching, he compared to a digestive apparatus, or to a railway marshalling yard. The kaleidoscope of perspective is assisted by metaphor, often of a surprising or discordant nature. In **'Crossroads Chapel'** the taking of the Host is a symbol of erotic defilement; in the hour of triumph Edison is like a novelist, an acrobat, a fisherman, a seducer. A shrewd contrast is achieved by the juxtaposition of the holy and the sexual, for example in the description of the city lights:

> the rosary above the river bridge,
> the halo of the daughters of the night.

The rapid movement from image to image gives an impression of vertigo; at times the poet leaves his subject and follows the images for their own sake. At the close of Part III of 'Edison' Nezval abandons himself to the wild dream and the borderland of the mind, and returns insensibly to the fount of his images, himself.

The combination of dissimilar images to make a poem is seen with brutal clarity in his 'Roofs of Marseilles' where the old woman, human, sentimental, decaying, yet set against a background of beauty, is contrapuntal to the steel splendour of the overhead line, that triumph of functional art. Sometimes the subjects of contrast are one: only the treatment is diachronic. In 'The Album' the radiant bride is one with the sexless hag; in 'The Unknown Girl' the girls who embody freshness and charm are transformed into creatures hideous with age. Our attention is demanded above all by a subject which becomes a bridge, linking diverse worlds. A child picks up a random piece of broken toy; holding it lovingly in his hand he sees the whole toy as it once was, a mass of memories delightful or sad. Others, who never knew the toy, see only a battered doll's head. The child sees the doll whole, in a variety of aspects; it is part of his past and his memory is the medium of creation. In the moment of blessed inspiration he sets the doll's head in the golliwog's broken body, closing the circle of recollection and creating a new world where two loves coalesce.

Nezval writes in his memoirs of the exquisite pang he first experienced at the linking by one motif of two worlds, hence at the formation of a third. It was, in this case, the sound of church bells in his childhood, drifting from the distant town over the homely world of his little village. The common chord, linking two places or people, is itself a symbol which joins two apparently mutually excluding elements, as Tragedy links beauty to suffering. The *leitmotiv* of 'Edison' is the alternation between loneliness and joy, dark and light, despair and triumph, the theme being worked out in infinite variations. The poet is intoxicated with the love of life, yet his other face is the suicide. At the touch of the inventor the lights go up on the world, a gift of beauty and a symbol of life: but the moth that flies from darkness to the flame will lose its wings, the eyes that strain into the sun will lose their sight. Using the common chord the poet reveals, with elaborate counterpoint, the dilemma of life as he saw it: the neurosis of intoxication and despair, the dialectic of darkness and light; the infinite sadness of the grey twilight, the terror of the darkness.

The achievement of strangeness by complexity of treatment and diversity of materials was a feature of the new poetry of which Nezval was, in the Czech field, a pioneer. The doctrine of strangeness and the cultivation of the surprise formed part of that technique which the critic Mukarovsky had in mind when he wrote that 'the norm is the breaking of the norm'. In one sense Nezval's aim was essentially romantic—the desire, as he said himself, to turn away from the academism of Czech literature, even as evidenced in the traditional poetry of revolt, and to sail without compass or plan, as in the intoxicated boat of Rimbaud, not knowing what fantastic islands lay in his path. It was in the yearning for the eternally new, the undiscovered horizons of art, that Nezval and his friends turned to the new primitivism: adjoining the sedate asphodel of Parnassus they plunged into the imaginary jungles of the far continents. While Nezval transplanted Luna Park to Moravia, and set lotuses and parakeets on the hillside of Prague, his friend Jezek was turning from the idiom of classical music to the syncopated rhythms of jazz.

How future generations will regard Nezval's work it is still impossible to judge with any confidence. We can say with certainty that because of immediate political preoccupations, or wholehearted adherence to still unformed artistic doctrines, some of Nezval's work is already dated. Yet among the poems which deserve to live are not only the highlights of his Poetist period, but a mass of exquisite cameos scattered throughout his life's work, and catching lucid and brilliant pictures of his real or imaginative work, as in a fragment of broken crystal. Critics are at one in stressing Nezval's artistry with words, of whose sound and associations he showed himself highly conscious. About the meaning of his poetry there is less agreement: its content is so vast that it is possible to read into it a more consistent philosophy than the poet ever dreamed of. One can identify, with reasonable confidence, the influence of the Czech folk tradition in literature and the romanticism of its great revival. Beside the critics who find in his work a steady driving force of social revolt are those who see in it no consistent message at all, only a sensitive expression of life's infinitely varied tones, glimpsed in the serene light of the ordinary world or reflected on the kaleidoscopic screen of his fevered imagination.

Death was a favourite theme with Nezval: the feverish search for light and life was the obverse to the melancholy certainty of darkness and death. The vision of a modern Atlantis, a world ruined by the blindness of its members, only exemplifies in a more startling form that end which waited inexorably for Nezval the individual. The bells which toll for Atlantis toll for Nezval, for his childhood, his youth, and his maturity. There is a certain luxuriance in his yearning for what is past, and in this he is essentially romantic. Primed with Freudian theory he delighted to explore his own subconscious mind, reaching for the chord which, once touched, set vibrating a long answering chain of echoes. From these explorations he would emerge with a whole arsenal of dazzling fireworks, each lighting the fuse to the next, so that the reader can hardly keep pace.

It was in his Surrealist period that Nezval pursued furthest the method of dream analysis, but other phases in his career are deeply coloured with this pre-occupation. The vision of his waking dreams was, as Nezval claimed, a lyricism translated into ordinary life, but it lends to his work an atmosphere of shadows, unstable, disturbing, and sometimes improbable. Yet the exploration of the subconscious was, to Nezval, merely another method of extending the province of poetry and art to the whole of life.

Thus even in the holiday atmosphere of *A Goodbye—a Handkerchief* his eye alights with equal pleasure on the conventionally beautiful and on the conventionally drab and ugly. One of the younger Czech poets remarked of Nezval that to him the rotten apple was as much a fitting object for poetry as the star.

Nezval's dissociation of the normally associated, by means of metaphor, reversed traditional usage. The great danger which the poet ran in such methods was obscurity, banality, and self-hypnotism, and when he falls into these traps he becomes decorative and cloying. In his early work Nezval is something of an illusionist, but the transformations which he presents are not necessarily escapist; his poetry does not try to deny life, but rather to show new angles upon it. A photograph appears flat because its focus is on one area only; the rest is dull background, hardly noticeable. Nezval changes the lens over and over again in bewildering succession so that the details of the familiar scenes loom up in new and queer focus: in this kaleidoscope of perspective, objects previously unnoticed become charged with significance, and the relationship of the details is bizarre. Nezval could do this with such ease only because he could shake himself free of the pre-conceptions which automatically arrange objects before our eyes in an accepted relationship. He was untraditional and anti-traditional in his attitude to the classical demands for stability, balance and restraint in art. Abandoning himself to the instincts, and adjuring intellectual restraint he achieved a disturbing freedom which enabled him in his poetry to reverse the order of nature and society in topsy-turvy fashion. With this freedom went that touch of irresponsibility, or anarchy, so typical of Nezval, the atmosphere of the pantomime, the circus, and the harlequinade.

Of Nezval's early work [Arne Novák] has written,

> Nezval has become the founder in this country, and at the same time the master, of the poetry of association; he has released a free play of imagination unrestrained by logic. In his work imagination is scarcely ever supported by the power of abstract thought or a feeling for any deep agreement between life and reality. There are limits to Nezval's sensitivity, which remains for the most part in the realm of instinct, even when he is at his most passionate. A poetic liberator of strange, sensuous charms, a revealer of dream-like fairytale wonders, untiringly inventive as a creator of metaphors, associations and oxymora, he is nevertheless not an artist who could stand above his own work and control it by the power of his aesthetic will.

The greatest of all modern Czech critics, F. X. Salda, paid high tribute to Nezval, regarding his place among the classics as assured.

> With amazing ease he throws out verses of great imaginative perception . . . fireworks of dazzling associations. . . . Everything he touches fleetingly, arousing a long chain of echoes. . . . A master of the echo which repeats in ever new intonations the original motif. . . . With a madly whirling needle he sews together from rainbow-coloured patches a fantastic harlequin

costume for his poetic masque of scattered instincts and earthy passions.

But perhaps Salda's greatest tribute was to claim for Nezval the role in which the latter had so often seen himself, that of the poet-liberator. 'He returned to poetry the lightness of wings, the feeling of bright daring, the atmosphere of delight . . . yes, the quality of mischievousness, without which it cannot exist.' (pp. 21-38)

> A. French, "The Czech Lyric Poet: Vítězslav Nezval," in Melbourne Slavonic Studies, No. 2, 1968, pp. 21-38.

Beatrice M. Nosco   (essay date 1968)

[*In the following review, Nosco focuses on the autobiographical prose writings collected in* Dílo XXVII-XXVIII-XXIX.]

Dílo XXVII-XXVIII-XXIX is part of a posthumous edition of Nezval's work in thirty-one volumes. This trilogy contains some of his prose writings, perhaps the most important ones, and surely the most autobiographical ones: *Kronika z konce století, Posedlost,* and *Dolce far niente.*

Nezval, known primarily as a lyric poet and an enchanting playwright, denies that this trilogy was an attempt at a novel. He had already begun it in 1927, and he finished its final version about thirty years later, shortly before his death. (p. 459)

In Nezval's own words, this trilogy was not to record the events of his life, but rather "the forgotten regions of my soul." Artistically speaking, there is little to be said about this trilogy. Its significance lies, indeed, in the light it sheds on the author's life and personality, since it is a rather curious confession not far removed from those heard in a psychiatrist's office, although Nezval assures us that he "in no way attempted to apply in this book Freudian or any other psychoanalysis" and that the only purpose of this writing is to make it possible for a reader to communicate with his own dark childhood, his own "Ideálno." "Ideálno," he goes on to explain, "is not a deer that stops regularly at a brook to drink," but "a deer that walks into our way, when we are set for a tiger hunt." Strange, too, is Nezval's use of the term for leisure: *dolce far niente.* According to his own explanation, he applies this term to "all metaphysical conditions of a soul," but later he reduces this statement to an Oriental attitude of detachment, and describes himself as "a pilgrim, who . . . without a desire for anything . . . not aware of his own existence . . . being only an observing eye . . . not asking anything from himself or life . . . sits in some kind of post-mortem bliss. This is my *dolce far niente.*" Yet the most memorable pages of this trilogy provide us with glimpses into Nezval's intense anxiety before death.

Nezval the poet and Nezval the playwright is a man in love with life and with love. This autobiographical document reveals to us that, behind the mask of poetism and *dolce far niente,* Nezval was a deeply troubled man. (pp. 459-60)

> *Beatrice M. Nosco, in a review of "Dílo XXVII-*

XXVIII-XXIX," in Books Abroad, *Vol. 42, No. 3, Summer, 1968, pp. 459-60.*

Arne Novák (essay date 1976)

[*In the following excerpt, Novák presents a brief overview of Nezval's career, discussing the style of his poetry and highlighting his major works.*]

Vítězslav Nezval heard the distant echoes of the First World War while still a young high-school student and attempted in several amorphous Surrealist novels to chronicle the atmosphere, inner life and sensuality of his childhood and adolescence, as if he had intended to indicate beforehand that in those early impressions and sensations lay the key to the poet he was ultimately to become. And it is true that one forceful and colorful wing of his lyrical poetry had its origin in a certain infantilism, and utilized with folklike naivete childhood memories and rural impressions. This side of Nezval's work, reflecting the poet's artificially-maintained illusion of perpetual boyhood—an illusion that filled him with delight and helped him in his romantic escape from reality, from contemporary problems and from himself—as exemplified by the series of books starting with *Most* (1922; *The Bridge*) and leading to *Pantomimy* (1924; *Pantomime*), *Menší růžová zahrada* (1926; *The Smaller Rose-garden*), and *Bliženci* (1927; *Twins*). A second source of Nezval's inspiration was the bliss of eroticism, playful, hedonistic, almost entirely physical and sensuous, without overtones of any higher emotion. The attempts of this poet of sensuality and reminiscence to write proletarian poetry and to take a radical social stance were mere modish self-deception. But there is one additional wellspring of inspiration which might well have been called ideological in another poet who did not reject intellectuality as vehemently as did Nezval: this was a longing for unity, a sense of solidarity born of participation in a common civilization which redeems man from individualistic isolation, from the dread of eternally fleeing time that burns up human lives, from the terrors of the infinite, of the deep, empty, silent night. In this mood Nezval was an elegiac poet reminiscent of [Karel Hynek] Mácha, and his verse—at other times often fragmented and short-winded—soars with lyrical expressiveness. Nezval grouped the best poems of this period into the book *Básně noci* (1930; *Poems of the Night*); in the foreground of this collection is the stirring hymn to civilization, **"Edison."** But a total lack of self-criticism, indifference to creative discipline, self-indulgent willingness to entertain all ideas and inspirational needs, a frivolously playful attitude toward words, images and sound—all these traits made it impossible for this disciple of form-for-its-own-sake to grow or even to mature. Thus, in books such as *Skleněný havelok* (1932; *The Glass Cape*), Nezval's rich lyrical gifts lie in ruin. His last poems originated under the influence of Breton's Surrealism as well as Freudian ideas about the effects of the subconscious on poetic imagination and the value of dream logic for poetic creation. Later collections included *Praha s prsty deště* (1936; *Prague with the Fingers of the Rain*) and *Absolutní hrobař* (1937; *The Absolute Gravedigger*). The cruel experience of Hitlerite oppression of his homeland and the struggle of the democra-cies for freedom inspired his historic vision, *Historický obraz* (1945; *A Historic Portrait*), in which the epic nature of the material somewhat disciplined this lyrical poet, endowed by God's grace with easy, unbounded creativity.

In his somber elegies about cosmic vanity and decay Nezval himself demonstrated that Poetism, with its method of imaginative free association, need not be limited to extolling the magic of sensuality and dreams, the foam of life and artistic novelties, erotic play and enticing fantasies, but that this method was also capable of treating the other side of life—the painful and even tragic aspects of existence. The young poets who followed him tried to free themselves from oppressive nihilism in a variety of ways. (pp. 320-21)

Arne Novák, "Modern Literature," in his Czech Literature, *edited by William E. Harkins, translated by Peter Kussi, Michigan Slavic Publications, 1976, pp. 255-332.*

> **"Only when one succeeds in breaking through all inner ties with morals and preconceived values, which picture for us an image of the human spirit in uniform, only when one escapes from the conventions of logical thought, can one reach the psyche. And love, because it is instinctive, helps us to break down these categories, in the same way as opium, alcohol, beauty, terror, and movement."**
>
> **—*Vítěslav Nezval, 1931***

Maria Němcová Banerjee (essay date 1979)

[*In the following excerpt, Banerjee discusses Nezval's contributions to Surrealism, focusing on* Prague with Fingers of Rain.]

The enthusiasm of Vítězslav Nezval for the theory and practice of Surrealism grew out of his contacts with the French leaders of the movement. He met Paul Eluard and André Breton in Paris and invited them to carry their "theses of hope" to Prague. In 1935, an international gathering of Surrealists was organized in Prague, with lectures by Breton and Eluard. The ground had been prepared by Nezval's own manifesto *Surrealismus v ČSR* a year earlier. Prague between the two wars was an obligatory stop for any literary leader with European ambitions. (p. 505)

For all its utopistic and scientific ambitions, Surrealism deserves attention primarily as a doctrine of literary renewal. Like Romanticism before it, and even Realism in its heroic infancy around 1848, Surrealism fought its battles for a new mode of literary expression, a new style in the arts, around the definition of what is real. But always in literature, a new gnosis begins with a reform of the morphology of poetic speech and a conquest of new territories of reality is made possible only by the destruction of old literary conventions, a substitution of new devices for the old. Breton's apparent denial of all aesthetic and moral concerns is almost a ritualistic disclaimer, for the invention of new poetic forms and the renewal of the lexicon led him to create a new beauty. Similarly, the utopian fervor of the manifestoes naturally translated into a new moral rhetoric.

Breton's example led Nezval away from Teige's play theory of the arts, with its emphasis on the purely sensuous values of phonetic experimentation. But in matters of literary technique, Nezval never forgot his debt to *Poetismus*. He makes it a point of honor to stress that some of the discoveries of Czech *Poetismus* in the formal aspects of poetry, such as the emphasis on free association of images and the organic nature of rhythm, had all ante-dated Breton's first manifesto, or evolved independently of it. Nevertheless, he considered Surrealism to be a more complete and more "scientific" doctrine of the Imagination. It helped turn his own poetry inward and provided him with important myths—the myth of woman, of childhood, and of revolution. The last was particularly useful to Nezval in the increasingly polarized political atmosphere of the thirties. Like his fellow poets Josef Hora and Jaroslav Seifert, Nezval felt the sentimental pull of the Bolshevik promise, but was unwilling to surrender his artistic autonomy to Moscow. Surrealism seemed to offer another, parallel way to the goal of social liberation, leading by the high road to free poetic imagination instead of the tunnels and smithies of the Proletarian poets. As Breton himself in the second manifesto (December 1929), Nezval could argue that it was absurd to talk of a proletarian art in a society which remained essentially bourgeois and that the acceptance of Freud's primacy of the inner man was a prerequisite of true liberation. Still, the attempts by Surrealists to gain admission on their own terms into the Marxist Church of Revolution proved a complete failure. At the 1934 Congress of Writers in Moscow, Nezval defended the Surrealist position as a synthesis of discipline and freedom, only to see his intervention omitted from the final report on the conference. Next year, when the representatives of the literary Left assembled in Paris, Nezval was denied a hearing for his views and Breton was expelled from the meeting.

Prague with Fingers of Rain (*Praha s prsty deště,* 1936) is Nezval's second Surrealist cycle of poems, coming a year after *Woman in Plural* (*Žena v množném čísle*) which he had dedicated to Paul Eluard. In the Prague cycle, Nezval creates a polythematic image of the city, whose "mysterious order" (*tajemné uspořádání*) and complex poetry have remained hidden under layers of conventional literary associations. As a Surrealist lover of Prague, Nezval has the magic task of awakening her dormant beauty by the fiat of his rhythmic speech. The liberation of Prague from the bondage of literary convention is inaugurated in the lead poem of the cycle, **"The City of Towers" ("Město věží").** The invocation of Prague deliberately begins with a banal association. "Prague of a thousand towers" (*Stověžatá Praho*), a postcard epithet whose visual potency has been worn down by promiscuous use. The qualifying aposition "With fingers of all saints" (*S prsty všech*

svatých) opens the way for a hypnotic litany of images, evolving from each other in an apparently random sequence by free association. The rhythmic dynamo of the poem is the anaphoric repetition "With fingers" (*S prsty*), as if in an utterance that accompanies some magic ritual. This shift of rhythmic intensity from the traditional mnemotic, backward-looking end marker of the rhyme (there is no rhyming in the poem) to the beginning of the line creates a powerful forward thrust for the leap from the automatism of the audio-verbal formula into the realm of the sensuous image. The anaphora "With fingers" has a tactile suggestiveness which alludes simultaneously to the erotic and the investigative functions of a caress under which Prague materializes before us, as a sensuous and sentient being. The litany culminates in the evocation of the gesture of a flawed ritual, "With fingers of the desecrated host" (*S prsty znesvěcené hostie*), in which the flaw or, if you will, the creative subversion of the gesture, vibrates back to the more conventional visual closeup of a Prague Baroque statue in "With fingers of all saints" (*S prsty všech svatých*). This gesture of a lost or devalued ritual ushers in the last image of the series, in which the poet achieves the illusion of "open form." "With fingers of inspiration / With long fingers without joints / With fingers that write this poem" ("S prsty inspirace / S dlouhými prsty bez článku / S prsty jimiž píši tuto báseň") surrenders the secret of the poem's alchemy. We have indeed been privy to a magic ritual, the raising of the real Prague from the deadness of convention and now, in the climactic ending of the poem, the sensuous image of the city, the miracle of her flesh, is held up for our adoration in the fluid fingers of the poet-magician.

The second poem, **"The Walker of Prague" ("Pražský chodec"),** further develops the *persona* of the poet-magician as an explorer of the city's hidden life. This *persona* links together the poems of the cycle, providing a semblance of narrative continuity. The Surrealists, Breton in particular, while openly contemptuous of the sequential order of official time, often developed their poetic explorations as a fantastic narrative built around the "I" of the explorer and celebrant. Indeed it might be argued that the Surrealists were in line with the Romantics and the Symbolists in their fascination with the drama of knowledge and revelation, adding still one deeper level to the inward journey of the subject which, paradoxically, was also meant to lead him to new discoveries in the outer realm of reality. If dream is to be a new and all-powerful discipline, then the dreamer himself must be at the very center of the Surrealist quest, since there can be no dream without him, nor any magic without a magician, nor divination without a *voyante.*

In **"The Walker of Prague"** Nezval begins his double journey at a single point in official time: "One day in April 1920 I arrived / For the first time in Prague" ("Jednoho dne v dubnu 1920 jsem přijel / po prvé do Prahy"). The precision of the reference is nothing but a mystification, a deliberate false lead to confuse the *vulgus profanus.* The speaker of the poem is pursuing the subjective chronology of desire, measured only by the intensity of the illuminations it yields. The explorer of Prague is also an initiate of a new art of love, the seeker of a new "convulsive beauty" (*křečovitá krása*), which comes in Surrealistic objects, those "casual objects discovered by our desire." Words are this lover's true medium and he makes love to Prague by means of devices such as analogy and metonymy. The basic analogical equation of Prague with Woman, a none too original simple substitution, comes alive in newly invented metaphors, which dominate the lover's discourse throughout the cycle. The association is further complicated by the substitution of a part for the whole in both objects, the woman's body and the city, a metonym grafted on a metaphor, as in: "You looked for an embrace finding balconies" ("Hledal jsi náruč nalézáš balkony"), in the poem **"Balconies" ("Balkony")** or, in **"Wanderings" ("Procházky")**, "the street which unexpectedly telescopes for you Hradčany / You feel in her windblown hair the same freedom" ("ulice jejímž průhledem vidíš znenadání Hradčany / Cítíš v jejích rozevlátých účesech tutéž volnost"). In the second, more complex image, the relation of identity is deepened by synaesthesia. This sophisticated interplay of tropes, far from making the city more distant, achieves almost the primitive physical intensity of fetish.

"The Night of Acacias" ("Noc akátů") is a poem in which the identification of the *persona* of the walker of Prague with that of lover turns ecstatic. The erotic ecstasy is enacted as the mystical event of crossing the bridge over the river Vltava from Smíchov to Nové Město. The time context is particularly important, since it is assumed that the event can be mystical only once a year, on a particular night in June, "when acacias bloom and die" ("červnová noc kdy kvetou a umírají akáty"). That incandescent night which brings forth an agonistic fulfillment accompanied by death first figures in the poem as a setting for the action. It is a semi-magical setting in which the object of the vision (presumably Prague) can materialize as on a stage: "The streets are suddenly wide and glitter like perfume shops" ("Ulice jsou náhle široké a třpytí se jak parfumerie"). But in the middle section of the poem, the sudden apostrophe, "Night of acacias of fountains in luring pianissimo / linger" ("O akátová noci fontán a záludného pianissima / trvej dlouho"), transforms the stage into an addressee, turning the magic night, the original vehicle of ecstatic fulfillment, into the personified object of that ecstasy. This new mythical figure, "night which brought forth the summer" ("ó noci jež přivezlas léto"), born of the sudden switch in syntactic mode and feminine by the grace of Czech grammar, is the true daughter of the artifice of poetic speech, combining in her allure artificiality with naturalness, "acacias" and "bees" versus "diamonds" and "perfume shops." Her life is precariously sustained by the rhythmic magic of the rising and falling intonation in each line. Unmarked by rhyme, the line is here a natural unit of articulation, suggesting the rise and fall of heightened breathing. Once more, the primacy of the audio-verbal imagination has yielded a rich harvest of visual images.

Earlier, reference was made to the two great Surrealist myths—the myth of woman and the myth of childhood—which Nezval took over along with the related doctrine of love as the ultimate method of knowledge. He dedicated an entire cycle of poems to that theme, ***Woman in Plural*** (1935), whose vision seems to derive almost entirely from

Breton's poem-definition "L'Union libre" (1931). In the Prague cycle, Woman is ever-present by analogy, but she becomes the proper subject in one of the most original pieces, **"The Market" ("Tržnice")**, dedicated to Nezval's contemporary, the great experimental writer of Czech prose, Vladislav Vančura. Since the entire poem is built on the subtle manipulation of levels of reality, the compliment to Vančura is particularly apt, as he also, in his narrative style, strove to eradicate the traditional distinction between the language of poetry and of prose. **"The Market"** reorganizes our perception of everyday reality by infusing it with an unexpected and ominous sense of mystery. The poem opens with a simple but somewhat quaint invocation, "Gentle lady" ("Líbezná ženo"), of a housewife on her way to shop for food. This manner of address evokes a desirable but accessible being, until the qualifying terms of the apostrophe, "your breasts play with the morning sun / They rise" ("tvá ňadra si hrají s dopoledním sluncem / Vznášejí se ve výši"), raise the verbal stakes of the image, injecting a mythical potency into the figure of the walking woman, by alluding to her intimacy with the sun and her fabulous motherhood. This is the first signal directing us to read the shopping expedition of the housewife "who left the stove cooling" ("jež nechala vychladnout plotnu") as a mysterious script for some atavistic ritual, the meaning of which must forever remain hidden from males. "Locked in offices" ("Zavřeni v kanceláři"), men are excluded from the ceremonies of blood of a "world born of eggs" ("svět který se rodí z vajec"), in which the butcher's block becomes a place of execution ("popraviště"). When the woman, "elegant like an axeman pulls down her gloves" ("elegantní jak kat stahuje žena rukavice"), to palpitate a fish or a fowl, it is a ritualistic gesture of great and cruel beauty, matching some of the images of Cocteau's films. Yet it is important to keep in mind that the brilliant image of the mythical woman of blood is always tempered in this poem by a light, almost tongue-in-cheek humor, more reminiscent of Apollinaire's mock hyperboles and mock myths, such as that of "l'ange Hurtubise," than of Cocteau's theater of cruelty.

Verbal signs can, of course, be pointed downward as well as upward and, if everyday reality can be mythified, myths in their turn can be disintegrated by the Surrealist imagination. Nezval achieves that effect in what is probably the most ambitious and sustained piece of writing in the cycle, the long poem **"Trojsky Bridge" ("Trojský most")**. Dedicated to the memory of a friend, Bedrich Feuerstein, who apparently died in early youth by suicide, the poem is a Surrealistic reinterpretation of the elegy, as well as an exposure of the mystification of time. The traditional mood of nostalgia, characteristic of the elegiac mode, modulates the deceptively straight opening lines: "Prague of our youth the witnesses are disappearing / It will be evening" ("Praha naší mladosti svědkové se stráceji / bude večer"). Then follows an appealing evocation of the lost world of the 1920s, as the poem seems to accept the *ubi sunt* theme of elegy. But the hidden layer underneath the play-world of artifice and exuberance of the twenties, that marvelous *panoptikum* animated by Chaplinesque clowns and Futuristic bicycle riders, was the nightmare of the Great War: "It would be best by far to straddle the bicycle like our /

older comrades who then died in the war" ("Nejlépe by bylo usednout na bicykl jak naši / starší kamarádi kteří zemřeli pak ve válce"), and later, "It would be best by far to straddle that machine of infancy / And keep riding by the sunny sidewalk / Until again it is after the war" ("Nejlépe by bylo usednout na ten dětský stroj / a tak dlouho jét podél slunečního chodníku / až bude opět po válce"). World War I is known to the speaker only at secondhand, as the ordeal of older brothers, a tragedy as poetically distant from him as the suicide of the young friend. The war and the suicide derive their significance in the poem from their metaphoric, interchangeable relation to each other, a notion that brings to mind the quasi-symbolic suicide of Breton's war-time friend Jacques Vaché, one of the patron-saints of the Surrealist movement, whom Breton called "l'esprit même de l'humour." The Great War as the dark matrix of the play-world of the twenties and the implied motif of the passing of generations seem to give substance to the *ubi sunt* theme and lead us to expect a meditation on the mystery of time. The time mystery is further strengthened by several allusions to divination: "I pass a crone who mumbles to herself see a waiter from the night shift / O night of August 1899 why did you give birth to a poet" ("Míjím babku říká si hleďme noční číšník / srpnovánoc z roku 1899 proč jsi zrodila básníka"), and "I read in his palm long voyages" ("Věštím mu z ruky že bude cestovat"). However, the motif of divination, applied both to the speaker and his lost friend, is toppled from its seriousness by humor: "the crone" ("babka"), a midwife or a Sybil who meets a poet on a dark street, is capable of mistaking him for a night waiter hurrying home from work. As the elegiac question turns upon the speaker himself, the Surrealistic legerdemain takes over. Divination, as Breton had pointed out in his *Lettre aux voyantes* (1925), manipulates temporal sequence, making the future present in an act of consciousness, just as a poem makes the past present in lyric instance. Divination and poetry are thus related activities, inasmuch as both seek mastery over time. In this poem, the twin visionary activities of divination and lyricism are subtly attacked and corroded by humor. The elegiac quest for a lost time is translated into a childish search for an insignificant and even slightly ridiculous object: "I looked for a bit of checkered cloth / Such as was worn before the war / It was suspenseful like a detective novel" ("Hledal jsem kousek pepitové látky / jaká se nosila před válkou / bylo to napínavé jak detektivní román"). But the childish motif of the play-object gradually expands into a fullfledged apologia of childhood, in usurpation from the dark theme of war and suicide. The finality of time figures now as a shadow cast over the brightness of the super-real world of the child. In the *consolatio* coda of the poem, the speaker resolutely rejects the seduction of the elegiac theme, which carries in its wake an old hankering for immortality, by whatever means or myth available, be it the myth of religion or the myth of poetry. The refusal in "I do not lament the years gone by" ("Neoplakávám uplynulá léta") is not that of a Stoic: it is a verbal signal for a characteristically Nezvalian retreat from pain and tragedy into the paradise of childhood, as rehearsed by his imagination. The sorrows of childhood are also caused by loss—loss of magic objects which Nezval enumerates with loving wonder: "the thimble" ("náprstek"), "the sponge" ("houba"), "a bit of checkered cloth" ("kus pepitové látky"). The disarmed state of childhood, a surrender to all the contingencies of hazard and fantasy, is offered as an almost programmatic substitute for the consolation of immortality, an old poetic myth exploded here along with the other mystifications of time.

The last poem of the series, **"Prague with Fingers of Rain" ("Praha s prsty deště"),** fully develops the epiphany hinted at throughout and suggested in the very title of the cycle. A poem-definition, it is also a poem of celebration, almost a Surrealist ode. It celebrates simultaneously the object (Prague) and the subject (the poet as lover), as well as the cycle's poetic method. All the levels of the Surrealist quest are brought together, as the poet engages in the difficult but triumphant task of forging a negative definition of Prague, borrowing a device from the mystics: "It is nothing one can tear down it is nothing / One can build again" ("Není to v ničem co lze zbourat není to v ničem / co lze znovu postavit"); "There is no way to describe you there is no way to paint you there is no way / To hold a mirror to you" ("Nelze tě popsat nelze tě nakreslit nelze ti / nastavit zrcadlo"); "It is nothing / Nothing one infers / From beauty or style" ("Neni to v ničem / v ničem co lze vyložiti / z krásy nebo ze slohu"). After the sweeping negatives, the poet begins his task *ab nihilo,* deploying a succession of images which combine visual and other sensuous impressions with epigrammatic and witty *aperçus.* The effect is of a sensual gloss on the central definition of Prague's secret, her "mysterious order," which the poem weaves out of repetition and modification of the cycle's leitmotifs. Yet there is a distinct new progression from touch to speech, as if the added value of rain in the modified formula "with fingers of rain" carried with it the power of a new verbal harvest. In the peroration, the poet becomes the city's tongue: "I am the tongue of your bells but also of your rain" ("Jsem jazyk tvých zvonů ale také tvého deště"). This turns the homage to Prague into a celebration of the poet's craft and, indirectly, of the vitality and resourcefulness of the Czech language. As the private confession of love suddenly goes public and consolidates into a hymnal utterance, a premonition from the sphere of "official" time begins to cast its shadow on the processional of praise. It is, after all, 1936—"Time flies like a swallow and ignites old stars / Above Prague" ("Čas letí jak vlaštovka a rozžehuje staré hvězdy / nad Prahou"), and even the magic of this cycle of poems cannot hex away the nightmare gathering against the city. With the sudden humility of the speaker—"and so far I have said so little about you" ("a já jsem toho dosud o tobě málo řekl"), a note of defensiveness creeps into the ode. Retrospectively, this heightens for us the historical pathos of these poems which held out so stubbornly against sequential time. (pp. 506-12)

Maria Němcová Banerjee, "Nezval's 'Prague with Fingers of Rain': A Surrealistic Image," in Slavic and East-European Journal, *Vol. 23, No. 4, Winter, 1979, pp. 505-14.*

Milan Blahynka (essay date 1987)

[*In the essay excerpted below, Blahynka discusses anti-war sentiment in Nezval's poetry.*]

A typical feature of Czech poetry during its more than thousand-year-long development is its characteristic devotion to the Czech land, its closest bonds with the fate of a small nation proud of its culture, its share in the fund of European learning and the task assigned to it by history. There has not been a great Czech poet who is not concerned for his nation and its longings. (p. 86)

Masterpieces imbued with an active creative love of the nation, the country, the history and mother tongue include the lyrical-epic poem "May" by Karel Hynek Mácha, a romantic poet from the first half of the 19th century, the rebellious *Silesian Songs* by Petr Bezruč from the beginning of the 20th century, a book of sharp protest against oppression, both national and social, or the lyrics by Jaroslav Seifert, a poet of the charming Czech countryside and of Prague. **"A Song of Peace" ("Zpěv miru")** is one of them, a poetic composition written by the "remarkable wizard" of Czech poetry, Vitězslav Nezval, in 1950—at the time of the Korean war, a poem translated soon after it was written into more languages than any previous book of Czech verse.

Vitězslav Nezval prepared for **"A Song of Peace"**, written when he was fifty years old, with all his previous work, with all his life. Since his childhood spent in the country in peaceful patriotic surroundings—his father being a well-educated teacher, a lover of music and art, and Leoš Janáček's pupil, Nezval's character and vital prospects were formed in such a way that his lifelong work can be called "a song of peace". Nezval became a poet of peace as soon as he began to write. The sharply antimilitary **"War Ballad"** has been found among the manuscripts preserved of his earliest works written by the beginning author, then a pupil at the grammar school in Třebíč, when his father was placed in an Austro-Hungarian internment camp for his patriotic feelings. In the last year of the First World War, Vitězslav Nezval was conscripted into the army, too. He had no intention of dying for the interests of the hated empire and so, by cleverly simulating illness, he escaped being sent to the front and returned to civilian life before the end of the war.

A distinctive antimilitaristic tone marked his works even in the nineteen-twenties, when Nezval, himself one of the creators of avant-garde poetism, took part together with his companions in the international avant-garde art movement. Being a consistent, inventive and militant enemy of war, soldiers and militarism, he breathed an antiwar spirit not only into his poems but dramatic works and essays too. The pioneering "first radio scenario" Mobilization as well as the mime History of an Ordinary Soldier or the short story **"Little Soldiers"** prove that the young poet, who could learn antimilitarism from his older comrades, e.g. Fráňa Šrámek, sought new means of expression for the traditionally negative attitude of Czech poets towards war.

In the nineteen-thirties, when the existence of the Czechoslovak Republic began to be threatened by the expansiveness of aggressive German fascism, Nezval further stepped up his antiwar course. In many verses and also in theatrical pieces he noted and reminded of the danger of an approaching "future war", showing at the same time that the last war had not ended as long as "a single man was hungry". The poem, openly named **"Future War"** and published in book form in his collection *The Glass Havelock (Skleněný havelok,* 1932), tried "to wake up the conscience of those who do not think" and expressed the real, though unfortunately finally unfulfilled, hope of averting a new war.

In the second half of the nineteen-thirties, Nezval's peace "theme" grew together with his home "theme", especially that of Prague, in books of verse and prose. The poetry collection *Prague with Fingers of Rain (Praha s prsty deště,* 1936) culminated in the poem **"Prague, When You Are In Danger"**. The poet also wrote of the war danger nearing his beloved town in his prose book of reminiscences and reflections, *The Prague Pedestrian (Pražský chodec,* 1938). And when war broke out, the poet in his verses compiled in the collection *Five Minutes Beyond the City (Pět minut za městem,* 1940) called to peace—"the stray lamb"—to come back and fill the granaries again with "golden grain".

The evident peace character of Nezval's work deepened still further after the Second World War, especially in the poet's last years. The idea of peace, inseparable with Nezval from the idea of happiness and from his active fondness of love and freedom, permeates a poetic composition about the village of his childhood, *From the Homeland (Z domoviny,* 1951), and the collections *The Wings (Křídla,* 1952) and *Cornflowers and Cities (Chrpy a města,* 1955), but also the warning play *Today the Sun Still Sets Over Atlantis (Dnes ještě zapadá slunce nad Atlantidou,* 1956), and the poet's many essay-style speeches and lectures, delivered on all sorts of occasions in Czechoslovakia and abroad. In them Nezval disseminated the knowledge that "the reasons for peace are in fact the reasons for life" and "life itself in its fulness is really the most poetic thing imaginable". During his visit to France in 1954, Nezval presented the peace message of poetry as its most natural one:

> Bakeries, houses at the roadside, people in the fields and on the beaches, they all want peace. Poetry which expresses their longing is the most natural poetry. It is the very poetry of life, the poetry in defence of life, in defence of life against destruction. The great majority of mankind cooperates with this poetry in their efforts to prevent death and destruction, in their resolution to defend peace successfully. Thus, big and small nations have formed a bond of solidarity and their poets speak for this solidarity, knowing that they speak for life itself, for poetry in its most proper essence. If the beauty of life often seems to create idyllic images in poetry, the defence of human happiness and the defence of peace have nothing to do with an idyll. I don't like the weaponry with which the heroes of *Iliad* march before us. At the same time I'm aware that the shepherd's pipe from Virgil's *Bucolics,* though very poetic, is not a sufficient instrument

for the poets of peace. What is to be defended, is delightful and comely.

To defend peace means to defend Praxiteles' statues, the Louvre, people and fish, children of the whole world, roses and one's own present and future. Everything that great poetry has ever included and still can include in its unforeseen development, belongs to those values that should and must be saved by world peace.

The mission of poetry, its most natural mission is to strengthen life and place in a dazzling light everything that creates it, its beauty, grace and strength. It is a mission in the sign of peace—and the sacred dove should become the poets' emblem. It is becoming so and enjoins them to be willing to sacrifice all their strength for this emblem.

Nezval placed all his creative and civic experience into **"A Song of Peace"**, his constant hatred of war destroying lives and cultural values, his love of his homeland and of the world, too. **"A Song of Peace"** is Czech in many motifs. There is the village of the poet's childhood, the orchards in the region around the river Elbe, the Prague alleys wind through it and the Prague bells resound in it. However, not only the river Vltava but also the Rhine and the Yellow River flow through it, the mountain ranges of India appear on its horizon, as well as the Lake of Geneva and the ultramarine of Venice. (pp. 86-7)

"A Song of Peace", in which a Czech poet reacted to the world situation in 1950, develops the thousand-year-old tradition of the struggle of Czech culture and the Czech nation for a just, honourable and dignified peace. It is firmly established in our national culture, grows out of it organically and expresses the universal longing of honest people all over the world.

It is no chance whatsoever that it was just by this poem that Czech poetry overcame the language barrier separating it from the rest of the world. The composition, awarded a gold medal of the World Peace Council in 1953, has won popularity for the same reason as Jaroslav Hašek's *The Good Soldier Švejk*, Karel Čapek's humanist stories and plays, and Julius Fučík's *Report from the Gallows*. Through **"A Song of Peace"** Czech literature has spoken to the world about things that worry everyone, has expressed feelings and wishes that are the most widespread and yet very concrete and still topical. (p. 87)

> *Milan Blahynka, "Vítězslav Nezval," in* Panorama of Czech Literature, *Vol. 9, 1987, pp. 86-7.*

Peter Hruby (essay date 1990)

[*In the excerpt below, Hruby considers Nezval's literary contributions to the Communist movement during the 1920s.*]

The *enfant terrible* of the Communist movement and its poetic vanguard was a gifted but un-self-critical poet, Vítězslav Nezval. This *bon vivant* needed the red flag of collectivism to save himself from suicidal tendencies and obsessive and terrifying hallucinations. A long poem of

his, written in 1921, was published the next year in his first collection of verse, *Most* (*Bridge*), under the title **"Podivuhodný kouzelník"** (**"Amazing Magician"**). Karel Teige used this poem as a demonstration of the new movement, *Poetism,* which was replacing the short Proletarian phase. In it Nezval wildly combines strong eroticism with revolution. The fourth canto is called **"Revolution"**:

> A green table supports the hands of the old government
> fifteen thousand revolutionaries stand at the barricade. . . .
> Give me a weapon so I may also stand!
> Order me the largest cockade.
> Something overcomes me, something is amiss.
> I really like the Communist Manifesto . . .
> The magician has once more laid aside his grief
> and mixes with his comrades. . . .
> Nursing hatred in their hearts
> one two
> Nursing hatred in their hearts
> who will feed the little ones?

Nezval later admitted that his "holy man" had been the anarchist [Prince Pyotr Alekseyevich] Kropotkin, who supposedly helped him to understand Marx's and Engels' *Communist Manifesto* which he, rather incongruously, claimed he read and reread until he managed to lead his life in accordance with it.

But as the chances of a revolution in Czechoslovakia receded and Proletarian poets discovered that the workers were much less interested in poetry about factories than their bourgeois readers and publishers were, the poets now claimed that the task of writers was to prepare a socially liberated man for the future. They would free him from inhibitions of logic, form, tradition and any other order. Still swearing allegiance to Marx and Lenin, to the red flag and revolution, they proclaimed *hedonism* to be their goal. As an Australian observer remarked, "with this freedom went that touch of irresponsibility, of anarchy, so typical of Nezval, the atmosphere of the pantomime, the circus, and the harlequinade."

The poets of Prague were, in reality, much more influenced by modern trends in film, visual arts, jazz and literature, coming from Western countries, than by the Leninist revolution and its promises *cum* horrors. But for these typical bourgeois addicts of Prague night life it was tempting to fight, with their pens, for the new world that would emerge from revolution. In the style of *Proletkult* Nezval wrote a **"March of the Red International"**:

> . . . Proletariat
>   already
>   marching
>   terrible
>   rebellion
> Europe
>   is
>   cracking
>   Europe
>   is
>   crumbling
> Barbarian

comes
    against
        barbarian
            resist
                resist

Barbarism
    the
        weapon
            barbarism
                the
                    weapon

Barbarism
    the
        weapon
            barbarism
                the
                    weapon

So will flee
    the
        burning
            bourgeois
                moth

So will come
    the dictatorship
            so will come
                the dictatorship

[Two times more the same slogan, etc.]

The Marxist literary critic Bedřich Václavek, in 1925, welcomed "in the art of Vítězslav Nezval . . . a barbarian invasion of creative, indeed poetic energy into art. This invasion of barbarians into art, prophesized by Ch. L. Philippe, spiritually parallels the vital energy of the revolutionary masses awakened by war and the Russian Revolution." (pp. 29-31)

Peter Hruby, "Czech Poets' Post-World War I

Mésalliance: French Avantgarde and Russian Communism," in his Daydreams and Nightmares: Czech Communist and Ex-Communist Literature 1917-1987, *East European Monographs, 1990, pp. 21-39.*

FURTHER READING

French, Alfred. "Wolker and Nezval." In *Czechoslovakia Past and Present, Volume II: Essays on the Arts and Sciences,* edited by Miloslav Rechcigl, Jr., pp. 983-92. The Hague: Mouton & Co., 1968.

    Comparison of Jírí Wolker and Nezval, arguing that "the times had made them both revolutionaries, yet, as artists, they were in many respects at opposite poles, and their very divergence reveals how broad was the revolutionary platform of their time."

————. *The Poets of Prague: Czech Poetry Between the Wars.* London: Oxford University Press, 1969, 129 p.

    Includes discussion of Nezval's contributions to literary movements including Proletarianism, Poetism, and Surrealism, asserting that "to Nezval revolution was almost a way of life, an instinctive expression of his unruly nature which fled from conformity and preferred the outrageous to the conventional."

————. "Nezval's *Amazing Magician:* A Czech Shamanist Epic." *Slavic Review* 32, No. 2 (June 1973): 358-69.

    Detailed critical analysis of *The Amazing Magician,* asserting that it was "the first of the great Poetist works."

David Graham Phillips

1867-1911

American novelist, journalist, dramatist, and short story writer.

INTRODUCTION

A leading figure in the muckraking movement in American literature and journalism during the early twentieth century, Phillips is remembered as a novelist whose works drew public attention to political corruption and the role of women in American society. Employing his journalistic skills and experiences, he created "problem novels" in which he documented the social, economic, and political ills of his time.

Phillips was born in Madison, Indiana, the son of an upper-class family. Intending to become a banker, he entered Asbury College, later known as DePauw University, where he met Alfred J. Beveridge, who became his lifelong friend and a United States senator. Phillips subsequently transferred to Princeton, and, after graduating in 1887, he pursued a career as a journalist, working for the *Cincinnati Commercial Gazette,* the *New York Sun,* and eventually Joseph Pulitzer's *New York World.* At this time he began writing fiction and in 1901 published his first novel, *The Great God Success,* using the pseudonym John Graham because Pulitzer's employees were not allowed to free-lance. After Phillips left the *World* in order to devote more time to writing novels, he frequently contributed essays and fiction to *McClure's, Munsey's,* and the *Saturday Evening Post.* In *The Treason of the Senate,* a series of articles commissioned by William Randolph Hearst, he accused such prominent senators as Chauncey Depew and Nelson W. Aldrich of graft and fraud. Although this work led President Theodore Roosevelt to single out Phillips as the most gratuitously sensationalistic of the muckrakers, critics have asserted that Phillips's nonfiction, though melodramatic and occasionally embellished, was based on documented research and, like his novels, related his belief that moral leadership was lacking in government and industry. Phillips ultimately produced more than twenty novels, numerous essays, and one play. He was murdered in 1911 by Fitzhugh Coyle Goldsborough, a mentally unstable musician who believed that his sister's reputation had been maligned in Phillips's novel *The Fashionable Adventures of Joshua Craig.*

Phillips considered himself "just a novelist, telling as accurately as I can what I see." His narratives reflect events of his time and his own experiences as a reporter. Thus, the protagonists of his early novels, *The Great God Success* and *A Woman Ventures,* are successful journalists who reported on many of the events that Phillips himself had covered. Phillips also based characters in his novels on public figures. For example, Senator Beveridge became the

model for Hampden Scarborough, the hero of *The Cost* and *The Plum Tree,* and the socialist leader Eugene V. Debs was the prototype for a character in *The Conflict.* Faulting his conspicuous allusions to contemporary figures and events, some critics have dismissed Phillips as an editorialist whose fictional treatments of topical issues were absent of artistry. Phillips was more interested in fiction as a means of inspiring social reform than he was with the literary quality of his works. He was particularly concerned that the profit motive was destroying American society, a situation symbolically illustrated in *The Cost* when a Wall Street financier is choked to death with one of his own ticker tapes. Phillips also attributed America's decline to parasitic, wealthy, and materialistic women, whom he perceived as having no useful function to perform in society. This issue was introduced in Phillips's novels through romantic subplots and soon evolved into frank depictions of the relationship between the sexes and the topical "women's problem" or "female question."

In *A Woman Ventures, Old Wives for New, The Hungry Heart,* and *The Worth of a Woman: A Play in Four Acts,* followed by *A Point of Law: A Dramatic Incident,* Phillips focused on the role of women and their need for independent and productive lives. This theme culminated in *Susan Lenox: Her Fall and Rise,* which Phillips considered his masterpiece and which was released in 1931 as a major motion picture. Published posthumously, *Susan Lenox* chronicles the life of a woman who tries to obtain financial independence and emotional security only to become the victim of forced prostitution, drug addiction, and poverty. While the Society for the Suppression of Vice censored portions of the book, deeming them pornographic, critics saw the novel as an attempt to portray prostitution as a form of capitalism. Critics praised the novel's social relevance as well as Phillips's vivid descriptions of life in a small town, the effects of industrialization, and urban violence.

Phillips's reputation greatly diminished in the decades after his death. While H. L. Mencken viewed him as "America's leading novelist" and John C. Underwood described him as the "American Balzac," Granville Hicks called him a "non-subject" in American literature, stating that "so far as journalistic talent could make him so Phillips was a good novelist, but he could not go beyond that point." Other critics have argued that Phillips merely placed ideology over artistry, noting his work was a timely and convincing reflection of American society and the desires of his middle-class audience.

PRINCIPAL WORKS

The Great God Success (novel) 1901
Her Serene Highness (novel) 1902
A Woman Ventures (novel) 1902
Golden Fleece (novel) 1903
The Master Rogue (novel) 1903
The Cost (novel) 1904
The Deluge (novel) 1905
The Mother-Light (novel) 1905
The Plum Tree (novel) 1905
The Reign of Gilt (essays) 1905
The Social Secretary (novel) 1905
The Fortune Hunter (novel) 1906
Light-Fingered Gentry (novel) 1907
The Second Generation (novel) 1907
Old Wives for New (novel) 1908
The Worth of a Woman: A Play in Four Acts, followed by a Point of Law: A Dramatic Incident (dramas) 1908
The Fashionable Adventures of Joshua Craig (novel) 1909
The Hungry Heart (novel) 1909
The Husband's Story (novel) 1910
White Magic (novel) 1910
The Conflict (novel) 1911
The Grain of Dust (novel) 1911
George Helm (novel) 1912
The Price She Paid (novel) 1912
Degarmo's Wife, and Other Stories (short stories) 1913
Susan Lenox: Her Fall and Rise (novel) 1917
*The Treason of the Senate (journalism) 1953

**This work first appeared in *Cosmopolitan* in 1906

B. O. Flower   (essay date 1906)

[*As editor of the* Arena, *a popular magazine of the early twentieth century known for its dissenting viewpoints, Benjamin Orange Flower has been described by Arthur and Lila Weinberg as a "tireless agitator for social reform." In the following excerpt, Flower provides an overview of Phillips's novels and essays.*]

[David Graham Phillips's] style is always bright, epigrammatic and fascinating; on occasions it is bold and trenchant. He possesses the rare power of instantly arresting the attention and holding the interest of the reader. This is as true of his essays as of his novels. His latest work, **The Reign of Gilt,** is made up of a series of chapters dealing with plutocracy and democracy. In the hands of many writers these essays, however important in their facts, would be dry reading. Under Mr. Phillips' treatment each chapter is as absorbingly interesting as a well-written short story. Indeed, we believe that for the intelligent readers, even among those who delight in stories, most of these chapters will prove more compelling in interest than nine out of ten of the short stories that are appearing in our leading literary magazines.

It is, however, through his long stories that our author is best known. Here he is doing his greatest work for the cause of democracy and here also he is, we believe, destined to do some work that will place him among the greatest of our novelists and give him a permanent place in the literature of the world. His early novels, **A Woman Ventures** and **The Great God Success,** were promising but immature. They showed the pen of a man of imagination with brain trained to alertness, and here also was the human quality and the ethical impulse; but though they promised much they lacked the finished touch of the master. All his later books, **Golden Fleece, The Cost, The Plum-Tree, The Social Secretary** and **The Deluge,** have, however, showed a steady advance in many respects; and what is still more significant of greater things in the future, each evinces in a marked degree some special excellence which illustrates the versatility of the author and his capacity to do great work. (p. 256)

All [Phillips's] best writings reveal the requisites of a great novelist. First, he possesses the imagination that enables him to project his consciousness so as to see, feel and understand precisely what his typical creations are cognizant of, in all the varied walks of life. This seeing eye, this hearing ear, this feeling heart, constitute the first and supreme requisite for the novelist of the first rank. In the second place, our author possesses idealism, a sense of moral proportion and the rationalistic intellect that enables him to see great problems in a fundamental way. Furthermore, he possesses the human quality; he knows how to touch the heart-chord, to give to fiction that interest that appeals compellingly to the popular imagination. His style is plain, direct, attractive. Often his sentences are as epigrammatic as were Hugo's. He throws out thoughts that stick like burrs in the mind. He is versatile—very versatile. In **Golden Fleece** we have the finest satire that has appeared on the craze of the newly-rich and the American snobs in general to marry into the broken-down aristocratic families of the Old World, while incidentally with a master-hand he hits off the peculiar characteristics, and especially the weaknesses, of the rich and fashionable in such leading cities as New York, Boston, Washington and Chicago.

In *The Social Secretary* he gives a vivid picture of the undemocratic trend of life in our national capital under the imperialistic administration of the present incumbent, with a striking picture of the morally enervating and anti-democratic general conditions that are transforming the republic into a class-ruled government. All this is presented with charming realism through the vehicle of a pleasing story.

In *The Cost* we find the human and love interest very strong. This story displays the development of powers essential to great novels and which have only been foreshadowed in his previous romances. It also gives some splendid examples of character drawing in which colossal typical figures are introduced. Dumont and Scarborough represent the incarnation of the forces that are struggling for supremacy in the republic to-day. On the one hand is a powerful individuality overmastered by a sordid egoism, by a craze for gold and for the ease, comfort, gratification and power which it will give the individual, unattended by any recognition of moral responsibility or the dignity and duty of life. Here is the typical modern money magnate, crazed by the materialism of the market, insane with the gambler's frenzy. And in juxtaposition to this great typical character we have in Scarborough the type of the clean-souled, high-minded nature, touched, illuminated and glorified by the highest idealism—a man dominated by the spirit of freedom, democracy and human enlightenment, as were Jefferson and Lincoln; incorruptible and true, yet withal very human.

In *The Plum-Tree* a startling and compellingly realistic picture is presented of the overthrow of democracy and the enthronement of plutocracy or privileged wealth, and the degradation of the political life of the nation through the corrupt party-boss and the money-controlled machine. It is a powerful story of contemporaneous conditions, almost as compelling in its influence as the later novels of Zola, such as *Truth, Labor* and *Fecundity.*

The Deluge is a companion romance quite as strong as *The Plum-Tree.* It tears away the mask from our American Monte Carlo, the gambling hell of Wall street, and introduces the reader to the money-mad princes of privilege who pose as the pillars of society while playing with stacked cards and loaded dice and oppressing the masses of the nation and debauching the business and political life of America.

Now each of these works reveals some special excellence, some element of strength, power and popularity less marked in the others, and shows the power of the author to handle life in all its phases and in such varied manner as to make a distinctly great novel when the hour arrives in which the author will be able or wise enough to retire into some secluded fastness of nature and there amid solitude and natural grandeur permit his imagination to create a rich background for a cast that shall be as full of

great living, typical figures as *Les Miserables, Vanity Fair, David Copperfield,* or any other of the supreme works in the world of fiction.

Mr. Phillips possesses all the elements essential to the creation of great and immortal fiction. All that is necessary is time and patience in the composition of some great work. (pp. 256-58)

> B. O. Flower, "David Graham Phillips: A Twentieth-Century Novelist of Democracy," in The Arena, *Boston, Vol. XXXV, No. CXCVI, March, 1906, pp. 252-58.*

Frederic Taber Cooper   (essay date 1911)

[*An American educator, biographer, and editor, Cooper served for many years as literary critic at the* Bookman. *In the following excerpt, he examines the strengths and weaknesses of Phillips's novels.*]

In any critical analysis of the life work of the late David Graham Phillips, it is well to recognize frankly at the outset that he has been a rather important figure in the development of American fiction in recent years. We could name on the fingers of one hand the contemporary novelists who, like Mr. Phillips, have devoted themselves to depicting and studying the big ethical and social problems of their own country and generation, and doing it in a broad, bold, comprehensive way, with a certain epic sweep and magnitude. And among these few none was more deeply in earnest than Mr. Phillips, none strove more patiently to do his work in the best, most forceful, most craftsman-like manner. Having made these concessions, we are free to recognize that his results fell somewhat behind his intentions, that with all his industry he developed his technique rather slowly, and that while just a few of his novels are of a quality which no serious student of present-day fiction can afford to neglect, a large proportion of the remainder may conveniently be set aside as merely tending to increase the bulk of a critical analysis without contributing any light of real importance.

Now, in saying that Mr. Phillips was slow in acquiring the technique of construction, it behooves a critic to define rather carefully just wherein he showed himself defective. It certainly was not due to any lack of willingness or ability to practise infinite pains. On the contrary, the habit of making the act of writing a slow and conscientious toil grew upon him year by year. Few novelists of his degree of success have accepted adverse criticism in a more tolerant spirit; but there was one thing that he resented, and that was the charge of careless haste. "People sometimes say that I write too fast," he protested not long before his death. "They said so about my *Light-Fingered Gentry.* They don't know anything about it! I don't believe any one ever wrote more slowly and laboriously. Every one of my books was written at least three times—" He paused a moment, then added in correction, "And when I say *three times,* it really means nine times, on account of my system of copying and revision." When once under full headway in a book, he worked immoderately, producing an actual bulk of material far in excess of what was needed for the limits of the story. "I have writer's cramp every spring," he said with a laugh. As he became better acquainted with the characters and situations in a book, his great difficulty lay in confining himself to such details as were strictly relevant to his central purpose. He was hampered by knowing too much about his people, their habits of life and methods of thought. They were all the time taking matters into their own hands, and insisting upon his setting down upon paper all sorts of happenings quite extraneous to the story. According to his own estimate, he usually ended by discarding, not only in paragraphs and episodes, but also in whole chapters, from two to three times as much as he retained in the published volume.

Nor are his faults of construction due to a lack of acquaintance with the best methods of the modern schools of fiction, abroad as well as at home. There are certain qualities in his later volumes, such as **Old Wives for New** and **The Second Generation,** which are to be explained only through the influence of the best French realism—qualities which, on the one hand, are not the result of a conscious and deliberate imitation; but on the other, cannot possibly have been an independent and spontaneous creation. The broad, Zolaesque sweep of phrase and action, the sense of jostling crowds and ceaseless activity, the endless panorama of city streets, the whole trick of treating humanity in ranks and battalions, as though the crowd were a natural unit of measurement,—these are things which Mr. Phillips learned to do as just a few other American writers, Frank Norris, for instance, and Robert Herrick, have learned to do them: and necessarily he must have studied at the fountain head. Indeed, his whole conception of what a novel should be was French rather than Anglo-Saxon. When one discussed with him about theories of fiction he would admit frankly, on the one hand, that he had small use for such artificial devices for giving unity to a series of volumes as Balzac's scheme of the *Comédie Humaine* or Zola's complicated family tree of the Rougon-Macquart. But he did insist upon seeing every human story as a cross-section of life; and by a cross-section of life he did not mean a little local slice carefully measured to fit the dimensions of the particular story he happened to be telling. On the contrary, if he was narrating the simple love affair of a boy and girl in some small town of the Middle West, he was always conscious, even though he had no need of bringing this out in the story, that there was between that boy and girl and all the other people in that town an inevitable and all-pervading human relationship; that that town was not an isolated community, but was itself only a link in the vast network of social and industrial life stretching over the wide continent from the Atlantic to the Pacific, with endless miles of railroad intersecting it, with a centralized government, a President and Congress at Washington and with countless lines of steamers keeping it in touch with the other world powers. All this helps in a measure to show what to Mr. Phillips was a very vivid actuality. And of course the writer who always sees each little human happening, not as an isolated incident but as a detail in a tremendous and universal scheme, necessarily has a wider outlook upon life and necessarily communicates to his readers a similar impression of bigness and of vitality.

This brings us directly to the question: Why is it that so many of Mr. Phillips's books contain more of promise than of fulfilment? Why is it that, starting as they do with big ethical problems and a broad epic treatment, they are so apt at the end to leave rather the impression of having given us an isolated and exceptional human story than of having symbolized some broad and universal principle? The answer, I think, is simply this: that there was a curious anomaly in the manner in which Mr. Phillips's mind worked when in quest of the germ idea of a new story. In spite of the fact that his instinct led him to write purpose novels, and that his interest in social and economic problems was in some respects keener than his interest in people; yet, according to his own admission, no story ever began to shape itself in his mind in the form of an abstract principle, an ethical doctrine. Reversing the usual process followed by writers of the epic type, he always started from a single character or episode and built from these,—sometimes indeed from nothing more definite than a face glimpsed for a moment in a crowd. A striking case in point is the origin that he assigned to one of the novels left unpublished at the time of his death. The theme of this story was the outgrowth of Mr. Phillips's deep interest in the economic independence of the modern woman, and more especially in the peculiar dangers and temptations which beset her, as contrasted with the more sheltered lives of her mother and grandmother. He had been deeply stirred by recent statistics regarding the influx of refined young Southern women into New York, so many of them fated to be swept under by the surge of city life. He wanted to know whether such a girl could, by her own efforts, struggle up, out of the depths, to a position of independence and social standing. Such, in substance, is the longest book that Mr. Phillips ever wrote, a book that in the form in which he left it ran to considerably more than three hundred thousand words. The title of the book has not yet been made public; but it is probably safe to conjecture that it is the volume which he intended to call "Susan." At all events, it is utterly unlike any of his previous efforts, and the author himself confessed that it baffled his powers of self-criticism. But, like all his other books, it received its first impetus, not from economics, but from a trivial incident: namely, a passing glimpse of a young woman seated in a wagon.

The incident in question occurred when the author was a lad of fourteen. It was in a Western town, where he chanced to be staying at the time; and the face of the young woman in the farm-wagon haunted him long afterward. It was a beautiful face, a face indicating breeding and culture, but it bore the stamp of dumb, hopeless tragedy. As he stood gazing at her, a gaunt, elderly man, rugged and toil-stained, with the hall-mark of the well-to-do farmer plainly visible upon him, climbed to the seat beside her, gathered up the reins and drove off. Mr. Phillips, boy though he was, noticed how the girl shrank and whitened as her companion's shoulder touched her. He heard the girl's story afterward. She belonged to a family of local prominence; but there had been a scandal, sordid, notorious, unforgettable. The girl herself was probably the one person in the community who did not know the facts. She could not understand why her people were shunned socially, nor why they welcomed the chance of providing for her by marriage with an illiterate but prosperous old farmer, who lived at a desirable distance from town. The girl's story has nothing to do with Mr. Phillips's novel, but the suffering on her face was his inspiration after the lapse of a quarter-century.

It is the logical result of Mr. Phillips's method of working from the concrete to the abstract, from the specific to the general, that his big underlying principle, whatever it may be, is never personified with that graphic visualization that makes it everywhere and at all times loom up portentously, as, for instance, in Zola's *L'Argent,* the Bourse looms up, in *Le Ventre de Paris,* the Halles, in *L'Assommoir,* the Wine-shop, like so many vast symbolic monsters wreaking their malignant pleasure upon mankind. In Mr. Phillips's books one feels the ethical purpose far more vaguely; he is always stimulating, he sets us thinking deeply over big problems—most deeply, perhaps, when he most strongly antagonizes us; but it is difficult to say with precision, or, at all events, to say within the limits of ten words just what principle any one book of his stands for. Take, for instance, the best and strongest of all his books, *The Husband's Story:* even here the general public has groped rather helplessly to decide just what the author meant. It must be admitted that on the whole the general public has in this particular case been rather stupid in failing to recognize that when Mr. Phillips chose to see this particular story through the eyes of a certain shrewd and unscrupulous financier, he deprived himself of the chance of expressing his own ideas directly, and was obliged to give us every detail strongly colored by its passage through another man's temperament. Nevertheless, it is undoubtedly to some extent Mr. Phillips's own fault that a majority of his readers assumed that *The Husband's Story* was an indictment of the American woman as a whole, and not simply of one limited and ultra-snobbish type of American woman. And the same question of his meaning is raised with considerably more justice in every one of his earlier books. Is *Old Wives for New* a protest against girl-and-boy marriages, or an indorsement of divorce, or both? Is *The Hungry Heart* an arraignment of the *Doll's House* treatment of a wife, or a plea for equal standards for man and woman in questions of morality? And is *The Second Generation* to be taken mainly as a protest against inherited fortunes, a glorification of work, or as a satire upon the snobbery of America's idle class? In other words, had Zola written this book, would his symbol for it have been the Probate Court, the Dinner Pail, or the Powdered Flunkey? It was part and parcel of Mr. Phillips's habitual tendency to see his cross-section of life in its entirety, that he found himself unable to do one thing at a time, found himself obliged to complicate and obscure his central purpose by having in reality several simultaneous central purposes.

This brings us face to face with the real fault of Mr. Phillips's method of work, the real weakness of even his best achievements. He was not merely the clear-eyed and impartial observer of life; he was always a partisan and a reformer. His interest was so keen in the problems he was seeking to set forth that he found it impossible to keep himself and his ideas out of them. Of course when you take one of Mr. Phillips's novels to pieces you discover that in its essence it is a problem novel; but this side of his work

he had learned to disguise pretty cleverly. It is not so much the way in which he twisted the lives of his characters in order to point a moral, as it is the slight running comment going all through the narrative portions of his stories that keeps us reminded both of his personal outlook upon life and of the annoying fact that he is trying to do our thinking for us. Here, for instance, is a trivial little example that may stand as typical of his method: in *White Magic* he had occasion to tell us, as evidence of the expensive scale on which his heroine's mother ran her summer home, that she had no less than five footmen in attendance at the front door. Now, some of us may think this mere foolishness; others may wax indignant over it as a criminal extravagance; and others again simply regard it as no more than what was proper for a person in her position of life. Mr. Phillips had as good a right as anybody else to his own opinion about it, but it was not good art for him to force that opinion upon the reader by couching this little fact in the following terms: "Five lackeys . . . five strapping fellows with dumb faces and the stalwart figures that the rich select as menial show pieces." There is a veiled sneer in the very intonation of such a sentence that is incompatible with the best art.

It is this uncontrolled tendency to inject the personal equation into his books that every now and then sets the reader tingling with sudden antagonism in the midst of some of his strongest scenes. His outlook upon life was extremely clear-eyed and broad; and if he had been content to give us the uncolored facts and let us think what we would about them, we should get considerably more benefit as well as enjoyment out of contact with his people and their histories. That there is a good deal of snobbery among our wealthy and fashionable class, our imitation aristocracy of money, is undoubtedly true. And to the average sane-minded American there is something distinctly foolish in the sight of an American mother trailing her daughters through Europe with the open and unashamed intention of selling them to a title. But, after all, questions of this kind are largely a matter of the point of view. There is no useful purpose served in waxing indignant over people who happen to regulate their lives somewhat differently from the way in which you or I would regulate our lives. It is always worth while to set forth as strongly as possible in a story certain existing social conditions which the author in his secret heart condemns, but there is nothing gained by insisting that the reader must condemn them also. It may very well happen that the reader does not at all share the author's views, and in that case such an attempt to prejudice him is fully as irritating as is the coloring given to news in a paper of the opposite political party to your own.

This interference on the part of Mr. Phillips, born as it was of over-earnestness, produced upon the types of his people and the construction of his plots certain modifications which are precisely what a shrewd judge of books might have expected in advance to find there. In the first place, it led him quite frequently to picture, not what average people are doing under existing conditions, but what somewhat unusual people would in his opinion have done under conditions just the reverse of those that exist—as, for instance, in *The Second Generation,* not what happens to the inefficient heirs of great wealth, when the hardworking father dies, but to the distinctly exceptional and self-sufficient children of a rich man who, for their own good, deliberately disinherits them. Or again, in **White Magic,** he studied not the typical case of the girl reared in wealth and luxury who, upon losing her heart to an impecunious artist, fights a long battle with herself because she cannot go against her training; but the exceptional case of the girl who flings such training to the winds and brazenly offers her heart and hand to the penniless artist in question, who, being himself equally an exception, repulses her because he selfishly thinks that she will interfere with his art.

And, secondly, this tendency to tell us what we ought to think has its effect upon the individualization of his characters, and more especially upon his women. What I mean here is best illustrated by taking for a moment a book from which this particular fault is absent, *The Husband's Story.* The fact that this book was written in the first person made it of course impossible for Mr. Phillips to obtrude directly his own opinions; and probably it is due to this fact quite as much as to any other that, artistically speaking, this is the best book that he produced. The character of the wife Edna we get entirely as colored by the husband's eyes—as strongly colored as though we were looking at her through a piece of stained glass. The admirable thing about it is that the color is uniformly and consistently maintained from start to finish—a bit of craftsmanship that requires a rather masterly touch. In turning from this book to others that are not written in the first person we realize that a good deal of the time Mr. Phillips was coloring his women, not so strongly to be sure, but none the less to a noticeable extent—in other words, that he was forcing us to see them through the medium of his own eyes instead of directly from life. We become aware of this by finding that he quite frequently expects us, indeed demands of us, to admire things that his heroines do and say which we ourselves cannot find at all admirable; and sometimes he is led into making them take certain actions that we are quite sure the women that we ourselves think they are would not have been guilty of taking. But questions of this kind are not a matter for generalization; they can be better understood when we proceed to take up for separate analysis a few of the more significant of Mr. Phillips's novels.

During the dozen years that represent the period of his activity as a writer of fiction, Mr. Phillips produced somewhat less than a score of volumes. To analyze these books one by one in the order of their appearance, beginning with **The Great God Success** and **A Woman Ventures** and coming steadily down the list through **Golden Fleece** and **The Cost** and all the rest of them, would be not only tiresome but futile. It would be simply one of the many ways of making it impossible to see the woods because of the trees. Mr. Phillips was striving from the start to do pretty much the same sort of thing in all his work; and the only practical difference between his later volumes and his earlier is that he was steadily learning to do the same sort of thing considerably better. For this reason there is no more point in spending time on those earlier volumes than, if one were writing an analysis of Zola, it would be worth while to waste space on *Madeleine Férat* and *Nantas* and *Thérèse Raquin.* In point of fact, one gets quite effectively

the whole range of Mr. Phillips's powers and also of his weaknesses in the volumes that belong to his period of mature development, the volumes produced within the last four or five years.

The Second Generation is probably the best book to recommend to a reader approaching Mr. Phillips for the first time, because, on the one hand, it contains less than most of his books that is likely to arouse antagonism; and, on the other, it admirably illustrates his strongest qualities, his ability to give you the sense of life and motion and the clash of many interests. The substance of it can be told in rather fewer words than is usual with Mr. Phillips's novels. Old Hiram Ranger, millionaire manufacturer of barrels in a small Western town, suddenly makes two rather painful discoveries. First, he learns that his remarkable physical strength, which has never once failed him throughout all his years, is at last breaking and that he has not many days in which to "set his house in order." And his second and even more painful discovery is that for twenty years he has unwittingly been harming his son and his daughter by over-indulgence, allowing them to grow up in idleness, to form foolish and extravagant tastes, to choose their friends exclusively from the ultra-fashionable circles and to learn to despise the humble beginnings from which he himself sprang and from which the money that they thoughtlessly waste has come. He decides in bitter agony of soul that there is at this late date only one thing that he can do to repair his huge mistake: and that is to deprive his children of the inheritance on which they have counted. The act hurts him more cruelly than it can possibly hurt them—it hurts him through his love for them, through his pride in them and through his desire for public esteem and approval, since he foresees that such an act will be misunderstood and disapproved. All of this part of the story, the old man's sturdy courage and shrewd common sense, contrasted with the weak vanity and costly luxury of the son and daughter, is given with graphic truth, rugged strength, and a sure swiftness of movement. But from the middle point of the story we get a rather exasperating impression that we are being allowed to behold not so much a cross-section of life as an up-to-date morality play. Old Hiram Ranger has chosen rather drastic methods to teach his son and daughter a lesson, to reform their characters, practically to make them over. No one can say that a situation thus created is without interest; but it becomes exasperating to find that the old man has made his calculations with the sureness of omnipotence, that his plan succeeds even in all its minor details and that the son and daughter repent of all their errors, reform themselves completely, are to all intents and purposes born anew. Mr. Phillips was probably not conscious of it when he wrote the book, but none the less it is to all practical intents a grown-up version of the story of the bad little boy who went fishing on Sunday and was drowned and the good little boy who went to church and was rewarded with plum pudding.

A dozen different readers would probably give a dozen different statements of the central theme of **Old Wives for New.** The real importance of this book—for among Mr. Phillips's books it is unquestionably one of the important ones—is that it sets forth quite pitilessly the gradual estrangement that arises between a husband and wife in the course of long years through the woman's sloth and self-ishness and gratification of all her whims. It is an open question whether Mr. Phillips's method of presenting this problem might not have been improved upon. What he has done is to show us first in a brief prelude the sudden ardor of a boy-and-girl attachment, each caught by the mere physical charm of youth and health and high spirits and rushing into a marriage with no firm basis of mutual understanding. Then he skips an interval of about twenty years and takes us into the intimate life of this same couple, showing us with a frankness of speech and of thought that is almost cruel in its unsparing realism the physical and mental degeneration of the woman, fat and old and slovenly before her time, and the unspoken repulsion felt by the man who has kept himself young, alert and thoroughly modern in outward appearance as well as in spirit. The situation is complicated by the presence of two grown children, a son and a daughter, who see unwillingly the approaching crisis and realize their helplessness to ward it off. Such a situation in real life may solve itself in any one of fifty different ways. What Mr. Phillips has chosen to do is to bring the husband in contact with a young woman who represents everything in which his own wife is lacking. And although the man fights for a long time against temptation, in the end he obtains freedom from the old wife through the divorce court, and promptly replaces her with the new. There is probably no other American novel that gives us with such direct and unflinching clairvoyance the sordid, repellent, intimate little details of a mistaken marriage that slowly but surely culminates in a sort of physical nausea and an inevitable separation. What a good many of us are apt to resent in the book is the stamp of approval that the author seems to place upon the man who deliberately discards a wife after her youth and beauty are gone, not because he thinks it for their mutual welfare, but for the cold-blooded reason that he wants to marry somebody else. There is a sort of heartless immorality about the whole proceeding that makes us feel that the slovenly, faded wife, with her shallow pretense of having worn herself out with household cares, her gluttony that has been the ruin of health and beauty, her peevish temper and ridiculous vanity, makes on the whole a rather better showing than the husband. One cannot leave this book without adding just a word of protest against what may seem a trivial detail, yet is the sort of detail in which Mr. Phillips's technique sins rather frequently. The husband has met the woman who embodies his ideal of feminine perfection quite by chance in the woods, where he and his son are camping out. In the course of three weeks, almost without their knowing it, they have fallen in love with each other; then comes the awakening, and they go their separate ways, the man still knowing nothing of the woman's identity, of her station in life or of the particular corner of America which is her home. Several chapters later the man is in New York helping his daughter buy her trousseau. There are a thousand shops in New York from which she might choose, but purely by chance she takes her father to the one shop which happens to be presided over by the woman with whom he is in love. A coincidence of this sort is bad enough when it seems to be more or less of a structural necessity; but when, as in this case, one can

think of a dozen simple ways of avoidance, it becomes unpardonable.

There is only one excuse for pausing to speak of Mr. Phillips's next volume, *The Fashionable Adventures of Joshua Craig,* namely, that it shows that even yet the author was weak in the power of self-criticism. How it was possible for a writer possessing the breadth of view and the power of expression that have gone into the making of at least four or five of Mr. Phillips's best novels to put forth seriously a piece of cheap caricature like *Joshua Craig* quite passes the understanding of the ordinary impartial outsider. *Joshua Craig* is simply an exaggerated specimen of a rather exasperating type of novel which has unfortunately become far too common in American fiction: the novel which shows the refined and carefully nurtured American girl, usually from the East, belying all her inherited instincts and acquired training by marrying the rugged, virile, usually rather vulgar man of the people who, for the purposes of this type of novel, is generally represented as coming from the West. The whole type seems to have originated at about the time that Owen Wister made Mollie's New England conscience capitulate to *The Virginian;* and the type has steadily degenerated year by year. But of course it is never fair to quarrel with an author simply because one does not happen to like what he has tried to do. The trouble with *Joshua Craig* is that he has so obviously failed to do what he tried. Joshua is not merely bluff and rugged and primitive of manner; he is loud-mouthed and vulgar and deliberately discourteous. Margaret Severance, the reigning beauty of Washington, whom he decides in his stormy, violent, irresistible way to marry—not because he loves her, but because he conceives the idea that she loves him—is in point of manners pretty nearly his match. She has a way of looking at people "with a lady's insolent tranquillity"; and on one occasion, when she receives a letter that angers her, and her maid happens at the same moment to be buttoning her shoes, she relieves her feelings by springing up and bringing her sharp French heel down with full force on the back of her maid's hand, leaving it skinned and bleeding. She is distinctly an unpleasant personality, yet even so, to marry her to such a cyclonic boor as Joshua Craig does seem rather like making the punishment exceed the crime.

Passing over *White Magic,* which is simply an innocuous little love story told with rather more explosive violence than the theme warrants, we come to the two books that exhibit Mr. Phillips's ripest powers, *The Hungry Heart* and *The Husband's Story. The Hungry Heart* is a sincere and detailed study of a marriage that threatens to be a failure because the man adheres to old-fashioned standards regarding women, while the wife, with her modern education and progressive views, finds it impossible to accept the rôle of domesticity and inaction to which he would assign her. As a piece of careful construction this volume deserves frank praise. The entire action takes place within the house and grounds of the husband's ancestral home; the cast of characters is limited to just four people—two men and two women; we hardly get even a passing glimpse of any outsiders, friends or relatives, or even servants. And yet within this little world of four people we get a sense of universality of theme and interest, an impression not of learning the secrets of a few isolated lives, but of learning much that is big and vital about man and woman. There is nothing essentially new in the specific story; it is simply one of the many variants of the familiar triangle—the husband and wife who drift apart, the other man who takes advantage of a woman's loneliness to persuade her that she is in love when really she is only bored; and finally the inevitable discovery by the husband of his wife's infidelity. What gives the book its value is not the episode of the wife's frailty, but the wise, far-sighted understanding of the way in which two people, physically, mentally and morally well equipped to make each other happy, gradually drift apart through stubborn adherence to foolish prejudices, mistaken reticence, petty misunderstandings, and a hundred and one trivialities, no one of which by itself is worth a second thought, while the cumulative effect of them all becomes fatal. Mr. Phillips's solution of the story, in which he makes the wife experience a revulsion of feeling that drives her from her lover back to her husband, while the husband, after hearing her confession, not only forgives her but practically admits that he is glad everything has happened as it has, because the effect upon him is to have reawakened his love—this solution comes as a disappointment. One feels it to be in the nature of an anticlimax to an exceptionally fine piece of work. That a man of this husband's conventional, conservative type could bring himself to pardon and receive back the woman who admits her guilt with a frankness of speech that makes one wince, rings false. Forgiveness under such circumstances is a delusion and a blunder. The ghost of such a past would simply refuse to be laid.

An interesting side light on the concluding chapters of *The Hungry Heart,* which in point of fact came near to being the author's favorite among all his books, is shed by the following anecdote: it was pointed out to him one day in friendly criticism that a woman such as the heroine was portrayed to be throughout the first half of the story would neither have remained with her lover nor gone back to her husband, but would have lived alone unless some third man eventually came into her life. This comment impressed Mr. Phillips to an extent which seemed disproportionate, until he confessed that the solution of a third man was precisely what he had planned from the start as definitely as it lay in him to plan anything in advance. But, he explained, when he had reached the midway point, his characters took the matter quite out of his hands. He suddenly awoke to a realization that his heroine was quite a different woman from what he had all along supposed her to be; she made it clear to him that she was not the kind either to hold to the old lover or to take a new one; she was the type of woman who would have the courage to go back. "If I have not made her convincing," he concluded, "to that extent *The Hungry Heart* is a failure—but," he added undauntedly, "I know the type of woman I was after and I know she would have done just what I made this woman do."

Lastly, we have *The Husband's Story,* which is the type of book that we had long had the right to expect from Mr. Phillips, and which if he had been spared might have been the first of a long series of equal strength and bigness. Like all of this author's best previous work, it is a study of a marriage that failed. And the reason that it is a better and bigger book than any of his others is not because of his theme, but because of his workmanship: the thing is better done, in its underlying structure, in its working out of details, in all that goes to make up good technique. Robert Herrick, when he wrote *The Diary of an American Citizen,* attempted to handle much the same subject in the same way—but that book, clever though it was, hardly did more than scratch the surface of the opportunity lurking in his theme. Mr. Phillips dug deeper: he has shown us, in the lives of a certain couple, Godfrey Loring and Edna, his wife, all the artificiality and selfishness, the empty ambitions and false ideals that lie behind the tinsel and glitter of the so-called "Four Hundred." The husband tells the story with great simplicity and directness. He makes no secret of the utter sordidness of their origin in Passaic, New Jersey; of Edna's father, the undertaker, known as Old Weeping Willy; and his own father, "honest innocent soul, with a taste for talking what he thought was politics." He makes it clear that Edna married him, not for love, but because he was getting the biggest salary of any of the young fellows whom she knew and so offered her the best chance of advancement. She deliberately intended, when she married him, to get as much out of him as could be gotten by clever driving; nor could she have planned the thing more ruthlessly had she been acquiring a beast of burden, instead of a husband. Now, the one thing that saves the story and renders it at all possible is the fact that the husband is an exceptional man with that extra sense which constitutes the business instinct, and coupled with it a saving sense of humor. The early chapters, picturing the transition period while Edna was floundering out of the half-baked standards of Passaic into the midway stage of Brooklyn, are full of those wonderful little flashes of first-hand observation that seem like fragments filched, if not directly out of your life and mine, at least from that of the family next door or of the neighbor across the street. This husband is never for an instant under any illusion about his wife; he realizes her incompetence—the incompetence of thousands of young American wives for the particular work they have undertaken: the work of wife and of mother and of housekeeper. He realizes too her craving for social advancement; and, in a half-confessed way, he sympathizes with her and is willing to accept the fruits of her social conquests, although he will not raise a finger toward helping her. This perhaps is the cleverest touch in Mr. Phillips's satire. He does not tell us in so many words that the husband is just as much at fault as the wife, just as unfitted for his task of husband, and father and master of the house as she is for her duties,—but he makes this perfectly clear and distributes the blame with an admirable equity. If she has been cold and calculating and dishonest in her social life, he has been cold and calculating and dishonest in his business life; if she is meanly and snobbishly ashamed of the people from whom she sprang, so also is he; if she has been too absorbed in her schemes for advancement to give him the companionship due from a wife, he in turn is too absorbed in huge financial deals to give her the love and care due from a husband. In other words, this book might be defined as an indictment of the "high life" American marriage, on the ground of the woman's vaulting ambition and overweening self-importance, and the man's inertia, coupled with his absorption in the busy game of chasing dollars. A large part of the merit of this undeniably big novel lies in what it merely implies rather than in what it says. To conceive a story of this sort is something in itself to be proud of; but to conceive of telling it through the husband's lips was a stroke of genius. To have told it in any other way would have been to rob it of its greatest merit, the all-pervading sting of its satire.

As I have tried frankly to recognize, Mr. Phillips was a writer with many qualities and some defects—like all men who have it in them to do big things. But it would have been easy to forgive more serious faults than his in any one possessing his breadth and depth of interest in the serious problems of American life and his outspoken fearlessness in handling them. There are, unfortunately, few in this country to-day who are even trying to do the sort of work that he was doing. And the fact that he did it with apparent ease and that he had reached a point where he had begun to do it with triumphant strength multiplies tenfold the tragedy of his untimely death. The interruption of fate at the midpoint in his career has entailed a loss to American fiction not only irreparable but one which can never be accurately measured. (pp. 112-39)

> *Frederic Taber Cooper, "David Graham Phillips," in his* Some American Story Tellers, *Henry Holt and Company, 1911, pp. 112-39.*

John Curtis Underwood   (essay date 1914)

[*In the following excerpt, Underwood provides an overview of Phillips's fiction and, in responding to a review written by "Calvin Winter," the pseudonym of Frederic Taber Cooper, describes Phillips as an artist, scientist, and partisan who prescribed "practical politics" for the American public.*]

It is significant that in the year of this present writing, the story of the passing of the idle rich has been told by a man from their own ranks. It is an admitted fact that of the idle rich and near-rich in America, fully nine-tenths are women, many of them with fathers or husbands risen from the ranks. It is still more significant that, among the mob of more than five thousand women writers of some note in America to-day, not one has seen fit to enlarge upon this state of affairs successfully; and that it has been left to a novelist like David Graham Phillips to demonstrate conclusively the spiritual and mental poverty of the women of our conventional upper class, and to make both money and a lasting reputation through the most unmistakable and uncompromising handling of this phase of our national life.

There is very little evidence that Mr. Phillips began of set purpose to specialize on this theme. The conviction has been gradually forced on him, as it has been forced on the majority of his male contemporaries. He has been one of the few strong men in American fiction who have consistently had the courage of their convictions and the fitness to make these convictions carry through. He has at one time or another attacked and exposed successfully other special interests that the American people as a whole feel

least proud of to-day. It was left for him, in two of his most notable and most mature novels, *Old Wives for New* and *The Husband's Story,* to settle once and for all the pretensions of American femininity "higher up" to the unearned increments of sweetness and light, and the fine flowering into nothing of the culture, which he has stigmatized as that of a fog bank.

Few will be found to dispute the fact that Mr. Phillips has been, from first to last, consistently a radical in politics, in journalism and in literature. Like all successful radicals, he struck at the roots of things, he hewed to the lines, he never ceased to strike till his axe went to the mark and stayed there.

In spite of his early and tragic taking off, he attained success in his main line of attack, he made an indelible impression on the minds and hearts of his country men and country women while he was still a comparatively young man. The very suddenness and spectacular nature of his death deepened and fixed this impression while it was still in the fixative state. His loss remains the nation's gain. The negative suspensions of indifference and reaction towards the issues raised by him have been in innumerable cases developed into a positive appreciation of the man's sincerity and strength. In the racial advertising programme and cosmic scheme of things, the account has been already balanced; the picture of the Truth as he saw it and set forth has been already, in less than two years, permanently developed and enlarged in the gallery of our national literary and temperamental types.

It is proper to speak of Mr. Phillips in the terms of photography. His likenesses were so life-like that there was no getting by them. His art was no more that of either the miniaturist or the pastellist, than it was that of the genre or mural painter of classic tradition. He dealt in essentials, not nuances; in facts, not conventions. At times he transcended the range of the ordinary social camera of fiction and achieved the very X-ray of photography of the American mind and soul of to-day. Like the big business men who are his strongest male characters and most successful masculine portraits, he was out for results, and he got them.

Never in the history of fiction had there been a series of books—literary in the sense that much of the most virile parts of the Bible, Shakespeare and Ibsen are literary; popular and *sui generis* as a great modern railroad bridge or a skyscraper are popular and unmistakably distinguished—containing so many paragraphs, so many pages, of unmistakable truth, truth that hits one between the eyes, and makes one say, "I always knew that" or "Why didn't I ever see that before?" as Mr. Phillips achieved at the height of his powers, in half a dozen of the more notable and readable novels.

It was stated at the time of his death that he had decided to shift his attack from fiction to the stage. If *The Worth of a Woman,* which was produced at the Madison Square Theater, New York, in February, 1908, is any criterion, there is little doubt that before long he would have won the same success in the new field as in the old.

The time was ripe for it just as it was ripe for the extension of Colonel Roosevelt's policies during the seven years that our greatest living ex-president held the center of our political stage. Phillips may justly be called the Roosevelt of American literature.

Both have, at their best, been the product of a will power and an energy specialized to the limit by the individual, and reënforced consciously or insensibly by the unparalleled intensity of the American character and the American social and political conditions that have made themselves heard and felt through them. Both have been characteristic products of American environment. Both have as characteristically reacted on the environment that produced them.

Phillips, like Mark Twain, Howells, Frank Norris, Harold Frederic and Stephen Crane, was in the beginning a newspaper man. Like the first three, he was born in or near the middle West.

He came to New York in 1896 from Princeton, the most democratic of our typical Eastern Universities, with a point of view differing little in essentials from that expressed in 1905 in *The Reign of Gilt.*

It may be news to many that this book is not a novel. It is a brief and comprehensive statement of his social and political creed, and the evolutionary reasons on which he bases it. It is as unsparing in its denunciations of the things he sees fit to denounce as any of his later or earlier books; at the same time, like the rest of them, it is constructively and inspiringly optimistic.

It tells us:

> It is as exact a truth as any in chemistry or mechanics that Aristocracy is the natural, the inevitable sequence of widespread ignorance, and Democracy the natural, the inevitable, sequence of widespread intelligence. . . . New conditions may produce new and subtle tyrannies that seem stronger than the old. All in vain. As well might a concourse of parliaments and tongues resolve that the heat of the sun be reduced one-half. . . . The story of history, rightly written, would be the story of the march of Democracy, now patiently wearing away obstacles, accelerated there, now sweeping along upon the surface, again flowing for centuries underground, but always in action, always the one continuous, inevitable force. There has never been any more danger of its defeat than there has been danger that the human brain would be smoothed of its thought-bearing convolutions and set in retreat through the stages of evolution back to protoplasm.

> Because of these spectacles of sloth, incompetence and corruption in public officials, it is charged by many persons of reputation as "publicists" that Democracy is a breeder of public corruption! The truth is just the reverse. Democracy drags public corruption out of its mole tunnels where it undermines society, drags it into the full light of day. . . . The truth is, steam and electricity have made the human race suddenly and acutely self-conscious as a race for the first time of its existence. They have constructed a

mighty mirror wherein humanity sees itself, with all its faults and follies and diseases and deformities. And the sudden, unprecedented spectacle is so startling, is in such abhorrent contrast with poetical pictures of the past, painted in school and popular text books, that men of defective perspective shrink and shriek: "Man has become monstrous!" But not so, Man, rising, rising, rising through the ages, is not nearer to the dark and bloody and cruel place of his origin than to the promised land toward which his ideals are drawing him. . . .

> What our grandfathers regarded as the natural and just demands of employers upon employé are now regarded as rigorous and tyrannous exactions of a brute. . . . False weights were found in the ruins of the oldest city that has been exhumed. . . . It is no new thing for a man to be admired and envied for wealth and station, regardless of how he got them. But it is a new thing in the world for the public conscience to be so sensitive that a man in possession of wealth and station, got not by open and outright robbery—methods not long ago regarded without grave disapproval—but by means that are questionable and suspicious merely, should be in an apologetic attitude, should feel called upon to defend himself, and to give large sums in philanthropy in the effort to justify and rehabilitate himself. . . .

> And more than ninety per cent. of our business is done upon credit. Under the old order the very laws and customs, the very morality taught by the church was grounded upon the justice of the unjust distribution of the products of labor; under the new régime, under business enterprise, law and custom and religion teach only value for value received.

Mr. Phillips believed in value received, and practiced what he preached in literature as well as in journalism and other walks of life. (pp. 180-85)

In literature, as in journalism, he was out for results from start to finish, and he invariably got them. His native dramatic sense and his newspaper training taught him to specialize in stories of strong human interest, told in the kind of English that appeals lastingly to the better sort of newspaper readers in every large American city. In the course of time, from the plainest kind of statement of the plainest kind of facts, he evolved a technique that began to be big enough for his own art and the problems he handled; his last and best books are not only admirable examples of the art that conceals art, but they are veritable advances in the progress of constructive fiction, evolved and adapted to meet the literary and vital needs of the greatest number of readers on the broadest and firmest possible ground of inspiration and interest.

The art of Mr. Phillips grew with his life, and modern literature grew with it in no inappreciable or insignificant degree. In a widely quoted interview shortly before his death he said: "I have no mission, no purpose, no cult; I am just a novelist, telling as accurately as I can what I see and trying to hold my job with my readers." (p. 186)

In the interval of ten years between his death and the publication of his first work of fiction, besides numerous short stories and special articles, *The Worth of a Woman, The Treason of the Senate* and *The Reign of Gilt,* he managed to turn out nearly twenty novels. The majority of these average at least 100,000 words.

It is questionable if in the whole history of modern fiction since Balzac's time and Zola's, ten years' product of such solid, concentrated, comprehensive, far reaching and inspiring work has ever issued from the pen of any one man.

There is a closer kinship between the greater Frenchman and the American than mere passionate concentration in the work in hand year by year that Zola shared with both.

Phillips did not set to work of fixed purpose to construct a "Comedie Humaine," as did Balzac. None the less, in his novels viewed as a whole, he has achieved almost as comprehensive and constructive an account of early twentieth century American fundamentals as Balzac did of early nineteenth century life in France, in twice the number of volumes. Both have the same artist's and craftsman's conscientiousness, the same love of truth and its portrayal, the same directness of vision and clarity of style. Phillips, like his century, has the truer sense of cosmic proportion and the keener eye for essentials. Balzac wrote as an artist for aristocrats. Phillips wrote for the people as a trained newspaper man, in whom the science of journalistic and literary construction rapidly developed into an art and artistry of his own.

Any examination of the mere titles of his books—*The Great God Success, A Woman Ventures, Golden Fleece, The Master Rogue, The Plum Tree, The Deluge, The Cost, The Social Secretary, The Fortune Hunter, Her Serene Highness, The Second Generation, Light-Fingered Gentry, Old Wives for New, The Hungry Heart, White Magic, The Fashionable Adventures of Joshua Craig, The Husband's Story, The Grain of Dust,* and *The Price She Paid*—will go far to substantiate a part of these claims.

He began with the newspaper life that he knew from the inside out and the bottom up. His first novel, *The Great God Success,* 1901—which, in freshness, vigor, sincerity, literary finish and general human interest, ranks not only among the author's best books, but stands on its own merits as one of the important novels of late nineteenth century fiction in America—tells the story of a young newspaper man who went through the mill much as Mr. Phillips himself did. It is said that many of his own personal professional experiences are woven into the story.

Aside from the book's merit as mere literature, we recognize for the first time, as a new force in fiction, the author's sincere and uncompromising hatred of snobbery, of pretense, of conventional lies, of plutocratic and machine-made social distinctions, which in its intensity and breadth of scope is only rivaled in American letters by that of Mark Twain and [Frank] Norris. (pp. 187-89)

[*A Woman Ventures,* 1902], while well above the average of current American fiction, is comparatively unimportant as a literary product and a new indication of growth. In some ways it strikes one as younger and cruder than its predecessor; at the same time, it is significant of the author's point of view, the intense sincerity of his purpose and the effective democracy of his literary and personal standard.

For some time after this Mr. Phillips was at a loss to find himself. However, one feels instinctively as one reads book after book of his middle period, that the man's one aim is to tell the truth simply and effectively as he sees it; that sooner or later he is going to convince his readers that the real tragedies of life are not its melodramatic ones, but the tragedies of character and of economics: infinitely little, or infinitely degrading in their wholesale effect, which, consciously or unconsciously, are forming the very pattern and fabric of the lives of us all, through every waking and sleeping hour.

This period in the author's life coincided with one in the lives of his contemporaries, when the literature of the muck-rake got its name and its first intelligent and sympathetic hearing at the bar of public opinion.

If *Golden Fleece* [1903], *The Plum Tree,* [1905], *The Master Rogue,* [1903], *The Deluge,* [1905], and the rest of Mr. Phillips' muck-rake novels were temporarily symptomatic of the period and the campaign of popular education in things that concern us all; if as literature they were no better and no worse than *The Thirteenth District,* by Brand Whitlock, *The Memoirs of an American Citizen,* by Robert Herrick, *The Henchman,* by Mark Lee Luther, *The Minority,* by Frederic Trevor Hill, *The Boss,* by Alfred Henry Lewis, *J. Devlin, Boss,* by Churchill Williams, and dozens more of the same period and phase of American fiction, they would none the less deserve a more serious and extensive study both as literature and as human and sociological documents than there is space for here.

Considered separately, some of them, both as literature and as journalism, fall below the highest standard of the books by other authors quoted above; taken as a whole, they exhibit admirably Mr. Phillips' supreme capacity for getting hold of the essential facts in contemporary American life and translating them into a readable and stimulative popular language in the form of fiction.

It is easy to pick flaws in these books; it is easy to condemn them in one way or another on purely literary grounds; but when one considers that they form primarily a series of text-books for beginners in practical politics, it becomes plain that they are admirably adapted to their purpose.

The author is as sure of his facts as he is of the interest of the majority of his readers. He does not overstate diseased social and political conditions. He does not have to. He does not make his grafters and snobs in chief impossible or unconscionable variants of the average human type in America to-day. He makes them like his other characters, natural, human, interesting, and essentially characteristic products of a modern American environment for which the people in the mass are quite as much responsible as the men and women higher up.

The moral of the whole series, reiterated by Mr. Phillips, his contemporaries and predecessors from Lincoln down, is that the people in the long run get the kind of government they deserve; that snobbery is far more the product of those below, who look up to artificial standards, than of those above, who look down from them; that graft is the price that the people pay as a whole for individual indifference and inefficiency in public affairs.

In some ways, in these political novels, Mr. Phillips makes us out a pretty hard lot of citizens. At the same time he draws us true to life in our capacity to wake up to the facts that he sets forth, to appreciate them, and to act on them progressively. And the fact that this series of books, few of which showed any perceptible literary or sociological advance on the main arguments of their predecessors, were able to interest the American book-buying public so far and so long as they did, may be taken as fairly conclusive evidence of the man's own power of writing straight from the shoulder and the carrying force of the insurgent movement in American literature, which he as much as any man helped to start.

According to Mr. Calvin Winter, in *The Bookman* for February, 1911, "one gets quite effectively the whole range of Mr. Phillips' powers and also his weaknesses in the volumes that belong to the period of his mature development, the volumes produced within the last four or five years."

It is indicative of Mr. Winter's point of view that he attributes the real fault of Mr. Phillips' method of work, the real weakness of even his best achievements, to the fact

> that he is not merely the clear-eyed and impartial observer of life; he is always a partisan and reformer . . . of course, when you take one of Mr. Phillips's novels to pieces you discover that in its essence it is a problem novel; but this side of his work he has learned to disguise pretty cleverly. It is not so much the way in which he twists the lives of his characters in order to point a moral, but rather . . . the somewhat annoying fact that he is trying to do our thinking for us. . . . "

It does not take the experience of a critic like Mr. Winter to discover that the majority of Mr. Phillips's books are problem novels. A child could see it; and one of the facts that has probably escaped Mr. Winter's notice is that Mr. Phillips is writing not only for adults whose knowledge of the best fiction, ancient and modern, is inferior to that of the average well-read child of fourteen or fifteen, but also for the young Americans of to-day and to-morrow who are born to be partisans and reformers, in literature and out of it, as inevitably as men of Mr. Winter's type are born to be mildly pretentious spectators of life and art, sitters on the literary fence, and ineffectively destructive critics and cumberers of the earth.

Mr. Winter, in an essay of several thousand words— written shortly before the author's death—in which he finds himself forced to admit the novelist's breadth and depth of interest in the serious problems of life, and his outspoken fearlessness in handling them, shows small signs of appreciating Mr. Phillips' cumulative growth in power and fineness of craftsmanship.

He does suggest that Mr. Phillips must have learned something about the best French realism at the fountain head.

He tells us that the author's whole conception of what a novel should be is French rather than Anglo-Saxon; that he insists on seeing every human story as a cross-section of life—not as a little local cross-section, but as a part of a big inevitable and all-pervading human relationship stretching from the Atlantic to the Pacific. He says that the writer who sees each little human happening not as an isolated incident but as a detail, necessarily communicates to his readers an impression of bigness and vitality.

At the same time he asks why it is that so many of Mr. Phillips's books, starting with big ethical problems and a broad epic treatment, are so apt in the end to leave the impression of an isolated and exceptional human story instead of symbolizing some broad and universal principle.

He is inclined to quarrel with Mr. Phillips because he fails to symbolize, as Zola does in *L'argent, Le ventre de Paris* and *L'assommoir,* "vast symbolic monsters wreaking their malignant pleasure upon mankind." He suggests that Mr. Phillips reverses the usual process followed by writers of the epic type; that he finds his germ idea in a single character or incident, and builds from these, instead of starting with some ethical principle or psychological problem and then searching for characters and incidents that would best illustrate it. He complains that the novelist quite frequently pictures not what average people are doing under existing conditions, but what somewhat unusual people would in his opinion do under conditions just the reverse of those that exist. He instances, in support of this, the development under pressure of the heirs of the rich middle Western Manufacturer in *The Second Generation,* who disinherits his children (his son conditionally), for their own good; and the daughter of the New York capitalist who insists on marrying the young artist who has made up his mind to let no woman interfere with his work till he has reached a certain definite measure of success in his art.

It is possible that types like the young artist in question are more common even in New York than Mr. Winter seems to imagine; that girls like the one he eventually marries are on the increase there and elsewhere, and that rich men farther West who disinherit sons and daughters in a fair way to become worthless are not yet wholly obsolete.

Mr. Phillips was enough of a scientist to know that the type is sometimes best defined by its variants.

Mr. Winter is not yet enough of a critic to realize that Mr. Phillips's books are primarily novels of character and of American human nature evolved under contemporary economic storm and stress.

In his later books he has very little use for the more commonplace and subordinate types that go down, or barely hold their own in the struggle; or that remain stagnant on the surface of the social crust, as hopelessly slaves to conventions and artificial social distinctions as those that never emerge from below.

Quite as justly, both as man and artist, he has no more use for those Zolaesque "epic" themes, tending to emphasize an inevitable page of existence and an artificial fixity of social and economic conditions, which even to-day are still more characteristic of Europe than of America.

There is something about the atmosphere and the spirit of America to-day, outside New York and the adjacent Atlantic seaboard, that still justifies the proverb: "From shirt sleeves to shirt sleeves in three generations."

Mr. Phillips has seized upon this force and formula of the racial smelting pot, and has made it his own in his stories of the struggle to break through the barriers of caste and artificiality from below upward, and from above down.

Many of his characters begin as the victims of caste. Frequently we find these products of an environment of elaborate uselessness. Quite as frequently circumstances and their own desires force them to assert and develop themselves. The women that he chooses for his heroines go to work. The men that typify his heroes learn eventually that money, like the pursuit of it and its most obvious results, is not the only thing in life, and never can be. In the long run the stronger characters rise superior to their environment. In direct contrast, each book that follows this formula delineates other weaker and slighter personages who remain submerged, and the author's cross-section of life, in spite of apparent abnormalities to the superficial reader's mind, remains constructively true to life as the great majority of the plain people of America still see it to-day.

Mr. Phillips is here far more than an accurate and painstaking artist, handling with commendable thoroughness and increasing power the raw material of the life closest to him. He is a pioneer of that new movement in fiction of which Arnold Bennett in England and Herman Suderman in Germany are also notable examples. Such men deal with life directly and freely as an elementary fusion of environment and character, unhampered by any ultra-realistic, romantic, classical, epic or academic tradition or preconceived scheme of any sort, fostered or thrust upon them by third-rate critics or fourth-rate producers.

Such men, from Rabelais and Cervantes down to the present day, aim to get at the basic facts of life in the way most essential to the comprehension of the vast democratic majority of their readers, present and future. If they live, they evolve eventually a technique fit for their task, and the world stands eternally the richer for their works. If they die before the full fruition of their powers, as Frank Norris and David Graham Phillips did, none the less they have served to pioneer the way for others: their loss may be the world's gain by leaving their ultimate achievement not too hopelessly far in advance of the majority of their readers, the academic critics and partisans, and the young men and women who write, born to follow in their steps.

When Mr. Winter tells us that *The Second Generation,* 1907, is probably the best book to recommend to a reader approaching Mr. Phillips for the first time, because it is less likely to arouse antagonism than many others, and because it illustrates his strongest qualities, "his ability to give you the sense of life and action and the clash of many interests," we may have our reasonable doubts of the facts of the case and of Mr. Winter's appreciation of them. Similarly, when he says that the book "is to all practical interests a grown-up version of the story of the bad little boy

who went fishing on Sunday and was drowned and the good little boy who went to church and was rewarded with plum pudding."

It is true that before this he admits that the "graphic truth, rugged strength and sure swiftness of movement of the first part of the book show one that Mr. Phillips is one of the few contemporary American novelists that deserve to be taken seriously."

The theme of the book is stated in the language of the older generation ten or twenty years ago:

> It is the curse of the world, this inherited wealth. . . . Because of it humanity moves in circles instead of forward. The ground gained by the toiling generations is lost by the inheriting generations. And this accursed inheritance tempts men ever to long for and hope for that which they have not earned. God gave man a trial of the plan of living in idleness upon that which he had not earned, and man fell. Then God established the other plan, and through it man has been rising—but rising slowly and with many a backward slip, because he has tried to thwart the divine plan with the system of inheritance. Fortunately the great mass of mankind has nothing to leave to heirs, has no hope of inheritance. Thus no leaders have ever been developed in place of those destroyed by prosperity. . . . No wonder progress is slow when the leaders of each generation have to be developed from the bottom over again, and when the ideal of useful work is obscured by the false ideal of living without work.

Stated in more modern language we have here the biological truth that the fittest survive only through struggle, and that man, like all other animals, makes his best records under handicaps. Where the necessity for struggle is removed, the species or the race degenerates and inevitably falls a prey to those that are still struggling. This is as true in the world of character as in that of material things. (pp. 191-200)

Few men have written the literature of democracy more convincingly. Altogether *The Second Generation* is a big and inspiring book. Its one apparent defect in construction, the tragic and uncalled for death of one of the most lovable characters through the act of a madman, has a curious and convincing parallel in the life and death of the author himself. Mr. Phillips wrote of life not according to any artificial and pre-arranged literary or social scheme; but of life as it actually happens everywhere around us, day by day, in an America that the greed and negligence of the American people have filled with by-products of fanatic hatred and irresponsibility; products that the people of America are forced to-day, in one way or another, to pay for and reckon with.

This is the theme of *Light-Fingered Gentry,* 1907, which deals with the recent investigation into the scandals connected with the great insurance companies of New York City. (pp. 207-08)

Mr. Phillips postulates as his first principle of life and art that, in order to write a literature of contemporary American life which shall be real and lasting, one is forced to study and to represent the industrial conditions and the economic forces that have that life in the making. In this book he puts it in this way:

> To understand a human being in any or all of his or her aspects, however far removed from the apparently material, it is necessary to understand how the man or woman comes by the necessities of life—food, clothing, shelter. To study human nature either in the broad or in detail, leaving these matters out of account, is as if an anatomist were to try to understand the human body, having first taken away the vital organs and the arteries and veins. It is the method of the man's income that determines the man; and his paradings and posturings, his loves, hatreds, generosities, meannesses, all are either unimportant or but the surface signs of the deep, the real emotions that constitute the vital nucleus of the real man.
>
> In the material relations of a man or a woman, in the material relations of husband and wife, of parents and children, lie the ultimate, the true explanations of human conduct. This has always been so, in all ages and classes, and it will be so until the chief concern of the human animal, and therefore its chief compelling motive, ceases to be the pursuit of the necessities and luxuries that enable it to live from day to day and that safeguard it in old age. The filling and emptying and filling again of the purse perform towards the mental and moral life a function as vital as the emptying and filling again of the heart and lungs perform in the life of the body.
>
> (pp. 211-12)

If *The Second Generation* is a big, a significant, and an inspiring book, *Light-Fingered Gentry* is on the whole a bigger, a more significant, and a more inspiring one.

Mr. Winter passes over *White Magic* [1910] as "simply an innocuous little love story told with rather more explosive violence than the theme warrants."

The book's publishers have different views. According to them, Mr. Phillips shows us in his grim, humorous way some sketches of a portion of society life that many people fail to see the humor of at all.

Similarly with *The Fashionable Adventures of Joshua Craig* [1909]. Mr. Winter calls it a piece of cheap caricature. The publishers suggest that when Margaret Severance, reigning society beauty of Washington, marries her untamed Western politician, partly because she can't help it, and partly with the idea of civilizing him, and quite unexpectedly goes West with him to live, the *denouement,* while not pleasant from one point of view, is absolutely true. There is no doubt that here, as elsewhere at times, Mr. Phillips' social satire is both pointed and pitiless. It is no more than fair to suggest that as such it is on a par with the social commonplaces of the people that he attacks; and that to make an attack of the sort at all effective at headquarters, some such vigorous method was necessary to prick the thick hides and the insufferable self-complacency of the people at whom the satire was aimed.

Mr. Winter considers *The Hungry Heart* [1909], like *The Husband's Story* [1910], one of the two books that exhibit Mr. Phillips' ripest powers, possibly because it is conceived and executed more in the conventional French style and method of the eternal triangle, than in the manner that Mr. Phillips has made distinctively American and his own. According to Mr. Winter, this book deserves high praise as a piece of careful construction. Later he proceeds to quarrel with the author because, unconventionally, in the French sense, the husband takes his wife back after she has proved the worthlessness of the other man.

As a matter of fact, this book is one of Mr. Phillips' comparative failures, because the careful construction, which Mr. Winter praises, cramps the author's talent for large effects and restricts the action of a long book to a little rural world of four characters. The drifting apart of the husband and wife through his absorption in science, and his failure to see that she needs some vital interest in her life beyond dress and housekeeping, is carefully worked out—too carefully. The reader is inclined to sympathize with the wife's monotony and impatience through the early part of the book. The climax and the reconciliation are admirably executed. The husband, contrary to Mr. Winter's opinion, is less "a conventional, conservative type" than a man of science. As such he has sense enough to see that what has happened has been quite as much his own fault as his wife's, and to realize at the end that they have both grown stronger and better for the experience.

This book, while hardly fitted in itself to appreciably increase Mr. Phillips' popularity or rank in the literary world, forms an interesting connecting link between *Old Wives for New,* 1908, and *The Husband's Story.*

The former book is not a pleasant one. It is frankly realistic, at times brutally so. According to Mr. Winter, the real importance of this book is that

> it sets forth quite pitilessly the gradual estrangement that arises between a husband and wife in the course of long years through the woman's sloth and selfishness and gratification of all her whims. . . . What he has done is to show us first in a brief prelude the sudden ardor of a boy-and-girl attachment, each caught by the mere physical charm of youth and health and high spirits and rushing into a marriage with no firm basis of mutual understanding.
>
> Then he skips an interval of about twenty years and takes us into the intimate life of this same couple, showing us with a frankness of speech and of thought that is almost cruel in its unsparing realism, the physical and mental degeneration of the woman, fat and old and slovenly before her time, and the unspoken repulsion felt by the man who has kept himself young, alert and thoroughly modern in outward appearance as well as in spirit.
>
> The situation is complicated by the presence of two grown children, a son and a daughter, who see unwillingly the approaching crisis and realize their helplessness to ward it off. Such a situation in real life may solve itself in any one of fifty different ways.

What Mr. Phillips has chosen to do is to bring the husband in contact with a young woman who represents everything in which his own wife is lacking. And although the man fights for a long time against temptation, in the end he obtains freedom from the old wife through the divorce court and promptly replaces her with the new.

There is probably no other American novel that gives us with such direct and unflinching clairvoyance the sordid, repellent, intimate little details of a mistaken marriage that slowly but surely culminates in a sort of physical nausea and an inevitable separation.

Mr. Winter is inclined to feel that there is a heartless immorality in the story of the husband's deliberate and unrelenting progress towards freedom.

Judged by the modern test, that the difference between morality and immorality is that between construction and destruction of power, the wife in question is quite as immoral as the husband, if not more so. Their eventual separation, in one way or another, is inevitable; and here again it is evident that Mr. Phillips has meant to symbolize by these two characters an increasing class of American husbands and wives. Mr. Phillips tells the story with the terse impartiality of the star reporter on a conservative sheet. He recognizes that certain causes produce certain results, and that it is his business to make us see this. And he does make us see it, in this case as well as in the case of the husband's business associate, who is murdered in a Tenderloin resort as a result of a life of periodic licentiousness, carefully calculated and concealed.

The story of the decline and fall of the cast-off wife is focussed in two words: candy and corsets. Here again one is forced to realize that this woman is typical of a large and increasing class of American women who may be briefly characterized as home breakers rather than home makers. When not on dress parade, she slumps and slouches inevitably. She is slovenly, she is gluttonous, she is helpless and inert, in mind, body and soul.

When at last, warned by threats of her husband's desertion, she rouses herself feebly to try to win him back, the account of her own, her maid's and her *corsetières'* maneuvers with an impossible cage of silk and steel that is a very straight-jacket of torment to her, is at once ludicrous and tragic. Perusal of this part of the book is far from pleasant: people who enjoy the doubtful felicity of living in the part of the world here portrayed have ample reason to know that the reality is still less so.

Old Wives for New is Mr. Phillips' strongest piece of realism. For concentrated and consistent power in this respect, outside of Frank Norris's *McTeague,* there is not another American novel to equal or rival it. In many ways it is a far more artistic book, judged from a purely literary standpoint, than may appear superficially on a first or a second reading. It ranks easily among the three or four best and strongest of his books.

The same may be said of *The Husband's Story* though here the realism is modified and colored by its telling in the first person in the mouth of a New York captain of industry, the father of an American duchess, and the former husband of an Italian princess.

Mr. Winter says of this book:

> A large part of the merit of this undeniably big novel lies in what it merely implies, instead of what it says. To conceive a story of this sort is something in itself to be proud of, but to conceive of telling it through the husband's lips was a stroke of genius. . . . It is a ruthless indictment of the unfitness of a certain type of American woman to undertake the duties of wife and mother and housemaker . . . the whole intimate drama of a pushing, climbing couple, who start from sordid beginnings in an obscure little town in New Jersey . . . is given from the husband's point of view with a grim and unsparing irony.

Mr. Winter thinks that the irony lies in the husband's unconscious portrayal of himself. He believes that Mr. Phillips thought so too, and considers this a point that few readers detect. He considers the husband equally responsible with the wife for the failure of their marriage, and thinks this was the impression that Mr. Phillips intended to convey.

The fact is that Edna Loring typifies a class of American women who have become impossible to everyone who is not content to take them at their own valuation, or to pretend to. Her husband typifies a class of American business and professional men who have become guilty, through contributory negligence, of the supreme uselessness and artificiality displayed by their wives and daughters, and who are rapidly waking up to the fact.

In this case Mr. Phillips chooses to represent Godfrey Loring, a man who outgrows his wife and his own early standards, who is shrewd enough to see through them both, who is acute enough to realize that anywhere short of a desert island Edna Loring, New York society leader and mother of her American duchess, is hopeless as a life companion for him, who is sane enough after this realization to appreciate the advantages of a real wife and a real home and children, and who is determined enough, once his wife has given him a legitimate excuse for seeking them elsewhere, to hold her to the bond of the contract of separation she has herself proposed.

In this section of the book, before and after, there is abundant room for irony. Most of it, however, is irony of which the author, the man who tells the story, and the average reader are equally and at once aware. (pp. 216-22)

Mr. Winter has tried, inconclusively, to interpret *The Husband's Story* from a woman's point of view. Later we see what a woman has to say about it. In a letter to the *New York Times'* Literary Supplement for January 29th, 1911, Mrs. Annie Nathan Meyer declares:

> Here are three quotations from David Graham Phillips's latest novel, *The Husband's Story.* I could cull any number like them. In fact, there are so many, and they are so trenchant, so searching, that one almost wonders that the shot which cut short the career of the brilliant author was fired by a man:

"Probe to the bottom of any of the present-day activities of the American woman—I care not what it may be, church or lecture, suffrage movement or tenement reform—and you will discover the bacillus of society position biting merrily away at her.

"The cruellest indictment of the intellect of woman is the crude, archaic, futile, and unimaginative way in which is carried on the part of life that is woman's peculiar work—or, rather, is messed, muddled, slopped, and neglected.

"It may be that woman will some day develop another and higher sphere for herself. But first she would do well to learn to fill the sphere she now rattles round in, like one dry pea in a ten-gallon can."

How the American woman is taking what is to me the most poignant arraignment of her that has yet appeared I do not know. Private mutterings of wrath I have heard, but no more. . . . Unfaltering, mercilessly, Mr. Phillips has exposed the absurd pretentions of the American woman. His heroine and her kind are held up as bungling housekeepers, callous seekers after their own pleasure, ignorant mothers, slave-drivers to their good-natured, indifferent, woman-worshiping, woman-despising, money-making husbands. Furthermore, they are empty-headed and frivolous, both vain and colossally conceited. Of course, it is easy to call names. But Mr. Phillips does much more than that: he gives us a living, breathing woman, clean-cut in outline, yet amazingly subtle. He is not content, for instance, with painting his heroine as lazy, for the American woman is anything but lazy. He is penetrating enough to know that she is lazy only where she is indifferent. He does not paint her as hopelessly stupid, for he knows that in her own little line of social activities she is a general—Napoleonic even if Lilliputian. How well he hits the nail on the head:

"It was impossible to interest her in anything worth while. But as to the things in which she was interested, none could have thought more clearly or keenly, or could have acted with more vigor and effect."

In nothing else does he show better his skillful handling of the queer contradictions of woman than in making his wife at the beginning utterly indifferent to the food she provides for the bread-winner of the family, reducing him to the tender mercies of the delicatessen dealer, tackling the intricate problems of cooking with the serene cocksureness of complete ignorance, and yet strangely capable of self-denial and a devoted, conscientious study of nutriment for herself and daughter when she discovers that both complexion and figure depend on it. . . .

In one way the book is peculiarly impressive. If it dealt with one stratum of society alone, it would be easy to let it pass as an indictment of a small number of women only. But the first chapter starts with the squalor of Edna Wheatlands' childhood, shows her jilted by an eight-dollar-a-week clerk, takes her through the period of her honeymoon in the "forty-dollar flat," gorgeous with "its brave show of red plush," carries her along through middle-class gentility, thence by the leaps and bounds of a successful business man to the lower fringe of society, painfully working up to the upper crust, and finally bursting through into the aristocracy of Europe. And in each setting it is undeniable that the strictures on the "eternal feminine" ring equally true.

The characterization is superb. Difficult as it is, he has made us feel that the slatternly, down-at-the-heels bride of the early chapters is the same woman who later relentlessly carves the resplendent future of herself and daughter. The husband's cynical wonder at the extraordinary incompetence of women is the same whether it is aimed at the servantless mistress of the stuffy flat or the elegant dame of the fashionable mansion, helpless under the sway of her thirty-five minions. "A wife," he cries, "no more fitted to be a wife than the office-boy is fitted to step in and take the president's job."

Into one tradition after another he has charged with his gall-steeped pen. The woman is no homemaker, only a brazen schemer to achieve a more and more costly environment of discomfort. She is no mother; she knows nothing about the real needs of children, she is keen only for their world success. She is not the inspirer of her husband; she likes to pose as such, but she is interested in his business only for what there is in it for her, and in a crisis she is the last person to whom he would appeal for comfort, idealism, or even plain, business honesty.

And, finally, he boasts that he "has pricked the bubble of the American woman's pretense of superior culture." This undoubtedly took more courage than anything else he has done. Strangely enough, women are not so ashamed to admit that they are poor wives, and worse mothers; but when you take from them the glory of upholding the tradition of refinement and culture, then the blow hurts. How he laughs at those "expert smatterers," "with a little miseducation befogging their mind." But the deepest sting is here:

"The American woman fancies she is growing away from the American man. The truth is, that while she is sitting still, the American man is growing away from her."

Of course, as I intimated at the beginning, this is not pleasant reading for smug women, bursting with self-praise and scorn of the other sex. It is certainly much pleasanter to be assured (as they will find plenty of books to assure them) that the American women are the most wonderful women in the world, than to be told the plain truth that they are the most spoiled, the most incompetent in the things that count, and the hardest on their husbands, demanding more and giving less than any other women in the world.

These are the views of a woman that is well known in New

York, as an anti-woman-suffragist and educator of prominence. (pp. 223-27)

It is this same philosophy that *The Grain of Dust,* 1911, helps to exemplify.

The sale of this novel, published as a serial in *The Saturday Evening Post* at the time of the author's death, already threatens to equal or exceed that of any of Mr. Phillips' former works. Dramatized by Louis Evan Shipman, its success as a play in Chicago has been immediate and meteoric.

Save *The Worth of a Woman* [1908], Mr. Phillips has never written anything that appeals more directly and dramatically to all sorts and conditions of Americans of both sexes than this story of a New York corporation lawyer who comes within an ace of wrecking himself hopelessly through his infatuation for a stenographer in his own office, and who "comes back" after his long deferred marriage to her with increased power and usefulness in both harsher and more humane business and social relations.

Opinions, critical and commonplace, may vary considerably about the character of Frederic Norman, and the possible exaggeration of the faults and virtues of the type that Mr. Phillips has focussed in this extremely interesting and individualized American.

There can be but one verdict, however, as to the author's success with Dorothy Hallowell. In all his long gallery of American women of to-day she shines supreme. It is hardly too much to say that in all American fiction since Hester Prynne there are few women in the same class with her as a masterly example of character-drawing, reflecting perfectly the environment of which she is herself a part.

One may go further and suggest that, as a literary creation, she challenges comparison with Becky Sharp and the best of Balzac's women, or those of any novelist with whom accurate fidelity to life is the first and the final motive and accomplishment.

Almost equally admirable are the character-drawings of Norman's sister and his fiancée in his own class at the beginning of the story. The men in the book, with the exception of Norman himself—Dorothy's father, who bears a striking resemblance to the father of Neva Armstrong in *Light-Fingered Gentry,* and Fred Tetlow, Norman's partner and financial lifeline—are little more than sharply delineated figures in the background or middle distance. Tetlow, like Dorothy, is wonderfully human, and an admirable example of the pressure of Broadway and Wall Street environment upon human material commonplace in its strength and weakness to-day.

Just how far or how much Mr. Phillips intended to symbolize in him, in Norman, in the women of Norman's class, in Dorothy and her father, does not concern us intimately at present. The story as a story stands by itself. As such it is Mr. Phillips' most fascinating and brilliant effort since *The Great God Success.* At the same time, in common with *Old Wives for New* and *The Husband's Story,* it affords an adequate vehicle for the diffusion of the author's ideas of human nature under pressure in New York

and elsewhere in Twentieth Century America. (pp. 233-35)

Beside it *The Conflict,* 1911, judged as literature and a contemporary document of wide human appeal and assisting human interest, is inconsiderable. As a sociological tract, where the author, violating his own published creed of an impartial interpreter of life as he sees it, preached flatfooted Socialism in everything but the name, it reminds us uninspiringly of the later literary failures of Zola and Tolstoy.

The old sincerity is there still. The old dexterity in adapting situations and evolving characters to voice the author's views is still apparent. The old shrewdness and directness in unmasking the social and political shams of America in the making may stimulate and divert us by the way.

But at the end of the long journey of nearly four hundred close pages, we find ourselves, if we reach the end at all, at practically the same place where we started from in the first quarter of the book; and there is a disposition to ask ourselves whether the author has not wasted his time and our own.

As a piece of special pleading, his apparent intolerance of every phase of modern life, save those represented directly by the work of scientists and the manual labor that he tends to deify, defeats itself; and to any candid mind, disposed to accept gradually the sort of Socialism that evolves and proves its fitness to survive and to adapt itself to Twentieth Century conditions, Mr. Phillips' social criticism and philosophy, as voiced in *The Conflict,* displays itself as far more destructive than constructive; far more characteristic of the intolerant and unbalanced fanatic than of the shrewd and penetrating critic and interpreter of life that he has proved himself in the best of his earlier books.

Characters as pronounced as that of David Graham Phillips are certain to have the defects of their qualities. The man's characteristic and intense hatred of injustice, snobbery, pretentiousness, cruelty and falsehood was ingrained in the very fiber of him and was inevitably constrained to color everything that he wrote.

If in *The Conflict,* whose keynote is "Civilization means property as yet. And it doesn't mean men and women as yet. So to know the men and the women we look at the property"; the author's sincere and militant passion on behalf of the fundamental human rights and the Square Deal for those who are farthest from it, has led him to overstate his case. No such fault can be found with *George Helm,* 1912, first published as a series of short stories in *The Cosmopolitan.* (pp. 237-38)

The Price She Paid, 1912, is the story of an American girl who raises herself from fashionable obscurity to success as a singer of grand opera in the high places where sex and the world's applause are mere incidents in the day's work. It is a modern version, intensely interesting and readable from cover to cover, of "many are called, but few are chosen"—and fewer still choose and sustain themselves. (p. 239)

Mildred Gower, like the other characters in the book, does not cover the whole ground; she does not answer every demand; she does not solve or throw light upon every problem of the women with careers and without them, in New York and elsewhere, of whom and for whom Mr. Phillips wrote.

At the same time, she comes nearer perhaps to doing all this than any character in any twentieth century novel. The author has made of her not only a very exceptional and inspiring heroine, but also a tremendously and intensely natural and interesting character, and a human personality far more real, far more vital, far more modern and American in the best sense of the words, than nine-tenths of the women of flesh and blood who fail or succeed, or seem to succeed, at her own or any other calling or profession.

From first to last, even more than in his other books, he is absolutely merciless to every shred and symptom of hypocrisy, of self-deception, of self-excuse and self-indulgence.

It is more than the very X-ray photography of truth, warped and disguised in a welter of human meannesses, human prejudices, human intolerances and human ineptitudes: it is a virtual vivisection of human motives—the muscles of the mind and the soul, their underlying bony structure and basic instincts, and their overlapping and superficial adipose tissue of habit and impulse. It is sordid and revolting in some details at first. Later it is less and less brutally compelling, more and more intellectually satisfying and fascinating, as wider areas and more and more intricately ramifying networks of social and individual motor and sensory nerves are exposed. Finally the book becomes illuminating and ennobling in greater or less degree, according to the capacity of the reader to bring much or little to the reading of this modern masterpiece.

Through Mildred and the rest; through her mother, who is weakly and pretentiously ladylike in the most superficially snobbish acceptance of the term *lady* that Mr. Phillips has always abhorred; through Presby, her father-in-law, who is weakly and maliciously masculine; through General Bill Siddall, who knows no limits beyond which his egotism will not go when anyone or anything stands in its way, and who is at least made to seem possible if not probable; through Stanley Baird, who is a fair example of New York clubman and snob, naturally rather fine than coarse, rather adequate than futile, with too much money and too little incentive; through Agnes Belloc, who is one of the best characters in the book and a very significant sign of the times in New England and New York to-day; through Cyrilla Brindley, who is about as near perfect in the human and literary sense as any character one meets or reads about; through Jennings, Crossley and Ransdell, all admirably conceived and executed types and products of their peculiar environments; through Donald Keith, who at first, like Bill Siddall, seems keyed a bit too high, conceived in extremes a bit too glaring and impossible for mere flesh and blood, and who yet, like the little general of the sky-blue pajamas and the needle-sharp mustache and imperial points, is somehow made to compare with the others and blend admirably in the general grouping; through Mildred herself; through the three Mildreds: the first Mildred that we know and read about (or do not care to know and read about) everywhere in American life and literature and journalism to-day; the Mildred of the reconstruction period—inconsistent, capricious, luxurious, idle, industrious, determined, panic-stricken and trembling, eminently impressive and successful at moments in the reaction from sheer terror and despair and in the peculiar blend of knowledge and ignorance that carries her blindly past certain pitfalls and makes light of others; the Mildred of the last two chapters, as she emerges and stands the acid test of seeing and feeling fully how life may be good though it may seem to be based on evil, how it may be ideal and idealized through the translation of the most prosaic details of the home and marketplace into inspired and inspiring action and aspiration: in these the author strips off all masks, bares the meanest and most remote of motives, shows us human and bestial nature in all its blindness and deformity, its inveterate and ineradicable vanity and slant towards self-deception and self-excuse.

He handles self-conceit and self-sufficiency, pretense and plausible egotism as a great surgeon does a cancer. He dissects its widely branching roots and rootlets to the limit. And then, when he has demonstrated, step by step and inch by inch, the nature and the full extent of the disease, with a logic, an intuition and a human sympathy that no novelist has ever shown before; when he has shown all this to all whose gray matter, whose nerves, whose vitality, are still sufficiently unimpaired to render hope of a cure possible or probable, then he shows them what may gradually be done in the way of building up new tissue to take the place of that which has been diseased and excised.

Mr. Phillips's style and general method has been sufficiently commented on already. Here, as in many of his other books, one might start at the first chapter and quote through to the last, paragraph after paragraph and page after page of shrewd common sense, sound philosophy and social insight that, standing alone, sufficiently explains and justifies itself; that, read in the ordinary course of the narrative, fits into the general design as a gem into its setting, as a pregnant mouth or eye into the vital expression of a strong and noble face. (pp. 244-47)

Perhaps the characters that fit themselves best to play the large parts in life, and certainly the minds of something like the first order, are those that react best on environment as they move and grow; those that have the Cosmos in themselves most highly evolved and sensitized in an infinity of directions as a planet has sides; that are superficial in their sensory impressions and more or less immediate reactions to sense only in so far as such sudden reactions serve to inform and stimulate the larger forces lying latent beneath into transient stages of growth.

Minds and characters of the first order of effectiveness, ancient and modern, like Cecil Rhodes and Theodore Roosevelt, Cæsar and Alexander (whom Mr. Phillips instances), and the notable women who have had at once the most feminine and masculine egos of all history, may be cited in this category.

The mind of David Graham Phillips was of this order, at

least in its deep and broad humanity and in its vital and immediate response to certain of the most pressing and appalling problems of the life of his day in Twentieth Century America. Within his limitations, he fashioned for himself and for others the supremely efficient art and the instrument that Frank Norris has defined the novel in the hands of a modern master to be; and to this task he gave himself according to the best traditions of his country and his time; strenuously, unsparingly, humanly, justly, freely, fairly and effectively in the service of his art and the larger service of life that art interprets.

He learned to write through long toil and methodical daily and nightly application, very much as he makes his latest heroine learn to sing—as the birds sing naturally, freely with a vital fullness and intensity of tone that can appeal at once to the ear and heart of child and savant, of musical or literary critic, of tired business man and worldly woman, of saint and sinner, of the idle and frivolous, and the acknowledged specialists of the world's first fighting lines in other successful professional work.

This he did not all at once, not spectacularly at the start, nor perfectly in his technique as the greatest opera singers have sung at their débuts. His style was still a bit crude at the last—often purposely so, in view of the audience he had to reach. His range and flexibility of attack was still a bit limited. The rôles in which his chief characters were cast still showed the promise rather than the performance of variation that might in time have made of his novels a completer and more representative comedy of the human life of his time than Balzac or any other novelist ever wrote or tried to write.

As it was, the strength and intensity, the courage of his convictions, the depth and breadth and warm human passion of his sympathies, have saved him at his best to America and the world for all time. Where Balzac failed, he succeeded, largely as his opera singers succeed—through eternal daily and nightly discipline and slowly increasing power of working intelligently and pertinaciously—until he evolved in himself the genius which he himself defines as not only the infinite capacity for taking pains (that goes without saying in his scheme of life), but the habit of colossal self-denial intelligently directed to a vital and inspiring end.

Balzac, as Mr. James has pointed out, loved his characters, as a craftsman does—for themselves and what he made of them.

Phillips has some share of this artist-affection for his human mouthpieces, but over and above and beyond this, he loves them and he uses them, and the novels of which they form the exponents but not the main argument, to testify to the truth that appears in and through and beyond them.

Balzac saw life as an artist, Phillips as an artist and scientist. And any intelligent and comprehensive reading or re-reading of Balzac first amuses and stimulates, then saddens; that of Phillips first saddens, then liberates and inspires. Like all great artists, both reflect admirably the divine and changing tempers of their times and environments.

Balzac wrote in an era of reaction and in a city of cynicism and sophistication that saw life as Mr. James and any worldly woman see it—thrilling in its trivialities, but intensely interesting and shamefully human in its decadence.

Phillips' moral vivisections are those of the surgeon and scientist who sees in disease a symptom of vitality, of health and strength renewed. As such he is characteristically American, an intensely modern exemplar and prophet of twentieth century unrest and reconstruction.

Like the majority of the men and women who have done things in America in the past, and in the present century, he was out for results. And he did not fail to find them. Even among the American women of the conventional upper class that he hit the hardest, he gradually won to a partial recognition of his sincerity and breadth and depth of social analysis. Mrs. Meyer has already testified to this forcibly.

It is to another American woman, Mrs. Anna S. Walling, who was privileged to know him, that we owe the most searching analysis of his character and ideals of service to his country and his century that has yet been published.

In an article published in *The Saturday Evening Post* of October 21, 1911, Mrs. Walling tells us:

> He was a radical. Yet, living among radicals as we did, I found him different from them in that he was objective and held himself aloof from clique, party or even movement. His radicalism was a thing apart from his life, and not life itself. Where they were merged in their cause, abandoned without reserve to the exigencies of the movement, he was always himself, with a programme of his own, one not dependent on any outside force. But his individualism was not of the kind that made him put his ambitions before his ideals. He was an idealist, as are all radicals. One could say his work chose him, so great was his devotion to the ideas he promulgated. Unlike some other writers who go farther than he and call themselves Socialists, but whose subjects are conventional or in contradiction to the basic principles of progressive thought, he in all his work had one aim—to unmask his time and to pursue it to the bitter end.

(pp. 248-52)

Certainly, since the days of Emerson, no American writer of wide circulation has spoken with so inspiring and so searching a voice to the hearts and minds of his fellow-countrymen and women.

During his lifetime he got his grip unmistakably upon the pulse of our national consciousness. Though he is dead, his grasp on it still remains.

And it is probable that Emerson himself will be ranked no higher by posterity, as a prophet of America and democracy and a regenerative force and stimulus, than this trained reporter and journalist and middle-Western product of Princeton and Park Row, who made himself a world novelist by main force, and who, true to the best ethics of his breed and profession, went for legitimate results and got them. (p. 253)

John Curtis Underwood, "David Graham Phillips and Results," in his Literature and Insurgency: Ten Studies in Racial Evolution, *Mitchell Kennerley, 1914, pp. 179-253.*

The New Republic   (essay date 1917)

[*In the following excerpt, the critic contends that despite its faults* Susan Lenox *is Phillips's best novel.*]

It is a deep experience to read **Susan Lenox.** Not every one can give time to a novel so prodigiously long, especially by a writer who never ceased to be boyishly melodramatic, but for all its thousand pages and for all its imperfections **Susan Lenox** is one story in a myriad. It is a study that one feels impelled to criticize. To see it aright one must go to it with compensatory glasses, though the glare of it does not at all destroy the interest which Phillips arouses about his **Susan Lenox,** or the sense he creates of a character valuable and stimulating, or of an adventure plausible and grim. The flaws of David Graham Phillips appear in this book. They affect his work in such a manner that it seems merely loose-mouthed to call him great. But these defects simply impair the confidence and response necessary to a free enjoyment of any artist. It is only in youthfulness that creative half-gods, like Phillips, are treated harshly, that spirits struggling with the clay are easily and glibly disdained.

David Graham Phillips was a man of strong imagination and exceedingly vigorous sympathies, who undertook not merely to depict life but to determine the interpretation that one should put on it. He so far stepped beyond his function as an artist in imposing his interpretation that to read him is to be constantly aware of thumping philosophy and sophomoric excursions and alarums. One feels how tremendously in this instance he was seized by the reality of Susan Lenox, how her personality wrapt him, how her vividness and character and mystery became a personal epic on which he was rejoiced to lavish his powers. One also feels, however, a natural tendency in him to suppose that because he could imagine a thing vividly and "document" it, it must therefore have substance. He was capable of becoming quite possessed by anything that sprang out of his own so-called inner consciousness, and of inventing without regard for genuine ratification a swiftly moving drama that had everything but psychological specific gravity. He lacked, in short, the corrective of cool sense. He was not a complacent romancer. He was an intensely serious romancer, either vehemently asserting that people ought to be entirely different or that people cannot be expected to be different at all. But his imagination carried him off his feet so easily that he had no idea he was often railing against a world which was not really living according to his indictment. Nothing could have saved him but a sense of comedy which he probably would have deemed meanly disloyal to his own heroical expectations of life.

If there is one thing on earth that every one does feel is heroic it is self-reliance. It does not matter an atom whether it is Elbert Hubbard writing of the message to Garcia or Henry James portraying Newman in *The American,* every one is thrilled to discern at the core of a human being the clear, hard, jeweled integrity which means that in extremity a man can and will answer for himself. Phillips worshipped self-reliance and it gave him a chivalrous joy to write a book revealing it in a young American woman whom circumstances thrust through seven hells. Using all his documentary resources to bring out the hellishness that Susan Lenox encountered in narrow Indiana and Babylonish New York, Phillips sought to relate his notion of her heroism to his horror of woman's debased economic condition. The result, as Mr. R. W. Chambers says in his introduction, is stupendous and overwhelming; but it is derived from such complications of fact and fancy and requires assent to such queer psychology, one can scarcely swallow it without critical qualm.

The narrative of **Susan Lenox** must be reported if one is to grasp the bearing of any criticism. The author knew Indiana extremely well and he is at his happiest in opening the story at Sutherland, where Susan lives when the tale begins. Susan does not know she is an illegitimate child. She is being brought up in the bourgeois home of her aunt and uncle and has the same life as her cousin Ruth, both of them about seventeen. Susan is the beauty of the town, clear, direct, spirited, unspoiled. Her charm of mind and character is instantly conveyed. A youth makes love to her, her aunt and cousin are envious, the truth as to her illegitimacy is broken to her brutally, the youth's attitude is crass and disillusioning, she takes her fate bravely in her hands and strikes out to Cincinnati. She is dragged back next day to "Uncle Zeke's," on his remote farm, and is forced to marry an oaf of a farmer. On her bridal night she escapes. Thus within two days she is outraged in folkways that Phillips makes at once heartrending and credible.

On her escape she is aided by a newspaper man on vacation, Spenser, but by accident she loses him and the money he gave her and is forced to appeal to a river theatrical troupe. The kindly manager takes her on to sing ballads, and nothing worse than ordinary vagabondage befalls her until their theatre-barge is sunk in a collision and she and the elderly protective manager are stranded in Cincinnati. He becomes ill before he has placed her as a singer and to provide for him she tries the Cincinnati theatrical agents. The first is a repulsive, lecherous old man. He makes indecent advances to her. She then tries to get work in a department store, hopelessly fails, wanders to a park, is picked up by a friendly youth, goes to lunch with him, makes up her benumbed and desperate mind that she is an "outcast," and to get money for her benefactor goes to a "first-class quiet place" with the youth. With the money she has earned in the spirit of Monna Vanna she flies to the hospital, to find that her guide and philosopher is dead.

She is to meet the youth at the rendezvous-house again. "Free to soar or sink," she chooses the hard route, obtains work at a paper-box factory at $3 a week. Phillips indicates that her only alternative to slaving in the factory is slave-driving there, and emphasizes the sordid misery and helplessness of her detached position. She lives with a kind family in a loathsome tenement and stands it with her usual incommunicative calm until their house is burned out and the father and mother killed. The stolid son proposes to make her his mistress, but she decides instead, after a pitiless struggle, to go on the street with Etta, the sister. Her first man on the freezing night she starts is drunken. She earns $5. Then she and Etta meet two affluent college youths and spend a week with them. With a margin left after she has had the food and clothes she craved in the hideous tenement-life, she seeks her creditor, Spenser. Pride, which did not keep her from becoming a prostitute, restrained her from seeking him previously. Before their evening is over they plan to strike hands and risk their fortunes in New York.

Spenser wants to be a playwright and Susan wants to be an actress, but her love for him is darkened by his attitude toward her past. Her persuasion that she is dragging him down leads her to go away in search of work. She finds it as a cloak model. The first evening of her employment she is taken out to dinner by an important western buyer, and, fortified by champagne, acquiesces to his terms as a bargainer. Her disgust at this condition to her success as a cloak model causes her to accept factory work once more. She becomes a hat trimmer at $4 a week. After six months of this she is desperate and reckless. Her vision of the filth and drudgery of the future is too black to endure. She gets all her resources together and goes up town to try her fortune again. She picks up a man who takes her to Martin's. Later, at a dance, she acquires a new man, and as a result with $43 capital starts in the Tenderloin. Unable to go through with it, until all her reserve is gone, she is eventually taken in hand by a superb young Italian, who has an arrangement with the police; and on whisky, after he has beaten her up, she goes to work on the street. After five months of it she and he quarrel. He tries to beat her again, but she is more than his match in nerve and in the struggle she nearly kills him. She flees for safety to the Bowery. There she looks for a job as a singer in a café, is offered a try-out, is drugged that evening, imprisoned, and barely escapes. Her work as singer is not remunerative and now she becomes a Grand street prostitute. Her accumulation of $31 is stolen by a lobby gow. She sinks to opium. In a dreadful joint she comes across Spenser, now a bum through drink, and at last she has something to live for. He develops typhoid. To take care of him she has to earn $50 a week on the streets, but an introduction Spenser gives her throws her across the path of a great playwright, called Brent, who, for the first time in her twenty-one years of life, gives her a chance to earn an honest living wage.

Brent is interested in Susan as a human being. He wants to train her for the stage, and her self-reliance and practical imagination at last come into play. It is only the misfortune of his abrupt departure for Europe and Spenser's utter inadequacy that fling her back on sex as a source of income—this time as the cool and reasoning mistress of the Italian, who was once her "partner" and has become respectable and wants her as running mate. With his fortune to live up to they go to Paris together. They fall in with Brent eventually, and the climax of the story is her emergence as a deep, candid, firm, self-possessed individual, in her relations with these two exceptional men.

There is only one deadly charge to make against this story—it is an epic of feminine courage that required for its plausibility a consistent exaggeration of the difficulties of women in industry and a humorlessly romantic view of prostitution. It is easy to sympathize with David Graham Phillips in his desire to show what the filthy exigencies of a sub-minimum wage can be, and it is impossible not to join him at times in feeling to the limit a greater horror at economic prostitution than at any other. But is Phillips realistic about sexual prostitution in general, or in particular about Susan Lenox's supposedly insulated experience of it? Prostitution, says Abraham Flexner, is

> everywhere purely mercenary, everywhere rapacious, everywhere perverse, diseased, sordid, vulgar, and almost always filthy. In her bloom the Parisian cocotte possesses a bit of Gallic grace and verbal cleverness that is perhaps denied to English, German or Scandinavian women of the same class. But it is soon brushed away by excess, drink and perversion. The refined courtesan of the books is practically as rare in Paris as in London and Berlin.

Mr. Flexner asks:

> Why do we object to prostitution at all? Obviously, it is repugnant for one or more of several reasons: in the first place, because of the personal demoralization it entails; in the second, because of economic waste; again, because it is by far the main factor in the spread of venereal disease; finally, because of its intimate association with disorder or crime. . . . Part-time prostitution, occasional prostitution, pretentious prostitution—all the various kinds and grades above enumerated naturally and inevitably conduce to similar results.

It is the complete omission of several of these ungrateful considerations that marks the "fall" of Susan Lenox as a romanticism. Phillips was so enamored of his master-spirited girl that he was going to see Susan Lenox through the whole process without admitting one touch of weakness or deterioration, and if he kept her drunk a good deal of the time, and part of the time under morphine, he was careful to explain that she had a magnificent constitution, and rebounded into normal spirits and activities as soon as she got a good income.

Yet apart from these preposterous exaggerations, natural to a man who had no comedy, *Susan Lenox* is a story that moved and impressed this reader deeply. It may give a young reader an absurd idea of male voracity, or it may grievously disappoint a person in search of the erotic, otherwise it is a performance of indubitable vigor and valor and salience. When an author is dead and defenseless almost any trash he wrote may be published. It is the great fortune of David Graham Phillips, if the enhancement of one's memory is to be called fortunate, that the one big book he left unpublished was probably the best thing he ever did. It may be rash to say of any man who wrote over twenty novels that the particular one of them in hand surpasses the rest. One ought to read all of David Graham Phillips before offering such an opinion. On the basis of an ordinary acquaintance with his work, however, one is made bold to infer the superiority of *Susan Lenox* and to feel deeply consoled that the eternally lamentable insane act which killed Phillips did not intrude before he had had this full expression of his generous powers. (pp. 167-70)

F. H., *"Invicta," in* The New Republic, *Vol. X, No. 123, March 10, 1917, pp. 167-70.*

Phillips on his literary ideals:

I particularly abhor . . . the novels, histories, poems and every work of art that attribute to things that are essentially revolting, as war, tyranny, class distinctions, etc., qualities of beauty and charm which they do not in themselves possess. I think the artist should never lose sight of the truth that humanity is evolving—is on its way upward, that we must look in the past for the germs of the fine and the high which are budding in the present and will blossom in the future. In a word, I think the novel writer is under the universal obligation to tell the truth, and he should strive to add as little as his human frailties will permit to the fog of lies which becloud the path, and I think it is possible to put truth into the most fanciful romances, just as definitely as into the most realistic pictures of life accorded us. Finally it seems to me that every one, the novelists no less than other men, should strive to make most intelligible to as many of us fellow beings as possible, the fundamental truth that the universe is the common property of us all, and we should help each other to enter into our inheritance and enjoy the fulness of it.

David Graham Phillips, in an interview with B. O. Flower in The Arena, *1904.*

Granville Hicks   (essay date 1931)

[*With the publication of* The Great Tradition: An Interpretation of American Literature since the Civil War *(1933), Hicks became known as the author of "the first systematic analysis of American literature after the Civil War." An active member of the Communist Party in the 1920s and 1930s, Hicks is often credited as the first critic who called for a reevaluation of Phillips's fiction. In the following excerpt, he contends that Phillips was not a novelist, but a journalist, reformer, and muckraker who capitalized on popular interests in order to produce "documented fiction."*]

Phillips had, not unnaturally and certainly not unwisely, written his first novel on the subject that he knew best, journalism. The hero of *The Great God Success* wins his spurs with a story of a lost child, and doubtless many of his other adventures as closely parallel Phillips's own. As is so often true of first novels, *The Great God Success* indicates the direction in which Phillips was to move. It is in the new mood of the new century, the mood that Crane and Norris had done much to establish and that *Sister Carrie* was about to define. Unconventional in its treatment of the relations between men and women, candid in its portrayal of ruthlessness and chicanery in high places, naturalistic in its descriptions of newspaper work and city life, it bears little resemblance to either the classics or the popular fiction of preceding decades. And in its concern

with the conflict between liberalism and the desire for wealth in the individual and the conflict between democracy and plutocracy in the body politic, as well as in its concern with the relations between a man's domestic life and his financial success, it sounds the major themes not merely of Phillips's work but of a decade and a half of American literature.

But Phillips, not yet sure of himself, sought in his second novel to capitalize the already somewhat surfeited taste for Graustarkian romance. It is true that he balances the more picturesque elements in *Her Serene Highness* with sermons on and practical examples of the superiority of democratic Americans to the effete aristocrats of European countries, but the book is little more than a demonstration of his willingness to comply with the current demand, whatever its nature. Fortunately for him, that demand was already taking such form that his particular talents were not likely to be wasted. In *A Woman Ventures* he returned to journalism and in *The Golden Fleece* he aimed another blow at European aristocracy, but in *The Master Rogue* he established himself on the path that he was unhesitatingly, and most profitably, to follow.

The Master Rogue, a story of a great financier, appeared in 1903. In the autumn of 1902 *McClure's Magazine* had begun the publication of two series of articles, Ida Tarbell's on the Standard Oil Company and Lincoln Steffens's *The Shame of the Cities.* With the appearance of these articles, a new force came into American life; the muckraking movement had begun. Their success taught McClure and half a dozen other editors that Americans were becoming interested in the corruption that ever since the Civil War had accompanied industrial expansion. Within two or three years each issue of any one of eight of ten magazines contained two or three articles exposing corruption in business and government. This movement of criticism and exposure set the tone of the decade, a tone that Phillips altogether relished.

Into the movement Phillips plunged, not merely as a novelist but also as an active and none too gentle wielder of the muck-rake. He wrote articles on the dishonesty of officials, the crimes of financiers, and the extravagances of plutocrats, some of which he collected in *The Reign of Gilt.* But his most famous contribution, and one of the more notorious products of the entire decade, was *The Treason of the Senate,* published in the March, 1906, issue of the *Cosmopolitan* and subsequent issues. Genuinely horrified by what his perhaps none too thorough researches revealed, Phillips laid on the lash with a courageous disregard of personal consequences and a somewhat less admirable indifference to scientific accuracy. "From the steady, pointing finger of public scorn and contempt . . . ," he wrote in his first article, "[Senator Chauncey] Depew is not secure anywhere but in the Senate itself—when the galleries are closed and only his colleagues are there." Of [Senator Henry Cabot] Lodge he remarked, "We have seen enough to identify beneath the robe of the 'gentleman scholar' the familiar coarse type of machine politician. . . . To expect him to originate or to endorse any measure of democratic justice would be like looking for potatoes among the roots of a dock weed". He summarized his opinion of the group he was attacking by saying, "A scurvy lot they are, are they not, with their smirking and cringing and voluble palaver about God and patriotism. . . . The Senate is licensing and protecting the sneak-thieves that pilfer daily, hourly, from your wages, your savings, your till, your larder, your coal bin". This series, it has been claimed, helped to bring about the direct election of Senators; certainly it provoked threats of assassination against Phillips, an attack by name in the Senate, and President Roosevelt's speech that coined the term muckraker and made it current.

But, whatever his talents for frontal attack, Phillips preferred fiction as a vehicle for muckraking. After *The Master Rogue* came *The Cost,* another novel of the financial world; and after *The Cost* came *The Plum Tree. The Cost* is centrally concerned with the effect of an early and secret marriage, but inasmuch as Olivia's husband is a peculiarly unscrupulous financier and the man she loves an incredibly honest politician, the telling of her story involves Phillips in direct accounts of business fraud and political intrigue. Even more vigorously *The Plum Tree* leads us into the muckraking arena with the story Harvey Sayler tells of the methods by which he became the secret agent of a group of industrialists and finally a maker of presidents. Scarborough, the honest politician of *The Cost,* is the foil in this story as well, the spokesman of the forces of righteousness and the proponent of Phillips's own remedies for the evils he attacks.

The year 1905 witnessed the publication not only of *The Plum Tree* but of two other novels as well—*The Social Secretary,* which tells of love and snobbery in Washington, and *The Deluge,* which describes snobbery and love in New York and the warfare of Wall Street Titans. It is also the year of *The Reign of Gilt,* a collection of muckraking articles. No novel shows more clearly than does *The Deluge* Phillips's talent for timeliness. In July, 1904, *Everybody's* had begun the serialization of Thomas Lawson's sensational *Frenzied Finance,* and the articles were still appearing when *The Deluge* left the press. Without too closely paralleling Lawson's career, Phillips by no means concealed the resemblance between that spectacular performance and the conduct of his Matt Blacklock. Not only did his description of the pious Roebuck and the aristocratic Langdon—both characters he had introduced in earlier novels—give him opportunity for heavy-handed comments upon "the so-called 'organizers of industry' who bear about the same relation to industry that the boll weevil bears to the cotton crop"; his interpretation of Blacklock's motives must have impressed the pertinence of his novel upon the thousands of readers of *Frenzied Finance.*

After issuing but a single novel, *The Fortune Hunter,* in 1906, Phillips prepared himself for his farewell to muckraking. There is, of course, some muckraking in every book he wrote, but by 1907 he apparently judged that the market for the more slashing sort of fictional exposure was falling off. Making the best of the insurance scandals in *Light-Fingered Gentry,* he devoted his next novel to what he no doubt regarded as constructive criticism. *The Second Generation* is the story of Hiram Ranger, sturdy business man of the old school, diligent, honest, and democratic. His children, however, have been spoiled by education in the East and prolonged association with America's pseudo-aristocracy. Learning that he is fatally ill, Ranger resolves upon a desperate experiment and bestows his fortunes upon a local college. Immediately his son and daughter are jilted by the daughter and son of the Whitneys, another wealthy family of the same city. Arthur Ranger, quickly coming to his senses, goes to work in the factory his father had established, achieves financial success, and transforms the plant into a workers' paradise. Adelaide's progress is slower, but in the end she achieves sanity and becomes of great assistance to her husband in the educational enterprise in which he is engaged. The wealthy Whitney children, on the other hand, go rapidly and completely to the dogs.

The underlying theories of this novel are a fairly accurate measure of the profundity of Phillips's thinking on social problems. In the second part of *The Reign of Gilt* he had stated that the masses of the country's population were sound, that business was essentially honest, and that popular education was establishing a firm basis for national progress. Despite his obvious and detailed familiarity with the complexities of contemporary industrialism in all but especially in its political aspects, he was capable of attributing the evils he saw to the personal wickedness of a few individuals and of believing that the inculcation of honesty was the all-sufficient remedy for the country's ills. Though he could concretely describe the morals and methods of a Harvey Sayler, he saw no reason why an honest and altruistic Scarborough should not turn the rascals out. Fully aware of the methods by which the power of a Dumont or a Roebuck was won, he maintained that intelligent honesty "is the one competition in which a crook cannot survive", and found no obstacles to the success of a conscientious and public-spirited Arthur Ranger.

Of Phillips's sincerity and the genuineness of his crusading spirit there can be little question; equally evident are the superficiality of his diagnoses and the vagueness of his remedies. To the end of his life his thinking was incurably muddled. From his father, a Republican whose views had been formed in the atmosphere of idealism prevalent in the early days of the party, he had acquired a belief in plain living and high thinking, the rights and capacities of the common man, and the inevitability of democratic government. His journalistic experience led, on the other hand, to a confused Nietzscheanism. Not only did he make no attempt to reconcile these two sets of ideas; he seems to have been unaware of any conflict between them. Following whichever theory suited the moment's needs, he was predominantly the old-school Republican in his nonfiction and most of his muckraking novels, and the Nietzschean in his later work. But both attitudes are to be found in all his books, nor is it unusual to discover him on a single page employing the idea of the superman to defend one kind of ruthlessness and using his democratic theories as a stick with which to belabor a different kind. He was a fighter and hence he had to have a cause, but the cause interested him so much less than the fight that his vagueness with respect to the former is not surprising.

In his discovery of a new cause Phillips neatly anticipated, by a year or two, the sudden shift of the popular magazines from articles and stories of exposure to a more or less frank exploitation of sex themes. He boldly began his campaign with a not too memorable play called *The Worth of a Woman,* produced at the Madison Square Theatre in February, 1908. Rather more interesting than this drama of a woman who refuses to make pregnancy an excuse for marrying a man who does not love her—though he does, of course, realize his love just before the final curtain—is the note with which Phillips prefaced the printed version. "There are", he wrote,

> three ways of dealing with the sex relations of men and women—two wrong and one right. For lack of more accurate names the two wrong ways may be called respectively the Anglo-Saxon and the Continental. . . . The wishy-washy literature and the wishy-washy morality on which it is based are not one stage more—or less—rotten than the libertine literature and the libertine morality on which it is based. . . . They are twin sisters of the same horrid mother. . . . There is the third and right way of dealing with the sex relations of men and women. That is the way of simple candor and naturalness. Treat the sex question as you would any other question. Don't treat it reverently; don't treat it rakishly. Treat it naturally.

And so he set his jaw and went to work. *Old Wives for New,* with which he closely followed the play, defines his approach rather more exactly than the preface. Based on the familiar thesis that when women lose their beauty they lose their husbands, it shows Phillips writing with rather more frankness than at that time was fashionable and with the same sort of circumstantial definiteness one finds in his muckraking books; but it exhibits very little of that insight into women that Frank Harris has attributed to Phillips, and it suggests that his views on sexual problems were no clearer than his views on the economic order. In so far as it was novel to point out that women should be treated as human beings, that they are often aggressors in love, and that they have a preference for strong men, Phillips was blazing a new trail, but it can scarcely be maintained that he pursued his pioneering for any great distance.

The other novels that Phillips lived to see published treat the new theme. In *The Fashionable Adventures of Joshua Craig* he blended politics and love, relying chiefly on the latter ingredient. *White Magic* and *The Hungry Heart* are romances in which a lighter manner, clumsy though it actually is, seems skilful in comparison with the more customary blunderbuss methods. *The Husband's Story,* however, which returns to the sledge-hammer technique, is much the best of the group. Godfrey Loring, frequently interrupting himself to preach at the reader, tells the story of his career in business and his wife's career in society. It is an attack upon a certain type of ambitious woman, as thorough, as detailed, and as bitter as any Phillips ever directed against a corrupt politician or an unscrupulous financier. Compared with it, Robert Herrick's elaborations of a similar thesis are little less than complimentary to American womanhood. Yet it is the violence of feeling attributed to Loring that gives him a degree of vitality and

even lends to the silly woman who is the object of his disgust the appearance of reality.

Of the posthumous novels four are in the same vein; the other two, *George Helm* and *The Conflict* were probably written earlier. *Susan Lenox: Her Fall and Rise* is of course the best known of the four, but *The Price She Paid* has some interest because of its resemblance to the more famous book. Like *Susan Lenox* it is the story of a woman's struggle for independence, but its heroine is handicapped by early exposure to the customs of the idle rich and the ideology of the socially ambitious. Constantly betrayed by this training in her effort to become a singer, she finally rises above her weaknesses and achieves the spiritual independence that results in professional success.

Just as he classified politicians as either corrupt or honest, so Phillips classified women as either parasitical or independent. And he intended *Susan Lenox* to be the epic of a woman's struggle for independence. All his knowledge of American and European life he poured into this book, which moves from a small Indiana town to a Mississippi showboat, thence to Cincinnati tenements and factories, to New York theatres and cheap boarding-houses, to Paris, and back to New York. More courageous as well as more desperate than Mildred Gower in *The Price She Paid,* Susan more than once becomes a courtesan. Like Mildred, though after sinking to a lower level and experiencing greater hardships, she learns self-discipline and wins her independence. In an exquisitely sentimental passage at the end of the book, Phillips describes her appearance after her victory—her look of one who has suffered but stood fast, the "consummate fascination" of her "sensitive, strong yet gentle" mouth, the slightly tragic expression such as one always sees on the face of "any of the sons and daughters of men who is blessed—and cursed—with imagination".

Phillips intended *Susan Lenox,* on which he worked during most of his writing career and which he had just finished when he died, to be his masterpiece. Certainly, if he is to be remembered by only one book, it is well that this is the one. It is not merely his most serious effort; it is a completely representative work. Everything is here: the familiar theme of woman's place in the world, long muckraking episodes about factory and tenement conditions in Cincinnati and political corruption in New York, journalistically sensational episodes involving sudden death, sermons on the virtues of democracy and sermons on the creed of the superman. And through all its pages surge the twin impulses, the eagerness of the newspaper man to make a scoop and the zeal of the crusader to banish evil. To say that *Susan Lenox* is Phillips at his best is true, but it is not enough; the book is the whole of Phillips, the perfect product of all his talents and all his faults, apparently his only but his all-sufficient monument.

It would be difficult, despite the interest Arnold Bennett once expressed in his books and the enthusiasm with which Frank Harris calls him the greatest of American novelists, to maintain that Phillips is entitled to a higher place than the literary historians have given him. Most critics have dismissed him as a journalist, and the epithet, though perhaps there is more to be said for him *qua* journalist than has been said, is perfectly just. His subjects are as timely as front-page headlines; he bids for attention as boldly as a feature writer; his descriptions are as crisp and as superficial as a news report and his reflective comments as shallow as an editorial.

If a novelist cannot fashion plausible, self-consistent, well-rounded characters, it will scarcely matter what else he can do. Phillips, in his very first novel, clearly announced his failure in this respect by repeatedly pausing to explain his hero's motives. This habit he never outgrew, nor did he overcome the weakness it betrayed. At no point in his career, from *The Great God Success* to *Susan Lenox,* had he confidence enough in his characters to let them stand alone. When, by putting his story in the mouth of one of the actors, he chose a method that forced him to forego his commentaries, his deficiencies were baldly revealed. Matt Blacklock in *The Deluge* is, at least in the broader outlines of his character, self-consistent; but Godfrey Loring in *The Husband's Story* and Harvey Sayler in *The Plum Tree* shift as wantonly and bewilderingly as persons in a nightmare. Apparently it never occurred to Phillips that, however Sayler's ideas may have changed in the course of his life, he would necessarily have adopted a single point of view in writing his story. Instead, Sayler is allowed to speak on one page as if he were proud of his practices and on another as if he regarded them with Phillips's indignation; sometimes he is a boastful crook, sometimes a penitent crook, and sometimes in his own eyes no crook at all. Like the good journalist he was, Phillips wanted to put Sayler through his paces, using him to expose the ramifications of political corruption; like the crusader he was, he wanted to condemn the evils he exhibited; hence Sayler is whatever at the moment it suited Phillips's purpose for him to be.

Never was Phillips willing to let the logic of character shape a story; it is character that is moulded to meet other demands. Conversions such as those of Mildred Gower and Jane Hastings have no cause; sufferings such as those of Susan Lenox have no effect. Often it is eagerness to point a moral that dictates the treatment of character, but sometimes it is merely the desire for a happy ending. Harvey Sayler wins, for no good reason, the woman who has for years spurned him because of practices he never repudiates; Matt Blacklock's marital happiness requires a special miracle for him and another for his wife; Jack Dumont conveniently dies so that his long-suffering wife can marry Scarborough; the heroes of *Old Wives for New* and *The Husband's Story* secure the women they really love by virtue of strange coincidences as well as by recourse to divorce; even the stupid young fortune hunter in *The Golden Fleece* is provided, after his failure to get a rich wife, with a fortune that permits him to marry the English girl he had, so Phillips tells us, always loved.

After witnessing such performances, designed merely to gratify the sentimental reader, we cannot be surprised to discover Phillips manipulating his plots to prove his theses. The political triumphs of those paragons of virtue, Scarborough and Helm, are as patently made to order as the defeats of Roebuck, Dumont, Langdon, and other malefactors of great wealth. The way the rise of the Rangers is balanced by the fall of the Whitneys gives *The Second Generation* the appearance of a mathematical demonstration rather than that of a product of insight and imagination. Victor Dorn's political and personal successes in *The Conflict* have little relation to the kind of world that we happen to live in.

And Phillips could be as rankly emotional and as cheaply melodramatic as Robert W. Chambers or any other manufacturer of salable commodities. When Lorry is shot in *The Second Generation,* Phillips writes, "Lorry stood straight as a young sycamore for an instant, turned toward Estelle. 'Good-bye—my love!' he said softly, and fell, face downward, with his hands clasping the edge of her dress". There are long passages, indeed, on precisely this level, that make the reading of his books a not altogether painless proceeding. They suggest that nothing but his zeal for reform distinguishes Phillips from the purveyors of circulating library delicacies of his own day and ours.

Nothing but his zeal for reform and the excellence of his journalism. For Phillips was a good journalist. In *The Great God Success* the description of the mechanics of newspaper making is as impressive as the delineation of character is shoddy. *The Cost* and *The Deluge* describe in the most satisfying detail the operations by which fortunes are made and lost. *The Plum Tree* and *George Helm* omit none of the steps in the creation of political power. *Susan Lenox* is perfectly concrete, whether the heroine is playing on a showboat, working in a factory, walking the streets, or associating with gangsters. Phillips could describe the life of his times with the vigor and explicitness of a star reporter, and that is no mean gift. How many of our novelists from Howells on have fallen down at precisely this point! Phillips's contemporary, Robert Herrick, far more skilful as a novelist, failed again and again to achieve the solidity that his kind of fiction demands. If Phillips had written *The Memoirs of an American Citizen,* he would have ignored or misunderstood Van Harrington's spiritual decline, which Herrick so subtly analyzes, but he would have described Harrington's material rise so circumstantially that there could be no room for the scepticism Herrick's treatment arouses.

Phillips, like Dreiser and Upton Sinclair, gave us documented fiction. The documentation is not in itself particularly important, for it can only give his books a certain historical value. But the ability to document is evidence of familiarity with some of the complexities of American life, and without such familiarity American novelists, at least in so far as they deal with American subjects, are handicapped almost to the point of helplessness. At least a good journalist like Phillips shows what some of the material is and what its possibilities may be. So long as formal skill is divorced from intimate knowledge of American life, as it is today and for many decades has been, it will be necessary for critics to pay as much attention to those authors who have the knowledge but lack the skill as they pay to those who have the skill but lack the knowledge. Though Phillips's work seems crude when compared with the work of more polished novelists, and though admittedly it is upon a vastly lower level, it nevertheless, by indicating the tasks they have chosen to ignore, suggests a further comparison in which the stylists and technicians, the devotees of form and worshippers of the letter, do not fare so well. No one would maintain that such gifts as he had are enough to make a novelist, but they are gifts that would enrich a goodly number of our writers today. (pp. 260-66)

> Granville Hicks, "David Graham Phillips; Journalist," in The Bookman, *New York, Vol. LXXIII, No. 3, May, 1931, pp. 257-66.*

George Jean Nathan   (essay date 1935)

[*Nathan has been called the most learned and influential drama critic the United States has yet produced. He was a contributing editor to H. L. Mencken's magazine the* American Mercury *and coeditor of the* Smart Set. *With Mencken, Nathan belonged to an iconoclastic school of critics who attacked the vulgarity of accepted ideas and sought to bring a new level of sophistication to American culture, which they found provincial and backward. Throughout his career, Nathan shared with Mencken a gift for stinging invective and verbal adroitness, as well as total confidence in his own judgments. In the following excerpt, he attributes Phillips's literary attacks on the upper class to Phillips's desire to be a member of that class.*]

Although Phillips impressed the infrallectuals of his time as a gratifyingly well-barbered and well-tailored Dreiser, he was essentially little more than a Robert W. Chambers out of an Upton Sinclair. In even the best of his realistic writing a kind of pretty-pretty quality refractorily permeated the scene. And always one had the feeling—as one still has on re-reading him—that his realism was the residuum of suckled indignation rather than of actual experience. He was, as the more modern psychologists would quickly have observed, a snob who envied and even loved the things he professed to hate. He could write, but the blood in his eye blinded him to himself. He was, subconsciously, the squire of his worst villains.

These villains were (1) women, (2) money, and (3) the world of fashionable society. In one way or another, the bulk of his writing concerned the one or the other or all of them. His three earliest works, *The Great God Success, Her Serene Highness* and *A Woman Ventures,* consisted in a savage attack upon the American *haut monde* and the women who were part of it. *The Master Rogue* was a savage attack upon millionaires, as *The Social Secretary* was an attemptedly sardonic one. *Light-Fingered Gentry* again attacked the plutocratic *haut monde. Old Wives For New,* his best work, paid its author's usual compliments to the millionaire, and to woman. *The Fashionable Adventures of Joshua Craig* again touched upon money and ladies of high social standing, as *The Hungry Heart* had to do with a Southern mazuma magnifico and his disconsolate spouse. *The Husband's Story* hammered yet again at the rich American snob, chiefly female. And, *Susan Lenox: Her Fall and Rise,* written for one of the Hearst magazines, underneath its tin-pot movie melodrama plied the same old artillery against social and economic snobberies.

Whatever the variance of approach, the animus at the bottom of almost all these novels was generally the same: the animus of a somewhat bedraggled bird longing for a golden cage that was not open to it. Even when allowing, in a magnanimous gesture of fairness, glints of virtue to such rich and lofty personages as otherwise he literarily goosed, Phillips could barely conceal his disrelish in betraying even for a moment his own ingrained admiration of them. He performed constantly a vasectomy on his own secret personal ambitions, and the resulting pain became his sterile literary diatribes. That he could write, it must be repeated; but to strike a balance between what he passionately believed and what he passionately tried personally for his own obsequious comfort to forget, was within neither his power nor his talent. The self-depuratory faculty that is the gift of the true artist was denied him.

Phillips was, above all else, first and foremost simply an indignant melodramatist. In his attempted excursions into humor, traces of the indignant melodramatist still stubbornly revealed themselves. He was a blood-and-thunder show at five dollars a seat, doubling psychologically as the hero and villain, and sometimes even as Little Nell. It was natural, therefore, that in the turmoil his crusader self often confusedly presented itself in fierce black moustachios, the while his darker rôle surprised everyone with a beautiful curly blond wig. He was a realist self-manufactured in a stage dressing-room. The moment he emerged into the light of day, his make-up was disconcertingly evident. (pp. 80-2)

> George Jean Nathan, "Critical Presumptions—General," in his Passing Judgments, *Alfred A. Knopf, 1935, pp. 74-103.*

Eric F. Goldman   (essay date 1946)

[*Goldman is an American educator and historian. In the following excerpt, he contends that Phillips's muckraking articles, editorializing, and realistic depictions of American society led to his focus on the "woman's problem" and ultimately dated his work.*]

As a writer, Phillips became the muckraker incarnate. Like almost all the major figures in the muckraking movement, he came to it after striking success in conventional reportorial and editorial work. Three years in Cincinnati, seven years in New York, and Phillips had reached the pinnacle of journalism for his day—editorial writing for Joseph Pulitzer's New York *World.* While he was working on the *World,* his name began appearing regularly in *McClure's,* the *Cosmopolitan, Everybody's,* the *Saturday Evening Post,* and other mass circulation magazines that were featuring exposures of corruption in business and politics. **"Swollen Fortunes," "The Power Behind the Throne," "David B. Hill," "The Men Who Made the Money Trust," "The Madness of Much Power"**—Phillips' long list of magazine articles gave his name a sensational ring throughout the nation. None of the muckrakers, not even Lincoln Steffens, excelled him in a sense of where the muck could be found or in the flair for making each dirty detail carry a heavy onus of shame.

At the same time that Phillips was shocking his weekly readers, he began carrying muckraking over into novels.

In 1901 he made his first try, under the pseudonym of John Graham. *The Great God Success,* a novelized muckraking of journalism itself, went so well that the next year Phillips resigned from the *World* to stake his career on free-lance writing.

The words poured out at the rate of six to seven thousand every night—seventeen novels, averaging 100,000 words apiece, over fifty magazine articles, a play, and a book of nonfiction in the decade between his first novel and his death. Phillips' literary executor found in his desk the galley proofs of a two-volume novel and the completed manuscripts of four other novels and a dozen short stories. (pp. 320-21)

The result of Phillips' prodigious efforts was the same success as a novelist which he had enjoyed in everything else he tried. Most of his novels were serialized in mass circulation magazines, usually the *Saturday Evening Post.* When they appeared as books, they sold widely, often vaulting into the best-seller class. They were given extensive attention by the day's most prominent critics. Some of this attention was anything but flattering, but H. L. Mencken, in an unwonted burst of praise, flatly named Phillips the best American novelist of the period. Frank Harris went

Phillips at work in his sister's Gramercy Park apartment. He customarily wrote standing up.

still further. Having declared Phillips "the greatest writer of novels in English, with much of the power and richness and depth of Balzac in him," Harris added: "I would rather have written *The Hungry Heart* and *The Light-Fingered Gentry* than *Anna Karenina* itself." Today, when Phillips' novels lie untouched in second-hand stores, such praise sounds amazing. It leaves a reader of the novels incredulous, for the books are conspicuously mediocre in structure and style. They show a good newspaperman's sense of details and sometimes almost achieve a Zolaesque realism. But the plots are too often worked out by forced coincidences; the language is turgid even for the standards of the day; no character that Phillips created and very little of his dialogue is really convincing. Phillips could sound like the worst of the drug-store favorites of his time. There were many passages no better than the fatuous death scene in *The Second Generation:* "Lorry stood straight as a young sycamore for an instant, turned toward Estelle. 'Good-bye—my love!' he said softly, and fell, face downward, with his hands clasping the edge of her dress."

Obviously the enthusiasm for Phillips' novels came from the fact that he offered vigorous criticism of the *status quo* to a generation avid for revolt. *The Plum Tree* and *The Fashionable Adventures of Joshua Craig* muckraked national political corruption; *George Helm,* state corruption; and *The Conflict,* municipal corruption. The insurance scandals that made the investigating reputation of Charles Evans Hughes also formed the factual and emotional basis of *The Light-Fingered Gentry. The Second Generation* has quite accurately been called "an editorial in novel form" against the industrial ethics of the day. Other novels, notably *The Husband's Story, The Hungry Heart,* and *Old Wives for New,* blustered away at the institution of marriage as it existed among the rich. It is entirely appropriate that after five years as a novelist Phillips should have written a series of magazine articles which brought the whole literature of exposure the name by which it is known in history. (pp. 321-22)

The title of Phillips' series, *The Treason of the Senate,* represented the tone of the nine articles. "The Senate," Phillips wrote, "is the eager, resourceful, indefatigable agent of interests as hostile to the American people as any invading army could be, and vastly more dangerous; interests that manipulate the prosperity produced by all, so that it heaps up riches for the few; interests whose growth and power can only mean the degradation of the people, of the educated into sycophants, of the masses toward serfdom." Then, with a spectacular wealth of detail (Gustavus Myers, who was later to make his own reputation as a muckraker of the Supreme Court, did the research for Phillips), the articles went down the list of the Senate's biggest names and identified most of them with specific corporate interests. *The Treason of the Senate* was not always accurate; at times exclamation points had to serve for facts. But the series was accurate enough to infuriate conservatives more than any muckraking had done up to that time and to set off Theodore Roosevelt, who had heretofore been considered something of a muckraker's President. (pp. 322-23)

But muckraking itself, at least in the style of *The Treason of the Senate,* was on the way out. Whether Roosevelt had guessed the fact or not, the public was sated, and the New York banks, encouraged by the favorable reception of the President's attack, began cracking down on magazines which featured muckraking. Phillips was so upset by the train of events he had started that Charles Russell spent many an hour trying to convince him that the effects of *The Treason of the Senate* series were not all harmful to the reform movement. Russell was certainly right in the sense that most of the senators Phillips had assailed were soon retired from the Senate. Moreover, *The Treason of the Senate* is generally considered a major catalyst of the direct election of senators, which came by constitutional amendment eight years after the magazine series. But Russell's consolings and encouragements in 1905 did not accomplish much. The remaining five years of Phillips' life were dominated by a concern that had never been closely associated with muckraking. Somewhere in his thinking about the evils of a business civilization, Phillips' attention had been caught by the institution of marriage as it existed among the urban wealthy. He had touched upon this theme in some of his earlier novels. Now his more important novels were to focus on the "woman's problem." (pp. 323-24)

Without benefit of Freud, it is not difficult to see how Phillips drifted into feminism. Among all the causes pushing for reformist attention in the early twentieth century, none was more strident than that of the "emancipationists." A century of rapidly expanding industrialism had created thousands of leisure class families whose female members had time to think about how their time should be spent. In Phillips' novel-writing period the feminist movement had reached a particularly explosive stage—it had gone far enough to gather great force and not far enough to satisfy its zealots. The year 1900 was a long way from the 1860's, when ladies sometimes dined on roast beef in their boudoirs so that they might show a proper indifference to food at the table and when Lady Gough's *Etiquette* instructed: "The perfect hostess will see to it that the works of male and female authors be properly separated on her bookshelves. Their proximity unless they happen to be married should not be tolerated." But even in 1900, the suffragette movement had barely tasted its first American triumphs, women were barred by custom from most professional activities, and sex was still a subject for fantastic circumlocutions. In 1900 emancipating women seemed an exciting crusade, especially when the cause could be aided by blasts at the asininities of the newest newly rich.

Muckraker Phillips certainly managed to make his feminism emancipation by defamation. His favorite subjects were parvenus, and from them he generalized a picture of marriage among the rich that made it a gaudy restlessness for both wife and husband. The trouble started, Phillips was sure, from an education that prepared a woman neither for usefulness nor for genuine cultural interests. As a result, her adult interests were ramshackle and ridiculous, like those of Edna in *The Husband's Story,* who "took I don't know how many lessons a week for I don't know how many years. She learned nothing about music. She merely learned to strum on the piano. But, after all, the lessons attained their real object. They made Edna's

parents and Edna herself and all the neighbors feel that she was indeed a lady. She could not sew. She could not cook. . . . She didn't know a thing that would help her as a woman, wife, or mother. But she could play the piano!" The Ednas had nothing to offer in marriage except their bodies, and hence were party to an essentially fraudulent attitude,

> "the pretense of superhuman respect and deference the American man—usually in all honesty—affects toward woman—until he marries her, or for whatever reason becomes tired and truthful. . . . Beneath 'chivalry's' smug meaningless professions [are] the reality, the forbearance of 'strength' with 'weakness,' the graciousness of superior for inferior."

After a few years of living with such vapidity, Phillips insisted, the husband inevitably began to find his business and his business friends far more interesting than his wife. "The American woman fancies she is growing away from the American man," he said through one of his characters. "The truth is that while she is sitting still, playing with a lapful of artificial flowers of fake culture, like a poor doodle-wit, the American man is growing away from her. . . . He has no time or taste for playing with artificial flowers when the world's important work is to be done. So the poor creature grows more isolated, more neglected, less respected, and less sought, except in a physical way." To fill their minds and their days, wealthy women turned to money-squandering, feigned illnesses, vicious social climbing, bridge. And "if it weren't bridge," Phillips added, "it would be something else. Bridge is a striking example, but only a single example, of the results of feminine folly and idleness that all flow from the same cause."

So savage was Phillips' criticism of wealthy women that, standing alone, it would represent the very negation of feminism. But all the criticism was in a context that absolved women of guilt and placed it on a society which, Phillips emphasized again and again, was dominated by men. It was the men, his novels argued, who insisted that women be trained for perpetual childhood and banned from all experiences that might permit them to transcend their training; it was the men who then viewed with condescension, if not contempt, the products of their own demands. No feminine novelist of Phillips' day spoke more vigorously the feminist claim of mistreatment. To make the point more strongly, he usually picked not a boor but an intelligent, well-educated, likeable male to portray as an oppressor of his wife. The hunger in *The Hungry Heart* was created by just such a male, whose smile for his wife "was like a parent's at a precocious child. He kissed her, patted her cheek, went back to his work." When the wife grew restless, the husband had an easy explanation: "A few more years'll wash away the smatter she got at college, and this restlessness of hers will yield to nature, and she'll be content and happy in her womanhood. A few more children would have an excellent effect. She's suffering from the storing up of energy that ought to have outlet in childbearing. As grandfather often said, it's a dreadful mistake, educating women beyond their sphere." Like most reformers, Phillips had the social myopia which saw the issue reaching its climax in his own day. Mothers and daughters of the early twentieth century, he was sure, belonged to generations that were "perhaps further apart than any two in all human history." As a result the daughters were on their way "from vague restlessness to open revolt."

The emancipation these Phillips novels called for did not vary much from contemporary, middle-of-the-road feminism. He was demanding only a better education for women, the opening of professions to them, and, most important, the acceptance of women as persons capable of intelligent and mature action. The limitations of such feminism made it conspicuously dated in the short-hair enthusiasm of the 'twenties. If Phillips called for the opening of careers to females, he specifically condemned women who

> look down on housekeeping, on the practical side of life, as too coarse and low to be worthy their attention. They say all that sort of thing is easy, is like the toil of a day laborer. Men, no matter how high their position, weary and bore themselves every day, because they must, with routine tasks beside which dishwashing has charm and variety. Yet women shirk their proper and necessary share of life's burden, pretending that it is beneath them. . . . It may be that woman will someday develop another and higher sphere for herself. But first she would do well—in my humbly heretical opinion—to learn to fill the sphere she now rattles around in like one dry pea in a ten-gallon can. I want to see a few more women up to the modern requirements for wife and mother.

Similarly, in their handling of sex, Phillips' novels were a long way behind the four-letter words and single standard attitudes of a later form of feminism. They never questioned the double standard; indeed, most of what they said on the subject was a criticism of things that encouraged departures from the double standard. Their language carried a heavy aroma of the Victorian living room, the horrified titillation of phrases like "in frank invitation," "set him afire," "the bright, swift fading . . . flowers of passion." A prostitute was a "fast woman," and "her bloom was as evanescently tainted by her coarseness as is the bloom of the rose by the ugly worm that crawls across its petals and disappears." In tone, if not always in argument, the novels were a Victorian criticism of Victorianism.

But in a Victorian age, Victorian criticism can sound revolutionary. Phillips as a feminist excited almost as much controversy as Phillips the muckraker. Among the smart sets who were delighting in the ankle-revealing sheath gown or the first evidences of public smoking by respectable women, Phillips was hailed as an exciting new thinker. But to many a person along the Fifth Avenues of the nation, whose way of life was being made to appear stupid and vicious, he was another Eugene Debs or Emma Goldman. Every time a new Phillips novel appeared, some more of the Blue Book saw its leading character in their mirrors. (pp. 324-28)

For seven years [Phillips] wrote and rewrote the two volumes of **Susan Lenox: Her Fall and Rise,** working on it as a relaxation from his nightly stint of quickly published words. The book had been gradually taking shape in his

mind ever since the 'nineties when, walking down the street in his home town, he saw a beautiful girl sitting disconsolate beside a country lout. From the town gossips he learned all about this girl, including the stories that she was an illegitimate child and that she had been forced to marry the farmer to get a home and a respectable name. If Phillips had carried this girl's story forward along the pattern of his earlier novels, her chief problem as a woman would have been to hold her husband's interest, especially after the family achieved economic comfort. But as Phillips worked and reworked *Susan Lenox* in the last years of his life, his thought moved ahead with an advanced wing of the woman's movement. In the final product Susan's problem is not holding her husband's interest and she does not reach respectable comfort until the last part of the novel. Quickly leaving the farmer, she tries to make a living by herself. Failing, she resorts to prostitution and gets embroiled with machine politics in a red light district. When she attempts to break away from prostitution, she is defeated by the lack of economic opportunities, and only finally emerges as a respectable and wealthy actress. This story, so different from that of earlier Phillips novels about women, also carries within it the argument of a further stage in American feminism.

The focus of that argument was no longer the parvenu woman; it was all American womanhood. Before she lived through the 964 pages of the novel, Susan Lenox ran into practical and psychological difficulties at every economic level and became a deliberate symbol of the "hundreds, perhaps thousands of girls . . . [who] are caught in the same calamity every year, tens of thousands, ever more and more as our civilization transforms under the pressure of industrialism." At any economic level, the woman's problem now meant to Phillips far more than bad education, lack of professional opportunities, and male arrogance. It included a tying-in of the woman's problem with the conditions of all labor; an emphasis upon the joys of being a career woman; a more open, more belligerent insistence on the importance of sex and the open discussion of sex; an attack on the "hypocritical" double standard. *Susan Lenox* first appeared as a magazine serial, and the editors expurgated freely, but even in that form it divided public opinion like a manifesto. When Appleton finally published the book in 1917, *Susan Lenox* provoked one of the book battles of the century. It was taken up as a bible by the newest feminism, a feminism that had left the Victorian criticism of Victorianism for a Freudian and somewhat socialist criticism.

But the excitement over feminism was even shorter-lived than the muckraking era. In part, the explanation is the same. Feminism too had won enough notable victories to have the spring taken out of it, specifically in the Nineteenth Amendment and generally in every phase of American life. Yet success is hardly the entire explanation. *Susan Lenox* has a characteristic which might have served as a warning to its feminist enthusiasts—the same characteristic conspicuous in Lillian Smith's *Strange Fruit*, which in 1945 aroused a comparable enthusiasm among reformers concerned with another social problem. Miss Smith took a thoroughly untypical Negro girl, put her through a number of unusual situations, and emerged with a conclusion that depends more on the untypicality of the people involved than on any general social situation or general social program. Hence, the message of the novel has, in long-term reality, little to offer to the ordinary Negro or to the reformer concerned with the ordinary Negro. Phillips told the story of an extraordinarily beautiful, talented, strong-willed girl, and came out with conclusions similarly interesting, moving, and irrelevant to the general problem. Feminists who were enthusiastic about *Susan Lenox* failed to note that Phillips, having shown all the difficulties of a woman in society, finally gets his heroine out of them by a program for the elite alone: "If you want to do right, be strong or you'll be crushed; and if you want to do wrong, take care again to be strong—or you'll be crushed. My moral is, be strong! In this world the good weaklings and the bad weaklings had better lie low, hide in the tall grass. The strong inherit the earth." Susan was strong and she inherited the earth. Most of the feminists were not and they inherited a reaction from their ideas. As the Greenwich Village exuberance wore off, even strong women discovered that a single standard had its disadvantages, that a career meant a number of important sacrifices, that a woman was not simply a biological variant of a man and would not be too happy acting as one.

Depression and war speeded up the retreat from the extremes of feminism. The lean years of the 1930's shifted the attention of both sexes to desperately immediate problems of food and shelter and gave more than a tinge of the ridiculous to a movement that had never been entirely free of silliness. American entrance into World War II encouraged new laughter and some irritation at mention of the "woman's problem." War usually brings a reaction to older mores all along the line. Moreover, by increasing the seriousness of problems like juvenile delinquency, it reemphasized the traditional concern over the home and woman's place in it, while the departure of millions of males was arousing to a new high the instincts of femininity and of motherhood. As World War II ended, women of the most feminist of all professions, the social services, read approvingly works like Anna Freud and Dorothy Burlingham's *War and Children,* which emphasizes motherhood as much as any nineteenth century anti-feminist tract. Those who still talked of the "woman's problem" had, for the most part, reacted against the feminism of the *Susan Lenox* type except in its emphasis upon economic factors. They had gone back to a feminism better represented in the plea of *The Hungry Heart* and *The Husband's Story* for the treatment of woman as an equal, although still very much a woman.

But hardly anyone, feminist or anti-feminist, returned to *The Hungry Heart* or *The Husband's Story.* The reaction against the feminist crusade was no counter-crusade but a slow sliding back, and only a crusader's excitement could convert Phillips' novels into distinguished literature. So deficient is his writing in the qualities which make for literary permanence that even *Susan Lenox* commands few actual readers today. This book was, quite consciously, his magnum opus and it has generally been accepted as his best novel. Certainly Phillips' sense of detail never showed to better advantage, and Susan Lenox at times loves and hates with striking authenticity. But essentially the novel is the same as everything else Phillips wrote. It is a tract for the times, an editorial thinly veiled behind a novel. Always the great newspaperman, Phillips wrote with the brilliant evanescence of contemporaneity. His muckraking hit men and conditions so specifically that it passed into history with them; his feminism defined two stages of feminism and did little else. No doubt Phillips would have understood. Posterity, he used to say, has to take care of itself. (pp. 329-32)

Eric F. Goldman, "David Graham Phillips," in The Lives of Eighteen from Princeton, *edited by Willard Thorp, 1946. Reprint by Books for Libraries Press, 1968, pp. 318-32.*

B. O. Flower on Phillips as a reformer:

The present age is calling for strong, fine and fearless work, such as Mr. Phillips is giving the public. He is a man to whom the sturdy spirit of the old-time American democracy, the democracy of the Declaration of Independence and the fathers, appeals with overmastering force. He possesses the mental and imaginative power to carry forward the cause of human progress to a greater degree than he probably imagines, and at the same time to make contributions of permanent value to our literature. . . . Mr. Phillips is one of the few brilliant young novelists who not only "see things as the are," but who have the courage to depict them in their true colors.

B. O. Flower, in The Arena, *1904.*

Kenneth S. Lynn   (essay date 1955)

[*An American literary scholar whose works evidence his conservative principles, Lynn is the author of numerous essays and books on American life and letters. In the following excerpt, he relates Phillips's popularity to his depictions of the messianic reformer and to his appeal to the aspirations of the middle class.*]

In spite of Phillips's tremendous output, not one of his novels today gives substance to his ambitious boast that he would become the secretary of American society, that his fiction would mirror the secret history of the United States. If his name is now remembered at all, it is as the muckraking reporter whom the editor of Hearst's *Cosmopolitan* persuaded to write the sensational articles on *The Treason of the Senate.* His novels, always concerned with contemporary themes, always purporting to give the "true facts" and the "inside story," are as dead as yesterday's newspaper.

Yet Phillips is an interesting figure, even an important one. For through [the editor of the *Saturday Evening Post,* George Horace] Lorimer, Phillips made contact with the great middle-class audience which was, quite literally, waiting for him. Americans read his novels with weekly devotion in the *Post,* and then bought them in hard covers, because he lent to their anticlimactic lives a sense of excitement and achievement; in the midst of a strange new world Phillips brought them back the brave old world, *redivivus;* they were unsure of themselves . . . and his novels were filled with certainties. Thus—and this is what makes him important—Phillips actually did for a time become the secretary of American society, except that the "secret history of the United States" he wrote was not the Balzacian human comedy he had in mind. Phillips's novels, taken all in all, do compose a secret history—not, however, of the private lives of middle-class Americans, but of their private, innermost hopes and dreams. In pandering to those dreams, Phillips has managed to furnish us with an invaluable account of them.

Phillips the novelist, like Phillips the reporter, was an inside dopester. His novels tell not only a story but the "straight story." This was a fortunate circumstance, because what the troubled middle classes were looking for in their fiction was a description of who or what was causing all the trouble. Revelation by novel began with his very first book, *The Great God Success.*

The hero, a young man with the "energy of unconquerable resolution," has come to New York to enter the newspaper profession. He soon becomes a great reporter and is regarded along Park Row as a brilliant success. In his heart, however, he knows that he is a "brilliant failure"— he does his job without half trying, he is not really interested, he listlessly lets the chances "that are always thrusting themselves" at him slip by. "Will the stimulus to ambition," he wonders, "never come?" Finally, it does, in the shape of a political campaign. "The cause aroused his passion for justice, for democratic equality and the abolition of privilege." Henceforward, he works like a demon. He becomes editor in chief of the paper; he publishes exposés of corruption and professed reformers; he attacks the best people. Under his dynamic direction, circulation soars. His income mounts right along with the circulation, enabling him in a few years to buy the paper. More steadfastly than ever "an organ of the people," the paper grows more and more influential, and profitable. Then, once more, comes a political campaign, more crucial than the last. Both for "the people" and their journalistic champion, the eschatological moment has arrived:

> The great battle was on—the battle he had in his younger days looked forward to and longed for—the battle against Privilege and for a "restoration of government by the people." The candidates were nominated, the platforms put forward and the issue squarely joined.

So squarely, in fact, that the forces of Privilege are scared. The campaign has put their control of the country in jeopardy. They send an emissary to the hero with instructions to offer him an ambassadorship if he will shift his editorial position. The hero takes the bribe and political victory is once more snatched from the hands of the people.

The childlike naïveté of Phillips's "exposé"—a New York newspaper abruptly switches sides and a national election is lost—was nevertheless appealing because of its very simplicity. By reducing the meaning of modern America to a fight between two great opponents—the People versus Privilege—Phillips was using a common denominator already familiar to his readers: this was, all over again, the

Puritans' struggle against the forces of evil for control of the world; this was the polarized rhetoric familiar in every political campaign since Jackson.

If the combat was familiar, however, one of the combatants was not. There was no difficulty with "the People"— Phillips's middle-class readers, highly conscious that they were *echte Amerikaner,* readily defined the term as being coextensive with themselves. But beyond telling them that the forces of Privilege always preferred bribery and cheating to honest combat, Phillips had not, in this first novel, given them much more than a label. His books for the next few years were concerned with the task of further amplification.

Giving Privilege a local habitation as well as a name was easy; the address was, in the words of one of his characters, "That *damned* East!" Until the day he died Phillips blasted the East, particularly New York, with a steady stream of vituperation and abuse. Eastern businessmen were "respectable thieves" and "oily rascals," an "impudent and cowardly crowd." New York was corrupt, and corrupting, the siren city "that lures young men from the towns and the farms, and prostitutes them, teaches them to sell themselves with unblushing cheeks for a fee, for an office, for riches, for power." New York was no place to raise a child, no place indeed for any decent person to live—anyone doing so ran the risk of becoming fouled by the "slime of sordidness" which the city dabbled "on every flower in the garden of human nature."

Determining the identity of these Eastern cowards and rascals proved to be more difficult. Phillips was sure that a conspiracy of Privilege controlled the country, controlled its finances, its political parties, its destiny. But he could never quite decide who were the conspirators. In *The Cost,* Phillips talked darkly of "the half-dozen big corporations" which, by dominating both political parties, were exploiting the country, but did not specify any further. This was still terribly vague; if Phillips was to maintain his standing as an inside dopester, it was imperative that he do better. The following year he published two novels, each purporting to be the confessions of an ex-member of the conspiracy.

The Plum Tree enlarged upon the political machinations hinted at in *The Cost.* The narrator of the novel is an expert on such machinations, inasmuch as he has been until recently the political superboss charged with dispensing "the money that maintained the political machinery of both parties," buying off legislatures and purchasing election victories.

The forces of Privilege in *The Plum Tree* controlled affairs, but as Phillips was at pains to show, the conspiracy was a house divided against itself. The narrator is a Midwesterner, which is to say in a Phillips novel, a sensible man. His policy, albeit dishonest, is one of moderation— "to yield to the powerful few a minimum of what they could compel, to give to the prostrate but potentially powerful many at least enough to keep them quiet—a stomachful." He, and the corporations he represents, are thwarted in this plan, however, by the Eastern stockmarket crowd, which wants to milk the country dry. Thus, in

The Plum Tree, "the half-dozen big corporations" which had played the villain in *The Cost* emerge as rather less than ruthless in the matter of exploitation and rather less than dominant within the conspiracy. Business was apt to be Midwestern and therefore could be forgiven a certain amount of judicious corruption; Wall Street was indubitably Eastern and immoderate and culpable.

The "authentic" tone of the narration and the sensationally sordid portrayal of American politics gave the book a passing notoriety—Theodore Roosevelt said the novel had been very widely read, was very popular, and gave an entirely false impression—but when all was said *The Plum Tree* only amounted to an ordinary, run-of-the-mill diatribe against Wall Street, of the sort often voiced by Roosevelt himself, and before him by [William Jennings] Bryan and the Populists. But since Phillips desperately needed to expose the forces of evil in palpable form, apparently even a moth-eaten scapegoat was better than none.

After *The Plum Tree* came *The Deluge.* The confession in this instance is made by a former financial agent of the Wall Street conspiracy, the "seven cliques," said Phillips, which have "the political and industrial United States at their mercy." With the country "prostrate under their iron heels," the cliques are looting the nation at will. They have forcibly ejected "free American labor" from industry and substituted "importations of coolie Huns and Bohemians." They have for some time levied hidden taxes upon commodities all the way along the line from producer to consumer, so that the prices of "all the things for which . . . wages must be spent" are constantly being forced higher and higher. The seven cliques have also entered the business world, but not to manage, only to despoil. "They reaped only where and what others had sown; they touched industry only to plunder and blight it." While "torrents of unjust wealth" pour in upon the cliques, their systematic banditry continues to play havoc with the major industries of the country and to impoverish and demoralize the people still further. Who belonged to the seven cliques? Phillips's narrator confirmed *The Plum Tree* if not *The Cost;* the real conspirators weren't businessmen at all, they were "rascals of high finance."

But Phillips did not stick with his Wall Street story for long either. Only two years after *The Deluge* he was insisting that the insurance business was really the fount of all evil in America. As always, the new enemy was everywhere, and the cause of every wrong. The insurance trust, he claimed in *Light-Fingered Gentry,* "controlled about one half of the entire wealth of the country; not a blade was harvested, not a wheel was turned, not a pound of freight was lifted from Maine to the Pacific but that they directly or indirectly got a 'rake off.' "

Phillips's revelations did not vie merely with one another in these years; they also had to compete with those of other writers who were riding the crest of the sudden national craze over muckraking. (While, for example, Phillips was readying his insurance exposé for publication, Upton Sinclair was assuring the country that "a gigantic combination of capital" called the "Beef Trust," which had spread out from the stockyards of Chicago and now controlled "railroads and trolley lines, gas and electric franchises," was behind everything. The "incarnation of blind and insensate Greed," the Beef Trust ran the government of Chicago and dictated to that of the nation; it wiped out "thousands of businesses every year" and everywhere "drove men to madness and suicide.") The reasons for such competition were inherent in the exposé business itself; if one's revelations were not to become stale they perforce had to keep changing; and in order for the newest revelation to be considered important, omnipotent power and total depravity had to be claimed for each new villain. Eventually Phillips decided it was less hazardous to describe how the torrents of unjust wealth were spent than how they were come by, so that finally his novels became more concerned with the sociology of Privilege than with its economics or its politics.

The "reign of glitter" was also, of course, centered on New York, with outlying satrapies in Boston, Washington and the Harvard Yard. Throughout the East, said Phillips, "concentrated private wealth had been rising for a generation with amazing rapidity. Suddenly it overflowed in a waterfall of luxurious living . . . today the waterfall has become a Niagara"—and Manhattan Island was "the high-curving centre of the down-pouring, glittering stream." In New York there were more than two hundred private houses the equal of palaces in size and cost and showiness, more than five hundred imposing hotels and apartment houses built of marble or granite, hundreds of luxurious stores. In the best shops,

> you are dazzled and overwhelmed by the careless torrent of luxury . . . twenty-five dollars for a pair of shoes, fifteen dollars for a pair of stockings, two hundred dollars for a hat, one thousand dollars for a hat-pin or parasol, fifteen hundred for a small gold bottle for a woman's dressing table, thirty or forty thousand for a tiara, a hundred thousand for a string of pearls. . . .

Phillips's official attitude toward all this extravagance was extravagantly condemnatory, in much the same way as was his attitude toward New York in general. He found particularly offensive the pharisaical caste system of the newly risen American aristocracy. A professional Anglophobe, Phillips could think of nothing worse to say of New York's "gospel of snobbishness" than to denounce it as a "disease imported into this country from England." He raged at rich Americans for allowing English servants and English fortune hunters to make fools of them. In respect to the new pretentiousness Lorimer and Phillips were particularly close, and the *Post* published three serialized books and many articles by Phillips lampooning the social ambitions of Eastern snobs. American heiresses, affected and silly, with a fatal predilection for titled Europeans, were satirized by Phillips again and again.

The "rich" American who took the brunt of his abuse, however, was Theodore Roosevelt, whom Phillips loathed. Born to the manner of snobbish New York society, Roosevelt had been educated at what Phillips called that breeding ground of idiots, Harvard College, where men were taught "to use their lips in making words as a Miss Nancy sort of man uses his fingers in doing fancy work" and were urged "to believe themselves superior in intellectual knowledge." Worse, Harvard encouraged, as did all Eastern colleges, "that most un-American thing called class and culture." T. R. in the White House was simply the product of his environment. In *The Social Secretary* (another confessional novel), Phillips had his narrator remark that Europeans in the Washington embassies "laugh all day long at the President's queer manners and mannerisms—but then, so do we, for that matter." Phillips accused Roosevelt of transforming the White House into a Continental court. "The newly evolved notion of the Presidential office," Phillips wrote,

> is that it is the centre of political, intellectual and sociological authority and also of social honor. Not only must the democratic—or plutocratic—overlord, anointed with the new kind of divine oil, be the embodiment and exponent of the popular will; he must also be the source of honor, the recognizer of merit.

These changes were astounding, and yet they were only the beginning, a crude inaugural, Phillips felt, of the Washington of the future. "But it is a beginning—a most audacious move on the part of one of the most audacious men who ever rose to first place in the republic."

Thanks to the bad example of Roosevelt and other Eastern snobs, Phillips asserted, the worship of luxury was spreading across the entire continent. Even the Midwest showed signs of succumbing to the East's crazy passion for luxury and display. Like the plutocracy of business and politics, the plutocracy of society was everywhere. "The real people," (Phillips meant his readers) "those true Americans who think, who aspire, who advance, who work and take pleasure and pride in their work, the people who have built our republic," were surrounded. They could be destroyed, he cried, if such un-American activity continued unchecked.

Yet while Phillips gave voice to the middle classes' self-pity that they were not rich, he reinforced their optimism, too, with elaborate descriptions of the luckless fate of the wealthy. The rich in his novels lead a dog's life of broken marriages, lost friends, and spiritual boredom. The greatest of all sufferings visited upon the wealthy in Phillips's fiction is their children. In describing them, Phillips raised the success mythology's traditional contempt for poor little rich boys to a memorable pitch.

The children of wealth in his books are truly fearsome. They are a "self-intoxicated, stupid and pretentious generation, a polo-playing and racing and hunting, a yachting and palace-dwelling and money-scattering generation; a business-despising and business-neglecting, an old-world aristocracy-imitating generation." Phillips's rich children are ashamed of the crudity of their parents' conduct in front of the English servants; they speak to their fathers only to ask for larger allowances; they allow their mothers to wait on them. Not only do they not know how to think, they are so faint-hearted that the fathers must actually make their marriage proposals for them. Most important of all, they have no talent whatsoever for business, for "that is the rule—the second generation of a plutocrat inherits, with his money, the meanness that enables him to hoard it, but not the scope that enables him to make it."

That the children of wealth were incapable of earning a living was a generalization which had for Phillips all the certainty of a physical law.

> Just as soon as one of us becomes ashamed of his birth or of his own past, becomes infected with the cheap and silly vulgarisms that Europe is always thrusting upon us, just so soon does he or she begin to fall behind in the procession. Influential relatives will not long save him or her, nor inherited property. . . .

Only that part of the coming generation that was trained in "Democracy" would survive and prosper in the coming times. "The part that is bred in exclusiveness and caste feeling," he warned, "is going to be bitterly discontented and deplorably unprogressive certainly, and in all probability, except in a few rare cases, downright unprosperous."

One of Phillips's most important books, *The Second Generation,* was written to illustrate this thesis. It is the story of a father who gives away all his money for the sake of his children. If the novel is scarcely believable, it is fine fantasy. The father is a self-made man, a rich manufacturer, who in his declining years broods about the vanity and uselessness of his children. Especially is he worried about his son, a languid clotheshorse recently fired from Harvard, who is vastly insulted when his father suggests he get a job. Knowing that he will die soon, the father seeks the advice of a learned acquaintance, who tells him that wealth is a curse, that it stops the wheels of progress. A religious man, the acquaintance points to the Garden of Eden as an example of leisure-class living and reminds the father that when God saw what a bad idea Eden had turned out to be, God forthwith abandoned it. The analogy overpowers the old man; in his will he cuts off his son with five thousand dollars, leaving the bulk of his fortune to the welfare of the people. As it turns out, this plan benefits not only the public, but the son as well. Saying, "I've got to 'get busy' if I'm to pull out of this mess," the son enthusiastically pitches into his factory job. With a "thousand damn fool ideas" soon knocked out of his skull, he shows a great head for business. The end of the novel finds him happy, married, and in control of his father's old factory. The moral of the story could not have been more clear: the father's will had worked out beautifully for all concerned—therefore, would not all rich businessmen be advised to adopt it? Such a quick and painless solution to the problem of Privilege!

Time and again Phillips told the rich that work was the only way to salvation, as well as the only real earthly happiness man could know. "Remember," Phillips told them, "that working out a fixed purpose in life is just as amusing as drinking champagne and fox-hunting." Manifestly, however, they were too far gone, too stupid, to take his advice. Even the rich who enjoyed reading about the "gospel of work" still clung to their preference for the "gospel of snobbishness." James Hazen Hyde, the playboy who inherited the fortune which his father had amassed in the Equitable Life Assurance Society, was a Phillips fan—but Hyde still preferred throwing his fabulous parties to buckling down. Nor did their folly get the rich into trouble. Despite Phillips's predictions to the contrary, the plutocracy did not fall of its own weight, but obstinately continued to glitter and to control. It was all very frustrating.

From the depths of discouragement Phillips once wrote: "The Jews of ancient days are not the only people who have dreamed of a Messiah. The Messiah-dream, the Messiah-longing, has been the dream and the longing of the whole human race, toiling away in obscurity, oppressed, exploited, fooled, despised."

At the beginning of the twentieth century, there were two likely candidates for the job of Messiah of the American middle classes. Bryan could conceivably have filled the bill; certainly he stood on the side of the angels in the great battle against Privilege. But to the middle classes, Bryan's opposition to "government of, by and for plutocracy," had been, in Phillips's words, "fantastic, extreme, entangled with social, economic and political lunacies." Bryan had the look of a Messiah, but free silver was not a panacea which appealed to people who, like Phillips, had money in the bank and an income well above the national average. To some Americans, Theodore Roosevelt had the Messianic look, too, but Phillips was not one of them. The prince of snobs, he was sure, could not possibly represent the self-reliant middle classes. T. R. talked in a large way, but he was actually timid when it came to "really acting against rich people." In addition, Roosevelt was not the foe of bigness per se; he liked to make distinctions between good trusts and bad ones. Phillips, convinced that some supertrust of conspirators ran the whole show, considered distinctions between individual trusts patent nonsense. Indeed, in his eyes such talk only rendered Roosevelt suspect of being soft toward the conspiracy. As he told his friend Senator Albert J. Beveridge, Phillips was convinced that "Teddy is at heart with Wall Street," a conviction which was reinforced by the fact that the Roosevelt administration busted very few trusts.

Thus there existed the dream of a Messiah, yet for many Americans the dream had never materialized. In the absence of an actual Messiah, however, there was always the solace of Phillips's novels. For if the Saviour did not walk the earth, he did appear in fiction. Phillips's conjuration of the hero who would deliver middle-class America from the wilderness became the major activity of his writing career.

Phillips's Lochinvars all come out of the West, that "earnest, deeply religious" region where, although the cities might be tainted by wealth, there were still small towns and farms with "no tendencies toward the development of caste." More specifically, they have been born and bred in Indiana. This last detail was added by Phillips not simply because he himself happened to be a native of the state. He included it quite purposefully, for all of his saviors are in reality the same character, wearing various disguises from book to book, and this archetypal Messiah is the fused and terrifically romanticized image of two famous Hoosiers of the day: Albert J. Beveridge and the politician's "oldest and best-loved friend," Phillips himself. (pp. 128-41)

The Messiah of [Phillips's] novels acts like Beveridge, but, significantly, he looks like Phillips.

The Messiah plays two principal roles in Phillips's fiction, one political, the other economic.

The most important of the political figures is the character of Hampden Scarborough, who appears or is mentioned in several Phillips novels. Scarborough is first introduced in *The Cost* as a poor young man determined to work his way through college. He has a "look of superiority" and is yet the perfect democrat—a descendant of "men who had learned to hate kings in Holland in the sixteenth century, had learned to despise them in England." Phillips himself was six feet three, blond, and handsome, but Scarborough must be considered an instance of art improving upon nature: "The tall, powerful figure; the fair hair growing above his wide and lofty brow, with the one defiant lock; and in his aquiline nose and blue-gray eyes and almost perfect mouth and chin the stamp of one who would move forward irresistibly, moving others to his will."

Scarborough refuses to join one of the college fraternities—they are aristocratic—and he organizes a successful fight against them for control of the college literary society. The speech he makes at the height of the controversy already has the authentic ring: "It is time to rededicate our society to equality, to freedom of thought and speech. . . ." Scarborough's voice, even more than what he says, thrills the assembled throng. (He had been practicing in the woods every morning.)

From this triumph it is but an easy leap to reading law at night, and politics. Soon he is the leader of the "forces of honesty in his party," opposed to the "forces of the machine," which, like their opposite number in the other party, are controlled by the conspiracy of Privilege. Though the machine tries bribery to prevent it, Scarborough succeeds in winning his party's nomination for governor (his voice in the convention hall was "like magic, rising and falling in thrilling inflections as it wove its spell of gold and fire.") A few months later he is elected. "At last"—a phrase that longingly echoes again and again through Phillips's novels—"the people had in their service a lawyer equal in ability to the best the monopolies could buy, and one who understood human nature and political machinery to boot."

What does Scarborough do in office? How does he defeat the conspiracy—as he surely must? What happens next? The answers to these questions are strangely not to be found in *The Cost*. For, with his election, Scarborough abruptly disappears from the reader's sight, although the novel is far from concluded. After dominating the book for the first two thirds of its length, he is scarcely mentioned again in the concluding third. Nor is Scarborough allowed ever again to occupy the center of the stage of a Phillips novel for any length of time.

In *The Plum Tree* we learn that as governor Scarborough has got after "the monopolies," with the consequence that living costs are now a good 20 per cent lower in Indiana than in Ohio, but this interesting accomplishment is performed entirely offstage—we learn of it only secondhand, in a passing sentence. When Phillips finally does permit Scarborough to appear in the novel, his hero is, once again, a political candidate, this time for the Presidency.

He is depicted, as always, in the process of making a speech. Scarborough's voice is inevitably musical, and as he stands up on the platform, high above the throng, he seems "a sort of embodiment of fearlessness." His platform consists of a solemn promise to obey the Constitution and enforce the laws. When the people hear this they know that at last they have found the "firebrand to light the torch of revolution back toward what the republic used to be before differences of wealth divided its people into upper, middle and lower classes, before enthroned corporate combinations made equality before the law a mockery. . . . " But he is defeated—the election is bought. Scarborough carries the farms and small towns, just as he had done when he ran for governor, but the city machines and "other purchasable organizations" are enough to beat him. As in *The Cost,* he vanishes from the story after the election without explanation, then just as abruptly turns up again four years later, again as a candidate for President. This time he is elected—and the novel ends.

The hero of *The Fashionable Adventures of Joshua Craig* is subjected to the same now-you-see-him-now-you-don't treatment as Scarborough. The scene of the novel is the nation's capital, for Craig is Attorney General of the United States. As a cabinet officer, the "strenuous young Westerner" is invited to many parties at which he cuts a wide and scornful swath through the effete ranks of Washington society. Finally, Craig becomes thoroughly disgusted with the East and returns to the West, where he is destined to become, in the name of the people, the governor of his native state. But Craig's return to the West is a vanishing act; although he is presumably just entering on the major phase of his career, the novel ends with his departure from Washington.

What distinguishes *Joshua Craig* from *The Cost* and *The Plum Tree* is that more attention is paid in it to the appearance and personality of the Messiah. The fuller portrait is instructive. There is a narcissistic concentration on the details of Craig's physical person that far surpasses anything Phillips had allowed himself before. Craig's head "suggested the rude, fierce figurehead of a Viking galley; the huge, aggressively-masculine features proclaimed ambition, energy, intelligence." But this was just the beginning—Phillips could barely take his eyes off the man: his hero has "powerful shoulders," arms and legs which are "thick and strong, like a lion's or a tiger's" and a "fine head, haughtily set." Craig's eyes "emphasized the impression of arrogance and force. He had the leader's beak-like nose, a handsome form of it, like Alexander's, not like Attila's. The mouth was the orator's—wide, full, and flexible of lips, fluent." Lest the reference to Alexander prove confusing, Phillips hastened to add that Craig's appearance was democratically perfect. That full mouth, for example, was "distinctly not an aristocratic mouth," but one which "suggested common speech and common tastes." His hero's skin, too, lacked that aristocratic "finish of surface which . . . is got only by eating the costly, rare, best and best-prepared food."

To discuss Craig's personality is to describe one of the leading boors in American literature. He habitually insults the woman who loves him, he patronizes his friends because they are, after all, "inferior," to him; his characteristic manner is a "familiar, swaggering bustling braggadocio"; he talks, as someone admiringly tells him, "like Napoleon." What Phillips's attitude was toward all this is quite clear. Some time after the publication of the novel Phillips wrote a letter to a friend categorically denying that there was anything boorish about his hero. "Josh, it seems clear to me, is a worthy fellow. . . . I know him thoroughly. The ungentle way he acted with Margaret [the woman who loves him] was simply to impress her with his personality, his masculinity." How anyone could have failed to admire his hero was a complete mystery to Phillips.

From his tremendous faith in political solutions, Phillips was capable at times of switching to the position that mere laws could never do the job of protecting what rightfully belonged to the people. When this latter mood was upon him, Lochinvar became an economic not a political man, a business leader not a governor.

Phillips's businessmen, like his politicians, have no desire to be rich or even to make money. What they are interested in is power, and the excitement of winning. Although humbly born, and possessing neither money nor influence, they unfailingly prove themselves more than a match for the great plutocracy in any situation. The plutocracy had, according to Phillips, choked off all competition; its sway, he said, was unchallenged; yet for men like Matthew Blacklock in *The Deluge* and Horace Armstrong in *Light-Fingered Gentry,* men who had only "a will, a brain, courage—and nothing to lose," the forces of Privilege are a pushover. Undismayed by the odds which they face, these men evince nothing but a slightly murderous contempt for their plutocratic opponents. Blacklock, who is a Wall Street financier, boasts, "I'll strew the Street with their blood and broken bones"—and he does. In Armstrong the homicidal urge is even more marked. "The will to kill! To feel that creature [an evil plutocrat] under him, under his knees and fingers; to see eyes and tongue burst out; to know that the brain that dared conceive the thought of making a slave of him was dead for its insolence!" If such tendencies seem alarming to us, they were immensely satisfying to Phillips's readers. The middle classes of the time felt themselves being stifled by overwhelming forces and therefore took vicarious pleasure in reading about what it would be like to have their fingers around a plutocrat's throat. Beveridge, exclaiming over "its fierce climax of bayonet thrust and throat-clutch," called the account of Blacklock's career "mesmeric in its fascination." Phillips's business hero who slew the economic dragon embodied, even more than the politician who defeated the machines and was elected President, the most immediate kind of wish fulfillment.

In telling the story of a Blacklock or an Armstrong, Phillips was also attempting, once again, to give free advice to the rich. Just as they could make their children better people by giving away all their money when they died, so the rich could make more money while they lived if only they would run their businesses the way a Phillips hero did. The business leader of his novels refuses to indulge in "cheating and swindling, lying and pilfering and bribing"; instead of killing off competition, he encourages it; he constantly lowers prices. In the world of fiction, these policies pay off handsomely. "The Golden Rule is not a piece of visionary altruism, but a sound principle of practical self-interest"—and Blacklock and Armstrong wax fat on doing unto others as they would have others do unto them.

Phillips's confidence that the Golden Rule was the way to wealth comes out most clearly in his book of essays, *The Reign of Gilt,* wherein he devoted an entire chapter to advising a hypothetical son of John D. Rockefeller as to how he should act after his father is dead. First of all, said Phillips, Junior should immediately abandon all charitable enterprises—such benefactions were for "paupers, and panderers and parasites." Junior should then insist on selling commodities at fair prices and on paying a living wage. He should stop watering stocks and bribing legislatures. The plutocrats would denounce him for all this, Phillips predicted, but he would be "greatly cheered by the swelling, stentorian applause of the people." Next he should go into the squalid cities, tear down the tenements and erect clean houses, for which he should charge low rents. He should build "a huge department store" in every neighborhood, where, instead of shoddy clothes and "vile, poisonous, rotten meat and vegetables," he should sell decent goods and wholesome food at fair prices. The initial result of such a plan, Phillips was sure, would be that Junior would lose a great deal of money—in a sense become poor again—but he would then go on to compile an even vaster fortune than his father's. Everything he touched, said Phillips with breathless eagerness, would turn to gold. What a real opportunity big businessmen in America were missing! Why didn't they get smart?

Behind all of the energy and bustle of Phillips's Messiahs, with their sensational exposés of political graft and business corruption, lay a pathetic secret. Supposedly as modern as tomorrow, his heroes were in fact hopelessly anachronistic; in terms of the twentieth century, they were programmatically barren. (pp. 142-48)

As Theodore Roosevelt was the first to point out, Phillips the novelist, like Phillips the reporter, deified the past. Hampden Scarborough was not a prophet of the future, but a remembrance of things past. His political appeal is to the small towns and farms, not to the cities. His campaign promise is that he will lead the American people *back* to the good old days of 1870 when there had been competitive equality—or at least no trusts. Since, however, the untrammeled competition of the Alger era was precisely what had produced the plutocratic world of 1900, recapturing Alger could only lead inevitably back to the troubles of the present once again. But recapturing the past was not only futile, it was impossible. Such phrases as "enforcing the Constitution" and "equality before the law" could not dispel the twentieth century, and yet, when Phillips had pronounced those words he had exhausted his political ideas. Business had to be dominant, Phillips believed, for without business in the saddle America would lose its idealism and cease to be democratic—but it must be restrained. How to interfere with business and yet not interfere was, however, completely beyond him.

It is for these reasons that Phillips always depicted his Messiah making speeches but almost never showed him in power. When he did follow his hero into the governor's or the President's office, as he did in his last political novel, *George Helm,* the Messiah's program was revealed to consist of such measures as the enforced inspection of beer production, making railroads pay taxes, and compelling merchants to give honest weight—hardly a course of action designed to crush plutocracies or to help resuscitate the dear, dead past.

When Phillips found he had not the least idea how to restrain business, he invented the Alger hero who restrained himself. Blacklock, Armstrong, the hypothetical son of Rockefeller (who qualified as an Alger hero by initially losing his inherited fortune, then gaining it back tenfold) have, however, rather primitive conceptions of restraint. They strew the ground with the blood of plutocrats. Their labor policy is to fire idlers and to teach "thrift" to the workers who remain by squeezing out of them "full value for what they get." The fear of sinking to the bottom of the economic heap, said Phillips, was one of the greatest forces making for human betterment in the world, and the heroes of his novels do their best to encourage it. The abolition of poverty would be the "worst possible move" America could make, Phillips felt, and his business leaders restrain themselves admirably from making any moves in this direction. Phillips's idealized businessman, in sum, was pure robber baron out of the brave days of yore.

Phillips prided himself on the fact that his novels were up to date, hot off the press, the latest word. Yet there is nothing in them which goes beyond Alger. Even Phillips's rhetoric is, like his heroes, a relic of the past. Thus the advice he was so fond of handing out on the horrors of inheriting money and the like is not only Alger in substance, but is couched in the Alger vocabulary. His rhetorical indebtedness to the author of *Ragged Dick* can be first discerned in Phillips's newspaper days. When he worked for Pulitzer, Phillips wrote a column of "aphorisms for young men," which appeared at irregular intervals in the pages of the *World.* "Get a fixed purpose and never deviate from it." "Do not fancy that talent counts for so very much in the world. Persistence without intellect is better than an intellect without persistence." "Keep hard at it every waking hour, and when the time comes for sleep go to bed and stay there until it is time to get at it again." After he stopped writing the column, Phillips still went right on coining aphorisms, which he then sowed broadcast through his fiction. "Luck is a stone which envy flings at success," remarks the hero of *The Great God Success.* Hampden Scarborough and Victor Dorn (another of the political Messiahs) talk almost entirely in self-help maxims. Dorn, who is a socialist, affords a beautiful example of what could happen to the Communist Manifesto when it got into the mouth of an Alger hero:

> Organize! Think! Learn! Then you will rise out of the dirt where you wallow with your wives and your children. Don't blame your masters; they don't enslave you. They don't keep you in slavery. Your chains are of your own forging and only you can strike them off!

The American literary tradition of inspirational aphorisms which began with Puritan homilies was inherited by Benjamin Franklin in the eighteenth century and secularized, but it was with Alger in the post-Civil War years that the tradition reached the high point of its development; since then, there have only been variations on a theme, whether the author has been Andrew Carnegie or Dale Carnegie. Phillips's phrases are not only in the Alger vein, they are often direct steals. When a colleague of Horace Armstrong's tells him, "You're bound to win," or Joshua Craig is typified as a "hardy plotter in the arduous pathway from plowboy to President," Phillips was exploiting some of the most familiar of Alger's contributions to the American language.

The rhetoric of Phillips's novels held, as a result, a powerful appeal to a middle-class audience which had been raised on the Alger stories. Possibly the question of how any American could ever have believed in or even bothered to read the stories of Phillips's incredible heroes finds an answer here. The language of Alger, learned in childhood, exerted a hypnotic influence on Phillips's readers; they found his fantasies credible, and could will to believe in his Messiah, because of the overwhelming associations set in motion by the rhetoric. At the heart of Phillips's deification of the past lay an invocation of a childhood world.

One secret, then, behind the big modern front of Phillips's fiction was its anachronism, but there was a second secret, deeper and darker than the first. The denunciations of the American aristocracy, the abuse heaped upon the East, the celebration of small-town Indiana and "real people," were fraudulent from beginning to end. (pp. 148-52)

[Phillips's] Messiahs are men of the people, but they all want to become gentlemen. They hire instructors to train them in good form, good clothes and good grammar, and dancing masters to teach them how to walk. With their usual superiority, they quickly master all the details of aristocratic living; they are still scornful, but are henceforth better dressed and better housed than the plutocrats, who have money but no taste. Phillips's heroes have an instinct for the best in women as well as in clothes. Although contemptuous of society snobs and fortune hunters, they nevertheless all marry heiresses.

Having to cloak his interest in expensive things behind the excuse that he was merely demonstrating that an Alger hero could beat an aristocrat even at his own game eventually proved unsatisfying to Phillips. Posing as the perfect democrat with a distaste for what fascinated him grew as wearisome as always walking instead of riding must have. To fulfill himself, Phillips wrote a secret novel. He did not publish it, but kept it by him in his Gramercy Park apartment, writing it over and over and over again. Not until after he was dead did *Susan Lenox: Her Fall and Rise* see the light of day. Almost one thousand pages long, published in two volumes, *Susan Lenox* was Phillips's last will and testament.

The novel is the story of a prostitute. Susan is, however, not just another girl of the streets, but a special, demo-aristocratic kind of trollop. Born, inevitably, in a small Indiana city, she is raised by one of the more socially prominent families in town. The family, however, is not her own—Susan's origin was in democratic bastardy. Despite this, or rather because of it, Susan is superior to her contemporaries among the better families. Even as a small child she likes to walk by herself with no help from anyone; she is better-looking, has more fastidious taste in clothes and reads more difficult books than the other boys and girls in town. This combination of superiority and bastardy is too much for the other families and they jealously ostracize Susan from local society. Realizing she has no future in Indiana, Susan sets out "into the fascinating golden unknown."

At this point, Susan's endless series of falls and rises is set in motion. She becomes a successful riverboat singer, but her career is terminated when the boat burns. She finds work in a factory, then is finally reduced to streetwalking, whence the long climb back to the top is resumed. After a brief period of affluence, events drive her down to the bottom again. By this continuous sine wave of the plot action, Phillips's heroine is able to avoid the dilemma which plagued Sister Carrie. Carrie yearns for material things, but possession of them eventually bores her. Susan never has her desires fulfilled long enough to reach the point of satiation, and so she goes on and on and on, alternately yearning for and delighting in the jewelry and clothes and splendid apartment suites which Phillips never tired of describing.

Whereas Phillips's heroes had had to temper their rampant individualism with lip service to the public welfare, his secret heroine has only herself in mind. Susan has the "self-reliance and . . . the hardiness—so near akin to hardness" which "must come into the character before a man or a woman is fit to give and take in the combat of life." Abolishing inequality either by law or by Golden Rule Susan finds "fantastically false." Her tough philosophy of life is embodied in the advice she receives from one of the earliest of her men friends. "You're going to fight your way up to what's called the triumphant class—the people on top," he tells her,

> they have all the success, all the money, all the good times. Well, the things you've been taught—at church—in the Sunday School—in the nice story books you've read . . . they don't apply to people like you. . . . Once you've climbed up among the successful people you can afford to indulge—in moderation—in practicing the good old moralities. . . . But while you're climbing, no Golden Rule and no turning of the cheek. Tooth and claw then—not sheathed but naked—not by proxy, but in your own person.

Even as Susan falls for the first of so many times, she never takes her eye off the ball. In the factory she holds herself apart from the workers with the same aloofness that had characterized her among the better families in her home town. To Susan, they are not comrades, but people who smell bad. Although employed only a brief time, she becomes so skilled at her job that she turns out 25 per cent more work than the best hands in the plant. When someone tells her she is superior to "the rest of them dirty, shiftless mutton-heads," Susan blushes, but has to agree. Her descent to the streets does not in the least alter her consciousness of being a superior individual, for her decision to become a prostitute is not a mark of degradation, but a sign of her enormous self-reliance.

Susan's arduous career, extending over a period of years, has no deleterious effect whatsoever on Phillips's master-spirited girl. Her "iron strength" and "almost exhaustless endurance" are proof against all hazards. Fighting and clawing her way along, Susan at the end reaches the triumphant class. Like Carrie, she has become a famous actress. As lovely and unspoiled as the day she left Indiana, Susan is supremely happy, for at last she has reached "the world worth living in, the world from which all but a few are shut out." (pp. 153-56)

> Kenneth S. Lynn, "David Graham Phillips: The Dream Panderer," in his The Dream of Success: A Study of the Modern American Imagination, *Little, Brown and Company, 1955, pp. 121-57.*

David Mark Chalmers (essay date 1964)

[*Chalmers is an American critic and historian who has written, edited, and contributed to several studies of the muckrakers and their era. He is also the author of* Hooded Americanism: The History of the Ku Klux Klan *(1965) and has edited an abridged version of* Ida Tarbell's History of the Standard Oil Company *(1966). In the following excerpt, Chalmers examines Phillips's work in terms of the sociopolitical doctrines of socialism and Marxism.*]

[Muckrakers] Lincoln Steffens and David Graham Phillips went far along the path to socialism. They did not join the Party nor did they completely accept its doctrine, but their gravitation in that direction became the outstanding theme in their writing. It was natural that they should have to deal with such a problem. They believed that major reforms were absolutely essential, and the Marxian analysis of conditions seemed the most thorough. It recognized the growing extremes of wealth and the disturbing concentration of power in the economic world, and it offered a comprehensive solution. Thus, for those who believed that more was wrong than could be traced to individual transgressors or could be corrected by piecemeal legislation, the Socialist argument was one to be reckoned with.

Like almost all of the other muckrakers, David Graham Phillips and Lincoln Steffens moved in liberal and reform-minded circles, in which were numbered many Socialists. Phillips was greatly shaken when his intimate friend and former city editor on the *World,* Charles Edward Russell, joined the Party. Steffens, who knew almost all of the Socialist leaders, was confronted by Upton Sinclair demanding of him, "Don't you see it? Don't you see what you are showing?" Eugene V. Debs himself added, "You have written from and have been inspired by a social brain, a social heart, and a social conscience and if you are not a socialist I do not know one."

The Socialists seemed alive and eager in the struggle to create a better world; it was this spirit which had such great attraction for Ray Stannard Baker and seemed com-pelling to Phillips and Steffens. They admired this dedication to such a cause, and if Baker had been repelled by the materialism of the rank and file, Steffens and Phillips were captivated by the selflessness of the leaders. However for all that they found much that was desirable in socialism, they had serious doubts on important matters of theory. Emphasizing the political and social aspects of society, they were ill at ease when dealing with economic problems. They seemed inclined to equate their discomfort with the rejection of the Marxist doctrine. This helped them to maintain the line that they struggled to keep between themselves and the Party, but they were ideologically as uncomfortable outside of the movement as they probably would have been within it. David Graham Phillips and Lincoln Steffens were too individualistic to have been happy within any rigid mold, but in their writing they seemed to be asking themselves the question that Steffens had asked Ida Tarbell when Charles Edward Russell joined the Socialist Party, "Is that not what we should all be doing?" (pp. 75-6)

During the years 1902 and 1903, David Graham Phillips wrote more than twenty articles for the *Saturday Evening Post* picturing the grasp of commercialism and corporate influence in America. Even so, he believed that industry and democracy had produced a prosperous people despite the plutocracy balanced on top. His initial concern was with the influence of money on those who had it, but he soon became deeply upset over the results which touched the whole nation. The effect on the wealthy was developed most clearly in Phillips' early novels. The idle possessors of great fortunes were trying to create an American aristocracy, whose main characteristics were extravagance and ostentation. This was expressed in enormous mansions, foreign servants, the purchase of alien titles in the marriage market, snobbery, publicized philanthropy, and an insistence on artificial caste distinction. Cut off from the vital productive life of the nation, such existence was without real purpose and vulgar. It resulted in the destruction of the value in human relationships: friendship, trust, love and family.

At first Phillips attacked the men who pursued Mammon, but he soon shifted the blame to the women who worshipped the social snobbery that money purchased. Theirs was a meaningless world and they brought up their children to similar lives of vanity and uselessness; "the second generation of the rich," Phillips wrote [in ***The Second Generation***], "is rotten with the money cancer." By novel, play, and article he criticized the parasitic purposelessness of women who turned marriage into a calculated pursuit of social status, and he advocated the usefulness of divorce and the importance of sexual honesty. The vitality of a union came through a sharing and a partnership of equals. To go along with the masterful men of whom he always wrote, there was need for women of strength and integrity. In her own way the woman needed to have a creative personality in order to make her contribution. The conclusion of this line of thought was Phillips' vast posthumously-published novel ***Susan Lenox: Her Fall and Rise,*** which was the story of a woman who finally became great through breaking all bonds of conventionality.

Initially Phillips had disliked concentrated wealth because it destroyed democratic simplicity; in a short time he came to attack it for creating undemocratic poverty. As this happened his novels shifted from social to political themes. He pictured his friend and perpetual hero, Senator Albert J. Beveridge, as well as Senators Nelson Aldrich and Mark Hanna, President William McKinley, and the New York life insurance scandals. In *The Deluge* he presented an acute fictionalized biography of Thomas W. Lawson. In his articles and books, Phillips set forth the plutocratic control of the professional (medicine and law) and the articulate (press, colleges and churches) classes of the Republic by social and economic bribery. To share in the spoils, to shake the plum tree, had become the American dream, and the access to its favors was controlled by the political boss.

Central to this picture was the encroachment of the plutocracy on all branches of government: the courts, the Administration, the Congress, and especially the Senate of the United States. At the behest of William Randolph Hearst, he wrote a set of articles for *Cosmopolitan* on the corruption of the upper Chamber. Although this series [*The Treason of the Senate*] was the occasion for President Roosevelt's characterization of the "muckrakers," Phillips' effort was no wild polemic. Rather, it was a factually presented indictment of the role of wealth in the highest legislative body of the nation.

Phillips began each article with the Constitutional definition: "Treason against the United States shall consist only in levying war against them, or in *adhering to their enemies, giving them aid and comfort.*" He did not maintain that a large portion of the Senate was actually venal although five members were under indictment and others had been similarly accused. However, they owed their allegiance to the money power, rather than to the people whom they were supposed to represent. The greatest hold that the "interests" had was that they financed the Parties. Would the plutocracy supply the funds if they were to receive nothing in return? Senator Aldrich was "Boss" of the Senate because he was the representative of all of the interests. Arthur P. Gorman, the Democratic minority leader, was his right-hand man. Most of the Senators were lawyers, as were the state legislators who elected them. Almost all were eager for retainers from the big corporations, especially the railroads. The friends and acquaintances of the man in public life were drawn from the "exploiting" class. From these alliances he too often developed a misplaced sense of loyalty. The result was that wealth and power were put in the hands of a few, primarily by the failure of Congress to safeguard the people with necessary laws. This lack of suitable regulatory legislation was the basic factor in Phillips' analysis of plutocratic growth. The two best indications of the treason of big business against the American nation, he wrote, were to be found in tariff and in railway legislation. These were the chief ways in which "the interests" fattened upon the American people.

Although alarmed by the power and—to a lesser degree—by the results of the plutocracy, Phillips continually reaffirmed his belief in democracy and its two keys, education and the suffrage. In *The Reign of Gilt,* published in 1905, he had set forth the reasons for this faith. He believed that aristocracy and caste were the natural results of widespread ignorance and that democracy was the inevitable outcome of growing intelligence. Education was, for him, "democracy's dynamo." However he questioned the freedom of the universities, especially those of the East which his novels pilloried as snob factories swayed by the pressures of plutocratic philanthropy. The Middle West, he believed, was a healthier society.

While learning nourished the wisdom that was the raw material of progress, science and industrialism were creating a new political fluidity which would undermine the political bosses. At the same time, through increasing productivity, they were raising the standard of living. The immigrant was also a revitalizing stream in the democratic life. Those who came had believed so strongly in freedom that they crossed the oceans to seek it were a conscious, determined and dedicated force against oppression and aristocracy. The growing pressure of concentrated wealth was making the citizenry increasingly discontented; reactionary and aristocratic ideals had not caught on. In writing of the senatorial "treason" Phillips did not lose his belief in the inevitability of democracy. This faith remained with him throughout his life, but as he continued to write, he changed his conception of the nature of democracy.

At first he saw it as the treasured possession of the restless middle class. Socialism abroad, he maintained, was not radical but very much an approximation of the ideals of the American Republic. The "revolution" of which he frequently wrote would be caused not by mob rule but by mis-rule. It would be the result of bourgeois discontent rather than proletarian unrest.

The only way to end corruption, he felt, was for the government to take over such utilities as the railroads. Regulation had been worse than useless. On some occasions he was willing to call this step socialistic, but he usually avoided any labels. Although he praised the Socialists for seeing and grappling with the real issues of the distribution of wealth, he objected to their dogmatism. They were far too precise, he complained; their formulations were too much like prophecy. His principal motivation seemed to be that he felt himself uncomfortably close to their point of view and sought to avoid becoming so identified. As he came nearer to the Marxian doctrines in the last years of his life, Phillips refrained from any mention of socialism. In his two most radical novels, the term is never used.

With *The Second Generation* in 1907 Phillips centered his efforts on his novels. In this book, which many critics considered his best, he set forth a socialist panacea. No longer interested in the virtues of the bourgeoisie, he had worked out a theory of surplus value to show how a parasitic society robbed the toiler of his labor. The author's hero was a workingman who stuck by his class and refused to become a foreman because he couldn't "speed" the men: "Did you ever think, it takes one of us only about a day to make enough barrels to pay his week's wages, and that he has to donate the other five days' work for the privilege of being allowed to live? If I rose I'd be living off those five days of stolen labor." In Phillips' utopia, "profits" would be abolished and industry turned over to the workers in a gradually cumulative process. Factories were to be forced out of business by non-dividend-paying competition and taken over by the toilers. Phillips did not postulate transition from giant private to public trusts, for neither monopoly nor the national government seemed to be involved in this shop-by-shop process. When the change of ownership had been accomplished, the workers and their families would respond to their improved circumstances by learning to use their new leisure instead of merely existing to labor long hours for others. Culture was unproductive in the hands of the rich, he wrote, and meaningful only in those of the workers.

The analysis did not, however, absorb Phillips' full attention. The novels which he wrote between *The Second Generation* and his sudden death in 1911 usually dealt with the problems of marriage, divorce, and the range of man-woman relations and made no reference to his labor theories. However his posthumously published *The Conflict* plunged heavily into a dissertation on labor and on class divisions. The former was too powerful to be kept down while the latter were too strong to be crossed even by his hitherto omnipotent heroes and heroines. As an ideological manifesto, it was a bad book—or perhaps one which Phillips himself had not finished. It opposed strikes because they gave the capitalists an excuse to resort to force. He maintained that labor could prevail peacefully, but the book was not explicit about either the process or the results of power. The solidarity which it preached somehow looked more like an end than a means. The basic element of the book was a polemic emphasizing class conflict in vaguely Marxian terms.

This was not presented naked and unwashed, however, but only after having been bathed in the blood of the lamb. Along with his creation of a messianic hero—carpenter and son of a carpenter—Phillips had his heroine eulogize a Christ-like Karl Marx:

> And they were both labor leaders—labor agitators. The first proclaimed the brotherhood of man. But he regarded this world as hopeless and called on the weary and heavy-laden masses to look to the next world for the righting of their wrongs. Then—eighteen centuries after—came the second Jew—and he said 'No! not in the hereafter, but in the here. Here and now, my brothers. Let us make this world a heaven. Let us redeem ourselves and destroy this devil of ignorance who is holding us in this hell! It was three hundred years before the first Jew began to triumph. It won't be so long before there are monuments to Marx in clean and beautiful and free cities all over the earth.

The moving force of change set forth in *The Conflict* was the socialist spirit, analysis and movement, devoid of force and violence. It was moving toward an inevitable triumph within the democratic framework. (pp. 81-7)

> *David Mark Chalmers, "Travelers Along the Way: Lincoln Steffens and David Graham Phillips," in his* The Social and Political Ideas of the Muckrakers, *The Citadel Press, 1964, pp. 75-87.*

Elizabeth Janeway   (essay date 1977)

[Janeway, an American novelist, critic, lecturer, and author of children's books, is considered a major speaker for the woman's movement. She once wrote that in her work she is "exploring the interactions that are shifting our perceptions of gender roles and, indeed, of the entire political process through which our world is managed." In the following excerpt, written as an afterword for Susan Lenox, *Janeway examines the novel's implausibility in terms of the Nietzschean concept of the "superman."]*

On the basis of his output of fiction—more than twenty books which sold an average of one hundred thousand copies each—David Graham Phillips must be granted a novelist's place in the annals of American literature. Critically, however, he is much better regarded as an able, indeed an inspired, journalist. Today we might call him an investigative reporter. In his own time—from the 1890s to his death in 1911—he was a supreme example of the *muckracker,* a type made famous by Lincoln Steffens and Ida Tarbell. His *Treason of the Senate,* nearly as well known as Steffens's *Shame of the Cities,* helped to bring about the direct election of United States senators, and his work won praise from such a sophisticated critic as H. L. Mencken.

Susan Lenox: Her Fall and Rise was a posthumous novel: Phillips had met his death in a way that even a hardened author of melodrama would hesitate to use, shot to death by a paranoid reader who believed that his sister had been hostilely portrayed in one of Phillips's books. To be suspected of writing from life is a hazard that novelists expect, but few have paid so dearly for the convincing realism of their fiction. Phillips had worked long over this last novel, writing and rewriting, and when it finally appeared, after the censors of the Society for the Suppression of Vice had done their best to prevent its publication, it was hailed by *The New Republic* as "probably the best thing (Phillips) ever did," though the *New York Times* and the *Boston Transcript* piously sided with the censors in wishing that this "pornography" had "never been published." Two generations later we can still feel the force of Phillips's attack on the respectable and his revelations of the mean abyss of need in which the urban poor dwelt.

True, Phillips's characters are types and his narrative is not very plausibly sustained. But this tale of a nicely brought up girl whose life leads through the depths of poverty, drudgery and prostitution offers a hoard of minutely observed detail from the underside of that misnamed decade, The Gay Nineties. Nor does the author give us only a heap of data. Phillips intends to show us "how the system works": how wealth and respectability maintain themselves by exploiting the masses. He is neither socialist nor social scientist, but what he has to say about the background and the causes of poverty is relevant reading for both. In literary quality, Phillips's novel can't compare with the master realists like Zola, Balzac and Dreiser, but in observation it is not inferior. This is the sort of book that used to be called a "slice of life." It still is that.

The shape of Phillips's novel is familiar—the picaresque. *Susan Lenox* is a feminine version of *Tom Jones*. Like that hero, Susan was born "a love child" in a rural setting and raised in comfort and with seeming affection. Like Tom, she is good, innocent, fair of face and body and possessed of intelligence which is confounded only by her own goodness of heart. She is endowed with innate nobility and honesty which, though morally admirable, prevent her from seeing the envy and malice of others. True, Susan's Uncle Warren is no Squire Allworthy. It is not a jealous rival who persuades him that Susan is unworthy of his love (though one exists in her foster-sister, Ruth), but his own narrow bigotry. Nonetheless, the early world of trust and comfort vanishes quickly and even more brutally for Susan than for Tom. Like him, she is thrown on an uncaring society, to sink or swim. Survive she does. But it is clear that the recounting of her survival is a device that permits her creator to explore the dark corners of these lower depths. Susan's adventures, that is, take place at the pleasure of the journalist-author and not out of any real fictional development of character or situation.

Thus, some contemporary critics noted quite justly that Susan is spared the misfortunes of venereal disease and unwanted pregnancy which, in real life, might well have prevented the rise that follows her fall. And it is indeed implausible that a prostitute, alcoholic and opium addict could have escaped as easily as Susan did from the consequences of her life and achieved a brilliant stage career. Even if a few women managed to surmount such disasters, the plea that "it really happened" does not excuse fictional implausibility. Susan bears a charmed life for one simple reason: she is the instrument which allows Phillips to make the full ironic statement he has in mind. Only by surviving and rising from the depths can Susan condemn the way in which middle-class morality and the capitalist system both stack the cards against success for any outsiders—and then tolerate, if they do not direct, admiration for the maverick who breaks the rules and succeeds in spite of convention.

Phillips's emphasis on success is very turn-of-the-century, for what he is celebrating is not simply getting on and making a fortune. Nietzsche published his praises of the Superman, the unmoved individual hero, in the 1880s, but they were not put into English till the first decade of our century. At the same time appeared Shaw's *Man and Superman.* This distinction between the hero who controls life by his will and the ordinary indecisive majority of folk was exemplified in politics by Theodore Roosevelt, and it was a recurrent theme of the writing of the time. We should not misunderstand its implication. A Superman succeeds by no magic. He is created painfully, as the iron of his spirit is tempered by the hammer blows of fate.

Susan is toughened and enabled to survive the searching demands of her life in just such a way. The Superwoman theme is signalled early when, having learned from Ruth who she is and how society views her, she cries: "I'm done with God." As religion fails her and family affection vanishes before the threat of scandal, she comes to rely more and more on her own inner strength. True human kindness proves vulnerable to change—as when Burlingham, the producer who stood ready to help her, dies of typhoid, or as when in the case of Spenser it turns out to be only

a mask for lust and selfishness, since Spenser will save Susan only if she submits meekly to his domination.

Showing up the hypocrisy of American orthodoxy was not a new enterprise even two generations ago. The muckrakers, however, took on the job in a new way. They did not attack their targets with abstract moral arguments or theological principles, they collected the facts and heaped up masses of data on everyday life. The greatest value of Phillips's book lies in the cases he presents of human deprivation and degradation. Here are the factory girls struggling to live on $3.50 a week and so solve the impossible equation that should let them eat and sleep and clothe themselves, but never does. Paying sixty cents a week for carfare, Susan reflects in her paper-box factory days, would have sunk her. Here are the injured and old, thrown pensionless on the scrapheap, and the men who can save themselves if they desert their families. Here is the insidious offer of promotion from worker to foreman, which requires the new recruit to the "boss" class to wring more work out of his or her former colleagues. We learn how piece workers who contrive to turn out more finished goods than the norm find at once that the rate per piece goes down. And we are introduced to the miseries of a housing system in which owners, tenants, and servants—or slaveys—struggle to keep their heads above water at each other's expense under the relentless economic pressure of "the system."

This is the pressure, as Phillips documents, that leads young women into prostitution, since "the wages of sin" are higher, for a young and healthy girl, than the meager return on virtuous drudgery. Susan and her friend Etta are not only paid well by the "sports" they pick up on their first determined venture at selling their bodies, they are kept in comfort and enjoy good food and drink, entertainment and merry companionship. This idyll, of course, does not last. Etta is eventually able to persuade her "John" to marry her. (It's fascinating to find that term already in use.) But Susan could not, even if she wanted to. No doubt Phillips is once again manipulating the narrative: if Susan, not Etta, had married, we'd have had no story. But in fact, it's realistic to make clear that only a few street girls could have married a pick-up, as Etta did.

Susan's later experiences in New York show us the dark side of commercial sex. If at first it paid girls better than respectable work, "the system could not allow these benefits to accrue for long. Susan and Etta operated on their own for a short time in Cincinnati, but in New York, amateurs were quickly taken over by the professionals, the pimps. Phillips's study of the control of prostitution by an organized criminal network, in which police and the legal system play a regular part, is as up-to-date as *The Godfather,* and in some ways less sentimental. The girls were not only threatened with violence, they were controlled by prison sentences arranged by pimps and police for those who got out of line. These records were always available to blackmail any woman who tried to escape from the life. Phillips has seen and recorded it all. Indeed, there are times when the heaping up of repeated, grimy detail is almost too much, when the reader feels that the author is laboring his point beyond endurance; and yet the accumulation of horrors *is* telling. It emphasizes the depth of the swamp of poverty and the hungry clutch of the mud from which so few could entirely extricate themselves. In addition, we come to feel, I think, the hatred for such a life that those few carried with them out of the bog, and their rejection of those who were left behind.

Once again, the only salvation from these horrors, Phillips maintains, is strength: individual moral will. Susan repeats it over and over: only through pride and determination and a hard resolve to trust no one but herself can she achieve the rise which follows her fall. Which is not to say that she engineers this rise by herself. She is granted good fortune; chance smiles on her. But what she makes of her luck depends on herself. She refuses good fortune (sometimes implausibly) if it can be exploited only by continued dependence on someone else—that is, on some man or other, for what woman could or would help her? She turns down the Chicago buyer who would like to keep her in comfort; later she refuses to marry Freddie. Either arrangement would mean putting herself in the hands of the man, and she will not pay that price. Only to Spenser does she give up herself and her freedom, and that is out of love. She is not, that is, making the standard male-female bargain, in which affection and submission are exchanged for protection and support. Susan gives herself to Spenser for nothing, as a free gift, and by so doing she holds onto her pride because what she gives is given by her own free choice.

There is no doubt that Phillips's understanding of women's grievances is remarkable. He was writing, of course, at a time when the first feminist wave was beginning to make itself heard—but how many successful male authors were able to take in what theorists like Charlotte Perkins Gilman were saying? Phillips understood. Along with the documented evidence of the oppression of women, readers will find decisive statements of feminist ideas in this book. These range from the economic to the personal. Etta declares "Pa says the day's coming when women'll be like men, work at everything and get paid the same wages." Susan reflects on her middle-class upbringing. "I was raised as a lady and not as a human being." Perhaps the first is a commonplace, but the second shows true insight.

Yet it is clear that Phillips has not created "a new woman" in Susan. Certainly characterization is not his forte. He is a journalist who drapes the fabric of his wide experience on lay-figures. But Susan is not even a consistent type. What Phillips has done, I think, is to project himself—a young, talented, energetic man—into Susan's place, and to imagine what life there would have been like for him. Few men have ever attempted such a metamorphosis, and Phillips should be honored for the effort. It gave him a clarity of vision and an objectivity about women's real existence which is rare even now. There are, for example, no golden-hearted whores in the clutches of his pimps, only hard-pressed human beings. He finds feminine passivity unworthy and sees how the obligation of pleasing men has maimed and mutilated women's spirit. Phillips really made that long journey from taken-for-granted masculine dominance into women's place.

The one thing he could not do was to create a living human being in the center of these experiences; that would have taken not just talent, energy and honesty, but genius. We read about Susan Lenox because of what happens to her, not because of what she is. In fact, she is a double creature. When she is resigned she falls into stereotyped femininity and its synonym, weakness. When she acts, she becomes masculine. Phillips can conceive the idea of a strong woman, but when he tries to create such a character, it is a masculine personality that appears.

Thus, it is not a woman's voice that says "I'm done with God," or "Women are born weak and bred weaker. I've got to get over being a woman." It is a Nietzschean hero, a Superman, who speaks these words and who remarks ironically, "I'm not a sheltered woman. I've got no one to protect me from the consequences of doing nice, sweet, womanly things"; who asks "Why lean if I'm strong enough to stand alone?" Phillips here endows Susan with the masculine mystique of reckless individuality which rejects sharing and denies the validity of joint effort. Most people, he declares, float and drift through life like seaweed. To live, one must get away from them, break the bonds of common humanity. It is a queerly contradictory reaction for one who saw so clearly how "the system" worked against the weak. He recognized that the working class was at the mercy of their employers because they could be set against each other, but he preached neither unionism nor socialism, no coming together at all in opposition to the power-structure which he condemns.

And in the end, he can imagine no higher goal for Susan and the two strong and successful men who love her than absorption into the Establishment. Freddie, who started as a pimp, grows rich and becomes a political force: an early Mafia Don, one guesses. Brent, before his death, is acclaimed not just as a great playwright, but as a popular one whose earnings lift him to the upper class. Susan's rise makes her a brilliant Broadway star. Phillips might agree with Henry Adams that success is a "bitch goddess," but he can't find another divinity to put in her place.

It is this failure of imagination which limits Phillips's reach. He is a fine and very readable reporter, but he gets no further than that. Some of his contemporaries did: Dreiser and Willa Cather both created characters who not only struggled with the mire of poverty and managed to clamber out, they gave them a human sensibility and judgment that questioned the very success they wanted. Or these authors themselves questioned the values of the times: not simply the stereotyped clichés of the middle-class—Phillips did that too—but also the idealism of individuality. Because they were less single-minded, they were more far-sighted.

But we must not blame Phillips for what he did not see and could not, therefore, set down. He has given us a striking, indeed an unforgettable, view of the submerged life of the past, and it turns out to be a scene that merges imperceptibly into the present. Phillips painted his world in an old-fashioned style, but the figures and the action portrayed there grow more familiar and recognizable the longer we look at them. He wasn't a master, but I think he was entitled to repeat Isherwood's description of his own role in Berlin of the early Thirties: "I am a camera." (pp. xi-xix)

Elizabeth Janeway, in an afterword to Susan Lenox: Her Fall and Rise *by David Graham Phillips, Southern Illinois University Press, 1977, pp. xi-xix.*

Christopher P. Wilson   (essay date 1985)

[*In the following excerpt, Wilson relates Phillips's belief in political and economic doctrines of Progressivism to his ideals as a writer.*]

It was symptomatic of the times that Isaac Marcosson, the editorial lieutenant behind the publicity campaign of *The Jungle,* would also eventually become the biographer of reporter, muckraker, and novelist David Graham Phillips. . . . In Marcosson's memoirs, Jack London and Upton Sinclair come across as extravagant crusaders who were to be tolerated and prudently managed; Phillips, in contrast, is portrayed as the serene voice of the age.

Such hagiography symbolized the esteemed place the Phillips legend came to occupy in the mainstream culture of the Progressive era. It is not easy to recall, for instance, that commentators in these years habitually called the author of *The Treason of the Senate* (1905) and *Susan Lennox* (1917) the "dashing ideal journalist" with "exceptional news sense," the representative new novelist with "democratic ideals," or that no less an American critic than H. L. Mencken—certainly no Progressive himself—once called Phillips the "leading American novelist." Like London and Sinclair, Phillips was a devoted professional, a popular naturalist, and a political activist, yet he combined these cultural ingredients in a markedly more middle-class solution. His prominent position in the American mainstream, moreover, was a direct by-product of the progressive character of his market career. He began as a reporter for Joseph Pulitzer, was coaxed out into novel writing by Progressive Senator Albert Beveridge, who in turn introduced Phillips to Lorimer, and then made his mark writing for the *Post,* the *Cosmopolitan,* and Bobbs-Merrill as a muckraker and best-selling novelist. In short, Phillips was a man who had translated the power of the progressively managed marketplace into Progressive politics.

In particular, Phillips symbolized the new author's place in the strenuous and masculine style of the Progressive ethos. In adapting the literary marketplace's evocation of forceful prose, timeliness, and vigorous investigation, Phillips's manly prose and moral outrage resonated with a new American political style. When *Treason [of the Senate]* was published in the *Cosmopolitan,* for instance, the editors promised that it would be the "most vascular and virile" exposé of the Senate ever printed. Like his fellow popular naturalists, Phillips seemed to answer the contemporary chorus of new editors and publishers who belittled the feeble tastes of the Victorian "gentle reader" and who called for the "roast beef" of literature. Perhaps even more than the others, Phillips signified a cultural victory over what Ann Douglas and others have called the mid-Victorian "feminization" of American culture, that sentimental ethos which had stressed the cultural value of the

spirit over the material world, feminine nurture over masculine nature, influence rather than power.

There can be little doubt that the resurrection of this masculine style only helped to strengthen traditional patriarchal authority in our culture, and to perpetuate a gender imbalance with a long and often unfortunate history. A book like [Jack London's] *Martin Eden* [1908] . . . had definite misogynist themes. Additionally, it seems likely—though more research still needs to be done—that the popularity of this masculine style put constraints upon many female novelists and journalists. Certainly, someone like Ida Tarbell did make her mark as a muckraker, and was happy with the professional status she achieved. (pp. 141-42)

Of course, certain women spoke out vocally against the new masculine style. Charlotte Perkins Gilman, for instance, in a series of reviews and articles in her own *Forerunner* satirized the hegemony of masculine fantasies in popular fiction. Gilman argued that popular taste was dominated by fiction which created "predatory excitement" in its readers; she said contemporary novels were either "The Story of Adventure" or the "Story of Romance"—and that in fact, the latter was just a version of the former. "It is the Adventure of Him in Pursuit of Her," she said, "and it stops when he gets her." Gilman also wrote a rather scathing review of Phillips's own *Grain of Dust* [1911] in precisely these terms. Similarly, California novelist Gertrude Atherton, writing in the *New Republic* in 1915, lamented the demise of the "gentle reader," and her replacement by a creature with more "red-blooded tastes."

While not conclusive, these fragments suggest that the dominance of the masculine style may have compelled some serious female writers to resist the culturally legitimated professional style. On the other hand, we will oversimplify the significance of this masculine ethos—and indeed the popular appeal of a writer like Phillips—if we read the era's gender idiom too literally. That is, as Tarbell's case itself suggests, we must not lose sight of the fact that this masculine style spoke to a late-Victorian crisis which spanned even the gender gap. Like its feminine antecedent, the principal appeal of this masculine ethos lay not only in its fantasies of sexual dominance but in a broader palliative function. Within the revived masculine mythos lay a veiled promise that the individual would not be reduced to a social cipher by the stifling comfort, anxiety, and interdependence of modern life.

American elites at the close of the Victorian era were beset with a fear of becoming, in a word that had gained usage in the 1880s, "overcivilized." As many historians have written, for male and female members of the educated bourgeoisie alike, everyday life had become not only smothered by the advance of modernized comforts and leisure time, nor merely inundated with products, but morally "weightless," cut off from primary experience and serious moral choices. Thorstein Veblen's encyclopedic denunciation of the leisure class in 1899 only gave voice to anxieties within that class itself, a class convinced that its cultural traditions and self-reliance were being obliterated and displaced by the industrial dynamo. For males, these anxieties surfaced in Adamesque hand-wringing about psychic impotence; in women the generalized ailment was neurasthenia. Fearing the onset of decadence, often plagued by a sense of living on the periphery of life, many sought out more immediate contact with "real life" through the professions, politics, and similarly "other-directed" activities. What provided psychological salvation for so many late Victorians, in particular, was the saving grace of a masculine career in the muck of American life. It was altogether fitting, for example, that Upton Sinclair, once so prone to psychic depression and a sense of uselessness, should cross paths in Chicago with Jane Addams, who addressed her own "subjective necessity" in social work. It was in this fashion, then, that mass-market authorship played its part in the era's overall rehabilitation of bourgeois values—through a new and truly professional ethos. This version of professionalism was perhaps nowhere more vivified than in the case of a writer like Phillips himself.

For these reasons and others, Phillips's interest for us may be more than merely historical; in fact, his near-disappearance from our literary historics can be rather misleading. The fact of the matter is that he helped to craft a masculine and moralistic style which long outlived his martyrdom—indeed, a style that recurs today not only in our "big stick" policymakers, who are more indebted to T.R., but even in the manner of the modern newsman, who has Phillips as one of his progenitors. Moreover, the calling of the career is still with us. By populating his novels with effete, leisure-class youths transformed by an encounter with the world of work, Phillips helped to refashion an older myth of American regeneration into one of the most recurrent popular mythologies of our time: the tale of the modern son (or country) smothered by permissiveness, yet resurrected to timeless American self-reliance. Underneath all the masculine bluster and nostalgia, however, the inner life of this mythmaker took on the contours, and the contradictions, of a decidedly more modern nation. (pp. 143-44)

The novel [*The Great God Success* (1901)] . . . depicts the rise and fall of a Yale graduate named John Howard who, unlike Phillips himself, becomes trapped in a career in journalism. Essentially, the plot of the novel moves in two cycles: after initial success as a reporter, Howard falls into what Phillips calls a "bohemian quicksand" of love and stifling leisure; after succeeding again, he is ultimately corrupted by his own greed. From a vocational standpoint, the second cycle of the book is the more important. Howard, despite the fact that he converts his newspaper from tame Victorian elitism to exciting democratic service, finds his moral fiber in decay under the temptations of money and leisure. He is weakened by the contact with upper-class society that his notoriety brings him, and by a marriage that compromises both his intellectual and professional independence. The book ultimately closes with his corruption: he alters an editorial in order to protect his own financial investments and to snatch a political appointment.

Like *Martin Eden* and [Upton Sinclair's] *The Journal of Arthur Stirling* [1903], this novel obviously incorporates

autobiographical detail to enhance the impression of realism. Howard is drawn with Phillips's own temperament, a combination of "openness and reserve, friendliness and unapproachableness," a youth of wholly bookish upbringing who rises from his own psychological inertia by adopting the philosophy of self-help and hard work. In the same way, Howard's transformation of the *"News-Record"* applies direct factual detail, first from the *Sun,* and later, in the final section, from Pulitzer's *World.* Superficially, the novel reads rather like a historical parable, one which tries to chart the moral progress and eventual downfall of the new journalism.

In several ways, however, the novel is a good deal more ambitious, or indeed more ambiguous, than such a schematic reading might suggest. On the one hand, the novel was "progressive" enough that even Pulitzer himself, for instance, praised it. Indeed, Phillips seemed to view the older journalism with Pulitzerian disdain; one is inclined to call it a muckraking novel. In the older, genteel offices of the past, the profession of journalism is called a "dragon" demanding an annual sacrifice of youth—the office does seem clublike, yet it is criticized because it lacks room for advancement. As if drawn directly from contemporary debates about journalism schools and professional credentials, the old style seems anachronistic to the point of mummification. "Journalism is not a career," one reporter remarks prophetically. "It is either a school or a cemetery. A man may use it as a stepping-stone to something else. But if he sticks to it, he finds himself an old man, dead and done for to all intents and purposes years before he's buried."

At first, Howard's goal is to change the outdated attitudes of the *News-Record.* In time, he discovers that the key to the paper's regeneration is his own "work, incessant, self-improving, self-developing." At least from the narrator's explicit commentary, Phillips seems to have no qualms about Howard's goal of rehabilitating the paper:

> The theory of the *News-Record* staff was that their journal was too "respectable," too intelligent, to be widely read; that the "yellow journals" grovelled, "appealed to the mob," drew their vast crowds by the methods of the fakir and the freak. They professed pride in the *News-Record's* smaller circulation as proof of its freedom from vulgarity and debasement. They looked down upon the journalists of the popular newspapers and posed as the aristocracy of the profession.
>
> Howard did not assent to these self-complacent excuses. He was democratic and modern, and the aristocratic pose appealed only to his sense of humour and his suspicions. He believed that the success of "yellow journals" with the most intelligent, alert and progressive public in the world must be based upon solid reasons of desert, must be in spite of, not because of, their follies and exhibitions of bad taste. He resolved upon a radical departure, a revolution from the policy of satisfying petty vanity and tradition within the office to a policy of satisfying the demands of the public.

Howard thus seems to emerge as a hero Pulitzer would—

and did—adore: the *News-Record* becomes a democratic servant of a progressive public. The overriding impression this narrator leaves is that Howard's goal of reorienting the paper is all to the good.

What stands in the way of this rather pat interpretation, however, is that the resolution of the novel contradicts the narrator's confident assertions. Howard's conversion of the *News-Record*, in fact, lays the seeds of his downfall. Initially, Howard boasts that the paper, despite its profit motive, is free from entanglements; but later he falls victim to the very dependence created by his new affluence. In this way, the book seems to lend itself, paradoxically, to a conservative critique of the professional journalist's credo of independence. On these terms, quite clearly the novel became a rather traditional commentary on the cost of exchanging party politics for the imperatives of capital.

The heart of this apparent paradox was Phillips's own presentiment that the very success of the new journalism—and more particularly, of the new journalist—would be its undoing. As Howard leads a tour through his printing room, he is struck by the temporality of his work: the *Journal* is assembled by energy and sweat, and yet is a "corpse" the minute the news becomes old. Timeliness only invited this temporal limitation. Meanwhile, as he tracks down the plutocracy's sins in print, Howard's own success has similarly deadening results. He begins by disdaining the high style of the rich, yet over time he places a woman of culture as his goal of conquest—here, a socialite named Marian Trevor, already engaged to a plutocrat named Teddy. Although, like the character Ruth Morse in *Martin Eden*, Marian engages Howard in a Victorian and "Progressive" dialogue, she also symbolizes her hero's goal of status. Thus, though she initially succumbs to what Phillips calls "The Eternal Masculine" force represented by the rehabilitated Howard, ultimately Marian exerts a subtle influence on her mate that subverts his energy. Howard is debilitated by Marian's parlor world and weakened by a dependency on wealth, a fear of social pressure, and concern for his property. Paralleling his marital dependence with his professional compromises, he discovers: " 'A man who makes his living by the advocacy of principles should be wholly free. If he isn't, the principles are sure sooner or later to become incidental to the living, instead of the living being incidental to the principles'."

In sum, Phillips exposed the contradiction within the trade's tenuous equation of the journalist's moral integrity with its own. His paradoxical resolution underscored a modern crisis of dependence in a literary field that had supposedly released itself from Victorian elitism. At the same time his novel sanctioned activist journalism in political terms, it retreated from the professional and political compromises the new style engendered, particularly career stagnation and intellectual dependence. But the contradiction he had stumbled over was not merely professional, cultural, or political; rather, it was a combination of all three. What Phillips had done, in effect, was to extrapolate upon what began as essentially a literary crisis to a striking political point. The first step was his recognition that the impetus of the new journalism, especially in Pulitzer's hands, was to compel the reporter away from

his "literary" identity—which meant, specifically, his role as a discursive and autonomous observer of city life. The next step was to realize that this impetus was not, in its final outcome, wholly democratic—that in fact it drew the writer away from democratic "manners" in both the literary and social senses of the word. Ultimately, this novel—and indeed Phillips himself—testified to the tortured conscience the new professionalism could engender. At the level of narrative force and opinion, text and author sanctioned the displacement of the literary man. At another level, Phillips's funereal images evoked a spirit of mourning.

However torturous it had been, Phillips's apprenticeship in journalism revealed, in part, that he had approached the literary vocation with a particularly modern orientation: that is, as a rationalized career within a bureaucratized social structure. This orientation in itself affected the way Phillips adapted the pervasive rhetoric of literary professionalism to rather different political ends. London and Sinclair appropriated the ethos of literary labor as a source of solidarity with working-class Americans; they fashioned their craft in the terms of the artisan or the street. Yet Phillips, reflecting his more pious and middle-class perspective, imbued the professional ethos with the ideal of public service, and in so doing put his art at the service of middle-class Progressivism. As with the others, therefore, there was a traceable ideological current between Phillips's vocational ideology, his literary practice, and his political sympathies—one might say, a wave of value and sentiment which crested with *The Treason of the Senate*. At the same time, nonetheless, Phillips's success again undid him. The very public prominence of his muckraker role generated a personal and emotional undertow that ultimately pulled him out of the political arena altogether. (pp. 150-53)

What held this contradictory man together was the ideal of the career. In Phillips's eyes, professional novel writing was the logical summit of a structured occupational ladder. You acquired expertise in journalism's school of hard knocks; then you were entitled to sit upon a high pulpit and hold the public trust in your palms (or pen). The idea was well put by Frank Norris, whose viewpoints and apprenticeship were remarkably similar to Phillips's own. The novelist's vocation, Norris said, was defined by "responsibility," a sense of service and duty acquired by "the long grim grind of the years of his life that he has put behind him and the work that he has built up volume by volume, sincere work, telling the truth as he saw it.

Phillips's service orientation subtly altered the social connotations of his reverence for literary labor—a reverence which, superficially, looked quite like London's or Sinclair's. Although, like the others, Phillips spoke of the writer's duty to identify with the values of the common working populace, his was a decidedly more generalized empathy. When he spoke of himself as a "worker," he commonly made that nineteenth-century republican distinction that grouped businessmen with laborers as "working" people, in opposition to "parasitic" bankers or commercial elites. Really, Phillips took his place in a long middle-class tradition extending back to Howells and

Longfellow, both of whom had attempted to draw the literary vocation into the camp of everyday "common people." In other words, and again like Norris—who said the modern novelist should be a "Good Citizen" by aligning himself with "Common People"—Phillips's self-conception waffled on the issue of just how "common" a people he meant. Instead, his true intellectual touchstone was the professional notion of his public—in a sense, the literary contract with his readers. Denigrating the notion of literature as a divinely inspired or intrinsically noble calling, Phillips instead cast himself in a voice which evoked the rolled-up shirt-sleeves of the modern office employee. "I have no mission," he claimed, "no purpose, no cult. I am just a novelist, telling as accurately as I can what I see, and trying to hold my job with my readers." In sum, Phillips, much more than London or Sinclair, took the motive of the new market to heart: exchange and service, not labor per se, actually defined his literary selfhood.

Consequently, Phillips's acceptance of market standards was, at first, almost wholly uncritical. In public print Phillips ridiculed authors who could not "address large audiences," who chose to forgo publicity or monetary reward, or who (like Henry Holt) "rail[ed] against 'the commercialization of literature.'" Against this supposedly antiquated model Phillips posited a "democratic" notion of authorship. To use a phrase from Phillip Rieff, he cast his literary philosophy in "anti-creedal" rhetoric. "As for him," Phillips wrote, "who has as his ideal to speak what seems to him to be true, to speak it so that all can hear and understand, to seek out as his rostrum publicity's highest available hill—as for such a one, merely to utter the sacred word Art in his presence is desecration." In Phillips's eyes, the market secularized the literary enterprise, stripping it of high-cultural (and hence European) superstition and restoring it to political relevance. Making the impious sound pious, Phillips promoted authorship almost as civic religion, and again as an essentially classless enterprise.

Just as with London and Sinclair, labor did have its place. The writer earned his public trust internally, through a serious devotion to a disciplined work effort in which one did not wait upon inspiration. His literary discipline became legendary even in his own time. His output within a brief eleven-year career rivaled even London's and Sinclair's. In that time, Phillips wrote over twenty-six books, a play, and hundreds of short stories and articles. In one year (1905) he published five books. Having internalized the deadline regimen of metropolitan journalism, Phillips the novelist habitually wrote only at night, usually every day of the week, while standing at his "black pulpit," a writing stand that was itself a leftover from the Pulitzer years. He wrote in pencil in a minuscule hand on half-sheets of yellow-lined paper that even today show signs of considerable alteration, erasure, and editing. Adopting the practice of working on two manuscripts at once, he said he could "rest" by shifting from one to the other.

Nonetheless, there were differences in his use of the labor ideal. A man like Sinclair saw the regimen of work as an inescapable evil, though a means of emotional identification with the masses; Jack London saw it as his lot in life. But in Phillips's mind, labor was something to be recov-

ered, almost an American birthright to be restored. When asked, for instance, why young writers often did not succeed, Phillips had this ready quip:

> Because they are afflicted with what they call the artistic temperament. Now, the artistic temperament is nothing but idleness or dyspepsia. If any symptoms of artistic temperament appear, fight them to the death. Work, work, whether you want to or not. You must exercise your brain scientifically as you do your muscles. I throw away a whole day's writing sometimes, but I am satisfied at least. I've done a day's work, and it has kept my steam up, and prevented me from rusting, lagging behind.

Although fraught with several contradictions—which I will discuss momentarily—here Phillips not only secularized the literary vocation; in effect, he inoculated it with old American virtue. That is, he drew a therapeutic connection between literary labor and physical or moral health. Art and "literariness," in short, were not merely unmanly, but akin to spiritual disease such as had threatened him at Princeton. Again, his class roots were still evident: here, though he invokes the mystique of labor, he actually speaks of work almost as leisure—as a form of exercise. Literary composition is compared not so much to work as to a "work out," a means of keeping one's blood and "steam" going.

In that last image, of course, lurked only one of several contradictions. Leaving aside the problem of working "whether you want to or not," or the assumption that there was a "science" to writing well, Phillips's own externalization of literary labor had led him to visualize his composition process in quite mechanical terms. In the passage above, he quite literally thinks of himself as a machine subject to his own scientific management. He often seemed to view his literary ego at a distance, as if his own energies were workhorses that had to be harnessed—and managed. Therefore, it is perhaps not surprising that his literary thinking exhibited a certain compulsive strain. To [Joseph W. Piercy, one of his roomates at DePauw University], he wrote:

> I write *every* night, from about eleven until about four or five or six in the morning. Sometimes seven or eight. You can work in the day time. Let me urge you to work *the same hours* every day and *never, never, never* to let anything or anyone interfere between you and working at those hours. I write every night—seven days a week. I don't wait for mood or inspiration, and I don't give up because I don't begin right or am writing rubbish. I think it's fatal to give way to moods. And I'm not a bit afraid to throw away everything I've written, or to edit my stuff to the bone—"*Travailler, toujours travailler, encore travailler.*" I think that's the secret of developing whatever possibilities one may have.

Of course, both London and Sinclair had been driven to a similar compulsiveness. But in Phillips's case, the occasion was not the plight of the proletarian, nor the flights of poetic excess, but a decidedly white collar predicament: here, in short, was a rather striking echo of the modern workaholic. In fact, precisely *because* of his career orientation Phillips had been forced into his nighttime routine. His ambition forced him to do his regular job well and yet keep pushing ahead on the outside. Friends even noticed a secretiveness about what was literally a form of literary moonlighting.

Phillips's guiding aesthetic principles themselves reflected some of his ideological inconsistencies and excesses. Certainly to denigrate "art," or to speak rather generally about presenting the "truth," were not very specific literary guidelines. Nor were his poetics clarified by cloaking his technical precepts in nationalistic sentiments. The American "originals," he wrote, like all great writers, "simply put in words what they saw; what they felt, regardless of the methods that had been employed by the writers who had gone before them." To Phillips, the "society novel" was a dangerous European import; despite being a "great manufacturer of plots," Henry James was often singled out as an unfortunate "psychologizer." With an anti-intellectual flourish that even rivaled the more (in)famous proclamations of Frank Norris about letting "style go to the devil," Phillips often dismissed the issue of style itself with a wave of the wrist. In contrast to London, for instance, he disparaged Robert Louis Stevenson's advice to learn by mimicking other stylists. Conversely, Phillips spoke reverentially—and equally vaguely—about "ideas" in tones that echoed editors like [Edward] Bok and [George Horace] Lorimer. "I prefer ideas every time," the author wrote. "Ideas in any form are first rate. The style will come to a writer, but sometimes the ideas are lacking. . . . Writing is the result of thinking about things to write about and studying the most trivial details of action in contemporaneous life, so that you may set them down, not imaginatively, but accurately. . . . There isn't any time to waste on poses; you're too busy making notes."

Fortunately, even in these rather vague polemical proclamations, there was an implied aesthetic—again, a current between Phillips's vocational ideology and his literary style. In particular, a novel like *The Great God Success,* though it attacked the old style of journalism, showed a debt to the "note-taking" method of the reporter. The novel is dominated by dialogue (as if derived from remembered interviews), while scenes are set with the sparest of atmospheric details: a chair, a slant of light, a tea set. Particularly in his early writings, Phillips's reverence for moral strength and avoiding "moods," his claim to "speak . . . so that all can hear and understand," and his evocation of the professional's "calm, sure light of intellectual exercise," elicited a style which was direct and yet restrained. Good newspaper writers, he said, learned the value of "short, clear, and simple words—expressions of actual thought . . . words that the laboring men and humble people will not stumble over." This was how he described the style of his fictional surrogate, the young journalist John Howard:

> In all his better stories—for he often wrote poor ones—there was the atmosphere of sincerity, of realism, the marks of an acute observer, without prejudice and with a justifiable leaning toward a belief in the fundamental worth of humanity. Where others were cynical he was just. Where

others were sentimental, he had sincere, healthful sentiment. Where others were hysterical, he calmly and accurately described, permitting the tragedy to reveal itself instead of burying it beneath high-heaped adjectives. Simplicity of style was his aim and he was never more delighted by any compliment than by one from the chief political reporter.

> "That story of yours this morning . . . reads as if a child might have written it. I don't see how you get such effects without any style at all. You just let your story tell itself."

Phillips began, at least, with a rather different style than London or Sinclair's impassioned realism—or, rather, his passions were more subdued. Even though Phillips, like London, construed "sincerity" as an "atmosphere"— again, an externalization in his thinking that the market would later exploit—the bias of the prose was against excess. Phillips argued for warmth, understatement, evocation of moral health, balance. If Howard saw generosity, we are told, "he did not exaggerate it into godlike heroism"; if he saw sordidness, he incorporated "characteristics which relieved and partly redeemed it."

Descriptive passages from this novel give a good sense of Phillips's ideal method, and some of its better results. One instance occurs when Howard looks out his window on Washington Square and sees the panorama of the human race:

> After dusk from early spring until late fall a multitude of interesting sounds mingled with the roar of the elevated trains to the west and south and the rumble of carriages in "the Avenue" to the north. Howard, reading or writing at his window on his leisure days, heard the young men and young women laughing and shouting and making love under the trees where the Washington Arch glistened in the twilight. Later came the songs . . . or some other of the current concert-hall jingles. Many figures could be seen flitting about in the shadows. Usually these figures were in pairs; usually one was in white; usually at her waist-line there was a black belt that continued on until it was lost in the other and darker figure.

> Scraps of a score of languages—curses, jests, terms of endearment—would float up to him.

Here again, one feels the impact of the reporter's notebook: the cityscape is a collection of impressions, of sounds, simply rendered, gathered in piecemeal; the colors are pointedly "chromatic" (black and white), the language neutral ("interesting"). There are some conventional strokes here, but no pyrotechnics of tone. The passage aims, again, to appear virtually styleless and "anti-creedal."

Over time, of course, Phillips's literary ideology flowed into political Progressivism. His self-image as a public servant, his cloaking of literary endeavor in the language of strenuosity, and his reputation as a reporter seemed to make him a key role-player in the Progressive movement; that was obviously why Beveridge recruited him. Even *The Great God Success* evoked a typically Progressive theme: journalism's compromises were seen as part of a larger crisis of independence brought on by a society of trusts, unions, and irresponsible capital. Phillips's embrace of the literary profession as a form of moral health, in addition, reinforced his critique of "plutocrats," who were devoid of public utility and stultified by European culture. Work, in Phillips's political lexicon, was "the noble, dignified, the producer of civilization and self-respect." Though he disagreed with Thorstein Veblen on the value of the modern machine, Phillips's reverence for professional competence was not unlike Veblen's adoration of technical efficiency—and now, it brought with it a similar animus against the aristocratic culture of his own collegiate past. A book of essays like *The Reign of Gilt* (1905), in singling out the effete, aristocratic sons of inherited wealth, revealed some of these antipathies—indeed, the book might as well have been marginalia in Phillips's own diary. Describing the well-bred young man of the East, Phillips wrote that "in the place of a brain, the boy acquired at college and elsewhere a lump of vanities, affectations, and poses. Surrounded by hirelings from infancy, he became convinced that he was the handsomest in body and the most brilliant in mind that the world had in recent centuries produced. He thought . . . his taste was almost too fine for a coarse, commercial era." Here, professional values, which notably accepted the coarseness of commerce, were nonetheless contrasted with plutocratic gluttony. Like that of so many Midwestern Progressives, Phillips's critique was not so much political as moral. Money in abundance bred greed, corruption, moral decadence, and madness—a far cry from the supposed simplicity and sobriety of America's past, or indeed from its rural heartland. The difference between modern times and America's pioneer heritage, he wrote, was "chiefly in moral tone."

Indeed, as Phillips's career progressed, his social criticism only seemed to bring out his residual Midwestern piety, and hence to take on a religious and even strident tone. A critic (and member) of what one of his novels termed *The Second Generation* (1907), Phillips often turned his criticism into a jeremiad about the weakening of America's moral fiber. His social philosophy thus often took on nostalgic undertones. Undoubtedly drawing upon his own frustrations in the modern bureaucracy of journalism, Phillips invoked the irretrievable past of the self-made, independent man. "If we are to have freedom in this modern world," he wrote, "we must recreate the conditions . . . on which our own freedom of the period between the war of 1812 and the war of 1861 rested. We must establish conditions that will enable any and every American citizen willing to work and get work without any dependence on any master whatsoever, to get work as his right." As this "right to work" phrasing suggests, Phillips's insistence on self-sufficiency gave his philosophizing some conservative slants. Though he sympathized with socialism, he found it contrary to "the state of individual freedom which is America's gift to her children"; concerned with the plight of the poor, he denounced charity for undermining recipients' self-respect. Such fears about American self-reliance were essential even to his most famous muckraking piece, *The Treason of the Senate.* Here Phillips argued that Congress, particularly the Senate, had contributed to the creation of a plutocracy alongside "an equally amazing and equally unnatural descent of the masses, despite skill and industry . . . toward the dependence of wages and salaries."

Treason itself, of course, was a landmark in Phillips's career, and in American muckraking generally; [in the introduction to their 1964 edition of *The Treason of the Senate*] George Mowry and Judson Grenier have given us an exhaustive account of the series' precedents, immediate impact, and long-term consequences. What interests me here, however, is what we can learn from the exposé's rather remarkable departures in style from Phillips's early precepts about literary simplicity, balance, and stylelessness. *Treason* works, in contrast to those precepts, in the highly charged give-and-take of the evangelical sermons he must have heard as a boy. One by one, Phillips "calls out" the sinners in the Senate by name (usually followed by an exclamation point) and then chastises them with, by and large, the power of his rhetoric. The text is littered with emotionally charged diction like "vast," "sinister," "sycophant," and "parasite." Secrecy within committees commonly becomes obvious proof of wrongdoing; any apparently democratic statements are misleading sham. "A scurvy lot they are," Phillips writes at one point, " . . . with their smirking and cringing and voluble palaver about God and patriotism." In fact, dispensing with the reporter's notebook, Phillips seems to downplay the importance of presenting facts at all, citing a fear of testing the impatience of the masses. "Few among the masses have the patience to listen to these matters," he writes at one point; at another, he says "it takes an expert" to find the tedious details. In disdaining his own role as a *provider* of detail, and in reducing the relationship of wealth to political institutions to a matter of who knew whom, Phillips was perhaps polemically effective, yet in key moments his sermon style was rather more like caricature than sincere fidelity to fact. Chauncey Depew "presents a picture of himself," Phillips remarks, for instance, "the sly courtier agent, with the greasy conscience and the greasy tongue and the greasy backbone and the greasy hinges of the knees." The style dominates over the case at hand.

What caused such a departure in style? Perhaps the furor of the moment, or the importance of the cause. At another level, however, one might also be inclined to say that Phillips's masculine vocational precepts, indeed his compulsiveness, led naturally in the direction of overstatement and posturing. Even more fundamentally, perhaps, the way the series had been mapped out had itself denigrated Phillips into the role of stylist. As it turns out, though he himself had undertaken this particular muckraking assignment reluctantly, *Treason* was another instance of new progressive planning. The series had originally been the brainchild of muckraker Charles Edward Russell, who had passed it on to editor Bailey Millard, a longtime Hearst lieutenant. Phillips was then asked to conduct the series, but said he preferred to stick to fiction. Asking a price he hoped would be rejected—yet was not—Phillips then stipulated that he would write the piece only if someone else did the research. Subsequently, that assignment had been given to the socialist writer Gustavus Meyers. Phillips, partly due to his own reluctance to do the investigative prying, now found himself on the end of a literary assembly line—to apply Lorimer's definition of publishing, as the "hired" brain to carry out the editorial "idea." Phillips' own externalization of his "realism" into an "atmosphere" of "sincerity" made him vulnerable to just this kind of expropriation. Almost confessionally, his prose denigrated "facts" because he had not collected them; instead, he had been hired to make the facts "virile."

At an even deeper level, there may have been another, more complex reason for the hubris of Phillips's prose—a reason having to do with his original vocational hopes. One is struck, first of all, by how he had been dragged kicking and screaming into this series—and not by the intellectual merits of the case, but by a salary he originally had thought was absurd. Then, Phillips's anxiety over this new instance of dependence was probably not helped by the chorus of critics who pointed out that the *Cosmopolitan's* publisher, Hearst, was at the time seeking public office. Nor was his conscience eased by the fact that the catapulting circulation of the *Cosmopolitan* was up 50 percent over its average for that year. By the end of the series, in fact, Phillips regretted having even undertaken the assignment, and the last article ends, as Mowry points out, rather inconclusively. In other words, there is the possibility that Phillips argued so vehemently because he was, in part, arguing with his own conscience right from the start. In fact, his first novel had described just such a dilemma—and, moreover, how such a crisis played itself out:

> Sometimes, when [Howard] was talking to Marian or writing editorials, all in the strain of high principle and contempt for sordidness, he would flush at the thought that he was in reality a good deal of a hypocrite. "I'm expressing the ideals I ought to have, the ideals I used to have, not the ideals I have."
>
> But the clearer the discrepancy became to him and the wider the gap between what he ought to think and what he really did think, the more strenuously he protested to himself against himself, and the more fiercely he denounced in public the very poison he was himself taking.

This may seem a rather farfetched explanation for Phillips's vehemency at first. But it is no more arcane, or convoluted, than the confession above—nor than Lincoln Steffens's account of his own "shame." Even more suggestively, one has the outcome of the series to consider. It was telling, I think, how hard Phillips took Roosevelt's rather private, and indeed rather ambiguous, muckraker speech at the Gridiron Club, a speech which charged that journalists had their eyes only on the "muck" of material gain. Friends reported the author wandering aimlessly as if stricken, saying (rather lamely) he regretted his inability to have written in the first-person singular. Whereas some thinkers (like the *McClure's* crowd) readily adopted the intended epithet of muckraker, Phillips was driven out of political controversy for the rest of his career.

Unlike London, who recoiled from the rigors of work itself, Phillips again reflected his middle-class orientation in that he reacted primarily against a slur on his respectability. His "style," to use the term in both senses, had been questioned. One cannot help but feel Phillips recognized

he had come a long way from his original precepts about simplicity, balance, and stylelessness. Yet the abiding consequence of his own career orientation, and indeed his middle-class notion of labor itself, was the readiness with which he had externalized his work—and then his style—from his selfhood. Particularly in the way Phillips's vocational strategy externalized his literary practice into "exercise" and "atmosphere," his career vivified the powerful market forces which promoted the masculine style as something *independent* from true experience—as something which could be learned, and in his case applied, without much firsthand contact with the facts at all.

Our own inclination might not be to view Phillips's reluctant experience in exposé as harshly as he himself did. We might point to its democratic consequences in aiding the direct election of senators. What was at stake here, however, was also *continuity* of effort—and Phillips found himself forced to turn away from politics. In addition, there is the legacy of the style to consider. One cannot help but wonder how much a book like *The Treason of the Senate,* in its disdain for factuality and its reliance on style, looks forward to some of the more high-priced "prosecutorial" exposés of our own time—which have, let it be said, the same high "affect" but considerably less effect. Anticipating the assembly-line production of our modern newsroom, dispensing with the mundane details, Phillips's journalistic style achieved its effects, as Michael Arlen writes of modern TV investigations, by involving us mostly in the "thrill of the chase." In his style of masculine forcefulness, David Graham Phillips forecasts the modern anchorman's charade of toughness, the "hard news" style that takes on the policymakers in the "High Noon" of the staged interview.

Even if we credit Phillips with helping to formulate a popular style of exposé so recurrent in American life, on more literary grounds some might still be inclined to file him away in the footnotes of our cultural history. Indeed, that is the place he came to occupy in books as generally sympathetic to the realist cause as Alfred Kazin's *On Native Grounds* (1942), in which Phillips's writing is twice dismissed as depicting "stale scandal" with only "superficial distaste." In Kenneth Lynn's *The Dream of Success* (1955), Phillips fares little better, dismissed as a "dream merchant," and indeed, something of a hypocrite. My point in decoding the confessional dimension of *The Treason of the Senate,* however, is to suggest that in the final stages of his career Phillips became aware of his own failings. To [use] Raymond Williams's terms, Phillips recognized his own status of victim in the power he had helped to create. Consequently, in his private moments a subtle readjustment in his literary ideology began to make itself felt. In this regard, no portrait of Phillips would be complete without consideration of *Susan Lennox: Her Fall and Rise* (1917), the novel to which he devoted countless nights and spare moments over the last seven years of his life.

In the years after *Treason,* Phillips's self-banishment from the political pulpit only strengthened his earlier resolve to stick to fiction; harbingers of the move are visible even in the exposé itself. It is intriguing, for instance, that *Trea-*

son—like Steffens's *Shame of the Cities* (1904)—chastised the public as well as the plutocrats, and in a particularly telling way. "[The] people have neglected politics," Phillips wrote, "because they will not realize that *it is not enough to work, it is also necessary to think.*" This distinction between working and thinking was revealing in two senses. First, it suggested that Phillips's professional ideology, with its emphasis on the "clear light" of expertise, now only served to separate him from the supposedly muddled and money-oriented masses; Phillips's days of popular identification were over. Second, the distinction suggested that *within* his professional ideology Phillips himself now valued intellection more than the sheer discipline of labor. In other words, within his ideology one detects an important modification in his original professionalism. While he held fast to the design of the structured career, he continued to push onward, trying to escape the compromising predicaments of his middle years. Even as he continued to honor his professional contract with his audience—churning out nearly two books every year—Phillips had already begun the strategy of keeping a world elsewhere divorced from pure market engagement: this was *Susan Lennox*'s vocational significance. As the major literary figure of the novel remarks (echoing Martin Eden's desire to do "hackwork first, masterpieces after"), "it's my chromos that have earned me the means and the leisure to try oils."

Of course, *that* distinction was a bit more apparent than real. *Susan Lennox* does inherit a bit of the chromatic tone of Phillips's earlier works. Characters are still subject to rather miraculous transformations; the wisdom of prophets arises ingenuously from the victims of profit; and Phillips still often tends to treat psychology as some lower derivation of the larger science of gastronomy. He also still considers the mastery of life, even among the illiterate, as a matter of settling on the right philosophy. Nor does the plot seem, at first glance, too radical a departure. Susan Lennox, born illegitimate and forced, at seventeen, into an arranged marriage with an illiterate farmer, flees from her Midwestern home. After a brief stint as a singer in a riverboat theatrical troupe, she descends into the chaos of working-class life: tenement houses, the drudgery of factory labor, and struggling at below-subsistence levels. She is temporarily saved by a cynical reporter named Spenser, only to be abandoned for one of his flirtations. For a period of years Susan struggles between the hope of reviving Spenser's love and self-respect and the despair of drink, opium, and prostitution. Finally, she is taken up by a successful playwright named Brent, who cultivates her sense of mental discipline in order to make her an independent actress. In the end, though Brent is murdered by one of Susan's former boyfriends, the playwright has already left her a fortune in his will. Susan subsequently achieves success and independence in the theater, but her happiness is tempered by the loss of Brent, the only man she has truly loved.

At first reading, then, *Susan Lennox* continues to balance Phillips's primary themes: independence, labor, career, and success. But there had been a measurable shift in his ideological constellation—hence all the characters' emphasis on "philosophy." It is intriguing, first of all, that

the novelist whose idiom usually involved a character's resurrection of his (or her) class identity now begins with a classless soul, an outcast—who really stays that way. Susan acquires her outsider status at birth, in fact, when a doctor drags her into a world that felt it would have been more convenient for her to die; at the end of the novel, she is alone. Her status as female only doubles her desire to rebel from disadvantage and dependency. She is also no creature of "overcivilization." Rather, she exemplifies the "panics and collapses of recent years which have tumbled another and better section of the middle class into the abyss of the underworld." Having fully documented the perils of dependence on wealth in other books, Phillips now emphasized instead the subterranean threat of poverty, the experience of which only alienates his protagonist further from the middle-class mainstream.

At the same time, Phillips seems to dispense with his often-sentimental notion concerning the rehabilitating powers of work. Manual labor is no longer intrinsically ennobling; success comes not from work but, as a factory worker in the novel notes, from "makin' others work for you." The narrator repeatedly dismisses the reputed "dignity" of labor—a philosophy, Phillips now notes, appealing to those who do none. What replaced Phillips's usual therapeutic solution was a deeper and darker vision that gave this novel moments of real power. The broader canvas—one would be tempted to call the two-volume novel picaresque, were it not so humorless—opened up Phillips's plot structure away from the simple paralleling of a social institution and an individual (as in *The Great God Success*); now his voice (partly resurrecting the notebook style) was discursive, his reflections wide-ranging, and his perspective systemic and dark. Susan's experiences with poverty, for instance, increase her sympathy for the downtrodden: she passes beyond the bourgeois illusion that the ignorant lack the intelligence to suffer. But her underworld passage is also counterpointed by a cold Darwinian logic that sees poverty as "devoid of that dignity which is necessary to excite the deep pity of respect." Poverty was no longer a sign of mere moral collapse—though being poor surely made some people immoral—but, rather, a part of a seamless Draconian "system":

> The system ordained it all. Oppression and oppressed were both equally its helpless instruments. No wonder all the vast beneficent discoveries of science that ought to have made the whole human race healthy, long-lived and prosperous, are barely able to save the race from swift decay and destruction under the ravages of this modern system of labor worse than slavery—for under slavery the slave, being property whose loss could not be made good without expense, was protected in life and in health.

In passages like these, Phillips's mood was hardly a matter of superficial distaste; on the contrary, he drew a rather despairing portrait of a cycle of victimization between the equally ignorant rich and poor. Phillips's world was now seemingly unresponsive to most people's labor or will; for most, moral health was beyond resurrection. Hence Phillips's new disdain for reform. Susan considers staying on to help her poor companions, but decides one might as well "put out a conflagration barehanded and alone."

In part, this cycle of despair only illuminated Phillips's lifelong desire to surpass the run-of-the-mill life—a desire Susan herself vivifies. There are three classes of humanity, the narrator intones at one point: the arrived, those who will never arrive and never try, and those in a state of flux. This longing had been implicit in Phillips's professional ideology all along, but now his nostalgia for the self-made man led him to turn even more decisively from a society where such a figure was an anomaly. Consequently, Phillips now distinguished between "toil"—physical labor done in a dependent status—and a redefined idea of "work" rooted in an intellectual career. Brent, who rather obviously serves as Phillips's fictional spokesperson, explains. "Under this capitalistic system the whole working class is degraded. They call what they do 'work,' but that word ought to be reserved for what a man does when he exercises mind and body usefully. What the working class is condemned to by capitalism is not work but toil." Susan, like most of Phillips's protagonists, learns the multiple joys of "work congenial and developing"; yet now Phillips's idea emphasizes mental discipline not as an end in itself but as a means of rising above the "inert" crowd. The mind continues not to "rely upon any such rot as inspiration," but nonetheless uses the body as a trained instrument for its "genius."

This is why Susan is not the effete child of leisure—no fallen member of the second generation. Instead, Phillips's intention in portraying her as a classless spirit was partly to expose her exemption from a world of bourgeois conventionality. Her growth is achieved when she is finally able to accept her real mother's social stigma and to embrace it as a blessing that removed her from a commonplace existence. Now, therefore, Phillips's portrait of the middle class was hardly flattering. If he had not entirely dispensed with the sarcastic basting of high society reminiscent of Veblen, he nonetheless showed signs of moving towards something like the skewer of Sinclair Lewis. Susan's aunt and uncle, her guardians, are smug, conventional types, their midwesternism turned against them. In a striking departure from Phillips's primary myth, Susan aspires not to accept or redeem bourgeois values but to be "free from the bonds of convention—free to soar or to sink."

In time, Susan's outcast status slowly converts to a metaphor for the spirit of imagination. The text is replete with observations that Susan is a creature of talent, an original in embryo, one "of the few whose 'fancy' can soar." Brent, as her spiritual mentor, merely articulates her instincts, and when he dies she acts like his "reincarnation." What Brent leads Susan to discover is that she can, as Phillips writes, be a member of the exceptional "one class" not divided into slaves and owners. Susan's imaginative, creative spirit—what Phillips calls a "core of unsullied nature"—allows her to stand apart from her society, finally independent. Her real sense of identity arrives when she feels the interest of her career expanding within her.

On the one hand, it was remarkable here just *how* doggedly Phillips clung to the ideal of the independent career—even if his emphasis was now decidedly noninstitutional. Notably, however, Susan's spirit of imagination is also what brings her misery: her sense of separateness drives her onward, yet only renders her all the more alone. By the same token, Phillips's resolution shied away from seeing Susan's ultimate achievement as an actress as purely a victory. Reflecting on her outcome, the narrator ends on a guarded note. "Yes," he says, "she may be happy—doubtless is more happy than unhappy. But—I do not envy her—or any other of the sons and daughters of men who is blessed—and cursed—with imagination." The novel's last line: "Yes, she has learned to live. But—she has paid the price."

In the final analysis, Phillips's torturous career—and *Susan Lennox* itself—exposed a kind of price in the evolving national mythology of which he was a maker. Even in his reaching out for the ideal of a separate "talent class," certainly a departure from his earlier ideal of a literary employee, there are troubling impulses in his thinking all too familiar to the modern workaholic: a fear of a professional treadmill that only drives one faster; a fear that one will never really become one of the "arrived"; a fear that if one does, one will be alone. Phillips's own dream of "autonomy"—of waiting for the ship to finally come in—may have only made him work harder. Even as the new marketplace promoted a rhetoric of independence, responsibility, and masculinity, its own structure made the myth difficult to sustain, even among the most successful, like Phillips himself. To his credit, Phillips acknowledged the contradiction that his version of professionalism did not promise to cure overcivilization but to deepen it. Much as London and Sinclair had converted the ideology of labor into forms of political resistance, Phillips, the very symbol of the Progressive mainstream, now applied his professionalism to turn from the culture of his own class. Ultimately, his high regard for the professional ideal led him to reject a system where it was threatened, compromised, and "unmanned." (pp. 153-67)

As the capstone of Phillips's brief career, *Susan Lennox* thus set forth an intriguing final trinity of characters: Spenser, the egocentric and failed journalist; Brent, the machinelike artist; and Susan, the core of imagination. Susan, the survivor, is perhaps the best indicator of the direction of Phillips's thinking. Her novel revealed that Phillips's nostalgia for the self-made man had led him, albeit secretly, to harken to an ideal of autonomous imagination—in short, to the ideal of independent creation, though overshadowed by that sense of "price." In a sense, it was therefore altogether fitting that for the eternally masculine David Graham Phillips, his final protagonist would be not a hero but a heroine. This, in the end, was the outcome of his experience. (p. 167)

Christopher P. Wilson, "The Eternal Masculine: David Graham Phillips," in his The Labor of Words: Literary Professionalism in the Progressive Era, *The University of Georgia Press, 1985, pp. 141-67.*

FURTHER READING

Bibliography

Feldman, Abraham. "David Graham Phillips—His Works and His Critics." *Bulletin of Bibliography* 19, No. 6 (May-August 1948): 144-46.
　　Bibliography of works by and about Phillips.

Stallings, Frank L., Jr. "David Graham Phillips (1867-1911): A Critical Bibliography of Secondary Comment." *American Literary Realism* 3, No. 1 (Winter 1970): 1-35.
　　Annotated listing of books and articles about Phillips's life and work.

Biography

Filler, Louis. "Murder in Gramercy Park." *The Antioch Review* VI, No. 4 (December 1946): 495-508.
　　Recounts events surrounding Phillips's death.

———. "Legenda: The Daily Round of a Popular Novelist." *Journal of Popular Culture* X, No. 4 (Spring 1977): 732-40.
　　Describes Phillips's lifestyle, circle of friends, and writing habits.

———. "The Young Phillips: A Study in Roots and Influence." *The Old Northwest* 3, No. 2 (June 1977): 133-52.
　　Examines the impact Phillips's early childhood and adolescence had on his novels.

Marcosson, Isaac F. "Some Literary Friendships." In his *Adventures in Interviewing,* pp. 228-56. London: John Lane Company, The Bodley Head, 1919.
　　Brief anecdotes about Phillips and his writing habits.

McGovern, James R. "David Graham Phillips and the Virility Impulse of Progressives." *The New England Quarterly* XXXIX, No. 3 (September 1966): 334-55.
　　Provides psychological portrait of Phillips, claiming his "attitudes toward women reveal his own personality."

Criticism

"The Power Behind the Bosses and the Machines." *The Arena* XXXV (January 1906): 97-100.
　　Favorable review of *The Deluge,* claiming the novel foreshadowed many of the events of the Morgan ship-trust and Standard Oil Company scandals and marked Phillips's growth as a novelist.

Baldwin, Charles C. "David Graham Phillips." In his *The Men Who Make Our Novels,* pp. 423-26. New York: Dodd, Mead, and Co., 1919.
　　Brief synopsis of Phillips's life and career.

Filler, Louis. " 'The Treason of the Senate.' " In his *Crusaders for American Liberalism,* pp. 245-59. Yellow Springs, Oh.: Antioch Press, 1950.
　　Provides historical background for Phillips's *The Treason of the Senate.*

———. "The Reputation of David Graham Phillips." *The Antioch Review* XI, No. 4 (December 1951): 475-88.
　　Examines criticism of Phillips's work from a historical viewpoint.

———. "A Tale of Two Authors: Theodore Dreiser and David Graham Phillips." In *New Voices in American Studies,* edited by Ray B. Browne, Donald M. Winkelman, and Allen

Hayman, pp. 35-48. Lafayette: Purdue University Studies, 1966.
　　Compares Phillips's life and writings with those of Dreiser.

———. *Voice of the Democracy: A Critical Biography of David Graham Phillips: Journalist, Novelist, Progressive.* University Park: Pennsylvania State University Press, 1978, 206 p.
　　Critical survey of Phillips's life and writings.

Flower, B. O. "David Graham Phillips, a Novelist with Democratic Ideals." *The Arena* XXXI, No. 3 (March 1904): 236-43.
　　Relates Phillips's depiction of American society to an attempt "to carry forward the course of human progress" and democracy.

Harris, Frank. "David Graham Phillips: The Greatest American Novelist." In his *Latest Contemporary Portraits,* pp. 17-29. New York: Macaulay Co., 1927.
　　Recounts Harris's attempts to convince readers that Phillips was "the greatest American novelist."

Hatcher, Harlan. "Realism and the Public Taste: 1900-1921." In his *Creating the Modern American Novel,* pp. 21-33. Murray Hill, N. Y.: Farrar and Rinehart, 1935.
　　Concludes that Phillips's practice of writing thesis-dominated fiction was shared by his contemporaries.

Hicks, Granville. "The Years of Hope." In his *The Great Tradition: An Interpretation of American Literature since the Civil War,* pp. 164-206. New York: MacMillan Co., 1935.
　　Dismisses Phillips as merely a journalist who brought "to fiction the equipment of a highly trained reporter."

Higgins, William R. "David Graham Phillips, Robert Herrick and the Doctor: A Turn of the Century Dilemma." *American Transcendental Quarterly* 2, No. 2 (June 1988): 139-53.
　　Compares the role of medicine in the novels of Phillips and Herrick, claiming that both authors contrasted the doctor's "idealism, self-abnegation, and devotion to hard work with the money-grubbing attitude of the new businessman and the materialism of society in general."

———. *David Graham Phillips and His Times.* New York: Dodd, Mead, and Co., 1932, 308 p.
　　Study of Phillips's life and literary career.

Mencken, H. L. "The Leading American Novelist." *Smart Set* XXXIII (January 1911): 163-64.
　　Praises Phillips's novels.

Miller, Gabriel. "The New Woman Gets the Old Treatment." In his *Screening the Novel: Rediscovered American Fiction in Film,* pp. 19-45. New York: Frederick Ungar, 1980.
　　Compares *Susan Lenox* with the MGM 1931 film version.

Miraldi, Robert. "The Journalism of David Graham Phillips." *Journalism Quarterly* 62 (Spring 1986): 83-88.
　　Traces Phillips's career as a journalist.

"David G. Phillips's Novel." *The New York Times Saturday Review* XIL, No. 41 (12 October 1907): 615.
　　Review of *Light-Fingered Gentry* that contends the novel is merely "cousin to the special article of the

monthly magazine and the work of the star reporter on the daily newspaper."

Pollard, Percival. "Men and Manners." In his *Their Day in Court,* pp. 145-270. New York: Johnson Reprint Corporation, 1969.
    Reprints review of *Old Wives for New,* stating that with this work Phillips moved away from "the verbiage of journalism" and established himself as a novelist.

Ravitz, Abe. *David Graham Phillips.* New York: Twayne Publishers, 1966, 191 p.
    Biographical and critical study.

Russell, Charles Edward. "The Message of David Graham Phillips." *Book News Monthly* 25, No. 8 (April 1907): 511-13.
    Contends that Phillips's ability to describe events and the motives of individuals made him a great reporter and the "most truly American of all novelists."

Sinclair, Upton. "The Old-Fashioned American." In his *Mammonart: An Essay in Economic Interpretation,* pp. 353-57. Pasadena: Privately printed, 1924.
    Praises Phillips and *Susan Lenox* for challenging bourgeois values.

Additional coverage of Phillips' life and career is contained in the following sources published by Gale Research: *Contemporary Authors,* Vol. 108; and *Dictionary of Literary Biography,* Vols. 9 and 12.

Sapper

1888-1937

(Pseudonym of Herman Cyril McNeile) English novelist, short story writer, dramatist, and screenwriter.

INTRODUCTION

McNeile is best remembered for the popular detective novels he wrote during the 1920s and 1930s under the pseudonym "Sapper." These fast-paced thrillers feature Bulldog Drummond, a robust former officer of the English army who solves mysteries, rescues distressed heroines, and battles villainous "foreigners." Although McNeile's works are now considered outdated and full of ethnic and racial prejudices as well as sexism, he is nevertheless credited with creating a daring, witty hero who remains among the most memorable characters in the detective fiction genre.

McNeile was born in Bodmin, a small town in Cornwall, England. He trained as an officer at the Royal Military Academy and at nineteen joined the Royal Engineers. He served with distinction in World War I, earning the Military Cross and rising to the rank of lieutenant colonel. During the war, McNeile published several short story collections about his combat experiences under the pseudonym "Sapper," which was a military expression for an army engineer. He continued to write as Sapper after retiring from military life in 1919. His first novel, *Mufti,* was quickly followed by *Bull-Dog Drummond: The Adventures of a Demobilized Officer Who Found Peace Dull.* Based partly on McNeile and his friend and fellow writer Gerard Fairlie, Drummond was an immediate success among readers of detective fiction. The ensuing series of novels featuring Drummond, including *The Black Gang, The Final Count,* and *The Female of the Species,* enjoyed a loyal following and inspired several popular film and stage adaptations. While McNeile also wrote mysteries featuring Drummond's associate Ronald Standish and several novels outside the detective genre, he is chiefly remembered as the creator of Bulldog Drummond. Following McNeile's death in 1937, Gerard Fairlie continued the Drummond series as "Sapper" until 1954.

Critical discussions of McNeile's work have focused predominantly on the character of Hugh "Bulldog" Drummond. Critic Noel Behn has viewed him as the "granddaddy" of James Bond, the fictional character of Ian Fleming's spy novels. Like Bond, Drummond is an impeccably groomed gentleman who remains unperturbed in any situation, even when threatened with acid baths or by ferocious gorillas and poisonous asps. He is also a member of what McNeile terms "the Breed," a group of physically and morally courageous sportsmen whose patriotism and loyalty prompt them to risk their lives—almost eagerly at times—to defend their country. Drummond, however,

disdains such established institutions as the secret service or the police. He begins his career as a detective-for-hire by advertising: "Demobilized officer finding peace incredibly tedious, would welcome diversion. Legitimate, if possible; but crime, if of a comparatively humorous description, no objection. Excitement essential . . . Reply at once Box X10." And so begins Drummond's encounters with underworld criminals, solving murder mysteries, and foiling plots to destroy England. Drummond's widespread popularity has been attributed to his image as a man of action who unfailingly solves every mystery.

Drummond's other traits, however, are considered less appealing today. Specifically, critics have objected to the level of violence in the Drummond series. Unlike the more renowned fictional detective Sherlock Holmes, Drummond uses physical intimidation rather than logic or cunning to achieve his goals. Critics now regard the political and social views expressed in the works as antiquated and xenophobic; Drummond, for example, contemptuously views all non-English people as "foreigners" and battles villains whom he calls "Huns," "Wogs," "Dagoes," "niggers," "homicidal Jews," and "unwashed people of that type." These villains try to destroy England with political agitation—by preaching socialism, for example—or by concocting plots to embezzle government funds. Drummond invariably thwarts their plans, usually with the help of his loyal ex-army friends who detest foreigners as well. Most recent critics agree that because of the bigotry expressed in the Drummond novels, they have not survived as well as other works of detective fiction. Nevertheless Joan DelFattore reminds McNeile's detractors that the attitudes propounded in McNeile's work "were an accepted characteristic of his age and class and an accepted convention of the thriller literature of that period." She has added: "The Bulldog Drummond books make no claim to literary excellence; neither the characters nor the plots in which they appear can by any standard be considered original, plausible, or well rounded. They are, however, good, solid thrillers."

PRINCIPAL WORKS

The Lieutenant and Others   (short stories)   1915
Sergeant Michael Cassidy, R. E.   (short stories)   1915; also published as *Michael Cassidy, Sergeant,* 1916
Men, Women, and Guns   (short stories)   1916
No Man's Land   (short stories)   1917
The Human Touch   (short stories)   1918
Mufti   (novel)   1919
Bull-Dog Drummond: The Adventures of a Demobilized Officer Who Found Peace Dull   (novel)   1920
Bulldog Drummond [with Gerald du Maurier]   (drama) 1921
The Man in Ratcatcher, and Other Stories   (short stories) 1921
The Black Gang   (novel)   1922
The Dinner Club   (short stories)   1923
Jim Maitland   (short stories)   1923
The Third Round   (novel)   1924; also published as *Bulldog Drummond's Third Round,* 1924
Out of the Blue   (short stories)   1925
The Final Count   (novel)   1926
Jim Brent   (short stories)   1926
Shorty Bill   (short stories)   1926
Word of Honour   (short stories)   1926
The Saving Clause   (short stories)   1927
When Carruthers Laughed   (short stories)   1927
The Female of the Species   (novel)   1928; also published as *Bulldog Drummond Meets the Female of the Species,* 1943
John Walters   (short stories)   1928
Temple Tower   (novel)   1929
The Finger of Fate   (short stories)   1930
Sapper's War Stories   (short stories)   1930
Tiny Carteret   (novel)   1930
The Way Out   (drama)   1930
The Island of Terror   (novel)   1931; also published as *Guardians of the Treasure,* 1931
The Return of Bulldog Drummond   (novel)   1932; also published as *Bulldog Drummond Returns,* 1932
Knock-Out   (novel)   1933; also published as *Bulldog Drummond Strikes Back,* 1933
Ronald Standish   (short stories)   1933
51 Stories   (short stories)   1934

Bulldog Drummond at Bay   (novel)   1935
Bulldog Jack (Alias Bulldog Drummond) [with Gerard Fairlie and J. O. C. Orton]   (screenplay)   1935
Ask for Ronald Standish   (short stories)   1936
Bulldog Drummond Double-Header   (novel)   1937
Bulldog Drummond Hits Out [with Gerald Fairlie] (drama)   1937
Challenge   (novel)   1937
Sapper: The Best Short Stories   (short stories)   1984

The Times Literary Supplement   (essay date 1916)

[*In the following excerpt, the critic offers a mixed review of* Men, Women, and Guns, *stating that while Sapper's stories are "readable," they are not works of permanent value.*]

"Sapper" has been successful in previous volumes of war stories. In **Men, Women, and Guns** he carries on. When the time comes for picking out the writers whose war fiction has permanent value, his claim to be included in the list will call for serious examination. If posterity decides to "turn him down," that will probably be because his motives are apt to be ancient and conventional. Some of them—the *splendide mendax* motive, for example—have a history traceable through many generations of melodrama; and it may also be that his psychology is not much more subtle than that of Henry Pettit and Mr. George R. Sims. Perhaps, too, that is inevitable for those who write in the midst of the excitement, instead of waiting to remember their emotions in tranquillity. From that point of view these stories will not quite sustain the comparison which they tempt with Maupassant's stories of the war of 1870. Distance in that case helped memory to select, and the reader got the impression that the artist had invented nothing, but had only explored and analysed the minds of real men and women of a familiar type exposed to novel experiences and torn by strange emotions. That is a kind of praise which one cannot give to "Sapper's" work. He does not seem to have found his stories, but to have composed them. His emotional background is never so real as his descriptive detail. It is, indeed, so much less real that the author seems to have gone to look for it as for a peg on which the descriptive detail could be hung.

To say that sort of thing, however, is to apply the very severest test. Judged by any test less strict "Sapper's" stories are admirable. It must be very difficult indeed to pick out the dramatic individual from among such a crowd as that which now lines the trenches and presses behind them; and that "Sapper" succeeds in doing. He also knows what to describe and what to take for granted—what to eliminate and what to insist upon. His word-painting is not of the sort which lets the wood and the trees get in each other's way. We see the life in the trenches and the dug-outs in his lightning sketches as clearly as if they had been filmed; and we are also made to appreciate the difference between the points of view of a company officer of the new Army and a sergeant-major of the old one. Moreover, the tone of the book does more for realism than could be done by many pages of exact particulars, such as Zola used to delight in accumulating. Though the emotional situations are often melodramatic, there is little of melodrama in the actual narrative. Indeed, when the emotion gets too intense the author is apt to be looking the other way, as if he felt that he had no right to pry too deeply into his characters' private affairs. His own point of view is that of a British sportsman with a lively sense of humour. There are no heroics even in his chronicles of the most heroic deeds; no appeal to glory, or the flag, or the great issues at stake; no expression of hatred towards the enemy whom he overcomes, except when there is a woman in the case; no lust for blood on the one hand, and no war weariness on the other. His Englishmen go to war pretty much in the spirit in which they would play cricket; as lightheartedly, as determined to play the game, and with as little thought of stopping on account of a temporary setback until the proper time comes for drawing stumps. Probably there is no other country now at war in which a literary artist could adopt this nonchalant air and with so little disposition to let his concern with amusing trifles yield to his sense of his participation in a great national experience. It has always been our British way, however, to seem more nonchalant than we really are; and no one will blame "Sapper" for a manner which is characteristic of the race. The sportsman-like manner is just as bracing as the heroic manner, and most of us find it more readable. "Sapper," at any rate, is readable from the first page to the last; and his melodramatic background is not likely to impair his popularity.

> *"Men, Women, and Guns," in* The Times Literary Supplement, *No. 765, September 14, 1916, p. 439.*

The Spectator   (essay date 1917)

[*In the following excerpt, the critic praises McNeile's literary style in* No Man's Land.]

"Sapper" is among the very best of the writers who have tried to make people at home understand how our men in the trenches live and fight—and die. The war correspondents give us selected facts, anecdotes, and topography. "Sapper" prefers to present what he knows in the guise of fiction [in *No Man's Land*], and yet he often seems to come nearer to the truth than the precise reporter with his field-glasses and his notebook. Most people can only realize the war as it affects the individual fighting man. "**Seed Time**," "Sapper's" lively story of the evolution of Reginald Simpkins, shopwalker, into an expert sniper, is, we are sure, accurate in the little details of trench-fighting which our friends returning from the front never mention, though we long to ask for them. "Shorty Bill," who took Reginald in hand, was an old poacher. The patience and cunning that had served him against English gamekeepers helped him to outwit German patrols at night in No Man's Land. "Shorty," when Reginald encountered him, looked like a rubbish-heap; covered with sacking, on which bricks and grass were arranged with the art that conceals art, he had been lying out in front of the trench all day, waiting to get a shot at a German sniper in a ruin opposite to him. The innocent Reginald, peering over the sandbags, had de-

tected a movement in the rubbish-heap, and had begun to pelt it with bricks just before the critical moment came. But "Shorty" did not miss, and in his hour of triumph not only forgave Reginald but took him as his pupil. Then we are told how Reginald was trained to face the unknown terrors of the dark, how he was taught to use a knife, how he learned to control himself in a trench-raid when it was his duty as a sniper to stay well in the rear. Reginald, having been offered his stripe, referred the matter to "Shorty":—

> Shorty brought his fist down into his open palm. "I've been watching you lately, an' you're worth teaching—you've shown that. But now you've begun to feel your legs, you're inclined to think you're a bit bigger cheese-mite than you really are. You want a bit o' sobering up; an' there's nothing like taking on responsibility to sober up a man. As soon as you start looking after other fellows, you begin to realise you ain't the Lord High Emperor of the whole outfit." "But I don't want to look after the other fellows, Shorty." Our friend's tone was dubious. "Why, good Lord! I'd be bossing it over you if I took the stripe." An enigmatic smile wreathed gently over Shorty's face. "Don't you worry about that; I'll chance it." Then he turned suddenly on the man lying beside him. "You've got to take it— this bally little stripe in this funny old army. Otherwise you're a quitter—see? a quitter. You'd not be pullin' your weight. Do you get me?" "Right ho! Bill; I'll tell him I will." Reginald Simpkins stared silently at the football match for a while, and then a sudden thought struck him. "Say, why didn't *you* take it, Shorty?" "Never you mind; there are things as you can't get a hold of as yet. I pull more weight where I am, my son, than I would if I was the ruddy sergeant-major himself."

There, perhaps, lies the secret of the old soldier who, after serving for many years, never becomes even a lance-corporal and yet may be invaluable to his company. "**Seed Time**" is the longest story in the book, and the best. Some of "Sapper's" short stories are very funny. "**The Man-Trap**" relates how a too ingenious subaltern adapted a disused dug-out as a trap for over-curious Germans and caught in it his own General and Colonel. Incidentally we may remark that the war novelist must rid himself of the habit of describing all Generals as aged and rather decrepit gentlemen. The war has changed all that; indeed, we may soon expect to be told that Divisional Commanders are, like other people, "too old at forty." "**Bendigo Jones—his Tree**" is a whimsical extravaganza on a Post-Impressionist sculptor, who, not having been exempted through the united efforts of his misguided friends, finds himself in the trenches. Jones is given some clay and told to model a *camouflage* tree, for use as a sniper's station. The General coming on his rounds naturally takes the sculptor, mouthing over his work in the approved Post-Impressionist manner, to be a madman. In the midst of the confusion a shell carries away the original tree-stump in front of the line, and Bendigo presents the General with the misshapen clay, hurriedly rechristened "Children at play in Epping Forest." "Sapper" writes, too, on graver themes, such as the impressions of a man who rejoined what was left of his regiment in the early fighting at Ypres, and he has a dramatic little ghost-story of a German dug-out. But, as in most war fiction, humour predominates. The soldiers do not treat the war as a joke, but they are incurably light-hearted, and their laughter helps them to face things too deep for tears. "Sapper" as a jester is typical of a very large class of soldier-authors, but his literary quality is exceptional.

A review of "No Man's Land," in The Spectator, *Vol. 119, No. 4651, August 18, 1917, p. 169.*

Richard Usborne (essay date 1953)

[*An English critic, Usborne has written on and edited works by P. G. Wodehouse and is the author of* Clubland Heroes: A Nostalgic Study of Some Recurrent Characters in the Romantic Fiction of Dornford Yates, John Buchan and Sapper. *In the following excerpt from this work, he focuses on McNeile's portrayal of Bulldog Drummond and other protagonists as gentlemen and sportsmen.*]

In one of Sapper's 'Ronald Standish' short stories a dear old vicar in Cornwall is describing to Standish his excellent new curate. A fine young fellow, this curate, 'tall, upstanding, a typical British sportsman, and exactly the sort of man that we want today in the Church'.

It is left to Ronald Standish to prove that this particular 'curate' is an imposter, one of Snarkie Stenway's men, who is smuggling cocaine in tins of Cornish cream. He has kidnapped the real curate on his way down to Cornwall and got him out of the way. Now, ostensibly full of good works in the parish, and presumably well able to preach a sermon and teach at Sunday School, he's taking in consignments of 'snow' from ships offshore on moonless nights. Ronald Standish catches him with his surplice down.

There is no ironic intent in Sapper's mind when he makes the vicar say that the tall, upstanding, typical British sportsman is just the sort of man the Church needs today. In the world of Sapper's books the tall, upstanding sportsman type has a head start in any profession, the Church, soldiering, business, politics, the law and detection. Sapper's heroes are almost all exceptionally good at games, sports-men as well as sportsmen. To most of them a life of sport is a perfectly sufficient end in itself. If they are fortunate enough to be 'plentifully endowed with this world's goods', they make their H.Q. in Pall Mall and its western environs, and fill their week-days with playing or watching cricket and rugger, their weekends with country-house visits for shooting, fishing, hunting, golf and more cricket. And if their weekend host is troubled by a murder or two under his hospitable roof, so much the more exciting for his sportsmen guests.

The Sapper hero was the public school games-blood elevated, by age only, to Lord's, Twickenham, Hurlingham and Sunningdale. In his earlier books, about World War I, Sapper continually referred to the fighting as The Game, or The Great Game. The Celestial Umpire tended to give points to those (generally English, of course) who played The Game by public school rules. In after-the-war books The Game, or The Great Game, was more often the Secret Service. But note that almost all Sapper's heroes were members of that Sports Club in the south-west corner of St James's Square. And their rooms, in Clarges Street, Half Moon Street or Brook Street, were littered with cricket bags, golf-bags and gun-cases; the walls were hung with boxing-gloves, fencing foils and photographs of team-groups from schooldays onwards.

Jim Maitland himself was famous 'in three continents' as a big-game shot, and had been Amateur Heavyweight Boxing Champion of England. Drummond had been a sprinter and a boxer. He was a Free Foresters cricketer, a great revolver shot, a ju-jitsu expert and one of the best poker-players in London. Standish was a fine cricketer, scratch golfer, first class to hounds, and a first-class shot. Peter Darrell played Amateur Championship golf and cricket for Middlesex. Tiny Carteret had been capped seventeen times at rugger for England. Sport kept them fit, for more sport. If the routine dragged a bit, what they asked was stiffer shots of the old drug. In addition to games, they pined for The Game, sport with danger in it, sport with the killing of men in it. And, with the collusion of Scotland Yard, the Home Office or the War Office, they got what they pined for.

It was not enough for them to be individualists in their games of danger. Still trailing clouds of schoolboy glory, they formed easily into teams, and they acknowledged captains. Maitland was always captain of his team, even if the team consisted only of A. N. Other (the story-teller). Standish captained his own team, unless he was in Drummond's. Drummond was always captain of Peter, Algy, Ted, Toby and Co. The captain expected, and got, immediate obedience from his team when they were on the war-path. Any of his gang would gladly have died for Drummond on the job. Some of them suffered painful wounds, by revolver, horsewhip, dagger, bomb and lead piping, playing on Drummond's side. Drummond elected Peter Darrell as vice-captain. In one book, *The Female of the Species,* a system of presenting colours rears its puny schoolboy head. Joe Dixon, the clubman lawyer who gets dragged into the fray (and into writing the book), is inducted into the Order of Frothblowers, complete with song and cufflinks—the then audible and visible signs of being of Drummond's team. The lawyer had fought the good fight (if in something of a daze), and he was given his colours at the end. The public school Cock House system dies hard in Sapper, if it dies at all.

The team spirit is well enough for rough-house attacks and defences against villainy. But when the team, as a team, serves as judge and jury to punish the beaten opposing side, there is sometimes a whiff of bullying and, as we would say now, Fascism. *The Black Gang* especially shows the Clubland team acting as Gestapo, Storm Troopers *and* a People's Court. They even used a small island off the Scottish coast as a hard-labour—short-rations concentration camp for the captured foreign riff-raff. By public school and St James's Square standards the idea was sound. Taking the law temporarily into their own hands, these typical British sportsmen were giving these Bolshevik Jews a taste of their own medicine—a taste of the whip, of being dragged behind cars, of being let down, bound, into icy moats, of having half the head shaved and the equivalent of 'Dirty Foreigner' painted on it, of doing forced labour behind wire under orders of an ex-Guards sergeant-major. This was in 1923, a decade before Hitler became a headline. The Drummond team was justifying its solidarity. But it was carrying the Führer-principle from the school playing-field to St James's Square. It made good fulfilling reading for the schoolboy ambitious for colours and power. It appealed to the ambitious-schoolboy side of grown-ups. But private armies are dangerous things, in fact and fiction.

Only Ronald Standish, the best all-round games-player of the list of Sapper heroes, took to his own Game (detection and freelance M.I. work) because it appealed to his intellect. Maitland and Drummond could 'exercise the old grey matter' on their feet and in a crisis. But it was the rough-housing that they really liked. They revelled in rough-houses for the thrill of physical danger. Indeed, right to the last of Sapper's books on Bulldog Drummond, rough-housing was his hero's only real enthusiasm. It is touching to note that, in *Bulldog Drummond on Dartmoor,* the first Drummond book written by Sapper's coadjutor and successor, Gerard Fairlie, Drummond has been at last weaned away from 'sport' by his wife, Phyllis. That's to say he has acquired a new, real and non-lethal excitement in life. Pigs. The old Game, with fists, revolvers and lead piping, still attracts him when other people start playing it on the doorstep of his Dartmoor farm-house. But now that Drummond has got pigs in his supposed retirement, he only reaches for his revolver under strong pressure of events. Until Sapper died, Drummond, between lethal bouts with his Demon Kings, faced the bleak prospect of the London Season, Cowes, Scotland, hunting and night-clubbing.

Drummond married Phyllis at the end of the first book. And of course it was Phyllis who first lured him into the crime-busting game. Other Sapper heroes are unmarried. They live in rooms in London, W.1. Each has a 'man' to look after him. He eats a large breakfast. He then strolls to his club for beer at midday. A few martinis before lunch. Lunch. Then Lord's or the Oval or a game of golf at Roehampton. Dinner out, or at the club again. An evening's yarning, or playing poker. Perhaps a kipper at a night-club with a topping filly. Then home, and a bachelor bed in the 'rooms'.

Sapper's sympathetic women are of three types. There is the topping girl, Beryl, Marjorie or Molly, fit mate eventually for one of the sportsman heroes. She is straight, a sportsman, white clean through, a good companion. She probably calls the hero 'old man'. In a moment of emotion he may call her 'woman of mine'. Several clean-limbed young men are proposing marriage to her, fairly often. If a cad proposes to her, marriage or anything else, he gets his deserts from one of the decent fellows in the near hereafter. Decent fellows can adore, propose marriage to, and sometimes kiss their topping girls. To win them in marriage they must perform acts of courage. If by chance, in the performance of a courageous act, a decent fellow is found in a topping girl's bedroom (and in those country houses with calf-size mastiffs, baboons and legless monsters drifting around the grounds at night, a decent fellow never knows where he may find himself waiting, every sense alert), then the topping girl immediately informs the dressing-gowned house-party that she and the decent fellow are engaged. And they have to stay engaged.

The second type of Sapper girl is the same Beryl, Marjorie or Molly, but married. She is loyal to the core, but often, for pathos, to a rotter who's going downhill through drink; or to a decent fellow who has lost his memory during the war.

The third type is the elderly pensioned-off nurse, the 'man's' wife, the dear old deaf housekeeper. She's loyal to the core, too, and takes her druggings, gassings and lashings-up in good part. Drummond seems to have had two nannies at least when a boy. Both are useful to 'Master Hugh' in his energetic, grown-up, sportsman days. Standish has an old nannie too, Mrs Borden, in whose house in the Elephant and Castle district he makes Secret Service rendezvous. The 'dear old soul' type is good in emergencies.

In the short stories there are a few unsympathetic, hard, wicked Englishwomen. The callous Englishwoman who toys with a decent fellow's affection gets far less sympathy from Sapper than such foreign Demon Queens as Irma Peterson. Irma, being foreign, has no worthwhile side to let down. Lady Hounslow, in the *Jim Maitland* story, was letting down a man in the British Secret Service, and one who was ill, too. Lady Hounslow was therefore rotten to the core. Or take the case of the hard-hearted English beauty, perhaps the daughter of an earl, who lures some poor decent fellow into falling in love with her at Henley; she then laughs in his face and marries a profiteer. She gets her deserts in a miserable marriage, and the decent fellow goes out to a bungalow in Darkest Africa and, under a different name, drinks himself nearly to death. At the moment when, unshaven and sodden, he puts a photograph (from the *Tatler*) of the earl's daughter on the wall and shoots at it with his revolver, a topping girl called Beryl is probably riding over from a nearby bungalow to reclaim to manhood this thing that was once a man. As the sodden decent fellow totters sobbing into the night, or to his bedroom for a shave, Beryl cleans up his living-room and replaces the punctured photograph of the earl's daughter with another that she discovers among the empty whisky bottles: a photograph of the decent fellow winning the Grand National.

Loyal to the core, or rotten to the core, or just typical foreigners, Sapper's women exist solely to put his men through their paces. Only in Irma Peterson is there some slight subtlety of characterisation. Irma was loyal to the core to Carl Peterson and to his memory when he had gone. She was rotten to the core sociologically. And in her habit of turning up, jewel-encrusted and slinky, in most of the Ritz hotels of the world, she was a typical foreigner. Irma, bless her hard heart, is still putatively alive, and she hasn't forgiven Drummond the death of her Carl yet. He'll find her, disguised as a typical English shepherdess or something, feeding yew to his prize pigs one of these thundery summer evenings.

Irma is the girl who is constantly coming back. The Man Who Comes Back is a most important recurrent character in Sapper's short stories. The keen Sapper reader keeps a weather eye open for the tall stranger with a black beard in the bar. He may be the man who tried to get through the enemy's lines in Africa, and was missing, presumed dead. He may be the Lord Fauntleroy, presumed dead when his ship went down, leaving his little son to take over the old title. If so, he will be there just in time to prevent some fiendish cousin, next in line for the title, from killing little Lord Fauntleroy. In which case the bearded man and the fiendish cousin have a set-to, and both die, and little Lord Fauntleroy continues safely in his inheritance. Or it may be the man presumed killed in the war, who comes back with his memory missing, to grind a barrel-organ. Or the man who has been in gaol for something he didn't do, and comes back with the look of hell in his eyes, only to collect his dog and then to disappear. He finds that, on the morning of his leaving gaol, some cad has killed his dog with poison. And then he fights the cad, and this does him (the man who came back) a power of good. The look of hell goes out of his eyes. His girl kisses him above the grave of the dog, and all is well.

And the man in rat-catcher: his father had gone smash in some City job, and a lot of the family's friends had lost money. The son, who had been a wonderful man to hounds, disappears, but spends the next part of his life collecting enough money to pay off all the family friends (secretly: they don't know where this money is coming from). And, because the love of hunting is deep in him, he comes back for one final hunt with the old hounds. He comes under another name, and now, because he has spent all his money paying people back for his father, he can't afford a good hunter. He rides an old screw hireling from a livery stables. He is in rat-catcher, and he avoids the throng of the pink-coated. Some of these think they recognise him, but he says he is someone else. The hunt begins, and because he is a great horseman, he keeps his hireling out with those in front—with the master's daughter, who used to love him, and with some young puppy on a magnificent chestnut, who loves the master's daughter. Comes the kill, or a check. The man in rat-catcher has proved beyond doubt by his riding that he is the man he says he isn't. The master's daughter's horse suddenly bolts, towards an old disused quarry. The revenant seizes the young puppy's great chestnut, and rides after the girl. He rides her off the edge of the quarry, but he and the chestnut go over the edge. It is one of Sapper's best stories, and it gives its name to one of the several books of his collected short stories.

They led good lives, these decent fellows. They had had good wars, and used the slang of the trenches mixed up with the slang of sport. Their money was plentiful. They were footloose and quick on the trigger. Those who operated abroad were 'scornful men who diced with death under a naked sky'. Their test of friendship with another man was whether they'd like to be with him in a scrap. They carried the insularity of the Englishman with them to the ends of the earth, even if they had a gift for foreign lingos. In bush and kraal, Hoxton or Clarges Street, Valparaiso or Singapore, they stood up for 'The King', killed the dirty dago who called them 'dirty Englishman', treated women as sacred, kept fit, shot the pip out of the ace of diamonds at twenty paces, cultivated a pleasant, lazy drawl and a good pair of riding-boots, caught the flying knife in the bar-room brawl and hurled it back to pin the dago to the wall by the fleshy part of the arm. They mistrusted the Press, spoke curtly, turned on their heels and strode into the night, read Kipling and (I think) Robert Service, adopted frequent disguises, tore off the next two sheets of the telegraph-pad after they had sent wires, smoked pipes and many cigarettes and drank a great deal of beer.

They left it to the cads to bare their teeth in snarls, use blowpipes, dum-dum bullets and compressed-air rifles, shoot dogs, ask girls where their bedrooms were at country houses, send girls poisonous spiders in boxes marked 'Asprey's', pluck ceaselessly at their collars when the truth came out, consort with politicians, keep gorillas, Malay dwarfs and legless monsters, kick men in the ribs when unconscious, hit them across the face with sjamboks or kiss their wives when they are trussed up on chairs, use bayonets, thumbscrews and acid baths, and build into the walls of their Surrey homes jet-propelled swinging irons which lash out and back with ominous clangs.

Sapper's world was mostly England, and the home counties at that. Anything outside a radius of about 100 miles from St James's Square was tiger-country. Dagoes began at Calais. France was where, in 1914, the salt of the earth went to Play the Great Game, and where, afterwards, some of the few survivors of the great generation went, to gamble at Le Touquet or watch the Davis Cup in Paris. You didn't need to bother about its language, beyond the standard of Chardenal's *First French Course*. 'Nous avons craché dans les rognons', said Drummond, to everyone's delight, when his aeroplane came down in an onion-field. Beyond France you tried to go somewhere where the map was painted a comfortable British pink and the Loamshires had a battalion at the depot. There was champagne in the mess there, and polo on a field that had been cleared of its swarming arum lilies. Beyond again, beyond the reach of English law, in the islands of the Pacific or the ports of Dagoland, the Englishman kept a firm grasp of his revolver, but polished his riding-boots and eye-glass more scrupulously than ever. These were the places of bar-room brawls, when every man was your enemy who was not of your country. In the dance-hall you might find a soiled, or likely-to-be-soiled, English waif, the daughter of a Sussex vicar, the girl who had come out with a theatrical company and got stranded. You rescued her and sent her back to Sussex, her ticket bought, her eyes afloat with admiration for your gallantry. Your eye-glass got a little misty when you wished her Godspeed.

Or you might find a Balliol man drinking himself to death and being jeered at by dagoes. There are some things it is not good for a white man to look upon.

The Sapper canon, for the purpose of this survey, is all that he ever published in book form. In popularity I suppose his Bulldog Drummond books have been most successful. He tried Bulldog Drummond out in short stories for the *Strand Magazine,* but Drummond as a detective using his brain, rather than as a beefy extrovert using his fists, didn't work very well. The stories have not been published in book form. [Usborne adds in a footnote that "Sapper once admitted over the radio that the real-life character who had been his model for Hugh Drummond was Gerard Fairlie. This was a most odd and interesting literary involution, because Fairlie took over the task of writing the ever-popular Bulldog Drummond books. Fairlie was a regular soldier (though too young to fight in the 1914-18 war). He was a boxer of repute, and for twenty years a scratch golfer. He was a great friend of Sapper's. It is amusing to think that Drummond's prototype is a writer, because one feels that Drummond could hardly sign a cheque without making a blot and spelling his name wrong. And Drummond's *'Nous avons craché dans les rognons'* was hardly in the Fairlie manner. Fairlie was brought up in French, he broadcast to the French Resistance during the war, and was parachuted into France for a hair-raising Resistance job in Paris during the German occupation."]

Sapper was a regular soldier, and started writing during World War I. His short stories about that war are all interesting, and some of his heroes (I think here he must have been influenced by Kipling's *Soldiers Three*) were ranker-Cockneys, Irishmen and others who spoke in the not-very-well-handled vernacular. But already Sapper was building up to greater-than-life-size the white man proper, officer class, brave and loyal. Of such was The Breed.

> Before the war Derek Vane had been what is generally described as a typical Englishman. That is to say, he regarded his own country . . . whenever he thought about it at all . . . as being the supreme country in the world. He didn't force his opinion down anyone's throat; it simply was so. If the other fellow didn't agree, the funeral was his, not Vane's. He had to the full what the uninitiated regard as conceit; on matters connected with literature, or art, or music, his knowledge was microscopic. Moreover, he regarded with suspicion anyone who talked intelligently on such subjects. On the other hand he had been in the eleven at Eton, and was a scratch golfer. He had a fine seat on a horse and rode straight; he could play a passable game of polo, and was a good shot. Possessing as he did sufficient money to prevent the necessity of working, he had not taken the something he was supposed to be doing in the City very seriously. He had put in a periodical appearance at a desk and drawn pictures on the blotting paper; for the remainder of the time he had amused himself. He belonged, in fact, to the Breed; the Breed that has always existed in England, and will always exist to the world's end. You may meet its members in London and Fiji; in the lands that lie beyond the mountains and at Henley; in the swamps where the stagnant vegetation rots and stinks; in the great deserts where the night air strikes cold. They are always the same, and they are branded with the stamp of the breed. They shake your hand as a man shakes it; they meet your eye as a man meets it. Just now a genera-

tion of them lie around Ypres and La Bassée, Neuve Chapelle and Bapaume. The graves are overgrown and the crosses are marked with indelible pencil. Dead, yes; but not the Breed. The Breed never dies.

> *Mufti.*

Sapper goes on to say that The Breed has its critics, and that there are those who think that 'it would be a far, far better thing for mob adoration to be laid at the feet of the composer of the winning Greek Iambic rather than at the cricketing boots of the Captain of the Eleven.' But Sapper was not among those critics himself. He admired The Breed, and glorified it in his books. In his view its virtues were formed on the playing fields of the public schools, and in his thinking he never really cut the navel cord that joined his heroes to their schooldays. There are a few amiable professors (with pretty daughters) in Sapper's short stories, but generally the boys who would have been scholarship types at school (e.g. Carl Peterson and Henry Lakington) grew up to be fiends and villains.

If you're interested in the development of Sapper's ideas, read his early novel, *Mufti,* published in 1919. It may surprise you to find in it a wartime Labourite Trade Union leader treated with some sympathy, and the social problems of war discussed without dogmatism. I imagine that Sapper had been reading Wells's *Mr Britling,* and had been impressed by it. *Mufti* also contains two really good bits of reporting: the laying on of a gas attack on the Western Front, and the sinking of a passenger ship in the Irish Sea.

Mufti isn't a good book, because its two styles get in each other's light. About half of it is carefully written, by a young writer who is feeling his way, has ideas which he wants to discuss fairly, without giving the impression that his is the last word on them; a young writer who has been through the thick of the fighting, and wants to get the tension of nerves and the smell of fear through the medium of the printed word into the reader's mind and nostrils. That's the good part of the book. The other part is by the already self-assured Sapper, with an easy manner, a glib type-casting of characters, avoiding the problems of sensibility and motive, laying on the pathos, the tight-lipped nobility, the good-chappery. It was the latter mood of Sapper's that paid the ultimate dividend. He made his name and fortune with it.

There is a refreshing, if slight, air of: 'I may be wrong' in the long passage from *Mufti* quoted earlier. Sapper was saying the same thing, directly and by implication, for the rest of his writing life. But the air of uncertainty vanished. Sapper, when he hit his stride, was so certain of himself that he could drag you into his mood in the first paragraph, and hold you there till the last. Cliché after cliché, of phrase and thought, washes over your head. You don't want to argue. You just want to know what happened—to Jack Carruthers and his topping girl; to old Bimbo to get him his v.c. Sapper tells his stories so slickly that you race through them for their plots. You have a comfortable knowledge that you're never going to be surprised by the way anybody behaves. You want to know what happens. A cad's a cad, a white man's a white man, and, so long as the story's a good one, that's a blessed simplification. Sapper's stories were good. He always, within his own limitations, told them excellently. He developed into being one of the easiest authors to race through in the whole of English popular literature.

In several of his short stories, when he has to establish a man in a paragraph, you'll find this kind of thing: 'Mark Darrington had good looks and money. He played cricket for Middlesex, danced well and told a very good story.' (If the next word is 'But . . .', then Darrington may turn out to be a bad type.) Half a dozen times, in this or that tale, Sapper puts the ability to tell a good story among the social graces. It isn't mentioned in **Mufti** as being a prerequisite of The Breed, but Sapper might have put it in ten years later. He implied that the ability to tell a good story is something that the Gods bestow on their favourites: like good looks, a good eye for games and a good inherited income.

Sapper had the gift of story-telling on paper himself. He had it so abundantly that, as he became more and more successful, he acquired an extremely marked manner. In the end the manner never varied from plot to plot. His vocabulary diminished. He repeated situations. But he never failed to be readable. His story went with a swing, and for that you easily forgave the similarity of characters of his later, most famous and popular, books. Gerard Fairlie wrote that Sapper thought that the good short story should have a trajectory like that of a good iron shot to the green. It should get off the mark quickly, streak up to a climax and then fall quickly to a full-stop.

If you played the same sort of shot time and time again, it was always a good shot. Type-casting of heroes, women and villains didn't matter.

The Breed were English. It did not follow that all Englishmen were of The Breed. But Sapper did not waste much time opposing Englishmen to Englishmen. His villains were almost always foreigners, and foreigners, more often than not, were villains. Teutons, dagoes and Jews were the foreigners that The Breed particularly disliked.

The Drummond books, right from the start, had foreign villains who were trying to smash England. The dago, the Teuton, the Jew, the Russian—scratch a foreigner and you find an enemy of England. And the moral of that, in Sapper, was: the English should admit that they are a race apart; they should realise that foreigners will always, through jealousy, want to bring England to her knees; the English should, therefore, take strong measures to be strong. The country should re-arm, and the individual should keep fit. The working classes should be given a lead by sportsmen; not by politicians or intellectuals. As for pimply-faced undergraduates voting that they would not fight for King and Country, gad, sir, where's that rhinoceros-hide whip Drummond used on the hunchback Zadowa in **The Black Gang**?

The sportsmen who could, and should, be the aristocrats and leaders of post-war England, had returned to peace, and most of them to unimpaired wealth. But what did peace offer that was half as exciting as no-man's-land on a dark night in wartime? No wonder the sportsman's eyes

lit up when the rifle-shot cracked, the calf-sized hound bayed, the topping girl screamed (that was generally a trap), and the suave foreign millionaire's cigar and shirt-front gleamed in the Surrey gloaming by the electrified fence.

'Tall, upstanding, a typical British sportsman, and exactly the sort of man that we want today in the Church,' said the dear old Cornish vicar. Sapper would have put a full-stop after 'today'. And the schoolboy who had just got his house colours couldn't have agreed more.

The schoolboy who had not got his house colours, and never would, but who was in the Sixth-form Essay mood, might put away his set of Greek Iambics, and try to analyse the Sapper writing style.

In the bulk of the short stories, Sapper was the Kipling of the Lower Shell. Sapper must have read a great deal of Kipling in his impressionable years. He had the same gnomic didacticism as Kipling, the same exhibitionist aposiopeses. He beat the same nationalist drum (Hugh Drummond once applied the word 'patriot' to a Swiss for being pro-English). He sanctioned occasional bullying with the same implied justifications, 'animal spirits' or 'the greatest fun for the greatest number'. He overdid pathos. His women were cardboard.

In the Standish short stories, and occasional other tales of detection, Sapper showed that his memory of the Sherlock Holmes adventures were uncomfortably accurate. One does not for a moment suggest that Sapper consciously cribbed: only that character-types, incidents, plots and even names surged into his mind and out at his pen without his suspecting their Conan Doyle origins. For probably a dozen of Sapper's detective stories you could find close parallels in Conan Doyle. Incidentally, the Comte de Guy's dinner party in the Prologue to **Bulldog Drummond** is a remarkably close replica of a similar feast organised by Dr Nikola in Guy Boothby's *A Bid for Fortune*. Sapper could not remember that he was remembering.

Sapper's style suffers from repetitions of words (e.g. 'snarl', 'sneer', 'worthy'—meaning person), of phrases (e.g. 'his veins stood out like whipcord', 'and then it happened', 'wicked little automatic'), and inversions (e.g. 'loyal to the core was that old dear'). Sapper overdoes the guttural Teuton talk (e.g. 'hold him the arms of, and I will tear the throat out'), disguisings and lashings-up to chairs. Sapper is wonderfully forgetful, not only of the fact that someone else may have written the story before, but even of his own last book (e.g. Mrs Denny dead in one book, alive in the next).

In the Bulldog Drummond books Sapper tapped a head of steam that was waiting for someone to tap just after World War I. He glorified, in peacetime, the comradeship, leadership and bravery of the days in the trenches. Perhaps when Englishmen (in the light of the newspaper headlines of the period) were dividing themselves into strikers and world-weary decadents, it was salutary to read of sportsmen with money *and* guts, and still ready to fight for England. Sapper made hay while the sun still shone on the British Empire, and before the cold wind of overdrafts blew through London's clubland.

A scene from the movie adaptation of Bulldog Jack.

I remember that on my sixteenth birthday I received as presents a new Buchan, a new 'Berry' book and a new Bulldog Drummond book. And I remember which I grabbed for reading first. The Sapper.

There was another boy, of the same age, gulping down Sapper then. Ian Fleming. According to John Pearson in *James Bond,* Guy Burgess described James Bond as being Sapper down to the waist, Mickey Spillane from the waist downwards. Whether this definition is ascribed fictionally or factually to Burgess, it is a good one. (pp. 133-49)

> *Richard Usborne, "Sapper," in his* Clubland Heroes: A Nostalgic Study of Some Recurrent Characters in the Romantic Fiction of Dornford Yates, John Buchan and Sapper, *revised edition, Barrie & Jenkins Limited, 1974, pp. 133-49.*

Colin Watson   (essay date 1971)

[*Watson was an English mystery writer and critic. In the following excerpt from his study* Snobbery with Violence: Crime Stories and Their Audience, *he analyzes* the character of Bulldog Drummond and his widespread appeal in post-World War I Britain.]

There emerged from the British Army in 1919, with the rank of Lieutenant-Colonel, a man named Herman Cyril McNeile. In 1920, he published a book under the pseudonym 'Sapper', which had been bestowed upon him some years earlier by Northcliffe on his acceptance of a story for the *Daily Mail.* The book was entitled ***Bulldog Drummond.*** It was the prototype of a series that made McNeile one of the most avidly read authors in Britain.

McNeile himself seems to have had a personality closely akin to that of his hero. It was of the sort that can most kindly be described as ebullient. He had a loud voice and employed it unstintingly in company. His laugh was very loud indeed. He liked to enliven clubs and restaurants with the sight and sound of military good fellowship. The meals that he was able to order with part of his dividends from literary success always included immense quantities of caviare and were followed by equally generous intakes of vintage port. Lieutenant-Colonel 'Sapper' McNeile, as his friend and biographer, Gerard Fairlie, would later concede, was 'not everybody's cup of tea'.

And yet Bulldog Drummond—the fictional extension of

the man himself—proved as nearly universally popular as any creator of characters could desire. The books sold in huge numbers in their author's lifetime and even after his death in 1937, when the 'ghosting' of additions to the series was undertaken by Fairlie. This success confirmed the truth of Fairlie's declaration: 'Once a fan, always a fan.' One story, *The Final Count,* which was first published in 1926, went into no fewer than forty editions in the next twenty-five years. Drummond was put upon the stage and featured in films, receiving the accolade of the cinema industry in the form of portrayal by Ronald Colman. (It was Colman, incidentally, to whom the not dissimilar roles of 'Raffles' and 'Beau Geste' were assigned.)

Drummond is worth careful examination, for his popularity could only have been won by a character whose qualities made immediate and strong rapport with the ideas of the reading and, subsequently, the cinema-going public.

In the first place, he satisfied conventional British ideals of physique. He 'stood just six feet in his socks, and turned the scale at over fourteen stone'. He was 'hard muscle and bone clean through . . . a magnificent boxer, a lightning and deadly shot with a revolver, and utterly lovable'. His friends were happily aware of his propensity to 'burble at them genially, knock them senseless with a blow of greeting on the back, and then resuscitate them with a large tankard of ale'. They also recognized his deservedly good fortune in being 'married to an adorable wife'.

Such was Drummond's strength of personality that those he led into adventure 'never questioned, never hesitated'. He was invariably contemptuous of odds, which he countered with enormous personal strength and an armoury of assorted weapons that today would be considered distinctly anti-social in character. With the police he had very little patience and he would not hesitate to incapacitate any whose bumbling regard for the proprieties threatened to interfere with his fight for right.

His flamboyantly aggressive patriotism was matched by his loyalty to his friends. In moments of excitement, he found expression in the vocabulary of the public school First Fifteen changing room, using the word 'show' a great deal and occasionally crediting an enemy with taking 'a darned sporting chance'. Drummond's warning of the gravity of a situation was likely to be delivered as: 'You're up against something pretty warm, old lad . . . I take off my hat to 'em for their nerve.' The few occasions on which his loquacity failed included those when death seemed imminent and thoughts flew to loved ones—'You might-er-just tell-er-you know, Phyllis and all that . . .'

Drummond's reticence also applied to religion. It was, as doubtless his readers would have agreed, one of those things that one just didn't talk about. One rather curious feature of his speech, though, was the frequency of his use of the word 'devil' and its derivatives. It is true that this was a literary device of the time to signal conflict between tough heroes and unprincipled adversaries, but 'Sapper's' devotion to it was extreme, and perhaps psychologically significant. Another sphere in which Drummond preferred action to words was politics. His rare references to the subject were characteristically forthright. 'Years ago

we had an amusing little show rounding up Communists and other unwashed people of that type. We called ourselves the Black Gang, and it was a great sport while it lasted.'

Such were the chief idiosyncrasies built by Lieutenant-Colonel McNeile into a hero to whom millions responded sympathetically from 1920 onwards. Bulldog Drummond was a melodramatic creation, workable only within a setting of melodrama. The stories provided for that purpose were models of unselfconscious absurdity. They had been vigorously purged of likelihood and were uncontaminated by the slightest suggestion of subtlety of style. Perhaps the most splendidly ridiculous of the entire canon was *The Final Count.*

Robin Gaunt, a scientist, has perfected a poison capable of dealing 'universal, instantaneous death'. He believes that Britain should be prepared to use it in order to stop other nations going to war. The day before he is due to give a secret demonstration before the Army Council, he disappears. Two of his friends, John Stockton and Toby Sinclair, discover Gaunt's terrier, 'a topping little beast', dead in the scientist's rooms. A policeman who touches the dog dies at once in a paroxysm and his colleague exclaims: 'But it's devil's work. It ain't human.' Sir John Dallas, celebrated toxicologist, suggests the deaths have been caused by a poison known previously to the Borgias and to the Aztecs. Such a substance could be of great military importance.

At Toby Sinclair's rooms, Stockton meets Bulldog Drummond. The three friends proceed to lunch at Hatchett's, in Piccadilly, Drummond giving 'a grin of pure joy' and exclaiming: 'Is it possible, my jovial bucks, that once again we are on the war-path?' They reassemble in a low pub in the sinister London suburb of Peckham. Stockton is disguised as 'a mechanic with Communistic tendencies' and Sinclair as a 'nasty-looking little Jew'. They overhear an address, go to it, and notice strange noises. Drummond declares: 'I'm going in, trap or no trap; there's foul play inside that room.' They find a rat-faced man hanging, shoot a man who is about to syringe them with Gaunt's poison, and tangle with a dozen police led by Inspector MacIver, of Scotland Yard. Friendly relations are restored by Drummond's remark: 'The fact of the matter, MacIver, is that we're up against some unscrupulous swine.'

The rest of the evening is taken up by Drummond's disposal of two outsize tarantulas, delivered to his Mayfair home in separate boxes addressed to him and his wife, and accompanied by sarcastic notes. He drowns one spider and hits the other between the eyes with a poker while it is scuttling about, 'hissing loudly'.

Drummond recruits several more friends. After further violent encounters with Gaunt's kidnappers, the scene changes to Land's End, whither the gang has been traced thanks to a chance remark. Drummond and his forces arrive at Penzance in his Hispano-Suiza. Stockton notices odd comings and goings at a deserted tin mine. Drummond distributes ropes, gags, heavily loaded sticks and bottles of chloroform. They converge on the mine, disposing of sentries as they advance. One is 'put to sleep', another given 'a good biff' and a third 'dotted one'.

Confronting the rest of the gang at gun point in their hideout, Drummond says to the man he habitually addresses as 'fungus face': 'Only a keen sense of public duty restrains me from plugging you where you sit, you ineffable swine.' Less scrupulous, 'fungus face' floods the room with the 'universal death' liquid. Robin Gaunt, now insane, appears just in time to drain off the poison, before it rises to the level of Drummond's table-top refuge. An airship has arrived overhead and it is into its tanks that the poison is pumped by Gaunt.

Search reveals papers written by Gaunt before he lost his reason. They express his fear that his secret would fall into the hands of 'Russia, ruled by its clique of homicidal, alien Jews'. Also described is an attack by airship upon a yacht crowded with Society people wearing jewels, their deaths by poison, and the robbery of their corpses by Bolsheviks—'the most frightful gang of murderous-looking cutthroats I've ever seen (officers seem to have no control)'.

Drummond realizes that behind the whole affair is Carl Peterson, arch-criminal. It also dawns upon him that the airship is the same as that supposedly owned by a mysterious American millionaire calling himself 'Wilmot'. He remembers that he has been sent two complimentary tickets for a trip on 'Wilmot's' airship that very night. He drives his friends back to London. Gaunt is disposed of with the remark: 'Well, since the poor bloke is bug house, I suppose we'll have to stuff him in a home or something.'

The airship of 'Wilmot', who is really Peterson, is crowded with fashionably dressed guests, including at least one duchess. At dinner, Peterson asks 'the distinguished officer on my right' to propose the Loyal Toast in 'an old Chinese wine the secret of which is known only to a certain sect of monks'. Captain Drummond (for it is he) calls: 'The King!' Then he smells his glass. 'For God's sake don't drink! It's death!'

To Peterson, he cries: 'Drink, you foul brute: drink!' Peterson knocks the glass from his hand, spilling its contents upon his own wrist. Before he dies, the expression on his face reveals him for what he is. 'And of that revelation no man can write . . .'

Questioned by an earnest investigator of popular reading habits, such as Mrs Q. D. Leavis, the average Bulldog Drummond enthusiast would probably have asserted that he enjoyed the stories simply 'as good yarns' without for a moment giving them credence. They were, after all, in the tradition of all wildly extravagant tales designed to pass an idle hour and 'take people out of themselves'. The impossible was more fun than the all-too-probable.

This would have been true as far as it went. 'Sapper' was fulfilling a function defined by that writer in the *Quarterly* sixty years before who had declared that 'keepers of bookstalls, as well as of refreshment rooms, find an advantage in offering their customers something hot and strong, something that may catch the eye of the hurried passenger, and promise temporary excitement to relieve the dullness of a journey'. But not everything 'hot and strong' be-

comes an addictive taste. Reams of picaresque nonsense, more or less similar to the 'Raffles' and Drummond novels, were produced every month without promoting enough response to justify a second printing. What did they lack that gave something else, no better and no worse in terms of plot, subject and style, a runaway success?

Robert Standish wrote of E. Phillips Oppenheim: 'If he had his finger on the common pulse, it was because he had his finger on his own.' Again, 'There was in him, as there has been in almost every man or woman who has found a place in tens of millions of human hearts, a wide streak of mediocrity.' Those two statements could well be amalgamated to form a general First Law of bestsellers. 'Sapper' confirmed it to the letter.

Throughout his work there is discernible an inborn appreciation of what would excite his readers without disturbing them; what they were likely to admire or despise (as distinct from loving and hating, with which popular fiction has nothing to do); and what would make them feel flattered, but not patronized. There can be little doubt that such understanding was instinctive and not the product of a calculating intelligence. The public is remarkably sensitive to 'tongue in cheek' attitudes; it recognizes and rejects every attempt to write down by an author who does not himself share the popular ideas he pretends to approve.

If 'Sapper' had set about investing the character of Bulldog Drummond with qualities other than those he genuinely considered admirable, the books would never have succeeded. Whether his notions were sensible or silly, beneficent or vicious, has much less to do with the success that did come his way than the fact that they were sincerely held. C. Day Lewis called 'Sapper's' hero 'that unspeakable public school bully'. He was expressing the aversion that the arrogant, small-minded and aggressive Drummond was bound to arouse in anyone of a thoughtful and tolerant disposition and egalitarian leanings. But fantasy heroes usually *are* bullies. They must win, and since their opponents seem to enjoy a monopoly of cunning, sheer physical advantage has to be invoked.

Much play of this is made in the Bulldog Drummond saga. Some of the scenes are strongly reminiscent of rugby football scrums and the author's enjoyment of the portrayal of zestful mayhem communicates itself strongly. Drummond himself is the embodiment of 'hard muscle and bone' superiority. His consistently successful encounters clearly imply that the simple answer to evil is 'a good biff'.

Violence was not, in the 1920s, the psychological abstraction that has so deeply concerned social diagnosticians since the end of the second world war. Although millions had been slaughtered and more millions maimed, the survivors of the 1914-18 war saw no relationship between the ferocity on the battlefield and cruel behaviour elsewhere. Perhaps because the conflict had been mainly one of attrition, a static killing match geographically confined, civilians regarded its horrors as a special case—deplorable, certainly, but quite separate from domestic ills. Thus, the upsurge of pacifism that reached its peak in the Peace Pledge of the 1930s was essentially an anti-militarist reaction which had much narrower implication than the attempts by young people thirty years later to repudiate force as such and even to contract out of a society committed to the use of force.

Drummond's preference for the upper-cut as an effective and proper argument was by no means inconsistent with contemporary relief at the return of peace. The 'Hun' had been fairly beaten, if not by precisely the same mode of assault, at least in the same spirit. The feeling of a great number of ordinary people was that subsequent tiresome complications at home and abroad could have been avoided by the delivery of a few extra 'biffs' for good measure. Could the odious Peterson, archetypal scheming foreigner, have been given his quittance by the deliberations of the old men of Versailles? Of course not. Disposal of Peterson and like afflictions called for a strong arm propelled by simple resolution.

'Sapper' reminds his readers from time to time of Drummond's military antecedents by having other characters address him as 'Captain'. The choice of rank is interesting. It is high enough to suggest experience and prowess, without implying advanced years or too marked a social eminence. 'Captain' connotes good fellowship; it has something of dash about it. Generals scarcely ever appear in popular fiction: they sound old and forbidding. Colonels crop up frequently but they seem reserved for chief constableships or country character roles in detective novels. A major is only recruited when a dipsomaniac of private means is required by the plot. In Captain Drummond, however, we have a man with exactly the right status to appeal to a generation with a constitutional respect for titles and with minds in which the word 'ex-Service' had attained special emotional lustre to compensate for the drab realities of demobilization.

Emphasis is laid upon the fact that none of Drummond's companions ever questions the rightness of his decisions or fails to carry out his orders. There is no argument, no 'argy-bargy' of the kind that so unhappily complicates the business of getting things done in real life. Action throughout the novels flows straight from situation to situation and it gets all the right results in the end, despite the evasions and counter-attacks of the enemy. Not only is this satisfying in terms of the story, but it is pleasingly suggestive of the possibility of events in the actual world being amenable to a strong man's dealing. One of Britain's special misfortunes in the interwar years was to suffer a series of governments uniformly dim of intellect, unsure of purpose and inept in action. It was tempting in the atmosphere of frustration thus created to wonder whether dictatorial methods might not be preferable to the long-windedness and muddle of democratic administration. On the face of it, Bulldog cut a better figure than a MacDonald or a Baldwin, while Tiger Standish, Nayland Smith, Sanders (on home leave from The River) and the rest of popular fiction's go-getters each served in his way to underline the ineffectualness of Government as it actually existed.

Relevant, perhaps, to this aspect of leisure reading is the currency in the mid-1930s of the highly romantic notion that T. E. Lawrence of 'Lawrence of Arabia' fame, ought to be sent as plenipotentiary envoy to Hitler's Reich.

There was considerable confidence in his ability (at a single bound, no doubt) to settle the hash of the troublesome little German so far as Britain's interests were concerned. Before the theory could be put to the test, Lawrence's fatal motor-cycle accident supervened. An earlier and more mundane example of myth being harnessed to politics was the adoption of Edgar Wallace as one of the candidates for a parliamentary election. If his subsequent appearance at the bottom of the poll proved anything, it was that public readiness to identify an author with his creations is not to be relied upon.

The only national political development that could be suspected of indebtedness to Bulldog Drummond was the rise, after 1931, of the British Union of Fascists. The connection, though, was not one of cause and effect. Popular fiction is not evangelistic; it implants no new ideas. Fascism sprang, in Britain as elsewhere, from frustration caused by economic chaos and political ineptitude. That same frustration had made readers' minds receptive to tales of improbable heroics, but acknowledgement of a common source is not the same thing as saying Mosley's fascism derived from McNeile's fiction. They simply possessed a certain family resemblance. (pp. 63-71)

> *Colin Watson, "The Bulldog Breed," in his* Snobbery with Violence: Crime Stories and Their Audience, *Eyre & Spottiswoode (Publishers) Ltd., 1971, pp. 63-71.*

LeRoy L. Panek (essay date 1981)

[*An American critic, Panek has written several studies of detective fiction, including* Watteau's Shepherds: The Detective Novel in Britain, 1914-1940 *(1979) and* An Introduction to the Detective Story *(1987). In the following excerpt from his* The Special Branch: The British Spy Novel, 1890-1980 *(1981), he provides an overview of McNeile's work.*]

Captain Hugh "Bulldog" Drummond, D.S.O., M.C., late of His Majesty's Royal Loamshires: what a man! He focuses the attributes of the popular adventure hero from the teens and he becomes the model for the adventure heroes created in the forties and fifties. Today Hugh Drummond seems outdated and he is in disfavor among literary people: critics carp about Sapper's brash and sometimes trashy writing and his neolithic social attitudes. Nevertheless, Sapper's hero provides real energy and organization to the evolution of popular fiction in Britain. From 1920 to 1937, H. C. McNeile, using the pseudonym "Sapper" (i.e., Military Engineer), wrote ten Bulldog Drummond novels: *Bull-Dog Drummond* (1920), *The Black Gang* (1922), *The Third Round* (1924), *The Final Count* (1926), *The Female of the Species* (1928), *Temple Tower* (1929), *The Return of Bulldog Drummond* (1932), *Knockout* (1933), *Bulldog Drummond at Bay* (1935), and *Challenge* (1937). During the same period he wrote several miscellaneous novels which essentially reproduce the Bulldog Drummond material in another guise: *Tiny Carteret* (1930) deals with international intrigue, and *Guardians of the Treasure* (1931) tells a treasure hunt tale featuring Jim Maitland. Sapper also developed the same things in his collections of short stories (these sometimes have a frame story to give the illusion of continuity), including *Jim Maitland* (1923), *Ronald Standish* (1933), and *Ask for Ronald Standish* (1936). Bulldog Drummond, though, contributes most to the development of the spy novel. During the course of these books Sapper's purposes and practices vary a bit, but when we reduce them to their essentials, they all boil down to the forcefulness of the hero, the evil of the villain, exciting action, some boisterously rude comedy, and some clearly articulated social attitudes.

Let's start with the hero. McNeile began writing under the pseudonym of Sapper for a specific purpose. The pseudonym sounds like those classic letters to *The Times* which individuals sign with their professions in order to indicate that they represent a class and not a single writer. The military title, Sapper, points to the military subject matter of McNeile's early fictions. Thus his first collection of short stories, *Sergeant Michael Cassidy* (1915), contains vignettes, humorous and sentimental, from the trenches. The Bulldog Drummond books, particularly the early ones, have a specific military lure. When we first meet Hugh in *Bull-Dog Drummond,* we lear that he is a demobilized soldier rusting unused in the soft arms of civilian life. Throughout this first novel the narration constantly displaces the hero's name with "the soldier." The experience and peculiar skills which Hugh gained in France go a long way toward making him efficient in the new kind of warfare which nominal peace-time presents. Sapper dwells on this. Take the following passage from *Bull-Dog Drummond:*

> . . . Hugh had practiced in France till he could kill a man with his bare hands in a second. Olaki—a Japanese—had first taught him two or three secrets of his trade, and in the interludes of resting behind the lines he had perfected them until it was even money whether the Jap or he would win a practice bout.

> And there were nights in No Man's Land when his men would hear strange sounds, and knowing that Drummond was abroad on his wanderings, would peer eagerly over the parapet into the desolate torn-up waste in front. But they never saw anything . . .

> Perhaps a patrol coming back would report a German lying in a shell-hole, with no trace of a wound, but only a broken neck; perhaps the patrol never found anything. But whatever the report, Hugh Drummond only grinned and saw to his men's breakfasts . . .

> The result on Drummond was not surprising: as nearly as a man may be he was without fear.

Hugh Drummond is supposed to be the soldier's soldier who goes beyond the call of duty to master his craft. This is very much apparent in the early novels, but as he moved into the twenties, Sapper let it slide—in most books after *The Black Gang,* Sapper contents himself with briefly mentioning the hero's service record and lets his readers assume the details. The only really lasting result of Hugh's wartime expertise comes in his ability to move about unseen and unheard. We find little more about *ju-jitsu* after the first book and, in fact, Drummond's combats usually

reduce to Hugh grabbing the villain by the throat. Sapper also substitutes Hugh's skill as a boxer, with its vague public school connection, for the hand-to-hand combat, with its military connection. This change in the specifics of fighting corresponds with a growing public distaste for wartime memories, but Sapper, as the books proceed, does not completely eliminate Hugh's war-time experience.

Few ex-soldiers really want to relive the excitement of combat since it brings with its memories of blank fear and death. Neither do they want to recall the mindless regimen or inactivity of army life. More pleasant is the memory of the camaraderie of the trenches. We see this throughout all of Sapper's books. Hugh's man, Denny, is, of course, the cliche former batman with his lasting affection for his officer. In the novels Hugh never acts alone. He is always accompanied by a group of his fellow officers: Toby Sinclair, Algy Longworth, Ted Jerningham, and Peter Darrell. When Hugh stirs up a spot of trouble in *Bull-Dog Drummond,* his thoughts turn quickly to his fellow soldiers.

> Toby possessed a V.C., and a good one—for there are grades of the V.C., and those grades are appreciated to a nicety by the recipient's brother officers if not by the general public. The show would fit Toby like a glove. . . . Then there was Ted Jerningham, who combined the roles of an amateur actor of more than average merit with the ability to hit anything at any range with every conceivable type of firearm. And Jerry Seymour in the Flying Corps. . . . Not a bad thing to have a flying man—up one's sleeve. . . . And possibly someone versed in the ways of tanks might come in handy. . . . [Sapper's ellipses]

The soldiers' reunion sounds a bit like Hugh intends to start his own private army—which, in fact, he does—but more important from Sapper's point of view is the shared understanding and comradeship of these fellow officers. Outside the circle of soldier-friends Sapper tends to describe civilians as weak or debilitated. In the first two novels, Hugh also has at his beck loads of demobilized soldiers to provide troops in his battle against international hankypanky. Both the enlisted men and Hugh's fellow officers, moreover, show the virtues of military discipline and of Hugh's benevolent leadership: they follow him instinctively, as opposed to the minions of the villains who do their jobs out of greed, fear, or down right insanity. Sapper returns constantly to the camaraderie of soldiers. At every break in the action they congregate not only to plan the next attack—*toujours l'audace*—but to lower a pint or two and to chafe each other with good humor.

The war not only provided Hugh with his skills and his allies, it also formed some of his attitudes toward national and international politics. No burned-out intellectual like Owen or Sassoon, Hugh Drummond learned political reality in the war. He learned that one cannot mollycoddle evil: one must face it and destroy it. Thus in *Bulldog Drummond at Bay,* Hugh reads off a namby-pamby M.P. this way:

> "You did not go through the last war as—er—as a combatant. We did, and we don't want anoth-

er, any more than some of the pacifist young gentlemen to-day, who never heard a shot fired in anger. We know the horrors of it first-hand; we are all out to prevent it again if we can. But we maintain that the present policy of cutting down our fighting forces . . . is the most certain way of precipitating it . . . As you know, they intended to kill Waldron and Graham Cardwell, so that those two secrets would have been Kalinsky's sole property. Do you suppose he was going to use 'em [the military secrets] for shaving paper?"

The war has given the heroes what they perceive to be certain knowledge of the ways of evil and the only method of dealing with it—exterminate the brutes.

The military background also supplies a particular role for the structured authority in Sapper's books. Society does not depute Hugh Drummond and his chums to run down the bad folks of the world; they do it on their own time, using their own financial and personal resources, and out of their own initiative. Authority, this says, well-meaning as it sometimes is, cannot handle complex situations as well as vigilantes can. This motif of effective action and human feelings being limited to small groups versus the blindness, inefficiency, and hamstrung nature of high authority is a familiar one in literature about war: the General Staff, the men with the red tabs, sit on their duffs while the company or the platoon gets things done (or fails to get things done) and feels for each of its members. In this kind of book we also find that the real soldiers inevitably feel animosity or contempt for remote, structured authority. It is notable, in this connection, that Sapper only made Hugh a Captain as opposed to Buchan's elevation of Hannay to General's rank—Buchan was an armchair soldier. Sapper's hero, as the commander of the small group, gets things done and at the same time he gives authority the raspberry. This also connects Hugh to the tradition of the thriller. Thrillers habitually found ways of keeping established law-enforcement, the police, out of the action. They did this in order to boost the role of the amateur and to show that some problems present such grave peril to society that laws must be broken to solve them. Sapper combines these two anti-authority techniques and wrangles them into his plots. Not only does Hugh constantly break the law for what he believes to be the greater good—as in *The Black Gang,* where he kidnaps Marxists, ships them to a remote island, and shows them communism in action by making them work—he also mocks authority. Thus, also in *The Black Gang,* Hugh and his pals chloroform Inspector McIver and his policemen and leave them asleep on their own doorsteps. When this sort of hi-jinks comes up before authority, however, the powers in the society indulgently allow Hugh and his chums to keep up the good work—the justification of success is success. In both *The Black Gang* and *Bulldog Drummond at Bay,* therefore, Cabinet officials laughingly approve of Drummond's unorthodox methods of handling situations. Authority at the top remains inviolate, and individual initiative is praised and rewarded while the remote institution and lower-echelon managers take it on the chin.

In addition to the soldiering background, Sapper emphasizes Bulldog Drummond's size and strength. This largely occurs after the second novel, *The Black Gang,* where the narration partly replaces the repeated invocations of "the soldier" with repeated descriptions of Hugh as "huge" or "vast." In objective terms Bulldog Drummond is not all that big: he is just under *(Bull-Dog Drummond)* or precisely *(The Final Count)* six feet tall, and he weighs fourteen stone (one hundred ninety-six pounds). Today he would be a light heavy-weight—big, but hardly vast. But this is quibbling. If Sapper wants him to be huge there must be reasons for it. One of the reasons for Hugh's bulk comes as a logical conclusion to the gothic element in the novels. The evil people in Sapper's books live amidst gothic trappings (ostensibly haunted houses, etc.) and they use these things to terrify innocents. It is simple justice, therefore, that as part of their comeuppance they receive a good hearty dose of terror in return as earnest of their total punishment. Thus Hugh's huge hands come out of nowhere and grab the crook by the throat while his fellows cower in the corner. Hugh's physical size, for another thing, exists in order to underline his prowess as an action hero. Moving quickly and stalking silently seem the attributes of a smaller, lithe individual, but Hugh's ability to do these things and be the hulk that he is make him special. In the good-evil frame of these books, Hugh's size enables Sapper to play our giant against your giant, for he often introduces a figurative or, in the case of *The Black Gang,* literal gorilla to represent the awesome strength of the bad guys against which our champion must eventually do battle. Finally, Drummond's size exists to work a whole species of comedy. Hugh's gargantuan good humor and heartiness blow away gloom and bring in celebration. He is the big man who enjoys himself, his companions, and life in general to the fullest. It takes quarts of beer to satisfy his thirst, loads of friends to fulfill his gregariousness, and tons of excitement to keep him happy. Sapper uses this and, indeed, follows the comedy of size to absurd lengths. Thus in *Bulldog Drummond Returns,* the book opens with a narrative description of a whole country house being shaken to its foundations by the snores of the slumbering giant: it is a bit difficult to become seriously involved with the danger of adventure after such hyperbole.

Instead of being a grim-visaged avenger, Hugh Drummond is a sportsman from the leisure class. This leisure class business was an afterthought, but as the novels proceed, Sapper gives his readers more background on Hugh's family (he seems to be related to a Duke by the time of *The Black Gang,* and in later books, like *Temple Tower,* he numbers noblemen among his cronies) and his independent means (shown symbolically in his move to Brook Street in the second book). Sapper makes Inspector McIver type Hugh and his pals in *The Black Gang:*

> All of them built on the same pattern; all of them fashioned along the same lines. Talking a strange jargon of their own—idle, perfectly groomed, bored. As far as they were concerned, he [McIver] was non-existent save as the man who was with Drummond. He smiled a little grimly; he, who did more man's work in a week than the whole lot of them in a year. A strange caste, he reflected, as he sipped his drink; a cast which does not aim at, because it essentially is, good form; a caste which knows only one fetish—the

repression of all visible emotion; a caste which incidentally pulled more than its own weight in the war.

This may be a case of protesting too much, but we see Sapper's aim. These men do, though, have another fetish: sport and sportsmanship. While Sapper does not give Hugh much background as an actual sportsman, beyond telling us about his boxing and mentioning that he goes shooting, he makes up for it in the persons of Tiny Carteret, in whom Sapper essentially reproduces Hugh, and Ronald Standish. The former is an international at rugger and the latter is in constant demand for cricket elevens and golf matches. Even if Hugh does not often chase after balls of any size, he is still a sportsman. *Bull-Dog Drummond* tells us that normal varieties of sport offer no relief from boredom for Hugh. He looks for bigger game and consequently places his now-famous ad in the papers:

> Demobilized officer . . . finding peace incredibly tedious, would welcome diversion, legitimate, if possible; but crime, if of a comparatively humorous description, no objection. Excitement essential.

The same thing happens again and again in the Bulldog Drummond books: Hugh gets bored with shooting or golf or clubbing or country housing or just plain lolling about when, presto, a spot of real excitement crops up. In terms of sport and play, both the characters and narrators of the novels insist that the action rests on these things. Look at some of the titles—*The Third Round, The Final Count, Knockout, Challenge.* Boxing is sport, isn't it? Better yet, look into any of the books and you will find Hugh describing the action as a game. When Hugh, for instance, receives the second letter from Irma Peterson, who has kidnapped his wife, in *The Female of the Species,* Dixon, the narrator, describes the hero's reaction.

> "Absurd or not absurd," said Drummond gravely, "that is exactly what the woman has done. And from what I know of her it's going to be some chase."
>
> He got up, and suddenly to my amazement, and almost ecstatic grin spread over his face.
>
> "Gosh! boys," he said, "if it wasn't that it was Phyllis, what a glorious time we should have. Why did we never think of it before with Carl [the villain in the previous books]? We might have had two or three games in our spare time."

The ensuing action is, in fact, built on the game of Treasure Hunt. Risking one's life, grace and friendship under pressure all provide more pleasure than games like golf which mere burghers play. In *Temple Tower* Hugh and Peter pack their wives off to France under the pretext that they are going to play golf, but this is really a cover for getting mixed up with a bunch of French jewel thieves and gangsters. All of this sport carries with it its own set of rules: the reevaluation of fair play. The villains in all of these books play dirty; this shows particularly in their penchant for terrorizing and kidnapping helpless men and women. After raging about this lack of fair play, Drummond typically switches to their morality, usually murdering one of the villains at the close of the book—Lakington

in *Bull-Dog Drummond,* Yulowski in *The Black Gang,* Peterson in *The Final Count,* LeBossu in *Temple Tower,* Demonico in *Bulldog Drummond Strikes Back.* In the later books Hugh gives the villains a fighting chance, but, as we have seen above, he and his pals know that there is only one way to deal with evil. They do not, however, let this corrupt them, and when the next adventure comes along, they are ready to play the game with or without the rules of sportsmanship.

Some writers make the point that Bulldog Drummond represents the acme, or, if you will, nadir, of the traditions of the English public school. Now, seeing Sapper in the light of schoolboy fiction aids in understanding his books, but in fact Sapper makes surprisingly few explicit references to public school life in his novels. True, in *The Black Gang,* Hugh does refer to his "stinks" (Chemistry) master at school and wishes he had absorbed more of the fundamentals of science, and in the same book we learn that Hugh was Sir Brian Johnstone's fag at school. We never, however, learn the name of the school or get much more on school life than this. The most attention to schools and schoolboys enters with Joe Dixon, the narrator of *The Female of the Species,* who gets one of his old masters to help solve the riddle in one of Irma Peterson's cryptic letters. The schoolboy quality in Sapper's books depends very little upon any direct connection with school or memories of school life. Sapper, in fact, does not write for people who have memories of public school or the university, as do Buchan, Beeding, Coles, and other higher-brow writers. The schoolboy quality in his books comes rather from Sapper's use of certain well-known patterns and attitudes. First of all, through most of Sapper's books, the narrator or the villain insists on calling Drummond and his cronies young men, and the novels give us the impression that a group of good young men contends with a group of nasty old men. This is part of normal schoolboy fantasy. Second, there is the institution of fagging—the system of involuntary servitude in public schools which enslaves younger boys to older boys. As I noted above, in *The Black Gang* we learn that Hugh was Sir Brian Johnstone's fag at school. Here Sapper reverses the normal pattern and tells us that Hugh, the fag, defended and protected his studious and serious older friend from schoolboy calumny. This same pattern extends to adult life with Hugh continuing to fag for Sir Brian, now the Commissioner of Police, doing his real job for him and not seeking credit. The same relationship, only treated here in the conventional manner, exists between Hugh and his fags, Algy, Peter, Toby, Ted, etc. They drop everything and run to be of service to him and they obey his orders unquestioningly. The simple fact that Sapper inevitably uses the group of friends plus the hero, with all of its implicit and explicit lessons about cooperation and self-sacrifice, points to the schoolboy nature of these adventures. Further, through the filter of the schoolboy adventure, we get one more perspective on the nature of authority in these tales: Hugh and his chums, as the group of boys, do not go whining to the master when faced with a problem; instead they put their heads together and figure things out for themselves. Finally, some of the high jinks in the books derive from schoolboy pranks and schoolboy mentality. When Hugh first appears in *The Third Round,* he is standing by his window playing Beaver (i.e., counting the number of men with beards who pass by): hardly an adult pastime. In *Bulldog Drummond Returns* Irma Peterson achieves part of her long-sought revenge by causing Hugh to de-bag himself: getting caught with one's trousers down may, indeed, be embarrassing, but it is a schoolboy prank and hardly an action which we expect from a crazed Master Criminal. In all, it helps to understand the purpose of these books to view them as extended schoolboy or undergraduate rags.

Just two more items from the schoolboy tradition. First, women play a miniscule role in these stories, and Sapper avoids descriptions of love or domestic scenes. In the first novel Hugh meets and marries his Phyllis, but in subsequent novels she disappears a) because, playing the typical adventure heroine, she has been kidnapped by the villains; or b) because Sapper either sends her off to France or America or fails, as in *Challenge,* to mention her at all. As in the typical schoolboy story, women in Sapper serve as means of demonstrating the hero's chivalry or, in the case of the villainess, Irma Peterson, they demonstrate the writer's fundamental fear of women. The other important element from the schoolboy tradition is the prominent vein of anti-intellectualism running through these books. In every novel Sapper points out that Hugh is no genius: he has an average mind. Thus, in *The Third Round,* the narrator says

> Hugh Drummond laid no claim to being brilliant. His brain, as he frequently remarked, was of the "also-ran" variety. But he was undoubtedly the possessor of a very shrewd common sense, which generally enabled him to arrive at the same result as a far more brilliant man and, incidentally, by a much more direct route.

In addition to emphasizing his militant mediocrity, which is never converted as is Tom Brown's, Sapper makes Hugh into a defiantly insular Englishman. This shows best with his skill in foreign languages. In *Bull-Dog Drummond,* Hugh and his friends follow the villain to France, where they meet a policeman who wants to inquire about their unorthodox entry (they have crash-landed in an airplane) as well as the state of their passports:

> A Frenchman was advancing towards them down the stately vestibule of the Ritz waving protesting hands. He addressed himself in a voluble crescendo to Drummond, who rose and bowed deeply. His knowledge of French was microscopic, but such trifles were made to be overcome.

> "Mas oui, Monsieur mon Colonel," he remarked affably when the gendarme paused for lack of breath, "vous comprenez que notre machine avait crashe dans un field des turnipes. Nous avons lost notre direction. Nous sommes hittes dans l'estomacs . . . comme ci, comme ca. . . . Vous comprenez, n'est ce-pas, mon Colonel?" [Sapper's ellipses]

This from a man who supposedly spent a good deal of time in France during the Great War. Hugh does the same thing with fractured Italian in *The Black Gang.* The language business, of course, is part of the comedy upon which Sapper bases these books, but it also comes from the tradition of schoolboy ridicule of the grinds and the substantially educated. It also probably represents Sapper's reaction against the detective novel of the twenties, which was becoming increasingly complex and intellectual. In the late twenties, however, Sapper found it necessary to reverse himself on this, and he began to introduce into his novels intellectual problems (albeit sham ones) like riddles *(The Female of the Species)* and cipher *(Knockout).* To remain consistent, though, Sapper, rather than changing Hugh's mental make-up, introduced new characters, notably Ronald Standish (who appears in *Knockout, Bulldog Drummond at Bay, Challenge,* as well as in *Tiny Carteret* and his own series of short stories), who are allegedly competent at intellectual analysis.

Looking back for a moment at Hugh's fractured French, one of the prime reasons for the popularity of the Bulldog Drummond books stems from Sapper's combination of comedy and action. His main comic technique is the creation of comic diction. At first Sapper made this comic speech the province of the hero, but in the later novels it spread to other characters, including Carl Peterson, the villain in the first four books, only to fade in the thirties when Sapper seemed to tire of it, and then to return centered around Algy Longworth in *Challenge.* The creation of comic diction was one of the staples of popular writers between the wars in both Britain and America. P.G. Wodehouse was the most active and influential practitioner but he was followed by Bentley, Sayers, Allingham, Beeding, Coles and a bunch of others. As it is practiced by most of these writers, comic diction typically combines schoolboy lingo (Hugh's reference to chemistry as "stinks" for instance), American slang and underworld argot, casual upper class speech habits (dropping g's) and slang, hunting slang (yoicks), baby talk (Drummond frequently refers to himself as "little Willie"), as well as comic displacement, the absurd series, and other standard techniques of comic rhetoric. Sapper uses most of them, with the notable exception of the comic literary allusion (the skewed, inappropriate, or unexpected quotation), which points to the nature of his audience as opposed to Wodehouse's or Beeding's. Here is a representative sample of Hugh Drummond's conversation:

> "Which is where Ted comes in," said Hugh affably. "Does the Stomach-ache [Peter's airplane] hold two?" "My dear man," cried Jerningham, "I'm dining with a perfectly priceless she tonight."

> "Oh, no, you're not, my lad. You're going to do some amateur acting in Paris. Disguised as a waiter, or a chambermaid, or a coffee machine or something—you will discover secrets."

Much of the effect of this kind of speech is to give readers a dose of verbal comedy (which, considering its widespread nature in the twenties, readers wanted), but it also has a marked effect on character. Men who can be flippant and facetious in the face of danger or death simply ooze with nonchalance, and this, going back to McIver's description of Hugh and his chums, is one of the main elements which Sapper wanted to convey through Bulldog Drummond. It is also, incidentally, the main element which most detective and spy writers wanted to convey in their fictions in the twenties and early thirties.

Hugh Drummond, however, is not a terribly original character. We can trace much of what he does and is back to the adventures of Sherlock Holmes or Sexton Blake, or the exploits of other adventure heroes. Two of these have particular significance in respect to Sapper's place in the traditions of the spy novel. Bulldog Drummond is, first of all, Dick Hannay written down for tykes. Drummond takes over and magnifies Hannay's size and strength, he adventures with a gang of pals just as Hannay does in Buchan, and he learned his lessons in tracking people and animals from one Van Dyck who obviously comes from Peter Pienaar. In Hugh's gang Sapper only really differentiates one character, Algy Longworth. All of the others, Ted, Peter, and Toby, possess the same tongue, the same abilities, the same gung-ho spirit. Algy, though, in spite of the Wodehousean drivel added in *Challenge,* probably came from Archie Roylance in Hannay's tribe: they are both callow, girl crazy, and faintly bungling. Like Buchan, and perhaps more successfully, Sapper insists on making his sportsman hero into the Average Man.

The other important source for Bulldog Drummond can be found in the books of Baroness Orczy. Although she wrote a number of detective short stories, Orczy's fame rests on *The Scarlet Pimpernel* (1905). Sir Percy Blakeney, who masquerades as the Scarlet Pimpernel, seems a loutish bungler, sunk in the pleasures of life. In disguise, though, he zips over to France and rescues persecuted aristocrats from the guillotine. As Orczy describes him, Sir Percy is:

> Tall, above the average, even for an Englishman, broad-shouldered and massively built, he would have been called unusually good-looking, but for a certain lazy expression in his deep set blue eyes, and that perpetual inane laugh which seemed to disfigure his strong, clearly-cut mouth.

Hugh Drummond may not be good-looking, but he has most of the other qualifications in the Pimpernel line. Particularly in *The Black Gang,* Hugh pretends to be a jerk in order to mask his identity as the leader of the Black Gang which, like the Pimpernel and his followers, discomfits modern revolutionaries.

So much for heroes, though. Sapper's villains deserve some attention, too. Villains in popular fiction, like everything else, follow certain observable trends. Before the First World War, British writers leaned toward using the Master Criminal who wants to turn society to his own use: thus, *The Four Just Men* (1905), *The Insidious Fu Manchu* (1913), *The Power House* (1913), and other novels fostered this sort of villain. Books predicting war, as well as those written during the war itself, combined traditional elements of villainy with the identification of the villain with perceived weakness in German mentality and politics. Therefore Williams' *Okewood of the Secret Service* (1919) ropes in bits from the story of Mata Hari to color the evil against which the hero struggles. After the Armistice there was a widespread return to the Master Criminal-gangster motif: hence, Buchan's *The Three Hostages*

(1924), Beeding's *The Seven Sleepers* (1925), and *Bull-Dog Drummond.* Each of Sapper's novels, therefore, uses the Master Criminal as the antagonist. The first and most important of these is Carl Peterson, who appears in the first four Bulldog Drummond books. After Hugh calls Carl to his last reckoning in *The Final Count,* Sapper's villains go downhill: Peterson's mistress, Irma, prosecutes her revenge in *The Female of the Species,* but her villainy sadly falls off in *The Return of Bulldog Drummond.* The other villains, LeBossu, Zavier, Demonico, Kalinsky, Menalin, are all pretty much single shot, emaciated versions of Peterson. In spite of their real importance to character, plot, and theme, Sapper never hit his stride with his villains and kept on tinkering with their characters, trying to produce the desired effect. We find, for example, that in *The Third Round,* Sapper narrates in detail the villain's action while in the next book, *The Final Count,* the chief villain does not enter until the novel is nearly finished. Somehow Sapper never quite made his villains into the bogeys that he would have liked to portray.

At any rate, Sapper's villains do have a number of similarities, and they make pretty obvious character or thematic points. First, all of the villains create and use precise and carefully wrought plans and organizations. Peterson and Menalin write down every jot and title of their nasty plans, and all of the nefarious plots in the books turn on split-second timing. This, of course, gives easy access to their intent but, more importantly, it enhances the hero's nonchalance and quick intelligence in that he is able to thwart such finely-honed duplicity. Not only are the villains organizers, they are also part of the international capitalist conspiracy. Here Sapper taps into a theme that goes as far back as LeQueux's *The Red Room* (1911), which ascribes both international and domestic strife to the machinations of evil foreign capitalists (as opposed to good, honest, inventive British capitalists), and brings into fiction the progressive decline of British industry. Thus, in Sapper, we discover that it is not bolsheviks *qua* bolsheviks who aim to disrupt Britain in *Bull-Dog Drummond, The Black Gang,* and *Challenge,* but international capitalists who wish to stifle honest British labor and capital, or international fortune hunters like Peterson who want to cause unrest in order to line their own pockets. Likewise, in *Bulldog Drummond at Bay,* we find that nations' public policies will not bring on the next war but that the skulduggery of capitalist opportunists like Kalinsky will. The capitalist conspiracy meddles with warmongering in Sapper's early books and his late ones—those chronologically tied to the last and the next war.

In the middle books, Sapper reflects on the worsening economic climate in the world, and he posits Master Criminals who cause the disheartening fluctuations in the economy: Peterson aims to shake the international diamond market in *The Third Round,* Irma plans a stock scam in *The Return of Bulldog Drummond,* and Demonico plans to puncture confidence in sterling in *Knockout.* Capitalist greed stands behind most of the practical nastiness which the villains create in the novels (except for *Temple Tower,* which is a straight gangster plot). These monied bloodsuckers, though, never get their fingers dirty: they use loony, cunning, or misguided Marxists (see *Bull-Dog*

Drummond, The Black Gang and *Challenge*), common criminals, or psychologically-warped people who engage in crime for the thrills (as with Pendelton and Corinne Moxton in *Knockout*).

The machinery of Sapper's villains pretty much resembles the standard fare of the teens and twenties. In every case, the villains have numerous toadies who are usually identified by numbers rather than names, in order to stress not only the sterility of evil but also its organization and limitless supply of labor. They do tiresome jobs and supply answers to awkward plotting problems. Since Sapper frequently deals with continuing, series villains who jump from book to book (Carl and Irma Peterson), he introduces the evil second-in-command, like Lakington in *Bull-Dog Drummond,* who takes it in the neck at the end of the action, thereby showing the conquest of evil but allowing the series villain to toddle off-stage, ready to appear in the next book. Almost all of Sapper's antagonists take top honors for disguise, as Hugh does himself. Carl, Irma, Le-Bossu, and Demonico all pop up as unsuspected people—as does Hugh in *Bulldog Drummond at Bay,* where he is supposedly burned to a crisp. Sapper devotes a good deal of description in *The Third Round,* in fact, to Carl Peterson's disguising skill. Further, Sapper's villains usually possess some sort of hideout which is, at the same time, the hero's goal and his greatest peril. At the hideout the hero must deal with the gang, and he must surmount various perverse mechanical dangers in the place itself: the beheading staircase in *Bull-Dog Drummond,* the electrified fence in *The Black Gang,* the reservoir of poison in *The Final Count,* etc. This impinges on the Fu Manchuish elements in Sapper's antagonists. In a number of books the villains use exotic and weird threats. Thus, in *Bull-Dog Drummond,* Carl keeps a gorilla on the grounds of his headquarters, has a cobra slithering around in the draperies at night, and hires a pigmy with a blowgun to squat on top of Hugh's wardrobe and spit poisoned darts at the hero. In *The Final Count,* Carl sends a pair of horrible spiders to Hugh and Phyllis. Could Sax Rohmer do more?

Sapper's plots run pretty much along conventional adventure fiction lines. Typically, the villain and his minions plan some sort of nefarious business which will a) threaten England's stability, and b) boost their incomes and egos. Hugh Drummond accidentally stumbles across this plot, becomes interested in it as a potential adventure, and an initial skirmish occurs. The bad people then kidnap someone (Drummond's wife, a millionaire, or an inventor). Hugh attempts to rescue this hostage, but becomes a prisoner himself. Then he escapes, usually with the aid of his friends, and shortly afterward they finish off the bad guys and thwart their scheme. This pattern admits some variation—in *Bulldog Drummond at Bay,* for instance, readers do not learn about the motivation or objective of the villains until the middle of the book—but it remains Sapper's standard formula. The main feature of this pattern is that it contains numerous chances for capture and escape and, in turn, when faced with danger, capture and escape show best Hugh's physical virtues and his happy-go-lucky nonchalance. Sapper, though, has a gift for mucking up a perfectly good adventure plot by trying to include too much. Thus, in *Bull-Dog Drummond,* he clogs up the bolshevik

plot by including Lakington's theft of the Duchess' pearls, and in *The Return of Bulldog Drummond,* perhaps the most tedious of all the books, Sapper forgets about the murder at the start of the book when he introduces Irma Peterson and her swindling scheme. He could rarely leave well enough alone.

Other than showing his readers Hugh's character, Sapper never decided what effect he wanted his novels to produce. Sure, he wanted to produce laughs with the personalities and antics of Hugh and company. He also wanted to evoke gothic thrills and suspense, as witnessed by Stockton's "had I but known" narration in *The Final Count.* But Sapper never decided about the proper mix of these things or how to convey it to his readers; consequently, we witness him constantly tinkering with technique from book to book. In some novels he centers on the actions of the villains while in others he ignores them. In some he keeps the readers in the dark about the villain's plans (as in *Bulldog Drummond at Bay*) while in others we know about them from the start. For three books (*The Final Count, The Female of the Species,* and *Temple Tower*), he uses first person narration, but he cannot decide whether the narrator should be a novice being initiated into the world of chills and thrills, or one of the principal actors in the adventure. Occasionally Sapper's technical tinkering works and sometimes it does not. The effect is not one of planned experiment, but rather of the author charging more or less blindly about trying to find the proper vehicle for his character.

Whatever their level of craftsmanship or their sensitivity to humane values, though, Sapper's books rank among that small class of fictions in which the character grows out of the writer's hands and attains a place in the public consciousness. Bulldog Drummond survived Sapper and continued to affect the tradition of the spy story, not because of the films made about him or the novels written about him, after McNeile's death, by Gerald Fairlie, but because Hugh Drummond captured for the public the blend of brutality and nonchalance which sprang up in the twenties, and which later writers would look back upon with wistfulness or disgust. (pp. 68-82)

> *LeRoy L. Panek, "Sapper," in his* The Special Branch: The British Spy Novel, 1890-1980, *Bowling Green University Popular Press, 1981, pp. 68-83.*

Noel Behn   (essay date 1984)

[*A former counterintelligence officer in the U. S. Army, Behn is the author of several espionage novels. In the following excerpt, he examines the social and political climate in which McNeile wrote his Drummond stories.*]

Great apes and little pygmies with blow pipes, Bull Dog Drummond lives! Rereading *Bull Dog Drummond* stirs long dormant suspicions it is . . . for good and for bad . . . progenitor to a particular genre of contemporary espionage fiction; that the indomitable Hugh Drummond was none other than James Bond's granddaddy. Not that Bull Dog was a spy. He wasn't. He was, however, as unabashedly charming and ruthless an assassin as any killer in modern literature. And, like James Bond, Hugh Drummond was on the side of angels. Or at least the Empire.

Few authors have enjoyed the immediate popular success afforded H. C. McNeile for his novel *Bull Dog Drummond . . . The Adventures of a Demobilized Officer Who Found Peace Dull.* Rarer still are the fictional swashbucklers with the staying power of this title character. First published in England by Hodder and Stoughton in 1920 (and later that same year by New York's George H. Doran Company), the Drummond saga went on to include sixteen sequels . . . the last written in 1954 by McNeile's friend and biographer Gerard Fairlie, who is responsible for seven of the stories. The printed appeal of Bull Dog was compounded by the emerging media of World Wars I and II. Radio and television in both England and America presented weekly serialization. Motion pictures provided the most celebrated group of Drummond portrayers and thereby nurtured Hugh to near legendary status. Between 1922 and 1971, some twenty movies were produced in which Bull Dog was acted by the likes of Ronald Colman, Ralph Richardson, Ray Milland, Walter Pidgeon, Jack Buchanan, and many lesser-known actors. (For history buffs; the very first B-DD film, made in 1922 under the title *Bull-Dog Drummond,* had Carlyle Blackwell in the starring role.) Where movies left off, theatre picked up. In 1974, Alan Sherman appeared on Broadway in *Captain Hugh Bullshot Crummond,* a self-described "satiric reminder." New York City audiences have also seen an off-Broadway revival of the original dramatization, *Bull-Dog Drummond,* co-written by McNeile under his pseudonym "Sapper" and Gerald du Maurier. Produced in London in 1921, the play was presented in New York later that same year with A. E. Mathews starring.

Born in Bodmin, Cornwall, September 28, 1888, Herman Cyril McNeile was the son of a captain in the British Navy. After brief attendance at Cheltenham College, Gloucestershire, and the Royal Military Academy at Wolwich, McNeile in 1907, at the age of nineteen, joined the British Army. He served in the Royal Engineers for twelve years, inclusive of World War I. In 1914, he was both married and promoted to Captain . . . the same rank he would later bestow upon Hugh Drummond. Even before retiring in 1919 as Lieutenant Colonel, McNeile was writing military adventure stories. On accepting one of these pieces for publication in his *Daily Mail,* Lord Northcliffe assigned McNeile the pen name "Sapper" . . . a military slang expression of the day for "engineer." It is unclear if McNeile began *Bull Dog Drummond* before leaving the army in 1919, but that year his first novel *Mufti* was published. With *Mufti,* as well as *Bull Dog Drummond,* which appeared in 1920, the author forwent "Sapper" and used the name H. C. McNeile (though over the decade editions can be found credited to Cyril McNeile as well as to Sapper.)

As former naval officer Ian Fleming would 37 years later, Lieutenant Colonel "Sapper" McNeile returned to a postwar England different from the one he had left. Like his creator probably did, Captain Hugh Drummond, D.S.O., M.C., late of His Majesty's Royal Loamshires, finds post-

World War I London not only changed but boring . . . so boring that in the first chapter of the novel we learn Hugh has put this advertisement in the paper: "Demobilized officer finding peace incredibly tedious, would welcome diversion. Legitimate, if possible; but crime, if of a comparatively humorous description, no objection. Excitement essential . . . Reply at once Box X10." Many do reply, but only one is chosen—a damsel in the most insidious distress.

If a literary hero is best defined by the enemies his author seeks for him, then Hugh Drummond is every bit as jingoistic—and prejudiced—as McNeile. Granted, the Empire had been victorious in World War I, and Edwardian civility was generally intact, but at a devastating price. England and her allies were exhausted. Europe was sickly, ravaged, nearly bankrupt. Britain was beset by trouble (and, in the eyes of Drummond and McNeile, the troublesome). Economic trouble. Labor trouble. General unrest. New ideas. Worst of all, for Old Club, class-conscious military men such as Colonel Sapper McNeile and Captain Bull Dog Drummond, alien ideas. Ideas to imperil the fabric of Britannia. Meddle with the institutions. Alter the status quo. The Bolshevik revolution in Russia was filling far-off streets with blood, might be sweeping west across Europe at any moment . . . heading for you-know-where. Communists were boring from within. Along with socialists. Anarchists. Nihilists. The Jews were afoot as well. So were other foreigners. And industrialists. Particularly German industrialists who would wreak hideous revenge on Britannia for defeating the Hun Hordes.

These then were among the demonic forces many ordinary English men and women feared would destroy their nation. McNeile had a sense of the ordinary, of the common; possessed the skill to pestle such dreads into an odious concoction; equipped the horrors with every conceivable device of destruction from acid baths, which completely dissolved corpses, to apes and cobras and little pygmies with blow pipes. Galvanizing this layer cake of evil into a solitary reign of terror was an arch villain as multimalevolent as Professor Moriarty (and who was every bit as loathsome as a Communist or Jew or Pygmy . . . or worse: who was Irish)—Carl Peterson. Aiding Peterson are two sub-vipers, his beautiful mistress Irma, and a scientific genius gone wrong named Henry Lakington (who dreams up the acid bath plus drugs no civilized physician can counteract). Nothing on God's good earth or Victoria's Realm stood a chance against this juggernaut of venality . . . except McNeile's ultimate weapon, and alter ego . . . Hugh "Bull Dog" Drummond.

Like Fleming to come, McNeile opted for the urbane, was conversant with the trendy of his time . . . with middle class concepts of power and wealth and patriotism. Unlike Fleming, McNeile was sexually and morally a strict constructionist, Victorian to the never-unbuttoned britches. Drummond is a prototypical monogamist, the consummate anti-philanderer. Whereas Ian Fleming was physically attractive, the few photographs of McNeile show him somewhat less than comely. As was Drummond, whose "best friend would not have called him good looking, but he was the fortunate possessor of that cheerful

type of ugliness which inspires immediate confidence in its owner. His nose had never quite recovered from the final one year of Public Schools Heavy Weights; his mouth was not small . . . Only his eyes redeemed his face from being what is known in the vernacular as the Frozen Limit. Deep-set and steady, with eyelashes that many a woman envied, they showed the man for what he was . . . a sportsman and gentleman. And the combination of the two is an unbeatable product."

Thus we are left with possible meanings for Hugh Drummond's nickname . . . as ugly as a Bull Dog . . . as tenacious as a Bull Dog . . . as British as a Bull Dog.

His hero to the side, it was McNeile's flamboyant xenophobia that was to cast the die for Bondian spy fiction to come. If there is a difference between an adventure story and a romanticized espionage story, it is usually in the stakes each entity pursues. For the 007 breed of secret operative to rush into action, a cataclysm must be at hand; an entire nation, if not all of civilized mankind, must be on the brink of destruction or subjugation by some arch fiend . . . by Dr. No or Goldfinger or Blofeld. Civilized mankind, to McNeile, was the British Empire, and, in this first Drummond book, that is exactly what is at stake—derailing Peterson's plan to bring down the country.

Purists of espionage fiction are unremitting in their insistence that in a detective story you solve a crime and in a spy story you commit a crime . . . that espionage by definition is that illegal ten or fifteen percent of overall intelligence operations. Under these rules, neither the Bull Dog Drummond, Bond, nor most "spy books" would qualify. McNeile does do something else, however, that comes close to filling the bill. He allows his villain Peterson to concoct an international scheme to bring down England . . . a scheme the author lets his readers in on. To be technically correct, Hugh Drummond, as we see him in **Bull Dog Drummond,** might be one of the earliest counter-espionage agents.

Find a copy of **Bull Dog Drummond** and every now and then replace in your imagination the Bull Dog face with that of Sean Connery or Roger Moore, just to see what happens. Damn the anarchists and poison darts . . . full steam ahead! (pp. 368-69)

Noel Behn, "Britannia's Bull Dog," in The Armchair Detective, *Vol. 17, No. 4, Fall, 1984, pp. 368-69.*

FURTHER READING

Butler, William Vivian. "In Which Hugh Drummond Discusses Goldfish, and Carl Peterson is Icky-Boo." In his *The Durable Desperadoes,* pp. 58-65. London: Macmillan, 1973.
    Analyzes Bulldog Drummond's fascist tendencies and "brand of outlawry" in *The Black Gang* and *Bull-Dog Drummond.*

Connor, Edward. "The 12 Bulldog Drummonds." *Films in Review* 7, No. 8 (October 1956): 394-97.
    Discusses the portrayals of Bulldog Drummond on film by such actors as Ronald Colman and Ralph Richardson.

Review of *No Man's Land,* by Sapper. *The New York Times Book Review* (7 October 1917): 380-81.
    Praises McNeile's humorous and realistic portrayal of young soldiers during World War I in *No Man's Land.*

Penzler, Otto. "Bulldog Drummond." In his *The Private Lives of Private Eyes, Spies, Crimefighters, & Other Good Guys,* pp. 59-68. New York: Grosset & Dunlap, 1977.
    Examines the qualities that made Drummond one of the best-loved figures in detective fiction.

Review of *Men, Women, and Guns,* by Sapper. *The Spectator* 117, No. 4602 (9 September 1916): 292-93.
    Critiques the war stories in *Men, Women, and Guns* and concludes that "in the present volume [there is] an increasing tendency to enhance the tragedy or pitifulness of war by melodramatic or sentimental complications."

Additional coverage of Sapper's life and career is contained in the following source published by Gale Research: *Dictionary of Literary Biography,* Vol. 77.

Leo Tolstoy

Smert Ivana Ilyicha (The Death of Ivan Ilych)

(Also transliterated as Tolstoi and Tolstoj) Russian novelist, dramatist, short story writer, essayist, and critic.

The following entry presents criticism of Tolstoy's novella *Smert Ivana Ilyicha,* 1886 (*The Death of Ivan Ilych*). For discussion of Tolstoy's complete career, see *TCLC,* Volumes 4 and 11; for discussion of his novel *Anna Karenina,* see *TCLC,* Volume 17; for discussion of his novel *Voina i mir* (*War and Peace*), see *TCLC,* Volume 28.

INTRODUCTION

The Death of Ivan Ilych is considered one of Tolstoy's most important works of short fiction and a masterpiece of Russian literature. The short novel depicts the prolonged physical deterioration and ensuing spiritual rebirth of a man whose life was "most simple and most ordinary, and therefore most terrible." Significant as Tolstoy's first work of fiction to follow his moral and spiritual crisis of the 1870s, *The Death of Ivan Ilych* is cited by many critics as the work which marks the division of his literary career into two distinct phases. Frequently discussed as the fictional embodiment of Tolstoy's postconversion ideals, *The Death of Ivan Ilych* is also described as one of his most powerful and compelling tales.

Tolstoy's search for truth and meaning was intense and lifelong. As he approached middle age he became obsessed with attributing a purpose to existence in light of the inevitability of death. He sought answers through science, philosophy, and religion, eventually finding solace in the form of a radical Christianity whose doctrines included nonresistance to evil and complete abstinence from sex. He found inspiration in the simple, hard-working lifestyle of the Russian peasantry, admiring their ability to accept the often grim realities of life. Tolstoy's conversion led him to repudiate much of his previous work and profoundly influenced everything he wrote thereafter. Edward Wasiolek asserts that "no other author in the history of literature presents a change of such proportions as does Tolstoy during these years of spiritual crisis, with their isolating aftermath and the renewed creative energy." After nearly ten years of publishing only nonfiction works, including theological tracts and essays on art and moral conduct, Tolstoy published *The Death of Ivan Ilych* in 1886 to great popular acclaim.

Lionel Trilling has suggested that "perhaps no work of fiction is so painful to read as [*The Death of Ivan Ilych*]" due to its depiction of mental and physical anguish. Ivan Ilych is a self-centered and superficial man who conducts his life according to a strict social code, never deviating from what is proper or polite. In his professional life as a judge he adheres closely to the law, allowing no trace of compas-

sion to influence his decisions; in his personal life his contact with his wife and children is limited and shallow. His detachment from others and self-absorption serve him well when he is healthy, but when faced with death his loneliness overwhelms him. Ivan Ilych's fall from a ladder while hanging curtains is a pivotal event of the work, both because of its symbolic relation to the biblical fall from grace and because it results in the physical ailment which ultimately kills him. The pain in his side is at first just a minor annoyance, but eventually he realizes that his wound is fatal, and he is overcome with fear and despair in addition to physical pain: "And he had to live thus all alone on the brink of an abyss, while no one understood or pitied him." His physical deterioration is accompanied by a growing spiritual awareness: he begins to see the false values that had governed his adult life. His family and his doctors, however, continue to behave according to social decorum. His wife treats him with a detached courtesy, displaying an appropriate but insincere sympathy. His doctor treats him as an abstract case and adopts an air of joviality, refusing to admit the gravity of Ivan Ilych's illness. Their lack of compassion ironically recalls the manner in which Ivan Ilych dealt with the people who came before his bench in court. Only his young son, who has yet to adopt the artificiality of adult society, and his peasant servant Gerasim treat him with sincerity and understanding. Although Gerasim is a minor character whose physical presence is scarce and whose dialogue is minimal, his behavior has a significant impact on the work. Through him Tolstoy expresses his admiration of the Russian peasantry: Gerasim is the only adult in the story who acts selflessly and without pretense in his care of Ivan Ilych. Toward the end of his illness, Ivan Ilych evaluates his life and is overwhelmed by the fear that it was an existence without meaning or substance, despite his endless efforts to conduct himself in accord with social proprieties. Realizing the nearness of death, and riddled with doubt about the purpose of his life, Ivan Ilych experiences the sensation of being surrounded and trapped by a black sack. At this moment his son enters the room, and in a spontaneous gesture of love and pity, he kisses his father's hand. Ivan Ilych then feels released from the black sack, which is replaced by a light, and he dies without fear or anguish.

Critical commentary on *The Death of Ivan Ilych* often includes a discussion of Tolstoy's incisive depiction of society as an entity that is corrupt and in opposition to nature, but critics agree that the power of the tale lies primarily in the vivid and lengthy descriptions of Ivan Ilych's mental and physical agony. Several critics discuss *The Death of Ivan Ilych* as a parable due to its universal symbols and situations. Ivan Ilych's passage from life to death also entails a passage from falseness to truth, which is symbolically rendered in images of darkness and light. Some critics view the work as a tragedy, suggesting that Ivan Ilych's journey, though redemptive, is futile: he discovers his humanity too late and dies before aptly communicating his transformation to his surviving family members. Other commentators stress the religious themes of the work, particularly the concept of finding unity with God through selfless love for others, and assert that it ends on a somewhat hopeful tone.

Tolstoy, considered one of the world's greatest thinkers and scholars, has had a far-reaching influence among philosophers and authors. Critics specifically note the influence of *The Death of Ivan Ilych* on the short stories of Ernest Hemingway and on the works of existentialist philosopher Martin Heidegger. Many commentators also discuss the significance of the work in relation to the whole of Tolstoy's career. Wasiolek has described the years surrounding the composition of *The Death of Ivan Ilych* as "momentous for Tolstoy's moral and spiritual development. They are the difference between the 'first phase' and the 'second phase,' between the Tolstoy who captivated his readers with the power of his craft and his fictive vision, and the Tolstoy who captivated not only the Russians but the world with his theological and spiritual visions."

D. N. Ovsyaniko-Kulikovsky   (essay date 1905)

[*In the following excerpt, Ovsyaniko-Kulikovsky exam-*

ines what he considers the inflexible moral code underlying The Death of Ivan Ilych.]

Of what particularly is Ivan Ilich guilty before Tolstoy's moral code? His sins are as numerous as they are 'terrible'. Even in his youth,

> when he was a lawyer he was just as he was later, throughout his whole life: a capable man, cheerfully good-natured and sociable, but carrying out strictly what he considered his duty; *he considered his duty everything that people from the highest social strata considered to be his duty.* He was not ingratiating either as a boy or as a grown man, *but from his earliest years he was drawn to people from the highest social standing, like a fly is drawn to a light, he adopted their habits, their outlook on life and entered into friendly relations with them.*

Later when he was a civil servant charged with special duties in the provinces, this 'defect' took the form of fawning upon his superior and even his superior's wife. Furthermore his careerism did not cross the line of generally accepted respectability, like the misdemeanours of his youth, inasmuch as Ivan Ilich had a relationship with one of the ladies who thrust themselves on dandified lawyers; there was also a milliner; he had gone drinking with newly-arrived aides-de-camp and had 'gone to a street some way away after supper'. But 'none of this could be called by anything bad' for 'everything was done with clean hands, wearing clean shirts, speaking French and, most importantly, in the highest society and consequently with the approval of high-born people'.

Ivan Ilich is also guilty of not being a stoic but an epicurean; his ideal is an easy life, decent and pleasant. From this viewpoint he looked upon family life too. His marriage to Praskovya Fyodorovna seemed to him completely compatible with his 'programme'.

> To say that Ivan Ilich married because he loved his fiancée and found in her sympathy for his outlook on life, would be as unjust as to say that he married her because people in his social milieu approved the union. He married because of both these considerations: he made life pleasant for himself by taking such a wife and also did what high-society people considered correct. And so Ivan Ilich got married.

He is also guilty of treating everything in life, including both his work and even his family life, somewhat formally, one could say 'bureaucratically'. So, while serving as a civil servant charged with special duties and later as a coroner, he

> very quickly adopted the habit of keeping at a distance all circumstances which were not connected with his work and of clothing any highly complicated matter in such a way that it appeared on paper only in its external details, excluding completely his personal opinions, and, most importantly, observing all required formality.

It is exactly the same in his family life where Ivan Ilich finds it most convenient and pleasant to keep to the same system—to observe all the generally accepted 'formalities' of family life without participating in the intimate life of his family. In his family he is 'a civil servant'. Furthermore, he did not become like this at once, but after a year of marriage when spiritual discord developed between the couple and Praskovya Fyodorovna adopted the tactics of ceaselessly complaining, moaning and generally behaving badly. Then Ivan Ilich

> understood that married life, while offering a certain convenience to one's life, was a very complicated and serious affair, to which, in order to fulfil his duty, i.e. to lead a respectable life of which others would approve, it was necessary to work out a definite attitude, just as to his work. And this is just what he did. He demanded from family life only those comforts of dinner at home, of looking after the house, of bed, which she could give him and, most importantly, the proprieties of external forms which are set by social opinion.

Family life gave him annoyance and unpleasantness and contradicted his 'ideal of an easy, pleasant and respectable life'. And so he spiritually deserts his family and recognizes this desertion as something normal and even 'the object of his life'. 'His object consisted in freeing himself as much as possible from these unpleasantnesses and giving them the character of harmlessness and respectability.' He achieved this by spending as little time as possible in the family and also 'ensured it by having other people present'. It is unpleasant, cold and empty at home and he seeks some 'spiritual home' in his work, in his civic obligations. He becomes more and more ambitious. . . . But he shows himself as bankrupt in this as he does in family life—and again he is 'guilty'.

He is guilty in that he is incapable of introducing any, as it were, 'breath of life' into his civic obligations, that he has no calling for his work, but merely training, skill and official thoroughness; he only observes the rites of his work so as to receive his salary on the twentieth of the month and works only for promotion up the salary scale. In a word he is guilty of being a man of office routine and making a career. When he is unsuccessful in his work and looks for another post, he goes to St Petersburg

> for one thing: to obtain a post at 5,000-a-year. He was not choosy about any Ministry or any particular type of work. He only wanted a post, a post with 5,000, in the administration, banking, with the railways, in Empress Maria's household, even in the Customs—but certainly with 5,000, and certainly out of the Ministry where no one knew how to value him.

If we gather together all these factors of his guilt and then add them to all those little characteristics which Tolstoy so skilfully groups together in order to expose as clearly as possible the spiritual emptiness and vulgarity of Ivan Ilich, then we will have a conclusion as follows: Ivan Ilich is brought before the moral court because he is an average, ordinary man who has no 'divine spark'. The moral consequence, so artistically shown by Tolstoy, is that the defendant has no real love for his work, has no real feelings for his family; as a citizen, as a pillar of society he is a blank;

he has no convictions that he has worked out in his own head or from his own experience; as a moral individual he is nothing. From this spiritual poverty he is sentenced to death, and the heavy process of dying will be for him a kind of moral penalty and at the same time expiation. In dying he will gradually come to a realization of the emptiness, vulgarity and disorder of the life he has led, will see its nothingness and will feel all the horror of his spiritual loneliness. And he will die, transfigured and enlightened by the consciousness of the fact 'that his life had not been as it should' that his life had indeed been 'the most empty and commonplace' and also 'the most terrible'.

To discover and show this 'most terrible' in 'the most empty and commonplace life' was the object of the artistic experiment, carried out with such rare mastery. This is perhaps Tolstoy's most successful experiment.

But this 'most terrible' which Tolstoy found in the life of Ivan Ilich can possibly appear in various different lights, dependent upon the reader's particular point of view. One could profit from the results of Tolstoy's artistic experience without sharing the artist's dogma and without making such severe demands upon Ivan Ilich as Tolstoy makes. For him Ivan Ilich is a real moral freak who can 'be straightened out' only by death. For us this exclusive point of view is not obligatory. We meet people like Ivan Ilich on almost every corner but we do not at all consider them freaks. And actually Ivan Ilich is not a bad man, not an evil man; he is honourable, and incorruptible, etc. Although most of these characteristics are negative in that they show not so much the presence of good as the absence of bad, they none the less give us a picture of a very respectable person. Knowing that Ivan Ilich even before the Great Reforms when he served as a civil servant showed himself a man who could not be bought, that later in his position of coroner or procurator he did not misuse his power and even tried to soften its influence, etc., we have every right to include Ivan Ilich among so-called 'good people'. And the name of these good people is legion. And it seems to us that to investigate and judge these people from the standpoint of high religious and moral demands, as does Tolstoy, there are insufficient grounds. I dispute in the given circumstances the 'jurisdiction' and the 'choice of instances'. Tolstoy wants every such Ivan Ilich to be a fully developed moral and religious personality, rising above the given level of commonplace conceptions; he wants this average, morally insignificant man to be a participant in life, to react critically (and in this respect from a high moral standpoint) to established forms, morals and the accepted proprieties in order, in the end, to avoid being a petty egotist and not to look on life as a pleasant and orderly passing of the time, but see its meaning and value in serving some higher ideal. Tolstoy demands too much. . . . From the Ivan Iliches one can demand but one thing: that they do not descend below the average level, in a moral and civic sense, and do not prevent from living and acting those who rise above it. If they satisfy this modest, minimal requirement, we shall say to them: May health go with you! Labour and multiply! . . .

In describing the domestic disorder, the eternal arguments and disagreements between Ivan Ilich and his wife, in showing that 'arguments were always on the point of flaring up', Tolstoy gives us a type of abnormal family life, when there is no real love between the couple, only a sensual attraction in the satisfaction of which their mutual enmity flares up even more and takes on the explicit character of an organized loathing for each other. There were (in between the rows) a few periods of that mutual affection which comes over couples, but they did not last long. These were little islands at which they anchored for a time, but then again put out to their sea of suppressed hatred, expressed in their alienation one from the other. This serves as the starting-point for another artistic experiment in which the complicated question of the ethics of sexual relations in general and those of marriage in particular could be put point-blank. An adept at ascetic morals, Tolstoy will come to the dubious conclusion that sexual relations, no matter whether within or outside marriage, contradict man's ethical nature and that man, as a moral being, should abstain from them. The fact that the consequences of the carrying out of this principle would lead to the demise of the human race is of no concern to the moralist. For him the 'moral law' is superior to humanity and must triumph even at the price of the destruction of humanity—a point of view that humanity itself will never accept and which science and critical philosophy will refute and disprove. (pp. 420-24)

> *D. N. Ovsyaniko-Kulikovsky, in an extract in*
> Tolstoy: The Critical Heritage, *edited by A. V.*
> *Knowles, Routledge & Kegan Paul, Ltd.,*
> *1978, pp. 419-24.*

Temira Pachmuss (essay date 1961)

[*Pachmuss is an Estonian critic and educator. In the excerpt below, Pachmuss discusses* The Death of Ivan Ilych *as an expression of Tolstoy's despair at the thought of death.*]

In his *Ispoved'* (*Confession*), Tolstoy gives us a painful picture of a man who, in his search for a solution to the problems of human existence, experiences the same feelings as a man lost in a dense wood:

> He comes to an open plain, climbs up a tree, and sees around him endless space, but nowhere a house—he sees darkness, but again no house. Thus I lost my way in the wood of human knowledge, in the twilight of mathematical and experimental science, which opened before me a clear and distant horizon in the direction of which there could be no house, and in the darkness of philosophy, plunging me into a greater gloom with every step I took, until I was at last persuaded that there was, and could be, no way out. When I followed what seemed the bright light of learning, I saw that I had only turned aside from the real question. Notwithstanding the attraction of the distant horizon, unfolded so clearly before me, notwithstanding the charm of losing myself in the infinity of knowledge, I saw that the clearer it was, the less necessary it was to me, the less did it give an answer to my question.

Modern science has increased, rather than decreased, the need for speculation on being, truth, and knowledge: "Studying shadows instead of objects, men have quite forgotten the object whose shadow they are studying, and engrossing themselves more and more with the shadow, have reached complete darkness and rejoice that the shadow is so dense" [*On Life*]. Science, Tolstoy maintained, "perverts the conception of life by supposing itself to be studying life when it is studying merely the phenomena that accompany it. The longer it studies its phenomena, the farther does it diverge from the conception of life it wishes to study." Science does not give an answer to the question of our existence but only reasserts that we live in a world of outward appearances and illusions.

> If we turn to those branches of knowledge in which men have tried to find a solution to the problem of life—physiology, psychology, biology, sociology—we meet with a striking poverty of thought, with the greatest obscurity, with an utterly unjustifiable pretension to decide questions beyond their competence, and a constant contradiction of one thinker by another, and even by himself. If we turn to the branches of knowledge which are not concerned with the problem of life but find an answer to their own particular scientific questions, we are lost in admiration of man's mental powers; but we know beforehand that we shall get no answers to our questions about life itself, for these branches of knowledge directly ignore all questions concerning it. [*Ispoved'*]

Tolstoy's endeavors to solve the riddle of life and death originated not so much from his intellectual curiosity as from his deep spiritual fear of death. Tormented by the question "Is there any meaning in my life which can overcome the inevitable death awaiting me?" Tolstoy found himself on the brink of suicide. "There is nothing worse than death," he wrote in a letter from Nice to the poet Fet on October 17, 1860. "And when you fully realize that with it everything comes to an end, then there is nothing worse than life either." One night in 1869, while on a journey from Nizhnij Novgorod to Penza Province, Tolstoy had a harrowing experience which he recorded in his autobiographical *Zapiski sumasshedshego* (*Memoirs of a Madman*) some fifteen years later. On his trip he reached the town of Arzamas and spent the night in a small house where he actually saw and felt the approach of death; like some physical presence, it murdered his sleep and filled his mind with thoughts of dissolution and the end of all he held dear. In the depths of his thoughts there was always that terrible apparition of death, and in a few years it reappeared to demand an answer to his question: "Around me is death and destruction. Then why live? Why not die? . . . What is life for? To die?"

Countess S. A. Tolstoy, who knew of Tolstoy's ever-growing fear of death, recorded in her diaries that "his fear of death was enormous." We find a similar reference in the reminiscences of Mme Tatyana A. Kuzminskaya, Countess Tolstoy's sister, who wrote in May, 1866: "Tolstoy spoke often of death. I remember his saying once: 'Really, how peaceful is our life! Yet if one thinks deeply and pictures death vividly, then one cannot live!' " Many writers and scholars also commented on Tolstoy's anxiety.

Maxim Gorky, for example, wrote: "All his life Tolstoy feared and hated death, and all his life there throbbed in his soul the 'Arzamasian terror'—must he die?" Gorky aptly likened Tolstoy's fear of death to the feelings of "a young recruit who is beside himself with fear and anxiety at an unknown barracks." Analyzing Tolstoy's fear of death [in *Three Essays*] Thomas Mann wrote:

> Tolstoy's strongest, most tormenting, deepest, and most productive interest has to do with death. It is the thought of death which dominates his thoughts and writing, to such an extent that one may say no other great master of literature has felt and depicted death as he has—felt it with such frightful penetration, depicted it so insatiably often. . . . Death is a very sensual, very physical business; and it would be hard to say whether Tolstoy was so interested in death because he was so . . . interested in the body, and in nature as the life of the body, or whether it was the other way about.

Dmitrij Merezhkovskij claimed that Tolstoy tainted the soul of an entire generation with his fear of death:

> If in our time people are afraid of death, have such a convulsive fear of it, as no one had ever experienced before, if all of us in the depth of our hearts, in our flesh and blood feel this 'cold tremor,' a chill piercing to the marrow of our bones, it is Tolstoy whom we must chiefly thank for this fear. Tolstoy had no doubt, no hesitation, and no uncertainty about death, that it is a 'transition into nothingness,' a transition devoid of every mystery. His terror was inconsolable, fruitless, senselessly destructive and calculated to dry up the very springs of life. [*L. Tolstoj i Dostoevski*]

Many Tolstoy scholars believe that Tolstoy's fear of death was not so much spiritual as physical. They maintain that Tolstoy loved life so much that he feared to think of its end. The present writer does not attempt to challenge this view, especially since Tolstoy himself in his diaries, letters, and essays explained his fear of death in precisely that fashion, as we see, for example, in his essay *On Life:* "Indeed the fear of death is due only to the fear of losing the good of life at bodily death." However, even a thinking man is not always aware of the real causes of his fears. In *The Death of Ivan Ilyich,* the work that reveals Tolstoy's own state of despair at the thought of death, the hero's fear of death is caused by a feeling quite different from his love for life. Besides, Tolstoy himself in some of his works ascribed man's fear of death to his guilty conscience, as we can see again in his essay *On Life:* ". . . the fear of death is not in reality a fear of death but of false life. . . . Men are horrified at the thought of death not because they fear their life may end with it, but because physical death clearly shows them the necessity of the true life which they do not possess. And this is why men who do not understand life so dislike to think of death. For them to think of death is the same as to admit that they do not live as their reasonable consciousness demands that they should."

A critic as sensitive as Merezhkovskij, while recognizing the physical nature of Tolstoy's dread of death, maintained that this feeling did not originate in the novelist's "bodily fear," but had a metaphysical character: "This fear is of a more inward and profound kind, and its origin is abstract and metaphysical rather than animal." One of the most recent critics of Tolstoy, George Steiner, says:

> Like Goya and Rilke, Tolstoy was haunted by the mystery of death. This hauntedness deepened with the years . . . his whole being rebelled against the paradox of mortality. His terrors were not primarily those of the flesh . . . he suffered from a despair of reason at the thought that men's lives were doomed through illness or violence or the ravenings of time to irremediable extinction, to that inch-by-inch disappearance into the 'dark sack' which Ivan Ilyich records in his last agonized moments.

Tolstoy himself seemed to feel that man's fear of death was a result of sham civilization, which with its poisons affects the human mind and heart. Civilization, with its awakening of the individual and his self-assertion against the group, with its strife, division, and falsity, corrupts man's world outlook and nature. It spells moral ruin, universal egoism, spiritual disintegration, and the tormenting feeling of solitude. In the works of Tolstoy the theme of loneliness and isolation frequently forms the central point of his ethical speculations. Treating the various aspects of this problem, he shows isolation to be the logical consequence of man's selfishness and of the falsity of his life. Civilization teaches man to concentrate on his own personality, his own interests, and particularly on social decorum. He remains on the surface of life; incapable of profound experiences in his inner life, man lives in the illusion that if his existence is in accordance with social decorum, he lives an ideal life. In reality, however, Tolstoy warns, man's real life slips by. Such "civilized" people in most cases wake up only when they confront death and suddenly realize that their superficial life, devoid of any deep and genuine feelings, keeps them in inner isolation from their fellow men.

No careful reader of Tolstoy can miss the novelist's deeply felt conviction that the life of "civilized" man stands in flagrant opposition to human life as created by God and nature. The death of a "civilized" and conscious man is painful and ugly because he lives a false life, filled with the lies, artificiality, and corruption of modern cities. The descriptions of death scenes in Tolstoy's works strongly suggest that the novelist considered man's perverted world outlook his most serious disease and the greatest evil in his life. The writer made his beautiful adulteress, Anna Karenina, perish at the moment she became convinced that her life had been based on false assumptions, and that because of these she had been dragged into a blind alley from which she could find no way out. Polikushka, in the short story of the same title, was led into a false life because he was misunderstood by his fellow creatures, and was finally driven to suicide. In *Tri smerti* (*Three Deaths*), the spoiled upper-class lady—because of her "civilized Christianity," which according to Tolstoy engenders selfishness and self-centeredness—died a most painful death compared with the death of an old peasant and a felled birch tree. The main moral of these stories is the fallacy of modern civilization and the inferiority of the cultured and sophisticated man, with his sham values, to the illiterate peasant, with his innate wisdom and goodness. The primitive Russian man humbly accepts his death without undergoing the pangs of an inner struggle. Admiring, like Tolstoy, this feature of the Russian peasant, Turgenev exclaimed: "How wonderfully the Russian peasant dies! His condition before death can be called neither indifference nor insensitivity; he dies as if performing a ritual: coolly and simply." Like Tolstoy, Turgenev insisted that those just and righteous people who had lived close to nature and in complete harmony with it would die a beautiful and peaceful death.

In Tolstoy's *Krug chtenija* (*The Circle of Reading*) we find much evidence that the novelist's thoughts about death were strongly influenced by the philosophy of stoicism, especially by the views of Seneca and Marcus Aurelius, who maintained that the death of a man whose soul is infested with fears and lusts is accompanied by much suffering and pain, whereas the death of a righteous person is peaceful and quiet, despite the presence of tormenting physical pain. In *The Circle of Reading,* Tolstoy said: "The better a man's life the less dreadful death is to him and the easier it is for him to die." "One should live in such a way as not to fear death."

Tolstoy described a most terrifying agony in *The Death of Ivan Ilyich.* Ivan Ilyich also lived a false life, filled with lies and artificially multiplied needs. All his colleagues liked him, and yet, on receiving the news of his death, their first thoughts were of the changes and promotions it might occasion among themselves or their acquaintances. They gave no thought to the deceased himself, who had but recently lived among them. Even in the beginning of the work we may conjecture from Ivan Ilyich's feeling of loneliness that the sense of isolation while dying horrified Tolstoy as much as the thought of death itself. This isolation, the novelist warns, influences man's relationship with nature, which includes not only his life but his death. Affected by "civilization," Ivan Ilyich had escaped real life and failed to see his inner loneliness. He was completely absorbed in self, and this absorption, in turn, intensified the feeling of solitude he experienced at the approach of death. The very basis of Ivan Ilyich's relationship with nature was corrupt; however, although able to escape real life, he could not escape death.

We find the consciousness of this loneliness at the moment of dying not only in the works of Tolstoy but also in many other writings, such as the English morality play *Everyman* and Hugo von Hofmannsthal's adaptation *Jedermann.* When Everyman felt the approach of death, he sought desperately to find a companion for his last journey, and when he failed to do so, he was overwhelmed by despair at his terrible loneliness. A man like Ivan Ilyich, who during his life had no real contact with his closest relatives and was so alienated from nature that he could place no trust in it, had to experience his separateness in full measure. This same loneliness made him while dying want to weep: " . . . he wished most of all for someone to pity him as a sick child is pitied. He longed to be petted and comforted." As soon as he knew that death was approaching him, he felt "a loneliness, in the midst of a populous town and surrounded by numerous acquaintances and relations, yet which could not have been more complete anywhere—either at the bottom of the sea or under the earth." He wanted to be loved and to be pitied; he wanted others to feel and share his distress and sorrow: "And he had to live thus all alone on the brink of an abyss, while no one understood or pitied him." He remained alone with death: "And nothing could be done with it except to look at it and shudder." "He wept on account of this terrible loneliness . . . and the absence of God." Slowly Ivan Ilyich came to understand that loneliness had always been around him, but he had been blind to it because of his false ideas of life. He had always lived for himself alone, near his fellow creatures, yet never in real community with them. Tolstoy called these wrong ideas of life "falsity," describing "the approach of that ever-dreaded and hateful death which was the only reality, and always the same falsity." This "falsity," in Tolstoy's opinion, sprang from man's overrating himself. Ivan Ilyich's approach to life had always been completely egocentric; he considered his existence the center of the universe, never being able to understand that he, as a human being, was just a small particle in nature. His individualistic outlook was the trap in which he remained all his life. "Caius is a man, men are mortal, therefore Caius is mortal," argued Ivan Ilyich. "That Caius—man in general—was mortal was completely correct, but he wasn't Caius, not man in general, but a creature quite, quite different from all others."

This attitude was the reason why only "I" had meaning for Ivan Ilyich, never "you." As a result, his whole life was filled with unceasing care for himself and his own comfort, and this attitude even characterized his family life. He cared for his own feelings, never for those of his wife. Even the death of his children meant nothing more to him than an inconvenience. He always did what was considered decorous in his circle, yet always managed to connect what was considered necessary for "decorum" with what was pleasant for himself. Living this kind of life, Ivan Ilyich naturally lacked all sense of humility. He liked the feeling of possessing the power of crushing at his will people dependent on him, and yet, at the same time, it pleased him to think of himself as a generous and kind man. He deceived one feeling with another: he wanted as a *comme il faut* and decorous man to display his love and kindness toward human beings, but at the same time he was not prepared to renounce the heady feeling of possessing authority. Thus his kindness, all the enjoyments of his business and private life, his love for his wife and children, all these were falsity—the feeling that originated in his false attitude toward himself. All the people around him also lived the same kind of life and were involved in this same pretense. Like Ivan Ilyich, they accepted falsity as reality: " . . . I and all my friends felt that our case was quite different from that of Caius." In Tolstoy's words, "Ivan Ilyich's life had been most simple and most ordinary, and therefore most terrible." Tolstoy's words may seem paradoxical, but it was Ivan Ilyich and his associates who considered their lives to be simple and ordinary, and the very fact that their twisted and distorted lives should seem ordinary to themselves was in itself terrible.

Ivan Ilyich's physical sufferings were insignificant compared with his spiritual pain, which enabled him gradually to understand the complete falsity of his simple, ordinary, and therefore terrible life. While he lay dying he saw truth slowly supplanting falsity, yet all living people still kept on lying. Even in the presence of death they still lived in accordance with decorum, the master he had served all his life. His wife simulated sympathy and care for him because these belonged to that decorum; but now Ivan Ilyich was sick of falsity, and "while his wife was kissing him he hated her from the bottom of his soul and with difficulty refrained from pushing her away." "Those lies—lies enacted over him on the eve of his death and destined to degrade this awful, solemn act to the level of their visits, their curtains, their sturgeon for dinner—were a terrible agony for Ivan Ilyich," because now he understood that all their interests and enjoyments, which he had shared while healthy, were nothing but illusions created by his selfishness. With this discovery, life appeared unreal, in contrast to which stood death, the only reality, about which there could be no mistake: " . . . the approach of that ever-dreaded and hateful death which was the only reality, and always the same falsity."

Ivan Ilyich gained comfort only through his contact with Gerasim. Gerasim, a fresh peasant lad, knew nothing of the pretenses of the "civilized" life Ivan Ilyich had lived before his malady; on the contrary, his life had been more real because he sensed his minute part in the universe, that he was a human being just as any other human being. Because of his real humility he alone was able to grasp Ivan Ilyich's position: "We shall all of us die," said he, "so why should I grudge a little trouble?" Death was to him not only inevitable but also natural; he did not fear his dying master, and so Ivan Ilyich felt at ease only with him. Gerasim's assistance to him was not an act of hypocrisy; it was not burdensome work at all, but a service to life. Tolstoy thought the instinctive understanding of life and death that enabled Gerasim to do right naturally, to tell the truth, and to feel a deep sympathy for his fellow creatures was a result of Gerasim's identification with nature. His closeness to nature enabled him to live a life which, being foreordained by God, stood in striking opposition to Ivan Ilyich's life corrupted by culture and civilization. Culture and civilization were the poisons that filled Ivan Ilyich's soul and body all his life and became evident only through his malady and the torments caused by the prospect of death. "Ivan Ilyich was left alone with the consciousness that his life was poisoned and was poisoning the lives of others, and that this poison did not weaken but penetrated more and more deeply into his whole being."

For Tolstoy, death had a great metaphysical significance. Like Rainer Maria Rilke, the Russian novelist shows that death brings forth the conscious and subconscious aspects of human intellect. Death shows man the essence of his soul and teaches him to understand it; death compels man to review his life and to grasp its meaning. Death and the suffering preceding death are a means for knowing our own being, and through this we gain a consciousness of real existence. Tolstoy, however, goes further, since he interprets the knowledge of earthly existence as only the first stage of the death-experience, or what Jacqueline de Proyart de Bailescourt has called "an awakening of the con-

science." The second stage is a process of purification, through which man shakes off falsity together with his earthly existence. This is the stage reflected on the stern faces of the dying Prince Andrey Bolkonsky and Levin's brother, their faces reflecting their withdrawal from everything earthly. Ivan Ilyich underwent this process of purification when he had a feeling of being thrust into a dark sack by an invisible, irresistible force. Death itself compelled him to discard his conviction that he "lived a good life." At that moment when he "suddenly became aware of the real direction," the process of purification was accomplished. We might liken Ivan Ilyich's death to an antibody which is intended to kill the germs of a disease and to remove them from the diseased body, the disease representing Ivan Ilyich's corruption. The basis of his corruption is his inability to understand that since Caius is a man and therefore mortal, Ivan Ilyich is also mortal. Just as Caius is man in general, Ivan Ilyich is bound to be the same. As man in general, Caius is a part of the universe; as a man, Ivan Ilyich is bound to be the same. However, all his life he had lived as if he were not a part of anything, and his only purpose had been to protect his own well-being.

According to Tolstoy this process of purification through death does not apply to the Russian peasants because there is nothing to purify in the pure. Death, which is like a kernel that man carries with him all his life, purifies the consciousness only of the selfish, "civilized" people. Only these people have individuality, and the question of Christian love exists thus only for them because only they live individually. The Russian peasants, on the other hand, who are a mass and live closely together, are immersed in life as opposed to the "civilized" individual. The Russian peasants have no such concepts as "Christian love" or "Christian humility," but they have these qualities in the depths of their hearts. Gerasim understood instinctively that he was nothing but a Caius, and therefore also understood that the true meaning of a man's life is to render service to the whole world, of which he is but a minute part.

We can assume then that this part of Tolstoy's metaphysical concept agrees with the philosophy of Plato, Shakespeare, Dostoyevsky, and many others: that ultimate truth, as far as human beings can grasp it, is the harmonious relations of all beings and things—the ultimate all-embracing reality of the universe. On earth we call this relation love. This concept of love can be condensed to the idea that a living person appears real only in his relation to another living being. In accordance with this, Ivan Ilyich's fear of death, as far as it concerns the feeling of loneliness of a dying human being, is quite intelligible. We experience the reality of our existence only in our relation with others. Goethe, in his theory that polarities are the basis of all natural phenomena and of all relations between men, developed practically the same idea. In order to become fully conscious of his own reality, man seeks all his life, if only subconsciously, to establish a relationship with his fellow creatures that is quite free of egotism and selfishness. Since human love never reaches this purity, man must, as soon as he recognizes that he is a part of the harmonious unity of the whole, experience feelings of guilt toward the whole world. Tolstoy held that man attains this knowledge of his real self only at the moment of dying and that the feeling of emancipated love comes only after the realization of his inherent selfishness. "Forgive me," were the last words Ivan Ilyich wanted to say to his wife a few minutes before his death. The more selfish a man has been in life, the more conscience-stricken will he be at the moment of dying, or as Jacqueline de Proyart de Bailescourt put it: ". . . plus la vie conscience s'est égarée le rêve, plus est pénible le retour à la réalité." If we examine Ivan Ilyich's fear of death from this viewpoint, we see that nothing but his guilty conscience caused his agony as death approached. He died conscious of his guilt toward everybody and everything, ready to do penance for his "simple and most ordinary, and therefore most terrible" life.

It was love that Ivan Ilyich experienced after the realization of his guilt and the purification of his soul, and it was this love that enabled Ivan Ilyich to face death without fear. His pity for his family was part of his new relation to people—free of egotism and selfishness. "Love is the sole medicine against death," Unamuno maintained [in his *Tragic Sense of Life*], insisting, like Tolstoy or Thomas Mann, on the interrelation between love and death. Elsewhere in Tolstoy's works we find this feeling of love experienced by dying people. However, the sequence of the stages of death is somewhat vague, or perhaps is represented as just one step, including all three in one. At the time of writing *Three Deaths,* Tolstoy, it seems, lacked the spiritual maturity which permeates *The Death of Ivan Ilyich,* written some thirty years later.

Love is ultimate reality—this is Tolstoy's conclusion. As opposed to the primitive man, the "civilized" individual becomes a part of the harmonious whole only through death, or, during life, through love. Without love, Ivan Ilyich's life was empty and meaningless. With the discovery of love, Ivan Ilyich felt that his death was reduced to insignificance. He was allowed to become a part of the unity of the whole, an experience he described with the words: "Death is all over. It is no more."

It is, however, striking to note that despite Ivan Ilyich's perception of the mystery of death and his ultimate calm acceptance of it, the whole story reflects an icy coldness. Even kind and understanding Gerasim acts out of a sense of moral duty rather than from real love. Furthermore, Tolstoy is concerned here only with Ivan Ilyich; no one else matters. Ivan Ilyich's painful experience is over; his dead face does not express any pity for those who survive him, but a reproach and a warning. It seems that he has slipped back into his former remoteness from the world of mortals, of the Caiuses, those frightened and confused people who came to bid farewell to his coffin. There is no need for us, however, to dwell on Ivan Ilyich's facial expression in death as perceived by his relatives and colleagues, for the constructive principle of *The Death of Ivan Ilyich* requires concentration on the dying man rather than on those who surround him. The high point of the story is undoubtedly Ivan Ilyich's discovery of the ultimate reality which is love.

It is during the first stage of his death-experience that Tolstoy's "civilized" hero is compelled to review his whole life and grasp its meaning. Then follows a second stage—the process of purification. The hero withdraws from everything earthly and abandons the falsities of his life. In Tolstoy's interpretation, however, it is the third stage which is of utmost importance, since it is then that the hero becomes aware of his guilt toward the whole world and attains the knowledge of his own reality, that is, his meaning within the whole scheme of creation. This conclusion is in its essence deeply tragic, for man, according to Tolstoy, is given this precious knowledge only during the process of dying. Thus he cannot make use of this knowledge in the conduct of his life, cannot benefit from his new understanding of his place within the harmonious whole.

These two aspects of Tolstoy's search for truth—ethical and, in the writer's own terminology, "metaphysical"—underlie not only his religious and philosophical treatises but also many of his didactic and artistic works. It is mainly through his fiction that the reader is held tenaciously by the seriousness of the writer's efforts to reveal the fundamental principle of all-forgiving and all-embracing love. Although it is left to the reader's subjective comprehension to extract these ideas from Tolstoy's works, to make his own discoveries in the vast field of the novelist's speculations, there is no doubt that his message to mankind reveals in a gripping artistic form the core of the Christian teaching with all its implications—that a man must love his neighbor. (pp. 72-83)

> *Temira Pachmuss, "The Theme of Love and Death in Tolstoy's 'The Death of Ivan Ilyich',"* in The American Slavic and East European Review, *Vol. 20, No. 1, February, 1961, pp. 72-83.*

Irving Halperin   (essay date 1961)

[*Halperin is an American educator and critic. In the following excerpt, he examines the relationship between structure and theme in* The Death of Ivan Ilych.]

The power and profundity of *The Death of Ivan Il'ič* are so overwhelming that at first perusal the reader may not be sufficiently aware of its rare structural integrity. The component parts are closely knit, logically progressive; and the work as a whole has a design of luminous symmetry. This is not to suggest that Tolstoj consciously manipulated instruments of technique to achieve this design; here the familiar technical machinery and scaffolding of modern fiction are absent. For example, the author "tells" and does not "show" certain incidents; the point of view shifts between the author and main character; and the novel is without a "well-made" plot. However, the basis of unity in Tolstoj's masterpiece is in the increasingly intense and narrowing focus of its twelve narrative parts. And it is the purpose of this paper to examine the functional relationship between the novel's structural organization and the stages of Ivan Il'ič's metamorphosis.

The central function of Part I is to illustrate the falseness of the immediate society in which Ivan Il'ič had lived. This falsity is underscored by the reactions of colleagues, Petr Ivanovič and Švarc and of the widow to his passing. For

Petr Ivanovič nothing is more frightening than death: the smells of incense and carbolic acid intimidate him; the corpse's face seems a reproach to the living. To offset his horror, he attempts to view death as a kind of anomaly, something that had happened to Ivan Il'ič and not to *him*. He complies with the demands of propriety by feigning grief before the widow but is all the while impatient to join some friends at bridge. Duplicity is no less evident in Švarc, whom Tolstoj describes as one with a grave mouth but playful eyes; and his Piccadilly whiskers, top hat, and elegant evening dress give to this character a classically Mephistophelian presence. Similarly, the widow is hardly grief-stricken over her husband's death; indeed, she seems more concerned about the possible damage to a table by Ivan Ivanovič's cigarette ash and to a pouffe by his weight. The large failing of these colleagues and of the widow, then, is their essential lack of humanity; for them life is an agreeable rubber of bridge.

Here the question may occur—why does the novel open with minor characters on-stage? To begin with, this structural arrangement is in accord with the protagonist's ultimate discovery that the apparent end of human consciousness, death, is in reality the beginning of life. But, more important, if we first witness the actions of some people whose interests and values are very much like those that the dead man subscribed to, the typical values of average men in a quantitatively oriented society, we may more fully grasp the nature of Ivan Il'ič's failure as a man. And this is the salient function of Part II—to adumbrate his history of self-deception.

Throughout Part II Ivan Il'ič's life is described as filled with duplicity. He married because marriage was considered the "right thing" in his social set. Between husband and wife there had been little human connection; their essential attitude toward each other remained one of deep hostility. For the sake of mutual convenience, they sought to project the appearance of a happy marriage.

From an unhappy marriage, Ivan Il'ič retreated into his work; but there, as magistrate, he existed in an equally reprehensible state of falsity. Yet he is not to be criticized, Tolstoj seems to imply, simply for being attached to the baubles and trinkets of professional prestige and gain, but rather because he set himself up over others. Specifically, he did not turn a human face, as it were, toward those who were tried in his court; his most common attitude toward them was one of prideful condescension. Altogether, he prided himself on maintaining a public image of professional incisiveness and coolness.

Ivan Il'ič's mask resembles the one worn by his colleagues, Petr Ivanovič and Švarc. All three are self-centered and indifferent to humanity; they wish to lead lives of light-hearted agreeableness and decorum. And viewed within the frame of our larger consideration, the novel's structure, the likeness of the three men constitutes an important functional relationship between Parts I and II.

If it may be held that Part II sketches the lineaments of Ivan Il'ič's pride, the key purpose of Part III is to trace his Fall. Just as he chooses to *appear* before others as the prominent public official and the pleasant, well-bred social figure, he needs his house to lend proof to his professional attainments and aesthetic taste. In this perspective, his explosive reactions to the slightest disarrangement in the house's meticulously selected furnishings may be understood. For what is this compulsive orderliness if not the expression of a need to be on guard against the warm, spontaneous feelings of human affection? So it seems ironically fitting that during this cycle of preoccupation with material details (he *had* to show the upholsterer how the curtains were to be draped), Ivan Il'ič should suffer the accident which eventually resulted in his death. Accordingly, his fall was more than from a ladder, but, symbolically, from a pinnacle of pride and vanity. And from this point in Part III to the ending, the novel's narrative focus narrows in proportion to the contracting scope of Ivan Il'ič's delusion.

Enter the doctors of Part IV who pursue their profession in much the same way that he does his—from behind well-mannered masks. They appear to be self-assured but will not commit themselves on whether his condition is serious; instead they speculate that the cause of his pain may be a floating kidney or a defective appendix, perfunctorily referring to these organs as though they were separate from his total, sentient nature. The doctors' reluctance to commit themselves on his condition reduces him to a state of helplessness comparable to what, doubtless, was felt by some who had been tried in his court: "he had to live thus all alone on the brink of an abyss, with no one who understood or pitied him."

But if Ivan Il'ič is agitated and fearful, at least he is no longer playing at life. Suffering has humanized him; in consequence, he is able to look outside of himself. In contrast to the man of Part III who was obsessed with house furnishings, his chief interest now is in the health and ailments of others.

Until this stage in his illness, Ivan Il'ič has continued to hope that he would recover. Therefore, it is the function of Parts V-VI to shock him into emotionally recognizing that death is not simply a commonplace fact, something that happens to everyone—rather *it* is coming to him. Previously, he had manipulated the machinery of marriage and his official duties, but he will be unable to control death; this irrational force is coming to upset his temporal plans. He is especially fearful because dying appears to him to be a revelation of the nothingness of the self, a "dead emptiness." This awareness drives him into further despair, and yet is a requisite condition for his final illumination: for to the extent that despair scourges him of pride, he is vulnerable to self-scrutiny. Here one is reminded of Kierkegaard's statement in *Sickness Unto Death:* "One who without affectation says that he is in despair is after all a bit nearer, a dialectical step nearer to being cured than those who are not regarded and do not regard themselves in despair."

At this nadir (Part VII) in Ivan Il'ič's suffering, partial grace comes to him through the help of his servant Gerasim. The latter plays a very important part in the story, even though we see little of him and hear less of his direct voice than any other character. Nevertheless, the sparsity of his appearance invests him with a symbolic aura which in itself is a key to understanding his role in the redemption of Ivan Il'ič.

It is immediately significant that Gerasim comes from the country, from the fecund earth, as contrasted to the sterile urban backgrounds of Ivan Il'ič and his colleagues. Gerasim's clothes are clean, neat, and functional: his boots smell of tar and winter air. Thus he is literally and figuratively "a breath of fresh air" in the sick-room. Moreover, honest and self-sacrificing, Gerasim actuates the familiar Tolstoyan principle that the primary purpose of existence is to live for others and not merely, as did Ivan Il'ič, to gratify one's own will and desires. He does his work willingly and without lying to his master about the latter's hopeless condition. Hence Ivan Il'ič can abandon himself to Gerasim's care, and this is no small act for a man who hitherto had been given to placing himself over others, especially those of lower social stations. Implicit, too, in this relationship between master and servant is the suggestion of a generic interdependence between human beings which transcends considerations of worldly station and rank. Again, because of Gerasim's devotion, Ivan Il'ič becomes capable of extending compassion to his wife and son. In this overall perspective, then, Gerasim may be viewed as the true hero of the story.

In Parts VIII and IX, Ivan Il'ič is brought a step closer to his most important discovery. What impels him in this direction is the continuing duplicity of the doctors and the obtuseness (e.g., their desertion of him for Sarah Bernhardt's performance) of his family, who look on him with the humiliating pity of the living for the dying. Searching for an explanation to account for his suffering, he reflects on the past, concluding that his life had been going downhill for many years; his marriage, work, and social ties have not satisfied him. Altogether, his existence seems to him in this moment of "ontological shock" to have had no meaning. Only death looms as the *real*. He can not understand why such a meaningless, wretched ending ought to be for one who has conducted his life so properly. "Why, why dost Thou torment me so terribly?" he complains. "What for?" Yet though Ivan Il'ič has begun to pose questions about the past, he nevertheless avoids asking *the* crucial one.

The central effect of his physical and mental anguish in Parts X and XI is to edge him into asking the significant (for the older Tolstoj it was the "obsessive") question— "What if my whole life has really been wrong?" Then Ivan Il'ič finally perceives that amid the mechanics of familial, official, and social functions, he had been estranged from his essential nature, had shrunk from life itself. And though he had been driven by pride and vanity, these motives had not only been condoned but actually praised by his society. Following this admission, he is assailed by extreme torment and self-hatred, because he does not know how, in these last few hours of consciousness, to rectify the falseness of the past.

In Part XII, two hours before his death, he suddenly apprehends the "right thing" to be done. Death is inevitable but a man can choose to die loving instead of hating. The Christian principle of brotherly love, he now feels, as did Pierre in *War and Peace* and Nexljudov in *Resurrection,*

is the supreme human value. Here he seems to be in communion with the words Tolstoj himself dictated to his daughter, Aleksandra, a few days before his death—"The more a man loves the more real he becomes."

Acting out of conscious choice, Ivan Il'ič gestures to his wife and son to forgive him. Significantly, this gesture occurs at the moment he feels himself being thrust into a black hole. The point is that grace comes to him only when he is in a state of utter despair. Previously, in Part VII, we have noted this identical pattern of despair followed by grace (Gerasim's help). Now, too, grace comes from the outside in the form of his son's love. Moreover, it is revealing that directly following his son's kiss, Ivan Il'ič claims to see a light. For now the route of his metamorphosis becomes clearly visible—from despair (the black hole) to love (the son's kiss) to redemption (the light). Thus Ivan Il'ič's dialectical direction, so to speak, is from nothingness to meaning: he has learned that the one thing necessary for a man is to *be*.

With Ivan Il'ič's surrender of the last vestiges of a poisonous egoism, the novel makes its final leap. Standing face to face with death, Tolstoj's protagonist has confronted and defined his mortality, sounded the limits of fear. Now he is in accord with Spinoza's advice: "It is not good to fear death, nor yet to long for death. The scales must be so balanced that the pointer is vertical." In any event, Ivan Il'ič no longer views death as an end in itself ("Death is finished . . . It is no more."), but rather as a process which Tolstoj described to his wife in a letter of May 1898 as "the crossing-over from one consciousness to another, from one image of the world to another."

The tranquil tone of the final pages give measure to the spiritual distance separating the redemption of Ivan Il'ič in Part XII from the restive unawareness of his survivors in Part I. And looking back over the novel's pattern, one can see that the narrative focus, steadily narrowing since Part III, reaches its finest concentration at the ending. There, in the moment of Ivan Il'ič's self-realization, the coherent structure of Tolstoj's masterpiece is completed. (pp. 334-39)

Irving Halperin, "The Structural Integrity of 'The Death of Ivan Ilič'," in Slavic and East-European Journal, *n.s. Vol. V. No. 1, Spring, 1961, pp. 334-40.*

Lionel Trilling   (essay date 1967)

[*Trilling was one of the most significant and influential American literary and social critics of the twentieth century, and he is considered one of the most important critics to apply Freudian psychological theories to literature. In the essay below, he describes Tolstoy's religious conversion and examines the effect of this conversion on* The Death of Ivan Ilych.]

We all fear death and our imaginations balk at conceiving its actuality. We say readily enough that "all men are mortal," but like Ivan Ilych in Tolstoi's story, we say it as an abstract general proposition and each one of us finds it hard to believe that the generalization has anything to do with him in particular—with him personally, as we say. And literature tends to encourage us in our evasion. Not that literature avoids dealing with death—on the contrary, there is probably no subject to which it recurs more often. But even very great writers are likely to treat it in ways which limit its fearsomeness. The death of the hero of a tragedy, for instance, seldom seems terrible to us; we often think of it as making a moment of peace and beauty, as constituting the resolution of distressing conflicts. Literature inclines to soften death's aspect by showing it as through a veil, or by suggesting that it is sad and noble rather than terrifying, or by asking us to "accept" it as part of life.

This tendency is wholly reversed by *The Death of Ivan Ilych.* Tolstoi does not try to reconcile us to the idea of our extinction and he does not mask the dreadfulness of dying. Quite the contrary—not only does he choose an instance of death that is long drawn out and hideously painful, and dwell upon its details, but he emphasizes the unmitigated aloneness of the dying man, the humiliation of his helplessness, and his abject terror at the prospect of his annihilation, as well as his bitter envy of those who still continue in existence while he is in process of becoming nothing.

Tolstoi is explicit about these aspects of death as no writer before him had ever been, and the effect is excruciating. Perhaps no work of fiction is so painful to read as this story.

Why is this vicarious torture forced upon us? We can scarcely feel that the author's purpose was purely literary, that Tolstoi chose his subject as any writer chooses a subject, because it is interesting in and for itself. We cannot doubt that his intention was other than artistic, and we conjecture that it might well be religious, for religion often tries to put us in mind of the actuality of death, not in its terrors, to be sure, but in its inevitability, seeking thus to press upon us the understanding that the life of this world is not the sum of existence, and not even its most valuable part. And the circumstances of Tolstoi's life at the time he wrote *The Death of Ivan Ilych* confirm our sense of the story's religious inspiration.

Some eight years before writing *Ivan Ilych,* Tolstoi experienced a great spiritual crisis which issued in religious conversion and altered the whole course of his life. He abandoned the ways of the aristocratic class into which he had been born and undertook to live as a primitive Christian, committing himself to an extreme simplicity of life and to the service of mankind, especially the poor and the humble. He repudiated art and his own great achievements as a novelist and proposed the doctrine that artistic creation was justified only when it led men to morality and piety.

The particular nature of his crisis is most relevant to *The Death of Ivan Ilych.* At the age of fifty, Tolstoi was thrown into a state of despair by his insupportably intense imagination of mortality. It was not a new problem that he confronted—even in his youth he had known periods of black depression because he felt that the inevitability of death robbed life of all meaning. In *Anna Karenina,* the great novel he had completed shortly before the onset of

his crisis, Prince Levin, who closely resembles Tolstoi, cannot endure the thought that "for every man, and himself too, there was nothing but suffering, death, and oblivion." Death, he feels, makes life "the evil jest of some devil," and he must either learn to see human existence in some other way or commit suicide. Levin is able to pass beyond this terrible alternative; he overcomes his despair and accepts life for what good he may find in it. For a time it lay within Tolstoi's power to make a similar decision, but the period of calm was not of long duration; the horror of death again became unbearable and could be coped with only by the help of a religious faith.

And yet, despite this much ground for supposing that Tolstoi had an overt religious purpose in writing *The Death of Ivan Ilych,* it is not easy to show that the story itself supports the hypothesis. If we search it for religious doctrine, we find none. Nor can we even discover in it any significant religious emotion. Although it is true that the conclusion, the moment of Ivan Ilych's escape from pain into peace and even into "light," is charged with feelings and described in metaphors that are part of the Christian tradition, the passage can scarcely be taken as a genuinely religious affirmation or as effectually controverting the thoughts that the dying man has had about "the cruelty of God, and the absence of God."

On the contrary, it might well seem that Tolstoi, by his representation of death, is trying to win us not to the religious life but, rather, to a full acceptance of the joys of the life of this world. From the Christian point of view, his intention might even seem to be open to the charge of paganism. It was an ancient pagan custom to seat a human skeleton at a feast as *memento mori,* a reminder of death, to urge upon the revelers the idea that life is short and that the fleeting hours must be snatched; just so does Tolstoi use Ivan Ilych's death to shock us into awareness of what it means to be alive.

And it is not the virtuous life that Tolstoi has in mind or the pious life—he means life in any actuality, any life that is really lived. Ivan Ilych is remorseful not for the sins he committed but for the pleasures he never took. "Ivan Ilych's life had been most simple and most ordinary and therefore most terrible," says Tolstoi in a famous sentence, and as the reader follows Ivan Ilych's career as a "successful" person, he cannot but conclude that even if the poor man's taking of pleasure had involved his sinning, his life would have been less "ordinary" and therefore less "terrible."

And this would indeed seem to be a pagan conclusion. But perhaps it is not only pagan—perhaps it is also to be understood as Christian. For without life there cannot be a spiritual life, without the capacity for joy or delight there cannot be the conception of the happiness of salvation. The first inhabitants of Hell whom Dante meets on his journey are the Neutrals or Trimmers, the people who had lived "without disgrace and without praise"—those who, as Dante says of them, "were never alive." It was thus that Ivan Ilych had lived, without disgrace and without praise, as one who was never alive. In his maturity only three things had afforded him pleasure—his official position and the power over other men that it gave him; the decoration of his pretentious and conventional home; and playing whist. He had never known the joy of loving or of being loved. He had never felt the sting of passion or the energy of impulse. He had never experienced the calm pleasure of moral satisfaction such as might come from the consciousness of having been loyal or generous. He had never admired anyone or anything; he had never been interested in anything or anyone, not even, really, in himself. He had never questioned or doubted anything, not even himself.

Indeed he had lived without any sense that he had a self or was a self. He had assumed all the roles that respectable society had assigned to him: he had been a public official, a husband, a father. But a self he had never been, not between the time of his childhood (when there had been a little glow of pleasure and affection) and the time of his dying. Only at the point of his extinction is selfhood revealed to him. The means by which the revelation is effected are agonizing; it comes through pain and fear, through self-pity, through a hopeless childlike longing for comfort and love. Yet in his his awful dissolution, Ivan Ilych is more fully a human being than he had ever been in the days of his armored unawareness of himself. And it is when he has been tortured into an awareness of his own self that he can at last, for the first time, begin to recognize the actuality of other selves, that of the young peasant Gerasim and that of his poor sad son. (pp. 84-8)

> *Lionel Trilling, "Leo Tolstoi: 'The Death of Ivan Ilych',"* in his *Prefaces to The Experience of Literature, Harcourt Brace Jovanovich, 1979, pp. 84-8.*

James Olney   (essay date 1972)

[*Olney is an American critic and educator. In the following excerpt, he asserts that the focus of* The Death of Ivan Ilych *is not Ivan Ilych's death but his spiritual transformation.*]

"I felt very vividly," Tolstoy says in his last diaries (dated February 11, 1910, when he was in his eighties and within a few months of his death), "I felt very vividly how beneficial for life is the thought that death may occur every instant." Tolstoy's insight here sounds almost like a recollection of the meaning he had himself achieved some thirty-five years ealier in the fiction of *The Death of Ivan Ilych.* In the midst of life, Tolstoy had the peculiar experience of feeling himself always in death, and that changed for him the very meaning of life itself. Life would be one thing were we not all going to die; then it might be indulging in parties, cards, and pleasure every night, or tastefully decorating an apartment, or lying in bed reading French romances and eating gingerbread and honey (a pleasure Tolstoy once, as a boy, pursued for three days when the certainty of death and the vanity of life were especially vivid and present to him). But life, in fact and meaning, is something very different from this for Tolstoy, and different solely because we all exist under more or less immediate sentence of that death which, according to Tolstoy, worked as a great reordering power over life. And, since his experience was so intensely felt, so overwhelmingly immediate, Tolstoy could never quite understand how it was

that other men could blandly disregard, as they seemed to do, the imminence and terrible reality of death. This felt certainty of death gives the clue to the tone of exasperation and nervous urgency that one finds in Tolstoy, notably in his essays and moral writings. Men must be shown the folly of their ways and quickly, before it is too late; they must be made to feel how insane their concerns are, made to feel what is wrong and what is right in human life. The folly was only too pressingly alive to Tolstoy because he had participated in it, but other men—all men—must be made to *feel* what Tolstoy felt or his intuition, his insight, his vision would have come to nothing. And therein lay the joker: what Tolstoy would transmit or communicate or share was more a feeling than an idea, more a complex and subjective emotion than a rational and objective proposition. What he wanted to prove, and to prove on the pulse of his readers, had not come to Tolstoy only or primarily through rational processes but as the sum and result of his whole experience as a man, an experience which centered, as if hypnotized, around and around the conclusive fact of death.

The problem of communication (and communication, according to Tolstoy, is the artist's primary motive) was made enormously more complex for him precisely because of the nature of what he had to communicate. Tolstoy had little desire to persuade people logically; he wanted instead to make them experience with their entire being, as he himself had done. Capital punishment, for example, he says in *A Confession,* he "knew . . . to be unnecessary and bad" only when, as a spectator, he had shared the experience of an execution: "When I saw the head part from the body and how they thumped separately into the box, I understood, not with my mind but with my whole being. . . ." Being unique and subjective, however, experience, as such, is non-transferable. The experience of one man is not the experience of another man: it cannot be. A feeling, which in genesis and in expression involves the whole man, an emotion, simple or complex, cannot in itself be handed from man to man or from author to reader. Every man's emotional autobiography is irremediably his own. But that which he could share with no one, Tolstoy paradoxically felt the necessity to transmit to every one. It was finally in the metaphors of fiction that Tolstoy found what he sought and what was never there in the logic of moral philosophy: a bond or a bridge, not between one mind and another but between his experience as a human being and the experience of his readers.

"More than that of any other major novelist," Ernest Simmons quite rightly maintains, "Tolstoy's fiction is autobiographical. . . . The life he transposed into art was largely his own life of recorded experience and observation. . . ." And yet Tolstoy, who derived all that he knew and was, all the meaning that he would put into his writing, from his own ultimately lonely, subjective experience, begins and ends *The Death of Ivan Ilych* (in which the details of the life of the central figure are demonstrably drawn from Tolstoy's autobiographical experience) with the titular fact: the death of Ivan Ilych. If emotional experience is not directly transferable—and it certainly is not—and if, in any case, no one experiences death more than once, then how can Tolstoy, a living man, hope to evoke the emotion of death as a meaningful and real experience in his tale? The truth is that *The Death of Ivan Ilych* dramatizes a meaning which, achieved as it were through the metaphoric focus of death, has always to do with life. Ivan Ilych, a character drawn autobiographically from the life of his creator, and representing, together with the other elements of the complex presentation, the meaning of that life, stands in for the experience of every man, and in his death proves, for any reader, "beneficial for life."

Born as every individual is, however, waking up to himself willy-nilly at the center of phenomenal experience, there can never be, within life, a one-to-one correlation of experience and the kind of meaning Tolstoy sought to communicate. The individual has no Archimedean point, no perspective from without upon his own experience. Hence, though Ivan Ilych, like his creator, might be said to embody and dramatize truth or meaning, he does not and cannot (in a phrase from Yeats) "know" it as he embodies it—except, it may be, in the transfiguring moment of death, and then he is no longer limitedly "man" because he has gone beyond the living human condition. But the artist, in recreating his own experience in form, achieves this perspective from beyond or outside; and so art gives what life never can: simultaneous experience and meaning. Metaphor, which evokes an emotion (thus the experience) and which draws into significant focus and shape (thus the meaning), is of the essence of fictional art. It raises the artist above his experience in time as the expressive shaper and creator of his own self, for the self of the artist is the source of all metaphor.

One might thus summarize the conditions that Tolstoy assumes for the fiction of *Ivan Ilych:*

1. Having himself had a complex emotional experience, he would evoke that same total emotion in his reader (with a moral admonition implicit in the evocation);

2. He would do this, in the only way possible, not through logical argument but through fictional presentation;

3. Though Tolstoy has never experienced death himself, nor has his reader, he would center his tale around a man going through the experience of death in order to make the reader feel the meaning of life;

4. He would thus render simultaneously available to his reader life as experience (human) and life as meaning (superhuman).

Only in death and in art, it seems, is this reconciliation possible. Hence, *The Death of Ivan Ilych.*

It is a curious but, I believe, true observation that each of us ordinarily lives as if he were not going to die. I do not say that we live as if we should live forever—that is something else. The assumption is altogether implicit, unquestioning, negative: I am not going to live eternally—but neither am I going to die. Meursault, in Camus's *L'Etranger,* thinks of this psychological phenomenon as a personal lack of imagination. "J'écoutais mon cœur," he says.

Je ne pouvais imaginer que ce bruit qui m'accompagnait depuis si longtemps pût jamais cesser. Je n'ai jamais eu de véritable imagination. J'essayais pourtant de me représenter une certaine seconde où le battement de ce cœur ne se prolongerait plus dans ma tête. Mais en vain.

Another thing I did to deflect the course of my thoughts was to listen to my heart. I couldn't imagine that this faint throbbing which had been with me for so long would ever cease. Imagination has never been one of my strong points. Still, I tried to picture a moment when the beating of my heart no longer echoed in my head. But, in vain.

Heartbeat is clearly a metaphor for consciousness here, and Meursault cannot imagine that into non-existence; but his failure is not private or peculiar. None of us, I think, can imagine that consciousness, as we have always known it, could ever cease, or that the world would go on without our consciousness of it. In Ivan Ilych's thought about the possibility of his own death—thought which is quite like Meursault's or any man's—Tolstoy shows himself a very subtle, very exact psychologist:

> The syllogism he had learnt from Kiezewetter's Logic: "Caius is a man, men are mortal, therefore Caius is mortal," had always seemed to him correct as applied to Caius, but certainly not as applied to himself. That Caius—man in the abstract—was mortal, was perfectly correct, but he was not Caius, not an abstract man, but a creature quite, quite separate from all others. . . . "Caius really was mortal, and it was right for him to die; but for me, little Vanya, Ivan Ilych, with all my thoughts and emotions, it's altogether a different matter. It cannot be that I ought to die. That would be too terrible."

> Such was his feeling.

If it be granted that in ordinary consciousness every man lives as if he were not going to die, then each of us lives, in the terms of Tolstoy's story, as if there were no end to life and as if there were no pattern, for a series of unrepeated, discrete points is not a significant pattern but a mere heap and accumulation; as if, in sum, there were no meaning. But death is for Tolstoy rather a great reorganizer than a destroyer: it constitutes a total reordering of what we have been and done as well as what we are; it entirely refocuses the nature of what subjectively and eternally *is.* Men go on, however, from day to day forgetting or ignoring or denying their mortality; and this, to Tolstoy, is a fantastic, incomprehensible mistake. For, while it may be that the sane man would never choose death, yet, paradoxically, without death, life itself would hold no meaning. If individual life were infinite, then that might be its very meaning; if it were not a thing of disease, pain, dislocation, then one might say, "Life was given to live, and that is sufficient reason for activity." There would be no felt need for meaning but only a search for eternal pleasure. As man does die, however, that must be the unarguable condition of meaning for his existence. Death impresses us with the need to find a meaning, to find an end, in the sense of a goal or a purpose and not in the sense of a mere cessation or annihilation, for life. If the end of life (which would provide an answer without meaning) is pain, suffering, death, and annihilation, if we are set up as sawdust dolls merely to be knocked down, and knocked down only after much pummeling and pain, if we have nothing either inside or outside ourselves to discover an order in experience, then the "gift of life," as Tolstoy says in *A Confession,* is the meanest of things, and life itself is the grimmest joke in the worst of all possible worlds.

The reverse, however, is equally true: if meaning can be found, then all shall be well. "Meaning," as C. G. Jung says, reflecting on his own experiences, "Meaning makes a great many things endurable—perhaps everything." It was Tolstoy's assumption, logical or illogical and in any case largely unargued, that there must be a meaning for all we enjoy, for all we endure. His *Confession* records his search for just such a meaning to existence, his search for an answer to the insistent question, What for? A "What for" or a goal clearly implies a pattern, and a pattern implies a meaning. The meaning is not *in* the end (death is not the meaning of life), but existence of meaning is implied *by* an end, since a logical, foreseen end exists only if there has been beginning and middle. Meaning inheres not in the beginning alone or in the end alone, not in the single part at all, but in the whole pattern and in the entire, relational organization composing the pattern. If we see human existence in large perspective, of course, "beginning" and "end" apply only individually. We see individual beginnings and ends but not the beginning and not the end of life. Life, for Tolstoy, is synonymous with consciousness, and it is only resident in the conscious individual, but it is, at the same time, something much more than the individual. The paradox of the human dilemma, as Tolstoy resolves it, is that the pattern of life, which engages our finite, conscious being at every point in time and space, is only a pattern because it reaches into relation with eternity and infinity. Death is the given fact which determines the nature of the relation between human and superhuman and, rather than being something disconnected and disruptive, is one detail in an inclusive pattern of life. Meaning, then, lies in relation to the transcendent power which establishes death as a "given" of human existence, which appoints death as the end of individual being. Meaning, that is—and this holds good whether in life or in art—is not a thing or an object *within* the pattern, but is a process, a relation existing and evolving between the full pattern and the patterning or intending mind. This process, this patterning of experience to give it formal organization and relation to a shaping power which transcends the created experience, is precisely the mode of metaphoric art. In just this way, "All art," in D. H. Lawrence's phrase, "is *au fond* symbolic, conscious or unconscious"; and all life, insofar as it embodies truth and, for us, meaning, must be equally symbolic.

Let us examine rather more closely the significance of death in *A Confession* and in *The Death of Ivan Ilych:* we shall find the same thrust in the autobiographical piece as in the work of fiction. The argument (this may seem to contradict what I have said earlier but in fact, I believe, it does not) is this: the center of meaning in *Ivan Ilych,* the generating emotion and the culminating experience of the tale, is not death (which is seen finally as a mere physical and incidental fact, a literal metaphor for a state of the soul) but spiritual conversion (seen as essential transformation). "Conversion" one might describe briefly as "a transformation of self in response to a power that transcends the self." The metaphor on which the entire fiction of *Ivan Ilych* is based could be stated thus: death is the ultimate conversion. This conversion, like any conversion, affects the percipient self and not the perceived world; it alters the point of view on temporal details, not those details themselves. Death, in *Ivan Ilych,* transforms life from meaningless existence into a course of patterned significance. Or vice versa: any real spiritual conversion is necessarily a form of death, the new spirit or self signifying inevitable death for the old self. Tolstoy's vision is of life unitary and continuous: in the human state, no man shall be born to the new except as he simultaneously dies to the old. Life, then, is a matter of constant coming-into-being; when we are really alive (which is not the equivalent of "all our life"), we are in a state of continuous evolution. Essentially the self is always the same, but it realizes that essence in ever-changing temporal states. "I remembered very vividly that I am conscious of myself in exactly the same way now, at eighty-one, as I was conscious of myself, my 'I', at five or six years of age. Consciousness is immovable." Like all of Tolstoy's works, *A Confession* is an attempt to bring consciousness of evolving self to verbal expression.

Tolstoy begins *A Confession* with a sort of preamble, bringing the record of his experience up to that climactic moment that is the center of the work. It is the record of a life without meaning, of an existence dragged on according to the dictates of an immoral society, of individual being nullified by group morals. "Then," however, Tolstoy says, "occurred what happens to everyone sickening with a mortal internal disease." A profound lassitude, an undiagnosable psychic illness afflicted him and, he says, continued and worsened: "At first trivial signs of indisposition appear to which the sick man pays no attention; then these signs reappear more and more often and merge into one uninterrupted period of suffering. The suffering increases and, before the sick man can look round, what he took for a mere indisposition has already become more important to him than anything else in the world—it is death!" Eventually, Tolstoy came to a Carlylesque center of indifference, a sort of death in life: "My life came to a standstill." This, we see, points clearly to the metaphor informing *Ivan Ilych*—death is a conversion. But closer examination reveals that a significant reversal has been effected: in *A Confession* life without meaning figures as a disease, and death, as sheer annihilation, represents the climax of that life. Life, that is, is shown to us as death, and death, very shortly after, is seen to lead to life. So, while the metaphor of *A Confession* may be essentially the same as the metaphor of *Ivan Ilych,* yet, as a matter of fact, the subject and object of the metaphor (if we conceive the metaphoric process in those terms) are reversed in the work of autobiography; the flow of energy appears to be in the opposite direction: conversion is a form of death whereby we overcome meaningless life.

Metaphor, as here, is always a question of two terms *and their relation*—until finally the terms disappear, leaving, for metaphoric interest, the relation. The meaning of metaphor lies between the terms: in relation and only there—in form—do we find meaning. According to the metaphor of *Ivan Ilych,* "Death equals conversion." But meaning flows in either direction here, so that our understanding of "death" qualifies or defines our understanding of "conversion" as our understanding of "conversion" qualifies and defines our understanding of "death"—thus: "Death is conversion." The terms of the metaphor cannot be classified as primary or secondary; they are exactly and functionally equal. And the meaning derivable from the metaphor inheres not in the one or the other, not even simultaneously in both, but in the composite relation that this complex, whole pattern bears to the creative mind which intends and encompasses it. The meaning of *Ivan Ilych* lies in the equivalence of death and conversion, an equivalence which, in turn, represents the experience and meaning of the life of Leo Tolstoy. If this analysis is correct, then every work of art is doubly metaphoric: in detail, metaphoric elements evoke emotional experiences; in large, the composite metaphor of the work is a presentational image, or an expression, of the personality of its maker and of the meaning of his life. This points the last step in an analysis of metaphoric process. The equivalence of death and conversion in *Ivan Ilych* stands as a realized, dramatized metaphor for the being or the self of Leo Tolstoy, its creator and projector. The personal, private experience of spiritual conversion (which, as individual experience, is incommunicable) is metaphorized as death, here rendered as an insistently physical fact; the relation we perceive between the terms is the meaning we understand from the story; and the story, taken *in toto,* represents Tolstoy's understanding of his own life. "Reflecting on it in that way, regarding it, that is, from the standpoint of good and evil," Tolstoy says in the introduction to his *Recollections,*

> I saw that my whole long life falls into four periods: that wonderful period (especially in comparison with what followed) of innocent, joyful, poetic childhood up to fourteen; then the terrible twenty years that followed—a period of coarse dissoluteness, employed in the service of ambition, vanity, and above all of lust; then the eighteen-year period from my marriage to my spiritual birth—which from a worldly point of view may be called moral, that is to say, that during those eighteen years I lived a correct, honest, family life, not practising any vices condemned by social opinion, though all the interests of that period were limited to egotistic cares for the family, the increase of our property, the attainment of literary success, and pleasures of all kinds: and finally the fourth, twenty-year, period in which I am now living and in which I hope to die, from the standpoint of which I see the meaning of my past life, and which I should not wish to alter in any respect except for the effects of the evil habits to which I grew accustomed in the former periods.

The "recollection" is taken in tranquility—as it must be if any understanding is to attach to it; as also the recollection of Ivan Ilych's life is taken in the tranquility after his death. From a standpoint after conversion or from a standpoint after death—or better, from a standpoint after conversion/death—the whole pattern is available. And such a standpoint is, of course, transcendent. If the work of art or of autobiography is to have a moral effect, this must come from experience of complex relation existing within the work but perceived, as it were, from beyond the work rather than from experience of an emotion singly and directly transferred. Both death and conversion, in effect, are per se incommunicable experiences; but relation, which allows the reader to fill the terms of the metaphor from his own lived experience, is possible to the artist and is, in any case, his only way of meaning.

Life, considered alone, is meaningless; death alone is equally insignificant. Taken together, they point beyond either one to a meaning which embraces and transfigures both. Structurally, as well as thematically, *Ivan Ilych* is designed to draw life and death together; Tolstoy is at pains throughout never to give us one without a simultaneous awareness of the other. The two very clearly coincide in the conclusion of the novella where, in the death of Ivan Ilych, Tolstoy introduces a note of conversion and rebirth. The story begins, on the other hand, with death, because the point of view is focused on those still within life for whom, naturally, a transcendent perspective is impossible. Actors in a drama which they have not made and therefore do not understand, Praskovya Fedorovna, the self-pitying widow of Ivan Ilych, and Peter Ivanovich, one of his "nearest acquaintances," who has "sacrificed his usual nap" for the occasion of his friend's wake, can only live their lives in incomprehension: they are, and thankfully so, still alive. The reader, however, who is made to be conscious of life and death together, of the live widow and friend in one room and death, in the form of Ivan Ilych's body, in the next room understands their significance well enough; and it is a significance which lies in their lives' being uncomprehended and totally *in*significant. In them, in the broad and persistent irony with which Tolstoy characterizes them (the scene of the pouffe, the sympathetic signing, and the restrained weeping, for example), in their unconscious hypocrisy and petty selfishness, their laughable, hideous propriety and decorum, we are given the life of Ivan Ilych untransfigured by death. "Peter Ivanovich, like everyone else on such occasions, entered feeling uncertain what he would have to do. All he knew was that at such times it is always safe to cross oneself. But he was not quite sure whether one should make obeisances while doing so. He therefore [thus displaying, like the living Ivan Ilych, his wish to be the median or the abstract, average man] adopted a middle course. On entering the room he began crossing himself and made a slight movement resembling a bow." And in the midst of all this stingy self-interest lies the body, looking mysteriously as if a meaning beyond all this has been realized in death: "His face was handsomer and above all more dignified than when he was alive. The expression on the face said that what was necessary had been accomplished, and accomplished rightly. Besides this there was in that expression a reproach and a warning to the living. This warning seemed to Peter Ivanovich out of place, or at least not applicable to him." For the living this is a dead body, just that: unpleasant, indecorous, improper, messy; a distraction when they would prefer to be playing cards; and quite meaningless. It is dead, they are alive. And their kind of life draws all emotion to itself, asks that all fellow-feeling be directed toward them. "He screamed unceasingly," says Praskovya Fedorovna of Ivan Ilych's end, "not for minutes but for hours. For the last three days he screamed incessantly. It was unendurable. I cannot understand how I bore it; you could hear him three rooms off. Oh, what I have suffered!" With somewhat more of intelligence and tact, but equally motivated by a necessity to direct pity inward, Peter Ivanovich, momentarily terror-stricken with the "morbid" thought of his own end and the torment of being conscious that it *is* the end, responds, "Is it possible that he was conscious all that time?" Fortunately—for otherwise he would be propelled beyond his present life—Peter Ivanovich is soon able to believe that the only thing he has seen here is a dead body and not death itself; he leaves the house of death as he entered it, finding "the fresh air particularly pleasant after the smell of incense, the dead body, and carbolic acid."

With the knowledge that Ivan Ilych, in the very structure of the novella, is already dead before he lives, and with the knowledge that he screamed in agony and terror for three days before even that could be accomplished, the reader is prepared to understand the forty-five archetypically common years of Ivan Ilych's life in their true and deadly significance. With the smell of death in our nostrils and with Ivan Ilych's screams in our ears, Tolstoy abruptly begins the Life of Ivan Ilych, the quality of which is suggested by the flatness of Tolstoy's statement, seemingly inexorable in its logic: "Ivan Ilych's life had been most simple and most ordinary and therefore most terrible." There is no escape from that "and therefore": Ivan Ilych, like Praskovya Fedorovna and Peter Ivanovich, has handed over the only thing any man has—his life; and he has given it over to be shaped not by a living reality but by an abstraction—society. The life of Ivan Ilych, like the life of the preconversion Leo Tolstoy in *A Confession,* is rendered in the most grossly simplified outline. It proves to be a fantasy-like caricature of a life with all the implications and overtones of unrealistic fairy tale.

> So Ivan Ilych served for five years. . . .
>
> So at the end of an evening he sometimes danced with Praskovya Fedorovna. . . .
>
> So Ivan Ilych got married.
>
> After seven years' service in that town he was transferred. . . .
>
> So things continued for another seven years.
>
> So Ivan Ilych lived for seventeen years after his marriage.
>
> So he departed. . . .
>
> So they began living in their new home. . . .
>
> So they lived.
>
> So they lived, and all went well, without change, and life flowed pleasantly.

And so the grotesque fairy tale of *The Life of Ivan Ilych* continues until the reader expects—but, of course, never gets—"And so they lived happily even after." Directly

after the last "so they lived," chapter 4 begins ominously with the first signs of the "internal sickness," traceable to the injury suffered while decorating that house which "was just what is usually seen in the houses of people of moderate means who want to appear rich, and therefore succeed only in resembling others like themselves." From his efforts in decorating this little non-place, Ivan Ilych's mortal sickness begins and worsens, which returns us to the experience and the metaphor of *A Confession.* The same simple, archetypal pattern, the same death in life, determined and justified in the same terms by the approval of the same immoral society, is described there ("*Rien ne forme un jeune homme,*" that society tells Tolstoy, as it tells Ivan Ilych, "*comme une liaison avec une femme comme il faut*":

> So I lived for ten years.
>
> So I lived, abandoning myself to this insanity for another six years. . . .
>
> On returning from abroad I settled in the country. . . .
>
> Returning from there I married.
>
> So another fifteen years passed.
>
> So I lived. . . .
>
> Then occurred what happens to everyone sickening with a mortal internal disease.

This is death—or no, we recall, it is conversion. Tolstoy's conversion is Ivan Ilych's death—the real end of an unreal life.

Ivan Ilych's "most simple and most ordinary and therefore most terrible" life is also most typical, most attuned to social demands, individually most unreal, and therefore most immoral. The only reality in it is death, a reality ignored and evaded just as far as possible. His life is a social fairy tale, insistently *comme il faut,* shaped at every turn by "decorum" and "propriety," by pursuit of "pleasure" and finally by a desire for a salary of 5000 rubles. It is ruled, that is, by society, by sensual gratification, by materialistic motives, never by conscience, which Tolstoy conceives as a matter between the individual self and a power outside the self and beyond society. Ivan Ilych conducts his life so as to be the exactly expected average, the norm which would be discovered in a sociological survey. He becomes, in Tolstoy's working and by his own design, a type or an abstract average rather than a unique individual; he becomes, in effect, the Caius of Kiezewetter and so fits perfectly the terms of Cardinal Newman's ironically revised syllogism: "Man in the abstract is mortal; Ivan Ilych is abstract man; therefore Ivan Ilych is mortal."

Tolstoy's celebrated "realism," on the other hand, a technique which makes for uniqueness and individuality of characterization, is all exercised on the grim and literal, physical facts of death. We feel it, for example, in the sudden, and then continuing, nagging, gnawing pain of Ivan Ilych's "mortal internal disease"; in the degradation and humiliation of requiring help in his excretions; in the mental anguish which comes upon Ivan Ilych from behind with the pain—the "It" which gets worse whether admitted to consciousness or ignored; in the appearance and smell of Ivan Ilych's body. Except for the significant but generalized description of him as a mean within his family and society ("He had three sons, of whom Ivan Ilych was the second. . . . He was neither as cold and formal as his elder brother nor as wild as the younger, but was a happy mean between them. . . ."), the only physical description Tolstoy gives of Ivan Ilych is in the long process of his death. He is an individual presence only during and after his death: "Peter Ivanovich was immediately aware of a faint odour of a decomposing body. . . . The dead man lay . . . in a specially heavy way, his rigid limbs sunk in the soft cushions of the coffin, with the head forever bowed on the pillow. His yellow waxen brow with bald patches over his sunken temples was thrust up in the way peculiar to the dead, the protruding nose seeming to press on the upper lip." Passing time, too, in contrast to the dream quality of the years of physical health ("So Ivan Ilych lived for seventeen years"), is agonizingly real and particular in sickness. ("An hour and another pass like that.") Tolstoy spends about one-fourth of his pages on the forty-three-year dream of Ivan Ilych's life, about three-fourths on the painful reality of his death (which, in chronological time, covers fifteen or sixteen months). The result of all this is that Ivan Ilych, in dying, paradoxically becomes the individual that he never was in his typical life; and in becoming an individual, he becomes much more than merely individual.

When we come to Ivan Ilych's physical death, then, we find Tolstoy working in a very different way from the method used in presenting his cartoon-like life. From a death-in-life society, we proceed to a living individuation in death. Tolstoy has been called primarily a satirist, which is fair enough comment for a good part of *Ivan Ilych.* This limiting characterization of Tolstoy's art, however, offers no account of what the end of the story does; and surely the end of this novella is not only the end but also the climax. The tale, with its overview on both life and death, moves always in two opposed directions; it shows us, in image, gesture, and speech, a vision of life which is both negative and positive. Tolstoy, if he is a satirist, is a philosopher as well, and like any philosopher he would complete his picture of reality with implied moral imperative (but, being an artist, without going outside the frame of the picture). Being thus and so, we infer from the story, from the dramatization of meaning therein contained, that we should, as human beings, act in such and such a way. Latent within Tolstoy's tale is the philosopher's imperative: man is not like this, but like that; consequently, he should act not in this way, but in that way. As a satire (showing what man, in essence, is not and how he should not act), *Ivan Ilych* has a clearly defined, consistently delimited object of attack in a single social class—the *haute bourgeoisie.* Tolstoy's ironic commentary, which at once effectively destroys the pretensions of this dominant but hollow social caste and at the same time clears the ground for his own positive creation, his own enactment of reality, is directed with single-minded intensity against that class to which Ivan Ilych himself belongs: against lawyers and doctors (in *A Confession,* against artist and writers), against "educated" men of whatever profession who occupy self-perpetuating roles but perform no real and useful labor, all the while, however, holding power over those who do have a job to perform.

But I have said that the novella dramatizes a positive statement as well as this negative one. It is my experience that nearly every reader feels that Ivan Ilych is "saved" in the end and, further, that the servant Gerasim is somehow instrumental in his salvation. The exact nature of salvation in *Ivan Ilych,* however—what does it mean to be saved in the terms of the story?—seems to be obscure even for those who clearly feel it there. The negative part of salvation for Ivan Ilych is clearly enough spelled out: he must (and finally does) reject that false and unreal, socially-selfish and immoral "life" for which the only possible end is annihilation. Since such a life is all in and of this world, it must find its flat end also with the loss of this world. If a motive for continued life within the created universe is to be found, if a meaning, a value, a goal is to be discovered for life in time and in space, then that motive or that meaning must necessarily lie outside time and space. Society, of course, provides no such non-temporal, non-spatial motive; nor does sensual gratification; nor does any pursuit of material things. These all lie *within* the world, so cannot give a meaning *for* the world. Meaning is felt by mystic intuition in a union of different realms of being; it is not achieved by discursive intellect acting upon the objects within the realm of the created world. The positive vision which Tolstoy embodies in *Ivan Ilych* is, in fact, one of mystic union.

The clue to this positive enactment lies in the character of Gerasim and somewhat in the character of Vasya, "Ivan Ilych's schoolboy son, who was extremely like his father." The tone in which Tolstoy characterizes Gerasim, in notable contrast to the characterization of all those who share motivation and social rank with Ivan Ilych, is sympathetic, positive, un-ironic; we feel everywhere, in the way he is presented, the author's warm approval of all that he is and stands for. During Ivan Ilych's sickness only Gerasim acts naturally and efficiently, with a native honesty and intelligence and tact. He is "a clean, fresh peasant lad, grown stout on town food and always cheerful and bright"; he moves "with a firm light tread, his heavy boots emitting a pleasant smell of tar and fresh winter air," and he wears "a clean Hessian apron, the sleeves of his print shirt tucked up over his strong bare young arms," all the time carefully "refraining from looking at his sick master out of consideration for his feelings, and restraining the joy of life that beamed from his face. . . ." In short, with his "deft strong hands," his "fresh, kind, simple young face," and his "glistening white teeth," Gerasim, the state of whose soul is manifest in his appearance and his actions, represents the "health, strength, and vitality" of a class entirely separate from Ivan Ilych's class. And at the funeral service ("candles, groans, incense, tears, sobs") he alone has something human to do and does it, "stepping lightly in front of Peter Ivanovich" to strew "something on the floor."

Gerasim only enters the story of Ivan Ilych's life two-thirds of the way through (though he is presumably there in body earlier), after Ivan Ilych is well into the experience of his mortal sickness, "his ache, this dull gnawing ache that never ceased for a moment. . . . " It is only when death has pushed this far into his life and he begins to sense that his own individual life must not be all, that Ivan Ilych notices the servant. Only then does he feel the necessity to go beyond selfish, individual existence, for if he does not leave it, it will soon leave him. Gerasim, the single person to pity Ivan Ilych as he supposes he wants to be pitied, points the paradoxical way for Ivan Ilych out of his self-entanglement. What Ivan Ilych must eventually recognize is that he will not be freed by drawing a selfish emotional comfort from Gerasim but by imitating the servant's life. Taking Ivan Ilych's legs on his shoulders, Gerasim, a son of the soil, a peasant profoundly rooted in the land, provides his master with an Antaeus-like strength as he joins Ivan Ilych to the entire earth through his own person and the rooted peasantry. He represents for Ivan Ilych, in a quite literal sense, Yeats's "radical innocence."

> He saw that no one felt for him, because no one even wished to grasp his position. Only Gerasim recognized it and pitied him. And so Ivan Ilych felt at ease only with him. He felt comforted when Gerasim supported his legs (sometimes all night long) and refused to go to bed. . . .
>
> What most tormented Ivan Ilych was that no one pitied him as he wished to be pitied. At certain moments after prolonged suffering he wished most of all (though he would have been ashamed to confess it) for someone to pity him as a sick child is pitied. . . . And in Gerasim's attitude towards him there was something akin to what he wished for.

But Ivan Ilych fights a losing battle so long as he wishes to get and not to give. The direction of all pity inward leaves everything in the merely personal, worldly realm. To receive pity is human and mortal, to give pity immortal and divine. The human feeling in Gerasim's service gives a motive and a meaning to his life, but not to Ivan Ilych's.

One other character in the story, besides Gerasim, exhibits pity for Ivan Ilych: the son who, at the funeral, "seemed a little Ivan Ilych." When the family gathers around the sick bed, this reincarnation of Ivan Ilych's own childhood shows something of the peasant's pity for his father: " . . . the schoolboy crept in unnoticed, in a new uniform, poor little fellow, and wearing gloves. Terribly dark shadows showed under his eyes, the meaning of which Ivan Ilych knew well. His son had always seemed pathetic to him, and now it was dreadful to see the boy's frightened look of pity. It seemed to Ivan Ilych that Vasya was the only one besides Gerasim who understood and pitied him." When, later, Ivan Ilych thinks back over his own life, the only part of it which seems to him at all valuable or meaningful or real is the period up to the age of his son. In Vasya the dying man is reunited with his own childhood, "that wonderful period [as Tolstoy describes it in *Recollections*] of innocent, joyful, poetic childhood up to fourteen." At the time of Ivan Ilych's death, the boy has significantly reached the limit of this "joyful, poetic childhood"; he has reached the age of puberty, of the individual fall from innocence and out of union into the world of experience. "His tear-stained eyes," at the funeral, "had in

them the look that is seen in the eyes of boys of thirteen or fourteen who are not pure-minded." It is only in thoughts of the time before his own fall from innocence (paralleled but ironically reversed in the story of Ivan Ilych's death by his fall into the black sack) that Ivan Ilych can find anything at all to be called good.

> There also the further back he looked the more life there had been. There had been more of what was good in life and more of life itself. The two merged together. . . . "There is one bright spot there at the back, at the beginning of life, and afterwards all becomes blacker and blacker and proceeds more and more rapidly—in inverse ration to the square of the distance from death," thought Ivan Ilych. And the example of a stone falling downwards with increasing velocity entered his mind. . . . He stared at the back of the sofa and waited—awaiting that dreadful fall and shock and destruction.

In the son who has not fallen, a replica of his one-time self, and in the servant-peasant, who lives a life of natural union with the earth, Ivan Ilych sees symbols of the one possible good offered by the life around him.

What Ivan Ilych discovers, in the climactic experience of death, is that to reject the evil of his life and to embrace the good, to penetrate the blackness in the sack until he discovers light at the bottom mean rejecting a selfish life by paradoxically asserting a newfound selfhood and affirming individuality by paradoxically denying the all-importance of merely divisive personality. Impelled by their imminent failure, Ivan Ilych rejects all those things that he has sought in a continuously trivial life: personal pleasure, social approval, worldly advance. At the extreme limit of his individual life, he moves toward the childlike innocence and grace of Vasya and the natural simplicity of Gerasim, toward union with life at the beginning and life at its commonest, toward union, through the human and the natural, with the superhuman and the supernatural, the non-temporal and the non-spatial, the eternal and the infinite.

Ivan Ilych's sudden, complete movement toward union (and the change in his character, accomplished in one page, is less a steady development than a violent and thoroughgoing transformation) is a gesture of pity—of pity now, however, not for himself but for others. Pity, as Tolstoy says elsewhere, is that response in the human realm which is analogous to and leads toward love of God in another realm: "To love an individual one must be blinded. Without being blinded one can love only God, *but people can be pitied, which means, loved in a godly way.*" Gerasim, in his character and actions, enacts the message of pity; Vasya, in his being and situation, provides Ivan Ilych with the means or the object of pity. "This occurred at the end of the third day, two hours before his death. Just then his schoolboy son had crept softly in and gone up to the bedside. The dying man was still screaming desperately and waving his arms. His hand fell on the boy's head, and the boy caught it, pressed it to his lips, and began to cry." His childhood reclaims Ivan Ilych, and in this symbolic reunion with his own infancy and the infancy of humanity, Ivan Ilych passes out of individual life at either end as he shows his first sign of pity for another. "At that very moment Ivan Ilych fell through and caught sight of the light, and it was revealed to him that though his life had not been what it should have been, this could still be rectified. He asked himself, 'What *is* the right thing?' and grew still, listening. Then he felt that someone was kissing his hand. He opened his eyes, looked at his son, and felt sorry for him." With this first barrier overcome, having thereby broken from the prison of himself, Ivan Ilych can proceed to fuller, deeper responses of fellow-feeling, reaching even as far as his wife (who, in a significant detail, has "bad breath") with his pity. "His wife came up to him and he glanced at her. She was gazing at him openmouthed. . . . He felt sorry for her too. . . . With a look at his wife he indicated his son and said: 'Take him away . . . sorry for him . . . sorry for you too. . . . ' " On the final page of the novella, Ivan Ilych makes the conversion from self-pity to pity for others likewise trapped in the conditions of human life, and through that conversion, which is simultaneous death and reunion with an infinite other, he transcends his petty and meaningless, day-to-day, hand-to-mouth, merely personal and disjunct existence. His experience in death forces him to the realization that one must strive not for pleasure through self-seeking but for union through human pity and divine love. "To him all this happened in a single instant, and the meaning of that instant did not change." It is death which enforces the dictum, but the "meaning of that instant" is the eternal meaning of life itself. Pity, so long as we are human beings, is sufficient answer to the insignificance of life, for it puts us in relation to the divine; when we cease to be human, then love (pity *sub specie æternitatis*) will be known as the answer.

Tolstoy, in his *Last Diaries,* describes life, when experienced under human, finite conditions, as a continuous struggle of pure, nontemporal spirit against the limitations of the world and of the simply divisive personality. In the metaphoric transliteration of art, Tolstoy merges and unites these two poles of opposition, the physical or eventful and the spiritual or meaningful, so that the complex metaphor of *Ivan Ilych,* as a whole, unites the lived reality, the bodily-conscious experience of Ivan Ilych (which was also the experience of Tolstoy) with the theoretical statement dramatized by Gerasim (which is also Tolstoy's statement). The reader must be more subtle than to take Ivan Ilych as Tolstoy; he must also be suspicious of taking Gerasim as spokesman for the author. Tolstoy lives behind and in them both. The metaphor for experience with Tolstoy is not the one or the other but both and their relation. Art is here a fully human, living affair and in the achieved, expressive artifact, body and soul struggle—without that there would be no life—and yet coexist, cooperate to the artistic end. We might put the same idea another way: Ivan Ilych represents the way Tolstoy lived his life, at least up to a point (and there is, after all, a conversion for Ivan Ilych, generated by recognition of what Gerasim signifies, just as there was for Tolstoy in his unifying perception of the significance of peasant life); Gerasim, on the other hand, represents the way he feels, after conversion, that he should have lived his life. In drawing on the facts of his own experience, Tolstoy never forgot that a man is both what he would be and what circumstances have made him; in the metaphor of *Ivan Ilych,* consequently, he presents theoretical and actual, ideal and real, intention and fact, Gerasim and Ivan Ilych, meaning and experience. Every character in the fiction is finally Tolstoy himself, his experience and a perspective on that experience; all the characters, taken as a coherent metaphor, embody what and why Tolstoy was. Between the two in their struggle, metaphoric life is struck off, for life is exactly this struggle toward meaning between the way things are and the way things should be: the struggle—but also, here in the work of art, the fusion, the merger, the total and violently serene picture. Tolstoy's art gives us, then, what we have said life does not: simultaneous experience and meaning.

It is with a "complex feeling of delight" (as Wordsworth, in his Preface, calls the emotion of art) that the death and conversion of Ivan Ilych affects us. It is the happy end to a happy story, a story which can be seen as pathetic or unhappy—indeed, as anything but necessary—only if isolated details are separated from their contextual pattern.

> In place of death there was light.
>
> "So that's what it is!" he suddenly exclaimed aloud. "What joy!"
>
> To him all this happened in a single instant, and the meaning of that instant did not change. For those present his agony continued for another two hours. Something rattled in his throat, his emaciated body twitched, then the gasping and rattle became less and less frequent.
>
> "It is finished!" said someone near him.
>
> He heard these words and repeated them in his soul.
>
> "Death is finished," he said to himself. "It is no more!"
>
> He drew in a breath, stopped in the midst of a sigh, stretched out, and died.

Though Christ's name is never spoken in *Ivan Ilych,* yet one might maintain that the spirit is only there the more by the name's absence. "When Jesus therefore had received the vinegar, he said, It is finished: and he bowed his head and gave up the ghost" (John 19:30). *Consummatum est:* according to the Gospel, Christ died as a man to atone for man's sins, to redeem the fallen creature and restore him to immortal grace, to give, in effect, a meaning to human life. In the terms of Tolstoy's story, so must we all die to the body to be reborn to the spirit. Christ's life, in Tolstoy's dramatization, is every man's life, only intensely, supremely more individual, more real, more divine. Christ was simultaneously the most highly individuated man and the infinite God; his being was the bridge between a world in time and space and a realm of infinity and eternity. For Tolstoy, this signified simply that he was symbolic man, Ivan Ilych writ large. In this vision, each of us is (so far as we realize the condition) God incarnate, divine spirit under temporal and spatial limitations. Christ, according to Christian belief, is Love, and "Love," as Eliot says in *Four Quartets,*

> is itself unmoving,

Only the cause and end of movement,
Timeless, and undesiring
Except in the aspect of time
Caught in the form of limitation
Between un-being and being.

God took on the "form of limitation" as Christ—or as Ivan Ilych. To refuse to be what one cannot but be; to refuse the divine heritage; to refuse to realize one's self as God—this, for Tolstoy, was the ultimate denial, the denial of Ivan Ilych's life. In the death of Christ or of Ivan Ilych, however, life triumphs as the merely personal self is dissolved to be transcendently reunited with the inclusive and infinite source of all pity, of all love, of all life. Tolstoy's sense of the continuity of life, embodied in the metaphor of his fiction . . . is quite the same as Lawrence's: "You thought *Consummatum est* meant all is over. You were wrong. It means: *The step is taken.*" Death is the last, transfiguring step, the final conversion and ultimate transformation of the individual.

The twofold metaphoric process of *Ivan Ilych,* as we have described it, enables Tolstoy to achieve the transcendent vision; it allows him to see and to show us from beyond life and death. The perception of relation between death and conversion lifts us above the isolated experience; the perception of relation between *that* relation and an entire life raises us to a perspective on life itself and its meaning. Seen in this way, as it were from beyond, death is not the end nor an annihilation but an exfoliation and realization of full selfhood. "I am not living," Tolstoy said in his diary, "nor does the whole world live in time: an immutable universe in time, formerly unattainable to me, now unfolds itself. How much easier and more understandable this way! And from such a point of view how clearly is death not an end of something but its full unfolding." Death, then, is to be conceived of not as a cessation of consciousness (as in the end of Meursault's heartbeats) but as an elevation of consciousness to a new level to include within its purview all of past consciousness and its relation to a divine intention. Death is the moment of realization when the individual sees, truly according to Tolstoy, "that my soul is not 'divine,' as they say, but is God Himself." Ivan Ilych discovers in his conversion-death that the words ironically put into the mouth of Peter Ivanovich, as he leaves the room of death for a game of cards, are graciously true two hours before death: "It's not too late even now. . . ." Or, as the inscription on the medallion, which Ivan Ilych hangs on his watch chain, says, *Respice finem.* What is the end for which we are admonished to provide? The story proves that it is self-realization. And that is precisely what the fiction of *Ivan Ilych* does for Tolstoy himself: brings to conscious realization in a meaningful form that divine spirit momentarily resident in him. The complex metaphor of *Ivan Ilych* is spirit incarnate, meaning realized, truth embodied. For Tolstoy himself, as creator, and for his character Ivan Ilych, as creature, the death at the end of the story is a conversion of man into God. For either of them, in the completion of art and the completion of life, Hopkins's words are good. "Nature," Hopkins says, "is a Heraclitean fire" but the spirit of man, by "the Comfort of the Resurrection," will rise triumphant over the natural world in time and space.

Flesh fade and mortal trash
Fall to the residuary worm; world's wildfire,
   leave but ash:
      In a flash, at a trumpet crash,
I am all at once what Christ is, since he was what
   I am, and
This Jack, joke, poor potsherd, patch, match-
   wood, immortal diamond
      Is immortal diamond. .

But in Tolstoy's vision we are not given immortality: we create it. And as we create it, so shall it be. If we have a paucity of imagination, then our immortality will be poor and thin. If we create ourselves with intensity and so in fullness, then that is how we shall have it. Tolstoy did (or, more truly, *does*) so create his own immortality in his art and in his life. We realize ourselves, he says, and thereby realize God. Perhaps it is not so strange after all that the Orthodox Church excommunicated Tolstoy, for what his art and his life say is that man, in a continuing process, creates God, and creates him in man's own image. That, I suppose, is hardly orthodox, yet it is the claim of the artist's imagination. (pp. 101-13)

James Olney, "Experience, Metaphor, and Meaning: 'The Death of Ivan Ilych'," in The Journal of Aesthetics and Art Criticism, *Vol. XXXI, No. 1, Fall, 1972, pp. 101-14.*

Edward Wasiolek   (essay date 1978)

[*In the following excerpt, Wasiolek examines various critical perspectives on* The Death of Ivan Ilych, *concluding with a discussion of its central themes.*]

The Death of Ivan Ilych was Tolstoy's first published work after his conversion. It was written after almost a decade of immersion in theological reflection and writing, and indifference to the writing of fiction. More schematic and deliberate than the early tales, it is more pruned of descriptive and analytic detail. The density of circumstances is largely absent, and it reads like a distillation rather than a representation of life. Disdaining the verisimilitude that such density often confers upon an artistic work, Tolstoy makes his appeal by way of formulaic selection of essential detail. This gives the tale the air of a chronicle or parable. Such a manner could easily lead to abstract moralizing; yet, though the moralizing is there, the details and skeletal action have been so skillfully chosen that the distinctly uncontemporary mode of narration succeeds in an astonishing manner. There is, too, in *The Death of Ivan Ilych*—as there will be in the tales that follow—a punishing quality about Tolstoy's moral passion. He seems now more certain of the truth—more eager to castigate those who do not live by the truth. These are unpromising attitudes for the production of great art, but Tolstoy does not hesitate to express them. It must be remembered too that these are the years when Tolstoy's views on the uselessness and perniciousness of Western art, his own included, are maturing. The passions for moral truth and pedagogy cannot overcome his art, but they themselves are conquered and turned to the purposes of great art. It is to the art that we must turn in order to see how this had been accomplished.

The art of *The Death of Ivan Ilych* has affected widely diverse audiences and lent itself to various modes of dissection. The story is great enough to support the weight of different critical perspectives. It has the "transparency" that Roland Barthes has put forth as a mark of the greatest works of literature, permitting us to speak about it with the different critical languages of time, place, and critical intelligence. The Freudians, for example, have had little to do with Ivan Ilych, and Tolstoy's narrative manner as well as his philosophical convictions would seem to leave little terrain to work over. Tolstoy abjures ambiguity and symbolization; the intent of the narrative style is to lay everything out as clearly as possible. Nevertheless, Ivan Ilych's life may be described as a system of determined evasions of love, human contact, and self-knowledge. Because he has arranged his life in a rigid, ritualistic manner, it is easily unhinged by unexpected events, however trivial. There is nothing of the flexibility of interaction with reality that is the mark of a healthy man for Freud. Freud spoke of "love and work" as the two qualities of the healthy person. But Ivan Ilych has never learned to love and never learned to love work. He follows his career—in his father's footsteps—as one would a military campaign, with ramparts thrown up to keep him from contact with reality or human emotions, whether those of others or his own. It would take only a shift of vocabulary to see his rigidities and evasions as neurotic flight and defense.

Indeed, one can read this short novel as Ivan Ilych's attempt to appease one father and his discovery of another. Identification with his father and alienation from himself and real life by way of that identification constitutes the essence of his emotional life. He follows in his father's footsteps quite literally, imitating the relentless march toward the sinecure his father occupied and toward which his father has launched him. He is a "good boy," not only the *Phénix de la famille,* but also the "good boy" in the greater family of the bureaucratic and social circle in which he makes his career. He looks to his surrogate "fathers" with the same kind of attentiveness and pleas for approval as he had done apparently with his own father. Doing what is expected of him, he is rewarded for what he does. When he reflects on the various advantages of marrying Praskovya Fyodorovna, the most important is the approval of his superiors. What he does and what he feels have already been chosen for him. His greatest reward is to become one of the fathers—to enjoy what they had enjoyed.

In such a reading, Ivan Ilych's sickness would be a sign of his health, for the sickness (the bruise on his side), like a visitant from another world, would represent the return of the repressed, and as such would be perceived as painful. It is perhaps no accident that the pain that penetrates his body awakens in him memories of his childhood—of a sensuous and very personal nature. The personal life from which he had been deflected by identification with the life of the fathers is what returns to his consciousness; this for Tolstoy is a sign of health. The pain, which alienates him from the life of his fathers, returns him to his own forgotten, personal, and individualized life. This return is accompanied by what one would call "childhood" situations: Ivan Ilych is scolded by his doctors and by his wife; he becomes progressively helpless; Gerasim has to carry him from chamber pot to sofa as one would a child. One can even go so far as to say that he "progresses" back to "birth," for the symbolism of the black bag and the issuing into light is put in terms of birth pangs and giving birth.

The tale would seem too—in its evident philosophical and Christian intentions—to offer little for Marxist analysis; yet I am persuaded that it will bear a refined Marxist analysis—something that the Soviets have never given it. If we consider the tale in the light of Marx's propositions about the alienation man suffers in a commodity culture, the possibility of such a reading becomes evident. Things, it must be admitted, are prominent in the story, and Tolstoy plays stylistically on the density and power of possessions. Ivan Ilych is not ready to start his career—after being trained like a seal for it—until he has been provided with a portmanteau, an inscribed medallion for his watch chain, new linen, a traveling rug, and toilet accessories. He wants Praskovya Fyodorovna as much for her property as for her pretty face and correct social position. Things determine Ivan Ilych's feelings, his relationship with people, his pain and pleasure, his happiness and misery. His life has been environed by things: he is tucked in with them when he goes off to his first job; his marriage begins with conjugal caresses, new crockery, furniture, linen; his highest moment comes with the furnishing of a new house; and his fall comes from reaching to hang a drape. The whatnots, antiques, dishes, plates on the wall, bronzes, and upholstery which Ivan Ilych has bought, arranged, hung, and installed bring him and his wife and daughter to ecstasy and temporary harmony. But the same objects bring Ivan Ilych to irritation with every spot on the tablecloth, and to an explosive quarrel with his wife about expensive cakes left over from a party. Most of the characters in the novel relate to each other by way of what they possess. What they think, say, feel, and value has been congealed in what they own. They have become commodities, as is patently evident in the way the doctors handle Ivan Ilych's pain and the way that Ivan Ilych's dearest friends look upon his death. His death is an opportunity to be exploited, something to be measured by benefits or advantages. Indeed, the whole work may be read as a series of exploitations by Ivan Ilych and of him.

The novel lends itself magnificently, too, to a "formalist" or close linguistic analysis, for Tolstoy's art is rich in calculated linguistic effects. The power of the first line of the chronicle proper is unsurpassed in simple beauty: "Ivan Ilych's life had been the most simple and the most ordinary and therefore the most terrible" (*Proshedshaya istoriya zhizni Ivana Il'icha byla samaya prostaya i obyknovennaya i samaya uzhasnaya*). The line gets much of its beauty and power from the control the words exercise on the chronicle that follows. A range of possible meanings of the word simple (*prostaya*), in English and Russian, is artfully exploited. There is the intended meaning of "without complexity," but the word can also mean something left out, and there is also the hint of "foolish." The most powerful influence of the line comes from the juxtaposition of "simple" and "ordinary" (*obyknovennaya*) with the word "terrifying" (*uzhasnaya*). For if there is a dominant emotional effect in the novel it is the juxtaposition of common life with uncommon horror. We ordinarily expect horrible consequences from horrible causes. The horrible fate of Dostoevsky's characters, for instance, come from horrible crimes and guilts; even Anna Karenina's terrible fate comes from such proportionally terrible acts as leaving a husband and child for a guilty love. But Ivan Ilych's life is ordinary, structured on a few simple contrasts which are repeated with monotonous appropriateness: what is pleasant or unpleasant and what is proper or improper. In the course of the story the contrasts are confounded, so that the novel is based largely on a series of reversals. During the course of the tale, pleasure becomes pain, what is proper becomes what is not proper, approval of society becomes disapproval, the solidity of things becomes the spectrality of things, Ivan Ilych's well-regulated life becomes unregulated, and the common pleasure becomes the uncommon horror. The development of the story consists essentially of the progressive growth of Ivan Ilych's consciousness of the horror that lies below his well-regulated, pleasure-dominated, proper life. The story moves toward what the opening lines announce: the end is the beginning, and the beginning is the end. It is in keeping with this structure of ironic reversals that Tolstoy gives us the death of Ivan Ilych before telling us about his life.

Before Tolstoy gives us the chronicle of Ivan Ilych's life, he tells us what it was worth, how it should be judged. Irony is his weapon of judgment; we know immediately what we are supposed to be for or against. We are supposed to be against the predatory self-interest barely concealed beneath the routine expressions of condolence. The contrast between the conventional forms and private feeling is something Tolstoy has done many times before, but here he is doing a great deal more. The announcement of Ivan Ilych's death comes in one of those respites from judicial labor that Ivan Ilych loved so much, as is commented on later in the novel—when he was able to smoke, drink tea, talk about politics, general topics and most of all about official appointments. That is, we learn about his death in a situation that recalls one of the pleasures he enjoyed while he was alive, and the scene is the first of a series of identifications by which the life of Ivan Ilych before and after death is compared and analogized. The opening scene which presents Ivan Ilych in death is at the same time a representation of his life.

Tolstoy meticulously re-creates in the opening scene the atmosphere, conditions, values, and modes of behavior by which Ivan Ilych had lived, and the recreation in dramatic form is a judgment on Ivan Ilych in death. Life as Ivan Ilych had lived goes on after he is dead. As Ivan had a passion for bridge, so Pyotr Ivanovich, wearily performing the duty of paying respects to the dead, hurries away to meet the impish and impious Schwartz for a game of bridge. As Ivan Ilych had taken from Praskovya Fyodorovna only the conveniences of board and room, so Praskovya Fyodorovna in her tearful conversation with Pyotr Ivanovich reveals a predatory concern only with the monetary convenience she can gain from her husband's death. Ivan Ilych had labored to furnish his house with whatnots, antiques, dishes and plates on the walls, and Tolstoy goes to the point—in his recreation of Ivan Ilych's life—of drawing our attention to some of the commodities

that had ruled his life and which continue to exist after his death. The room in which Pyotr Ivanovich talks to Praskovya Fyodorovna is filled with furniture and bric-a-brac that Ivan Ilych had collected. Pyotr Ivanovich's attention is explicitly drawn to the upholstered furniture in pink cretonne that Ivan Ilych had consulted him about and to the antique clock that Ivan Ilych had liked so much.

As Ivan Ilych treated people before death, so they treat him after death. The "worth" of his colleagues was their capacity to advance his welfare and his pleasure, and the "worth" of Ivan Ilych in death is the opportunity his passing gives to others to advance their welfare and pleasure. He treated people impersonally and was indifferent to their vital interests. This was most evident in his relationship with his wife, with whom he talked at times only when a third person was present. She pays him back in death. We learn of his death in the opening scene by way of the formal obituary that Praskovya Fyodorovna has written, which Fyodor Vasilievich reads to his colleagues in the judicial chamber. The conventional expression of sorrow in the obituary is the precise correlative, in impersonality, of the actual emotions Praskovya Fyodorovna has toward her deceased husband. The items of description in this opening scene are a duplication of the kinds of feelings, human relationships, and objects in which Ivan Ilych had lived. Tolstoy is saying that Ivan Ilych's life is the ironical factor in his death.

The dramatized beginning casts its shadow over the chronicle that follows. We know that Ivan Ilych's life will be shallow, impersonal. The form of the narration that follows reinforces this judgment. Large blocks of Ivan Ilych's life are expressed in a few paragraphs, and Tolstoy deliberately mixes matters of consequence and inconsequence so as to reduce all the events to a kind of undifferentiated triviality. He tells us, for example: "The preparations for marriage and the beginning of married life, with its conjugal caresses, the new furniture, new crockery, and new linen, were very pleasant . . . ," mixing love and furniture in similar grammatical form and brevity. Later, the death of two children is reported in a subordinate clause, while the main clauses are retained for an account of the father's troubles.

The narration of the first seventeen years of Ivan Ilych's married life—an accounting of moves, promotions, successes—reads like an inventory rather than a life. The sameness of the events makes it difficult to remember what is individual, significant, or striking. Events of a significant personal nature do appear in his life, but Ivan Ilych manages, by adhering closely to the proper and decorous rules of his society, to avoid them. During the first months of her pregnancy, Praskovya Fyodorovna interrupts the even course of properness and pleasantness by irrational bursts of jealousy, by demands for his attention, and by coarse and ill-mannered scenes. But Ivan Ilych evades such pleas for sympathy by spending more time away from her; he evades her pleas as he evades similar pleas of the accused in his courtroom. All this is done in the name of good breeding, conformity to public opinion. The law of the society, to which Ivan Ilych subscribes enthusiastically, is the law of pleasantness and properness. What is disagreeable and improper has no place in this mode of life, and when it obtrudes itself—as had Praskovya Fyodorovna's behavior during pregnancy—it is ignored or relegated to irrationality.

Ivan Ilych's meaningless life takes on meaning only when the disagreeable that intrudes on his life cannot be ignored. When he is passed over for promotion, he is jolted out of mechanical complacency and projected into anger and self-evaluation. By happenstance, this intrusion in his well-planned and decorous life is quickly erased when Ivan Ilych manages to obtain a position better than the one he had been denied. His life resumes its decorous, pleasant course, but another disagreeable event, more fateful than the first, intrudes upon his life. He "falls," and the ambiguity of the word and its biblical connotations were probably intended by Tolstoy. The "fall," to be sure, is appropriately trivial: from a ladder and while he is occupied with the objects that are the explicit badge of his place in society. Ivan Ilych has climbed only as high as the drapery, but the fall is as deep as the abyss of death and the agonies of consciousness before death. This second accident with its attending misery brings Ivan Ilych to a kind of spiritual rebirth, to irritation, reflection, self-evaluation, and finally to an awareness of himself and of others. Little by little the pain, which penetrates his usual activities, excludes him from the unpainful lives of his associates, bringing him to isolation and to confrontation with that isolation. The pain in his side makes him different from others; it individualizes him.

The pain grows to affect his dinner, his bridge, his relations with his wife; it spoils his work and his enjoyment of his furniture. His pleasant, decorous life becomes unpleasant, indecorous. At first it affects only his outer life, but gradually it affects his inner life; it overcomes the resistances of self-satisfaction and self-exoneration and leads him to self-assessment and self-incrimination. Ivan Ilych comes finally to see that his life has been wrong, but he comes first to see that the lives of others are wrong. He notices that no one really cares that he is in pain. They ignore his pain; when they cannot ignore it, they trivialize it; and when this is no longer possible, they blame him for it. It is Ivan Ilych's pain, not theirs, and they want to be touched by it as little as possible. They give only what they have always given, which is what Ivan Ilych had always given when confronted with someone else's pain and someone else's appeal for compassion and love: pretended compassion and love, that is, the conventional forms of polite interest and concern. As Ivan Ilych earlier defended himself against involvement in his wife's pain by blaming her (she was irrational) and absenting himself, so now Praskovya Fyodorovna defends herself against involvement in his pain by blaming him (he was irrational in not following the doctor's orders) and by absenting herself with her opera, social life, and involvement in her daughter's coming marriage.

To the measure that Ivan Ilych's pain mounts and his behavior becomes disagreeable, the indifference of those about him becomes more determined. The weapons they use to protect themselves against his pain are the weapons

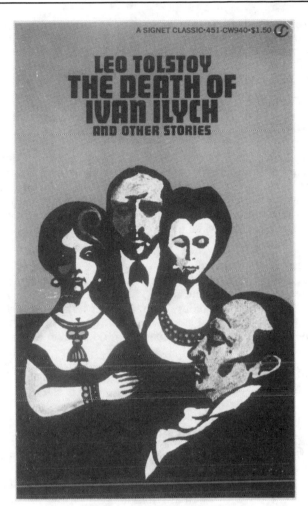

Cover illustration from the 1960 edition of The Death of Ivan Ilych, and Other Stories.

that Ivan Ilych used to protect himself from everything unpleasant. Schwartz continues to be impish; the bridge games go on; his wife, daughter, and the daughter's fiancé go to the theater and carry on the foolish conversations about art. Indeed, the tempo of enjoyment of those close to him seems to mount in inverse relationship to the increase of his pain. When he is about to lapse into the final day of unceasing pain, the daughter announces her engagement to the young examining magistrate, and the pleasure of Praskovya Fyodorovna and the daughter is at its apex.

Ivan Ilych comes to see their indifference and cruelty and he comes to blame them. He does not blame himself—not, at least, until the very end. Several times during his illness the thought comes to him that perhaps he has not lived his life well, but each time he dismisses the idea as nonsensical. He comes far enough in his forced, slow reassessment to admit that there had been little happiness in his life, and what there has been took place in childhood and has been decreasing ever since. But it is not until his final hours that Ivan Ilych sees the truth of his life. Undoubtedly the struggle he puts up in the black bag is a symbol of the struggle he maintains to justify his life. He slips through the bag and into the light only when, in his final hours, he stops justifying his life and listens, specifically when he himself feels pity for others: first for his son, who has come with eyes swollen with tears, and then for his wife.

It is hard to make artistic sense of Ivan Ilych's conversion, of the symbolism of the black bag, and the truth that he sees in the last moments of his life. The gradual reassessment of the worth of his life that he makes under the bludgeon of pain, the frustrated demands for compassion, the polite indifference to his plight from others, and his terrifying aloneness before impending death are all psychologically believable and well done by Tolstoy. But it is another matter to believe in the "revelation" that Ivan Ilych experiences when he slips through the bag and to believe artistically in a spiritual rebirth.

There is another difficulty, too, present throughout the long ordeal of Ivan Ilych's sickness. Ivan Ilych himself poses the problem one night about a month before his death when, exhausted by pain, he weeps "because of his helplessness, his terrible loneliness, the cruelty of man, the cruelty of God, and the absence of God." He cries out to God: "Why hast Thou done all this? Why hast Thou brought me here? Why, why dost Thou torment me so terribly?" The problem is correctly expressed in his anger against the senselessness of the suffering he undergoes, the lack of proportion between whatever he has done and what he has been forced to suffer, and against the contingency, accidentality, and senselessness of his fate.

If we ask with Ivan Ilych why he had to be bludgeoned by pain, we cannot say it is because he lived his life badly, although Tolstoy seems to be saying that. Even if we suppress the perfectly normal rejoinder that all the others in the society have lived lives just as badly but do not suffer, we still cannot find in any moral calculation a connection between the badly lived life and the physical pain. The life is not that bad, and the pain and terror are too much. The life is too trivial for the pain to be so great. We can make sense of the psychological pain—the loneliness, the suffering from lack of compassion, the humiliation of being treated as a thing by those about him—because these follow on the kind of life that Ivan Ilych has led. The lives of others in the society, like Ivan Ilych's, are trivial and terrifying, for reasons that are artistically believable. But we cannot make sense of the physical pain that Ivan Ilych suffers, nor, for that matter, why he and not others must suffer such pain.

If Tolstoy insists on the psychological suffering that Ivan Ilych undergoes after the "fall," he insists even more crudely on the sheer physical pain that Ivan Ilych endures. The unremitting howling of Ivan Ilych in the last three days of his life is a detail so monstrous that only Tolstoy's art could make it palatable. We know why Ivan Ilych suffers loneliness, fear, anger, resentment, depression after the "fall" but we do not know why he has to die. I believe that Tolstoy is conscious of the gulf between Ivan Ilych's behavior and his fate, and it is precisely the irrationality and the utter inexplicability of the gulf that he wants to express. Death exists, and it is the truth. It is something that Ivan Ilych has not believed in and that the others in

his society do not believe in. But it is the reality, nevertheless. The "pain" they so assiduously avoid, of which death is a summation, comes to be referred to as *ona* in Russian ("it" in the feminine gender), that is, both to pain (*bol'*) and death (*smert'*). It is this pain-death that makes Ivan Ilych's former life increasingly spectral, and that unmakes the pleasure he has guided his life by.

I am suggesting that it is the refusal to accept "death" as part of life that leads to the sterility of Ivan Ilych's life and the lives of those about him. Why this is so is something that follows upon Tolstoy's conception of death. The society is built upon a pursuit of well-being and an avoidance of discomfort. "Self-pleasure" is the law of society. The avoidance of "pain" and ultimately death explains the series of abstract and impersonal relations that obtain in the story. One protects oneself from involvement in the pain others suffer by formalizing and thus impersonalizing relations with others.

This process is illustrated in the relations between Ivan Ilych and his wife, in his indifference toward her pain in pregnancy and her later indifference toward his pain in his mysterious illness. Each blames the other. His friends act similarly; they want nothing to do with his pain, and when it obtrudes on their lives, they trivialize it, formalize it, and deny it. Ivan Ilych may be irascible, annoying, and embarrassing, but he is not dying. They will not accept his pain as part of their lives, nor will they accept his dying.

It is Gerasim alone who acknowledges the truth. He accepts the fact that Ivan Ilych is dying and cheerfully acts to make him comfortable. He breathes the health of youth and natural peasant life, lifts up the legs of the dying Ivan Ilych, cleans up after him with good humor, and in general shows him a kind of natural compassion. Expressly conjoining Gerasim's health and vitality with his acceptance of death, Tolstoy seems to be saying that death and life go together. But it is not immediately clear how they go together.

Death is for Tolstoy the supreme irrational event: an event impervious to human desire, understanding or the manipulation of will. It is also the summation of whatever is disagreeable in life—of every pain, sickness, and accident. Ivan Ilych's plea for justice from a seemingly cruel God may arouse our sympathy, but for Tolstoy the plea is an attempt to bring death into the realm of human understanding. There is no logic to Ivan Ilych's sickness and death, no accounting for the intrusion of such pain into his well-ordered life, and surely none that he rather than someone else be picked out for the special bludgeoning. The fact cannot be understood or justified. But it does make a difference, apparently, whether we acknowledge death. If we ignore it, then our lives are struck with sterility; our relations with others and ourselves become impersonal.

Why this should be so is not immediately clear, since the consciousness of death may lead to a whole range of attitudes, including despair and stoicism. It may lead and has led to the impoverishment as well as to the enrichment of life. The special tie that Tolstoy seems to see now between the conscious acceptance of death and fullness of life can be explained in part by turning back to his early work. Although *The Death of Ivan Ilych* signals a change in Tolstoy's view of the world, it also reaffirms the continuity of his thinking and his art. In the early writings, through *War and Peace,* Tolstoy had celebrated submission to the accidentality of circumstances and had satirized the attempt to control circumstances either by an outright act of will or by making subtle demands upon life. The withdrawal of control over life and the humility before the infinitude of circumstances was what revealed the manifold beauty, wealth, and significance of life; now, in *The Death of Ivan Ilych,* it is the consciousness and acceptance of death that reveals the significance of life. In this sense, then, we are beginning to see, beginning with this tale, a profound shift in his view of the world. Tolstoy is now saying that the acceptance of the world and the revelation of the complex purity of sensuous things are not enough, because the roots of the sensuous things are deeper than their flowering in this world. Without the consciousness of death, the things themselves become spectral, as indeed they become with Ivan's consciousness of his impending death.

The reasons for this change have to do with a great number of things among which Tolstoy's religious conversion, his advancing age, and the maturing of his philosophical views must count. It is probably impossible to separate cause from effect, nor may it matter. However, his concern with "brotherhood" seems to lie, at least in part, at the heart of the change. Critics have generally taken his concern with brotherhood as an indication that his view of truth has changed: that he sees it not as something individual but as something communal. This is the way, for example, that Janko Lavrin understands Tolstoy's religious thought in his later years. If one takes individualism to imply exploitation and selfishness, Lavrin is right. Still, Tolstoy had always been against these things, and the only difference with the later works would be one of emphasis and directness. But if one takes individualism as Tolstoy had defined it, in his early creative works through *War and Peace,* as the radically concrete at-one-ness with one's being and with the sensuous flow about one, then he continues to champion individualism. There is thus consistency and continuity in his thought and creation. The repeated refrain of his later works—whatever the collective words of brotherhood, sacrifice, giving—is that one comes to brotherhood by way of individual reason and consciousness. Tolstoy's Christian anarchism represents in one sense the most extreme individualism, because it makes one's being inviolate to the tamperings of secular authority of any kind. Society in the sense of abstract impositions of others on oneself was opposed to individualism in the early works, and it continues to be opposed to it in the later works. The point is that one comes to brotherhood by being oneself. And one comes to "false" brotherhood by being anti-individual, that is, by way of societies, abstract religious precepts, governments—in other words, by way of generalized feelings and choices above the concrete flow within one.

The sacramental moments in the early works had to do with some enriched individualism: a Natasha swimming in the happiness of her own being and indifferent to the society about her; a Nikolay cut off from the social forms of regiment, estate, and possible marriage and alone with the primal elements of field, sensation, desire, and wolf. The individual and society are opposed, but after the conversion Tolstoy needs to find some way to weld religious conviction with aesthetic and philosophic outlook to bring individual and society together. He does it on the theological and social levels by his exhortations to share one's goods, love one's fellow man, and resist no evil. He can make his exhortations directly in his expository works, but his artistic conscience works to preserve as well as to deny. Something of the same changes can be seen to operate in his artistic works, though in a form that preserves what he had said before the conversion. Society and the individual are still opposed in *The Death of Ivan Ilych* as they had been in the early works. It is through himself and his own suffering that Ivan Ilych comes to the truth about himself, and not through education, the imitation of others, or indoctrination by others. Natasha, Nikolay at the hunt, Andrey on the battlefield of Austerlitz come to the truth by way of individual consciousness as Ivan Ilych does. But whereas the consciousness of Natasha, Andrey, and Nikolay is one of immediate seizure of some pristine and personal perceptual and sensuous manifold, Ivan Ilych's consciousness is one of personal suffering. Pain and the consciousness of death are now the special conditions of perceiving truth, not happiness and absorption in sense. Death for Tolstoy now, as the supremely shared experience, is the model of all solidarity, and only the profound consciousness of its significance can bring one to the communion of true brotherhood. The sacramental individual moments of the early works brought one to communion with others only by way of the infectious spirit of such happiness: Andrey is drawn to Natasha because she is absorbed in her own immediate being, and Pierre is able to command the interest of the Mamantov sisters and of Villarsky because he looks at things only from his own point of view. Because such absorption in self implies respect for the selves of others, Tolstoy has a theoretical position for the infection of one being upon another. Yet the radical individualism on which these moments are based offer at best a limited communing effect. The consciousness of death, Tolstoy is convinced, is the cement of true brotherhood. Even while he continues to preach brotherhood and to portray the consciousness of it in his artistic works, Tolstoy continues to denounce false brotherhood (society). Such false brotherhood comes about and manifests itself in ways that are similar to those of the early works: by imitation, group control, education, that is, by way of nonindividual experience.

There is both continuity and change in Tolstoy's artistic works beginning with *The Death of Ivan Ilych.* The continuity is preserved in the "form" of experience, which continues as before to be radically individual and given, something prior to the educative influence of others; but the change lies in the character of that "given," which is no longer simply the purity of the instincts. Tolstoy would have said with Dostoevsky and father Zossima that the roots of sensuous things lie in other worlds. What is real and human for him is the consciousness of death; without such consciousness the experiences of this world are spectral. (pp. 167-79)

Edward Wasiolek, in his Tolstoy's Major Fiction, *The University of Chicago Press, 1978, 255 p.*

Robert Russell   (essay date 1981)

[*In the excerpt below, Russell examines* The Death of Ivan Ilych *as both a parable and a realistic narrative.*]

At one point in Tolstoy's *Smert' Ivana Il'icha* the hero recalls the feeling that he had always had with regard to the syllogism about death in Kiezewetter's textbook of logic: ' "Caius is a man, men are mortal, therefore Caius is mortal" had seemed to him all his life to be correct only as regards Caius, but certainly not as regards himself. As far as Caius was concerned—man in the abstract—this was perfectly just; but he was not Caius, not a man in the abstract; he had always been a creature, quite, quite distinct from all others.'

This passage encapsulates a fundamental point about *Smert' Ivana Il'icha*—one from which others stem, namely the distinction between the particular and the general. There is a gap between Ivan Il'ich's appreciation of the logic of the syllogism in general and his acceptance of the implications for his own life with its own unique experiences. This is, surely, a common enough aspect of human attitudes to mortality. As James Olney, writing about *Smert' Ivana Il'icha,* puts it: 'It is a curious but, I believe, true observation that each of us ordinarily lives as if he were not going to die. I do not say that we live as if we should live forever—that is something else. The assumption is altogether implicit, unquestioning, negative: I am not going to live eternally—but neither am I going to die' ['Experience, Metaphor, and Meaning: *The Death of Ivan Ilyich*', *Journal of Aesthetics and Art Criticism,* 1972].

My purpose . . . is to examine some aspects of *Smert' Ivana Il'icha* in the light of the distinction between general and particular that is the work's basic axis; and to show how one of Tolstoy's intentions throughout is to make the reader aware of what *he* was aware of—what Olney calls 'the felt certainty of death'—by constant movement back and forth between particular and general, individual and universal.

Several critics of *Smert' Ivana Il'icha* have commented on Tolstoy's realism in this tale, a technique which 'makes for uniqueness and individuality of characterization and which here is all exercised on the grim and literal physical effects of death' (Olney). Yet, one must also agree with those who have commented on the tale's resemblance to a parable: this is, indeed, one of the striking first impressions from the work. Edward Wasiolek, for example, writes: 'More schematic and deliberate than the early tales, it is more pruned of descriptive and analytic detail. It reads like a distillation rather than a representation of life. Tolstoy makes his appeal by way of the formulaic selection of essential detail. This gives the tale the air of a chronicle or parable' [*Tolstoy: The Major Fiction*].

Its simultaneous realistic and parabolic qualities contribute greatly to the power of *Smert' Ivana Il'icha;* and the methods used to achieve this can be distinguished by analysis of various levels of the work using techniques that could broadly be termed 'formalist'.

Leaving aside for the moment the first element in the tale—its title—let us pass on to the structure of the work. It is a very obvious feature of *Smert' Ivana Il'icha* that its first chapter is chronologically the final episode in the story. In other words, there is a gap between what has been called 'the dispositional sequence' (events as they actually occurred) and the 'compositional sequence' (events as presented by the author). In the first chapter Ivan Il'ich's colleagues learn of his death from a newspaper announcement, and one of his closest friends—a certain Pyotr Ivanovich—attends the requiem service. In the work's first draft the character who later became Pyotr Ivanovich attended the requiem service, and while there, was given Ivan Il'ich's diary by his widow. The diary then forms the rest of the draft. At this stage, therefore, the visit by a colleague to the home of the dead man had to come first in order to motivate the rest of the work. But the use of the diary did not survive into the final version, whereas the first chapter survives almost intact. Why has Tolstoy felt it necessary to depart from chronology by using this flashback technique? Several critics have given answers to this question. C. J. G. Turner, for example, writes: 'The reason for putting this chapter first is doubtless that at the end it would detract too much from the climax of Ivan's final vision and death'. And, most pertinently for the thesis of the present article, he sees the function of the first chapter as being 'that of generalizing. The contrast between norms of social behaviour and real feelings is generalized not only spatially, as it were, but also chronologically'. James Olney, addressing himself to the same problem, writes: 'Structurally, as well as thematically, *Ivan Ilyich* is designed to draw life and death together'. A. D. P. Briggs suggests that through this device 'Tolstoy removes much of the strain on his plot; by taking the risk of abandoning uncertainty and therefore suspense he avoids the meretricious and the melodramatic'. Finally, Wasiolek's view is that 'before Tolstoy gives us the chronicle of Tolstoy's life, he tells us what it was worth, how it should be judged . . . Tolstoy meticulously re-creates in the opening scene the atmosphere, conditions, values, and modes of behaviour by which Ivan Ilyich had lived, and the re-creation in dramatic form is a judgement on Ivan Ilyich in death'.

The transposition of what is chronologically the final episode to first position, then, allows Tolstoy to relate the life of Ivan Il'ich having already prepared the reader by presenting Ivan as a corpse; it also serves as an ironic judgement of Ivan's life, because the settings (the law courts, the detailed account of the furniture and fittings, the importance of cards)—are all situations which he valued and are now viewed in a satirical light. Moreover, the transposition allows Tolstoy to generalize by focusing attention not on Ivan Il'ich but on those who are still alive and whose lives are as sterile as that which has just ended. A detailed analysis of the first chapter would be too long for inclusion in this article, but the kind of effects achieved through the transposition can be assessed on the basis of three representative examples.

The first of these concerns the ironical evaluation by Tolstoy of Ivan Il'ich's colleagues' conception of pity, love, and friendship. On the first page of the story we read: 'Ivan Il'ich had been a colleague of the gentlemen gathered together [in Shebek's office] and they all liked him' (*i vse lyubili yego*). A few lines further on the passage continues: 'So that, on hearing of Ivan Il'ich's death, the first thought of each of the gentlemen gathered together in the office was of the possible effect that his death might have in the way of transfer or promotion for themselves or their acquaintances'. The first thoughts of those who liked Ivan Il'ich are for themselves, and cast doubt on the meaning of the verb 'to like' (*lyubit'*). This is a very clear example of Tolstoy's irony, but it does not rely for effect on the transposition of the chapter. It is, however, related to an example that does: the evaluation of the characters' feelings of pity through their use of the word 'pity' (*zhalko* and *zhalet'*). When Pyotr Ivanovich goes to the requiem at Ivan Il'ich's house he meets Gerasim on the way out: ' "Well, Gerasim, my friend", said Pyotr Ivanovich for something to say, "it's a pity [*zhalko*], isn't it?" "It's God's will. We'll all end up the same way", said Gerasim, showing his even, white, peasant's teeth . . . '. This little incident takes on its full significance only when the reader reaches the later chapters of the work and discovers firstly the role of Gerasim in Ivan Il'ich's last days and secondly the enormous importance which Ivan Il'ich came to attach to pity. As his illness progresses Ivan Il'ich feels increasingly the need to be loved, but the term that he uses is 'pity'—*zhalet'*—as he was pitied when he was ill as a child. The repetition of this term becomes quite striking. At the end of Chapter 7, for example, where the relations between Ivan Il'ich and Gerasim reach full maturity, the word *zhalet'* occurs six times in a passage of approximately two hundred words. Significantly, none of these occurrences is attributable to Gerasim, who, as he had done in Chapter 1, simply says 'we will all die one day'. Similarly, at the end of the final chapter the word *zhalko* occurs five times in a passage of approximately one hundred and forty words; this time Ivan Il'ich feels pity not for himself but for others—an important development for the story's meaning.

In the light of these clusters of the important word 'pity' the casual use of the word by Pyotr Ivanovich in Chapter I ('for something to say') takes on considerable importance. Tolstoy's evaluation of the word's meaning for members of Ivan Il'ich's social circle is achieved through the transposition of the chapter and the scope which this affords for irony.

The second example of the sort of effects achieved by the flashback technique involves the figure of Shvarts, a colleague of Ivan Il'ich's who attends the requiem and whose whole demeanour reveals him to be a flippant cynic. He does not even try to hide his amused satisfaction that it is Ivan Il'ich who has died, whereas he, Shvarts, is still alive. He is presented through the eyes of his colleague as being elegantly dignified and solemn and at the same time playful and flippant: 'Shvarts's face complete with English-style sidewhiskers, and his whole slim figure in a frock-coat had, as always, an air of elegant solemnity which constantly contrasted with his flippant character and had a special piquancy here'. Every time Shvarts is mentioned

in this chapter the elegance and flippancy are emphasized: 'with a playful glance' (*igrivym vzglyadom*); 'playing with both hands' (*igraya obeimi rukami*); 'he winked' (*podmignul*); and 'clean and elegant figure' (*chistoplotnaya i elegantnaya figura*).

As with the first example, this detail, which is full of irony even within the first chapter, is given a further ironical twist by a detail in a later chapter. In Chapter 4, when Ivan Il'ich is being isolated by his illness from his social life we read: 'In particular he was irritated by Shvarts with his playfulness, his vitality, and his correctness which reminded Ivan Il'ich of what he himself had been like ten years before'. In looking at Shvarts Ivan Il'ich is reminded of a younger version of himself. Like Shvarts, Ivan Il'ich had also played at life; indeed, in the previous chapter there is an extended image of Ivan Il'ich as a virtuoso player, artificially separating his official life from his private life, and through his great virtuosity, just occasionally allowing the two to mix a little.

There is one other reference to the characteristic mixture of solemnity and playfulness, namely in Chapter 8, when one of the doctors begins to treat Ivan Il'ich: 'And, discarding all of his former levity [*igrivost'*] the doctor begins to examine the patient with a serious expression on his face'. So then, Shvarts's attitude—the mixture of solemnity and flippancy that appears so callous in Chapter I—is in fact similar to Ivan Il'ich's attitude to life and to that of the doctor. Humanity is carefully excluded; the pose is all-important. The abominable Shvarts, whom some critics have seen as Mephistophelean, is largely a projection of Ivan Il'ich himself and of others in his social circle.

The third example of the function of transposition touches directly on the question of mortality and the tendency of the individual to deny its relevance for him. When Pyotr Ivanovich goes into the room where the body of Ivan Il'ich lies, his strongest impression is of the body as an object. Ivan Il'ich is nothing but a corpse. But then Pyotr Ivanovich notices something else about him: 'Moreover, in this expression there was a reproach or a reminder to the living. This reminder seemed to Pyotr Ivanovich to be out of place, or at any rate to have nothing to do with him'. Pyotr Ivanovich's feeling here anticipates Ivan Il'ich's feelings about death in general, or the death of Caius on the one hand, and his own death on the other. I use the word 'anticipates', because that is the case in the compositional sequence of the work; but of course in the fable Ivan Il'ich's thoughts about the Caius syllogism come before Pyotr Ivanovich's thoughts prompted by the sight of Ivan's body. Once again, the transposition of the final episode to the first position adds greatly to the sense of irony with which the work is imbued. By the time the reader reaches Ivan Il'ich's thoughts about Caius he already knows that Ivan is dead; and the similarity of Pyotr Ivanovich's thoughts in Chapter I serves to generalize the point, to show how the trap of self-deception ensnares all men.

These three examples, then, illustrate the effects achieved through the reverse structure of the tale. Links are forged between Ivan Il'ich and his colleagues, so that their behaviour reflects his own when alive. His life is therefore judged ironically before it is ever narrated to us. More-over, his attitudes to death, having been seen already in a colleague, are raised from the particular to the general. The structure fulfils part of the overall purpose of the work—the presentation of Ivan Il'ich's life as a parable. Significantly, the bridge between the transposed final episode and the straightforward narration of Ivan Il'ich's life is a resonant sentence proclaiming the universality of Ivan's story: 'The story of Ivan Il'ich's life was the simplest and most ordinary, and the most terrible'.

The setting of the work will be considered under the two headings of time and space. The most striking aspect of time in Tolstoy's work in general is the overwhelming preference for the present. As V. Dneprov writes in a recent essay: 'In Tolstoy's novels present time predominates. The novels cultivate in the reader the capacity to exist as fully as possible in the present.' This feature of Tolstoy's work has often been noted by critics. Perhaps one of the best known discussions (at least in this country) is that of Percy Lubbock, who rather takes Tolstoy to task for his failure to sketch in the past in **Anna Karenina.** For example, 'Given [Tolstoy's] reluctance to leave the actually present occasion . . . there is not room for the due creation of Anna's life.' Or again: 'Tolstoy's eye was infallibly drawn, whenever he wrote, to the instant aspect of his matter.' And finally, 'The whole of the book, very nearly, is scenic, from the opening page to the last; it is a chain of particular occasions, acted out, talked out by the crowd of people concerned.' [In his *The Craft of Fiction,* Percy] Lubbock makes the distinction between a 'scenic' and a 'panoramic' presentation of a story, and he suggests that Tolstoy overwhelmingly prefers the former. The distinction between 'scenic' and 'panoramic', between showing and telling, goes back, as Norman Friedman reminds us, as far as Plato, and 'the history of [literature's] aesthetic could in part be written in terms of this fundamental tension' ['Point of View in Fiction: The Development of a Critical Concept', *PMLA* 1955]. In Tolstoy's case, however, telling takes second place to showing; the scenic completely dominates the panoramic. This does not mean that there is no past whatsoever in Tolstoy, but in contrast to, say, Dostoyevsky, it plays very little part. Tolstoy rarely moves backward in time to draw some detail from his characters' past. In one or two later works, however, he breaks this habit and moves from the present into the past of a character's life, in order—as Dneprov puts it—'to hold that life up to examination'. Such is the case with **Smert' Ivana Il'icha.** The great preponderance of the present noted by Lubbock and others is not to be found in this work.

After the scenic first chapter the whole of Ivan Il'ich's life up to the onset of his illness is surveyed in a panoramic presentation. In this section Tolstoy tells us rather than showing us, and one of the clear markers of this mode of presentation is his indication of passing time. Ivan Il'ich's career and family life are narrated in stages, like the rungs of a ladder, with each new stage being marked by a summarizing phrase:

> Ivan Il'ich lived like this for five years.

> After two years service in the new town Ivan

Il'ich met his future wife. . . . after three years he was appointed assistant public prosecutor.

> After seven years service in the one town Ivan Il'ich was transferred to another province and appointed public prosecutor.

> He lived in this way for another seven years.

> Such was the course of Ivan Il'ich's life for a period of seventeen years after his marriage.

All of these examples are taken from Chapters 2 and 3. In the course of these chapters Ivan Il'ich makes steady progress in his career; he marries; children are born and die. Yet the panoramic presentation, in which the birth and death of children are seen more as markers of passing time than as important events in an individual's life, reduces everything to what has been called 'a kind of undifferentiated triviality' (Wasiolek). It is a nice ironical touch that the fall which precipitates Ivan Il'ich's illness and death takes place within the panoramic presentation of his life. It appears as trivial an event as the others in this account of a trivial life.

With the beginning of Chapter 4 and the onset of Ivan's illness, time in the novel appears to move into the present. Certainly its passing slows down. Chapters 5, 10, and 11 open with sentences similar in structure to those just quoted, but the timescale is now much smaller as the stages of Ivan Il'ich's life are replaced by the much more significant stages of his death:

> So one month went by, then two.

> Another two weeks went by.

> So two weeks went by.

Some clearly differentiated scenes now stand out: the arrival of Ivan's brother-in-law and the visit to the theatre by his wife and daughter, for example. Yet, even here panoramic presentation vies with scenic in a way which is uncharacteristic of the Tolstoy of the pre-***Ispoved'*** period. For instance, the 'scene' in which Ivan Il'ich plays cards, hoping thereby to take his mind off the gnawing pain is not really a scene at all. It is a representative incident, deliberately chosen to make a point. The particular scene in which Ivan Il'ich ruins a grand slam for his partner through his inability to concentrate on the cards is narrated partly in the present tense and it emerges from a passage containing verbs in the past imperfective:

> Friends would come for a game of cards. They would sit down. They would deal, bending the new cards to soften them. He sorted out his diamonds [*skladyvalis' bubny k bubnam*] there were seven of them. His partner said, 'No trumps' and supported him with two diamonds. What more could you ask? It should have been jolly and lively—they would make a grand slam. And suddenly Ivan Il'ich feels that gnawing pain, that taste in the mouth, and it seems to him grotesque that in these circumstances he can take pleasure in a grand slam.

For all its scenic quality, this episode is representative. The use of the present tense certainly makes the scene immediate; but, in combination with the earlier past imperfectives, it suggests possible repetition. The same device is used at the end of Chapter 7, when the visit of Shebek is narrated in the present tense so that it is both a scene and a typical episode in the progression of Ivan Il'ich's illness.

Tolstoy's treatment of time in *Smert' Ivana Il'icha*—the abandonment of his normal scenic method in favour of a summarizing or panoramic approach to the revelation of his characters' lives—derives largely from the intensity of his moral fervour. As the first sentence of Chapter 2 states, Ivan Il'ich's life is most simple and ordinary and therefore most terrible. As with his other techniques, Tolstoy adjusts his normal presentation of time in order to raise Ivan Il'ich's life from the particular to the general so that his fiction might alter the real lives of his readers.

As far as place is concerned, the setting of *Smert' Ivana Il'icha* is entirely social. By this I mean that the whole work is set indoors in the homes and offices of a particular social class, with the only excursion beyond these limits taking place within the equally restricting space of a railway carriage. Ivan Il'ich and his family and colleagues have no contact with the natural world, and so natural phenomena—trees, grass, even weather—are irrelevant to their socially motivated lives. Only at one point in the work does weather play any part, and even there it is an indirect one (related not so much to Ivan Il'ich as to Gerasim), namely the episode in Chapter 7 where the servant comes into Ivan's sick room, filling it with the pleasant smell of tar from his boots and with the freshness of the cold winter air. Here the reference to weather is appropriate, since it is a new element brought into Ivan Il'ich's life by the natural man, Gerasim. (It may also be significant in this connexion that Ivan Il'ich gains relief when he is supported by Gerasim. Like Antaeus he seems to gain strength through contact with the earth through the intermediary of the peasant servant.) For the rest, however, the settings are domestic or official.

Here again, as at other levels of analysis, Tolstoy creates a tension between the apparent individuality of Ivan Il'ich's surroundings and their actual universality—at least within the social class against which his satire is directed. Thus, Ivan Il'ich surrounds himself with objects which, he believes, help to define his uniqueness, his personal good taste. One thinks of the pink cretonne furnishings, of his medal, his fashionable clothes, the stylish old furniture which he managed to obtain cheaply. In fact, of course, as Tolstoy cannot forbear telling us directly (although there was no need): ' . . . it was exactly the same as in the houses of all people who are not very rich but who want to be like rich people, and who, as a result, are only like each other'.

Tolstoy's use of symbolism is not a feature unique to his later works. The example of the tree which Prince Andrey sees on his way to and from Otradnoye springs immediately to mind. Some critics of *Anna Karenina* have objected to the obtrusiveness of Tolstoy's 'novelish devices', 'the man killed on the line as Anna arrives in Moscow—or the schematization of "the peacemakers" ' [John Bayley, *Tolstoy and the Novel*]. If such devices seem occasionally to obtrude within the vast framework of *Anna Karenina,* they become more obvious in the smaller and more intense structure of *Kreytserova sonata* or *Smert' Ivana Il'icha.* When Ivan Il'ich graduates from the Law School he obtains for himself a medal with the slogan *Respice finem*—'Foresee the ending'. From his perspective these words refer to his career duties, but the reader, knowing from the work's title and first chapter what Ivan Il'ich's ultimate fate is to be, cannot but read them in another way. Ivan Il'ich patently lives his life in ignorance of the ending.

The furnishings of the house also take on a symbolic meaning in the light of Ivan Il'ich's fate. Ivan himself feels that he has sacrificed his life for the sake of furnishing his home, for he traces his illness to the apparently insignificant fall while hanging curtains. Some critics have seen the word 'fall' as particularly significant because of its additional biblical reference. Certainly, it seems highly appropriate to Tolstoy's design that Ivan Il'ich's life should enter its new and final phase as the result of his concern for the outward trappings of social success.

Ivan's furniture survives him and contributes to a ridiculous comedy of manners in the final episode, that is the first chapter, when the hypocritical decorum of Praskovya Fyodorovna and Pyotr Ivanovich is highlighted by a pouffe which 'rebels' against being sat on. This pouffe seems to come alive and assert its will as its former owner—the man who had chosen it as an object worthy of maintaining his own prestige—lies dead in the next room; and not simply dead, but completely depersonalized. The futility of Ivan Il'ich's life is captured in the contrast between his own stiff, waxy corpse and the lively, rebellious pouffe.

Finally, the moment of death is conveyed through the symbol of the black bag into which Ivan Il'ich feels himself thrust and in which he struggles because he cannot lose the conviction that his life had been a good one. This image can be read as a metaphor for birth-pangs, and in this reading the process of Ivan Il'ich's death, during which he regresses back to childhood situations—requiring help with defecation, for example—culminates in a repetition of the experience of birth. Given the importance of childhood within the tale, such a reading has some validity. The black bag image strikes John Bayley in another way, however. He compares the moment of Ivan Il'ich's death unfavourably with that of Khadzhi Murat precisely because of Tolstoy's determination to retain, through metaphor, control over the thoughts of the dying man. 'The description is too weighted, the power too authoritative' he says. And, indeed, one sees what he means. Symbols are a way of organizing and controlling experience; and whereas in the vastness of *Anna Karenina* such moments of determined authorial control are balanced by awareness of the uniqueness of individual responses, in the smaller confines of *Smert' Ivan Il'icha* the symbols are used to universalize. Tolstoy does not allow mystery to cloud his own certainty of death here. In this parable Tolstoy's didactic aim is too important for him to give up control—to 'blur in truthful doubt' as Barbara Hardy puts it [in her *The Appropriate Form*]—and so he uses metaphor to convince his readers of what their own deaths will inevitably be like. Once again, then, the movement from individual to universal can be seen to be Tolstoy's underlying intention at this level of the work.

As had been the case earlier with **Anna Karenina,** the original stimulus which led Tolstoy to write **Smert' Ivana Il'icha** was the death of an acquaintance, in this case a certain Ivan Il'ich Mechnikov, a prosecutor from Tula who died of cancer in July 1881 at the age of forty-five. Tolstoy met Mechnikov and liked him, describing him as 'a very nice man'. T. A. Kuzminskaya, Tolstoy's sister-in-law, recalls meeting Mechnikov at Yasnaya Polyana and comments on the good impression which he made on Tolstoy: 'I could see that during Mechnikov's stay at Yasnaya Polyana Lev Nikolayevich grew extremely fond of him, feeling with his artistic sensibility that here was an exceptional man'. Professor N. F. Golubov, author of an article on the medical aspects of **Smert' Ivana Il'icha,** states that the details of the illness and death of Tolstoy's hero coincide very closely with those of Mechnikov.

But, although Tolstoy's Ivan Il'ich is also a lawyer and although his illness and death closely resemble those of the real Ivan Il'ich Mechnikov, the fictional character is not essentially based on the prototype. For one thing, we are told both by Tolstoy and his sister-in-law that the writer liked Mechnikov. Moreover, if Kuzminskaya is to be believed, Mechnikov was an extraordinary man. Ivan Il'ich Golovin is the epitome of ordinariness, and Tolstoy certainly does not like his hero. One commentator has described **Smert' Ivana Il'icha** as a work of great rage; it is a rage directed at society in general, and at Ivan Il'ich in as much as he is a man who has been moulded entirely by society. However close may be the resemblances between the illnesses of the real Mechnikov and the fictional Golovin, there can be no doubt that the life of Ivan Il'ich is Tolstoy's invention. Surely Tolstoy was drawn to the story of Mechnikov—a man who apparently came to revise his view of the value of his life when faced with the prospect of death—not for its uniqueness, but because of the universality of 'the forty-five archetypically common years of Ivan Il'ich's life'.

At the level of character what we find in **Smert' Ivana Il'icha** is an archetype, almost a Russian Everyman, as many critics have pointed out. The first indication of what to expect comes with the title: **Smert' Ivana Il'icha.** Not Ivan Golovin (as Anna Karenina); not simply Ivan (as Gerasim); but somewhere in between. Ivan Il'ich's status as an ordinary member of a particular social class is implied in the title, and confirmed once it becomes clear that he is just one of many people called by their name and patronymic. We hear of Pyotr Ivanovich, Fyodor Vasil'yevich, Mikhail Mikhaylovich, Ivan Semyonovich, Pyotr Petrovich, Mikhail Danilovich, and Zakhar Ivanovich. At some remove from this inner circle of professional acquaintances—people who have evidently structured their lives on similar principles to Ivan Il'ich— there is another group of people who, while leading similar lives, are yet sufficiently distant or senior to be excluded from the coterie and called by their surnames: Shvarts, Alekseyev, Vinnikov, Shtabel', Goppe.

Ivan Il'ich is a representative member of a group with a set of values which is savagely satirized by Tolstoy. Even on a first reading, the frequent repetition of the words 'pleasant' (*priyatnyy*), 'decent' (*prilichnyy*) and cognates, together with 'falsehood' (*lozh'*) and 'deception' (*obman*), stands out. When the occurrence of these words is carefully analysed, as has been done by C. J. G. Turner, the extent to which Ivan Il'ich's life is shaped by social norms becomes evident. By submitting to the influence of society Ivan Il'ich has allowed his individuality, which was there in childhood, to seep away until he is a mere cipher, one of the countless number for whom a decent salary, the pursuit of pleasure, and an outward show of decorum are all that matter.

One of the distinguishing marks of Ivan Il'ich's type is the way in which he takes pride in his ability to split his character into two distinct halves: the urbane and flippant social being and the stern and incorruptible official being. In Chapter 3 Tolstoy lists the qualities of the type so schematically that they almost seem to form a balance-sheet:

Social Qualities

'pleasant' (*priyatno*)
'decent' (*prilichno*)
'made merry' (*veselilsya*)
'tendency to a light gaiety' (*sklonnost' k lyogkomu vesel'yu*)
'playful' (*igriv*)
'witty' (*ostroumen*)
'good natured' (*dobrodushen*)
'bon enfant'

Official Qualities

'exceptionally restrained' (*chrezvychayno sderzhan*)
'official' (*ofitsialen*)
'severe' (*strog*)
'dignity' (*dostoinstvo*)
'accurately' (*s tochnost'yu*)
'with incorruptible honesty' (*s nepodkupnoy chestnost'yu*)

What is striking in this catalogue is that neither in their social nor in their official lives do Ivan Il'ich and those like him accept other human beings simply as people. The carefully worked-out attitudes of social flippancy and official correctness preclude humanity. People are corpses, legal cases, appendixes, foul smells: anything rather than human beings. It is, of course, Gerasim's function to break this pattern and to reveal to Ivan Il'ich the folly of allowing his childish instincts of love to be submerged in society's mire.

Ivan Il'ich's family background adds greatly to the archetypical impression that he creates. As in a fairy-story, Ivan Il'ich is the most successful of three brothers, although not the youngest. It suits Tolstoy's purpose more to break the fairy-tale structure slightly in order to make the successful hero the middle brother—the mean between his brothers' excesses, for, after all, Ivan Il'ich is a typical man. If the description of Ivan Il'ich's early family life seems to come from a fairy-tale, so does the incident in which he sets off for Petersburg to complain to the ministry about their treatment of him. Like some mythical hero, Ivan Il'ich sets out in search of fortune, and finds it in the unlikely setting of a railway carriage, only to discover that it leads indirectly to his death. These examples show how Tolstoy presents Ivan's life so as to justify his opening remark that it was the most ordinary and therefore most terrible. Ivan Il'ich is a representative—almost an archetype.

Yet if this is so, what has happened to Tolstoy's supreme art of individualizing, of capturing the uniqueness of his characters' lives? Has it been sacrificed entirely to his need to make his moral point all-inclusive? It must be said first of all that even in *Voyna i mir* and *Anna Karenina* certain characters are satirically portrayed as having been moulded by social norms. One thinks of Berg for example. Such characters remain in the background of the great novels, whereas Ivan Il'ich is at the centre of the tale that bears his name. It is perhaps then unfair to compare Ivan Il'ich with any of the central characters of *Voyna i mir* or *Anna Karenina,* or even with the heroes of the non-satirical shorter works. Yet to a degree this proviso turns out to be unnecessary, for Tolstoy's ability to bring out a character's uniqueness is not entirely absent here. If Ivan Il'ich's life lacks individuality, his death—the process of his dying—does not. In a sense the fall that precipitates the onset of illness releases Ivan Il'ich from society's mould and allows him to become himself again. This has been recognized by Wasiolek when he writes: 'It is perhaps no accident that the plain that penetrates his body awakens in him memories of his childhood—of a sensuous and very personal nature'. It is in recollection of childhood that Ivan Il'ich re-establishes his unique vision of the world. A dulled sensibility re-awakens as he recalls the feel of a leather ball and the taste of prunes. Nor is his newly aroused sense of the physical world restricted to memory; we recall that he smells the tarry smell of Gerasim's boots and feels the freshness of the servant's clothes. Tolstoy undoubtedly intended Ivan Il'ich's death to put the reader in mind of his own coming death just as it does momentarily for Pyotr Ivanovich; but, artist that he is, he makes Ivan Il'ich's experience of dying simultaneously individual and universal. Only in the satirical scenes of the hero's early life is the balance between the particular and the general reduced to a schematic and undifferentiated picture.

The other characters need not delay us long, for they are mostly functional. Gerasim, for example, is characterized largely through the repetition of positive terms such as 'clean' (*chistyy*), 'joy' (*radost'*), 'life' (*zhizn'*), 'fresh' (*svezhiy*), 'strong' (*sil'nyy*), 'adroitly' (*lovko*), 'softly' (*myagko*). In this he resembles Platon Karatayev, who is equally functional, if a little more substantial. Praskovya Fyodorovna and Pyotr Ivanovich will be discussed briefly under the heading of point of view. That leaves the important minor figure of the son, Vasya. In Tolstoy's scheme, childhood is a golden age from which, if one belongs to a certain class, one is deflected by society. Through the recollections of Pyotr Ivanovich and the hero himself, we gain glimpses of Ivan Il'ich's own childhood, and we are told that Vasya is very like his father had been at that age. Vasya has, therefore, an important function to play as a figure standing at the threshold of adulthood, still capable of feeling love and pity, but no doubt about to be deflected by society as his sister already has been. Herein lies the significance of the twice underlined detail—the terrible blue shadows under the eyes—that suggests that Vasya has

reached puberty. It is significant that Ivan Il'ich's final salvation comes as a result of his pity initially for Vasya.

In a letter to Urusov of 22 August 1885 Tolstoy said that he wanted to write a 'description of the simple death of a simple man from his point of view' (*opisyvaya iz nego*). As we have already seen, the first draft of the work, which was probably begun that same month, consists of two first-person narratives, one in present time belonging to a colleague of Ivan Il'ich and the other consisting of the diary of the late Ivan Il'ich. In his account of point of view in fiction Norman Friedman reminds us that 'when an author surrenders in fiction he does so in order to conquer. He gives up certain privileges and imposes certain limits in order the more effectively to render his story-illusion, which constitutes artistic truth in fiction'. Tolstoy originally intended to make the kind of surrender of privilege discussed here by Friedman (in other words to use a first-person narrative) for the sake of immediate access to the mind of the dead hero and the colleague who is (in the first version) so affected by the dying man's diary. However, it seems reasonable to suppose that he found the price of surrendering his authorial privilege too high in this particular instance. As V. A. Zhdanov says, had Tolstoy kept to his original conception he would have been able to show us only a few scenes from Ivan Il'ich's past life: 'Naturally enough, the friend of his youth can remember only certain individual episodes from the life of Ivan Il'ich, the key moments of notable meetings or quarrels'.

So, we may suppose that, finding the first-person narrative mode too restrictive for his wide aims, Tolstoy rejected this mode in favour of what [M. Yeryomin] calls 'the objective mode of narration'. But, as almost always with Tolstoy, when analysed, the so-called 'objective form of narration' turns out to be, in Boris Uspensky's words, 'a sequence of several different first-person narratives . . . transformed into third-person narrative' [*A Poetics of Composition*]. Tolstoy thus retains many of the advantages of first-person narrative and combines them with the advantage of authorial omniscience when required.

Given the length of *Smert' Ivana Il'icha,* a detailed analysis of the shifts in point of view is clearly beyond the scope of the present article, and I will restrict myself to a few examples, mostly from Chapter I.

In the opening paragraph of the tale the point of view is that of one of the lawyers in Shebek's office or else of 'an observer who is invisibly present in the room' (Uspensky). The indicators that tell us that Tolstoy has here interposed an unseen narrator between himself and the characters described are, firstly, the use of the adjective 'famous' in the phrase 'conversation about the famous Krasovsky case', and secondly the use of first names and patronymics only of characters who are as yet unknown to the reader. The implications are that the Krasovsky case is well known to the narrator and that he is familiar with and of equal standing to the lawyers in the room. The use of this point of view in the opening paragraph has the advantage of taking us straight away into the enclosed world of this particular social group—one might almost say along with Yeryomin this 'caste'—in which Ivan Il'ich spent so much time. Because our narrator is implicitly a member of this caste we enjoy for a moment a privileged insider's view similar to that which Ivan Il'ich must have had. However, Tolstoy cannot remain inside the group for long, because he wishes to criticize this society, to show how it turns out people who are carbon-copies of each other. In order to reveal these lawyers' uniformity of response to the news of their colleague's death, Tolstoy has to step back from the limited position of his unseen observer and assume full omniscience for a moment. So we learn that they all liked Ivan Il'ich, and that the first thought of each of them was of his own possible transfer or promotion. After a passage of conversation between the lawyers which, inevitably, turns from the serious matter of Ivan Il'ich's death to trivial, materialistic questions, the omniscient narrator can once more be heard revealing their uniformity of thought. In one short paragraph we find 'in each of them' (*v kazhdom*), 'in all of them' (*vo vsekh*), and 'as always' (*kak vsegda*).

For the most part the scene in Ivan Il'ich's house is viewed through the eyes of Pyotr Ivanovich, and the narrative is full of terms of estrangement, such as 'as if' (*kak budto*), 'evidently' (*ochevidno*), and 'strangely' (*stranno*). As Uspensky says: 'The use of words of estrangement points to the presence of a synchronic narrator at the place of action'. Here it is Pyotr Ivanovich. Later in the work it will frequently be Ivan Il'ich himself.

Perhaps the most striking of the scenes narrated through the consciousness of Pyotr Ivanovich is the generalized description of the dead Ivan Il'ich, in which Pyotr Ivanovich does everything he can to depersonalize the corpse and separate it off from his own experience. The description of Praskovya Fyodorovna is also greatly estranged. She is first observed as 'a short, fat woman' (*nevysokaya, zhirnaya zhenshchina*), and towards the end of the chapter her every action is accompanied by an estrangement term, such as 'evidently', or 'as if'. Only in one short phrase does the point of view switch to Praskovya Fyodorovna; significantly, this is when her precious furniture appears to be under threat from Pyotr Ivanovich's ash. For the rest, she is observed at a distance, as indeed she is almost throughout the story. This constant estrangement undoubtedly contributes much to the unsympathetic impression which she makes.

Pyotr Ivanovich himself does not escape Tolstoy's irony. In the scene where he has difficulty with the pouffe the point of view switches from him to an invisible observer, so that Praskovya Fyodorovna and he appear equally ridiculous participants in this little farce. Moreover, Tolstoy may view the world for a while through Pyotr Ivanovich's eyes, but he most evidently does not share the character's values. The character is simultaneously the medium for perception and himself an object of evaluation. This technique is to be used extensively throughout the rest of the story, particularly in Chapters 2 and 3, where Ivan Il'ich is both the narrating consciousness and the object of Tolstoy's satire.

The pattern in point of view established in Chapter I is, in general, maintained throughout the work, with Tolstoy switching in sequence between a character's viewpoint, that of an invisible observer with limited knowledge, and a fully omniscient narrator. We have already seen that Chapter I contains many terms of estrangement; the same is true of the rest of the work, indicating Tolstoy's reliance for much of the time on a synchronic narrator, with an omniscient view interposed occasionally in order to generalize, and evaluate unambiguously.

In narrating through a character's consciousness Tolstoy uses a variety of modes of discourse, including reported speech and—very prominently—inner monologue and free indirect discourse (*nesobstvenno-pryamaya rech'*). As Roy Pascal indicates through the title of his recent book on free indirect discourse [*The Dual Voice*], this mode is a *dual* voice: it is simultaneously the character's and the authorial narrator's. This leads occasionally to passages where the two voices, though coalescing, appear to be straining against each other. For example, from the very first, doctors in **Smert' Ivana Il'icha** are linked with lawyers as equally pompous and inhuman. Whose voice do we hear in the following passage?

> He went. Everything was as he had expected; everything was as it always is. The waiting, and the doctor's important manner, which he was familiar with—it was the same manner that he himself adopted in court—and the sounding and listening, and the questions which demanded answers that were foregone conclusions and evidently unnecessary, and the weighty look which implied You just submit to us and we'll arrange it all, we know for sure how to arrange these things, we do it in the same way for everybody, no matter who. Everything was exactly the same as in court. Just as, in court, he adopted a pose with regard to the prisoners at the bar, so was the famous doctor adopting a pose with regard to him.

There are some indications that the point of view here is that of Ivan Il'ich ('as he had expected', 'he was familiar with', 'evidently'). But at this early stage of his illness would Ivan Il'ich really have an insight into the nature of his own legal profession such as that contained in the passage? Is the term 'important manner' (*vazhnost' napusknaya*) really used by Ivan Il'ich of himself at this stage? We are told so in the phrase 'which he himself adopted in court'. Yet psychologically this does not seem to ring true. Surely these judgements on the similarities between the medical and legal professions belong, at this stage of the work at any rate, to the authorial narrator. What we have here may well be a slip. A flaw in Tolstoy's artistry induced by the strength of his predjudice. Or it could be argued that in such a passage one cannot and should not look for one consistent viewpoint, since the mode is inherently dual—both the character's and the authorial narrator's voices can be heard. However one judges the quoted passage, it seems undeniable that the reliance throughout the tale on both a synchronic narrator and an omniscient one—usually sequentially but sometimes together—gives Tolstoy the capacity to move from the particular to the general in a way that the original conception of first-person narratives would not have done. The flexibility of the point of view in the final version suits Tolstoy's purpose better than that in the first draft.

Through an analysis of different levels of **Smert' Ivana Il'icha** we have seen that Tolstoy uses the story of Ivan Il'ich as a parable. Having, through the power of his writing, engaged the reader's attention in the fate of this man, he does everything he can to ensure that the reader perceives this man as Everyman. For some, such as John Bayley, the work, though initially impressive, is ultimately disappointing precisely because Tolstoy is too authoritative, because in seeking to make a universal point he seeks to do too much. Yet it is the case that the power of the work stems largely from the author's determination to venture beyond the life of his hero into the lives of his readers. **Smert' Ivana Il'icha** is a remarkable work by a great man for whom—by this stage of his life at any rate—fiction could not simply record the uniqueness of individual experience. (pp. 629-42)

> Robert Russell, "From Individual To Universal: Tolstoy's 'Smert' Ivana Il'icha'," in The Modern Language Review, *Vol. 76, No. 3, July, 1981, pp. 629-42.*

Michael V. Williams   (essay date 1984)

[*In the following essay, Williams relates Ivan Ilych's physical decline to the myth of the "fortunate fall," which suggests that a fall from innocence can result in greater self-awareness and spiritual rebirth.*]

Certainly a memorable image in Leo Tolstoy's **The Death of Iván Ilých** is that of the "dark sack" through which the stricken Iván passes shortly before death. In recent decades this narrative sequence has drawn the attention of critics who have seen in Tolstoy's sack image a dual suggestion of Iván's physical death and spiritual rebirth. This view is perhaps most succinctly summarized by W. R. Hirschberg, for whom the sack is a kind of uterus:

> The final expulsion through the 'hole at the end' [of the sack] into the world of truth and into a new consciousness coincides with the end of Ivan's earthly life. If death coincides with birth, then Ivan's struggles in the sack are those of a human being in labor; the uterus of Ivan's mind is about to give birth to a new consciousness. ["Tolstoy's 'The Death of Ivan Ilych,'" *Explicator,* 1969]

This interpretation seems reasonable given its limited focus, and it is not my object here to take issue with Hirschberg or others who have viewed the image in this way. I do believe, however, that critical preoccupation with Tolstoy's sack image and the familiar pattern of death and rebirth associated with it has obscured recognition of an equally significant and even more pervasive pattern, one related to the death-rebirth archetype and in fact subsuming it: the myth of the Fortunate Fall.

In his book *Some Versions of the Fall*, Eric Smith examines how, after Milton's *Paradise Lost,* the Fall myth becomes increasingly personalized, as the writer "creates, indeed grows, his own myth, although aware of the accepted versions and paralleling and commenting on them." An essentially Romantic and post-Romantic variation of the Fall myth is the *felix culpa,* or fortunate fall, in which

man's fall from innocence to the knowlege of sin and error is viewed ambivalently as both a curse and a blessing. In Milton, the fall from innocence into guilt and mortality means the loss of Eden, but the eventual gain of Heaven through Christ. On the other hand, the Romantics often equated the Fall with the self-conscious condition of modern man, and strove to transcend that self-consciousness via the imagination. Sharing the Romantic concern for right consciousness, Tolstoy fashioned a version of the Fall myth that retained contours familiar in European Romanticism while adapting to his own iconoclastic moral and psychological attitudes. Reduced to its baldest features, this version may be described as a four-stage process: an integrated condition of natural honesty and wholeness which Iván had known "at the beginning of life"; a subsequent fall into a false relation to life based on a mendacious denial of mortality and ironically coinciding with Iván's rise in the professional world; a second fall, marked by Iván's physical fall from a stepladder, into a conscious awareness of his low estate; and a final reintegration and moral regeneration enabled by this awareness. Thus Tolstoy divines in selfconsciousness both a problem and a solution. Iván awakens to his false relation to life, based on selfish egotism and denial of death, and subsequently adapts a new, right view made possible by a belated acceptance of death as life's ultimate reality. In accepting death, Iván becomes psychologically integrated, and finally capable of the truth and love he had previously forfeited. The catalyst of this change is the introspection and self-analysis which result from the consequences of a seemingly trivial household accident, his plunge from the stepladder. It is in this sense, then, that one may speak of a Fortunate Fall in **Iván Ilých.** I hope to show in what follows that the concept of the Fall is deeply embedded in Tolstoy's story and reflected in many of its narrative details.

The myth of the Fall is chiefly visible as two broad movements or verbal montages: repeated suggestions, especially at the level of worldly affairs, of height, ascent, and flight; and countervailing allusions, in the realm of the spirit, to depths, descent, and collision. These elements are frequently juxtaposed with ironic effect.

The story begins with an ending of sorts, the announcement in the law office of Iván's death. In the funeral scene which follows, Iván's body lies "in a specially heavy way . . . sunk in the soft cushions of the coffin." Iván's temples are "sunken," and Tolstoy twice depicts Iván's nose "seeming to press on [his] upper lip." These details, with their evocation of heaviness, sinking, and pressing, suggest the results of crash and impact, and prefigure the fuller development given the Fall myth in subsequent sections of the story; these recall Iván's domestic and professional life and the events leading to his death.

As a young man eager to follow in the footsteps of his father, a successful and secure government official, Iván is by nature attracted to people of "high" station. Unreflective but capable and industrious, he is known as *"le phènix de la famille"*; the designation is significant, for it points ironically to Iván's future condition as one destined, like the fabulous bird of mythology, to descend and self-destruct in connection with a regenerative process. After marrying and encountering domestic difficulties during his wife's first pregnancy, Iván becomes increasingly ambitious as he "transfer[s] the centre of gravity of his life more and more to his official work." (Of course to shift the center of gravity of anything is to risk upsetting it.) Following a brief occupational "stumble," Iván resumes his climb up the promotional ladder and ultimately attains a satisfactory post two stages "above" his former associates. Intent on arranging the smooth transfer of his family to a new town, Iván journeys there and purchases a splendid new home, one corresponding to his aspirations perfectly and having, among other desirable features, "spacious, lofty reception rooms." One day while attempting to show a workman how a drape should be arranged, Iván falls from a stepladder and knocks his side against a window frame. Apart from inflicting his ultimately fatal injury, Iván's fall precipitates a crisis of the psyche. His illness progresses, and his despair deepens, as the pleasant superficiality with which he has conducted his life gives way beneath the bludgeonings of pain and fear.

Iván's injury does not, however, seem serious at first. He laughs about his fall and shows his newly arrived family how he had frightened the workman when he had gone "flying," a word which recalls the phoenix image and ironically points to Iván's ignorance of the seriousness of his situation. For a while the pleasant decorum of Iván's life reasserts itself as he enjoys a domestic truce with his wife and revels in the satisfactions of home and job. Still, the discomfort in Iván's side does not go away, but gradually worsens. After consulting a physician Iván experiences the realization of his own precarious mortality as a kind of shock: he is "struck" to learn that his case is serious. His physical disorder is uncertainly diagnosed as a "floating kidney"; the designation is significant, for it suggests Iván's isolation and separation from those about him while pointing to a deeper sources of malaise. The most conventional of men, Iván has lived his simple life in pursuit of social decorum and professional success—a life, that is, without meaningful foundations, unattached to anything of transcendent, nurturing value. In Tolstoy's view such an existence is necessarily diseased.

The narration of Iván's final months continues the emphasis on verticality, or up-down relationships, allusions which occur with increasing frequency as his physical condition steadily worsens. Iván "jump[s] up" from his bed to light a candle, fails, and "f[a]ll[s] back on his pillow." In a subsequent effort, he "raise[s] himself," then "f[a]ll[s] on his back, expecting death to come immediately." His wife enters his room and finds him in darkness, staring "upwards." Later, he "drop[s]" into an armchair and must ask his servant Gerásim to "Lift me up."

Such allusions are especially evident in descriptions of Iván's mental state. His heart "s[i]nk[s]" with the return of his pain. He imagines himself being gradually drawn to a terrifying "abyss." His wife's indifference causes him to hate her "from the bottom of his soul" even as he knows "in the depth of his heart" that he is doomed. His efforts to find a mitigating consolation "f[a]ll to pieces." Picturing his life and death in terms of stasis and movement,

Iván tells himself that "life was there and now it is going, going and I cannot stop it. . . . I was here and now I'm going there." His desperate hopes are "shattered" when he remembers with what regularity he has been "going downhill." He feels that his loneliness could not be more complete "at the bottom of the sea or under the earth."

These references to depth and descent are reinforced when Iván, now desperately ill and struggling to make sense of his life, says

> 'There is one bright spot there at the back, at the beginning of life, and afterwards all becomes blacker and proceeds more and more rapidly—in inverse ratio to the square of the distance from death'. . . . And the example of a stone falling downwards with increasing velocity entered his mind.

Realizing that resistance is futile, Iván must simply await death, for him "that dreadful fall and shock and destruction." Significantly, the image of the stone falling with increasing velocity illustrates a fundamental principle of the work's narrative structure: succeeding chapters tend to be shorter than preceding ones, creating the effect of increasing speed. Thus the outer form of Tolstoy's story reflects its central and informing metaphor, the Fall, as the reader, like Iván, experiences events at an accelerating rate.

At times Iván finds some relief from his torment by resting his raised legs on the shoulders of his servant Gerásim. Mentioned several times in the narrative, this awkward position, in which Iván's feet are elevated above his head, suggests the attitude of one hurtling headlong through space.

Shortly before death, Iván feels himself being forced into a dark sack. After an exhausting struggle of three days, he feels himself "struck" in the chest and side and falls through the dreaded dark hole of the sack—only to find himself, after passing through the bottom, in a new world of peace and light. Here it should be noted that Hirschberg's interpretation of this sequence in the uterine terms of birth simply extends the Fall myth previously elaborated, for the birth process obviously involves a physical fall of sorts.

On the face of it, Iván's fall hardly seems fortunate, since it obviously results in intense physical suffering, intolerable mental anguish, and an agonizing sense of alienation from those about him. But in the moral terms in which this story is so largely cast, Iván's fall is a fall into self-consciousness, a new awareness of what he is as a man which ultimately brings a much needed inner regeneration. More specifically, Iván's plunge from the ladder is, as mentioned near the outset, a second fall, the first one having ironically accompanied his ascent in the world. Iván's professional rise had really been a descent because it had been bought at the price of self knowledge and represented a loss of that spontaneity and natural honesty which had been his as a child. Thus Iván later says "It is as if I had been going downhill while I imagined I was going up. . . . I was going up in public opinion, but to the same extent life was ebbing away from me." If Iván's worldly rise is really a descent, his fall from the ladder is, in moral terms, a kind of rise, being a necessary first step on the path toward recovering that natural honesty and wholeness of self best exemplified in the story by Gerásim, who "alone did not lie" and who alone successfully incorporates an acceptance of death in his approach to life. And for the later Tolstoy of *Iván Ilych* such an acceptance had become of paramount importance, since by then (1886) he had come to believe that it is only the pursuit of life in full consciousness and acceptance of death that results in full and worthwhile living.

In attaining his new view, Iván acquires a legitimate individuality which sets him apart from others of his milieu, to whose likeminded values and manners he had earlier thoughtlessly conformed. For if before his fall Iván had been capable and prudent, enjoying the approbation of superiors at work and conducting his decorous private life *comme il faut,* there was lacking in him any real sense of introspection; he had walled himself up in a thoughtless egotism which prevented an active, spontaneous love of others as surely as it obstructed a real comprehension of his own mortality. Now desperately ill, Iván discovers that further evasions are impossible, for "all that had formerly shut off, hidden, and destroyed, his consciousness of death, no longer had that effect." Dreading the inevitable, Iván is forced to reassess his life, which he ultimately apprehends as "not real at all, but a terrible deception which had hidden both life and death." The knowledge that he has wasted his life only intensifies Iván's suffering and further estranges him from his family. However, a sudden change occurs when Iván feels himself pulled through the black sack and emerges into a world of light; he now realizes that his mistaken approach to life can "still be rectified." As though to emphasize this emergence as a vindication of all that Iván has had to endure, Tolstoy compares it to "the sensation one sometimes experiences in a railway carriage when one thinks one is going backwards while one is really going forwards and suddenly becomes aware of the real direction." Purged of his selfish egotism, Iván for the first time feels genuine love and compassion for his wife and young son. Though unable to speak clearly, Iván resolves to act "so as not to hurt them: to release them and free himself. . . ." Accompanying this resolution is the fresh realization that what has been oppressing him is no longer doing so; instead, he experiences a new and liberating sense of joy and peace. That Tolstoy links these blissful feelings to Iván's new commitment to love and pity only underscores what is perhaps the major religious theme of this work: the discovery of God through the discovery of a selfless love of others. It seems significant that the emergence of Iván's new consciousness follows a final period of "three whole days, during which time did not exist for him." These three days during which time is seemingly suspended suggest the period between Christ's death and resurrection. In this connection the words of a bystander, which Iván repeats to himself, "It is finished," recall the final words of the crucified Jesus and likewise suggest Iván's own spiritual regeneration. Following the bystander's remark, Iván expires, at peace with the thought that "Death is finished." (pp. 229-34)

Michael V. Williams, "Tolstoy's 'The Death of
Iván Ilých': After the Fall," in Studies in Short

Fiction, *Vol. 21, No. 3, Summer, 1984, pp. 229-34.*

Rima Salys   (essay date 1986)

[*In the following essay, Salys asserts that Ivan Ilych's physical movements represent aspects and phases of a spiritual journey.*]

The narrator of **The Death of Ivan Il'ič** tells his hero's story with relentless and devastating assurance. He relates the steps leading to Ivan's death—his pleasant and decorous life, his illness, spiritual crisis, and conversion—with the absolute certainty of one who fully knows the nature and consequences of such a life: "most simple and ordinary and most dreadful." It is not immediately evident, however, that the imagery and metaphorical language of the narrative also tell and foretell Ivan's physical decline and spiritual renewal. The peripeteias of Ivan's progress are conveyed through a complex pattern of motion: as he traverses the road of life, his misdirection is suggested in the impedimenta of physical objects that clutter his path and by half-understood warnings in foreign languages, signs that point ironically toward his true destination. Critics have noted that Ivan gradually erects a series of screens to protect himself against all that is unpleasant in life. His work, faith in doctors, wonderworking icons, even the last rites, all provide a temporary protection that death inevitably penetrates. Among these screens against the fact of mortality are Ivan's beloved objects, the stock expressions in foreign languages, and his belief in the conventional road of life or career path. As these screens fall, it becomes clear that objects are also mortal, the stock phrases all have a second, telling meaning, and ultimately—that Ivan has been travelling in the wrong direction.

"Things" abound in **The Death of Ivan Il'ič** because of the acquisitiveness of the story's upper-class characters. Like their owners they are born, live, and die. Ivan's marriage is accompanied by new furniture, new dishes, and new linens. To the living, fresh, new things blunt or screen the awareness of mortality. Paradoxically, Ivan's death is announced by a "newborn" newspaper, fresh and still smelling of printer's ink. The living, however, see no paradox: to them Praskov'ja Fedorovna's announcement is "news" rather than a reminder of death. Ivan's death triggers only surprise and thoughts of their immediate, professional future, not of the day when their names will be announced in black borders. At the funeral service (*panixida*), they fail to heed the dead man's warning, and hastily return to the card game of life, reassured by four fresh candles (we recall the usual symbolism when Ivan drops his candle in chapter 5) and the pleasure of opening and snapping a brand-new deck of cards.

Other objects relate to their owners in a more complex, metonymical fashion. At Ivan's funeral, the rebellious pouffe—no longer new but not yet on its last legs—resembles the middle-aged Petr Ivanovič; giving voice to its decrepitude in an audible snap of its misaligned springs (*ščelknul*), the pouffe conveys perfectly the agitating consciousness of death which he struggles to subdue during his conversation with Praskov'ja Fedorovna ("puf stal volnovat'sja"). The lengthening ash on Petr Ivanovič's cigarette—another *memento mori*—likewise upsets the decorum of their conversation, when Praskov'ja Fedorovna is obliged to pass him an ashtray to protect Ivan's "new" antique table. Just as the cigarette threatens the table, the table endangers Praskov'ja Fedorovna's black lace mantilla, when she snags it on the carving—a rebellion analogous to the pouffe's assault on Petr Ivanovič. The snagging of the black mantilla, an obvious symbol of mourning, is emblematic of the ways in which objects or material concerns impede or screen even the formal expression of grief in the widow's conversation with Petr Ivanovič.

The ominous (if comical) interplay of table, pouffe, cigarette, and mantilla in Ivan's knickknack-cluttered living room prefigures his growing awareness of the mortality of objects during the time between his fall and the first unmistakable signs of illness. Every spot on the tablecloth or upholstery, every broken curtain cord begins to irritate him. Later, as Ivan is forced to face his own mortality, he wanders into his beloved living room and notices a scratch on the lacquered table. Ivan finds that his photo album ("expensive and lovingly compiled"—like his living room and his life) has damaged the table. The torn and topsy-turvy photos upset him because they are a record of his life (the formally posed Victorian album chronicling, among other things, his career progress, e.g., the group photo taken when he leaves his first job), and particularly important during his mortal illness as an attempt to freeze time. Like the family snapshots, his life has been turned upside down, and he is trying to right it. He fails, just as he fails to stop the progress of his illness. Ivan's growing, subconscious recognition of his impending death is reflected in his decision to shift the albums to another corner by the flowers, the very same flowers from which a moment later death peeps out at him. At the funeral service Praskov'ja Fedorovna, while justifying her unimpaired practical abilities to Petr Ivanovič, casually moves the albums to one side, as if to sweep aside the life Ivan had so carefully constructed. The dying man had called the table and albums "this whole établissement"; the foreign phrase (as we will see later) underscores the narrator's ironic view of Ivan's life.

In the same way, throughout the story the narrator takes a skeptical view of the euphemistic aspect of language, consistently removing its figurative screens to expose literal meanings, all of which convey a truth about Ivan. The French and Latin maxims and phrases in chapter 2 all have a second, "telling" meaning. Ivan Il'ič supposes that his wife is disrupting their pleasant and proper life purely on a whim (*de gaité de cœur*), when in fact she is hurt by his neglect and lack of sympathy for the complications of childbearing, and takes her revenge on purpose and out of "tristesse" rather than "gaité." The other foreign phrases all pertain to Ivan Il'ič, and just as death eventually penetrates all the screens in his existence, the reader notices that with Ivan's illness, all foreign expressions revert to their literal meanings. Ivan is *le phénix de la famille,* the well-adjusted middle child, who has revived the family's fortunes; yet the phrase ultimately points to his death and spiritual rebirth rather than to his material success. The *respice finem* medal he wears attached, appropriately, to

his watch is a lawyer's affectation, but also conveys a warning to "look to the end." Ivan's youthful sins are excused with a tolerant shrug—*il faut que jeunesse se passe* (the chic of a French phrase screens his ugly behavior all the better), yet the reader is warned that youth is passing too. In society Ivan is considered a good fellow (*bon enfant*). Years later, as he reviews the past, he sees that his morally good childhood was the only patch of light in a life which led inexorably into the black sack: "There had been one bright spot back there, at the beginning of life, and then everything got blacker and blacker." Ivan and his entire life are very much *comme il faut,* yet during his illness the affirmation of decorum reverses to doubt: "Perhaps I did not live as I *should* have [*ne tak kak dolžno*]?", and in death his face again reveals the literal meaning of the phrase: "The expression on the face said that what needed to be done [*čto nužno bylo sdelat'*], had been done, and done rightly."

Although objects and language both point the way to Ivan's destination, the central metaphor for his physical decline and spiritual renewal is the "road of life" must have attracted Tolstoj because of its accessibility to all readers—a major aim of his post-conversion writings. Walking, stepping, and other related metaphors consistently record Ivan's moral progress along the road of life and later, when he can no longer walk, mirror his shifting state of mind at different stages of his illness.

Ivan Il'ič is already dead as the story begins. Because his life's journey has been completed, his spatial immobility is emphasized: "The dead man lay, as dead men always lie, in an especially heavy way." Chapter 1 is, in fact, concerned with the living, the other characters, who either ignore Ivan's silent warning or are annoyed and discomfited by this indecorous reminder of their own mortality. Petr Ivanovič, another Ivan still en route to his destination, looks at his feet during the funeral service and then ignores the dead man's warning. Two other characters reflect Ivan's own evasions at different stages of his life. Entering Ivan's house, Petr Ivanovič sees the dapper Švarc, whom Ivan had earlier recognized as his double, at the head of the stairs. Having reached the pinnacle of worldly success, Švarc is in his prime, and therefore stands at the top of the staircase of life. Ivan's son, Vasja, just beginning his climb, materializes from under the lower part of the staircase. Each double recalls a different though already corrupt stage of the dead man's existence—Ivan as sex-obsessed but still sensitive adolescent and late as callous and complacent man of the world.

The rest of the story (chapters 2-12) chronicles Ivan's life, illness, and death. Commentators have pointed out that the content ironically reverses the meaning of the title. Ivan's existence turns out to have been a living death, while his death is a rebirth into a new spiritual life. In keeping with this reversal, Ivan sets out upon the path of (or rather *to*) life not in childhood or adolescence, but only when he falls ill and begins to question the ideas upon which his existence is predicted. In spite of all his "activity" on the conventional road of life in chapter 2 (schooling, love affairs, marriage, children, and career peripeteias), the stepping/walking imagery which appears later in the story is missing at this point because Ivan, before his illness, has been on the wrong road.

The first stage of his progress is marked by a step, albeit a false one. While showing the upholsterer how to hang curtains, the hero misses a step and falls, banging his side against the knob of the window frame. Ivan is injured by the naked reality of life—essentially indecorous, unbeautiful, and Darwinian—as seen through the bare window which he has just been trying to cover up with one of the many screens against reality he sets up in the course of his life. In his preoccupation with decorating the new apartment, which supersedes even his interest in the coveted appointment, Ivan reaches new heights of trivial and frivolous materialism (a judge concerning himself with pink cretonne and knickknacks), and it is just at this point, at the pinnacle of material success, recalling the staircase of chapter 1, that he stumbles and falls off the ladder. Ivan later boasts to his family about his lucky escape ("someone else would have been killed"), yet he is already morally dead.

The consequences of Ivan's fall, the first step toward a spiritual life, are at first suppressed; all is well for a time, or so Ivan wants to think. He feels well: "Čuvstvuju, čto s menja soskočilo let 15", but in its literal meaning, the phrase in fact hints at the 15 years of life he has lost through his fall. The narrator's simple but devastating summary conveys Ivan's complacent sense of invulnerability and tranquil motion: "And so they lived. And so everything went [*šlo*], without change, and everything was very good." Ivan realizes that he is dying only after his brother-in-law's visit, when the progress of his illness, as well as his own increasing superfluity to the world, are expressed in terms of walking, approaching ever closer to an unavoidable abyss: "I kept coming [*vse šel*] closer and closer"; "it happened step by step." Ivan tries twice to light a symbolic candle of life in the dark room, but fumbles and drops it, cannot find the matches, and finally throws himself back onto the bed in despair. As his wife brings him another candle, he lies panting, very much like one who is no longer walking the path of life, but is now running a race against time and death: "He lay there breathing heavily and quickly, like a man who had run a verst." As Ivan's disease progresses, physical movement become more difficult. Rising from the commode, he is horrified by the sight of his emaciated, weak thighs. When physical mobility (with its implied link to the outside world) is restricted, Ivan sets out upon the mental journey which will lead first to awareness of the hypocrisy of his past life and eventually to his conversion.

At the stage of his illness when he is no longer able to move about freely, Ivan requires the assistance of Gerasim, who serves as a model of Christian behavior. Unlike his physically and spiritually debilitated master, the kindhearted and cheerful peasant walks with a distinctively light step, an obvious metaphor for the way he goes through life—with the simplicity, ease, and acceptance of "God's will" born of religious faith. Gerasim half carries, half helps Ivan walk across the room from commode to bed and then spends hours holding Ivan's legs aloft on his shoulders. This is viewed as a sick man's eccentricity by those around Ivan; in reality Gerasim is helping (as if bearing) his master along the path to a new spiritual life. The narrator stresses metaphorical "carrying" in his explanation of Gerasim's motives: "He is not oppressed by his work precisely because he bears it [*neset ego*] for a dying man and hopes that when his time comes someone will also do the same [*poneset tot že trud*] for him." Gerasim's act is foreshadowed in the earlier reference to Princess Trufonova, the sister of the founder of the society *Unesi ty moe gore* (Carry away my sorrow). The parodistic name of the charitable organization, derived from a colloquial expression of disapproval, like all the foreign phrases pertaining to Ivan's earlier life, undergoes an ironic "unscreening" or literalizing in the context of his illness. It is the peasant Gerasim, close to the tradition of the folksong "Unesi ty moe gore, bystra rečenka, s soboj," and not the society ladies, who will bear the burden of Ivan's sorrow or misfortune.

Before Ivan Il'ič can be saved, he must recognize the moral wrongness of his entire adult life, a truth he resists and the last screen he maintains, up to the very moment of his death. The first step in the process is his gradually developing awareness of "the lie," the hypocrisy governing all levels of human contact which torments him even more than his physical pain. Chapter 8 distills and concentrates the various social screens (feigned conjugal love and society's refusal to acknowledge, i.e., speak about, death) which Ivan's heightened consciousness now penetrates.

Realizing the hypocrisy around him leads Ivan to doubt for the first time the direction of his past life, and once again his thought is expressed in terms of concrete physical motion: "It is as if I had been going [*šel*] steadily downhill while imagining that I was going uphill. . . . I was going uphill in public opinion, and to the same degree life was ebbing away from me [*rovno nastol'ko iz-pod menja uxodila žizn'*]." The mountain of worldly success here again recalls Švarc's complacent pose at the top of the staircase in chapter 1.

As Ivan's illness progresses, his living space contracts—from the world to his apartment, to his study, and finally to the sofa on which he dies. In the absence of external events, Tolstoj now turns to the movement of Ivan's mind to maintain the momentum of the story. Because Ivan can no longer walk, his movements on the sofa take on particular significance, although most of the "motion" of the story, the train of thought leading to his conversion, now takes place in his head. Beginning with Ivan's realization in chapter 5 that he is dying, that life is escaping him ("Da, žizn' byla i vot uxodit, uxodit"), the figurative phrases of mental motion ("train of thought or memory," "current of feeling") enter the text: "On pytalsja vozvratit'sja k prežnim xodam mysli"; "vmeste s ètim xodom vospominanija . . . .'

As Ivan's spiritual life intensifies in his steadily constricting physical space, mental motion increases (his struggles to get into and out of the black sack in the first dream). Simultaneously, his actual physical motion wanes: he awakens and lies looking at his emaciated legs. Ivan's shifting positions on the sofa also seem to relate to specific aspects of his mental perambulations. When he first begins to think about the reasons for his illness, he turns onto his side, weeps in self-pity and seeks from God an explanation of his torment. As the internal dialectic—really court briefs for and against the correctness of Ivan's life—intensifies, he turns over onto his other side, towards the wall, and begins to think. Refusing to believe his life could have been wrong, he reaches an impasse in his search for justification of his pain; literally and metaphorically he faces the wall: "No matter how much he thought, he did not find an answer."

For the entire next chapter, Ivan continues in the same position, his physical isolation now corresponding to his total estrangement from those around him. When he is completely confined to the sofa, his mental activity increases even more, as if the spatial compression engendered a previously unknown density of memories. Ivan now journeys in time (*xod vospominanij*) from the present to childhood and then back. The movement of Ivan's thoughts through time provides him with a perspective from which he can weigh the contrasting values of his childhood and maturity and come to see the direction of his entire life. A button on the sofa and wrinkles in the leather (an even narrower spatial focus) impel him on another journey from the materialistic present ("Morocco is expensive and flimsy; there had been a quarrel because of it") to his childhood and unselfish mother-love ("But there had been another morocco and another quarrel when we tore Father's briefcase and were punished, and Mama brought us tarts".

This "Recherche du temps perdu" leads to yet another train of thought about the progress of his illness: "vmeste s ètim xodom vospominanija, u nego v duše šel drugoj xod vospominanij—o tom, kak usilivalas' i rosla ego bolezn." Ivan identifies the course of his life—morally all downhill—with the course of his disease ("Just as the torments get [*idut*] worse and worse, so all of life got [*šla*] worse and worse"), thereby progressing toward an acknowledgement of spiritual death in life, the reversal implied by the story's title. Mental motion accelerates even more as Ivan compares his life to a stone gathering speed in its fall—another image of very concrete spatial movement. The inevitable progress of Ivan's life, its temporal and spatial movement toward death, has assumed the incontrovertible authority of physical law. Yet, in spite of his mental peregrinations, as the chapter concludes, Ivan is again at a dead end, facing the back of the sofa, because he still refuses to follow the line of thought and memory to its logical conclusion—the incorrectness of his life.

Two weeks later, on the crest of another wordly success (Petriščev's longawaited proposal to Liza), the sick man takes a turn for the worse (i.e., the better) and for the first time not only thinks, but also speaks the unscreened truth to his family and doctor: "Let me die in peace"; "you know you can't do anything to help." Both before and after this scene the narrator stresses that Ivan is now lying in a different position: "He lay down on his back and began to review his whole life in a completely new way." In its spatial "openness," Ivan's body position (the same as in his dignified coffin repose) clearly parallels his acknowledgement of the incorrectness of his life, and con-

trasts to his earlier doubts about its value and the rejection of these doubts while lying on his side, facing the wall.

Ivan's acceptance of his wasted life in chapter 11 is short-lived. Soon he is again assailed by doubts, abandons the "open" position, and begins to toss about on the sofa, as if in mental and physical uncertainty. The screen of religion soothes him temporarily, but the sight of Praskov'ja Fedorovna and his false answer to her query about his health ("You feel better, don't you?") place the lie squarely before him once again. By agreeing that he is better, Ivan actively participates in the deception, and consequently his spatial reaction is all the more extreme: "Having said 'yes,' looking her straight in the face, he turned face down with a rapidity unusual for his weak condition." In complete negation of the earlier "open" position, he turns over on his belly, just as he has once again turned away from an admission of guilt: "At the moment he answered his wife he understood that he was lost . . . that the end had come . . . and his doubts were still not resolved."

During the last three days of his life Ivan's space narrows to the tunnel of the black sack, but mental motion continues with even augmented intensity ("he struggled," "thrashed about," "can't squeeze through") in the decreasing area. Two related images of spatial motion express the final train of thought which leads to his change of heart. In the first, Ivan himself is trapped and finds release; he struggles inside the black sack and eventually falls out through a hole. At the same time, within Ivan exists a blockage which is eventually expelled: "What oppressed him and would not come out" suddenly was coming out all at once, from all sides. The images narrow in spatial sequence: Ivan is inside the sack struggling to escape; yet at the same time something is inside him and wants to come out.

The two parallel struggles represent Ivan's isolation in sickness and in health. All his life Ivan has set up screens between himself and others, practiced voluntary isolation, in effect a negative self-enclosure. With the onset of his illness, however, isolation is forcibly imposed from without: his space contracts from the total openness of life in the world to the progressively more constricted area of apartment and sofa. Confined to the sofa, turned to the wall, his forcible isolation (the opposite of his lifelong self-imposed isolation) leads to productive reflection upon the past and present.

Ivan's bad life has steadily darkened into the black sack of pain and doubt, the epitome of the isolation forced upon him by his illness; the blockage he labors to expel is the moral defect within Ivan—his self-absorption and subsequent lack of compassion for others that caused him to set up screens against them—which he has refused to recognize up to this moment. Ivan breaks out of the sack at the same time he admits the badness of his life and makes human contact, when his hand falls upon his son's head. His internal blockage dissipates when he stops thinking only of himself, asks forgiveness for his indifference toward his wife and son ("He wanted to say 'forgive,' but said, 'let me through' "—another way out of the sack), and acts to express compassion. The direction of both actions is from confinement (also implying darkness) to openness and light. When Ivan is able to pity someone other than himself, he breaks through the external barrier of the sack and at the same time breaks down the barrier within.

The moment of illumination in Ivan's journey, when he finally admits that he has lived badly, is expressed in a modern equivalent of the road of life metaphor: "What happened to him was what he used to experience in a railway car when you think you are going forward, but you are going backward, and suddenly you become aware of the real direction." Tolstoj had employed the same metaphor in **Anna Karenina:** returning to Petersburg after her first meeting with Vronskij, Anna thinks about him and gradually loses her moral bearings. Her confusion is reflected in her perception of the train's direction: "She continually had moments of doubt; was the car going forward or backward, or not moving at all?" When Ivan Il'ič recognizes the right direction, his journey comes to an end: "He inhaled, stopped in the middle of a sigh, stretched out and died." The climactic motion of Ivan's journey fulfils the logic of reversal that governs the story's structure. Having arrived at its destination, his body stretches out and relaxes, assuming the ease and natural dignity it lacked in a life constricted by the moral rigor mortis Ivan escapes only in the moment of death. (pp. 18-26)

Rima Salys, "Signs on the Road of Life: 'The Death of Ivan Il'ič'," in Slavic and East-European Journal, *Vol. 30, No. 1, Spring, 1986, pp. 18-28.*

FURTHER READING

Dayananda, Y. J. *"The Death of Ivan Ilych:* A Psychological Study *On Death and Dying." Literature and Psychology* XXII, No. 4 (1972): 191-98.
> Juxtaposes Tolstoy's conception of death in *The Death of Ivan Ilych* with that of the psychiatrist Elizabeth Kübler-Ross in her *On Death and Dying* (1969), observing that Ivan exemplifies all five of the psychological stages of the terminally-ill patient: Denial and Isolation, Anger, Bargaining, Depression, and Acceptance.

Glicksberg, Charles I. "Tolstoy and the Death of Ivan Ilyitch," In his *The Ironic Vision in Modern Literature,* pp. 81-86. The Hague, Netherlands: Martinus Nijhoff, 1969.
> Detects an essentially modern view of death in the work.

Hajnady, Zoltan. "Ivan Ilyich and Existence Compared to Death: Lev Tolstoj and Martin Heidegger." *Acta Litteraria* 27, Nos. 1-2 (1985): 3-15.
> Indicates parallels between *The Death of Ivan Ilych* and Martin Heidegger's existential philosophy.

Howe, Irving. Introduction to *The Death of Ivan Ilych,* by Leo Tolstoy. In *Classics of Modern Fiction: Eight Short Novels,* edited by Irving Howe, pp. 113-21. New York: Harcourt, Brace & World, 1968.
> Concise summary of the primary themes of *The Death of Ivan Ilych.*

Meyers, Jeffrey. "Tolstoy and Hemingway: *The Death of Ivan Ilych* and 'The Snows of Kilimanjaro'." In his *Disease and the Novel, 1880-1960,* pp. 19-29. London: Macmillan, 1985.
> Compares the two works as stories of "disease and dying, revelation and redemption," and discusses Tolstoy's influence on Ernest Hemingway.

Parthé, Kathleen. "The Metamorphosis of Death in Tolstoy." *Language and Style* 18, No. 2 (Spring 1985): 205-14.
> Discusses the literary devices employed by Tolstoy in *The Death of Ivan Ilych* which "create a compelling and unusual vision of death."

Perrett, Roy W. "Tolstoy, Death and the Meaning of Life." *Philosophy* 60, No. 232 (April 1985): 231-45.
> Examines Tolstoy's spiritual crisis and his subsequent views on death as expressed in both his nonfiction work *A Confession* and in *The Death of Ivan Ilych.*

Rahv, Philip. "The Death of Ivan Ilyich and Joseph K." In his *Image and Idea: Twenty Essays on Literary Themes,* pp. 121-39. Norfolk, Conn.: New Directions, 1957.
> Comparison of the protagonists and dramatic situations in *The Death of Ivan Ilych* and Franz Kafka's *The Trial.*

Rogers, Philip. "Scrooge on the Neva: Dickens and Tolstoj's *Death of Ivan Il'ič." Comparative Literature* 40, No. 3 (Summer 1988): 193-218.
> Focuses on Tolstoy's admiration for the novels of Charles Dickens and describes how Dickens's characterization, narrative technique, and themes influenced the writing of *The Death of Ivan Ilych.*

Speirs, Logan. "Chekhov and Later Tolstoy: Studies in Death." In his *Tolstoy and Chekhov,* pp. 141-53. London: Cambridge University Press, 1971.
> Compares *The Death of Ivan Ilych* to Chekhov's *A Dreary Story,* asserting that Tolstoy's story reflects a genuine despair and lack of faith, while Chekhov's story contains a degree of excitement and hope.

Turner, C. J. G. "The Language of Fiction: Word-Clusters in Tolstoy's *The Death of Ivan Ilyich." The Modern Language Review* 65, No. 1 (January 1970): 116-21.
> Analyzes how Tolstoy used two groups of "word-clusters"—"the groups consisting firstly of *priyatny* (pleasant), *prilichny* (proper) and cognate or related terms, and secondly of *lozh'* (falsehood), *obman* (deceit) and cognate or related terms"—to structure the narrative of *The Death of Ivan Ilych.*

Wasiolek, Edward. "Tolstoy's *The Death of Ivan Ilytch* and Jamesian Fictional Imperatives." In *Tolstoy: A Collection of Critical Essays,* edited by Ralph E. Matlaw, pp. 146-56. Englewood Cliffs, N.J.: Prentice-Hall, 1967.
> Contrasts Tolstoy's literary technique in *The Death of Ivan Ilych* with that of Henry James.

Wexelblatt, Robert. "The Higher Parody: Ivan Ilych's Metamorphosis and the Death of Gregor Samsa." *The Massachusetts Review* XXI, No. 3 (Fall 1980): 601-28.
> Extension of Philip Rahv's essay on "The Death of Ivan Ilych" and Franz Kafka (cited above), shifting the basis of comparison from *The Trial* to "The Metamorphosis," a work in which, Wexelblatt asserts, "Kafka [compress-

es] what Tolstoy has done more discursively into a pointed image."

Winn, Harbour. "Hemingway's African Stories and Tolstoy's 'Illich'." *Studies in Short Fiction* 18, No. 4 (Fall 1981): 451-53.

Compares *The Death of Ivan Ilych* to Ernest Hemingway's short stories "The Snows of Kilimanjaro" and "The Short Happy Life of Francis Macomber," citing parallels in their plots and themes.

Additional coverage of Tolstoy's life and career is contained in the following sources published by Gale Research: *Contemporary Authors,* Vols. 104, 123; and *Something about the Author,* Vol. 26.

Nathanael West

Miss Lonelyhearts

(Born Nathan Weinstein) American novelist, screenwriter, and editor.

The following entry contains criticism of West's novel *Miss Lonelyhearts* (1933). For discussion of West's complete career, see *TCLC,* Volumes 1 and 14.

INTRODUCTION

Miss Lonelyhearts is considered West's most artistically accomplished novel and an important early twentieth-century literary exploration of alienation and despair. The novel concerns the spiritual crisis of an advice columnist who becomes increasingly disturbed by the letters he receives and by his inability to help those who write to him. Focusing on human suffering and the range of individual responses to it, *Miss Lonelyhearts* asserts the futility of attempts to effect positive change in people's lives or to assign meaning and purpose to existence. In addition, West's use of grotesque, hallucinatory imagery and cruel humor in *Miss Lonelyhearts* has led critics to regard this novel as an important forerunner of Surrealism and black humor in American literature.

West reportedly conceived of *Miss Lonelyhearts* in 1929, when he and the humorist S. J. Perelman dined with an advice columnist who thought that Perelman could derive comic material from the correspondence she received. Perelman found the letters an unpromising source of comedy, but West was inspired by the material. He began to develop a novel focusing on an advice columnist while he sought publication of his first novel, *The Dream Life of Balso Snell,* which was accepted by a publisher in 1931. West continued to work on *Miss Lonelyhearts* while managing a hotel owned by relatives in New York City. The dramatist Lillian Hellman, a guest at the hotel during this period, later suggested that West partially based the letter-writers in *Miss Lonelyhearts* on lodgers he observed there. Early drafts of the novel, which West published in *Contact,* a little magazine he edited with the poet William Carlos Williams, attracted some favorable notice, including an appreciative essay by Ezra Pound in the Italian journal *Il mare.* West finished *Miss Lonelyhearts* in 1932, and it was published the following year.

The protagonist of *Miss Lonelyhearts* is an otherwise unnamed young male journalist who edits an advice column for a metropolitan newspaper. Initially unconcerned with the assignment, he grows increasingly distressed by the letters, which bespeak the suffering, despair, and violence that West perceived, according to Thomas H. Jackson, as "definitive qualities of modern life." Identifying himself as a lover of humanity with a "Christ complex," Lonelyhearts becomes obsessed with the misery of his correspon-

dents. He is tormented by the feature editor, Shrike, who savagely mocks the letter-writers and the columnist's messianic aspirations, and by his own inability to offer effective help. Seeking first-hand understanding of the problems that beset his correspondents, Lonelyhearts attempts to involve himself in their lives. These encounters yield disastrous results: one woman, for example, pursues an adulterous affair with Lonelyhearts, and, when an old man accosted at random is unwilling to discuss his life, the columnist beats him. Lonelyhearts gradually reaches a state of insanity in which he imagines God as his editor approving drafts of his column. In the climax of the novel Lonelyhearts is shot and killed during a struggle with a correspondent whom he had earlier embraced as an embodiment of suffering humankind.

The power and effectiveness of *Miss Lonelyhearts* has been largely attributed to West's ironic use of religious imagery and doctrines, substituting manufactured dreams promoted by the mass media for the eternal truths thought attainable through spiritual means. One by one the values in which Lonelyhearts has been taught to believe—love, success, religion—fail to alleviate his desperation. Other possible means of fulfillment, including primitivism, hedonism, or immersion in art and culture, are ridiculed and dismissed by Shrike in one of the novel's most renowned and powerful passages. The conclusion of *Miss Lonelyhearts* is often interpreted as an assertion that the love and compassion central to Judeo-Christian ethics are powerless and meaningless in a brutal, random world.

Much of the commentary on *Miss Lonelyhearts* focuses on the protagonist. The advice columnist, dispensing platitudes when confronted with genuine anguish, has been described as an apt embodiment of the socially and financially unstable 1930s, and most critics concur that West's decision to identify his protagonist only as Miss Lonelyhearts serves to underscore the dehumanizing temper of the times by equating the person with his public function. West initially planned Lonelyhearts's conflict to be primarily internal, and much of the dialogue assigned to Shrike was originally intended to be spoken by Lonelyhearts. The development of Shrike as the novel's antagonist and the scenes in which Lonelyhearts and Shrike are seen in opposition suggest that West intended the two to represent antithetical poles of faith and cynicism, or innocence and experience. Shrike, savagely fatalistic in his point of view, is commonly interpreted as a demon or antichrist figure, although some commentators have regarded him as an early example of the nihilistic antihero in twentieth-century American literature.

Miss Lonelyhearts is generally considered a small masterpiece, albeit one that has received divisive and contradictory critical assessments. Stanley Edgar Hyman, one of the earliest important critics to write extensively on West, suggested that *Miss Lonelyhearts* "seems to have come into the world with hardly a predecessor, but it has itself influenced a great many American novelists since." Others, however, have explored numerous influences on West's work. Fyodor Dostoevsky is among the most prominent literary influences cited, an influence whom critics have noted particularly in West's depiction of devotion to the teachings of Christ and in the dualistic presentation of good and evil within the protagonist, Lonelyhearts. Many critics also advance a Freudian psychosexual interpretation of the novel, while other commentators cite the influence of the philosopher William James's theoretical writings on the nature of religious experience. West's use of hallucinatory images and compressed language has been favorably compared to that of French Symbolists and Surrealists, most notably Charles Baudelaire. In addition, West's acute awareness of suffering in the modern world is often discussed as a more pessimistic vision of the perspective presented by T. S. Eliot in *The Waste Land. Miss Lonelyhearts,* however, is to most commentators almost unremittingly bleak, depicting modern life as a spiritual wasteland inhabited by stereotyped characters who represent various neurotic responses to the spiritual malaise of the twentieth century.

Florence Haxton Britten   (essay date 1933)

[*In the following review, Britten commends the original-*

ity of Miss Lonelyhearts *and notes that it is somewhat shocking and grotesque.*]

It is easy enough to indicate the materials which Mr. Nathanael West has used in his grotesquely beautiful novel **Miss Lonelyhearts.** But it is a far more difficult matter to convey some notion of the intensely original incandescence of spirit which fuses these simple elements. Chapter after brilliantly written chapter moving like a rocket in mid flight, neither falls nor fails. The book itself ends with the sudden, swift delumination of a light going out.

In **Miss Lonelyhearts** we have the story of a young man who is unable to catch hold of his spiritual destiny even by his fingernails. His plight is as ludicrous as it is pitiful.

The young crusader is a lineal descendant of the New England Puritan tradition. He has come to a dead-end road in front of the typewriter of Miss Lonelyhearts. He *is* Miss Lonelyhearts, editor of a column on a metropolitan daily newspaper. It is the fashion in the office to laugh at the letters. Shrike, the feature editor, a natural scoffer, leads the sardonic cheers over appeals signed Broken-hearted, Sick-of-it-all, Disillusioned. The woman who thinks she will kill herself rather than have another child, "her kidneys hurt so much"; the young girl who—like the pobbles, was it?—had no nose; the fifteen-year-old whose deaf and dumb sister has been precociously learning the facts of life, "so please what would you do if the same happened in your family?" and the woman wed to a cripple, who pines for a more vigorous love—all these, "stamped from the dough of suffering with a heart-shaped cookie knife," submerge Miss Lonelyhearts in their ridiculous sorrows. Neither naive nor a weakling, he is oppressed. He cannot forget them nor help them—nor help himself. He goes down, in the end, like a drowning man. And even that final involuntary gesture has its ironic humor.

Much of **Miss Lonelyhearts** is set in the speakeasy where the newspaper crowd does most of its drinking. It is drinking of the more serious sort, which enables a fellow to forget for a while a disorganized world. Under its stimulus our hero grows loud-mouthed and violent, with an absorbing aftermath of mystic wistfulness. Christ is a name which has subconscious magic for him, which expresses somehow his love and pity for humanity which he can't get hold of and grip and which slips off continually into futility and oblivion. A period of illness is a soothing escape for him—as he well knows. But love—he tries all kinds of it—seems to have no lift for him whatsoever. The intimate physical scenes, by the way, are boldly convincing. In technique they bear, in about equal proportions, resemblance to Ben Hecht and the Dadaists!

This literary comparison might perhaps be applied, without intent to depreciate, to the novel as a whole. If you are thoroughly shockproof **Miss Lonelyhearts** will richly reward your attention.

Florence Haxton Britten, "Grotesquely Beautiful Novel," in New York Herald Tribune Books, *April 30, 1933, p. 6.*

A. M. Tibbetts   (essay date 1960)

[*In the following excerpt, Tibbetts revaluates West's growing critical reputation, maintaining that West depicted a grotesque, unrealistic, and incomplete view of reality. Tibbetts pronounces* Miss Lonelyhearts *successful not because of its satire, which he considers flawed, but because of its compact structure, precise imagery, and judiciously employed elements of high comedy.*]

Nathanael West wrote four unsuccessful books before he died in 1940. As is so often the case, with his death came reappraisal; and although *The Dream Life of Balso Snell* and *A Cool Million* have been universally condemned, *Miss Lonelyhearts* and *The Day of the Locust* have risen in critical esteem, until now it appears that these two small books will give West a solid, lasting literary reputation—with the critics, if not with ordinary readers. Norman Podhoretz, for example, has remarked in the *New Yorker* that in his pursuit of "the big, significant things," West deserves more credit than either of his contemporaries, Hemingway or Fitzgerald.

It seems to me that some critical balance needs to be applied to Nathanael West before post-mortem adulation gets completely out of hand. West was simply not that good a writer; indeed in some ways he was a very bad writer. And I must throw in my lot with the "ordinary" book-buyers who may have sensed what was wrong with his art. The public will swallow a satirist's work if his world is complete and recognizable; West's was not. His world was cut in two—and half of it was missing.

West himself recognized this: "If I put into *The Day of the Locust* any of the sincere, honest people . . . those chapters couldn't be written satirically and the whole fabric of the peculiar half-world which I attempted to create would be badly torn by them. . . . " The trouble is (besides the fact that West did not understand the nature of satire) that the missing half is the most important part of an artist's invention—real people doing real things. There is simply not enough in West's two best novels about recognizable people and recognizable situations.

Consider [this plot]. . . . *Miss Lonelyhearts* is about a male writer of an advice-to-the-lovelorn-and-the-miserable column. Beyond the name, Miss Lonelyhearts, he is never identified. He takes his job far too seriously, is needled and harassed by his editor, Shrike. Stung by his knowledge that he is playing a journalistic Christ to near-illiterates, whom he very badly wants to help, he begins quietly to go insane. He tries various ways of escape: fresh, young love; organized religion; lechery; homosexuality; a return to Rousseau's Natural Man; and finally in a blaze of insane religiosity, gets himself murdered ("crucified") by a cripple he is trying to help. (p. 8)

As I said before, West's people are not real. They are not even physiologically real. When Miss Lonelyhearts takes a drink, the alcohol warms "only the lining of his stomach." . . .

West purposely distorted his characters, much as a cartoonist does, giving a personality a two-dimensional effect. (p. 9)

[The] fixed, mask-like quality of West's people has on the reader an effect like that on the theatre-goer of O'Neill's experimentations with masks in his plays. (pp. 9-10)

In a play, one can watch an actor move about the stage, perhaps take off his mask—at any rate, act like a human being. But in a novel a character is what the writer says he is; and if the writer describes someone, as West describes Shrike in *Miss Lonelyhearts,* as a mask-like figure, the reader must see him that way:

> Although his gestures were elaborate, his face was a blank. He practiced a trick used much by moving-picture comedians—the dead pan. No matter how fantastic or excited his speech, he never changed his expression. Under the shining white globe of his brow, his features huddled together in a dead, gray triangle.

Not only is this true of Shrike; other characters are similarly mask-like. There is the cripple who finally kills Miss Lonelyhearts:

> The cripple had a very strange face. His eyes failed to balance; his mouth was not under his nose; his forehead was square and bony; and his round chin was like a forehead in miniature. He looked like one of those composite photographs used by screen magazines in guessing contests.

Miss Lonelyhearts himself is a mask, and when he asks his girl to marry him, he sees only what stands for her—her "party dress": "He begged the party dress to marry him, saying all the things it expected to hear . . . "

It is probably to be expected, then, that since West's masks are not human they will not have human emotions. Their strongest non-human quality is that they cannot *love;* even the idea of love is torture. (p. 10)

It may be objected that in this very lack of humanity and love in West's books there lies his peculiar strength. In a sense, possibly, this is true: he tries to expose the sterility of modern life by creating sterile people in sterile situations; which, practically speaking, is similar to the theory that one shows boredom in a novel by boring the reader. Whether this idea is valid or not, and it is certainly arguable, I think that West's real excellence as an artist lies elsewhere, and can be found only in *Miss Lonelyhearts.* The power of this extremely short novelette comes not from its satire, but from its beautifully ordered, tight structure; its clean, brilliant imagery; and the traces of high comedy played out in its fine, sharp scenes.

Structurally, *Miss Lonelyhearts* is perfectly tight; there is no hole or flaw anywhere. In the beginning, Miss Lonelyhearts is a man who must help, metaphorically, all mankind; he must love these unlovable "proles" who write ungrammatically to him for spiritual aid. But he cannot. He can love nobody. From the beginning of the book, then, each chapter is part of his struggle to love somebody; and each chapter shows him trying a different path towards love: "Miss Lonelyhearts and the Clean Old Man," "Miss Lonelyhearts and the Cripple," "Miss Lonelyhearts and the Party Dress," until finally, in a parody of the crucifixion, "Miss Lonelyhearts Has a Religious Experience," and is murdered by the cripple.

The point of view of *Miss Lonelyhearts* is superbly consistent. The reader is always with the protagonist, and all characters are seen from the overlapping (but complementary and unifying) viewpoints of the main character and the omniscient author. (pp. 11-12)

The third good element in the structure of *Miss Lonelyhearts* is scenic. West tended to close his highly dramatic and well-knit chapters in a final culminating scene which can be very effective. For instance, at the end of the chapter on Shrike, called "Miss Lonelyhearts and the Dead Pan," Shrike is sitting at the back of a bar haranguing on religion and seducing a girl at the same time:

> "The Catholic hunts this bird [the soul] with bread and wine, the Hebrew with a golden ruler, the Protestant on leaden feet with leaden words, the Buddhist with gestures, the Negro with blood. I spit on them all. Phooh! And I call upon you to spit. Phooh! Do you stuff birds? No, my dears, taxidermy is not a religion. No! A thousand times no. Better, I say unto you, better a live bird in the jungle of the body than two stuffed birds on the library table."

> His caresses kept pace with the sermon. When he had reached the end, he buried his triangular face like the blade of a hatchet in her neck.

West's poetic imagery in *Miss Lonelyhearts* is as clear, cold and accurate as a dagger of ice. Miss Lonelyhearts

> entered the park at the North Gate and swallowed mouthfuls of the heavy shade that curtained its arch. He walked into the shadow of a lamp-post that lay on the path like a spear. It pierced him like a spear. . . . the gray sky looked as if it had been rubbed with a soiled eraser.

And:

> Miss Lonelyhearts went home in a taxi. He lived by himself in a room that was as full of shadows as an old steel engraving.

And:

> He tried to reply to her greeting and discovered that his tongue had become a fat thumb.

And:

> The whiskey was good and he felt warm and sure. Through the light-blue tobacco smoke, the mahogany bar shone like wet gold. The glasses and bottles, their high lights exploding, rang like a battery of little bells when the bartender touched them together.

There is something almost elegant about the glittering, slightly insane perfection of these images, set as they are in the bare formal structure of the novelette like finely-cut stones in an unornamented ring.

Contrasted to this poetry in *Miss Lonelyhearts* are a series of ironies which are sometimes close to comedy. Miss Lonelyhearts tries and tries to see, by looking down her blouse, what the medal is that Mrs. Shrike wears around her neck. After much teasing, it is brought out, and "he

was able to read the inscription: 'Awarded by the Boston Latin School for first place in the 100 yd. dash.' "

Miss Lonelyheart's bout with the elephantine Mrs. Doyle is high comedy:

> He had always been the pursuer, but now found a strange pleasure in having the roles reversed. He drew back when she reached for a kiss. She caught his head and kissed him on his mouth. . . .

> "Don't," she begged.

> "Don't what?"

> "Oh, darling, turn out the light."

> He smoked a cigarette, standing in the dark and listening to her undress. She made sea sounds; something flapped like a sail; there was the creak of ropes; then he heard the wave-against-a-wharf smack of rubber on flesh. Her call for him to hurry was a sea-moan, and when he lay beside her, she heaved, tidal, moon-driven.

> Some fifteen minutes later, he crawled out of bed like an exhausted swimmer leaving the surf. . . .

A part of the comic pattern, but more sardonic, are West's chapter titles—"Miss Lonelyhearts on a Field Trip" (in which he meets, by assignation, one of his readers, Mrs. Doyle); "Miss Lonelyhearts and the Fat Thumb" (in which he tries to communicate—his tongue is the Fat Thumb—with his girl); and "Miss Lonelyhearts Has a Religious Experience" (in which he is "crucified").

The Day of the Locust does not have these qualities that mark the other, shorter book, within its limits, as a successful tour de force. (pp. 12-13)

Locust lacks the lustrous imagery that so distinguishes *Miss Lonelyhearts.* The book is a dance of masks only, and this is not enough.

It is valuable, finally, to recall what West thought he was doing in these two books. He defended his literary "half-world," saying—"I believe there is a place for the fellow who yells fire and indicates where some of the smoke is coming from without actually dragging the hose to the spot. . . ." Although West quite apparently thought that he was a satirist, one must recognize that he was not. In order to be effective, a satirist must indicate explicitly or implicitly the standards of society which he considers good and bad. Swift did this. Voltaire did this. Modern and successful satirists like Evelyn Waugh do this. *The Day of the Locust* was originally called *The Cheated,* but West shows no person who is *not* cheated, nor does he imply that there are any. One cannot infer what West's standard of human fulfillment truly is. For Miss Lonelyhearts himself there can be no fulfilment, no possible escape, no right road to salvation. "Few things are sadder," said West, "than the truly monstrous," without realizing that the monstrous is sad only in comparison to the normal; and West in neither book showed normal people with normal emotions. A true satirist must put in his *grotesques* some recognizable humanity, or set beside them some characters with recognizable human feelings; otherwise, his books will be only a dance of masks.

West was not a successful satirist, and *The Day of the Locust* is not, as one critic has called it, "the greatest book to come out of Hollywood"; it is demonstrably a flawed book. *Miss Lonelyhearts* is a successful tour de force because it is a tour de force; it pretends to be nothing else. By itself, the latter book is a minor accomplishment; an art-form separated from life, placed firmly in the half-world. For *The Day of the Locust,* and for the rest of his work, Nathanael West wrote his own epitaph—

> . . . there is nothing to root for in
> my work and what is even worse, no rooters.
>
> (p. 14)

A. M. Tibbetts, "The Strange Half-World of Nathanael West," in Prairie Schooner, Vol. XXXIV, No. 1, Spring, 1960, pp. 8-14.

Stanley Edgar Hyman (essay date 1962)

[*A longtime literary critic for the* New Yorker, *Hyman was prominent in American letters during the mid-twentieth century. Believing that modern literary criticism should draw on disciplines outside the field of literature, Hyman often applied theories from cultural anthropology, comparative religion, and psychology to his critical assessments. In the following excerpt from his* Nathanael West, *Hyman offers a Freudian reading of* Miss Lonelyhearts *and identifies the novel's principal theme as that of human suffering.*]

When *Miss Lonelyhearts* was published . . . in 1933, West told A. J. Liebling that it was entirely unlike *Balso Snell,* "of quite a different make, wholesome, clean, holy, slightly mystic and inane." He describes it in **"Some Notes on Miss L."** as a "portrait of a priest of our time who has had a religious experience." In it, West explains, "violent images are used to illustrate commonplace events. Violent acts are left almost bald." He credits William James's *Varieties of Religious Experience* for its psychology. Some or all of this may be Westian leg-pull.

The plot of *Miss Lonelyhearts* is Sophoclean irony, as simple and inevitable as the plot of *Balso Snell* is random and whimsical. A young newspaperman who writes the agony column of his paper as "Miss Lonelyhearts" has reached the point where the joke has gone sour. He becomes obsessed with the real misery of his correspondents, illuminated for him by the cynicism of William Shrike, the feature editor. Miss Lonelyhearts pursues Shrike's wife Mary, unsuccessfully, and cannot content himself with the love and radiant goodness of Betty, his fiancée. Eventually he finds his fate in two of his correspondents, the crippled Peter Doyle and his wife Fay. Miss Lonelyhearts is not punished for his tumble with Fay, but when on his next encounter he fights her off, it leads to his being shot by Doyle.

The characters are allegorical figures who are at the same time convincing as people. Miss Lonelyhearts is a New England puritan, the son of a Baptist minister. He has a true religious vocation or calling, but no institutional church to embody it. When Betty suggests that he quit the column, he tells her: "I can't quit. And even if I were to quit, it wouldn't make any difference. I wouldn't be able to forget the letters, no matter what I did."

In one of the most brilliant strokes in the book, he is never named, always identified only by his role. (In an earlier draft, West had named him Thomas Matlock, which we could translate "Doubter Wrestler," but no name at all is infinitely more effective.) Even when he telephones Fay Doyle for an assignation, he identifies himself only as "Miss Lonelyhearts, the man who does the column." In his namelessness, in his vocation without a church, Miss Lonelyhearts is clearly the prophet in the reluctance stage, when he denies the call and tells God that he stammers, but Miss Lonelyhearts, the prophet of *our* time, is stuck there until death.

Miss Lonelyhearts identifies Betty as the principle of order: "She had often made him feel that when she straightened his tie, she straightened much more." The order that she represents is the innocent order of Nature, as opposed to the disorder of sinful Man. When Miss Lonelyhearts is sick, Betty comes to nourish him with hot soup, impose order on his room, and redeem him with a pastoral vision: "She told him about her childhood on a farm and of her love for animals, about country sounds and country smells and of how fresh and clean everything in the country is. She said that he ought to live there and that if he did, he would find that all his troubles were city troubles." When Miss Lonelyhearts is back on his feet, Betty takes him for a walk in the zoo, and he is "amused by her evident belief in the curative power of animals." Then she takes him to live in the country for a few days, in the book's great idyllic scene. Miss Lonelyhearts is beyond such help, but it is Betty's patient innocence—she is as soft and helpless as a kitten—that makes the book so heartbreaking. She is an innocent Eve to his fallen Adam, and he alone is driven out of Eden.

The book's four other principal characters are savage caricatures, in the root sense of "caricature" as the overloading of one attribute. Shrike is a dissociated half of Miss Lonelyhearts, his cynical intelligence, and it is interesting to learn that Shrike's rhetorical masterpiece, the great speech on the varieties of escape, was spoken by Miss Lonelyhearts in an earlier draft. Shrike's name is marvelously apt. The shrike or butcherbird impales its prey on thorns, and the name is a form of the word "shriek." Shrike is of course the mocker who hands Miss Lonelyhearts his crown of thorns, and throughout the book he is a shrieking bird of prey; when not a butcherbird, "a screaming, clumsy gull."

Shrike's wife Mary is one vast teasing mammary image. As Miss Lonelyhearts decides to telephone Mary in Delehanty's speakeasy, he sees a White Rock poster and observes that "the artist had taken a great deal of care in drawing her breasts and their nipples stuck out like tiny red hats." He then thinks of "the play Mary made with her breasts. She used them as the coquettes of long ago had used their fans. One of her tricks was to wear a medal low down on her chest. Whenever he asked to see it, instead of drawing it out she leaned over for him to look. Although he had often asked to see the medal, he had not yet found out what it represented." Miss Lonelyhearts and Mary go out for a gay evening, and Mary flaunts her breasts while talking of her mother's terrible death from cancer of the breast. He finally gets to see the medal, which reads "Awarded by the Boston Latin School for first place in the 100 yd. dash." When he takes her home he kisses her breasts, for the first time briefly slowing down her dash.

The Doyles are presented in inhuman or subhuman imagery. When, in answer to Fay's letter of sexual invitation, Miss Lonelyhearts decides to telephone her, he pictures her as "a tent, hair-covered and veined," and himself as a skeleton: "When he made the skeleton enter the flesh tent, it flowered at every joint." Fay appears and is a giant: "legs like Indian clubs, breasts like balloons and a brow like a pigeon." When he takes her arm, "It felt like a thigh." Following her up the stairs to his apartment, "he watched the action of her massive hams; they were like two enormous grindstones." Undressing, "she made sea sounds; something flapped like a sail; there was the creak of ropes; then he heard the wave-against-a-wharf smack of rubber on flesh. Her call for him to hurry was a sea-moan, and when he lay beside her, she heaved, tidal, moon-driven." Eventually Miss Lonelyhearts "crawled out of bed like an exhausted swimmer leaving the surf," and she soon drags him back.

If Fay is an oceanic monster, Peter Doyle is only a sinister puppy. In bringing Miss Lonelyhearts back to the apartment at Fay's order, he half-jokes, "Ain't I the pimp, to bring home a guy for my wife?" Fay reacts by hitting him in the mouth with a rolled-up newspaper, and his comic response is to growl like a dog and catch the paper with his teeth. When she lets go of her end, he drops to his hands and knees and continues to imitate a dog on the floor. As Miss Lonelyhearts leans over to help him up, "Doyle tore open Miss Lonelyhearts' fly, then rolled over on his back, laughing wildly." Fay, more properly, accepts him as a dog and kicks him.

The obsessive theme of *Miss Lonelyhearts* is human pain and suffering, but it is represented almost entirely as female suffering. This is first spelled out in the letters addressed to Miss Lonelyhearts: Sick-of-it-all is a Roman Catholic wife who has had seven children in twelve years, is pregnant again, and has kidney pains so excruciating that she cries all the time. Desperate is a sixteen-year-old born with a hole in her face instead of a nose, who wants to have dates like other girls. Harold S. writes about his thirteen-year-old deaf-and-dumb sister Gracie, who was raped by a man when she was playing on the roof, and who will be brutally punished if her parents find out about it. Broad Shoulders was hit by a car when she was first pregnant, and is alternately persecuted and deserted by an unbalanced husband, in five pages of ghastly detail. Miss Lonelyhearts gets only two letters about male suffering, one from a paralyzed boy who wants to play the violin, the other from Peter Doyle, who complains of the pain from his crippled leg and the general meaninglessness of life.

The theme of indignities committed on women comes up in another form in the stories Miss Lonelyhearts' friends tell in Delehanty's. They seem to be exclusively anecdotes of group rape, of one woman gang-raped by eight neighbors, of another kept in the back room of a speakeasy for three days, until "on the last day they sold tickets to niggers." Miss Lonelyhearts identifies himself with "wife-torturers, rapers of small children." At one point he tries giving his readers the traditional Christian justification for suffering, that it is Christ's gift to mankind to bring them to Him, but he tears up the column.

Ultimately the novel cannot justify or even explain suffering, only proclaim its omnipresence. Lying sick in bed, Miss Lonelyhearts gets a vision of human life: "He found himself in the window of a pawnshop full of fur coats, diamond rings, watches, shotguns, fishing tackle, mandolins. All these things were the paraphernalia of suffering. A tortured high light twisted on the blade of a gift knife, a battered horn grunted with pain." Finally his mind forms everything into a gigantic cross, and he falls asleep exhausted.

The book's desperate cry of pain and suffering comes to a focus in what Miss Lonelyhearts calls his "Christ complex." He recognizes that Christ is the only answer to his readers' letters, but that "if he did not want to get sick, he had to stay away from the Christ business. Besides, Christ was Shrike's particular joke." As Miss Lonelyhearts leaves the office and walks through a little park, the shadow of a lamppost pierces his side like a spear. Since nothing grows in the park's battered earth, he decides to ask his correspondents to come and water the soil with their tears. He imagines Shrike telling him to teach them to pray each morning, "Give us this day our daily stone," and thinks: "He had given his reader many stones; so many, in fact, that he had only one left—the stone that had formed in his gut."

Jesus Christ, Shrike says, is "the Miss Lonelyhearts of Miss Lonelyhearts." Miss Lonelyhearts has nailed an ivory Christ to the wall of his room with great spikes, but it disappoints him: "Instead of writhing, the Christ remained calmly decorative." Miss Lonelyhearts recalls: "As a boy in his father's church, he had discovered that something stirred in him when he shouted the name of Christ, something secret and enormously powerful." Unfortunately, he recognizes, it is not faith but hysteria: "For him, Christ was the most natural of excitements."

Miss Lonelyhearts tells Betty he is "a humanity lover," but Shrike more aptly identifies him a "leper licker." "If he could only believe in Christ," Miss Lonelyhearts thinks, "then everything would be simple and the letters extremely easy to answer." Later he recognizes that "Shrike had accelerated his sickness by teaching him to handle his one escape, Christ, with a thick glove of words." He decides that he has had a part in the general betrayal of suffering mankind: "The thing that made his share in it particularly bad was that he was capable of dreaming the Christ dream. He felt that he had failed at it, not so much because of Shrike's jokes or his own self-doubt, but because of his lack of humility." Miss Lonelyhearts concludes that "with him, even the word Christ was a vanity." When he gets drunk with Doyle, he calls on Christ joyously, and goes home with Doyle to bring the glad tidings to both Doyles, to heal their marriage. He preaches "love" to them and realizes that he is only writing another column, switches to preaching Christ Jesus, "the black fruit that hangs on the crosstree . . . the bidden fruit," and realizes that he is only echoing Shrike's poisoned rhetoric.

What Miss Lonelyhearts eventually achieves, since he cannot believe in the real Christ, and refuses to become a spurious Christ, is Peter's condition. He becomes the rock on which the new church will be founded, but it is the church of catatonic withdrawal. After three days in bed Miss Lonelyhearts attains a state of perfect calm, and the stone in his gut expands until he becomes "an ancient rock, smooth with experience." The Shrikes come to take him to a party at their apartment, and against this rock the waves of Shrike dash in vain. When Mary wriggles on Miss Lonelyhearts' lap in the cab, "the rock remained perfect." At the party he withstands Shrike's newest mockery, the Miss Lonelyhearts Game, with indifference: "What goes on in the sea is of no interest to the rock." Miss Lonelyhearts leaves the party with Betty: "She too should see the rock he had become." He shamelessly promises her marriage and domesticity: "The rock was a solidification of his feeling, his conscience, his sense of reality, his self-knowledge." He then goes back to his sickbed content: "The rock had been thoroughly tested and had been found perfect."

The next day Miss Lonelyhearts is burning with fever, and "the rock became a furnace." The room fills with grace, the illusory grace of madness, and as Doyle comes up the stairs with a pistol Miss Lonelyhearts rushes downstairs to embrace him and heal his crippled leg, a miracle that will embody his succoring all suffering mankind with love. Unable to escape Miss Lonelyhearts' mad embrace, terrified by Betty coming up the stairs, Doyle tries to toss away the gun, and Miss Lonelyhearts is accidentally shot. He falls dragging Doyle down the stairs in his arms.

It is of course a homosexual tableau—the men locked in embrace while the woman stands helplessly by—and behind his other miseries Miss Lonelyhearts has a powerful latent homosexuality. It is this that is ultimately the joke of his name and the book's title. It explains his acceptance of teasing dates with Mary and his coldness with Mary; he thinks of her excitement and notes: "No similar change ever took place in his own body, however. Like a dead man, only friction could make him warm or violence make him mobile." It explains his discontent with Betty. Most of all it explains his joy at being seduced by Fay—"He had always been the pursuer, but now found a strange pleasure in have the roles reversed"—and how quickly the pleasure turns to disgust.

The communion Miss Lonelyhearts achieves with Doyle in Delehanty's consists in their sitting silently holding hands, Miss Lonelyhearts pressing "with all the love he could manage" to overcome the revulsion he feels at Doyle's touch. Back at the Doyles, after Doyle has ripped open Miss Lonelyhearts' fly and been kicked by his wife, they hold hands again, and when Fay comes back in the room she says "What a sweet pair of fairies you guys are." It is West's ultimate irony that the symbolic embrace they

manage at the end is one penetrating the body of the other with a bullet.

We could, if we so chose, write Miss Lonelyhearts' case history before the novel begins. Terrified of his stern religious father, identifying with his soft loving mother, the boy renounces his phallicism out of castration anxiety—a classic Oedipus complex. In these terms the Shrikes are Miss Lonelyhearts' Oedipal parents, abstracted as the father's loud voice and the mother's tantalizing breast. The scene at the end of Miss Lonelyhearts' date with Mary Shrike is horrifying and superb. Standing outside her apartment door, suddenly overcome with passion, he strips her naked under her fur coat while she keeps talking mindlessly of her mother's death, mumbling and repeating herself, so that Shrike will not hear their sudden silence and come out. Finally Mary agrees to let Miss Lonelyhearts in if Shrike is not home, goes inside, and soon Shrike peers out the door, wearing only the top of his pajamas. It is the child's Oedipal vision perfectly dramatized: he can clutch at his mother's body but loses her each time to his more potent rival.

It should be noted that if this is the pattern of Miss Lonelyhearts' Oedipus complex, it is not that of West, nor are the Shrikes the pattern of West's parents. How conscious was West of all or any of this? I would guess, from the book's title, that he was entirely conscious of at least Miss Lonelyhearts' latent homosexuality. As for the Oedipus complex, all one can do is note West's remarks in **"Some Notes on Miss L.":** "Psychology has nothing to do with reality nor should it be used as motivation. The novelist is no longer a psychologist. Psychology can become much more important. The great body of case histories can be used in the way the ancient writers use their myths. Freud is your Bulfinch; you can not learn from him."

The techniques West uses to express his themes are perfectly suited to them. The most important is a pervasive desperate and savage tone, not only in the imagery of violence and suffering, but everywhere. It is the tone of a world where unreason is triumphant. Telling Miss Lonelyhearts that he is awaiting a girl "of great intelligence," Shrike "illustrated the word *intelligence* by carving two enormous breasts in the air with his hands." When Miss Lonelyhearts is in the country with Betty, a gas station attendant tells him amiably that "it wasn't the hunters who drove out the deer, but the yids." When Miss Lonelyhearts accidentally collides with a man in Delehanty's and turns to apologize, he is punched in the mouth.

The flowering cactus that blooms in this wasteland is Shrike's rhetoric. The book begins with a mock prayer he has composed for Miss Lonelyhearts, and every time Shrike appears he makes a masterly speech: on religion, on escapes, on the gospel of Miss Lonelyhearts according to Shrike. He composes a mock letter to God, in which Miss Lonelyhearts confesses shyly: "I read your column and like it very much." He is a cruel and relentless punster and wit. In his sadistic game at the party, Shrike reads aloud letters to Miss Lonelyhearts. He reads one from a pathetic old woman who sells pencils for a living, and concludes: "She has rheum in her eyes. Have you room in your heart for her?" He reads another, from the paralyzed boy who wants to play the violin, and concludes: "How pathetic! However, one can learn much from this parable. Label the boy Labor, the violin Capital, and so on . . . " Shrike's masterpiece, the brilliant evocation of the ultimate inadequacy of such escapes as the soil, the South Seas, Hedonism, and art, is a classic of modern rhetoric, as is his shorter speech on religion. Here are a few sentences from the latter: "Under the skin of man is a wondrous jungle where veins like lush tropical growths hang along overripe organs and weed-like entrails writhe in squirming tangles of red and yellow. In this jungle, flitting from rock-gray lungs to golden intestines, from liver to lights and back to liver again, lives a bird called the soul. The Catholic hunts this bird with bread and wine, the Hebrew with a golden ruler, the Protestant on leaden feet with leaden words, the Buddhist with gestures, the Negro with blood."

The other cactus that flowers in the wasteland is sadistic violence. The book's most harrowing chapter, "Miss Lonelyhearts and the lamb," is a dream or recollection of a college escapade, in which Miss Lonelyhearts and two other boys, after drinking all night, buy a lamb to barbecue in the woods. Miss Lonelyhearts persuades his companions to sacrifice it to God before barbecuing it. They lay the lamb on a flower-covered altar and Miss Lonelyhearts tries to cut its throat, but succeeds only in maiming it and breaking the knife. The lamb escapes and crawls off into the underbrush, and the boys flee. Later Miss Lonelyhearts goes back and crushes the lamb's head with a stone. This nightmarish scene, with its unholy suggestions of the sacrifices of Isaac and Christ, embodies the book's bitter paradox: that sadism is the perversion of love.

Visiting Betty early in the novel, aware "that only violence could make him supple," Miss Lonelyhearts reaches inside her robe and tugs at her nipple unpleasantly. "Let me pluck this rose," he says, "I want to wear it in my buttonhole." In "Miss Lonelyhearts and the clean old man," he and a drunken friend find an old gentleman in a washroom, drag him to a speakeasy, and torment him with questions about his "homosexualistic tendencies." As they get nastier and nastier, Miss Lonelyhearts feels "as he had felt years before, when he had accidentally stepped on a small frog. Its spilled guts had filled him with pity, but when its suffering had become real to his senses, his pity had turned to rage and he had beaten it frantically until it was dead." He ends by twisting the old man's arm until the old man screams and someone hits Miss Lonelyhearts with a chair.

The book's only interval of decency, beauty, and peace is the pastoral idyll of the few days Miss Lonelyhearts spends with Betty in the country. They drive in a borrowed car to the deserted farmhouse in Connecticut where she was born. It is spring, and Miss Lonelyhearts "had to admit, even to himself, that the pale new leaves, shaped and colored like candle flames, were beautiful and that the air smelt clean and alive." They work at cleaning up the place, Betty cooks simple meals, and they go down to the pond to watch the deer. After they eat an apple that has ominous Biblical overtones, Betty reveals that she is a virgin and they go fraternally to bed. The next day they go

for a naked swim; then, with "no wind to disturb the pull of the earth," Betty is ceremonially deflowered on the new grass. The reader is repeatedly warned that natural innocence cannot save Miss Lonelyhearts: the noise of birds and crickets is "a horrible racket" in his ears; in the woods, "in the deep shade there was nothing but death—rotten leaves, gray and white fungi, and over everything a funereal hush." When they get back to New York, "Miss Lonelyhearts knew that Betty had failed to cure him and that he had been right when he had said that he could never forget the letters." Later, when Miss Lonelyhearts is a rock and leaves Shrike's party with Betty, he tries to create a miniature idyll of innocence by taking her out for a strawberry soda, but it fails. Pregnant by him and intending to have an abortion, Betty remains nevertheless in Edenic innocence; Miss Lonelyhearts is irretrievably fallen, and there is no savior who can redeem.

The book's pace is frantic and its imagery is garish, ugly, and compelling. The letters to Miss Lonelyhearts are "stamped from the dough of suffering with a heart-shaped cookie knife." The sky looks "as if it had been rubbed with a soiled eraser." A bloodshot eye in the peephole of Delehanty's glows "like a ruby in an antique iron ring." Finishing his sermon to the "intelligent" girl, Shrike "buried his triangular face like the blade of a hatchet in her neck." Miss Lonelyhearts' tongue is "a fat thumb," his heart "a congealed lump of icy fat," and his only feeling "icy fatness." Goldsmith, a colleague at the paper, has cheeks "like twin rolls of smooth pink toilet paper." Only the imagery of the Connecticut interlude temporarily thaws the iciness and erases the unpleasant associations with fatness and thumb. As Miss Lonelyhearts watches Betty naked, "She looked a little fat, but when she lifted something to the line, all the fat disappeared. Her raised arms pulled her breasts up until they were like pink-tipped thumbs."

The unique greatness of *Miss Lonelyhearts* seems to have come into the world with hardly a predecessor, but it has itself influenced a great many American novelists since. *Miss Lonelyhearts* seems to me one of the three finest American novels of our century. The other two are F. Scott Fitzgerald's *The Great Gatsby* and Ernest Hemingway's *The Sun Also Rises.* It shares with them a lost and victimized hero, a bitter sense of our civilization's falsity, a pervasive melancholy atmosphere of failure and defeat. If the tone of *Miss Lonelyhearts* is more strident, its images more garish, its pace more rapid and hysterical, it is as fitting an epitome of the thirties as they are of the twenties. If nothing in the forties and fifties has similarly gone beyond *Miss Lonelyhearts* in violence and shock, it may be because it stands at the end of the line. (pp. 16-28)

There is humor but little joy in West's novels, obsessive sexuality but few consummations. . . . The world West shows us is for the most part repulsive and terrifying. It is his genius to have found objective correlatives for our sickness and fears: our maimed and ambivalent sexuality, our terror of the idiot mass, our helpless empathy with suffering, our love perverted into sadism and masochism. West did this in convincing present-day forms of the great myths: the Quest, the Scapegoat, the Holy Fool, the Dance of Death. His strength lay in his vulgarity and bad taste, his pessimism, his nastiness. West could never have been the affirmative political writer he sometimes imagined, or written the novels that he told his publisher, just before his death, he had planned: "simple, warm and kindly books." We must assume that if West had lived, he would have continued to write the sort of novels he had written before, perhaps even finer ones.

In his short tormented life, West achieved one authentically great novel, *Miss Lonelyhearts,* and three others less successful as wholes but full of brilliant and wonderful things. He was a true pioneer and culture hero, making it possible for the younger symbolists and fantasists who came after him, and who include our best writers, to do with relative ease what he did in defiance of the temper of his time, for so little reward, in isolation and in pain. (pp. 45-6)

> *Stanley Edgar Hyman, in his* Nathanael West, *University of Minnesota Press, Minneapolis, 1962, 48 p.*

Victor Comerchero (essay date 1964)

[*Comerchero's* Nathanael West: The Ironic Prophet *has been assessed as a daringly original, ambitious, and controversial critical survey. In the following excerpt from that work, Comerchero discusses what he perceives as the influence of Freud as well as French Surrealists and Symbolists on* Miss Lonelyhearts, *highlighting elements of classical quest and wasteland mythology in the novel.*]

Stanley Edgar Hyman has called *Miss Lonelyhearts* "one of the three finest American novels of our century" [*Nathanael West*]; though an extreme claim, it is not a foolish one. A small, apparently simple novel with a very hard finish, *Miss Lonelyhearts* is West's masterpiece and the novel that most clearly reveals his singular sensibility. In no other novel are the tragic, comic, pathetic, and satiric so inseparably fused; in no other novel has he so nicely balanced the three emotional attitudes which are reflected in his novels—compassion, contempt, and suffering; and in no other novel has he developed such complex harmonics of meaning—harmonies resulting from the counterplay of the literal and the symbolical. Strident and garish as it is, *Miss Lonelyhearts* is a novel most delicately poised between agonizing pessimism and ironic amusement. It was a balance too fine for West to achieve in any other novel. Perhaps he achieved it in *Miss Lonelyhearts* because in it he first gives voice to violent despair and because, though it is his most personal, subtle, and important philosophic statement of life, it followed too soon after *Balso Snell* to escape that novel's broad comic irony.

Though clearly unique among West's novels, *Miss Lonelyhearts* reflects little change in West's world view; in retrospect, one sees much in *Balso Snell* that foreshadows the novel. Thus, in addition to the dream, search, isolation, and communication—or lack of communication—themes; the conflict between illusions and reality; self-dramatization; the analysis of man's spiritual nature; and the similarity between Shrike, Miss Lonelyhearts, John Gilson, and Beagle Hamlet Darwin, there are verbal echoes: the *"Anima Christi"* in *Balso Snell* becomes Shrike's prayer to Miss Lonelyhearts, the jokes at the expense of religion in *Balso Snell* are paralleled by Shrike's numerous ones, the murder of the idiot with a knife parallels the murder of the lamb both descriptively and in its psychosexual implications, and the staginess of John Gilson and B. Hamlet Darwin's speech is echoed constantly in Shrike's and occasionally in Miss Lonelyhearts'. But if some of the devices are old, the artistry is new.

By polishing and artistically reworking themes dealt with in his earlier experimental novel, West begins a pattern that applies as well to *A Cool Million* and *The Day of the Locust.* It is as if he had to experiment once before he discovered the vehicle which would artistically sustain his concern. More important, it suggests that West's anxieties persisted until they were resolved esthetically. *The Dream Life of Balso Snell—Miss Lonelyhearts* and *A Cool Million—The Day of the Locust* form pairs; hence, after the completion of *Miss Lonelyhearts,* and presumably after *The Day of the Locust,* West tended to seek out a new conceptual center. Thus, despite certain prevalent motifs in all four novels, the first two are personal, psychological, and philosophical; the latter two, more social-psychological and political. Moreover, the second novel in each pair treats the problem in a darker, less comic fashion. The skepticism and nihilism that found such personal and boisterous expression in *Balso Snell* is in *Miss Lonelyhearts,* muted but intensified and made moving by its more serious treatment. The vision, however, has changed little. One errs if he fails to see this fundamental truth merely because in *Balso Snell* West aroused laughter, and in *Miss Lonelyhearts* the laughter is "too deep for tears." It is not the problem that determines one's response, it is the treatment.

Unlike the picaresque formlessness of *Balso Snell*—a construction admirably suited to comedy—structurally *Miss Lonelyhearts* has a composition similar to that of tragic drama. In its movement from ignorance through experience to discovery—a movement similar to that in *Balso Snell*—it approximates Francis Fergusson's "tragic rhythm of action . . . Purpose, Passion (or Suffering) and Perception" [*The Idea of a Theater: A Study of Ten Plays*]. The purpose: to answer the letters; the passion: Miss Lonelyhearts' agonizing realization of the reality of human suffering; the perception: his vision of God and his acceptance of Him. West, however, does not tell the whole story of Miss Lonelyhearts; one never sees him in his "innocent" state. Instead, the novel concentrates on the last weeks of his life, thereby crystallizing the reader's impressions into a single one of enormous power.

Even more dramatic in technique is West's use of discovery and reversal; perhaps here it will help to draw parallels. In most conventionally structured modern drama, the nature of the problem is presented as soon as possible; the first act curtain rarely rings down before it is clearly known. West proceeds to do the same thing and does it with stunning brilliance. Within two pages after the novel begins, and certainly within twelve, the nature of Miss Lonelyhearts' problem is quite clear: how does he answer the letters when the letters are "no longer funny"?

In the second and third acts of this kind of dramatic structure, the protagonist struggles to resolve his problem. This struggle usually consumes most of the stage action; and in *Miss Lonelyhearts,* the bulk of the novel is concerned with Miss Lonelyhearts' struggles to escape, to find an answer that will ease his readers' suffering and his own. The dramatist, in constructing his play, is constantly trying to create suspense as to how the protagonist will resolve his problem. He does this by delaying the resolution, which is usually achieved by a discovery and a reversal, as long as possible. An attempt is made by the dramatist to have his discovery and reversal come as near to the end of the play as possible. (pp. 72-4)

West delays Miss Lonelyhearts' discovery until the last fifteen or twenty pages of the novel. It is a gradual, groping, uncertain realization, but this merely increases the tension and the reader's interest. Only two pages before the end is the final ironic "discovery" made that "Christ is life and light." The reversal is instantaneous; "his identification with God was complete" and his acceptance total. Death follows three hundred words later and the "tragedy" is ended.

What is important about *Miss Lonelyhearts* is the superimposition of comedy upon its tragic structure. It cannot

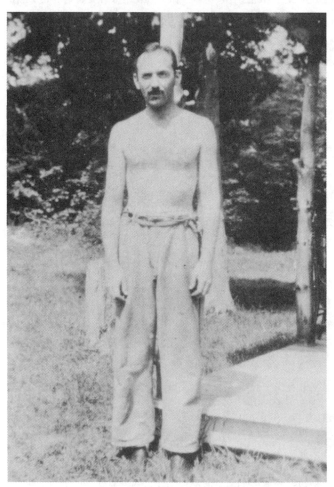

West at a rented cabin in the Adirondacks in 1931, where he retreated to work uninterrupted on Miss Lonelyhearts.

be insisted too strongly that if one is to use such terms, in a sense inappropriate ones, *Miss Lonelyhearts* is a comedy with tragic overtones rather than a tragedy with comic overtones. In reality, these terms lose their meaning when discussing a novel such as *Miss Lonelyhearts:* is Beckett, to name another apostle of the absurd, writing a tragedy in *Waiting for Godot* or a comedy? Horace Walpole's remark that "the world is a comedy to those that think, a tragedy to those who feel" fails utterly to describe West's peculiar sensibility. It does, however, help illuminate West's "unified sensibility," and by extension, that of many other exponents of the Absurd.

Whatever one may think of the novel, it is clear that it is not a conventional tragedy; not merely because Miss Lonelyhearts lacks tragic stature—he is fundamentally heroic in conception if not in execution—but because the very fabric of the novel is invaded by comic irony and incongruity. Thus, despite a natural wish to read *Miss Lonelyhearts* as moral, even Christian, tragedy, one can only do so by doing violence to West's pessimistic belief that life is without discernible order or meaning.

Divergent readings are inevitable, for, contrary to appearances, *Miss Lonelyhearts* is not a simple or "easy" novel. Perhaps it is misread more often than not. An article by James F. Light ["Violence, Dreams, and Dostoevsky: The Art of Nathanael West," *College English,* February 1958] offers a characteristic example:

> These letters ask the eternal question of crippled humanity: "What is the whole stinking mess for?" To the question Miss Lonelyhearts can find no answer. He therefore must try to find the true Christ. By the end of the novel Miss Lonelyhearts has, through the negation of his personality, gained a mystical union with God and the peace that comes with grace. But to the contemporary materialistic world, Miss Lonelyhearts has become hysterical, become "sick." . . . The moral is obvious. Only through the perfect love of Christ can the pain of man be alleviated; only through faith can the conflict between the evil in the universe and the goodness of God be reconciled. Christ gave these answers; the letters have forced Miss Lonelyhearts to them. But just as the world of Christ was not ready, so the world of today is still unready.

Light is not quite so unequivocal in his major study of West [*Nathanael West: An Interpretive Study*]; but despite his recognition that West doubted Christ's divinity, his reading changed but little:

> Miss Lonelyhearts is shot by Doyle, destroyed, like Christ, by the panic and ignorance of those whom he would save. Doyle, and in him suffering man, shatters the only solution to the intolerableness of man's pain, destroys the Christlike man who perceives that love and faith are the only answers to man's pain in a universe he cannot understand.

> True belief in the Christian answers, however, rest upon the dissolution of the self and the subsequent mystical experience of God's love and grace. . . . After God's love and grace, the per-

sonal ecstacy they bring is a "reality," but the reality is incommunicable.

Such a reading attempts to make a Christian of West, something very difficult to do for more than one reason. But even more disturbing, such a reading is diametrically opposed to everything West believed. It offers a solution to the human dilemma when it is clear that West had none and never attempted to pose one. Moreover, one cannot so read the novel without ignoring West's finest achievement—his control of irony.

Even on the purely narrative level, as distinct from the various symbolic ones, ironies permeate the novel. They begin on the first page:

> The Miss Lonelyhearts of The New York *Post-Dispatch* (Are-you-in-trouble?—Do-you-need-advice?—Write-to-Miss-Lonelyhearts-and-she-will-help-you) sat at his desk and stared at a piece of white cardboard.

Not only is the Miss an uncertain Mr., but soon, even before realizing the source of his suffering, one learns that, besides being incapable of helping anyone, Miss Lonelyhearts is badly in need of help himself:

> Although the deadline was less than a quarter of an hour away, he was still working on his leader. He had gone as far as: "Life *is* worth while, for it is full of dreams and peace, gentleness and ecstacy, and faith that burns like a clear white flame on a grim dark altar." But he found it impossible to continue. The letters were no longer funny. He could not go on finding the same joke funny thirty times a day for months on end. And on most days he received more than thirty letters. . . .

Miss Lonelyhearts is tortured by two questions: Why doesn't God make manifest the higher order which governs man's existence? And, if there is no higher order—if God does not exist—how does one respond to suffering and injustice in this world?

The problem of man's response to suffering is raised in the first chapter. West ironically counterpoints Miss Lonelyhearts' platitudes about life's being beautiful with sordid reality. In three letters, he captures the essence of a pervasive, inexplicable human suffering that afflicts guilty and innocent, pious and impious alike; and in response to the letters, Miss Lonelyhearts has to fight "himself quiet."

While there is little irony in the letters, just as in *Balso Snell,* much of West's commentary in *Miss Lonelyhearts* is developed by means of ironic contrasts and associations. Perhaps *Miss Lonelyhearts* is West's greatest work because in it the ironies are the most subtle and the most poetically conceived. Sometimes they are simple ironies intended to point out the impossibility of communication, to show that hell is other people. Hence the incompatabilities that permeate the novel: Shrike the "satyr" wedded to Mary, who has been fighting to remain a virgin ever since she married; tortured Miss Lonelyhearts, whose "confusion was significant," paired with Betty, whose "order was not"; and crippled Doyle, who is "all dried

up" and "isn't much" in bed, married to Fay Doyle, who is insatiable.

At other times, the ironies are merely verbal, as when West conveys how Miss Lonelyhearts, in desperation to escape, will clutch at any straw: "although he had tried hot water, whiskey, coffee, exercise, he had completely forgotten sex." It is one of the novel's cruelest ironies that sex actually does lead him out of the world, not, however, in the way he thought it would. For just as Oedipus' act ultimately led him out of the city, Miss Lonelyhearts' problem leads him to withdraw, but not with Betty to the country: the withdrawal is a catatonic one.

Once aware that " 'the majority of the letters are profoundly humble pleas for moral and spiritual advice, that they are inarticulate expressions of genuine suffering . . . [Miss Lonelyhearts] is forced to examine the values by which he lives. This examination shows him that he is the victim of the joke and not its perpetrator.' " The ironic depth of this joke is fearful, for Miss Lonelyhearts is not a godless man seeking faith: that search is altogether too trivial and trite. He is a fallen man who would seek a reassuring word from God. The horror of *Miss Lonelyhearts* proceeds from one's awareness of how Miss Lonelyhearts has fallen and of the agony of his fall. In his naked need to embrace God, this "son of a Baptist minister" arouses genuine pity and terror. Miss Lonelyhearts—this man in whom "something secret and enormously powerful" stirred when "he shouted the name of Christ"—is West's modern (fallen) Myshkin, West's "holy fool." He is the first and most memorable of West's scapegoats. The symbolic cry that rings throughout the novel is the loud cry of Christ crucified, "My God, my God, why hast thou forsaken me?" (Matt. 27:46) From the beginning, Miss Lonelyhearts realizes that "Christ was the answer, but, if he did not want to get sick, he had to stay away from the Christ business. Besides, Christ was Shrike's particular joke."

Shrike is a bird of prey. Again and again he impales Miss Lonelyhearts on the barbed edge of his rhetoric. " 'The same old stuff,' " he remarks upon reading one of Miss Lonelyhearts' columns. " 'Why don't you give them something new and hopeful?' " In passages full of the brilliant puns, clichés, and rhetoric in which West excelled, he cruelly and systematically destroys one of Miss Lonelyhearts' potential escapes after another: first; "the soil" (". . . you turn up the rich black soil, the wind carries the smell of pine and dung across the fields and the rhythm of an old, old work enters your soul"); then, "the south seas" ("You live in a thatch hut with the daughter of the king. . . . Her breasts are golden speckled pears, her belly a melon" . . .); then the pursuit of pleasure ("You fornicate under pictures by Matisse and Picasso, you drink from Renaissance glassware, and often you spend an evening beside the fireplace with Proust and an apple"); and finally, just before "the First Church of Christ Dentist" ("Father, Son and Wirehaired Fox Terrier"), art:

> Tell them that you know that your shoes are broken and that there are pimples on your face, yes, and that you have buck teeth and a club foot, but that you don't care, for tomorrow they are playing Beethoven's last quartets in Carnegie Hall

and at home you have Shakespeare's plays in one volume.

Calling Christ "the Miss Lonelyhearts of Miss Lonelyhearts," he relegates Christ to the same meaningless class as Miss Lonelyhearts. As a result, the ivory Christ nailed to Miss Lonelyhearts' wall with large spikes fails to stir: "Instead of writhing, the Christ remained calmly decorative."

Miss Lonelyhearts tries to escape by ridiculing the problem out of existence. " 'Ah, humanity . . . ' " he says mockingly. "But he was heavy with shadow and the joke went into a dying fall. He tried to break its fall by laughing at himself." That West is intent on demonstrating Miss Lonelyhearts' disintegration as a result of his search is early made apparent, for he describes Miss Lonelyhearts' desire to believe in Christ in the terrifying snake image of insanity.

Hoping by association to regain a sense of order, he seeks out Betty. Yet, she cannot console him; for the more desperate, helpless, and alone he feels, the more hostile and violent he becomes: " 'I've got a Christ complex,' " he shouts. But his shouts are accompanied by "gestures that were too appropriate, like those of an old-fashioned actor." They are not completely false, but are no longer simple and true; introspection, self-consciousness, and isolation have corrupted his emotions: even in counterfeit responses he cannot escape from his fallen state.

" 'What's the matter sweetheart?' " he asks, again burlesquing the mystery of feeling at its source. " 'Didn't you like the performance?' " He is sick; and, unable to free himself from the cause of his sickness, he tries to revenge himself for the suffering he is undergoing. His revenge manifests itself childishly like that of his friends in Delehanty's who "did not know how else to revenge themselves." "Like Shrike, the man they imitated, they were machines for making jokes."

Again he seeks out Christ: "If only he could believe in Christ . . . then everything would be simple and the letters extremely easy to answer." But he cannot believe; Shrike has not allowed it. Instead, "Shrike had accelerated his sickness by teaching him to handle his one escape, Christ, with a thick glove of words."

The country interlude with Betty further hastens his disintegration, for there he learns that nature does not cleanse. A vision of Eden changes nothing in the Bronx slums; he discovers this fact as soon as he returns:

> When they reached the Bronx slums, Miss Lonelyhearts knew that Betty had failed to cure him and that he had been right when he had said that he could never forget the letters. He felt better, knowing this, because he had begun to think himself a faker and a fool.

Once Miss Lonelyhearts acknowledges that "he could never forget the letters," all avenues of escape are cut off to him but Christ. His disintegration is swift. He reads one long, incredibly horrifying letter by "Broad Shoulders" and is in ruins within a week. Striving for humility, he dodges Betty "because she made him feel ridiculous." Un-

able to shake her innocence—she still lives in a Connecticut Garden of Eden—and unable to play at house any longer, he must avoid her. Miss Lonelyhearts' catatonic escape has begun; Shrike has cut off all others.

The withdrawal is foreshadowed by the number of times West refers to Miss Lonelyhearts' search for Christ as an escape. Moreover, as will be illustrated more clearly later, the abnormal nature of the withdrawal is built into the novel's imagery. Not only is the hollowness of his solution ironically suggested by the rock that he becomes, but the escapist nature of his "rocklike" tranquility is counterpointed against the true immersion of oneself in the sea of human suffering: "What goes on in the sea is of no interest to the rock." Further, if the description of Miss Lonelyhearts standing naked—indifferent to Shrike and four others—carefully examining "each cracker before popping it into his mouth" is not enough to point out his growing loss of contact with reality, one has only to note the way West refers to Miss Lonelyhearts' plans for the future—to get a new job and marry Betty—as "a castle in Spain."

Miss Lonelyhearts is sick because any affirmation of traditional values—represented in a soft and pure form by Betty—makes him feel absurd, and because he can discover no other values by which to live. He cannot accept Betty's world, a world in which she is a "party dress" and he is "just what the party dress wanted him to be: simple and sweet, whimsical and poetic, a trifle collegiate yet very masculine."

The scenes with Betty, amusing as they are, are genuinely poignant. They temper the novel's stridency, and they supply it with some of its warmth and tenderness, with a bittersweet suffering which contrasts sharply with the sordid and grotesque suffering of the letter writers. It is the novel's most heartbreaking irony that Betty's patient and innocent efforts to retrieve Miss Lonelyhearts make her pregnant and ultimately destroy him; for her final visit, apparently to plan "their life after marriage," by cutting off the cripple's escape results in his death. As in *Oedipus Rex,* the ironies are bitter ones: innocence and good intentions are not enough.

Such a literal reading of the novel, though satisfying to many readers and probably favored by most, ultimately fails to illuminate the novel's peculiar resonances. The novel seems to, and does, contain deeper symbolic and ironic reverberations. Some of these symbols and ironies are indicated in West's explanation of what he was trying to do in the novel:

> Miss Lonelyhearts became the portrait of a priest of our time who has a religious experience. His case is classical and is built on all the cases in James' *Varieties of Religious Experience* and Starbuck's *Psychology of Religion.* The psychology is theirs not mine. The imagery is mine. Chapt. I—maladjustment. Chapt. III—the need for taking symbols literally is described through a dream in which a symbol is actually flashed. Chapt. IV—deadness and disorder; see Lives of Bunyan and Tolstoy. Chapt. VI—self-torture by conscious sinning: see life of any saint. And so on.

The "portrait" is an ironic one, but it is not strange that the irony should go unnoticed, or that West's description of Miss Lonelyhearts as "a priest of our time" should trigger stock responses of respect and compassion in the reader. West obviously wished to elicit such responses, for he takes pains to make clear Miss Lonelyhearts' priestlike role at several points in the novel. The note is struck early:

> On seeing him [Miss Lonelyhearts] for the first time, Shrike had smiled and said, "The Susan Chesters, the Beatrice Fairfaxes and Miss Lonelyhearts are the priests of twentieth-century America."

The metaphor is repeated again and again in various remarks by Shrike and then finally crystallized in the image describing Miss Lonelyhearts as he listens to the cripple's disjointed, abused outburst: "Like a priest, Miss Lonelyhearts turned his face slightly away." West, however, goes further and develops the character of Miss Lonelyhearts as a Christ figure. This identity, as well as the central theme of the novel—man in search of God—is suggested on the first page by the parody of the *"Anima Christi"* or "Soul of Christ" from Loyola's *Spiritual Exercises:*

> Soul of Miss L, glorify me.
> Body of Miss L, nourish me
> Blood of Miss L, intoxicate me.
> Tears of Miss L, wash me.
> Oh good Miss L, excuse my plea,
> And hide me in your heart,
> And defend me from mine enemies.
> Help me, Miss L, help me, help me.
> In saecula saeculorum. Amen.

Lest the reader miss the point, on page six West thrusts upon him the image of a lamp post piercing Miss Lonelyhearts "like a spear," an image so obvious that he cannot ignore it. And, at the end, Miss Lonelyhearts is shot, with his arms "spread," ready for the martyrdom.

Throughout the novel, West continues the theme of man in search of God and uses Christian images to suggest Miss Lonelyhearts' emotional state. He is, at the same time, trying to indicate Miss Lonelyhearts' preoccupation with Christ and the impossibility of finding Him in this modern age. But this quest is merely part of the irony. Not only must the reader never forget *Miss Lonelyhearts'* link with *Balso Snell*—that "rejection of . . . the spiritual pretensions of man"—he must never forget that the Miss Lonelyhearts *are* the priests of his time.

"God," Nietzsche said metaphorically, "is dead"; and with Him, West adds, died the priest. In his place has arisen that peculiarly modern corruption, the advice columnist—the new father confessor and pastoral guardian. So essential to West is his readers' awareness of the identity of this modern debasement that he feels compelled to have Shrike establish the *equation* of twentieth-century priest to traditional priest seven pages after the novel begins: " 'the Susan Chesters . . . are the priests of twentieth-century America.' " Only by recognizing the true identity of the subject in the portrait can one dissociate the novel from certain prevalent prejudices and preconceptions.

Christianity has lost its vital center; as a viable force it is dead. As he has before, and as he will again later, West

here seizes upon an image or an objective correlative—Miss Lonelyhearts or his like—to symbolize the corruption in the palace of religion and, therefore, in the society. The religion Gibbon charged with causing the decline of the Roman Empire is itself declining, and with it—though not because of it—the West. In essence, Miss Lonelyhearts becomes an archetypal symbol of the decline of the West. The vision is Spenglerian to be sure, but one for which West had a great affinity, as [indicated by James F. Light in his *Nathanael West: An Interpretive Study*]:

> As Spengler and Valery had suggested (and West had read their criticisms), man's "progress" is leading to the end of Western civilization. West agreed with such viewpoints, though perhaps more emotionally than intellectually.

The materialistic nature of that "progress" and West's hatred of it are revealed again and again, as Light also points out. (Significantly, Chief Satinpenny in *A Cool Million* refers specifically to Spengler and Valery in his diatribe against Western civilization.)

As a result of his Spenglerian vision and religious skepticism, West is placed in the paradoxical position of debunking religion while using the decline of Christianity to symbolize the decline of the West. On the surface, it appears to be an impossible task; closer examination reveals a logical, but no inherent, artistic contradiction. West's opposition, if one can use so strong a word, to Christianity is doctrinal or theological, not ethical. Moreover, West is not lamenting the decline of Christianity as much as he is using that decline as an archetypal symbol of the decline of Western civilization.

It seems impossible to explain the novel's peculiar reverberations without turning to the complex texture established by interweaving a comic and a tragic vision of Miss Lonelyhearts and Western society. Much of one's failure to sense the bitter comic irony of the novel results from the mythic conception of the novel and from West's capacity to feel compassion for basically unlovely types. Thus, despite his purpose—to analyze ironically Miss Lonelyhearts' "religious experience"—West is able to charge Miss Lonelyhearts with such genuine anguish that the reader is overwhelmed with compassion. One should not be led by a tender response to Miss Lonelyhearts' *angst* to ignore the novel's comic aspects, for in addition to, or maybe as part of, its symbolic intention, the novel is a case study of a modern Oedipus. West has taken a "classical" case history—an Oedipus complex—and, by the use of brilliant imagery, translated it into a work of art.

Stanley Edgar Hyman has neatly described Miss Lonelyhearts' Oedipus complex [in his *Nathanael West*]:

> Terrified of his stern religious father, identifying with his soft loving mother, the boy renounces his phallicism out of castration anxiety—a classic Oedipus complex. In these terms the Shrikes are Miss Lonelyhearts' Oedipal parents, abstracted as the father's loud voice and the mother's tantalizing breast. The scene at the end of Miss Lonelyhearts' date with Mary Shrike is horrifying and superb. Standing outside her apartment door, suddenly overcome with pas-

sion he strips her naked under her fur coat while she keeps talking mindlessly of her mother's death, mumbling and repeating herself, so that Shrike will not hear their sudden silence and come out. Finally Mary agrees to let Miss Lonelyhearts in if Shrike is not home, goes inside, and soon Shrike peers out the door, wearing only the top of his pajamas. It is the child's Oedipal vision perfectly dramatized; he can clutch at his mother's body but loses her each time to his more potent rival.

The tidiness with which Hyman is able to describe Miss Lonelyhearts' complex is evidence of West's success. He was not, of course, trying to keep the complex or Miss Lonelyhearts' latent homosexuality a mystery.

The parallels between the two Oedipuses are striking: like Oedipus of old, this modern Oedipus tries to ease the suffering of his subjects; like him, he engages in a quest which ultimately and ironically results in the discovery of his true identity. However, as is to be expected of a modern Oedipus, the problem of identity is a sexual one: "who am I?" becomes "what am I?" Finally, both Oedipuses are scapegoats. In addition, there are numerous other parallels; for though comic in execution, Miss Lonelyhearts is heroic and archetypal in conception. . . . There is no twentieth-century dragon, though there is a shrike; but nevertheless, the land is blighted:

> As far as he could discover, there were no signs of spring. The decay that covered the surface of the mottled ground was not the kind in which life generates. Last year, he remembered, May had failed to quicken these soiled fields. It had taken all the brutality of July to torture a few green spikes through the exhausted dirt.

> What the little park needed, even more than he did, was a drink.

The theme of a parched earth in need of water occurs repeatedly:

> A desert, he was thinking, not of sand, but of rust and body dirt, surrounded by a back-yard fence on which are posters describing the events of the day. Mother slays five with ax, slays seven, slays nine. . . . Inside the fence Desperate, Broken-hearted, Disillusioned-with-tubercular-husband and the rest were gravely forming the letters MISS LONELYHEARTS out of white-washed clam shells, as if decorating the lawn of a rural depot.

West's vision of the people who populate this wasteland does not alter in his last three novels. The apocalyptic riot that ends *The Day of the Locust* is foreshadowed in *Miss Lonelyhearts* in the shattered letter writers and in a furtive glimpse of Tod Hackett's "torchbearers":

> Crowds of people moved through the street with a dream-like violence. As he looked at their broken hands and torn mouths he was overwhelmed by the desire to help them, and because this desire was sincere, he was happy despite the feeling of guilt which accompanied it.

> He saw a man who appeared to be on the verge of death stagger into a movie theater that was showing a picture called Blonde Beauty. He saw a ragged woman with an enormous goiter pick a love story magazine out of a garbage can and seem very excited by her find.

The echoes from Eliot's *Waste Land* have already suggested that the novel is a moving modernization of the Grail legend. Perhaps only the solidity and intensity of West's vision have prevented the recognition that the world of *Miss Lonelyhearts* is the fallen world of myth. Adam and Eve in Eden are glimpsed in the pastoral interlude, but in the context of the novel, it is an unreal Eden. Betty, unconscious of the symbolic curse that afflicts the land, is not burdened with the mysterious, mythic sense of guilt that troubles Miss Lonelyhearts. At this mythic level, Betty seems to symbolize the restorative feminine principle in nature. Under her urging, after Miss Lonelyhearts' illness, they plan to take a trip to Connecticut.

> She told him about her childhood on a farm and of her love for animals, about country sounds and country smells and of how fresh and clean everything in the country is. She said that he ought to live there and that if he did, he would find that all his troubles were city troubles.

First they convalesce at the zoo: "He was amused by her evident belief in the curative power of animals. She seemed to think that it must steady him to look at a buffalo."

Betty's mythic function exists mainly to punctuate ironically Miss Lonelyhearts' failure, the exact nature of which can only be explained by perceiving the myth and the novel as an organic whole. While the main elements of the Grail legend are familiar—the wasteland, Fisher King, quest, lance and Grail—only a close, somewhat technical examination of the mythic parallels in the novel will reveal the brilliance of West's achievement. West, who probably knew Jessie L. Weston's work on the Grail legend [*From Ritual to Romance*] more than casually (he was probably introduced to it through Eliot), seems to have felt free to depart from Miss Weston's interpretation when he found it useful. Thus, despite Miss Weston's convincing argument for a ritualistic rather than a Christian reading, West makes use of both interpretations; while the quest for the Grail is interpreted sexually, the Fisher King is not a life or fertility symbol so much as Christ, the "King of the Fishermen."

The novel's mythic characteristics begin at once. From the parody of the *"Anima Christi,"* it is apparent that Miss Lonelyhearts is on a quest, the precise nature of which is as vague as the original. One soon realizes it is to give "the dead world . . . a semblance of life . . . [by] bringing it [Christ] to life." The parallels with Miss Weston's description of a variant of the Grail quest are clear. In both, the hero is oppressed by a sense of urgency; in both, he understands neither the nature of the task nor how to perform it; in both, there is the insistence upon the sickness of the Fisher King; in both, there is a suggestion that the death of the Fisher King is the "direct cause of the wasting of the land"; and in both, "the task of the Quester [is] that of restoring him to life."

Though West has occasionally departed from Miss Weston's interpretation in adding other mythic elements to the central Grail quest, he seems to have followed her closely. Miss Weston connects a procession or nature ritual—a "resuscitation ceremony"—with the Grail legend: "The Vegetation Spirit appears in the song as an Old Man, while his female counterpart, an Old Woman, is described. . . . " In a note, Miss Weston adds: "besides the ordinary figures of the Vegetation Deity, his female counterpart, and the Doctor, common to all such processions, we have Phallus, Frog, and Horse." The parallels of this ritual with the chapter "Miss Lonelyhearts and the Clean Old Man" are ingenious but unmistakable.

Miss Lonelyhearts and Ned Gates, alias Havelock Ellis and Krafft-Ebing (obvious surrogates for the doctor), encounter a "clean old man" who, as a homosexual, is not only a "defunct Vegetation Spirit" but one who will serve to suggest his female counterpart as well. In his avowed purpose "to help," *i.e.,* to revitalize the old man, Miss Lonelyhearts' behavior parallels an early preliterary version of the Gawain variant: "he [Gawain] played the *role* traditionally assigned to the Doctor, that of restoring to life and health the dead, or wounded, representative of the Spirit of Vegetation."

Is it too ugly to see the old man as a Christ figure? Perhaps ugly, but quite probable. Not only does he "love mankind," but, like the Fisher King, he is sick, unvital, and literally, because of his sickness, sterile. This identification of both Miss Lonelyhearts and the old man as a Christ figure is suggested closely by a parallel identification in the Gawain legend: "In the final development of the story the *Pathos* is shared alike by the representative of the Vegetation Spirit, and the Healer. . . . " The pathos of this identification of the two will be dealt with later from a psychoanalytic perspective, for it is operative upon that level as well. The brilliance of West's achievement, as has been suggested elsewhere, lies not only in the subtle working out of the Grail parallels, but in the working out of other meanings at the same time. It is the Kafkaesque ability to create layers of meaning.

It may be straining to suggest that the horseplay substitutes for the presence of the horse, and perhaps straining to see the cane as a phallus, but not necessarily; for as an accessory of the old man which he is ready to use, the cane is a nice symbolic substitute for the phallus he is unwilling to use. It is impossible, however, to dismiss the prominence rightly given the frog, for it has great symbolic importance, not only in underlining the Grail parallels but in other ways. It is important to note that already, at the end of the fifth chapter, the failure of the quest is suggested: the old man is not rejuvenated. Moreover, the element of perversion dramatizes the enormity of the blight that afflicts the land.

Such pessimistic foreshadowing gains intensity when one realizes that immediately preceding this scene, West has presented a hopeful sign: the children "gravely and carefully" dancing, "a simple dance yet formal." West apparently wished to counterpoint youthful hope and innocence with aged despair and perversion. The description of the dance ("square replacing oblong and being replaced by circle") also can be read as a traditional symbolic state-

ment of order and harmony replacing disorder. More importantly, the dance is a remarkable recreation of the ritual sword dance performed by the youthful Maruts who "were, by nature and origin, closely connected with spirits of fertility of a lower order." Miss Weston describes the dances as "solemn ceremonial," and notes that a variation of the ritual existed in "the belief among Germanic peoples . . . in a troop of Child souls . . . closely connected with the dominant spirit of Vegetation."

It was naturally impossible for West always to establish exact parallels without rending the fabric of his novel. Nor does he seem to have attempted to match the Grail legend episode for episode: perhaps he felt a too blatant parallel would obscure his other intentions; moreover, perhaps like Joyce he merely wished to universalize his material by fixing it in archetypal forms. That he chose the Grail legend seems in part the result of his own preoccupation with the quest motif, in part the result of the religious subject matter of the novel. Perhaps it pleased West's ironic, pessimistic turn to discover that even this most sacred of Christian stories upon examination revealed the inevitable sexual dynamic.

What should be stressed is that even if West does not follow the legend's chronology of events, even if he has modernized those events and modified them under the influence of his peculiar temperament, he has nevertheless used nearly all of them. The conviction that Miss Weston's book was something of an idea book for West just as it had been to a lesser degree earlier, for Eliot, is inescapable. Only such an explanation helps one to understand the subtle transformations West has worked upon variations of the legend, transformations suggested by Miss Weston's analysis.

The most substantial transformation occurs in the chapter "Miss Lonelyhearts and the Lamb," a chapter which parallels the episode of the Perilous Chapel in the Grail romances. (pp. 74-89)

After an all-night college drinking bout, Miss Lonelyhearts and two other boys buy a lamb to barbecue in the woods. First, however, they intend to sacrifice it to God. Traditionally, sacrifice has been a ritual form of penance or purification or an attempted initiation "into the Spiritual Divine Life, where man is made one with God." This sacrifice has more than spiritual overtones, for the lamb, "a little, stiff-legged thing," and the sacrifice are described in language suggesting virgin rape. After picking "daisies and buttercups" (the semipagan element), the boys proceed with the business at hand:

> When they had worked themselves into a frenzy, he [Miss Lonelyhearts] brought the knife down hard. The blow was inaccurate and made a flesh wound. He raised the knife again and this time the lamb's violent struggles made him miss altogether.

If Freud has not, Miss Weston has made it clear that the lance and cup are sex symbols representing male and female, respectively. It is difficult to conceive of a scene which could have fulfilled the varied criteria of Miss Weston's initiation as well as this one does, for this "initiation carried out on the astral plane" (or its equivalent—a dream) reacts upon, or at least mirrors, a "fatal" flaw (Miss Lonelyhearts' sexual anxieties and disturbance) upon the physical. Moreover, West has not violated the novel's beautifully balanced symbolic structure: the scene carries equally well its narrative, religious, and psychoanalytic weight. Meaning on one level is not sacrificed for meaning on another level.

There are other examples of West's employment of the legend or of Miss Weston's theses, such as the use of fishing imagery to describe Miss Lonelyhearts' religious experience. (This employment of fishing imagery is not an isolated, final occurrence; fishing imagery abounds in the novel.) With respect to such imagery, Miss Weston notes:

> We can affirm with certainty that the Fish is a Life symbol of immemorial antiquity, and that the title of Fisher has, from the earliest ages, been associated with Deities who were held to be specially connected with the origin and preservation of Life.

In *Miss Lonelyhearts,* West has seized upon a myth, just as Joyce and Eliot had in *Ulysses* and *The Waste Land,* in an attempt to bring order to a disordered world, and to give the action a timeless truth. In the legend of the dead Fisher King he found a myth which was rather perfectly suited to his heightened sensitivity to despair and decay.

Although dealing with legend or myth, West does not allow himself to be restricted by it. *Miss Lonelyhearts* is the symbolist masterpiece that it is precisely because West has merely incorporated the Grail and Oedipal legends into a larger conception. More than a modernization of a legend, *Miss Lonelyhearts* is a modern myth.

The myth was ironically conceived; any other conception was probably impossible in a scientific world where the inherited, enduring universe of symbols has collapsed. Dream-bounded societies "within a mythologically charged horizon . . . no longer exist" [Joseph Campbell, *The Hero with a Thousand Faces*]. West's sensibility—a strange blend of irony and faintly mystic intensity—was perhaps a necessary one for the modern mythmaker. Moreover, "humor [being] the touchstone of the truly mythological as distinct from the more literal-minded and sentimental theological mood," West, as evidenced by the novel, was at home in the mythic mode.

In his study of the archetypal hero, Joseph Campbell defines a composite adventure of the hero which bears a striking resemblance to Miss Lonelyhearts' experience:

> . . . the *separation* or *departure:* . . . (1) "The Call to Adventure," or the signs of the vocation of the hero; (2) "Refusal of the Call," or the folly of the flight from the god; (3) "Supernatural Aid," the unsuspected assistance that comes to one who has undertaken his proper adventure; (4) "The Crossing of the First Threshold"; and (5) "The Belly of the Whale," or the passage into the realm of night. The stage of *the trials and victories of initiation:* . . . (1) "The Road of Trials," or the dangerous aspect of the gods; (2) "The Meeting with the Goddess" (*Magna Mater*), or the bliss of infancy regained; (3)

"Woman as the Temptress," the realization and agony of Oedipus; (4) "Atonement with the Father"; (5) "Apotheosis"; and (6) "The Ultimate Boon."

In warning against overly literal readings, Mr. Campbell notes that "the changes rung on the simple scale of the monomyth defy description." The warning notwithstanding, with the exception of a slight modification of order, the composite monomyth describes *Miss Lonelyhearts* so strikingly as scarcely to need comment: The "Call" is the Miss Lonelyhearts job which leads to a priestlike vocation; his fear of hysteria, the "snake," is his "Refusal"; and his ultimate capitulation to God reveals the "folly of his flight." The symbolic "Supernatural Aid," according to Campbell, is often provided by "a little old crone or old man"; and in *Miss Lonelyhearts* the "clean old man," who is associated with a frog (a symbol for the unconscious), provides the hero with an unconscious insight into himself which hastens his "Atonement with the Father." "Crossing the First Threshold" occurs in the chapter "Miss Lonelyhearts and the Dead Pan." Campbell notes: "The Arcadian god Pan is the best known Classical example of this dangerous presence dwelling just beyond the protected zone of the village boundary." And Miss Lonelyhearts' growing catatonia is described in sea imagery clearly suggesting the "night journey" or the descent into the "belly of the whale." Campbell notes, significantly, that the passage of the mythological hero is fundamentally inward.

Miss Lonelyhearts' *trials* or "initiations"—they can hardly be called *victories* in the novel—begin with the dream sacrifice of the lamb. The beginning of his night journey, it has obvious parallels with the following description by Campbell of "The Road of Trials":

> And so it happens that if anyone . . . undertakes for himself the perilous journey into the darkness by descending, either intentionally or unintentionally, into the crooked lanes of his own spiritual labyrinth, he soon finds himself in a landscape of symbolical figures (any one of which may swallow him).

The meaning of West's description of Chapter Three [in **"Some Notes on Miss L.,"** *Contempo* III, 13 May 1933]— "the need for taking symbols literally is described through a dream in which a symbol is actually flashed"—begins to become clear. Campbell then adds a remark that not only explains West's meaning but also becomes of great importance when discussing the dream sacrifice of the lamb from a psychoanalytical viewpoint: "The specific psychological difficulties of the dreamer frequently are revealed with touching simplicity and force."

The pastoral interlude with Betty, who is an obvious surrogate for the *Magna Mater,* conveys the "bliss of infancy regained"; that it is a false or, at best, temporary bliss does not thereby invalidate this element of the monomyth. The next characteristic, his encounter with "Woman as Temptress"—Fay Doyle's seduction—induces in him an "Oedipus-Hamlet revulsion." Campbell, in his discussion of "Woman as the Temptress," notes that when this "revulsion remains to beset the soul . . . the world, the body, and woman above all, become the symbols no longer of victory but of defeat." In the novel, after the seduction, is the following passage:

> Soon after Mrs. Doyle left, Miss Lonelyhearts became physically sick . . . his imagination began to work.
>
> He found himself in the window of a pawnshop full of fur coats, diamond rings, watches, shotguns, fishing tackle, mandolins. All these things were the paraphernalia of suffering. . . .
>
> He sat in the window thinking. Man has a tropism for order. Keys in one pocket, change in another. Mandolins are tuned G D A E. The physical world has a tropism for disorder, entropy. Man against nature . . . the battle of the centuries. Keys yearn to mix with change. Mandolins strive to get out of tune. Every order has within it the germ of destruction. All order is doomed. . . .

Finally, Campbell's description of "The Atonement with the Father" is a comment on Miss Lonelyhearts' religious conversion as well:

> The problem of the hero going to meet the father is to open his soul beyond terror to such a degree that he will be ripe to understand how the sickening and insane tragedies of this vast and ruthless cosmos are completely validated in the majesty of Being. The hero transcends life with its peculiar blind spot and for a moment rises to a glimpse of the source. He beholds the face of the father, understands—and the two are atoned.

Ultimately, what is so remarkable about the novel is the range and depth of its archetypal conception. Apparently casual responses are far from casual. The richness of the novel resides in symbolic or archetypal dimension residing in almost every detail. Note, for example, how Campbell's description of the hero who refuses the summons describes Miss Lonelyhearts' responses: "Walled in boredom, hard work, or 'culture,' the subject loses the power of significant affirmative action and becomes a victim to be saved. His flowering world becomes a wasteland of dry stones and his life feels meaningless."

Miss Lonelyhearts is the near perfect work it is because as a myth, it is not a dream—not even a grotesque nightmare. Its pattern, like that of myth, is consciously controlled. Intended to "serve as a powerful picture language for the communication of traditional wisdom," myths "are not only symptoms of the unconscious . . . but also controlled and intended statements of certain spiritual principles" [Campbell]. That West consciously constructed his myth to give "certain spiritual principles" a bitter, ironic twist is not only characteristic, but revealing; it suggests that West, like many moderns, was prone to a psychological interpretation of myth. Since Freud's Oedipal studies and Jung's analysis of the collective unconscious, such psychological interpretation has become widespread. West's success in adding this psychoanalytic dimension to the classic archetypal drama of *Miss Lonelyhearts,* in psychoanalyzing Miss Lonelyhearts *imagistically,* is his most

brilliant achievement, and so subtle an accomplishment that his method is worth some discussion.

West revealed the heart of his psychological method in **"Some Notes on Miss L.":**

> Psychology has nothing to do with reality nor should it be used as a motivation. The novelist is no longer a psychologist. Psychology can now become something much more important. The great body of case histories can be used in the way the ancient writers used their myths. Freud is your Bullfinch; you can not learn from him.

Freud (psychoanalysis) has delved so deeply into the human psyche that the analytic novel has been rendered sterile. "The novelist is no longer a psychologist," because the novelist can offer no new psychological insights. Instead, "psychology can now become something much more important." "The great body of case histories" can now be used in an archetypal sense. They have already taken on the elements of legend and should be so used. West's assertion that Miss Lonelyhearts' "case is classical" was not mere legpull, for West has taken a "classical case history"—an Oedipus complex—and, by the use of brilliant imagery, translated it into a work of art. (pp. 90-5)

Miss Lonelyhearts may strike many, particularly religious readers, as an unpleasant, even ugly novel, and not without some justification. Nevertheless, despite its many unfortunate anti-religious overtones, one misunderstands West and does him a disservice if one fails to realize that the attack is against that kind of religiosity which seeks to escape involvement in human suffering by explaining and justifying its existence. If *Miss Lonelyhearts* upsets its readers, it is because in various forms it reveals the cancerous deceits by which men disguise their indifference, by which they escape involvement in, as W. H. Auden put it, the "human position" of suffering. *Miss Lonelyhearts* is a moving, powerful novel because it is the comic, pathetic, and perhaps even tragic story of a holy fool, who as quester is ultimately made scapegoat by his inability to fathom the mystery of human suffering or to forget it.

Still the novel, another example of West's "particular kind of joking," is much more. The subtle symbols, the allusive conception, and the bitter ironies are all part of West's attempt to disguise his emotional involvement in an agonizing perception, and are his way of preventing the novel from being sentimental. They make a simple reading impossible. *Miss Lonelyhearts* is an enormously compressed and complex novel; to pretend that it is simple is to pretend that West was neither a symbolist nor a highly allusive writer.

Perhaps the novel's conception precludes a widely agreed-upon interpretation; even now West's sensibility as reflected in the novel is beyond the purview of most of his readers. However, with effort, and with an awareness of what is being done in post-World War II European and American fiction and drama, they can now begin to read rather than misread the novel. (p. 101)

The layers of meaning in the novel do not, as they might seem to, sit on top of one another as oil sits on water; they dissolve into each other. More than a mechanical sum of its parts, the novel is a *Gestalt* and must be seen as one. A symbolist prose poem, it is neither as moving and religious as its simple narrative suggests; as grand, heroic, and affirmative as its mythic conception indicates; nor as thoroughly savage, cynical, and obscene as its psychological dimension leads one to believe. The purity of each line has been blurred by the others.

In its poignant evocation of religious atrophy, its ironic anti-heroism, and its pervasive and faintly sickening psychological reduction of human behavior, **Miss Lonelyhearts** is a summation of our time. It is an affirmation of despair and a protest—a raging, mythic, mocking, agonizing protest against a world so flattened and absurd that true compassion is unendurable. (pp. 101-02)

> *Victor Comerchero, in his* Nathanael West: The Ironic Prophet, *Syracuse University Press, 1964, 189 p.*

Randall Reid (essay date 1967)

[*Reid, an American short story writer, educator, and critic, is the author of* The Fiction of Nathanael West: No Redeemer, No Promised Land. *A chapter devoted to* Miss Lonelyhearts *discusses major themes, structure, imagery, characterizations, narrative technique, and the influence of such authors as Fyodor Dostoevsky, Aldous Huxley, and Charles Baudelaire on its composition. In the following excerpt, Reid rejects Freudian interpretations of* Miss Lonelyhearts *as applied by Stanley Edgar Hyman and Victor Comerchero. For a discussion by Hyman, see the excerpt dated 1962; for Comerchero's views, see the excerpt dated 1964.*]

> Psychology has nothing to do with reality nor should it be used as motivation. The novelist is no longer a psychologist. Psychology can become something much more important. The great body of case histories can be used in the way the ancient writers used their myths. Freud is your Bulfinch; you can not learn from him.—
> West, **"Some Notes on Miss L."**

Though they may be unnecessarily epigrammatic, these remarks clearly repudiate psychology—any psychology—as a system of revealed truth. It is therefore interesting that two of the three long studies on West which have appeared should expound psychoanalytic readings of **Miss Lonelyhearts.** [In a footnote the critic cites Stanley Edgar Hyman's *Nathanael West* and Victor Comerchero's *Nathanael West: The Ironic Prophet.*] It is even more interesting—or odd—that West's comments should be cited to support them, but that is exactly what has happened. Here, for example, is the way Victor Comerchero has construed West's remarks: "Freud (psychoanalysis) has delved so deeply into the human psyche that the analytic novel has been rendered sterile. 'The novelist is no longer a psychologist,' because the novelist can offer no new psychological insights." Following Stanley Edgar Hyman, Comerchero then asserts that Miss Lonelyhearts embodies, in orthodox Freudian terms, an Oedipal case history of repressed homosexuality, and he concludes with this description of Miss Lonelyhearts' religious experience:

What Miss Lonelyhearts *really* accepts is his castration. The religious conversion is *really* a conversion from latent to overt homosexuality; so is the ending. The final embrace between Miss Lonelyhearts and Doyle is, as Stanley Edgar Hyman has noted, "a homosexual tableau—the men locked in embrace while the woman stands helplessly by."

The emphasis upon the "really's" is mine. I supply it for two reasons: to underscore Comerchero's flat contradiction of West's own statement ("Psychology has nothing to do with reality") and to underscore the assumption behind too many exercises in "Freudian" literary criticism—that Freudian theory is not just an interpretive method but reality itself. Whatever the merits of such an assumption, West did not share it. His remarks indicate that we should regard Freud the way modern intellectuals regard classic fables, not the way devout believers regard their scriptures.

West's remarks do not, of course, prove that Freudian interpretation is irrelevant to **Miss Lonelyhearts.** The test of any interpretation is its ability to illuminate a text, not its endorsement by the author. But we need not invoke West's authority to demonstrate that the Hyman-Comerchero reading fails even that fundamental test. Hyman offers this hypothetical case history for Miss Lonelyhearts:

Terrified of his stern religious father, identifying with his soft loving mother, the boy renounces his phallicism out of castration anxiety—a classic Oedipus complex. In these terms the Shrikes are Miss Lonelyhearts' Oedipal parents, abstracted as the father's loud voice and the mother's tantalizing breast. The scene at the end of Miss Lonelyhearts' date with Mary Shrike is horrifying and superb. Standing outside her apartment door, suddenly overcome with pas-

West posing on a Hollywood movie set, 1933.

sion, he strips her naked under her fur coat while she keeps talking mindlessly of her mother's death, mumbling and repeating herself, so that Shrike will not hear their sudden silence and come out. Finally Mary agrees to let Miss Lonelyhearts in if Shrike is not home, goes inside, and soon Shrike peers out the door, wearing only the top of his pajamas. It is the child's Oedipal vision perfectly dramatized: he can clutch at his mother's body but loses her each time to his more potent rival.

This sounds plausible enough, but it contains a disconcerting number of inventions, misstatements, and omissions. From the novel, we know only that Miss Lonelyhearts' father was a minister, not that he was stern or loud-voiced or that Miss Lonelyhearts was terrified of him. The only evidence that Miss Lonelyhearts even had a mother—hard or soft, loving or cruel—is the fact of his own existence. Further, Miss Lonelyhearts is not "suddenly overcome with passion." Instead, he is trying "to work this spark [of desire] into a flame," trying "desperately to keep the spark alive." Mary is so far from being the object—maternal or otherwise—of his desire that his sexual response is an effort of the will, not a passionate act. Her "tantalizing breast" fails to tantalize. And the case history ignores the connivance of the Shrikes in the comedy enacted, a comedy in which Miss Lonelyhearts is perhaps the most passive and innocent party. The comedy's chief author is, of course, Shrike himself. Mary tells Miss Lonelyhearts that Shrike lets her go out with other men because "He knows that I let them neck me and when I get home all hot and bothered, why he climbs into my bed and begs for it." In the hallway she says: "We can't stop talking. We must talk. Willie probably heard the elevator and is listening behind the door. You don't know him. If he doesn't hear us talk, he'll know you're kissing me and open the door. It's an old trick of his." It is indeed. And if we want to identify latent homosexuals, I suggest that Shrike is a far more obvious suspect than Miss Lonelyhearts.

Hyman's interpretation requires him to read the novel's ending as a revelation of repressed desire.

> It is of course a homosexual tableau—the men locked in embrace while the woman stands helplessly by. . . .
>
> It is West's ultimate irony that the symbolic embrace they manage at the end is one penetrating the body of the other with a bullet.

Again, this is persuasive until one reads the novel. The embrace is "symbolic" enough, but it is hardly suggestive of homosexuality. Doyle shouts a warning, but Miss Lonelyhearts "did not understand the cripple's shout and heard it as a cry for help from Desperate, Harold S., Catholic-mother, Broken-hearted, Broad-shoulders, Sick-of-it-all, Disillusioned-with-tubercular-husband. He was running to succor them with love." Miss Lonelyhearts has clearly lost all sense of particular identity. The object of his embrace has neither sex nor substance. It is an abstraction, a compound illusion projected upon a real person whom Miss Lonelyhearts barely recognizes. And Doyle, the other party to the "homosexual tableau," tries to escape the embrace and also tries to get rid of the gun. It is the

entry of the "helpless" Betty, "cutting off his escape," which leads to the grotesque accident of Miss Lonelyhearts' death.

The homosexual interpretation is, then, so weak that it requires us to ignore many of the novel's details and invent others. It is also quite irrelevant to the novel's issues. Nothing in the diagnosis explains the fact of mass suffering or the reasons for Miss Lonelyhearts' response to that suffering or the ultimate failure of his mission. Heterosexuality is no doubt desirable, but it is hardly sufficient to permit the successful imitation of Christ, and in the world of Miss Lonelyhearts nothing less than the imitation of Christ can really help. [The critic adds in a footnote that: "Significantly, neither Hyman nor Comerchero is able to relate the homosexual interpretation to any important aspect of the novel. Its essential irrelevance can easily be demonstrated. For example: let us assume that 'latent homosexuality' is an accurate diagnosis, and let us assume that Miss Lonelyhearts is either 'cured' of his repressed tendencies or brought to accept them. He could then marry Betty and go into advertising or marry Doyle and go into interior decorating. What effect would either resolution have? None at all. Hyman and Comerchero do not, of course, pretend that homosexuality is Miss Lonelyhearts' only problem, but I do not think they have demonstrated that it is, in terms of the novel's major themes, any kind of problem at all."] To read the novel as a case of repressed homosexuality is to read it as though Betty had written it. The clinical attitude mimics Betty's blindness to evil and her insistence upon regarding Miss Lonelyhearts as an isolated specimen of morbid illness, not as a man responding intelligibly to a real external situation. "No morality, only medicine." Significantly, Hyman becomes tone deaf to irony whenever Betty appears. He speaks of Betty's "Edenic innocence," of her "patient innocence . . . that makes the book so heartbreaking," and concludes that "she represents . . . the innocent order of Nature, as opposed to the disorder of sinful Man." This is nonsense. It is the "innocent order of Nature," of course, which produces the cruel disorder of a girl born with no nose, an idiot child, an unwanted pregnancy. And Betty's innocence is hardly Eve-like. Though she means well and deserves some sympathy, she is unintelligent and even somewhat corrupt. Her "patient innocence" ignores not only mass suffering but the meaning of this suffering to Miss Lonelyhearts, and her devotion to him is therefore not impressive. And her formula for successful living—country idylls supported by a job in advertising—does not strike me as Edenic. [The critic adds in a footnote that "Hyman, however, is so infatuated with Betty, that he offers repressed homosexuality to explain Miss Lonelyhearts' discontent with her. Betty's triviality and incomprehension are surely sufficient explanations in themselves."]

West's own remarks on psychology are interesting apart from the question of clinical interpretation. We should note initially that he did not introduce his notes as the credo of a lifetime, but as "some of the things I thought when writing [*Miss Lonelyhearts*]." We have no right, therefore, to assume that they were more than working principles for a single book. Yet those working principles are important. "Psychology has nothing to do with reality nor should it be used as motivation." This statement implies an absolute distinction between reality and psychological interpretations of it. It explicitly denies that any psychological theory reveals the "real" motives for behavior. "The novelist is no longer a psychologist"—no longer, that is, a fabricator and explainer of motives. "Psychology can become something much more important. The great body of case histories can be used in the way the ancient writers used their myths." How did the ancient writers use their myths? As established stories whose plausibility did not have to be justified. Sophocles, for example, does not have to convince his audience that the murder of Laius and the marriage of Oedipus and Jocasta are plausible. Both events have the status of facts for which Sophocles does not have to account—not, at least, in the way that George Eliot has to account for the marriage of Dorothea and Causabon. Further, he need not laboriously explain what happened because the audience already knows what happened—the writer can focus on the critical issues in his story without having to document it or rationalize it. The resulting gain in economy is obvious. In one sense, therefore, West's remarks on psychology are only a particular application of his general theory of the lyric novel. West wanted to relieve the novel of its burden of documentation, and the use of familiar materials was fundamental to this aim. "The novelist is no longer a psychologist" in the sense that he no longer has to contrive and heavily document his own case histories; instead, he can borrow his stories from sources which are as familiar to modern readers as myths were to the ancients. But the case history is all he should borrow. "Freud is your Bulfinch; you can not learn from him"—a remark which reduces Freud to the status of an anthologist. We could paraphrase it as "take the data and let the interpretations go." West's attitude may be extreme but it is also extremely clear: Freudian theory can teach you nothing about reality. Freudian case histories, however, like any collection of familiar stories, can be both useful and important to a writer. And West implies that a writer should exercise the same freedom in his use of borrowed case histories that Euripides did in his use of traditional myths.

West's use of psychology relies, however, on more than the familiarity of particular materials. He said that Miss Lonelyhearts' "case is classical and is built on all the cases in James' *Varieties of Religious Experience* and Starbuck's *Psychology of Religion*," and I have [in an unexcerpted portion of this essay] argued that it is built on other case histories—notably Raskolnikov's—as well. The generic quality of this method is crucial. A classical case history is a type; it is formed by abstracting the common features from many histories until a pattern emerges, a pattern which will be familiar even if the particular materials from which it is formed are not. And the pattern is likely to be persuasive apart from its familiarity. The logic of character becomes, in West's hands, almost musical. It rests upon the internal rhythm and harmony of a sequence of behavior, not upon assignable motives taken from depth psychology or from "rational" theories about human personality. "Psychologizing" can therefore be cut out of the novel. A "classical" pattern of behavior does not need to

be explained to be believed; its ubiquity is ample proof of its plausibility.

But what of its meaning? The question is treacherous. It cannot be answered by any psychological analysis which ignores the novel's principal themes. Take, for example, that sexual deadness in Miss Lonelyhearts which both Hyman and Comerchero regard as presumptive evidence of homosexuality. The deadness is certainly there. Though Mary's excitement is revealed in the changed scent of her body, "no similar change ever took place in his own body, however. Like a dead man, only friction could make him warm or violence make him mobile." He tries to "excite himself . . . by thinking of the play Mary made with her breasts. . . . But the excitement refused to come. If anything, he felt colder than before he had started to think of women. It was not his line." And when he tries to tease himself with the prospect of Fay Doyle, he remains "as dry and cold as a polished bone."

The evidence is abundant, but what does it mean? If the deadness were limited to Miss Lonelyhearts' sexuality, diagnosis might be simple—but it is not. Deadness pervades all his responses. When he tries to preach the gospel of divine love, he can only produce the mock rhetoric of Shrike, and he feels "like an empty bottle, shiny and sterile." Even his sympathy is deadened by "the stone that had formed in his gut," a stone which, by the novel's end, has become an impervious Gibraltar: "He did not feel guilty. He did not feel. The rock was a solidification of his feeling, his conscience, his sense of reality, his self-knowledge." And deadness is as pervasive in Miss Lonelyhearts' world as it is in Miss Lonelyhearts himself. The newspapermen in the speakeasy are just "machines for making jokes." Shrike is a master of the "dead pan" whose features "huddled together in a dead, gray triangle," and Mrs. Doyle's massive hams are "like two enormous grindstones." In the park, "the decay that covered the surface of the mottled ground was not the kind in which life generates." Even the country idyll has its images of deadness: "In the deep shade there was nothing but death—rotten leaves, gray and white fungi, and over everything a funereal hush."

The world of Miss Lonelyhearts is a waste land. Its psychology owes far more to regenerative myths than to Freud and far more to ascetic or apocalyptic Christianity than to Jessie L. Weston. The world confirms the saint's anguished vision of this life. It reaches but to dust. Nature and sexuality are agents of death, alive only in their power to hurt. Though latent homosexuality is not relevant to the novel's major themes, universally crippled and malignant sexuality is. The two representatives of fleshly love— Shrike and Mrs. Doyle—are described in imagery which is grotesquely symbolic. Shrike's name, for example, comes from the butcher bird which impales its living prey on thorns, and the sense of murderous penetration is in his every act. Mrs. Doyle, however, is omnivorously engulfing. The sexes are thereby given nightmarish attributes: the phallus is just an instrument of sadistic impalement, and the female genitalia are a smothering, swallowing, devouring sea. Miss Lonelyhearts is quite properly terrified of both sexes. And quite properly sympathetic to both. Like all the other forces in the novel, the sexes are, in their active forms, irreconcilable and mutually destructive. But in their passive forms, both sexes are victims—Doyle, Mary Shrike, the idiot girl, even Shrike himself. " 'She's selfish. She's a damned selfish bitch. . . . Sleeping with her is like sleeping with a knife in one's groin.' " Miss Lonelyhearts is therefore like a child with parents so vicious and so unhappy that identifying with either sex is impossible. And, conversely, identifying with both is inevitable. He is the child in whom all the destructive and conflicting demands of the parents meet. Unless he can reconcile the sexes to each other, they will destroy themselves and him. His own sexual behavior exhibits the same duality of active cruelty and passive suffering. With both Mary Shrike and Betty, for example, he is sometimes as compulsively destructive as Shrike. Sexuality therefore arouses in Miss Lonelyhearts both personal terror and moral horror. His acceptance of "castration" at the moment of conversion is a fantasy of deliverance, not a resignation to loss.

There is, in the saint's vision, no real love but divine love, no real life but eternal life. When God is withdrawn, only deadness remains. Miss Lonelyhearts muses upon "how dead the world is . . . a world of doorknobs," and he dreams of playing the redeemer and bringing the doorknobs to life. "At his command, they bled, flowered, spoke." Regeneration is a classic problem. Its important realities here are the fact of Miss Lonelyhearts' condition and the implications of his role. His dilemma is that of a man with a religious vocation—"for him, Christ was the most natural of excitements"—in which he cannot believe. He knows that his strongest desire leads only to hysteria, that his deepest tendencies have no outlet except in delusion. The frustrations inherent in this condition alone would explain much of his paralysis, and frustration in general would explain the rest. The alternate deadness and violence in Miss Lonelyhearts are a familiar psychological state, a state which can be induced by any combination of unremitting stimulus and thwarted response. It does not matter what the stimulus is—hunger, repressed homosexuality, physical pain—so long as it is inescapable and unrelieved. Nor does it matter what the barriers are so long as they are insurmountable. In *Miss Lonelyhearts,* constant pain and constant thwarting are universal. They are conditions of living, not symptoms of individual neuroses, and "latent homosexuality" is therefore neither a necessary explanation nor a meaningful definition of Miss Lonelyhearts' problem. If there is no health in us, diagnosis of specific pathologies is irrelevant, for the real disease is life itself. And the classic conversion experience derives from exactly this perception—that both one's own nature and the nature of mortal life are composed of irreconcilable contradictions, contradictions which are experienced as sin or inherent evil. There is no escape from these contradictions except by escaping the conditions of mortality. One must be reborn. The terrible paradox of *Miss Lonelyhearts* is that it accepts the saint's definition of this life but denies the saint's alternative to it. This world is indeed corrupt, dead, and irreconcilably evil, but this world is all there is.

The classic problem of misery is, in *Miss Lonelyhearts,* combined with a modern corollary—the puerility and exhaustion of all classic responses. The implications of this

corollary are everywhere in West, firmly embodied in each of the deliberately artificial techniques he employed. (pp. 72-84)

Randall Reid, in his The Fiction of Nathanael West: No Redeemer, No Promised Land, *The University of Chicago Press, 1967, 174 p.*

James F. Light   (essay date 1971)

[*Light is an American educator and critic and the author of* Nathanael West: An Interpretive Study *(1961; revised edition, 1971). In the following excerpt from that study, he examines West's treatment in* Miss Lonelyhearts *of the inadequacy of socially conditioned dreams and expectations in a decaying, violent world. Light concludes with a discussion of West's principal influences in writing* Miss Lonelyhearts.]

Miss Lonelyhearts tells the story of a young man who writes a sob-sister column for the newspapers. Miss Lonelyhearts (in the original manuscript West had named his hero Thomas Matlock) gives advice in his column to desperate and helpless people who have no other place to turn. Miss Lonelyhearts has taken the job as a joke, and he hopes it will lead to his writing a gossip column. After a while the pathetic letters addressed to him make him feel that the joke has turned upon him. Here the novel really begins, and the action treats Miss Lonelyhearts' attempts to come to terms with his own helplessness. This he can do in no easy way. Instead he must go through what might be called a program for the attainment of salvation. This program, or pilgrimage, eventually leads to a mystical experience, but by the time it has reached this culmination Miss Lonelyhearts has become completely alienated from those around him; in the eyes of the world, he has become "sick." Though tragically ironic, it is only fitting that he should be killed by one of those desperate creatures who have led him to his ordeal and his mystical experience. The novel, as West claimed [in **"Some Notes on Miss L.,"** *Contempo* III, 15 May 1933], is the "portrait of a priest of our time who has had a religious experience." The portrait is painted in a succinct, imagistic style, and it attempts to fulfill West's claim that

> Lyric novels can be written according to Poe's definition of a lyric poem. The short novel is a distinct form especially suited to use in this country. France, Spain, Italy have a literature as well as the Scandinavian writers. For a hasty people we are far too patient with the Bucks, Dreisers, and Lewises. Thank God we are not all Scandinavians.

> Forget the epic, the master work. In America fortunes do not accumulate, the soil does not grow, families have no history. Leave slow growth to the book reviewers, you only have time to explode.

From the point of view of Miss Lonelyhearts, this priest of twentieth-century America, the American scene is a desolate one. Its basic components are decay and violence and pain. In this American wasteland, the decay is extreme. Though the action takes place in the spring, the air seems waxy and artificial, while the dirt of the city appears without possibility of generation. Even in the country, the vision is of death and rot. For Miss Lonelyhearts, the entire world is dead, and only through hysteria, brought on by the name of Christ, can the "dead world take on a semblance of life."

In this decayed world, violence exists everywhere. Partly its source is the Darwinistic struggle for survival; partly it stems from the unsatisfied spiritual needs of man. Through violence, modern man comes alive; it is the salt by which he savors an existence without the Saviour. Before attaining grace, Miss Lonelyhearts thinks that "only violence could make him supple"; or, comparing himself to a dead man, he feels that "only friction could make him warm or violence make him mobile."

Man is caught in a viselike trap: in a sterile world he would still be alive, but only through violence can he feel himself potent. The world of *Miss Lonelyhearts* is, therefore, filled with violence. Its everyday presence is suggested by innumerable actions and images and by casual understatement. "Violent images are used to illustrate commonplace events. Violent acts are left almost bald."

Man's desire for life leads to his seemingly instinctive preoccupation with sexual violence, the type most intimately associated with life. The letters to Miss Lonelyhearts are permeated with sexual suffering, from the nightmarish epistle of Broad Shoulders to the pathos of Sick-of-it-all, who writes that she is expecting her eighth child in twelve years "and I don't think I can stand it. . . . I cry all the time it hurts so much and I don't know what to do." Miss Lonelyhearts' newspaper associates gain vicarious life from the violence of the sexual gang-shag tales they love to tell. Even Miss Lonelyhearts at one time tugs sadistically at a woman's nipples, at another time tears at an unwilling woman's clothes.

This emphasis on violence was in every novel West wrote. Even before the publication of *Miss Lonelyhearts,* West stated his defense:

> In America violence is idiomatic. . . . What is melodramatic in European writing is not necessarily so in American writing. For a European writer to make violence real, he has to do a great deal of careful sociology and psychology. He often needs three hundred pages to motivate one little murder. But not so the American writer. His audience has been prepared and is neither surprised nor shocked if he omits artistic excuses for familiar events ["**Some Notes on Violence,**" *Contact,* October 1932].

In this world of decay and violence man is able to exist only through dreams. The search for a dream to believe in is right—and in this contention *Miss Lonelyhearts* and *Balso* agree—for it is only through dreams that men can fight their misery. However, the commercialization and stereotyping of man's dreams have led to a weakening of their power, a puerility in their content. This is the worst betrayal of modern man.

Typically betrayed is Mary Shrike, the wife of Miss Lonelyhearts' chief tormentor. In her early childhood she has been familiar with violence and suffering, but she romantically transforms her past when she speaks of it. Her alterations of reality make Miss Lonelyhearts realize that "People like Mary were unable to do without such tales. They told them because they wanted to talk about . . . something poetic." This desire for the beautiful attracts Mary to El Gaucho, and it is her poetic longing which explains the medallion she wears between her breasts. Both suggest romance, but both are obvious fakes. El Gaucho, with its romantic atmosphere, is only a commercialized dream, just as the medallion has no religious significance but is an award for a childhood racing contest. These small dreams are betrayals of man's true spiritual needs, but despite their limitations Mary must cling to them. Through such fantasies she attempts to satisfy her psychological need for mystery and romance. Her need unites her with the unfortunate correspondents who seek help from Miss Lonelyhearts.

Perhaps even more than the letter writers, Mrs. Shrike needs the help of Christ, the Miss Lonelyhearts of Miss Lonelyhearts. Not really able to believe in her tiny dreams, she, nevertheless, needs something on which to dream. The split personality which results can be seen in her inner conflict. On the one hand, she is pulled by the head's knowledge and fears; on the other, she instinctively reacts according to the body's desires. When Miss Lonelyhearts kisses Mary, she reacts with sexual grunts and scents; but never will her mind allow her to submit wholly to the sexual act. Because of the body-mind conflict, with the fears of the mind in eventual control, she will not sleep with Miss Lonelyhearts and cannot respond sexually to her husband. Being divided, Mary can submit totally to no one, and paradoxically one must give oneself to gain oneself. Mary becomes the eternal virgin; and the head, or reason, is the villain that makes her so. Rationalism dooms Mary, and much of modern man, to dream the small dreams rather than the big Christ dream; but the small dreams are psychologically inadequate to the spiritual needs of man.

A more powerful dream might have saved Mary by giving her a mystery and romance worthy of belief. But in this commercialized world the needs of the spirit have been betrayed. The modern dream merchants do not offer love as the dream by which man can conquer suffering. They do not even justify human suffering by stating that it is Christ's gift to man and that by suffering man comes to know Christ. Instead they offer the easy Technicolor evasions (from Art to the South Seas) that man so much wants to believe in. Unfortunately none of these escapes is powerful enough to salve for long the pain of existence.

In this world of decay and violence and pain, man can react in only a limited number of ways. He can, like Mary Shrike, who wavers between acceptance and non-acceptance of a lesser dream than Christ, become a split personality. By distortion and simplification, he can so blind himself to the suffering of man that he is capable of accepting a lesser dream. He can reject all dreams. He can accept the Christ dream of faith and universal love.

Miss Lonelyhearts' girl friend, Betty, follows the second of these paths. By her excessive simplification of the world, she is able to bring order out of chaos. When Miss

Lonelyhearts first thinks of her, he muses "that when she straightened his tie, she straightened much more." Later on, when Betty visits Miss Lonelyhearts while he is ill, she puts the jumbled confusion of his room in order. This same ability to put her universe in order leads Betty to an inner peace that is reflected even in her physical smoothness. Because of Miss Lonelyhearts' own unsuccessful attempts to attain this harmony, he feels Betty is a Buddha, lacking only the potbelly.

For Miss Lonelyhearts, Betty's order is a false one. It excludes not only suffering but also the spiritual needs of man. It degrades man to a mere body and assumes that all his ailments can be cured by such drugs as aspirin. Still, while basically false, Betty's ability to limit experience allows her to retain her innocent, natural speech, and laugh. Such naturalness is more related to the primal simplicities of nature than to the elaborate artificiality, both physical and psychological, of the city. Inevitably Betty combats Miss Lonelyhearts' spiritual sickness by taking him to the zoo and talking of the country's sounds and smells. Then she takes him to the country. Though the visit does not cure Miss Lonelyhearts, Betty becomes an "excited child, greeting the trees and grass with delight."

Betty's vision of the way of the world is one of childlike order and harmony. It is akin to one of the childhood memories of Miss Lonelyhearts:

> One winter evening . . . he had . . . gone to the piano and had begun a piece by Mozart. His sister left her picture book to dance to his music. She had never danced before. She danced gravely and carefully, a simple dance yet formal. . . . As Miss Lonelyhearts stood at the bar, swaying slightly to the remembered music, he thought of children dancing. Square replacing oblong and being replaced by circle. Every child everywhere; in the whole world there was not one child who was not gravely, sweetly dancing.

Such a world of simple patterns, however, is the world of childhood only; that it is based on children's limited, and therefore false, experience is suggested by what immediately follows: an unjustified punch in the mouth from a stranger loosens one of Miss Lonelyhearts' teeth. Violence and suffering exist in the real universe, and any harmony which eliminates these elements is false.

Though Betty's world is one of Buddhistic blindness, it can, through its limitations, become a universal of personal love, of "his job and her gingham apron, his slippers beside the fireplace and her ability to cook." This simplification makes Betty oblivious both to the world of suffering humanity and to the things of the spirit. The possibility of such a limited outlook continuing throughout life is slim.

Because the dreams sold by the modern dream merchants offer no adequate solution for conquering or justifying suffering in a world of rot and violence, some cynical sophisticates react toward dreams in still a third way. They reject all dreams. Shrike, Miss Lonelyhearts' chief tormentor, has made such a rejection. So have most of the newspapermen with whom Shrike associates. Once these men had felt that their devotion to Beauty and self-expression justi-

fied their existence, but under the commercialized mold of the news story they have lost all faith in Beauty. Shrike, as feature editor, has especially seen culture and Beauty and self-expression corrupted by commercialism. The loss of faith in Beauty deafens these men, whom Shrike epitomizes, to the call of any faith. Mechanically and cynically, they make jokes of man's dreams about the soil, the South Seas, Hedonism, and Art. The biggest joke, however, is the Christ dream, and Shrike reserves his most brutal attacks for man's aspirations toward Christ. Shrike sends a parodied prayer of the *"Anima Christi"* to Miss Lonelyhearts:

> Soul of Miss L, glorify me
> Body of Miss L, nourish me
> Blood of Miss L, intoxicate me. . . .

Or Shrike makes vulgar jokes about Christianity: "I am a great saint. I can walk on my own water." Or Shrike reads and shows others a news story concerning a condemned robber and murderer for whom a goat-and-adding-machine service, a religious ceremony, is to be held. Shrike proclaims that such a service embodies the true American religion. This assertion shows that Shrike has become dominated by the lust of the goat and the mechanicalness of the adding machine. To Shrike man is a thing of chemistry alone.

Except about the sexual reluctance of his wife, Shrike is as emotionless as a machine. His lack of emotion dominates the chapter entitled "Miss Lonelyhearts and the Dead Pan." The dead pan refers to Shrike's lack of facial expression, but the word *pan* also suggests the dead nature-god of flocks and pastures. In Shrike, *Pan* is dead, and Shrike is identified with the new mechanical world based on the emotionless physical sciences. These sciences, in their purest form, exist in the "triangles" of mathematics, and these triangles are symbolized in the novel by the triangular, hatchetlike face of Shrike. These triangles, representing the physical sciences with their tendency to destroy the world of spirit, perpetually bury themselves, as Shrike does, in the neck of mankind.

Shrike's lack of emotion determines his action throughout the book. He laughs at humanity by laughing at the pathos of Doyle. He invents a game which has laughter at the letters of the helpless as its purpose, and that game indicts him as the inhuman joke-machine he is. This lack of love and pity justifies the name Shrike, suggestive as it is of the bird that impales its prey upon a cross of thorns. Shrike has become the anti-Christ, crucifying those who strive for faith.

The final alternative to the inadequacy of modern dreams is to attempt the Christ dream, which was once capable of alleviating man's suffering. Miss Lonelyhearts attempts this dream. Puritanical in appearance, he has a "bony chin . . . shaped and cleft like a hoof." The boniness connotes the man of spirit rather than flesh. The cleft chin indicates the split between the spirit and the flesh, between the devil and the saint. This opposition creates barriers to the Christ dream, and they crop up at every milestone of the spiritual journey.

One of the basic obstacles is materialism. Early in the novel Miss Lonelyhearts, like Shrike, accepts the idea of a materialistic and indifferent universe. He feels that if there were some spiritual manifestation, he could show his contempt by casting a stone. But in the indifferent sky there are "no angels, flaming-crosses, olive-bearing doves, wheels within wheels." Wanting to escape from a world dominated by decay and pain, a creation without spiritual manifestation, Miss Lonelyhearts, in true Shrike fashion, starts for a speakeasy.

Two other similarities between Shrike and Miss Lonelyhearts stem from materialism. Like Shrike, Miss Lonelyhearts attempts to become a worshiper of the flesh. Though without great enthusiasm, Miss Lonelyhearts pursues Betty and Mrs. Shrike. Later, he experiences a sexual act with Mrs. Doyle, who embodies primal, carnal, sealike sexuality, and when it is over, he knows that for him flesh-worship is no escape. A more important similarity between Shrike and Miss Lonelyhearts is that for a while Miss Lonelyhearts too attempts to become a joke-machine by laughing at his own sympathetic heart. For Miss Lonelyhearts the laugh is at first bitter and then dies in his throat. It is no wonder that West changed an early draft of the manuscript, in which he had Miss Lonelyhearts express the indictment of escapes found in "Miss Lonelyhearts in the Dismal Swamp," and placed the indictment where it really belonged: in the mouth of Shrike.

Materialism, with its corollaries of carnal love and cynicism, is no solution to Miss Lonelyhearts' need for an answer to the letters. Because of the failure of materialism, Betty, with her faith in personal love and a benevolent, therapeutic nature, finally succeeds in persuading Miss Lonelyhearts to go with her to the country. Momentarily he is able to accept Betty's limited world, but only momentarily. Violence quietly insists upon its existence, for in the country Miss Lonelyhearts sees in stark relief the ever-present animal struggle for survival. The ignorance and viciousness of man also persist; they are personified in the bigotry of a garage attendant who proclaims that it is not hunters but "yids" who have driven the deer from the countryside. Once back in the city, Miss Lonelyhearts realizes that "Betty had failed to cure him . . . he had been right when he said he could never forget the letters."

The ultimate barrier to the realization of the Christ dream is neither Shrike's materialism nor Betty's simplified world. That barrier is pride, and it resides in Miss Lonelyhearts as in all men. Its simplest manifestation is in man's revulsion from his fellow man, his unwillingness to lick lepers, as the saints of old had licked them, out of sheer humility and love. Though Miss Lonelyhearts "wants to lick lepers," he finds it difficult to attain sufficient humility. Rather than uniting himself to the unfortunate, he pities them. The first time he achieves identification is with the cripple, Doyle. The embodiment of broken humanity, Doyle has a primitive pathos that is totally repellent. When Miss Lonelyhearts, striving for complete humility, touches Doyle's hand, he instinctively "jerked away, but then drove his hand back and forced it to clasp the cripple's . . . he did not let go, but pressed it firmly with all the love he could manage." With this handclasp Miss Lonelyhearts symbolically licks his first leper.

This humility leads from the acceptance of Doyle, who represents suffering humanity, to the faith that some order, some pattern, does exist in the universe. There follows an interior calm so perfect that it seems either that of the dead man or of the religious fanatic who, in the perfectness of his faith, is in full accord with his universe. Miss Lonelyhearts' monastic retreat from the world further likens him to the ascetic religious. His asceticism, however, is clearly of the modern world: he not only drinks water and eats crackers but also smokes cigarettes. Still, his is a sainted calm, resting on the "rock" of Christ-like love and faith. Miss Lonelyhearts has achieved a life-in-death serenity, where "what goes on in the sea is of no interest to the rock."

Christ-like love and faith become the rock which leads to Miss Lonelyhearts' alienation from the sea of life. No longer is Miss Lonelyhearts bothered by intellectual problems such as the existence of pain and violence in a world created by a benevolent God, or the lack of order in a universe which, were it created by a purposeful God, should have order and harmony. The philosophic drama of the novel grows primarily from the first problem, but the lack of visible order has also affected Miss Lonelyhearts. He develops a need for order that he himself sees borders on insanity. He recognizes the sad truth that "Man has a tropism for order. . . . The physical world has a tropism for disorder." Man's intellect is constantly frustrated. Its human limitations make the mind unable to see the infinite order, yet its desires toward God demand that it seek a significant pattern. Philosophically Miss Lonelyhearts justifies his futile search: "All order is doomed, yet the battle is worth while."

Though the battle of the intellect is worthwhile in its direction toward the infinite, it is only by faith, by the abdication of the intellect, that the infinite order is perceived by man. Through humility Miss Lonelyhearts attains this simplified outlook. Now nothing remains of Miss Lonelyhearts save love and faith. Through humility he has united himself to suffering humanity, has accepted a universe whose order he cannot comprehend, and consents to marry Betty. The loss of all things save love and faith leaves "his mind free and clear. The things that had muddled it had precipitated out into the rock." After Betty tells him she is pregnant, he shows no emotional response and asks no questions about the future. In his faith, his loss of intellectual questioning, he can become the kind of person that Betty wishes him to be and can accept a future life circumscribed by her innocent but limited dreams: personal love, children, a farm in Connecticut.

Through his humility Miss Lonelyhearts has become dead to this world. Following Christ's injunction that whosoever would find his life must first lose it, Miss Lonelyhearts can now attain a mystical union with God. Transcending the fevered sickness of his body through a transforming grace of light and perfumed cleanliness, he becomes "conscious of two rhythms that were slowly becoming one. When they became one, his identification with God was complete. His heart was the one heart, the heart of God. And his brain was likewise God's."

In this moment of hallucinatory ecstasy the cripple, Doyle, rings Miss Lonelyhearts' doorbell. Miss Lonelyhearts, wishing to succor with love all the desperate of the universe and expecting to perform a miracle by which the cripple will be cured, runs rapturously toward Doyle. But there is no miracle. Instead Miss Lonelyhearts is shot by Doyle, destroyed, like Christ, by the panic and ignorance of those whom he would save. Doyle, and in him suffering man, shatters the only solution to the intolerableness of man's pain, destroys the Christ-like man who perceives that love and faith are the only answers to man's pain in a universe he cannot understand.

True belief in the Christian answers, however, rests upon the dissolution of the self and the subsequent mystical experience of God's love and grace. Until such experiences (the price of which is alienation from this world), the very name of Christ, as Miss Lonelyhearts had felt before his "sickness," is a vanity on the lips of man. After God's love and grace, the personal ecstasy they bring is a "reality," but it is founded upon an insane delusion and even then the "reality" is incommunicable. Thus Miss Lonelyhearts runs toward Doyle with love in his heart, while the cripple, filled with hatred, makes his way up the stairs. In the ironic lack of communication, Doyle's gun, the symbol of a mechanical, loveless world, goes off, and the two men roll down the stairs together.

Although Doyle is the actual murderer of Miss Lonelyhearts, Betty is also indirectly responsible. She comes in while Miss Lonelyhearts and Doyle are grappling, and Doyle feels she is cutting off his escape. He tries to get rid of his gun, but in his panic at seeing Betty he causes the gun to explode. This involvement of Betty is meaningful, for Betty's fragmentary view of the universe would leave out pain and violence. With her belief that man's needs are always bodily ones and his ills are easily cured by aspirin, Betty would destroy the spiritual in man. Her approach to life would negate the need for Christ. It would kill the Christ dream, for without pain and violence there is no need for the relief of Christ-like love, no need for faith to reconcile unjustified suffering with the existence of a good God.

Betty's fragmentary view is false and cannot endure. Witnessing the murder of her unborn child's father, she will need an even greater blindness than she has shown before if she is to disregard the existence of violence. The pain of childbirth, which West emphasizes in the novel, will impress upon her the fact of suffering. Then she, like so many others, will have to reconcile pain and violence with a godly universe. Though there are answers that bring no peace, the love and faith of Christ could make for a better world, one founded on Dostoevsky's Christianity. Truly man needs Christ—witness the cry for "help" on which the novel begins—but Christ in our time has been dwarfed to a lovelorn columnist, his message has become a cliché, and his "agony" is a parody of the Christian myth. Even more ironically and horribly, the only "solution" for man's pain is Christian faith, yet that "solution" does not ease the pain of the letter writers, and it leads Miss Lonelyhearts to hallucinations, insanity, and death. That is the absurdity which illumines contemporary man's pilgrimate and quest.

In its fusion of form and content, *Miss Lonelyhearts* is the best novel West was ever to write. To the novel nothing should be added and nothing could be taken away. Its stark simplicity of language and sentence structure, a bareness achieved by continual pruning and sharpening through six revisions of the novel, creates a peculiarly nightmarish etching of shadows and decay unlike the art of any other American novelist. In addition the book has a warmth, a compassion, which exceeds that of West's other novels. The warmth is especially apparent in the increased depth with which West treats the dilemma of humankind in its need for a dream. Earlier, in **Balso Snell,** West had implied that the wisest thing man can do is to accept himself as an animal and to avoid dreams completely, for in dreams there is only misery. Such an attitude was naïve: an oversimplified solution of a very young man. In **Miss Lonelyhearts,** West probes deeper. The horror of a life lived without any dream is illustrated by the joke-machine called Shrike. Terrible as it is, even a bad dream is better than no dream at all, and this idea, from **Miss Lonelyhearts** on, is constant in West. Faye Greener, in West's last novel, **The Day of the Locust,** puts the insight most bluntly: "She said that any dream was better than no dream and beggars couldn't be choosers." Undoubtedly it would be better for mass man if he wanted a worthy dream instead of the nonsense offered to him by Hollywood or love story magazines, just as it would be better for him to like great art rather than the trash he prefers. His tragedy is that he doesn't make intelligent choices, and he doesn't because of what he is. The pathos of his need to dream, while forced by his nature to choose dreams that will not soothe his pain, is explored with both horror and compassion in **Miss Lonelyhearts,** and in **Miss Lonelyhearts,** unlike **The Day,** the pity is greater than the horror.

While **Miss Lonelyhearts** is wholly unique, one cannot leave it without being aware of how much West is indebted to other writers. Two of the more obvious are T. S. Eliot and William James. Like Eliot, West sees the world as a wasteland, though he is less optimistic than Eliot that a knight, a new Christ, may transform the land and its hollow men into human beings with purpose and direction. Like Eliot, West emphasizes the loss of love in this world, but West intensifies the pain of sex until it becomes a frightening, devouring nightmare—a vision that may be related less to Eliot than to the fact that West himself, while being treated for gonorrhea, sustained a slight injury to his prostate gland and thereafter suffered recurrent pain from the wound. Like Eliot's poem, West's novel takes the form of a Quest, and quite possibly West drew upon Eliot's chief source, Jessie L. Weston's *From Ritual to Romance,* for some of the details of Miss Lonelyhearts' trials; but unlike the "shantih, shantih, shantih" on which *The Waste Land* ends, West's novel ends in a total lack of communication between the "inspired" savior, Miss Lonelyhearts, and the earthbound man, Mr. Doyle. The final effect of the novel is less one of peace than of a confused universe in which the end of the Quest is meaningless, absurd death.

Just as obvious a source is James's *The Varieties of Religious Experience.* In that work James noted the classic states that precede religious conversion—from a feeling of deadness and disorder to despair and eventual submission to God—and that diagnosis accurately describes the psychological movement of Miss Lonelyhearts' mentality. For James the ultimate core of the problem of religion is the cry for "Help! Help!" that the victims of life call out, and that cry is the one that leads Miss Lonelyhearts to his agony. For James, men can be categorized into those who are healthy-minded (and see good as the essential quality of life) and those who are morbid-minded (and see evil as fundamental), and in the way in which she excludes evil, Betty is undoubtedly healthy-minded (and philosophically shallow), while Miss Lonelyhearts, who cannot limit his vision, is morbid-minded (and, for James as well as West, religiously profound).

More important than these influences are those of Dostoevsky, the French symbolists, and the French surrealists. None of these influences is surprising. West himself would have quickly admitted the influence of Dostoevsky, a fact brought out by John Sanford's comment that West had a constant "little brag that he could rewrite Dostoevsky with a pair of shears." Josephine Herbst also remembers the numerous conversations she and West held upon Dostoevsky: how West commented on the power of *The Possessed,* with its grotesqueness and its violence, and how Stavrogin's rape of a young child tormented West.

In *Miss Lonelyhearts,* the Dostoevskyan influence is apparent in the character of Miss Lonelyhearts: he reads and ponders Dostoevsky; he wears the same hair shirt of guilt that tortures so many of Dostoevsky's heroes; he wears the hair shirt because he, like Dostoevsky's heroes, feels his inability to aid the helpless of the universe. Another Dostoevskyan concept is the dualism of good and evil which tugs at the heart of Miss Lonelyhearts and which fills him with the dream of attaining the love and humility of Christ and at the same time permits him sadistically to twist the arm of the clean old man.

Dostoevsky's influence on West is also shown in a letter West once wrote. In it he stated his conviction that the survival of humanity depended upon its acceptance of the Christian ideals of Dostoevsky. This Christianity is probably best defined by Dostoevsky himself when he says: "If we do not follow Christ we shall err in everything. The way to the salvation of mankind leads through his teachings alone." This is to say that whatever reservations he might have about whether God created man or man created God, Dostoevsky had no reservations about the perfect love and humility which Christ preached and lived. West understood Christ and his teachings in just the same way.

Whether West believed in the probability of man's free survival, however, is open to doubt. Always in West's writing, and above all in his last novel, there is the fear that there may be truth in Dostoevsky's "Legend of the Grand Inquisitor" in *The Brothers Karamazov.* In Dostoevsky's masterpiece, the Grand Inquisitor charges that God has given man not happiness but freedom. This freedom only the few can bear; for the many it leads only to untold suffering. The Grand Inquisitor, by enslaving man, has taken the burden of freedom from his shoulders; he has given man the semblance of earthly happiness even though at the cost of eternal joy.

In *Miss Lonelyhearts* and the novels which followed, this same freedom causes the suffering of West's characters. They strive for something to worship completely, yet never find anything which will wholly enslave them. There is no Grand Inquisitor in West's world to give the mass of men earthly happiness by giving them total enslavement. Most men are thoroughly contemptible creatures, doomed to misery, without a nature capable of choosing a dream worthy of dreaming. In their misery West's creatures turn to mere parodies of something to worship. In the world of the Grand Inquisitor, Christ at least exists as an attainable ideal for the few who can worship Christ by their own free choice. In West's world there is no such possibility. For the modern world, the big dream, the Christ dream, is just an ironic joke. Few men can even conceive of such a dream. He who dares to dream it dies clutching with Christ-like love the cripple, who is man, in his arms; but the darer dies in the most meaningless of ways, killed accidentally by a mechanical thing in the hands of the cripple he would save.

The French symbolist influence upon *Miss Lonelyhearts* manifests itself generally in the bareness and concentration of the action and the writing, as well as in the epigrammatic style and satiric manner. In addition certain of West's ideas are more common perhaps to French symbolism than to any other literature: for instance the flesh-spirit opposition, or the concept that the world is a hospital or a madhouse from which man cannot escape save by death. Villiers de l'Isle Adam, one of the symbolists whom West discussed with Saul Jarcho, uses both concepts in *Axël:* though Axël and Sara, at the end of the play, may have dominion over every earthly desire, they prefer to escape by suicide from this world of flesh and pettiness. Joris-Karl Huysmans, to whom West refers in *Balso,* dramatizes both ideas in *Là Bas.* Huysman's major character, the writer Durtal, wants to escape the humdrum, to get *out of the world,* and Huysmans' villains, Marshall Gilles de Rais and Mme. Chantelouve, are satanists whose evil stems from the same out-of-the-world desire. (The latter phrase is repeated often in the novel.) Durtal, however, learns, through a sexual rendezvous with Mme. Chantelouve, "that the flesh domineers the soul and refuses to admit any schism." Therefore, the out-of-the-world dream is but a fantasy for either the religious or the satanist. (pp. 83-101)

The symbolist whom West's writing most reflects is Charles Baudelaire. The influence of Baudelaire's prose poem "Anywhere Out of this World" is clearly seen in *Miss Lonelyhearts.* West's reference to the poem in *Balso Snell* indicates that West knew the poem well. Its influence in *Miss Lonelyhearts* is especially apparent in the chapter "Miss Lonelyhearts in the Dismal Swamp." Baudelaire's poem compares life to a hospital in which all the patients long to change their beds. In the poem Baudelaire and his soul discuss the question of moving elsewhere. To his soul, Baudelaire suggests various possibilities of escape: Lisbon for its warmth, Holland for its tranquillity, Batavia for its tropical beauty, Tornéo, the Baltic, the Pole. To all of these escapes the soul is silent until at the end of the poem it explodes: "N'importe où! pourvu que ce soit hors de ce monde!" In almost exactly the same way

Shrike offers escapes to Miss Lonelyhearts: the South Seas, Art, Hedonism, Suicide, Art, and Drugs. At the very last, Shrike mockingly offers the escape of Christ. It is after Shrike's mockery that Miss Lonelyhearts most desperately strives for the love and humility and faith of Christ. His growing involvement with the Christian dream leads to his alienation from the rest of the world, his mystical experience, and eventually his death. Ironically, the big dream will not work in this loveless world, and so can only lead *out of the world.*

Most important to the eventual impact of ***Miss Lonelyhearts*** are the images that West creates. These images owe a good deal stylistically to the surrealists—probably more than West himself realized. The nihilistic side of surrealism wished to destroy the world of rationalism, to replace it with the surrealistic world of individual perceptions. This world at its most truthful was the product of dreams and visions. The rational relationship of objects was replaced by the subconscious and truer vision, where Dali clocks hung without suspension in varicolored skies, where an umbrella and a sewing machine copulate on an operating table, where the symbol of the surrealistic is the *sur réalité* of the objects in a drugstore: douche bags piled against aspirin bottles and both outlined against a toothpaste ad. In this kind of surrealistic perception, suggestive of the cosmic chaos, the surrealists felt that there was a shocking humor, the humor of the Jacobean writer of conceits. It is this kind of humor, destroying the stereotyped perceptions, laughing at the normal human relationships, that the surrealists strove for in their work. This humor of conceits is shown in Picabia's painting of "A Young American Girl in a State of Nudity," in which the girl is portrayed as a clean, dry spark plug. It was even better illustrated by Dali, who painted a pair of scales to fulfill a teacher's assignment to paint a Gothic virgin. When the teacher expressed astonishment, Dali replied by saying that although others might have seen a virgin, he saw a pair of scales. This same desire for conceits led to the search for new images in literature, for the revolution of the word that Eugene Jolas preached so often in *Transition.* The revolution was to be accomplished by new arrangements of words, and the search for the new sometimes led to strange literary amusements: for instance, some writers plucked by chance, out of a paper bag or a newspaper, two or more words and then yoked them together to create a shocking effect. The chance combinations eventually bore fruit in such weirdly titled, surrealistic poetic texts as "L'Homme Approximatif," "Mouchoir de Nuages," and "Les Vases Communicants," such a startlingly titled painting as Dali's "Debris of an Automobile Giving Birth to a Blind Horse Eating a Telephone."

This metaphysical humor of conceits is at the root of West's macabre wit in ***Miss Lonelyhearts.*** Even the basic concept suggests the metaphysical in its yoking of Christ to an advice-to-the-lovelorn columnist. The progress of Miss Lonelyhearts toward his "sickness" leads to distorted, unique perceptions: a man's tongue is seen as a fat thumb, and a man's cheeks as rolls of toilet paper; a woman's buttocks are seen as enormous grindstones and a woman's nipples as little red hats; a woman is seen as a tent, veined and covered with hair, and a man as a skeleton in a closet; the stone shaft of a war memorial becomes a penis, sexually dilated and ready to spout seeds of violence.

As a writer, West took great pride in his image-making ability. His pictorial eye was active as far back as college, where he spent a good deal of time drawing. His interest in painting lasted throughout his life, and shortly after college he began his collection of Max Ernst's surrealistic prints. That West was proud of the images he created is evident in his statement that ***Miss Lonelyhearts*** is indebted for its psychology to William James's *Varieties of Religious Experience,* but "The immagery [sic] is mine." This pride in his imagery is again evident in his statement that he had originally intended to subtitle ***Miss Lonelyhearts***

> "A novel in the form of a comic strip." The chapters to be squares on which many things happen through one action. . . . I abandoned this idea, but retained some of the comic strip technique: Each chapter instead of going forward in time, also goes backward, forward, up and down in space like a picture.

In these imagistic terms the characters subordinate to Miss Lonelyhearts become merely simplified states of mind. Juxtaposed pictorially against the growing alienation of Miss Lonelyhearts from the world of reality, the minor characters serve primarily as contrast and chiaroscuro. This static, pictorial quality is also true of the actions, which seem like candid snapshots of people caught in mid-air against a background of dull sky and decaying earth. Each action becomes a symbol of an abstract state of mind and heart, and leaves one remembering a series of almost independent pictures rather than with a memory of the developing actions: Miss Lonelyhearts bringing the knife down upon the lamb; Miss Lonelyhearts twisting the arm of the clean old man; Miss Lonelyhearts entwined about Doyle while Betty watches the two roll down the stairs. The pictures are, in reality, sensory portrayals of the inner heart and mind of Miss Lonelyhearts. They portray in archetypal imagery Miss Lonelyhearts' guilty mind (the murder of the lamb); his self-torturing, flagellating heart (the beating of the clean old man); his deluded, mystical vision (the entwined pair). In West's hands the case histories of James and Starbuck and Freud become merely the necessary folklore tradition, the Bullfinch, that instigates him not to psychologize but to pictorialize. This pictorialization, West felt, was the writer's fulfillment:

> Psychology has nothing to do with reality nor should it be used as motivation. The novelist is no longer a psychologist. Psychology can become much more important. The great body of case histories can be used in the way the ancient writers use their myths. Freud is your Bullfinch; you can not learn from him.

This use of Freud as the inspirer of images revealing states of heart and mind is continually apparent in the novel. A simple illustration is the deliberately sinning mind of Miss Lonelyhearts which envisions sex as a way of escape from the letters and then involuntarily pictorializes the sex act in the tent-and-skeleton image of Mrs. Doyle. In a more extended way, this imagistic style is shown in the description of Miss Lonelyhearts' feeling that in sex is the core

of pain: a mental state objectified in Miss Lonelyhearts'
image of himself

> in the window of a pawnshop full of fur coats,
> diamond rings, watches, shotguns, fishing tack-
> le, mandolins. All these things were the para-
> phernalia of suffering. A tortured high light
> twisted on the blade of a gift knife, a battered
> horn grunted with pain.

Later on this imagistic, surrealistic style is evident in the
externalization of Miss Lonelyheart's feeling of himself as
a rock unaffected by the sea of life. Miss Lonelyhearts visualized that

> a train rolled into a station where he was a re-
> clining statue holding a stopped clock, a coach
> rumbled into the yard of an inn where he was sit-
> ting over a guitar, cap in hand, shedding the rain
> with his hump.

Or again this use of Freud as Bullfinch is suggested in Miss
Lonelyhearts' inner sensation of himself as a dead man, in
a world of dead things, being reborn through grace. The
feeling is pictorialized in the vision of

> the Christ that hung on the wall opposite his
> bed. As he stared at it, it became a bright fly,
> spinning with quick grace on a background of
> blood velvet sprinkled with tiny nerve stars.

> Everything else in the room was dead—chairs,
> tables, pencils, clothes, books. He thought of this
> black world of things as a fish. And he was right,
> for it suddenly rose to the bright bait on the wall.
> It rose with a splash of music and he saw its shin-
> ing silver belly.

These images make the abstract concrete. They pictorialize the inner feelings. They partially explain the peculiar
power of West's writing, with its nightmarish involvement
in a world of hallucinations and shadows. In this approach
to writing, West owes a good deal to surrealism. In the
success with which he makes his distorted world of half-
light come alive, perhaps more alive than the world of everyday toast and tea, he is indebted only to the intensity
and power of his own imagination. (pp. 101-06)

> *James F. Light, in his* Nathanael West: An In-
> terpretative Study, *second edition, Northwest-
> ern University Press, 1971, 236 p.*

Jeffrey L. Duncan   (essay date 1972)

[*In the following essay, Duncan explores West's thematic and textual use of language in* Miss Lonelyhearts.]

Almost halfway through his story Miss Lonelyhearts gets
sick. His sickness is essentially spiritual—he is, the chapter title says, "in the Dismal Swamp"—and it has been
brought on by his job. His girl friend, Betty, brings him
some hot soup and advice: quit, try another line of work.
He tells her that quitting would not help much because he
would still remember the letters. She does not understand,
so he offers her an explanation of unusual length and for-
mality:

> Perhaps I can make you understand. Let's start

from the beginning. A man is hired to give advice to the readers of a newspaper. The job is a
circulation stunt and the whole staff considers it
a joke. He welcomes the job, for it might lead to
a gossip column, and anyway he's tired of being
a leg man. He too considers the job a joke, but
after several months at it, the joke begins to escape him. He sees that the majority of the letters
are profoundly humble pleas for moral and spiritual advice, that they are inarticulate expressions of genuine suffering. He also discovers that
his correspondents take him seriously. For the
first time in his life, he is forced to examine the
values by which he lives. This examination
shows him that he is the victim of the joke and
not its perpetrator.

Here he stops, satisfied it seems that there is no more to
say. Betty still does not understand, to no one's surprise,
but we do: Miss Lonelyhearts cannot answer the letters because he has found that his values do not, cannot, justify
genuine suffering, including his own. (For he is suffering
too, languishing in the dismal swamp.) Hence he is the victim of the joke: the advice-giver is himself sick-of-it-all, in
desperate need of advice.

He does not say what his values are (or were), but he does
not really need to. He has found them, he implies, not just
wanting, but false. His crisis then is intensely personal, because *he* has been false, and still is. He no longer claims
a proper name, and he wears at all times his workaday non
de plume, a women's at that. But not only is he no lady,
he cannot fulfill the requirements, as he construes them,
that his pseudonym entails. He has become a misnomer.
In one sense, though, the name suits him: he is as lonely
a heart as any of his correspondents. Accordingly, the
only identity he feels entitled to is the same one they assume, the victim. Better any identity than none, we might
say, but not so. For he has come to doubt all values and
therefore the value of suffering itself. If it has no value, neither does the role of victim. One simply suffers, that's all,
without upshot or significance, the butt of a joke.

What makes the joke *bad* is the fact, as Miss Lonelyhearts
sees it, that the suffering his correspondents express is genuine. Others have agreed. In his review of the novel, for
instance, William Carlos Williams protested, "The letters
which West uses freely and at length must be authentic.
I can't believe anything else. The unsuspected world they
reveal is beyond ordinary thought" ["Sordid? Good God!"
Contempo III, 25 July 1933]. Thirty some years later Randall Reid said the same thing [in his *The Fiction of Nathanael West: No Redeemer, No Promised Land*]: "They
[the letters] have the vividness and the unarguable reality
of a revelation." Both statements, cueing off Miss Lonelyhearts, couple authenticity and revelation. The letters reveal a reality that is unarguable. They are, like revelation,
their own evidence. Upon seeing them one believes them,
if not instantaneously, like Williams, then slowly, gradually like Miss Lonelyhearts. Their truth, in other words, is
not a matter of fact, but an article of faith, and no one has
questioned it. I think we should, just as I think that, deep
down, Miss Lonelyhearts himself does. At issue is a central concern, the nature of language, both as a theme and
as the medium of West's novel.

Miss Lonelyhearts deals primarily not with people, but with letters, with various orders and disorders of words. In his personal relations he is not engaged in dialogue, the language of spontaneous give and take, nearly so much as he is confronted with speeches, with words as deliberately composed as those of the letters, if not more so. Notably, in the two days (and chapters) before he beds himself in the dismal swamp, he hears two speeches, one by Mary Shrike, then one by Fay Doyle, that amount to letters in the flesh. "People like Mary were unable to do without such tales. They told them because they wanted to talk about something besides clothing or business or the movies, because they wanted to talk about something poetic." Like Mary like Fay: they simply have different poetics. Understandably Miss Lonelyhearts listens to neither. They reveal a reality, unarguably, but it is hardly one of genuine suffering, much less of profound humility. Instead they betray mere attitudes struck, postures assumed, poses wantonly displayed, a comic pornography of suffering and trouble. If they express anything authentic—though it is doubtful that these women give a fig about authenticity—it is a desire for suffering, for indisputable reality, personal significance. And if they are to be pitied, it is because they do not, perhaps cannot, suffer.

That is, they have nothing really to speak of, Mary and Fay. Their words merely fill in their blanks. And what is true of them may also—since West's characters are consistently thin—be true of the others, of Betty, of Desperate, of Broad Shoulders, of Shrike, of Miss Lonelyhearts himself. For that reason, if no other, Shrike can burlesque the letters, the expressions of undeserved, unmitigated suffering, just as effectively as he can parody the conventional formulae of value, of the life worth living:

> This one is a jim-dandy. A young boy wants a violin. It looks simple; all you have to do is get the kid one. But then you discover that he has dictated the letter to his little sister. He is paralyzed and can't even feed himself. He has a toy violin and hugs it to his chest, imitating the sound of playing with his mouth. How pathetic! However, one can learn much from this parable. Label the boy Labor, the violin Capital, and so on . . .

> So you buy a farm and walk behind your horse's moist behind, no collar or tie, plowing your broad swift acres. As you turn up the rich black soil, the wind carries the smell of pine and dung across the fields and the rhythm of an old, old work enters your soul. To this rhythm, you sow and weep and chivy your kine, not kin or kind, between the pregnant rows of corn and taters.

Shrike can handle them with equal facility because he insists that they bear the same message, and that it is their only message: the human race is a poet that writes the eccentric propositions of its fate, and propositions, fate, the race itself amount only to so much noisy breath, hot air, flatulence.

Miss Lonelyhearts reluctantly suspects as much. That is why he can find no sincere answers, why he can take nothing he says or thinks seriously, why he lacks the courage of his clichés, why he converts even an original formula-tion immediately into a cliché. "Man has a tropism for order," he thinks to himself; "The physical world has a tropism for disorder, entropy. Man against Nature . . . the battle of the centuries." A capital "N" no less. Four sentences later he dismisses it for good: "All order is doomed, yet the battle is worthwhile." No wonder then that only a little while later he casts his explanation to Betty in the third person—it accommodates exactly his ironic self-consciousness, the distance between what he wants to believe and what he suspects. No wonder as well that his explanation sounds like another speech, one that he has often rehearsed to himself; it is so pat, so articulate, the cool, collected rhetoric of desperation, of futile resolves, private last-stands. For if he can only bring himself to believe what he says, that the suffering is genuine, he may yet hope to believe that it can be justified. That is, faith, once succumbed to, may wax and multiply like irony succumbed to. But the "if " is difficult; it requires breaking the force of irony, which is considerable. Not only can it move mountains, it can annihilate them. And people, too.

Irony is not always humorous, but humor is always ironic. And the letters in the book are humorous.

> I am in such pain I dont know what to do sometimes I think I will kill myself my kidneys hurt so much. . . . I was operated on twice and my husband promised no more children on the doctors advice as he said I might die but when I got back from the hospital he broke his promise and now I am going to have a baby and I don't think I can stand it my kidneys hurt so much.

The writers have had nothing to do with the terrible turns their fates have taken—they are innocent—and neither they nor anyone else can do a thing about their difficulties. Their problems are, by their own terms, insoluble; they themselves are, by their own accounts, schlmiels with Weltschmerz; "I don't know what to do," concludes Sick-of-it-all. "Ought I commit suicide?" queries Desperate. "What is the whole stinking business for?" muses Peter Doyle. They are actually seeking confirmation, not advice; they want someone else to see them as they see themselves. Also, the letters are all graced by the common touch, illiteracy. The writers seem sublimely unaware that their words, like double agents, constantly betray them. "But he [Broad Shoulders' boarder] tries to make me bad and as there is nobody in the house when he comes home drunk on Saturday night I dont know what to do but so far I didnt let him." Betrayal is revelation, but of a fundamentally ambiguous sort: we cannot say whether the words of the letters misrepresent or faithfully execute their authors as they really are. Either way, though, they are funny. The slip of the tongue, Freudian or otherwise, reliably gets a laugh.

Miss Lonelyhearts, however, no longer finds the letters funny because he assumes they are authentic. Genuine suffering, he tells Betty, is no joke. This difference between his response and ours gets us at last into the troubled heart of the novel. Suffering is not funny, certainly, but it has been since Eden, no less than vanity and folly, the very stuff of humor. Pathos, too, of course, and tragedy, but we pay for the loss of Paradise with laughter as well as tears, and comedy is one of the more common forms of man's inhumanity to man. But nothing is more human, for we are considering one application of our capacity for abstraction, our ability to translate instances of suffering and pain into symbol systems that go absurdly awry. Humor is a function of symbolic consciousness. It involves the displacement if not the annihilation of persons, their particular reality, by words, a particular scheme of concepts. The unnamed perpetrator of the joke is language, like West's, for example, when he describes the letters as all alike, "stamped from the dough of suffering with a heart-shaped cookie knife." Just as West's words undercut the letters, so the letters' words displace their writers: "it dont pay to be innocent and is only a big disappointment." Miss Lonelyhearts no longer finds the letters funny because he refuses to consent to this displacement, to bless this annihilation with a laugh. He looks over or through their words to their writers, as he imagines them: profoundly humble, genuinely suffering, terribly real.

But Shrike recognizes a laugh when he sees one, and Miss Lonelyhearts knows it. That is why he has to insist that the letters are not funny: they are not because in truth they are, and that, in his opinion, is wrong, all wrong. For it is not just the letters—he doesn't find anything funny. He will not be a party to humor per se, and therefore, consistently enough, he tries to leave the premises of language altogether, in violence, in women's flesh, in a rural retreat, and in a hand-holding soul-session in a speakeasy.

His expeditions fail, hardly to his surprise, because in them he only finds himself engaged face-to-face with more words on the loose. Sometimes they are spoken, sometimes they are enacted, but they are always there, inescapable. "With the return of self-consciousness, he knew that only violence could make him supple." Spiritually speaking, I take it. His violence serves a metaphysical cause self-consciously conceived. Instead of delivering him from language into whatever—say reality—it necessarily forces him into obeisance to language. For language is its maker. He works over the clean old man for his story, the dubious words of his life—"Yes, I know, your tale is a sad one. Tell it, damn you, tell it"—and sees him at last as the embodiment of his correspondents, his letters. Mary gives him a little of her body to tell him all of her tale; Fay uses her story as a pretext for sex, but she also uses sex as a pretext for her story. Betty believes in a *Sunset* version of *Walden*, and for a while Miss Lonelyhearts is able to relax in her belief, but when they get back to the city he realizes that "he had begun to think himself a faker and a fool." So he is back in language again, and not at all sure that he ever really left it. Like violence, his session of silence with Doyle serves a metaphysical purpose self-consciously forced to its crisis: "He . . . drove his hand back and forced it to clasp the cripple's . . . pressed it firmly with all the love he could manage." This may be a flight of the alone to the alone, but the wings are words, words like "love" and "communion," like "together" and "alone." His only real hope, then, as he has seen it all along, is Christ, appropriately enough.

Let us go back to the dismal swamp. "He was thinking of how Shrike had accelerated his sickness by teaching him to handle his one escape, Christ, with a thick glove of words." Shrike does not get his entire due: he has taught Miss Lonelyhearts to handle everything with a thick glove of words, to suspect that there may be nothing really for the glove to handle, nothing for it to do but make figures of itself, or that the glove, like a magician's white one, renders whatever reality it handles null and void. Genuine magic, though, not legerdemain. Destructive force. The word "escape," in this context, usually means a flight from reality to some more tenable opposite. In Miss Lonelyhearts' case, however, it seems to mean a flight from words in and of themselves to that only (as he sees it) which can redeem them, put them in their proper place—a flight from the terrible logic of Shrike to the Logos itself, Christ, the Word made flesh. The Word informs flesh, flesh substantiates the Word: reality then carries a life-time guarantee, its value insured by language. Then tropes can become unironic Truth, victims can become martyrs, and Paradise, that place of complete integration, can be regained.

Or so a Christian might have it: not an escape, like Tahiti, the soil, hedonism, or art, but a redemption. West's script, however, follows the Christian's with a thumb on its nose and its fingers sadly crossed. Peter Doyle's letter moves Miss Lonelyhearts to holding hands. Later, though, Doyle's hearthside demeanor bankrupts the credibility of his prose, so much that Miss Lonelyhearts takes himself to bed. This time, however, instead of languishing in despair, he becomes the rock. In that metaphor of the Church he has finally, he solipsistically thinks, found himself. "The rock was a solidification of his feeling, his conscience, his sense of reality, his self-knowledge." Thus solidified, though, he feels nothing, and nothing (except the rock) seems real. Betty is a party dress to whom he can say anything without deliberately lying because there is no one to lie to and nothing to lie about. "He could have planned anything. A castle in Spain and love on a balcony or a pirate trip and love on a tropical island." He has changed the game from show-and-tell to play-pretend. As a preliminary to his union with Christ he seems to have gained himself by renouncing words and the world, as he had apparently hoped. But he has actually done nothing of the sort: Miss Lonelyhearts, a pseudonym, has merely become a metaphor, the rock, in a world that was never his.

Up to this point he has always been afraid of Christ. "As a boy in his father's church, he had discovered that something stirred in him when he shouted the name of Christ, something secret and enormously powerful." Later he construes this thing in clinical terms, as hysteria, though he wishes he could believe that it is more than that, that it is actual divinity. Whatever it actually is, his fear is the traditional one of self-relinquishment, of letting go. But now that he has such a definitive sense of self—a rock is definite, if nothing else—he is ironically no longer afraid, and silently shouting the name Christ to himself, he gives himself up and over and has his union. "Christ is life and light." He is also love and Miss Lonelyhearts' new feature editor.

He is, in other words, yet another metaphor, a whole string of them—not the Word, but a word, signifying neither more nor less than any other. Nothing is redeemed, least of all language. Doyle arrives, bad poetry on a field rampant. He has come in the name of secular romantic love to avenge Miss Lonelyhearts' alleged insult to his wife's honor. The allegation is hers, of course, and it is as false as her honor, as her husband's love, as his mission's motive. Miss Lonelyhearts sees him as a sign and, mistaking his warning for a humble plea, goes in the name of divine love to perform a literal miracle, to save Doyle, to save all his correspondents in Doyle's figure, just as he had sought to hurt them all in the figure of the clean old man. Doyle loses heart, so to speak, and tries to flee. Betty, the idle figure of Miss Lonelyhearts' secular fancy, blunders in. Doyle's gun accidentally goes off, and Miss Lonelyhearts meets his end at last, not as martyr, but as unwitting victim, and not as victim of "reality" but of a symbol system gone absurdly awry—of a joke, if you will—because there is no other way for it to go. There is no truth for Miss Lonelyhearts, only words.

It may seem then that Shrike has the last word. All we really have, all we really are, says Shrike, is words, but he does not stop there. There is no cause for grief, he consistently implies, only occasion for jokes. Jokes are his form of prophecy, and they are self-fulfilling. Their form is their content, for their only point is the perfect pointlessness of it all. Nothing is wrong because nothing ever was or could be right. Nothing really matters, not even the fact that nothing really matters. This second step, though, Shrike follows by choice, not of logical necessity. He pronounces "truth" only in order to evade it, to protect himself from pain. Between nothing and grief he will take nothing, not because it is true, finally, but because it is easier.

But while Shrike may take this second step for the sake of comfort, one could argue that the novel takes it of necessity. In open concord with Shrike, it depicts language as radically false, a fundamentally misleading order of being, or nonbeing, as the case may be. Yet the novel is itself a form of language. It would seem then that either the theme must render the form futile, a design of dumb noise, or the form must render the theme gratuitous. But if the theme is gratuitous, the form is perforce futile: it is predicated on counterfeit, a phony issue. Either way (or both ways?) the novel would amount to a display in negation, like the self-dismantling sculpture of Tinguely, like the jokes of Shrike. But Shrike is good only for a laugh, whereas the last elaborate joke of the novel occasions dismay. That is, we respond as if both the statement and the structure were ontologically sound. Now it could be that West has misled us to the very end, that we, to the extent that we care about the outcome, are the unwitting butts of his joke and he is snickering up his sleeve. If so, then West's novel would seem to give us the void as a stripper, taking it all off. On the other hand, our response may be warranted. Curiously enough, we have the same problem with the book that Miss Lonelyhearts has with the letters: whatever we finally deem it, we are necessarily engaged in an act of faith. But we need not, as a consequence, simply toss the book up for grabs.

For the sake of his faith, Miss Lonelyhearts must ignore the bad language of the letters. We enjoy the same lan-

guage because it is so good: "I bought a new sowing machine as I do some sowing for other people to make both ends meet . . . ." The paradox is simple yet profound. All of the demonstrations of bad language—the letters, Miss Lonelyhearts' awful answers, Shrike's parodies—all involve not only an exhibition of West's skill, but of the adequacy of language to his skill. In order to make humorous "nonsense" (as in the quote just cited), language must be able to make common sense. Further, it must make both kinds at once, since it is precisely the play of the one off the other that is funny. A joke reveals the meaningfulness of language. And like revelation, it constitutes its own evidence: the simple fact that it is funny, that *we* laugh, makes the case.

Now we can understand why Shrike is such a desperate character, inistent, shrill. He cannot make his point—the meaninglessness of it *all* —without contradicting himself. Jokes are his form of prophecy, and they betray him every time. He is the victim of his own success. He grieves, in his fashion, that he cannot have nothing.

But the fact that language is meaningful does not necessarily mean that it is significant, any more than a correct sentence is necessarily true. A philosophical idealist might disagree, of course, but West's characters are not idealists. They want some words that signify something beyond their own sound and sense, something, preferably a redemptive Absolute, that can be empirically ascertained. Miss Lonelyhearts, for example, has no quarrel with the coherence of Betty's "world view," but with its significance. Her order, as far as he is concerned, does not match reality—they are an odd pair—whereas his own disorder does. His experience tells him so, or so he thinks. However, we cannot say whether his confusion results from or produces the confusion he perceives, nor whether the world he perceives is in fact a disorder. For it is not the relation between words and reality that West depicts, it is the disjunction: his characters cannot find out what, if anything, lies on the other side of their words. As a bridge, language breaks; as a window, it shuts out, like stained glass, and keeps his characters in. But it does not become genuinely false, actually misleading, until West's characters believe the bridge is sound, the window perfectly transparent, their words reliably significant, true. As, for instance, when Shrike insists there is nought beyond, and when Miss Lonelyhearts insists there is confusion, or Christ, the Word intact. They do not know, literally, what they are talking about.

Words in the novel fail to do the job West's characters assign them—to reveal a reality beyond themselves. But at the same time the words of the novel, West's words, manage quite successfully to do their job, to reveal all they need to, the patterns their sound and sense make: "the gray sky looked as if it had been rubbed with a soiled eraser. It held no angels, flaming crosses, olive-bearing doves, wheels within wheels. Only a newspaper struggled in the air like a kite with a broken spine." These words do not match reality, fit any empirical facts. Neither do they distort any facts or displace reality. They are not *about* something beyond themselves, an actual person's experience, a historical event. They constitute, rather, their own reality, and their only job is to be true to the structure of which they are a part, that is, to be right, self-consistent, aesthetically correct. Were it some other character than Miss Lonelyhearts sitting there, the sky might very properly contain angels, crosses, doves, wheels, a cloud that speaks, a breeze that inspires, a pulse that beats. In art, language is free of obligation to referents; it is free to be strictly itself, and it stands or falls entirely on its own. And when it stands, it satisfies the idealist and the empiricist alike, for it is simultaneously as conceptual as any law and as phenomenal as an apple falling. It is completely sensible. The poet, as Emerson happily put it, "adorns nature with a new thing" ["The Poet," in *Selected Writings of Ralph Waldo Emerson*].

Our relationship with the novel, then, is not exactly analogous to Miss Lonelyhearts' with the letters. The language of each (even when it is the same) draws different duty. For that reason, the demonstrable error of his and his companions' ways does not necessarily compromise the validity of ours. We place our bets on a different thing, and we have demonstrably good grounds for our wager, namely, the novel's coherence. Being or nonbeing, it is an *order* of experience. Thus the novel's theme does not necessarily undermine its form. Still, we must recognize that the center of the analogy holds: the novel's coherence depends upon our faith. The world seems able to survive capricious gods, but a work of fiction cannot survive an unreliable third-person narrator. (First-person narrators are a different story, of course, but their implied third-person narrators are not.) Try to imagine, for instance, the last passage I quoted as misleading, false, the sky as actually blue, bearing crosses, wheels, and so forth. The whole show stops; all bets are off. But we in fact read on because we trust the narrator. In order to read on, we must. And in reading on we find constant justification of our faith: the novel elaborates its problem without sentimental dodges or cheap solutions. True to itself, it is true to us. As for those novels that self-consciously make even their third-person reliability suspect, our willing suspension of belief amounts to a working agreement based on the same trust, that they will prove to be meaningful orders of experience. But by meaningful I do not want to suggest comfortable or reassuring. On the contrary, almost all art worth the name repays our faith by raising hell within us, with our cherished assumptions and secret illusions, with our workaday values and beliefs. For it takes us as far as words can go, and thus brings us face-to-face, finally, with silence, mystery. "Emotion" comes from *emovere,* "to move out of," "disturb." Let us momentarily suppose that West has conned us at the end. Now that we are on to it, we can easily dismiss the book, for he has given us the void *merely* as a stripper, a tease, not a real threat but a pretence of one. "Ah," we can say in relief, "he didn't mean it after all."

But West's novel does disturb us, threaten, because its form makes its theme intensely meaningful, utterly real. Here we witness words falling short of reality, and here, and here, and we watch their continual shortcomings compose an actual pattern of doom. We are unsettled because most of us are, like Dr. Johnson, rock-kickers—we ordinarily assume that our words signify something be-

yond themselves—and reading this story forces us to face the possibility that they do not. The story defines the issue that has become major in certain circles, "the problem of language." But West simultaneously solves the problem *in* the form, every word of the way. For unlike his characters, malpracticing empiricists all, and unlike most of us, West was, as an artist, a practicing idealist. We know that he got the idea for his novel from seeing actual letters to an advice columnist. Had he been concerned with historical-empirical fidelity, he could have used them more-or-less intact. But we also know that he changed them radically, that he in truth wrote his own letters, to make them right, aesthetically correct. All artists, of course, change things to suit their purposes, but their purposes have a single premise, that the work of art must be absolutely true to itself, self-integral, one. Then it can stand and unfold itself, an articulated body of ideas, an avatar of Being.

The novel is an order of being, finally, because in it West shows us that words realize our possibilities as well as define our limits. Miss Lonelyhearts looks at a gray sky and, empiricist that he is, sees only a dirty *tabula rasa.* Against that he sees the most referential and hence ephemeral of all literature, a newspaper, failing (naturally) to soar. But West's words lift nicely, bearing for the space of our imagination all the significance Miss Lonelyhearts misses in his, not in the form of crosses and doves, to be sure, but in the form of figures, of ideas, of words touched with life and touching us with the same.

West's other three stories suffer to varying degrees in comparison with *Miss Lonelyhearts.* They demonstrate a precise but simplistic satire, a sentimental obsession with easy pickings: in *The Dream Life of Balso Snell,* the contrived labyrinths of literary journeys, in *A Cool Million,* the Horatio Alger myth, in *The Day of the Locust,* the Hollywood motif. The unreality of West's marks is patent, their exposure therefore, funny or not, perfunctory: "The fat lady in the yachting cap was going shopping, not boating; the man in the Norfolk jacket and Tyrolean hat was returning, not from a mountain, but an insurance office . . . ." They expose bills of fraudulent goods that we, his readers, declined to buy in the first place; hence they do not disturb, they merely confirm our glib assumptions. *Miss Lonelyhearts,* on the other hand, makes us reconsider.

Here is the difference I mean:

> It is hard to laugh at the need for beauty and romance, no matter how tasteless, even horrible, the results of that need are. But it is easy to sigh. Few things are sadder than the truly monstrous.
> (*The Day of the Locust*)

> . . . I would like to have boy friends like other girls and go out on Saturday nites, but no boy will take me because I was born without a nose—although I am a good dancer and have a nice shape and my father buys me pretty clothes.
> (*Miss Lonelyhearts*)

A girl without a nose is monstrous, truly, yet it is hard not to laugh, particularly when she expresses her need for beauty and romance. A nice shape does not compensate for a noseless face. Perhaps it should, but it does not. Perhaps we should not laugh, either, but we do. Perhaps words should not take precedence over persons, but here (pretending for the moment the girl is real) they do. On the other hand, West does not permit us to indulge in cant. The letter's words spell out a troublesome truth, that this girl, however unfortunate, has tacky values. She would give a great deal to be Homecoming Queen. Victims can be insufferably vain, no less than Presidents, and pity can be primarily self-gratifying. My point is that in the first passage West is keeping certain suppositions intact—the value, for instance, of pity—while in the second he orders his words so that we have to recognize ourselves as we truly are, not as we might prefer to suppose we are. It is recognizing this difference that makes us laugh, and our laughter implies a major admission: that the idealist's absolute may finally be more significant, more real, than we mere mortals are.

We regard West loosely as a writer ahead of his time. I would say that it is specifically *Miss Lonelyhearts* that warrants this reputation, and that it anticipates in particular the work of Barth, Barthelme, Coover, Elkin, Gardner, Pynchon, of all those writers loosely bunched as comic whose humor, by trying its own limits, examines how language does and undoes us, what it gives and what it takes, what it may mean and what it may not, and if we are at last full of fear and wonder, we should be: Being is finally awful, no matter how we look at it. (pp. 116-27)

> *Jeffrey L. Duncan, "The Problem of Language in 'Miss Lonelyhearts'," in* The Iowa Review, *Vol. 8, No. 1, Winter, 1972, pp. 116-28.*

Marcus Smith   (essay date 1973)

[*Smith is an American educator and critic. In the following essay, he examines West's ambiguous portrayal of the protagonist of* Miss Lonelyhearts.]

Criticism of Nathanael West's *Miss Lonelyhearts* seems stymied by the question of whether his protagonist, Miss Lonelyhearts, is sympathetically presented as a viable modern priest or saint, or whether he is merely a demented fool and meant to be regarded ironically. This dilemma seems irreconcilable by appeal to external criteria, such as sources, literary precedents, or moral and philosophic standards of any sort. Indeed, my present view is that the ambiguous effect of *Miss Lonelyhearts* is intentional and I think I can point to the precise technical features in the novel which produce it and the subsequent critical debate.

Miss Lonelyhearts is established as the "center of consciousness" in the novel's opening sentence: "The Miss Lonelyhearts of The New York *Post-Dispatch* . . . sat at his desk and stared at a piece of white cardboard." Thus we are immediately "locked into" Miss Lonelyhearts' "consciousness," and with very few (but crucial) exceptions our vision and experience in the novel are coincident with his. It is through his eyes that we read the grotesque, agonized letters and see a sky that "looked as if it had been rubbed with a soiled eraser." Indeed, the sky *is* soiled because we see it through Miss Lonelyhearts' anhedonic eyes.

Only once does West himself "enter" the novel to comment directly—in the opening chapter when he describes Miss Lonelyhearts' appearance: "Although his cheap clothes had too much style, he still looked like the son of a Baptist minister. A beard would become him, would accent his Old-Testament look. But even without a beard no one could fail to recognize the New England puritan. His forehead was high and narrow. His nose was long and fleshless. His bony chin was shaped and cleft like a hoof." West's stance here is authoritative and his description establishes the basic flesh-spirit conflict in Miss Lonelyhearts' character. But this solitary passage does little to shape our attitude towards Miss Lonelyhearts, which is determined subsequently by the novel's pattern of events.

At times Miss Lonelyhearts evokes our sympathy and compassion. His response to the letter-writers is humane and moving. Whenever he is with Shrike, for example, he emerges in a much more favorable moral position: Shrike's glib cynicism is a completely irresponsible alternate to the problem of evil in the world established by the letters. Moreover, Miss Lonelyhearts strikes us as a "larger" person than Betty whose "sureness was based on the power to limit experience arbitrarily." We cannot agree

---

Ezra Pound comments on early drafts of chapters from *Miss Lonelyhearts* published in 1932:

The special strength of West, apart from his ability to maneuver words, is that he has taken seriously a theme of great importance so trite that all of us thought there would be no life in it: I mean the terrible moral impoverishment of our youth in the cities.

But to do that he has discovered that the way to treat this theme is to use the dialect natural to such a condition. Since the newspapers are the principal corruptors of all that has value in language, it is through the use of this very journalistic perspective and everyday speech that language must be regenerated. West has taken as his material the idiom of the reporters, the tough men of the newspapers, and has counterpointed it with the pathetic letters and the emotions of the poor and the ignorant city dwellers who write to the newspapers to obtain counsel for their afflictions and poverty.

After all, what is the urban population made up of? Of seduced and corrupted, nothing more. They have been gathered together so that they may be better exploited, and this is West's material. But no, his "material" is writing itself—he has invented a new manner, he has invented a means that allows him the full expression of his sentiments in a language that a journalist would recognize. It conveys the real, incredibly dead life of the people and the incredibly dead atmosphere of the book itself and—my God!—we understand what scoundrels we've become in this century. "Don't be deceived" could be West's motto.

> *Pound in a 1932 issue of the Italian journal* Il mare, *translated by Edmundo Dodsworth and published in Jay Martin's* Nathanael West: The Art of His Life, *1970.*

Photograph of West used on the dust jacket of Miss Lonelyhearts.

with Betty when she suggests that Miss Lonelyhearts settle for a job in an advertising agency; we sympathize instead with his defense:

> A man is hired to give advice to the readers of a newspaper. The job is a circulation stunt and the whole staff considers it a joke. . . . He too considers the job a joke, but after several months at it, the joke begins to escape him. He sees that the majority of the letters are profoundly humble pleas for moral and spiritual advice, that they are inarticulate expressions of genuine suffering. He also discovers that his correspondents take him seriously. For the first time in his life, he is forced to examine the values by which he lives.

Miss Lonelyhearts, however, is not always so favorably presented. At times West cruelly undercuts him and shows him to be ridiculous and hypocritical. When he visits Betty he abuses her physically and emotionally, just as later he torments the "clean old man" in the speakeasy: "He was twisting the arm of all the sick and miserable, broken and betrayed, inarticulate and impotent." With both Betty and the old man, Miss Lonelyhearts reacts to the evil in the world by sadistically contributing to it. Likewise, Miss Lonelyhearts' sexual adventures with Shrike's wife, Mary, and with Mrs. Doyle, are selfish and

bizarre and they are presented to us as such. His handling of Mrs. Doyle's letter is a clear example. The letter is filled with suggestiveness which he instantly picks up: "*I need some good advice bad but cant state my case in a letter as I am not good at letters and it would take an expert to state my case. I know your a man and am glad as I dont trust women.*" Miss Lonelyhearts tries to disarm the leering Goldsmith by dropping the letter in the wastepaper basket. As soon as Goldsmith leaves, however, he retrieves it and betrays the thinness of his morality by thinking that "If he could only believe in Christ, then adultery would be a sin, then everything would be simple and the letters extremely easy to answer." But he cannot find any reason for avoiding adultery and so arranges a rendezvous, which leaves him "physically sick."

The question is raised, therefore, very early in the book: just where is the reader supposed to stand in relation to Miss Lonelyhearts? Is the reader supposed to be with him or against him? Is Miss Lonelyhearts meant to be seen as seriously coming to terms with "the values by which he lives" or as a pretentious and deluded fool? To use Wayne Booth's terms it is a question of ironic versus sympathetic "norms."

The dilemma becomes more obvious (and even more irreconciliable) later in the novel when Miss Lonelyhearts decides in favor of the "Christ dream." This occurs when he returns from the trip to Connecticut with Betty. He discovers that he has not been cured of his *angst* and that after all he is capable of "dreaming the Christ dream," which he has failed at previously, "not so much because of Shrike's jokes or his own self-doubt, but because of his lack of humility."

Miss Lonelyhearts, therefore, sets out to become a humble man. But humility is an extremely paradoxical virtue in that it must be achieved without calculation. Thus, a character consciously trying to achieve humility is ripe for the irony caused by "grotesque disparity between word and word or word and deed." This is Miss Lonelyhearts' situation: he "dodged Betty because she made him feel ridiculous. He was still trying to cling to his humility, and the farther he got below self-laughter, the easier it was for him to practice it." "Humility" for Miss Lonelyhearts means withdrawal into the self, into a state of ultra-self-consciousness. The next time it is mentioned, when he and Doyle are leaving the speakeasy, Miss Lonelyhearts is completely preoccupied with "the triumphant thing his humility had become."

In short, Miss Lonelyhearts' "humility" is false humility—and West seems to intend it to be seen this way, for when Miss Lonelyhearts goes to the Doyles' apartment he launches into a plea to Mrs. Doyle to love her crippled husband. Miss Lonelyhearts' style is bizarre and messianically hysterical: " 'You can take the chill out of his bones. He drags his days out in areaways and cellars, carrying a heavy load of weariness and pain. You can substitute a dream of yourself for this load. A bouyant dream that will be like a dynamo in him. You can do this by letting him conquer you in your bed. he will repay you by flowering and becoming ardent over you . . .'." Despite the genuine appeal in this exhortation (again a tension between sympathy and irony), the chapter ends in violence. Miss Lonelyhearts rejects Mrs. Doyle's sexual advances and, in frustration, beats her and flees back to his bed.

Miss Lonelyhearts then withdraws even further into himself and becomes an impersonal "rock" in the sea of humanity. When Shrike appears, he is merely a "clumsy" gull "trying to lay an egg in the smooth flank" of the rock. And Betty is merely a "little wave" splashing at his feet. Shrike drags Miss Lonelyhearts to his apartment to play a game: "Everyman his own Miss Lonelyhearts." Shrike has taken a batch of letters from the files and distributes them to the assembled drunks. Miss Lonelyhearts, the rock, is unmoved by all this: when Shrike hands him a letter he drops it to the floor without reading it and when Betty leaves he goes after her. West, however, maintains the party scene. This is the only instance in the novel when Miss Lonelyhearts is not dramatically present, not the "center of consciousness."

There is an important reason for Miss Lonelyhearts' departure at this point, for the letter which Shrike handed him is from Peter Doyle. Shrike picks it up from the floor:

> He took the letter out of its envelope, as though he had not read it previously, and began:
> " 'What kind of a dirty skunk are you? When I

got home with the gin, I found my wife crying on the floor and the house full of neighbors. She said that you tried to rape her you dirty skunk and they wanted to get the police but I said that I'd do the job myself you. . . . So that's what all your fine speeches come to, you bastard, you ought to have your brains blown out'."

Shrike continues his drunken ramble for another two paragraphs, but West has already clearly set up the dramatic irony of the novel's ending by having Shrike read Doyle's threat. The reader knows what Miss Lonelyhearts does not know, that Peter Doyle is out to kill him. Two chapters later when Miss Lonelyhearts gets out of bed and sees Doyle climbing the stairs he thinks he will perform a miracle: "He would embrace the cripple and the cripple would be made whole again. . . ." The reader, however, knows that Miss Lonelyhearts will get his "brains blown out."

If West had maintained the ironic distance established by Doyle's letter, then despite his previous engagement of our sympathies the novel would have ended on a bitter but clearly ironic note. West, though, draws us closely into Miss Lonelyhearts' "religious experience" just before he is shot. It is difficult to focus ironically on the description of Miss Lonelyhearts' conversion:

> "Christ! Christ!" This shout echoed through the innermost cells of his body.
>
> He moved his head to a cooler spot on the pillow and the vein in his forehead became less swollen. He felt clean and fresh. His heart was a rose and in his skull another rose bloomed.
>
> The room was full of grace. A sweet, clean grace, not washed clean, but clean as the inner sides of the inner petals of a newly forced rosebud.
>
> Delight was also in the room. It was like a gentle wind, and his nerves rippled under it like small blue flowers in a pasture.
>
> He was conscious of two rhythms that were slowly becoming one. When they became one, his identification with God was complete. His heart was the one heart, the heart of God. And his brain was likewise God's.

This passage (only a page before Miss Lonelyhearts' death) can be read ironically, as the hysterical ravings of a megalomaniac. But its lyricism does not compel our ironic response. Instead, it erases the ironic distance established by Doyle's letter in the previous chapter. Thus the reader's final emotion is extremely complicated. His sympathy for Miss Lonelyhearts wars with the irony of Miss Lonelyhearts' death, his compassion is mingled with his awareness of Miss Lonelyhearts' folly.

While the discussion above has described the reason for the ambiguous effect of **Miss Lonelyhearts,** we must ask whether such an effect is warranted. A neo-Aristotelian such as Wayne Booth would perhaps conclude that **Miss Lonelyhearts** is a flawed work because it does not control its irony and establish clear and consistent (or at least ultimate) norms for the reader's response.

In *The Rhetoric of Fiction,* Booth argues that the modern

novel's tendency towards "objectivity" through "impersonal narration" (especially the third person "center of consciousness" method which West employs in *Miss Lonelyhearts*) leads frequently to confusion of effect and unintentional ambiguity. The "deep inside view of the center of consciousness" method tends, because of the very closeness of the "center" to the reader, to make the intelligent character appealing: as Booth says, "inside views can build sympathy even for the most vicious character." At the same time, the modern writer's penchant for irony (and the modern reader's responsiveness to it) creates difficulties, for when an author selects an impersonal narrative method and does not directly establish ironic norms for the reader, then the author must resort to "grotesque disparity between word and word or word and deed" to warn his reader that irony is intended. A problem arises, however, when we follow Booth into the arena of judgment. "In most works of any significance," argues Booth, "we are made to admire or detest, to love or hate, simply to approve or disapprove of at least one central character, and our interest in reading from page to page, like our judgment upon the book after reconsideration, is inseparable from this emotional involvement."

Booth's argument would seem to apply to *Miss Lonelyhearts,* and from a purely descriptive standpoint his insights are extremely useful. Yet I am unable to agree with the implied censure which would seem to follow when dealing with West's novel. In the first place, after careful reconsideration, I find that the great appeal of *Miss Lonelyhearts* is due precisely to the careful balance West establishes and maintains between ironic and sympathetic norms. The fact that Miss Lonelyhearts is *both saint and fool* has a great deal to do with his contemporary relevancy. In the best sense of the absurd term, he is "absurd" and few writers, in America or elsewhere, have succeeded as well as West in dramatizing the absurd. Another objection to Booth's demand for an ultimate "norm" in fiction is that, while this sounds like a good thing, to take this seriously would result in remaindering many of the best works of modern fiction. What is the ultimate norm in, say, *Lord Jim, Portrait of the Artist as a Young Man, Lord of the Flies* or *The Magus?* Do the protagonists of these works emerge as ultimately sympathetic or ironic? I would argue neither side, but would propose that our proper response is an unresolved tension between the two emotions. The reason for this (I cannot justify it aesthetically) lies in the modern reader himself and in the dilemmas of his time. (pp. 103-09)

> *Marcus Smith, "The Crucial Departure: Irony and Point-of-View in 'Miss Lonelyhearts',"* in Nathanael West, the Cheaters and the Cheated: A Collection of Critical Essays, *edited by David Madden, Everett/Edwards, Inc., 1973, pp. 103-09.*

Kingsley Widmer (essay date 1982)

[*Widmer is an American educator and critic. In the following excerpt, he interprets* Miss Lonelyhearts *as a skewed religious fable and an indictment of traditional Christianity.*]

The Double Play of Profoundity and Pathology

Miss Lonelyhearts (1933), West's second novella, is often, and I think rightly, viewed as his finest work. Possibly some of its superiority to his first novella can be related to the more serious pessimism and concern with commonplace suffering of the depression during which it was written. Certainly it attempts far more than the solipsistic dream-onanism of art of *The Dream Life of Balso Snell. Miss Lonelyhearts* is a richly aslant religious fable. The entitling figure, a twenty-seven-year-old newspaper reporter, remains otherwise unnamed than by his advice column appelation, probably to emphasize the forced role he plays. Midway in the narrative, Lonelyhearts tries to explain to his conventional fiancée, Betty, his dilemma:

> A man is hired to give advice to the readers of a newspaper. The job is a circulation stunt and the whole staff considers it a joke. He welcomes the job, for it might lead to a gossip column, and anyway he's tired of being a leg man. He too considers the job a joke, but after several months of it, the joke begins to escape him. He sees that the majority of the letters are profoundly humble pleas for moral and spiritual advice, that they are inarticulate expressions of genuine suffering. He also discovers that his correspondents take him seriously. For the first time in his life, he is forced to examine the values by which he lives. This examination shows him he is the victim of the joke and not its perpetrator.

Betty still does not understand his anguish, and in her naive but not altogether imperceptive way, thinks that he is sick, suffering from "city troubles," an unhealthy life. But at this point the reader may also not quite understand this slightly stiff passage of the reporter's schematic rationalization. A larger and more perplexed personal and cultural "joke" has also been made evident under the guise of this role-playing.

Part of the Lonelyhearts' victimization comes from responding to the "profoundly" pathetic pleas, the self-parodying letters to his advice column of physical and psychological cripples crying for help: "Desperate, Harold S., Catholic-mother, Broken-hearted, Broad-shoulders, Sick-of-it-all, Disillusioned-with-tubercular-husband," and the many other laments, "all of them alike, stamped from the dough of suffering with a heart-shaped cookie knife." But his situation, on an exploitative periodical in a megapolitan wasteland and under an hysterical cynical-mocking feature editor, Willie Shrike (perhaps named after the predatory bird), makes acceptance nearly impossible, even if he had moral clarity and religious solace to offer.

Nor is any real alternative presented by his fiancée, Betty, "the girl in the party dress" who believes in curative chicken soup, therapeutic visits to nature, boy buys girl a soda, an ordinary dishonest job in advertising, and conventionally cute suburban marital bliss and order. She cannot understand the Lonelyhearts dilemma, nor can all the Betty-moralists of the bland world. For, as Lonelyhearts comments, her "answers were based on the power to limit experience arbitrarily. Moreover, his confusion was significant while her order was not." As long as he takes his role at all seriously, he feels the demands of real suffering. And the lack of adequate answers to it.

West seriously presents the Lonelyhearts dilemma of solacing commonplace anguish; he is a self-defined tormented "humanity-lover." But he is also presented as a grotesque joke, a victim of his own, and traditional Christianity's, pathology. In the third of the fifteen brief chapters that make up the fiction, "Miss Lonelyhearts and the lamb," some of the religious mania appropriate to the "born again Christian" (as we now call it) is compactly annotated. Lonelyhearts has returned to his rather monastic room, solely decorated with "an ivory Christ that hung opposite the foot of the bed," nailed directly to the wall with large spikes, and reads from Dostoyevsky's *The Brothers Karamazov* a passage by the saintly Zossima advocating "all embracing love." Reflecting on his sense of "vocation" as son of a New England Baptist minister, he recalls that "something stirred in him when he shouted the name of Christ, something secret and enormously powerful." Now he knows what the "thing" is—"hysteria, a snake whose scales are tiny mirrors in which the dead world takes on a semblance of life. And how dead the world is . . . a world of doorknobs. He wondered if hysteria were really too steep a price to pay for bringing it to life." Though his intelligent self-consciousness seems considerably greater than the usual born-again religious devotee, the next dozen chapters provide the logic, of his dilemmas and his compulsions, for the concluding "Miss Lonelyhearts has a religious experience" where he feverishly reaches the hysteria of "Christ! Christ!" and "his identification with God was complete." He turns his doorknob and goes forth to "perform a miracle" to test his "conversion," to embrace not only a confusedly vengeant cripple but to "succor . . . with love" all the suffering. But the immediate grotesque result is his semiaccidental death and the messing up of several lives since there is no place for the Christ-vision in the real modern world. Such hysteria really is too steep a price for bringing the world to purposive life since it entails madness, death, and further suffering.

Conversion to faith is the snake-induced sin in our dead world. Lonelyhearts's religious experience comes from a self-cultivated hysteria, aided by fasting, fever, psychic paralysis, hallucinations, added to his personal history of an obsessional "Christ-complex" (his phrase), a tormenting sexual ambivalence, and genuine moral anguish. Also in the third chapter, where Lonelyhearts still just plays with his conversion hysteria, he cuts short his chant of "Jesus Christ" when "the snake started to uncoil in his brain," and pushes himself into an amnesiac sleep. There, however, he dreams that he is "a magician who did tricks with doorknobs . . . [which] bled, flowered, spoke." His dream then shifts from such Daliesque surrealism to a Buñuelish hyper-realism in which he recapitulates a college prank. He and several student buddies had argued all night about "the existence of God," then drunkenly gone out to barbeque a lamb, though on Lonelyhearts's "condition that they sacrifice it to God" first. Singing an "obscene version of 'Mary had a Little Lamb,'" they take one purchased alive to a field where Lonelyhearts botches the butchering and the injured lamb escapes. Deserted by the others, he has

to messily smash the lamb with a stone, ending with a grotesque Beelzebub image of gruesome sacrifice with flowers, blood, and flies. That stone he will later metaphorically translate into the "rock of faith" so that he can sacrificially offer himself to botched suffering.

Underneath, then, the earnest newspaper columnist resides a sick Jesus-freak, as we would now say. Clinically astute West emphasizes other pathological elements in his protagonist, especially his sexual contradictions. Not only has Lonelyhearts identified with his womanish role-name as lovelorn columnist but his relation to women is peculiar. Much of his treatment of fiancée Betty is hostile, from pinching her nipples to meanly ignoring her to making the virginal girl pregnant to savagely putting her down. Clearly, he does not really like her. He also rather passively lets himself be seduced by an impotent cripple's unfeminine wife, Fay Doyle, though a gross character whom he finds repulsive and frightening (her "massive hams . . . were like two enormous grindstones"; "she looked like a police captain"; etc.). She sexually exhausts him, and later arouses his total revulsion. In a final scene with her, supposedly acting out one of his Christian love-roles, he ends roughly dropping her to the floor and blindly beating her "again and again" in the face before fleeing.

He had previously focused on her husband, Peter Doyle, as his Christian love-object, solacing him and holding hands. All Lonelyhearts's sexuality seems messily ambivalent. With Mary Shrike, sex-teasing (and apparently frigid) wife of his editor, he hypes himself into compulsive but always failing attempts at seduction. Several peculiar obscenities appear here, including perhaps an Oedipal twisting, as in paternalistic Willie Shrike's complaining to his reporter of his wife's sexual coldness before sending her off with him. Apparently, also, in sly lubricity, Mary has Lonelyhearts pet her into sexual response, and then runs in to her waiting husband. But even when thinking of Mary, Lonelyhearts "felt colder than before he had started to think of women. It was not his line." His sexual line seems to be disguised and displaced homoeroticism. While his warmly holding hands with the crippled Peter Doyle might be taken as confused Christian compassion, or at least playing at it, an earlier chapter emphasizes something else. In "Miss Lonelyhearts and the clean old man," the protagonist, after leaving the girl friend he was abusing, goes to Delehanty's, a bar frequented by newspaper people (a pre-1933 prohibition "speakeasy"), where he listens to other reporters tell stories of gang rapes of resented female writers. Then, with another drunken reporter, he torments a gay elderly man they forcibly pull out of a public toilet. Lonelyhearts ends up twisting and twisting the screaming "old fag's" arm until someone smashes him in the head. The sexual fascination has turned into guilty rage. Various other detailing also underlines the sexual ambivalence, such as Shrike shrewdly noting, earlier, to Lonelyhearts, "so you don't care for women, eh? J. C. is your only sweetheart, eh?" (With bemused double play, which West frequently uses, the woman, Farkis, who shows up for Shrike's predatory ministrations right after this is described as an exaggeratedly mannish figure.) As one can confirm in the often effete iconography of the Protestant churches of West's time, much about the traditional Jesus might appropriately suggest a covertly homosexual response. That, of course, should not be separated from the general sexual repression of puritanized Christianity, especially strong in that direction in America, or from the admixture with a guiltily sadistic misogyny. Thus West has larger grounds for strongly implying homoeroticism in the love of Jesus, including the longing for sexual mergence for the born-again in the guise of submission to compassionate feeling. When Lonelyhearts is being most Christian, as with Peter Doyle, he is also being most homoerotic. J. C. does become this terribly ambivalent fellow's deathly sweetheart.

Before turning to other aspects of West's analysis of the Lonelyhearts's syndrome, including the compulsion to order, the violent self-laceration, and the hallucinatory longings, I think it crucial to emphasize the double nature of West's treatment, some of which I have been summarizing. Lonelyhearts is clearly presented by West as thoughtfully earnest about the serious moral dilemma of how to answer and solace hardly remediable human suffering. Other details and tropes confirm that we are to see the young man as sincerely searching for a religious answer to human anguish and pervasive modern disorder. But the reader is also carefully, indeed almost gleefully, provided with the details of guilty sexual confusion, long inculcated religious hysteria, and a religiousized suicidal loss of all reality. The protagonist, and the issues, must be seen as *simultaneously* morally profound and clinically pathological. A good many misreadings result from failing to recognize the careful and thorough *doubleness* of West's perceptions and art. We must see Lonelyhearts as *both* sick and saintly. To West's sardonic non-Christian eye, Lonelyhearts, and much of his religion, can only be viewed as inseparably earnest and grotesque, a pious illness. Modern religiousness is a sadly serious disease masquerading as an answer to the impossible.

Otherwise put, Lonelyhearts is a "case" of denied and twisted homoeroticism, a compulsive-obsessional neurosis, even finally an hysteric-schizophrenic psychosis—a not untypical "Christ complex." But he also reveals the moral quester, the sensitively compassionate man seeking to answer the deepest moral cruxes of human disorder and suffering. He is, indeed, as I first quoted him, the victim of a bad joke, but it is finally a cultural and cosmic one. I think it is this doubleness of view, however finally dissolving into the ironies of the sick saint, which not only produces the intensely paradoxical stylization of the work—combining earnest speech, gross wisecracks, surreal dreams, illiterate letters, witty conceits, serious cultural critiques, clinical detailing, and religious visions—but which gives it much of its distinctive brilliance of perception.

If one seeks the most pertinent literary analogue (the stock literary criticism device), *Miss Lonelyhearts* might well be viewed as a Dostoyevskian fiction. But this would not relate to the Russian's Christian apologetics (a bit mocked with the Zossima passage quoted earlier) but his feverish atheism. Thus Lonelyhearts parallels in part the "antihero" of *Notes from Underground,* another nameless figure also simultaneously a clinical case (sadomasochistic,

sexually troubled, guiltily anguished) and a profound existential metaphysician of the limits of rationality and the nature of freedom in an absurdist universe. Both novellas end without any possibility of redemption or regeneration, paradoxical explorations of a fated modernist self-consciousness.

Where Dostoyevsky provocatively indicted the disease of Western rationality as unable to order the self and the world, West provocatively indicted Christian religiousness as masquerading the self and the world. Double playing his material into both a clinical case and a moral exemplum, into a poignant tale and a horrendous joke, West went deeper than either iconoclasm or compassion. It is a profound response to a central issue of our culture.

The Order of Suffering

Suffering is real. Part of what this means for the author of ***Miss Lonelyhearts*** is that much of human pain, misery, and despair cannot readily be resolved, ameliorated, cured, solaced, dissolved by usual human efforts. In the novella's first chapter, "Miss Lonelyhearts, help me, help me," part of the issue gets established through West's mimicry of three semiliterate letters to an advice columnist: one from an eight-time pregnant Catholic mother in constant pain from her kidneys but piously denied an abortion; one from a yearning sixteen-year-old girl thinking of suicide because "born without a nose"—she wants love but finds that even her mother "crys terrible" when looking at her, her father thinks "maybe I was being punished for his sins," and boys won't go out with her ("although I am a good dancer and have a nice shape") because "I have a big hole in the middle of my face which scares people even myself"; and one from the concerned adolescent brother of a retarded deaf and dumb thirteen-year-old girl, with brutally punitive parents, who has been sexually molested. Later letters in the story come from the wife of an impotent cripple, the frightened wife of an unemployed abusive psychopath, a cripple with an unfaithful wife ("what I want to no is what is the whole stinking business for"), an impoverished widow who has lost her son, and a paralytic boy who wants to be a violinist. The problems given are predominantly female and sexual, around physical or psychological crippling, in a context of the moralistically punitive. Such miseries cannot be readily ameliorated, often not genuinely assuaged, and traditionally call for a religious answer.

Alternatively, we find the typical modern response of viewing all such miseries as "illness" which reduce to ostensible corrections by expertise of therapy, trivial psuedo-change, institutional device, or obtuse pity. So with the figure of conventional order, Betty. Even when Lonelyhearts behaves outrageously to her, she assures him that he is just "sick." All suffering comes from a temporary condition of illness. He shouts back at her in moral-religious indignation, though since it is self-conscious it, too, becomes a forced role-playing "with gestures that were too appropriate, like that of an old fashioned actor"—the always insistent Westean point about masquerading. Says Lonelyhearts, "What a kind bitch you are. As soon as anyone acts viciously, you say he's sick. . . . No morality, only medicine." This is the modern "liberal" refusal disguised as tolerance, the denial of the moral sensibility and of responding to suffering, the failure to recognize the unredeemable disorder in the moral universe.

The metaphysical pathos of wishing to restore order, which must of course include responding to suffering, also gets presented in a double way by West. His reporter clearly shows a compulsion, in the clinical sense, for order, an obsessional need to ritually compose things, to restrictively confine sensations, to limit reality. For example, in the chapter "Miss Lonelyhearts and the fat thumb," he found himself "developing an almost insane sensitiveness to order. Everything had to form a pattern . . . ," whether personal efforts, objects in hand, or even the view from the window. But such self-conscious mania leads to an insistent rigidity in which things tend to fall, break, clash, go out of control, as, threateningly, all reality does. In the street the "chaos" seems overwhelming once one becomes so sensitive to ordering: "Broken groups of people hurried past. . . . The lamp-posts were badly spaced and the flagging was of different sizes. Nor could he do anything with the harsh clanging sounds of streetcars and the raw shouts of hucksters. No repeated group of words would fit their rhythm and no scale could give them meaning." Like common little compulsions of counting left steps, avoiding sidewalk cracks, pairing or counting-off objects, etc., the patterned responses will not long hold. The man's awareness of the insistent disharmonies of modern urban sensations is true but has become a madness. All one can finally do with the surreal jumble and cacophony of sights and sounds is, like the desperate Lonelyhearts, try "not to see or hear." Intense awareness, which most of us protectively refuse to have most of the time, becomes a paralyzing condition.

Be it the urban street sights and sounds, a media format (such as the front page of a newspaper, or, now, an ad-announcement-fantasy riddled segment of television programming), or our reality-and-dream garbled mental states, painful chaos threatens if we fully recognize and respond. In a later chapter of despair, "Miss Lonelyhearts and the dismal swamp," the reporter, withdrawn into bedridden physical illness after sex with Fay Doyle, slides into a surreal fantasy, the slough of despond of the modern Bunyan:

> He found himself in the window of a pawnshop full of fur coats, diamond rings, watches, shotguns, fishing tackle, mandolins. All of these things were the paraphernalia of suffering. A tortured high light twisted on the blade of a gift knife, a battered horn grunted with pain.

> He sat in the window thinking. Man has a tropism for order. Keys in one pocket, change in another. Mandolins are tuned G D A E. The physical world has a tropism for disorder, entropy. Man against nature. . . . Keys yearn to mix with change. Mandolins strive to get out of tune. Every order has within it the germ of destruction. All order is doomed. . . .

> A trumpet, marked to sell for $2.49, gave the call to battle and Miss Lonelyhearts plunged into the fray. First he formed a phallus of old watches

and rubber boots, then a heart of umbrellas and trout flies, then a diamond of musical instruments and derby hats, after these a circle, triangle, square, swastika. But nothing proved definitive and he began to make a gigantic cross. When the cross became too large for the pawnshop, he moved it to the shore of the ocean. There every wave added to his stock faster than he could lengthen its arms. His labors were enormous. He staggered from the last wave to his work, loaded down with marine refuse. . . .

His psychological tics of compulsion, brilliantly extended in conceits by West, merge with religious mania, the phallus become a cross, and all reality "the paraphernalia of suffering" in a grandiloquent attempt to order our trashy world. Sex and religion and junk become one tidal-wash of chaos. Against our pathetic futility of order, entropy wins.

While this compulsion to order comes close to madness, yet the mania also should be seen as heroic, ideal. In an earlier episode, Lonelyhearts recalled an incident from his adolesence with his younger sister in which "he had gone to the piano and begun a piece by Mozart. . . . His sister left her picture book to dance to his music. She had never danced before. She danced gravely and carefully, a simple dance, yet formal. . . ." Though drunk in a speakeasy, Lonelyhearts is also having a vision: "swaying slightly to the remembered music, he thought of children dancing. Square replacing oblong and being replaced by circle. Every child, everywhere; in the whole world there was not one child who was not gravely, sweetly dancing." The attempt in this, as in the previously quoted passage, to give geometrical shape and a lyrical and symbolical ordering, Mozartean or Christian, aesthetic and religious, to our messy world serves high poignancy. And gross irony, since Lonelyhearts gets in an accidental bar brawl in the middle of his meditations, and the main real shaping is that his "anger swung in large drunken circles." He ends up gruesomely assaulting someone, beaten, hungover. Formal and sweet order can have little place in this world.

A psychologically forced ordering provides the substitute. Religion, in a view such as West's, provides some of the most ornate forms of a compulsion mania, as with hynotically chanting the holy name (Jesus), imposing on all the flotsam and jetsam of disintegrating reality the symbolic self-castrating form (a phallus become a cross), and shaping anxiety with a ritualized routine (the imitation of Christ). By the thirteenth chapter, after ragingly beating Fay Doyle in sexual revulsion (and perhaps for not responding to his guilty role-playing with the "love-fruit" of Christian rhetoric), Lonelyhearts retires to his bed for a purgative three days, living on crackers, water, cigarettes, and hysteria. In religious crisis and personal breakdown, he attempts to heighten the paralytic Christian humility he took on a few days earlier by identifying himself as the impervious "rock of faith." No longer responding with anger, sex, pity, thought, he wills but one thing in mad purity of heart, his compulsive rockness. Humility, as so often, has become hardness. In the extended play with the conceit of the rock, West suggests how self-demands based on compassionate sensitivity become its antithesis. Part of the technique here is to sympathetically see most of the compulsions from inside, from Lonelyhearts's viewpoint (as with most of the narration, with the early exception of the physical-religious description of him, and the late exception of Shrike's last party after Lonelyhearts leaves—both rather pat foreshadowing devices).

In one of Shrike's shrewd but flamboyantly self-parodying metaphors, Lonelyhearts has become a rock-head, a "swollen Mussolini of the soul." (Fascist dictator-poseur Mussolini had a very large, completely bald, and imperviously arrogant dome.) Lonelyhearts's caring self has become untouchable—it was only "his mind that was touched, the instrument with which he knew the rock"—so all subserves the compassionate mania to escape from compassion's suffering. His "rock of faith" extends the earlier "stone" of Shrike's advice: when your readers "ask for bread, don't give them crackers as does the Church, and don't, like the State, tell them to eat cake. Explain that man cannot live by bread alone. . . . Teach them to pray each morning, 'Give us this day our daily stone.' " Lonelyhearts's daily "stone that had formed in his gut" of moral anguish defensively becomes an all-consuming petrification disguised as faith. He can now desperately but blandly play the calm martyr with all his mockers, even masquerade as the charmingly conventional husband-to-be in advertising-and-suburb with Betty. The obsessional image protects him from all mere reality. "He did not feel guilty. He did not feel. The rock was a solidification of his feeling, his conscience, his sense of reality, his self-knowledge. He could have planned anything." With an amazing doubleness of empathy and mockery, West shows how the call to feeling and genuineness gets compulsively transposed into nonfeeling and masquerade.

In sympathetically savaging the Lonelyhearts mania, West also double plays the culminating religious experience. Back in his ascetic bed and desperation in the final chapter, Lonelyhearts's quest-compulsion reaches madness in which he "welcomed the arrival of fever. It promised heat and mentally unmotivated violence. The promise was soon fulfilled; the rock became a furnace." He is disassociating, a very sick man, and a mystic. The compulsion to order becomes hallucinatory. The decorative Christ figure on his wall becomes moving, animate, Lonelyhearts's "life and light," even apparently his pattern of nerves, as well as the "bright bait" for the dead fish things of this world. Then "the room was full of grace," and he becomes, heart and mind, the fresh "rose" of the mystic tradition of beatitude (and of feminine vulnerability to the masculine deity), and thus completes his "identification with God." The beatitude turns, of course, into a regressive oneness which denies all discrimination of reality and must be fatal.

As I read the Westean metaphors, drawn from the ecstatic Christian tradition, they are both earnest in their intensity and ironic in their jumbling (Christ is bait instead of fish; what the quester seeks is more feverish violence than true serenity; God becomes an approving editor). Lonelyhearts's compulsive imposition on himself of metaphors of divine order complete, he goes forth to impose them on the world, to embrace the crippled Peter (Doyle), the impo-

tent phallus he has betrayed with his wife, arriving on the stairs to threaten Lonelyhearts with a gun to play-the-man in retaliating for the misunderstood beating of Fay Doyle. That, indeed, will be the "miracle" of love. Doyle, confusedly caught between the ecstatic Lonelyhearts he does not understand and the arrival of Betty, accidentally fires the gun, finishing off Lonelyhearts in the gratuitously grotesque way which is the only final order in this world. Compulsive manias, such as born-again religion, can only feverishly disguise the world until violence sunders all, returning the masquerade to the reality of suffering.

The Solace of Fantasy

Along the way of his quest for religious transformation, and the fatal masquerade of personal and social realities, Lonelyhearts tries a pastoral recuperation, a few days in the country with Betty, at her insistence. Returning from that, especially when they "reached the Bronx slums," he knew that she and nature "had failed to cure him" of his vision of human suffering and the need to answer it:

> Crowds of people moved through the street with a dreamlike violence. As he looked at their broken hands and torn mouths he was overwhelmed by the desire to help them, and because this desire was sincere, he was happy despite the feeling of guilt which accompanied it.
>
> He saw a man who appeared to be on the verge of death stagger into a movie theater that showed a picture called *Blonde Beauty*. He saw a ragged woman with an enormous goiter pick a love story magazine out of a garbage can and seem very excited by her find.
>
> Prodded by his conscience, he began to generalize. Men have always fought their misery with dreams. Although dreams were once powerful, they have been made peurile by the movies, radio and newspapers. Among many betrayals, this one is the worst.

This point about the violence implicit in ordinary suffering (the hyperbolic surreal images) is presented seriously. Since Lonelyhearts feels himself "capable of dreaming the Christ dream," once one of the most serious, he has a fervent stake in the solacing process, and, as a yellow journalism advice columnist, a guilty share in its corruption.

Dream-fantasies, whether of art (the preceding *The Dream Life of Balso Snell*) or of the American gospel of success (the following *A Cool Million*), dominate West's concern. *Miss Lonelyhearts* does not confine itself to the central Christian fantasy; it also surveys, as part of its imaginative argument, other dream escapes. The main vehicle for this is Lonelyhearts's editor, Shrike, a somewhat diabolical hysteric-cynic, a compulsive machine for making jokes—a not uncommon repressed type—who exacerbates the Christ-complex by making Lonelyhearts the butt of ornate parodies, though hardly more grotesque than the commonplace scene just quoted. Shrike, too, insists on the fusion of the great dreams of the culture and the debasing media—the "Suzan Chesters, the Beatrice Fairfaxes and the Miss Lonelyhearts are the priests of twentieth-century America," which we might update with the whole range of nostrum peddlers of religiosity and psychiatry. Shrieking Shrike is the angry-hurt idealist about it.

And it is Shrike who, at the end of the opening chapter, mockingly dictates the start of an alternative column of advice: *"Art Is a Way Out."* Eight chapters later, in a series of parody dream-escapes, Shrike proposes more personally to Lonelyhearts "Art! Be an artist or a writer. When you are cold, warm yourself before the flaming tints of Titian, when you are hungry, nourish yourself with great spiritual foods by listening to the noble periods of Bach . . . ," and so on through a nonsense purple-passage and Beethoven and Shakespeare as compensation for poverty and crippling. Thus West continues the mockeries of cultural pretension he presented with his *Balso Snell,* but now the psuedo-compensatory media culture is viewed, as in the earlier quote above, as gross "betrayal." The exploitative debasement so integral to most of modern culture-marketing has, as with the Christ dream, essentially destroyed the ideal possibility for both actor and audience. Thus we generally recognize that however important the fantasies, the religious, the romantics, the aesthetes, etc., do not really lead lives much different than the rest of us. The great cultural ideals come out as mere diversions, entertainments, psychic and moral masturbations. But is this the *"worst"* of all the many "betrayals" of our humanity? As his examples suggest, West further indicts the processed culture, the exploited fantasy, for a denial of actual reality, of authentic being. Religion, art, and other fantasies now become vicious masquerades in the deepest sense, denying recognition and change of the self and the world.

Denatured religion and art falsify all. So do the other fantasy-answers (though oddly West leaves out our processed politics). Shrike, in the same section as on art as a way out of actual miseries, also provides Lonelyhearts sick-a-bed with other burlesqued escape alternatives. The life of "the soil": "You are fed up with the city and its teeming millions. The ways and means of men, as getting and lending and spending . . . are too much with you" and so you go back to the ancient rural ways and "sow and reap and chivy your kine, not kin or kind, between the pregnant rows of corn and taters. Your step becomes the heavy sexual step of a dance-drunk Indian and you tread the seed down into the female earth. . . ." The hyped-up euphoniousness, the aslant allusions (including Wordsworth, Tolstoy, and Hart Crane), and the emphasis on sexual displacement are all heavily self-parodying. So, too, with escape to the South Seas: "You live in a thatch hut with the daughter of the king. . . . Her breasts are golden speckled pears, her belly a melon. . . . In the evening, on the blue lagoon, under the silvery moon, to your love you croon in the soft sylabelew and vocabelew . . . and when a beautiful society girl comes to your hut . . . you send her back to her yacht that hangs on the horizon like a nervous racehorse. . . ." (Allusions here may include several pop songs of the period and a standard romantic movie formula.) Shrike concludes that the South Seas stuff is done with and that "there's little use in imitating Gauguin" anymore—just more arty masquerade. But let us "now examine Hedonism, or take the cash and let the credit go. . . ." Then follows a cataloging of what we

might now call "The *Playboy* Philosophy," with superficial doses of sports, stock vices, faddish paraphernalia, and trite culture ("You fornicate under pictures by Matisse and Picasso, and often you spend an evening beside the fireplace with Proust and an apple.") For your last party, "the table is a coffin carved for you by Eric Gill" (an early twentieth-century English craftsman of neo-medievalizing piety), and you finish with a speech: " 'Life,' you say, "is a club . . . where they deal you only one hand and you must sit in. So even if the cards are cold and marked by the hand of fate . . . play up like a gentleman and a sport. Get tanked, grab what's on the buffet, use the girls upstairs, but remember . . . don't squawk." Shrike annotates for Lonelyhearts this parody (it may partly mock Hemingwayesque American he-man-stoicism) with "you haven't the money, nor are you stupid enough to manage it."

Then follows the parody of art as compensation and passing references to the options of suicide and drugs, concluding, "God alone is our escape. The Church is our only hope, the First Church of Christ Dentist, where He is worshipped as Preventer of Decay. . . ." (While Christian Science provides the shape of the rhetoric, many varieties of faith-healing and escapist rhetoric are at issue, here and elsewhere.) Shrike finishes with a parodistic letter to J. C., the "Miss Lonelyhearts of Miss Lonelyhearts," decrying the difficulty of faith and life "in this day and age," and jokily begging for reassurance.

While this mockery of escapist fantasies has its points, the burlesque testifying to mass-culture vulgarization and exploitation, the manner seems a bit thick, too much in the style of collegiate humor, or *Saturday Night Live,* or certain stand-up comedians. It is an hysterically compulsive humor, a mechanical jokiness—as Lonelyhearts elsewhere comments on professional-journalist humor—out of control in pathetic disillusionment. While appropriate to Shrike in his sexual and moral hysteria (and also to part of the known character of Nathanael West), it is too shallow, too pat, to be really witty.

Shrike's "thick glove of words," typical to a stock type of compulsive joker, self-revealingly culminates in his role as Lonelyhearts's alter ego in his charade party, "Every man his own Miss Lonelyhearts." Also a pathetically anxious sore-rubbing are Lonelyhearts's other desperate efforts at escapism—drunkenness, predatory sex, psychosomatic illness, violent outbursts. In his messy little effort at revenge against the tormenting Willie Shrike, he takes Mary Shrike to a nightclub, El Gaucho. He recognizes the phony romantic atmosphere as "part of the business of dreams," of the exploited fantasies of those "who wanted to write and live the life of an artist," or other fantasy modes of adventure, prowess, beauty, success, love—just variations on "those who wrote to Miss Lonelyhearts for help." Mary's insistent fantasized tales of her past and her heritage are just another sad effort at "something poetic" in a meanly empty life. With mechanical desperation, she would do anything to be "gay" (in the older sense)— "Everyone wants to be gay—unless they're sick"—in that saddest of all fantasy compulsions, the anxious search for a "good time." For Lonelyhearts, and the perceptive reader, such efforts can only heighten the "feeling of icy fatness."

Part of the persuasiveness, the seriousness, of the figure of Lonelyhearts comes from West giving him his own sharply intelligent sense of our fraudulent mass culture. Though West shortly later went to work in the Hollywood dream factory, his sense of the "betrayal" by sleazy romanticizing remained constant—the genuine evil which encourages masquerading.

To pursue romanticizing in a slightly different sense, West, in the chapter following Shrike's burlesque of the escape fantasies, "Miss Lonelyhearts in the country," has his protagonist try Betty's therapy of a few spring days with her at an unused farm, her childhood home in Connecticut. This pastoral interlude, which is also the only bit of affectionate sex in West, is more positive than any other scene. Even so, Lonelyhearts finds in a walk in the spring woods destructive entropy at work: "in the deep shade there was nothing but death—rotten leaves, gray and white fungi, and over everything a funereal hush." And even at Lonelyhearts's most vital moment, his copulating in the grass with virginal "little girl" Betty (thus seeing her, he escapes feminine power), he also notes that the small green leaves hung in the hot still day "like an army of little metal shields," and he heard a singing thrush sound like "a flute choked with saliva." While this may partly be understood as West's further characterization of Lonelyhearts's megapolitan morbidity even when in a pastoral love scene, I think it also typically reveals the Westean sensibility. No nature-romantic, he insistently, even incongruously, displays modernist sensibility in its concern with entropic mechanisms.

The pastoral-sexual peace, of course, can only be a regenerative interlude—that is the nature of pastoral—and one hardly answering the "Bronx slums," the letters witnessing horrible commonplace anguish, the betrayed culture, and the megapolitan malaise. A series of ironically surreal scenes in a "little park" in New York City reenforces the point with "waste land" imagery. The park was a self-parody of one, desolate, its ground "not the kind in which life generates," its "gray sky looked as if it had been rubbed with a soiled eraser. It held no angels, flaming crosses, olive-bearing doves, wheels within wheels. Only a newspaper struggled in the air like a kite with a broken spine." For Lonelyhearts, it is a dead land (properly marked by spineless media) but full of inhuman crucifying threats. As he walks through the park, even the shadow of a lamp post "pierced him like a spear." In another nightmarish extension of his anguished psyche in the park, looking toward a memorial obelisk he saw its "rigid shadow . . . lengthening in rapid jerks"; looking at the monument itself, it "seemed red and swollen in the dying sun, as though it were about to spout a load of granite seed." Waiting another sexual rendezvous near the obelisk, "he examined the sky," with the continuation of the same metaphor he had been applying to a woman (a recurrent psychological point in West) "and saw that it was canvas covered and ill-stretched." Trying to fathom its unnaturalness, he "examined it like a detective who is searching for a clue to his own exhaustion." In the "tons

of forced rock and tortured steel" that makes up the menacingly surrounding skyscrapers, he discovered his "clue." "Americans have dissipated their radical energy in an orgy of stone breaking . . . hysterically, desperately, almost as if they knew the stones would some day break them." Lonelyhearts's tortured psyche reflects the hard hysterical reality, its revulsive stone becoming the rock that will break him. The park, like the dreams, provides no real solace, only frightening human constructs, stone city and stoned soul.

The mechanically hard and violent order overwhelms all. The solacing fantasies of religion provide no exception. The obsessive Shrike produces a news clipping in a bar—"ADDING MACHINE USED IN RITUAL OF WESTERN SECT. . . . *Figures Will be Used for Prayers for Condemned Slayer of Aged Recluse. . . .*" Dreams of hope have turned into mechanical bad jokes, media hypes like the Lonelyhearts column, willed and destructive hysteria like the Lonelyhearts "religious experience." They are also grotesquely irrelevant to most of actuality which West, with the pessimistic refusal of solace central to modernist sensibility, sees as harsh, random, breaking.

Violent Tropes

One of the most striking characteristics of ***Miss Lonelyhearts,*** it should be evident, is the drastic metaphor, the shocking figure of speech. To note a few more. When Lonelyhearts's smug colleague Goldsmith smiled, he was "bunching his fat cheeks like twin rolls of smooth pink toilet paper." When the crippled Doyle hobbled across the barroom, "he made many waste motions, like that of a partially destroyed insect." When hostile-joker Shrike, whose "dead pan" face has been geometrically as well as punningly described, finishes his preliminary seduction speech (religious parody, of course) to a Miss Farkis, he "buried his triangular face like the blade of a hatchet in her neck." Later, when the hysterically joking Shrike tries to persuade the near-catatonic Lonelyhearts, now rocklike in faith, to play one of his mocking games, he "was a gull trying to lay an egg in the smooth flank of a rock, a screaming, clumsy gull." When Lonelyhearts despairingly looks out the window after failing to polish off his column (partly because his religious rhetoric is too drippingly artificial to even be convincing to himself), a "slow spring rain was changing the dusty tar roofs below him to shiny patent leather . . . slippery . . . he could find no support for either his eyes or his feelings." Often surrealistically hyper-lucid and extreme, the tropes resonate with the themes of mechanical artifice, hysterical masquerade, and violent breakdown.

A number of West's metaphors are extended, in the sense of seventeenth-century poetic conceits. Bemusedly, we hear gross Fay Doyle undressing in the dark for sex: "She made sea sounds; something flapped like a sail; there was the creak of ropes; then he heard the wave-against-a-wharf smack of rubber on flesh. Her call for him to hurry was like a sea-moan, and when he lay beside her, she heaved, tidal, moon driven." And then, as they say of comic routines, the topper: "Some fifteen minutes later, he crawled out of bed like an exhausted swimmer leaving the surf. . . ." (Some critics, again missing the mockery and

West's double play, have earnestly misread the metaphoric point as sexual vitality or the maternal sea, but most of West's maritime figures are negative, here and elsewhere, ironic play with the inhuman and gratuitous.)

Some figures more slyly continue. When Lonelyhearts fails to communicate with the embittered Doyles though he has hysterically poured out his Christian-love message (ironically, a parody of Shrike's parodies), he "felt like an empty bottle, shiny and sterile." Half a dozen paragraphs later, his message totally misunderstood by the lascivious and voracious Fay, she attempts to sexually arouse him and he "felt like an empty bottle that is being slowly filled with warm, dirty water." He finally overflows with violent rage.

The elaboration of metaphors, whether of the psyche-stone-skyscraper-city-religious-rock, of the compulsive metaphysic of geometrical and symbolic shapes, of Lonelyhearts phallic fears, breast fixations and homoerotic confusions, or of the parodistic images of media romanticism and debased religiosity, heightens, incises, almost takes over the fiction. Highly artful work, we can certainly believe the reports that West rewrote and rewrote *Miss Lonelyhearts* with a rather un-American sense of craft quite antithetical to the vulgar romanticism of pouring out warmly dirty "self-expression." Curiously, he countered "confessional" subject matter—the dream life of the artist, religious conversion, fantasy-dominated people—with rigorous craft. Almost uniquely in his time and place, West combined self-conscious strict artistry with intense immediate concern.

Some of that self-consciousness deserves further emphasis. West's writing shows an exacerbated visual imagination, beyond his evident fascination with painting, especially surrealism. The hyperlucid visualization organizes, disciplines, objectifies the concern with extreme subjectivity. Aesthetically, no doubt, West is heir to the symbolists' "correspondences" (Baudelaire), the modernist Anglo-American poets' "objective correlative" (Eliot), and the surrealists' disjunctive images of "dream lucidity" (Breton). But those are pedantic considerations. More interestingly, the self-conscious tropes do something else; they carry out and reenforce the dominant issue of self-consciousness, which is what forces the masquerading. I have noted a few instances in which Lonelyhearts, for all his sincere anguish, is so aware of what he is doing that he has taken on a pose, actor's gestures, a willed role. Even his final desperate escape from consciousness and role-playing by hysteria and hallucination seems incomplete, yet more wilful masquerading. Still another example: in one of his most sincere conversations with fiancée Betty, Lonelyhearts plays what he acknowledges to be a "trick" in speech; "he stumbled purposely, so that she would take his confusion for honest feeling." Ironically, she is too simple and sincere to be taken in. Of course part of Lonelyhearts's difficulty in role-playing here (and with Mary Shrike and Fay Doyle) comes, as I noted earlier, from hostility to women and ambiguous homoeroticism. But it clearly goes beyond that. His self-induced hysterical conversion experience attempts to break through his tormenting self-consciousness in costuming as Miss Lonelyhearts.

If he can only become the true believer, the ultimate Miss Lonelyhearts, J. C., he can become real and one, transcend the masquerade.

This I take to be West's crux. Whether Lonelyhearts holds Doyle's hand as expression of compassion, pursues sex, advises the lovelorn, plans the future with Betty, or withdraws to his rock of faith, he is, as an examination of each scene will show, role-playing, masquerading. The ills of such divided consciousness, and the consequent forced pretending of a role, apply, of course, to Lonelyhearts's alter ego, Shrike, and his ornate joking, gaming, parodies. The "acting" also applies to others, even the inchoate simple cripple Doyle (his pretense at a leering manner in the speakeasy, his playing "dog" for his wife, his later playing the injured husband). Lonelyhearts also applies the point to the disillusioned tough-guy pretenses of the other reporters in the speakeasy. They return the perception by seeing Lonelyhearts's religiousness as put on, made up, "too damn literary." In both details and style West ironically confirms their point. One of Lonelyhearts's colleagues notes that even if the character were to achieve "a genuine religious experience, it would be personal," only, and thus end up "meaningless," incomprehensible, which in fact it does. Another replies that the trouble with Lonelyhearts, "the trouble with all of us, is that we have no outer life, only an inner one, and that by necessity." Then the reporters turn back to compulsively defensive jokes as usual disguises for their irrelevant feelings. But that division between inner and outer life, between human feeling and the compulsive order surrounding it, remains central throughout the novella as the condition of anguished self-consciousness and consequent role-playing—theirs, Shrike's, Lonelyhearts's, and not least the oh so self consciously artful author's. Our world violates us and we escape into unreality.

Miss Lonelyhearts is also full of small and large violence; stylistically as well as dramatically. Violence marks the essential breaking out of self-consciousness and through the masquerade, a desperate assertion against alienation, helplessness, inauthenticity. In his final effort toward religious experience, as I previously noted, Lonelyhearts explicitly wants "unmotivated violence" to restore life to the dead world. And he gets it. Earlier, despairingly drinking and thinking of sex, he summarizes: "Only friction could make him warm or violence make him mobile." And in yet another passage, he notes of himself: "With the return of self-consciousness, he knew that only violence could make him supple."

Alive, "mobile," "supple"—these are, in the biblical phrase, the difference between "the quick and the dead." West, preoccupied with violence in all his works, which he presents as quintessentially American, serves it as the assertion of life against suffering: as when Lonelyhearts recalls accidentally stepping on a frog, and then frenziedly eliminating its misery by crushing it, or when he smashed with a stone the misbutchered lamb, or when he twists and twists the arm of "the clean old man," or when his suffering over his failure of charity with the Doyles turns to his ragingly beating Fay, or when his guilty misery over Betty turns to giving her pain ("like a kitten whose soft helplessness makes one ache to hurt it"), or when his compassion for the hurt in the lovelorn letters turns to rage, or when his own total misery leads to the violent denial of himself. This violently hallucinatory denial of all reality is the destructive religious fallacy. Violence becomes the crucial assertion through suffering of life, only to end as its final masquerade, death.

Among the masquerades which West pursues, one of the most violating tropes, of course, is the entitling one—the hysterical need for the ultimate Miss Lonelyhearts. That savage metaphor for Christianity is truly violent to the heritage, a really "sick" joke. I suppose that in a vestigially Christian culture it should be offensive to many—if they do not willfully misread or disguise their responses—perhaps even more so than the fervent blasphemy in D. H. Lawrence's *The Man Who Died* (a novella written not long before *Miss Lonelyhearts*) where a Christ copulates on an altar with a priestess. Perhaps West's more cynical fiction also offends more supposedly tolerant folk, those from the likes of William James (*Varieties of Religious Experience* was one of West's acknowledged sources) to current agnostics. These would grant that religious fervors have a decently pragmatic side; it is nice to believe: it may help one feel good, or bear the world, or endure suffering, or "get through the night," or add other poetic flavor to existence. Nonsense. For from the Westean view, they may discover that the joke is on them. Betraying self-consciousness and inauthentic role-playing will result in a cosmic pratfall.

While West may be no more sardonically atheistic in his savaging of religious grotesquery than some fo his fine aristic contemporaries (for example, Céline or Buñuel), he leaves no room for displaced piety. The role-playing religious order madly violates the (dis)ordering that is. Religion, by the same logic with which it provides acceptance or solace, anesthetizes the essential human and defeats the actual. Instead of answering misery, despair, unmerited suffering, suicide, religion often creates them. To be "born again," as was Miss Lonelyhearts, is to be dead—and quite literally—to the truth. It destroys him, hurts others, answers nothing. Faith is a grotesque disease, however much we are aware, as West was, of the poignant imperatives to it. To falsely order suffering takes the heart out of the human, which would better remain lonely in its unacceptable universe. That is the unmasqueraded message of *Miss Lonelyhearts.*

Miss Lonelyhearts is an exceptionally intense very short novel, yet in the fundamental sense Nathanael West's largest work. Appropriately to its time of depression disillusion (perhaps *the* twentieth-century revelation, so far, that the American system doesn't work), and to its place as a somewhat marginal American's response to the mainline mythologies (Menckenism cum brilliance?), it is a compassionately savage piece of iconoclasm. At the level of stock cultural history, I suppose it can be viewed as combining the zesty art of negation that partly characterized the 1920s with some of the more grimly sordid realities of the following time. As with many of the more interesting achievements in literary history, it does not quite categorize and can be viewed in later perspective as a document

of cultural "transition." It seems to precariously fuse two kinds of sensibility—a "hinge" work—with both the artful modern expressiveness of the period after the Great War and the depressed social actualities of the following period—a literary flying fish.

But more importantly, *Miss Lonelyhearts* may be *sui generis,* a striking literary act intriguing in its very exceptionalness for both the times and the author. West's novella may be one of those unique works (one thinks of others by Laclos, Corbière, Lermontov, Zamiatin, Melville, and Hart Crane) which stands beyond its genesis, beyond its author—a one-time only achievement, the small odd masterpiece. Indeed, to continue a discussion of West beyond *Miss Lonelyhearts* must have more than a little of the tone of anticlimax. West was never again to achieve such shaping intensity. *Miss Lonelyhearts* might thus be said to overreach its author as well as times, arriving at that kind of impersonality which certain self-contained works seem to acquire. The "Miss Lonelyhearts" paradigm, as it were, remains a permanent expressive accounting of the religious masquerade, and its relentless unmasking. (pp. 26-50)

Kingsley Widmer, in his Nathanael West, *Twayne Publishers, 1982, 146 p.*

Robert Emmet Long   (essay date 1985)

[*In the following excerpt from a chapter in his* Nathanael West *devoted to the imagery, satire, characterization, symbolism, and themes of* Miss Lonelyhearts, *Long comments on West's revisions of the novel from original conception to publication and suggests that F. Scott Fitzgerald's 1925 novel* The Great Gatsby *was a literary forerunner of West's novel.*]

West's initial conception of *Miss Lonelyhearts* grew out of an incident that occurred in March 1929. S. J. Perelman invited West to join him at Siegel's restaurant in Greenwich Village where he was to have dinner with a newspaperwoman who wrote a lovelorn column for the *Brooklyn Eagle* under the name "Susan Chester." At the restaurant, "Susan Chester" read aloud some of the letters from her readers, thinking that Perelman might be able to put them to comic use. He did not find them especially promising as material for satire, but West was moved, and intrigued, by them; and they became the starting point for his novel, which evolved slowly, passing through six different drafts, before being completed in December 1932.

Although the earliest drafts of the novel have not survived, the later stages of West's revision can be glimpsed in five next-to-final chapter drafts published in *Contact* and *Contempo* magazines in 1932, a year before the publication of the work. They reveal that even in this later stage of composition he was still attempting to resolve the problem of how best to present the protagonist. In the February 1932 issue of *Contact,* the third-person protagonist is called Thomas Matlock, but in the May issue West's narration shifts to the first person, and in the October issue back again to the third. Clearly, a first-person narration would have diminished the author's ironic judgment of the hero—and proved unmanageable at the end, when he is killed. Clearly, too, while using the name Thomas Matlock in the first segment, West had decided to dispense with a name for him at all, other than Miss Lonelyhearts, as the work progressed, thus achieving additional irony—a relentless challenging of the hero's identity.

Another conspicuous feature of West's revision is that in the earlier version Miss Lonelyhearts and Shrike were not as absolutely antithetical as they later became. The earlier Miss Lonelyhearts indulged in moments of self-mockery that, in revision, were rewritten as a mockery of him by Shrike. Indeed, a whole sequence in the first draft of "Miss Lonelyhearts in the Dismal Swamp," in which Miss Lonelyhearts ponders, only to reject as fruitless, avenues of escape from his despair (the South Seas, the arts, the farm), was later given to Shrike. Moreover, this lengthy, rather lushly parodic passage is out of key stylistically with the rest of the work. In rewriting, West reduced the length and tone of the passage considerably, making it suitable to be spoken mockingly by Shrike as Miss Lonelyhearts's alter ego.

West's revisions almost always work toward greater cohesiveness and concreteness, as can be seen in the opening sentences in the February 1932 and April 1933 versions:

February 1932

> Thomas Matlock, the Miss Lonelyhearts of the New York Evening Hawk (Are you in trouble? Do you need advice? Write to Miss Lonelyhearts and she will help you) decided to walk from the Hawk Building across the park to Delehanty's speakeasy.

April 1933

> The Miss Lonelyhearts of the New York Herald *Post-Dispatch* (Are-you-in-trouble?-Do-you-need-advice? Write-to-Miss-Lonelyhearts-and-she-will-help-you) sat at his desk and stared at a piece of white cardboard.

Not only has the actual name for Miss Lonelyhearts been removed, but the name of the newspaper has also been changed for the sake of greater realism; and the lines lead directly to the blasphemous prayer Shrike has had printed, bringing the reader immediately to the heart of the conflict within the hero. Elsewhere, in the first-person draft, the hero attempts to explain himself to the reader: "Don't misunderstand me. My Christ has nothing to do with love. Even before I became Miss Lonelyhearts, my world was moribund. I lived on a deserted stairway of ornate machinery. I wrote my first love letters on a typewriter. . . . I turned to Christ as the most familiar and natural of excitants. I wanted him to destroy this hypnosis. He alone could make the rock of sensation bleed and the stick of thought flower." This explanatory passage was deleted in revision, allowing the reader more dramatically to grasp Miss Lonelyhearts's mental state through understatement.

The revisions also show West confronting and overcoming problems of diffuseness. In the early draft of the opening chapter Miss Lonelyhearts prepares to go to Delehanty's, and on the way pauses to rest for a moment on a bench in the small park. But here he decides against going to the speakeasy after all, returns home, goes to bed, and reads Father Zosima's sermon in *The Brothers Karamazov,* after which he falls asleep and has a dream in which he and two other college friends, on a drinking spree, decide to sacrifice a lamb in a quasi-religious ceremony, a botched attempt that turns into sordid cruelty. In revision, Miss Lonelyhearts, in his office, is reading the letters from Sick-of-it-all and Desperate when Shrike appears, and their first confrontation concludes the chapter dramatically. In the second chapter he not only prepares to go but does go to Delehanty's, where he meets Shrike and Miss Farkis, a strikingly self-contained "scene." Only in the next chapter does Miss Lonelyhearts return home to read the Father Zosima passage and have the dream. With far greater concentration of effect, West finds the proper place for the lamb incident, which dominates the chapter in which it appears.

Other revisions reveal West's attention to nuance. In the early part, for example, the mirror on the wall of Miss Lonelyhearts's room, an emblem of his introspection, is removed. The sacrifice of the lamb scene is bathed in blood in the early draft ("A thick stream of blood pumped over their heads and clothes"), but is muted in the later one. A dream in which he appears as a child in a flannel nightgown, with his head bent in prayer on the knees of the mother he innocently "loved," a scene which precedes his later rage over the loss of love, is removed as being too explicit. In the early draft, the letter from Broad Shoulders contains more pedestrian details and is less powerful than the letter as it appears in the final version, an indication of how carefully West weighed every word, how he built up effects in revision as well as toned them down.

All the magazine-draft chapters contain lines and passages that were refined upon in the book version. In certain cases names were changed. Fay Doyle's husband was named Martin before becoming Peter, and her daughter Lucy was at first named Mary. In some instances, gross touches were softened. The "clean old man" at the comfort station is said to turn away "to wipe himself with some paper from the roll beside the seat," but in the book version he turns away "to wipe his mouth." In the seduction scene, Fay Doyle "caught [Miss Lonelyhearts's] head and put her tongue into his mouth"—which in the book version becomes, "and kissed him on the mouth." The revisions include scores of minor alterations, all of which contribute to the polish of the final draft. In general, West's tendency is to abbreviate, foreshorten, and to avoid direct statement or explanation; and in this way the novel becomes not only more certain in its tone but also more cryptic and mysterious.

If the revisions reveal West's refinement upon his conception, they do not, of course, explain the conception. West himself has commented on the composition of **Miss Lonelyhearts** in **"Some Notes on Miss L.,"** published in *Contempo* magazine in 1933, but it is difficult to know how seriously to take what he says. He explains that **Miss Lonelyhearts** "became the portrait of a priest of our time who has a religious experience. His case is classical and is built on all the cases in James' *Varieties of Religious Experience* and Starbuck's *Psychology of Religion.* The psychology is theirs not mine. The imagery is mine." He also remarks that while writing the novel, he conceived of it as a comic strip:

> The chapters to be squares in which many things happen through one action. The speeches contained in conventional balloons. I abandoned this idea, but retained some of the comic strip technique: Each chapter instead of going forward in time, also goes backward, forward, up and down in space like a picture. Violent images are used to illustrate commonplace events. Violent acts are left almost bald.

Miss Lonelyhearts does have something of the nature of a comic strip or cartoon. Each chapter is dramatically focused by a single event or brief sequence of events, comparable to the series of pictorial frames of a comic strip. Like the figures in a cartoon, West's characters are stripped down to the sharp outline of a few traits. Pete Doyle is a cripple, his wife is sexually devouring, Betty is simple and unworldly, Shrike is a mocker. They have also been strongly visualized (Miss Lonelyhearts's long, bony "biblical" face, and Pete Doyle's built-up shoe which he drags after him), and West makes frequent use of the tableau. The endings of the chapters, particularly, often use framing tableaux that bring the chapters to visual climaxes. The novel's denouement also has the graphic, pictorial quality of a comic strip ending—Miss Lonelyhearts's fall on the staircase a visual analogue of his fall from the grace he had just imagined.

But if *Miss Lonelyhearts* is a comic strip, it is a distinctly sinister one. A death theme runs through it, evoking a dead world that cannot be brought to life, and the novel ends with death. One of the prominent features of *Miss Lonelyhearts,* as compared to *Balso Snell,* is the manner in which West moves from an indeterminate interior landscape that can be located nowhere in time and space to a concrete social setting of the thirties. Its setting, with the exception of a brief visit to the Connecticut countryside, is New York, which has been created with a harsh stylization that could be compared to the hard-boiled detective fiction of Dashiell Hammett. Hammett, in fact, was West's guest at the Sutton Hotel when *Miss Lonelyhearts* was being written, and he read the novel in an early draft. West, in turn, had read Hammett's detective novels, as well as many of the issues of *Black Mask,* the great magazine forum for hard-boiled detective fiction of the thirties. When *Miss Lonelyhearts* was published, Josephine Herbst called it a "moral detective story"—and it does give the impression of a raw world in which values have disappeared, and in which violence is sudden and frequent. As in Hammett's fiction, the quester figure is alone in what is essentially an irrational world; and curiously, in the early draft, but later removed, Miss Lonelyhearts is even compared to a detective. As he waits in the park for Mrs. Doyle to appear, he examines the sky "like a stupid detective who is searching for a clue to his own exhaustion." A few minutes later, "the detective saw a big woman enter the park and start in his direction." Miss Lonelyhearts is evoked here as a man who searches for clues to the mystery of an absent God, and in his later wanderings he attempts but fails to unravel the mystery.

The hard-boiled aspect of *Miss Lonelyhearts* can be noticed in chapter 5, which begins in Delehanty's speakeasy as a group of nameless, dimensionless men assault women verbally, particularly women writers who pretend to one aesthetic ideal or another. One of the men tells of a woman writer who was hurt "by beauty," and is taken "into the lots" one night by eight men and gang raped, presumably as a curative for her illusions. Another man relates a story about a female writer who cultivated "hard-boiled stuff," and is assaulted and sexually abused for three days by a group of hardened, low-life men who resent her glamorization of the primitive and physical. Not only is violence recounted by these men in the accents of a calloused dehumanization, it also erupts in fact. Miss Lonelyhearts is struck suddenly in the face at one point, and by the end of the chapter, in another speakeasy, he is hit over the head with a chair. The chapter ends with his loss of consciousness. West's characters, in fact, show very little consciousness of any kind, whether social, aesthetic, or political.

Although *Miss Lonelyhearts* is not a political novel, a criticism of capitalism does enter into it. In *Miss Lonelyhearts,* unlike *Balso Snell,* West is unusually conscious of the life of the masses, of a suffering that he has related to society's complicity in the dehumanization of its members, its trashing of their very dreams. Miss Lonelyhearts's girl friend Betty, who represents the status quo and does not question it, wants him to go to work for an advertising agency, where he will be a manipulator of dreams for commercial ends. As it is, as a newspaper columnist, he offers mere palliatives for suffering, all that his spiritually deadened society can provide its members.

About the role of society in the manipulation of dreams, West is quite explicit. "Men have always," he writes, "fought their misery with dreams. Although dreams were once powerful, they have been made puerile by the movies, radio and newspapers. Among many betrayals this one is the worst." Miss Lonelyhearts often seems, powerlessly, like a man in a cage. His solitary room and office at the newspaper are like boxes; and in an earlier draft the street upon which he looks from his office window is "walled at both ends." In his office he meditates on life as a desert, a place of inertia, animality, and violence, which are part of everyday life. His petitioners for help seem to him to live in little enclosed spaces, surrounded by commercial billboards that serve as reminders of violated values. In such a meaningless world, violence is a logical outcome.

Elsewhere, in a dream sequence, Miss Lonelyhearts is in the window of a pawnshop, where he attempts to create order out of the paraphernalia around him. He tries to assemble stable shapes from the musical instruments, umbrellas, and derby hats, and eventually forms a large cross. When the cross becomes too large for the pawnshop, he moves it, in his imagination, to the shore of the ocean. But here each wave throws up more debris, adding to the stock of the cross faster than he can extend its arms, and he becomes a kind of Sisyphus struggling with an impossible task. The sequence implies the impossibility of Miss Lonelyhearts's effort to create order out of chaos; but the pawnshop image is particularly interesting, since it evokes the discarding or destruction of dreams in a commercial society. When West refers to "the business of dreams," he implies that human dreams are an industry for capitalist exploitation. In an early section, Shrike produces a newspaper clipping about a religious sect that will hold a "goat and adding machine ritual" for a man about to be executed in a Colorado prison. The clipping is of course a parody of American religious sects that have become "worldly" and incoherent. But it also suggests that the prisoner, who slew another man in an argument over a small amount of money, is a "goat," or scapegoat of the society, in which spiritual reality is no more meaningful than the figures in an adding-machine tally.

Although West does not refer specifically to the Depression, it is an unnamed presence in the novel. When Miss Lonelyhearts returns from his escape vacation in the country, the first thing he notices as he drives into the city are the Bronx slums. It is at this point that he recognizes the hopelessness of his "mission." People wander the streets with "broken hands" and "torn mouths." A man on the verge of death staggers into a movie theater showing a film called *Blonde Beauty,* an escapist sexual fantasy; and a ragged woman with "an enormous goiter" gleefully picks a love-story magazine out of a garbage can. These are the betrayed ones, betrayed by their culture—the spiritually beggared.

West's portrait of Miss Lonelyhearts, however, is less a social than a psychological study, one which is indebted particularly to Dostoyevsky. Dostoyevsky's "underground man" supplies the model for Miss Lonelyhearts's self-division and psychological suffering; and Raskolnikov in *Crime and Punishment* especially prepares for him—in his impulse to play a heroic role for which he is not necessarily qualified, his fevered dreams, isolation within an oppressive society, and obsession. As if to make the Russian analogy unmistakable, West has Goldsmith, an underling of Shrike's, address Miss Lonelyhearts by asking "How now, Dostoievsky?" Dostoyevsky is referred to again when Miss Lonelyhearts withdraws to his room to read *The Brothers Karamazov,* and Father Zosima's sermon is quoted: "Love the animals, love the plants, love everything. If you love everything, you will perceive the divine mystery in things. Once you perceive it, you will begin to comprehend it better every day. And you will come at last to love the whole world with an all-embracing love." It is this vision of an all-embracing love that torments Miss Lonelyhearts with its unattainability, and is part of his "Christ complex."

Miss Lonelyhearts is also similar in a number of essentials to Prince Myshkin, in *The Idiot,* who yearns for a community of Christian love and brotherhood in a society that would seem to deny its possibility absolutely. Alone, in a deeply disillusioning world, Prince Myshkin finds that he can only be misunderstood, and becomes increasingly estranged. In the end his retirement to the Swiss sanitarium indicates the futility of his quest. Like Myshkin, Miss Lonelyhearts is set apart from others by his spiritual aspiration that is out of key with the materialistic world in which he lives, so that he is regarded as a freak and suffers the torment of the misfit. To his friend John Sanford, West

Drawing of West by David Schorr.

boasted that he could rewrite Dostoyevsky "with a pair of shears"; and remarkably he has done just that, reproducing Dostoyevsky in miniature in an American Depression setting.

Miss Lonelyhearts's dreams are inner psychological dramas, like the dreams in Dostoyevsky, but they have also been influenced by Freud and the surrealists. Freudian symbolism is apparent, for example, in the scene in which Miss Lonelyhearts meditates in the little park near a Mexican War obelisk. "He sat staring at [the obelisk] without knowing why," West comments, "until he noticed that it was lengthening in rapid jerks, not as shadows usually lengthen. He grew frightened and looked up quickly at the monument. It seemed red and swollen in the dying sun, as though it were about to spout a load of granite seed." A moment later, his thoughts turn to the desire for sex that he has been suppressing. The scene is not actually a dream but it is something like a dream state, and another dream state occurs when Miss Lonelyhearts drives through the Bronx slums, where "crowds of people moved through the street with a dream-like violence," an image that might have come from a surrealist canvas. In an actual dream late in the novel, West's imagery is oddly reminiscent of a Salvador Dali painting: "A train rolled into a station, where [Miss Lonelyhearts] was a reclining statue holding a stopped clock, a coach rumbled into the yard of an inn where he was sitting over a guitar, cap in hand, shedding the rain with his hump."

Miss Lonelyhearts takes much of its life from West's striking and haunting imagery. It is difficult to say how West learned to use imagery to such effect, but he may well have been influenced by the poetry of the period—by the Imagists, Ezra Pound, and William Carlos Williams, in whose verse the image takes on a luminous life of its own. He was undoubtedly influenced by T. S. Eliot, since the symbolism of *The Waste Land* is apparent in the novel. *The Waste Land* theme is particularly evident in West's depiction of the small, barren park, which ought to be a spiritual oasis in the city but is instead a miniature wasteland—a setting of dessication and blight. Describing the little park, West writes: "The decay that covered the surface of the mottled ground was not the kind in which life generates. Last year, he remembered, May had failed to quicken these soiled fields. It had taken all the brutality of July to torture a few green spikes through the exhausted dirt." In this wasteland park, Miss Lonelyhearts waits for a spring that does not come—until the end, when it brings only death.

Although hardly noted in the past, Fitzgerald's *The Great Gatsby* is also a decided influence on West's novel. Both are classic works of miniaturization that are tragic and comic at once, and end with the death of the heroes, who have been obsessed with an illusion of spiritual transcendence. If *Miss Lonelyhearts* has a cartoon quality, its characters limned in sinister caricature, so does *The Great Gatsby.* Myrtle Wilson, in *The Great Gatsby,* establishes the type of the cheap, sexual woman, preposterous in her vulgarity, who is reimagined exuberantly by West in Fay Doyle. Fay has, in fact, the name of another character in Fitzgerald's novel, Daisy Fay, whose beguiling sexuality proves to be sterile illusion; and this instance of common naming is given increased importance by its appearance again in *The Day of the Locust,* in which Faye Greener is a vacant Venus.

Myrtle Wilson, like Fay Doyle, is married to a pathetic failure of a man. Wilson pumps gas, and Pete Doyle reads gas meters, but neither is fueled with any vitality or has any sense of direction in his life. Wilson, according to Myrtle, "doesn't even know he's alive," and Doyle, as his wife says, "is all dried up." Their sexually starved wives cheat on them, and then, in the grotesque endings the husband-failure insanely shoots the hero. The absurdist climax of *The Great Gatsby* becomes the ultimate absurdist joke of *Miss Lonelyhearts.* A death theme is pervasive in *The Great Gatsby,* as it is again in *Miss Lonelyhearts,* not only because the heroes must die but also because the cultures themselves are dead, and any attempt to transcend them is doomed to failure.

V. S. Pritchett has described *Miss Lonelyhearts* as an "American fable," and it is as a fable, with an intricate miniaturization of effect, that frequently calls *The Great Gatsby* to mind. Quite apart from the similarity of at least two of the principal characters and of the endings, the novels group together as very artful works belonging to a special, very limited tradition in modern American fiction. The fable dimension of the novels derives in part from their quest themes and quester heroes whose failures reveal the most elemental truths of their cultures. But it is

insinuated, too, in the dream forms of the works, the "magical" realism they employ. The real worlds they explore seem distorted, so that the meanness of life becomes almost incredibly mean, menacing, evil—although comic too. Meyer Wolfsheim, with his cuff buttons made of human molars, becomes a plausible figure in the bizarre world in which he appears. The sexually devouring Fay Doyle, whose arm is like a "thigh," can be credited in *Miss Lonelyhearts,* with its vision of radical dislocation. In each novel a limited number of characters drawn in caricature interact in a morally charged atmosphere. Good and evil are constantly involved in the tensions of the works, in which values have become inverted. Both "fables" have a quality of lightness and grace, yet have been intensely and powerfully focused, and are modern moralities.

Miss Lonelyhearts can be compared to *The Great Gatsby* in still other ways. Both are strongly visualized and imagistic, and are structured dramatically, developing in a series of distinct scenes, with many chapters dominated by a single episode. Both are elegantly satirical, and show special finesse in their reproduction of vulgar people and their banal speech. Scenes in *The Great Gatsby* are comic and horrible at once, as in the scene at the Washington Heights apartment; and this dual quality informs *Miss Lonelyhearts*—in the letters written to Miss Lonelyhearts, for example, and in Miss Lonelyhearts's seduction by Fay Doyle. The sterility of women in *The Great Gatsby* is striking, and it is again in *Miss Lonelyhearts,* in which, as in Fitzgerald, sexuality is linked with death. In all of these respects Fitzgerald is a presence in the background of *Miss Lonelyhearts,* which, remarkably original as it is, yet does have a context in the American literature that immediately precedes it. (pp. 44-56)

Robert Emmet Long, in his Nathanael West, *Frederick Ungar Publishing Co., 1985, 202 p.*

Rebecca R. Butler   (essay date 1985)

[*In the following essay, Butler demonstrates that* Miss Lonelyhearts *meets Tzvetan Todorov's criteria for fantastic literature as presented in his* The Fantastic: A Structural Approach to a Literary Genre, *despite Todorov's insistence that fantastic literature ended in the nineteenth century. She also places the novel in Wolfgang Kayser's aesthetic category of the grotesque which he established in his* The Grotesque in Art and Literature.]

In his theoretical study *The Fantastic: A Structural Approach to a Literary Genre,* Tzvetan Todorov put forward some provocative hypotheses toward a systematic definition of the *fantastic.* He hoped, if successful, to be able to identify and predict the progress of a work of fantastic fiction if given no more than a single element from the narrative, much the same way that a famous anthropologist, with a single bone, identifies a particular animal and reconstructs its entire skeleton. As he pursued this ambitious undertaking Todorov became guilty of some awkward swings between the extremes of sweeping generalization and suffocating narrowness, and his seemingly absent-minded self-contradiction casts doubt occasionally on his credibility as a critic. Despite some weaknesses in presentation, the specific conditions he established and the frequent illustrations he developed make an appealing, indeed, an exciting, case for his definition, which would, if useful, allow us to discuss with some precision the nature of a great many works whose effects and contents are now vaguely called "weird, improbable, bizarre, unearthly, extravagant, eerie, or peculiar," for lack of better terminology. However, Todorov eventually limited the arena of the fantastic so strenuously that he called into question the usefulness of that definition. In his view the fantastic occupies a period that lasted only from the late eighteenth to the late nineteenth century and no longer exists in the twentieth century. He attempted to support his point with a discussion of *The Metamorphosis,* showing that Gregor Samsa, instead of continuously feeling some hesitation, confusion, or indecision about the unnatural change that has overtaken him, works to adapt to his new condition. "With Kafka," Todorov wrote, "we are thus confronted with a *generalized* fantastic which swallows up the entire world and the reader along with it." Apparently, in an attempt to rescue the term from that meaningless (especially in fiction) designation of everything that does not belong to the category of the real, Todorov has excluded too much from the province of the fantastic.

It seems unlikely that fantastic fiction ended abruptly with the tales of Guy de Maupassant. A twentieth-century novel that comes to mind as meeting Todorov's conditions for the fantastic is *Miss Lonelyhearts,* by Nathanael West. Moreover, it illustrates a great many parallels between Todorov's description of the fantastic and the aesthetic category of the grotesque as discussed by Wolfgang Kayser in *The Grotesque in Art and Literature.* Such a comparison may provide some evidence that the fantastic operates on a wider stage than Todorov has claimed for it and not unquestionably as a separate genre.

In fantastic fiction as Todorov described it there occurs at least one event whose cause is uncertain; the reader as well as the character involved hesitates in understanding the situation as having a natural or a supernatural explanation. Because the fantastic exists only as long as this hesitation lasts, the doubt and indecision about the nature of the extraordinary circumstance lingers, ideally, even when the story is finished. If a natural solution to the ambiguity is offered (as in detective stories), the fiction belongs to the neighboring genre of the "uncanny." But if the explanation is definitely supernatural (as it may be in a ghost story), the other neighboring genre of the "marvelous" exercises dominion. Whatever themes or contents the fiction may include, this hesitation must occur for the reader if the story is to belong to Todorov's category of the fantastic. Beyond this requirement there are the more general effects of an intensity of feeling, usually some fear, horror, or suspense; an experience of limits or of the crossing of natural limits; the blurring of ordinary boundaries; a sense of the excessive; a perception of the uncanny, the mysterious. Perception actually becomes a theme of the fantastic, as do metamorphosis; the collapse of the boundaries between mind and matter and between the word and the thing it denotes; madness; multiple personalities; a fusion of human and inhuman; all kinds of distortions of time

and space; the demonic, particularly sexual demonism; and sadism.

Miss Lonelyhearts seems to be a good test case for the fantastic, because never has a novelist more delicately avoided a resolution and retained the ambiguity of his fiction more scrupulously than in this "portrait of a priest of our time," created by West from saints' legends and psychological case histories. With masterful balance and deliberation West maneuvered his conscientious columnist through a nightmarish Depression-era New York City made peculiarly unbearable by his verbally sadistic feature editor Shrike and the shocking letters it is his job to answer for his newspaper's lonelyhearts column. Not only does Miss Lonelyhearts hesitate in interpreting the cause of some of his extraordinary experiences, he is uncertain about his own perceptions, about the possibility that he is suffering delusions, is going mad. Although Miss Lonelyhearts finally abandons his doubt, this uncertainty persists for the reader throughout the course of the narrative.

As the novel begins, Miss Lonelyhearts sits reading the morning's letters, one of which is from a sixteen-year-old girl born without a nose, who is considering the possibility that some supernatural causation is at work: "What did I do to deserve such a terrible bad fate?" she writes. She wonders if she "did something in the other world" before she was born for which she is being punished. The other letters are equally troubling. Miss Lonelyhearts, too, considers a spiritual solution: "Christ was the answer," he immediately thinks. But he hesitates to accept that explanation, fearing that he will lose control, that he will become "sick" if he gives in to the supernatural. This character is peculiarly suited to the experience of the fantastic, because he takes symbols very seriously, we gradually learn, and even searches the sky for signs of superhuman agency. But there the besieged columnist sees "no angels, flaming crosses, olive-bearing doves, wheels within wheels." In fact, Miss Lonelyhearts tries to avoid the supernatural explanation, seeking normality in drink, in sex, in a retreat to country living. Nevertheless, his hesitation persists when he cannot escape what Todorov called "the brutal intrusion of mystery into the context of real life." Miss Lonelyhearts becomes frighteningly aware that he cannot depend on a reliable order when one day "all the inanimate things over which he had tried to obtain control took the field against him." His ordinary possessions seem animated with a life of their own and finally drive him out onto the street, where "chaos was multiple." This is what Todorov described as the intense forcing of limits, the experience of the extreme, and a fusion or blurring of boundaries between ordinarily separate categories, here the animate and the inanimate. Again, while resting in the park, the distraught young man suddenly becomes aware that the shadow of a monument is moving forward across the ground in great jerks, "not as shadows usually lengthen." This uncanny sight sends him hurrying away, attempting to rationalize his strange experience. Of course, the letters themselves represent a distorted, nightmarish existence, and one of those letter writers, Mr. Doyle, illustrates, in his person, the blurring of boundaries and the failure of conventional order: "The cripple had a very strange face. His eyes failed to balance; his mouth was not under his nose; his forehead was square and bony; and his round chin was like a forehead in miniature. He looked like one of those composite photographs used by screen magazines in guessing contests."

In the face of such a repellent natural world, Miss Lonelyhearts turns gradually toward a supernatural source of order and meaning. Even though he fears that the mysterious power that stirs within him when he chants the name of Christ is actually hysteria, both his waking and his dream worlds attest that the risk is worthwhile. The physical world seems dead, "a world of doorknobs"; spring has come but no vegetation grows in the park, and in the country woods "there was nothing but death—rotten leaves, gray and white fungi, and over everything a funereal hush." In one of many revealing dreams, Miss Lonelyhearts sees himself as a magician who makes doorknobs flower, speak, and bleed. In another he finds himself, first in a pawnshop window, surrounded by discarded objects, then on a beach where this inanimate flotsam "yearns" and "strives" with a will of its own to undo the order imposed on it by humans. These dreams intensify rather than dispel the fantastic, because they are elaborations on the very ambiguity that occupies Miss Lonelyhearts's waking life.

When he returns to New York from the country, he looks out where crowds of people move through the street with a "dream-like violence" and sees "their broken hands and torn mouths." He wants to find some redemptive solution for them, knowing, he thinks to himself, that "dreams were once powerful," and "that he was capable of dreaming the Christ dream." Not at this point, or even when Miss Lonelyhearts rushes out to heal the crippled Doyle, is the reader invited to understand that this character is simply mad; on the contrary, his world and the people who inhabit it are so forbidding, so bizarre, so ominous, that Miss Lonelyhearts's desire to invoke a sacred dimension, while possibly a symptom of a disintegrating mind, responds to a universal need for a meaningful order. In fact, this turn of events answers to one of Todorov's themes of the fantastic, that of "madness viewed as, perhaps, a higher reason."

At last we reach what Todorov identified as the culminating scene of intense and ambiguous mystery. In the final chapter, "Miss Lonelyhearts Has a Religious Experience," not only does a peculiar metamorphosis take place, but the collapse of the separation between mind and matter seems complete. Miss Lonelyhearts now thinks of himself as "the rock," having internalized the notions of indestructibility, immovability, and calm. He has retreated to his room, where he "rides" his bed like a flying carpet, in search of vision. As he stares at the ivory Christ nailed to the wall, it begins to spin like a bright fly while the dead contents of the room rise to it like a fish to bait. Miss Lonelyhearts's heart becomes a rose, "and in his skull another rose bloomed." Gradually, he realizes that his heart is becoming one with God's, and finally, "his brain was likewise God's." At this enigmatic juncture the doorbell rings, and Miss Lonelyhearts uncannily knows that it is Doyle, sent by God, he believes, to prove his conversion. But in-

stead of a miraculous healing, the would-be savior is inadvertently shot by the cripple.

With even so selective an illustration as this, it is clear that this novel meets the criteria established in Todorov's theory. It is certainly not a story that stays within the bounds of the uncanny, nor can it be called a tale of the marvelous. It pursues a hesitation between the natural and the supernatural as far as it can be followed. Yet once we turn to Kayser's wide-ranging analysis of the grotesque, completed in 1957, we may be less satisfied that we have been on the right track. For one thing, the language of Kayser and the language of Todorov are often identical: both wrote of the "uncanny," "distortion," "uncertainty," "confusion," and the "fusion" of ordinarily separate realms. For Todorov's term *hesitation* we read in Kayser "transitional moments"; both examined "metamorphosis," "madness," "dreams," "horror," and the "demonic." Kayser, in fact, used the term *fantastic grotesque* and made this one of two subdivisions of the aesthetic category of the grotesque.

The primary effect of the grotesque as Kayser explained it is a "sense that the natural order of things has been subverted." Whether inanimate objects themselves or the character's reaction produces this perception, an alienation and estrangement from the world results. Ominous and sinister elements intrude into an otherwise realistic setting. There is a blurring of distinction between animate and inanimate realms; the laws of statics, symmetry, and proportion are invalid. The fusion of mutually incompatible worlds becomes a picture of our world, which is breaking apart.

To return to Miss Lonelyhearts, sitting at his desk, reading his morning's letters: In those letters Miss Lonelyhearts is catching disconcerting glimpses of what Kayser called the "sinister background of the brighter and rationally organized world." The willful animation of the contents of his room, the unnatural movement of the shadow in the park, the hideously incongruous face of his correspondent, Mr. Doyle, are grotesque experiences, producing, as they do, the sense of surprise, confusion, and the ominous that accompanies Miss Lonelyhearts's growing conviction that the natural order of things is dissolving. Even so apparently small a thing as the failure of new vegetation to appear with the spring, when perceived in combination with these other disorienting events, contributes to Miss Lonelyhearts's anxiety that vitality and stability have abandoned the natural world, leaving behind a ghastly mixture of demonic things and monstrous people where there had been, he thought, logic, proportion, and meaning. West called his novel a "moral satire," and Kayser discussed the role that disillusionment such as Miss Lonelyhearts feels plays in the satiric grotesque, quoting from Goethe: "Looked at from the height of reason, life as a whole seems like a grave disease, and the world like a madhouse." Writers with satiric purposes use the grotesque not only to mock tradition and society's cherished ideals but to demolish complacent categories, to deprive the apparently meaningful of meaning, and to shake the reader's confident expectations about his world. Except for suicide, Miss Lonelyhearts has no practical advice to give his pathetic correspondents.

It is no wonder that Miss Lonelyhearts seeks meaning elsewhere when the natural world fails him. As Kayser explained, "We are so strongly affected and terrified because it is our world which ceases to be reliable, and we feel that we would be unable to live in this changed world. The grotesque instills fear of life rather than fear of death." That is a striking inversion and one that Todorov touched upon when he discussed the incompatibility that often exists between sex and religion in fantastic fiction, where the general rule is that "one world must die that the other may live." In grotesque literature the entire living world may seem to die, and in *Miss Lonelyhearts* it gives place to a macabre, a ghostly, or a monstrous world in which street crowds with broken hands and torn mouths move trance-like and violent in search of a sustaining dream from the marquee of a movie house or from a love-story magazine. In his dreams and in his chanting the name of Christ, Miss Lonelyhearts is clearly motivated by this fear of life. The desperate man attempts to invoke a transcendent order. His apparent madness is a theme, as already noted, found in both fantastic and grotesque art. Insanity, in Kayser's view, is the ultimate estrangement, self-estrangement; and "the encounter with madness," he continued, "is one of the basic experiences of the grotesque which life forces upon us." Whether Miss Lonelyhearts's belief that he experienced a mystical union with God is a delusion or whether it is genuine, the loss of identity that accompanies it undercuts the very foundations of personality, of human nature.

There is one last feature of the grotesque, as Kayser defined it, that must be matched with its counterpart from Todorov's thesis on the fantastic, and this is the inexplicability of the perceived fundamental dislocation. As Kayser concluded his investigation of a topic that he pursued through several centuries of European and American painting and literature, he emphasized that a crucial requirement of the grotesque is that it must, finally, point to no meaning. More exactly, the artist employing the grotesque must imply no cause, no source, no meaningfulness, no purpose guiding and reconciling us to this subversion of the natural order of things; otherwise the grotesque vanishes. Neither physical disfigurement, nor the living dead, nor animation of the inanimate, nor religious visions, nor miracles may be explained or evaluated within the purview of the grotesque. What Kayser, looking into the incomprehensible heart of disorientation and dislocation, called "inexplicable" and "meaningless" answers to Todorov's condition of "indecision." The reader experiences that all-important "hesitation" or "indecision," as Todorov explained it, because he cannot be certain whether some peculiar circumstances have a supernatural or a natural explanation, and ideally, this indecision continues indefinitely. In that masterfully ambiguous conclusion to *Miss Lonelyhearts* we can watch Todorov's "indecision" and Kayser's "inexplicability" converge. When Miss Lonelyhearts, rushing down the stairs with arms outstretched, is shot by Doyle, the reader is being invited to view the story's denouement through bifocals, as it were, to entertain a doubled, a split, perspective, in other words, to hesitate indefinitely between two explanations, both having been made equally valid: (1) Miss Lonelyhearts dies a martyr, the mistaken victim of one he came to save;

(2) Miss Lonelyhearts's ludicrous end is pathetically and grimly suited to the peculiarities of his religio-sexual pathology. The first meaning answers to a supernatural interpretation; the second, to a natural. There is a third meaning, that sheer random bad luck put the clumsy Doyle on the stairs when the overwrought columnist was ill with a raging fever. If the story is to exert its full power, all of these possible explanations, no single one of them, must be allowed. To assign any definite cause, meaning, or purpose would minimize the sense of an awesome and dreadful mystery that it is the goal of the writer to prolong. Once more we find Todorov and Kayser in agreement—whether this style, structure, or effect is called fantastic or grotesque—that in this kind of fiction the brutal intrusion of mystery is paramount, and that mystery must be deliberately preserved.

This single test case is not meant to be taken as sufficient grounds for discarding Todorov's thesis, nor is it intended to challenge any of the details of his description of the fantastic, but it is meant to place his analysis within a broader perspective. Indeed, some significant exceptions to his theory seem to have arisen. First, although it has been demonstrated how completely West's novel meets Todorov's major and minor criteria for the fantastic, this demonstration conflicts both with Todorov's conception of the fantastic as a genre existing within the bounds of the eighteenth and nineteenth centuries and with the prevailing critical views of *Miss Lonelyhearts,* all of which recognize the novel's irony, satire, and grim humor, and none of which considers the novel fantastic. Therefore, Todorov's expectation of picking up at random a thread in a narrative and from it identifying and reconstructing the whole, the way that the anthropologist he mentioned worked with a single bone, would seem doomed to disappointment.

In speculating why and how Todorov's theory may have been undermined, the failure may be located somewhere between two of the limiting conditions he set on this so-called genre: the specified historic period and the dichotomy of natural-supernatural that fields the important "hesitation" response. Perhaps because from the mid-eighteenth to the late nineteenth century the supernatural was gradually losing its unquestioned status as an actual reality, and coming to be understood as an imaginary realm, the "hesitation" that Todorov found is largely a function of that cultural shift, evidence of external influence rather than inherent to an aesthetic structure. What makes *Miss Lonelyhearts* seem to be an example of the fantastic, then, may be this issue of belief, of supernatural versus natural agency, which is the book's subject. Still another explanation for this novel's seeming to fit into a category otherwise unsuited to it lies in Eric Rabkin's more expansive analysis of the fantastic. The extremity of Miss Lonelyhearts's experience is chiefly satiric, and "satire," according to Rabkin in *The Fantastic in Literature,* "is inherently fantastic," because it depends upon the reversal of perspectives and is usually ironic in tone. Finally, the large territory of overlapping and duplicated terminology, themes, purposes, effects, motifs, and techniques that exists between Todorov's mapping of the fantastic and

Kayser's study of the grotesque makes the usefulness of Todorov's definition all the more doubtful.

Perhaps it is unfair to compare one critic's very early work with the seasoned product of another, but the comparison here is instructive. While identifying clear and reasonable criteria, Kayser established a broad base for his subject, historically, geographically, in terms of artistic media, and he designated the grotesque an "aesthetic category." Todorov, in *The Fantastic,* radically limited the range and effect of the fantastic, which he called a genre, and regularly interspersed his explication with leading statements such as this: "Any discription of a text, by the very fact that it is made by means of words, is a description of a genre." Whereas Kayser recognized the relatedness of the fantastic and the grotesque modes and provided an appropriate category for their conjunction, which he named the fantastic grotesque, Todorov never mentioned the grotesque at all. Without a doubt, Todorov's theoretical approach is stimulating and therefore entirely worthwhile. Let the explorer in pursuit of the fantastic, however, follow it advisedly and not overlook the rich terrain of the twentieth century, even though it is not shown on Todorov's map. (pp. 41-8)

> *Rebecca R. Butler, "Todorov's Fantastic, Kayser's Grotesque, and West's 'Miss Lonelyhearts',"* in The Scope of the Fantastic— Theory, Technique, Major Authors: Selected Essays from the First International Conference on the Fantastic in Literature and Film, *edited by Robert A. Collins and Howard D. Pearce, Greenwood Press, 1985, pp. 41-8.*

FURTHER READING

Bibliography

White, William. *Nathanael West: A Comprehensive Bibliography.* Kent, Ohio: Kent State University Press, 1975, 209 p.
Contains both primary and secondary bibliographic material. An appendix lists West's uncollected writings.

Biography

Caldwell, Erskine. "The Middle Years." In his *Call It Experience: The Years of Learning How to Write,* pp. 81-166. New York: Duell, Sloan and Pearce, 1951.
Recounts his acquaintance with West in 1931, when Caldwell lived at the Sutton residential hotel at a reduced rate arranged by West who, at the time, was working on *Miss Lonelyhearts.*

Martin, Jay. *Nathanael West: The Art of His Life.* New York: Farrar, Straus and Giroux, 1970, 435 p.
Provides a broad social and cultural history of West's era, drawing on interviews with West's friends and family members as well as letters and other unpublished private papers.

Criticism

Abrahams, Roger D. "Androgynes Bound: Nathanael West's *Miss Lonelyhearts.*" In *Seven Contemporary Authors: Essays on Cozzens, Miller, West, Golding, Heller, Albee, and Powers,* edited by Thomas B. Whitbread, pp. 49-72. Austin: University of Texas Press, 1966.
Identifies the protagonist's search for life's meaning as the central theme of *Miss Lonelyhearts* and maintains that the character of Betty represents a childlike, presexual state of androgyny that the protagonist desires but cannot attain.

Allen, Walter. "The Thirties: American." In his *The Modern Novel in Britain and the United States,* pp. 138-87. New York: E. P. Dutton & Co., 1964.
Discusses West, together with Henry Roth and Daniel Fuchs, as important delineators of the human condition whose works contrast with the didactic politicization of much American literature of the 1930s. Allen identifies *Miss Lonelyhearts* as West's most important work.

Andreach, Robert J. "Nathanael West's *Miss Lonelyhearts:* Between the Dead Pan and the Unborn Christ." *Modern Fiction Studies* XII, No. 2 (Summer 1966): 251-60.
Identifies antagonism between paganism and Christianity as the unifying principle of *Miss Lonelyhearts.*

Baxter, Charles. "Nathanael West: Dead Letters and the Martyred Novelist." *West Coast Review* 9, No. 2 (October 1974): 3-11.
Identifies the inadequacy of language as a means to alleviate suffering as the central theme of *Miss Lonelyhearts* and suggests that the protagonist's self-sacrifice is necessary because he is unable to help the letter-writers through written replies.

Betsky-Zweig, S. "The Cannonballed of Popular Culture: Nathanael West's *Miss Lonelyhearts* and *The Day of the Locust.*" *Dutch Quarterly Review* 4, No. 4 (1974): 145-56.
Describes West's novels as "cannonballs" shot in anger and sadness against American culture of the 1930s and attributes the effectiveness of *Miss Lonelyhearts* to the novel's basis in the mass media, particularly comic strips, animated cartoons, soap operas, magazines, and newspapers.

Bush, C. W. "This Stupendous Fabric: The Metaphysics of Order in Melville's *Pierre* and Nathanael West's *Miss Lonelyhearts.*" *Journal of American Studies* I, No. 2 (October 1967): 269-74.
Compares the artistic ordering of experience in novels by West and Herman Melville.

Cohen, Arthur. "Nathanael West's Holy Fool." *The Commonweal* LXIV, No. 11 (15 June 1956): 276-78.
Cites the protagonist of *Miss Lonelyhearts* as a modern example of the "holy fool," a traditional figure in Russian literature whose protests against social conditions are tolerated because he is believed to be both mad and sanctified.

Conroy, Mark. "Letters and Spirit in *Miss Lonelyhearts.*" *The University of Windsor Review* XVII, No. 1 (Fall-Winter 1982): 5-20.
Explores ways in which the exchange of letters and words between Miss Lonelyhearts and his correspondents, coworkers, and acquaintances reflect a continuous process of self-definition and attempts to define others in comprehensible terms.

"Miss Lonelyhearts Is Reviewed." *Contempo* III, No. 11 (25 July 1933): 1, 4-5, 8.

>Symposium of important early reviews and commentary by Bob Brown, Angel Flores, Josephine Herbst, S. J. Perelman, and William Carlos Williams.

Cowley, Malcolm. "No Escape." In his *Exile's Return: A Literary Odyssey of the 1920s,* pp. 235-45. New York: Viking Press, 1951.

>Identifies escape from the status quo of American society as a prevalent theme in American literature, and discusses a scene from *Miss Lonelyhearts* in which the editor Shrike ridicules conventional escapes into art, hedonism, religion, or primitivism.

Daniel, Carter A. "West's Revisions of *Miss Lonelyhearts.*" *Studies in Bibliography* XVI (1966): 232-43.

>Analyzes West's revisions of the chapters from *Miss Lonelyhearts* that appeared in periodicals before the novel was published in 1933 in order "to clarify the author's aims, some features of his thought, and the technical means by which he solved certain problems of style and structure."

DiStasi, Lawrence W. "Nowhere to Throw the Stone." In *Nathanael West: The Cheaters and the Cheated,* edited by David Madden, pp. 83-101. Deland, Fla.: Everett/Edwards, 1973.

>Asserts that West's use of violence in *Miss Lonelyhearts* reflects his insight into the fundamental role of aggression in human relationships.

Foulkes, A. Peter. "Nathanael West: *Miss Lonelyhearts.*" In *Der Amerikanische Roman im 19. und 20. Jahrhundert: Interpretationen,* edited by Edgar Lohner, pp. 309-19. Berlin: Erich Schmidt, 1974.

>Identifies suffering and the range of responses to suffering as important aspects of West's novels, particularly in *Miss Lonelyhearts,* maintaining that West's pessimistic vision of suffering as endemic to the human condition sprang directly from his observations of twentieth-century American society.

Frank, Mike. "The Passion of Miss Lonelyhearts According to Nathanael West." *Studies in Short Fiction* X, No. 1 (Winter 1973): 67-73.

>Rejects the interpretation that the characters of Betty and Miss Lonelyhearts represent two polarized attitudes toward life—innocence and experience—arguing that Betty is identified with the natural world, which in the novel is presented as cruel, random, and violent.

Gorak, Jan. "The Art of Significant Disorder: The Fiction of Nathanael West." In his *God the Artist: American Novelists in a Post-Realist Age,* pp. 37-58. Urbana: University of Illinois Press, 1987.

>Characterizes *Miss Lonelyhearts* as a novel about the diminishing power of religious values in American lives in which the mass media has supplanted organized religion.

Hand, Nancy Walker. "A Novel in the Form of a Comic Strip: Nathanael West's *Miss Lonelyhearts.*" *The Serif* V, No. 2 (June 1968): 14-21.

>Discusses West's structuring of his novel "in the form of a comic strip," with each chapter functioning as the equivalent of a cartoon panel in which one action instigates many reactions.

Hanlon, Robert M. "The Parody of the Sacred in Nathanael West's *Miss Lonelyhearts.*" *The International Fiction Review* 4, No. 2 (July 1977): 190-93.

>Examines how West parodied Christian myth and ritual in *Miss Lonelyhearts* for ironic, satiric, and comic effect.

Herbst, Josephine. "Nathanael West." *The Kenyon Review* XXIII, No. 4 (Winter 1961): 611-30.

>Biographical and critical essay that includes a discussion of West's revisions of *Miss Lonelyhearts,* individual chapters of which appeared in the journals *Contact* and *Contempo* before the book's publication.

Hickey, James W. "Freudian Criticism." In *Nathanael West: The Cheaters and the Cheated,* edited by David Madden, pp. 111-150. Deland, Fla.: Everett/Edwards, 1973.

>Dismisses Freudian interpretations of *Miss Lonelyhearts* by Stanley Edgar Hyman, Randall Reid, and Victor Comerchero and offers "some new constructive insights about the main character and central issues" of the novel, based on "the legitimate place of Freudian theory as a tool of literary criticism."

Jackson, Thomas H., ed. *Twentieth Century Interpretations of "Miss Lonelyhearts": A Collection of Critical Essays.* Englewood Cliffs, N.J.: Prentice-Hall, 1971, 112 p.

>Compilation of previously published essays by James F. Light, Josephine Herbst, Arthur Cohen, Robert Andreach, Robert I. Edenbaum, Stanley Edgar Hyman, Edmond L. Volpe, Randall Reid, Angel Flores, and William Carlos Williams.

Jacobs, Robert G. "Nathanael West: The Christology of Unbelief." *Iowa English Yearbook* 9 (Fall 1964): 68-74.

>Suggests that West deliberately introduced ambiguity into *Miss Lonelyhearts* by portraying the protagonist as a Christ figure in an age that has largely rejected Christian myth.

Jones, Beverly. "Shrike as the Modernist Anti-Hero in Nathanael West's *Miss Lonelyhearts.*" *Modern Fiction Studies* 36, No. 2 (Summer 1990): 218-24.

>Maintains that in his relentless exposure of the hypocrisy and irrationality of Miss Lonelyhearts's impulses toward religion, the editor Shrike functions not as an antichrist or demon figure but as a nihilistic Modernist antihero.

Keyes, John. " 'Inarticulate Expressions of Genuine Suffering?': A Reply to the Correspondence in *Miss Lonelyhearts.*" *University of Windsor Review* 20, No. 1 (Fall-Winter 1987): 11-25.

>Offers sustained analysis of the letters to Miss Lonelyhearts, maintaining that they have been consistently misinterpreted as expressions of authentic suffering when in fact they convey the irony and even humor of the human condition.

Laurenson, Diana. "Alienation, Reification, and the Novel: Sartre, Camus, Nathanael West." In *The Sociology of Literature,* by Diana Laurenson and Alan Swingewood, pp. 207-48. London: MacGibbon & Kee, 1971.

>Identifies *Miss Lonelyhearts* as an important early twentieth-century literary presentation of alienation.

Lewis, R. W. B. "Days of Wrath and Laughter." In his *Trials of the World: Essays in American Literature and the Human-*

istic Tradition, pp. 184-235. New Haven: Yale University Press, 1965.

Includes mention of the editor Shrike in a discussion of the antichrist or Satan figure in twentieth-century American literature.

Lorch, Thomas M. "West's *Miss Lonelyhearts:* Skepticism Mitigated?" *Renascence* XVIII, No. 2 (Winter 1966) 99-109.

Discusses the influence of William James's *Varieties of Religious Experience* and Starbuck's *Psychology of Religion* on *Miss Lonelyhearts,* and the nature of Miss Lonelyhearts's religious experiences.

———. "Religion and Art in *Miss Lonelyhearts.*" *Renascence* XX, No. 1 (Autumn 1967): 11-17.

Suggests that *Miss Lonelyhearts* treats both religious belief and art as means whereby the individual can achieve self-realization, give order and meaning to existence, and establish relationships with others.

Malin, Irving. *"Miss Lonelyhearts."* In his *Nathanael West's Novels,* pp. 31-66. Carbondale and Edwardsville: Southern Illinois University Press, 1972.

Relates *Miss Lonelyhearts* to West's career and discusses the novel's plot, structure, characterizations, and imagery.

May, John R. "Words and Deeds: Apocalyptic Judgment in Faulkner, West, and O'Connor." In his *Toward a New Earth: Apocalypse in the American Novel,* pp. 92-144. Notre Dame: University of Notre Dame Press, 1972.

Posits that the theme of judgment is central to the plot of *Miss Lonelyhearts,* in which the protagonist seeks an answer to the problem of human suffering, aspires to godlike status, is found deficient in word and deed, and dies at the hands of one he intended to cure.

Mott, Frank Luther. Review of *Miss Lonelyhearts,* by Nathanael West. *Journalism Quarterly* X, No. 2 (June 1933): 170-71.

Dismisses *Miss Lonelyhearts* as a badly written, "maudlin, hysterical, bawdy" novel and pronounces both the protagonist and the author capable of only ignoble responses to human suffering.

Nelson, Gerald B. "Lonelyhearts." In his *Ten Versions of America,* pp. 77-90. New York: Alfred A. Knopf, 1972.

Impressionistic account of *Miss Lonelyhearts,* identifying the clash between the protagonist's religious mania and Shrike's cynical self-absorption as the novel's central conflict.

Nilsen, Helge Normann. "A Novel of Despair: A Note on Nathanael West's *Miss Lonelyhearts.*" *Neophilologus* LXX, No. 3 (July 1986): 475-78.

Terms *Miss Lonelyhearts* a novel of "metaphysical absurdity" that conveys a more effective vision of despair than the social protest novels of the period, and suggests that this novel's greatest horror "lies in its demonstration of how human beings will go on searching for faith and love even when it seems obvious that the process is pointless."

Olsen, Bruce. "Nathanael West: The Use of Cynicism." In *Minor American Novelists,* edited by Charles Alva Hoyt, pp. 81-94. Carbondale and Edwardsville: Southern Illinois University Press, 1970.

Maintains that although West has come to be "a repre-

sentative figure" and "an emblem of an era of violent exploitation," it is only with *Miss Lonelyhearts* that he achieved the objectivity necessary to create a literary masterpiece, calling this the only work "in which West succeeded in using his views instead of declaring them."

Orvell, Miles D. "The Messianic Sexuality of Miss Lonelyhearts." *Studies in Short Fiction* X, No. 2 (Spring 1973): 159-67.

Contends that *Miss Lonelyhearts* exemplifies one kind of response to modern life—the urge to replace eros with agape, or to transcend the human and attain the divine.

Palumbo, Ronald J. "Stone and Rock in West's *Miss Lonelyhearts.*" *American Notes and Queries* XIV, No. 5 (January 1976): 74-5.

Asserts that two Biblical allusions involving stone and rock imagery in West's novel provide reference points for assessing the development of the protagonist's obsession with Christ.

Pinsker, Sanford. "Charles Dickens and Nathanael West: Great Expectations Unfulfilled." *Topic* 18 (1969): 40-52.

Suggests that West and Dickens similarly employed satire based on failed expectations in their novels.

Poznar, Walter. "The Apocalyptic Vision in Nathanael West's *Miss Lonelyhearts.*" In *Apocalyptic Visions Past and Present,* edited by JoAnn James and William J. Cloonan, pp. 111-19. Tallahassee: Florida State University Press, 1988.

Maintains that West's "apocalyptic vision" moves beyond repudiation of the spiritual barrenness of the American Dream to a relentless assessment of human nature itself as sterile, empty, and apathetic. Poznar suggests that West's bleak vision is somewhat ameliorated by his avoidance of facile, sardonic cynicism and the depth of his concern for the human condition.

Raban, Jonathan. "A Surfeit of Commodities: The Novels of Nathanael West." In *The American Novel and the Nineteen Twenties,* edited by Malcolm Bradbury and David Palmer, pp. 215-31. London: Edward Arnold, 1971.

Includes discussion of *Miss Lonelyhearts* in a chapter noting that West has been retrospectively pronounced a forerunner of "the comic apocalyptic novel" of the 1950s.

Richardson, Robert D., Jr. *"Miss Lonelyhearts."* *The University Review* XXXIII, No. 2 (December 1966): 151-57.

Terms *Miss Lonelyhearts* a novel about the disintegration of sanity in American life and discusses the novel's imagery, plot, and prose style, contending that its chief interest lies in its brilliant communication of a story that is about the absence of meaningful communication.

Robinson, Douglas. "The Ritual Icon." In his *American Apocalypses: The Image of the End of the World in American Literature,* pp. 198-232. Baltimore: Johns Hopkins University Press, 1985.

Includes discussion of *Miss Lonelyhearts* in a chapter devoted to religious imagery in apocalyptic American fiction.

Schulz, Max F. "Nathanael West's 'Desperate Detachment'." In his *Radical Sophistication: Studies in Contemporary Jewish-American Novelists,* pp. 36-55. Athens: Ohio University Press, 1969.

Commends *Miss Lonelyhearts* as the most subtle and complex of West's novels.

Schwartz, Edward Greenfield. "The Novels of Nathanael West." *Accent* XVII, No. 4 (Autumn 1957): 251-62.

Comments on some prominent themes of *Miss Lonelyhearts* in a review of the *Complete Works of Nathanael West.*

Scott, Nathan A., Jr. *Nathanael West: A Critical Essay.* Grand Rapids, Mich.: William E. Eerdmans, 1971, 47 p.

Includes discussion of the plot, imagery, and narrative style of *Miss Lonelyhearts* in a biographical and critical survey of West's life and career.

Seymour-Smith, Martin. "Prophet of Black Humour." *Spectator* 221, No. 7308 (19 July 1968): 94-5.

Reviews West's collected works, maintaining that in writing *Miss Lonelyhearts* West "discovered the methods most suitable to his genius."

Simonson, Harold P. "California, Nathanael West, and the Journey's End." In his *The Closed Frontier: Studies in American Literary Tragedy,* pp. 99-124. New York: Holt, Rinehart and Winston, 1970.

Includes discussion of *Miss Lonelyhearts* in a chapter devoted to American frontier mythology in West's fiction.

Swan, Michael. Review of *Miss Lonelyhearts,* by Nathanael West. *The New Statesman and Nation* XXXVIII, No. 961 (6 August 1949): 153-54.

Commends "the spirit of the book, the toughness, the touch of sentimentality, its vitality and the audacious passion with which it attacks the vast problem of human suffering."

Tropp, Martin. "Nathanael West and the Persistence of Hope." *Renascence* XXXI, No. 4 (Summer 1979): 205-14.

Contends that in *Miss Lonelyhearts* particularly, and to a lesser extent in his last two novels, West suggested that alternatives to suffering exist.

Troy, William. Review of *Miss Lonelyhearts,* by Nathanael West. *The Nation* (New York) CXXXVI, No. 3545 (14 July 1933): 672-73.

Commends West's avoidance of the political didacticism that infuses much contemporaneous fiction and terms *Miss Lonelyhearts* "one of the most readable and one of the most exceptional books of the season" despite West's tendency toward baroque prose.

Wexelblatt, Robert. "*Miss Lonelyhearts* and the Rhetoric of Disintegration." *College Literature* XVI, No. 3 (Fall 1989): 219-31.

Examines West's formal strategies for presenting a novel about disorder and disintegration in a rigorously ordered and integrated manner.

Wilson, T. C. "American Humor." *The Saturday Review of Literature* IX, No. 43 (13 May 1933): 589.

Terms *Miss Lonelyhearts* a "robust satire" and a "comedy with tragic implications."

Zlotnick, Joan. "Nathanael West and the Pictorial Imagination." *Western American Literature* 9, No. 3 (Fall 1974): 177-85.

Discusses the "striking pictorial effects" that West achieves in his prose.

Additional coverage of West's life and career is contained in the following sources published by Gale Research: *Concise Dictionary of American Literary Biography, 1929-1941; Contemporary Authors,* Vols. 104, 125; *Dictionary of Literary Biography,* Vols. 4, 9, 28; and *Major 20th-Century Writers.*

Twentieth-Century
Literary Criticism

Cumulative Indexes
Volumes 1-44

This Index Includes References to Entries in These Gale Series

Children's Literature Review includes excerpts from reviews, criticism, and commentary on works of authors and illustrators who create books for children.

Classical and Medieval Literature Criticism offers excerpts of criticism on the works of world authors from classical antiquity through the fourteenth century.

Contemporary Authors series encompasses five related series. **Contemporary Authors** provides biographical and bibliographical information on more than 97,000 writers of fiction, nonfiction, poetry, journalism, drama, and film. **Contemporary Authors New Revision Series** provides completely updated information on active authors covered in previously published volumes of *CA*. **Contemporary Authors Permanent Series** consists of updated listings for deceased and inactive authors removed from the original volumes 9-36 when those volumes were revised. **Contemporary Authors Autobiography Series** presents specially commissioned autobiographies by leading contemporary writers. **Contemporary Authors Bibliographical Series** contains primary and secondary bibliographies as well as analytical bibliographical essays by authorities on major modern authors.

Contemporary Literary Criticism presents excerpts of criticism on the works of novelists, poets, dramatists, short story writers, scriptwriters, and other creative writers who are now living or who have died since 1960.

Dictionary of Literary Biography comprises three related series. **Dictionary of Literary Biography** furnishes illustrated overviews of authors' lives and works and places them in the larger perspective of literary history. **Dictionary of Literary Biography Documentary Series** illuminates the careers of major figures through a selection of literary documents, including letters, interviews, and photographs. **Dictionary of Literary Biography Yearbook** summarizes the past year's literary activity and includes updated and new entries on individual authors. A cumulative index to authors and articles is included in each new volume. **Concise Dictionary of**

American Literary Biography, a six-volume series, collects revised and updated sketches on major American authors that were originally presented in *Dictionary of Literary Biography*.

Drama Criticism provides excerpts of criticism on the works of playwrights of all nationalities and periods of literary history.

Literature Criticism from 1400 to 1800 compiles significant passages from the most noteworthy criticism on authors of the fifteenth through the eighteenth centuries.
Nineteenth-Century Literature Criticism offers significant passages from criticism on authors who died between 1800 and 1899.

Poetry Criticism presents excerpts of criticism on the works of poets from all eras, movements, and nationalities.

Short Story Criticism combines excerpts of criticism on short fiction by writers of all eras and nationalities.

Something about the Author series encompasses three related series. **Something about the Author** contains well-illustrated biographical sketches on authors and illustrators of juvenile and young adult literature from all eras. **Something about the Author Autobiography Series** presents specially commissioned autobiographies by prominent authors and illustrators of books for children and young adults. **Authors & Artists for Young Adults** provides high school and junior high school students with profiles of their favorite creative artists.

Twentieth-Century Literary Criticism contains critical excerpts by the most significant commentators on poets, novelists, short story writers, dramatists, and philosophers who died between 1900 and 1960.

Yesterday's Authors of Books for Children contains heavily illustrated entries on children's writers who died before 1961. Complete in two volumes.

Literary Criticism Series
Cumulative Author Index

This index lists all author entries in the Gale Literary Criticism Series and includes cross-references to other Gale sources. References in the index are identified as follows:

AAYA: *Authors & Artists for Young Adults,* Volumes 1-7
CA: *Contemporary Authors* (original series), Volumes 1-135
CAAS: *Contemporary Authors Autobiography Series,* Volumes 1-14
CABS: *Contemporary Authors Bibliographical Series,* Volumes 1-3
CANR: *Contemporary Authors New Revision Series,* Volumes 1-35
CAP: *Contemporary Authors Permanent Series,* Volumes 1-2
CA-R: *Contemporary Authors* (first revision), Volumes 1-44
CDALB: *Concise Dictionary of American Literary Biography,* Volumes 1-6
CLC: *Contemporary Literary Criticism,* Volumes 1-69
CLR: *Children's Literature Review,* Volumes 1-25
CMLC: *Classical and Medieval Literature Criticism,* Volumes 1-8
DC: *Drama Criticism,* Volume 1-2
DLB: *Dictionary of Literary Biography,* Volumes 1-112
DLB-DS: *Dictionary of Literary Biography Documentary Series,* Volumes 1-9
DLB-Y: *Dictionary of Literary Biography Yearbook,* Volumes 1980-1990
LC: *Literature Criticism from 1400 to 1800,* Volumes 1-18
NCLC: *Nineteenth-Century Literature Criticism,* Volumes 1-34
PC: *Poetry Criticism,* Volumes 1-3
SAAS: *Something about the Author Autobiography Series,* Volumes 1-13
SATA: *Something about the Author,* Volumes 1-66
SSC: *Short Story Criticism,* Volumes 1-9
TCLC: *Twentieth-Century Literary Criticism,* Volumes 1-44
YABC: *Yesterday's Authors of Books for Children,* Volumes 1-2

Beckett, Samuel (Barclay)
1906-1989 ..... **CLC 1, 2, 3, 4, 6, 9, 10,**
11, 14, 18, 29, 57, 59
See also CA 5-8R; DLB 13, 15

Beckford, William 1760-1844 .... **NCLC 16**
See also DLB 39

Beckham, Barry 1944-
See also BLC 1; CANR 26; CA 29-32R;
DLB 33

Beckman, Gunnel 1910- .... **CLC 26**
See also CANR 15; CA 33-36R; SATA 6

Becque, Henri 1837-1899 .... **NCLC 3**

Beddoes, Thomas Lovell
1803-1849 .... **NCLC 3**

Beecher, Catharine Esther
1800-1878 .... **NCLC 30**
See also DLB 1

Beecher, John 1904-1980 .... **CLC 6**
See also CANR 8; CA 5-8R;
obituary CA 105

Beer, Johann 1655-1700 .... **LC 5**

Beer, Patricia 1919?- .... **CLC 58**
See also CANR 13; CA 61-64; DLB 40

Beerbohm, (Sir Henry) Max(imilian)
1872-1956 .... **TCLC 1, 24**
See also CA 104; DLB 34

Behan, Brendan
1923-1964 .... **CLC 1, 8, 11, 15**
See also CA 73-76; DLB 13

Behn, Aphra 1640?-1689 .... **LC 1**
See also DLB 39, 80

Behrman, S(amuel) N(athaniel)
1893-1973 .... **CLC 40**
See also CAP 1; CA 15-16;
obituary CA 45-48; DLB 7, 44

Beiswanger, George Edwin 1931-
See Starbuck, George (Edwin)

Belasco, David 1853-1931 .... **TCLC 3**
See also CA 104; DLB 7

Belcheva, Elisaveta 1893-
See Bagryana, Elisaveta

Belinski, Vissarion Grigoryevich
1811-1848 .... **NCLC 5**

Belitt, Ben 1911- .... **CLC 22**
See also CAAS 4; CANR 7; CA 13-16R;
DLB 5

Bell, Acton 1820-1849
See Bronte, Anne

Bell, Currer 1816-1855
See Bronte, Charlotte

Bell, James Madison 1826-1902 ... **TCLC 43**
See also BLC 1; CA 122, 124; DLB 50

Bell, Madison Smartt 1957- .... **CLC 41**
See also CA 111

Bell, Marvin (Hartley) 1937- ..... **CLC 8, 31**
See also CA 21-24R; DLB 5

Bellamy, Edward 1850-1898 ...... **NCLC 4**
See also DLB 12

Belloc, (Joseph) Hilaire (Pierre Sebastien
Rene Swanton)
1870-1953 .... **TCLC 7, 18**
See also YABC 1; CA 106; DLB 19

Bellow, Saul
1915- ..... **CLC 1, 2, 3, 6, 8, 10, 13, 15,**
25, 33, 34, 63
See also CA 5-8R; CABS 1; DLB 2, 28;
DLB-Y 82; DLB-DS 3;
CDALB 1941-1968

Belser, Reimond Karel Maria de 1929-
See Ruyslinck, Ward

Bely, Andrey 1880-1934 .... **TCLC 7**
See also CA 104

Benary-Isbert, Margot 1889-1979 ... **CLC 12**
See also CLR 12; CANR 4; CA 5-8R;
obituary CA 89-92; SATA 2;
obituary SATA 21

Benavente (y Martinez), Jacinto
1866-1954 .... **TCLC 3**
See also CA 106

Benchley, Peter (Bradford)
1940- .... **CLC 4, 8**
See also CANR 12; CA 17-20R; SATA 3

Benchley, Robert 1889-1945 .... **TCLC 1**
See also CA 105; DLB 11

Benedikt, Michael 1935- .... **CLC 4, 14**
See also CANR 7; CA 13-16R; DLB 5

Benet, Juan 1927- .... **CLC 28**

Benet, Stephen Vincent
1898-1943 .... **TCLC 7**
See also YABC 1; CA 104; DLB 4, 48

Benet, William Rose 1886-1950 ... **TCLC 28**
See also CA 118; DLB 45

Benford, Gregory (Albert) 1941- .... **CLC 52**
See also CANR 12, 24; CA 69-72;
DLB-Y 82

Benjamin, Walter 1892-1940 ..... **TCLC 39**

Benn, Gottfried 1886-1956 .... **TCLC 3**
See also CA 106; DLB 56

Bennett, Alan 1934- .... **CLC 45**
See also CA 103

Bennett, (Enoch) Arnold
1867-1931 .... **TCLC 5, 20**
See also CA 106; DLB 10, 34

Bennett, George Harold 1930-
See Bennett, Hal
See also CA 97-100

Bennett, Hal 1930- .... **CLC 5**
See also Bennett, George Harold
See also DLB 33

Bennett, Jay 1912- .... **CLC 35**
See also CANR 11; CA 69-72; SAAS 4;
SATA 27, 41

Bennett, Louise (Simone) 1919- ..... **CLC 28**
See also Bennett-Coverly, Louise Simone
See also BLC 1

Bennett-Coverly, Louise Simone 1919-
See Bennett, Louise (Simone)
See also CA 97-100

Benson, E(dward) F(rederic)
1867-1940 .... **TCLC 27**
See also CA 114

Benson, Jackson J. 1930- .... **CLC 34**
See also CA 25-28R

Benson, Sally 1900-1972 .... **CLC 17**
See also CAP 1; CA 19-20;
obituary CA 37-40R; SATA 1, 35;
obituary SATA 27

Benson, Stella 1892-1933 .... **TCLC 17**
See also CA 117; DLB 36

Bentley, E(dmund) C(lerihew)
1875-1956 .... **TCLC 12**
See also CA 108; DLB 70

Bentley, Eric (Russell) 1916- .... **CLC 24**
See also CANR 6; CA 5-8R

Beranger, Pierre Jean de
1780-1857 .... **NCLC 34**

Berger, John (Peter) 1926- ...... **CLC 2, 19**
See also CA 81-84; DLB 14

Berger, Melvin (H.) 1927- .... **CLC 12**
See also CANR 4; CA 5-8R; SAAS 2;
SATA 5

Berger, Thomas (Louis)
1924- .... **CLC 3, 5, 8, 11, 18, 38**
See also CANR 5; CA 1-4R; DLB 2;
DLB-Y 80

Bergman, (Ernst) Ingmar 1918- ..... **CLC 16**
See also CA 81-84

Bergson, Henri 1859-1941 .... **TCLC 32**

Bergstein, Eleanor 1938- .... **CLC 4**
See also CANR 5; CA 53-56

Berkoff, Steven 1937- .... **CLC 56**
See also CA 104

Bermant, Chaim 1929- .... **CLC 40**
See also CANR 6; CA 57-60

Bernanos, (Paul Louis) Georges
1888-1948 .... **TCLC 3**
See also CA 104; DLB 72

Bernard, April 19??- .... **CLC 59**

Bernhard, Thomas
1931-1989 .... **CLC 3, 32, 61**
See also CA 85-88,; obituary CA 127;
DLB 85

Berriault, Gina 1926- .... **CLC 54**
See also CA 116

Berrigan, Daniel J. 1921- .... **CLC 4**
See also CAAS 1; CANR 11; CA 33-36R;
DLB 5

Berrigan, Edmund Joseph Michael, Jr.
1934-1983
See Berrigan, Ted
See also CANR 14; CA 61-64;
obituary CA 110

Berrigan, Ted 1934-1983 .... **CLC 37**
See also Berrigan, Edmund Joseph Michael,
Jr.
See also DLB 5

Berry, Chuck 1926- .... **CLC 17**

Berry, Wendell (Erdman)
1934- .... **CLC 4, 6, 8, 27, 46**
See also CA 73-76; DLB 5, 6

Berryman, John
1914-1972 ..... **CLC 1, 2, 3, 4, 6, 8, 10,**
13, 25, 62
See also CAP 1; CA 15-16;
obituary CA 33-36R; CABS 2; DLB 48;
CDALB 1941-1968

Bertolucci, Bernardo 1940- .... **CLC 16**
See also CA 106

Bertrand, Aloysius 1807-1841 .... **NCLC 31**

Bertran de Born c. 1140-1215 ..... **CMLC 5**

Bottoms, David 1949-.............. CLC 53
See also CANR 22; CA 105; DLB-Y 83

Boucolon, Maryse 1937-
See Conde, Maryse
See also CA 110

Bourget, Paul (Charles Joseph)
1852-1935 .... TCLC 12
See also CA 107

Bourjaily, Vance (Nye) 1922- .... CLC 8, 62
See also CAAS 1; CANR 2; CA 1-4R;
DLB 2

Bourne, Randolph S(illiman)
1886-1918 .... TCLC 16
See also CA 117; DLB 63

Bova, Ben(jamin William) 1932-.... CLC 45
See also CLR 3; CANR 11; CA 5-8R;
SATA 6; DLB-Y 81

Bowen, Elizabeth (Dorothea Cole)
1899-1973 ..... CLC 1, 3, 6, 11, 15, 22;
                                       SSC 3
See also CAP 2; CA 17-18;
obituary CA 41-44R; DLB 15

Bowering, George 1935-........ CLC 15, 47
See also CANR 10; CA 21-24R; DLB 53

Bowering, Marilyn R(uthe) 1949-... CLC 32
See also CA 101

Bowers, Edgar 1924- .... CLC 9
See also CANR 24; CA 5-8R; DLB 5

Bowie, David 1947- .... CLC 17
See also Jones, David Robert

Bowles, Jane (Sydney)
1917-1973 .... CLC 3, 68
See also CAP 2; CA 19-20;
obituary CA 41-44R

Bowles, Paul (Frederick)
1910- .... CLC 1, 2, 19, 53; SSC 3
See also CAAS 1; CANR 1, 19; CA 1-4R;
DLB 5, 6

Box, Edgar 1925-
See Vidal, Gore

Boyd, William 1952-........... CLC 28, 53
See also CA 114, 120

Boyle, Kay 1903- .. CLC 1, 5, 19, 58; SSC 5
See also CAAS 1; CA 13-16R; DLB 4, 9, 48

Boyle, Patrick 19??-.............. CLC 19

Boyle, Thomas Coraghessan
1948- .... CLC 36, 55
See also CA 120; DLB-Y 86

Brackenridge, Hugh Henry
1748-1816 .... NCLC 7
See also DLB 11, 37

Bradbury, Edward P. 1939-
See Moorcock, Michael

Bradbury, Malcolm (Stanley)
1932-.................... CLC 32, 61
See also CANR 1; CA 1-4R; DLB 14

Bradbury, Ray(mond Douglas)
1920- .... CLC 1, 3, 10, 15, 42
See also CANR 2; CA 1-4R; SATA 11;
DLB 2, 8

Bradford, Gamaliel 1863-1932..... TCLC 36
See also DLB 17

Bradley, David (Henry), Jr. 1950- .. CLC 23
See also BLC 1; CANR 26; CA 104;
DLB 33

Bradley, John Ed 1959-........... CLC 55

Bradley, Katherine Harris 1846-1914
See Field, Michael

Bradley, Marion Zimmer 1930-..... CLC 30
See also CANR 7; CA 57-60; DLB 8

Bradstreet, Anne 1612-1672......... LC 4
See also DLB 24; CDALB 1640-1865

Bragg, Melvyn 1939- .... CLC 10
See also CANR 10; CA 57-60; DLB 14

Braine, John (Gerard)
1922-1986 .... CLC 1, 3, 41
See also CANR 1; CA 1-4R;
obituary CA 120; DLB 15; DLB-Y 86

Braithwaite, William Stanley 1878-1962
See also BLC 1; CA 125; DLB 50, 54

Brammer, Billy Lee 1930?-1978
See Brammer, William

Brammer, William 1930?-1978 ..... CLC 31
See also obituary CA 77-80

Brancati, Vitaliano 1907-1954..... TCLC 12
See also CA 109

Brancato, Robin F(idler) 1936- ..... CLC 35
See also CANR 11; CA 69-72; SATA 23

Brand, Millen 1906-1980........... CLC 7
See also CA 21-24R; obituary CA 97-100

Branden, Barbara 19??-........... CLC 44

Brandes, Georg (Morris Cohen)
1842-1927 .... TCLC 10
See also CA 105

Brandys, Kazimierz 1916-........ CLC 62

Branley, Franklyn M(ansfield)
1915-.................... CLC 21
See also CLR 13; CANR 14; CA 33-36R;
SATA 4

Brathwaite, Edward 1930-........ CLC 11
See also CANR 11; CA 25-28R; DLB 53

Brautigan, Richard (Gary)
1935-1984 .... CLC 1, 3, 5, 9, 12, 34, 42
See also CA 53-56; obituary CA 113;
SATA 56; DLB 2, 5; DLB-Y 80, 84

Braverman, Kate 1950- .... CLC 67
See also CA 89-92

Brecht, (Eugen) Bertolt (Friedrich)
1898-1956 .... TCLC 1, 6, 13, 35
See also CA 104; DLB 56

Bremer, Fredrika 1801-1865 ..... NCLC 11

Brennan, Christopher John
1870-1932 .... TCLC 17
See also CA 117

Brennan, Maeve 1917-............. CLC 5
See also CA 81-84

Brentano, Clemens (Maria)
1778-1842 .... NCLC 1
See also DLB 90

Brenton, Howard 1942-........... CLC 31
See also CA 69-72; DLB 13

Breslin, James 1930-
See Breslin, Jimmy
See also CA 73-76

Breslin, Jimmy 1930-........... CLC 4, 43
See also Breslin, James

Bresson, Robert 1907-............ CLC 16
See also CA 110

Breton, Andre 1896-1966... CLC 2, 9, 15, 54
See also CAP 2; CA 19-20;
obituary CA 25-28R; DLB 65

Breytenbach, Breyten 1939-..... CLC 23, 37
See also CA 113, 129

Bridgers, Sue Ellen 1942- .... CLC 26
See also CANR 11; CA 65-68; SAAS 1;
SATA 22; DLB 52

Bridges, Robert 1844-1930........ TCLC 1
See also CA 104; DLB 19

Bridie, James 1888-1951 .... TCLC 3
See also Mavor, Osborne Henry
See also DLB 10

Brin, David 1950-................. CLC 34
See also CANR 24; CA 102

Brink, Andre (Philippus)
1935- .... CLC 18, 36
See also CA 104

Brinsmead, H(esba) F(ay) 1922- .... CLC 21
See also CANR 10; CA 21-24R; SAAS 5;
SATA 18

Brittain, Vera (Mary) 1893?-1970... CLC 23
See also CAP 1; CA 15-16;
obituary CA 25-28R

Broch, Hermann 1886-1951....... TCLC 20
See also CA 117; DLB 85

Brock, Rose 1923-
See Hansen, Joseph

Brodkey, Harold 1930-............ CLC 56
See also CA 111

Brodsky, Iosif Alexandrovich 1940-
See Brodsky, Joseph (Alexandrovich)
See also CA 41-44R

Brodsky, Joseph (Alexandrovich)
1940- .... CLC 4, 6, 13, 36, 50
See also Brodsky, Iosif Alexandrovich

Brodsky, Michael (Mark) 1948- .... CLC 19
See also CANR 18; CA 102

Bromell, Henry 1947-.............. CLC 5
See also CANR 9; CA 53-56

Bromfield, Louis (Brucker)
1896-1956 .... TCLC 11
See also CA 107; DLB 4, 9

Broner, E(sther) M(asserman)
1930- .... CLC 19
See also CANR 8, 25; CA 17-20R; DLB 28

Bronk, William 1918-............. CLC 10
See also CANR 23; CA 89-92

Bronte, Anne 1820-1849.......... NCLC 4
See also DLB 21

Bronte, Charlotte
1816-1855 .... NCLC 3, 8, 33
See also DLB 21

Bronte, (Jane) Emily 1818-1848 .. NCLC 16
See also DLB 21, 32

Brooke, Frances 1724-1789 .... LC 6
See also DLB 39

Brooke, Henry 1703?-1783 .... LC 1
See also DLB 39

Brooke, Rupert (Chawner)
1887-1915 .... TCLC 2, 7
See also CA 104; DLB 19

Brooke-Rose, Christine 1926-...... CLC 40
See also CA 13-16R; DLB 14

Caballero, Fernan   1796-1877 . . . . .   **NCLC 10**

Cabell, James Branch   1879-1958 . . . **TCLC 6**
See also CA 105; DLB 9, 78

Cable, George Washington
1844-1925 . . . . **TCLC 4; SSC 4**
See also CA 104; DLB 12, 74

Cabrera Infante, G(uillermo)
1929- . . . . **CLC 5, 25, 45**
See also CANR 29; CA 85-88

Cade, Toni   1939-
See Bambara, Toni Cade

CAEdmon   fl. 658-680 . . . . **CMLC 7**

Cage, John (Milton, Jr.)   1912- . . . . . **CLC 41**
See also CANR 9; CA 13-16R

Cain, G.   1929-
See Cabrera Infante, G(uillermo)

Cain, James M(allahan)
1892-1977 . . . . **CLC 3, 11, 28**
See also CANR 8; CA 17-20R;
obituary CA 73-76

Caldwell, Erskine (Preston)
1903-1987 . . . . **CLC 1, 8, 14, 50, 60**
See also CAAS 1; CANR 2; CA 1-4R;
obituary CA 121; DLB 9, 86

Caldwell, (Janet Miriam) Taylor (Holland)
1900-1985 . . . . **CLC 2, 28, 39**
See also CANR 5; CA 5-8R;
obituary CA 116

Calhoun, John Caldwell
1782-1850 . . . . **NCLC 15**
See also DLB 3

Calisher, Hortense   1911- . . . . **CLC 2, 4, 8, 38**
See also CANR 1, 22; CA 1-4R; DLB 2

Callaghan, Morley (Edward)
1903-1990 . . . . **CLC 3, 14, 41, 65**
See also CANR 33; CA 9-12R;
obituary CA 132; DLB 68

Calvino, Italo
1923-1985 . . . . **CLC 5, 8, 11, 22, 33, 39;
SSC 3**
See also CANR 23; CA 85-88;
obituary CA 116

Cameron, Carey   1952- . . . . **CLC 59**

Cameron, Peter   1959- . . . . **CLC 44**
See also CA 125

Campana, Dino   1885-1932 . . . . **TCLC 20**
See also CA 117

Campbell, John W(ood), Jr.
1910-1971 . . . . **CLC 32**
See also CAP 2; CA 21-22;
obituary CA 29-32R; DLB 8

Campbell, Joseph   1904-1987 . . . . **CLC 69**
See also CANR 3, 28; CA 4R;
obituary CA 124; AAYA 3

Campbell, (John) Ramsey   1946- . . . . **CLC 42**
See also CANR 7; CA 57-60

Campbell, (Ignatius) Roy (Dunnachie)
1901-1957 . . . . **TCLC 5**
See also CA 104; DLB 20

Campbell, Thomas   1777-1844 . . . . **NCLC 19**

Campbell, (William) Wilfred
1861-1918 . . . . **TCLC 9**
See also CA 106

Camus, Albert
1913-1960 . . . **CLC 1, 2, 4, 9, 11, 14, 32,
63, 69; DC 2; SSC 9**
See also CA 89-92; DLB 72

Canby, Vincent   1924- . . . . **CLC 13**
See also CA 81-84

Canetti, Elias   1905- . . . . **CLC 3, 14, 25**
See also CANR 23; CA 21-24R; DLB 85

Canin, Ethan   1960- . . . . **CLC 55**

Cape, Judith   1916-
See Page, P(atricia) K(athleen)

Capek, Karel
1890-1938 . . . . **TCLC 6, 37; DC 1**
See also CA 104

Capote, Truman
1924-1984 . . . . . **CLC 1, 3, 8, 13, 19, 34,
38, 58; SSC 2**
See also CANR 18; CA 5-8R;
obituary CA 113; DLB 2; DLB-Y 80, 84;
CDALB 1941-1968

Capra, Frank   1897- . . . . **CLC 16**
See also CA 61-64

Caputo, Philip   1941- . . . . **CLC 32**
See also CA 73-76

Card, Orson Scott   1951- . . . . **CLC 44, 47, 50**
See also CA 102

Cardenal, Ernesto   1925- . . . . **CLC 31**
See also CANR 2; CA 49-52

Carducci, Giosue   1835-1907 . . . . . . **TCLC 32**

Carew, Thomas   1595?-1640 . . . . **LC 13**

Carey, Ernestine Gilbreth   1908- . . . . **CLC 17**
See also CA 5-8R; SATA 2

Carey, Peter   1943- . . . . **CLC 40, 55**
See also CA 123, 127

Carleton, William   1794-1869 . . . . . . **NCLC 3**

Carlisle, Henry (Coffin)   1926- . . . . . . **CLC 33**
See also CANR 15; CA 13-16R

Carlson, Ron(ald F.)   1947- . . . . **CLC 54**
See also CA 105

Carlyle, Thomas   1795-1881 . . . . . . **NCLC 22**
See also DLB 55

Carman, (William) Bliss
1861-1929 . . . . **TCLC 7**
See also CA 104

Carpenter, Don(ald Richard)
1931- . . . . **CLC 41**
See also CANR 1; CA 45-48

Carpentier (y Valmont), Alejo
1904-1980 . . . . **CLC 8, 11, 38**
See also CANR 11; CA 65-68;
obituary CA 97-100

Carr, Emily   1871-1945 . . . . **TCLC 32**
See also DLB 68

Carr, John Dickson   1906-1977 . . . . . . **CLC 3**
See also CANR 3; CA 49-52;
obituary CA 69-72

Carr, Virginia Spencer   1929- . . . . **CLC 34**
See also CA 61-64

Carrier, Roch   1937- . . . . **CLC 13**
See also DLB 53

Carroll, James (P.)   1943- . . . . **CLC 38**
See also CA 81-84

Carroll, Jim   1951- . . . . **CLC 35**
See also CA 45-48

Carroll, Lewis   1832-1898 . . . . **NCLC 2**
See also Dodgson, Charles Lutwidge
See also CLR 2; DLB 18

Carroll, Paul Vincent   1900-1968 . . . . **CLC 10**
See also CA 9-12R; obituary CA 25-28R;
DLB 10

Carruth, Hayden   1921- . . . . **CLC 4, 7, 10, 18**
See also CANR 4; CA 9-12R; SATA 47;
DLB 5

Carter, Angela (Olive)   1940- . . . . . **CLC 5, 41**
See also CANR 12; CA 53-56; DLB 14

Carver, Raymond
1938-1988 . . . **CLC 22, 36, 53, 55; SSC 8**
See also CANR 17; CA 33-36R;
obituary CA 126; DLB-Y 84, 88

Cary, (Arthur) Joyce (Lunel)
1888-1957 . . . . **TCLC 1, 29**
See also CA 104; DLB 15

Casanova de Seingalt, Giovanni Jacopo
1725-1798 . . . . **LC 13**

Casares, Adolfo Bioy   1914-
See Bioy Casares, Adolfo

Casely-Hayford, J(oseph) E(phraim)
1866-1930 . . . . **TCLC 24**
See also BLC 1; CA 123

Casey, John   1880-1964
See O'Casey, Sean

Casey, John   1939- . . . . **CLC 59**
See also CANR 23; CA 69-72

Casey, Michael   1947- . . . . **CLC 2**
See also CA 65-68; DLB 5

Casey, Patrick   1902-1934
See Thurman, Wallace

Casey, Warren   1935- . . . . **CLC 12**
See also Jacobs, Jim and Casey, Warren
See also CA 101

Casona, Alejandro   1903-1965 . . . . . . **CLC 49**
See also Alvarez, Alejandro Rodriguez

Cassavetes, John   1929-1991 . . . . **CLC 20**
See also CA 85-88, 127

Cassill, R(onald) V(erlin)   1919- . . . **CLC 4, 23**
See also CAAS 1; CANR 7; CA 9-12R;
DLB 6

Cassity, (Allen) Turner   1929- . . . . **CLC 6, 42**
See also CANR 11; CA 17-20R

Castaneda, Carlos   1935?- . . . . **CLC 12**
See also CA 25-28R

Castedo, Elena   1937- . . . . **CLC 65**
See also CA 132

Castellanos, Rosario   1925-1974 . . . . . **CLC 66**
See also CA 131; obituary CA 53-56

Castelvetro, Lodovico   1505-1571 . . . . . **LC 12**

Castiglione, Baldassare   1478-1529 . . . **LC 12**

Castro, Rosalia de   1837-1885 . . . . . **NCLC 3**

Cather, Willa (Sibert)
1873-1947 . . . . . . **TCLC 1, 11, 31; SSC 2**
See also CA 104; SATA 30; DLB 9, 54;
DLB-DS 1; CDALB 1865-1917

Catton, (Charles) Bruce
1899-1978 .... CLC 35
See also CANR 7; CA 5-8R;
obituary CA 81-84; SATA 2;
obituary SATA 24; DLB 17

Cauldwell, Frank 1923-
See King, Francis (Henry)

Caunitz, William 1935- .... CLC 34

Causley, Charles (Stanley) 1917-..... CLC 7
See also CANR 5; CA 9-12R; SATA 3;
DLB 27

Caute, (John) David 1936-......... CLC 29
See also CAAS 4; CANR 1; CA 1-4R;
DLB 14

Cavafy, C(onstantine) P(eter)
1863-1933 .... TCLC 2, 7
See also CA 104

Cavanna, Betty 1909-............. CLC 12
See also CANR 6; CA 9-12R; SATA 1, 30

Caxton, William 1421?-1491? .... LC 17

Cayrol, Jean 1911-................ CLC 11
See also CA 89-92; DLB 83

Cela, Camilo Jose 1916-...... CLC 4, 13, 59
See also CAAS 10; CANR 21; CA 21-24R

Celan, Paul 1920-1970 ...... CLC 10, 19, 53
See also Antschel, Paul
See also DLB 69

Celine, Louis-Ferdinand
1894-1961 ..... CLC 1, 3, 4, 7, 9, 15, 47
See also Destouches,
Louis-Ferdinand-Auguste
See also DLB 72

Cellini, Benvenuto 1500-1571 .... LC 7

Cendrars, Blaise 1887-1961 .... CLC 18
See also Sauser-Hall, Frederic

Cernuda, Luis (y Bidon)
1902-1963 .... CLC 54
See also CA 89-92

Cervantes (Saavedra), Miguel de
1547-1616 .... LC 6

Cesaire, Aime (Fernand) 1913-.. CLC 19, 32
See also BLC 1; CANR 24; CA 65-68

Chabon, Michael 1965?-............. CLC 55

Chabrol, Claude 1930- .... CLC 16
See also CA 110

Challans, Mary 1905-1983
See Renault, Mary
See also CA 81-84; obituary CA 111;
SATA 23; obituary SATA 36

Chambers, Aidan 1934- .... CLC 35
See also CANR 12; CA 25-28R; SATA 1

Chambers, James 1948-
See Cliff, Jimmy

Chambers, Robert W. 1865-1933... TCLC 41

Chandler, Raymond 1888-1959 ... TCLC 1, 7
See also CA 104

Channing, William Ellery
1780-1842 .... NCLC 17
See also DLB 1, 59

Chaplin, Charles (Spencer)
1889-1977 .... CLC 16
See also CA 81-84; obituary CA 73-76;
DLB 44

Chapman, Graham 1941?- .... CLC 21
See also Monty Python
See also CA 116; obituary CA 169

Chapman, John Jay 1862-1933 ..... TCLC 7
See also CA 104

Chappell, Fred 1936- .... CLC 40
See also CAAS 4; CANR 8; CA 5-8R;
DLB 6

Char, Rene (Emile)
1907-1988 .... CLC 9, 11, 14, 55
See also CA 13-16R; obituary CA 124

Charles I 1600-1649 .... LC 13

Chartier, Emile-Auguste 1868-1951
See Alain

Charyn, Jerome 1937- .... CLC 5, 8, 18
See also CAAS 1; CANR 7; CA 5-8R;
DLB-Y 83

Chase, Mary (Coyle) 1907-1981 ...... DC 1
See also CA 77-80, 105; SATA 17, 29

Chase, Mary Ellen 1887-1973....... CLC 2
See also CAP 1; CA 15-16;
obituary CA 41-44R; SATA 10

Chateaubriand, Francois Rene de
1768-1848 .... NCLC 3

Chatier, Emile-Auguste 1868-1951
See Alain

Chatterji, Bankim Chandra
1838-1894 .... NCLC 19

Chatterji, Saratchandra
1876-1938 .... TCLC 13
See also CA 109

Chatterton, Thomas 1752-1770 .... LC 3

Chatwin, (Charles) Bruce
1940-1989 .... CLC 28, 57, 59
See also CA 85-88,; obituary CA 127

Chaucer, Geoffrey c. 1340-1400 ..... LC 17

Chayefsky, Paddy 1923-1981....... CLC 23
See also CA 9-12R; obituary CA 104;
DLB 7, 44; DLB-Y 81

Chayefsky, Sidney 1923-1981
See Chayefsky, Paddy
See also CANR 18

Chedid, Andree 1920-............. CLC 47

Cheever, John
1912-1982 ..... CLC 3, 7, 8, 11, 15, 25,
64; SSC 1
See also CANR 5, 27; CA 5-8R;
obituary CA 106; CABS 1; DLB 2;
DLB-Y 80, 82; CDALB 1941-1968

Cheever, Susan 1943-........... CLC 18, 48
See also CA 103; DLB-Y 82

Chekhov, Anton (Pavlovich)
1860-1904 ...... TCLC 3, 10, 31; SSC 2
See also CA 104, 124

Chernyshevsky, Nikolay Gavrilovich
1828-1889 .... NCLC 1

Cherry, Caroline Janice 1942-
See Cherryh, C. J.

Cherryh, C. J. 1942-.............. CLC 35
See also CANR 10; CA 65-68; DLB-Y 80

Chesnutt, Charles Waddell
1858-1932 .... TCLC 5, 39; SSC 7
See also BLC 1; CA 106, 125; DLB 12, 50,
78

Chester, Alfred 1929?-1971 .... CLC 49
See also obituary CA 33-36R

Chesterton, G(ilbert) K(eith)
1874-1936 .... TCLC 1, 6; SSC 1
See also CA 104; SATA 27; DLB 10, 19,
34, 70

Chiang Pin-Chin 1904-1986
See Ding Ling
See also obituary CA 118

Ch'ien Chung-shu 1910-........... CLC 22

Child, Lydia Maria 1802-1880 .... NCLC 6
See also DLB 1, 74

Child, Philip 1898-1978 .... CLC 19
See also CAP 1; CA 13-14; SATA 47

Childress, Alice 1920-......... CLC 12, 15
See also BLC 1; CLR 14; CANR 3, 27;
CA 45-48; SATA 7, 48; DLB 7, 38

Chislett, (Margaret) Anne 1943?-... CLC 34

Chitty, (Sir) Thomas Willes 1926-.. CLC 11
See also Hinde, Thomas
See also CA 5-8R

Chomette, Rene 1898-1981
See Clair, Rene
See also obituary CA 103

Chopin, Kate (O'Flaherty)
1851-1904 .... TCLC 5, 14; SSC 8
See also CA 122; brief entry CA 104;
DLB 12, 78; CDALB 1865-1917

Christie, (Dame) Agatha (Mary Clarissa)
1890-1976 ..... CLC 1, 6, 8, 12, 39, 48
See also CANR 10; CA 17-20R;
obituary CA 61-64; SATA 36; DLB 13

Christie, (Ann) Philippa 1920-
See Pearce, (Ann) Philippa
See also CANR 4; CA 7-8

Christine de Pizan 1365?-1431?....... LC 9

Chulkov, Mikhail Dmitrievich
1743-1792 .... LC 2

Churchill, Caryl 1938-......... CLC 31, 55
See also CANR 22; CA 102; DLB 13

Churchill, Charles 1731?-1764........ LC 3

Chute, Carolyn 1947-............. CLC 39
See also CA 123

Ciardi, John (Anthony)
1916-1986 .... CLC 10, 40, 44
See also CAAS 2; CANR 5; CA 5-8R;
obituary CA 118; SATA 1, 46; DLB 5;
DLB-Y 86

Cicero, Marcus Tullius
106 B.C.-43 B.C.............. CMLC 3

Cimino, Michael 1943?-........... CLC 16
See also CA 105

Cioran, E. M. 1911-............... CLC 64
See also CA 25-28R

Cisneros, Sandra 1954-........... CLC 69
See also CA 131

Clair, Rene 1898-1981 .... CLC 20
See also Chomette, Rene

Clampitt, Amy 19??-.............. CLC 32
See also CA 110

Clancy, Tom 1947-................ CLC 45
See also CA 125

Clare, John 1793-1864 .... NCLC 9
See also DLB 55

Clark, Al C. 1937?-1974
See Goines, Donald

Clark, (Robert) Brian 1932-....... **CLC 29**
See also CA 41-44R

Clark, Eleanor 1913- .... **CLC 5, 19**
See also CA 9-12R; DLB 6

Clark, John Pepper 1935- .... **CLC 38**
See also BLC 1; CANR 16; CA 65-68

Clark, Mavis Thorpe 1912?- .... **CLC 12**
See also CANR 8; CA 57-60; SAAS 5;
SATA 8

Clark, Walter Van Tilburg
1909-1971 .... **CLC 28**
See also CA 9-12R; obituary CA 33-36R;
SATA 8; DLB 9

Clarke, Arthur C(harles)
1917- ...... **CLC 1, 4, 13, 18, 35; SSC 3**
See also CANR 2; CA 1-4R; SATA 13

Clarke, Austin 1896-1974......... **CLC 6, 9**
See also BLC 1; CANR 14; CAP 2;
CA 29-32; obituary CA 49-52; DLB 10,
20, 53

Clarke, Austin (Ardinel) C(hesterfield)
1934- .... **CLC 8, 53**
See also CANR 14; CA 25-28R; DLB 53

Clarke, Gillian 1937- .... **CLC 61**
See also CA 106; DLB 40

Clarke, Marcus (Andrew Hislop)
1846-1881 .... **NCLC 19**

Clarke, Shirley 1925-............ **CLC 16**

Clash, The .... **CLC 30**

Claudel, Paul (Louis Charles Marie)
1868-1955 .... **TCLC 2, 10**
See also CA 104

Clavell, James (duMaresq)
1924- .... **CLC 6, 25**
See also CANR 26; CA 25-28R

Clayman, Gregory 1974?-......... **CLC 65**

Cleaver, (Leroy) Eldridge 1935- .... **CLC 30**
See also BLC 1; CANR 16; CA 21-24R

Cleese, John 1939-............... **CLC 21**
See also Monty Python
See also CA 112, 116

Cleland, John 1709-1789 .... **LC 2**
See also DLB 39

Clemens, Samuel Langhorne
1835-1910 ..... **TCLC 6, 12, 19; SSC 6**
See also Twain, Mark
See also YABC 2; CA 104; DLB 11, 12, 23,
64, 74; CDALB 1865-1917

Cliff, Jimmy 1948-............... **CLC 21**

Clifton, Lucille (Thelma)
1936- .... **CLC 19, 66**
See also BLC 1; CLR 5; CANR 2, 24;
CA 49-52; SATA 20; DLB 5, 41

Clough, Arthur Hugh 1819-1861.. **NCLC 27**
See also DLB 32

Clutha, Janet Paterson Frame 1924-
See Frame (Clutha), Janet (Paterson)
See also CANR 2; CA 1-4R

Coburn, D(onald) L(ee) 1938- ...... **CLC 10**
See also CA 89-92

Cocteau, Jean (Maurice Eugene Clement)
1889-1963 .... **CLC 1, 8, 15, 16, 43**
See also CAP 2; CA 25-28; DLB 65

Codrescu, Andrei 1946- .... **CLC 46**
See also CANR 13; CA 33-36R

Coetzee, J(ohn) M. 1940-.... **CLC 23, 33, 66**
See also CA 77-80

Cohen, Arthur A(llen)
1928-1986 .... **CLC 7, 31**
See also CANR 1, 17; CA 1-4R;
obituary CA 120; DLB 28

Cohen, Leonard (Norman)
1934- .... **CLC 3, 38**
See also CANR 14; CA 21-24R; DLB 53

Cohen, Matt 1942-................ **CLC 19**
See also CA 61-64; DLB 53

Cohen-Solal, Annie 19??-.......... **CLC 50**

Colegate, Isabel 1931- .... **CLC 36**
See also CANR 8, 22; CA 17-20R; DLB 14

Coleman, Emmett 1938-
See Reed, Ishmael

Coleridge, Samuel Taylor
1772-1834 .... **NCLC 9**

Coleridge, Sara 1802-1852....... **NCLC 31**

Coles, Don 1928- .... **CLC 46**
See also CA 115

Colette (Sidonie-Gabrielle)
1873-1954 .... **TCLC 1, 5, 16**
See also CA 104; DLB 65

Collett, (Jacobine) Camilla (Wergeland)
1813-1895 .... **NCLC 22**

Collier, Christopher 1930-......... **CLC 30**
See also CANR 13; CA 33-36R; SATA 16

Collier, James L(incoln) 1928- ..... **CLC 30**
See also CLR 3; CANR 4; CA 9-12R;
SATA 8

Collier, Jeremy 1650-1726.......... **LC 6**

Collins, Hunt 1926-
See Hunter, Evan

Collins, Linda 19??- .... **CLC 44**
See also CA 125

Collins, Tom 1843-1912
See Furphy, Joseph

Collins, (William) Wilkie
1824-1889 .... **NCLC 1, 18**
See also DLB 18, 70

Collins, William 1721-1759 .... **LC 4**

Colman, George 1909-1981
See Glassco, John

Colter, Cyrus 1910- .... **CLC 58**
See also CANR 10; CA 65-68; DLB 33

Colton, James 1923-
See Hansen, Joseph

Colum, Padraic 1881-1972......... **CLC 28**
See also CA 73-76; obituary CA 33-36R;
SATA 15; DLB 19

Colvin, James 1939-
See Moorcock, Michael

Colwin, Laurie 1945- .... **CLC 5, 13, 23**
See also CANR 20; CA 89-92; DLB-Y 80

Comfort, Alex(ander) 1920-........ **CLC 7**
See also CANR 1; CA 1-4R

Compton-Burnett, Ivy
1892-1969 .... **CLC 1, 3, 10, 15, 34**
See also CANR 4; CA 1-4R;
obituary CA 25-28R; DLB 36

Comstock, Anthony 1844-1915 .... **TCLC 13**
See also CA 110

Conde, Maryse 1937-............. **CLC 52**
See also Boucolon, Maryse

Condon, Richard (Thomas)
1915- .... **CLC 4, 6, 8, 10, 45**
See also CAAS 1; CANR 2, 23; CA 1-4R

Congreve, William 1670-1729 ... **LC 5; DC 2**
See also DLB 39, 84

Connell, Evan S(helby), Jr.
1924- .... **CLC 4, 6, 45**
See also CAAS 2; CANR 2; CA 1-4R;
DLB 2; DLB-Y 81

Connelly, Marc(us Cook)
1890-1980 .... **CLC 7**
See also CA 85-88; obituary CA 102;
obituary SATA 25; DLB 7; DLB-Y 80

Conner, Ralph 1860-1937........ **TCLC 31**

Conrad, Joseph
1857-1924 ...... **TCLC 1, 6, 13, 25, 43;
SSC 9**
See also CA 104, 131; SATA 27; DLB 10,
34, 98

Conrad, Robert Arnold 1904-1961
See Hart, Moss

Conroy, Pat 1945-................ **CLC 30**
See also CANR 24; CA 85-88; DLB 6

Constant (de Rebecque), (Henri) Benjamin
1767-1830 .... **NCLC 6**

Cook, Michael 1933- .... **CLC 58**
See also CA 93-96; DLB 53

Cook, Robin 1940- .... **CLC 14**
See also CA 108, 111

Cooke, Elizabeth 1948- .... **CLC 55**

Cooke, John Esten 1830-1886..... **NCLC 5**
See also DLB 3

Cooney, Ray 19??- .... **CLC 62**

Cooper, Edith Emma 1862-1913
See Field, Michael

Cooper, J. California 19??- .... **CLC 56**
See also CA 125

Cooper, James Fenimore
1789-1851 .... **NCLC 1, 27**
See also SATA 19; DLB 3;
CDALB 1640-1865

Coover, Robert (Lowell)
1932- .... **CLC 3, 7, 15, 32, 46**
See also CANR 3; CA 45-48; DLB 2;
DLB-Y 81

Copeland, Stewart (Armstrong)
1952- .... **CLC 26**
See also The Police

Coppard, A(lfred) E(dgar)
1878-1957 .... **TCLC 5**
See also YABC 1; CA 114

Coppee, Francois 1842-1908 ...... **TCLC 25**

Coppola, Francis Ford 1939-.... **CLC 16**
See also CA 77-80; DLB 44

Corcoran, Barbara 1911- . . . . CLC 17
See also CAAS 2; CANR 11; CA 21-24R;
SATA 3; DLB 52

Corman, Cid 1924- . . . . CLC 9
See also Corman, Sidney
See also CAAS 2; DLB 5

Corman, Sidney 1924-
See Corman, Cid
See also CA 85-88

Cormier, Robert (Edmund)
1925- . . . . CLC 12, 30
See also CLR 12; CANR 5, 23; CA 1-4R;
SATA 10, 45; DLB 52

Corn, Alfred (Dewitt III) 1943- . . . . . CLC 33
See also CA 104; DLB-Y 80

Cornwell, David (John Moore)
1931- . . . . CLC 9, 15
See also le Carre, John
See also CANR 13; CA 5-8R

Corso, (Nunzio) Gregory 1930- . . . CLC 1, 11
See also CA 5-8R; DLB 5, 16

Cortazar, Julio
1914-1984 . . . . . CLC 2, 3, 5, 10, 13, 15,
33, 34; SSC 7
See also CANR 12; CA 21-24R

Corvo, Baron 1860-1913
See Rolfe, Frederick (William Serafino
Austin Lewis Mary)

Cosic, Dobrica 1921- . . . . CLC 14
See also CA 122

Costain, Thomas B(ertram)
1885-1965 . . . . CLC 30
See also CA 5-8R; obituary CA 25-28R;
DLB 9

Costantini, Humberto 1924?-1987 . . . CLC 49
See also obituary CA 122

Costello, Elvis 1955- . . . . CLC 21

Cotter, Joseph Seamon, Sr.
1861-1949 . . . . TCLC 28
See also BLC 1; CA 124; DLB 50

Couperus, Louis (Marie Anne)
1863-1923 . . . . TCLC 15
See also CA 115

Courtenay, Bryce 1933- . . . . CLC 59

Cousteau, Jacques-Yves 1910- . . . . . . CLC 30
See also CANR 15; CA 65-68; SATA 38

Coward, (Sir) Noel (Pierce)
1899-1973 . . . . CLC 1, 9, 29, 51
See also CAP 2; CA 17-18;
obituary CA 41-44R; DLB 10

Cowley, Malcolm 1898-1989 . . . . CLC 39
See also CANR 3; CA 5-6R;
obituary CA 128; DLB 4, 48; DLB-Y 81

Cowper, William 1731-1800 . . . . NCLC 8

Cox, William Trevor 1928- . . . . . . CLC 9, 14
See also Trevor, William
See also CANR 4; CA 9-12R

Cozzens, James Gould
1903-1978 . . . . CLC 1, 4, 11
See also CANR 19; CA 9-12R;
obituary CA 81-84; DLB 9; DLB-Y 84;
DLB-DS 2; CDALB 1941-1968

Crabbe, George 1754-1832 . . . . NCLC 26

Crace, Douglas 1944- . . . . CLC 58

Crane, (Harold) Hart
1899-1932 . . . . TCLC 2, 5; PC 3
See also CA 127; brief entry CA 104;
DLB 4, 48; CDALB 1917-1929

Crane, R(onald) S(almon)
1886-1967 . . . . CLC 27
See also CA 85-88; DLB 63

Crane, Stephen
1871-1900 . . . . . TCLC 11, 17, 32; SSC 7
See also YABC 2; CA 109; DLB 12, 54, 78;
CDALB 1865-1917

Craven, Margaret 1901-1980 . . . . . . CLC 17
See also CA 103

Crawford, F(rancis) Marion
1854-1909 . . . . TCLC 10
See also CA 107; DLB 71

Crawford, Isabella Valancy
1850-1887 . . . . NCLC 12
See also DLB 92

Crayencour, Marguerite de 1903-1987
See Yourcenar, Marguerite

Creasey, John 1908-1973 . . . . CLC 11
See also CANR 8; CA 5-8R;
obituary CA 41-44R; DLB 77

Crebillon, Claude Prosper Jolyot de (fils)
1707-1777 . . . . LC 1

Creeley, Robert (White)
1926- . . . . CLC 1, 2, 4, 8, 11, 15, 36
See also CANR 23; CA 1-4R; DLB 5, 16

Crews, Harry (Eugene)
1935- . . . . CLC 6, 23, 49
See also CANR 20; CA 25-28R; DLB 6

Crichton, (John) Michael
1942- . . . . CLC 2, 6, 54
See also CANR 13; CA 25-28R; SATA 9;
DLB-Y 81

Crispin, Edmund 1921-1978 . . . . CLC 22
See also Montgomery, Robert Bruce
See also DLB 87

Cristofer, Michael 1946- . . . . CLC 28
See also CA 110; DLB 7

Croce, Benedetto 1866-1952 . . . . . . TCLC 37
See also CA 120

Crockett, David (Davy)
1786-1836 . . . . NCLC 8
See also DLB 3, 11

Croker, John Wilson 1780-1857 . . NCLC 10

Cronin, A(rchibald) J(oseph)
1896-1981 . . . . CLC 32
See also CANR 5; CA 1-4R;
obituary CA 102; obituary SATA 25, 47

Cross, Amanda 1926-
See Heilbrun, Carolyn G(old)

Crothers, Rachel 1878-1953 . . . . . . TCLC 19
See also CA 113; DLB 7

Crowley, Aleister 1875-1947 . . . . . . TCLC 7
See also CA 104

Crowley, John 1942-
See also CA 61-64; DLB-Y 82

Crumb, Robert 1943- . . . . CLC 17
See also CA 106

Cryer, Gretchen 1936?- . . . . CLC 21
See also CA 114, 123

Csath, Geza 1887-1919 . . . . TCLC 13
See also CA 111

Cudlip, David 1933- . . . . CLC 34

Cullen, Countee 1903-1946 . . . . . TCLC 4, 37
See also BLC 1; CA 108, 124; SATA 18;
DLB 4, 48, 51; CDALB 1917-1929

Cummings, E(dward) E(stlin)
1894-1962 . . . . . . CLC 1, 3, 8, 12, 15, 68
See also CANR 31; CA 73-76; DLB 4, 48;
CDALB 1929-1941

Cunha, Euclides (Rodrigues) da
1866-1909 . . . . TCLC 24
See also CA 123

Cunningham, J(ames) V(incent)
1911-1985 . . . . CLC 3, 31
See also CANR 1; CA 1-4R;
obituary CA 115; DLB 5

Cunningham, Julia (Woolfolk)
1916- . . . . CLC 12
See also CANR 4, 19; CA 9-12R; SAAS 2;
SATA 1, 26

Cunningham, Michael 1952- . . . . CLC 34

Currie, Ellen 19??- . . . . CLC 44

Dabrowska, Maria (Szumska)
1889-1965 . . . . CLC 15
See also CA 106

Dabydeen, David 1956?- . . . . CLC 34
See also CA 106

Dacey, Philip 1939- . . . . CLC 51
See also CANR 14; CA 37-40R

Dagerman, Stig (Halvard)
1923-1954 . . . . TCLC 17
See also CA 117

Dahl, Roald 1916- . . . . CLC 1, 6, 18
See also CLR 1, 7; CANR 6; CA 1-4R;
SATA 1, 26

Dahlberg, Edward 1900-1977 . . . CLC 1, 7, 14
See also CA 9-12R; obituary CA 69-72;
DLB 48

Daly, Elizabeth 1878-1967 . . . . CLC 52
See also CAP 2; CA 23-24;
obituary CA 25-28R

Daly, Maureen 1921- . . . . CLC 17
See also McGivern, Maureen Daly
See also SAAS 1; SATA 2

Daniken, Erich von 1935-
See Von Daniken, Erich

Dannay, Frederic 1905-1982
See Queen, Ellery
See also CANR 1; CA 1-4R;
obituary CA 107

D'Annunzio, Gabriele
1863-1938 . . . . TCLC 6, 40
See also CA 104

Dante (Alighieri)
See Alighieri, Dante

Danziger, Paula 1944- . . . . CLC 21
See also CLR 20; CA 112, 115; SATA 30,
36

Dario, Ruben 1867-1916 . . . . TCLC 4
See also Sarmiento, Felix Ruben Garcia
See also CA 104

Darley, George 1795-1846 . . . . NCLC 2

Ende, Michael 1930-.............. CLC 31
See also CLR 14; CA 118, 124; SATA 42;
DLB 75

Endo, Shusaku 1923- ..... CLC 7, 14, 19, 54
See also CANR 21; CA 29-32R

Engel, Marian 1933-1985......... CLC 36
See also CANR 12; CA 25-28R; DLB 53

Engelhardt, Frederick 1911-1986
See Hubbard, L(afayette) Ron(ald)

Enright, D(ennis) J(oseph)
1920- .... CLC 4, 8, 31
See also CANR 1; CA 1-4R; SATA 25;
DLB 27

Enzensberger, Hans Magnus
1929- .... CLC 43
See also CA 116, 119

Ephron, Nora 1941- .... CLC 17, 31
See also CANR 12; CA 65-68

Epstein, Daniel Mark 1948- .... CLC 7
See also CANR 2; CA 49-52

Epstein, Jacob 1956- .... CLC 19
See also CA 114

Epstein, Joseph 1937-............ CLC 39
See also CA 112, 119

Epstein, Leslie 1938- .... CLC 27
See also CANR 23; CA 73-76

Equiano, Olaudah 1745?-1797....... LC 16
See also BLC 2; DLB 37, 50

Erasmus, Desiderius 1469?-1536..... LC 16

Erdman, Paul E(mil) 1932- .... CLC 25
See also CANR 13; CA 61-64

Erdrich, Louise 1954-.......... CLC 39, 54
See also CA 114

Erenburg, Ilya (Grigoryevich) 1891-1967
See Ehrenburg, Ilya (Grigoryevich)

Erickson, Steve 1950-............. CLC 64
See also CA 129

Eseki, Bruno 1919-
See Mphahlele, Ezekiel

Esenin, Sergei (Aleksandrovich)
1895-1925 .... TCLC 4
See also CA 104

Eshleman, Clayton 1935-........... CLC 7
See also CAAS 6; CA 33-36R; DLB 5

Espriu, Salvador 1913-1985......... CLC 9
See also obituary CA 115

Estleman, Loren D. 1952- .... CLC 48
See also CA 85-88

Evans, Marian 1819-1880
See Eliot, George

Evans, Mary Ann 1819-1880
See Eliot, George

Evarts, Esther 1900-1972
See Benson, Sally

Everett, Percival L. 1957?- .... CLC 57
See also CA 129

Everson, Ronald G(ilmour) 1903- ... CLC 27
See also CA 17-20R; DLB 88

Everson, William (Oliver)
1912- .... CLC 1, 5, 14
See also CANR 20; CA 9-12R; DLB 5, 16

Everyman 1495- .... DC 2

Evtushenko, Evgenii (Aleksandrovich) 1933-
See Yevtushenko, Yevgeny

Ewart, Gavin (Buchanan)
1916- .... CLC 13, 46
See also CANR 17; CA 89-92; DLB 40

Ewers, Hanns Heinz 1871-1943 ... TCLC 12
See also CA 109

Ewing, Frederick R. 1918-
See Sturgeon, Theodore (Hamilton)

Exley, Frederick (Earl) 1929- .... CLC 6, 11
See also CA 81-84; DLB-Y 81

Ezekiel, Nissim 1924-............. CLC 61
See also CA 61-64

Ezekiel, Tish O'Dowd 1943- .... CLC 34

Fagen, Donald 1948-.............. CLC 26

Fair, Ronald L. 1932-............. CLC 18
See also CANR 25; CA 69-72; DLB 33

Fairbairns, Zoe (Ann) 1948- .... CLC 32
See also CANR 21; CA 103

Fairfield, Cicily Isabel 1892-1983
See West, Rebecca

Fallaci, Oriana 1930-............. CLC 11
See also CANR 15; CA 77-80

Faludy, George 1913-............. CLC 42
See also CA 21-24R

Fanon, Frantz 1925-1961
See also BLC 2; CA 116; obituary CA 89-92

Fante, John 1909-1983 .... CLC 60
See also CANR 23; CA 69-72;
obituary CA 109; DLB-Y 83

Farah, Nuruddin 1945-............. CLC 53
See also BLC 2; CA 106

Fargue, Leon-Paul 1876-1947 ..... TCLC 11
See also CA 109

Farigoule, Louis 1885-1972
See Romains, Jules

Farina, Richard 1937?-1966........ CLC 9
See also CA 81-84; obituary CA 25-28R

Farley, Walter 1920- .... CLC 17
See also CANR 8; CA 17-20R; SATA 2, 43;
DLB 22

Farmer, Philip Jose 1918-....... CLC 1, 19
See also CANR 4; CA 1-4R; DLB 8

Farrell, J(ames) G(ordon)
1935-1979 .... CLC 6
See also CA 73-76; obituary CA 89-92;
DLB 14

Farrell, James T(homas)
1904-1979 .... CLC 1, 4, 8, 11, 66
See also CANR 9; CA 5-8R;
obituary CA 89-92; DLB 4, 9, 86;
DLB-DS 2

Farrell, M. J. 1904-
See Keane, Molly

Fassbinder, Rainer Werner
1946-1982 .... CLC 20
See also CA 93-96; obituary CA 106

Fast, Howard (Melvin) 1914- ...... CLC 23
See also CANR 1; CA 1-4R; SATA 7;
DLB 9

Faulkner, William (Cuthbert)
1897-1962 .... CLC 1, 3, 6, 8, 9, 11, 14,
18, 28, 52, 68; SSC 1
See also CANR 33; CA 81-84; DLB 9, 11,
44, 102; DLB-Y 86; DLB-DS 2;
CDALB 1929-1941

Fauset, Jessie Redmon
1882-1961 .... CLC 19, 54
See also BLC 2; CA 109; DLB 51

Faust, Irvin 1924-................. CLC 8
See also CA 33-36R; DLB 2, 28; DLB-Y 80

Fearing, Kenneth (Flexner)
1902-1961 .... CLC 51
See also CA 93-96; DLB 9

Federman, Raymond 1928- ...... CLC 6, 47
See also CANR 10; CA 17-20R; DLB-Y 80

Federspiel, J(urg) F. 1931-........ CLC 42

Feiffer, Jules 1929-........... CLC 2, 8, 64
See also CANR 30; CA 17-20R; SATA 8,
61; DLB 7, 44; AAYA 3

Feinberg, David B. 1956-.......... CLC 59

Feinstein, Elaine 1930-............ CLC 36
See also CAAS 1; CA 69-72; DLB 14, 40

Feke, Gilbert David 1976?- .... CLC 65

Feldman, Irving (Mordecai) 1928-.... CLC 7
See also CANR 1; CA 1-4R

Fellini, Federico 1920-............ CLC 16
See also CA 65-68

Felsen, Gregor 1916-
See Felsen, Henry Gregor

Felsen, Henry Gregor 1916- .... CLC 17
See also CANR 1; CA 1-4R; SAAS 2;
SATA 1

Fenton, James (Martin) 1949-...... CLC 32
See also CA 102; DLB 40

Ferber, Edna 1887-1968........... CLC 18
See also CA 5-8R; obituary CA 25-28R;
SATA 7; DLB 9, 28, 86

Ferguson, Samuel 1810-1886..... NCLC 33
See also DLB 32

Ferlinghetti, Lawrence (Monsanto)
1919?- .... CLC 2, 6, 10, 27; PC 1
See also CANR 3; CA 5-8R; DLB 5, 16;
CDALB 1941-1968

Ferrier, Susan (Edmonstone)
1782-1854 .... NCLC 8

Ferrigno, Robert 19??-............ CLC 65

Feuchtwanger, Lion 1884-1958 ..... TCLC 3
See also CA 104; DLB 66

Feydeau, Georges 1862-1921...... TCLC 22
See also CA 113

Ficino, Marsilio 1433-1499 .... LC 12

Fiedler, Leslie A(aron)
1917- .... CLC 4, 13, 24
See also CANR 7; CA 9-12R; DLB 28, 67

Field, Andrew 1938-.............. CLC 44
See also CANR 25; CA 97-100

Field, Eugene 1850-1895 .... NCLC 3
See also SATA 16; DLB 21, 23, 42

Field, Michael.................. TCLC 43

Fielding, Henry 1707-1754 .... LC 1
See also DLB 39, 84

Freneau, Philip Morin   1752-1832 .. **NCLC 1**
See also DLB 37, 43

Friedman, B(ernard) H(arper)
1926- .... **CLC 7**
See also CANR 3; CA 1-4R

Friedman, Bruce Jay   1930- .... **CLC 3, 5, 56**
See also CANR 25; CA 9-12R; DLB 2, 28

Friel, Brian   1929- .... **CLC 5, 42, 59**
See also CA 21-24R; DLB 13

Friis-Baastad, Babbis (Ellinor)
1921-1970 .... **CLC 12**
See also CA 17-20R; SATA 7

Frisch, Max (Rudolf)
1911- .... **CLC 3, 9, 14, 18, 32, 44**
See also CA 85-88; DLB 69

Fromentin, Eugene (Samuel Auguste)
1820-1876 .... **NCLC 10**

Frost, Robert (Lee)
1874-1963 ... **CLC 1, 3, 4, 9, 10, 13, 15,**
                        26, 34, 44; PC 1
See also CA 89-92; SATA 14; DLB 54;
DLB-DS 7; CDALB 1917-1929

Fry, Christopher   1907- .... **CLC 2, 10, 14**
See also CANR 9; CA 17-20R; DLB 13

Frye, (Herman) Northrop   1912- .... **CLC 24**
See also CANR 8; CA 5-8R; DLB 67, 68

Fuchs, Daniel   1909- .... **CLC 8, 22**
See also CAAS 5; CA 81-84; DLB 9, 26, 28

Fuchs, Daniel   1934- .... **CLC 34**
See also CANR 14; CA 37-40R

Fuentes, Carlos
1928- ...... **CLC 3, 8, 10, 13, 22, 41, 60**
See also CANR 10; CA 69-72

Fugard, Athol   1932- ... **CLC 5, 9, 14, 25, 40**
See also CA 85-88

Fugard, Sheila   1932- .... **CLC 48**
See also CA 125

Fuller, Charles (H., Jr.)
1939- .... **CLC 25; DC 1**
See also BLC 2; CA 108, 112; DLB 38

Fuller, John (Leopold)   1937- .... **CLC 62**
See also CANR 9; CA 21-22R; DLB 40

Fuller, (Sarah) Margaret
1810-1850 .... **NCLC 5**
See also Ossoli, Sarah Margaret (Fuller
marchesa d')
See also DLB 1, 59, 73; CDALB 1640-1865

Fuller, Roy (Broadbent)   1912- .... **CLC 4, 28**
See also CA 5-8R; DLB 15, 20

Fulton, Alice   1952- .... **CLC 52**
See also CA 116

Furabo   1644-1694
See Basho, Matsuo

Furphy, Joseph   1843-1912 .... **TCLC 25**

Futabatei Shimei   1864-1909 ...... **TCLC 44**

Futrelle, Jacques   1875-1912 ...... **TCLC 19**
See also CA 113

Gaboriau, Emile   1835-1873 ...... **NCLC 14**

Gadda, Carlo Emilio   1893-1973 .... **CLC 11**
See also CA 89-92

Gaddis, William
1922- .... **CLC 1, 3, 6, 8, 10, 19, 43**
See also CAAS 4; CANR 21; CA 17-20R;
DLB 2

Gaines, Ernest J.   1933- ...... **CLC 3, 11, 18**
See also BLC 2; CANR 6, 24; CA 9-12R;
DLB 2, 33; DLB-Y 80;
CDALB 1968-1988

Gaitskill, Mary   1954- .... **CLC 69**
See also CA 128

Gale, Zona   1874-1938 .... **TCLC 7**
See also CA 105; DLB 9, 78

Gallagher, Tess   1943- .... **CLC 18, 63**
See also CA 106

Gallant, Mavis
1922- .... **CLC 7, 18, 38; SSC 5**
See also CA 69-72; DLB 53

Gallant, Roy A(rthur)   1924- .... **CLC 17**
See also CANR 4; CA 5-8R; SATA 4

Gallico, Paul (William)   1897-1976 ... **CLC 2**
See also CA 5-8R; obituary CA 69-72;
SATA 13; DLB 9

Galsworthy, John   1867-1933 .... **TCLC 1**
See also CA 104; DLB 10, 34

Galt, John   1779-1839 .... **NCLC 1**

Galvin, James   1951- .... **CLC 38**
See also CANR 26; CA 108

Gamboa, Frederico   1864-1939 ..... **TCLC 36**

Gann, Ernest K(ellogg)   1910- ...... **CLC 23**
See also CANR 1; CA 1-4R

Garcia Lorca, Federico
1898-1936 ..... **TCLC 1, 7; DC 2; PC 3**
See also CA 131; brief entry CA 104;
DLB 108

Garcia Marquez, Gabriel (Jose)
1928- ... **CLC 2, 3, 8, 10, 15, 27, 47, 55,**
                           68; SSC 8
See also CANR 10, 28; CA 33-36R;
AAYA 3

Gardam, Jane   1928- .... **CLC 43**
See also CLR 12; CANR 2, 18; CA 49-52;
SATA 28, 39; DLB 14

Gardner, Herb   1934- .... **CLC 44**

Gardner, John (Champlin, Jr.)
1933-1982 .... **CLC 2, 3, 5, 7, 8, 10, 18,**
                         28, 34; SSC 7
See also CA 65-68; obituary CA 107;
obituary SATA 31, 40; DLB 2; DLB-Y 82

Gardner, John (Edmund)   1926- ..... **CLC 30**
See also CANR 15; CA 103

Gardons, S. S.   1926-
See Snodgrass, W(illiam) D(e Witt)

Garfield, Leon   1921- .... **CLC 12**
See also CA 17-20R; SATA 1, 32

Garland, (Hannibal) Hamlin
1860-1940 .... **TCLC 3**
See also CA 104; DLB 12, 71, 78

Garneau, Hector (de) Saint Denys
1912-1943 .... **TCLC 13**
See also CA 111; DLB 88

Garner, Alan   1935- .... **CLC 17**
See also CLR 20; CANR 15; CA 73-76;
SATA 18

Garner, Hugh   1913-1979 .... **CLC 13**
See also CA 69-72; DLB 68

Garnett, David   1892-1981 .... **CLC 3**
See also CANR 17; CA 5-8R;
obituary CA 103; DLB 34

Garrett, George (Palmer, Jr.)
1929- .... **CLC 3, 11, 51**
See also CAAS 5; CANR 1; CA 1-4R;
DLB 2, 5; DLB-Y 83

Garrick, David   1717-1779 .... **LC 15**
See also DLB 84

Garrigue, Jean   1914-1972 .... **CLC 2, 8**
See also CANR 20; CA 5-8R;
obituary CA 37-40R

Garvey, Marcus   1887-1940 .... **TCLC 41**
See also BLC 2; CA 124; brief entry CA 120

Gary, Romain   1914-1980 .... **CLC 25**
See also Kacew, Romain

Gascar, Pierre   1916- .... **CLC 11**
See also Fournier, Pierre

Gascoyne, David (Emery)   1916- .... **CLC 45**
See also CANR 10; CA 65-68; DLB 20

Gaskell, Elizabeth Cleghorn
1810-1865 .... **NCLC 5**
See also DLB 21

Gass, William H(oward)
1924- .... **CLC 1, 2, 8, 11, 15, 39**
See also CA 17-20R; DLB 2

Gates, Henry Louis, Jr.   1950- ...... **CLC 65**
See also CANR 25; CA 109; DLB 67

Gautier, Theophile   1811-1872 ..... **NCLC 1**

Gaye, Marvin (Pentz)   1939-1984 ... **CLC 26**
See also obituary CA 112

Gebler, Carlo (Ernest)   1954- .... **CLC 39**
See also CA 119

Gee, Maggie   19??- .... **CLC 57**

Gee, Maurice (Gough)   1931- .... **CLC 29**
See also CA 97-100; SATA 46

Gelbart, Larry   1923?- .... **CLC 21, 61**
See also CA 73-76

Gelber, Jack   1932- .... **CLC 1, 6, 14, 60**
See also CANR 2; CA 1-4R; DLB 7

Gellhorn, Martha (Ellis)   1908- .. **CLC 14, 60**
See also CA 77-80; DLB-Y 82

Genet, Jean
1910-1986 ... **CLC 1, 2, 5, 10, 14, 44, 46**
See also CANR 18; CA 13-16R; DLB 72;
DLB-Y 86

Gent, Peter   1942- .... **CLC 29**
See also CA 89-92; DLB 72; DLB-Y 82

George, Jean Craighead   1919- ...... **CLC 35**
See also CLR 1; CA 5-8R; SATA 2;
DLB 52

George, Stefan (Anton)
1868-1933 .... **TCLC 2, 14**
See also CA 104

Gerhardi, William (Alexander)   1895-1977
See Gerhardie, William (Alexander)

Gerhardie, William (Alexander)
1895-1977 .... **CLC 5**
See also CANR 18; CA 25-28R;
obituary CA 73-76; DLB 36

Gertler, T(rudy)   1946?- .... **CLC 34**
See also CA 116

Gessner, Friedrike Victoria   1910-1980
See Adamson, Joy(-Friederike Victoria)

Ghelderode, Michel de
1898-1962 .... **CLC 6, 11**
See also CA 85-88

Author Index

Josipovici, Gabriel (David)
1940- .... CLC 6, 43
See also CAAS 8; CA 37-40R; DLB 14

Joubert, Joseph 1754-1824 .... NCLC 9

Jouve, Pierre Jean 1887-1976...... CLC 47
See also obituary CA 65-68

Joyce, James (Augustine Aloysius)
1882-1941 ...... **TCLC 3, 8, 16, 26, 35;**
SSC 3
See also CA 104, 126; DLB 10, 19, 36

Jozsef, Attila 1905-1937......... TCLC 22
See also CA 116

Juana Ines de la Cruz 1651?-1695 .... LC 5

Julian of Norwich 1342?-1416?....... LC 6

Just, Ward S(wift) 1935- .... CLC 4, 27
See also CA 25-28R

Justice, Donald (Rodney) 1925- .. CLC 6, 19
See also CANR 26; CA 5-8R; DLB-Y 83

Juvenal c. 55-c. 127 .... CMLC 8

Kacew, Romain 1914-1980
See Gary, Romain
See also CA 108; obituary CA 102

Kacewgary, Romain 1914-1980
See Gary, Romain

Kadare, Ismail 1936- .... CLC 52

Kadohata, Cynthia 19??- .... CLC 59

Kafka, Franz
1883-1924 .... **TCLC 2, 6, 13, 29; SSC 5**
See also CA 105, 126; DLB 81

Kahn, Roger 1927- .... CLC 30
See also CA 25-28R; SATA 37

Kaiser, (Friedrich Karl) Georg
1878-1945 .... TCLC 9
See also CA 106

Kaletski, Alexander 1946- .... CLC 39
See also CA 118

Kallman, Chester (Simon)
1921-1975 .... CLC 2
See also CANR 3; CA 45-48;
obituary CA 53-56

Kaminsky, Melvin 1926-
See Brooks, Mel
See also CANR 16; CA 65-68

Kaminsky, Stuart 1934-........... CLC 59
See also CANR 29; CA 73-76

Kane, Paul 1941-
See Simon, Paul

Kanin, Garson 1912-.............. CLC 22
See also CANR 7; CA 5-8R; DLB 7

Kaniuk, Yoram 1930-............. CLC 19

Kant, Immanuel 1724-1804 ...... NCLC 27

Kantor, MacKinlay 1904-1977 ...... CLC 7
See also CA 61-64; obituary CA 73-76;
DLB 9

Kaplan, David Michael 1946- ...... CLC 50

Kaplan, James 19??-.............. CLC 59

Karamzin, Nikolai Mikhailovich
1766-1826 .... NCLC 3

Karapanou, Margarita 1946-....... CLC 13
See also CA 101

Karl, Frederick R(obert) 1927-..... CLC 34
See also CANR 3; CA 5-8R

Kassef, Romain 1914-1980
See Gary, Romain

Katz, Steve 1935-................ CLC 47
See also CANR 12; CA 25-28R; DLB-Y 83

Kauffman, Janet 1945-............ CLC 42
See also CA 117; DLB-Y 86

Kaufman, Bob (Garnell)
1925-1986 .... CLC 49
See also CANR 22; CA 41-44R;
obituary CA 118; DLB 16, 41

Kaufman, George S(imon)
1889-1961 .... CLC 38
See also CA 108; obituary CA 93-96; DLB 7

Kaufman, Sue 1926-1977 .... CLC 3, 8
See also Barondess, Sue K(aufman)

Kavan, Anna 1904-1968......... CLC 5, 13
See also Edmonds, Helen (Woods)
See also CANR 6; CA 5-8R

Kavanagh, Patrick (Joseph Gregory)
1905-1967 .... CLC 22
See also CA 123; obituary CA 25-28R;
DLB 15, 20

Kawabata, Yasunari
1899-1972 .... CLC 2, 5, 9, 18
See also CA 93-96; obituary CA 33-36R

Kaye, M(ary) M(argaret) 1909?-.... CLC 28
See also CANR 24; CA 89-92

Kaye, Mollie 1909?-
See Kaye, M(ary) M(argaret)

Kaye-Smith, Sheila 1887-1956..... TCLC 20
See also CA 118; DLB 36

Kaymor, Patrice Maguilene 1906-
See Senghor, Leopold Sedar

Kazan, Elia 1909-........... CLC 6, 16, 63
See also CA 21-24R

Kazantzakis, Nikos
1885?-1957............. TCLC 2, 5, 33
See also CA 105

Kazin, Alfred 1915- .... CLC 34, 38
See also CAAS 7; CANR 1; CA 1-4R;
DLB 67

Keane, Mary Nesta (Skrine) 1904-
See Keane, Molly
See also CA 108, 114

Keane, Molly 1904- .... CLC 31
See also Keane, Mary Nesta (Skrine)

Keates, Jonathan 19??-............ CLC 34

Keaton, Buster 1895-1966 .... CLC 20

Keaton, Joseph Francis 1895-1966
See Keaton, Buster

Keats, John 1795-1821...... NCLC 8; PC 1

Keene, Donald 1922- .... CLC 34
See also CANR 5; CA 1-4R

Keillor, Garrison 1942- .... CLC 40
See also Keillor, Gary (Edward)
See also CA 111; SATA 58; DLB-Y 87;
AAYA 2

Keillor, Gary (Edward)
See Keillor, Garrison
See also CA 111, 117

Kell, Joseph 1917-
See Burgess (Wilson, John) Anthony

Keller, Gottfried 1819-1890....... NCLC 2

Kellerman, Jonathan (S.) 1949-..... CLC 44
See also CANR 29; CA 106

Kelley, William Melvin 1937-...... CLC 22
See also CANR 27; CA 77-80; DLB 33

Kellogg, Marjorie 1922-............ CLC 2
See also CA 81-84

Kelly, M. T. 1947- .... CLC 55
See also CANR 19; CA 97-100

Kelman, James 1946-............. CLC 58

Kemal, Yashar 1922- .... CLC 14, 29
See also CA 89-92

Kemble, Fanny 1809-1893 .... NCLC 18
See also DLB 32

Kemelman, Harry 1908-............ CLC 2
See also CANR 6; CA 9-12R; DLB 28

Kempe, Margery 1373?-1440? .... LC 6

Kempis, Thomas á 1380-1471 .... LC 11

Kendall, Henry 1839-1882....... NCLC 12

Keneally, Thomas (Michael)
1935- ...... CLC 5, 8, 10, 14, 19, 27, 43
See also CANR 10; CA 85-88

Kennedy, Adrienne 1931-
See also BLC 2; CANR 26; CA 103;
CABS 3; DLB 38

Kennedy, Adrienne (Lita) 1931- .... CLC 66
See also CANR 26; CA 103; CABS 3;
DLB 38

Kennedy, John Pendleton
1795-1870 .... NCLC 2
See also DLB 3

Kennedy, Joseph Charles 1929-...... CLC 8
See also Kennedy, X. J.
See also CANR 4, 30; CA 1-4R; SATA 14

Kennedy, William (Joseph)
1928-.......... CLC 6, 28, 34, 53
See also CANR 14; CA 85-88; SATA 57;
DLB-Y 85; AAYA 1

Kennedy, X. J. 1929-............ CLC 8, 42
See also Kennedy, Joseph Charles
See also CAAS 9; DLB 5

Kerouac, Jack
1922-1969 .... CLC 1, 2, 3, 5, 14, 29, 61
See also Kerouac, Jean-Louis Lebris de
See also DLB 2, 16; DLB-DS 3;
CDALB 1941-1968

Kerouac, Jean-Louis Lebris de 1922-1969
See Kerouac, Jack
See also CANR 26; CA 5-8R;
obituary CA 25-28R; CDALB 1941-1968

Kerr, Jean 1923-.................. CLC 22
See also CANR 7; CA 5-8R

Kerr, M. E. 1927-............... CLC 12, 35
See also Meaker, Marijane
See also SAAS 1; AAYA 2

Kerr, Robert 1970?- .... CLC 55, 59

Kerrigan, (Thomas) Anthony
1918-.................... CLC 4, 6
See also CAAS 11; CANR 4; CA 49-52

Kesey, Ken (Elton)
1935- ...... CLC 1, 3, 6, 11, 46, 64
See also CANR 22; CA 1-4R; DLB 2, 16;
CDALB 1968-1987

Kesselring, Joseph (Otto)
1902-1967 .... CLC 45

Kessler, Jascha (Frederick) 1929-.... CLC 4
See also CANR 8; CA 17-20R

Kettelkamp, Larry 1933-.......... CLC 12
See also CANR 16; CA 29-32R; SAAS 3;
SATA 2

Kherdian, David 1931-.......... CLC 6, 9
See also CLR 24; CAAS 2; CA 21-24R;
SATA 16

Khlebnikov, Velimir (Vladimirovich)
1885-1922 ....TCLC 20
See also CA 117

Khodasevich, Vladislav (Felitsianovich)
1886-1939 ....TCLC 15
See also CA 115

Kielland, Alexander (Lange)
1849-1906 ....TCLC 5
See also CA 104

Kiely, Benedict 1919-.......... CLC 23, 43
See also CANR 2; CA 1-4R; DLB 15

Kienzle, William X(avier) 1928-.... CLC 25
See also CAAS 1; CANR 9; CA 93-96

Kierkegaard, SOren 1813-1855... NCLC 34

Killens, John Oliver 1916-........ CLC 10
See also CAAS 2; CANR 26; CA 77-80,
123; DLB 33

Killigrew, Anne 1660-1685.......... LC 4

Kincaid, Jamaica 1949-........ CLC 43, 68
See also BLC 2; CA 125

King, Francis (Henry) 1923-..... CLC 8, 53
See also CANR 1; CA 1-4R; DLB 15

King, Martin Luther, Jr. 1929-1968
See also BLC 2; CANR 27; CAP 2;
CA 25-28; SATA 14

King, Stephen (Edwin)
1947-.............. CLC 12, 26, 37, 61
See also CANR 1, 30; CA 61-64; SATA 9,
55; DLB-Y 80; AAYA 1

Kingman, (Mary) Lee 1919-........ CLC 17
See also Natti, (Mary) Lee
See also CA 5-8R; SAAS 3; SATA 1

Kingsley, Sidney 1906-........... CLC 44
See also CA 85-88; DLB 7

Kingsolver, Barbara 1955-........ CLC 55
See also CA 129

Kingston, Maxine Hong
1940-................ CLC 12, 19, 58
See also CANR 13; CA 69-72; SATA 53;
DLB-Y 80

Kinnell, Galway
1927-.......... CLC 1, 2, 3, 5, 13, 29
See also CANR 10; CA 9-12R; DLB 5;
DLB-Y 87

Kinsella, Thomas 1928-...... CLC 4, 19, 43
See also CANR 15; CA 17-20R; DLB 27

Kinsella, W(illiam) P(atrick)
1935-............... CLC 27, 43
See also CAAS 7; CANR 21; CA 97-100

Kipling, (Joseph) Rudyard
1865-1936 .... TCLC 8, 17; PC 3; SSC 5
See also YABC 2; CANR 33; CA 120;
brief entry CA 105; DLB 19, 34

Kirkup, James 1918- .... CLC 1
See also CAAS 4; CANR 2; CA 1-4R;
SATA 12; DLB 27

Kirkwood, James 1930-1989 .... CLC 9
See also CANR 6; CA 1-4R;
obituary CA 128

Kis, Danilo 1935-1989 .... CLC 57
See also CA 118, 129; brief entry CA 109

Kivi, Aleksis 1834-1872......... NCLC 30

Kizer, Carolyn (Ashley) 1925-... CLC 15, 39
See also CAAS 5; CANR 24; CA 65-68;
DLB 5

Klabund 1890-1928.............. TCLC 44
See also DLB 66

Klappert, Peter 1942-........... CLC 57
See also CA 33-36R; DLB 5

Klausner, Amos 1939-
See Oz, Amos

Klein, A(braham) M(oses)
1909-1972 .... CLC 19
See also CA 101; obituary CA 37-40R;
DLB 68

Klein, Norma 1938-1989 .... CLC 30
See also CLR 2, 19; CANR 15; CA 41-44R;
obituary CA 128; SAAS 1; SATA 7, 57;
AAYA 2

Klein, T.E.D. 19??-............... CLC 34
See also CA 119

Kleist, Heinrich von 1777-1811.... NCLC 2
See also DLB 90

Klima, Ivan 1931-............... CLC 56
See also CANR 17; CA 25-28R

Klimentcv, Andrei Platonovich 1899-1951
See Platonov, Andrei (Platonovich)
See also CA 108

Klinger, Friedrich Maximilian von
1752-1831 .... NCLC 1

Klopstock, Friedrich Gottlieb
1724-1803 .... NCLC 11

Knebel, Fletcher 1911-........... CLC 14
See also CAAS 3; CANR 1; CA 1-4R;
SATA 36

Knight, Etheridge 1931-1991...... CLC 40
See also BLC 2; CANR 23; CA 21-24R;
DLB 41

Knight, Sarah Kemble 1666-1727 ..... LC 7
See also DLB 24

Knowles, John 1926- ...... CLC 1, 4, 10, 26
See also CA 17-20R; SATA 8; DLB 6;
CDALB 1968-1987

Koch, C(hristopher) J(ohn) 1932-... CLC 42
See also CA 127

Koch, Kenneth 1925- .... CLC 5, 8, 44
See also CANR 6; CA 1-4R; DLB 5

Kochanowski, Jan 1530-1584....... LC 10

Kock, Charles Paul de
1794-1871 .... NCLC 16

Koestler, Arthur
1905-1983 .... CLC 1, 3, 6, 8, 15, 33
See also CANR 1; CA 1-4R;
obituary CA 109; DLB-Y 83

Kohout, Pavel 1928-.............. CLC 13
See also CANR 3; CA 45-48

Kolmar, Gertrud 1894-1943....... TCLC 40

Konigsberg, Allen Stewart 1935-
See Allen, Woody

Konrad, Gyorgy 1933-.......... CLC 4, 10
See also CA 85-88

Konwicki, Tadeusz 1926-..... CLC 8, 28, 54
See also CAAS 9; CA 101

Kopit, Arthur (Lee) 1937- .... CLC 1, 18, 33
See also CA 81-84; CABS 3; DLB 7

Kops, Bernard 1926-.............. CLC 4
See also CA 5-8R; DLB 13

Kornbluth, C(yril) M. 1923-1958.... TCLC 8
See also CA 105; DLB 8

Korolenko, Vladimir (Galaktionovich)
1853-1921 .... TCLC 22
See also CA 121

Kosinski, Jerzy (Nikodem)
1933- .... CLC 1, 2, 3, 6, 10, 15, 53
See also CANR 9; CA 17-20R; DLB 2;
DLB-Y 82

Kostelanetz, Richard (Cory) 1940- .. CLC 28
See also CAAS 8; CA 13-16R

Kostrowitzki, Wilhelm Apollinaris de
1880-1918
See Apollinaire, Guillaume
See also CA 104

Kotlowitz, Robert 1924-........... CLC 4
See also CA 33-36R

Kotzebue, August (Friedrich Ferdinand) von
1761-1819 .... NCLC 25

Kotzwinkle, William 1938- ... CLC 5, 14, 35
See also CLR 6; CANR 3; CA 45-48;
SATA 24

Kozol, Jonathan 1936-............ CLC 17
See also CANR 16; CA 61-64

Kozoll, Michael 1940?-............ CLC 35

Kramer, Kathryn 19??-............. CLC 34

Kramer, Larry 1935-.............. CLC 42
See also CA 124, 126

Krasicki, Ignacy 1735-1801....... NCLC 8

Krasinski, Zygmunt 1812-1859 .... NCLC 4

Kraus, Karl 1874-1936......... TCLC 5
See also CA 104

Kreve, Vincas 1882-1954......... TCLC 27

Kristofferson, Kris 1936-.......... CLC 26
See also CA 104

Krizanc, John 1956-.............. CLC 57

Krleza, Miroslav 1893-1981........ CLC 8
See also CA 97-100; obituary CA 105

Kroetsch, Robert (Paul)
1927-................ CLC 5, 23, 57
See also CANR 8; CA 17-20R; DLB 53

Kroetz, Franz Xaver 1946- .... CLC 41
See also CA 130

Kropotkin, Peter 1842-1921....... TCLC 36
See also CA 119

Krotkov, Yuri 1917-.............. CLC 19
See also CA 102

Krumgold, Joseph (Quincy)
1908-1980 .... CLC 12
See also CANR 7; CA 9-12R;
obituary CA 101; SATA 1, 48;
obituary SATA 23

Krutch, Joseph Wood 1893-1970.... CLC 24
See also CANR 4; CA 1-4R;
obituary CA 25-28R; DLB 63

Krylov, Ivan Andreevich
  1768?-1844 . . . . NCLC 1

Kubin, Alfred 1877-1959 . . . . TCLC 23
  See also CA 112; DLB 81

Kubrick, Stanley 1928- . . . . CLC 16
  See also CA 81-84; DLB 26

Kumin, Maxine (Winokur)
  1925- . . . . CLC 5, 13, 28
  See also CAAS 8; CANR 1, 21; CA 1-4R;
    SATA 12; DLB 5

Kundera, Milan
  1929- . . . . CLC 4, 9, 19, 32, 68
  See also CANR 19; CA 85-88; AAYA 2

Kunitz, Stanley J(asspon)
  1905- . . . . CLC 6, 11, 14
  See also CANR 26; CA 41-44R; DLB 48

Kunze, Reiner 1933- . . . . CLC 10
  See also CA 93-96; DLB 75

Kuprin, Aleksandr (Ivanovich)
  1870-1938 . . . . TCLC 5
  See also CA 104

Kureishi, Hanif 1954- . . . . CLC 64

Kurosawa, Akira 1910- . . . . CLC 16
  See also CA 101

Kuttner, Henry 1915-1958 . . . . TCLC 10
  See also CA 107; DLB 8

Kuzma, Greg 1944- . . . . CLC 7
  See also CA 33-36R

Kuzmin, Mikhail 1872?-1936 . . . . . TCLC 40

Labrunie, Gerard 1808-1855
  See Nerval, Gerard de

La Bruyere, Jean de 1645-1696 . . . . . . LC 17

Laclos, Pierre Ambroise Francois Choderlos
  de 1741-1803 . . . . NCLC 4

La Fayette, Marie (Madelaine Pioche de la
  Vergne, Comtesse) de
  1634-1693 . . . . LC 2

Lafayette, Rene
  See Hubbard, L(afayette) Ron(ald)

Laforgue, Jules 1860-1887 . . . . NCLC 5

Lagerkvist, Par (Fabian)
  1891-1974 . . . . CLC 7, 10, 13, 54
  See also CA 85-88; obituary CA 49-52

Lagerlof, Selma (Ottiliana Lovisa)
  1858-1940 . . . . TCLC 4, 36
  See also CLR 7; CA 108; SATA 15

La Guma, (Justin) Alex(ander)
  1925-1985 . . . . CLC 19
  See also CANR 25; CA 49-52;
    obituary CA 118

Lamartine, Alphonse (Marie Louis Prat) de
  1790-1869 . . . . NCLC 11

Lamb, Charles 1775-1834 . . . . NCLC 10
  See also SATA 17

Lamming, George (William)
  1927- . . . . CLC 2, 4, 66
  See also BLC 2; CANR 26; CA 85-88

LaMoore, Louis Dearborn 1908?-
  See L'Amour, Louis (Dearborn)

L'Amour, Louis (Dearborn)
  1908-1988 . . . . CLC 25, 55
  See also CANR 3, 25; CA 1-4R;
    obituary CA 125; DLB-Y 80

Lampedusa, (Prince) Giuseppe (Maria
  Fabrizio) Tomasi di
  1896-1957 . . . . TCLC 13
  See also CA 111

Lampman, Archibald 1861-1899 . . NCLC 25
  See also DLB 92

Lancaster, Bruce 1896-1963 . . . . CLC 36
  See also CAP 1; CA 9-12; SATA 9

Landis, John (David) 1950- . . . . CLC 26
  See also CA 112, 122

Landolfi, Tommaso 1908-1979 . . . CLC 11, 49
  See also CA 127; obituary CA 117

Landon, Letitia Elizabeth
  1802-1838 . . . . NCLC 15

Landor, Walter Savage
  1775-1864 . . . . NCLC 14

Landwirth, Heinz 1927-
  See Lind, Jakov
  See also CANR 7; CA 11-12R

Lane, Patrick 1939- . . . . CLC 25
  See also CA 97-100; DLB 53

Lang, Andrew 1844-1912 . . . . TCLC 16
  See also CA 114; SATA 16

Lang, Fritz 1890-1976 . . . . CLC 20
  See also CANR 30; CA 77-80;
    obituary CA 69-72

Langer, Elinor 1939- . . . . CLC 34
  See also CA 121

Lanier, Sidney 1842-1881 . . . . NCLC 6
  See also SATA 18; DLB 64

Lanyer, Aemilia 1569-1645 . . . . LC 10

Lao Tzu c. 6th-3rd century B.C. . . . . CMLC 7

Lapine, James 1949- . . . . CLC 39
  See also CA 123, 130

Larbaud, Valery 1881-1957 . . . . TCLC 9
  See also CA 106

Lardner, Ring(gold Wilmer)
  1885-1933 . . . . TCLC 2, 14
  See also CA 104; DLB 11, 25, 86;
    CDALB 1917-1929

Larkin, Philip (Arthur)
  1922-1985 . . . CLC 3, 5, 8, 9, 13, 18, 33,
                                    39, 64
  See also CANR 24; CA 5-8R;
    obituary CA 117; DLB 27

Larra (y Sanchez de Castro), Mariano Jose de
  1809-1837 . . . . NCLC 17

Larsen, Eric 1941- . . . . CLC 55

Larsen, Nella 1891-1964 . . . . CLC 37
  See also BLC 2; CA 125; DLB 51

Larson, Charles R(aymond) 1938- . . . CLC 31
  See also CANR 4; CA 53-56

Latham, Jean Lee 1902- . . . . CLC 12
  See also CANR 7; CA 5-8R; SATA 2

Lathen, Emma . . . . CLC 2
  See also Hennissart, Martha; Latsis, Mary
    J(ane)

Latsis, Mary J(ane) . . . . CLC 2
  See also Lathen, Emma
  See also CA 85-88

Lattimore, Richmond (Alexander)
  1906-1984 . . . . CLC 3
  See also CANR 1; CA 1-4R;
    obituary CA 112

Laughlin, James 1914- . . . . CLC 49
  See also CANR 9; CA 21-24R; DLB 48

Laurence, (Jean) Margaret (Wemyss)
  1926-1987 . . CLC 3, 6, 13, 50, 62; SSC 7
  See also CA 5-8R; obituary CA 121;
    SATA 50; DLB 53

Laurent, Antoine 1952- . . . . CLC 50

Lautreamont, Comte de
  1846-1870 . . . . NCLC 12

Lavin, Mary 1912- . . . . . . CLC 4, 18; SSC 4
  See also CA 9-12R; DLB 15

Lawler, Raymond (Evenor) 1922- . . . CLC 58
  See also CA 103

Lawrence, D(avid) H(erbert)
  1885-1930 . . . . TCLC 2, 9, 16, 33; SSC 4
  See also CA 104, 121; DLB 10, 19, 36

Lawrence, T(homas) E(dward)
  1888-1935 . . . . TCLC 18
  See also CA 115

Lawson, Henry (Archibald Hertzberg)
  1867-1922 . . . . TCLC 27
  See also CA 120

Laxness, Halldor (Kiljan) 1902- . . . . CLC 25
  See also Gudjonsson, Halldor Kiljan

Laye, Camara 1928-1980 . . . . CLC 4, 38
  See also BLC 2.; CANR 25; CA 85-88;
    obituary CA 97-100

Layton, Irving (Peter) 1912- . . . . . CLC 2, 15
  See also CANR 2; CA 1-4R; DLB 88

Lazarus, Emma 1849-1887 . . . . NCLC 8

Leacock, Stephen (Butler)
  1869-1944 . . . . TCLC 2
  See also CA 104; DLB 92

Lear, Edward 1812-1888 . . . . NCLC 3
  See also CLR 1; SATA 18; DLB 32

Lear, Norman (Milton) 1922- . . . . . . CLC 12
  See also CA 73-76

Leavis, F(rank) R(aymond)
  1895-1978 . . . . CLC 24
  See also CA 21-24R; obituary CA 77-80

Leavitt, David 1961?- . . . . CLC 34
  See also CA 116, 122

Lebowitz, Fran(ces Ann)
  1951?- . . . . CLC 11, 36
  See also CANR 14; CA 81-84

Le Carre, John 1931- . . . CLC 3, 5, 9, 15, 28
  See also Cornwell, David (John Moore)
  See also DLB 87

Le Clezio, J(ean) M(arie) G(ustave)
  1940- . . . . CLC 31
  See also CA 116, 128; DLB 83

Leconte de Lisle, Charles-Marie-Rene
  1818-1894 . . . . NCLC 29

Leduc, Violette 1907-1972 . . . . CLC 22
  See also CAP 1; CA 13-14;
    obituary CA 33-36R

Ledwidge, Francis 1887-1917 . . . . . . TCLC 23
  See also CA 123; DLB 20

Lee, Andrea 1953- . . . . CLC 36
  See also BLC 2; CA 125

Lee, Andrew 1917-
  See Auchincloss, Louis (Stanton)

Milner, Ron(ald) 1938-............ CLC 56
See also BLC 3; CANR 24; CA 73-76;
DLB 38

Milosz Czeslaw
1911-.......... CLC 5, 11, 22, 31, 56
See also CANR 23; CA 81-84

Milton, John 1608-1674............. LC 9

Miner, Valerie (Jane) 1947-........ CLC 40
See also CA 97-100

Minot, Susan 1956- .... CLC 44

Minus, Ed 1938-................ CLC 39

Miro (Ferrer), Gabriel (Francisco Victor)
1879-1930 .... TCLC 5
See also CA 104

Mishima, Yukio
1925-1970 .... CLC 2, 4, 6, 9, 27; DC 1;
SSC 4
See also Hiraoka, Kimitake

Mistral, Gabriela 1889-1957 .... TCLC 2
See also CA 104

Mitchell, James Leslie 1901-1935
See Gibbon, Lewis Grassic
See also CA 104; DLB 15

Mitchell, Joni 1943-.............. CLC 12
See also CA 112

Mitchell (Marsh), Margaret (Munnerlyn)
1900-1949 .... TCLC 11
See also CA 109, 125; DLB 9

Mitchell, S. Weir 1829-1914 ..... TCLC 36

Mitchell, W(illiam) O(rmond)
1914-....................... CLC 25
See also CANR 15; CA 77-80; DLB 88

Mitford, Mary Russell 1787-1855.. NCLC 4

Mitford, Nancy 1904-1973........ CLC 44
See also CA 9-12R

Miyamoto Yuriko 1899-1951...... TCLC 37

Mo, Timothy 1950-................ CLC 46
See also CA 117

Modarressi, Taghi 1931- .... CLC 44
See also CA 121

Modiano, Patrick (Jean) 1945-..... CLC 18
See also CANR 17; CA 85-88; DLB 83

Mofolo, Thomas (Mokopu)
1876-1948 .... TCLC 22
See also BLC 3; brief entry CA 121

Mohr, Nicholasa 1935-............ CLC 12
See also CLR 22; CANR 1; CA 49-52;
SAAS 8; SATA 8

Mojtabai, A(nn) G(race)
1938- .... CLC 5, 9, 15, 29
See also CA 85-88

Moliere 1622-1673 .... LC 10

Molnar, Ferenc 1878-1952........ TCLC 20
See also CA 109

Momaday, N(avarre) Scott
1934- .... CLC 2, 19
See also CANR 14; CA 25-28R; SATA 30,
48

Monroe, Harriet 1860-1936....... TCLC 12
See also CA 109; DLB 54, 91

Montagu, Elizabeth 1720-1800 .... NCLC 7

Montagu, Lady Mary (Pierrepont) Wortley
1689-1762 .... LC 9

Montague, John (Patrick)
1929- .... CLC 13, 46
See also CANR 9; CA 9-12R; DLB 40

Montaigne, Michel (Eyquem) de
1533-1592 .... LC 8

Montale, Eugenio 1896-1981... CLC 7, 9, 18
See also CANR 30; CA 17-20R;
obituary CA 104

Montesquieu, Charles-Louis de Secondat
1689-1755 .... LC 7

Montgomery, Marion (H., Jr.)
1925- .... CLC 7
See also CANR 3; CA 1-4R; DLB 6

Montgomery, Robert Bruce 1921-1978
See Crispin, Edmund
See also CA 104

Montherlant, Henri (Milon) de
1896-1972 .... CLC 8, 19
See also CA 85-88; obituary CA 37-40R;
DLB 72

Monty Python .... CLC 21

Moodie, Susanna (Strickland)
1803-1885 .... NCLC 14

Mooney, Ted 1951-.............. CLC 25

Moorcock, Michael (John)
1939- .... CLC 5, 27, 58
See also CAAS 5; CANR 2, 17; CA 45-48;
DLB 14

Moore, Brian
1921- .... CLC 1, 3, 5, 7, 8, 19, 32
See also CANR 1, 25; CA 1-4R

Moore, George (Augustus)
1852-1933 .... TCLC 7
See also CA 104; DLB 10, 18, 57

Moore, Lorrie 1957-........ CLC 39, 45, 68
See also Moore, Marie Lorena

Moore, Marianne (Craig)
1887-1972 ... CLC 1, 2, 4, 8, 10, 13, 19,
47; PC 4
See also CANR 3; CA 1-4R;
obituary CA 33-36R; SATA 20; DLB 45;
DLB-DS 7; CDALB 1929-1941

Moore, Marie Lorena 1957-
See Moore, Lorrie
See also CA 116

Moore, Thomas 1779-1852........ NCLC 6

Morand, Paul 1888-1976 .... CLC 41
See also obituary CA 69-72; DLB 65

Morante, Elsa 1918-1985........ CLC 8, 47
See also CA 85-88; obituary CA 117

Moravia, Alberto
1907- .... CLC 2, 7, 11, 18, 27, 46
See also Pincherle, Alberto

More, Hannah 1745-1833 .... NCLC 27

More, Henry 1614-1687............. LC 9

More, Sir Thomas 1478-1535 ...... LC 10

Moreas, Jean 1856-1910 .... TCLC 18

Morgan, Berry 1919-.............. CLC 6
See also CA 49-52; DLB 6

Morgan, Edwin (George) 1920-..... CLC 31
See also CANR 3; CA 7-8R; DLB 27

Morgan, (George) Frederick
1922- .... CLC 23
See also CANR 21; CA 17-20R

Morgan, Janet 1945- .... CLC 39
See also CA 65-68

Morgan, Lady 1776?-1859 ...... NCLC 29

Morgan, Robin 1941-.............. CLC 2
See also CA 69-72

Morgan, Seth 1949-1990 .... CLC 65
See also CA 132

Morgenstern, Christian (Otto Josef Wolfgang)
1871-1914 .... TCLC 8
See also CA 105

Moricz, Zsigmond 1879-1942 ..... TCLC 33

Morike, Eduard (Friedrich)
1804-1875 .... NCLC 10

Mori Ogai 1862-1922............. TCLC 14
See also Mori Rintaro

Mori Rintaro 1862-1922
See Mori Ogai
See also CA 110

Moritz, Karl Philipp 1756-1793 ...... LC 2

Morris, Julian 1916-
See West, Morris L.

Morris, Steveland Judkins 1950-
See Wonder, Stevie
See also CA 111

Morris, William 1834-1896 .... NCLC 4
See also DLB 18, 35, 57

Morris, Wright (Marion)
1910- .... CLC 1, 3, 7, 18, 37
See also CANR 21; CA 9-12R; DLB 2;
DLB-Y 81

Morrison, James Douglas 1943-1971
See Morrison, Jim
See also CA 73-76

Morrison, Jim 1943-1971.......... CLC 17
See also Morrison, James Douglas

Morrison, Toni 1931-..... CLC 4, 10, 22, 55
See also BLC 3; CANR 27; CA 29-32R;
SATA 57; DLB 6, 33; DLB-Y 81;
CDALB 1968-1987; AAYA 1

Morrison, Van 1945- .... CLC 21
See also CA 116

Mortimer, John (Clifford)
1923- .... CLC 28, 43
See also CANR 21; CA 13-16R; DLB 13

Mortimer, Penelope (Ruth) 1918-.... CLC 5
See also CA 57-60

Mosher, Howard Frank 19??- ...... CLC 62

Mosley, Nicholas 1923-........... CLC 43
See also CA 69-72; DLB 14

Moss, Howard
1922-1987 .... CLC 7, 14, 45, 50
See also CANR 1; CA 1-4R;
obituary CA 123; DLB 5

Motion, Andrew (Peter) 1952-...... CLC 47
See also DLB 40

Motley, Willard (Francis)
1912-1965 .... CLC 18
See also CA 117; obituary CA 106; DLB 76

Mott, Michael (Charles Alston)
1930-.................... CLC 15, 34
See also CAAS 7; CANR 7, 29; CA 5-8R

Mowat, Farley (McGill) 1921- ..... CLC 26
See also CLR 20; CANR 4, 24; CA 1-4R;
SATA 3, 55; DLB 68; AAYA 1

Author Index

Powell, Anthony (Dymoke)
1905- .... CLC 1, 3, 7, 9, 10, 31
See also CANR 1; CA 1-4R; DLB 15

Powell, Dawn 1897-1965 .... CLC 66
See also CA 5-8R

Powell, Padgett 1952-............. CLC 34
See also CA 126

Powers, J(ames) F(arl)
1917- .... CLC 1, 4, 8, 57; SSC 4
See also CANR 2; CA 1-4R

Powers, John J(ames) 1945-
See Powers, John R.

Powers, John R. 1945-........... CLC 66
See also Powers, John J(ames)
See also CA 69-72

Pownall, David 1938-............. CLC 10
See also CA 89-92; DLB 14

Powys, John Cowper
1872-1963 .... CLC 7, 9, 15, 46
See also CA 85-88; DLB 15

Powys, T(heodore) F(rancis)
1875-1953 .... TCLC 9
See also CA 106; DLB 36

Prager, Emily 1952-............. CLC 56

Pratt, E(dwin) J(ohn) 1883-1964.... CLC 19
See also obituary CA 93-96; DLB 92

Premchand 1880-1936 .... TCLC 21

Preussler, Otfried 1923-.......... CLC 17
See also CA 77-80; SATA 24

Prevert, Jacques (Henri Marie)
1900-1977 .... CLC 15
See also CANR 29; CA 77-80;
obituary CA 69-72; obituary SATA 30

Prevost, Abbe (Antoine Francois)
1697-1763 .... LC 1

Price, (Edward) Reynolds
1933- .... CLC 3, 6, 13, 43, 50, 63
See also CANR 1; CA 1-4R; DLB 2

Price, Richard 1949- .... CLC 6, 12
See also CANR 3; CA 49-52; DLB-Y 81

Prichard, Katharine Susannah
1883-1969 .... CLC 46
See also CAP 1; CA 11-12

Priestley, J(ohn) B(oynton)
1894-1984 .... CLC 2, 5, 9, 34
See also CA 9-12R; obituary CA 113;
DLB 10, 34, 77; DLB-Y 84

Prince (Rogers Nelson) 1958?- ..... CLC 35

Prince, F(rank) T(empleton) 1912-.. CLC 22
See also CA 101; DLB 20

Prior, Matthew 1664-1721.......... LC 4

Pritchard, William H(arrison)
1932-....................... CLC 34
See also CANR 23; CA 65-68

Pritchett, V(ictor) S(awdon)
1900- .... CLC 5, 13, 15, 41
See also CA 61-64; DLB 15

Probst, Mark 1925- .... CLC 59
See also CA 130

Procaccino, Michael 1946-
See Cristofer, Michael

Prokosch, Frederic 1908-1989.... CLC 4, 48
See also CA 73-76; obituary CA 128;
DLB 48

Prose, Francine 1947-............ CLC 45
See also CA 109, 112

Proust, Marcel 1871-1922 .. TCLC 7, 13, 33
See also CA 104, 120; DLB 65

Pryor, Richard 1940-............. CLC 26
See also CA 122

Przybyszewski, Stanislaw
1868-1927 .... TCLC 36
See also DLB 66

Puig, Manuel
1932-1990 .... CLC 3, 5, 10, 28, 65
See also CANR 2, 32; CA 45-48

Purdy, A(lfred) W(ellington)
1918- .... CLC 3, 6, 14, 50
See also CA 81-84

Purdy, James (Amos)
1923- .... CLC 2, 4, 10, 28, 52
See also CAAS 1; CANR 19; CA 33-36R;
DLB 2

Pushkin, Alexander (Sergeyevich)
1799-1837 .... NCLC 3, 27

P'u Sung-ling 1640-1715 .... LC 3

Puzo, Mario 1920-......... CLC 1, 2, 6, 36
See also CANR 4; CA 65-68; DLB 6

Pym, Barbara (Mary Crampton)
1913-1980 .... CLC 13, 19, 37
See also CANR 13; CAP 1; CA 13-14;
obituary CA 97-100; DLB 14; DLB-Y 87

Pynchon, Thomas (Ruggles, Jr.)
1937- ..... CLC 2, 3, 6, 9, 11, 18, 33, 62
See also CANR 22; CA 17-20R; DLB 2

Quarrington, Paul 1954?-......... CLC 65
See also CA 129

Quasimodo, Salvatore 1901-1968 ... CLC 10
See also CAP 1; CA 15-16;
obituary CA 25-28R

Queen, Ellery 1905-1982 .... CLC 3, 11
See also Dannay, Frederic; Lee, Manfred
B(ennington)

Queneau, Raymond
1903-1976 .... CLC 2, 5, 10, 42
See also CA 77-80; obituary CA 69-72;
DLB 72

Quir, Ann (Marie) 1936-1973 .... CLC 6
See also CA 9-12R; obituary CA 45-48;
DLB 14

Quinn, Simon 1942-
See Smith, Martin Cruz
See also CANR 6, 23; CA 85-88

Quiroga, Horacio (Sylvestre)
1878-1937 .... TCLC 20
See also CA 117

Quoirez, Francoise 1935-
See Sagan, Francoise
See also CANR 6; CA 49-52

Rabe, David (William) 1940-... CLC 4, 8, 33
See also CA 85-88; CABS 3; DLB 7

Rabelais, Francois 1494?-1553........ LC 5

Rabinovitch, Sholem 1859-1916
See Aleichem, Sholom
See also CA 104

Rachen, Kurt von 1911-1986
See Hubbard, L(afayette) Ron(ald)

Radcliffe, Ann (Ward) 1764-1823 .. NCLC 6
See also DLB 39

Radiguet, Raymond 1903-1923 .... TCLC 29
See also DLB 65

Radnoti, Miklos 1909-1944 .... TCLC 16
See also CA 118

Rado, James 1939-............... CLC 17
See also CA 105

Radomski, James 1932-
See Rado, James

Radvanyi, Netty Reiling 1900-1983
See Seghers, Anna
See also CA 85-88; obituary CA 110

Rae, Ben 1935-
See Griffiths, Trevor

Raeburn, John 1941- .... CLC 34
See also CA 57-60

Ragni, Gerome 1942-............. CLC 17
See also CA 105

Rahv, Philip 1908-1973 .... CLC 24
See also Greenberg, Ivan

Raine, Craig 1944-............... CLC 32
See also CANR 29; CA 108; DLB 40

Raine, Kathleen (Jessie) 1908- ... CLC 7, 45
See also CA 85-88; DLB 20

Rainis, Janis 1865-1929.......... TCLC 29

Rakosi, Carl 1903- .... CLC 47
See also Rawley, Callman
See also CAAS 5

Ramos, Graciliano 1892-1953 ..... TCLC 32

Rampersad, Arnold 19??-.......... CLC 44

Ramuz, Charles-Ferdinand
1878-1947 .... TCLC 33

Rand, Ayn 1905-1982........ CLC 3, 30, 44
See also CANR 27; CA 13-16R;
obituary CA 105

Randall, Dudley (Felker) 1914-...... CLC 1
See also BLC 3; CANR 23; CA 25-28R;
DLB 41

Ransom, John Crowe
1888-1974 .... CLC 2, 4, 5, 11, 24
See also CANR 6; CA 5-8R;
obituary CA 49-52; DLB 45, 63

Rao, Raja 1909- .... CLC 25, 56
See also CA 73-76

Raphael, Frederic (Michael)
1931- .... CLC 2, 14
See also CANR 1; CA 1-4R; DLB 14

Rathbone, Julian 1935- .... CLC 41
See also CA 101

Rattigan, Terence (Mervyn)
1911-1977 .... CLC 7
See also CA 85-88; obituary CA 73-76;
DLB 13

Ratushinskaya, Irina 1954- .... CLC 54
See also CA 129

Raven, Simon (Arthur Noel)
1927- .... CLC 14
See also CA 81-84

Rawley, Callman 1903-
See Rakosi, Carl
See also CANR 12; CA 21-24R

Rawlings, Marjorie Kinnan
1896-1953 .... TCLC 4
See also YABC 1; CA 104; DLB 9, 22

Ray, Satyajit 1921-.............. CLC 16
See also CA 114

Read, Herbert (Edward) 1893-1968 .. CLC 4
See also CA 85-88; obituary CA 25-28R;
DLB 20

Read, Piers Paul 1941- ...... CLC 4, 10, 25
See also CA 21-24R; SATA 21; DLB 14

Reade, Charles 1814-1884 .... NCLC 2
See also DLB 21

Reade, Hamish 1936-
See Gray, Simon (James Holliday)

Reading, Peter 1946- .... CLC 47
See also CA 103; DLB 40

Reaney, James 1926- .... CLC 13
See also CA 41-44R; SATA 43; DLB 68

Rebreanu, Liviu 1885-1944 .... TCLC 28

Rechy, John (Francisco)
1934- .... CLC 1, 7, 14, 18
See also CAAS 4; CANR 6; CA 5-8R;
DLB-Y 82

Redcam, Tom 1870-1933 .... TCLC 25

Reddin, Keith 1956?- .... CLC 67

Redgrove, Peter (William)
1932- .... CLC 6, 41
See also CANR 3; CA 1-4R; DLB 40

Redmon (Nightingale), Anne
1943- .... CLC 22
See also Nightingale, Anne Redmon
See also DLB-Y 86

Reed, Ishmael
1938- .... CLC 2, 3, 5, 6, 13, 32, 60
See also BLC 3; CANR 25; CA 21-24R;
DLB 2, 5, 33; DLB-DS 8

Reed, John (Silas) 1887-1920 ...... TCLC 9
See also CA 106

Reed, Lou 1944-................. CLC 21

Reeve, Clara 1729-1807 .... NCLC 19
See also DLB 39

Reid, Christopher 1949-........... CLC 33
See also DLB 40

Reid Banks, Lynne 1929-
See Banks, Lynne Reid
See also CANR 6, 22; CA 1-4R; SATA 22

Reiner, Max 1900-
See Caldwell, (Janet Miriam) Taylor
(Holland)

Reizenstein, Elmer Leopold 1892-1967
See Rice, Elmer

Remark, Erich Paul 1898-1970
See Remarque, Erich Maria

Remarque, Erich Maria
1898-1970 .... CLC 21
See also CA 77-80; obituary CA 29-32R;
DLB 56

Remizov, Alexey (Mikhailovich)
1877-1957 .... TCLC 27
See also CA 125

Renan, Joseph Ernest
1823-1892 .... NCLC 26

Renard, Jules 1864-1910 .... TCLC 17
See also CA 117

Renault, Mary 1905-1983 .... CLC 3, 11, 17
See also Challans, Mary
See also DLB-Y 83

Rendell, Ruth 1930-.......... CLC 28, 48
See also Vine, Barbara
See also CA 109; DLB 87

Renoir, Jean 1894-1979 .... CLC 20
See also CA 129; obituary CA 85-88

Resnais, Alain 1922-............. CLC 16

Reverdy, Pierre 1899-1960 .... CLC 53
See also CA 97-100; obituary CA 89-92

Rexroth, Kenneth
1905-1982 ...... CLC 1, 2, 6, 11, 22, 49
See also CANR 14; CA 5-8R;
obituary CA 107; DLB 16, 48; DLB-Y 82;
CDALB 1941-1968

Reyes, Alfonso 1889-1959 .... TCLC 33

Reyes y Basoalto, Ricardo Eliecer Neftali
1904-1973
See Neruda, Pablo

Reymont, Wladyslaw Stanislaw
1867-1925 .... TCLC 5
See also CA 104

Reynolds, Jonathan 1942?- ...... CLC 6, 38
See also CANR 28; CA 65-68

Reynolds, Michael (Shane) 1937-... CLC 44
See also CANR 9; CA 65-68

Reynolds, Sir Joshua 1723-1792..... LC 15

Reznikoff, Charles 1894-1976 ...... CLC 9
See also CAP 2; CA 33-36;
obituary CA 61-64; DLB 28, 45

Rezzori, Gregor von 1914-........ CLC 25
See also CA 122

Rhys, Jean
1890-1979 ...... CLC 2, 4, 6, 14, 19, 51
See also CA 25-28R; obituary CA 85-88;
DLB 36

Ribeiro, Darcy 1922- .... CLC 34
See also CA 33-36R

Ribeiro, Joao Ubaldo (Osorio Pimentel)
1941- .... CLC 10, 67
See also CA 81-84

Ribman, Ronald (Burt) 1932- .... CLC 7
See also CA 21-24R

Rice, Anne 1941- .... CLC 41
See also CANR 12; CA 65-68

Rice, Elmer 1892-1967.......... CLC 7, 49
See also CAP 2; CA 21-22;
obituary CA 25-28R; DLB 4, 7

Rice, Tim 1944- .... CLC 21
See also CA 103

Rich, Adrienne (Cecile)
1929- .... CLC 3, 6, 7, 11, 18, 36
See also CANR 20; CA 9-12R; DLB 5, 67

Richard, Keith 1943- .... CLC 17
See also CA 107

Richards, David Adam 1950-....... CLC 59
See also CA 93-96; DLB 53

Richards, I(vor) A(rmstrong)
1893-1979 .... CLC 14, 24
See also CA 41-44R; obituary CA 89-92;
DLB 27

Richards, Keith 1943-
See Richard, Keith
See also CA 107

Richardson, Dorothy (Miller)
1873-1957 .... TCLC 3
See also CA 104; DLB 36

Richardson, Ethel 1870-1946
See Richardson, Henry Handel
See also CA 105

Richardson, Henry Handel
1870-1946 .... TCLC 4
See also Richardson, Ethel

Richardson, Samuel 1689-1761 ...... LC 1
See also DLB 39

Richler, Mordecai
1931- .... CLC 3, 5, 9, 13, 18, 46
See also CLR 17; CA 65-68; SATA 27, 44;
DLB 53

Richter, Conrad (Michael)
1890-1968 .... CLC 30
See also CANR 23; CA 5-8R;
obituary CA 25-28R; SATA 3; DLB 9

Richter, Johann Paul Friedrich 1763-1825
See Jean Paul

Riddell, Mrs. J. H. 1832-1906..... TCLC 40

Riding, Laura 1901-............. CLC 3, 7
See also Jackson, Laura (Riding)

Riefenstahl, Berta Helene Amalia
1902-....................... CLC 16
See also Riefenstahl, Leni
See also CA 108

Riefenstahl, Leni 1902- .... CLC 16
See also Riefenstahl, Berta Helene Amalia
See also CA 108

Rilke, Rainer Maria
1875-1926 .... TCLC 1, 6, 19; PC 2
See also CA 104, 132; DLB 81

Rimbaud, (Jean Nicolas) Arthur
1854-1891 .... NCLC 4; PC 3

Ringwood, Gwen(dolyn Margaret) Pharis
1910-1984 .... CLC 48
See also obituary CA 112

Rio, Michel 19??-................ CLC 43

Ritsos, Yannis 1909-........ CLC 6, 13, 31
See also CA 77-80

Ritter, Erika 1948?-.............. CLC 52

Rivera, Jose Eustasio 1889-1928... TCLC 35

Rivers, Conrad Kent 1933-1968...... CLC 1
See also CA 85-88; DLB 41

Rizal, Jose 1861-1896.......... NCLC 27

Roa Bastos, Augusto 1917- .... CLC 45

Robbe-Grillet, Alain
1922- ...... CLC 1, 2, 4, 6, 8, 10, 14, 43
See also CA 9-12R; DLB 83

Robbins, Harold 1916-............. CLC 5
See also CANR 26; CA 73-76

Robbins, Thomas Eugene 1936-
See Robbins, Tom
See also CA 81-84

Robbins, Tom 1936-........ CLC 9, 32, 64
See also Robbins, Thomas Eugene
See also CANR 29; CA 81-84; DLB-Y 80

Robbins, Trina 1938- .... CLC 21

Author Index

Roberts, (Sir) Charles G(eorge) D(ouglas)
1860-1943 . . . . TCLC 8
See also CA 105; SATA 29; DLB 92

Roberts, Kate 1891-1985 . . . . CLC 15
See also CA 107; obituary CA 116

Roberts, Keith (John Kingston)
1935- . . . . CLC 14
See also CA 25-28R

Roberts, Kenneth 1885-1957 . . . . . . TCLC 23
See also CA 109; DLB 9

Roberts, Michele (B.) 1949- . . . . CLC 48
See also CA 115

Robinson, Edwin Arlington
1869-1935 . . . . TCLC 5; PC 1
See also CA 104; DLB 54;
CDALB 1865-1917

Robinson, Henry Crabb
1775-1867 . . . . NCLC 15

Robinson, Jill 1936- . . . . CLC 10
See also CA 102

Robinson, Kim Stanley 19??- . . . . CLC 34
See also CA 126

Robinson, Marilynne 1944- . . . . CLC 25
See also CA 116

Robinson, Smokey 1940- . . . . CLC 21

Robinson, William 1940-
See Robinson, Smokey
See also CA 116

Robison, Mary 1949- . . . . CLC 42
See also CA 113, 116

Roddenberry, Gene 1921- . . . . CLC 17
See also CANR 110; SATA 45

Rodgers, Mary 1931- . . . . CLC 12
See also CLR 20; CANR 8; CA 49-52;
SATA 8

Rodgers, W(illiam) R(obert)
1909-1969 . . . . CLC 7
See also CA 85-88; DLB 20

Rodman, Howard 19??- . . . . CLC 65

Rodriguez, Claudio 1934- . . . . CLC 10

Roethke, Theodore (Huebner)
1908-1963 . . . . . . CLC 1, 3, 8, 11, 19, 46
See also CA 81-84; CABS 2; SAAS 1;
DLB 5; CDALB 1941-1968

Rogers, Sam 1943-
See Shepard, Sam

Rogers, Thomas (Hunton) 1931- . . . . CLC 57
See also CA 89-92

Rogers, Will(iam Penn Adair)
1879-1935 . . . . TCLC 8
See also CA 105; DLB 11

Rogin, Gilbert 1929- . . . . CLC 18
See also CANR 15; CA 65-68

Rohan, Koda 1867-1947 . . . . TCLC 22
See also CA 121

Rohmer, Eric 1920- . . . . CLC 16
See also Scherer, Jean-Marie Maurice

Rohmer, Sax 1883-1959 . . . . TCLC 28
See also Ward, Arthur Henry Sarsfield
See also CA 108; DLB 70

Roiphe, Anne (Richardson)
1935- . . . . CLC 3, 9
See also CA 89-92; DLB-Y 80

Rolfe, Frederick (William Serafino Austin
Lewis Mary) 1860-1913 . . . . . . TCLC 12
See also CA 107; DLB 34

Rolland, Romain 1866-1944 . . . . . . TCLC 23
See also CA 118; DLB 65

Rolvaag, O(le) E(dvart)
1876-1931 . . . . TCLC 17
See also CA 117; DLB 9

Romains, Jules 1885-1972 . . . . CLC 7
See also CA 85-88

Romero, Jose Ruben 1890-1952 . . . TCLC 14
See also CA 114

Ronsard, Pierre de 1524-1585 . . . . LC 6

Rooke, Leon 1934- . . . . CLC 25, 34
See also CANR 23; CA 25-28R

Roper, William 1498-1578 . . . . LC 10

Rosa, Joao Guimaraes 1908-1967 . . . CLC 23
See also obituary CA 89-92

Rosen, Richard (Dean) 1949- . . . . . . CLC 39
See also CA 77-80

Rosenberg, Isaac 1890-1918 . . . . . . TCLC 12
See also CA 107; DLB 20

Rosenblatt, Joe 1933- . . . . CLC 15
See also Rosenblatt, Joseph

Rosenblatt, Joseph 1933-
See Rosenblatt, Joe
See also CA 89-92

Rosenfeld, Samuel 1896-1963
See Tzara, Tristan
See also obituary CA 89-92

Rosenthal, M(acha) L(ouis) 1917- . . . CLC 28
See also CAAS 6; CANR 4; CA 1-4R;
SATA 59; DLB 5

Ross, (James) Sinclair 1908- . . . . CLC 13
See also CA 73-76; DLB 88

Rossetti, Christina Georgina
1830-1894 . . . . NCLC 2
See also SATA 20; DLB 35

Rossetti, Dante Gabriel
1828-1882 . . . . NCLC 4
See also DLB 35

Rossetti, Gabriel Charles Dante 1828-1882
See Rossetti, Dante Gabriel

Rossner, Judith (Perelman)
1935- . . . . CLC 6, 9, 29
See also CANR 18; CA 17-20R; DLB 6

Rostand, Edmond (Eugene Alexis)
1868-1918 . . . . TCLC 6, 37
See also CA 104, 126

Roth, Henry 1906- . . . . CLC 2, 6, 11
See also CAP 1; CA 11-12; DLB 28

Roth, Joseph 1894-1939 . . . . TCLC 33
See also DLB 85

Roth, Philip (Milton)
1933- . . . . . CLC 1, 2, 3, 4, 6, 9, 15, 22,
31, 47, 66
See also CANR 1, 22; CA 1-4R; DLB 2, 28;
DLB-Y 82; CDALB 1968-1988

Rothenberg, James 1931- . . . . CLC 57

Rothenberg, Jerome 1931- . . . . CLC 6, 57
See also CANR 1; CA 45-48; DLB 5

Roumain, Jacques 1907-1944 . . . . . . TCLC 19
See also BLC 3; CA 117, 125

Rourke, Constance (Mayfield)
1885-1941 . . . . TCLC 12
See also YABC 1; CA 107

Rousseau, Jean-Baptiste 1671-1741 . . . LC 9

Rousseau, Jean-Jacques 1712-1778 . . . LC 14

Roussel, Raymond 1877-1933 . . . . . TCLC 20
See also CA 117

Rovit, Earl (Herbert) 1927- . . . . CLC 7
See also CANR 12; CA 5-8R

Rowe, Nicholas 1674-1718 . . . . LC 8

Rowson, Susanna Haswell
1762-1824 . . . . NCLC 5
See also DLB 37

Roy, Gabrielle 1909-1983 . . . . CLC 10, 14
See also CANR 5; CA 53-56;
obituary CA 110; DLB 68

Rozewicz, Tadeusz 1921- . . . . CLC 9, 23
See also CA 108

Ruark, Gibbons 1941- . . . . CLC 3
See also CANR 14; CA 33-36R

Rubens, Bernice 192?- . . . . CLC 19, 31
See also CA 25-28R; DLB 14

Rubenstein, Gladys 1934-
See Swan, Gladys

Rudkin, (James) David 1936- . . . . . . CLC 14
See also CA 89-92; DLB 13

Rudnik, Raphael 1933- . . . . CLC 7
See also CA 29-32R

Ruiz, Jose Martinez 1874-1967
See Azorin

Rukeyser, Muriel
1913-1980 . . . . CLC 6, 10, 15, 27
See also CANR 26; CA 5-8R;
obituary CA 93-96; obituary SATA 22;
DLB 48

Rule, Jane (Vance) 1931- . . . . CLC 27
See also CANR 12; CA 25-28R; DLB 60

Rulfo, Juan 1918-1986 . . . . CLC 8
See also CANR 26; CA 85-88;
obituary CA 118

Runyon, (Alfred) Damon
1880-1946 . . . . TCLC 10
See also CA 107; DLB 11

Rush, Norman 1933- . . . . CLC 44
See also CA 121, 126

Rushdie, (Ahmed) Salman
1947- . . . . CLC 23, 31, 55, 59
See also CA 108, 111

Rushforth, Peter (Scott) 1945- . . . . . CLC 19
See also CA 101

Ruskin, John 1819-1900 . . . . TCLC 20
See also CA 114; SATA 24; DLB 55

Russ, Joanna 1937- . . . . CLC 15
See also CANR 11; CA 25-28R; DLB 8

Russell, George William 1867-1935
See A. E.
See also CA 104

Russell, (Henry) Ken(neth Alfred)
1927- . . . . CLC 16
See also CA 105

Russell, Mary Annette Beauchamp 1866-1941
See Elizabeth

Russell, Willy 1947- . . . . CLC 60

Author Index

Sitwell, (Dame) Edith
　　1887-1964 . . . . CLC 2, 9, 67; PC 3
　　See also CA 11-12R; DLB 20

Sjoewall, Maj　1935-
　　See Wahloo, Per
　　See also CA 61-64, 65-68

Sjowall, Maj　1935-
　　See Wahloo, Per

Skelton, Robin　1925- . . . . CLC 13
　　See also CAAS 5; CA 5-8R; DLB 27, 53

Skolimowski, Jerzy　1938- . . . . CLC 20

Skolimowski, Yurek　1938-
　　See Skolimowski, Jerzy

Skram, Amalie (Bertha)
　　1847-1905 . . . . TCLC 25

Skrine, Mary Nesta　1904-
　　See Keane, Molly

Skvorecky, Josef (Vaclav)
　　1924- . . . . CLC 15, 39, 69
　　See also CAAS 1; CANR 10, 34; CA 61-64

Slade, Bernard　1930- . . . . CLC 11, 46
　　See also Newbound, Bernard Slade
　　See also DLB 53

Slaughter, Carolyn　1946- . . . . CLC 56
　　See also CA 85-88

Slaughter, Frank G(ill)　1908- . . . . . . CLC 29
　　See also CANR 5; CA 5-8R

Slavitt, David (R.)　1935- . . . . CLC 5, 14
　　See also CAAS 3; CA 21-24R; DLB 5, 6

Slesinger, Tess　1905-1945 . . . . TCLC 10
　　See also CA 107

Slessor, Kenneth　1901-1971 . . . . CLC 14
　　See also CA 102; obituary CA 89-92

Slowacki, Juliusz　1809-1849 . . . . . NCLC 15

Smart, Christopher　1722-1771 . . . . LC 3

Smart, Elizabeth　1913-1986 . . . . CLC 54
　　See also CA 81-84; obituary CA 118;
　　DLB 88

Smiley, Jane (Graves)　1949- . . . . CLC 53
　　See also CA 104

Smith, A(rthur) J(ames) M(arshall)
　　1902-1980 . . . . CLC 15
　　See also CANR 4; CA 1-4R;
　　obituary CA 102; DLB 88

Smith, Betty (Wehner)　1896-1972 . . . CLC 19
　　See also CA 5-8R; obituary CA 33-36R;
　　SATA 6; DLB-Y 82

Smith, Cecil Lewis Troughton　1899-1966
　　See Forester, C(ecil) S(cott)

Smith, Charlotte (Turner)
　　1749-1806 . . . . NCLC 23
　　See also DLB 39

Smith, Clark Ashton　1893-1961 . . . . CLC 43

Smith, Dave　1942- . . . . CLC 22, 42
　　See also Smith, David (Jeddie)
　　See also CAAS 7; CANR 1; DLB 5

Smith, David (Jeddie)　1942-
　　See Smith, Dave
　　See also CANR 1; CA 49-52

Smith, Florence Margaret　1902-1971
　　See Smith, Stevie
　　See also CAP 2; CA 17-18;
　　obituary CA 29-32R

Smith, Iain Crichton　1928- . . . . CLC 64
　　See also DLB 40

Smith, John　1580?-1631 . . . . LC 9
　　See also DLB 24, 30

Smith, Lee　1944- . . . . CLC 25
　　See also CA 114, 119; DLB-Y 83

Smith, Martin Cruz　1942- . . . . CLC 25
　　See also CANR 6; CA 85-88

Smith, Martin William　1942-
　　See Smith, Martin Cruz

Smith, Mary-Ann Tirone　1944- . . . . . CLC 39
　　See also CA 118

Smith, Patti　1946- . . . . CLC 12
　　See also CA 93-96

Smith, Pauline (Urmson)
　　1882-1959 . . . . TCLC 25
　　See also CA 29-32R; SATA 27

Smith, Rosamond　1938-
　　See Oates, Joyce Carol

Smith, Sara Mahala Redway　1900-1972
　　See Benson, Sally

Smith, Stevie　1902-1971 . . . . CLC 3, 8, 25, 44
　　See also Smith, Florence Margaret
　　See also DLB 20

Smith, Wilbur (Addison)　1933- . . . . . CLC 33
　　See also CANR 7; CA 13-16R

Smith, William Jay　1918- . . . . CLC 6
　　See also CA 5-8R; SATA 2; DLB 5

Smolenskin, Peretz　1842-1885 . . . . NCLC 30

Smollett, Tobias (George)　1721-1771 . . LC 2
　　See also DLB 39

Snodgrass, W(illiam) D(e Witt)
　　1926- . . . . CLC 2, 6, 10, 18, 68
　　See also CANR 6; CA 1-4R; DLB 5

Snow, C(harles) P(ercy)
　　1905-1980 . . . . CLC 1, 4, 6, 9, 13, 19
　　See also CA 5-8R; obituary CA 101;
　　DLB 15, 77

Snyder, Gary (Sherman)
　　1930- . . . . CLC 1, 2, 5, 9, 32
　　See also CANR 30; CA 17-20R; DLB 5, 16

Snyder, Zilpha Keatley　1927- . . . . . . CLC 17
　　See also CA 9-12R; SAAS 2; SATA 1, 28

Sobol, Joshua　19??- . . . . CLC 60

Soderberg, Hjalmar　1869-1941 . . . . TCLC 39

Sodergran, Edith　1892-1923 . . . . . . TCLC 31

Sokolov, Raymond　1941- . . . . CLC 7
　　See also CA 85-88

Sologub, Fyodor　1863-1927 . . . . TCLC 9
　　See also Teternikov, Fyodor Kuzmich
　　See also CA 104

Solomos, Dionysios　1798-1857 . . . NCLC 15

Solwoska, Mara　1929-
　　See French, Marilyn
　　See also CANR 3; CA 69-72

Solzhenitsyn, Aleksandr I(sayevich)
　　1918- . . . CLC 1, 2, 4, 7, 9, 10, 18, 26, 34
　　See also CA 69-72

Somers, Jane　1919-
　　See Lessing, Doris (May)

Sommer, Scott　1951- . . . . CLC 25
　　See also CA 106

Sondheim, Stephen (Joshua)
　　1930- . . . . CLC 30, 39
　　See also CA 103

Sontag, Susan　1933-. . . CLC 1, 2, 10, 13, 31
　　See also CA 17-20R; DLB 2, 67

Sophocles
　　c. 496? B.C.-c. 406? B.C. . . . . . CMLC 2;
　　　　　　　　　　　　　　　　　　　DC 1

Sorrentino, Gilbert
　　1929- . . . . CLC 3, 7, 14, 22, 40
　　See also CANR 14; CA 77-80; DLB 5;
　　DLB-Y 80

Soto, Gary　1952-. . . . . CLC 32
　　See also CA 119, 125; DLB 82

Soupault, Philippe　1897-1990 . . . . . . CLC 68
　　See also CA 116; obituary CA 131

Souster, (Holmes) Raymond
　　1921- . . . . CLC 5, 14
　　See also CANR 13; CA 13-16R; DLB 88

Southern, Terry　1926- . . . . CLC 7
　　See also CANR 1; CA 1-4R; DLB 2

Southey, Robert　1774-1843 . . . . NCLC 8
　　See also SATA 54

Southworth, Emma Dorothy Eliza Nevitte
　　1819-1899 . . . . NCLC 26

Soyinka, Wole
　　1934- . . . . CLC 3, 5, 14, 36. 44; DC 2
　　See also BLC 3; CANR 27; CA 13-16R;
　　DLB-Y 86

Spackman, W(illiam) M(ode)
　　1905- . . . . CLC 46
　　See also CA 81-84

Spacks, Barry　1931- . . . . CLC 14
　　See also CA 29-32R

Spanidou, Irini　1946- . . . . CLC 44

Spark, Muriel (Sarah)
　　1918- . . . . CLC 2, 3, 5, 8, 13, 18, 40
　　See also CANR 12; CA 5-8R; DLB 15

Spencer, Elizabeth　1921- . . . . CLC 22
　　See also CA 13-16R; SATA 14; DLB 6

Spencer, Scott　1945-. . . . . CLC 30
　　See also CA 113; DLB-Y 86

Spender, Stephen (Harold)
　　1909- . . . . CLC 1, 2, 5, 10, 41
　　See also CA 9-12R; DLB 20

Spengler, Oswald　1880-1936 . . . . . . TCLC 25
　　See also CA 118

Spenser, Edmund　1552?-1599 . . . . LC 5

Spicer, Jack　1925-1965 . . . . CLC 8, 18
　　See also CA 85-88; DLB 5, 16

Spielberg, Peter　1929- . . . . CLC 6
　　See also CANR 4; CA 5-8R; DLB-Y 81

Spielberg, Steven　1947- . . . . CLC 20
　　See also CA 77-80; SATA 32

Spillane, Frank Morrison　1918-
　　See Spillane, Mickey
　　See also CA 25-28R

Spillane, Mickey　1918- . . . . CLC 3, 13
　　See also Spillane, Frank Morrison

Spinoza, Benedictus de　1632-1677 . . . . LC 9

Spinrad, Norman (Richard)　1940-. . . CLC 46
　　See also CANR 20; CA 37-40R; DLB 8

Spitteler, Carl (Friedrich Georg)
    1845-1924 .... **TCLC 12**
    See also CA 109

Spivack, Kathleen (Romola Drucker)
    1938- .... **CLC 6**
    See also CA 49-52

Spoto, Donald 1941- .... **CLC 39**
    See also CANR 11; CA 65-68

Springsteen, Bruce 1949- .... **CLC 17**
    See also CA 111

Spurling, Hilary 1940- .... **CLC 34**
    See also CANR 25; CA 104

Squires, (James) Radcliffe 1917- .... **CLC 51**
    See also CANR 6, 21; CA 1-4R

Stael-Holstein, Anne Louise Germaine Necker,
    Baronne de 1766-1817 .... **NCLC 3**

Stafford, Jean 1915-1979 ... **CLC 4, 7, 19, 68**
    See also CANR 3; CA 1-4R;
    obituary CA 85-88; obituary SATA 22;
    DLB 2

Stafford, William (Edgar)
    1914- .... **CLC 4, 7, 29**
    See also CAAS 3; CANR 5, 22; CA 5-8R;
    DLB 5

Stannard, Martin 1947- .... **CLC 44**

Stanton, Maura 1946- .... **CLC 9**
    See also CANR 15; CA 89-92

Stapledon, (William) Olaf
    1886-1950 .... **TCLC 22**
    See also CA 111; DLB 15

Starbuck, George (Edwin) 1931- .... **CLC 53**
    See also CANR 23; CA 21-22R

Stark, Richard 1933-
    See Westlake, Donald E(dwin)

Stead, Christina (Ellen)
    1902-1983 .... **CLC 2, 5, 8, 32**
    See also CA 13-16R; obituary CA 109

Steele, Sir Richard 1672-1729 ...... **LC 18**
    See also DLB 84, 101

Steele, Timothy (Reid) 1948- .... **CLC 45**
    See also CANR 16; CA 93-96

Steffens, (Joseph) Lincoln
    1866-1936 .... **TCLC 20**
    See also CA 117; SAAS 1

Stegner, Wallace (Earle) 1909- ... **CLC 9, 49**
    See also CANR 1, 21; CA 1-4R; DLB 9

Stein, Gertrude 1874-1946 ... **TCLC 1, 6, 28**
    See also CA 104; DLB 4, 54, 86;
    CDALB 1917-1929

Steinbeck, John (Ernst)
    1902-1968 ..... **CLC 1, 5, 9, 13, 21, 34,
                                 45, 59**
    See also CANR 1; CA 1-4R;
    obituary CA 25-28R; SATA 9; DLB 7, 9;
    DLB-DS 2; CDALB 1929-1941

Steinem, Gloria 1934- .... **CLC 63**
    See also CANR 28; CA 53-56

Steiner, George 1929- .... **CLC 24**
    See also CA 73-76; DLB 67

Steiner, Rudolf(us Josephus Laurentius)
    1861-1925 .... **TCLC 13**
    See also CA 107

Stendhal 1783-1842 .... **NCLC 23**

Stephen, Leslie 1832-1904 .... **TCLC 23**
    See also CANR 9; CA 21-24R, 123;
    DLB 57

Stephens, James 1882?-1950 .... **TCLC 4**
    See also CA 104; DLB 19

Stephens, Reed
    See Donaldson, Stephen R.

Steptoe, Lydia 1892-1982
    See Barnes, Djuna

Sterchi, Beat 1949- .... **CLC 65**

Sterling, George 1869-1926 .... **TCLC 20**
    See also CA 117; DLB 54

Stern, Gerald 1925- .... **CLC 40**
    See also CA 81-84

Stern, Richard G(ustave) 1928- ... **CLC 4, 39**
    See also CANR 1, 25; CA 1-4R; DLB 87

Sternberg, Jonas 1894-1969
    See Sternberg, Josef von

Sternberg, Josef von 1894-1969 ..... **CLC 20**
    See also CA 81-84

Sterne, Laurence 1713-1768 .... **LC 2**
    See also DLB 39

Sternheim, (William Adolf) Carl
    1878-1942 .... **TCLC 8**
    See also CA 105

Stevens, Mark 19??- .... **CLC 34**

Stevens, Wallace 1879-1955 ..... **TCLC 3, 12**
    See also CA 104, 124; DLB 54

Stevenson, Anne (Katharine)
    1933- .... **CLC 7, 33**
    See also Elvin, Anne Katharine Stevenson
    See also CANR 9; CA 17-18R; DLB 40

Stevenson, Robert Louis
    1850-1894 .... **NCLC 5, 14**
    See also CLR 10, 11; YABC 2; DLB 18, 57

Stewart, J(ohn) I(nnes) M(ackintosh)
    1906- .... **CLC 7, 14, 32**
    See also CAAS 3; CA 85-88

Stewart, Mary (Florence Elinor)
    1916- .... **CLC 7, 35**
    See also CANR 1; CA 1-4R; SATA 12

Stewart, Will 1908-
    See Williamson, Jack
    See also CANR 23; CA 17-18R

Still, James 1906- .... **CLC 49**
    See also CANR 10, 26; CA 65-68;
    SATA 29; DLB 9

Sting 1951-
    See The Police

Stitt, Milan 1941- .... **CLC 29**
    See also CA 69-72

Stoker, Abraham
    See Stoker, Bram
    See also CA 105; SATA 29

Stoker, Bram 1847-1912 .... **TCLC 8**
    See also Stoker, Abraham
    See also SATA 29; DLB 36, 70

Stolz, Mary (Slattery) 1920- .... **CLC 12**
    See also CANR 13; CA 5-8R; SAAS 3;
    SATA 10

Stone, Irving 1903-1989 .... **CLC 7**
    See also CAAS 3; CANR 1; CA 1-4R, 129;
    SATA 3

Stone, Robert (Anthony)
    1937?- .... **CLC 5, 23, 42**
    See also CANR 23; CA 85-88

Stoppard, Tom
    1937- ... **CLC 1, 3, 4, 5, 8, 15, 29, 34, 63**
    See also CA 81-84; DLB 13; DLB-Y 85

Storey, David (Malcolm)
    1933- .... **CLC 2, 4, 5, 8**
    See also CA 81-84; DLB 13, 14

Storm, Hyemeyohsts 1935- .... **CLC 3**
    See also CA 81-84

Storm, (Hans) Theodor (Woldsen)
    1817-1888 .... **NCLC 1**

Storni, Alfonsina 1892-1938 .... **TCLC 5**
    See also CA 104

Stout, Rex (Todhunter) 1886-1975 ... **CLC 3**
    See also CA 61-64

Stow, (Julian) Randolph 1935- .. **CLC 23, 48**
    See also CA 13-16R

Stowe, Harriet (Elizabeth) Beecher
    1811-1896 .... **NCLC 3**
    See also YABC 1; DLB 1, 12, 42, 74;
    CDALB 1865-1917

Strachey, (Giles) Lytton
    1880-1932 .... **TCLC 12**
    See also CA 110

Strand, Mark 1934- .... **CLC 6, 18, 41**
    See also CA 21-24R; SATA 41; DLB 5

Straub, Peter (Francis) 1943- ...... **CLC 28**
    See also CA 85-88; DLB-Y 84

Strauss, Botho 1944- .... **CLC 22**

Straussler, Tomas 1937-
    See Stoppard, Tom

Streatfeild, (Mary) Noel 1897- ..... **CLC 21**
    See also CA 81-84; obituary CA 120;
    SATA 20, 48

Stribling, T(homas) S(igismund)
    1881-1965 .... **CLC 23**
    See also obituary CA 107; DLB 9

Strindberg, (Johan) August
    1849-1912 .... **TCLC 1, 8, 21**
    See also CA 104

Stringer, Arthur 1874-1950 .... **TCLC 37**
    See also DLB 92

Strugatskii, Arkadii (Natanovich)
    1925- .... **CLC 27**
    See also CA 106

Strugatskii, Boris (Natanovich)
    1933- .... **CLC 27**
    See also CA 106

Strummer, Joe 1953?-
    See The Clash

Stuart, (Hilton) Jesse
    1906-1984 .... **CLC 1, 8, 11, 14, 34**
    See also CA 5-8R; obituary CA 112;
    SATA 2; obituary SATA 36; DLB 9, 48;
    DLB-Y 84

Sturgeon, Theodore (Hamilton)
    1918-1985 .... **CLC 22, 39**
    See also CA 81-84; obituary CA 116;
    DLB 8; DLB-Y 85

Styron, William
    1925- .... **CLC 1, 3, 5, 11, 15, 60**
    See also CANR 6; CA 5-8R; DLB 2;
    DLB-Y 80; CDALB 1968-1987

Thiele, Colin (Milton) 1920- .... CLC 17
See also CANR 12; CA 29-32R; SAAS 2;
SATA 14

Thomas, Audrey (Grace)
1935- .... CLC 7, 13, 37
See also CA 21-24R; DLB 60

Thomas, D(onald) M(ichael)
1935- .... CLC 13, 22, 31
See also CANR 17; CA 61-64; DLB 40

Thomas, Dylan (Marlais)
1914-1953 ..... TCLC 1, 8; PC 2; SSC 3
See also CA 104, 120; SATA 60; DLB 13,
20

Thomas, Edward (Philip)
1878-1917 .... TCLC 10
See also CA 106; DLB 19

Thomas, John Peter 1928-
See Thomas, Piri

Thomas, Joyce Carol 1938- .... CLC 35
See also CLR 19; CA 113, 116; SAAS 7;
SATA 40; DLB 33

Thomas, Lewis 1913- .... CLC 35
See also CA 85-88

Thomas, Piri 1928-................. CLC 17
See also CA 73-76

Thomas, R(onald) S(tuart)
1913- .... CLC 6, 13, 48
See also CAAS 4; CA 89-92; DLB 27

Thomas, Ross (Elmore) 1926- ...... CLC 39
See also CANR 22; CA 33-36R

Thompson, Ernest 1860-1946
See Seton, Ernest (Evan) Thompson

Thompson, Francis (Joseph)
1859-1907 .... TCLC 4
See also CA 104; DLB 19

Thompson, Hunter S(tockton)
1939- .... CLC 9, 17, 40
See also CANR 23; CA 17-20R

Thompson, James Meyers 1906-1976
See Thompson, Jim

Thompson, Jim 1906-1976........ CLC 69

Thompson, Judith 1954-........... CLC 39

Thomson, James 1700-1748........ LC 16
See also DLB 95

Thomson, James 1834-1882...... NCLC 18
See also DLB 35

Thoreau, Henry David
1817-1862 .... NCLC 7, 21
See also DLB 1; CDALB 1640-1865

Thurber, James (Grover)
1894-1961 .... CLC 5, 11, 25; SSC 1
See also CANR 17; CA 73-76; SATA 13;
DLB 4, 11, 22

Thurman, Wallace 1902-1934 ...... TCLC 6
See also BLC 3; CA 104, 124; DLB 51

Tieck, (Johann) Ludwig
1773-1853 .... NCLC 5
See also DLB 90

Tilghman, Christopher 1948?- ...... CLC 65

Tillinghast, Richard 1940-........ CLC 29
See also CANR 26; CA 29-32R

Timrod, Henry 1828-1867 .... NCLC 25

Tindall, Gillian 1938-.............. CLC 7
See also CANR 11; CA 21-24R

Tiptree, James, Jr. 1915-1987... CLC 48, 50
See also Sheldon, Alice (Hastings) B(radley)
See also DLB 8

Tocqueville, Alexis (Charles Henri Maurice
Clerel, Comte) de 1805-1859.. NCLC 7

Tolkien, J(ohn) R(onald) R(euel)
1892-1973 .... CLC 1, 2, 3, 8, 12, 38
See also CAP 2; CA 17-18;
obituary CA 45-48; SATA 2, 24, 32;
obituary SATA 24; DLB 15

Toller, Ernst 1893-1939 .... TCLC 10
See also CA 107

Tolson, Melvin B(eaunorus)
1898?-1966................. CLC 36
See also BLC 3; CA 124;
obituary CA 89-92; DLB 48, 76

Tolstoy, (Count) Alexey Nikolayevich
1883-1945 .... TCLC 18
See also CA 107

Tolstoy, (Count) Leo (Lev Nikolaevich)
1828-1910 ..... TCLC 4, 11, 17, 28, 44;
SSC 9
See also CA 104, 123; SATA 26

Tomlin, Lily 1939- .... CLC 17

Tomlin, Mary Jean 1939-
See Tomlin, Lily
See also CA 117

Tomlinson, (Alfred) Charles
1927- .... CLC 2, 4, 6, 13, 45
See also CA 5-8R; DLB 40

Toole, John Kennedy
1937-1969 .... CLC 19, 64
See also CA 104; DLB-Y 81

Toomer, Jean
1894-1967 ..... CLC 1, 4, 13, 22; SSC 1
See also BLC 3; CA 85-88; DLB 45, 51;
CDALB 1917-1929

Torrey, E. Fuller 19??-........... CLC 34
See also CA 119

Tosei 1644-1694
See Basho, Matsuo

Tournier, Michel 1924- ...... CLC 6, 23, 36
See also CANR 3; CA 49-52; SATA 23;
DLB 83

Townsend, Sue 1946- .... CLC 61
See also CA 119, 127; SATA 48, 55

Townshend, Peter (Dennis Blandford)
1945- .... CLC 17, 42
See also CA 107

Tozzi, Federigo 1883-1920....... TCLC 31

Traill, Catharine Parr
1802-1899 .... NCLC 31
See also DLB 99

Trakl, Georg 1887-1914........... TCLC 5
See also CA 104

Transtromer, Tomas (Gosta)
1931- .... CLC 52, 65
See also CA 129; brief entry CA 117

Traven, B. 1890-1969 .... CLC 8, 11
See also CAP 2; CA 19-20;
obituary CA 25-28R; DLB 9, 56

Tremain, Rose 1943-............ CLC 42
See also CA 97-100; DLB 14

Tremblay, Michel 1942-.......... CLC 29
See also CA 116; DLB 60

Trevanian 1925- .... CLC 29
See also CA 108

Trevor, William 1928- ..... CLC 7, 9, 14, 25
See also Cox, William Trevor
See also DLB 14

Trifonov, Yuri (Valentinovich)
1925-1981 .... CLC 45
See also obituary CA 103, 126

Trilling, Lionel 1905-1975 .... CLC 9, 11, 24
See also CANR 10; CA 9-12R;
obituary CA 61-64; DLB 28, 63

Trogdon, William 1939-
See Heat Moon, William Least
See also CA 115, 119

Trollope, Anthony 1815-1882 .. NCLC 6, 33
See also SATA 22; DLB 21, 57

Trollope, Frances 1780-1863 ..... NCLC 30
See also DLB 21

Trotsky, Leon (Davidovich)
1879-1940 .... TCLC 22
See also CA 118

Trotter (Cockburn), Catharine
1679-1749 .... LC 8
See also DLB 84

Trow, George W. S. 1943-........ CLC 52
See also CA 126

Troyat, Henri 1911-.............. CLC 23
See also CANR 2; CA 45-48

Trudeau, G(arretson) B(eekman) 1948-
See Trudeau, Garry
See also CA 81-84; SATA 35

Trudeau, Garry 1948-............ CLC 12
See also Trudeau, G(arretson) B(eekman)

Truffaut, Francois 1932-1984....... CLC 20
See also CA 81-84; obituary CA 113

Trumbo, Dalton 1905-1976 .... CLC 19
See also CANR 10; CA 21-24R;
obituary CA 69-72; DLB 26

Trumbull, John 1750-1831....... NCLC 30
See also DLB 31

Tryon, Thomas 1926-........... CLC 3, 11
See also CA 29-32R

Ts'ao Hsueh-ch'in 1715?-1763........ LC 1

Tse, Isaac 1904-1991
See Singer, Isaac Bashevis

Tsushima Shuji 1909-1948
See Dazai Osamu
See also CA 107

Tsvetaeva (Efron), Marina (Ivanovna)
1892-1941 ....TCLC 7, 35
See also CA 104, 128

Tunis, John R(oberts) 1889-1975 ... CLC 12
See also CA 61-64; SATA 30, 37; DLB 22

Tuohy, Frank 1925- .... CLC 37
See also DLB 14

Tuohy, John Francis 1925-
See Tuohy, Frank
See also CANR 3; CA 5-8R

Turco, Lewis (Putnam) 1934- ... CLC 11, 63
See also CANR 24; CA 13-16R; DLB-Y 84

Turgenev, Ivan
1818-1883 .... NCLC 21; SSC 7

Turner, Frederick 1943-.......... CLC 48
See also CANR 12; CA 73-76; DLB 40

Weiss, Theodore (Russell)
1916- .... CLC **3, 8, 14**
See also CAAS 2; CA 9-12R; DLB 5

Welch, (Maurice) Denton
1915-1948 .... TCLC **22**
See also CA 121

Welch, James 1940- .... CLC **6, 14, 52**
See also CA 85-88

Weldon, Fay
1933- .... CLC **6, 9, 11, 19, 36, 59**
See also CANR 16; CA 21-24R; DLB 14

Wellek, Rene 1903- .... CLC **28**
See also CAAS 7; CANR 8; CA 5-8R;
DLB 63

Weller, Michael 1942- .... CLC **10, 53**
See also CA 85-88

Weller, Paul 1958- .... CLC **26**

Wellershoff, Dieter 1925-........ CLC **46**
See also CANR 16; CA 89-92

Welles, (George) Orson
1915-1985 .... CLC **20**
See also CA 93-96; obituary CA 117

Wellman, Mac 1945- .... CLC **65**

Wellman, Manly Wade 1903-1986 .. CLC **49**
See also CANR 6, 16; CA 1-4R;
obituary CA 118; SATA 6, 47

Wells, Carolyn 1862-1942 .... TCLC **35**
See also CA 113; DLB 11

Wells, H(erbert) G(eorge)
1866-1946 ...... TCLC **6, 12, 19; SSC 6**
See also CA 110, 121; SATA 20; DLB 34,
70

Wells, Rosemary 1943-............ CLC **12**
See also CLR 16; CA 85-88; SAAS 1;
SATA 18

Welty, Eudora (Alice)
1909- .... CLC **1, 2, 5, 14, 22, 33; SSC 1**
See also CA 9-12R; CABS 1; DLB 2;
DLB-Y 87; CDALB 1941-1968

Wen I-to 1899-1946 ....CENTURY TCLC **28**

Werfel, Franz (V.) 1890-1945 ...... TCLC **8**
See also CA 104; DLB 81

Wergeland, Henrik Arnold
1808-1845 .... NCLC **5**

Wersba, Barbara 1932-............ CLC **30**
See also CLR 3; CANR 16; CA 29-32R;
SAAS 2; SATA 1, 58; DLB 52

Wertmuller, Lina 1928- .... CLC **16**
See also CA 97-100

Wescott, Glenway 1901-1987....... CLC **13**
See also CANR 23; CA 13-16R;
obituary CA 121; DLB 4, 9

Wesker, Arnold 1932- .... CLC **3, 5, 42**
See also CAAS 7; CANR 1; CA 1-4R;
DLB 13

Wesley, Richard (Errol) 1945-....... CLC **7**
See also CA 57-60; DLB 38

Wessel, Johan Herman 1742-1785 .... LC **7**

West, Anthony (Panther)
1914-1987 .... CLC **50**
See also CANR 3, 19; CA 45-48; DLB 15

West, Jessamyn 1907-1984 ...... CLC **7, 17**
See also CA 9-12R; obituary CA 112;
obituary SATA 37; DLB 6; DLB-Y 84

West, Morris L(anglo) 1916-..... CLC **6, 33**
See also CA 5-8R; obituary CA 124

West, Nathanael
1903-1940 .... TCLC **1, 14, 44**
See also CA 104, 125; DLB 4, 9, 28;
CDALB 1929-1941

West, Paul 1930- .... CLC **7, 14**
See also CAAS 7; CANR 22; CA 13-16R;
DLB 14

West, Rebecca 1892-1983 .. CLC **7, 9, 31, 50**
See also CANR 19; CA 5-8R;
obituary CA 109; DLB 36; DLB-Y 83

Westall, Robert (Atkinson) 1929-... CLC **17**
See also CLR 13; CANR 18; CA 69-72;
SAAS 2; SATA 23

Westlake, Donald E(dwin)
1933- .... CLC **7, 33**
See also CANR 16; CA 17-20R

Westmacott, Mary 1890-1976
See Christie, (Dame) Agatha (Mary
Clarissa)

Whalen, Philip 1923- .... CLC **6, 29**
See also CANR 5; CA 9-12R; DLB 16

Wharton, Edith (Newbold Jones)
1862-1937 .... TCLC **3, 9, 27; SSC 6**
See also CA 104; DLB 4, 9, 12, 78;
CDALB 1865-1917

Wharton, William 1925-........ CLC **18, 37**
See also CA 93-96; DLB-Y 80

Wheatley (Peters), Phillis
1753?-1784................. LC **3; PC 3**
See also BLC 3; DLB 31, 50;
CDALB 1640-1865

Wheelock, John Hall 1886-1978.... CLC **14**
See also CANR 14; CA 13-16R;
obituary CA 77-80; DLB 45

Whelan, John 1900-
See O'Faolain, Sean

Whitaker, Rodney 1925-
See Trevanian

White, E(lwyn) B(rooks)
1899-1985 .... CLC **10, 34, 39**
See also CLR 1; CANR 16; CA 13-16R;
obituary CA 116; SATA 2, 29, 44;
obituary SATA 44; DLB 11, 22

White, Edmund III 1940-......... CLC **27**
See also CANR 3, 19; CA 45-48

White, Patrick (Victor Martindale)
1912-1990 .. CLC **3, 4, 5, 7, 9, 18, 65, 69**
See also CA 81-84; obituary CA 132

White, T(erence) H(anbury)
1906-1964 .... CLC **30**
See also CA 73-76; SATA 12

White, Terence de Vere 1912-...... CLC **49**
See also CANR 3; CA 49-52

White, Walter (Francis)
1893-1955................... TCLC **15**
See also BLC 3; CA 115, 124; DLB 51

White, William Hale 1831-1913
See Rutherford, Mark
See also CA 121

Whitehead, E(dward) A(nthony)
1933- .... CLC **5**
See also CA 65-68

Whitemore, Hugh 1936-.......... CLC **37**

Whitman, Sarah Helen
1803-1878 .... NCLC **19**
See also DLB 1

Whitman, Walt
1819-1892 .... NCLC **4, 31; PC 3**
See also SATA 20; DLB 3, 64;
CDALB 1640-1865

Whitney, Phyllis A(yame) 1903-.... CLC **42**
See also CANR 3, 25; CA 1-4R; SATA 1,
30

Whittemore, (Edward) Reed (Jr.)
1919- .... CLC **4**
See also CAAS 8; CANR 4; CA 9-12R;
DLB 5

Whittier, John Greenleaf
1807-1892 .... NCLC **8**
See also DLB 1; CDALB 1640-1865

Wicker, Thomas Grey 1926-
See Wicker, Tom
See also CANR 21; CA 65-68

Wicker, Tom 1926-................ CLC **7**
See also Wicker, Thomas Grey

Wideman, John Edgar
1941- ....CLC **5, 34, 36, 67**
See also BLC 3; CANR 14; CA 85-88;
DLB 33

Wiebe, Rudy (H.) 1934-...... CLC **6, 11, 14**
See also CA 37-40R; DLB 60

Wieland, Christoph Martin
1733-1813 .... NCLC **17**

Wieners, John 1934-............... CLC **7**
See also CA 13-16R; DLB 16

Wiesel, Elie(zer) 1928-..... CLC **3, 5, 11, 37**
See also CAAS 4; CANR 8; CA 5-8R;
SATA 56; DLB 83; DLB-Y 87

Wiggins, Marianne 1948-.......... CLC **57**

Wight, James Alfred 1916-
See Herriot, James
See also CA 77-80; SATA 44

Wilbur, Richard (Purdy)
1921- .... CLC **3, 6, 9, 14, 53**
See also CANR 2; CA 1-4R; CABS 2;
SATA 9; DLB 5

Wild, Peter 1940-................. CLC **14**
See also CA 37-40R; DLB 5

Wilde, Oscar (Fingal O'Flahertie Wills)
1854-1900 .... TCLC **1, 8, 23, 41**
See also CA 119; brief entry CA 104;
SATA 24; DLB 10, 19, 34, 57

Wilder, Billy 1906-............... CLC **20**
See also Wilder, Samuel
See also DLB 26

Wilder, Samuel 1906-
See Wilder, Billy
See also CA 89-92

Wilder, Thornton (Niven)
1897-1975 ..... CLC **1, 5, 6, 10, 15, 35;
DC 1**
See also CA 13-16R; obituary CA 61-64;
DLB 4, 7, 9

Wiley, Richard 1944-.............. CLC **44**
See also CA 121, 129

Wilhelm, Kate 1928-.............. CLC **7**
See also CAAS 5; CANR 17; CA 37-40R;
DLB 8

Author Index

Literary Criticism Series
Cumulative Topic Index

This index lists all topic entries in the Gale Literary Criticism Series *Contemporary Literary Criticism, Literature Criticism from 1400 to 1800, Nineteenth-Century Literature Criticism,* and *Twentieth-Century Literary Criticism.*

Topic Index

TCLC Cumulative Nationality Index

AMERICAN

Adams, Henry **4**
Agee, James **1, 19**
Anderson, Maxwell **2**
Anderson, Sherwood **1, 10, 24**
Atherton, Gertrude **2**
Austin, Mary **25**
Barry, Philip **11**
Baum, L. Frank **7**
Beard, Charles A. **15**
Belasco, David **3**
Bell, James Madison **43**
Benchley, Robert **1**
Benét, Stephen Vincent **7**
Benét, William Rose **28**
Bierce, Ambrose **1, 7, 44**
Black Elk **33**
Bodenheim, Maxwell **44**
Bourne, Randolph S. **16**
Bradford, Gamaliel **36**
Bromfield, Louis **11**
Burroughs, Edgar Rice **2, 32**
Cabell, James Branch **6**
Cable, George Washington **4**
Cather, Willa **1, 11, 31**
Chambers, Robert W. **41**
Chandler, Raymond **1, 7**
Chapman, John Jay **7**
Chesnutt, Charles Waddell **5, 39**
Chopin, Kate **5, 14**
Comstock, Anthony **13**
Cotter, Joseph Seamon, Sr. **28**
Crane, Hart **2, 5**
Crane, Stephen **11, 17, 32**
Crawford, F. Marion **10**
Crothers, Rachel **19**
Cullen, Countee **4, 37**
Davis, Rebecca Harding **6**
Davis, Richard Harding **24**

Day, Clarence **25**
DeVoto, Bernard **29**
Dreiser, Theodore **10, 18, 35**
Dunbar, Paul Laurence **2, 12**
Dunne, Finley Peter **28**
Fisher, Rudolph **11**
Fitzgerald, F. Scott **1, 6, 14, 28**
Flecker, James Elroy **43**
Fletcher, John Gould **35**
Forten, Charlotte L. **16**
Freeman, Douglas Southall **11**
Freeman, Mary Wilkins **9**
Futrelle, Jacques **19**
Gale, Zona **7**
Garland, Hamlin **3**
Gilman, Charlotte Perkins **9, 37**
Glasgow, Ellen **2, 7**
Goldman, Emma **13**
Grey, Zane **6**
Guiney, Louise Imogen **41**
Hall, James Norman **23**
Harper, Frances Ellen Watkins **14**
Harris, Joel Chandler **2**
Harte, Bret **1, 25**
Hawthorne, Julian **25**
Hearn, Lafcadio **9**
Henry, O. **1, 19**
Hergesheimer, Joseph **11**
Higginson, Thomas Wentworth **36**
Hopkins, Pauline Elizabeth **28**
Howard, Robert E. **8**
Howe, Julia Ward **21**
Howells, William Dean **7, 17, 41**
James, Henry **2, 11, 24, 40**
James, William **15, 32**
Jewett, Sarah Orne **1, 22**
Johnson, James Weldon **3, 19**
Kornbluth, C. M. **8**
Kuttner, Henry **10**

Lardner, Ring **2, 14**
Lewis, Sinclair **4, 13, 23, 39**
Lewisohn, Ludwig **19**
Lindsay, Vachel **17**
Locke, Alain **43**
London, Jack **9, 15, 39**
Lovecraft, H. P. **4, 22**
Lowell, Amy **1, 8**
Marquis, Don **7**
Masters, Edgar Lee **2, 25**
McCoy, Horace **28**
McKay, Claude **7, 41**
Mencken, H. L. **13**
Millay, Edna St. Vincent **4**
Mitchell, Margaret **11**
Mitchell, S. Weir **36**
Monroe, Harriet **12**
Muir, John **28**
Nathan, George Jean **18**
Nordhoff, Charles **23**
Norris, Frank **24**
O'Neill, Eugene **1, 6, 27**
Oskison, John M. **35**
Phillips, David Graham **44**
Porter, Gene Stratton **21**
Post, Melville **39**
Rawlings, Marjorie Kinnan **4**
Reed, John **9**
Roberts, Kenneth **23**
Robinson, Edwin Arlington **5**
Rogers, Will **8**
Rölvaag, O. E. **17**
Rourke, Constance **12**
Runyon, Damon **10**
Saltus, Edgar **8**
Santayana, George **40**
Sherwood, Robert E. **3**
Slesinger, Tess **10**
Steffens, Lincoln **20**

Nationality Index

TCLC Title Index to Volume 44

Title Index

485

ISBN 0-8103-2426-1

90000